AF673732

AN ORIENTAL BIOGRAPHICAL DICTIONARY

AN ORIENTAL BIOGRAPHICAL DICTIONARY

FOUNDED ON MATERIALS COLLECTED

BY THE LATE

THOMAS WILLIAM BEALE,

AUTHOR OF THE MIFTAH-UL-TAWARIKH.

A NEW EDITION REVISED AND ENLARGED

BY

HENRY GEORGE KEENE, C.I.E., M.A., OXON,

FELLOW OF THE UNIVERSITY OF CALCUTTA;
AUTHOR OF *The Fall of the Moghul Empire*, ETC.

MANOHAR
2004

First published, London, 1894
Reprinted in India, 2004

ISBN 81-7304-525-9

Published by
Ajay Kumar Jain for
Manohar Publishers & Distributors
4753/23 Ansari Road, Daryaganj
New Delhi 110 002

Printed at
Print Perfect
New Delhi 110 064

PREFATORY NOTICE.

The substance of this Dictionary was collected by Mr. T. W. Beale, formerly a Clerk in the office of the Board of Revenue, N.W.P., at a time when the Secretary was Henry Myers Elliot, afterwards well known as Sir H. M. Elliot, K.C.B. It is probable that, in preparing his extracts from the Muhammadan Histories of India, Elliot availed himself of the aid of Mr. Beale, of whose scholarship Prof. Dowson makes justly deserved mention in the eighth volume of his valuable edition of Elliot's work.* Mr. Beale died at Agra, at a very advanced age, in the summer of 1875; having before his death expressed a wish that I would see his MS. through the press, and reduce the transliteration into conformity with the system then recently adopted by the Government of India, and founded (as I need hardly observe) upon the system of Sir W. Jones.

Accordingly, on the 5th October of that year I laid the MS. before Sir John Strachey, the then Lieut.-Governor, in a letter from which the following is an extract:—

"This is no ordinary book. I have used it as a work of reference for years: and have lately had an opportunity of showing it to the eminent scholar Mr. E. B. Eastwick, C.B., who, I am authorised to say, concurs with me in thinking that the Dictionary will be of unique value to oriental students."

Sir J. Strachey took up the subject with that enlightened energy which always actuated him in dealing with the past history of the country over whose administration he then presided. The MS. and copyright were acquired at the expense

* "The History of India, by its own Historians," Trübner and Co., 1877.

of Government; and it was ultimately resolved—in view of the importance of the work and my own official occupations—that the editing should be entrusted to the Asiatic Society of Bengal.

The Society confided the labour of seeing the Dictionary through the press to their Philological Secretary, Principal Blochmann, of whose qualifications it would be presumptuous to say more than that they have an œcumenical reputation. That distinguished man (of whom it has been observed by Count von Noer that he united the enthusiasm of an artist to the most patient accuracy of research*) undertook the task with his characteristic earnestness and ability. But unhappily for oriental scholarship Mr. Blochmann's lamented death occurred before he had completed the preparation of more than a few sheets; and the duty ultimately reverted to the present Editor.

The substance, as already stated, is almost entirely Mr. Beale's; and I cannot close this notice more fitly than by giving the following extract from the preface originally drafted by himself:—

"In preparing a work of this nature, intended to be used as a work of reference on matters connected with Oriental History, it is proper to state that the greatest care has been taken to ensure accuracy in the narrative, as also in the dates of births, deaths, and other events recorded. . . . Various MSS. have been collated whenever discrepancy was observed . . . . To remove all doubt, chronograms indicating the dates with a certainty not to be found by any other method and written when the events were fresh in the minds of men, have been inserted, when available."

I may, however, add that it has been judged expedient to omit these chronograms, for the most part, in printing the book. In the chapter of Mr. Dowson's book already cited, will be found an account of this species of *memoria technica*. But it is chiefly

* "Kaiser Akbar," Leyden, 1880. [Since the above was written the illustrious author quoted has himself died.]

interesting as machinery for producing a certain result; and when the result has been produced is not of much more use than the scaffolding of a building when the building is complete.

This notice may well terminate with a repetition of Mr. Beale's guarantee of accuracy: and with an appeal to scholars of larger leisure and opportunities for an indulgent treatment of a work originated by a man who had never been in Europe nor enjoyed the use of a complete Library. Mr. Beale had, however, drawn up a list of more than thirty books in various languages which had furnished him with materials. In addition I have from time to time referred to the translation of the *Ain Akbari* and its invaluable notes by the late Mr. Blochmann, of which the First Volume (never, alas, continued) was published in Calcutta some years ago; also to the works of Garcin de Tassy and the Baron McG. de Slane.

One word more as to the inexhaustible subject of transliteration. The English, as is well-known, have three methods; the Haphazard (which indeed is no method at all); the Gilchristian; and the popularised Jonesian introduced by the Government of India under the inspiration of Sir W. W. Hunter. None of these is quite satisfactory. The French adopt a system of their own, and so do the Germans. Mr. Beale had followed an orthography, compounded of the two first-named elements, which has been conformed to the third method in printing these pages. The principle is, mainly, to accentuate the long vowels and to express the other vowels by the English sounds in "r*u*m*i*n*a*nt" and "*o*b*e*y." *G* is always to be pronounced hard, as in "*g*ive." For the convenience of Continental European scholars the names have also been printed in the Persian character: and it is hoped that no practical difficulty will be experienced by those who may have occasion to use the Dictionary.

A

A'azz-Uddin (اعز الدين), Prince, second son of Shāh 'Ālam Bahādur Shāh. He was born on the 17th Ẕī-Qa'da 1074, and appears to have died early.

A'azz-Uddin (اعز الدين), son of Mu'izz-uddīn Jahāndār Shāh, emperor of Dehlī. He was blinded and imprisoned by Farrukh-siyar, in the end of A.H. 1124.

Aba Bakr (ابا بکر), Mirzā or Sulṭān, the son of Shāhrukh Mirzā, the son of Amīr Timur. He was murdered by order of his brother Mirzā Ulugh Beg, A.D. 1448 (A.H. 852).

Aba Qaan or Abqa Khan or Abaqa Khan (ابا قاآن or ابقا خان), a king of Persia, of the tribe of Mughuls or Tartars, and descendant of Chingiz Khān, succeeded his father Hulākū Khān in February, A.D. 1265 (Rabī'-uṣ-Ṣānī, A.H. 663), and was crowned on Friday the 19th June following (3rd Ramaẓān). He was a prince who added to the qualifications of courage and wisdom those of moderation, clemency, and justice. His ambassadors were introduced in 1274 to the ecclesiastical Synod at Lyons. He proved a somewhat formidable neighbour to the Christians who settled at Jerusalem. The intrigues of his court embittered the latter years of his reign; and his days were believed by many to have been shortened by poison given to him by his minister Khwāja Shams-uddīn Muhammad, which occasioned his death on Wednesday the 1st April, A.D. 1282 (20th Ẕil-ḥijja, A.H. 680), after a reign of 17 years and some months. He had married the daughter of Michael Palæologus, emperor of Constantinople, who had been betrothed to his father, but arrived at Marāgha in Tabrīz, the seat of his government, after the death of that prince. Abā Khān was succeeded by his brother, Nekodar Khān (*q.v.*), who embraced Muhammadanism, and took the title of Aḥmad.

'Abbas (عباس), the son of 'Abd-ul-Muttalib, and uncle of the prophet Muhammad. He at first opposed the ambitious views of his nephew, but when defeated in the battle of Badr, he was reconciled to him, warmly embraced his religion, and thanked heaven for the prosperity and the grace which he enjoyed as a Musalmān. He served the cause of Muhammad at the battle of Ḥunain by recalling his dismayed troops to the charge, and inciting them boldly to rally round their prophet, who was near expiring under the scimitars of the Ṣakafites. He died on the 21st of February, A.D. 653 (17th Rajab, A.H. 32); and 100 lunar years after Abul-'Abbās, surnamed As Saffāḥ, one of his descendants, laid the foundation of the 'Abbāsī or Abbaside family of the Caliphs in Baghdād, which continued for 524 lunar years. The tomb of 'Abbās is in Madīna.

'Abbasa (عباسه), a sister of Hārūn-ur-Rashīd, the Khalīfa of Baghdād, who bestowed her hand on Ja'far Barmakī, his minister, on condition that she abstained from the marriage rights. The promise was forgotten, and the husband's life was sacrificed by the tyrant, and 'Abbāsa was reduced to poverty. This circumstance took place in A.D. 803 (A.H. 187). There are still extant some Arabic verses which beautifully celebrate her love and her misfortunes. [*See* Ja'far ul-Barmakī.]

'Abbas 'Ali (عباس علی), a physician, and one of the Persian magi, who followed the doctrines of Zoroaster. He wrote, A.D. 980, a book called *Royal Work*, at the request of the son of the reigning Khalīfa of Baghdād, to whom it was dedicated. It was translated into Latin by Stephen of Antioch in A.D. 1127.

'Abbas 'Ali (عباس علی), Mirzā, whose poetical name was Betāb, the son of Nawāb Sayādat 'Alī Khān, son of Ghulām Muhammad Khān, the son of Faiẓ-ullah Khān, Nawāb of Rāmpūr in the 18th century.

'Abbas Bin-'Ali Shirwani (عباس بن علی شروانی), author of a history, containing the narrative of Sher Shāh the Afghān, who drove Humāyūn from Hindūstān, A.D. 1539, and mounted the throne of Dehlī. This work was dedicated to the emperor Akbar, and is called *Tuḥfa-i-Akbar-shāhī*. The first part of this work was translated into Urdū by Maẓhar 'Alī Khān in the time of Lord Cornwallis, and is entitled *Tārīkh-i-Sher Shāhī*.

[*Vide* Dowson, *Elliot's History of India*, iv. p. 301.]

'Abbas Mirza (عباس مرزا), a Persian prince, son of Fatḥ 'Alī Shāh, was born in 1783. He died in 1833. His death was a great loss to his country, although he could not prevent the encroachments of Russia. His eldest son, Muhammad Mirzā, mounted the throne in 1834, on the death of Fatḥ 'Alī, under the united protection of England and Russia.

'Abbas Mirza (عباس مرزا), whose title was Nawāb Iqtidār-uddaula, was the author of a Masnawī in Urdū verse, containing a history of Christ. He was living in Lucknow in A.D. 1849, and was then about eighty years of age.

'Abbas (Shah) I. (عباس شاه), surnamed the Great, and seventh king of Persia of the Ṣafawī family, was born on Monday the 29th of January, A D. 1571 (1st Ramaẓān, A.H. 978). He was proclaimed king of Persia, in his sixteenth year, by the chiefs of Khurāsān, and took possession of the throne during the lifetime of his father, Sulṭān Sikandar Shāh, surnamed Muhammad Khudābanda, A.D. 1588, (A.H. 996). He was the first who made Iṣfahān the capital of Persia. He was brave and active, and enlarged the boundaries of his dominions. He took, conjointly with the English forces, in A.D. 1622, the island of Ormuz, which had been in the possession of the Portuguese for 122 years. He reigned 44 lunar years, was contemporary with Akbar and Jahāngīr, and died on Thursday the 8th of January, A.D. 1629 (24th Jumāda I., A.H. 1038). His grandson succeeded him and took the title of Shāh Ṣafī.

[He was a bigoted Shī'a. In later histories he is generally called ماضي *māẓī ; vide* Blochmann's *Aīn Translation*, i. pp. 445, 453.]

'Abbas (Shah) II. (عباس شاه ثانی), great grandson of Shāh 'Abbās I. succeeded his father Shāh Ṣafī on the throne of Persia in the month of May, A.D. 1642 (Ṣafar A.H. 1052), when he was scarcely ten years old. Qandahār, which was lost by his father, was recovered by this prince before he was sixteen years of age. Shāh Jahān made many efforts to recover this city, but with no success. He reigned 25 lunar years, and was cut off by the *lues venerea* in his 34th year, on the 26th August, A.D. 1666 (5th Rabī'-ul-awwal, A.H. 1077). He was succeeded by his son Safī Mirzā, who took the title of Shāh Sulaimān. According to Chardin, he died on the 25th September which corresponds with the 5th Rabī'-uṣ-Ṣānī.

[Vide *Orme's Historical Fragments of the Mogul Empire*, p. 196.]

Abdal (ابدال), son of 'Alī Rāī, ruler of Little Tibet during the reign of Shāh Jahān. He was captured, and Adham Khān was appointed governor of Little Tibet.

[*Vide* Dowson, *Elliot's History of India*, vii. p. 63.]

Abdal Chak (ابدال چک), uncle of Yūsuf Khān Chak (last King of Kashmīr, who succumbed to the emperor Akbar).

[Vide *Āīn Translation*, i. p. 478.]

Abdali (ابدالي), *vide* Ahmad Shāh Abdālī.

Abdals, the Forty, hence called *Chihiltanān*. After Muhammad's death, the Earth complained to God that she would henceforth be no longer honored by prophets walking on her surface. God promised that there should always be on earth forty (or, according to some, seventy-two) holy men, called *Abdāls*, for whose sake he would not destroy the earth. The chief of the Forty is called 'Ghauṣ.'

Abdar Begam (آبدار بيگم), one of the concubines of the emperor Akbar.

'Abdi (عبدي), his proper name is not known. He is the author of the work called *Tarjami-i-Takmila*, a translation of *Yāfi'ī's Legends of Qādiriya saints* into Persian verse, completed in A.D. 1641, A.H. 1051, under Shāh Jahān.

'Abdi of Tun (عبدي), a poet who had a predilection for Masnawīs, and is the author of the *Gauhar-i Shāh-wār*, which is in the style of Niẓāmī's *Makhzan-ul-Asrār*. He came to celebrity in Khurāsān in A.D. 1545, A.H. 950.

[*Vide* Khwāja Zain-ul-'Ābidīn 'Alī 'Abdī, who appears to be the same person.]

'Abdi (عبدی), **and Nawedi** (نویدی), *vide* Khwāja Zain-ul-'Ābidīn 'Alī 'Abdi.

Abdi (ابدی), author of a heroic poem called *Anwar nāma* in praise of Nawāb Anwar-uddīn Khān of the Karnātik, in which the exploits of Major Lawrence and the first contests between the English and French in India are recorded with tolerable accuracy.

[*Vide* Abjadī.]

'Abdul-'Ali (Maulana) (عبد العلي), entitled Baḥrul-ulūm (i.e., The Sea of Knowledge), the son of Mullā Niẓām-uddīn Sihālī. He is the author of the *Arkān Arba' Fiqah'* and several other works. He died A.D. 1811, A.H. 1226.

'Abdul-'Aziz bin 'Umar (عبد العزيز بن عمر), son of 'Umar (Omar), the second Khalīfa after Muhammad. He did not succeed his father in the khilāfat. The Muhammadans consider him a great lawyer.

'Abdul-'Aziz (عبد العزيز), author of the *Tārīkh-i-Husainī*, containing the Life of the famous Ṣadr-uddīn Muhammad Husainī Gesū-Darāz, whose tomb is held in the highest veneration at Kulbarga in the Deccan. This work was dedicated to Ahmad Shāh Bahmanī in A.D. 1445.

'Abdul-'Aziz bin-Ahmad Dairini (Shaikh) (ديريني), an Arabian author who died A.D. 1294.

'Abdul-'Aziz Khan, *vide* 'Azīz.

'Abdul-'Aziz (Maulana Shah), son of Shāh Walīullah, a learned Musalmān of Dehlī. He is the author of a Persian commentary on the Qurān, entitled *Tafsīr Fath-ul-'Aziz*, and several other works. His death took place in June A.D. 1824 (7th Shawwāl, A.H. 1239).

'Abdul-'Aziz, emperor of Turkey, son of Sulṭān Mahmūd, succeeded his brother Sulṭān 'Abdul-Majīd on the 25th June, 1861, A.H. 1277; deposed in 1875.

'Abdul-'Aziz (Shaikh) (عبد العزيز شيخ), of Dehlī, a learned man who died in the time of the emperor Akbar, A.D. 1567, A.H. 975. 'Abdul-Qādir of Badāoṇ found the chronogram of his death in the following words—"Quṭb-i-Ṭariqat-numā."

'Abdul-'Aziz (Shaikh) (عبد العزيز شيخ). His poetical name was 'Izzat. He held a manṣab of 700 in the reign of Aurangzīb, and died in the year A.D. 1680, A.H. 1091. He is the author of a poem called *Sāqī-nāma*.

[For a detailed biography *vide* the *Maja'-un-Nafāis*.]

'Abdul-Baqi (عبد الباقى), author of the *Maāṣir-i-Rahīmī*, or *Memoirs of 'Abdur-Rahīm Khān, Khān-Khānān*, and of all the illustrious nobles, authors, and poets, who resided at the court of Akbar. He completed his work in A.D. 1616, A.H. 1025, and died about the year A.D. 1642, A.H. 1052, in the reign of Shāh Jahān.

[For further notes *vide* Dowson, *Elliot's History of India*, vi. 237.]

'Abdul-Baqi (Maulana). He was a *Ṣadr* (or Judge) in the beginning of Akbar's reign.

'Abdul Basit (Maulana) (عبد الباسط مولانا), the son of Rustam 'Alī. He wrote a commentary on the Qurān which he left incomplete. He also wrote a work called *'Ajīb-ul-Bayān fī 'ulūm-il-Qurān*. He died in A.D. 1808, A.H. 1223.

'Abdul-Fattah (عبد الفتاح), author of the Persian work called *Aurād-i-Ghauṣiya'* on Ṣufīsm, and of one entitled *Jawā-hir-ul-Kāyināt*.

'Abdul-Ghaffar (عبد الغفار), whose full title is Shaikh Najmuddīn 'Abdul-Ghaffār ush-Shāfi'ī Qazwīnī, is the author of the *Ḥāwī*, *Fiqah*, *Lubāb*, and *Sharḥ Lubāb*. He died in the year A.D. 1265, A.H. 663.

'Abdul-Ghafur, of Lahor (عبد الغفور لاهورى), was an author and a pupil of 'Abdur-Rahmān Jāmī. He died in the year A.D. 1506, A.H. 912.

'Abdul-Ghafur (Shah) (عبد الغفور شاه), commonly called Bābā Kapūr, a saint whose tomb is at Gwāliār. He was a native of Kālpī, and a disciple of Shāh Madār. He died in the year A.D. 1571, A.H. 979.

[Vide *Āīn Translation*, i. p. 539.]

'Abdul-Ghafur (Shaikh), of Āzampūr in Sambhal, a pupil of 'Abdul Quddūs. He died in A.H. 995.

'Abdul-Ghani (Mirza) (عبد الغنى مرزا), a native of Kashmīr, wrote under the name of Qabūl. He died in the year A.D. 1726, A.H. 1139.

[*Vide* Qabūl.]

'Abdul-Haqq (Shaikh) (عبد الحق دهلوى شيخ), of Dehlī, surnamed "Muhaddiṣ," son of Saif-uddīn, son of Sa'd-ullah Turk. He was a descendant of one of Amīr Timur's followers, who had remained at Dehlī, after the return of the conqueror to his native land. He is the author of the *Tārīkh-i-Haqqī*, which is more frequently styled *Tārīkh-i-'Abdul-Haqq*, compiled in the 42nd year of the emperor Akbar's reign, A.D. 1596, A.H. 1005. He went on a pilgrimage to Mecca and Madīna, where he dwelt for a long time, and wrote works upon many subjects—Commentaries, Travels, Ṣūfī Doctrines, Religion and History, and his different treatises amount altogether to more than one hundred. The best known are the *Madīna Sakīna*, *Matla'-ul-Anwār*, *Madārij-un-Nubuwwat*, *Jazb-ul-qulūb*, *Akh-bār-ul-Akhyār*, a book on the saints. He was born in the month of January, A.D. 1551, Muharrum, A.H. 958. In the year A.D. 1637, although he was then nearly ninety years old, he is said to have been in possession of his faculties. He died in the year A.D. 1642, A.H. 1052, aged ninety-four lunar years; lies buried on the bank of the Ḥauẓ Shamsī in Dehlī, and now holds a high rank among the saints of Hindūstān. His son Shāikh Nūr-ul-Haqq is the author of the *Zubdut-ut-Tawārīkh*.

[For further notes *vide* Dowson, *Elliot's History of India*, vi. pp. 175, 483.]

'Abdul - Hakim of Siyalkot (عبد الحکیم) was a pupil of Maulānā of Kamāl-uddīn of Kashmīr. He wrote the *Hāshiya*, or marginal commentary, on the *Tafsīr Baizāwi*, and a *Hāshiya* on the marginal notes of 'Abdul-Ghaffar. He died in the year A.D. 1656, A.H. 1066.

'Abdul-Halim bin-Muhammad (عبد الحلیم), surnamed "Kanalizāda," an Arabian author, who died in the year A.D. 1589, A.H. 997.

'Abdul - Hamid, *vide* Ahmad IV, emperor of Turkey.

'Abdul - Hamid of Lahore was the author of the *Pādshāh-nāma-i-Shāhjahāni*.

[Regarding this history, *vide* Dowson, *Elliot's History of India*, vii. p. 3.]

'Abdul - Hasan (Kazi), author of an Arabic work on Jurisprudence called *Ahkām-us-Sultānī*.

'Abdul-Hay (Mir) Sadr (عبد الحی صدر میر), a learned man who wrote a chronogram on the death of the emperor Humāyūn, and one on the accession of Akbar in A.D. 1556, A.H. 963.

[Vide *Āīn Translation* i. p. 480.]

'Abdul-Jalil (Mir or Sayyid) (عبد الجلیل بلگرامی میر), of Bilgrām in Audh. He was a great scholar and an elegant poet, and his poetical name was Wāsitī. In A.D. 1699, A.H. 1111, he visited the camp of Aurangzīb at Bījāpūr; and being presented to that monarch by Mīrzā 'Alī Beg, the royal intelligencer, obtained a mansab and jāgīr, with the joint offices of Bakhshī (Paymaster) and News-writer of Gujrāt; from which place he was removed to Bhakar in Sindh, with similar appointments. Through some intrigues at court, he was recalled from Bhakar in the reign of Farrukh-siyar in A.D. 1714, A.H. 1126, but upon circumstances being explained, he was restored in the most honourable manner, and was at length permitted to officiate by deputy, whilst he himself remained at Dehlī until A.D. 1721, A.H. 1133, when he resigned in favour of his son, Mīr Sayyid Muhammad. He was the son of Sayyid Ahmad of Bilgrām, was born on the 2nd June, A.D. 1661; 13th Shawwāl 1071, and died on Monday the 28th December, A.D. 1724; 23rd Rabbī' I. 1137; aged 66 lunar years, and is buried at Bilgrām close to his father's tomb. He is the author of several works, one of which containing letters written in Persian is called *Ādāb-ul-Mursilīn*.

[For a detailed biography, *vide* Āzād's *Sarw-i-Āzād*, and the *Tabsirat-un-Nāzirīn* by 'Abdul-Jalīl's son.]

'Abdul - Qadir (Sultan) was the descendant of a Marabaut family of the race of Hāshim, who trace their pedigree to the Khalīfas of the lineage of Fātima. His father died in 1834. His public career began at the time of the conquest of Algiers by the French. In 1847, he was defeated and surrendered himself, but was afterwards permitted to reside in Constantinople. He died in 1873.

'Abdul-Qadir bin-Abil-Wafa al-Misri (Shaikh Muhiy-Uddin) (عبد القادر بن ابی الوفا مصری شیخ محی الدین), author of the *Jawāhir-ul-Maziya fī Tabaqāt-il Hanafiya*, a biographical dictionary giving an account of the Hanafī lawyers, arranged in alphabetical order. He died in A.D. 1373, A.H. 775.

'Abdul-Qadir Badaoni (Shaikh) (عبد القادر بداؤنی شیخ) was the son of Mulūk Shāh of Badāon and pupil of Shaikh Mubārak of Nāgor. He is the author of a work called *Muntakab-ut-Tawārīkh*. He was a very learned man, and was frequently employed by the emperor Akbar to make translations into Persian from the Arabic and Sanskrit, as in the case of *Mu'jam-ul-Buldan, Jāmi-ur-Rashīdī*, and the *Rāmāyan*. He also composed a moral and religious work, entitled *Najāt-ur-Rashīd*, and translated two out of the eighteen Sections of the *Mahābhārat*, and made an abridgement of the *History of Kashmīr* in A.D. 1591, A.H. 999. The year of his death is not known, but he was living in A.D. 1596, A.H. 1004, in which year he completed the *Muntakhab-ut-Tawārīkh*. His poetical name was Qādirī.

[He died at Badāon, in 1004. For a detailed biography, vide *Jour. As. Sc.*, Bengal, 1869, pt. i. p. 118; and Dowson, v. p. 477.]

'Abdul-Qadir Suhrawardi (عبد القادر سہروردی), author of the work called *Ādāb-ul-Murid*.

'Abdul - Qadir Bedil (Mirza) (عبد القادر بیدل مرزا), a celebrated poet, better known by his poetical name of Bedil or Mirzā Bedil. He was a Tartar of the tribe of Birlās; in his youth he was employed by prince A'zam Shāh, son of Aurangzīb, but being one day ordered by the prince to write a panegyric in his praise, he resigned the service and never afterwards served any one. He is the author of several works, such as *Muhīt A'zam; Chār 'Unsur; Inshā-i-Bedil,* also called *Ruq'āt-i-Bedil*; and of a Dīwān or book of Odes in Persian, containing 20,000 couplets. He died in the commencement of the reign of Muhammad Shāh, on the 24th November, O.S. 1720; 4th Ṣafar, A.H. 1133. He is also the author of a work called *Nukāt-i-Bedil*, containing the memoirs of Shaikh Junaid, third in descent from the celebrated Shaikh Ṣafī, and grandfather of Shāh Ismā'īl Ṣafavi, king of Persia.

[*Vide* Sprenger, *Catalogue of Oudh MSS.*, p. 379.]

'Abdul-Qadir Gilani or Jilani or Jili (Shaikh), also called Pīr-i-Dastgīr and Ghauṣ-ul-A'zam Muḥiy-ud-dīn, a saint, who is said to have performed a number of miracles during his lifetime. He was born in Gīlān or Jīlān in Persia, in the year A.D. 1078, A.H. 471, and was greatly revered for his learning, his piety, and the sanctity of his manners. He died on the 22nd February, A.D. 1166, 17th Rabi' II. 561, aged 91 lunar years, and is buried at Baghdād, where he held the place of guardian of Abū-Hanīfa's tomb. The order of Dervishes, called after him the Qādirīs acknowledge him as founder. His tomb is held in high veneration amongst the Muhammadans. He is said to have written many books on Mystical Theology, amongst which are the *Futūḥ-ul-Ghaib, Malfūzāt-i-Qādirī* in Arabic, and a translation of the same in Persian, named *Malfuzāt-i-Jīlāni*. Another work of his in Arabic on Jurisprudence is called *Ghunyat-ut-Ṭālibīn*, and another work on Sufism is entitled *Bahjat-ul-Asrār*, and a book of Odes called *Dīwān-i-Ghauṣ-ul-A'zam*.

[*Vide* Muhammad Qāsim (Sayyid) and Abdāls.]

Some say that he was born at Jīl, a village near Baghdād; hence he should be called Jīlī.

'Abdul-Qadir (Maulana) (عبد القادر دهلوی مولانا), of Dehlī, the son of Maulawī Walī-ullah. He is the author of an Urdū commentary on the Qurān, entitled *Tafsīr Mūziḥ-ul-Qurān*. He made an Urdū translation of the Qurān, which was finished 1803.

[*Vide* Abdullah Sāyyid.]

'Abdul-Qadir Naini (Maulana) (عبد القادر نائینی), a poet who was a native of Nāīn near Iṣfahān, and contemporary with Shaikh Sa'dī.

'Abdul-Qadir, a resident of Devi, a village in the district of Lucknow. From the *Jāmi'-ut-Tawārikh of Rashīd-uddīn* he translated that portion which is called the book of Patanjalī into easy Persian, at the request of Major Herbert, in May, 1823. It is a collection of all the sciences, and one of the most valuable works of the sages of Hind. It contains an account of their various sects, and the history of their ancient kings, also the life of Sākyamuni.

'Abdul-Qahir Jurjani (Shaikh) (عبد القاهر جرجانی), son of 'Abdur-Rahmān, was the author of the book called *Da ăil-ul-I'jaz*, and several other works. He died in A.D. 1081, A.H. 474.

'Abdul-Karim (عبد الكريم), surnamed Imām-uddīn Abul-Qāsim, author of the *Sharh Kabīr* and *Sharḥ Ṣaghīr*.

'Abdul-Karim bin-Muhammad al-Hamadani, author of a Persian Commentary on the Sirājiya of Sajāwandī, entitled *Farāiz-ut-Tājī Sharḥ Farāiz-is-Sirājī*.

'Abdul-Karim Sindhi (Mulla) (عبد الكريم سندهی), a native of Sindh who served under Khwāja Mahmūd Gāwān in the Deccan, and was living about the year A.D. 1481, A.H. 886. He is the author of the history of Sulṭān Mahmūd Bahmanī, entitled *Tārīkh-i-Mahmūd-Shāhi*.

'Abdul-Karim, a native of Dehlī, who accompanied Nādir Shah to Persia, and wrote a history of that conqueror about the year A.D. 1754, A.H. 1168, entitled *Bayān-i-Wāqi*.

[Regarding this work, *vide* Dowson, *Elliot's History of India*, viii. p. 124.]

'Abdul-Karim, Mīr, of Bukhārā, who died at Constantinople about A.H. 1246, A.D. 1830. He is the author of a history of Afghānistān and Turkistān (A.D. 1740 to 1818), translated into French by C. Schefer, Paris, 1876.]

'Abdul-Karim, Munshi, who died about thirty years ago. He is the author of the *Tārīkh-i-Ahmad*, a history of Ahmad Shah Durrānī and his successors. The Persian text was lithographed in 1266, and an Urdū translation under the title of *Wāqi'āt-i-Durrānī* was issued at Kānhpūr in A.H. 1292 (A.D. 1875). 'Abdul-Karim also wrote a larger work, entitled *Muhāraba-i-Kābul o Qandahār* (H. 1265), which contains the heroic deeds of Akbar Khān, son of Dost Muhammad Khān, and is chiefly based on the Akbar-nāma written in verse by Munshī Qāsim Jān; and the *Tārīkh-i-Panjāb tuhfatan lil-aḥbāb* (A.H. 1265) on the Sikh wars.

'Abdul - Quddus Gangohi (Shaikh) (عبد القدوس گنگوهی شیخ), a native of Gangoh, near Dehlī, was a descendant of Abū-Ḥanīfa Kūfa, and a famous saint of India. He died on the 27th November, A.D. 1537, 23rd Jumāda II. A.H. 944, the chronogram of the year of his death being "Shaikh-i-ajall." His grandson Shaikh 'Abdun-Nabī held a high post in the reign of Akbar, but was subsequently imprisoned and murdered.

'Abdullah (عبدالله بن عبد المطلب), the father of Muhammad the Prophet, was a younger son of 'Abdul-Muttalib the son of Hāshim. He was remarkable for his beauty, and though a driver of camels, he is said to have possessed such merits, that his hand was solicited in marriage by the fairest and the most virtuous of the women of his tribe. He was so universally admired, that on the night of his nuptials one hundred young females expired in despair. His wife Āmina, though long barren, at last became the mother of Muhammad. 'Abdullah died during the lifetime of his father, eight days (some say eight years) after the birth of his son, and left his widow and infant son in very mean circumstances, his whole substance consisting of only five camels and one female Ethiopian slave. 'Abdul-Muttalib, his father was therefore obliged to take care of his grandson Muhammad, which he did and at his death enjoined his eldest son Abū-Tālib to provide for him for the future. 'Abdullah died about the year A.D. 571.

'Abdullah bin-'Ali al-Halabi was one of the first writers on Shīfa jurisprudence, as he was amongst the earliest compilers to the traditions of that sect. It does not appear that any of his legal compositions are extant.

'Abdullah (عبدالله بن رواحه), son of Rawāḥa, was an Arabian poet, who signalized himself in arms as well as poetry. He became an associate of Muhammad and was sent with the army, of which Zaid was the chief, against the Greeks, and was killed at Mūta in Syria with Zaid and Ja'far the brother of 'Alī, in A.D. 629, A.H. 8.

'Abdullah, son of Zubair (عبدالله بن زبیر) was a Musalmān born at Madīna amongst those who were called "Muhājirīn," that is to say, fugitives from Mecca. After the battle of Karbalā in A.D. 680, in which Husain the son of 'Alī was slain, the inhabitants of Mecca and Madīna, perceiving that Yazīd did all that lay in his power to suppress the house of 'Alī, made an insurrection against Yazīd, the second khalīfa of the house of Umayya, and proclaimed 'Abdullah khalīfa in the city of Mecca. The Musalmāns of Syria also, after the death of Yazīd and Mu'āwiya the 2nd, acknowledged him for the space of 128 days, after which time Marwān the son of Ḥakam was proclaimed khalīfa in the city of Damascus. 'Abdullah still remaining in the city of Mecca, was besieged there in A.D. 691, A.H. 72, by Ḥajjāj, general of the khalīfa 'Abdul-Malik. The siege lasted 8 months and 17 days, after which 'Abdullah made a sally upon the enemy, destroyed a great number of them with his own hand, and was at length killed fighting valiantly in A.D. 692, A.H. 73. His head was cut off and sent to the khalīfa 'Abdul-Malik.

'Abdullah (عبدالله بن مسعود), son of Mas'ūd, companion of Muhammad. He died in A.D. 652, A.H. 32.

'Abdullah (عبدالله بن عباس), son of 'Abbās, the uncle of Muhammad, was distinguished as a teacher of the sacred book. Before he was ten years of age, he is said to have received inspiration from the angel Gabriel. He was born in A.D. 619, three years before the Hijra (622), and was considered the ablest interpreter of the Qurān then in existence. He was appointed governor of Basra, by the khalīfa 'Alī, and remained there for some time. He then returned to Ḥijāz, and died at Ṭāyif, a town lying 60 miles eastward of Mecca, in A.D. 687, A.H. 68, aged 70 years. His mother Umm-ul-Fazl was the sister of Maimūna, one of the wives of Muhammad.

'Abdullah (عبدالله بن عمر), son of 'Umar the second khalīfa after Muhammad, was one of the most learned Arabians amongst the contemporaries of Muhammad. He died in A.D. 692, A.H. 73. He is famous for his liberality.

'Abdullah (عبدالله بن يزيد), son of Yazīd, was celebrated as a lawyer in the 7th century. He was the disciple of Abū-Huraira and Abū-'Abbas, companions of Muhammad, and lived till the hundredth year of the Hijra, or A.D. 718, A.H. 100.

'Abdullah (عبدالله بن علی), the son of 'Alī, son of 'Abdullah, son of 'Abbās, the uncle of Muhammad, was the uncle of the first two khalīfas of the Abbasides, viz., Abul-'Abbās al-Saffāḥ and Al-Manṣūr, under whom he served as general against the khalifa Marwān, and having vanquished that prince, proclaimed his nephew Al-Saffāḥ. He was guilty of horrible cruelties on the family of the Ommaides. When his eldest nephew died, his brother Al-Manṣūr took upon him the government, which displeased 'Abdullah so much, that he raised an army against him, but was defeated and afterwards perfidiously murdered in A.D. 754, A.H. 137.

'Abdullah (عبدالله بن راوند), the son of Rāwand, was the founder of an impious sect, who were called after him the Rāwandites, during the Khilāfat of Al-Manṣūr the Abbaside, about the year A.D. 776.

'Abdullah (عبدالله), the son of Shams-uddīn, author of the marginal notes on the *Talwīḥ*, entitled *Ḥāshiya bar Talwīḥ*, a work on jurisprudence.

'Abdullah (عبدالله بن طاهر), the son of Ṭāhir, the general of Al-Māmūn. He succeeded his brother Ṭalḥa in the government of Khurāsān about the year A.D. 828, A.H. 213, reigned 17 years, and died in A.D. 844, A.H. 230. He was succeeded by his son Ṭāhir II.

'Abdullah (عبدالله بن طيب السرخسى), the son of Tayyib al-Sarakhsī, preceptor to the Khalīfa Mu'tazid Billah, by whom he was put to death A.D. 899, A.H. 286. He is the author of the *Bahr-ul-Mantiq*, and *Isāghjī* (a commentary on the *Isagoge* of Porphyras).

'Abdullah (عبدالله بن عدى), the son of 'Adiy, author of the *Kitāb Kāmil*. He died in A.D. 975, A.H. 365.

'Abdullah, author of a collection of Letters, entitled *Inshā-i-'Abdullah*.

'Abdullah (عبدالله بن مسلم بن قتيبه), the son of Muslim, the son of Qutaiba, was the author of the work called *Kitab-ul-ma'ārif*, and several other works. He died in A.D. 889, A.H. 276.

'Abdullah (عبدالله), author of the Persian work on jurisprudence, called *Aḥkām us-Ṣalāt*.

'Abdullah (عبدالله كلبرگى), of Kulbarga, author of a work called *Fars-nāma*, written in A.D. 1407.

'Abdullah (Maulana) (عبدالله مولانا), son of Ilahdād. He is the author of *Sharḥ Mīzān-il-Mantiq*, and several other works. He was a native of Dehlī, flourished in the reign of Sulṭān Sikandar, and died in A.D. 1516, A.H. 923.

'Abdullah (Maulana), of Sulṭānpūr, a learned bigoted Sunnī at Akbar's Court. He had the title of "Makhdum-ul-Mulk." He played a prominent part in the religious discussions which led Akbar to renounce Islām. He died, or was poisoned, in A.H. 990.

[Vide *Āīn Translation*, p. 544, and p. vii. of *Abub-Fazl's Biography*.]

'Abdullah (عبدالله بن سلام), the son of Salām, author of the questions which Muhammad was asked on the subject of his prophecy. He is also the author of a work called *'Azmat-ul-Manqūl*. Another work, called *Hazār Masāyil*, is ascribed to him.

'Abdullah (عبدالله بن محمد), son of Muhammad, surnamed Qalānisī, an Arabian author. He died in A.D. 1121, A.H. 515.

'Abdullah (عبدالله ابن اليافعى شافعى), the son of 'Al-Yāfi'ī Shāfi'ī, author of the Arabic work called *Rauzat-ur-Rayāḥ n*, containing a detailed account of the lives of Muhammad, the twelve Imāms, and of all the saints of Arabia, Persia, and Hindūstān.

'Abdullah Abu-Muslim (عبدالله ابو مسلم), author of the Commentary on the Qurān, called *Ṣaḥīḥ Muslim*. He was born in A.D. 817, A.H. 202, and died in the year A.D. 875, A.H. 261. He is called by some writers Abul-Husain Muslim bin-al-Ḥajjāj bin Muslim al-Qushairī, and by others Muslim bin-Ḥajjāj Nīshāpūrī, which see.

'Abdullah Ahrar (عبدالله احرار), author of the *Malfū-zūt-i-Khwāja 'Abdullah*, containing the doctrines of the Naqshbandīs, and of the *Anīs-us-Sālikīn*.

'Abdullah Ansari (Khwaja) (عبدالله انصاري), surnamed Shaikh Abū Ismā'īl, the son of Abū-Manṣūr, the son of Abū-Ayyūb. He was born at Hirāt in May, A.D. 1006, Sha'bān, A.H. 396, and is the founder of the sect called 'Anṣārīs in Hirāt and Khurāsān. He died on the 2nd July, A.D. 1088, 9th Rabī' I. A.H. 481, aged 84 lunar years, and is buried at Hirāt, in a place called Gāzurgāh. 'Abdullah was struck with stones by the boys when he was doing penance, and expired.

'Abdullah bin-'Ali bin-Abu-Shu'ba al-Halabi (عبدالله بن على بن ابو شعبه الحلبى). One of the earliest writers both on the Ḥadṣī and Law of the Imāmiya sect. His grandfather, Abū-Shu'ba, is related to have collected traditions in the time of the Imāms Hasan and Husain. 'Abdullah wrote down these traditions, and presented his work, when completed, to the Imām Ja'far Ṣādiq, by whom it is said to have been verified and corrected.

'Abdullah bin-'Ali, author of the work called *Sīrak-ul-Hind*, which he paraphrased from the Persian into the Arabic, for it had been originally translated from Sanskrit into the Persian.

'Abdullah bin-Fazl-ullah, of Shīrāz, author of the *Tārīkh-i-Waṣṣāf.*

[The first four volumes of this work, which may be looked upon as a continuation of the *Jahān-kushā'*, go as far as Sha'bān, 690 (March, 1300). Subsequently, the author added a fifth volume which relates the events down to the year 728 (A.D. 1328); vide *Elliot's History of India*, iii. p. 24. 'ABDULLAH is also the name of the author of the *Tārīkh-i-Dāūdī*, an Afghān History, written during the reign of Jahāngīr; *vide* Dowson, iv. p. 434.]

'Abdullah Hatifi, *vide* Hātifī.

'Abdullah Khan Uzbak (عبدالله خان أزبک) was a renowned officer in the time of Akbar. He was made governor of Mandū (Mālwā) in A.D. 1562, and afterwards rebelled against the king, but was defeated and compelled to leave the country.

[For further notes, vide *Āīn Translation*, i. p. 320.]

'Abdullah Khan (عبدالله خان أزبک), chief of the Uzbaks, was the son of Sikandar Khān, the son of Jānī Beg Khān, a descendant of Jūjī Khān, son of Chingiz Khan. After the death of his father (during whose life he had several battles with him), he ascended the throne of Samarqand and Bukhārā in A.D. 1582, A.H. 990, invaded Khurāsān, and took Hirāt after a siege of nine months in A.D. 1585, A.H. 993. Its governor, 'Alī Qulī Khan, with several other chiefs were put to death, and the city was plundered. He was contemporary with Shāh 'Abbas of Persia and Akbar Shāh, and died after a reign of 15 years, aged 66, on the 12th February, A.D. 1597, 5th Rajab A.H. 1005. The chronogram of the year of his death is "qiyāmat qāyim shud." He was succeeded by his son 'Abdul-Mūmin Khān.

'Abdullah Khan Firuz-Jang (عبدالله خان فیروز جنگ), a descendant of Khwāja 'Abdullah Aḥrār. He came to India in the latter end of the reign of the emperor Akbar, was raised to the rank of 6000 by the emperor Jahāngīr, and died in the time of Shāh Jahān, A.D. 1644, 17th Shawwāl 1054, aged nearly 70 years.

'Abdullah Khan (Sayyid) (عبدالله خان سید), styled Quṭbul-Mulk, was governor of Allāhābād from the time of Bahādur Shāh, emperor of Dehlī, and his younger brother Sayyid Husain 'Alī Khān, that of Bihār. These brothers sprung from a numerous and respected family of the descendants of the prophet, who were settled in the town of Bārha, and in consequence of this origin, they are best known in India by the name of Sādāt, or Sayyids, of Bārha. Farrukh-siyar, who by the aid of these two brothers had ascended the throne of Dehlī, on his accession in January, A.D. 1713, A.H. 1125, made the former his prime minister, with the title of Quṭb-ul-Mulk, and appointed the latter Amīr-ul-Umarā. Husain 'Alī Khān was assassinated by Mīr Ḥaidar Khān, at the instigation of the emperor Muhammad Shāh, on the 18th September, O.S. 1720, 27th Ẕil-qa'da 1132, and his brother, 'Abdullah Khān, who made some resistance, was defeated and taken prisoner on the 4th November following, 14th Muḥarram 1133, and died in confinement, after three years, on the 19th September, O.S. 1723, 30th Ẕil-ḥijja 1135. The remains of Husain 'Alī Khān were transferred to Ajmīr for burial. His brother 'Abdullah was buried at Dehlī.

[Regarding the Sayyids of Bārha, vide *Āīn Translation*, i. p. 390; and for 'Abdullah Quṭb-ul-Mulk, *vide* Dowson, vii. 447ff.]

'Abdullah Qutb-Shah (عبدالله قطب شاه), the sixth Sulṭān of the Qutb-Shāhī dynasty of Golkonda in Ḥaidarābād, Deccan. He succeeded Muhammad Quṭb-Shāh, and reigned many years under the protection of the emperor Shāh Jahān, to whom he acknowledged himself tributary, and paid an annual sum; but in the year A.D. 1656, A.H. 1066, he displeased that monarch, and brought upon himself much trouble. The emperor had commanded him to permit his prime minister, Mīr Muhammad Sa'īd, and his son Muhammad Amīn, to repair with their effects to court. Quṭb-Shah disobeyed the mandate, and confining Muhammad Amīn, then at Ḥaidarābād, seized part of his wealth. The prince Aurangzīb, then governor of the imperial territories in the Deccan, enraged at this conduct, marched to Ḥaidarābād, which he took and plundered. 'Abdullah was obliged to purchase pardon by a contribution of a crore of Rupees, and the gift of his daughter in marriage to the son of his enemy, the prince Sulṭān Muhammad. From this time 'Abdullah, during the remainder of his life, was, in fact, a vassal of the empire. 'Abdullah Quṭb-Shāh died in June, A.D. 1674, Rabī I., A.H. 1085, and was succeeded by his son-in-law, Abul-Hasan.

'Abdullah Mansur (عبدالله منصور), author of the *Tarjama-i-Ṭabaqāt-i-Sūfiya*, containing the lives of the most celebrated Ṣūfīs and Shaikhs.

'Abdullah Mirza (عبدالله مرزا) was the son of Ibrāhīm Mirzā, the son of Shāhrukh Mirzā, and great-grandson of Amīr Timur. Upon his father's death (about the year A.D. 1443), he became possessed of the sovereignty of Fārs, or Persia; but, four years after, he was dispossessed by one of his cousins-german, named Mirzā Abū-Sa'īd, and was obliged to fly to his uncle Mirzā Ulugh Beg, who then reigned in Transoxiana, and who gave him his daughter in marriage. Some time after, Ulugh Beg having been defeated in a battle against his son Mirzā 'Abdul-Laṭīf, and afterwards put to death by him in October, A.D. 1449, Ramaẓān, A.H. 853, and the latter not enjoying the success of his parricide above six months, 'Abdullah, as son-in-law to Ulugh Beg, took possession of his dominions; but Mirzā Abū-Sa'īd, his cousin-german, declared war against him, and defeated him in a pitched battle, in which he perished. This event took place in the year A.D. 1451, A.H. 855.

'Abdullah Sayyid, son of Bahādur 'Alī, a native of Sawāna, near Thanesar, and a prominent disciple of Sayyid Ahmad (*q.v.*), under whose inspiration he published Abdul Kādīr's Urdu version of the Korān, with commentary, 1822.

'Abdullah Shattari (Shaikh) (عبدالله شطاری), a descendant of Shaikh Shihāb-uddin Suhrawardī. He came from Persia to India, and died in Mālwā, A.D. 1406, A.H. 809, and is buried there.

[Regarding the Shaṭṭārīs vide *Jour. As. Soc. Bengal*, 1874, pt. i. p. 216.]

'Abdullah Tamimi (عبدالله تمیمی), author of the Arabic work called *Rauẓat-ul-Abrār*, which contains the history of Muhammad, and Memoirs of many of his companions.

'Abdullah Tirmizi (Mir) (عبدالله ترمذي) was an elegant poet and wrote an excellent Nasta'līq hand, for which he received from the emperor Jahāngīr the poetical name of Wasfī, or praiseworthy, and the title of Mushkīn-Qalam, that is to say, out of whose pen flowed musk. He is the author of several poems. His death happened in the year A.D. 1626, A.H. 1035. His tomb stands at a place in Agra, called Naglā Jawāhir.

[For the inscription on his tomb, and his son Muhammad Ṣāliḥ Kashfī, vide *Proc. As. Soc. Bengal*, 1874, p. 162.]

'Abdul-Latif (عبد اللطيف), a cele-brated physician born at Baghdād, A.D. 1261, A.H. 660. To the acquirement of medical knowledge, he applied himself with diligence; and it was chiefly with this view that, in his 28th year, he left Baghdād in order to visit other countries. Having spent a year in Mauṣil, he removed to Damascus in Syria and thence to Egypt, where the people of the highest rank continued to vie with each other in cultivating his friendship. He afterwards travelled to Aleppo, and resided several years in Greece. Of 150 treatises which he composed on various subjects, only one, entitled *Historiæ Ægypti Compendium*, has survived the ravages of time. He died suddenly at Baghdād in his 65th year.

'Abdul-Latif (عبد اللطيف), a great-grandson of Amīr Timur. In October A.D. 1449, he defeated his father Mirzā Ulugh Beg in an action near Samarqand, took him prisoner and put him to death. He did not long enjoy his success, for he had scarcely reigned six months, when he was murdered by his own soldiers on the 9th May, 1450, 26th Rabī I. A.H. 854. His head was separated from his body and sent to Hirāt, where it was placed on the gate of the college built by his father.

'Abdul-Latif (عبد اللطيف), a native of Qazwīn, and author of the work entitled *Lubb-ut-Tawārīkh*, a history of Persia, written in the middle of the 16th century.

'Abdul-Latif (Mulla) (عبد اللطيف ملا) of Sulṭānpūr, was the tutor of the prince Auranzīb. In the last years of his life he became blind, received from the emperor Shāh Jahān a few villages free of rent for his support, and died in the year A.D. 1632, A.H. 1042.

'Abdul-Latif, author of a collection of Letters called *Inshā-i-'Abdul-Laṭif*.

'Abdul-Latif (عبد اللطيف), author of the work called *Laṭāif-i-Ma'nawī*, a commentary on the difficult passages of the Masnawī or Maulānā Rūm, written in A.D. 1640. He also is the author of a Dictionary called *Laṭāif-ul-Lughāt*.

[Regarding the author vide *Jour. As. Soc.* for 1868, p. 32.]

'Abdul-Maal (عبد المعال), author of a system of Geography, written in the Persian Language, and entitled *Masāḥat ul-Arẓ*, or the survey of the earth.

'Abdul-Majid Khan (عبد المجيد), the Turkish emperor of Constantinople, was born on the 23rd April, 1823, and succeeded his father Mahmūd II. on the 2nd July, A.D. 1839, A.H. 1277. He died on the 25th June, 1861, aged 39 years, and was succeeded by his brother 'Abdul-'Azīz.

'Abdul-Majid Khan (عبدالمجيد خان), entitled Majd-ud daula, a nobleman who was promoted by Ahmad Shāh of Dehlī to the post of 3rd Bakhshigarī or paymastership, in A.D. 1748, A.H. 1161. He died in the year 1752, A.H. 1165.

'Abdul-Majid (Shaikh) (عبد المجيد شيخ), a learned man who flourished in the time of Shāh Jahān, and wrote a history of that emperor entitled *Shāh Jahān-nāma*.

[This seems to be a mistake for 'Abdul-Ḥamīd.]

'Abdul-Malik (عبد الملک بن مروان), the son of Marwān I. and the 5th Khalīfa of the house of Umayya (Ommaides). He succeeded his father at Damascus, on the 13th April, A.D. 685, 3rd Ramaẓān, A.H. 65, surpassed his predecessors in military exploits, and extended his power as far as Spain in the west, and India in the east. He was so generous as not to take a church from the Christians, which they had refused to grant him when he requested it. He was called Abul-Ẓubāb or "father of flies," because his breath was so offensive, that it killed the very flies that settled on his lips. He reigned upwards of 21 lunar years and died in October, A.D. 705, Shawwāl, A.H. 86. He was succeeded by Walīd I. the eldest of his sixteen sons, who greatly extended the Moslem dominions.

'Abdul-Malik (عبد الملک بن صالح), the son of Ṣaliḥ, the son of 'Abdullah, the son of 'Abbās, was related in blood to the prophet Muhammad; was invested by Hārūn-ur-Rashīd, the Khalīfa of Baghdad, with the government of Egypt, in which he continued till about the year A.D. 794, A.H. 178, when Harūn, suspecting that he was engaged in some cabals, in order to obtain the empire, threw him into prison, where he remained till Hārūn's death. His son released him, and invested him with the govern-of Syria, A.D. 809, A.H. 193.

'Abdul-Malik (عبد الملک ابن ظهر), the son of Ẓuhr, an eminent Arabian physician, commonly called by Europeans Avenzur, a corruption of Ibn-Ẓuhr. His full name is Abū-Marwān 'Abdul-Malik ibn-Ẓuhr. He flourished about the end of the 11th or the beginning of the 12th century. He was of noble descent, and born at Sevilla, the capital of Andalusia, where he exercised his profession with great reputation. His grandfather and father were both physicians. It is said that he lived to the age of 135; that he began to practice at 40 or, as others say, at 20; and had the advantage of a longer experience than almost any one ever had, for he enjoyed perfect health to his last hour. He left a son, also known by the name of Ibn-Ẓuhr, who followed his father's profession, was in great favour with Al-Manṣūr, emperor of Morocco, and wrote several treatises on physic. Avenzur wrote a book, entitled *Tayassur fi-l-mudāwāt wat-tadbīr*, which is much esteemed. This work was translated into Hebrew in A.D. 1280, and thence into Latin by Paravicius, whose version has had several editions. The author added a supplement to it, under the title of *Jāmi'*, or Collection. He also wrote a treatise *Fil-adwiyat wal-aghziyat*, *i.e.*, of medicines and food, wherein he treats of their qualities. Ibn-Ẓuhr was contemporary with Ibn-Rashīd (Averroes), who more than once gives him a very high and deserved encomium, calling him admirable, glorious, the treasure of all knowledge, and the most supreme in medicine from the time of Galen to his own.

'Abdul-Malik (عبد الملک), king of Fez and Morocco, was dethroned by his nephew Muhammad, but he afterwards defeated Sebastian, king of Portugal, who had landed in Africa to support the usurper. The two African monarchs and Sebastian fell on the field, A.D. 1578 (A.H. 986).

'Abdul-Malik (Khwaja), a native of Samarqand who held the office of Shaikh-ul-Islām in that city in the reign of Amīr Timur.

'Abdul-Malik Samani I. (عبد الملک سامانی), a king of the house of Sāmān, and son of Amīr Nūḥ I., whom he succeeded in A.D. 954 (A.H. 343). He reigned in Khurāsān and Māwarān-nahr seven and a half years, and was killed by a fall from his horse while playing at ball in A.D. 961 (A.H 350). He was succeeded by his brother Amīr Manṣūr I.

'Abdul-Malik Samani II. (عبد الملک سامانی), an Amīr of the house of Sāmān, was elevated to the throne of Khurāsān, after his brother Amīr Manṣūr II. in A.D. 998 (A.H. 388). He was the last Amīr, or king, of the race of the Samanides. He reigned only a few months, and was defeated in battle against Sulṭān Mahmūd of Ghaznī in A.D. 999, who took possession of his country. 'Abdul-Malik was shortly after murdered.

'Abdul-Manaf (عبد المناف), or 'Abd-Manāf, (*i.e.* slave of the idol Manāf) the great-great-grandfather of Muhammad, was the son of Quṣayy, who aggrandised the tribe of the Quraish by purchasing the keys of the Ka'ba from Abū-Ghassān, a weak and silly man, for a bottle of wine. Quṣayy was succeeded by his second son 'Abdul-Manāf, to whom the prophetic light, which is said to have manifested itself in his face, gave the right of primogeniture. After his death his son Hāshim, the father of 'Abdul-Muttalib, succeeded.

['ABD-MANĀF is also the name of a son of the Prophet, who died in infancy.]

'Abdul-Mannan (Mir) (عبد المنان میر), son of Mīr Nu'mān Khān, son of Khwāja 'Abdur-Raḥīm Khān of Andijān. He served under the celebrated Niẓām-ul-Mulk Āṣaf-Jāh in the Deccan for several years, was an excellent poet, and is known under the poetical name of 'Ibrat.

'Abdul-Mumin (عبد المومن), a man of obscure origin and son of a potter, who seized the crown of Morocco, after destroying the royal family. He extended his dominions by the conquest of Tunis, Fez, and Tremezen. He meditated the invasion of Spain, when death stopped his career in A.D. 1156. His son Yūsuf who succeeded him, carried his ambitions into effect.

'Abdul-Mumin Khan (عبد المومن خان), the son of 'Abdullah Khān, chief of the Uzbaks, was raised to the throne after the death of his father at Samarqand in the year A.D. 1597, A.H. 1005. He took Mashad and put the inhabitants to the sword. He was soon after assassinated by his own officers in A.D. 1598, A.H. 1006; the chronogram of his death being contained in the words "Badbakht-i-sar-burīda." After his death, Dīn Muhammad Khan, the son of 'Abdullah Khān's sister, was placed on the throne; but he fell shortly after, in a battle fought at Hirāt, against Shāh 'Abbas, king of Persia.

'Abdul-Muttalib (عبد المطلب), the grandfather of Muhammad, the son of Hāshim of the tribe of Quraish. He is said to have been extremely affable and easy of access, as well as just and generous. The well which God shewed Hagar the mother of Ishmael, in the wilderness, is said to have been miraculously discovered to 'Abdul-Muṭṭalib, about five hundred years after it had been filled up by 'Amr, prince of the Jorhomites. The well is called Zamzam by the Arabs and is on the east side of the Ka'ba, covered with a small building and cupola. Its water is highly reverenced, being not only received with particular devotion by the pilgrims, but also sent in bottles as a great rarity to most parts of the Muhammadan dominions. 'Abdul-Muṭṭalib had ten sons whose names are as follows: Abū-Tālib, the father of 'Alī; 'Abbās, the ancestor of the Abbasides who reigned at Baghdād; Ḥamza; Hāriṣ; Abū-Lahab; Abdullah, the father of Muhammad; Al-Maqawwam; Zubair; Zirār; Quṣam. His younger son 'Abdullah, the father of Muhammad, dying eight days after the birth of his son, 'Abdul-Muṭṭalib was obliged to take care of his grandson Muhammad, which he not only did during his life, but at his death enjoined his eldest son Abū-Ṭalib to provide for him for the future. 'Abdul-Muṭṭalib died about the year A.D. 579, at which time Muhammad was about eight years old.

'Abdul-Nabi (Shaikh) (عبد النبي شيخ), son of Shaikh Ahmad, and grandson of Shaikh 'Abdul-Quddūs of Gangoh. He was the tutor of the Emperor Akbar, and was honoured with the post of Ṣadr-us-Ṣadūr (Chief Justice). No Ṣadr during any former reign had so much favour. The Emperor was for some time so intimate and unceremonious with him that he would rise to adjust the Shaikh's slippers when he took his leave. At last, through the enmity of Maulānā 'Abdullah Makhdūm-ul-Mulk (*vide* p. 6) and others, he fell in Akbar's estimation, and began to be treated very differently. He was banished to Mecca, and after his return was murdered in the year A.D. 1583 (A.H. 991).

[Vide *'Āīn Translation*, i. pp. 538, 546, and p. xiii *(Abul-Fazl's Biography)*; and *Proc. As. Soc. Bengal*, January, 1876.]

'Abdul-Nabi Khan served under Aurangzīb, and built the large Mosque at Mathurā.

[Vide *Proc. As. Soc. Bengal*, 1873, p. 12.]

'Abdul-Rahim bin-Ahmad Sur (عبد الرحيم بن احمد سور), author of the Persian Dictionary *Kashf-ul-Lughāt*.

[Vide *Jour. As. Soc. Bengal*, for 1868, p. 9.]

'Abdul-Rahim Khan (عبد الرحيم خان خان خانان), Khān Khānān, commonly called Khān Mirzā, was the son of Bairām Khān, the first prime-minister of the emperor Akbar. He was born on the 17th December, A.D. 1556 (14th Ṣafar A.H. 964) and was only four years old when his father was assassinated. When of age, he received a command in the force attached to the emperor's person. In 1584 he was one of the commanders of the army sent to Gujarāt, and on the conclusion of the campaign, was made head of the army. On Todar Mal's death (1589) he was made prime-minister. His daughter Jānī Begam was married to prince Dānyāl in the year A.D. 1599 (A.H. 1007). He translated the *Wāqi'āt-i-Bābarī* (Memoirs of the emperor Bābar) from Turkī into Persian. After Akbar's death he served under Jahāngīr for 21 years, and died a few months before that emperor, shortly after the suppression of Mahābat Khān's rebellion, in the year A.D. 1627 (A.H. 1036), aged 72 lunar years, and lies buried at Dehlī near the Dargāh of Shaikh Niẓām-uddīn Auliyā, where his tomb is to be seen to this day. His poetical name was Raḥīm.

[For a detailed biography, vide *Āīn Translation*, i. p. 334.]

'Abdul-Rahim (عبد الرحيم), one of the principal nobles who joined Prince Khusrau in his rebellion against his father Jahāngīr in A.D. 1606. He was taken prisoner with the prince and brought to the emperor at Lāhor; by whose order he was sewn up in the raw hide of an ass, kept constantly moist with water, in which miserable condition he remained twenty-four hours. He was afterwards pardoned.

[Vide *Āīn Translation*, i. p. 455.]

'Abdul-Rahim Khan (Khwaja) (عبد الرحيم خان خواجه), the son of Abul-Qāsim. He was a native of Andijān in Farghāna, came to India in the reign of the emperor Shāh Jahān, and served under Aurangzīb for several years. He died in A.D. 1692 (A.H. 1103.)

'Abdul-Rahman (عبد الرحمن ابن ملجم), the son of Muljim, the murderer of 'Alī, son-in-law of Muhammad. He was killed by Hasan, son of 'Alī, in January, A.D. 661 (Ramazān A.H. 40).

[No Shī'a would now-a-days call his son 'Abd-ul Rahmān, just as no orthodox Muhammadan would call his son Yazīd.]

'Abdul-Rahman (عبد الرحمن ابن ابوبكر), the son of Abū-Bakr, first Khalīfa after Muhammad, and brother to 'Āyisha, the favourite wife of the prophet. He died in the same year that his sister died, *i.e.*, in A.D. 678, A.H. 58.

'Abdul-Rahman (عبد الرحمن بن محمد حنيف), the son of Muhammad Hanīf son of 'Alī. He raised a formidable power against Hajjāj, the governor of Arabia, defeated him in several battles, and at last, rather than fall into his hands, threw himself from a house and died, A.D. 701, A.H. 82.

'Abdul-Rahman, a popular Afghān poet of Peshāwar. His verses are written with fiery energy, which has made them popular amongst a martial people, and yet with natural simplicity which is charming to the lover of poetry. Not far from the city is his grave, situated on the road to Hazārkhāna, the poet's native village.

'Abdul-Rahman (عبد الرحمن), a Saracen general of the Khalīfa Hishām (called by some of our authors Abderames) who penetrated into Aquitain and Poitou, and was at last defeated and slain by Charles Martel near Poiters, in A.D. 732, A.H. 114.

'Abdul-Rahman Mustafa (عبد الرحمن مصطفى), who in Watkin's Biographical Dictionary is called Babacauschi, was muftī of the city of Caffa, in Tauris. He wrote a book called *The Friend of Princes.* He died in A.D. 1381, A.H. 783.

'Abdul-Rahman (عبد الرحمن), also called by old writers Abderames, a descendant of the Khalīfas of the house of Umayya. He was invited to come to Spain, in A.D. 756, A.H. 139, by the Saracens who had revolted; and after he had conquered the whole kingdom, he assumed the title of king of Cordova. He was the founder of the Ommaides of Spain, who reigned above two hundred and fifty years from the Atlantic to the Pyrenees. He died in A.D. 790, A.H. 174, after reigning 32 years.

'Abdul-Rahman Ichi (عبد الرحمن ايجي), or Ījī, the father of 'Qāzī 'Azd-uddīn of Shīrāz, a learned man and native of Īch, a town situated 40 farsakhs from Shīrāz.

'Abdul-Rahman (عبد الرحمن), called by us Abderames, a petty prince in the kingdom of Morocco, who murdered 'Imād-uddīn, his predecessor and nephew, and was himself after a long reign assassinated by a chieftain whose death he meditated, A.D. 1505, A.H. 911.

'Abdul-Rahman, the Sultān of Fez and Morocco, born 1778, was rightful heir to the throne when his father died; but was supplanted by his uncle, after whose death he ascended the throne in 1823. His eldest son Sīdī Muhammad (born 1803) is heir to the throne.

'Abdul-Rahman Khan (عبد الرحمن خان), Nawāb of Jhajjar, who on account of his rebellion during the mutiny of the native troops in A.D. 1857, A.H. 1274, was found guilty and executed at Dehlī before the Kotwālī on the 23rd December of the same year. He was a descendant of Najābat 'Ali Khān, to whom in 1806, when Sir G. Barlow was Governor-General of India, were granted the large territorial possessions held by the late Nawāb, yielding a yearly revenue of 12½ lacs, and consisting of Jhajjar, Badlī, Karaund with its fort, Nārnaul, etc. In addition to these, expressly for the purpose of keeping up 400 horsemen, the territory of Badwān and Dadrī was granted. Up to May, 1857, he had always been looked upon as a staunch friend of the British Government; but when the rebellion burst forth, he forgot all his obligations to the British, and sided with the rebels.

'Abdul-Rahman Khan (عبد الرحمن خان), Sadr-us-Sudūr of Kānhpūr (Cawnpore), a rebel and a staunch supporter of Nanā Ṣāḥib, when that rebel commenced his career. He was hanged at Kānhpūr, in June, 1858, A.H. 1274.

'Abdul-Rahman Sulami (Shaikh), author of the *Ṭabaqāt Ṣufiya*, a work on Sufism. He died in A.D. 1021, A.H. 412. He is also called Abū-'Abdur-raḥmān.

'Abdul-Rahman, son of 'Abdul-'Azīz Naqshbandī, the father-in-law of Salaimān Shikoh, who married his daughter in A.H. 1062, the 25th year of Shāh Jahān.

'Abdul-Rahman Chishti (عبد الرحمن چشتي), author of the *Mir-āt-i-Mas'ūdī*, which contains the legendary history of Sālār Mas'ūd Ghāzī, buried at Bahrāich in Audh. 'Abur-raḥmān died during the reign of Aurangzīb in A.H. 1094.

[For extract translations *vide* Dowson, *Elliot's History of India*, ii. p. 513. An Urdū translation of the *Mir-āt-i-Mas'ūdī* was lithographed at Kānhpūr A.H. 1287, under the title of *Ghazā-nāma-i-Mas'ūd*.]

'Abdul-Rashid (عبد الرشيد), was the son of Sulṭān Mas'ūd, of Ghaznī. He began to reign, after deposing and confining his brother 'Alī, in A.D. 1052, A.H. 443. He had reigned but one year, when Ṭughril, one of his nobles, assassinated him and mounted the throne of Ghaznī. Ṭughril reigned only forty days, and was murdered on the Persian New Year's day in March A.D. 1053, A.H. 444, when Farrukhzād, a brother of 'Abdur-Rashīd, succeeded him.

'Abdul-Rashid (Mir) (عبد الرشيد مير), son of 'Abdul-Ghafūr-ul-Husainī. He lived in the time of the emperor Shāh Jahān, and wrote chronograms on his accession to the throne of Dehlī in A.D. 1628, A.H. 1037. He is the author of the Persian Dictionary called *Farhang-i-Rashīdī*, also of the *Muntakhab-ul-Lughāt*, a very useful Arabic Dictionary, with Persian explanations, dedicated to the emperor Shāh Jahān. Another work of his is called *Risāla-i-Mu'arrabāt*.

The *Farhang-i-Rashīdi*, which was written in 1064 (A.D. 1653), is the first critical dictionary of the Persian language, and has been printed by the Asiatic Society of Bengal.

[Vide *Jour. As. Soc. Bengal*, 1868, p. 20.]

'Abdul-Rashid Khan (عبد الرشيد خان), son of Sultān Abū-Sa'īd Khān, king of Kāshghar. He was the contemporary of Humāyūn, the emperor of Dehlī. Mīrzā Ḥaidar, author of the *Tārīkh-i-Rashīdī*, dedicated his work to him.

[*Vide* Dowson, *Elliot's History of India*, v. p. 127; and *Aīn Translation*, i. p. 460.]

'Abdul-Razzaq (عبد الرزاق), a chief of the Sarbadāls of Sabzwār. He was at first employed by Sulṭān Abū-Sa'īd Khān as a Yasāwal, or mace-bearer, but after his death, when confusion took place, he possessed himself of Khurāsān in A.D. 1336, A.H. 737, and was slain, after one year and two months, by his brother, Wajīh-uddīn Mas'ūd, in September, 1337, Ṣafar A.H. 738. Mas'ūd reigned seven years, and was deposed by his brother Shams-uddīn, who after a reign of four years and nine months was slain at Sabzwār by Ḥaidar Qaṣṣāb. After him Amīr Yahya Qirātī made himself master of Khurāsān, and gave the command of his troops to Ḥaidar Qaṣṣāb. In the month of December A.D. 1353, A.H. 754, Yahya slew Tughān Timur, a descendant of the Mughul kings, in battle, and was himself slain by his nobles, after he had reigned four years and eight months. After him they raised Khwāja Luṭf-ullah, the son of Khwāja Mas'ūd to the masnad. He was slain after a short time by Hasan Dāmghānī, who reigned four years and four months, when Khwāja 'Alī Muāyyad slew him, and reigned eighteen years in Khurāsān, after which he made over his country to Amīr Timur, who passed Khurāsān in A.D. 1380, A.H. 782. 'Alī Muayyad was killed in a battle in the year 1386, A.H. 788, and with him terminated the power of the Sarbadāls.

'Abdul-Razzaq, Kamāl-uddīn, son of Jalāl-uddīn Is-hāq, born at Hirāt on the 12th Sha'bān, 816 (6th November, 1413). He is author of the historical work entitled *'Maṭla'-us-sa'-dain.* He died in 887 (A.D. 1482).

[*Vide* below *in voc.* Kamāl, and Dowson, iv. p. 90.]

'Abdul-Razzaq, the son of Mirzā Ulugh Beg, the emperor Bābar's uncle. He was killed by the command of that monarch, before his invasion of India, for raising disturbances at Kābul, about A.D. 1509, A.H. 915.

'Abdul-Razzaq (Mulla) (عبد الرزاق ملا), of Lāhijān, author of the *Gauhar-i-Murād*, a dissertation on the creation of the world, and the pre-eminence then given by God to man, dedicated to Shāh Abbās II. of Persia. He lived about the year A.D. 1660, A.H. 1072. His poetical name is Fayyāz.

'Abdul-Salam (عبد السلام بن محمد), son of Muhammad, a celebrated learned man, and author of the *Tafsīr Kabīr*, a commentary on the Qurān. He died in the year A.D. 1095, A.H. 488.

'Abdul-Salam (Qazi) (عبد السلام قاضي بداوني), of Badāon, son of 'Atā-ul-Haqq. He is the author of the commentary called *Tafsīr Zād-ul-Akhirat*, in Urdū, consisting of 200,000 verses, which he completed about the year A.D. 1828, A.H. 1244, as the name of the work shows.

'Abdul-Salam, a famous philosopher and physician, who died at Damascus in A.D. 1443, A.H. 847.

'Abdul-Salam (Mulla) (ملا عبد السلام), of Lāhor, a pupil of Amīr Fath-ullah Shīrāzī. He died in the year A.D. 1628, A.H. 1037.

[Vide *Aīn Translation*, i. p. 545.]

'Abdul-Salam (Mulla), of Dehlī, was the pupil of Mullā 'Abdus-Salām of Lāhor. He wrote the Sharh, or marginal notes, on the commentaries called *Tahzīb*, *Manār*, etc., and is also the author of the work on Sufism, in Arabic, called *Hall-ur-Rumūz*.

'Abdul Samad (عبد الصمد), uncle of the two first Khalīfas of the house of 'Abbās, died at a great age during the khilāfat of Hārūn-ur-Rashīd, in the year A.D. 801, A.H. 185. It is said of him that he never lost a tooth, for both the upper and lower jaws were each of one single piece.

'Abdul-Samad (Khwaja) (عبد الصمد خواجه), a noble of Akbar's court, also well-known as a caligrapher. He was the father of Sharīf, Amīr-ul-Umarā, under Jahāngīr (vide *Aīn Translation*, i. pp. 495, 517), and had the title of "Shīrīn-Qalam," or sweet-pen.

'Abdul-Samad, nephew of Shaikh Abul-Fazl, secretary to the emperor Akbar. He is the compiler of the work called *Inshā-i-Abul-Fazl*, which he collected and published in the year A.D. 1606, A.H. 1015.

'Abdul-Samad Khan (عبد الصمد خان), styled Nawāb Samsām-uddaula Bahādur-Jang, was the son of Khwāja 'Abdul-Karīm, a descendant of Khwāja 'Ubaid-ullah Ahrār. The native country of his father was Samarqand, but he was born at Āgra. In his childhood, he went with his father to Samarqand, where he completed his studies. In the reign of Aurangzīb he returned to India, and was, at his first introduction to the emperor, raised to the rank of 600, and after a short time to that of 1500, with the title of Khān. In the reign of Jahāndār Shāh, the rank of 7000 and the title of 'Alī-Jang were conferred on him. He was made governor of Lāhor, in the time of Farrukh-siyar, and was sent with a great army against the Sikhs, whom he defeated and made prisoners with Bānda their chief. He was made governor of Multān by the emperor Muhammad Shāh, with the title of Samsām-uddaula, and his son, Zakariyā Khān, Sūbadār of Lāhor. He died in A.D. 1739, during the invasion of Nādir Shāh.

[The histories call him "Diler-jang," not "Ālī-jang"; *vide* also Dowson, vii. pp. 456, 491, 511.]

'Abdul-Samad Khan (عبد الصمد خان), Faujdār of Sarhind, distinguished himself in the Maratha Wars, and was at last beheaded by Bhāo in A.H. 1174 (A.D. 1760).

[*Vide* Dowson, viii. p. 278.]

'Abdul-Shukur (Maulana) (عبد الشكور مولانا). His poetical name was Bazmī [*q.v.*], and he was killed, or mortally wounded, in a skirmish near Karnal, 16th February, A.D. 1634.

'Abdul Wahhab (Qazi) (عبد الوهاب قاضي) lived in the time of the emperor 'Ālamgīr, and died on the 26th November, A.D. 1675, 18th Ramazān, A.H. 1086, at Dehlī. He is the author of a *Dastūr-ul-'Amal*, which he dedicated to that monarch.

'Abdul Wahhab (Mir) (عبد الوهاب مير), author of the *Tazkira-i-Benazīr*, which he wrote about the year A.D. 1758, A.H. 1172.

'Abdul-Wahhab, author of the *Manāqib-i Maulawī Rūm*, containing the memoirs of the celebrated Jalāl-uddin Rūmī.

'Abdul-Wahhab bin-Ahmad (عبد الوهاب بن احمد), author of the Arabic work on theology, called *Anwār Ahmadiya*, written in A.D. 1548.

'Abdul-Wahhab, or Muhammad bin-'Abdul-Wahhāb, founder of the sect of the Wahhābīs, was born at Huraimala, in the province of Najd, in Arabia, about the year A.D. 1750.

'Abdul-Wahid (عبد الواحد), author of the *Sab'a Sanābil*, essays on the duties of Instructor and Student, written in the year A.D. 1561, A.H. 969.

'Abdul-Wahid (Mir) (عبد الواحد مير), a native of Bilgrām, in Audh, whose poetical name was Shāhidī. He died in his native country on the 11th of December, A.D. 1608, 3rd Ramazān, A.H. 1017. His son's name was Mīr 'Abdul-Jalīl the father of Sayyid Uwais, whose son's name was Sayyid Barkat-ullah.

'Abdul-Wahid (Mir), of Bilgrām. He wrote under two assumed names, viz.: Wāhid and Zauqī, was an excellent poet in Persian and in Hindī, and is the author of a work in prose and verse, called *Shakar-istān-i-Khayāl*, wherein he has mentioned the names of all kinds of sweetmeats. He was killed on the 13th October, A.D. 1721, Friday, 2nd Muharram, A.H. 1134, in an affray with the Zamīndārs of Rāhūn, in the Panjāb, the settlement of which place was entrusted to his father Sayyid Muhammad Ashraf.

'Abdul-Wahidi, a Turkish poet, author of a Dīwān, comprising 30 Qasīdas, 200 Ghazals, 29 Tārīkhs, and 54 Rubā'īs.

'Abdul-Wasi' of Hansi (عبد الواسع هانسوی), author of a Persian grammar, called after his name, *Risāla-i-'Abdul-Wāsi.* He flourished in the last century, and is also the author of a Hindūstanī Dictionary, entitled *Gharaib-ul-Lughāt.*

[For further notes, vide *Proc. As. Soc. Bengal*, for 1887, p. 121.]

'Abdul-Wasi' Jabali (عبد الواسع جبلي), a celebrated poet of Persia, who flourished about the year A.D. 1152, A.H. 547, in the time of Sultān Bahrām Shāh, son of Sultān Mas'ūd, of Ghaznī, and Sultān Sanjar Saljūqī, in whose praise he wrote several beautiful panegyrics. He died in the year A.D. 1160, A.H. 555. "Jabal" means a mountain, and as he was a native of Ghurjistān, a mountainous country, he chose "Jabalī" for his poetical title; *vide* Jabalī.

[*Vide* Sprenger, *Catalogue of Oudh MSS.* p. 443.]

Abengnefil (a corruption of an Arabian name, spelt so in Lemprière's Biographical Dictionary), was an Arabian physician of the 12th century, and author of a book, the translation of which, entitled *De virtutibus medicinarum et ciborum*, was printed at Venice in 1851: folio.

'Abhai Singh (راجه ابهی سنگه), Rājā of Jodhpūr, who had acquired his power by the murder of his father, Rājā Ajit Singh Rāthaurī in the beginning of the reign of Muhammad Shāh, emperor of Dehlī, about the year A.D. 1726, A.H. 1139. He served under the emperor, and having in a battle defeated Sarbaland Khān, the usurper of Gujrāt, was appointed governor of that province in A.D. 1727, A.H. 1140; but his younger brother Bakht Singh succeeded his father to the Rāj of Jodhpūr. Abhai Singh was poisoned in A.D. 1752, and after his death his son Bijai Singh succeeded him.

'Abi Bakr, author of the *Jawāhir-ul-Ganj*, and of another work on Sufism, called *Marsād-ul-'Ibād.*

'Abi Bakr Muhammad (ابی بکر محمد), author of an Arabic work in prose entitled *Adīb-ul-Kitāb*, written in A.D. 984, A.H. 374.

'Abid Khan (عابد خان), a nobleman on whom Aurangzīb conferred the Sūbadārship of Multān.

Abjadi (ابجدی), the poetical name of Mīr Muhammad Ismā'īl Khān, tutor of the Nawāb 'Umdat-ul-Umarā of the Karnatik, who made him a present of 6700 Rs. on the completion of the history, called *Anwar-nāma*, a masnawī, or epic, containing an account of the exploits of Nawāb Anwar Khān, the father of the patron of the author. It was completed in A.D. 1760 (A.H. 1174), and in 1774 the title of Malik-ush-shu' arā, or poet laureate, was conferred on the author.

[*Vide* Abdī.]

'Abqa Khan (ابقا خان), *vide* Abā Qāān.

Abrakh Khan (ابرخ خان) (the son of Qizilbash Khān Afshār, governor of the fort of Ahmadnagar, who died there in the 22nd year of Shāh Jahān) was a nobleman of high rank in the time of 'Ālamgīr. A few years before his death, he was appointed governor of Barār, where he died on the 24th of July, A.D. 1685, 3rd Ramazān, A.H. 1096.

Abru (آبرو), *vide* Hāfiz Ābrū.

Abru (آبرو), poetical name of Shāh Najm-uddīn, of Dehlī, *alias* Shāh Mubārak, who flourished in the reign of the emperor Muhammad Shāh. He died in A.H. 1161.

[*Vide* Sprenger, *Oudh MSS.*, p. 196.]

Abtin (آبتین), the father of Farīdūn, seventh king of Persia of the first, or Peshdādian, dynasty. Ābtin pretended that he derived his origin from Jamshed, king of Persia of the same dynasty.

Abu-'Abbas (ابو عباس), the first khalīfa of Baghdād, of the race of 'Abbās.

[*Vide* Abul-'Abbās.]

Abu-'Abdullah (ابو عبدالله). There are three Muhammadan saints of this name, whose lives are written by Abū-Ja'far. The first is surnamed Quraishī, because he was of the family of the Quraishites, and a native of Mecca. The second bore the name of Iskandar, and the third that of Jauharī.

Abu-'Abdullah Bukhari, *vide* Muhammad Ismā'il Bukhārī.

Abu-'Abdullah, Muhammad Fāẕil, son of Sayyid Ahmad, the son of Sayyid Hasan of Āgra, author of the poem called *Mukhbir-ul-Wāṣil'n*, written in praise of Muhammad and his descendants, with the dates of their respective deaths in verse. The title of the book is a chronogram for A.H. 1106, in which year it was completed, corresponding with A.D. 1650. He flourished in the time of 'Alamgīr, and died in the year A.D. 1694. He is also called Maẕhar-ul-Haqq, which see.

Abu-'Abdullah (ابو عبدالله ابن مالک), commonly called Ibn-Mālik, author of the *Sharḥ Saḥīḥ Bukhārī*. He died at Damascus in A.D. 1273 (A.H. 672).

Abu-'Abdullah, the surname of Shāfi'ī, which see.

Abu-'Abdullah (ابو عبدالله بن احمد انصاری قرطبی), the son of Ahmad Anṣārī, an author, of Cordova, who died A.D. 1272 (A.H. 671).

'Abu-'Abdullah (ابو عبدالله حمیدی), Ḥamīdī, son of Abū-Naṣr, author of the work called *Jam'baina-l-Ṣaḥīḥain*, and the history of Andalusia, called *Tārīkh Undulus*. The former comprehends the collections of al-Bukhārī and Muslim, and has a great reputation. He died in A.D. 1095 (A.H. 488).

Abu-'Abdullah Maghribi (ابو عبدالله مغربی), named Muhammad bin-Ismā'īl, tutor of Ibrāhīm Khawās, Ibrahīm Shaibān of Kirmānshāh, and of Abū-Bakr of Bīkand, and pupil of Abul-Husain Zarrīn of Hirāt. Abū-'Abdullah died in the year A.D. 911 (A.H. 299), and was buried on Mount Sinai.

Abu-'Abdullah Muhammad (ابو عبدالله محمد), son of Sufyān, a native of Qairuwān in Africa. He is the author of the work called *Hādī*. He died in A.D. 1024 (A.H. 415.)

Abu-'Abdullah Muhammad bin-'Ali ar-Rahibi (ابو عبدالله محمد), author of a short treatise, entitled the *Bighyat-ul-Bāḥiṣ* consisting of memorial verses, which give an epitome of the law of inheritance according to the doctrine of Zaid bin-Ṣābit.

Abu-'Abdullah Muhammad Ha'kim Kabir (ابو عبدالله محمد حاکم کبیر), author of the work called *Mustadrik*. He died in A.D. 1014, A.H. 405.

Abu-'Abdullah Muhammad bin-Muhammad al-Nu'mani, surnamed Shaikh Mufīd and Ibn-Mu'allim, was a renowned Shī'a lawyer. Abk-J'afar ut-Ṭūsī describes him in the *Fihrist* as the greatest orator and lawyer of his time, the most ancient Mujtahid, the most subtle reasoner, and the chief of all those who delivered Fatwas. Ibn-Kaṣīr-ush-Shāmī relates that, when he died, Ibn-Naqīb, who was one of the most learned of the Sunnī doctors, adorned his house, told his followers to congratulate him, and declared that, since he had lived to see the death of Shaikh Mufīd, he should himself leave the world without regret. Shaikh Mufīd is stated to have written 200 works, amongst which one, called the *Irshād*, is well-known. He also wrote many works on the law of inheritance. His death took place in A.D. 1022, A.H. 413, or as some say A.D. 1025, A.H. 416.

Abu-'Abdullah Muhammad bin-'Umar al-Waqidi (ابو عبدالله محمد بن عمر الواقدی), an author who wrote in Arabic the work, called *Ṭabaqāt Wāqidī*, containing the history of the conquest of Syria by the generals of 'Umar during the years A.D. 638-9. He is said by some to have died in the year A.D. 824, A.H. 219, but as he makes mention of Al-Mu'taṣim Billah, whose reign began in 833, he must have died about the year 834 and not A.D. 824, A.H. 209.

[*Vide* Wāqidī.]

Abu-'Abdullah Muhammad bin-Husain al-Shaibani (ابو عبدالله محمد بن حسین الشیبانی), commonly called Imām Muhammad, was born at Wāsiṭ in 'Irāq-'Arab in A.D. 749, A.H. 132, and died at Rai, the capital of Khurāsān in A.D. 802, A.H. 187. He was a fellow pupil of Abū-Yūsuf, under Abū-Ḥanīfa, and on the death of the latter pursued his studies under the former. His chief works are six in number of which five are considered of the highest authority, and cited under the title of the *Ẓāhir-ur-Riwāyāt*; they are *Jāmi'-ul-Kab r*, *Jāmi'-us-Ṣaghīr*, the *Mabsūt fī furū'-il-Ḥanafiya* the *Ziiyādāt fī furū'-il-Ḥanafiya, the Siyar-ul-Kabīr wal Ṣaghīr*; and the *Nawādir*, the sixth and last of the known compositions of Imān Muhammad, which, though not so highly esteemed as the others, is still greatly respected as an authority.

Abu-'Abdullah Salih, *vide* Abū-'Alī, Wazīr of Manṣūr I.

Abu-'Abdul-Rahman Ahmad bin-'Ali bin-Shu'aib al-Nasai (ابو عبد الرحمن احمد نسائی), author of the works called *Sunan Kubra* and *Sunan Sughra'*. The first is a large work on the traditions; but as Nasāī himself acknowledged that many of the traditions which he had inserted, were of doubtful authority, he afterwards wrote an abridgement of his great work, omitting all those of questionable authenticity; and this abridgement which he entitled *Al-Mujtaba* and is also called *Sunan Sughra*, takes its rank as one of the six books of the Sunna. Al-Nasāī was born at Nasā a city in Khurāsān, in A.D. 830, A.H. 303, and died at Makka in A.D. 915.

Abu-'Abdul-Rahman Sulami. *Vide* 'Abdul-Raḥmān Sulamī.

Abu-'Abdul-Rahman Yunas (عبد الرحمن یونس), the son of Ḥabīb, an excellent grammarian who died in the year A.D. 798, A.H. 182.

Abu-'Abdul-Wahid (ابو عبد الواحد), an elegant Turkish poet who flourished in Constantinople in the earlier part of the seventeenth century.

Abu-Ahmad (ابو احمد بن قاسم), the son of Qāsim, was born in the city of Amasia in Natolia A.D. 1483, A.H. 888; he publicly explained the book written by his father Aḥmad bin-'Abdullah ul-Kirmī on the fundamental points of Muhammadanism.

Abu-'Ali (ابو علی مهندس), surnamed Muhandis, "the Geometrician," who excelled in that science. He flourished A.D. 1136, A.H. 530, in the time of Al-Ḥāfiẓ li-dīn-illah, Khalīfa of Egypt, and Al-Rāshid Billah, the son of Al-Mustarshid of Baghdād.

Abu-'Ali (ابو علی), the wazīr of Manṣūr I. the son of Nūḥ, prince of the Samanian dynasty of Khurāsān. In A.D. 963, A.H. 352, he translated the *Tārīkh Ṭabarī* into the Persian language from the Arabic. It is a general history from the creation of the world, down to the 300th year of the Hijra. In the course of eight centuries the language of Abū-'Alī having become obsolete, Abū-'Abdullah Sālih bin-Muhammad was persuaded by Nūrullah Khān, prince of Tūrān, to put it into modern Persian.

[*Vide* Abu Jā'far at-Ṭabarī, and Ṭabarī.]

Abu-'Ali Ahmad bin-Muhammad, the son of Ya'qūb bin-Maskawaihi Khāzin of Rai, author of the Arabian work entitled *Kitāb-ut-Ṭahārat*, which was translated in Persian by Nāṣir-uddīn Ṭūsī, and named *Akhlāq i-Nāsirī*. He flourished about the 12th century.

Abu-'Ali Ismail (ابو علی اسمعیل), an Arabian author who died in A.D. 967, A.H. 356.

Abu-'Ali Qalandar (Shaikh) (ابو علی قلندر), commonly called Bū-'Alī Qalandar Shaikh Sharaf-uddīn Pānīpātī, a celebrated and highly respected Muhammadan saint, who is said to have performed numerous miracles during his life. He was born at 'Irāq in Persia, but came to India and fixed his residence at Pānīpat, where he died, aged about 100 years, on the 30th August, A.D. 1324, 9th Ramazān A.H. 724. His tomb is held sacred and is visited by the Musalmans to this day.

[Vide *Proc. As. Soc. Bengal*, for 1870, p. 125, and for 1873, p. 97.]

Abu-'Ali Sina (ابو علی سینا). *Vide* Abū-Sīnā.

Abu-'Ali 'Umar (ابو علی عمر بن محمد), son of Muhammad, was the author of the commentary, called *Sharḥ Kabīr* and *Shruḥ Saghīr*. He died in the year A.D. 1247, A.H. 645.

Abu-Ayyub (ابو ایوب), a companion of the prophet Muhammad, who had been with him in the battles of Badr and Uḥud, and lost his life in the expedition of Constantinople (A.D. 668, A.H. 48) in the reign of Mu'āwiya, the first Khalīfa of the house of Umayya. His tomb is held in such veneration by the Muhammadans, that the Sulṭāns of the 'Uṣmān, or Ottoman, dynasty gird their swords on at it on their accession to the throne.

Abu-Bakr (ابو بکر بن ابی شیبة), son of Abū-Shaiba, an Arabian author who died in the year A.D. 849, A.H. 235.

Abu-Bakr Ahmad (ابو بکر احمد), son of Husain Baihaqī, *vide* Baihaqī.

Abu-Bakr Ahmad bin'Umar al-Khassaf (ابو بکر احمد بن عمر الخصاف), author of several treatises, known by the name of *Ādāb-ul-Qāẓī*. Hājī Khalīfa speaks very highly of this work. It contains 120 chapters, and has been commented upon by many learned jurists: the most esteemed commentary is that of 'Umar bin-'Abdul-'Azīz bin-Māja, commonly called Ḥusām-ush-Shahīd, who was killed in A.D. 1141. Al-Khaṣṣāf died in A.D. 874, A.H. 261.

Abu-Bakr Baqalani (ابو بكر باقلانی), son of Tayyib. He was of the sect of Imām Mālik, and author of the work called *Al-Tauhīd*, and several other works. He died in A.D. 1012, A.H. 403. See Bāqalānī.

Abu-Bakr Bikandi, a pupil of Abū-'Abdullah Maghribī. He lived about the year A.D. 900.

Abu-Bakr bin-Mas'ud al-Kashani (ابو بکر بن مسعود الکاشانی), author author of the work on jurisprudence, entitled *Badā'i'*. It is also called *Badā'i-us-Sanāi'*. He died in A.D. 1191, A.H. 587.

Abu-Bakr Kattani, Shaikh Muhammed bin-'Alī Ja'far, a famous saint, who was born at Baghdād, and died in A.D. 954, A.H. 322.

Abu-Bakr Muhammad al-Sarakhsi (ابو بکر محمد السرخسی), whose title was Shams-ul-Aïmma; he composed, whilst in prison at Uzjand, a law book of great extent and authority, entitled the *Mabsūt*. He was also the author of the celebrated *Al-Muhīt*. He died in A.D. 1096, A.H. 490.

Abu-Bakr, or Aba-Bakr (ابو بکر or ابا بکر), son of Mīrānshāh, was killed in battle A.H. 810, A.D. 1407.

Abu-Bakr Shadan (Shaikh) (ابو بکر شادان شیخ), of Qazwīn, a celebrated pious Musalmān who died at Qazwīn in the year A.D. 1137, A.H. 531.

Abu-Bakr Shashbani (ابوبکر ششبانی), a valiant commander, born in a village called Shasbān in the province of Māzandarān. He was one of the greatest opponents of Amīr Timur in his conquest of Asia.

Abu-Bakr Shibli (Shaikh) (ابو بکر شبلی شیخ), a celebrated doctor of divinity, born and brought up at Baghdād, but the native country of his parents was Khurāsān. This Sūfī followed the doctrines of the sect of Imān Mālik, and had for his masters Junaid and other holy men of that epoch. He died at Baghdād on Friday 31st July, A.D. 946, 27th Zil-hijja A.H. 334, aged 87 years.

Abu-Bakr Siddiq (ابو بکر صدیق), the father of 'Āyisha, the wife of Muhammad the prophet, by whom he was so much respected that he received from him the surname of Siddīq, which signifies in Arabic "a great speaker of truth," and at the Prophet's death, in June, A.D. 632, he was elected Khālīf in opposition to 'Ālī, the son-in-law of the prophet. He supported with energy the new faith, and reduced several of the Arabian tribes who wished to abandon the new doctrines and return to the religion of their fathers. Afterwards he turned his arms against foreign nations, and by the valour of his active general Khālid, he defeated an army of 200,000 men, whom the Greek emperor Heraclius had sent to ravage Syria. He did not long enjoy his victories: a slow fever wasted his vigour, and he died the very day that Damascus was taken; but before he died he appointed for his successor 'Umar (Omar) the son of Khattāb. He reigned two lunar years three months and nine days, and expired in his 63rd year on Friday the 23rd August, A.D. 634, 22nd Jumāda II. A.H. 13. He was buried close to the tomb of Muhammad in Madīna.

Abu-Bakr Tughluq (ابو بکر تغلق), the son of prince Zafar Khan, and grandson of Fīrūz Shāh Tughluq, was raised to the throne of Dehlī after the assassination of his cousin Ghiyās-uddīn Tughluq, in February, A.D. 1389, Safar, A.H. 791. He reigned one year and six months, after which his uncle Prince Muhammad Tughluq, the son of Fīrūz Shāh, who was at Nagarkot (Kāngra), proclaimed himself king, and proceeded with an army towards Dehlī. After some repulses he was victorious, entered Dehlī, and ascended the throne in the month of August, A.D. 1390, Ramazān, A.H. 792. Abū-Bakr who had fled towards Mewāt, was taken prisoner on the 29th November of the same year, 20th Zil-hijja, and sent to the fort of Mīrath (Meerut), where he died some years after.

[*Vide* Dowson, iv. p. 20.]

Abu-Bakr Yahya (ابو بکر یحیی), author of the *Bahjat-ul-ul-Mahāfil*, or the Delight of Assemblies, containing various anecdotes recorded of Muhammad, the four Khalīfas, and other illustrious persons, in Arabic.

Abu-Bakr Zain-uddin (Maulana) (ابو بکر زین الدین مولانا), surnamed Zain-uddīn, a learned Musalmān, who died at Tāibād, on Thursday the 28th of January, A.D. 1389, 30th Muharram, A.H. 791.

[For further notes, vide *Āīn Translation*, i. p. 366.]

Abu-Bakr Zangi (ابو بکر بن سعد بن زنگی), son of Sa'd, son of Zangī, one of the Atābaks of Persia, who reigned at Shīrāz for thirty-five years, and died in the year A.D. 1260, A.H. 658. The celebrated Shaikh Sa'dī of Shīrāz dedicated his Gulistān to him in A.D. 1258.

Abu-Darda (ابو دردا), a companion of Muhammad, who was governor of Syria in the time of the Khalīfa 'Umar.

Abu-Daud Sulaiman bin-al-Ash'as (ابو داؤد سلیمان بن الاشعث), surnamed Al-Sijistānī, author of a *Kitāb us-Sunan*, which contains 4,800 traditions, selected from a collection made by him of 500,000. It is considered the fourth book of the Sunna. He was born in A.D. 817, A.H. 202, and died at Baṣra in A.D. 888, A.H. 275.

Abu-Daud Sulaiman bin-'Uqba (ابو داؤد سلیمان بن عقبه الظاهری), surnamed Az-Ẓāhirī. He is the translator and commentator of Euclid in Arabic. He was also the founder of a Sunnī sect, but had few followers, and was called Az-Ẓāhirī, because he founded his system of jurisprudence on the exterior (*ẓāhir*), or literal meaning of the Qurān and the traditions, rejecting the qiyās. He was born at Kūfa A.D. 817, A.H. 202, and died at Baghdād in A.D. 883, A.H. 270. Some authors say that he died A.H. 275 (A.D. 888). He was a great partisan of Shāfi'ī.

Abu-Hafs al-Bukhari (ابو حفص البخاری), a muftī of Bukhārā, and a very rigid Musalmān. He was surnamed Al-Kabīr, the Great, to distinguish him from his son, who was surnamed Al-Ṣaghīr, the Little, or the Younger, and was also a learned teacher, but not so famous as his father.

Abu-Hafs Haddad, 'Amr, son of Salama, of Nīshāpūr, a saint, who died in A.H. 264.

Abu-Hafs 'Umar (ابو حفص عمر بن احمد), son of Aḥmad, author of 330 works, among which are *Targhib* and *Tafsīr* and *Masnad*. He died in A.D. 995, A.H. 385.

Abu-Hafs 'Umar al-Ghaznawi (ابو حفص عمر الغزنوی سراج الدین), surnamed Sirāj-uddīn, a follower of Abū-Ḥanīfa, and author of the Arabic work called *Zubdat-ul-Aḥkām*, which expounds the practical statutes of the different doctrines of the four Sunnī sects. He died in A.D. 1371, A.H. 773.

Abu-Hamid (Imam) (ابو حامد امام بن محمد غزالی), son of Muhammad, surnamed Ghazzālī. He is the author of the Arabic work on theology, called *Iḥyāu-'ulūm-id-dīn*, and of many other works. He died in A.D. 1111, A.H. 505.

[*Vide* Ghazzālī.]

Abu-Hamza bin-Nasr al-Ansari (ابو حمزه بن نصر الانصاری), surnamed Aus bin Mālik, was one of the six authors most approved for Muhammadan traditions. He died at Baṣra, in the year A.D. 710, A.H. 91, aged 103 years, after having begot 100 children. He was the last that was styled Ṣaḥāba, that is to say, friends, companions, and contemporaries of Muhammad.

Abu-Hanifa (Imam) (ابو حنیفه امام), *Vide* Ḥanīfa.

Abu-Haraira (ابو هریره), that is "father of the kitten," so nicknamed by Muhammad, because of his fondness for a cat, which he always carried about with him. He was so constantly called by this name, that his true name is not known, nor his pedigree. He was such a constant attendant upon Muhammad, that a great many traditions go under his name; so many, indeed, that the multitude of them make people suspect them. Nevertheless, others receive them without hesitation as of undoubted authority. He was Qāẓī of Mecca in the time of 'Uṣmān. He died in the year A.D. 679, A.H. 59.

Abu-Husain Zarrin (ابو حسین زرین), of Hirāt, and master of Abū-'Abdullah Maghribī. He died at the age of 120.

Abu-Hatim (ابو حاتم), a celebrated Musalmān lawyer.

[*Vide* Ḥātim, surnamed Al-Aṣamm.]

Abu-Ibrahim Ismail (ابو ابرهیم اسمعیل بن یحیی المزنی), son of Yaḥya al-Mazanī, a distinguished disciple of Imām Shāfi'ī, and author of the *Jāmi' Ṣaghhir* and other works. He died in the year A.D. 878, A.H. 264. He was the most celebrated amongst Shāfi'ī's followers for his acquaintance with the legal system and juridicial decisions of his preceptor, and for his knowledge of the traditions. Amongst other works, he wrote the *Mukhtaṣir*, the *Manṣūr*, the *Rasāil-ul-Mu'tabira*, and the *Kitāb-ul-Waṣāiq*. The *Mukhtaṣir* is the basis of all the treatises composed on the legal doctrines of Shāfi'ī, who himself entitled Al-Mazanī "the champion" of his doctrine.

Abu-Is-haq, son of Alptigīn, independent governor of Ghaznī. Abū-Is-ḥāq handed over the reigns of the government to Subuktigīn, who, on Is-ḥāq's death, in A.D. 977, A.H. 367, usurped the throne.

Abu-Is-haq (ابو اسحق بن محمد), the son of Muhammad, an inhabitant of Syria, who wrote an excellent commentary to Mutanabbī. He died in A.D. 1049, A.H. 441.

Abu-Is-haq Ahmad (ابو اسحق احمد) or Abul-Is-hāq Ibrāhīm bin-Ismā'īl, author of the *Qiṣaṣ-ul-Anbiyā*, which contains an account of the creation of the world, and a history of all the prophets preceding Muhammad; also the history of Muhammad till the battle of Uḥud, A.D. 623. He died in A.D. 1036, A.H. 427.

Abu-Is-haq al-Kaziruni (ابو اسحق الكازرونى), a Muhammadan saint who, they say, lighted a lamp in the mosque of the college called "Takht Sirāj," which continued burning for four hundred years till the time of Bin-Qāsim.

Abu-Is-haq Hallaj (ابو اسحق حلاج اطعمه). *Vide* Is-ḥāq.

Abu-Is-haq Isfaraini (ابو اسحق اسفراینی), son of Muhammad, author of the *Jāmi'-ul-Jila*, which refutes the doctrines of various sects. He died in A.D. 1027, A.H. 418.

Abu-Is-haq (Shah Shaikh) (ابو اسحق شاه شیخ). His father Amīr Muhammad Shāh, a descendant of Khwāja 'Abdullah Anṣārī, was governor of Shīrāz in the reign of Sultān Abū-Sa'īd Khān, and was murdered during the reign of Arpā Khān, in A.D. 1335, A.H. 736. His son, Amīr Mas'ūd, who succeeded him, was also slain shortly after, when his brother, Abū-Is-hāq, took possession of Shīrāz in 1336. He reigned 18 years; but when Amīr Muhammad Muẓaffar besieged Shīrāz, in A.D. 1353, A.H. 754, Abū-Is-hāq fled to Iṣfahān, where he was slain four years after, on Friday the 12th May, A.D. 1357, 21st Jumāda I. A.H. 758.

Abu-Is-haq Shami, of Syria, a famous saint, who died on the 14th Rabī' II. 329, and lies buried at 'Akka.

Abu-Is-haq Shirazi (ابواسحق شیرازی), author of the *Ṭabaqāt ul-Fuqahā*, a collection of the lives of celebrated lawyers. He died A.D. 1083, A.H. 476.

Abu-Ismail Muhammad (ابو اسمعیل محمد), author of the history called *Tārīkh Futūḥ-il-Shām*, the conquest of Syria by the generals of 'Umar in forty-two battles, during the years 638 and 639 of the Christian era, translated and abridged from the *Ṭabaqāt Wāqidī*.

Abu-Ja'far (ابو جعفر). *Vide* Al-Manṣūr.

Abu-Ja'far Ahmad bin-Muhammad Tahawi (ابو جعفر احمد بن محمد طحاوي), an inhabitant of Ṭaḥā, a village in Egypt. He was a follower of the Ḥanafiya sect, and is the author of the commentary on the Qurān, called *Aḥkām-ul-Qurān*, and other works, called *Ikhtilāf-ul-'ulamā, Ma'ānī-l-Āsār, Nāsikh and Mansūkh*, all in Arabic. He died in the year A.D. 933, A.H. 321. He also wrote an abridgment of the Ḥanafī doctrines, called the *Mukhtaṣir ut-Ṭaḥāwī*.

Abu-Ja'far al-Haddad (ابو جعفر الحداد), **Abu-Ja'far al-Saffar** (ابو جعفر الصفار), two great teachers of the spiritual life; one was a locksmith, and the other a brazier. The latter is called "Al-Haffār," *i.e.*, gravedigger, in Jāmī's Nafḥāt-ul-Uns.

Abu-Ja'far al-Tabari (ابو جعفر الطبری ابن جریر), son of Jarīr, author of the *Tārīkh Ṭabarī*, a very authentic history in Arabic, which he wrote in the year A.D. 912. This work was translated and continued by Abū-Muhammad of Tabrīz in Persian. Ṭabarī was the founder of the seventh Sunnī sect, which did not long survive the death of its author. He was born at Āmul in Ṭabaristān in A.D. 838, A.H. 224, and died at Baghdād in A.D. 922, A.H. 310. He was also the author of a commentary to the *Qurān*. His son, Muhammad Ṭabarī, was also an author, and died about twenty years later.

Abu-Ja'far Muhammad bin-'Ali bin-Babwaihi al-Kumi (ابو جعفر محمد بن علی بن بابویه الصدوق), surnamed As-Ṣadūq, one of the earliest of the many writers on the *Qurān* among the Shī'as. He lived in the fourth century of the Hijra, and was a contemporary of Rukn-ud-daula Dailamī. He was one of the greatest of the collectors of Shī'a traditions, and the most celebrated of all the Imāmiya lawyers of Qum in Persia. This writer composed a large and a small Tafsīr. There is considerable uncertainty as to the exact time when he lived. Shaikh Ṭūsi says in the *Fihrist* that Abū-Ja'far died at Rai in A.H. 331, A.D. 942, but this appears to be erroneous. Shaikh Najāshī, who died in A.D. 1014, states that Abū-Ja'far visited Baghdad whilst yet in the prime of life, in A.H. 355, A.D. 965, which might well have been the case, since Abul-Hasan 'Alī bin-Bābwaihi, the father of Abū Ja'far, did not die until A.H. 329, A.D. 940. In addition to this, Nūr-ullah relates, on the authority of the Shaikh ad-Dūrysatī (Dūryast, a village near Rai, which is now called Durasht), that Abū-Ja'far lived in the time of Rukn-ud-dauln Dailamī, and had repeated interviews with that prince, who, as is well-known, reigned from A.H. 338 to A.H. 336, A.D. 949—976. He is also the author of the *Man lā yahzarhu al-Faqīh*, which is the fourth of the four authentic books on Shī'a tradition, called "Kutab Arba." He is said to have written in all 172 works, and to have been specially skilled in Ijtihād (jurisprudence, *q.v.*).

Abu-Ja'far Muhammad bin-Hasan al-Tusi Shaikh, who was one of the chief Mujtahids of the Imāmiya or Shī'a sect, is the author of the work entitled *Fihristu-Kutub-ish-Shī'a wa Asmā-il-Muṣannifīn.* It is a bibliographical dictionary of Shī'a works, together with the names of the authors. The greater part of this author's works were publicly burnt in Baghdād in the tumult that arose between the Sunnīs and Shī'as in A.D. 1056, A.H. 448—460, Abū-J'afar died in A.D. 1067. He is also the author of a very extensive commentary on the *Qurān*, in twenty volumes, which is generally called the *Tafsīr-ut-Ṭūsī*, though it was entitled by its author the *Majma'-ul-Bayān li-'ulūm-il-Qurān.* Among the Four Books on Shī'a Ḥadīs, called *Kutab Arba'*, the two first in order were composed by him entitled *Tahzīb-ul-Aḥkām*, and *Istibṣār*. His chief works are the *Mabsūt* and *Khilāf*, which are held in great estimation, as are also the *Nihāya* and the *Muḥīṭ* by the same author. The *Risāla-i-Ja'fariya* is likewise a legal treatise by at-Ṭūsī, which is frequently quoted.

Abu-Jahl (ابو جهل), the uncle of 'Umar ibn-ul-Khaṭṭab ("Father of ignorance." Jahl means theological ignorance, or unbelief). He was one of the most inveterate enemies of Muhammad and his religion. Though his son 'Ikrima became a convert to the tenets of Muhammad, yet the father was for ever shut out from paradise; and so violent is the resentment of the Musalmans against this first enemy of their prophet, that they call the colocynth, in contempt, the melon of Abū-Jahl. Abū-Jahl was slain in the battle of Badr, which he fought against Muhammad, together with Al-Āṣ, his brother, in the 70th year of his age, in the month of March, A.D. 624, Ramazān A.H. 2.

Abu-Lahab (ابو لهب), the uncle of Muhammad, also called 'Abdul-'Uzza, was the son of 'Abdul-Muṭṭalib and one of the bitterest enemies of Muhammad and his doctrines. He died of grief within a week after the defeat of Abū-Sufyān in the battle of Badr, which took place about the beginning of the year A.D. 624, A.H. 2. He was a man of wealth, of proud spirit, and irritable temper. His son 'Utba was engaged, or according to some, married to, Muhammad's third daughter Ruqayya, but when Muhammad appeared as a prophet, the contract was dissolved, and Ruqayya married her lover 'Uṣmān. Abū-Lahab was also allied to the rival line of Quraish, having married Umm-Jamīl, sister of Abū-Sufyān.

Abu-Lais Nasir Samarkandi, author of the work on jurisprudence in Arabic called *Fiqh Abu-Laiṣ*, and the *Ghunyat-ul-Mubtadī.*

Abul-'Abbas, surnamed Al-Saffāḥ, which see.

Abul-'Abbas Ahmad bin-Muhammad, commonly called Ibn-'Uqda, was one of the greatest masters of the science of traditions, and was renowned for his diligence in collecting them, and the long and frequent journeys which he undertook for the purpose of obtaining information on the subject. Al-Dārquṭnī, the Sunnī traditionist, is reported to have said that Ibn-'Uqda knew 300,000 traditions of the Ahl-i-Bait and the Banū-Hāshim. He died in A.D. 944, A.H. 333.

Abul-'Abbas bin-Muhammad (ابو العباس بن محمد), author of the Arabic work *Ma'rifat-us-Ṣaḥāba*, and other books. He died in A.D. 1041, A.H. 432.

Abul-'Abbas Fazl, bin-Ahmad, of Isfarāīn, was minister to Mahmūd of Ghazni.

Abul-'Aina (ابو العينا), a Musalmān lawyer, celebrated for his wit. When Mūsa, son of the khalīfa 'Abdul Malik, put to death one of Abul-'Ainā's friends, and afterwards spread a report that he had escaped, Abul-'Ainā said in the words of the Lawgiver of the Hebrews, "Moses smote him and he died." The sentence was reported to the prince, and Abul-'Ainā was summoned to appear. Instead of dreading the threats of the tyrant, he boldly replied in the words of the following verse in Exodus, "Wilt thou kill me to-day as thou killedst the other man yesterday?" The ingenuity of the expression disarmed the anger of Mūsa, who loaded him with presents.

Abul-'Ala (ابو العلا), entitled Malik-ush-Shu'arā, or royal poet, of Ganja, flourished in the time of Manūchihr, ruler of Shirwān. The poets Falakī and Khāqāni were his pupils, and to the latter he gave his daughter in marriage.

Abul-'Ala Ahmad bin-'Abdullah al-Ma'arri (ابو العلا احمد بن عبدالله المعری), a celebrated Arabian philosopher, free-thinker and poet, born at

Ma'arra in Syria on Friday the 26th December, A.D. 973, 1st Rabi' I. A.H. 363. Though he lost his sight in the third year of his age by the small-pox, his poetry is animated and his descriptions are beautiful and striking. He died on Friday the 9th of May, A.D. 1057, 1st Rabi' I. A.H. 449. He was the panegyrist of Al-qāyim Billah, the khalīfa of Baghdād, and has left a Dīwān in Arabic.

[Vide *Zeitschrift*, D.M.G. xxix. p. 304.]

Abul-'Ala Mir (میرابو العلااکبرابادی), (Mīr), son of Mīr Abul-Wafā Hasanī, of Āgra, was born in the year A.D. 1582, A.H. 990. His grandfather Mir 'Abd-us-Salām came to India from Samarqand, and went on a pilgrimage to Mecca, and died after some years. His father Mīr Abul-Wafā died at Fatḥpūr Sīkrī, from which place his remains were conveyed to Dehlī and buried close to the college situated near the Lāl Darwāza. When Rāja Mān Singh was appointed governor of Bengal, Mīr Abul-'Alā accompanied him, and was honored with the rank of 3000, but he soon left him and proceeded to Ajmīr, and thence to Āgra, where he passed the remainder of his life, and is said to have performed many miracles. He died on Friday the 21st January, A.D. 1651, 9th Ṣafar, A.H. 1061, aged 71 lunar years, and lies buried at Āgra, at a place near the karbalā, where every year on the anniversary of his death a great number of people assemble together and worship his tomb.

He was a Naqshbandī and a descendant of Khwāja Aḥrār.

Abul-Barakat 'Abdullah bin-Ahmad (ابو البرکات عبدالله بن احمد), *vide* Nasafī.

Abul-Barakat Nishapuri (ابو البرکات نیشاپوری), author of the work called *Dastūr-ul-Kitābat.*

Abul-Barakat, Shaikh, brother of Abul-Fazl, born A.D. 1552.

[*Vide* Blockmann's *Āīn Translation*, p. xxxiii.]

Abul Farah, of Wāsiṭ, the ancestor of the Sayyid families of Bārha, Bilgrām, Khairābād, Fatḥpūr, Hanswa, and other places.

[Vide *Āīn Translation,* i. p. 390.]

Abul-Faraj (ابو الفرج), who in some of our Biographical Dictionaries is called Abulfaragius (George), was the son of Aaron, a Christian physician, born at Malatia in Armenia, near the source of the Euphrates in A.D. 1226. He followed his father's profession, but afterwards studied the Eastern languages and divinity, and was ordained bishop of Guba in his 20th year, from whence he was translated to Lacabena and Aleppo. He wrote a work on history, called *Mukhtaṣir-ud-Dawal*, divided into dynasties, which is an epitome of universal history from the creation to his own time. The most excellent part of the work is that which relates to the Saracens, Mughuls, and the conquests of Chingiz Khān. Dr. Pococke, Professor of Hebrew and Arabic at Oxford, published this work in 1663, in the original Arabic, with a Latin version to it. Abul-Faraj died in A.D. 1286, A.H. 685.

Abul-Faraj 'Ali (ابو الفرج علی بن حسین), the son of Husain bin-Muhammad Quraishī Iṣfahānī, was born in the year A.D. 897, A.H. 284, and was brought up at Baghdād. He is the author of a famous work called *Kitāb-ul-Aghānī*, or Book of Songs, an important biographical dictionary, notwithstanding its title, treating of grammar, history, and science, as well as of poetry. The basis is a collection of one hundred Arabian songs, which he presented to Saif-ud-daula, prince of the race of Ḥamdān, who ordered him a thousand dīnārs. The minister of that prince, thinking this sum too small for the merit of the work, on which the author had laboured fifty years, doubled it. The author of this celebrated work died in A.D. 967, A.H. 356, having lost his reason previous to his death.

Abul-Faraj al-Khalidi (ابو الفرج الخالدي), **Abul-Faraj al-Baghawi** (ابو الفرج البغوی), two great poets, who lived at the court of the Sultān Saif-ud-daula of the house of Ḥamdān, who was a protector of men of letters, on whom he bestowed large pensions.

Abul-Faraj ibn-Jauzi (ابو الفرج ابن جوزی), surnamed Shams-uddīn, was the most learned man, the ablest traditionist, and the first preacher of his time. He compiled works on a variety of subjects, and was the tutor of the celebrated Shaikh Sa'dī of Shīrāz. He died on the 16th June, A.D. 1201, 12th Ramaẓān, A.H. 597, and is buried at Baghdād. His father's name was 'Alī, and that of his grandfather Jauzī. One of his works is called *Talbīs Iblīs, The Temptation of Satan.*

Abul-Faraj Runi (ابو الفرج رونی), of Rūn, said to be near Lāhore. He is the author of a Dīwān, and was the panegyrist of Sulṭān Ibrāhīm (the grandson of Sulṭān Mahmūd of Ghaznī) who reigned from A.D.

1059 to 1088, A.H. 451 to 481. Anwarī imitated his style.

[*Vide* Sprenger, *Oudh MSS.*, p. 308. He is often wrongly called Abul-Faraḥ Ruwainī; *vide* Dowson iv. p. 205.]

Abul-Faraj Sanjari (ابو الفرج سنجری), a Persian poet who lived in the time of the great irruption of the Tartars under Chingiz Khān.

[*Vide*, however, Sprenger, *Oudh MSS.* p. 308, from which it appears that Sanjarī is a mistake for Sijizī, *i.e.* of Sijistān.]

Abul-Fath, author of a Persian work called *Chahār Bāgh* or *The Four Gardens*, containing forms of letters on different subjects.

Abul-Fath, Muhammad bin-Abū-Bakr al-Marghīnānī al-Samarqandī, author of the *Fuṣūl-ul-'Imādiya*, which comprises forty sections containing decisions respecting mercantile matters, and being left incomplete at the author's death, which took place in A.D. 1253, A.H. 651, was finished by Jamāl-uddīn bin-'Imād-uddīn.

Abul-Fath Bilgrami Qazi (ابو الفتح), commonly called Shaikh Kamāl. It is mentioned in the work called *Sharāif-i-'Usmānī*, that he was born in the year A.D. 1511, A.H. 917, and that in the reign of the emperor Akbar he held the situation of Qāẓī of Bilgrām, and died in the year A.D. 1592, A.H. 1001. Mullā Fīrūz 'Usmānī found the chronogram of the year of his death in the letters of his name, viz.: Shaikh Kamāl.

Abul-Fath Busti Shaikh (ابو الفتح بستی), a learned Musalmān of Bust, who lived in the time of Sulṭān Mahmūd of Ghaznī, wrote excellent poetry on divinity, and died in July, A.D. 1039, Shawwāl, A.H. 430. He is the author of a Dīwān in Arabic.

Abul-Fath Gilani (ابو الفتح گیلانی), surnamed Masīḥ-uddīn, the son of 'Abdur-Razzāq, a nobleman of Gīlān, was a physician in the service of the emperor Akbar. In the year A.D. 1589 he proceeded to Kashmīr with that monarch, and during the emperor's progress from Kashmīr to Kābul, he died at a place called Dhantūr, on the 20th June of the same year, 16th Sha'bān, A.H. 997, and was buried at Bābā Ḥasan Abdāl. He had come to India with his two brothers Ḥakīm Humām and Ḥakīm Nūr-uddīn Qarārī about the year A.D. 1567, A.H. 974.

[For further notes, vide *Aīn Translation*, i. p. 424.]

Abul-Fath Lodi, chief of Multān. Sulṭān Mahmūd of Ghaznī took Multān in A.D. 1010, and carried away Abul-Fatḥ as prisoner to Ghaznī.

Abul-Fath Muhammad al-Shahristani (ابو الفتح محمد الشهرستانی), author of the Arabic work called *Kitāb ul-Milal wan-Nihal*, or the *Book of Religious and Philosophical Sects.* This book, which gives a full account of the various Sunnī sects, was translated into Latin and published by Dr. Haarbrücker, in A.D. 1850, and into English by the Rev. Dr. Cureton. Shahristānī died in A.D. 1153, A.H. 548.

Abul-Fath Nasir bin-Abul-Makarim Mutarrizi (ابو الفتح ناصر بن ابو المكارم مطرزی), author of the Arabic Dictionary called *Mughrib*. He died in A.D. 1213, A.H. 610 in Khwārazm. He was a Mu'tazilite and invited people to that faith. He is also the author of the *Sharḥ Maqāmāt Harīrī*, and of another work called *Kitāb Azharī*. The inhabitants of Khwārazm used to call him the master of Zamaqhsharī, and on his death the poets wrote more than seven hundred elegies in his praise.

Abul-Fath Nasir bin-Muhammad (ابو الفتح ناصر), author of the *Jāmi'-ul-Ma'ārif*.

Abul-Fath Rukn-uddin bin-Husam Nagori (ابو الفتح رکن الدین), author of a work on jurisprudence, entitled the *Fatāwa Ḥammādiya*, which he composed and dedicated to his tutor, Ḥammād-uddīn Ahmad, chief-qāẓī of Naharwāla (Paṭan) in Gujrāt. This work was lithographed in the original Arabic at Calcutta in A.D. 1825.

Abul-Fath 'Usman (ابو الفتح عثمان), surnamed Malik ul-'Azīz 'Imād-uddīn, second king of Egypt of the Ayyūbite dynasty. He acted as viceroy of Egypt during the absence of his father, Sulṭān Ṣalāḥ-uddīn Yūsuf ibn-Ayyūb, in Syria. On the demise of his father at Damascus in A.D. 1193, he took possession of the supreme power with the unanimous consent of the great military officers of the empire. He was born at Cairo on the 7th of January, A.D. 1172, 8th Jumādạ I., A.H. 567, reigned about five years, and died at Cairo on the 23rd November, A.D. 1198, 21st Muḥarram, A.H. 595.

Abul-Fazl 'Abdul-Malik bin-Ibrahim al-Hamadani al-Mukaddasi (ابو الفضل عبد الملک), author of the *Farāiẓ-ul-Muqaddasī*, a treatise on the law of inheritance according to the Shāfi'ī doctrine. He died A.D. 1095, A.H. 489.

Abul-Fazl Baihaki (ابو الفضل بیہقی), author of several works on history. *Vide* Baihaqī.

Abul-Fazl Ja'far (ابو الفضل جعفر), son of the khalīfa Al-Muktafī, was a great astronomer. *Vide* Al-Mutawakkil.

Abul-Fazl Muhammad (ابو الفضل محمد), author of the Arabic Dictionary called *Ṣurāḥ-ul-Lughāt*.

Abul-Fazl (Shaikh) (ابو الفضل شیخ), Akbar's favorite Secretary and Wazīr. His poetical name was 'Allāmī. He was the second son of Shaikh Mubārak of Nāgor, and brother of Shaikh Faiẓī. He was born in the year A.D. 1551, A.H. 958, and was introduced to the emperor in the 19th year of his reign. His writings prove him to have been the most learned and elegant writer then in the East. He is celebrated as the author of the *Akbarnāma* and the *Āīn-Akbarī*, and for his letters, called *Maktūbāt-i-'Allāmī*, which are considered in India models of public correspondence. The history of the Mughul emperors he carried on to the 47th year of Akbar's reign, in which year he was murdered. He was deputed with prince Sulṭān Murād in A.D. 1597, A.H. 1006, as Commander-in-Chief of the army of the Deccan, and on his being recalled five years after, he was advancing towards Narwar with a small escort, when he fell into an ambuscade laid for him by Birsingh Deo Bundelā, rājā of Urchā in Bundelkhand, at the instigation of Prince Salīm (afterwards Jahāngīr) on suspicion of being the occasion of a misunderstanding between him and the emperor his father; and although Abul-Faẓl defended himself with great gallantry, he was cut off with most of his attendants, and his head was sent to the prince, who was then at Allāhābād. This event took place on Friday the 13th of August, A.D. 1602, 4th Rabī' I, A.H. 1011. Akbar was deeply afflicted by the intelligence of this event; he shed abundance of tears, and passed two days and two nights without food or sleep. Abul-Fazl is also the author of the *'Ayār-Dānish*, which is a translation of Pilpay's Fables in Persian.

[For a detailed biography, vide *Āīn Translation*, i. pp. 1 to 36.]

Abul-Fazl Tahir bin-Muhammad Zahir-uddin Faryabi (ابو الفضل محمد), a Persian poet. *Vide* Ẓahīr.

Abul-Fida Ismail Hamawi (ابو الفدا اسمعیل حموی), whose full name is Malik Muayyad Ismā'īl Abul-Fidā, son of Malik-ul-Afẓal, a learned and celebrated prince, who succeeded his brother Ahmad as king of Ḥamāt, in Syria, in the year A.D. 1342, A.H. 743. When a private man, he published in Arabic an account of the regions beyond the Oxus called *Taqwīm-ul-Buldān*, which was first edited by Grævius, with a Latin translation, London, 1650, and by Hudson, Oxford, 1712. Abul-Fidā died in 1345, aged 72, at Ḥamāt. The principal of Abul-Fidā's other works is his abridgment of Universal History down to his time, called *Tārīkh Mukhtaṣir*. He is very exact, and his style is elegant, on which account his works are very much esteemed.

Abul-Faiz (ابو الفیض). *Vide* Faiẓī.

Abul-Faiz Muhammad bin-Husain bin-Ahmad, surnamed Al Kātib, or the Writer, is better known by the name of bin-Ahmad. He was a wazīr of Sulṭān Rukn-ud-daula, of the Boyides. He was a great orator and a poet, and brought Arabian caligraphy to perfection. He died in A.D. 961, A.H. 360.

Abul-Futuh Razi Makki (ابو الفتوح رازی مکی), author of the Arabic work called *Risāla*, or *Kitāb Hasaniya*, which has a great reputation amongst the Shī'as, particularly in Persia. It consists of an imaginary disputation between a Shī'a slave-girl and a learned Sunnī lawyer, on the merits of their respective doctrines, in which, as a matter of course, the girl utterly discomfits her opponent. The argument is very ingenuously managed, and the treatise, taken altogether, furnishes a good and concise exposition of the tenets of the Shī'as, and the texts on which their belief is founded. This work was translated from Arabic into Persian by Ibrāhīm Astarābādī, in A.D. 1551.

Abul-Ghazi Bahadur (ابو الغازی بہادر), Khān of the Tartars, was descended from the great Chingiz Khān. He came to the sovereignty of Khwārazm on the death of his brother; and after 20 years, during which he was respected at home and abroad, he resigned the sovereignty to his son, Anūsha Muhammad, and retired to devote himself to literature. He wrote a valuable genealogical history of the Tartars, the only Tartar history known in Europe, but did not live to finish it. He died A.D. 1663, A.H. 1074, and on his death-bed charged his son and successor to complete his history, which he performed in two years after his father's death. This valuable work was translated in to German by Count Strahlenberg, and a French translation appeared at Leyden in 1726.

Abul-Ghazi Bahadur. *Vide* Sulṭān Husain Mirzā.

Abul-Haras (ابو الحرث المشهور به ذو الرمه بن عقبه), or Ḥaraṣ, commonly called Ẕul-Rama, son of 'Uqba. He was an Arabian poet, and was contemporary with Farazdaq. He died in A.D. 735, A.H. 117.

Abul-Husain Ahmad bin-'Ali al-Najashi, author of a biographical work entitled *Kitāb-ur-Rijāl*, comprising the lives of eminent Shī'as. Najāshī died in A.H. 405 (A.D. 1014).

Abul-Husain 'Ali bin-'Umar al-Darqutni (ابو الحسين على بن عمر دارقطنى), a Sunnī traditionist, whose collection of traditions, like those of Abū-Bakr Ahmad-bin-al-Husain al-Baihaqī, are of the highest authority. He died in A.D. 995, A.H. 385.

Abul-Husain bin-Abu-Ya'la al-Farra (Kazi) (ابو الحسين بن ابو يعلى), author of the *Ṭabaqāt-ul-Ḥanbaliya*, which comprises the lives of the most famous lawyers of the sect of Ibn-Ḥanbal; it was commenced by our author, continued by Shaikh Zain-uddīn 'Abdur-Raḥmān bin-Aḥmad, commonly called Ibn-Rajab, and concluded by Yūsuf bin-Hasan al-Muqaddasī; these three writers died respectively in A.D. 1131, 1392, and 1466, A.H. 526, 795, and 871.

Abul-Husain Kharqani (ابو الحسين خرقانى), author of the *Sharḥ-i-Makhzan-ul-Asrār*, and *Mir-āt-ul-Muḥaqqiqīn*, containing an explanation of the ceremonies used on the induction of a Ṣūfī, and the rules of the order. He died A.D. 986, A.H. 376.

Abul-Husain Zarrin. *Vide* Abū-Husain Zarrīn.

Abul-Hasan (ابو الحسن), author of the *Siyar Nūr Maulūd*, a heroic poem on the wars of the prophet Muhammad.

Abul-Hasan (ابو الحسن), a poet who wrote a commentary on the Dīwān of Anwarī, called *Sharḥ-i-Dīwān-i-Anwarī*.

Abul-Hasan (Shah) (ابو الحسن شاه), son of the famous Shāh Ṭāhir, of Ahmadnagar, in the Deccan, and minister of 'Alī 'Adil Shāh I., about the year A.D. 1572, A.H. 980.

Abul-Hasan, the son of I'timād-ud-daula, prime minister of the emperor Jahāngīr, had three daughters, viz. Arjmand Bānū, also called Mumtāz-Maḥall, married to the emperor Shāh Jahān; Sulṭān Zamānia, the second daughter, was married to Sulṭān Parwīz; and the third, Badr-uzzamānia, to Shāh 'Abdul-Laṭīf, the spiritual guide of the emperor 'Ālamgīr. *Vide* Āṣaf Khān.

Abul-Hasan 'Abdullah (Imam) (ابو الحسن عبدالله بن مقنع), son of Muqanna'. He translated Pilpay's Fables from the Pahlawī language into Arabic by order of Abū-Ja'far Manṣūr, the second khalīfa of the house of 'Abbās, who reigned at Baghdād from A.D. 754 to 775. The book is called *Kalīla Damna*.

Abul-Hasan 'Ali (ابو الحسن على), author of the works called *Sunan* and *'Ilal*. He died A.D. 990, A.H. 380.

Abul-Hasan 'Ali bin-al-Husain al-Kumi (ابو الحسن بن جسين القمى بابويه), commonly called Bābwaihi, who is said to have died in A.D. 940, A.H. 329, was the author of several works of note, one of which is called *Kitāb-ush-Sharī'a*. This writer is looked upon as a considerable authority, although his fame has been almost eclipsed by his more celebrated son, Abū-Ja'far Muhammad Ibn-Bābwaihi (p. 14). When these two writers are quoted together, they are called the two Ṣadūqs. He is also the author of the *Kitāb-ul-Mawāriṡ*, a treatise on the law of inheritance.

Abul-Hasan 'Ali (ابو الحسن على بن سلطان مسعود), the son of Sulṭān Mas'ūd I., ascended the throne at Ghaznī, on Friday 29th December, A.D. 1049, 1st Sha'bān, A.H. 441, reigned little more than two years, and was deposed by his brother, 'Abdur-Rashīd, in A.D. 1052, A.H. 443.

Abul-Hasan Ash'ari (ابو الحسن اشعرى ابن اسمعيل), son of Ismā'īl. He was a Mu'tazilite, but afterwards became a Sunnī. He is the author of nearly 400 works. He died in the year A.D. 936, A.H. 324.

Abul-Hasan Jurjani (ابو الحسن جرجانى), a celebrated lawyer, a native of Jurjān or Georgia. *Vide* Jurjānī.

Abul-Hasan Qhan (Mirza) (ابوالحسن خان مرزا), Persian ambassador to the British Court in 1809 and 1819. He is the author of a work called *Ḥairat-nāma*, or book of wonders, which title was given to it by Fatḥ 'Alī Shāh, king of Persia. It contains a long account of the Khān's travels in India, Turkey, Russia, England, etc.

Abul-Hasan Qutb-Shah (ابو الحسن قطب شاه), whose literary name was Tānā Shāh, was the son-in-law of 'Abdullah Quṭb-Shāh, after whose demise, about the year A.D. 1672, A.H. 1083, he succeeded to the throne of Golkonda in Haidarābād, Deccan. This place was conquered by 'Ālamgīr, after a siege of seven months, on the 22nd September, A.D. 1687, 24th Ẓil-qa'da, A.H. 1098, and Abul-Hasan was taken prisoner and confined for life in the citadel of Daulatābād. Golkonda was then reduced to a province of the empire of Hindūstān. Abul-Hasan died in confinement about the year A.D. 1704. He was the last Sulṭān of the Quṭb-shāhī dynasty, and a famous poet in the *Dakini*, or dialect of the Deccan.

Abul-Hasan Razin bin-Mu'awiya al-'Abdari (ابو الحسن رضين بن معاويه العبدرى), author of a collection of traditions bearing the same title as the one written by Baghawī, namely *Jāmi' baina-l-Ṣaḥīḥain*. It comprises the works of Al-Bukhārī and Muslim, the Muwaṭṭā of Mālik ibn-Aus, the Jāmi'-ut-Tirmizī, and the Sunans of Abū-Dāūd, and Al-Nasāī. He died in A.D. 1126, A.H. 520.

Abul-Hasan Turbati (ابو الحسن تربتی), entitled Rukn-us-Salṭanat, an Amīr who held the rank of 5,000 in the reign of the emperor Jahāngīr, and died in the sixth year of Shāh Jahān, A.D. 1632, A.H. 1042, aged 70 years.

Abul-Qasim al-Sahrawi (ابو القاسم الصحراوی), called in Lempriere's English Biographical Dictionary "Alsaharavius," an Arabian physician who lived about the year A.D. 1085, A.H. 478, and is the author of the *Al-Taṣrīf*, a treatise in thirty-two books on medical practice.

Abul-Qasim Namakin (ابو القاسم نمكين), a Sayyid of Hirāt, served with distinction under Akbar and Jahāngīr, and became a rich landowner in Bhakar, in Sindh. He built the great mosque in Sakhar. His descendants served under Shāhjahān, 'Ālamgīr, and Farruk-siyar.

[Vide *Āīn Translation*, i. p. 470.]

Abul-Qasim Nishapuri (ابو القاسم نيشاپورى), author of a Persian work on Ethics, called *Ganj-i-Ganj*, and of another work, entitled *Ḥulyat-ul-Muttaqīn*.

Abul-Qasim 'Abdullah (ابو القاسم عبدالله), son of Muhammad Baghawī, author of the book called *Mu'jam*, and several other works. He died in the year A.D. 929, A.H. 317.

Abul-Qasim Isma'il bin-'Abbad (ابو القاسم اسمعيل), wazīr of the Boyide prince Fakhr-ud-daula. One of the most splendid libraries ever collected by a private individual in the East was that of this nobleman. Ibn-Aṣīr relates that four hundred camels were required to remove the books.

Abul-Qasim Mirza, son of Kāmrān Mirzā, brother of the emperor Humāyūn. In the year A.D. 1557, A.H. 964, he was confined in the fort of Gwāliār by the emperor Abkar, who, when going to punish Khān Zamān, ordered him to be murdered.

Abul-Qasim Kahi (ابو القاسم كاهى), of Isfahān, though it is usually said that he was of Kābul. He died at Āgra. *Vide* Qāsim-i-Kāhī.

Abul-Qasim of Hilla (ابوالقاسم الحلى), commonly called Shaikh Muayyad, author of the *Sharāi'-ul-Islām*, a treatise on lawful and forbidden things. This book is of great authority amongst the Muhammadans professing Shī'a doctrines. He is also called Shaikh Najm-uddīn Abul-Qāsim Ja'far bin-Muayyad. He died A.D. 1277, A.H. 676.

Abul-Qasim 'Ubaidullah bin-'Abdullah bin-Khurdadbih, died A.H. 300, A.D. 912. He is best known as Ibn-Khurdādbih. He wrote the *Kitāb-ul-Masālik wal-Mamālik*, the *Book of Roads and Kingdoms*.

[*Vide* Khurdādbih, and Dowson, i. p. 12.]

Abul-Khair Maulana of Khwarazm (ابو الخير خوارزمى مولانا), a physician and poet, whose poetical name was 'Āshiq. From his native country he went to Hirāt in the latter part of the reign of Sulṭān Husain Mirzā, and was there till Muhammad Shaibānī, commonly called Shāhī Beg Khān Uzbak, conquered that province, and took him to Māwarān-nahr, or Transoxiana, where he died in A.D. 1550, A.H. 957. The chronogram of the year of his death is "Faut-i-'Āshiq," the death of 'Āshiq.

Abul-Ma'ali, whose proper name is Muhammad Ṣadr-uddīn, is claimed by the Turks as the first of their poets, though his labours were not confined to their language alone, for he wrote in Arabic also, and was in Persian the rival and opponent of Nāṣir-uddīn. He was contemporary with Jalāl-uddīn Rūmī and his son Walad, and died about the year A.D. 1270. He is not, however, according to Baron von Hammer, to be strictly considered a Turkish poet by his countrymen; but the mystic tone which he adopted from Persian literature, and which he was undoubtedly the first to impress upon the national mind, gives him an unquestionable right to the place assigned him. The names of his works, such as the *Seal of Perfection*, and the *Key of Mysteries*, indicate the peculiarity of his taste and genius; but amidst all the confusion of style and thought some passages of great beauty and even simplicity are found in his works. He is lost, however, in the fame of his successor 'Āshik.

Abul-Ma'ali (ابو المعالی بن عبد المجید), the son of 'Abdul-Majīd, the most eloquent of the Persians, who flourished in the time of Sulṭān Bahrām Shāh Ghaznawī, by whose order, in the year A.D. 1118, A.H. 512, he wrote in prose his *Kalīla Damna* (or *Pilpay's Fables*) from a copy which Rūdakī, the celebrated poet, had formerly used for poetry. This version continued in vogue till the time of Sulṭān Husain Mirzā, fourth in descent from 'Umar Shaikh, the second son of Amīr Timur, when his prime minister Amīr Shaikh Ahmad Suhailī got Husain Wā'iẓ to modernize it, in A.D. 1505, A.H. 910, under the name of *Anwār Suhailī*, or the *Rays of Canopus*. Abul-Fazl, the able prime minister of Akbar, compressed this work, and gave it the name of *'Ayār-Dānish*, or the *Touch-stone of Knowledge*. He is called by Daulat Shāh, Hamīd-uddīn Naṣr-ullah. *Vide* Naṣr-ullah, the son of 'Abdul Ḥamīd.

Abul-Ma'ali (Shah) (ابو المعانی شاه), a chief in the service of the emperor Akbar, who having revolted was compelled to seek safety in Kābul, where Mirzā Muhammad Ḥākim, the brother of Akbar, gave him his sister, named Mihr-un-Nisā Begam, in marriage, and raised him to the first office in that kingdom. The ungrateful refugee, however, had not been many months in office, before he aspired to the kingdom of Kābul, and in March A.D. 1564, Sha'bān, A.H. 971, basely assassinated Mirzā Muhammad Ḥākim's mother, his own mother-in-law, who was a woman of uncommon abilities, and might with truth be said to have ruled that kingdom. He then pretended to act as regent to the young prince, who was still in his minority, with a view to get rid of him as soon as he could conciliate the Umarās. In the meantime Mirzā Sulaimān, prince of Badakhshān, attacked him, and slew him in a battle on the 13th May, A.D. 1564, 1st Shawwāl, A.H. 971, and took possession of that country, which he held for two years. Abul-Ma'ālī was an elegant poet, and his poetical name was Shahbadī.

Abul-Ma'ali (Shaikh) (ابو المعالی الله آبادی شیخ), of Allāhābād, author of the work called *Tuḥfat-ul-Qādiriya*, or the life of Shaikh 'Abdul-Qādir Gīlānī. He resided in Lahore, and died there on the 6th April, A.D. 1615, 16th Rabī' I., A.H. 1024.

Abul-Mafakhir Razi (ابو المفاخر رازی), a poet who flourished in the reign of Sulṭān Muhammad Saljūqī.

Abul-Mahasin (ابو المحاسن), author of the work called *Manhal-i-Ṣāfī*.

Abul-Makarim bin-'Abdullah. There are three comments on the Niqāya of 'Ubaidulla bin-Mas'ūd, which are much esteemed; they were written respectively by Abul-Makārim in A.D. 1501, A.H. 907; Abū-'Alī bin-Muhammad al-Birjindī in A.D. 1528, A.H. 935; and Shams-uddīn Muhammad al-Khurāsānī in A.D. 1534, A.H. 941.

Abul-Ma'shar (ابو المعشر), who is called by some older authors Albumassar and Albumazar, was a learned Arabian astronomer, who flourished in the ninth century in the reign of the khalīfa Al-Māmūn of Baghdād, and wrote a treatise on the revolutions of the years. His full name is Ja'far bin-Muhammad bin-'Umar Abul-Ma'shar. He is called the prince of the Arabian astrologers. He was born in Balkh. In his famous work, called *Ulūf* or *Kitāb-ul-Ulūf*, which he wrote from a Sanskrit work on astronomy, he asserts that, when the world was created, the seven planets were together in the first point of the sign of Aries, and that it will end when the same planets shall meet again in the last point of Pisces in their exaltation or Dragon's head. He died in A.D. 885, A.H. 272. His works were printed in Latin at Venice in 1586, 8vo.

Abul-Najib al-Bukhari (ابو النجیب البخاری), poetically called also 'Am'aq, was a Persian poet who flourished in the fifth century of the Hijra at the court of the Sulṭān Qadr Khān, king or khāqan of Turkistān, who made him president of the academy of poets which he had established. His poem of the loves of Yūsuf and Zalīkhā, which can be read in two different metres, is much admired. He was particularly famous for his elegies. He lived nearly 100 years. Daulat Shāh says, he lived in the time of Sulṭān Sanjar, who requested him to write an elegy on the death of his daughter Malik Khātūn, which he did, although he was then blind on account of old age. He appears to have died some years before or after A.D. 1145, A.H. 540.

Abul-Sa'adat Mubarak Ibn-Asir (ابوالسعادت مبارک ابن اثیر الجزری), al-Jazarī, author of an Arabic Dictionary called *Al-Nihāya fī gharīb-il-Hadīs*. He died in A.D. 1209, A.H. 606. *Vide* Ibn-Asīr.

Abul-Wafa (Khwaja), one of the great saints of Khwārazm, and author of several works on Sufism. He died A.D. 1432, A.H. 835.

Abu-Maaz Muslim (ابو معاذ مسلم), an Arabian grammarian, who died in A.D. 803, A.H. 187.

Abu-Mansur, surnamed al-Ḥākim bi-amr-illah, succeeded his father Al-'Azīz to the throne of Egypt in A.D. 990, A.H. 381, when only 11 years of age. In the latter part of his reign he fancied himself a god, and found no fewer than 16,000 persons who owned him as such. These were mostly the Darārians, a new sect sprung up about this time, who were so called from their chief, Muhammad Ibn-Ismā'īl, surnamed Darārī. He is supposed to have inspired the mad khalīfa with this impious notion; and as Darārī set up for a second Moses, he did not scruple to assert that Abū-Manṣūr was the great creator of the universe. He was assassinated in the year A.D. 1020. His son Ṭāhir succeeded him.

Abu-Mansur (ابو منصور), author of the *Kitāb-ut-Tauḥīd*, and several other works.

Abu-Mansur 'Abdul-Kahir al-Baghdadi, author of a treatise on the law of inheritance according to Shāfi'ī. He died A.D. 1037, A.H. 429.

Abu-Mas'ud, surnamed Shaikh-ul-Islām, a native of Constantinople, and author of the valuable commentary on the Qurān, entitled *Irshād-ul-'aql*, flourished in the reign of Sulṭān Salīm Khān, emperor of Constantinople, and died in A.D. 1516, A.H. 922.

Abu-Muhammad (ابو محمد مکی), of Mecca, son of Abū-Ṭālib, author of a commentary on the Qurān, and several other works. He died in A.D. 1045, A.H. 437.

Abu-Muhammad, son of 'Abbās, the son of a sister of Abū-Ja'far bin-Muhammad bin-Jarīr al-Ṭabarī. It is said that he had by heart 100,000 verses of different authors. He died in A.D. 993, A.H. 383, and was a contemporary of the author of the *'Ayyār*.

Abu-Muhammad Husain bin-Mas'ud Farra al-Baghawi (ابو محمد حسین ابن مسعود فراء البغوی), author of a collection of traditions called the *Maṣābīḥ*, in Arabic; also of the *Ma'ālim-ut-Tanzīl*, and *Sharḥ-us-Sunnat*. He died in A.D. 1122, A.H. 516. He was a vendor of furs, consequently he was called Farrā. Baghāwī also wrote a *Jāmi' baina-l-Ṣaḥīḥain*.

Abu-Muhammad Hisham bin-al-Hakim al-Kindi al-Shabani, who lived in the time of the Khalīfa Hārūn-ur-Rashīd, and died in A.D. 795, A.H. 179, is famed as one of the first compilers of Shī'a traditions.

Abu-Muhammad Nasihi (ابو محمد ناصحی), was a man of eminent learning in the time of Sulṭān Mas'ūd I., of Ghaznī. He wrote a book entitled *Mas'ūdī*, in support of the doctrine of Abu-Ḥanīfa, which he presented to the king. He flourished about the year A.D. 1035.

Abu-Muhammad Rozbihan Bakali Shirazi (ابو محمد روزبهان بقلی شیرازی), author of the *Ṣafwat-ul-Mashārib*. He died in July, A.D. 1209, Muḥarram, A.H. 606. *Vide* Rozbihān (Shaikh).

Abu-Muhammad Shatibi (ابو محمد شاطبی), a very learned Musalmān and author of the *Qasīda Shāṭibiya*. He died in A.D. 1194, A.H. 590. His proper name was Qāsim; he was born at Shāṭibiya, in Andalusia, from which he derived his title of Shāṭibī. He is also the author of several other works.

Abu-Muhammad Tabrizi, author of the Persian history called *Tārīkh-i-Ṭabarī*. The original of this book was written in Arabic by Abū-Ja'far bin-Jarīr Ṭabarī, in A.D. 912, A.H. 300, and was afterwards translated into Persian and continued by Abū-Muhammad, and dedicated to Abū-Ṣāliḥ bin-Nūḥ, about the year A.D. 1118, A.H. 512.

Abu-Musa Ja'far al-Sufi, whose poetical name is Jabar, was the founder of the Arabian school of chemistry, flourished towards the end of the eighth, or the commencement of the ninth century. According to the majority of authorities, he was born at Ṭūs, in Khurāsān. He wrote an immense number of treatises on alchemy, also a work on astronomy. An edition of his works in Latin was published at Dantzic, in 1662, and another in English by Russel, in 1678.

Abu-Musa al-Ash'ari (ابو موسی الاشعری), one of the arbitrators between 'Alī and Mu'āwiya I., by whose decision 'Alī was deposed in the year A.D. 658, A.H. 37. Eight months after the battle of Ṣiffīn between 'Alī and Mu'āwiya, the two arbitrators, Abū-Mūsa and 'Amr, the son of 'Aṣ, met at a place between Mecca and Kūfa, where a tribunal was erected. Abu-Mūsa first ascending it, pronounced these words with a loud voice: "I depose 'Alī and Mu'āwiya from the Khilāfat (or government) to which they pretend, after the same manner as I take this ring from my finger," and immediately came down. 'Amr then went up and said: "You have heard how Abū-Mūsa has on his part deposed 'Alī; as for my part I depose him too, and I give the Khilāfat to Mu'āwiya, and invest him with it after the same manner as I put this ring upon my finger; and this I do with so much the more justice, because he is 'Usmān's heir and avenger, and the worthiest of all men to succeed him."

Abu-Muslim, a great general, to whom the Abbasides entirely owed their elevation to the Khilāfat, for which he is commonly called Ṣāhib-ud-Da'wat, or author of the vocation of the Abbasides. For his good conduct and bravery, he occupied the first posts in the service of the Ommaides. He was governor of Khurāsān, A.D. 746, when he proclaimed the Abbasides the lawful heirs of the Khilāfat, and in A.D. 749 transferred the dignity of Khalīfa from the family of Umayya to that of the Abbasides. This revolution occasioned the death of above 600,000 men; and when Abū-Ja'far Al-Manṣūr, the second Khalīfa of the race of 'Abbās, was opposed on his accession by his uncle 'Abdullah, son of 'Alī, 'Abū-Muslim was despatched against him. This general having harassed him for five months together, at last brought him to a general action, and having entirely defeated him, forced him to fly to Baṣra. Notwithstanding all his services, however, Abū-Muslim was soon after, on Thursday the 13th February, A.D. 755, 24th Sha'bān, A.H. 137, ungratefully and barbarously murdered by Al-Manṣūr, and his body was thrown into the Tigris. Abū-Muslim took his origin (as Iṣfahānī, a Persian historian relates) from Ḥamza, who pretended to descend from Gaudarz, one of the ancient kings of Persia.

Abu-Na'im (ابو نعیم بن عبدالله), son of 'Abdullah, author of the works *'Ulyā* and *Dalāil-i-Nubuwwat*. He died in the year A.D. 1012, A.H. 403.

Abu-Nasr Farabi (ابو نصر فارابی). *Vide* Fārābī.

Abu-Nasr, author of a Persian work on Sufism, called *Anīs-ul-Ṭālibīn*.

Abu-Nasr Farahi (ابو نصر فراهی), flourished about the year A.D. 1220, in the time of Bahrām Shāh, son of Tāj-uddīn, ruler of Sīstān (also called Nīmrūz), who began to reign in the year A.D. 1215. He is the author of a vocabulary in verse, called *Niṣāb-us-Ṣibyān*. His real name is Muhammad Badr-uddīn, and he belongs to Farāh, a town in Sijistān.

[Vide *Āīn Translation*, i. note 41.]

Abu-Nasr Isma'il bin-Hammad al-Jauhari (ابو نصر اسمعیل بن حماد الجوهری) is the author of the Dictionary called *Ṣiḥāḥ-ul-Lughāt*. He was born at Fārāb, and died about the year A.D. 1003, A.H. 394.

Abu-Nasr Khan (Nawab) (ابو نصر خان نواب), an amīr of the reign of the emperor 'Alamgīr. The mosque of Jājnagar, in Orīsa, was built by him in the year A.D. 1687, A.H. 1098.

Abu-Nasr Maskati (ابو نصر مسکطی), a native of Maskaṭ, and author of the book called *Maqāmāt*.

Abu-Nasr Sabur (Shapur), son of Ardsher. He built in the year A.D. 954, an edifice at Baghdād, dedicated to scientific and literary exercises, and collected a large quantity of books, designed for the use of Musalmāns; there were, it is said, upwards of 10,400 volumes of all kinds, including a hundred Qurāns, copied by the celebrated caligrapher Ibn-Muqla.

Abu-Nawas (ابو نواس), al-Hasan bin-Hānī, a celebrated Arabian poet, born in the city of Baṣra. His merit was acknowledged at the court of Hārūn-ur-Rashīd. His principal works have been collected by several persons, on which account there is a great difference between the copies of his works. His proper name is Abū-'Alī. He died A.D. 810, A.H. 195.

Abu-Raihan al-Biruni (ابو ریحان البیرونی), or Abū-Raiḥān Muhammad bin-Ahmad al-Bīrūnī, was born about the year A.D. 971, in the town of Bīrūn, said to be situated in the province of Khwārazm. He was astronomer, geometrician, historian, scholar, and logician. Besides metaphysics and dialectics, he studied, and appears to have drawn his chief lustre from, attainments in the magical art. Of this the following instance is related. One day Sulṭān Mahmūd ordered him to deposit with a third person a statement of the precise manner in which the monarch would quit the hall where he then was sitting. The paper being lodged, the king, instead of going out by one of the numerous doors, caused a breach to be made in the wall, by which he effected his exit; but how was he amazed, when, on the paper being examined, there was found in it a minute specification of the precise spot through which he penetrated! Hereupon the prince with horror denounced this learned man as a sorcerer, and commanded him to be instantly thrown out of the window. The barbarous sentence was presently executed; but care had been taken to prepare beneath a soft cushion, into which the body of the sage sank without sustaining any injury. Abū-Raiḥān was then called before the monarch, and was required to say whether by his boasted art he had been able to foresee these events, and the treatment through which he had that day passed. The learned man immediately desired his tablets to be sent for, in which were found regularly predicted the whole of these singular transactions. He travelled into different countries, and to and from India for the space of 40 years. He wrote many works, and is said to have executed several translations from the Greek, and epitomized the Almajest of Ptolemy. His works are said to have exceeded a camel load. The most valuable of all his works is the *Tārīkh-ul-Hind*. Another of his works is the *Qānūn Mas'ūdī*, dedicated to Sulṭān Mas'ūd of Ghaznī, for which he received an elephant-load of silver coins. He lived in the time of Sulṭāns Mahmūd and Mas'ūd Ghaznawī, and died in the year A.D. 1039, A.H. 430.

[For further notes *vide* Dowson, *Elliot's History of India*, ii. p. 1.]

Abu-Sa'id (ابو سعيد بن عبدالله), the son of 'Abdullah, an Arabian poet who flourished in the court of Ṣalāḥ-ud-dīn, (Saladin), and was his prime minister. He died in the year A.D. 1201, A.H. 597.

Abu-Sa'id (ابوسعيد بن كليب شاشى), the son of Kulaib Shāshī, author of the book called *Masnad Kabīr*. He died in A.D. 946, A.H. 335.

Abu-Sa'id 'Abdul-Malik bin-Quraib (ابو سعيد عبد الملك بن قريب), commonly called Aṣma'ī, celebrated for his grammatical knowledge and eloquence. He was born in the year A.D. 740, A.H. 122, and flourished in the time of Al-Manṣūr, khalīfa of Baghdād (who reigned from A.D. 754 to 775), and died at Baṣra during the reign of Hārūn-ur-Rashīd, or, as some authors say, in A.H. 216 (A.D. 832).

Abu-Sa'id 'Abdur-Rahman bin-Mamun al-Mutawalli, author of the *Farāiz Mutawallī'*, a treatise on the law of inheritance according to Shāfi'ī's doctrine. He died A.D. 1085, A.H. 478.

Abu-Sa'id Baizawi (ابوسعيد بيضاوى), or Qāẓī Abū-Sa'īd 'Abdullah Baiẓāwī, author of the work called *Niẓām-ut-Tawārīkh*, an epitome of Oriental History from Adam to the overthrow of the Khilāfat by the Tartars under Hulākū Khān, A.D. 1258, A.H. 674, written about the year 1275. *Vide* Baiẓāwī.

Abu-Sa'id Fazl-ullah (ابو سعيد فضل الله), son of Abul-Khair, a great Ṣūfī, of Mahna. His spiritual guide was Abul-Faẓl Luqmān of Sarakhs. He devoted himself to ascetic exercises, and spent fourteen years in the wilderness. He is the author of the Quatrains, called Rubā'iyāt-i-Abū-Sa'īd Abul-Khair. He died at the age 44 in the year A.D. 1068, A.H. 440.

Abu-Sa'id Khan Bahadur (ابو سعيد خان بهادر بن الجايتو), a Sulṭān of the family of Hulākū Khān, was the son of Oljāitū, commonly called Muhammad Khudā-banda, whom he succeeded to the throne of Persia in December, A.D. 1316, Shawwāl, A.H. 716, when he was only twelve years of age. In his time Rashīd-ud-dīn, the author of the *Jāmi'-ut-Tawārīkh*, was put to death. This monarch may be termed the last of the dynasty of Hulākū Khān who enjoyed any power. The few princes of that sovereign's family who were raised to the throne after Abū-Sa'īd were mere pageants, whom the nobles of the court elevated or cast down as it suited the purposes of their ambition. Abū-Sa'īd reigned 19 lunar years, and died of fever on the 30th November, A.D. 1335, 13th Rabī' II., A.H. 736. The following is a list of the princes of the family of Chingiz Khān, who were raised to nominal power after the death of Abū-Sa'īd Khān:-

Arpā Khān (Mu'izz-uddīn) was crowned in 1335, reigned five months, and was killed in battle in A.D. 1336.

Mūsa Khān was elevated in 1336, reigned two years, and was murdered in A.D. 1338.

Sākī, sister of Abū-Sa'īd Khān, was elevated to the throne in 1338. She was married to Jahān Timur, who got the kingdom as her dowry, but was deposed the same year. After him

Sulaimān Khān was declared king; he left the kingdom and went to Diyār-bakr in 1344.

Nausherwān was elevated in 1334.

Abu-Sa'id Mirza (Sultan) (ابو سعيد مرزا سلطان), the son of Sulṭān Muhammad Mirzā, son of Mīrānshāh, son of Amīr Timur (Tamerlane). He was born in A.D. 1427. After the death of his father in 1441, he continued to live with Mirzā Ulugh Beg, son of Mirzā Shāhrukh, at Samarqand, and served in his army when he was at war with his son Mirzā 'Abdul-Laṭīf; but when that prince was murdered by his unnatural son, in October, A.D. 1449, Ramazān, A.H. 353, and he in his turn was slain after six or seven months by his own soldiers, and Samarqand was taken possession of by Mirzā Abdullah, son of Mirzā Ibrāhīm, and grandson of Mirzā Shāhrukh, Abū-Sa'īd, with the assistance of Abū-Khair Uzbak, having defeated and taken 'Abdullah prisoner in a battle, put him to death and ascended the throne of Samarqand in A.D. 1451, A.H. 855. He also took possession of Khurāsān after the death of Bābar Sulṭān, son of Bāyasanghar Mirzā, in A.D. 1457, A.H. 861, and greatly extended his dominions, but was at last taken prisoner in an ambuscade, and put to death on the 8th February, A.D. 1469, 25th Rajab, A.H. 873, after he had reigned 18 years. After his death, Sulṭān Husain Bāiqrā, surnamed Abul-Ghāzī, a descendant of Amīr Timur, made himself master of the empire. Abū-Sa'īd at his death left eleven sons, viz.: Mirzā Sulṭān Ahmad, Mirzā Sulṭān Mahmūd, Mirzā Sulṭān Muhammad, Mirzā Shāhrukh, Mirzā Ulugh Beg, Mirzā 'Umar Shaikh, Mirzā Abā-Bakr, Mirzā Sulṭān Murād, Mirzā Sulṭān Khalīl, Mirzā Sulṭān Walīd, and Mirzā Sulṭān 'Umar; of whom four arrived to the dignity of kings, viz.: Mirzā Ulugh Beg to the throne of Kābul; Mirzā Sulṭān Ahmad to the kingdom of Samarqand; Mirzā 'Umar Shaikh to the united thrones of Andijān and Farghāna; and Mirzā Sulṭān Mahmūd to those of Kunduz and Badakhshān. Abū-Sa'īd Mirzā, says Bābar Shāh, though brought up in the city, was illiterate and unrefined.

[*Vide* Genealogical Table attached to Āīn Translation.]

bu-Sina Muhammad, author of the Arabic work called *Daqāiq-ul-Ḥaqāiq*, containing a collection of traditions.

bu-Sina (ابو سینا), or Abū-'Alī Sīnā, whom we call Avicenna, was a famous Muhammadan physician and philosopher, who early applied himself to literature, botany, and mathematics. At the age of eighteen he began to practise, and with such success that he became physician to the court at Baghdād. He was born in the city of Bukhārā, in A.D. 983, A.H. 373, and died at Hamadān in July, A.D. 1037, A.H. 427, aged 54 lunar years, with the character of a learned man, but too much addicted to wine and effeminating pleasures. His books on Medicine, etc., were in number 100, now nearly all lost. He is also called Ibn-Sīnā. The following are the titles of his works: Of the Utility and Advantages of Sciences, 20 books; of Innocence and Criminality, 2 books; of Health and Remedies, 18 books; on the means of Preserving Health, 3 books; Canons of Physic, 14 books; on Astronomical Observations, 1 book; on Mathematical Sciences; of Theorems, or Mathematical and Theological Demonstrations, 1 book; on the Arabic Language, 10 books; on the Last Judgment; on the Origin of the Soul, and the Resurrection of Bodies; of the end we should propose to ourselves in Harangues and Philosophical Arguments; Demonstrations of the collateral lines in the sphere; abridgment of Euclid; on Finity and Infinity; on Physics and Metaphysics; on Animals and Vegetables, etc.; Encyclopædia, 20 volumes. Avicenna is also credited with an Arabic redaction of some of the works of Aristotle, and with some Persian quatrains in the style afterwards popularized by Umar Khāyyām (*q.v.*).

Abu-Sufyan (ابو سفیان بن حرب), the son of Ḥarb, the grandson of Umayya, and great-grandson of 'Abdul-Shams. He was an able and ambitious man, of great wealth and influence, and one of the most persevering and powerful opponents of Muhammad. He was the father of Mu'āwiya, the first khalīfa of the house of Umayya, and one of the heads of the tribe of Quraish, to which Muhammad also belonged. When Muhammad took up arms for the propagation of his faith, Abū-Sufyān was made generalissimo of his enemies against him; and after the battle of Badr, he stood very fair for the headship of that tribe. But he was at last convinced (as it seems, by a signal victory gained by Muhammad over his enemies) of the truth of the prophet's pretensions, and was converted in the 8th year of the Hijra, A.D. 629.

Abu-Sulaiman Daud (ابو سلیمان داؤد), bin-Abul-Fazl bin-Muhammad Fakhr Binākitī, so called from having been born at Binākit, or Fīnākit, a town in Transoxiana, afterwards called Shāhrukhiya. He is the author of the *Tārīkh-i-Binākitī*. Its correct name in full length is *Rauzatu ūlī-l-albāb fī Tawārī -il-Akābir wal-Ansāb*, i.e. the garden of the learned in the histories of great men and genealogies. It is chiefly an abridgment of the *Jāmi'-ur-Rashīdī*, and was compiled by the author only seven years after that work, in A.D. 1317, A.H. 707, and is dedicated to Sulṭān Abū-Sa'īd, the ninth Mughul king of Persia. The author was a poet as well as an historian, and was appointed by Sulṭān Ghāzān Khān, poet laureate of his court. He died in or about the year A.D. 1330, A.H. 731.

[*Vide* Dowson, *Elliot's History of India*, iii. p. 55.]

Abu-Tahir (ابو طاهر), of Tortosa, in Spain, author of the *Dārāb-nāma*, an abridgment of Oriental Biography, containing the Lives of Zuḥāk, of Darius, of Philip of Macedon, and of Alexander the Great; also Memoirs of Galen and other Greek Philosophers, etc.

Abu-Tahir Khatuni (ابو طاهر خاتونی), a poet who flourished in the twelfth or thirteenth centuries of our era. He is the author of the History of the Saljūqī kings, entitled *Tārīkh-ul-Saljūqī*, and of another work, called *Manāqib-ush-Shu'arā*.

Abu-Talib (ابو طالب) was the father of 'Alī, and the uncle of Muhammad the prophet. He died three days before Khadīja, the first wife of Muhammad, in August, A.D. 619, aged 80 years.

Abu-Talib Husaini, author of the *Tuzuk-i-Timūrī*. This work contains an account of the first forty-seven years of the life of Tamerlane, written by himself in Chaghtāi Turkī, and translated into Persian by Abū-Ṭālib, who dedicated it to Shāh Jahān. It has been translated into English by Major Charles Stewart.

[*Vide* Dowson, iii. p. 389.]

Abu-Talib Kalim (ابو طالب كليم همداني), whose poetical name was Kalīm, was a great poet of Hamadān in Persia, and came to India, the first time in the reign of the emperor Jahāngīr, and returned home in A.D. 1619, A.H. 1028. After some years he again visited India in time of Shāh Jahān, who employed him, and conferred on him the title of "Malik-ush-Shu'arā," or Poet Laureate. He was twice weighed against gold and silver, and the amount was given to him as a reward for his poetical talents. He died at Lahore on the 19th November, A.D. 1651, 15th Ẕil-ḥijja, A.H. 1061. He is the author of a poem called *Ẕafar-nāma-i-Shāh Jahān*, or the conquests of Shāh Jahān, and of a Dīwān in Persian.

Abu-Talib Khan (Mirza) (ابو طالب خان مرزا), the son of Ḥājī Muhammad Beg Khān, by descent a Turk, was born at Lucknow in the year A.D. 1752, A.H. 1165. He was appointed by Mukhtār-ud-daula, the prime minister of Nawāb Aṣaf-ud-daula of Lucknow, in A.D. 1775, 'Amaldar of Iṭāwa and several other districts situated between the rivers Jamunā and Ganges. In this situation he continued for two years; but, after the death of his patron, and the appointment of Ḥaidar Beg Khān to his office, he was superseded, and repaired to Lucknow, and was allowed by the Nawāb 60,000 rupees per annum for his support. After the expiration of one year, Colonel Alexander Hannay, having been appointed Collector of Gorakhpūr, requested the Nawāb's leave to take him as an assistant, in which situation he continued for three years. He was afterwards employed by Mr. Middleton, the Resident of Lucknow, in reducing the rebel Rājā Balbhaddar Singh, whom, during two years, he frequently defeated and pursued. At length, the Rājah, being surprised in his camp, was killed in endeavouring to make his escape. Abū-Ṭālib, after this falling into distress for some years, embarked for Europe with Captain David Richardson, a British officer, and left Calcutta in February, 1799, Ramaẕān A.H. 1213. He visited England and other parts of Europe, and was well known in London under the title of the Persian Prince. During his travels he wrote a Journal in which he daily inserted every event, and committed to writing such reflections as occurred to him at the moment. On his return to Calcutta in 1803, A.H. 1218, having revised and abridged his notes, he published them under the title of *Maāṣir-ut-Ṭālibī fī Bilād-i-Ifranjī*. This work was translated by Charles Stewart, and published in London in the year 1814. Abū-Ṭālib died about the year A.D. 1806, A.H. 1221. He is also the author of the *Khulāṣat-ul-Afkār*.

[*Vide* Dowson, viii. p. 298.]

Abu-Talib Mirza. *Vide* Shāista Khān.

Abu-Talib (Shaikh) (ابو طالب شيخ), the father of Shaikh Muhammad 'Alī Ḥazīn. He died at Iṣfahān, in A.D. 1715, A.H. 1127, and was interred in the cemetery, called Mazār Bābā Rukn-uddīn, close to the tomb of the learned Maulānā Hasan, Shaikh-ul-Islām of Gīlān.

Abu-Tammam Habib ibn-Aus al-Tai (ابو تمام حبيب ابن اوس الطائى), an Arabian poet. Having arrived in the city of Hamadān, he was received with great distinction by Abul-Wafā bin-Salama. When about to depart, a heavy fall of snow made the roads for a long time impassable. Abul-Wafā conducted the poet to his library, and placed it entirely at his disposal. Surrounded with these literary treasures, Abā-Tammām forgot his journey, read the precious volumes with avidity, and devoted his time to the composition of several works. The poetical collection entitled *Khamsa* was the principal fruit of these researches, and attests the indefatigable attention with which the learned writer had ransacked this rich library. Amongst the other works that he wrote, one is called *Fuḥūl-ush-Shu'arā*. He was born in A.D. 804, A.H. 188, at Jāsim, near Damascus, and died in A.D. 845, A.H. 231.

Abu-Tayyib al-Mutanabbi (ابو طيب المتنبي). *Vide* Mutanabbī.

Abu-Turab (Mir) (ابو تراب مير), a Salāmī Sayyid of Shīrāz, who served, with his son Mīr Gadāī, in Gujrāt, and then under Akbar. He died in A.H. 1005, and lies buried in Ahmadābād.

[Vide *Āīn Translation*, i. p. 506.]

Abu-'Ubaida (ابو عبيده) a friend and associate of Muhammad, who had the command of the Moslem army in the time of Abū-Bakr, the first Khalifa, but being defeated in a battle against the troops of the Greek emperor, he was deprived of the command, which was given to Khālid. 'Umar, on his accession to the khalifāt, replaced 'Abū-'Ubaida in the command of the army in Syria, being greatly displeased with the cruel and blood-thirsty disposition of Khalid. 'Abū-'Ubaida extended his conquests over Palestine and Syria, and drove the Greeks out of the whole country extending from the Mediterranean to the Euphrates. This conquest was completed in A.D. 639, A.H. 18, in which year Syria was visited by a dreadful plague, in which the Moslems lost 25,000 men, among whom were Abū-'Ubaida himself, Yazīd ibn Abū-Sufyān, and many other men of distinction.

Abu-'Ubaida ibn-Mas'ud (ابو عبیده ابن مسعود), a general in the time of the khalīfa 'Umar. He was defeated and killed in battle by Farrukhzād, who commanded the army of Tūrān-Dukht, queen of Persia, about the year A.D. 635.

Abu-'Ubaida Kam bin-Salam, author of a work on *Qarāat*.

Abu-'Ubaida Ma'mar bin-Al-musanni (ابو عبیده معمر بن المثنی), a famous Arabian grammarian, born in Baṣra, who lived in the time of Hārūn-ur-Rashīd, and died A.D. 824, A.H. 209, aged 99 lunar years.

Abu - 'Umar Minhaj al - Jurjani (ابو عمر منهاج الجرجانی), author of the *Ṭabaqāt-i-Nāṣirī*, a celebrated history, written in A D. 1252, A.H. 650, and dedicated to Sulṭān Nāṣir-uddīn Mahmūd of Dehlī. *Vide* Minhāj-i-Sirāj.

Abu-Yahya bin-Sanjar (ابو یحیي ابن سنجر), author of a Dīwān in Arabic. He died in A.D. 1234, A.H. 632.

Abu - Yahya Ahmad bin - Daud al - Farazi al-Jurjani (ابو یحیی احمد بن داؤد), who was originally a Sunnī, but became a convert to the Imāmiya or Shī'a faith, is the author of a biographical work, entitled *Kitāb fī ma'rifat-ir-Rijāl*, containing the lives of eminent Shī'as.

Abu-Ya'qub al-Warraq (ابو یعقوب الوراق). *Vide* Muhammad bin-Is-ḥāq an-Nadīm.

Abu - Yazid (Maktabdar) (ابو یزید مکتبدار), secretary of state in Egypt, who rebelled against Qāim, the second khalīfa of the race of the Faṭimites. He was not punished for his rebellion till Ismā'īl al-Manṣūr defeated him, and confined him in an iron cage, where he ended his days.

Abu-Yusuf (Imam) (ابو یوسف امام) bin-Ḥabīb al-Kūfī, a celebrated Qāẓī of Baghdād, and one of the first pupils of Abū-Ḥanīfa, dignified with the title of Qāẓī-l-Quẓāt, or supreme judge, in the reigns of Hādī and Hārūn-ur-Rashīd, khalīfas of Baghdād. He supported the tenets of Abū-Ḥanīfa, and maintained the dignity of his office by impartiality. When one day reproached for his ignorance of one of the causes brought before him, for the decision of which he received an ample allowance, he jocosely replied, that he received in proportion as he knew; but, said he, "If I were paid for all I do not know, the riches of the khilāfat itself would not be sufficient to answer my demands." He was born A.D. 731, A.H. 113, and died on the 13th September, A.D. 798, 27th Rajab, A.H. 182, at the age of 69 years, at Baghdād. The only work known to have been written by him, treats of the duties of a Magistrate, and is entitled *Ādāb-ul-Qāẓī*. The reputation of this work has been eclipsed by that of another, having a similar title, by al-Khaṣṣāf.

Abu-Yusuf Ya'kub bin-Sulaiman Isfaraini (ابو یوسف یعقوب بن سلیمان), author of the *Sharāiṭ-ul-Khilāfat*. He died in A.D. 1095, A.H. 488.

Abu - Zakariya Yahya al - Nawawi. *Vide* Nawawī.

Abu-Zarr (ابو ذر قرمطی), the father of the Karamatians in Arabia, who not only opposed the religion of Muhammad, but plundered and insulted the temple of Mecca, and carried away the black stone which was believed to have fallen from heaven. He died A.D. 953, A.H. 342. *Vide* Qarmaṭ.

Abu-Zarr Yaqut Mausili (ابوذر یاقوت موصلی), a celebrated caligrapher.

Abu-Zubaid (ابو زبید), an author who has written on the lion and all its names in the Arabic language.

Achaemenes, old Persian Hakhāmanis; founder of the dynasty of kings called after him, viz.:

	B.C.	
Cyrus I. ?		(*v.* Kai Kobād).
Cambyses I. ?		
Cyrus II. d. 529		
Cambyses II. d. 522		
Darius I. d. 485.		
Xerxes (?), d. 465 (*v.* Isfandyār).		
Artaxerxes, d. 425.		
Darius II. d. 405		(*v.* Dārā).
Darius III. d. 330		

Achanak Begam, one of the concubines of the emperor Akbar. She had built a garden on the banks of the Jamunā, at Āgra, called Achānak Bāgh. Some traces of it are yet to be seen.

Achchhe (اچهے), the poetical name of prince Baland-Akhtar, a brother of the emperor Muhammad Shāh of Dehlī. He was familiarly called Achchhe Ṣāḥib, and therefore chose Achchhe for his "takhalluṣ." He is the author of a beautiful poem, called *Nāhīd-o-Akhtar*, i.e. Venus and the Star, containing 355 verses, which he completed in the year A.D. 1726, A.H. 1139.

Adam, the first man. The Muhammadans place Ādam's Paradise in heaven; hence after the fall Ādam and Ḥawwā (Eve) were hurled down to earth. As this event happened about 7,000 years before the Hijra, Ādam is often called haft-hazārī.

Adam Khan Gakkhar (آدم خان گکهر), chief of the Gakkhars, who defied the power of the emperor Akbar. In 970, at the instigation of Kamāl Khān Gakkhar, Ādam was attacked, and defeated and captured at Hīlān, south of Chiliānwālā, near Dāṇgalī, Ādam's stronghold.

[Vide *Āīn Translation*, i. p. 457.]

Adham (ادهم), the poetical name of Mirzā Ibrāhīm, a Sayyid of the Ṣafawī race. He came to India in the time of the emperor Shāh Jahān. He died, or was put to death in prison, in the year A.D. 1650, A.H. 1060. He is the author of a Dīwān, and also of a Maṣnawī, called *Rafīq-us-Sālikīn*, and a Sāqī-nāma.

Adham Artamani (ادهم ارتمانی), author of a Dīwān in Persian.

Adham (ادهم). *Vide* Ibrāhīm-i-Adham.

Adham Khan (ادهم خان), the son of Māhum Anaga. He appears to have been an illegitimate son of the emperor Hamāyun. His mother Māhum was one of Akbar's nurses (*anaga*), who attended on Akbar "from the cradle till after his accession." She played a considerable part in bringing about Bairām's fall. Adham Khān (*i.e.* the Black Khān) was a commander of 5,000, and distinguished himself in keeping the rebellious Bhadauriya clan, near Hatkānth, south-east of Āgra, in order. In A.H. 968, he defeated Bāz Bahādur of Mālwā, whose female favourite was the poetess Rupmati (*q.v.*). In the following year, A.D. 1562, he stabbed at court his enemy Atgah Khān, Akbar's foster-father, and was killed by the emperor's order. Māhum Anaga died forty days after from grief, and was buried with her son in Dehlī, in a Mausoleum erected by Akbar. Adham's brother Bāqī Khān, or Khān Bāqī Khān, died in the 30th year of Akbar's reign, as Governor of Gaṛha-Katanga (Central Provinces).

Vide Keene's *History of Hindustan*.

Adhan (Shaikh) (ادهن), a Chishtī saint, who died at Jaunpūr in A.H. 970.

Adib (ادیب), the poetical name of Abū-Hasan 'Alī bin-Naṣr, an excellent philosopher, who was a judge in Egypt, under the khilāfat of Ammār the Fāṭimite.

Adib (ادیب), surnamed Ṣābir, a poet who was contemporary with Aṣīr-uddīn Futūḥī and Anwarī. *Vide* Shihāb-uddīn Adīb Ṣābir.

'Adil Khan (عادل خان فاروقی), Fārūqī I., ruler of Khandesh, who is also called Mīrān Ghanī, which see.

'Adil Khan II, Faruqi (عادل خان فاروقی ثانی), entitled A'ẓam Humāyūn, son of Hasan, and grandson of Naṣīr Khān Fārūqī by the daughter of Mahmūd Shāh, of Gujrāt. He succeeded to the throne of Khāndesh after the death of Dāūd Khān Fārūqī, in August, A.D. 1510, Jumādạ I., A.H. 916, and removed from Tālner to Burhānpūr, which place he made the seat of his government, and died there, after a reign of nine or ten years, in A.D. 1520, A.H. 926, and was succeeded by Mīrān Muhammad, his eldest son by the sister of Bahādur Shāh of Gujrāt.

'Adil Khan (عادل خان), the eldest brother of Sulṭān Islām Shāh, king of Dehlī. He fled to Patna after his defeat in a battle against his brother, but he soon disappeared, and was never heard of afterwards.

Adina Beg Khan (آدینه بیگ خان), son of Channū, an Arāin by caste, was born at Sarakpūr, near Lahore. He was brought up in a Mughul family, became a soldier, but devoted himself to accounts. He was Governor of Sulṭānpūr when Nādir Shāh invaded India. Subsequently, he became Governor of the Panjāb. In 1758 he defeated the Afghans near Lahore. Soon after this he died, without heirs, at Khānpūr, near Hoshyārpūr, where a fine tomb was erected over his remains.

'Adli (عدلی), the nickname of Muhammad 'Ādil Shāh, king of Dehlī. His name was Mubāriz Khān, son of Niẓām Khān. He succeeded Islām Shāh in the very end of A.H. 960, defeated with the help of his general Hīmū, in 962, Muhammad Shāh of Bengal at Chhapparghatta, east of Kālpī, and was at last, in 964, one year after Akbar's accession, defeated and killed in the battle of Sūrajgarh, near Munger, by Bahādur Shāh, Sulṭān of Bengal. His nickname 'Adlī was often further corrupted to "Andhlī'," the blind woman.

'Adnan (عدنان), one of the descendants of Ismā'īl, the son of Abraham, with whom the genealogies of the Arabians, and also that of Muhammad, terminate. For reckoning up from 'Adnān to Ismā'īl, the descents are very uncertain, and the best historians confess that there is nothing certain beyond 'Adnān.

Afi (آفی), poetical name of Ahmad Yār Khān, author of a small poem in Persian called *Masnawī Gulzār-i-Khayāl*, containing the story of Shāhzāda and Gadā, written in 1848.

'Afif. *Vide* Shams Sirāj 'Afīf.

Afrasyab (افراسیاب), an ancient, if not mythic, king of Tūrān, the son of Pashang. He overcame Nauzar, king of Persia of the Peshdādian dynasty, and having killed him, ruled over Persia for twelve years. He was subsequently defeated in a battle against Kai-khusrau, king of Persia, of the second or Kaiānian dynasty.

Afrasyab Khan, adopted son of Mirza Najaf Khān (*q.v.*), became Amīr-ul-Umra on the death of his master, A.D. 1782. Intriguing with Madhuji Sindhia, he was over-reached, and was assassinated near Āgra, October, 1783.

Afrin (آفرین), poetical name of Shaikh Qalandar Bakhsh, of Sahāranpūr, who is the author of a work called *Tuḥfat-us-Ṣanāi'*.

Afrin (آفرین), the poetical name of Shāh Faqīr-ullah, of Lahore. He was a Gūjar, embraced Muhammadanism, and is the author of a Dīwān, and of an epic, called *Hīr-wa-Rānjhā*. Some say that he died in A.D. 1730, and others in 1741, A.H. 1143, or 1154.

Afsah (افصح), Shāh Faṣīh, a pupil of Mirzā Bedil, died at Lucknow in A.H. 1192, and left a Dīwān.

Afsari (افسری), the poetical name of a poet.

Afshin (افشین), the surname of Ḥaidar ibn-Kāūs, a general of the khalīfa al-Mu'taṣim Billah, of Baghdād. He was a Turk by origin, and had been brought up a slave at the khalīfa's court, and having been employed in disciplining the Turkish militia, had acquired the reputation of a great captain. He was, however, executed about the year A.D. 840, by the khalīfa, being accused of holding correspondence with the khalīfa's enemies.

Afsos (افسوس), the poetical name of Mīr 'Alī, son of S. Muzafar Alī Khān, claiming descent from Imām Jāfar (*q.v.*), born at Dehlī, where his grandfather had been in the imperial service; author of the *Ardish*, a sort of Urdu Gazetteer, admired for its style. He was first in the service of Nawāb Is-ḥāq Khān, the uncle of Āṣaf-ud-daula, of Lucknow, and subsequently of Mirzā Jawān-Bakht, and was finally recommended to Lord Wellesley, and appointed a Munshī of the College of Fort William. He is the author of the *Ārāish-i-Maḥfil*, in Urdū, and of the *Gulistān*, translated by him into the same language. He died in Calcutta in A.D. 1806, A.H. 1221.

Aftab (آفتاب), the Takhallus, or poetical name of Shāh 'Ālam, king of Dehlī, who died in the year A.D. 1806. The following couplet is a sample of his Majesty's poetry:

> "The forenoon with the wine-cup, the evening with the wife;
> The rest is known to God alone; meantime I live my life."
> (Shāh 'Ālam.)

Afzal, the poetical name of Shāh Ghulām A'ẓam, which see.

Afzal 'Ali Khan (Nawab). *Vide* Afẓal Khān (p. 36), whose original name was Shukr-ullah.

Afzal, the poetical name of Muhammad Afẓal, which see.

Afzali (افضلی), the poetical name of Shaikh Muhammad Nāṣir, son of Shaikh Khūb-ullah, of Allāhābād. He died in A.D. 1750, A.H. 1163.

Afzal Khan (افضل خان), or Mīr Muhammad Afẓal. He flourished in the reign of the emperor Muhammad Shāh, of Dehlī, and died in the year A.D. 1735 or 1738, A.H. 1148 or 1151. His poetical name was Ṣābit, which see.

Afzal Khan (افضل خان), Shaikh 'Abd-urraḥmān, son of the celebrated Shaikh Abul-Fazl, minister and secretary to the emperor Akbar, was Jahāngīr's governor of Bihār in A.D. 1610, and died at Āgra in 1613.

[Vide *Āīn Translation*, p. xxxv. (Abul-Fazl's Biography), and Dowson, vi. p. 205.]

Afzal Khan (افضل خان), whose original name was Mullā Shukr-ullah, the son of 'Abdul-Haqq, came from Shīrāz to the Deccan, and was introduced by 'Abdur-Raḥīm Khān, Khānkhānān, to the emperor Jahāngīr, who conferred on him the rank of an Amīr. In the second year of Shāh Jahān, A.D. 1628, A.H. 1038, the office of Wizārat-i-kull having become vacant by the dismissal of Irādat Khān, the brother of Āṣaf Khān Ja'far Beg, he was honoured with that appointment. In the eleventh year of the emperor, the manṣab of 7,000 and 4,000 sawārs was conferred upon him, but he died the next year at Lahore, on the 7th January, 12th Ramazān, A.H. 1048, O.S. 1639, aged 70 years. His poetical name was 'Allāmī. His tomb, called Chīnī Rauza, is in Āgra, on the left bank of the Jamnā.

Afzal-ud-daula (Nawab), Nizām of Ḥaidarābād, succeeded his father, Nawāb Naṣīr-ud-daula, in May, A.D. 1857, 15th Zil-qa'da, A.H. 1285, and departed this life on the 26th February, 1869, aged 44 years, leaving an infant son, who, according to the succession guarantee granted by Lord Canning, is now his successor.

Afzal-uddin (Mir), Nawāb of Sūrat. He died on the 7th August, 1840, at the age of 59 years, after enjoying his nominal nawābship about 21 years. His son-in-law, Mīr Ja'far 'Alī, succeeded him.

Agah (آگاه), the poetical name of Maulawī Muhammad Bāqir. His parents were of Bījāpūr, but he was born at Elloṛa in A.D. 1745, A.H. 1158, and died on the 3rd March, A.D. 1806, 14th Zil-ḥijja, A.H. 1220. He is the author of a Dīwān.

[He was a Nāita (pl. *Nawāit*, said to be a corruption of the Persian *nau-āmad*, a "new arrival"), a name given to certain seafaring Arabs, settled in Western India.]

Agah Khan, a eunuch of the emperor Shāh Jahān, who died on the 9th Rabī' I., A.H. 1067. His tomb is near the Mumtāz-Maḥall, in Tājganj.

Agha Ahmad 'Ali, poetically styled Ahmad, son of of Āghā Shajā'at 'Alī, of Dhākā, a Persian grammarian of note, who successfully defended, in his *Muayyid-i-Burhān*, and the *Shamsher-i-Teztar*, the author of the *Burhān Qāṭi'*, a Persian Dictionary, against the famous Dehlī poet Ghālib. He also published the *Risāla-i-Ishtiqāq*, the *Risāla-i-Tarāna*, *Haft Āsmān*, *A History of the Persian Masnawī*, and edited several works for the Asiatic Society of Bengal. He was a Persian teacher in the Calcutta Madrasa when he died, June, 1873.

Agha Husain Khwansari (آغا حسین خوانساری). *Vide* Husain Khwānsārī.

Agha Mir (آغا میر), entitled Mu'tamad-ud-daula, minister of Ghāzī-uddīn Ḥaidar, king of Audh. He was dismissed in A.D. 1826, A.H. 1242, and retired to Kānhpūr, where he died on Monday 7th May, A.D. 1832, 5th Zil-ḥijja, A.H. 1247.

Agha Muhammad Khan (آغا محمد خان). *Vide* Āqā Muhammad Khān Qājār.

Agha Mulla (آغا ملا), surnamed "Dawātdār," "the inkstand-holder," the ancestor of the three Āṣaf Khāns who served under Akbar and Jahāngīr. His genealogical table is given in *Āīn Translation*, i. p. 369.

Aghar Khan (اغر خان), Pīr Muhammad, who served during the reign of Aurangzīb against Prince Shujā', in Āsām, and in Kābul. He died in A.H. 1102. His son, Aghar Khān II., was still alive during the reign of Muhammad Shāh. The family traced their descent from Aghar, a descendant of Yāfiṣ (Japhet), son of Nūḥ. Their villa, Agharābād, near Dehlī, is often mentioned in the histories.

Ahi (آهی), a poet who was a chief of one of the Chaghtāi hordes, and had assumed originally the poetical name of "Nargisī," but changed it into "Āhī," because he found that another poet of his time had adopted it. He is the author of a Dīwān, which he dedicated to prince Gharīb Mirzā, the son of Sulṭān Husain Mirzā Bāiqrā. He died in the year A.D. 1520, A.H. 927.

Ahl-i-Bait (اهل بیت), "the people of the house," a general name for the descendants of Muhammad, the Sayyids.

Ahl-i-Kitab (اهل کتاب), "the people of the book," a collective name for the Jews, Christians, and Muhammadans, who received a book, *i.e.* revealed religion from heaven.

Ahli Khurasani (اهلئ خراسانی), a poet who died at Tabrīz in the year A.D. 1527, A.H. 934. He must not be confounded with Ahlī-i-Tūrānī, a Chaghtāī nobleman of profligate character, who lived at the court of Sulṭān Husain Mirzā, and died in A.D. 1497, A.H. 902.

Ahli Shirazi (Maulana) (اهلئ شیرزای), of Shīrāz, an elegant poet in the service of Shāh Isma'īl Ṣafawī I. He is the author of several poems, amongst which are the *Siḥr-i-Ḥalāl*, *Sham' wa Parwāna*, *Risāla-i-Naghz*, *Sāqīnāma*, and *Fawāid-ul-Fawāid*. He died in the year A.D. 1535, A.H. 942, and is buried at Shīrāz, close to the tomb of Ḥāfiẕ.

Ahlia Bai, the wife of Madhu Rāo Peshwā, built a ghāt at Āgra, in the time of Shāh 'Ālam, called Bisnān Ghāṭ, or a bathing-place for all men, on the banks of the river Jamnā. It extended from the trench of the fort to the house of Dārā Shikoh, and was in good preservation in the year A.D. 1830 On one of the corners a large gun of iron was then lying, under the Hawelī of Dārā Shikoh, called Dhaul Dahanī.

Ahlia Bai (اهلیه بائی), the wife of Khānde Rāo, the son of Malhār Rāo Holkar I., of Indor, after whose death, in A.D. 1766, she had a jāgīr allotted to her, yielding an annual revenue of 1,500,000 rupees. Her husband, Khānde Rāo, was killed in battle at Dīg against Sūrajmal Jāṭ, in 1754. Her son Malī Rāo, who had succeeded his grandfather Malhār Rāo in 1766, died nine months after. She was a woman of spirit and ability, and reserved in her own hands the right of nominating a successor, and elected Tukajī to the rāj.

Ahmad al-Makkari (احمد), author of the *History of the Muhammadan Dynasties in Spain*. This work was translated by M. Pascual de Gayangos, an erudite Spaniard, London, 1810, in 4to. Vol. I. He was born in the 16th century, and died in Damascus in the year A.D. 1631, A.H. 1041. After having composed a very detailed biography of the celebrated and learned wazīr of Granada, Muhammad Ibn-ul-Khaṭīb, he added to it, in the form of an introduction, a general history of the Arabs in Spain from the conquest to their final expulsion.

Ahmad I. (احمد بن محمد), emperor of Turkey, son and successor of Muhammad III., whom he succeeded in January, A.D. 1604, Sha'bān, A.H. 1012. This prince was of a good constitution, strong and active; he would throw a horseman's mace, of nine or ten pounds weight, farther than any of his court. He was much given to sensual pleasures, and had 3,000 concubines. He died on the 15th November, A.D. 1617, 15th Ẕil-qa'da, A.H. 1025, at the age of thirty, having reigned fourteen years. He was succeeded by his brother Muṣṭafa I.

Ahmad II. (احمد بن ابراهیم), son of Ibrāhīm, succeeded on the death of his brother Sulaimān II., in A.D. 1691, A.H. 1103, to the throne of Constantinople, and died in A.D. 1695, A.H. 1106. He was succeeded by Muṣṭafa II., son of Muhammad IV.

Ahmad III. (احمد بن محمد), son of Muhammad IV., was placed on the throne of Constantinople in A.D. 1703, A.H. 1115, by the heads of a faction which had deposed his brother Muṣṭafa II. He granted a friendly asylum to Charles XII. of Sweden, after the battle of Pultowa; and the kindness and the hospitality which marked the whole of his intercourse with that unfortunate monarch, are entitled to the highest encomium. He was preparing an expedition against Persia, when an insurrection hurled him from his throne, and exalted his nephew Mahmūd I. from a prison to the sovereign power in A.D. 1730, A.H. 1142. He died of apoplexy in 1736, aged 74 years, A.H. 1148.

Ahmad IV. (احمد بن احمد), (also called 'Abdul-Ḥamīd), son of Ahmad III., emperor of Turkey, succeeded his brother Muṣṭafa III. in A.D. 1774, A.H. 1188. He died, after a reign of 15 years, on the 7th April, 1789, Rajab A.H. 1203, and was succeeded by Salīm III.

Ahmad (احمد), an Arabian author who is known as the writer of a book on the interpretation of dreams, a translation of which, in Greek and Latin, was published with that of Artemidorus on the same subject, at Paris, by Rigault, A.D. 1603. He lived in the 4th century of the Hijra.

Ahmad Abu-Tayyib al-Mutanabi (احمد ابو طیب المتنبی), a celebrated Arabian poet whom none excelled in poetry. He is the author of a Dīwān. He died in the year A.D. 965, A.H. 354. *Vide* Mutanabbī.

Ahmad al-Ghaffari (احمد الغفاري). *Vide* Ahmad bin-Muhammad al-Ghaffārī, p. 26.

Ahmad 'Ali Hashimi (Shaikh) (احمد علی هاشمی شیخ), author of the Biographical Dictionary, called *Makhzan-ul-Gharāib*, dedicated to Nawāb Ṣafdar-Jang, of Faizābād, who died in A.D. 1754, A.H. 1167. His poetical name was Khādim.

Ahmad 'Ali Khan, Nawāb of Rāmpūr. *Vide* Faiz-ullah Khān.

Ahmad 'Ali Khan (احمد علی خان نواب), Nawāb of Karnāl. A remission of revenue to the extent of 5,000 rupees per annum was granted to him in perpetuity by the British Government, and a khil'at of the value of 10,000 rupees was conferred on him, in July, 1858, for his distinguished loyalty, and for the eminent services rendered by him during the rebellion of 1857. In 1806, the Pargana of Karnāl consisted of a number of villages, yielding a revenue of 40,000 rupees per annum. It was conferred by Lord Lake in jāgīr on three Mandal chiefs, named Muhammadī Khān, Ghairat 'Alī Khān, and Is-ḥāq Khān, for their lives, and after their death to descend to their heirs, subject to the payment of 15,000 rupees per annum in perpetuity. Nawāb Ahmad 'Alī Khān is the lineal descendant of Muhammadī Khān, and holds 24 entire villages, besides a third share in four others. These lands are assessed at 24,000 rupees, on which the Nawāb has hitherto paid a quit rent of 5,000 rupees, payment of which sum the Government has now remitted.

Ahmad 'Ali Khan (Sayyid) (احمد علی خان سید), Nawāb-Nāzim of Bengal, succeeded his brother 'Alī-Jāh. He died on the 30th October, A.D. 1824.

Ahmad 'Ali Khan, and Walīdād Khān, the rebel Nawābs of Mālāgaṛh.

Ahmad Ayaz, Malik Khwāja Jahān, served with distinction under Muhammad Shāh bin-Tughluq, of Dehlī. On the death of the king at Tatta, in A.D. 1352, A.H. 752, he tried to set up at Dehlī a son of the late king, but had to submit to Fīrūz Shāh III., who allowed the nobles to execute him before he himself entered Dehlī.

Ahmad Bakhsh Khan (Nawab), entitled Fakhr-ud-daula, was the jāgīrdār of Fīrūzpūr and Lohārū, in the district of Dehlī, after whose death his son, Nawāb Shams-uddīn Khān, succeeded him. The latter was executed for murder in October, 1835.

Ahmad Barani (احمد برنی), author of a Persian work called *Sifr-us-Siyar*.

Ahmad Beg Kabuli, served in Kabūl under Muhammad Ḥakīm, Akbar's brother, and later under Akbar and Jahāngīr. He was for some time governor of Kashmīr. He died about A.D. 1614.

Ahmad Beg Khan, a son of (Muhammad Sharīf) Nūr Jahān's brother. He served under Jahāngīr in Bengal, assisted Prince Shāhjahān during his rebellion, and was subsequently made, by Shāhjahān Governor of Tatta, Sīwistān, and of Multān. He received as jāgīr Jāis and Ameṭhī, in Audh, where he died.

Ahmad bin-'Abdullah al-Kirmi (احمد بن عبدالله), author of a work on the fundamental points of Muhammadanism. *Vide* Abū-Ahmad, the son of Qāsim.

Ahmad bin-Abu-Bakr, (احمد بن ابو بکر), an Arabian author who wrote the *Mashra'-ul-Manāqib*, a minute account of the events of Muhammad's life, with memoirs of his successors and companions.

Ahmad bin-Abu-Bakr bin-Nasir Mustafa al-Kazwini (احمد بن ابو بکر), author of the *Tārīkh-i-Guzīda*, which contains the history of the four ancient Persian Dynasties, viz. Peshdādians, Kaiānians, Ashkānians, and Sāsānians, that is, from the year B.C. 890 to A.D. 636, and memoirs of the several dynasties who ruled over Persia, Tartary, etc., during the khilāfat, and to the year A.D. 1329. See also called Ḥamd-ullah Mustaufī.

Ahmad bin 'Ali Razi (Shaikh) (احمد بن علی رازي شیخ), surnamed Jassās, a famous lawyer. He was born in the year A.D. 917, A.H. 305, and died in A.D. 980, A.H. 370, aged 65 lunar years.

Ahmad bin-'Ali al-Khatib Kastalani (احمد بن علی الخطیب). *Vide* Qasṭalānī.

Ahmad bin-Hasan Maimandi (Khwaja) (احمد بن حسن میمندی), foster brother and fellow student of his sovereign Sulṭān Mahmūd, of Ghaznī. On the removal of Abul-'Abbās Fazl, two years after the succession of Mahmūd, Khwāja Ahmad was appointed prime minister, which office he held uninterruptedly for a period of eighteen years, when Altūntāsh, the commander-in-chief, and a number of other Amīrs, brought before the court of the king charges against him. He was in consequence disgraced and imprisoned for thirteen years in one of the forts of India. He was released by Sulṭān Mas'ūd, son and successor of Mahmūd, and reinstated in the responsible office of minister, which he held for some time. He died a natural death in the year A.D. 1033, A.H. 424.

Ahmad bin-Idris (احمد بن ادريس), a lawyer of the sect of Mālik, was the author of many works, and died about the year A.D. 1285, A.H. 684.

Ahmad bin-Israil (احمد بن اسرائيل), a great astrologer who lived under the khilāfat of Wāṣiq Billah, of Baghdād.

Ahmad bin-Kasir (احمد بن كثير), also called Muhammad bin-Kaṣīr and Kaṣīr al-Farghānī, is the same person whom we call Alfaraganius, a great astronomer, who lived during the reign of the khalīfa al-Māmūn. *Vide* Farghānī.

Ahmad bin-Khizrawaih (احمد بن خضرويه), a celebrated Muhammadan saint, was the disciple of Khwāja Ḥātim Aṣamm. He died in the year A.D. 854, A.H. 240, and is buried at Balkh.

Ahmad bin-Muhammad al-Ghaffari al-Kazwini (احمد بن محمد الغفارى), a qāẓī, and a descendant of 'Abdul-Ghaffār, the author of the *Ḥāwī*. He is the author of the work called *Naskh-i-Jahān-ārā*, which he composed in the year A.D. 1563, A.H. 971, of which number the title forms the chronogram. It is also called *Tārīkh-i-Mukhtaṣir*, an abridged history of Asia, from Ādam down to Shāh Ṭahmāsp of Persia, A.D. 1525. It also contains memoirs of the Muhammadan kings of Spain, from A.D. 755 to 1036. It was dedicated to Shāh Ṭahmāsp. We are also indebted to him for the better known work entitled *Nigāristān*. We learn from the *Tārīkh Badāonī* that, having resigned his employment in Persia, he went towards the close of his life on a pilgrimage to Mecca, and that, landing in Dībal in Sindh, for the purpose of paying a visit to Hindūstān, he died at that port in A.D. 1567, A.H. 975.

[*Vide* Dowson, *Elliot's History of India*, ii. p. 504.]

Ahmad bin-Muhammad al-Qastalani (احمد بن محمد القسطلانى), an author who died in the year A.D. 1527, A.H. 933. *Vide* Qasṭalānī.

Ahmad bin-Muhammad Quduri (احمد بن محمد قدوري), author of a work on jurisprudence, called *Qudūrī*, and several other works. He died in A.D. 1046, A.H. 438.

Ahmad bin-Muhammad bin-'Ali Bakr al-Hanafi, author of the *Khazānat-ul-Fatāwa*, a collection of decisions made towards the end of the eighth century of the Hijra, and comprising questions of rare occurrence.

Ahmad bin-Tulun (احمد بن طولون), the founder of the Ṭūlūnide dynasty in Egypt. *Vide* Ahmad Ibn-Ṭūlūn.

Ahmad bin-Yahya bin-Jabir al-Biladuri (البلادرى or البلاذرى), surnamed also Abū-Ja'far and Abul-Hasan, was the instructor to one of the princes of the family of al-Mutawakkil, and died in A.D. 892, A.H. 279. His *Futūḥ-ul-Buldān* is one of the earliest Arabic chronicles. He also wrote a geographical work entitled *Kitāb-ul-Buldān*, the Book of Countries.

Ahmad bin-Yahya (احمد بن يحيى), author of the marginal notes on the *Wiqāya*, a work on jurisprudence.

Ahmad bin-Yusuf (احمد بن يوسف), an historian, and author of the *Akhbār-ud-dawal*, written in A.D. 1599, A.H. which is said to be an abridgment of Janābī's *Tārīkh-ul-Janābī*, called also *Bar-uzh-Zakhkhār*.

Ahmad Chap, Malik, was Nāib-Bārbak under Fīrūz Shāh II. (Khiljī), of Dehlī, whom he warned in vain against 'Alā-uddīn. He was blinded by 'Alā-uddīn after his accession.

Ahmad Ghaffari. *Vide* Ahmad bin-Muhammad al-Ghaffārī.

Ahmad Ghazzali. *Vide* Ghazzālī (Ahmad).

Ahmadi (احمدى), a Turkish poet, whose proper name was Khwāja Ahmad Ja'farī, and of whom we have the following anecdote: The great Tartar conqueror Amīr Timur (Tamerlane) being on his march through Anadoli, halted for awhile at Amasia, where Ahmadī lived; and the poet took the opportunity of presenting him with an ode. This led to further intimacies, Timur being a patron of literary men; and one day when both were in the bath, the monarch amused himself by putting crotchetty questions to Ahmadī, and laughing at his answers. "Suppose now," said he, pointing to the surrounding attendants, "you were required to value these beautiful boys, how much would you say each was worth?" Ahmadī answered with becoming gravity, estimating one at a camel-load of silver, another at six bushels of pearls, a third at forty gold wedges, and so made the circuit of the ring. "Very fair," said Timur, "and now tell me, What do you value Me at?" "Four and twenty aspers," replied the poet, "no more and no less." "What!" cried Timur, laughing, "why the shirt I have on is worth that." "Do you really think so?" asked Ahmadī, with the greatest apparent simplicity—"at that rate you must be worth nothing, for I included the shirt in the valuation!" Much to his credit, Timur, instead of being angry, applauded and rewarded the wit and boldness of the poet. Ahmadī was a contemporary of Shaikhī, and is the author of the *Kulliyāt-i-Khwāja Ahmad Ja'farī*. He also composed a heroic poem on the actions of Tamerlane, and a Sikandar-nāma in the Turkish language. He died in A.D. 1412.

Ahmadi (احمدى), the poetical name of Mīr Sayyid Luṭf-ullah, who died in A.D. 1633, A.H. 1043.

Ahmad Ibn-'Arab-Shah. *Vide* 'Arab-Shāh.

Ahmad Ibn-Hanbal. *Vide* Ḥanbal (Imām).

Ahmad Ibn-Tulun (احمد ابن طولون), the founder of the Ṭūlūnide dynasty in Egypt, a Turkish slave, who, being entrusted by al-Mu'tamid, the khalīfa of Baghdād, with the government of that country and Syria in A.D. 879, set up for himself, and maintained his authority notwithstanding all attempts to depose him. He reduced Damascus, Ḥimṣ, Ḥamāt, Ḳinnisrīn, and ar-Raqqa, situated upon the eastern banks of the Euphrates. His mosque in Cairo may be seen to this day. He died in A.D. 884, A.H. 270, and was succeeded by his son Khumārwaih. Egypt continued to be governed by his successors for several years, when it was again reduced in A.D. 905 by Muhammad, general of the khalīfa of Baghdād al-Muktafī; the last khalīfa of Egypt having assassinated his predecessor, and thereby rendered himself very odious. In the year 933, Muhammad, the son of Tāj, or Tājīl, surnamed al-Ashhad, seized upon Syria and Egypt in the khilāfat of ar-Rāẕī Billah, and his family retained the whole of it, except a small part which 'Ubaid-ulla al-Mahdī, the first of the Fāṭimite dynasty (the seat of whose empire was at Qairuwān, near Tunis) had conquered in A.D. 910. His successor, Abū-Tamīm Ma'd, surnamed Mu'izz li-dīn-illah, conquered the rest of Egypt about the year 970, by his general Ja'far, who built the city of al-Qāhira, commonly called Grand Cairo, whither his master soon removed his court. The Fāṭimite dynasty ended in A.D. 1176, when, upon the death of the last prince of this family, the kingdom was usurped by the famous Ṣalāḥ-uddīn (Saladin).

List of the Khalīfas of Barbary.

'Ubaid-ullah al-Mahdī, first of the Fāṭimite race.

Al-Qāim Mahdī, his son.

Ismā'īl, surnamed al-Manṣūr, son of al-Qāim.

Mu'izz li-dīn-illah, son of al-Manṣūr, who conquered Egypt and became the first khalīfa of the Fāṭimite dynasty in that country.

Ahmad Ilkani (احمد ايلكانى), also called Ahmad Jalāyir. *Vide* Hasan Buzurg.

Ahmad Jafari (Khwaja) (احمد جعفرى). *Vide* Ahmadī.

Ahmad Jalal Bukhari (Sayyid), son of Sayyid Muhammad Bukharī.

Ahmad Jalayir (احمد جلاير), also called Ahmad Īlkānī, a descendant of Hasan Buzurg, which see.

Ahmad Jam (Shaikh ul-Islam) (احمد جام), entitled Abū-Naṣr and Zinda-Pīl, a celebrated Muhammadan saint of Nīshāpūr, born in the year A.D. 1049 A.H. 441. He passed 18 years of his life in devotion in wilds and mountains. He subsequently got married, and was blessed with thirty-nine sons and three daughters. At the time of his death, besides the three daughters, fourteen of his sons were living, all of whom became men of learning and authors of several works. Ahmad Jām himself was an author, and among the different works that he wrote are the following: *Risāla Samarqandī*, *Anīs-ut-Ṭālibīn*, *Miftāḥ-un-Najāt*, *Bahr-ul-Ḥaqīqat*, and *Sirāj-us-Sāyirīn*. He died in the reign of Sulṭān Sanjar, in February, A.D. 1142, Rajab, A.H. 536.

Ahmad Jan (Sultan), of Hirāt. He died about the 6th April, A.D. 1863, 17th Shawwāl, A.H. 1279, and was succeeded by his son, Shāh Nawāz Khān.

Ahmad Kabir (Sayyid) (احمد كبير سيد), a Musalmān saint, whose tomb is at Uchcha in Multān. He is the son of Sayyid Jalāl, and the father of two other saints, Sayyid Jalāluddīn, surnamed Makhdūm Jahāniyān Jahān-gasht, and Rājū Qattāl. Numerous miracles were wrought by these two brothers.

Ahmad Khan (احمد خان), surnamed Nekodār (or Nicholas), was raised to the throne of Persia after the death of his brother Abāqā Khān, the son of Hulākū Khān, in April, A.D. 1282, Ẕil-ḥijja, A.H. 680, and was the first emperor of the race of Chingiz Khān who embraced the Muhammadan religion. He is said to have been baptized in his youth by the name of Nicholas, but policy, or conviction, led him to abandon the doctrine of Christ for that of Muhammad, when he assumed the name of Ahmad Khān. In the first year of his reign, Majd-ul-Mulk Yazdī, a nobleman of his court, being accused of sorcery, lost his life. He put his own brother to death, and was successful in obtaining possession of the person of his nephew, Arghūn Khān; but that prince was not only rescued from his violence by the Mughul nobles, but by their aid was enabled to deprive him of his crown and life on the night of Thursday 11th August, A.D. 1284, 26th Jumādạ I., A.H. 683, and become his successor.

Ahmad Khan Bangash (احمد خان بنگش), second son of Muhammad Khān Bangash, Nawāb of Farrukhābād. When the Wazīr Ṣafdar-Jang, after the death of Qāim-Jang, the brother of Ahmad Khān, confiscated his estates in December, A.D. 1749, A.H. 1163, he (Ahmad Khān) collected an army of Afghāns, defeated rājā Nawal Rāi, the Wazīr's deputy, who was slain in the action, and recovered the territories lately seized from his family. This circumstance took place on Friday the 2nd August, 1750, 10th Ramaẓān, A.H. 1163. After this, Ahmad Khān governed his country about 22 lunar years, and died in November, 1771, Sha'bān, A.H. 1185, when he was succeeded by his son, Diler Himmat Khān, who received the title of Muẓaffar-Jang from the emperor Shāh 'Ālam, who was then on his way to Dehlī from Allāhābād.

Ahmad Khan Mewati, one of the petty rulers *(mulūk-i-ṭawāif)* who had usurped the chief parts of the Dehlī empire during the Sayyid dynasty (beginning of the fifteenth century). Ahmad Khān held Mewāt, his frontier coming close up to Dehlī. He had to submit to Buhlūl Lodī.

Ahmad Khan (Sayyid), C.S.I., of 'Alīgaṛh, a distinguished Muhammadan reformer. He wrote a book on the life and work of the Prophet, and founded the 'Alīgaṛh College. (See Sayyid Ahmad.)

Ahmad Khan Sur. *Vide* Sikandar Khān Sūr.

Ahmad Khattu (Shaikh) (احمد کهتو شیخ), surname of Wajīh-uddīn Ahmad Maghribī, who was the son of Malik Ikhtiyār-uddīn, a nobleman at the court of Sulṭān Fīrūz Shāh Tughluq of Dehlī, and related to him. After the death of his father, having squandered his wealth in pleasure and dissipation, he became a disciple of Shaikh Bābā Is-ḥāq Maghribī, and turned very pious and journeyed to Gujrāt, where he acquired great fame. During his residence at that place, he obtained such celebrity, that Sulṭān Muẓaffar Gujrātī became his disciple. He died in that country in the reign of Sulṭān Muhammad of Gujrāt, on Thursday 6th of January, 1446, 8th Shawwāl, A.H. 849, aged 111 years, and was buried at Sarkich, near Ahmadābād. Khaṭṭū is a place in Nāgor, where Shaikh Ahmad was born.

Ahmad Maghribi. *Vide* Ahmad Khaṭṭū (Shaikh).

Ahmad Mirza (Sultan) (احمد مرزا سلطان), son of Abū-Sa'īd Mirzā, after whose death, in A.D. 1469, he took possession of Samarqand, and died about the year 1495.

Ahmad (Mulla) (احمد ملا), the son of a qāẓī of Tatta. His ancestors, who resided in Sindh, were Fārūqīs of the Ḥanīfa sect, but he was a Shī'a. He is the author of a work called *Khulāṣat-ul-Ḥayāt*, the Essence of Life. He came from the Deccan to the court of the emperor Akbar, in the year A.D. 1582, A.H. 990, and when that monarch ordered the *Tārīkh-i-Alfī* to be compiled, several authors were employed in the compilation, but subsequently the chief labour devolved upon Mullā Ahmad. The compilation of the first two volumes up to the time of Chingiz Khān was just finished by him, when Mīrzā Fūlād Birlās, during the month of January, 1588, Ṣafar, A.H. 996, persuaded the Mullā, who was always openly reviling the first khalīfas, to leave his own house at midnight on some pretence, and then murdered him in a street at Lahore. For this act Mīrzā Fūlād was sentenced to death, was bound alive to the leg of an elephant in the city of Lahore, and dragged along till he died. The Mullā expired three or four days after the Mīrzā. After the death of Mullā Ahmad, the remainder of the work was written by Āṣaf Khān Ja'far Beg, up to the year A.H. 997, or A.D. 1589. Mullā Ahmad was buried at Lahore, but being a Shī'a who openly used to revile the first khalīfas, the people of Lahore exhumed his remains and burnt them.

[Vide *Āīn Translation*, i. p. 206.]

Ahmad Nizam Shah Bahri (احمد نظام شاه), the founder of the Niẓām-Shāhī dynasty of the Deccan, was the son of Niẓām-ul-Mulk Baḥrī, prime minister to Sulṭān Mahmūd Shāh Bahmanī. He had conquered many places in the vicinity of his father's jāgīr, and was besieging the fort of Dundrājpūr about the year A.D. 1486, A.H. 891, when he received intelligence of the assassination of his father, and immediately returned and assumed the titles of the deceased, and was generally known by those of Ahmad Niẓām-ul-Mulk Baḥrī, to which the people of the Deccan added the title of Shāh. As he had distinguished himself repeatedly as a general in the field, though the Sulṭān wished to remove him from power, none of his nobility would accept the task of reducing him. He, however, on the 3rd May, 1490, 3rd Rajab, A.H. 895, gained a victory over the army of the Sulṭān, and from that time he sat without opponent on the masnad of royalty, and by the advice of Yūsuf 'Ādil Shāh, who had already become independent, having discontinued to read the khuṭba in the name of the king, put in his own and spread a white umbrella over his head. He laid the foundation of the city of Ahmadnagar in A.D. 1495, A.H. 900, which was completed in two years, and became the first of the Niẓām-Shāhī kings of Ahmadnagar. He died in A.D. 1508, A.H. 914, and was succeeded by his son, Burhān Niẓām Shāh I. The following is a list of the Niẓām-Shāhī kings of Ahmadnagar:

Ahmad Niẓām Shāh I., A.D. 1490.
Burhān Niẓām Shāh, 1508.
Husain Niẓām Shāh I., 1553.
Murtaẓa Niẓām Shāh, 1565.
Mīrān Husain Niẓām Shāh, 1587.
Ismā'īl Niẓām Shāh, 1589.
Burhān Niẓām Shāh II.
Ibrāhīm Niẓām Shāh, 1594.
Ahmad Niẓām Shāh II., son of Shāh Ṭāhir, 1594.
Bahādur Niẓām Shāh, 1595.
Murtaẓa Niẓām Shāh II., 1598.

The Niẓām Shāhī dominions fall under the control of Malik 'Ambar, 1607.

Ahmad Pasha (احمد پاشا), a general of Sulaimān I., emperor of Turkey, who, when appointed Governor of Egypt, revolted from his sovereign in A.D. 1524. He was soon after defeated by Ibrāhīm, the favourite of Sulaimān, and his head was sent to Constantinople.

Ahmad Rumi (احمد رومي), author of the *Fāiq-ul-Ḥaqāiq*, a work written in imitation of the *Masnawī* of Jalāl uddīn Rūmī.

Ahmad Samani (Amir) (احمد ساماني امير), second king of the race of Sāmān (Samanides), succeeded his father Amīr Ismā'īl in the provinces of Khurāsān, etc., in A.D. 907, A.H. 295. He was a cruel prince, and contended with his uncle, his brothers, and other relations, for the extensive possessions of his father, more by intrigues at the court of Baghdād than by arms. After a reign of seven years, he was murdered by some of his domestics on Thursday 30th January, A.D. 914, 23rd Jumādạ I., A.H. 301, and his son, Amīr Naṣr, then only eight years of age, was placed upon the throne of Khurāsān and Bukhārā. Ahmad was buried in Bukhārā, and they gave him the title of Sulṭān Shahīd, *i.e.* the martyred king.

Ahmad Sarhindi (Shaikh) (احمد سرهندی شیخ), entitled Mujaddid-i-Alf-i-Ṣānī, a dervish celebrated for his piety and learning, was the son of Shaikh 'Abdul-Wāḥid Fārūqī, and was born at Sarhind in A.D. 1563, A.H. 971. He was a disciple of Khwāja Bāqī, a celebrated saint of Dehlī, and is the author of several works. He died on Tuesday 29th November, A.D. 1624, the last Tuesday in the month of Safar, A.H. 1034, and is buried at Sarhind. He was called "Mujaddid-i-Alf-i-Ṣānī, or the "Renewer of the second Millennium," because he adopted the general belief that every thousand years a man was born who has a thorough knowledge of the Islām, and whose vocation it is to revive and strengthen it. He believed that he was the man of the second *(ṣānī)* Millennium *(alf)*.

Ahmad, Sayyid, of Bārha, brother of Sayyid Mahmūd Bārha, served under Akbar in Gujrāt. He was in charge of Akbar's hunting leopards. His son, Sayyid Jamāluddīn, was killed by the explosion of a mine before Chītor.

Ahmad, Sayyid, of Bukhārā, father of the renowned Shaikh Farīd-i-Bukhārī. *Vide* below.

Ahmad Shah (احمد شاه), entitled Mujāhid-ud-dīn Muhammad Abun-Naṣr Ahmad Shāh Bahādur, was the son of Muhammad Shāh, emperor of Dehlī, whom he succeeded on the 15th April, A.D. 1748, 27th Rabī' II., A.H. 1161. His mother's name was Udham Bāī. He was born in the fort of Dehlī on Tuesday 14th December, A.D. 1725, 17th Rabī' II., A.H. 1138, and crowned in Pānīpat on Monday 19th April, A.D. 1748, 2nd Jumādạ I., A.H. 1161. After a reign of 6 years 3 months and 8 days, he was deposed and imprisoned, and afterwards blinded, together with his mother, by his prime minister, 'Imād-ul-Mulk Ghāzī-uddīn Khān, on Sunday 2nd June, N.S. 1754. After this, he lived more than 21 years, and died on the 1st January, A.D. 1775, from bodily disease. He was buried in front of the mosque of Qadam-Sharīf in Dehlī, in the mausoleum of Maryam-Makānī. After his imprisonment, 'Ālamgīr II., son of Jahāndār Shāh, was raised to the throne.

[Vide *Proc. As. Soc. Bengal*, for 1874, p. 208.]

Ahmad Shah Abdali (احمد شاه ابدالی), commonly called Shāh Durrānī, was the son of a chief of the Afghān tribe of Abdāl, in the vicinity of the city of Hirāt. He was taken prisoner in his infancy by Nādīr Shāh, who gave him the post of a mace-bearer, and by degrees promoted him to a considerable command in the army. The morning after the assassination of Nādīr Shāh, which took place in the night of the 12th May, 1747, O.S., he made an attack, supported by a corps of Uzbeks, upon the Persian troops, but was repulsed. He then left the army, and proceeding by rapid marches to Qandahār, not only obtained possession of that city, but took a large convoy of treasure which was coming from

Kābul and Sindh to the Persian camp. By the aid of these means, he laid the foundation of a kingdom, which soon attained a strength that rendered it formidable to the surrounding nations. He not only subdued Qandahār and Kābul, but took Peshāwar and Lahore; and emboldened by this success, and the weakness of the empire, he resolved the conquest of the capital of Hindūstān. In the beginning of the year A.D. 1748, A.H. 1161, he began his march from Lahore. Muhammad Shāh, the emperor of Dehlī, being at this time too indisposed to take the field, despatched his only son, prince Ahmad, against the enemy, under the command of the wazīr Qamar-uddīn Khān, Safdar-Jang, governor of Audh, and several other chiefs, with a great army. For some days several skirmishes took place between the two armies near Sarhind. At length, on Friday 11th March, A.D. 1748, 22nd Rabī' I., A.H. 1161, Qamar-uddīn Khān, the wazīr, being killed as he was at his devotion in his tent by a cannon ball, a panic prevailed in the Mughul army; the battle, however, continued till a magazine of rockets taking fire in the enemy's camp, numbers of the troops were wounded by the explosion; and Shāh Abdālī, either disheartened by the loss, or satisfied by the plunder gained at Sarhind, thought it proper to retreat towards Kābul, which he did unmolested. In the year, A.D. 1757, A.H. 1170, he again advanced as far as Dehlī and Āgra, and after having plundered and massacred the inhabitants of Mathurā, he returned to Qandahār. About the year A.D. 1758, A.H. 1172, the Maratha power had spread itself in almost every province of Hindūstān, when Najīb-ud-daula, the Rohela, Shujā'-ud-daula Nawāb, of Audh, and not only the Musalmāns, but Hindūs also, joined in petition to Ahmad Shāh Abdālī, that he would march and assume the throne of Dehlī, in which they promised to support him. The Abdālī, enraged at the seizure of Lahore by the Marāthas, rejoiced at the invitation, and advanced without delay across the Indus, and driving the Marathas before him, he did not stop till they reached the vicinity of Dehlī. He engaged the Marathas in several battles, and attained the highest renown among Muhammadans by the memorable defeat that he gave the hostile army on the plains of Pānīpat. This famous action was fought in January, 1761. After this victory, Durrānī Shāh returned to his own country, but before his departure he acknowledged Shāh 'Ālam, then in Bengal, as emperor of Hindūstān, and commanded Shujā'-ud-daula and other chiefs to submit to his authority. He died after a reign of 26 years in A.D. 1772, A.H. 1182, aged 50 years, and was succeeded by his son, Timur Shāh. His tomb, covered with a gilt cupola, stands near the king's palace, and is held sacred as an asylum.

Ahmad Shah Bahmani II. (Sultan) (احمد شاه بهمنی). On the death of his father, Sultān Mahmūd Shāh II., in October, A.D. 1518, Shawwāl, A.H. 924, Amīr Barīd, his prime minister, dreading that the surrounding powers would attack him should he assume open independence, placed prince Ahmad, son of the late king, upon the throne at Ahmadābād Bīdar, leaving him the palace, with the use of the royal jewels, and a daily allowance of money for his support. The sum not being equal to his expenses, the king broke up the crown, which was valued at 400,000 huns, or £160,000, and privately sold the jewels. He died two years after his accession to the throne, in the year A.D. 1521, A.H. 927. After his death Amīr Barīd raised Sultān 'Alā-uddīn III., one of the princes, on the throne. Two years after he was imprisoned, and another son of Mahmūd Shāh, named Walī-ullah Shāh, was placed in his room. Three years after his accession, the minister conceiving a passion for his wife, he caused him to be poisoned, and espoused the queen. He then placed Kalīm-ullah, the son of Ahmad Shāh II., on the throne. This prince enjoyed nothing but the name of sovereign, and was never allowed to leave the palace. He was afterwards treated with great rigour by Amīr Barīd, whereupon he made his escape, first to his uncle Ismā'īl 'Ādil Shāh to Bījāpūr, and thence to Burhān Nizām Shāh of Ahmadnagar, where he resided till his death. With him ended the dynasty of the Bahmanī kings of the Deccan. In fact, before this event, the Deccan was divided into five kingdoms—'Ādil-Shāhī, or kings of Bījāpūr; Qutb-Shāhī, or kings of Golkonda; 'Imād-Shāhī, or kings of Barar; Nizām-Shāhī, or kings of Ahmadnagar; and Barīd-Shāhī, kings of Ahmadābād Bīdar.

Ahmad Shah I. (احمد شاه), second king of Gujrāt, was the son of Tātār Khān and grandson of Muzaffar Shāh, whom he succeeded as king of Gujrāt. The author of the *Muntakhab-ut-Tawārīkh* states that his grandfather placed him on the throne during his lifetime, in the year A.H. 813, A.D. 1410, and that he survived that measure five months and sixteen days. In the same year he laid the foundation of a new city on the banks of the Sābarmatī, which he called after his own name, Ahmadābād, and which afterwards became the capital of the kings of Gujrāt. The date of the laying of the foundation of this city is contained in the words "Bā-khair," *i.e.* all well. He died after a reign of nearly 33 years, on the 4th July, A.D. 1443, 4th Rabī' I., A.H. 847, and was succeeded by his son, Muhammad Shāh.

Ahmad Shah II. (احمد شاه ثاني), king of Gujrāt. After the death of Mahmūd Shāh III., there being no relation on whom the succession might devolve, I'timād Khān, the prime minister, resolved rather than see the kingdom in absolute anarchy, to elevate a youth, whom he asserted to be the son of prince Ahmad Khān, formerly governor of Ahmadābād, and declared him the legal successor to the crown of Gujrāt. He was forthwith placed on the throne on the 18th

February, A.D. 1554, 15th Rabī' I., A.H. 961. He reigned seven years and some months, and was found murdered one morning at the foot of the palace wall. This event took place on Monday the 21st April, A.D. 1561, 5th Sha'bān, A.H. 968. He was succeeded by Muzaffar Shāh III.

[*Vide* *Āīn Translation*, i. p. 335.]

Ahmad Shah of Bengal (احمد شاه), succeeded his father, Jalāl-uddin, to the throne of Bengal in A.H. 834, or A.D. 1430, reigned about 16 years, and died about the year A.D. 1446, A.H. 850. He was succeeded by Nāẓir-uddīn Mahmūd Shāh I., a descendant of Shams-uddīn Ilyās Shāh.

Ahmad Shah, or Ahmad-ullah Shah (احمد شاه), commonly called "The Maulawī," a prominent character in the neighbourhood of Shahjāhānpūr and Muhammadī during the mutiny of 1857. He is said to have been the inspired Faqīr who travelled through the upper provinces, a few years ago, on a miraculous mission. He made a pretty long stay at Āgra, astonishing the natives and puzzling the authorities. It seems probable that he was even then busy in sowing the seeds of rebellion. He held great power within the city of Lucknow, in March, 1858, when the Commander-in-chief entered that city and commanded a stronghold in the very heart of the city. He was slain at Pawain, on the 15th June, 1858, sixteen miles north-east of Shāhjahānpūr, and the rājā of that place sent the head and trunk to Mr. Gilbert Money, the Commissioner.

Ahmad Shah Wali Bahmani I. (Sultan) (احمد شاه ولی بهمنی), was the second son of Sulṭān Dāūd Shāh of the Bahmanī race. He ascended the throne of the Deccan on the 15th September, A.D. 1422, 5th Shawwāl, A.H. 825, ten days before the demise of his brother, Sulṭān Fīrūz Shāh, who had resigned the crown in his favour. He is the founder of the city and fort of Ahmadābād Bīdar, the foundation of which he laid in the year A.D. 1432, A.H. 836. It is said that the Sulṭān, on his return from a war at Bīdar, took to the amusement of hunting; and coming to a most beautiful spot, finely watered, resolved to build upon it a city, to be called after his name, Ahmadābād. A citadel of great extent and strength was erected on the very site of Bīdar, the ancient capital of princes, who, according to the Hindū books, 5,000 years back, possessed the whole extent of Mīrhat, Karnatik, and Talingāna. Rājā Bhīm Sen was one of the most celebrated of this house, and the history of the loves of his daughter and Rājā Nal, king of Mālwā, are famous through all Hindūstān. Their story was translated from the Sanskrit by Shaikh Faiẓī, under the title of *Nal Daman*, into Persian verse, at the command of the emperor, Akbar Shāh. Ahmad Shāh reigned 12 lunar years and 10 months, and died on the 19th February, A.D. 1435, 18th Rajab, A.H. 838. He was buried at Ahmadābād Bīdar, and was succeeded by his son, Sulṭān 'Alā-uddīn II.

Ahmad (Shaikh) (احمد غزنوی شیخ), of Ghaznī, author of the work entitled *Maqāmāt-i-Shaikh Ahmad*, containing the Life of Ahmad Jām, Shaikh-ul-Islām, of Nīshāpūr; with a minute account of the miracles performed by him. *Vide* Ahmad Jām.

Ahmad (Shaikh) (احمد امیٹھی شیخ), commonly called Mullā Jīwan, of Amethī, was the tutor of the emperor 'Ālamgīr, and author of the *Tafsīr-i-Ahmadī*. He died in A.D. 1718, A.H. 1130. *Vide* Mullā Jīwan.

Ahmad (Shaikh), second son of Shaikh Salīm Chishtī, of Fathpūr Sīkrī. He served under Akbar, and died in A.H. 985.

Ahmad Shihab-uddin Talish (احمد شهاب الدین تالش). *Vide* Shihāb-uddīn Ahmad Tālish.

Ahmad Suhaili (Amir) (احمد سهیلی امیر), seal-bearer to Sulṭān Husain Mirzā of Hirāt, to whom several of the poets of his time dedicated their works. Husain Wāiẓ dedicated his *Anwār Suhailī* to him. *Vide* Suhailī.

Ahmad-ullah Shah, commonly called "The Maulawī"; see **Ahmad Shah.**

Ahmad Yadgar (احمد یادگار), author of the *Tārīk-i-Salāṭīn-i-Afāghina*, a history of the Afghān kings of India from Buhlīd Lodī, composed by order of Dāūd Shāh, last king of Bengal.

[*Vide* Dowson, v. p. 1.]

Ahmad Yar Khan (احمد یار خان), whose poetical name is Yaktā, was of the tribe of the Turks called Birlās. His father, Allah Yār Khān, held at different periods the sūbadārī of Lahore, Tatta, and Multān, and was afterwards appointed to the Faujdarī of Ghaznī. Ahmad Yār Khān also held the Sūbadārī of Tatta in the latter part of the reign of 'Ālamgīr. He was an excellent poet, and is the author of several poems. He died on the 21st September, A.D., O.S. 1734, 23rd Jumāda I., A.H. 1147.

Ahmad Yar Khan (Nawab), of Barelī, the son of Nawāb Ẕul-fiqār-ud-daula Muhammad Zul-fiqār Khān Bahādur Dilāwar-Jang of Barelī. He was alive in A.D. 1815, A.H. 1230.

Ahmad Zarruq (احمد زروق), surname of Abul-'Abbās Ahmad bin-Ahmad bin-Muhammad bin-'Isā Barallusī, author of the commentary called *Sharḥ Asmā'il-Ḥusnạ*. He died in A.D. 1493, A.H. 899.

Ahsan (احسن), poetical name of 'Ināyat Khān, the son of Nawāb Ẕafar Khān. He was Governor of Kābul in the reign of 'Ālamgīr, and is the author of a Dīwān. *Vide* Āshnā.

Ahsan-ullah Khan (Hakim) (احسن الله حكيم), so well-known at Dehlī, died in September, 1873, in that city.

'Ain-uddin (Shaikh) (عين الدين شيخ), of Bījāpūr, author of the *Mulḥaqāt*, and *Kitāb-ul-Anwār*, containing a history of all the Muhammadan saints of India. He flourished in the time of Sulṭān 'Alī-uddīn Hasan Bahmanī.

'Ain-ul-Mulk (Hakim) (عين الملك حكيم), a native of Shīrāz, and a well-educated and learned Musalmān, was an officer of rank in the time of the emperor Akbar. He was an elegant poet, and his poetical name was Wafā. He died in the 40th year of the emperor's reign in A.D. 1594, A.H. 1003.

[For further notes, vide *Āīn Translation*, i. p. 481.]

'Ain-ul-Mulk (Khwaja) (عين الملك خواجه), a distinguished nobleman of the court of Sulṭān Muhammad Shāh Tughluq and his successor Sulṭān Fīrūz Shāh, kings of Dehlī. He is the author of several works, one of which is called *Tarsīl 'Ain-ul-Mulkī*. He also appears to be the author of another work called *Fatḥ-nāmā*, containing an account of the conquests of Sulṭān 'Alā-uddīn, who reigned from A.D. 1296 to 1316.

'Aish (عيش), the poetical name of Muhammad 'Askarī, who lived in the reign of the emperor Shāh 'Alam.

'Aishi (عيشى), a poet, who is the author of a Masnawī called *Haft Akhtar*, or the seven planets, which he wrote in A.D. 1675, A.H. 1086.

Ajaipal, the rājā who founded Ajmīr about A.D. 1183.

Ajit Singh, a Sikh chief and murderer of Mahārājā Sher Singh of Lahore. He also slew Dhaiān Singh, another chief, and was himself seized by Hira Singh, the son of Dhaiān Singh, and put to death together with Lena Singh and others. This took place in September, 1843.

Ajit Singh (Raja) (اجيت سنگه راجه), a Rāṭhaurī Rājpūt, and hereditary zamīndār of Mārwār, or Jodhpūr, was the son of Rājā Jaswant Singh Rāṭhaurī. He was restored in A.D. 1711 to the throne of his ancestors, and gave his daughter in marriage to the emperor Farrukhsiyar in the year A.D. 1716. He was murdered one night, when fast asleep, at the instigation of his son, Abhai Singh, who succeeded him. This took place in the beginning of the reign of the emperor Muhammad Shāh, about A.D. 1724.

'Ajiz (عاجز), the poetical name of 'Ārif-uddīn Khān, who lived about A.D. 1754, A.H. 1168.

'Ajiz, the poetical name of Lālā Gangā Bishn, father of Rāmjas Munshī, which see.

Ajmal (Shah) (اجمل), or Shāh Muhammad Ajmal, a Pīrzāda of Allāhābād, was a descendant of Shāh Khūb-ullah, and younger brother of Shāh Ghulām Quṭb-uddīn, the son of Shāh Muhammad Fākhir, the respectability of whose family is well-known at Allāhābād. He died in the year A.D. 1821, A.H. 1236.

Ajmiri Khan, an inhabitant of Ajmīr. He walked with the emperor Akbar from Āgra to Ajmīr, on which account he received the title of Ajmīrī Khān from that emperor. He had built a garden on a spot of 28 bīghas of ground at Āgra. This place is now called Ajmīrī Khān-kā Tīla.

Aka Rihi, of Nishāpūr, an author.

Akbarabadi Mahall (اكبرابادى محل), A'azz-un-Nisā Begam, was the name of one of the wives of the emperor Shāh Jahān. The large red stone mosque at Faiẕbāzār, in Dehlī, was built by her in the year A.D. 1651, A.H. 1060, at a cost of 150,000 rupees. She died on the 29th January, A.D. 1677, 4th Ẕil-ḥijja, A.H. 1087, in the reign of 'Ālamgīr. There is also a masjid inside the city of Āgra built by her, called Akbarābādī Masjid. She had a villa also built at Āgra.

Akbar 'Ali Tashbihi (اكبر علي تشبيهي). He is mentioned in the Khulāṣat-ul-Ash'ār to have been the son of a washerman. He went to India, and turned faqīr, but, as he was an infidel, his ascetic exercises cannot have been of much use to his soul. He left a dīwān of about 8000 verses, and a maṣnawī, called *Zarra wa Khurshed.* He was alive in A.D. 1585, A.H. 993.

[Regarding this poet, vide *Āīn Translation*, i. p. 956.]

Akbar Khan, the son of Dost Muhammad Khān, ruler of Kābul, by his first wife. He shot Sir W. H. Macnaghten on the 26th December, 1841, when his father, Dost Muhammad Khān, was a State prisoner in India. When his father, Dost Muhammad Khān, came in possession of Kābul after the retreat of the English in 1842, he was appointed heir-apparent in preference to Muhammad Afzal Khān, his eldest son by his second wife. He died in 1848, when his full brother, Ghulām Haidar Khān, was nominated heir-apparent, after whose death, in 1858, Sher 'Ali, his brother, was nominated.

Akbar (Prince), the youngest son of the emperor 'Alamgīr, was born on the 10th September, O.S. 1657, 11th Ẕil-ḥijja, A.H. 1067, raised the standard of rebellion against his father, and joined the Maratha chief Sambhujī in June, 1681. He afterwards quitted his court, and repaired to Persia, where he died in A.D. 1706, A.H. 1118, a few months before his father, and was buried at Mashhad, in Khurāsān. 'Ālamgīr, at one time, intended to make Akbar his successor, and this preference arose from Akbar being the son of a Muhammadan mother, the daughter of Shāh Nawāz Khān; whereas his brothers, Sulṭāns Mu'azzam and A'ẓam, were born of Rājpūt princesses.

Akbar Shah (اكبر شاه), the Great, emperor of Hindūstān, surnamed Abul-Fatḥ Jalāl-uddīn Muhammad, was the eldest son of the emperor Humāyūn, and was born in Amarkoṭ in the province of Sindh, on Sunday the 15th October, A.D. 1542, 5th Rajab, A.H. 949, at a time when his father, after being defeated by Sher Shāh, had taken refuge with Rānā Prashād. At the time of his father's death, Akbar was at Kālānūr, where he had been deputed by his father with a considerable force to expel the ex-king Sikandar Shāh Sūr from the Siwālik mountains. When information reached the prince of this mournful event, Bairām Khān, and other officers who were present, raised him to the throne on Friday 14th February, A.D. 1556, 2nd Rabī' II., A.H. 963, Akbar being then only 13 years and 9 months old. He enlarged his dominions by the conquest of Gujrāt, Bengal, Kashmīr, and Sindh. Besides the forts of Aṭak, Agra, and Allāhābād, many military works were erected by him. He also built and fortified the town of Fathpūr Sīkrī, which was his principal residence, and which, though now deserted, is one of the most splendid remains of former grandeur of India. He died after a prosperous reign of 51 lunar years and 9 months, on Wednesday the 16th October, O.S. 1605, 13th Jumāda II., A.H. 1014, aged 64 lunar years and 11 months. The words "Faut-i-Akbar Shāh" (the death of Akbar Shāh), are the chronogram of his death. He was buried in the village of Sikandra, in the environs of Agra, where a splendid mausoleum was built over his remains by his son Jahāngīr, which is still in a high state of preservation. He received after his death the title of "Arsh-'Ashyānī," and was succeeded by his son Sulṭān Salīm, who assumed the title of Jahāngīr. His mother's name was Ḥamīda Bānū, commonly called Maryam-Makānī. The history of this potentate has been written, with great elegance and precision, by his wazīr Abul-Fazl, in the work entitled *Akbar-nāma.* In order to keep his turbulent Umarās, Turks, and Afghans, in check, Hindū chiefs were encouraged by Akbar, and entrusted with the highest powers, both military and civil, as was the case with Rājā Māldeo of Māṛwāṛ, Bhagwān Dās of Amber, Mān Singh, his son, and Rājā Todar Mal. He also connected himself and his sons with them by marriage. Both Akbar and his successor, Jahāngīr, had amongst their wives several of Hindū origin. Towards the middle of his reign, Akbar became dissatisfied with the Muhammadan religion, and invited to his court teachers of the Christian, Hindū, and Parsī religions, and took an interest in their discussions. He adopted, however, none of them, but attempted to found a new system of belief, called "Dīn-i-Ilāhī," which acknowledged one God, and the king as his vice-regent.

[Vide *Elphinstone's History of India*, and *Kaiser Akbar*, by the late Graf v. Noer (Prince Frederick of Schleswig-Holstein).]

Akbar Shah II. (اكبر شاه ثانى), king of Dehlī, whose title in full is Abul-Naṣr Mu'in-uddīn Muhammad Akbar Shāh, was the son of the nominal emperor Shāh 'Ālam; was born on Wednesday 23rd April, N.S. 1760, 7th Ramaẓān, A.H. 1173, and succeeded his father at the age of 48, on the 19th November, A.D. 1806, 7th Ramāẓān, A.H. 1221, as titular king of Dehlī. On his accession he made some weak attempts to increase his influence and power. These were properly resisted, but at the same time the pledge given by Lord Wellesley, to increase the allowance of the imperial family when the revenue of the country improved, was redeemed by an act of politic liberality. An augmentation of 10,000 rupees per mensem was appropriated for the support of his eldest son, whom he had declared heir-apparent. He sat on the throne of his ancestors nearly 32 lunar years; died on Friday 28th

September, A.D. 1837, 28th Jumāda II., A.H. 1253, aged about 80 lunar years, and was buried at Dehlī, close to the tomb of Bahādur Shāh. His son Bahādur Shāh II., the last king of Dehlī, succeeded him. Akbar sometimes wrote poetry, and used the word Shu'ā for his poetical name.

Akhfash Ausat (اخفش اوسط), was called Akhfash, because he had small eyes. His proper name is Abul-Hasan Sa'īd. He was an author, and died in the year A.D. 830. Some say he was born at Balkh, and died in A.H. 376. There were three persons of this name, all of whom were authors. Akhfash Asghar, or the lesser, died in A.D. 845.

Akhtar (اختر), the poetical name of Qāzī Muhammad Ṣādiq Khān, an excellent writer of prose and verse.

Akhtar (اختر), the poetical name of Wājid 'Alī Shāh, the last king of Audh, now of Garden Reach, Calcutta.

Akmal-uddin Muhammad bin-Mahmud (Shaikh), author of a commentary on the Hidāya, entitled *'Ināya*, or *al-'Ināya*. There are two commentaries on the Hidāya, commonly known by that name, but the one much esteemed for its studious analysis and interpretation of the text, is by this author; it was published in Calcutta in 1837. This author died in the year A.D. 1384, A.H. 786.

'Akrima, or more correctly **'Ikrima** (عکرمه), surname of Abū-'Abdullah, who was a freed slave of Ibn-'Abbās, and became afterwards his disciple. He was one of the greatest lawyers. He died in the year A.D. 725, A.H. 107.

Aksir, or more correctly, **Iksir (Mirza)** (اکسیر اصفهانی مرزا), of Iṣfahān, author of a book of elegies. He served under Nawāb Niẓām-ul-Mulk Āṣaf-Jāh and Ṣafdar-Jang, and died in Bengal in N.S. 1756, A.H. 1169.

Alahdad Sarhindi, or more correctly, **Ilahdad**, poetically styled Faizi, a native of Sarhind, and author of a Persian Dictionary called *Madār ul-Afāẓil*.

[Regarding this dictionary and its author, vide *Jour. As. Soc. Bengal*, 1868, p. 10.]

Al-Ahnaf (الاحنف), uncle of Yazid, the second khalīfa of the house of Umayya. At the battle of Ṣiffīn he had fought on the side of 'Alī. Several sayings of this celebrated chief are recorded in the Biographical Dictionary of Ibn Khallikān. He outlived Mu'āwiya.

Alahwirdi Khan (الهوردی خان), or more correctly, **Ilahwirdi Khan**, a nobleman of the reign of the emperor Jahāngīr. He was raised to the rank of 5,000 in the time of Shāh Jahān, and held several offices of importance. He was appointed Governor of Patna, and espoused the cause of Sulṭān Shujā', brother of Aurangzīb, A.D. 1658, A.H. 1068, and after the defeat of Shujā', accompanied him to Bengal, where he was slain, together with his son Saif-ullah, by order of that prince, in July, A.D. 1659, Ẕil-qa'da, A.H. 1069.

[The word *wirdī* or *wirdī* means "a rope," God being the *ḥabl-i-matīn*, the strong rope which the faithful seize so as not to perish.]

Alahwirdi Khan (الهوردی خان), or more correctly, **Ilahwirdi Khan**, title of Ja'far Khān, the son of Ilāhwīrdī Khān the first. He was raised to the rank of an amīr by 'Ālamgīr, with the title of Ilahwardī Khān 'Ālamgīr-Shāhī. He was appointed Sūbadār of Allāhābād, where he died A.D. 1669, A.H. 1079. He was an excellent poet, and has left a Dīwān.

Alahwirdi Khan, (اللهوردی خان مهابت جنگ), or more commonly, **Allahwirdi Khan**, styled Mahābat-Jang, the usurper of the government of Bengal, was originally named Mīrzā Muhammad 'Alī. His father, Mīrzā Muhammad, a Turkmān, an officer in the service of the prince A'ẓam Shāh, on the death of his patron in A.D. 1707, falling into distress, moved from Dehlī to Kaṭak, the capital of Orīsā, in hopes of mending his fortune under Shujā'-uddīn, the son-in-law of Nawāb Murshid Qulī Ja'far Khān, Sūbadār of Bengal, who received him with kindness, and after some time bestowed on his son the Faujdārī of Rājmaḥall, and procured for him from the emperor a manṣab and the title of Allahwīrdī Khān, and afterwards that of Mahābat-Jang. After the death of Shujā'-uddīn, and the accession of his son, Sarfarāz Khān, to the government of Bengal, Allahwīrdī overthrew the Nawāb, in an action in which the latter was slain, in A.D. 1740, A.H. 1153, and ursurped the government. He reigned sixteen years over the three provinces of Bengal, Bihār, and Orīsā, and died on Saturday the 10th April, N.S. 1756, 9th Rajab, A.H. 1169, aged 80 years. He was buried in Murshidābād, near the tomb of his mother, in the garden of Khush-Bāgh, and was succeeded by his grand-nephew and grandson, Mīrzā Mahmūd, better known by his assumed name of Sirāj-ud-daula. It does not appear that Allahwirdī ever remitted any part of the revenue to Dehlī after payment of the first instalment, of which the bulk went to the Maraṭha Government at Puna.

Alah Yar Khan (الله یار خان شیخ), or more correctly, **Ilah Yar Khan (Shaikh)**, son of Shaikh ʻAbdus-Subḥān, was formerly employed by Nawāb Mubāriz-ul-Mulk Sarbaland Khān, Governor of Gujrāt, and in the reign of the emperor Farrukhsiyar was raised to the rank of 6,000, with the title of Rustam Zamān Khān. In the time of the emperor Muhammad Shāh, when Rājā Abhai Singh, the son of Rājā Ajīt Singh Māṛwāṛī, was appointed Governor of Gujrāt in the room of Nawāb Sarbaland Khān, the latter made some opposition to his successor; a battle ensued, and Shaikh Ilāh Yār, who was then with the Nawāb, was killed in the action. This took place on the day of Dasahrā, 5th October, o.s. 1730, 8th Rabī II., A.H. 1143.

Alah Yar Khan (الله یار خان ابن افتخار خان), or more correctly, **Ilah Yar Khan**, son of Iftikhār Khān Turkmān, a nobleman of the court of Shāh Jahān. He died in Bengal in A.D. 1650, A.H. 1060.

Alah Yar Khan Mir-Tuzuk (الله یار خان میر توزک), or more correctly, **Ilah Yar Khan**, a nobleman in the time of the emperor ʻĀlamgīr, who held the rank of 1,500, and died A.D. 1662, A.H. 1073.

Alamayo (Prince), the son of king Theodore of Abyssinia. After the fall of Magdala and the death of his father, 10th April, 1868, he was sent to England to be educated, where he died.

Al-Amin (الامین), the 6th khalifa of the house of ʻAbbās, succeeded his father, Hārūn-ur-Rashīd, to the throne of Baghdād, in March, A.D. 809, A.H. 193. He was no sooner seated on the throne than he formed a design of excluding his brother, al-Māmūn, from the succession. Accordingly, he deprived him of the furniture of the imperial palace of Khurāsān; and in open violation of his father's will, who had bestowed on al-Māmūn the perpetual government of Khurāsān and of all the troops in that province, he ordered these forces to march directly to Baghdād. Upon the arrival of this order, al-Māmūn expostulated with the general al-Fazl Ibn Rabīʻa, who commanded his troops, and endeavoured to prevent his marching to Baghdād; but without effect, for he punctually obeyed the orders sent by the khalīfa. Al-Fazl having ingratiated himself with the khalīfa by his ready compliance with his orders, was chosen prime minister, and governed with absolute sway, al-Amīn abandoning himself entirely to drunkenness. Al-Fazl was a very able minister; but fearing al-Māmūn's resentment, if ever he should ascend the throne, he gave al-Amīn such advice as proved in the end the ruin of them both. He advised him to deprive al-Māmūn of the right of succession that had been given him by his father, and transfer it to his own son Mūsa, though then but an infant. Agreeable to this pernicious advice, the khalīfa sent for his brother al-Qāsim from Mesopotamia, and recalled al-Māmūn from Khurāsān, pretending he had occasion for him as an assistant in his councils. By this ill-treatment al-Māmūn was so much provoked, that he resolved to come to an open rupture with his brother. A war soon after broke out between them. Ṭāhir ibn-Husain, the general of al-Māmūn, laid siege to Baghdād, took it, and having seized al-Amīn, cut off his head, and exposed it to public view in the streets of Baghdād. Afterwards he sent it to al-Māmūn in Khurāsān, together with the ring or seal of the khilāfat, the sceptre and the imperial robe. At the sight of these, al-Māmūn fell down on his knees, and returned thanks to God for his success, making the courier who brought the insignia a present of a million dirhams. The death of al-Amīn took place on the 6th October, A.D. 813, 6th Ṣafar, A.H. 198. He was then 30 years of age, and had reigned but four years and some months.

ʻAlamgir I. (عالمگیر پادشاه), emperor of Hindūstān, surnamed Abul-Ẓafar Muhi-uddīn Muhammad Aurangzīb, took the title of ʻĀlamgīr on his accession to the throne. He was the third son of the emperor Shāh Jahān, born on Sunday 10th October, o.s. 1619, 11th Ẓil-qaʻda, A.H. 1028. His mother's name was Arjmand Bānū, surnamed Mumtāz-Maḥall. In his youth, he put on the appearance of religious sanctity, but in June, A.D. 1658, Ramẓān, A.H. 1068, during his father's illness, he, in conjunction with his brother, Murād Bakhsh, seized Āgra, and made his father prisoner. Murād was soon after imprisoned by ʻĀlamgīr, who marched to Dehlī, where he caused himself to be proclaimed emperor on the 21st July of the same year, 1st Ẓil-qaʻda, A.H. 1068, but was not crowned till the first anniversary of his accession, a circumstance which has introduced some confusion in the chronology of his reign. Soon after, he put Murād Bakhsh and his eldest brother, the heir-apparent, Dārā Shikoh, to death. He greatly enlarged his dominions, and became so formidable that all Eastern princes sent ambassadors to him. He was an able prince, but a bigoted Sunnī, and attempted to force the Hindūs to adopt that faith, destroying their temples, and levying the capitation tax (*jizya*) from every Hindū. The feudatory chiefs of Rājpūtānā successfully resisted the impost. He died after a reign of 50 lunar years at Ahmadnagar, in the Deccan, on Friday the 21st February, O.S. 1707, 28th Ẕil-qa'da, A.H. 1118, aged 90 lunar years and 17 days, and was interred in the court of the mausoleum of Shaikh Zain-uddīn, in Khuldābād, eight *kos* from the city of Aurangābād. After his death, he received the title of "Hazrat Khuld-Makān" (*i.e.* He whose place is in paradise). He was married in the 19th year of his age to a daughter of Shāhnawāz Khān, the son of 'Āsaf Khān, the prime minister of the emperor Jahāngīr, by whom he had five sons and four daughters. His eldest son, named Sultān Muhammad, died before his father; his second son was Muhammad Mu'azzam, who succeeded him with the title of Shāh 'Ālam Bahādur Shāh; the third, A'zam Shāh, was slain in battle fought against the latter; the fourth, Muhammad Akbar, who revolted against his father, took refuge in Persia, and died there; the fifth, Kām Bakhsh, who was also slain in battle. The names of his four daughters are: Zeb-un-Nisā, Zīnut-un-Nisā, Badr-un-Nisā, and Mihr-un-Nisā.

'Alamgir II., 'Azīz-uddīn, was the son of the emperor Jahāndār Shāh by Anūp Bāī; was born in A.D. 1688, A.H. 1099, and raised to the throne, in the fort of Dehlī, by 'Imād-ul-Mulk Ghāzī-uddīn Khān the wazīr, on Sunday the 2nd June, N.S. 1754, 10th Sha'bān, A.H. 1167, after the deposition and imprisonment of Ahmad Shāh, the son of the emperor Muhammad Shāh. He was, after a nominal reign of five years and some months, assassinated by the same person who had placed him on the throne, on the 29th November, N.S. 1759, 8th Rabī' II. A.H. 1173, and was interred in the platform before the mausoleum of the emperor Humāyūn. His son 'Ālī Gauhar (afterwards Shāh 'Ālam) being then in Bengal, Muḥiy-ul-Sunnat, son of Kām Bakhsh, the son of the emperor Aurangzīb, was seated on the throne, with the title of Shāh Jahān, and insulted by the empty name of emperor for some months, after which, on the 10th October, N.S. 1760, 29th Ṣafar, A.H. 1174, the Marathas having plundered Dehlī, prince Mīrzā Jawān Bakht, the son of 'Ālī Gauhar, was placed on the throne by the Maratha chief Bhāo, as regent to his father, who was still in Bengal.

Alap Arsalan. *Vide* Alp Arsalan.

Alaptigin or **Alptigin** (البتگين), one of the chief nobles of Bukhārā, and Governor of Khurāsān during the reign of the house of Sāmān. Having, in A.D. 962, renounced his allegiance to that court, he retired, with his followers, to Ghaznī, then an insignificant town, to escape the resentment of Amīr Manṣūr Sāmānī, whose elevation to the throne he had opposed, on the ground of his extreme youth. He established a petty principality, of which Ghaznī became the capital. He died A.D. 976, A.H. 366, when his son, Abū-Is-ḥaq, succeeded him; but that weak and dissipated prince survived his father but a short time; and the suffrage of all ranks gave the rule to Subiktagīn, a chief in the service of Alaptigīn, in A.D. 977, A.H. 367.

Al-Aswad (الاسود), an impostor. *Vide* Musailama.

'Ala-ud-daula (Prince) (علاؤالدوله نواب), the son of Bāisanghar Mirzā, and grandson of Shāhrukh Mirzā, after whose death, in A.D. 1447, he ascended the throne at Hirāt, but was soon driven from it by his uncle, Ulugh Beg. After the death of Ulugh Beg, A.D. 1449, he was imprisoned and blinded by his brother, Ṣultān Bābar. He died in A.D. 1459, A.H. 863.

'Ala-ud-daula (نواب علاؤالدوله), a Nawāb of Bengal. *Vide* Sarfarāz Khān.

'Ala-ud-daula (Mir or Mirza) (علاؤالدوله مير), a poet whose poetical name was Kāfī. He is the author of a biography of those poets who flourished in the reign of the emperor Akbar. The time of his death is not known, but he was living at the time of the conquest of Chītor by Akbar in A.D. 1567, A.H. 975. There is some mistake in his poetical name; he appears to be the same person who is mentioned under the poetical name of Kāmī, which see.

'Ala-ud-daula Samnani (علاؤالدوله سمناني), one of the chief followers of the Ṣūfī Junaid Baghdādī. In his youth he served Arghūn Khān, the Tartar king of Persia, and his uncle Sharaf-uddīn Samnānī was a nobleman at the court. He died on Friday the 8th March, A.D. 1336, 23rd Rajab, A.H. 736, aged 77 lunar years, six years before Khwajā Kirmānī.

'Ala-uddin (علاؤالدين), a Muhammadan prince of the Arsacides or Assassins, better known by the appellation of "The old man of the mountains." His residence was a castle between Damascus and Antioch, and was surrounded by a number of youths, whom he intoxicated with pleasures, and rendered subservient to his views, by promising still greater voluptuousness in the next world. As these were employed to stab his enemies, he was dreaded by the neighbouring princes.

[*Vide* Hasan Sabbāḥ.]

'Ala - uddin (Khwaja) (علاؤالدين خواجه عطاملک), surnamed 'Atā Mālik, was the brother of Shams-uddīn Muhammad Ṣāḥib, dīwān, and is the author of a history called *Jahānkushā*.

'Ala-uddin 'Ali al-Quraishi ibn-Nafis (علاؤالدين علي القريشي ابن نفيس), author of the commentary termed *Mūjiz-ul Qānūn fil-Ṭibb*, being an epitome of the canons of Avicenna. He died A.D. 1288.

'Ala-uddin Ali Shah (علاؤالدين على شاه), king of Western Bengal. He usurped the government of that country after defeating Fakhr-uddīn Mubārak Shāh, and was assassinated, about A.H. 746, by the instigation of Khwāja Ilyās, who succeeded him under the title of Shams-uddīn Ilyās Shāh.

'Ala-uddin Atsiz (علاؤالدين التسز), the son of 'Alā-uddīn Hasan Ghorī. He defeated Bahā-uddīn Sām in A.D. 1210, and reigned four years in Ghōr. He fell in battle against Tāj-uddīn Ildūz, A.D. 1214, and was the last of the kings of Ghōr, of the family of 'Alā-uddīn Hasan.

'Ala-uddin Hasan (علاؤالدين حسن غوري), prince of Ghōr, entitled Jahān-sōz. His elder brother, Quṭb-uddīn, prince of Ghōr, was publicly executed by his brother-in-law, Bahrām Shāh of Ghaznī, in A.D. 1119, A.H. 513. Saif-ud-daula, brother of the deceased, took possession of Ghaznī in A.D. 1148, A.H. 543, but afterwards was defeated, taken prisoner, and put to death by Bahrām Shāh in A.D. 1149, A.H. 544. When the mournful news of his brother's death reached 'Alā-uddīn, he burnt with rage, and being determined to take revenge, invaded Ghaznī with a great army. He defeated Bahrām Shāh, who fled to Lāhore, took possession of Ghaznī, in A.D. 1152, A.H. 574, and gave up the city to flames, slaughter, and devastation for several days, on which account he is known by the epithet of "Jahān-sōz," or the burner of the world. He carried his animosity so far as to destroy every monument of the Ghaznī emperors with the exception of those of Sulṭān Mahmūd, Mas'ūd, and Ibrāhīm; but he defaced all the inscriptions, even of their times, from every public edifice. 'Alā-uddīn died in the year A.D. 1156, A.H. 549, after a reign of six years, and was succeeded by his son Malik Saif-uddīn, or Saif-ud-daula, who in little more than a year fell in battle with the Ghiza Turkmāns. He was succeeded by his eldest cousin, Ghiyās-uddīn Muhammad Ghorī. The following is a list of the kings of Ghōr:

1. 'Alā-uddīn Hasan Ghorī.
2. Malik Saif-uddīn, son of 'Alā-uddīn Hasan Ghorī.
3. Ghiyāṣ-uddīn Muhammad Ghorī, son of Bahā-uddīn Sām, the younger brother of 'Alā-uddīn.
4. Shihāb-uddīn, brother of Ghiyāṣ-uddīn.
5. Ghiyāṣ-uddīn Mahmūd, son of Ghiyāṣ-uddīn.
6. Bahā-uddīn Sām, son of Ghiyāṣ-uddīn Mahmūd.
7. Atsiz, son of Jahān-sōz, and last of the kings of Ghōr of this branch.

'Ala-uddin I. (علاؤالدين حسن كانگوه بهمني), Hasan Kāngoh Bahmanī, the first Bahmanī king of the Deccan. He was a native of Dehlī, and in the service of a Brahmanical astrologer named Kāngoh, or Gāngoh, enjoying high favour with the prince Muhammad Tughluq, afterwards king of Dehlī. This Brahman assured Hasan that he perceived from his horoscope that he would rise to great distinction, and be eminently favoured of the Almighty; and made him promise that if he ever should attain regal power, he would use the name of Kāngoh and employ him as his minister of finance, a request with which Hasan readily complied. The Governor of Daulatābād and others having revolted took possession of the place, and selected Hasan (who had then the title of Ẓafar Khān and a jāgīr in the Deccan) to be their king. On Friday the 3rd August, A.D. 1347, 24th Rabī' II. A.H. 748, they crowned him and raised him on the throne, with the title of 'Alā-uddīn Hasan Kāngoh Bahmanī at Kulbarga, which place became the royal residence and capital of the first Muhammadan king of the Deccan, and was named Ahsanābād. Towards the end of the reign of Muhammad Tughluq of Dehlī, he subdued every part of the Deccan previously subject to the throne of Dehlī. The death of 'Alā-uddīn Hasan happened ten years, ten months, and seven days after his accession to the throne, about the 10th February, A.D. 1358, 1st Rabī' I. A.H. 759. He was succeeded by his son, Muhammad Shāh I. Bahmanī. The following is a list of the kings of the Bahmanī dynasty of Kulbarga or Ahsanābād with the years of their accessions:

'Alā-uddīn Hasan I.	A.H. 748,	A.D. 1347.
Muhammad Shāh I.	A.H. 759,	A.D. 1358.
Mujāhid Shāh	A.H. 776,	A.D. 1375.
Daūd Shāh	A.H. 780,	A.D. 1378.
Mahmūd Shāh	A.H. 780,	A.D. 1378.
Ghiyāṣ-uddīn	A.H. 799,	A.D. 1397.
Shams-uddīn	A.H. 799,	A.D. 1397.

Fīrūz Shāh Roz-afzūn A.H. 800, A.D. 1397.
Ahmad Shāh Walī . . A.H. 825, A.D. 1422.
'Alā-uddīn Ahmad II. A.H. 838, A.D. 1435.
Humāyūn the cruel.
Nizām Shāh.
Muhammad Shāh II.
Mahmūd II.
Ahmad Shāh II.
'Alā-uddīn III.
Walī-ullah.
Kalīm-ullah, with whom the Bahmanī dynasty terminates, and is succeeded by Amīr Barīd at Ahmadābād Bidar.

'Ala-uddin II. (Sultan) (علاؤالدين ثاني سلطان), son of Sultān Ahmad Shāh Walī Bahmanī, ascended the throne at Ahmadābād Bīdar in the Deccan, in the month of February, A.D. 1435, A.H. 838, and died after a reign of 23 years, 9 months, and 20 days in the year A.D. 1457, A.H. 862. He was succeeded by his son, Humāyūn, a cruel prince.

'Ala-uddin Khilji (Sultan) (علاؤالدين خلجى سكندر ثانى سلطان), styled Sikandar-i-Sānī, "the second Alexander," was the nephew and son-in-law of Sultān Jalāl-uddīn Fīrūz Shāh Khiljī, whom he murdered at Kara-Mānikpūr, in the province of Allāhābād, on the 29th July, A.D. 1296, 17th Ramazān, A.H. 695, and marching thence with his army ascended the throne of Dehlī in the month of October the same year, Zil-hijja, A.H. 695, after having defeated and removed Rukn-uddīn Ibrāhīm, the son of Fīrūz Shāh. He was the first Musalmān king who made an attempt to conquer the Deccan. He took the fort of Chītor in August, A.D. 1303, 3rd Muharram, A.H. 703. It is said that the empire never flourished so much as in his reign. Palaces, mosques, universities, baths, mausolea, forts, and all kinds of public and private buildings, seemed to rise as if by magic. Among the poets of his reign, we may record the names of Amīr Khusrau, Khwāja Hasan, Sadr-uddīn 'Alī, Fakhr-uddīn Khawās, Hamīd-uddīn Rājā, Maulānā 'Ārif, 'Abdul-Hakīm, and Shihāb-uddīn Sadr-Nishīn. In poetry, Amīr Khusrau and Khwāja Hasan had the first rank. In philosophy and physic, Maulāna Badr-uddīn Dāmishqī. In divinity, Maulānā Shitābī. In astrology, Shaikh Nizām-uddīn Auliyā acquired much fame. 'Alā-uddīn died, according to Firishta, on the 6th Shawwāl, A.H. 716, or 19th December, A.D. 1316, after having reigned more than twenty years. He was buried in the tomb which he had constructed in his life-time near the Manihār Masjid in Old Dehlī. Amīr Khusrau, in that part of his Dīwān called *Baqiya-i-Naqiya*, says that he died on the 6th Shawwāl, A.H. 715, *i.e.* about the 30th December, A.D. 1315. After his death, Malik Nāib Kāfūr, one of the eunuchs of the king, placed his youngest son, Sultān Shihāb-uddīn 'Umar, who was then only seven years old, on the throne. After a short time, however, the eunuch Kāfūr was slain, and Shihāb-uddīn was set aside, and his elder brother, Mubārak Khān, under the title of Mubārak Shāh, ascended the throne on the 1st April, A.D. 1316, 7th Muharram, A.H. 716, but according to Firishta in 1317. It was the boast of 'Alā-uddīn that he had destroyed one thousand temples in Banāras alone. He is best known now by the beautiful gateway to the Kutb Mosque, and the unfinished tower by which he hoped to rival the Kutb Minār.

'Ala-uddin 'Imad Shah (علاؤالدين عماد شاه) succeeded to the government of Barār in the Deccan after the death of his father, Fath-ullah 'Imād Shāh, about the year A.D. 1513, and following the example of other chiefs of the house of Bahmanī, declared himself king of Barār, and established his royal residence at Gawal. He contracted an alliance by marriage with the sister of Ismā'īl 'Ādil Shāh, named Khadīja, in A.D. 1528, A.H. 935, and died some time about the year A.D. 1532, A.H. 939. He was succeeded by his son Daryā, 'Imād Shāh.

'Ala-uddin Kaiqubad (Sultan) (علاؤالدين كيقباد), a prince of the Saljūqian dynasty. When Sultān Malik-Shāh conquered Rūm or Anatolia, in Asiatic Turkey, he conferred on Sulaimān, the son of Kutlumish, that kingdom, whose descendants reigned there till the time of Abāqā Khān, the Tartar king of Persia. 'Alā-uddīn Kaiqubād was a descendant of Sulaimān Shāh, and died about the year A.D. 1239, A.H. 637. *Vide* Sulaimān bin-Kutlumish.

'Ala-uddin Majzub (Shah) (علاؤالدين مجذوب شاه), a Muhammadan saint of Āgra, commonly called Shāh 'Alāwal Balāwal, son of Sayyid Sulaimān. He died in the beginning of the reign of Islām Shāh, son of Sher Shāh, in the year A.D. 1546, A.H. 953. His tomb is in Āgra, at a place called Nāī-kī Mandī, where crowds of Musalmāns assemble every year to worship it. The adjacent mosque has sunk into the ground to the spring of the arches.

'Ala-uddin Mas'ud (علاؤالدين مسعود), Sultān of Dehlī, was the son of Sultān Rukn-uddīn Fīrūz, and grandson of Shams-uddīn Iltitmish, was raised to the throne of Dehlī after the murder of Bahrām Shāh, in May, A.D. 1242, Zil-qa'da, A.H. 639. He died on the 10th June, A.D. 1246, 23rd Muharram, A.H. 644, after a reign of four years, and was succeeded by his brother (or uncle), Sultān Nāzir-uddīn Mahmūd.

'Ala-uddin Muhammad al-Samarqandi (Shaikh) (علاؤالدين محمد السمرقندي), author of a compendium of Al-Qudūrī's Mukhtaṣir, which he entitled the *Tuhfat-ul-Fukahā*. This work was commented upon by his pupil Abū-Bakr bin-Mas'ūd al-Kāshānī, who died in A.D. 1191, A.H. 587. This comment is entitled al-Badāi' as-Ṣanāi'

'Ala-uddin Husain Shah (علاؤالدين حسين شاه), king of Bengal. He was the son of Sayyid Ashraf, and after defeating Muẓaffar Shāh at Gaur in A.H. 899, ascended the throne of Bengal. He reigned with justice for a considerably longer period than any of his predecessors until the year A.D. 1521, A.H. 927, when he died a natural death, after a reign of 28 years. His son Nuṣrat Shāh succeeded him.

'Ala-uddin (Sultan) (علاؤالدين سلطان سلجوقى), a king of the race of Saljūq, who reigned in Iconium, and died in the year A.D. 1301, A.H. 700.

'Ala-uddin (Sultan) (علاؤالدين سلطان پادشاه دهلى), the last king of Dehlī of the Sayyid dynasty, succeeded his father Sulṭān Muhammad Shāh to the throne in January, A.D. 1446, Shawwāl, A.H. 849. Bahlōl Lodī, in A.D. 1451, A.H. 855, at the instigation of Ḥamīd Khān wazīr, took possession of Dehlī during the absence of the king, who was then at Badāoṇ. 'Alā-uddīn continued to reside at Badāoṇ unmolested till his death, which happened in the year A.D. 1478, A.H. 883; his reign at Dehlī being about six years, and his government at Badāoṇ 28 years.

'Ala-uddin (Sayyid), of Oudh, whose poetical name was Wāṣilī, is the author of a Tarjī'band, commonly called *Māmuqīmān*, with which word it commences. He was a native of Khurāsān, came to India about the year A.D. 1300, became a disciple of Niẓām-uddīn Auliā, and fixed his residence in Oudh.

'Ala-uddin Takash (علاؤالدين تكش), a Sulṭān of Khwārizm. *Vide* Takash.

'Ala-ul-mulk Kotwal (Malik) (علاؤ الملك كوتوال ملک). He served under Sulṭān 'Alā-uddīn Khiljī, king of Dehlī, and was the uncle of Ziyā-uddīn Barni, the author of the *Tārīkh Fīrūz-Shāhī*. He was then very old and so fat that he was not able to attend the court more than once a month. He was living in A.D. 1300, A.H. 699.

'Al-Aziz Billah Abu-al-Mansur Tarar (العزيز بالله ابو المنصور طرار), son of Mu'izz-ud-dīn-allah, second khalīfa of Egypt the Fāṭimite dynasty, succeeded his father in A.D. 976, and committed the management of affairs entirely to the care of Jauhar, or Ja'far, his father's long-experienced general and prime minister. This famous warrior, after several battles with Al-Aftakīn, the amīr of Damascus and the Karmatians, died in A.D. 990, A.H. 381. 'Al-Aziz died on his way to Syria, in the 21st year of his reign and 42nd of his age, and was succeeded by his son, Abul-Manṣūr.

Al-Baghawi (البغوى). *Vide* Abul-Faraj-al-Baghawī and Abū-Muhammad Farrāī ibn-Mas'ūd al-Baghawī.

Al-Batani (البطني), commonly called by European writers Albategnius, was an Arabian astronomer who wrote a treatise on the knowledge and the obliquity of the Zodiac of the stars. He died in 929. He greatly reformed astronomy, comparing his own observations with those of Ptolemy. This book was printed at Nüremberg, in 1537, 4to., and at Bologna in 1545. He died A.D. 929.

Al-Biruni (البروني), an Arabian author, whose original work, entitled *Tārikh Hind*, was compiled in India in about A.D. 1030–33. *See* Abū-Raiḥān.

Al-Bukhari (البخارى), who received this name from Bukhārā, the place of his birth or his chief residence, was a famous lawyer by name of Muhammad Ismā'īl. His collection of traditions on the Muhammadan religion, commonly called *Ṣaḥīḥ-ul-Bukhārī*, is of the greatest authority of all that have ever been made; he called it *Al-Ṣaḥīḥ*, i.e. genuine, because he separated the spurious ones from those that were authentic. He says, he has selected 7,275 of the most authentic traditions out of 10,000, all of which he looked upon to be true, having rejected 200,000 as false. He died at Bukhāra in the year A.D. 870, A.H. 256. *Vide* Muhammad Ismā'īl Bukhārī.

Al-Dawani. *Vide* Dawānī.

Al-Farghani (الفرغاني), surname of Ahmad ibn Kathīr or Kaṣīr, an Arabian astronomer of the ninth century, author of an introduction to astronomy.

[*Vide* Farghānī.]

'Alha and Udal (آلها و أودل), princes of Mahōba. There is a heroic ballad sung or recited by the Hindū sepoys in a kind of monotonous, but not unmusical sort of chaunt, accompanied by a sotto voce beat of the dhōl, which rise to a constrepito in the pause between the verses. Whoever has resided in a military cantonment must have frequently observed the sepoys, when disengaged from military duty, collected in small knots, listening to one of the party reciting some poem or tale to a deeply interested audience. The subject of this lay is the prowess of 'Alhā', the Rāja of Mahōba, a town in Bundelkhand, of which extensive ruins remain. The hero is described as the terror of the Muhammadans; his triumphs over whom are attributed not only to his own valour, but the favour of the goddess Kālī, whom he had propitiated by the offering of his life. There are many songs, it is said, of this prince, and his brother Udal, a warrior of equal estimation; but they are preserved only traditionally by the Powārs, and their amateur students. The verses are in Bhakha.

Al-Hadi (الهادی), the fourth khalīf of the house of 'Abbās, succeeded his father, al-Mahdī, on the 4th August, A.D. 785, 23rd Muharram, A.H. 169, to the throne of Baghdād. He reigned one year and one month, and having formed a design to deprive his younger brother, Hārūn-al-Rashīd, of his right of succession, and even to assassinate him, was poisoned by his prime minister about the month of September, A.D. 786, Rabī I. A.H. 170. On his death his brother, the celebrated Hārūn-al-Rashīd, ascended the throne.

Al-Hakm, also called ibn Abdūl Hakm, an Arabian author, who (according to the chronological arrangement of the Arab authorities by Howard Vyse and Dr. Sprenger, in the former's second volume of *The Pyramids of Gizeh*) lived about A.D. 1450, or six hundred years after the death of the khalīf al-Mamūn of Baghdād, but by a manuscript note recorded by a gentleman of the British Museum 1868), it appears that al-Hakm was nearly contemporary with that prince, who flourished between A.D. 813 and 843. Al-Hakm writes that the Great Pyramid in Egypt was built by a certain antediluvian king Saurid, and filled by him chiefly with celestial spheres and figures of the stars, together with the perfumes used in their worship; and that khalīfa al-Mamūn found the body of a man deposited, with jewels, arms, and golden writing, in the coffer, when he broke into the king's chamber of the Great Pyramid. But neither Abū Mūshar Jāfar bin Muhammad Balkhi, who wrote in about A.D. 890, nor ibn Khurdalbeh, in A.D. 920, have one word about al-Mamūn, or any opening of the pyramid. But when we descend to Masaūdi, in A.D. 967, he, after an astonishing amount of romancing on what took place at the building of the pyramids 300 years before the Flood, mentions that, not al-Mamūn, but his father, khalīfa Harūn-al-Rashīd, attempted to break into the Great Pyramid; and after penetrating 20 cubits, found a vessel containing 1000 coins of the finest gold, each just one ounce in weight, and making up a sum which exactly repaid the cost of his operations, at which, it is added, he greatly wondered. About the year A.D. 1170, or 340 years after al-Mamūn's age, that prince is mentioned by Abū Abd-ullah Muhammad bin Abdur Rahīm Alkaisi, who states that he was informed that those who went into the upper parts of the Great Pyramid in the time of al-Mamūn, came to a small passage, containing the image of a man in green stone, and within that a human body with golden armour, etc., etc.

Al-Hasan (الحسن), an Arabian who wrote on optics, about the year A.D. 1100.

'Ali (علی ابن ابو طالب), son of Abū-Ṭalib, was the cousin and son-in-law of Muhammad. He was born 23 years before the Hijrī, *i.e.*, in the year A.D. 599, at the very temple itself. His mother's name was Fāṭima, daughter of Asad the son of Hāshim. After the death of Muhammad, he was opposed in his attempts to succeed the prophet by 'Uṣmān and 'Umar, and retired into Arabia, where his mild and enlarged interpretation of the Qurān, increased the number of his proselytes. After the death of 'Uṣmān, the 3rd khalīfa, he was acknowledged khalīfa by the Egyptians and Arabians in July, A.D. 655, but in less than five years after he was compelled to resign that title, and Mu'āwiya was proclaimed khalīfa at Damascus. 'Alī was subsequently wounded by 'Abdur-Rahmān ibn-Muljim in a mosque at Qūfa, whilst engaged in his evening prayers, on Friday the 22nd January, A.D. 661, 17th Ramaẓān, A.H. 40, and died four days after. 'Alī, after the decease of his beloved Fāṭima, the daughter of the prophet, claimed the privilege of polygamy, and had 18 sons and 18 daughters. The most renowned of them are the two sons of Fāṭima, viz., Hasan and Husain, as also Muhammad Ḥanīf, by another wife. Among the many surnames, or honorable titles bestowed upon 'Alī, are the following: Wasī', which signifies "legatee and heir;" Murtaẓa, "beloved by God;" Asad-ullah-ul-Ghālib, "the victorious lion of God;" Ḥaidar, "a lion;" Shāh Mardān, "king of men;" Sher Khudā, "the lion of God." His memory is still held in the highest veneration by the Muhammadans, who say that he was the first that embraced their religion. They say, moreover, that Muhammad, talking of him, said, "Alī is for me and I am for him; he stands to me in the same rank as Aaron did to Moses; I am the town in which all knowledge is shut up, and he is the gate of it." However, these great eulogies did not hinder his name, and that of all his family, from being cursed, and their persons from being excommunicated through all the mosques of the empire of the khalīfas of the house of Umayya, from Mu'āwiya down to the time of 'Umar ibn-

'Abdul-'Azīz, who suppressed the solemn malediction. There were besides several khalīfas of the house of 'Abbās, who expressed a great aversion to 'Alī and all his posterity; such as Mu'tazid and Mutawakkil. On the other hand, the Fāṭimite khalīfas of Egypt caused his name to be added to that of Muhammad in the call to prayer *(azān)*, which is chaunted from the turrets of the mosques. He is the first of the twelve Imāms, eleven of whom were his descendants. Their names are as follows:

1. 'Alī, the son of Abū-Ṭālib.
2. Imām Hasan, eldest son of 'Alī.
3. ,, Husain, second son of 'Alī.
4. ,, Zain-ul-'Ābidīn, son of Husain.
5. ,, Muhammad Bāqir, son of Zain-ul-'Ābidīn.
6. Imām Ja'far Sādiq, son of Muhammad Bāqir.
7. Imām Mūsạ Kāẓim, son of Ja'far Sādiq.
8. ,, Alī Mūsạ Raẓa, son of Mūsạ Kāẓim.
9. Imām Muhammad Taqī, son of Mūsạ Raẓa.
10. Imām 'Alī Naqī, son of Muhammad Taqī.
11. Imām Hasan 'Askarī, son of 'Alī Naqī.
12. ,, Mahdī, son of Hasan 'Askarī.

As to the place of 'Alī's burial, authors differ; but the most probable opinion is, that he was buried in that place which is now called Najaf Ashraf, in Kūfa, and this is visited by the Muhammadans as his tomb.

The followers of 'Alī are called Shī'as, which signifies sectaries or adherents in general, a term first used about the fourth century of the Hijra.

Alī is reputed the author of several works in Arabic, particularly a collection of one hundred sentences (paraphrased in Persian by Rashīd-uddīn-Waṭwaṭ), and a Dīwān of didactic poems, often read in Madrasahs.

In mentioning 'Alī's name, the Shī'a use the phrase "'alaihi as-salām," which is used after the names of prophets; the Sunnīs say, "karrama allāhu wajhahu," may God honour his face.

'Ali (علی بن احمد بن ابو بکر کوفی), son of Ahmad bin-Abū-Bakr Kūfī, a resident of Ūch and author of the history of Sindh in Arabic called *Tuḥfat-ul-Kirām*. This work was translated into Persian and called *Chāch Nāma*, a translation of which was made in English by Lieutenant Postans and published in the *Jour. As. Soc.* in 1838.

'Ali (علی بن احمد المشهوربو احدی), son of Ahmad, commonly called Wāḥidī, was an Arabian author who wrote three Commentaries, viz.: *Wasīṭ*, *Zakīr*, and *Basiṭ*, and also *Kitāb Nuzūl*. He died in A.D. 1075, A.D. 468.

'Ali (علی بن حمزه), son of Ḥamzā, author of the *Tārīkh Iṣfahānī*.

'Ali (علی بن حسین واعظ), son of Husain Wāiẓ Kāshifī, the famous writer of the *Anwār-i-Sohaili*, author of the work called *Laṭāif-uz-Ẓarāif*, containing the anecdotes of Muhammad, of the twelve Imāms, of the ancient kings of Persia, and of various other persons. He is also the author of another work entitled *Rushḥāt*, containing the Memoirs of the Ṣūfī Shaikhs of the Nakshbandī order. 'Alī died in A.D. 1532, A.H. 939. He is also called 'Alī Waez.

[*Vide* Ṣafī-uddīn Muhammad.]

'Ali (علي بن محمد قوسنجي), son of Muhammad Qūsanjī, an astronomer, and author of the *Sharḥ-ul-Jadīd*, the new commentary. He died A.D. 1474, A.H. 879.

'Ali (علی بن عثمان), son of 'Usmān Gīlānī, author of the *Kashf-ul-Maḥjūb*, containing a minute description of the twelve orders of Ṣūfīs, etc., written in A.D. 1499, A.H. 905. He is also called Pīr 'Alī Hajwīrī.

'Ali (علی ملقب به ابو الحسن), surnamed Abul Hasan. *Vide* Abul-Hasan 'Alī.

'Ali (علی تخلص ملا ناصرعلی), the poetical name of Mullā Nāṣir 'Ali, which see.

'Ali (علی), the poetical name of a poet who converted the Ghazals of Ḥāfiz into Mukhammas.

'Ali 'Adil Shah I. (علی عادل شاه بیجاپوری), of Bījāpūr, surnamed Abul-Muẓaffar, succeeded to the throne of that kingdom after the death of his father Ibrāhīm 'Adil Shāh I, in A.D. 1558, A.H. 965. He reigned about 22 lunar years, and as he had no son, he appointed in the year A.D. 1579 his nephew, Ibrāhīm, son of his brother Ṭahmāsp, his successor; and the following year on the night of Thursday the 10th April, 1580, 23rd Ṣafar, A.H. 988, he was assassinated by a young eunuch. He was buried in the city of Bījāpūr, where his tomb or mausoleum is called by the people, "Rauẓa Alī."

[Vide *Āīn Translation*, i. p. 545.]

'Ali 'Adil Shah II. (علی عادل شاه ثاني بيجاپوری), of Bījāpūr, succeeded his father Muhammad 'Adil Shāh in his childhood in November, A.D. 1656, Muharram, A.H. 1067, and was unable to remedy the disorders which had occurred in his kingdom, by the rebellion of the celebrated Marhatta chief Sewājī, who had possessed himself of all the strongholds in the Kokan country, and erected several new forts. Under pretence of making his submissions to the Sulṭān, he begged an interview with the Bījāpūr general, Afzal Khān, whom he treacherously stabbed in an embrace. Rustam Khān was afterwards sent against him, and defeated. 'Alī 'Adil Shāh died in the year A.D. 1672, A.H. 1083, after a turbulent reign of eleven or twelve years. He was succeeded by his son Sikandar 'Adil Shāh.

'Ali Ahmad (Shaikh) (علي احمد شيخ), the son of Shaikh Husain Naqshī, a learned man and engraver who died suddenly on hearing a verse of the poet Khwāja Hasan of Dehlī repeated in the presence of the emperor Jahāngīr on the 13th April, O.S. 1609, 18th Muharram, A.H. 1018.

'Ali Akbar (علي اكبر), the eldest son of Imām Husain, killed in battle together with his father on the 10th October, A.H. 680.

'Ali Akbar (علي اكبر), author of the work called *Majma'-ul-Auliā*, containing a detailed account of all the Muhammadan saints, dedicated to the emperor Shāh Jahān, who was a great admirer of saints, A.D. 1628, A.H. 1038.

'Ali Akbar (علي اكبر الهٰه‌ابادی), of Allahābād, author of the *Fasūl Akbarī* and *Usūl Akbarī*, and several other works.

'Ali Asghar (علي اصغر), proper name of Imām Zain-ul-'Ābidīn, which see.

'Ali Asghar (علي اصغر قنوجی), of Qanauj, author of a commentary on the Qurān called *Sawākib-ut-Tanzīl.* He died in the year A.D. 1727, A.H. 1140.

'Ali Bahadur (علی نواب بهادر), Nawāb of Banda, eldest son of Shamsher Bahādur I. and grandson of the Marhatta chief Bājī Rāo Peshwā I. He received the investiture of Bundelkhand from Nānā Farnawīs, the Pūna minister, about the year A.D. 1790, and accompanied by his brother Ghāni Bahādur, and supported by a powerful army, invaded Bundelkhand, but was opposed by Nāna Arjun (the guardian of Bakhat Singh, a descendant of Rāja Chatursāl), who falling in the contest, and Rāja Bakhat Singh being taken prisoner, Alī Bahādur acquired the whole of that part of the rāj of Banda which belonged to Bakhat Singh and all the rāj of Panna. He reigned about eleven or twelve years, and as at the time of his death, which happened in A.D. 1801 or 1802, his eldest son, Shamsher Bahādur II. was absent at Pūna, his youngest son Zulfikār Alī was proclaimed (in violation of the title of his eldest brother) as his successor by his uncle Ghānī Bahādur and his Dīwān Himmat Bahādur Goshāīn. Ghānī Bahādur, however, was soon after expelled by Shamsher Bahādur, who took possession of the rāj.

'Ali Bahadur Khan (علی بهادرخان), the last Nawāb of Banda and son of Zulfikar Alī Khān Bahādur. He is the author of a dīwan and a masnawī called *Mehrūllah.* He was removed for alleged complicity in the rebellion of 1857.

'Ali Bai (علي بای), (whose name is spelt in our English Biographical Dictionaries Alī Bey) was a native of Natolia, son of a Greek priest. In his thirteenth year he was carried away by some robbers as he was hunting, and sold to Ibrahīm, a lieutenant of the Janissaries, at Grand Cairo, who treated him with kindness. 'Alī distinguished himself against the Arabs, but when his patron was basely assassinated in A.D. 1758, by Abrahīm the Circassian, he avenged his death, and slew the murderer with his own hand. This violent measure raised him enemies, and his flight to Jerusalem and to Ptolemais or Acre with difficulty saved him from the resentment of the Ottoman Porte, that had demanded his head. Time, however, paved the way to his elevation. Those who had espoused the cause of the Circassian were sacrificed to the public safety; and 'Alī, recalled by the public voice, governed the country with benevolence and equity. In a battle fought against a rebellious Mamlūk to whom he had entrusted part of his army, 'Ali saw some of his troops desert, and unwilling to survive a defeat, he defended himself with the fury of a lion, till he was cut down by a sabre and carried to the conqueror's tent, where eight days after he expired of his wounds, April 21st, A.D. 1773, in his 45th year, and left behind him a character unrivalled for excellence, for courage, and magnanimity.

'Ali Bai (علي بائي). The titles by which he was known in the Muhammadan countries were al-Amīr, al-Hakīm, al-Faqīh, al-Sharīf, al-Hāj 'Alī Bāi ibn Usmān Bāi al-Abbās, Khādim Baitullāh al-Harām, *i.e.* the prince, the learned, doctor of the law, of the blood of Muhammad, pilgrim, 'Ali Bāī, son of Usmān Bāi, of the race of the Abbasidesī, servant of the house of God. He was master of the Arabic language, and had carefully studied the mathematical and natural branches of science and knowledge. It was in A.D. 1802 that he visited England. In June, A.D. 1803, he sailed from Spain to Morocco, and travelled through Tripoli, Cyprus, Egypt, Arabia, Syria, and Turkey, and wrote a history of his travels, which was translated into English and published in London in the year A.D. 1816, entitled *The Travels of 'Alī Bāi.* In his visit to the isle of Cyprus he surveyed some curious remains of antiquity that have been usually overlooked. Having been admitted in his character of a Muhammadan prince to sweep the interior of the Ka'ba at Mecca, the most sacred office that a Musalmān can perform, and to visit it repeatedly, he has given, from personal inspection, a more minute and exact account of the Temple of Mecca than other travellers could lay before the public. His notice of the venerated mountain beyond Mecca, the last and principal object of the pilgrimage to that city, and his description of the interior of the Temple of Jerusalem, which no Christian is permitted to enter, is said to contain much new information.

'Ali Barid I. (علی برید) succeeded his father, Amīr Barīd, to the throne of Ahmadābād Bīdar in the Deccan in the year A.D. 1542, and was the first of this family who assumed royalty. He died after a reign of more than twenty years in A.D. 1562, A.H. 970, and was succeeded by his son Ibrāhīm Barīd.

'Ali Barid II. succeeded his father Kasim Barīd II. in the government of Ahmadābād Bīdar in A.D. 1572, and was deposed in A.D. 1609 by his relative Amīr Barīd II. who succeeded him, and was the last of this dynasty.

'Ali Beg (علی بیگ), a Pole, born of Christian parents. When young he was made prisoner by the Tartars and sold to the Turks, who educated him in the Muhammadan faith. He rose in the Turkish court, and was appointed interpreter to the Grand Signior, and translated the Bible and the English Catechism into the Turkish language. His great work is on the liturgy of the Turks, their pilgrimages to Mecca, and other religious ceremonies, translated into Latin by Dr. Smith. He died A.D. 1675.

'Ali Beg (Mirza) (علی بیگ مرزا), a native of Badakhshān who held a high rank in the service of the emperor Akbar; and was honoured with the office of 4,000 in the reign of Jahāngīr. He accompanied the emperor one day to visit the shrine of the celebrated saint, Shaikh Maīn-uddīn Chishtī at Ajmir, and happening to see the tomb of Shāhbāz Khān Kambū, he embraced it, and crying out with a loud voice, that "he, when living, was one of his oldest and best friends," gave up the ghost. This happened on the 11th March, O.S. 1616, 2nd Rabī I. A.H. 1025.

'Ali bin al-Husain al-Masa'udi al-Hudaili (علی بن الحسین مسعودی), the far-famed author of the Marūj-uz-Zahab, and who has been, with some justice, termed the Herodotus of the East, was also a writer on the Shia' traditions. He died A.D. 957, A.D. 346.

'Ali Buya or Ali ibn Buya (علی بویه), entitled 'Imād-ud-daula, the first of a race of kings of Fars and 'Irāk. The flatterers of this family, which is called Dīlamī or Diālima (from the name of their native village, Dīlam) and Buya or Buyites (from that of one of their ancestors named Buya), trace their descent to the ancient kings of Persia; but the first of this race that history notices was a fisherman of Dīlam whose name was Buya. His eldest son, 'Ali Buya, was employed by a governor of his native country, named Murawij, and was in the command of the chief part of his army, with which he encountered and defeated Yākūt, the governor of Isfahān, and by the immense plunder that he obtained from that victory, he became at once a leader of reputation and of power. He pursued Yākūt into Fars, defeated him again, and took possession of the whole of that province as well as those of Kirmān, Khūzistān and 'Irāq in A.D. 933, A.H. 321. This chief was afterwards tempted by the weak and distracted state of the Khilāfat or Caliphate, to a still higher enterprise; accompanied by his two brothers, Hasan and Ahmad, he marched to Baghdād. The Khalīf al-Rāzī Billāh fled, but was soon induced to return, and his first act was to heap honours on those who had taken possession of his capital. 'Alī Buya, on agreeing to pay annually 600,000 dīnars of gold, was appointed viceroy of Fars and 'Irāq, with the rank of Amīr-ul-Umrā, and the title of 'Imād-ud-daula. His younger brother Ahmad received the title of Maizz-ud-daula, and was nominated wazīr to the khalīf. Hasan, who was his second brother, received the title of Rukn-ud-daula, and acted, during the life of 'Alī Buya, under that chief. 'Alī Buya fixed his residence at Shīrāz, and died on Sunday the 11th November, A.D. 949, 16th Jamad I. A.H. 338, much regretted by his soldiers and subjects. He was succeeded by his brother Rukn-ud-daula.

Sulṭāns of the race of Buya, who reigned 108 *lunar years in Persia.*

- 'Imād-ud-daula 'Alī Buya; Maizz-ud-daula Ahmad; Rukn-ud-daula Hasan, sons of Buya.
- Azd-ud-daula; Mouyyad-ud-daula; Fakhr-ud-daula Abūl Hasan, sons of Rukn-ud-daula.
- Majd-ud-daula, son of Fakhr-ud-daula.
- Izz-ud-daula Bakhtyār, son of Maizz-ud-daula.

'Ali Durdazd (Moulana) (علی دردزد مولانا استرابادي), of Astarābad. A poet who was contemporary with Katibī Tarshīzī, who died in A.D. 1435, A.H. 840. He is the author of a dīwān. He was living in A.D. 1436, in which year his wife died, on which account he wrote a beautiful elegy.

Alif bin Nur Kashani (الف بن نورکاشني), author of another *Matla-ul-Anwār*, besides the one of the same name written by Mullā Husain Wāez. This is a complete history of Muhammad, his descendants, with Memoirs of the khalīfs.

'Ali Ghulam Astarabadi (علی غلام استرآبادي), a poet who served under the kings of Deccan and was living in A.D. 1565, A.H. 972, in which year Rāmrāj the rāja of Bījānagar was defeated and slain in a battle against the Muhammadan princes of Deccan, of which event he wrote a chronogram.

'Ali Hamdani (علي همداني). *Vide* Sayyid 'Alī Hamdānī.

'Ali Hamza (علي حمزه), author of the *Jawāhir-ul-Asrār*, a commentary on the abstruse meaning of the verses of the Qurān, etc., being an abridgment of the *Miftāh-ul-Asrār*, written in A.D. 1436. 'Alī Hamza's poetical name is 'Azurī, which see.

'Ali Hazin (Shaikh Muhammad) (علي حزين). *Vide* Hazīn.

'Ali ibn Isa (علي ابن عيسیٰ), general of the khalīf al-Amīn, killed in battle against Ṭāhir ibn Husain, the general of the khalīf al-Māmūn, in the year A.D. 811, A.H. 195, and his head sent as a present to the khalīf.

'Ali ibn ul-Rijal (علي ابن الرجال), author of the Arabic work on astronomy called *Albāra' ahkām Najūm.*

'Ali Ibrahim Khan (علي ابراهيم خان), a native of Patna, who became judge of Banaras. He was the author of twenty-eight mans and several other works, and a tazkira or biography of Urdū poets, which he wrote about the year A.D. 1782, A.H. 1196, and which he entitled *Gubzār-i-Ibrāhim.* His poetical name is Khalīl. He is called Hāl by Ishki (*q.v.*).

'Ali Jah (علي جاه), the eldest son of the Nizām of Haidarābād. He rebelled against his father in June, A.D. 1795, was defeated and made prisoner, and died shortly after.

'Ali Lala (Shaikh Razi-uddin), a native of Ghaznī. His father Sayyid Lālā was the uncle of Shaikh Sanāī the poet. He was a disciple of Najm-uddīn Kubrā and his title Shaikh-ul-Shaiukh. He died A.D. 1244, A.H. 642, aged 76 lunar years.

'Ali Mahaemi (علي مهايمي), a native of Mahāem in the Deccan, was the son of Shaikh Ahmad, and is the author of the commentary on the Qurān entitled *Tafsīr Rahmānī.* He died A.D. 1431, A.H. 835.

'Ali Mardan Khan (علي مردان خان), Amīr-ul-Umra, was a native of Persia and governor of Qandahār on the part of the king of Persia, but finding himself exposed to much danger from the tyranny of his sovereign Shāh Safī, he gave up the place to the emperor Shāh Jahān, and himself took refuge at Dehlī in the year A.D. 1637, A.H. 1047. He was received with great honour, was created Amīr-ul-Umrā, and was, at different times, made governor of Kashmīr and Kābul, and employed in various wars and other duties. He excited universal admiration at the court by the skill and judgment of his public works, of which the canal which bears his name at Dehlī still affords a proof, and the taste and elegance he displayed on all occasions of show and festivity. He died on his way to Kashmīr, where he was going for change of air, on the 16th April, A.D. O.S. 1657, 12th Rajab, A.H. 1067, and was buried at Lāhore in the mausoleum of his mother. He left three sons, *viz.*, Ibrāhīm Khān, Isma'īl Beg and Is-ḥāq Beg, of whom the two last were slain in the battle which took place between Dāra Shikōh and 'Alamgīr at Dhaulpūr on the 29th May, O.S. 1658, 7th Ramazan, A.H. 1068. He is believed to have introduced the bulbous Tartar dome into Indian architecture.

'Ali Mosi Raza (علي موسیٰ رضا), the eighth Imām of the race of Alī, and the son of Mūsī Kāzim the seventh Imām. His mother's name was Umm Sayyid; he was born in the year A.D. 764 or A.D. 769, A.H. 147, and died on Friday the 12th August, A.D. 818, 9th Safar, A.H. 203. His wife's name was Umm Habīl, the daughter of the Khalīf al-Māmūn. His sepulchre is at Tūs in Khurāsān. That town is now commonly called Mash-had, that is, the place of martyrdom of the Imām. To the enclosure wherein his tomb is raised, the Persians give the name of "Rauzat Rizawī," or the garden of Razā, and esteem it the most sacred spot in all Persia. The chief ornament and support of Mash-had is this tomb, to which many thousands of pious pilgrims annually resort, and which had been once greatly enriched by the bounty of sovereigns. Nasīr-ullah Mirzā, the son of Nādir Shāh, carried away the golden railing that surrounded the tomb, and Nādir Mirzā, son of Shāh-rukh Mirzā and grandson of Nādir Shāh, took down the great golden ball which ornamented the top of the dome over the grave, and which was said to weigh 60 maunds or 420 pounds. The carpets fringed with gold, the golden lamps, and everything valuable were plundered by these necessitous and rapacious princes. Alī Mūsī Razā was poisoned by the khalīf al-Māmūn, consequently is called a martyr.

'Ali Muhammad Khan (علي محمد خان), founder of the Rohila government. It is mentioned in Forster's Travels, that in the year A.D. 1720 Bashārat Khān and Dāūd Khān, of the tribe of Rohilas, accompanied by a small number of their adventurous countrymen, came into Hindūstan in quest of military service. They were first entertained by Madan Shāh, a Hindū chief of Seraulī (a small town on the the north-west quarter of Rohilkhand) who by robbery and predatory excursions maintained a large party of banditti. In the plunder of an adjacent village, Dāūd Khān captured a youth of the Jāṭ sect, whom he adopted and brought up in the Muhammadan faith, by the name of 'Alī Muhammad, and distinguished this boy by pre-eminent marks of paternal affection. Some years after, the Rohilas quarrelling with Madan Shāh, retired from his country, and associating themselves with Chānd Khān, the chief of Barelī, they jointly entered into the service of Azmat Khān, the governor of Moradābād. After the death of Dāūd Khan, who was slain by the mountaineers in one of his excursions, the Rohila party in a short space of time seized on the districts of Madan Shāh and 'Alī Muhammad Khān was declared chief of the party. From the negligence of government and the weak state of the empire of Dehlī in the reign of Muhammad Shāh, he possessed himself of the district of Katir (now called from the residence of the Rohilas, Rohilkhanḍ) and assumed independence of the royal authority. He was besieged in March, A.D. 1745, Safar, A.H. 1158, in a fortress called Bankar and 'Aoulā and taken prisoner, but was released after some time, and a jāgīr conferred on him. The emperor Muhammad Shāh died in April, A.D. 1748, A.H. 1161, and 'Alī Muhammad Khan some time after him in the same year at 'Aoulā, which he had ornamented with numerous public and private edifices. He left four sons, viz., Sa'd-ullāh Khān, Abdullāh Khān, Faiz-ullāh Khān, and Dūnde Khān. Sa'd-ullāh Khān succeeded to his father's possession, being then twelve years old.

[*Vide* Sa'd-ullah Khān.]

'Ali (Mulla) (علي ملا), Muhaddis or the traditionist, whose poetical name was "Tārī," died in the year A.D. 1573, A.H. 981, and Mullā 'Alam wrote the chronogram of his death.

'Ali Murad Khan (علي مراد خان), a king of Persia of the Zand family. He succeeded to the throne after the death of Sādiq Khān in March, A.D. 1781, and assumed the title of wakīl. He reigned over Persia five years, and was independent of the government two years prior to this period. Persia during this time enjoyed a certain degree of peace. He continued to confine his rival 'Akā Muhammad Khān to the province of Māzindarān. He died in A.D. 1785.

'Ali Murad (Mir), present chief of Khairpūr (1869).

'Ali Naqi (Imam) (علي نقي امام) was the tenth Imām of the race of 'Alī, and the son of Imām Muhammad Taqī, who was the ninth Imām. He was born in the year A.D. 828, A.H. 213, and died on the 17th June, A.D. 869, 3rd Rajab, A.H. 255. His tomb is in Sarmanrāe (which is also called Sāmira) in Baghdād, where his son Muhammad Askarī was also buried afterwards.

'Ali Naqi Khan (Nawab) (علي نقي خان نواب), the father-in-law and prime minister of Wājid 'Alī Shāh, the last king of Lucknow. He died at Lucknow of cholera about the 1st December, 1871, 17th Ramzān, A.H. 1278.

'Ali Naqi (علي نقي), Dīwān of Prince Murad Bakhsh, son of Shalyahī, whom he slew with his own hand.

'Ali Nawedi (علي نويدى), a poet and pupil of Shāh Ṭāhir Andjānī, came to India, where he was patronized by Abūl Fatha Husain Nizām Shāh I. in the Deccan. For some time he was in disgrace with his patron and changed his Takhallus or poetical name from Nawedī to Nā-umaidī (or hopeless). He died in A.D. 1567, A.H. 975, at Ahmadnagar in the Deccan.

'Ali Quli Beg. *Vide* Shāh Afghān Khān.

'Ali Quli Beg of Khurasan (علي قلي بيگ), author of a tazkira or biography of poets.

'Ali Quli Khan (Nawab) (علي قلي خان). *Vide* Ganna Begam.

'Ali Qusanji (Mulla) (علي قسانجي). *Vide* Mullā 'Ali Qūsanjī.

'Ali Qusanji (Mulla) (علي قوسنجي), author of the *Sharah Tajrīd*, and *Hāshia Kashshāf*. He died in A.D. 1405, A.H. 808.

'Ali Shahab Tarshizi (علي شهاب ترشيزى), a poet who was a native of Tarshish. He flourished in the reign of Shāh-rukh Mirzā, and found a patron in his son Muhammad Jogī, in whose praise he wrote several panegyrics. He was contemporary with the poet Azurī, who died A.D. 1462, A.H. 866.

'Alisher (Amir) (عليشير امير), surnamed Nizām-uddīn, was the prime minister of the Sulṭān Husain Mirzā (*q. v.*), ruler of Khurāsān. He sprang from an illustrious family of the Jaghtaī or Chaghtaī tribe. His father, Gajkīna Bahādur, held one of the principal offices of government during the reign of Sulṭān Abūl Qāsim Bābar Bahādur, great grandson of Amīr Taimūr. His grandfather, by his mother's side, was one of the principal Amīrs of Sulṭān Bāiqara Mirzā, the grandfather of Sulṭān Husain Mirzā. 'Alīsher, who was born A.D. 1440, and educated at the same school as his future patron, attached himself originally to Sulṭān Abūl Qāsim Bābar Mirzā, who was greatly attached to him, and called him his son. After his death he retired to Mash-had and continued his studies there; which place he subsequently quitted for Samarqand, on account of the disturbances which broke out in Khurāsān, and applied himself diligently to the acquirement of knowledge in the college of Khwāja Fazl-ullāh. When Sulṭān Husain Mirzā became uncontrolled ruler of Khurāsān (A.D. 1469), he requested Sulṭān Ahmad Mirzā, at that time ruler of the countries beyond the Oxus, to send 'Alīsher to him. On his arrival he was received with the greatest distinction, and raised to the highest posts of honour. 'Alīsher's palace was open to all men of learning: and notwithstanding that the reigns of government were placed in his hands, in the midst of the weightiest affairs, he neglected no opportunity of improving both himself and others in the pursuit of knowledge. He was not only honoured by his own Sulṭān and his officers, but foreign princes also esteemed and respected him. After being employed in the capacity of dīwān and prime minister for some time, love of study induced him to resign, and bidding a final adieu to public life, he passed the remainder of his days in composing Turkish and Persian works, of which Sām Mirzā recounts the names of no less than twenty-one. Daulat Shāh, the biographer, Mīrkhūnd and his son Khūndamīr, the historians, dedicated their works to him, and amongst other men of genius who were cherished by his liberality may be mentioned the celebrated poet Jāmī. His collection of Odes in the Chaghtaī or pure Turkish dialect, which he wrote under the poetical name of Nawāī, amounts to 10,000 couplets, and his parody of Nizāmī's five poems, containing nearly 30,000 couplets, is universally admired by the cultivators of Turkish poetry, in which he is considered to be without a rival. In the Persian language also he wrote a collection of Odes, under the poetical name of Fānī or Fanāī, consisting of 6000 distiches. He was also a proficient in painting and some of the plastic arts. 'Alīsher died on Sunday the 6th December, A.D. 1500, 15th Jamad I. A.H. 906, five years before his royal friend and master Sulṭān Husain Mirzā. Khūndamīr has recorded the year of his death in an affectionate chronogram: "His highness the Amīr, the asylum of divine guidance, in whom all the marks of mercy were conspicuous, has quitted the thorny brake of the world, and fled to the rose-garden of compassion. Since the 'light of mercy' has descended on his soul, those words represent the year of his departure." One of his works is called *Majālis-ul-Nafāes*.

'Ali Tabar (Prince) (على طبار شهزاده), was the son of prince 'Azim Shāh, and grandson of the emperor 'Alamgīr. He died in the year A.D. 1734, A.H. 1147.

'Ali Waez (على واعظ), the son of the famous Husain Wāez Kāshifī of Hirāt.

[*Vide* 'Alī, son of Husain Wāez.]

'Ali Wardi Khan (على وردى خان), also called Alahwardī Khān, which see.

'Ali Yezdi (علي يزدى). *Vide* Sharaf-uddīn 'Alī Yezdī.

Aljaitu (الجايتو), a Tartar king of Persia, who assumed the title of Muhammad Khudā Bandā on his accession to the throne, which see.

Al-Khassaf (الخصاف). *Vide* Abū Bakr Ahmad bin-'Umar al-Khaṣṣāf.

'Allama Dawani. *Vide* Dawānī.

'Allama Hilli (Shaikh) (علامه حلى شيخ), the great Shia lawyer, whose full name is Shaikh al-'Allāma Jamāl-uddīn Hasan bin Yūsuf al-Mutakhir Hillī, was the author of the *Khulāsat-ul-Aqwāl*, a biography of eminent Shias. His chief works on the subject of traditions are the *Istiksā al-Ya'tbār*, the *Masābīh al-Anwār*, and the *Durar-wa al-Marjān*. He died in A.D. 1326, A.H. 726.

[*Vide* Jamāl-uddīn Hasan bin Yūsuf.]

'Allami. *Vide* Afzal Khān.

'Allami (علامي), the poetical name of Shaikh Abūl Fazl, the favorite wazīr and secretary of the emperor Akbar.

'Allami Shirazi (علامي شيرازي), or the philosopher of Shīrāz, a very learned man, so generally called that his proper name is almost forgotten. He is the author of a celebrated collection of tracts on pure and mixed mathematics, entitled *Durrat-ut-Tāj*.

Al-Mahdi (المهدي), the third khalīf of the race of Abbās, succeeded his father, Abū Ja'far al-Mansūr, to the throne of Baghdād, and was inaugurated on Sunday the 8th October, A.D. 775, 6th Ẕil-hijja, A.H. 158. From the accession of al-Mahdī to the year A.D. 781, A.H. 164, the most remarkable event was the rebellion of al-Maqna (or al-Maqanna), which see. All this time war had been carried on with the Greeks, but without any remarkable success on either side. But after the suppression of the rebellion of al-Maqna, the khalīf ordered his son Harūn-'al-Rashīd to penetrate into the Greek territories with an army of 95,000 men. Harūn then, having entered the dominions of the empress Irene, defeated one of her commanders that advanced against him; after which he laid waste several of the imperial provinces with fire and sword, and even threatened the city of Constantinople itself. By this the empress was so terrified, that she purchased a peace with the khalīf by paying him an annual tribute of 70,000 pieces of gold, which for the present at least delivered her from the depredations of these barbarians. After the signing of the treaty, Harūn returned home laden with spoils and glory. This year (*i.e.* the 164th year of the Hijrī or A.D. 781) according to some of the oriental historians, the sun one day, a little after his rising, totally lost his light in a moment without being eclipsed, when neither any fog nor any cloud of dust appeared to obscure him. This frightful darkness continued till noon, to the great astonishment of the people settled in the countries where it happened. Al-Mahdī was poisoned, though undesignedly, by one of his concubines, named Hasana. She had designed to destroy one of her rivals whom she imagined to have too great an ascendancy over the khalīf, by giving her a poisoned pear. This the latter, not suspecting anything, gave to the khalif; who had no sooner eaten it than he felt himself in exquisite torture, and soon after expired. This event took place on the eve of Thursday the 4th August, A.D. 785, 23rd Muhurram, A.H. 169, in a village called Ar Rād in the dependencies of Māsabadān. He was succeeded by his eldest son al-Hādi.

Al-Mahdi (المهدي), a khalīf of Barbary. *Vide* Obeid-ullah al-Máhdī and Muhammad al-Mahdī.

Al-Mamun (المامون), surnamed 'Abdullāh, was the seventh khalīf of the race of the Abbasides, and the second son of Harūn-al-Rashīd. He was proclaimed khalīf at Baghdād on the 6th October, A.D. 813, 6th Safar, A.H. 198, the day on which his brother al-Amīn was assassinated. He conferred the government of Khurāsān upon Ṭāhir ibn Husain, his general, and his descendants with almost absolute and unlimited power. This happened in the year A.D. 820, A.H. 205, from which time we may date the dismemberment of that province from the empire of the khalīfs. During the reign of this khalīf nothing remarkable happened; only the African Moslems invaded the island of Sicily, where they made themselves master of several places. Al-Māmūn conquered part of Crete, had the best Greek writers translated into Arabic, and made a collection of the best authors. He also calculated a set of astronomical tables and founded an academy at Baghdād. In Khurāsān he made Tūs, at that time the capital of the kingdom, his place of residence. Under his patronage Khurāsān became the resort of learned men; and the city of Tūs, the great rival of Baghdād. He died of a surfeit on the 18th August, A.D. 833, 17th Rajab, A.H. 218, after a reign of 20 years and some months in Asia Minor, aged 48 years, and was buried at Tarsus, a city on the frontiers of Asia Minor. His wife named Būrān, daughter of Hasan ibn Sahl, his prime minister, out-lived him 50 years, and died on Tuesday the 22nd September, A.D. 884, 27th Rabī I. A.H. 271, aged 80 years. Al-Māmūn was succeeded by his brother al-Mo'tasim Billah.

Al-Mansur (المنصور), 2nd khalīf of Barbary of the Fatimite race. *Vide* Ismāīl, surnamed al-Mansūr.

Al-Mansur (المنصور), whose former name was Abū Ja'far, was called al-Mansūr, the victorious, by his overcoming his enemies. He was the second khalīf of the noble house of Banī Abbās or Abbasides, and succeeded to the throne of Irak at Baghdād after the death of his brother Abūl Abbās surnamed al-Saffāh, in A.D. 754, A.H. 136. He was opposed by his uncle, 'Abdullāh, son of Alī, who caused himself to be proclaimed khalīf at Damascus, but was defeated by al-Mansūr's general, Abū Muslim. He laid the foundation of the city of Baghdād on the banks of the Tigris in A.D. 762, and finished it four years after. He was a prince of extraordinary talent and taste, and an ardent lover of science and literature. He got the Pahlawī copy of Pilpay's Fables translated into Arabic. In the year A.D. 775, A.H. 158, the khalīf set out from Baghdād in order to perform the pilgrimage to Mecca; but being taken ill on the road, he expired at Bīr Maimūn, whence his body was carried to Mecca, where, after 100 graves had been dug, that his sepulchre might be concealed, he was interred, having lived, according to some 63, according to others 68 years, and reigned 22 lunar years. He is said to have been extremely covetous, and to have left in his treasury 600,000,000 dirhams and 24,000,000 dīnars. He is reported to have paid his cook by assigning him the heads and legs of the animals dressed in his kitchen, and to have obliged him to procure at his own expense all the fuel and vessels he had occasion for. He was succeeded by his son al-Mahdī. A Christian physician, named Bactishua, was very eminent at the court of al-Mansūr, who understanding that he had an old infirm woman for his wife, sent him three beautiful Greek girls and 3,000 dīnars as a present. Bactishua sent back the girls and told the khalīf that his religion prohibited his having more than one wife at a time; which pleased the khalīf so much, that he loaded him with presents, and permitted him, at his earnest request, to return to his own country of Khurāsān.

Al-Maqna or al-Maqanna (المقنع),

a famous impostor of Khurāsān who lived in the reign of al-Mahdī the khalīfa of Baghdād. His true name was Hākam ibn Hāsham, and he had been an under-secretary to Abū Muslim, governor of that province. He afterwards turned soldier, and passed thence into Māwarunnahr, where he gave himself out as a prophet. The name of al-Maqna, as also that of al-Burqaī, that is, the veiled, he received from his custom of covering his face with a veil or girdle-mask, to conceal his deformity; he having lost an eye in the wars, and being otherwise of a despicable appearance, and a stutterer; though his followers pretended he did this for the same reason that Moses did, *viz.*, lest the splendour of his countenance should dazzle the eyes of his beholders. In some places he made a great many proselytes, deluding the people with a number of juggling tricks which they swallowed as miracles, and particularly by causing the appearance of a moon to rise out of a well for many nights together; whence he was also called in the Persian tongue, Sāzinda Māh, or the Moon-maker. This wretch, not content with being reckoned a prophet, arrogated to himself divine honours; pretending that the Deity resided in his person. He had first, he said, assumed the body of Adam, then that of Noah, and subsequently of many other wise and great men. The last human form he pretended to have adopted was that of Abū Muslim, a prince of Khurāsān, from whom it proceeded to him. At last this impostor raised an open rebellion against the khalīf, and made himself master of several fortified places in Khurāsān, so that al-Mahdī was obliged to send one of his generals with an army against him about the year A.D. 780, A.H. 163. Upon the approach of the khalīfa's troops, al-Maqna retired into one of his strong fortresses which he had well provided for a siege. But being closely besieged by the khalīfa's forces, and seeing no possibility of escaping, he gave poison in wine to his whole family and all that were with him in the castle; when they were dead, he burnt their bodies, together with all their furniture, provisions, and cattle; and lastly he threw himself into the flames. He had promised his followers, that his soul should transmigrate into the form of an old man riding on a greyish coloured beast, and that after so many years he would return and give them the earth for their possession; which ridiculous expectation kept the sect in being for several years. English readers will remember the use made of this story by the author of Lallah Rookh.

Al-Mo'tamid Billah (المعتمد بالله),

the fifteenth khalīf of the house of Abbās, was the son of al-Mutwakkil Billāh. He was raised to the throne of Baghdād by the Turks after the murder of al-Muhtadī in A.D. 870, A.H. 256. This year the prince of the Zanjians, Alī or al-Habīb, made incursions to the very gates of Baghdād, doing prodigious mischief wherever he passed. In the year A.D. 874, Ya'kūb-bin-Lys having taken Khurāsān from the descendants of Tāhir, attacked and defeated Muhammad ibn Wāsil (who had killed the khalīf's governor of Fars, and afterwards made himself master of that province), seizing on his palace, where he found a sum of money amounting to 40,000,000 dirhams. In the year A.D. 879, A.H. 265, Ahmad ibn Tūlan rebelled against the khalīf and set up for himself in Egypt. There were now four independent powers in the Moslem dominions, besides the house of Umyya in Spain, *viz.*, the African Moslems, or Aghlabites, who had for a long time acted independently; Ahmad ibn Tūlan in Syria and Egypt; Ya'kūb ibn al-Lys in Khurāsān, and al-Habīb in Arabia and I'rāq. In the year A.D. 883, A.H. 270, al-Habīb was defeated and slain by al-Muwafiq, the khalīf's brother and coadjutor, who ordered his head to be cut off, and carried through a great part of that region which he had so long disturbed. In the year A.D. 891, A.H. 278, the Qarmatians first made their appearance in the Moslem empire, and gave almost continual disturbance to the khalīfs and their subjects. Al-Mo'tamid reigned 22 lunar years 11 months and some days, and died in the year A.D. 892, A.H. 279. He was succeeded by his nephew, al-Mo'tazid Billah, the son of al-Muwafiq.

Al-Mo'tasim Billah (المعتصم بالله)

was the fourth son of Harūn-al-Rashīd, and the eighth khalīf of the house of Abbās. He succeeded to the throne by virtue of his brother al-Mamūn's express nomination of him to the exclusion of his own son al-'Abbās, and his other brother al-Qāsim, who had been appointed by Harūn-al-Rashīd. In the beginning of his reign, A.D. 833, A.H. 218, he was obliged to employ the whole forces of his empire against one Bābak, who had been for a considerable time in rebellion in Persia and Persian Irāq, and had taken upon himself the title of a prophet. He was, however, defeated and slain. In the year A.D. 838, A.H. 223, the Greek emperor Theophilus invaded the khalīf's territories, where he behaved with the greatest cruelty, and, by destroying Sozopetra, the place of al-Mo'tasim's nativity, notwithstanding his earnest entreaties to the contrary, occasioned the terrible distinction of Amorium. He is said to have been so robust, that he once carried a burden of 1,000 pounds weight several paces. As the people of Baghdād disturbed him with frequent revolts and commotions, he took the resolution to abandon that city, and build another for his own residence. The new city he built was first called Sāmira, and afterwards Sarmanrī (for that which gives pleasure at first sight), and stood in the Arabian 'Irāq. He was attached to the opinion of the Matazalites who maintain the creation of the Qurān; and both he and his predecessor cruelly persecuted those who believed it to be eternal. Al-Mo'tasim died on Thursday the 5th January, A.D. 842, 18th Rabī I. A.H. 227. He reigned eight years, eight months and eight days, was born in the eighth month (Shaban) of the year, was the eighth khalīf of the house of Abbās, ascended the throne in the 218th year of the Hijrī, died on the eighteenth of Rabī I. lived forty-eight years, fought eight battles, built eight palaces, begat eight sons and eight daughters, had 8,000 slaves, and had 8,000,000 dīnars, and 80,000 dirhams in his treasury at his death, whence the oriental historians gave him the name of al-Musamman, or the Octonary. He was the first khalīf that added to his name the title of *Billāh*, equivalent to the *Dei Gratia* of Christian sovereigns. He was succeeded by his son al-Wāthiq or Wāsiq Billāh.

'Al-Mo'tazid Billah (المعتضد بالله), the son of al-Muwafiq, the son of al-Mutwakkil Billah, was the sixteenth khalīf of the race of Abbas. He came to the throne of Baghdād after the death of his uncle al-Mo'tamid Billāh in A.D. 892, A.H. 279. In the first year of his reign, he demanded in marriage the daughter of Khamarawia, Sultān or khalīf of Egypt, the son of Ahmad ibn Tūlan; which was agreed to by him with the utmost joy, and their nuptials were solemnized with great pomp in the year A.D. 895, A.H. 282. He carried on a war with the Qarmatians, but very unsuccessfully, his forces being defeated with great slaughter, and his general al-Abbās taken prisoner. The khalīf some time after his marriage granted to Hārūn, son of Khamarawia, the perpetual prefecture of Awāsam and Kinnisrin, which he annexed to that of Egypt and Syria, upon condition that he paid him an annual tribute of 45,000 dīnars. He reigned nine years, eight months and twenty-five days, and died in A.D. 902, A.H. 289. His son al-Muktafī Billāh succeeded him.

Al-Mughira (المغيرة), the son of Sayyid and governor of Kūfa in the time of Mū'āwia, the first khalīf of the house of Umyya. He was an active man, and of very good parts; he had lost one of his eyes at the battle of Yersnouk, though some say that it was with looking at an eclipse. By the followers of Alī he was accounted to be of the wrong party, and one of the chief of them. For thus they reckon: There are five elders on Alī's side: Muhammad, Alī, Fātima, Hasan and Husain; and to these are opposed Abū Bakr, 'Umar, Muāwia, Amrū and al-Mughīra. He died in the year A.D. 670, A.H. 50, at Kūfa. A great plague had been raging in the city, which made him retire from it; but returning upon its violence abating, he nevertheless caught it, and died of it.

Al-Muhtadi (المهتدي), the fourteenth khalīf of the Abbasides, was the son of one of Wāthiq's concubines named Kurb, who is supposed by some to have been a Christian. Al-Muhtadī was raised to the throne of Baghdād after the dethronement of al-Muttai'z Billāh in A.D. 869, A.H. 255. The beginning of his reign is remarkable for the irruption of the Zanjians, a people of Nubia, Ethiopia, and the country of Caffres, into Arabia, where they penetrated into the neighbourhood of Basra and Kūfa. The chief of this gang of robbers was 'Alī ibn Muhammad ibn Abdūl Rahmān, also called al-Habīb, who falsely gave himself out to be of the family of Alī ibn Abū Taleb. This made such an impression upon the Shīas in those parts, that they flocked to him in great numbers; which enabled him to seize upon the cities of Basra and Ramla, and even to pass the Tigris at the head of a formidable army. In the year A.D. 870, A.H. 256, al-Muhtadī was barbarously murdered by the Turks who had raised him to the throne. He reigned only eleven months and was succeeded by al-Mo'tamid.

Al-Mukhtar (المختار), a celebrated Muhammadan chief who had beaten all the generals of the khalīfs Yezīd, Marwān, and Abdūl Mālik, and had made himself sole master of Babylonian I'rāq, whereof Kūfa was the capital. He persecuted all those he could lay his hands on, who were not of Husain's party; he never pardoned any one of those who had declared themselves enemies to the family of the prophet, nor those who, as he believed, had dipped their hands in Husain's blood or that of his relations. He sent an army against Ubeid-ullah the son of Zayād, who was sent by the khalīf Abdūl Mālik towards Kūfa with leave to plunder it for three days, and slew him in battle in August, A.D. 686, Muharram, A.H. 67. Al-Mukhtār was killed at Kūfa in a battle fought with Misaa'b, the brother of Abdullāh, the son of Zuber, governor of Basra, in the month of April, A.D. 687, Ramzan, A.H. 67, in the 67th year of his age. It is said that he killed nearly 50,000 men.

Al-Muktafi Billah (المكتفي بالله) was the seventeenth khalīf of the house of Abbās who reigned in Baghdād. He succeeded his father, al-Mo'tazid Billāh, in A.D. 902, A.H. 289, and proved a warlike and successful prince. He gained several advantages over the Qarmatians, but was not able to reduce them. The Turks, however, having invaded the province of Māwarunnahr, were defeated with great slaughter; after which al-Muktafī carried on a successful war against the Greeks, from whom he took Seleucia. After this he invaded Syria and Egypt, which provinces he recovered from the house of Ahmad ibn Tūlan in A.D. 905, A.H. 292; he then renewed the war with success against the Greeks and Qarmatians.

Al-Muktafī died in A.D. 908, A.H. 295, after a reign of about six years and a half. He was the last of the khalīfs who made any figure by their warlike exploits. His successors al-Muqtadir, al-Qāhir, and al-Rāzī, were so distressed by the Qarmatians and numberless usurpers who were every day starting up, that by the 325th year of the Hijrī, A.D. 937, they had nothing left but the city of Baghdād.

Al-Muqtadi Billah (المقتدي بـالـلـه), surnamed Abūl Qāsim Abd-ullāh, the son of Muhammad, and grandson of al-Qāem Billāh, was raised to the throne of Baghdād after the death of his grandfather in A.D. 1075, A.H. 467, by orders of Sultān Malikshāh Saljūkī, who was then the real master of the empire. He was the 27th khalīf of the race of Abbās, reigned 19 lunar years and 5 months and died A.D. 1094, A.H. 487. His death induced Barkayāraq the Saljūkī, the reigning Sultān of Persia, whose brother Mahmūd had died about the same period, to go to Baghdād, where he confirmed al-Mustazhir, the son of the late khalīf, as his successor, and was himself hailed by the new lord of the faithful, as Sultān of the empire.

Al-Muqtadir Billah (المقتدر بـالـلـه), the eighteenth khalīf of the house of Abbās, was the son of al-Mo'tazid Billāh. He succeeded his brother al-Muktafī to the throne of Baghdād in A.D. 908, A.H. 295. He reigned 24 lunar years 2 months and 7 days, and was murdered by a eunuch on the 29th October, A.D. 932, 25th Shawwal, A.H. 320. He was succeeded by his brother al-Qāhir Billāh.

Al-Muqtafi Bi-amr-illah (المقتفي بامرالله), the son of al-Mustazahr, was the 31st khalīf of the house of Abbās. He succeeded his nephew al-Rāshid in A.D. 1136, A.H. 530, reigned about 24 lunar years and died in A.D. 1160, A.H. 555, leaving his kingdom to his son al-Mustanjad.

Al-Mustaa'li Billah (المستعلى بالله), the sixth Fatimite khalīf, succeeded his father, al-Mustanasar Billāh, in the government of Egypt and Syria. During his reign, the power of that dynasty was impaired, and its authority weakened, their political influence having ceased in most of the Syrian cities, and the provinces of that country having fallen into the possessions of the Turkmans on one hand, and the Franks on the other. This people (the Crusaders) entered Syria and encamped before Antioch in the month of October, A.D. 1097, Zil-qada, A.H. 490; they obtained possession of it on the 20th June, 1098, 16th Rajab, A.H. 491; the following year they took Maaratun Nomān, and in the month of July, 1099, Sha'ban, A.H. 492, they became masters of Jerusalem, after a siege of more than 40 days. This city was taken on a Friday morning; during the ensuing week a great multitude of Moslems perished, and upwards of 70,000 were slain in the Masjid al-Aqsā (or mosque of Umar) —— al-Musta-a'lī was born at Cairo on the 24th August, A.D. 1076, 20th Muharram, A.H. 469, proclaimed khalīf on Thursday the 28th December, A.D. 1094, 18th Zil-hijja, A.H. 487, and died in Egypt on the 10th December, A.D. 1101, 16th Safar, A.H. 495. His son Amar bi Ahkām-ullāh Abū Alī Mansūr succeeded him.

Al-Mustaa'sim Billah (المستعصم بالله), surnamed Abū Ahmad Abdullāh, was the thirty-seventh and last khalīf of the race of Abbās. He succeeded his father, al-Mustanasar, to the throne of Baghdād in A.D. 1242, A.H. 640. In his time Halakū Khān Tartar, emperor of the Mughals and grandson of the great conqueror Changiz Khān, besieged Baghdād for two months, and having taken that place, seized al-Mustaa'sim and his four sons, whom he put to a most cruel death with 800,000 of its inhabitants. Halākū Khān was very desirous of seizing upon Baghdād, and of adding the whole kingdom of Mesopotamia to his already vast and numerous conquests; but, partly on account of his own scruples, and partly from fear of offending the prejudices of his Sunnī followers, who were all of the same faith with the khalīf, he refrained for a time from entering the sacred dominion of one who was considered as the head of their holy religion, and the true representative of their beloved prophet. But the glorious days of the house of Banī Abbās had already been numbered, the effeminate Mustaa'sim had personal vices enough to lead to and excuse the final extinction of his race! Ibn al-Qama, his prime minister (who hated him more than any other of his oppressed subjects) from within, and Nasīr-uddīn Tūsī, the preceptor of the Mughal prince (who owed him an old grudge) from without, urged the conqueror to the gates of Baghdād. Nasīr-uddīn had a few years before been at Baghdād, seeking shelter from persecution, and when he was introduced to Mustaa'sim, the latter asked him to what country he belonged? "Tūs, please your holiness," answered Nasīr-uddīn. "Art thou of the asses, or of the oxen of Tūs?" said the khalīf (meaning the two principal branches of the Shia faith—Akhbarīs and Usūlīs). Mortified as the illustrious refugee was at this inhospitable insult, he still submissively answered, "Of the oxen of Tūs, please your highness." "Where, then, are thy horns," said the insolent buffoon. "I have them not with me," replied Nasīr-uddīn, "but if your holiness permit, I will go and fetch them." "Make haste, hence, thence, thou deformed animal," said the khalīf, "and never again appear in my presence in so imperfect a state!" Nasīr-uddīn kept his promise well, for, at the moment when Baghdād was on the point of being surrendered, and the khalīf driven to the last extremity, he sent him a message to the effect that the ox of Tūs was at the gate with *his horns*, and inquiring, when it would please his holiness to receive him? Nasīr-uddīn had in the city another old offender, whom he was anxious also to chastise. This was ibn Hājib, also one of the khalīf's ministers, and a person of great reputation for his learning; but being an Arabian Sunnī, and a very bigoted one too, he had behaved still more cruelly than his master to the distressed Persian Shia when he sought protection at Baghdād. Ibn Hājib, having been seized with depression of spirits, the physicians had recommended him (and the priests had granted him dispensation) to take, occasionally, a little wine. This happened when Nasīr-uddīn was at Baghdād. One day, ibn Hājib feeling himself particularly melancholy, and having, in consequence, taken a larger dose than usual, he became unusually merry, and requested Nasīr-uddīn to accompany him on the Tigris. Having reached the middle of the stream, he stopped the boat, and produced the several volumes of Nasīr-uddīn's works, which the learned refugee had presented to the khalīf—some of them in the original manuscript, and not yet transcribed, and in the presence of their anxious author, he threw them all, one after another, into the river, with such spiteful force, that the water was splashed about in every direction; when turning himself, on each occasion, to his mortified guest, he exclaimed with a sarcastic smile of triumph, "How wonderfully it bubbles!" When the turn of Nasīr-uddīn came he, too, gave full vent to his revenge. He ordered ibn Hājib to be cased up to his neck, in an ox's hide, just taken off the animal, and, having filled the skin with air, he laid it for a few hours in the sun, till it became quite dry, and sounded like a drum. Then the victor advanced close to his half exhausted enemy, gave him a kick of triumph, and, as he rolled on the ground, exclaimed, "How wonderfully it rattles!" The fall of Baghdād took place on Sunday the 10th February, A.D. 1258, 4th Safar, A.H. 656, from which time Baghdād was added to the other conquered provinces of this proud emperor. Al-Mustaa'sim reigned 15 lunar years and 7 months.

Al-Musta'in Billah (المستعين بالله), the son of Muhammad, the son of al-Mo'tasim Billāh, was the twelfth khalīf of the race of Abbās. He ascended the throne of Baghdād in A.D. 862, A.H. 248, after the death of his cousin or brother al-Mustanasar Billāh, but was forced to abdicate the throne in A.D. 866, A.H. 252, by his brother al-Mo'tiz Billāh, who afterwards caused him to be privately murdered.

Al-Mustakfi Billah (المستكفى بالله) was the 22nd khalīf of the Abbaside family, and the son of al-Muktafī, the son of al-Mō'tazid Billāh. He succeeded his uncle al-Muttaqī in A.D. 945, A.H. 333, reigned in Baghdād one year and four months, and was deposed by his wazir in A.D. 946, A.H. 334. After him al-Mutīa' Billāh was raised to the throne.

Al-Mustanasar Billah (المستنصر بالله), the son of Tāhir, was the fifth khalīf of Egypt of the Fātimite race. He succeeded his father A.D. 1036, and with the assistance of a Turk named Basāsirī, conquered Baghdād and imprisoned al-Kāem Billāh about the year A.D. 1054, and for a year and a half was acknowledged the only legitimate chief of all the Musalmāns. Basāsirī was defeated and killed by Tughral Beg A.D. 1059, A.H. 487.

[*Vide* Basāsirī. Al-Mustanasar died in 1094, having reigned 60 years; and was succeeded by his son al-Mustaa'lī Billāh Abūl Qāsim.]

Al-Mustansir Billah I. (المستنصر بالله), the eleventh khalīf of the race of Abbās, ascended the throne of Baghdād after the murder of his father, al-Mutwakkil, in December, A.D. 861, Shawwal, A.H. 247, and had reigned only six months, when he was cut off by the hand of death in A.D. 862, A.H. 248. He was succeeded by his cousin al-Musta'īn Billāh.

Al-Mustansir Billah II. (المستنصر بالله), surnamed Abū Ja'far al-Mansūr, ascended the throne of Baghdād after the death of his father, al-Tāhir, in A.D. 1226, A.H. 623. He was the 36th khalīf of the house of Abbās, reigned about 17 years, and died A.D. 1242, A.H. 640, leaving his kingdom to his son al-Mustaa'sim Billāh, the last of the khalīfs.

Al-Mustanjid Billah (المستنجد بالله), the 32nd khalīf of the race of Abbās, succeeded to the throne of Baghdād after the death of his father al-Muktafī, in A.D. 1160, A.H. 555, reigned 11 lunar years and died in A.D. 1171, A.H. 566, when his son al-Mustazī succeeded him.

Al-Mustarashid Billah (المسترشد بالله), the twenty-ninth khalīf of the Abbaside family, succeeded his father, al-Mustazahr, to the throne of Baghdād in A.D. 1118, A.H. 512. It is related by ibn Khallikān that when Sultān Masaūd, the son of Muhammad, the son of Malikshāh Saljūkī, was encamped outside the town of Marāgha in Azurbejān, al-Mustarashid was then with him, and on Thursday the 28th or, according to ibn Mustaufī, the 14th or 28th Zil'qada, A.H. 529 (corresponding with the 24th August or 7th September, A.D. 1135), a band of assassins broke into the khalīf's tent and murdered him. Al-Mustarashid reigned 17 lunar years and some months, and was succeeded by his son al-Rāshid Billāh.

Al-Mustazhir Billah (المستظهر بالله), the son of al-Muqtadī, was the twenty-eighth khalīf of the dynasty of Abbās. He was placed on the throne of Baghdād after the death of his father in A.D. 1094, A.H. 487, by Barkyaraq Saljūkī, the Turkish Sultān of Persia. He reigned 25 lunar years and some months, and at his death, which happened in the year A.D. 1118, A.H. 512, he was succeeded by his son al-Mustarashid.

Al-Mustazi Bi-amr-illah (المستضي بامر الله), the thirty-third khalīf of the Abbaside family, succeeded his father, al-Mustanjad, to the throne of Baghdād in A.D. 1171, A.H. 566. He reigned about seven years and died in A.D. 1179, A.H. 575, when his son al-Nāsir Billāh succeeded him.

Al-Mutaa'zz Billah (المتعز بالله), the son of al-Mutwakkil, was the 13th khalīf of the race of Abbās. He deposed his brother al-Mustaīn in A.D. 866, A.H. 252, and having caused him to be murdered privately, ascended the throne of Baghdād. He did not, however, long enjoy the dignity of which he had so iniquitously possessed himself, being deposed by the Turkish Militia (who now began to set up and depose khalīfs as they pleased) in the year A.D. 869, A.H. 255. After his deposition, he was sent under an escort from Sarr Manrae to Baghdād, where he died of thirst and hunger, after a reign of three years and about seven months. The fate of this khalīf was peculiarly hard: the Turkish troops had mutinied for their pay; and al-Mutaa'zz not having money to satisfy their demands, applied to his mother, named Kabīha, for 50,000 dīnars. This she refused, telling him that she had no money at all, although it afterwards appeared that she was possessed of immense treasure. After his deposition, however, she was obliged to discover them, and even deposit them in the hands of the new khalīf al-Muhtadī. They consisted of 1,000,000 dīnars, a bushel of emeralds, and another of pearls, and three pounds and three quarters of rubies of the colour of fire.

Al-Mutia' Billah (المطيع بالله), the twenty-third khalīf of the race of Abbās, was the son of al-Muqtadir Billāh. He ascended the throne of Baghdād after al-Mustakfī in A.D. 946, A.H. 334, reigned 29 lunar years and 4 months, and died in A.D. 974, A.H. 363. It was in his time that the temporal power of the khalīfs of Baghdād, after having been long sustained by Turkish mercenaries, was completely and finally broken by the Byzantine Romans, led by Nicephorus Phocas and John Zimisces. [Smith's Gibbon (ed. 1862), vi. pp. 106, 422, 427–8.] His son al-Taya' succeeded him.

Al-Muttaqi Billah (المتقى بالله), the son of al-Muqtadir, was the twenty-first khalīf of the dynasty of Abbās. He succeeded his brother al-Rāzī Billāh to the throne of Baghdād in A.D. 941, A.H. 329, reigned 3 years 11 months and 15 days, and died in A.D. 945, A.H. 333. He was succeeded by his nephew al-Mustaqfī, the son of al-Muktafī.

Al-Mutwakkil 'Al-allah (المتوكل على الله). This was the name and title assumed by Abūl Fazl Ja'far on his accession to the throne of Baghdād. He was the tenth khalīf of the house of Abbās, and the son of al-Mō'tasim Billāh. He succeeded his brother al-Wāthik or Wāsiq in the year A.D. 847, A.H. 232, and began his reign with an act of the greatest cruelty. The late khalīf's wazīr having treated al-Mutwakkil ill in his brother's lifetime, and opposed his election to the khilāfat, was on that account now sent to prison, and afterwards thrown into an iron furnace lined with spikes or nails heated red hot, where he was miserably burnt to death. During this reign nothing remarkable happened, except wars with the Greeks, which were carried on with various success. He was very intolerant, especially of the Jews and Christians, on whom he heaped many indignities. He did not stop there. In his imbecility and ferocity he forbade the pilgrimage to Karbala, and caused the sacred repository of the ashes of Husain and the other martyrs interred there to be razed. He reigned 14 years 9 months and 9 days, and was assassinated and cut into seven pieces on the 24th December, A.D. 861, 17th Shawwal, A.H. 247, at the instance of his son al-Mustanasar, who succeeded him.

Al-Muwaffiq Billah (الموفق بالله), the son of al-Mutwakkil Billāh, the khalīf of Baghdād and brother and coadjutor of the khalīf al-Ma'tamid, to whom he was of much service in his battles against his enemies. He died of elephantiasis or leprosy in the year A.D. 891, A.H. 278, and while in his last illness could not help observing that of 100,000 men whom he commanded, there was not one so miserable as himself. His son Mō'tazid, after the death of his brother al-Mō'tamid in A.D. 892, succeeded to the throne of Baghdād.

Al-Muwyyid (Isma'il) (الموید اسمعیل), whose name is spelt in Lempriere's *Universal Biographical Dictionary* "Alombuadad," and in Watkin's *Biographical Dictionary* "Almuvadad," was an Arabian historian, who gave a chronological account of the Saracen affairs in Sicily from A.D. 842 to 904. This MS. is in the Library of the Escurial, in Spain, and a Latin version of it is inserted in Muratori's *Rerum Italicarum Scriptores*.

Al-Muzani (المزنی). *Vide* **Abū** Ibrāhīm Ismaīl.

Al-Nasir Billah (الناصر بالله), or al-Nasir-uddin allah, the son of al-Mustazī, succeeded his father to the throne of Baghdād in A.D. 1179. He professed the Shia' faith, and after a long reign of 46 lunar years and 11 months, died in the year A.D. 1225. He was the 34th khalīf of the house of Abbās, and was succeeded by his son al-Tāhir Billāh.

Alp Arsalan (الپ ارسلان), (which means in the Turkish language "the valiant lion"), was a king of Persia of the Seljūkian dynasty, and the son of Dāūd Beg Saljūkī. He succeeded his uncle Tughral Beg in A.D. 1063, A.H. 455, married the sister of the khalīf Qāim Billāh, and his name was pronounced in the public prayers of the Muhammadans after that of the khalīf. He was a warlike prince; and, having spoiled the Church of St. Basil in Cæsarea, defeated Romanus Diogenes, Emperor of the Greeks in A.D. 1068, A.H. 460, who was seized and carried to the conqueror. Alp Arsalan demanded of his captive, at the first conference, what he would have done if fortune had reversed their lot. "I would have given thee many a stripe," was the imprudent and virulent answer. The Sultān only smiled and asked Romanus what he expected would be done to him. "If thou art cruel," said the Emperor, "put me to death. If vainglorious load me with chains, and drag me in triumph to thy capital. If generous, grant me my liberty." Alp Arsalan was neither cruel nor vain-glorious, he nobly released his prisoner, and, giving all his officers who were captives dresses of honour, sent them away to their homes. Alp Arsalan after a reign of more than nine years was stabbed about the 15th December, A.D. 1072, 30th Rabī I. A.H. 465, by a Khwārizmian desperado whom he had taken prisoner and sentenced to death. He was buried at Marv in Khurāsān, and the following is the translation of the inscription engraved on his tomb: "All ye who have seen the glory of Alp Arsalan exalted to the heavens, come to Marv, and you will behold it buried in the dust." He was succeeded by his son Malikshāh.

Alp Arsalan, who is by some called Apal Arsalan, was the son of Atsiz, a Sultān of Khwārizm, whom he succeeded in A.D. 1166, A.H: 551-557, and died in A.D. 1162.

Alptakin or **Alptagin** (الپتكين). *Vide* Alaptakīn.

Al-Qadir Billah (القادر بالله), the twenty-fifth khalīf of the Abbaside family, was the son of Is-ḥāq, the son of Muqtadir Billah. He ascended the throne of Baghdād after the dethronement of al-Taya' in A.D. 991, A.H. 381. He was a contemporary of Sultān Mahmūd of Ghazni; reigned 41 lunar years and 3 months, and died A.D. 1031, A.H. 422. He was succeeded by al-Qāimbi-amr-illāh.

Al-Qadiri or **Qadiri** (القادري), a sect of Muhammadans. These are a branch of the Muetazillīs, and differ in their opinions from the orthodox Musalmāns, in that they deny God's decree, and assert free will; affirming that the contrary opinion makes God the author of evil.

Al-Qahir Billah (القاهر بالله), the nineteenth khalīf of the race of the Abbasides, and the third son of al-Mo'tazid Billāh, succeeded his brother al-Muqtadir to the crown of Baghdād in October, A.D. 932, Shawwāl, A.H. 320. He had reigned only one year, five months and twenty-one days when his wazīr ibn Maqla deprived him of his sight with a hot iron on Wednesday the 23rd April, A.D. 934, 6th Jamad I. A.H. 322, and raised al-Rāzī Billāh, the son of Muqtadir, to the throne. It is said that al-Qāhir, after this, as long as he lived, was obliged to beg for charity in the mosque at Baghdād, calling out to the people that assembled there, "Have pity and give charity to one, who had once been your khalīfa."

Al-Qaim (القايم), second khalīf of the Fātimite race of Barbary; he succeeded his father Obeid-ullah al-Mahdī A.D. 924, A.H. 312. During his reign we read of nothing remarkable, except the revolt of Yezīd ibn Kondat, a man of mean extraction. Al-Qāim reigned nearly 12 years and died in A.D. 945, A.H. 334. His son Ismaīl al-Mansūr succeeded him.

'Al-Qama (علقمه), son of Qys, was one of the pupils of Abdullah bin Masaūd, and an eminent man. He died in A.D. 681, A.H. 61.

Al-Qaim Billah or **Al-Qaim-bi-amr-illah** (القايم بالله), surnamed Abū Ja'far Abdullāh, the 26th khalīf of the house of 'Abbās. He succeeded his father Qādir Billāh to the throne of Baghdād in A.D. 1031, A.H. 422, reigned 44 lunar years and 8 months, and died in A.D. 1075, A.H. 467, which was soon after Sultān Malikshāh the Seljūkī had ascended the throne of Persia, and as that monarch was the real master of the empire, the nomination of a successor was deferred till he was consulted. He deputed a son of his prime minister Nizām-ul-Mulk to Baghdād with orders to raise al-Muqtadī, the grandson of al-Qāim, to the (nominal) rank of the commander of the faithful.

Al-Rashid or **Harun al-Rashid** (هارون الرشيد), the celebrated hero of the Arabian Nights, was the fifth khalīf of the race of Abbās and son of al-Mahdī; he succeeded his eldest brother al-Hādī to the throne of Baghdād in A.D. 786, A.H. 170. This was one of the best and wisest princes that ever sat on the throne of Baghdād. He was also extremely fortunate in all his undertakings, though he did not much extend his dominions by conquest. In his time the Moslem empire may be said to have been in its most flourishing state, though, by the independency of the Moslems in Spain, who had formerly set up a khalīf of the house of Umyya, his territories were not quite so extensive as those of some of his predecessors. He possessed, however, the provinces of Syria, Palestine, Arabia, Persia, Armenia, Natolia, Media or Azurbejān, Babylonia, Assyria, Sindh, Sijistan, Khurāsān, Tabristān, Jurjān, Zābulistān, Māwarunnahr, or great Bukhāria, Egypt, Libya, Mauritania, etc., so that his empire was still by far the most powerful of any in the world, and indeed extended farther than the Roman empire ever had done.

In the beginning of the year A.D. 802, A.H. 186, he divided the government of his extensive dominions among his three sons in the following manner: To al-Amīn the eldest, he assigned the provinces of Syria, Irāk, the three Arabias, Mesopotamia, Assyria, Media, Palestine, Egypt, and all the part of Africa extending from the confines of Egypt and Ethiopia to the Straits of Gibraltar, with the dignity of khalīf; to al-Māmūn the second, he assigned Persia, Kirmān, the Indies, Khurāsān, Tabristān, Kābulistān and Zabulistān, together with the vast province of Māwarunnahr; and to his third son al-Qāsim, he gave Armenia, Natolia, Jurjān, Georgia, Circassia, and all the Moslem territories bordering upon the Euxine sea. As to the order of succession, al-Amīn was to ascend the throne immediately after his father's decease; after him al-Māmūn; and then al-Qāsim, whom he had surnamed al-Mō'tasim.

The most considerable exploits performed by this khalīf were against the Greeks, who by their perfidy provoked him to make war upon them, and whom he always overcame. In the year A.D. 803, A.H. 187, the khalīf received a letter from the Greek Emperor Nicephorus, commanding him to return all the money he had extorted from the Empress Irane, or expect soon to see an Imperial army in the heart of his territories. This insolent letter so exasperated Hārūn, that he immediately assembled his forces and advanced to Heraclea, laying the country through which he passed waste with fire and sword. For some time also he kept that city straitly besieged, which so terrified the Greek Emperor that he submitted to pay an annual tribute.

In the year A.D. 804, A.H. 188, war was renewed with the Greeks, and Nicephorus with a great army attacked the khalīf's forces with the utmost fury. He was, however, defeated with the loss of 40,000 men, and received three wounds in the action; after which the Moslems committed terrible ravages in his territories, and returned home laden with spoils. The next year Hārūn invaded Phrygia; defeated an Imperial army sent to oppose him, and having ravaged the country, returned without any considerable loss. In the year A.D. 806, A.H. 190, the khalīf marched into the Imperial territories with an army of 135,000 men, besides a great number of volunteers and others who were not enrolled among his troops. He first took the city of Heraclea, from which he is said to have carried 16,000 prisoners; after which he made himself master of several other places, and, in the conclusion of the expedition, he made a descent on the island of Cyprus, which he plundered in a terrible manner. This success so intimidated Nicephorus, that he immediately sent the tribute due to Hārūn, the withholding of which had been the cause of the war; and concluded a peace upon the khalīf's own terms. Charlemagne respected his character, and Hārūn in token of his friendship presented to the European prince a clock, the mechanism and construction of which were regarded among the prodigies of the age. Hārūn reigned 23 years, and died in Khurāsān on the eve of Saturday the 24th March, A.D. 809, 3rd Jamad II., A.H. 193, and was buried at Tūs, which is now called Mashhad. He was succeeded by his eldest son, al-Amīn.

Al-Rashid Billah (الراشد بالله), the thirtieth khalīf of the Abbasides, succeeded his father, al-Mustarashad, in August or September, A.D. 1135, Zil'kad, A.H. 529, and died in the year A.D. 1136, A.H. 530. He was succeeded by al-Muqtafī, the son of al-Mustazahir.

Al-Razi. See Rāzī.

Al-Razi Billah (الراضى بالله), the son of al-Muqtadir and the twentieth khalīf of the house of Abbās, was the last who deserved the title of the Commander of the Faithful. He was raised to the throne of Baghdād, after the dethronement of his uncle al-Qāhir Billāh by the wazīr Ibn Maqla in April, A.D. 934, Jamad I. A.H. 322. In the year 936, the khalīf finding himself distressed on all sides by usurpers, and having a wazīr of no capacity, instituted a new office superior to that of wazīr, which he entitled Amīr-ul-Umra. This great officer, Imād-ud-daula Alī Bōya, was trusted with the management of the finances in a much more absolute and unlimited manner than any of the khalīf's wazīrs ever had been. Nay, he officiated for the khalīf in the great mosque at Baghdād, and had his name mentioned in the public prayers throughout the kingdom. In short the khalīf was so much under the power of this officer, that he could not apply a single dīnār to his own use without the leave of the Amīr-ul-Umra. In the year A.D. 937, the Moslem empire so great and powerful, was shared among the following usurpers:

The cities of Wasat, Basra, Kūfa with the rest of the Arabian Irāq, were considered as the property of the Amīr-ul-Umra, though they had been in the beginning of the year seized upon by a rebel called al-Baridi, who could not be driven out of them.

The country of Fars, Faristan, or Persia properly so called, was possessed by Imad-ud-daula Alī ibn Boya, who resided in the city of Shīrāz.

Part of the tract denominated al-Jabal, together with Persian Irāq, which is the mountainous part of Persia, and the country of the ancient Parthians, obeyed Rukn-ud-daula, the brother of Inad-ud-daula, who resided at Isfahān. The other part of the country was possessed by *Washmakin* the Dīlamite.

Dayār Rabia, Dayār Bikr, Dāyār Modar, and the city of Musal, acknowledged for their sovereign a race of princes called Hamdanites.

Egypt and Syria no longer obeyed the khalīfs, but Muhammad ibn Tāj, who had formerly been appointed governor of those provinces.

Africa and Spain had long been independent.

Sicily and Crete were governed by princes of their own.

The provinces of Khurāsān and Malvarunnahr were under the dominions of al-Nasr ibn Ahmad, of the dynasty of the Samānians.

The provinces of Tabristān, Jurjan or Georgia, and Māzindarān, had kings of the first dynasty of the Dīlamites.

The province of Kirmān was occupied by Abū Alī Muhammad ibn Eylia al-Sāmānī, who had made himself master of it a short time before. And

Lastly, the provinces of Yemama and Bahryn, including the district of Hajr, were in the possession of Abū Tāhir the Karmatian.

Thus the khalīfs were deprived of all their dominions, and reduced to the rank of sovereign pontiffs; in which light, though they continued for some time to be regarded by the neighbouring princes, yet their power never arrived to any height. In this low state the khalīfs continued till the extinction of the Khilāfat by Halākū Khān the Tartar in the year A.D. 1258, A.H. 656.

Al-Rāzī Billāh reigned 7 years 2 months and 11 days, and died in A.D. 941, A.H. 329. He was succeeded by his brother al-Muttaqī.

Al-Saharawi (الصحراوی). *Vide* Abūl Qāsim.

Al-Saffah (السفاح), surname of Abūl Abbās, the son of Muhammad, the son of Alī, the son of 'Abdullāh, the son of Abbās, the uncle of the prophet. He was proclaimed khalīfa by the inhabitants of Kūfa on Friday the 29th November, A.D. 749, 13th Rabī II., A.H. 132, upon which a battle took place between him and Marwān II., the last khalīfa of the house of Umyya and Ommaides, in which the latter was slain, 5th August, A.D. 750, 26th Ẓil-ḥijja, A.H. 132. Al-Saffāh after this victory investing himself with sovereign power, laid the foundation of the dynasty of the Abbasides, which continued to be transmitted to his family from father to son for 524 lunar years, during a succession of 37 khalīfs, till they were dispossessed by Halākū Khān the Tartar king of Persia in A.D. 1258, A.H. 656. By the elevation of the house of Abbās to the dignity of khilāfat, began that glorious period during which Arabic and Persian literature reached its highest perfection. With some few exceptions these khalīfas were the noblest race of kings that ever adorned the throne of sovereignty. Abūl Abbās died, after a reign of more than four years, of the small-pox, on Sunday the 9th June, A.D. 754, 13th Ẓil-ḥijja, A.H. 136, and was succeeded by his brother Abū Ja'far Almansūr.

List of the khalīfas of the race of Abbās who reigned at Baghdād.

1. Al-Saffāh, or Abūl 'Abbās al-Saffāh.
2. Al-Mansūr.
3. Al-Mahdī, son of al-Mansūr.
4. Al-Hādī, son of al-Mahdī.
5. Al-Rashīd, or Hārūn al-Rashīd, son of al-Mahdī.
6. Al-Amīn, son of Hārūn.
7. Al-Mamūn, son of Hārūn.
   Ibrahīm, son of Mahdī, competitor.
8. Al-Mo'tasim Billāh, son of Hārūn.
9. Al-Wāthiq, or Wāsiq, son of Mo'tasim.
10. Al-Mutwakkil.
11. Al-Mustanasar Billāh.
12. Al-Mustāīn Billāh.
13. Al-Mo'tia' Billāh.
14. Al-Muhtadī Billāh.
15. Al-Mo'tamid.
16. Al-Motazid Billāh.
17. Al-Muktafī Billāh.
18. Al-Muqtadir Billāh.
19. Al-Kahir Billāh.
20. Al-Rāzī Billāh.
21. Al-Muttakī Billāh.
22. Al-Mustakfī Billāh.
23. Al-Mutīa Billāh.
24. Al-Tāyā Billāh.
25. Al-Qādir Billāh.
26. Al-Qāim bi-amr-ullāh.
27. Al-Muqtadī Billāh.
28. Al-Mustazahir Billāh.
29. Al-Mustarashid Billāh.
30. Al-Rashid Billāh.
31. Al-Muktafī bi-amr-ullāh.
32. Al-Mustanjad Billāh.
33. Al-Mustazī bi-amr-ullāh.
34. Al-Nāsir Billāh.
35. Al-Tāhir bi-amr-ullāh.
36. Al-Mustanasar Billāh II.
37. Al-Mu'tasim Billāh, the last khalīf.

Al-Tahir bi-amr-illah Muhammad (الطاهر بامرالله محمد) succeeded his father, al-Nāsir Billāh, to the throne of Baghdād in A.D. 1225, A.H. 622. He was the thirty-fifth khalīf of the house of Abbās, reigned 9 months and 11 days, and died in A.D. 1226, A.H. 623. His son al-Mustanasar II. succeeded him.

Al-Taya' (or **al-Tayi'**) **Billah** (الطايع بالله), the son of al-Mutīa' Billāh, was the twenty-fourth khalīf of Baghdād. He succeeded his father in A.D. 974, reigned 17 years and 4 months, and was deposed by Bahā-ud-daula in A.D. 991, when Qādir Billāh, the son of Is-ḥāq, the son of Muqtadir, was raised to the throne.

Altimsh (التمش). *Vide* Shams-uddīn Altimsh.

Al-Walid (الوليد). *Vide* Walīd.

Al-Wathik or **al-Wasik Billah** (الواثق), the ninth khalīf of the family of the Abbasides, succeeded his father, al-Mō'tasim Billāh, on the 5th January, A.D. 842, 18th Rabī I., A.H. 227, to the throne of Baghdād. The following year, he invaded and conquered Sicily. Nothing remarkable happened during the rest of his reign. He reigned 5 lunar years 7 months and 3 days, and died in A.D. 847, A.H. 232. He was succeeded by his brother al-Mutwakkil. He is the *Vathek* of Beekford's well-known tale.

'Alwi (علوی), poetical name of Shaikh Wajī-uddīn, which see.

'Alwi (علوی), poetical name of Mīr Tāhir 'Alwi, who died at Kashmīr previous to the year A.D. 1723, A.H. 1136. He is the author of a dīwan and a Masnawī; the latter contains the story of the blacksmith and the cotton cleanser called Qissae Haddād wa Hallāj.

'Alwi Khan (Hakim) (علوی خان), a physician, who was invited from Persia by the Emperor Muhammad Shāh, and died at Dehlī in A.D. 1748, A.H. 1161. His title was Mō'tmid-ul-Malūk Sayyid 'Alwī Khān Hakīm. He is the author of a medical work called *Jāma'-ul-Jawa'ma'*.

'Amad (عماد), 'Amād Shāh, 'Amād-uddīn, etc. *Vide* Imād, Imād Shāh, etc.

'Ama-'aq or **Uma-'aq Bukhari** (عمعق). *Vide* Abūl Najīb-al-Bukhārī.

Amanat (امانت), poetical name of Sayyid Aghā Hasan, son of Āghā Razwī, author of a Dīwān.

Amanat 'Ali (Maulwi) (امانت علی), author of a small work entitled *Bahār Ajam*, containing 121 letters written by him to different persons, in pure Persian.

Amanat Khan Mirak (امانت خان میرک), title of Mīr Ma'īn-uddīn Ahmad Khān Khwāfī, a native of Khwāf in Khurāsān. He was a nobleman of high rank in the time of the Emperor 'Alamgīr, and died in the year A.D. 1684, A.H. 1095, at Aurangābād. He is the author of the work called *Shariat ul-Islām*.

Amanat Khan (امانت خان), title of Mīr Husain, son of Amānat Khān Khwāfī. He was honoured with the title of his father about the year A.D. 1688, A.H. 1100, by the Emperor 'Alamgīr, and raised to the rank of a nobleman. He held different offices under that Emperor, and died at Surat A.D. 1699, A.H. 1111.

Amanat Khan (امانت خان), a celebrated Nastāliq writer, who in the 11th year of the reign of the Emperor Shāh Jahān wrote the inscriptions on the Tāj at Āgra.

Amani (Mir) (امانی میر), of Kābul, died in A.H. 981, or A.D. 1573.

Amani (اماتی), poetical name of Mirzā Amān-ullāh, the eldest son of Mahabat Khān. He flourished in the time of the Emperor Shāh Jahān, and died in the year A.D. 1637, A.H. 1047. He is the author of a dīwān.

[*Vide* Khān Zamān Bahādur and Mahābat Khān.]

Aman-ullah (Hafiz) (امان الله حافظ), of Benares, was an author and Qāzi of Lucknow in the time of the Emperor 'Alamgīr. He died in A.D. 1721, A.H. 1133.

Aman-ullah Husaini (امان الله حسيني), author of an Insha which goes by his name, *Inshāe Amān-ullāh Husainī*.

Ahmad Shah Abdali (احمد شاه ابدالي) on his seventh invasion of Hindustan arrived at the Satlaj in A.D. 1764. Amar Singh waited on him, but was ordered to shave his head and beard before entering the royal presence. By a nazarana or present of a lac of rupees, he purchased permission to appear bearded and unshorn, and received investiture with the title of Maha Raja Rājagān Mahindar Bakashr, which title is now borne by the head of the Patiala family.

Amar-ibn-obaid. *Vide* Umar-ibn-ubaid.

Amar Singh (امر سنگه), Rāja of Patiala, was the son of Sardal Singh, who survived his father, Rājā Ala Singh, two or three years. Ahmad Amar Singh, *vide* Rana Amar Singh.

Amar Singh Rana, son of Rama Pallal Singh of Chittore, died in A.H. 1028

Amar Singh (امر سنگه), son of Gaj Singh, a rajpūt chief of the tribe of Rāṭhor. He killed Salābat Khān Mīr Bakhshī in the 17th year of Shāh Jahān in the presence of the Emperor, on Thursday evening the 25th July, O.S. 1644, 30th Jamadi I., A.H. 1054, and was by the order of the Emperor pursued and cut to pieces after a gallant defence near one of the gates of the fort of Agra, which is to this day called Amar Singh Darwāza or Amar Singh Gate. An account of this prince's early history will be found in Tod's *Rājasthān*.

Amar Singh (امر سنگه), of Benares, whose poetical name was Khushgō, held a government appointment in the Koel district. He compiled a short history of Akbar's palace and of the Tāj of Agra, and put the Bahār Dānish into verse and called it *Tarjuma Bahār Dānish*. This book is to be distinguished from the Izhār Dānish, an Urdū translation of *Bahār Dānish* by Mullazāda at Palnar.

Amar Singh (Rana), son of Rana Purtab Singh. *Vide* Rana Sankar.

Ambaji Inglia, a general of the Gwaliar State who served under Mahādaji Sindhia from 1787, and who continued his services, both military and political, under his nephew Daulat Rao. The last mention of him is in Lake's war in Hindustan, in which he succeeded Gen. Perron [Keene's *History of India*, i. pp. 274, 360, 372].

Amili (آملي), a poet who was the author of a Dīwān. This person appears to be the same with Shaikh Baha-uddīn 'Amilī.

Amin (امين), the sixth khalīf of the house of Abbās. *Vide* al-Amīn.

Amin (امين), poetical name of Shāh Amīn-uddīn of Azīmābād, who flourished about the year A.D. 1715, A.H. 1127, and left a dīwān of Ghazals, etc.

Amina (آمنه), the wife of 'Abdullah, and mother of Muhammad the prophet of the Musalmāns. She was the daughter of Wahab the son of 'Abdul Manāf. She is represented as the most beautiful, prudent, and virtuous lady of her tribe, and consequently the most worthy of such an extraordinary person as 'Abdullah. She died six years after the birth of her son Muhammad, about the year A.D. 577.

Amina Begum (امينه بيگم). *Vide* Ghasītī Begum.

Amin Ahmad or **Amin Muhammad Razi** (امين احمد رازى), the author of the Biographical Dictionary called *Haft Aklīm*. (The seven climates.) This book, which he finished in the time of the emperor Akbar in A.D. 1594, A.H. 1002, contains a short description of the seven climates of the Temperate Zone, and the Topography of their principal cities; with memoirs of the illustrious persons and eminent poets which each has produced.

Amin-uddin Khan, Nawāb of Lohārū, descended from Ahmad Bakhsh, a Minister of the Alwar State in 1803-1826. The Nawāb succeeded his unhappy brother Shams-ul-din (*q.v.*) in 1835; and died on the 31st December, A.D. 1869, aged 70 years. His eldest son, Mirzā 'Ala-uddīn Khān, succeeded to his estates at Lohārū, on the 11th January, 1870.

Amini (اميني), poetical name of Amīr Sultān Ibrahīm, a contemporary of Khwāja 'Asafī, who died in A.D. 1520, A.H. 926. Amīnī wrote a chronogram on that occasion.

Amin-uddin (Mir) (امين الدين مير), a poet and a great jester, was contemporary with the poets Moulana Alī Kāhi and Khwāja Alī Shahāb.

Amin-uddin (Amir) (امين الدين امير). *Vide* Yemīn-uddīn (Amīr) and Tughrāi.

Amin-ud-daula Abul Jin (امين الدوله ابوالجن), surnamed the Samaritan, was a physician, and had been wazīr to Mālik Sālah Isma'īl. He was strangled at Cairo in A.D. 1250, A.H. 648, and there were found in his house, amongst other precious articles, about 10,000 volumes of valuable works, copied by the most celebrated caligraphers.

Amin-ud-daula Khan (امين الدوله خان), a rebel, was blown from the mouth of a gun on the 3rd August, 1857, at Āgra.

Amir bi Ahkam Allah (امر حكام الله), surnamed Abū Alī Mansūr, seventh khalīf of the Fatimite dynasty of Egypt, succeeded his father, al-Mustaa'lī Billāh, in December, 1101. From this time to the reign of 'Azid li-dīn Allah, during which period five khalīfs ascended the throne of Egypt, the history of that country affords little else than an account of the intestine broils and contests between the wazīrs or prime ministers, who were now become so powerful, that they had in a great measure stripped the khalīfs of their civil power, and left them nothing but a shadow of spiritual dignity. These contests at last gave occasion to a revolution, by which the race of Fatimite khalīfs were totally extinguished.

[*Vide* 'Azid li-dīn Allah.]

Amir (امير), poetical name of Amīr-uddaulā Nasīr Jang, commonly called Mirza Mendhū, son of Nawāb Shuja-ud-daulā and brother to Nawāb Asaf-ud-daulā.

Amiran Shah (اميران شاه). *Vide* Mīrān Shāh.

Amira Singh Tappa (اميره سنگه تپه), also called Amar Singh, a Gurkha general. He was the highest in rank and character of all the military chiefs of Nipāl. In 1814 during his campaign against Sir David Ochterlony in the Kamāon hills, he evinced equal valour and patriotism; but was compelled to surrender, at Malaun near Simla, 10th May, 1815.

[Keene's *History of India*, ii. p. 21.]

Amir Barid I. (امير بريد), the son of Qāsim Barīd, whom he succeeded in the government of Ahmadābād Bīdar in A.D. 1504, A.H. 910. During his rule the king Sultān Mahmūd Shāh Bahmanī died in A.D. 1517, A.H. 923, when Amīr Barīd placed Sultān 'Alā-uddīn III. on the throne, and after his death Sultān Kalīm Ullah, who being treated with great rigour by the Amīr, fled from Bīdar to Ahmadnagar, where he died shortly after. With Kalīm Ullāh ended the dynasty of the Bahmanī kings of Deccan. Amīr Barīd reigned over the territories of Ahmadābād Bīdar with full power more than 25 years, and died at Daulatābād in A.D. 1542, A.H. 949. He was buried at Ahmadābād Bīdar, and succeeded by his son Alī Barīd.

Amir Barid II. (امير بريد ثاني) succeeded to the government of Ahmadābād Biwar after deposing his relative Alī Barīd Shāh II. in A.D. 1609, and was the last of the Barīd Shahī dynasty.

Amiri (اميري), the poetical name of Maulāna Sultān Muhammad, a distinguished man who lived in the time of Shāh Tahmasp Safwī I. He praised this sovereign in his poems, and is the translator of Amīr Alī Sher's Tazkira, called *Majālis-ul-Nafāes*, from Turki into Persian. He is also the author of the *Bostān ul-Khayāl*.

Amir Khan (امير خان), title of Mīr Abūl Wafā, the eldest son of Mīr Qāsim Khān Namkīn, was a nobleman in the time of the emperors Jahangīr and Shāh Jahān. At the time of his death he was governor of Thatta, where he died A.D. 1647, A.H. 1057, aged more than 100 years. His former name was Mīr Khān, but having made a present of one lac of rupees to Shāh Jahān, he was honoured with the title of Amīr Khān.

Amir Khan (امير خان ميير ميران), surnamed Mīr Mīrān, the son of Khalīl-ullāh Khān Yezdī, was a nobleman of high rank in the time of the emperors Shāh Jahān and 'Alamgīr, and a great favourite of the latter. He died at Kābul on the 28th April, A.D. 1698, 27th Shawwal, A.H. 1109, and the emperor conferred the title of Amīr Khān on his son.

Amir Khan (Nawab) (اميرخان نواب), entitled U'mdat-ul-Mulk, was the son of the principal favourite of the emperor 'Alamgīr, of the same name, and a descendant of the celebrated Shāh Na'mat-ullāh Walī. He was himself a favourite of the emperor Muhammad Shāh; was appointed governor of Allahabad in A.D. 1739, A.H. 1152, and re-called to court in A.D. 1743, A.H. 1156. He was naturally free of speech, and the emperor, fond of his repartee, had allowed him more license in his conversation than was consistent with respect to his own dignity, when he was on business with the emperor, which by degrees disgusted Muhammad Shāh and made him wish his removal from office. He was consequently, with the consent of the emperor, stabbed with a dagger by a person who had been discharged from his service, and fell down dead on the spot. This circumstance took place on Friday the 26th December, 1747, 23rd Zil-hijja, A.H. 1159. He was buried after four days in the sepulchre of Khalīl-ullāh Khān his grandfather, which is close to the Sarāe of Rūh-ullāh Khān at Dehlī. His poetical name was Anjām. He composed logographs, and has left Persian and Rekhta Poems. There is a full account of Amīr Khān in the *Sujar-ul-Mutūkharin*, where he is said to have died in the same year as the emperor.

Amir Khan (امير خان), the famous ally of the Pindarīs and ancestor to the present Nawab of Tonk. He was originally in the service of Jaswant Rāo Holkar, who becoming insane in 1806 and incapable of the administration of his own affairs, this Muhammadan chief endeavoured to establish an ascendancy at his court, but soon left it with the army he commanded to pursue the separate object of his own ambition, and became the chief supporter of the Pindarīs. A treaty was ratified with him by the British Government on the 19th December, 1817. He had on various pretexts avoided the ratification of the engagements which his agent had concluded with the resident of Dehlī, but the movement of troops to his vicinity, and their occupation of positions which left him only the option between engaging in an unequal conflict and signing this treaty, induced him to adopt the safer course. He was confirmed in the possession of all the territories he held from the Holkar family, but compelled to surrender his large trains of artillery to the English Government, and to disband that great body of plunderers which had been for more than two years the scourge of Mālwa and Rājputāna. Amīr Khān died A.D. 1834, A.H. 1250. His *Life* was written by a Hindu named Basāwan Lāl; and the Memoir was translated into English by the late Thoby Prinsep.

Amir Khan (اميرخان), whose proper name was Mīr Khān, but was changed by the emperor 'Alamgīr by adding an alif to it into Amīr Khān. On a spot of seven bīghas of ground, he had built his house close to the place called Guzur Tijara, including the mahalla of Chhīpitolā. In the first year of the emperor 'Alamgīr he was appointed governor of the fort of Shāhjahanabad, and in the eleventh year of the reign of the emperor he was appointed Sūbadār of Kābul.

Amir Khan Sindhi (اميرخان سندهي), title of Mīr Abdul Karīm, son of Amīr Khān, the son of Mīr Abul Qāsim Namkīn. He was employed in various offices during the reign of 'Alamgīr, Bahādur Shāh and Farrukhsiyar, and died some time before the accession of Muhammad Shāh to the throne of Dehlī.

Amir Khond (امیر خوند). *Vide* Mīr Khūnd or Khawind Shāh.

Amir Khusru (امیر خسرو). *Vide* Khusro (Amīr).

Amir Mahmud (امیر محمود فخر الدین), surnamed Fakhr-uddīn, and commonly called Ibn-Yemīn, was the son of Amīr Yemīn-uddīn, entitled Mālik-ul Fuzlā, *i.e.*, the prince of the learned. Amīr Mahmūd was an excellent poet, and died on Saturday the 29th January, A.D. 1368, Jumāda II. A.H. 769, in Persia. He is mentioned in Dr. Sprenger's Catalogue, p. 67, to have died in 749 Hijrī corresponding with A.D. 1348, and in the *Tazhira Daulat Shahī* it is mentioned that he died in A.H. 745, A.D. 1344. He has left a Dīwān.

Amir Mirza (Nawab) (امیر میرزا نواب) was the son of George Hopkins Walters, a pensioned European officer, who, with his family, consisting of a wife, two daughters and one son, had established himself in Lucknow as a merchant many years ago. After his death his family, through the intrigues of one Bakhsh Alī Khān, embraced the Muhammadan religion, and the younger daughter not long after was consigned to the Seraglio of king Nasīr-uddīn Hydar and became one of the queens of that monarch, under the title of Wilayetī Mahal, or the King's European consort. The elder daughter also received the name and title of Ashraf-un-nisa Begam. She remained unmarried all her life. The brother, Joseph Walters, received the name of Amīr Mirzā. He was brought up as a Musalmān of the Shī'a sect, and always took a pride in showing himself as an orthodox follower of the Crescent. After Wilayetī Mahal's death, her elder sister Ashraf-un-nisa Begam succeeded to her estate, consisting of Government Securities valued at 11,400,000 rupees besides jewellery, movable and immovable property of considerable value. In 1832 Ashraf-un-nisa died, and was succeeded by Amīr Mirzā, her brother, who squandered almost the whole property by his reckless prodigality. Amīr Mirzā died on the 10th January, 1870, in his 66th year.

Amir Mo'izzi (امیر معزی), a celebrated poet of Samarqand, who served under Sultān Malik Shāh and Sultān Sanjar Saljūkī, and was honoured with the title of Mālik-ush-Shua'rā, or the Royal Poet. He was accidentally killed by an arrow shot by the latter prince. His Dīwān contains 15,000 verses. His death happened in the year A.D. 1147, A.H. 542. His proper name was Amīr Alī.

Amir Shahi (امیر شاهی سبزواری), of Sabzwār, a poet who flourished in the time of Shāhrukh Mirzā, about the year A.D. 1436. *Vide* Shāhī (Amīr).

Amir Taimur (امیر تیمور صاحبقران), styled Sāhib Qirān, because he reigned more than 30 years, or because he was born in a conjunction of the planets so called. He is also called Timurlang (Tamerlane) from some defect in his feet; was born at Kush in ancient Sogdania on Tuesday, the 9th April, A.D. 1336, 27th Sha'bān, A.H. 736. Some say he was the son of a shepherd, and others that he was descended in a right line from Qājulī Bahādur, son of Tūmana Khān, of the same lineage with Changez Khān, the celebrated conqueror of Persia. His father's name was Amīr Turāghāī and mother's Takīna Khātūn; however, his obscurity was soon forgotten in the glory of his exploits. Distinguished by his courage and unbounded ambition, he gained a number of faithful adherents, and seized the city of Balkh, the capital of Khurāsān, and having put to death Amīr Husain, the ruler of that place, whose sister he had married, he ascended the throne on Wednesday the 10th April, A.D. 1370, 12th Ramzān, A.H. 771. He then subdued Kandahār, Persia and Baghdād, and seconded by an enthusiastic army he penetrated to India, took Dehlī on Tuesday the 17th December, A.D. 1398, 7th Rabī II. A.H. 801, with its immense treasures, and returned to punish Baghdād that shook off his yoke. The offending city was given up to pillage, and 80,000 of her inhabitants put to the sword. Now master of the fairer part of Asia, he interfered, at the request of the Greek emperor, in the affairs of Bāiazīd (Bajazet), emperor of the Turks, and commanded him to abandon the siege of Constantinople. The message roused the indignation of Bāiazīd; he marched against the new enemy, and was defeated by him in Phrygia, after a battle of three days, on Friday the 21st July, A.D. 1402, 19th Zil-hijja, A.H. 804. Bāiazīd fell into the hands of the emperor, and was carried about in mockery in an iron cage. To these conquests Taimūr added Egypt and the treasures of Cairo, and then fixed the seat of his empire at Samarqand, where he received the homage of Manuel Palæologus, emperor of Constantinople, and of Henry III. King of Castile, by their ambassadors. Taimūr was preparing fresh victories by the invasion of China, when death stopped his career on Wednesday the 18th February, A.D. 1405, 17th Sha'-bān, A.H. 807, in the 36th year of his reign, aged 71 years, and was buried at Samarqand. He was the ancestor of Bābar, who founded the dynasty of the Mughul emperors of Dehlī. After his death he received the title of "Firdaus Makānī," *i.e.*, "May paradise be his place of residence." He had four sons, *viz.*, Jahāngīr Mirzā, Umar Shaikh Mirzā, Mīrān Shāh and Shāhrukh Mirzā. Tamerlane on his death-bed named his grandson Pīr Muhammad, son of Jahāngīr Mirzā, the universal heir of all his dominions; but the contempt with which his will was treated after death was equal to the veneration which had been paid to his authority during his life. The Sultān Khalīl, another of his grandsons, immediately took possession of the capital of Samarqand, and proclaimed himself emperor. Pīr Muhammad did not live long enough to assert his rights, but was assassinated six months after the death of his grandfather. After his death, Shāhrukh Mirzā, the youngest of the two surviving sons of Tamerlane, succeeded to the inheritance assigned for Pīr Muhammad.

List of the kings of Samarqand of the race of Amir Taimūr.

Khalīl Sulṭān, the son of Mīrān Shāh.
Shāhrukh Mirzā, son of Amīr Taimūr.
Ala-ud-daula Mirzā.
Ulugh Beg Mirzā, son of Shāhrukh.
Mirzā Babar, who subsequently conquered Dehlī, and became the first emperor of the Mughuls in India.
Mirzā Abdul-Latīf.
Mirzā Shāh Muhammad.
Mirzā Ibrahīm.
Sulṭān Abū Sayyid.
Mirzā Yādgār Muhammad.

Amir Yemin-uddin (امیر یمین الدین), entitled Mālik-ul-Fuzlā, *i e.*, the prince of the learned, was a Turk and an excellent poet. He flourished in the time of Sulṭān Muhammad Khudā Banda, and died in A.D. 1324, A.H. 724. [*Vide* Tughardī.]

Amjad 'Ali Shah (امجد علي شاه) was the son of Muhammad Alī Shāh, whom he succeeded on the throne of Lucknow as king of Oudh, with the title of Suriā Jāh, on the 17th May, A.D. 1842, 5th Rabī II. A.H. 1258, and died on the 16th March, A.D. 1847, 26th Safar, A.H. 1263. He was succeeded by his son Wājid Alī Shāh, in whose time Oudh was annexed to the British Government on the 7th February, A.D. 1856.

'Ammar ibn Hissan (عمّار ابن حسان) was Alī's general of the horse, and was killed in battle fought by Alī against Mu'āwia, the first khalīf of the house of Umaia, in the month of July, A.D. 657, Safar, A.H. 37. He was then about 90 years of age, and had been in three several engagements with Muhammad himself. He was one of the murderers of Usmān, the third khalīf after Muhammad.

Amra-al Qais (امراء القيس), the son of Hajar, one of the most illustrious poets the Arabians had before Muhammadanism. He is one of the seven poets whose poems have, for their excellency, been hung in the temple of Mecca. These poems were called *Muallakat* (suspended), and as they were written in letters of gold, they were also called *Muzahhibāt*. The names of these seven celebrated poets are Amra-al-Qais, Tarafa, Zuhīr, Labīd, Antār, Amrū and Hārath.

[Amra-al-Qais is the same person who is commonly called Majnūn, the lover of Laila, and Labīd was his friend and master. Amīr Khussu's *Loves of Majnun and Laila* has been translated into English.]

Amrit Rao (امرت راو), a Mahṛattā chief who had been placed on the masnad of Pūnā by Holkar in A.D. 1803, but deposed by the British, and a pension of 700,000 rupees was assigned for his support annually. He was the son of Raghunāth Rāo, commonly called Raghoba. For some time he resided at Banaras and then in Bundelkhand, and died at the former station in A.D. 1824.

'Amru bin Mua'wia (عمرو بن معاويه), an ancient Arabian poet whose collection of poems are to be found in the Royal Library at Paris, No. 1120.

'Amru ibn Al-'As (عمرو ابن لعاص), a celebrated Muhammadan, at first the enemy and afterwards the friend of Muhammad, of whom it is reported by tradition that Muhammad said, "There is no truer Musalman, nor one more steadfast in the faith than 'Amrū." He served in the wars of Syria, where he behaved with singular courage and resolution. Afterwards Umar the khalīf sent him into Egypt, which he reduced in A.D. 641, A.H. 20, and became lieutenant of the conquered country. Usmān continued him in that post four years, and then removed him; whereupon he retired to Palestine, where he lived privately till Usmān's death. Upon this event, he went over to Mu'āwia upon his invitation, and took a great part in the dispute between 'Alī and Mu'āwia. The latter restored him to the lieutenancy of Egypt, and continued him in it till his death, which happened in A.D. 663, A.H. 43. Before he turned Muhammadan he was one of the three poets who were famous for writing lampoons upon Muhammad, in which style of composition 'Amrū particularly excelled. There are some fine proverbs of his remaining, and also some good verses. He was the son of a courtezan of Mecca, who seems to have numbered some of the noblest of the land among her lovers. When she gave birth to this child, the infant was declared to have most resemblance to 'As, the oldest of her admirers, whence, in addition to his name of Amrū, he received the designation of Ibn-al-'As.

'Amru (عمرو بن سعيد), the son of Sa'īd, was a cousin of the khalīf 'Abdul-Malik. In the year A.D. 688, A.H. 69, the khalīf left Damascus to go against Misaa'b, the son of Zuber, and appointed Amrū to take care of Damascus, who seized upon it for himself, which obliged 'Abdul-Malik to return. After three or four days the khalīf sent for him and killed him with his own hand.

'Amru bin Lais (عمرو بن ليث), brother of Ya'kūb ibn Lais, whom he succeeded in the government of Khurāsān, etc., in A.D. 878, A.H. 265, and ruled over those countries for 23 years. He was at last seized by Amīr Isma'īl Sāmānī in A.D. 900, A.H. 288, and sent to Baghdād, where he was confined for some time; his execution was the last act of the Khalīf Al-Mo'tazid, who gave orders for it a few months before his own death in A.D. 901, A.H. 289. He was blind of one eye. With Amrū fell the fortunes of his family. His grandson Tāhir struggled for power in his native province; but after a reign of six years, during which he conquered Fārs, his authority was subverted by one of his own officers, by whom he was seized and sent prisoner to Baghdād. The only other prince of the family of Banī Lais that attained any eminence was a chief of the name of Khalāf, who established himself in Sīstān and maintained his power over that province till the time of Sultān Mahmūd of Ghaznī, by whom he was defeated and made prisoner.

Amurath, names of several emperors of Turkey, as written by English writers, being a corruption of Murād, which see.

Anandpal (انندپال), son of Jaipāl I., rāja of Lāhore, whom he succeeded about the year A.D. 1001, and became tributary to Sultān Mahmūd of Ghaznī. He died about the year 1013, and was succeeded in the government by his son Jaipāl II.

Anarkali (اناركلي), the name of a lady, otherwise "Nadira Begam," who lived in the time of the emperor Jahāngīr. Her mausoleum is at a place called Anārkalī in Lāhore, which has been recently used as a church. Different stories are told concerning the name Anārkalī, by which the mausoleum as well as the station in its vicinity is known. According to some, it was the name of a princess in Jahāngīr's time, while others say that Anārkalī was a beautiful handmaid with whom Jahāngīr fell in love, and who, on Akbar becoming aware of it, was buried alive. These stories may not be true; but this much is at least certain, that the woman after whose name the building is called, lived in the time of Akbar, or his son Jahāngīr, that Jahāngīr or some other prince was madly in love with her, and that her death took place under such mournful circumstances as broke the heart of the fond lover, and led him to compose the following couplet, still found engraved on her tombstone: "Oh! could I see again the face of my lost friend, I would thank my God until the day of judgment."

Anand Rao, Gaikwar (انند راو گيكوار), a Marhattā chief of Barōda, with whom the English Government had in 1812 concluded a subsidiary alliance. Before the treaty he was a nominal dependant of the Peshwa.

Anas (آنس), a poet of Arabia.

'Andalib (عندليب). *Vide* Khwāja Nāsir.

Anis (انس), poetical name of Mohan Lāl, which see.

Anisi Shamlu (انيس شاملو), a poet named Yūl Qulī Beg. He was an intimate friend and constant companion of prince Ibrāhīm Mirzā, a grandson of Shāh Isma'īl Safwī, consequently took the takhallas of Anīsī. When 'Abdullah Khān Uzbaq took Hirāt he made a proclamation in his army, that the life of Anīsī be spared, and treated him with great respect. He came to India and received a salary of 50,000 rupees and a jagīr. He died at Barhānpūr in A.D. 1605, A.H. 1014, and has left a Dīwān and a Masnawī called *Mahmūd Aiāz*.

Ang or **Ungh Khan**, a king of the Trit Tartars, who resided at Karakoram, and to whom the celebrated Jangez Khān was at one time a tributary. He is also called Prester John by the Syrian Missionaries. Jangez Khān having thrown off his allegiance, a war ensued, which ended in the death of Ang Khān in A.D. 1202.

Anjam (انجام), the poetical name of Nawāb Umdat-ul-Mulk Amīr Khān. *Vide* Amīr Khān.

Anup Bai (انوپ بائي), the wife of the emperor Jahāndār Shāh, and mother of Alamgīr II. king of Dehlī.

Anushtakin (انوشتكين), the cup-bearer of Sultān Sanjar, and father of Sultān Qutb-uddīn Muhammad of Khwārizm.

Ans bin Malik (آنس بن مالک). *Vide* Abu Hamza bin Nasr-al-Ansārī.

'Ansuri (عنصري), a poet of the court of Sultān Mahmūd. *Vide* Unsarī.

Antar (انتار), one of the seven Arabian poets, whose poems were hung up in the temple of Mecca in golden letters, and from that circumstance were called Mua'llakāt (suspended), or Muzahhibāt (golden). The first volume of the history of Antār, called *The Life and Adventures of Antār*, was translated into English and published in December, A.D. 1818, in England.

[*Vide* Amra-al-Kais.]

Anwari (انوري), a famous Persian poet surnamed Ashad-uddīn. He formerly took for his poetical name "Khāfwarī," but he changed it afterwards to "Anwarī." From the superiority of his poetical talents he was called the king of the poets of Khurāsān. He was a native of Abiward in Khurāsān, was the favourite of Sulṭān Sanjar Saljūkī, and the rival of the poet Rashīdī surnamed Watwāt, who espoused the cause of Atsiz, the Sulṭān of Khwārizm. Whilst the two princes were engaged in war, the two poets assailed one another by rhymes sent on the point of arrows. He is also said to have been the greatest astronomer of his age. It so happened in the year A.H. 581 or 582, September, A.D. 1186, that there was a conjunction of all the planets in the sign of Libra; Anwarī predicted a storm which would eradicate trees and destroy every building. When the fatal day arrived it was perfectly calm, and there was the whole year so little wind, that the people were unable to winnow their corn. He was therefore accused for his predictions as an astrologer, and was obliged to fly to Balkh, where he died in the reign of Sulṭān Alāuddīn Takash in A.D. 1200, A.H. 596. His death is mentioned in the Khulāsat-ul-Asha'ār to have taken place in A.H. 587, and others have written A.H. 592. Anwarī, when very young, was sitting at the gate of his college, called Mansūria in Tūs, when a man richly dressed rode by him on a fine horse, with a numerous train of attendants; upon his asking who it was, he was told that it was a poet belonging to the court. When Anwarī reflected on the honour conferred on poetry, for which art he had a very early bent, he applied himself to it more ardently than ever, and having finished a poem, presented it to the Sulṭān, who approved the work and invited him to his palace, and raised him even to the first honours of the State. He found many other poets at court, among whom were Salmān, Zahīr and Rashīdī, all men of wit and genius. Anwarī has left us a collection of highly esteemed poems on various subjects, called *Dīwān Anwarī*. Verses from his poems are quoted by Sa'dī in his Gulistān.

Anwari Khan (انوري خان), a corruption of Abū Raihān, which see.

Anwar-uddin Khan (انور الدين خان), Nawāb of the Carnatic, a soldier of fortune, who had attained power by treacherous connivance to the murder of the legitimate heir, a child whose guardian he had been appointed by Nizām-ul-Mulk. He at first served under one of the emperors of Dehlī, and was appointed governor of Korā Jahānābād. Ill success, or perhaps ill conduct, preventing him from being able to pay the usual revenues of his government to the throne; he quitted it privately, and went to Ahmadābād, where Ghāzī-uddīn Khān, the father of Nizām-ul-Mulk, gave him a post of considerable trust and profit in the city of Sūrat. After the death of Ghazī-uddīn, his son, who had succeeded in the Sūbadarī of the southern provinces, appointed him Nawāb of the Carnatic, or Vellore and Rājmandrum, countries which he governed from A.D. 1725 to 1741, and in A.D. 1744 he was formally created governor of the country. He was killed in battle fought against Muzaffar Jang, the grandson of Nizām-ul-Mulk, on the 23rd July, O.S. A.H. 1162, who took possession of the Carnatic. Anwar-uddīn was then 107 years old. His eldest son was made prisoner and his second son, Muhammad Alī, fled to Trichinopoly. A heroic poem called *Anwar Nāma*, in praise of this Nawāb was written by Abdī, in which the exploits of Major Lawrence, and the first contests between the English and French in India are recorded with tolerable accuracy. (*Vide* Sa'ādat-ullah Khān.) His son Muhammad Alī was confirmed by Nawāb Nasir Jang in the government of the Carnatic in A.D. 1750.

Aohad Sabzwari (Khwaja) (اوحد سبزواري خواجه), poetical name of Khwāja Fakhr-uddīn, a physician, astronomer, and poet, of Sabzwār. He died A.D. 1463, A.H. 868, aged 81 lunar years, and left a Dīwān in Persian containing Ghazals, Qasīdas, etc.

Aohadi (اوحدي), the poetical name of Shaikh Aohad-uddīn of Isfahān or Marāgha, a celebrated Persian poet who put into verse the *Jām-i-Jam*, a book full of Muhammadan spirituality, which he wrote in imitation of the Hadīqa of Sanāī; he also wrote a Dīwān containing verses. He was liberally rewarded by Arghūn Khān, the king of the Tartars. He was a pupil of Aohad-uddīn Kirmānī; died in A.D. 1337, A.H. 738, and was buried at Marāgha in Tabreiz.

Aohad-uddin Isfahani (Shaikh) (اوحدالدين اسفهانى), a Persian poet. *Vide* Aohadī.

Aohad-uddin Kirmani (Shaikh) (اوحدالدين كرماني), author of the *Misbah-ul-Arwāh*. He flourished in the reign of Al-Mustanasar Billāh, khalīf of Baghdād, and died in the year A.D. 1298, A.H. 697. His poetical name is Hāmid. He was a contemporary of Shaikh Sa'dī of Shīrāz.

Aohad-uddin (اوحدالدين), the surname of the celebrated Anwarī, which see.

Aoji (اوجى), a poet who died in A.D. 1640, A.H. 1050.

'Apa Sahib (آپا صاحب), a nephew of Rāghōjī Bhonsla II. and cousin to Parsarām Bhonsla, commonly called Bālā Sāhib, rāja of Nāgpūr or Berār. The latter succeeded his father in March, A.D. 1816, but being an idiot and unfit to rule, 'Apā Sāhib assumed the chief authority under the title of Regent, and had the sole conduct of the public affairs. Although he was in a great degree indebted for his elevation to the English Government, he early evinced a disposition as inconsistent with the gratitude which he owed to that State, as with the obligations of good faith. It was also discovered that he had secretly murdered his predecessor, Bālā Sāhib (Parsarām), in order to obtain that elevation which he had so disgraced. He was consequently seized in the beginning of the year A.D. 1818, and brought to the Residency, where he continued in confinement till directed to be sent under a strong escort to the Company's territories. When arrived at Raichora, a village within one march from Jabalpūr, he contrived, by bribing some of his guards, to make his escape. It is believed that after having for a short period found a refuge in Asīrgurh, he fled to the Panjāb, where he remained a miserable dependant on the charity of Rāja Ranjīt Singh. After the dethronement of 'Apā Sāhib, the grandson of Rāghōjī Bhonsla was raised to the masnad of Nāgpūr.

[*Vide* Keene's *India*, ii. 34, f. f.]

Apa Sahib (آپا صاحب), also called Shalyi, third brother of Partāp Singh Narāyan, rāja of Satāra. After the dethronement of his brother in A.D. 1839, he was placed on the masnad of Satāra by the British Government, and died on the 5th April, 1848. Before his death he expressed a wish that he might adopt as a son, a boy by name Balwant Rāo Bhonsla. It was, however, determined to annex Satāra.

Aqa Muhammad Khan Qajar (آقا محمد خان قاجار), king of Persia, of the tribe of Qājār, and son of Muhammad Hasan Khān Qājār, ruler of Māzanderān. He was made an eunuch in his childhood by 'Ādil Shāh, the nephew and immediate successor of Nādir Shāh. After the death of 'Ādil Shāh he obtained his release, and joined his father, who was afterwards slain by Karīm Khān Zand, king of Persia. Āghā, or Āqā Muhammad, was obliged to surrender himself to him, and was a prisoner in the city of Shīrāz. He had for some time been very strictly guarded, and was never allowed to go beyond the walls of the town, but afterwards he was permitted to go a-hunting. When the last illness of Karīm Khān assumed a dangerous appearance, he contrived to leave that city on the usual pretext of hunting. When intelligence was brought to him that the founder of the Zand dynasty was no more, accompanied by a few attendants, he commenced his flight, and, favoured by the confusion of the moment, he reached his province of Māzandarān in safety, and proclaimed himself one of the competitors for the crown of Persia. Soon after the death of 'Alī Murād Khān, ruler of Persia, in A.D. 1785, he made himself master of Iṣfahān without a battle, but had for several years to contend with Luṭf 'Alī Khān, the last prince of the Zand family, before he became sole master of Persia. Luṭf 'Alī Khān was put to death by him in A.D. 1795, 14th Muḥarram, A.H. 1212. Āqā Muhammad Khān was murdered on the 10th July, A.D. 1797, by two of his attendants, whom he had sentenced to death, in the 63rd year of his age. He had been a ruler of a great part of Persia for 20 years, but had only for a short period enjoyed the undisputed sovereignty of that country. He was succeeded by his nephew, Fatḥ 'Alī Shāh, who died in A.D. 1834, A.H. 1250. After him, his grandson, Muhammad Shāh, the son of 'Abbās Mirzā, mounted the throne, and died in 1847, when his son, Nāṣir-uddīn Ahmad Shāh, the present king of Persia, succeeded him.

Aqa Razi (آقا رضی), a poet of Persia, who came to India, and after his return home, died in A.D. 1615, A.H. 1024.

'Aqidat Khan (عقیدت خان), title of Mīr Mahmūd, brother of Aṣālat Khān Mashhadī. He came to India in the 14th year of 'Ālamgīr, A.D. 1670, and was raised to the rank of 1,000 and 400 sawārs.

'Aqil (عقیل), 'Aqil the brother of 'Ali. There is a story of him that being displeased with his brother 'Alī the Khalīfa, he went over to Mu'āwiya, who received him with great kindness and respect, but desired him to curse 'Alī; and as he would not admit of any refusal, 'Aqīl thus addressed the congregation: "O people, you know that 'Alī, the son of Abū-Ṭālib, is my brother; now Mu'āwiya has ordered me to curse him, therefore, may the curse of God be upon him." So that the curse would either apply to 'Alī or to Mu'āwiya.

'Aqil Khan (عاقل خان), 'Āqil Khān, nephew of Afzal Khān wazīr, a nobleman of 3,000, who served under the emperor Shāh Jahān, and died A.D. 1649, A.H. 1059.

'Aqil Khan (Nawab) (عاقل خان نواب), the title of Mīr 'Askarī. He was a native of Khawāf, in Khurāsān, and held the office of wizārat in the time of the emperor 'Ālamgīr. He was an excellent poet; and as he had a great respect for Shāh Burhān-uddīn, entitled Rāz-i-Ilāhī, he chose the word Rāzī for his poetical title. He is the author of several works, among which are a Masnawī and Dīwān. He died A.D. 1695, A.H. 1108. *Vide* Rāzī.

'Arabshah (عربشاه), author of a history of Amīr Taimūr (Tamerlane) called *Ajāeb-ul-Maqdūr*, and of a treatise on the unity of God. He was a native of Damascus, where he died in A.D. 1450, A.H. 854. He is also called Ibn 'Arabshāh and Ahmad Ibn Arabshāh.

Aram Bano Begam (آرام بانو بیگم), a daughter of the emperor Akbar, who died in the 40th year of her age in A.D. 1624, A.H. 1033, during the reign of Jahāngīr, her brother, and is buried in the mausoleum of Akbar at Sikandra in Agra. Her tomb is of white marble. Her mother's name was Bībī Daulat Shad, and her sister's name Shakr-un-nisa Begam.

Aram Shah (Sultan) (آرام شاه), king of Dehlī, succeeded his father, Sulṭān Qutb-uddīn Aibak, in A.D. 1210, A.H. 607, and had scarcely reigned one year when he was deposed by Altimsh (the adopted son and son-in-law of Qutb-uddīn) who assumed the title of Shams-uddīn Altimsh.

Araru (آرارو), a zamīndār of Koṛā in the province of Allahābād, was of the tribe of K͟hīchaṛ, who, taking advantage of the weakness of the empire, slew Nawāb Jān Nisār K͟hān (brother to the wazīr's wife), chakladār of that district in A.D. 1731, A.H. 1144, upon which 'Azim-ullāh K͟hān, the son of the deceased, was sent with an army to chastise him, but the zamīndār took refuge in his woods, and for a long while eluded his pursuer, who, tired out, returned to Dehlī, leaving his army under the command of K͟hwārizm Beg K͟hān. Aṛāṛū, emboldened by the Nawāb's retreat, attacked and slew the deputy; upon which the wazīr Qamar-uddīn K͟hān applied for assistance to Burhān-ul-Mulk Sa'ādat K͟hān Sūbadār of Oudh, for the reduction of the rebel. Sa'ādat K͟hān marched against Aṛāṛū in A.D. 1735, A.H. 1148, killed him in a battle and sent his head to the emperor Muhammad Shāh. The skin of his body was flayed off, and sent stuffed with straw to the wazīr.

Ardai Viraf (اردي وراف), a priest of the Magian religion, who lived in the time of Ardisher Bābagān, king of Persia, and is the author of the *Ardai Virāf Nama*, which he wrote in the Zend, or the original Persian language.

[See Nousherwān Kirmānī.]

Ardisher Babakan (اردشیر بابکان), or Bābagān, the son of Bābak, was, we are told, a descendant of Sāsān, the son of Bahman and grandson of Isfandiār. He was the first king of the Sāsānian dynasty. His father Bābak, who was an inferior officer in the public service, after putting to death the governor appointed by Ardawān (Artabanes) made himself master of the province Fars. The old man survived but a short time. His son Ardisher, after settling the affairs of Fars, not only made himself master of Isfāhān, but of almost all Irāq, before Ardawān, who was the reigning prince, took the field against him, about the year A.D. 223. The armies met in the plains of Hurmuz, where a desperate battle ensued, in which Ardawān lost his crown and his life; and the son of Bābak was hailed in the field with the proud title of Shāhan Shāh, or King of kings. He was contemporary with Alexander Severus, the Roman emperor. Ardisher (whom the Roman historians call Artaxerxes) having reigned fourteen years as absolute sovereign of Persia, resigned the government into the hands of his son, Shāhpūr, called by the Romans Sapor or Sapores, in the year A.D. 238.

The following is a list of the kings of Persia of the Sāsānian race:—

1. Ardisher.
2. Shāhpūr I.
3. Hurmuzd I.
4. Bahrām I.
5. Bahrām II.
6. Bahrām III.
7. Narsī.
8. Hurmuzd II.
9. Shāhpūr II.
10. Ardisher II.
11. Shāhpūr III.
12. Bahrām IV.
13. Yezdijard I.
14. Bahrām Gōr.
15. Yezdijard II.
16. Hurmuz, or Hurmuzd III.
17. Fīrōz.
18. Balas or Palash.
19. Kubād.
20. Jāmāsp.
21. Naushirwān (Kasra).
22. Hurmuzd.
23. K͟husro Parwez.
24. Sherōya.
25. Ardisher III.
26. Shahriār.
27. Tūrān, or Pūrān Duk͟ht.
28. Azarmī Duk͟ht.
29. Farruzk͟hād Bak͟htiār.
30. Yezdijard III.

Ardisher (اردشیر), (or Artaxerxes) II. succeeded his father Shāhpūr II. in the year A.D. 380, and sat on the throne of Persia only four years, during which period no event of consequence occurred. He was deposed in A.D. 384 by his brother Shāhpūr III. who succeeded him.

Ardisher (اردشیر), (or Artaxerxes) III. a king of Persia, of the Sāsānian race, who reigned about the year A.D. 629, after Sheroyā.

Ardisher Darazdast (اردشـــيـــر درازدسـت), an ancient king of Persia, the Artaxerxes Longimanus of the Greeks, surnamed Bahman, was the son of Isfandiār. He succeeded his grandfather, Gashtasp, as king of Persia in B.C. 464. He is celebrated for the wisdom he displayed in the internal regulation of his empire. In the commencement of the reign of this monarch, the celebrated Rustam was slain by the treachery of his brother. This prince is supposed to be the Ahasuerus of Scripture, who married Esther, and during the whole of his reign shewed the greatest kindness to the Jewish nation. The long reign of this monarch includes that of two or more of his immediate successors, who are not noticed by Persian writers. According to them, he ruled Persia 112 years, and was succeeded by his daughter Queen Humāi.

Arghun Khan (ارغون خان), the son of Abākā Khān and grandson of Halākū Khān, was raised to the throne of Persia after the murder of his uncle Ahmad Khān, surnamed Nekōdār, in August, A.D. 1284, Jamad I. A.H. 683. His reign was marked by few events of consequence. He recalled the celebrated Shams-ud-dīn Muhammad Sāhib Dīwān, his father's wazīr, who, disgusted with court, had retired to Isfahān: but this able minister was hardly re-established in his office, before his enemies persuaded the prince that he had actually poisoned his father; and the aged wazīr was in the same year made over to the public executioner. Amīr Būkā, the rival of Shams-ud-dīn, rose, upon his fall, to such power that he was tempted to make a grasp at the crown; but he was unsuccessful, and lost his life in the attempt. Arghūn Khān died on Saturday, the 10th March, A.D. 1291, 5th Rabī I. A.H. 690, after a reign of 6 years and 9 months, and was succeeded by his brother Kaijaptū or Kaikhatū. His mother was a Christian.

[*V. Sup.* Aba Kaan.]

Arghun Shah Jani Qurbani (Amir) (ارغون شاه جاني قرباني اميرا), who reigned in Naishapūr and Tūs about the year A.D. 1337, and was defeated by the Sarbadals of Sabzwār.

'Arif (عارف), the poetical name of the son of Ghulām Husain Khān. He was an excellent Urdū poet of Dehlī, and died in A.D. 1852, A.H. 1268.

'Arifi (Maulana) (عارفي), a Persian poet who flourished in the time of the wazīr khwāja Muhammad bin Is-hāq, and wrote a work in his name called *Dah Nāma*. He lived in the 9th century of the Hijrī era.

'Arifi (Maulana) (عارفي), son of Mubārik Maskhara, was a learned Musalmān, and was living in A.D. 1580, A.H. 988, when he wrote a chronogram on the death of Qāsim Kāhī, who died in that year, during the reign of the emperor Akbar.

Arjumand Bano Begam (ارجمند بانو بيگم), entitled Mumtāz Mahāl (now corrupted into Tāj Mahāl and Tāj Bībī) was the favourite wife of the emperor Shāh Jahān, and daughter of 'Asaf Khān, wazīr, the brother of the celebrated Nūr Jahān Begam. She was born in the year A.D. 1592, A.H. 1000, and married to the prince Mirzā Khurram (afterwards Shāh Jahān) in A.D. 1612, A.H. 1021, by whom she had several children. She died in child-bed a few hours after the birth of her last daughter, named Dahar Ārā, on the 7th July, O.S. 1631, 17th Zil-hijja, A.H. 1040, at Burhānpūr in the Deccan, was at first buried there in a garden called Zainābād, but afterwards her remains were removed to Āgra, where a most splendid mausoleum was built over her tomb, with a coating of white marble decorated with mosaics, which for the richness of the material, the chasteness of the design, and the effect at once brilliant and solemn, is not surpassed by any other edifice either in Europe or Asia. It was completed in A.D. 1645, A.H. 1055, and is now called the "Tāj," or "Tāj Mahāl," which is said to have cost the enormous sum of £3,000,000. The chronogram of her death contains the date in the word "Gham," or Grief. She was also called Kudsia Begam and Nawāb 'Alia Begam.

Arjun Singh (ارجن سنگه) was one of the three sons of Rāja Mānsingh.

[Vide *Āīn Translation*, i. p. 485.]

Arpa Khan (اربا خان), one of the princes of the Tartar family, was crowned king of Persia after the death of Abū Saīd Khān Bahādur, in November, A.D. 1335, A.H. 736. He reigned five months and was killed in battle against Mūsī Khan in A.D. 1336, who succeeded him.

[*Vide* Abū Saīd Khān Bahādur.]

Arsalan Khan (ارسلان خان), title of Arsalān Qulī, the son of Alahwardī Khān I., was a nobleman in the service of the emperor Alamgīr, and was living about the year A.D. 1696, A.H. 1108.

Arsalan Shah (ارسلان شاه), the son of Sultān Masa'ūd III. of Ghaznī. He murdered his brother Sherzād in A.D. 1115, A.H. 509, and having ascended the throne, he imprisoned all his other brothers excepting Bahrām Shāh, who fled to Khurāsān and sought assistance of Sultān Sanjar his uncle.

Sanjar in the year A.D. 1118, A.H. 512, marched to Ghaznī, and in a battle defeated Arsalān Shāh, who made his escape to Lāhore, but was soon after taken prisoner and put to death, when Bahrām Shāh ascended the throne.

Arsalan Shah (ارسلان شاه), a king of Khwarizm, and son of Atsiz. *Vide* Alp Ārsalān.

Arsalan Shah Saljuki (ارسلان شاه سلجوقي), the son of Tughral II and grandson of Sultān Muhammad, brother to Sultān Sanjar. Arsalān Shāh died in January, A.D. 1176, A.H. 571. His son Tughral III. who succeeded him, was the last Sultān of the family of the Saljūkides, who reigned in Persia.

'Arsh-Ashaiani (عرش آشياني), the title given to the emperor Akbar I. after his death.

'Arshi (عرشي), whose proper name was Mīr Muhammad Momin, was a brother of Mīr Sālah Kashifī, the son of Mīr Abdullāh Mushkīn Qalam Husainī, who was a celebrated caligrapher under Jahāngīr. Arshī is the author of a poem called *Shāhid-Arshī*, composed in the year A.D. 1659, A.H. 1070, also of another work entitled *Mehr wa Wafā*, and of a Dīwān.

Artaxerxes. *Vide* Ardisher.

Arzami Dukht (ارزمي دخت), a queen of the Persians, whose general named Mehrān being killed in a battle against the Saracens, she was deposed by the people, who placed Yezdijard III. upon the throne in her stead, a young man of the royal family. But this did not much mend the matter, the government of the new king of theirs being even more inauspicious than that of the queen; for in her reign the confines of the empire were only invaded, but in his all was entirely lost, and the whole kingdom and country of the Persians fell into the hands of the Musalmāns. The accession of Yezdijard is placed by Sir John Malcolm in A.D. 632, A.H. 11, but Major Price fixes it in A.D. 635, A.H. 14.

[*Vide* Taurāndukht.]

Arzani Begam (ارزاني بيگم) was the daughter of Shahriar, who was married, in the 16th year of Jahāngīr's reign, to Mihr-un-nīsā, the daughter of Nur Jahān.

[Vide *Āīn Translation* i. p. 331.]

Arzu (آرزو), the poetical name of Sirāj-ud-dīn Alī Khān, which see.

Asa Ahir (آسا اهير), a shepherd chief, who built the fortress of Asīrgarh in the Deccan in the 14th century; he had some 2000 retainers. The hill had long before been encircled by a wall to protect the cattle, and it was to employ the poor that Āsā constructed, instead of the fortifications, which still remain, beyond all comparison, the strongest native built fortress in India. Āsā was put to death by Malik Nasīr, the Muhammadan chief Khandais, who possessed himself of the stronghold by treachery, and completed the fortifications. Two centuries later Asīrgarh and all Nimar were conquered by Akbar and incorporated with the Mughal empires. It was taken by the British in 1817.

Asad (اسد), the poetical name of Mirzā Asad-ullāh Khān, usually called Mirzā Noushāh. His ancestors were of Samarqand, but he was born at Āgra; but was brought up and lived at Dehlī, where he rose to great fame as a poet and writer of the Persian language, whilst his compositions in Urdū were not less admired. He won the favour of Bahādur Shāh, the last king of Dehlī, who conferred upon him the title of Nawāb, and appointed him royal preceptor in the art of poetry. He is the author of a Persian Inshā, a Masnawī in praise of 'Alī, and a Dīwān in Persian and another in Urdū. Both have been printed. He was in A.D. 1852, when sixty years of age, living at Dehlī, and was engaged in compiling a history of the Mughal emperors of India His poetical name is Ghālib, which see. He died in the year A.D. 1869, A.H. 1285.

Asadi Tusi (اسد طوسي), a native of Tūs in the province of Khurāsān, and one of the most celebrated Persian poets at the court of Sultān Mahmūd of Ghaznī, whom the Sultān often entreated to undertake the legendary history of Persia, but he excused himself on account of his age. His best work is supposed to be lost. He was the master of Firdausī, who afterwards composed the Shāh Nāma. It is said that Firdausī on his departure from Ghaznī requested him to finish the Shāh Nāma, which was yet incomplete, and that Asadī composed that part of the poem between the Arabian conquest of eastern Persia under the khalīf 'Umar, to the end, consisting of 4000 couplets. The year of Asadī's death is unknown, but it appears from the above circumstance that he was living in A.D. 1010, A.H. 401, in which year Firdausī departed from Ghaznī. The most celebrated of the other works of Asadī now extant is his dispute between Day and Night, a translation of which in English verse is to be found in the *Rose Garden of Persia*, by Louisa Stuart Costello, published, London, 1845.

Asad Khan (Nawab) (اسد خان نواب), entitled Asāf-ud-daula and Jumlat-ul-Mulk, was descended from an illustrious family of

Turkmans. His father, who fled from the oppressions of Shāh Abbās, of Persia, into Hindūstan, was raised to high rank by the emperor Jahāngīr with the title of Zulfiqār Khān, and married to the daughter of a new relation to his empress Nūr Jahān. His son Asad Khān (whose former name was Ibrahīm) was very early noticed by Shāh Jahān, who married him to a daughter of his wazīr 'Asaf Khān, and promoted him to the office of second Bakhshī, which he held till the 15th year of 'Alamgīr (A.D. 1671), when he was raised to the rank of 4000, and a few years afterwards to the office of wazīr and highest order of nobility, seven thousand. In the reign of Bahādur Shāh he was appointed Wakīl Mutlaq (an office superior to wazīr), and his son Isma'īl made Mīr Bakhshī or chief paymaster, with the title of Amīr-ul-'Umra Zulfikār Khān; but on the accession of Farrukhsiar, he was disgraced, his estates seized, and his son put to death. After that period, he lived upon a scanty pension in a sort of confinement, but much respected by all ranks. He died in the year A.D. 1717, A.H. 1129, aged 90 lunar years, and was buried with great funeral pomp at the expense of the emperor, in a mausoleum, erected by his father for the family.

Asad-ullah al-Ghalib (اسدالله الغالب), the conquering lion of God, an epithet of Alī the son-in-law of Muhammad.

Asad-ullah Asad Yar Khan (Nawab) (اسد الهه اسد یار خان); he lived in the time of the emperor Muhammad Shāh, and died in A.D. 1745, A.H. 1158. His poetical name was Insān, which see.

Asad-ullah Khan (Mirza) (اسد الهه خان میرزا). *Vide* Asad and Ghālib.

Asaf (آصف), a native of Qumm in Persia, who came to India in the reign of the emperor Shāh Jahān, and is the author of a Dīwān. [The name comes from the legendary minister of Solomon, who appears to have been merely a musician; *vide* I. Chron. c. xvi. 7.]

Asafi (Khwaja) (آصفي خواجه), son of Khwaja Na'mat-ul-lāh, was an elegant poet. Āsafī is his poetical name, which he took on account of his father having served in the capacity of wazīr to Sultān Abū Sa'īd Mirzā; for, they say, Āsaf or Asaph of the Scriptures, was wazīr to king Solomon. He was one of the contemporaries and companions of Jāmī, and took instructions from him in the art of poetry. He died about the month of August, A.D. 1520, 16th Shaban, A.H. 926, aged more than 70, and was buried at Herat; but according to the work called *Khulāsat-ul-Asha'ār*, he died in A.H. 920. He is author of a Dīwān or book of Odes called *Dīwān Āsafī*, and a Masnawī in the measure of *Makhzan-ul-Asrār*.

Asaf Jah (آصف جاه), the title of the celebrated Nizām-ul-Mulk of Haidarābād.

Asaf Khan I. (آصف خان), surnamed Abdul Majīd, was a nobleman in the time of the emperor Akbar, who in A.D. 1565, A.H. 973, distinguished himself by the conquest of Garrakōṭa, a principality on the Narbada, bordering on Bundelkhand. It was governed by a Queen or Rānī named Durgāwatī, who opposed the Muhammadan general in an unsuccessful action, and when seeing her army routed and herself severely wounded, she avoided falling into the hands of the enemy by stabbing herself with a dagger. Her treasures, which were of great value, fell into the hands of Āsaf Khān; he secreted a great part, and the detection of this embezzlement was the immediate cause of his revolt. He was, however, subsequently pardoned, and after the conquest of Chittour, that country was given to 'Asaf Khān in jāgīr.

Asaf Khan II. (آصف خان), title of Khraj-Ghayas-ud-dīn Alī Qaiwanī, the son of Āqā Mullānd, uncle to Āsaf Khān Jāfar Beg. He held the Bakhshīgarī in the time of the emperor Akbar, and after the conquest of Gujrat in A.D. 1573, A.H. 981, in which he distinguished himself, the title Abbās Khān was conferred on him. He died at Gujrat in A.D. 1581, A.H. 989, and after his death his nephew Mirzā Jāfar Beg was buried with the title of Āsaf Khān.

Asaf Khan III. (آصف خان جعفر بیگ), commonly called Mirzā Ja'far Beg, was the son of Mirzā Badī-uz-Zamān and grandson of Aqā Mullā Qazwīnī. He was born at Qazwīn, and came to India in his youth, A.D. 1577, A.H. 985. At the recommendation of his uncle Mirzā Ghaiās-ud-dīn, who was a nobleman at the court of the emperor Akbar, and bore then the title of Asaf Khān, was received with honour, and after the death of his uncle the office of Bakhshīgarī was conferred on him with the title of Āsaf Khān, A.D. 1581, A.H. 989. He was an excellent poet, and was one of the many that were employed by the emperor in compiling the *Tārīkh Alfī*, and after the assassination of Mullā Ahmad in A.D. 1588, A.H. 996, the remainder of the work was written by him up to the year A.H. 997. He is also called Āsaf Khān Mirzā Ja'far Bakhshī Begī, and is the author of a poem called *Shīrīn wa Khusro*. The office of chief Dīwān was conferred on him by the emperor in A.D. 1598, A.H. 1007, and in the reign of Jahāngīr he was raised to the high post of wazārat. He died in the year A.D. 1612, A.H. 1021. In his poetical compositions he used the name of Ja'far. One of his sons, who also bore the name of Ja'far, became an excellent poet and died in the time of 'Alamgīr, A.D. 1682, A.H. 1094.

Asaf Khan IV. (آصف خان), the title of 'Abūl Hasan, who had several other titles conferred on him at different times, such as Ya'tqād Khān, Yemīn-ud-daula, etc., was the son of the celebrated wazīr Ya'tmād-ud-daula, and brother to Nūr Jahān Begam. After his father's death in A.D. 1621, A.H. 1030, he was appointed wazīr by the emperor Jahāngīr. His daughter Arjumand Bāno Begam, also called Mumtāz Mahal, was married to the prince Shāh Jahān. 'Asaf Khān died at Lāhore in the 15th year of Shāh Jahān on the 10th November, o.s. 1641, 17th Sha'ban, A.H. 1051, aged 72 lunar years, and was buried there on the banks of the Rāwī opposite to the city of Lāhore. Besides Mumtāz Mahal, he had four sons, *viz.*, Shāista Khān; Mirzā Masīh, who was drowned in a drunken frolic in the river Behat in Kashmīr; Mirzā Husain, of moderate abilities and little note; and Shāhnawāz Khān, who rose to much reputation and distinction.

Asaf-ud-daula (آصف الدوله), a title of Asad Khān, which see.

Asaf-ud-daula (Nawab) (اصف الدوله نواب), the eldest son of Nawāb Shujāa'-ud-daula of Audh, after whose death in January, A.D. 1775, Zil-qada, A.H. 1188, he succeeded to his dominions, and made Lucknow the seat of his government, which formerly was at Faizābād. He died after a reign of twenty-three lunar years and seven months on Friday the 21st September, A.D. 1797, 28th Rabī I. A.H. 1212, and was buried in the Imām Bāra at Lucknow, of which he was the founder. His eldest adopted son, Wazīr Alī Khān, agreeably to his request, was placed on the masnad, but was after four months deposed by Sir John Shore, then Governor of Calcutta, and Sa'ādat Alī Khān, the brother of the deceased, raised to the masnad. Asaf-ud-daula is the author of a Dīwān in Urdū and Persian.

Asalat Khan (اصالت خان), title of Mīr Abdul Hādī, son of Mīr Mīrān Yezdī, was a nobleman in the service of the emperor Shāh Jahān. He died in the year A.D. 1647, A.H. 1057.

Asalat Khan (اصالت خان), title of Mirzā Muhammad, son of Mirzā Badīa' of Mashhad. He came to India in the 19th year of Shāh Jahān, A.D. 1645, A.H. 1055, and was raised to the rank of 5,000 by the emperor 'Alamgīr, in whose time he died, A.D. 1666, A.H. 1076.

Asam or Atham (اثم), poetical name of Hafīz-ullāh, which see.

Asar (اثر), poetical name of Akhūnd Shāfa'ī or Shafīa'āī of Shīrāz, who died at Lār in the year A.D. 1701, A.H. 1113, and left a Dīwān containing 10,000 verses.

Asar (اثر), poetical name of Nawāb Husain Alī Khān, son of Amīr-ud-daula Haidar Beg Khān. He is the author of a Dīwān.

Asghar (اصغر حسین خان), Husain Khān (Nawāb) of Furrukhābād, in 1874, went to Bombay, intending to proceed to Mecca on a pilgrimage.

Asha'ri (اشعري), the surname of one of the most celebrated doctors among the Musulmāns, named Abūl Hasan Alī bin-Isma'īl. Originally a resident of Bassora and a teacher of the sect which flourished there in the tenth century A.D.; he publicly renounced their doctrines and finally removed to Baghdād, where he died in his 70th year, after writing more than half a hundred works on the side of orthodoxy. He died about 952.

[*Vide* Mu'tazila.]

'Ashiq (عاشق), poetical name of Mahdī Alī Khān, grandson of Nawāb Alī Mardān Khān. He is the author of three Dīwāns in Urdū, two in Persian, a book called ***Hamla Haidari***, and several works.

'Ashiq (عاشق), poetical name of Shaikh Nūr-ud-dīn Muhammad, the author of the Masnawī called ***Aish wa Tarab*** (Enjoyment and Merriment), composed in A.D. 1668, A.H. 1079.

'Ashiq Pasha (عاشق پاشا), a Turkish poet, who was born at Hirshari, in the reign of Sultān Orkhan, the successor of Othman, and died at no very advanced age, in the reign of Murād I. He was, says Von Hammer, one of the richest Shaikhs of his time, but lived nevertheless the life of a simple darvesh, from conscientious motives. His Dīwān or great work, in imitation of Jalal-ud-dīn Rūmī's, is a collection of mystical poetry, exceeding ten thousand distichs, and divided into ten books, each book into ten parts.

'Ashiq (عاشق), poetical name of Maulānā Abūl Khair of Khwārizm, which see.

Ashir-ud-din (اشير الدين), pronounced by the Indians Asīr-ud-dīn, which see.

Ashk (اشک), poetical name of Muhammad Khalīl-ullah Khān, which see.

Ashna (آشنا), poetical name of Mirzā Muhammad Tāhir, who had the title of Ināit Khān. He was a son of Nawāb Zafar Khān Ihsān, and died in A.D. 1666, A.H. 1077. His complete work is called *Kulliāt 'Ashnā*, in which Kasīdas are to be found in praise of Shāh Jahān and Dārā Shikōh.

Ashna (آشنا), poetical name of Ghaiās-ud-dīn, who died in A.D. 1662, A.H. 1073.

Ashob (آشوب), poetical name of Muhammad Bakhsh, a poet who flourished in Audh during the reign of Āsaf-ud-daula and his father Shujāa'-ud-daulā. He is the author of a Dīwān.

Ashraf (اشرف), or Darwesh Ashraf. He flourished under Bāisanghar's son, and has left a Dīwān.

Ashraf Ali Khan Koka (اشرف علي خان كوكه). *Vide* Fighān.

Ashraf (اشرف), poetical name of Mirzā Muhammad Sa'īd of Māzandarān, son of Mullā Muhammad Qāna'. He came to India and was appointed to instruct Zebun Nisā Begam, the daughter of the emperor 'Alamgīr. He died at Mūngair. He is the author of a Dīwān and several Masnawis.

Ashraf (اشرف), poetical name of Muhammad Hasan, son of Shāh Muhammad Zamān of Allahābād. He was probably alive in A.D. 1852, and is the author of a Masnawī called *Ma'dan Faiz*.

Ashraf (اشرف), a chief of the Afghāns of the tribe of Ghilzaī, who was elected on the 22nd April, o.s. 1725, by the Afghāns as successor of his cousin or uncle Mahmūd, another chief of the same tribe, who had usurped the throne of Persia in the time of Sultān Husain Safwī, whom he kept in confinement. Ashraf on his accession murdered the latter, and sent his corpse to be interred in Qumm. He was defeated by Nādir Qulī (afterwards Nādir Shāh) in A.D. 1729, A.H. 1142, who placed Shāh Tahmāsp II. son of Sultān Husain on the throne. Ashraf was afterwards seized and murdered by a Billoch chief between Kirmān and Qandahār in January, A.D. 1730, A.H. 1143, and his head sent to Shāh Tahmāsp.

Ashraf Khan (اشرف خان), title of Mirzā Muhammad Ashraf, the son of Islām Khān Mashhadī. In the reign of Shāh Jahān he held the rank of 1500, and the title of Ya'tmād Khān. In the time of 'Alamgīr he was raised to the rank of 3000 with the title of Ashraf Khān, and died five days after the conquest of Bījāpūr on the 17th September, A.D. 1686, 9th Zil-qada, A.H. 1097.

Ashraf Khan (اشرف خان), whose proper name was Muhammad Asghar, was a Sayyad of Mashhad, and held the office of Mīr Munshī in the time of the emperor Akbar. He wrote a beautiful hand, and was an excellent poet. He composed a chronogram on the death of Muhammad Yūsaf in A.D. 1562, A.H. 970; another on the completion of the mosque of Shaikh Salīm Chishtī at Fathapūr Sīkrī in A.D. 1571, A.H. 979; and one on the conquest of Sūrat by Akbar on the 1st January, A.D. 1573, 25th Sha'bān, A.H. 980. He accompanied Munaim Khān Khānkhānān to Bengal and died at Lakhnautī in the year A.D. 1575, A.H. 983. At the time of his death he held the rank of 2,000.

'Ashrat (عشرت). *Vide* Ishrat.

'Ashrati (عشرتي). *Vide* Ishratī.

'Ashrati (عشرتي), the name of a poet. *Vide* Ishratī.

'Asi (عاصي), the poetical name of Ghulām Sarwar, author of the Qāf Nāma, which consists of Ghazals, all the verses of which end in Qāf, hence the name; another peculiarity is that the first letter of every verse of the first Ghazal is Alif, of the second Be, of the third Te, etc., a ghazal for every letter of the alphabet.

'Asif Khan. *Vide* Āsaf Khān.

'Asimi (عاصمي), an Arabian poet who lived in the time of Khwāja Nizām-ul-Mulk, and wrote beautiful panegyrics in his praise.

Asir (اسير), poetical name of Sayyid Gūlzar Alī, the son of Nazīr, a poet of Āgra. He is the author of an Urdū Dīwān, and is still living in Āgra (1878).

Asir (اسير), commonly called Mirzā Jalāl Āsīr, a celebrated poet of Persia and a relation of Shāh Abbās the great. He flourished about the year A.D. 1600, never came to India, and is the author of a Dīwān in Persian. He died in A.D. 1630, A.H. 1040.

Asir-ud-din Akhsikati (اسير الدين اخسيكتي), a native of Akhsīkat, a city in the province of Farghāna, was an excellent poet and contemporary with Khākānī. He died in A.D. 1211, A.H. 608. He spent the greatest part of his life at the courts of the Atābaks, and stood in high favour with Arsalān Shāh, the son of Tughral, Eldiguz and Qizil Arsalān.

Asir-ud-din Aomani or Aamani (اسیر الدین اوماني), a poet of Hamdān, who was a pupil of Nasīr-ud-dīn Tūsī. He is the author of a Dīwān in Persian and Arabic.

Asir-ud-din ibn-Umar al-Abhari (اسیر الدین ابن عمر الابهري), author of the *Kashf*, *Zubda*, and *Hidāya*, which is also called *Hidāyei-ul-Hikmat, the Guide to Philosophy*. He died in A.D. 1344, A.H. 745.

'Asjudi (عسجدی), a powerful poet at the court of Sultān Mahmūd of Ghaznī, was a native of Mary, and one of the scholars of 'Unsarī. He evinced in his works much genius; but they are scarce, and the greatest part of them are lost.

Askaran (Raja) (اسکرن راجه), brother of Rāja Bihārī Mal Kachhwāha. He served under the emperor Akbar for several years, and died some time after the year A.D. 1588, A.H. 996. After his death, his son Rāj Singh was raised to high rank and honours.

'Askari (Imam) (عسکري امام). *Vide* Hasan Askarī.

'Askari (Mirza) (عسکري مرزا), third son of the emperor Bābar Shāh. On the accession of his eldest brother, Humāyūn, to the throne of Dehlī, the district of Sarkār Sambhal was conferred on him as jāgīr. He was subsequently kept in confinement for some time on account of his rebellious conduct by Humāyūn on his return from Persia. He afterwards obtained permission to go on a pilgrimage to Mecca, but died on his way across the deserts of Arabia in the year A.D. 1554, A.H. 961. He left one daughter, who was married to Yūsaf Khān, an inhabitant of Mashhad.

Asmai (اصمعي), surname of Abū Saīd Abdul Malik bin Qureb, which see.

'Asmat (عصمت), or Ismat, poetical name of Khwāja Asmat-ullah of Bukhāra. He was descended from a noble family of Bukhāra tracing his ancestry to Ja'far, the son of Abū Tālib, the father of Alī. He was successful in all kinds of poetical composition; and flourished in the time of prince Mirzā Khalīl, the grandson of Amīr Taimūr, whom he instructed in the art of poetry. He died in the year A.D. 1426, A.H. 829, and has left a Dīwān consisting of 20,000 verses.

'Asmat-ullah (عصمت الهه). *Vide* Asmat.

'Asmat-ullah (Mulla) (عصمت الهه ملا), of Sahāranpūr, was the author of the work called *Shurah Khulāsat ul-Hisāb*. He died in A.D. 1626, A.H. 1035.

Asoka (اسوکه), the son of Bindusāra and grandson of Chandragupta, rāja of Patali-putra in Magadha. He reigned for about forty years, until the year B.C. 223. His reign is most important. Numerous inscriptions made by his order have been discovered in various parts of India. In his edicts he styles himself "Pīyadāsi."

'Assar (عسار) (oil-presser), the poetical name of Shams-ud-dīn Muhammad. He was a native of Tabrez, and author of a romantic poem called *Mehr wa Mushtarī*, the Sun and Jupiter, which he completed on the 20th February, A.D. 1377, 10th Shawwāl, A.H. 778, and died in the year A.D. 1382, A.H. 783.

Aswad (اسود), or Al-Aswad. *Vide* Musailima.

'Ata (عطا), the poetical name of Shaikh Atā-ullāh, a pupil of Mirzā Bedil. He died at Dehlī in A.D. 1723, A.H. 1135.

Atabak (اتابک), or Atābeg. This is a Turkish title, formed from the word Atā, father or tutor, and Beg, lord; and signifies a governor or tutor of a lord or prince. From the time of the decline of the dynasty of Saljūk to the conquest of Persia by Halākū Khān (which occupies a period of more than a century), that country was distracted by the contests of a number of petty princes, or governors, called Atābaks; who, taking advantage of the weakness of the last monarchs of the race of Saljūk, established their authority over some of the finest provinces of the empire. One of the most distinguished of these Atābegs was Eldiguz, a Turkish slave, whose descendants reigned over 'Azurbejān. The Atābegs of Fars were descended from Salghur, a Turkish general.

[*Vide* Eldiguz and Salghur, also 'Imad-ud-dīn Zangī. There were four dynasties of these Atābaks.]

Atabak Abu Bakr (اتابک ابو بکر), the son of Atābak Muhammad, the son of Eldiguz, succeeded his uncle Qizal Arsalān as prime minister to Tughral III. Saljūkī, in A.D. 1191, A.H. 587. He appears to have contented himself with the principality of 'Azurbejān, and fixed his residence at Tabrez. His long reign was only disturbed by one war with his brother Qutalaq, in which he was victorious. Qutlaq fled into Khwarizm and encouraged Ala-ud-dīn Takash to advance against Tughral III. whom he defeated and slew in A.D. 1194, A.H. 590. Abū Bakr died in A.D. 1210, A.H. 607, and was succeeded by his brother Atābak Muzaffar.

Atabak Abu Bakr bin-Sa'd bin-Zangi (اتابک ابو بکر بن سعد بن زنگي). *Vide* Sunqar.

Atabak 'Ala-ud-daula (اتابک علاء الدوله), the son of Atābak Sām, one of the Atābaks of Isfahan of the race of the Dīlamites. He died in A.D. 1227, A.H. 624, aged 84 years.

Atabak Eldiguz (اتابک يلدگز). *Vide* Eldiguz.

Atabak Muhammad (اتابک محمد) was the eldest son of Eldiguz, whom he succeeded as prime minister in A.D. 1172, A.H. 568. When Tughral III. a prince of the Saljūkian dynasty (who was a child of seven years of age), was placed on the throne in A.D. 1176, Muhammad, who was his uncle, became the actual ruler of Persia. This chief after enjoying power 13 years died in March, A.D. 1186, Zil-hijja, A.H. 581, in which year the conjunction of all the planets took place. He was succeeded by his brother Qizal Arsalān.

Atabak Muzaffar (اتابک مظفر), the son of Atābak Muhammad. He succeeded his brother Abū Bakr in A.D. 1210, A.H. 607, and not only inherited Azurbejān, but a considerable part of 'Iraq. He enjoyed this power 15 years; after which 'Azurbejān was invaded and conquered by Sultān Jalāl-ud-dīn, the monarch of Khwārizm, A.D. 1225, A.H. 622. Muzaffar shut himself up in the fort of Alanjaq, where he died; and with him perished the power of the family of Eldiguz.

Atabak Muzaffar-ud-din Zangi (اتابک مظفر زنگي), a prince of Shīraz, and brother of Sunqar, which see.

Atabak Sa'd bin-Zangi. *Vide* Sunqar.

'Ata Husain Khan (عطا حسين خان), whose poetical name was Tahsīn, is the author of the *Nautarz Murassa'*, an Urdū translation of the *Chahār Darwesh*. He flourished in the time of Nawāb 'Asaf-ud-daula of Lucknow, about the year A.D. 1776, A.H. 1189. As a specimen of the Urdū language the *Nautarz Murassa'* was rendered objectionable for students, by his retaining too much of the phraseology and idiom of the Persian and Arabic. On this account a simple version was executed by Mīr Amman of Dehlī in A.D. 1802, A.H. 1217, which is styled the *Bāgh-o-Bahār*.

[*Vide* Tahsīn.]

Atal (اتل), a name assumed by Mīr Abdul Jalīl Dehlī in his poetical compositions, who gave out that he was by inspiration the pupil of Ja'far Zatallī, and wrote poetry in Persian and Arabic.

'Ata Malik (عطا ملک). *Vide* Atā-ud-dīn surnamed 'Atā Malik.

Atash (آتش), poetical name of Khwāja Haidar Alī of Lucknow, who is the author of two Dīwāns or books of Odes consisting of Persian and Urdū verses. He died in A.D. 1847, A.H. 1263.

'Ata-ullah (عطا الهه), surname of several Musalmān authors, but particularly of Tāj-ud-dīn Muhammad bin-Ahmad bin-Atā-ullāh, who is the author of a book entitled *Hakam-ul-Atia*, which treats on Musalmān law, and is to be found in the Royal Library at Paris, No. 672. There is one Atā-ullāh who is the author of a dictionary called *Firdaus-ul-Lughāt*.

'Ata-ullah (عطا الهه), bin-Muhammad-al-Husainī Naishāpūrī, author of the *Rauzat-ul-Ahbāb*, containing the history of Muhammad, of his companions, and of the twelve Imāms. This book was written at Herāt and dedicated to Amīr 'Alīsher in A.D. 1494, A.H. 899. He is also called Amīr Jamāl-ud-dīn Atā-ullāh. He also wrote another work on the art of writing poetry, entitled *Kitāb Takmīl-us-Sanaa't*, dedicated to the same Amīr, in which he calls himself 'Atā-ullāh bin-Muhammad-al-Husainī Naishāpūrī. He was wazīr to Sultān Husain Mirzā of Herāt, and died in the beginning of the year A.H. 917.

At-har or **Athar Khan** (اطهر خان), the son of Amīr Nizām-ud-dīn Razwī; he was a native of Bukhāra, and came to India in the time of the emperor 'Alamgīr, where he collected his poems into a Dīwān.

Atma' (اطمع), a poet whose proper name is Abū Is-hāq Hallāj, which see.

Atsiz (اتسز), one of the Sultāns of Khwārizm called Atsiz ibn-Auk by Ibn Khallikān. Tutush or Turtush, son of Alp Arsalān, who was lord of the countries to the east of Syria, caused him to be arrested, and having put him to death on the 21st October, A.D. 1078, 11th Rabī II. A.H. 471, took possession of his kingdom.

Atsiz (اتسز), a Sultān of Khwārizm called by ibn-Khallikān, Atsiz, the son of Qutb-ud-dīn Muhammad, the son of Anushtakīn. He was contemporary with Sultān

Sanjar Saljūkī, with whom he had several battles. He died in A.D. 1166, 6th Jamad II. A.H. 551, and was succeeded to the throne by his son Alp Arsalān, who is also called Apa Arsalān. He died in A.D. 1162, 19th Rajab, A.H. 557.

Atsiz (اتسز), son of Ala-ud-dīn Hasan Jahān Sōz, king of Ghōr. He reigned after Bahā-ud-dīn Sām, and was killed in a battle against Tāj-ul-dīn Eldūz, prince of Ghaznī, some time about the year A.D. 1211, A.H. 608. He was the last of the kings of Ghōr of this branch.

'Attar (عطار), poetical name of Farīd-ud-dīn Attār, which see.

Aurang (اورنگ), name of a lover whose mistress was Gulchehra.

Aurangabadi Begam(اورنگابادي بيگم), one of the wives of the emperor Aurangzeb 'Alamgīr.

Aurangzeb (اورنگزيب), the son of Shāh Jahān, emperor of Dehlī. On his accession to the throne, he took the title of 'Alamgīr, agreeably to the custom of the Eastern princes, who always assume a new one on that occasion.

[*Vide* 'Alamgir.]

Aurangzeb (اورنگزيب), private name of the emperor 'Alamgīr I. which see. The Mughal Emperors changed their names on accession, like the Popes of modern times.

Avank Khan (اونک خان), or Ung Khān, a prince of the tribe of Karit or Kirit, a tribe of Mughals or Oriental Tartars, who made profession of the Christian religion. He was surnamed Mālik Yūhannā, or king John. From the name of this prince we have made John the Priest, who was stripped of his dominions by Changez Khān in A.D. 1202, A.H. 599. They have since applied the name of John the Priest or Prestre John to the king of Ethiopia, because he was a Christian. Avank Khān is by some authors called Avant Khān. He was a very powerful sovereign, and the greatest part of Tartary was tributary to him; but he was defeated and put to death by Changez Khān.

Aven Rosch. *Vide* Ibn Rashīd.

Avenzur. *Vide* Abdul Malik bin-Zohr

Averroes. *Vide* Ibn Rashīd.

Avicenna. *Vide* Abū Sīna.

Aweis Qarani (Khwaja) (اويس قرني), an upright Musalmān of the Sūfī sect, who had given up the world, used to say to those that sought him, "Do you seek God? If you do, why do you come to me? And if you do not seek God, what business can I have with you?" He was an inhabitant of Yeman and of the tribe of Qāran. He was slain in a battle fought by Alī against Mu'āwia I. in A.D. 657, 17th Shawwal, A.H. 37. This man had never seen Muhammad, and yet the Musalmāns say, that when he heard that Muhammad had lost a tooth in battle, and not knowing which, he broke all his teeth.

Aweis Jalayer (Sultan) (اويس جلاير سلطان) succeeded his father, Amīr Hasan Buzurg, as king of Baghdād in July, A.D. 1356, Rajab, A.H. 757, and after a reign of nearly nineteen lunar years died on Tuesday the 10th October, A.D. 1374, 2nd Jamad I. A.H. 776. He was succeeded by his son Sultān Husain Jalāyer.

Aweis Mirza (اويس مرزا), a prince nearly related to Baiqara Bahādur, was nephew to Abūl Ghāzī Sultān Husain Bahādur. He was murdered by Sultān Abū Sāid Mirzā, between the years A.D. 1451 and 1457.

'Ayani (عياني), whose proper name was Abū Is-hāq Ibrāhīm, probably flourished previous to the 8th century of the Hijrat. He is the author of a Masnawī called *Anbia Nāma*, a history of the prophets who preceded Muhammad.

Ayaz (اياز), a slave of Sultān Mahmūd of Ghaznī who, being a great favourite of his master, was envied by the courtiers; they therefore informed the Sultān that they frequently observed Ayāz go privately into the Jewel office, whence they presumed he had purloined many valuable effects. The next time when the slave had entered the treasury, the Sultān followed by a private door, and, unobserved, saw Ayāz draw from a large chest a suit of old dirty garments, with which having clothed himself, he prostrated himself on the ground and returned thanks to the Almighty for all the benefits conferred on him. The Sultān, being astonished, went to him, and demanded an explanation of his conduct. He replied, "Most gracious Sire, when I first became your Majesty's servant, this was my dress, and till that period, humble had been my lot. Now that, by the grace of God and your majesty's favour, I am elevated above all the nobles of the land, and am intrusted with the treasures of the world, I am fearful that my heart should be puffed up with vanity; I therefore daily practise this humiliation to remind me of my former insignificance." The Sultān being much pleased, added to his rank, and severely reprimanded his slanderers.

'Ayaz (Qazi) (عیاض قاضی), son of Mūsa, and author of the *Sharah Salīh Muslim, Mashāriq-ul-Anwār*, and several other works. He died in A.D. 1149, A.H. 544.

'Ayesha (عایشه), daughter of Abū Bakr, and one of the most beloved wives of Muhammad, though she bore him no child. She was his third wife, and the only one that was a maid, being then only seven years of age; on which account (some say) her father, whose original name was Abdullāh, was named Abū Bakr, that is to say, the father of the virgin. An Arabian author, cited by Maracci, says, that Abū Bakr was very averse to giving him his daughter so young, but that Muhammad pretended a divine command for it; whereupon he sent her to him with a basket of dates, and when the girl was alone with him, he stretched out his hand, and rudely took hold of her clothes; upon which she looked fiercely at him, and said, "People call you the faithful man, but your behaviour to me shews you are a perfidious one." But this story is most probably one of those calumnies against Muhammad which were invented and found favour in the Middle Ages. After the death of her husband she opposed the succession of Alī, and had several bloody battles with him; although violent, her character was respected, and when taken prisoner by Alī she was dismissed without injury. She was called prophetess and mother of the faithful. She died, aged 67, in the year A.D 678, A.H. 58. Her brother Abdur Rahmān, one of the four who stood out against Yezīd's inauguration, died the same year. There is a tradition that 'Ayesha was murdered by the direction of Mu'āwia I. and the following particulars are recorded:—'Ayesha having resolutely and insultingly refused to engage her allegiance to Yezīd, Mu'āwia invited her to an entertainment, where he had prepared a very deep well or pit in that part of the chamber reserved for her reception, and had the mouth of it deceptively covered over with leaves and straw. A chair was then placed upon the fatal spot, and 'Ayesha, on being conducted to her seat, instantly sank into eternal night, and the mouth of the pit was immediately covered with stones and mortar. There is, however, no trustworthy authority in support of this story.

'Ayn-uddin (Shaikh) (عین الدین شیخ), of Bījāpūr, author of the *Mulhiqat*, and *Kitāb-ul-Anwār* containing a history of all the Muhammadan saints of India. He flourished in the time of Sultān Ala-uddīn Hasan Bahmanī.

'Ayn-ul-Mulk (Hakim) (عین الملک حکیم), a native of Shīrāz, and a well-educated and learned Musalmān, was an officer of rank in the time of the emperor Akbar. He was an elegant poet, and his poetical name was Wafā. He died in the 40th year of the emperor in A.D. 1594, A.H. 1003.

'Ayn-ul-Mulk (Khwaja) (عین الملک خواجه), a distinguished nobleman in the court of Sultān Muhammad Shāh Tughlaq and his successor Sultān Fīroz Shāh Bārbak, kings of Dehlī. He is the author of several works, one of which is called *Tarsīl 'Ayn-ul-Mulkī*. He also appears to be the author of another work called *Fatha Nāma*, containing an account of the conquests of Sultān 'Alā-uddīn Sikandar Sānī, who reigned from A.D. 1296 to A.D. 1316.

'Aysh (عیش), poetical name of Muhammad 'Askarī, who lived in the reign of the emperor Shāh 'Alam.

'Ayshi (عیشي), a poet who is the author of a Masnawī called *Haft Akhtar*, or the seven planets, which he wrote in A.D. 1675, A.H. 1086.

Azad (آزاد), poetical name of Mīr Ghulām Alī of Bilgrām, born about 1703. His father Sayyad Nūh, who died in A.D. 1752, A.H. 1165, was the son of the celebrated Mīr Abdūl Jalīl Bilgrāmī. He was an excellent poet and is the author of several works in Persian and Arabic, among which are *Qasāid 'Uzzā, Sab-hat-ul-Mirjān, Khazāna 'Amira*, and *Tazkira Sarv 'Azād*. He died in the year A.D. 1786, A.H. 1200.

Azad (آزاد), the poetical name of Captain Alexander Hiderley, in the service of the rāja of Alwar. He was a good poet and has left a small Dīwān in Urdū. His father's name was James Hiderley, and his brother's Thomas Hiderley. He died on the 7th July, 1861, Zilhij, A.H. 1277, at Alwar, aged 32 years.

Azad Khan (آزاد خان), governor of Cashmere, of the Afghān tribe, succeeded his father, Hājī Karīm Dād, a domestic officer of Ahmad Shāh Abdālī, and who was at the death of that prince advanced to the government of Cashmere by Taimūr Shāh, as a reward for quelling the rebellion of Amīr Khān, the former governor. Azād Khān was only 18 years of age (in 1783) when he was governor of Cashmere, but his acts of ferocity exceeded common belief.

'Azaeri (عضایری). *Vide* Uzāerī.

Azal (ازل), poetical name of Mirzā Muhammad Amīn, who died in A.D. 1728, A.H. 1141.

'Azam Shah (اعظم شاه), the third son of the emperor Alamgīr, was born on the 11th July, o.s. 1653, 25th Shābān, A.H. 1063. After his father's death (his eldest brother Bahādur Shāh being then at Kābul) he was crowned in the garden of Shālimar at Ahmadābād in the Deccan on the 4th March, o.s. 1707, 10th Zil-hijja, A.H. 1118, but was soon after slain, together with his two sons, Bedār Bakht and Wālājāh, in a battle fought against his eldest brother at Jajowan between Āgra and Dholpur. This took place on Sunday the 8th June, o.s. 1707, 18th Rābī' I. A.H. 1119, three lunar months and eighteen days after his father's death. His mother's name was Bāno Begam, the daughter of Shāhnawāz Khān. He was buried in the mausoleum of Humāyūn at Dehlī. His two youngest sons who survived him were 'Alī Tabār and Bedar Dil.

Azdihak. *Vide* Zuhāk.

'Azd-ud-daula (عضد الدوله), a Sultān of the Boyites, succeeded his father, Rukn-ud-daula, in September, A.D. 976, Muharram, A.H. 366, to the government of Fars and 'Irāk, as well as in the office of wazīr or Amīr-ul-Umrā to the khalīf Al-Tāya Billāh of Baghdād, in the room of his cousin Izz-ud-daula, the son of Maizz-ud-daula, whom he killed in battle in A.D. 978, A.H. 367. He built the mausoleum of 'Alī at Najaf Ashraf, embellished Baghdād and other places by magnificent public buildings, and died on Monday the 27th March, A.D. 983, 8th Shawwal, A.H. 372, aged 47 lunar years. At his death the reigning khalīf read the prayers at the funeral of this good and great man. His name is still fondly cherished in a country over which he endeavoured during the reign of his father and his own, being a space of 34 years, to diffuse prosperity and joy. His power and possessions became from the moment of his death a subject of contest between his brothers and nephews.

'Azd-uddin (Qazi) (عضد الدين قاضي), of Shīrāz, author of several works, one of which is called the *Muwāqif 'Azdia*, a celebrated work in Arabic on Jurisprudence. He flourished in the time of Shāh Abū Is-hāq, governor of Shīrāz, to whom he dedicated the above work. He died A.D. 1355, A.H. 756.

'Azid la din-allah-bin-Yusaf-bin-Hafiz (عاضد لدين الله بن يوسف بن حافظ), the eleventh and last khalīf of Egypt of the Fātimite dynasty, succeeded his father, Fāez-bi-nasr-allāh Īsā bin-Zāfir, in the year A.D. 1158, A.H. 553. But the state of affairs in Egypt was now tottering to its fall. The descendants of 'Alī from the death of Al-Musta'alī Billāh, A.D. 1101, had become puppets in the hands of their wazīr or Amīr-ul-Jayūsh (generalissimo), who wielded all the regal authority of the state: two Amīrs, Dargam and Shāwar, had contested in arms this high dignity; and the latter, defeated and expelled from Egypt, sought refuge and aid from Nūr-uddīn, styled Mālik-ul-'Adil Nūr-uddīn Mahmūd, the celebrated ruler of Syria. The sovereign of Damascus eagerly embraced the opportunity of obtaining a footing in Egypt, and in A.D. 1163, A.H. 558, despatched a force under Asad-ud-dīn Shirakoh (the brother of Aiyūb) and his nephew Sālah-uddīn to reinstate Shāwar, whose rival called in the Christians of Palestine to his support; but ere Amaury (the brother and successor of Baldwin III.) could enter Egypt, Dargam had been overpowered and slain by Shirakoh, who replaced Shāwar in his former power. But Shāwar, faithless alike to friend and foe, now entered into arrangements with the Franks in order to elude the fulfilment of his engagements with Nūr-uddīn; and Shirakoh, after maintaining himself for some time in Belbes against the joint forces of Jerusalem and Egypt, was compelled to enter into a convention with Amaury and evacuate the country. But he was soon recalled by Shāwar to deliver him from the vengeance of his new allies, to whom he had proved as perfidious as to those of his own faith; Cairo was closely besieged by the Franks, and the Fātimite khalīf, 'Azid le-dīn-allah, sent the hair of his women, the extreme symbol of Oriental distress, to implore the succour of Nūr-uddīn (A.D. 1168). Shirakoh again entered Egypt with an army, forced Amaury to retreat, and after beheading the double traitor Shāwar, installed himself in the twofold office of wazīr to the Fātimite khalīf and lieutenant of Egypt in the name of Nūr-uddīn; but dying the same year, was succeeded in his dignities by his famous nephew Sālah-uddīn, who, after the death of Nūr-uddīn in May, A.D. 1173, Shawwal, A.H. 569, became the sole master of Egypt and Syria. The khalīf 'Azid died in A.D. 1171, A.H. 567, and the name of the Abbaside khalīf Mustazī was substituted in the public prayers till the death of Nūr-uddīn.

'Azim (عظيم), the son of Mullā Qaidī, and a nephew of Mullā Nazīri, was a Persian poet of Naishāpūr. He flourished about the year A.D. 1663, A.H. 1074, and is the author of a Dīwān, and a Masnawī called *Fauz Azīm*.

[*Vide* Azīm Naishāpūrī.]

'Azim (اعظم), poetical name of Sirāj-ud-daula Muhammad Ghaus Khān, Nawāb of the Karnatic.

'Azim (اعظم), poetical name of Sayyad 'Azim 'Alī of Allahābād, author of a Dīwān in Urdū, composed in A.D. 1855.

'Azim Ali (Mir) (اعظم علي مير), of Āgra, author of a Sikandar Nāma in Urdū verse, translated from the one in Persian, in A.D. 1844.

'Azim Humayun (اعظم همايون). *Vide* Adil Khān Fārūqī II.

'Azim Humayun Shirwani (اعظم هماون شرواني), a nobleman of the court of Sulṭān Sikandar Shāh Lōdī. He was imprisoned by Sulṭān Ibrāhīm and died in prison.

'Azim Jah (عظيم جاه), Nawāb of Arkat, died 14th January, 1874, aged 74. He was the second son of Azim Jāh, one of the Nawābs of the Carnatic, and the uncle of the late Nawāb Ghulām Muhammad Ghaus Khān. He received a pension of 2500 rupees from the Government.

'Azim Jah (Nawab) (عظيم جاه نواب), Sirāj-ul-Umrā, the son of Azīm-ud-daula, Nawāb of the Karnatic, was installed by the British Government as Nawāb on the 3rd February, 1820. He died on the 12th November, 1825, aged 34 years.

'Azim Khan (اعظم خان), or Khān 'Azim, an officer of state in the time of Humāyūn and Akbar, emperor of Dehlī. He was commonly called Anka Khān, surnamed Shams-uddīn Muhammad, and was the father of Mirzā Azīz Kōka, who also afterwards held the title of 'Azim Khān. He was a native of Ghaznī, and formerly served under Prince Kāmrān Mirzā. It is said that he saved the life of Humāyūn, or had been of some service to him after his defeat by Sher Shāh at Kanauj; for which service he was handsomely rewarded by that emperor after his having recovered the kingdom. He accompanied the emperor to Persia, and as his wife, Jījī Begam, became the wet-nurse of Akbar, the emperor's son, he was consequently called Atyak Khān. He was the first person that was honoured with the rank of "Haft Hazārī," or Seven Thousand, by Akbar. The office of Wakīl Mutlaq, which was taken away from Māham Anka, was also conferred on him; on which account, Adham Khān Kokaltāsh (*q.v.*), the son of Māham Anka, took offence, and assassinated Khān 'Azim on Monday the 18th May, A.D. 1562, 12th Ramzan, A.H. 969, in a room adjoining to that occupied by the emperor. Adham Khān was immediately bound hand and foot by order of the emperor, and thrown down headlong from a window of the court at Āgra, where this circumstance had taken place, and crushed to death. The remains of Khān 'Azim were sent to Dehlī, and buried in the vicinity of the Dargāh of Nizām-uddīn Auliā, where a mausoleum was erected over his grave by his son Mirzā Azīz Kōka, which is still to be seen at Dehlī. Māham Anka died with grief one month after the death of his son Adham Khān. The tomb of Adham Khān, who is also buried at Dehlī, is called Bhūl Bhuliān.

'Azim Khan (اعظم خان). The inhabitants of the town of Azimgaṛh, which is near Jaunpūr, say that the fortress and town of Azimgaṛh was founded by a person who belonged to the family of the Rājas of that place, and who was forced by the emperor Jahāngīr to become a Muhammadan, and received the title of Azim Khān.

'Azim Khan (اعظم خان), commonly called Mirzā Azīz Kōkā or Kokaltāsh, was the son of 'Azim Khān or Khān 'Azim. He was called Kōkā or Kokaltāsh on account of his being foster-brother and playmate of Akbar; for his mother, whose name was Jījī Begam, was Akbar's wet-nurse. He was one of the best generals of the emperor, who, in the 16th year of his reign, conferred on him the title of 'Azim Khān. He held the government of Gujrāt for several years together, and being absent from the presence for a long period, was summoned to court by Akbar in A.D. 1592, A.H. 1001, but as that chief had always entertained the wish to proceed on a pilgrimage to Mecca, and his friends representing to him that the king was displeased with him, and merely sought an opportunity to imprison him, he placed his family and treasure on board a vessel, and on the 13th March, O.S. 1594, 1st Rajab, A.H. 1002, set sail for Hejāz without leave or notice. In a short time, however, he found his situation irksome in that country, and returned to India, where he made his submission, and was restored at once to his former place in the emperor's favour and confidence. He died at Ahmadābād Gujrāt in the 19th year of the reign of Jahāngīr, A.D. 1624, A.H. 1033. His remains were transported to Dehlī and buried close to his father's mausoleum, where a splendid monument was erected over his tomb all of marble. It consists of sixty-four pillars, and is called by the people "Chaunsa'th Khambh."

'Azim Khan (اعظم خان), title of Mīr Muhammad Bāqir, the brother of 'Asaf Khān Jāfar Beg. In the second year of the reign of the emperor Jahāngīr, A.D. 1606, A.H. 1015, he was honoured with the mansab of 1000 and title of Irādat Khān. In the first year of Shāh Jahān, A.D. 1628, A.H. 1037, the rank of 2000 was conferred on him with the office of Wizārat Kull; in the third year of his reign he received the title of 'Azim Khān. He was appointed at different times governor of Bengal, Allahābād, Gujrāt and latterly of Jaunpūr, where he died in A.D. 1649, A.H. 1059, aged 76 lunar years, and was buried there. After his death the title of 'Azim Khān was conferred on his eldest son, who was slain in the battle which took place between Dārā Shikoh and his brother Alamgīr in A.D. 1658, A.H. 1068, at Āgra. His second son, Mīr Khalīl, was honoured with the title of Khān Zamān. During the government of this viceroy in A.D. 1634, the English obtained permission to trade with their ships in Bengal by the emperor Shāh Jahān, but were restricted to the port of Pipley, where they established their factory.

'Azim Khan (اعظم خان), ex-amīr and a brother of Sher Alī Khān, Amīr of Kabul, died at Shāh Rūd on the 6th October, 1869.

'Azim Khan Koka (اعظم خان كوكه), the title of Muzaffar Husain, commonly known by the appellation of Fidāī Khān, a title conferred on him by the emperor Shāh Jahān. His elder brother held the title of Khān Jahān Bahādūr Kokaltāsh, and were both foster-brothers to the emperor Alamgīr. Fidāī Khān was honoured with the title of 'Azīm Khān by Alamgīr about the year A.D. 1676, A.H. 1086, and appointed governor of Bengal in A.D. 1676, A.H. 1087, which situation he held for a whole year, and died on his way to Behar on the 21st April, O.S. 1678, 9th Rabī I. A.H. 1089.

'Azim Naishapuri (اعظم نیشاپوری) author of a Dīwān found in the Library of Tīpū Sultān.

'Azim-ud-daula (Nawab) (عظم الیدوله نواب), of the Carnatic, was the son of Nawāb Amīr-ul-Umrā, the brother of Umdat-ul-Umrā. On the death of Umdat-ul-Umrā, the English resolved to take the functions of government into their own hands. 'Alī Husain, the next heir, refused to comply, consequently Ayīm-ud-daula, the nephew of the deceased, was placed on the masnad by the British Government on the 31st August, A.D. 1801. He died on the 2nd August, A.D. 1819. His son 'Azīm Jāh was installed as Nawāb of the Carnatic on the 3rd February, A.D. 1820.

'Azim-ul-Umra (عظیم الامرا), minister of the Nizām of Hydarābād. He succeeded Rukn-ud-daula about the year A.D. 1794.

'Azim-ullah Khan (عظیم الله خان), says Mr. Sheppard in his Narrative of the Mutiny, was a charity boy, having been picked up, together with his mother, during the famine of 1837-1838, when they were both in a dying state from starvation. The mother being a staunch heathen, she would not consent to her son being christened. He was adopted in the Cawnpore Free School under Mr. Patan, schoolmaster. After ten years he was raised to be a teacher. After some years he attached himself to the Nāna, who sent him to England for the purpose of bringing his case before the Home Government. He became a favourite in English society, and visited the camp before Sevastopol, returning to India in 1856. He intrigued with Dehlī, and persuaded the Nāna to join the mutinous Sepoys in 1857. He is believed to have instigated the Cawnpore massacre. He fled on the re-occupation of the place, and his further fate is unknown.

'Azimush Shan (عظیم انشان), second son of the emperor Bahādur Shāh of Dehlī. He was appointed by his grandfather, the emperor 'Alamgīr, governor of Bengal; he made Patna the seat of his government and named it Azīmābād. On the news of his grandfather's death, leaving his own son Farrukhsiar (afterwards emperor) to superintend the affairs of that country, he came to Āgra, and was present in the battle which took place between his father and his uncle 'Azam Shāh, in June, A.D. 1707, A.H. 1119. He was slain in the battle which ensued after his father's death between Jahāndār Shāh and his other brothers, in the month of February, O.S. 1712, Muharram, A.H. 1124. His second son, Muhammad Karīm, was taken prisoner after the battle and murdered by order of Jahāndār Shāh, who ascended the throne.

'Aziz (عزیز), whose proper name was Abdūl Azīz Khān, was a native of Deccan. He is the author of a Dīwān, also of a prose composition called *Gulshān Rang*.

'Aziz Koka (Mirza) (عزیز کوکه مرزا), the foster-brother of the emperor Akbar. *Vide* 'Azim Khān, the son of Khān 'Azim, commonly called Anka Khān.

'Aziz-ullah Zahidi (عزیز الله زاهدی), author of a Masnawī, which he composed in the year A.D. 1407, A.H. 810. He is commonly called Azīz.

'Azmat-ullah (Shah) (عظمت الله), author of the *Mazhar-ul-Asrār*, being a long dissertation on the nature of the divinity, the soul, and other abstruse subjects on Sūfiism.

'Azra (عذرا), name of the celebrated mistress of Wāmiq.

Azraqi (ازرقي حكيم), commonly called Hakīm Arzaqī or Azraqī, was a physician and a poet. He was a native of Mars, and flourished in the reign of Tughral III. Saljūkī, king of Persia, in whose name he wrote several books. Arzaqī died in A.D. 1189, A.H. 585. His Dīwān contains nearly 2000 verses. He is also said to be the author of a work called *Kitāb Sindbād*. His proper name is Abū'l Mahāsin Abū Bakr Zain-ud-dīn, son of Isma'īl Warrāq. He introduced himself into the society and confidence of the Saljūkī prince Tughān Shāh I. the seat of whose government was Naishapūr, by the composition of a most obscene book, which he called *Alfia Shalfia*, illustrated with pictures. This book appears to be a version of the Kōk Shāshtar. He is called Azraqī in the *Jour. As. Soc.* of Bengal for 1844, vol. xiii. part ii. p. 520, and stated to be the author of a history of Mecca, of which ancient work several MSS. are in Europe, especially one at Cambridge, formerly the property of Dr. Burckhardt, who in the preface to his *Travels in Arabia* professes to have largely made use of it.

Azur (آذر), the poetical name of Lutf 'Alī Beg, author of the Tazkira called *Ataishkada Azur*. He was engaged in the compilation of this work in A.D. 1765, A.H. 1179, and was alive in A.D. 1782, A.H. 1196. He never came to India.

Azuri Razi (آذری رازی), a native of Rei in Persia, was a celebrated poet who lived at the court of Sultān Mahmūd of Ghaznī. On one occasion he received a present of 14,000 dirhams from the Sultān for a short panegyric.

Azuri (Shaikh) (آذری شیخ), Isfarāenī, whose original name was Jalāl-uddīn Hamza, was a pious Musalmān and an excellent poet. He came to the Deccan from Persia in the reign of Sultān Ahmad Shāh Walī Bahmanī, A.D. 1432, A.H. 835, and returned again to Khurāsān, his native country, where he died in the year A.D. 1462, A.D. 866, aged 82 lunar years. He is the author of several works, among which are *Jawāhir-ul-Asrār*, *Tughrāe Humāyūn*, and *Samrāt Fruits*, which consists of four books, viz., *Almakrī Tāma*, *Ajāeb-ud-dunia*, *Ajāeb-ul-'Ala* and *Sa'ī-us-Safā*. He also left a Dīwān of 30,000 verses. He adopted the poetical name of 'Azurī, because he was born in the Persian month of Azur. His tomb is at Isfarāen, and was at the time of Daulat Shāh so sacred, that convicts found an asylum there from the hands of justice. He is also the author of another poetical work, called *Bahman Nāma*.

[*Vide* Alī Hamza.]

'Azz-uddin Abdul Aziz (عز الدین عبد العزیز). *Vide* 'Izz-uddīn.

B

BABA

Baba (بابا), a Turkish imposter, who announced himself in A.D. 1260 as the messenger of God; and collected a number of adherents, at whose head he laid waste Anatolia. He was at last overpowered and his sect dispersed.

Baba Afzal Kashi (بابا افضل کاشے), an author.

Baba Fighani (بابا فغاني), a poet of Persia who served under Sulṭān Ya'qūb, the son of Uzzan Hasan, and died in the year A.D. 1519, A.H. 925, at Khurasān. He has left a Dīwān containing 6000 verses.

Baba 'Isa (بـابـا عـيـسـى), or 'Īsa Langotesband. His tomb is in Tatta in Sindh. The inscription gives the year A.D. 1514, A.H. 920.

Babak (بابک), the father of Ardsher Bābākān, which see.

Babak (بابک), an impostor, who first appeared in A.D. 816, A.H. 201, when he began to take upon him the title of a prophet. What his particular doctrine was, is now unknown; but his religion is said to have differed from all others then known in Asia. He gained a great number of proselytes in 'Azarbāījān and Persian 'Irāq, where he soon grew powerful enough to wage war with the khalīf Al-Atāmūn, whose troops he often beat, so that he was become extremely formidable in the beginning of the khalīf Al-Mu'ta'ṣim's reign. The general sent by the khalīf to reduce him was Ḥaidar-ibn-Kāūs, surnamed Afshīn (*q.v.*), a Turk by birth. By him Bābak was defeated with prodigious slaughter, no fewer than 60,000 men being killed in the first engagement. The next year, A.D. 835, A.H. 220, he received a still greater overthrow, losing 100,000 men either killed or taken prisoners. By this defeat he was obliged to retire into the Gordian mountains, where he fortified himself in such a manner that Afshīn found it impossible to reduce him till the year A.D. 837, A.H. 222, when he was forced to surrender to Afshīn upon that general promising him pardon. But Afshīn no sooner had him in his power, than he first caused his hands and feet, and afterwards his head to be cut off. Bābak had supported himself against the power of the khalīfs for upwards of 20 years, during which time he had cruelly massacred 250,000 people, it being his custom to spare neither man, woman, nor child of the Muhammadans or their allies.

Baba Kaikhusiz (بابا کیخوسز) (Father without Anxiety), a dervish who flourished in the reign of Murād III. and was author of the '*Abdullah-Nāma*.

Baba Lal Guru (بابا لال گورو), a Hindū of the tribe of Khattrīs, who was a Hindī poet, and flourished in the time of Jahāngīr. He was an inhabitant of Mālwa.

Baba Ratan (بابا رتن ابو رضا), surnamed Abū Razā, a pious Musalmān, who is said, by Daulat Shāh, to be one of the disciples of Jesus Christ, and that he lived to the advanced age of 1400 years, and died about the beginning of the 13th century of the Christian era.

Babar Shah (بابرشاه ظهير الدين محمد), surnamed Zahīr-ud-dīn Muhammad, the ancestor of the Mughal emperors of Dehlī, was the sixth in descent from Amīr Taimūr (Tamerlane). His father 'Umar Shaikh Mirzā, was the son of Abū Sa'īd Mirzā, the son of Muhammad Mirzā, the son of Mīrānshāh, the son of Amīr Taimūr. His mother's name was Kutlagh Nigār Khānam, daughter of Yūnas Khān, king of Mughālistān and sister to Mahmūd Khān, a descendant of the famous Changez or Jenghiz Khān. He was born on the 15th February, A.D. 1483, 6th Muharram, A.H. 888, and succeeded his father in the government of Farghāna, the capital of which is Andjān, in June, A.D. 1494, Ramazān, A.H. 899. During eleven years he fought several battles with the Tartar and Uzbak princes, but was at last obliged to leave his country and fly towards Kābul, which place he conquered, without opposition, together with Qandahār and Badakhshān. He reigned for 22 years over those countries before his conquest of India. He then proceeded to Hindūstān, slew Ibrahīm Husain Lodī, the Pathān king of Dehlī, in a battle at Pānīpat on Friday the 20th April, A.D. 1526, 7th Rajab, A.H. 932, and became the founder of the Mughal dynasty of India, which ended in 1857. Babar wrote his own life—*Tuzak-*

i-Bābari—in the Turkish language, with such elegance and truth, that the performance is universally admired. It was translated in the reign of his grandson Akbar, by Abdūl Rahīm Khān Khānkānān into Persian, and recently into English from the Jaghatai Turkī, by Dr. Leyden and Mr. W. Erskine. This monarch ascended the throne in his 12th year, and reigned 38 lunar years, *viz.:* at Andjān 11 years, at Kābul 22, and nearly 5 years in India, and died in Āgra on Monday the 26th December, A.D. 1530, 6th Jamād I. A.H. 937. He was at first buried in a garden on the left bank of the Jamna, then called the Nūr Afshān, and now Rāmbāgh, from which place his remains were transported after six months to Kābul, where a splendid mausoleum was built over his tomb by his great-great-grandson, the emperor Shāh Jahān, in A.D. 1646. His tomb on a hill near the city, surrounded by large beds of flowers, commands a noble prospect. The chronogram of the year of his death was found to consist in the words "Bahisht-rozībād," or "May heaven be his lot." After his death, he received the title of "Firdaus-Makānī." He was succeeded on the throne of Dehlī by his eldest son, the emperor Humāyūn. His three other sons were Mirzā Kāmrān, Mirzā 'Askarī, and Mirzā Handāl. Firishtā says that Bābar, who was much addicted to women and wine, on occasions when he was inclined to make merry, used to fill a reservoir in a garden in the neighbourhood of Kābul with wine, over which was inscribed a verse to this purpose :

Bright Spring blooms here, from day to day,
Young girls stand by, old wine to pour;
Enjoy them, Babar, while you may—
Your Spring, once gone, returns no more.

Babar (Sultan) (بابر سلطان), surnamed Abūl Qāsim, was the son of Mirzā Baisanghar and grandson of Shāhrukh Mirzā. After the death of Mirzā Ulagh Beg and his son 'Abdūl Latīf, he succeeded in January, A.D. 1452, Ẕil-ḥijja, A.H. 855, in murdering his own brother Sulṭān Muhammad and establishing himself in the government of Khurāsān and the neighbouring countries. A few months before his death, the comet of A.D. 1456, A.H. 860, made its appearance and alarmed the inhabitants of Khurāsān. He died at Mashhad on Tuesday the 22nd March, A.D. 1457, 25th Rabī II. A.H. 861. After his death Khurāsān was taken possession of by Mirzā Abū Sa'īd, the grandfather of the emperor Bābar Shāh of Dehlī.

Baba Soudai. *Vide* Soudāī (Bābā) (بابا سودائي).

Babawia (بابويه), or Bin Bābawia, father of Ibn Babawia. *Vide* Abū'l Hasan Alī Bin-al-Husdin at Kumarī.

Badakhshi (بدخشي), a Persian poet who was a native of the province of Badakhshān. He flourished in the reign of the khalīf Al-Muktafī, about the year A.D. 905, A.H. 294. His Dīwān or collection of poems is written upon the fortunes of the great men of the court; and he says that the varied scene in human affairs ought not to create surprise as we see that life is measured by an hour-glass, and that an hour is always above and the other below in alternate succession.

Badakhshi (Maulana) (بدخشي مولانا سمرقندی), of Samarqand, flourished in the reign of Ulagh Beg Mirzā, the son of Shāhrukh Mirzā, and is the author of a dīwān.

Badan Singh Jat (بدن سنگه جاٹ), the son of Chūrāman Jāt, a rāja of Bhartpūr and the founder of the fort at Ḏīg. He was living at the time of Nādir Shāh's invasion of India in A.D. 1739, A.H. 1152. After his death his son Sūrajmal Jāṭ succeeded him.

[*Vide* Chūrāman Jāt.]

Badaoni (بداؤني). Abdūl Kadīr of Badaon (*q.v.*).

Badi-uddin (بدع الدين). *Vide* Shāh Madār.

Badi-uddin (Shaikh) (بدع الدين شيخ), of Sahāranpūr, was a disciple of Shaikh Ahmad Sarhindī. He died in the year A.D. 1632, A.H. 1042, and lies buried in the yard of the masjid erected by him at Sahāranpūr.

Badi'-Uzzaman Mirza (بديع الزمان مرزا), was the eldest son of Sultān Husain Mirzā, after whose death in A.D. 1506, A.H. 912, he reigned conjointly with his younger brother, Muzaffar Husain Mirzā, over Khurāsān. He was subsequently compelled by the victorious Uzbaks, and the usurpation of his brother, to take refuge in 'Irāq; and in the year A.D. 1514, A.H. 920, went to the court of the Ottoman Sulṭān, Salīm I. where, after a few months' residence, he died of the plague. He was the last of the race of Taimūr who reigned in Persia. In a work called *Ship of the Time*, a Persian Anthology, there are to be found verses of the royal poet's composition. The following is a translation of a few lines—

Since not for me thy cheek of roses shines,
My bosom like the fading tulip pines;
Who in his burning heart conceals its flame,
And mine, in absence, perishes the same.
Pour wine—and let me, as I drink, suppose
I see the colours of that blushing rose;
Pour wine—and let it borrow every hue
Born in the tulip's petals wet with dew;
Till I believe thou may'st e'en yet be mine—
And let me never wake, nor that sweet
dream resign.

Badr (بدر), poetical title of Gangā Parshād, a Hindū.

Badr Chachi (بدر چاچي), surnamed Fakhr-uz-zamān, a celebrated poet of Chāch (the ancient name of Tāshkand), who flourished in the reign of Sulṭān Muhammad Tughlaq Shāh, king of Dehlī, and died some time after the year A.D. 1344, A.H. 745.

Badr Muhammad (بدر محمد دهلوي), of Dehlī, author of the Persian Dictionary called *Adāb-ul-Fuzalā*, dedicated to Qadr Khān bin Dilāwar Khān, written in A.D. 1419, A.H. 822.

Badr Shirwani (Maulana) (بدر شيرواني مولانا), a Musalmān scholar and poet, who was contemporary with Kātibī, who died in A.D. 1435.

Badr (Pir). *Vide* Pīr Badar.

Badr-uddin Aintabi(بدرالدين اينتبى), an historian, who relates that the Qāzī Ibn-al-Maghūlī, who died in A.D. 1231, A.H. 628, bequeathed a part of his vast collection of books to the library of the college founded in Cairo by Mālik 'Ashraf Borsabaī.

Badr-uddin (Balbaki) (بدر الدين بعلبكى), a Syriac physician, who wrote a book called *Musarrah-al-Nafs*. He lived in the 7th century of the Hijrah.

Badr - uddin, Isma'il - al - Tabrizi (بدر الدين اسمعيل التبريزي), an Arabian author, surnamed Bāzil.

Badr-uddin Jajurmi (بدر الدين جاجرمى), an author who died in A.D. 1287, A.H. 686, in which year also died Majd-uddīn Hamkar. He was a contemporary of Shams-uddīn Muhammad Sāhib Dīwān, and of Sa'dī.

Badr-uddin Lulu (بدر الدين لولو), ruler of Mausal, who was living in the reign of Halākū Khān, the Tartar, in A.D. 1258, and was in his 90th year.

Badr-uddin Mahmud (بدر الدين محمود), known by the name of Ibn-al-Qāzī Simāwana, is the author of the *Jāma'-al-Fusulain*, a collection of decisions on mercantile matters. He died A.D. 1420, A.H. 823.

Badr-uddin Mahmud Bin Ahmad-àl-'Aini (بدر الدين محمود بن احمد العيتى), author of a commentary on the *Kanz-ul-Daqīeq*, called *Ramz-ul-Haqāeq*. He died in A.D. 1451, A.H. 855. He is also the author of a collection of decisions entitled the *Masāel-al-Badria*.

Badr-uddin Muhammad Bin Abdur Rahman-al-Dairi (بدر الدين محمد بن عبدالرحمان الديري), author of a commentary on the *Kanz-ul-Daqīeq*, entitled *Matlab-ul-Fāeq*, which is much esteemed in India.

Badr-uddin Shashi Shirwani (بدر الدين شاشي شيرواني), died in A.H. 754 or 854.

Badr-uddin Sufi (بدر الدين صوفى), author of the *Bahr-ul-Hayāt* (the sea of life), containing many good rules for moral conduct.

Badr-uddin (بدر الدين), of Sarhind, author of a Persian work called Hazrāt-ul-Quds, containing the miracles performed by Ahmad Sarhindī.

Badr-un-nisa Begam (بدر النسا بيگم), the daughter of 'Ālamgīr, died in March, A.D. 1670, Zi-Qa'da, A.H. 1080.

Badshah Bano Begam (بادشاه بانو بيگم), one of the wives of the emperor Jahāngīr. She died in A.D. 1620, A.H. 1029.

Badshah Begam (بادشاه بيگم), wife of the emperor Jahāngīr, died in the year A.H. 1029.

Baghdad Khatun (بغداد خاتون), a daughter of Amīr Chobān or Jovian, who governed the empire of the Tartars in the reign of Sulṭān Abū Sa'īd, the son of Aljāitū. Her father refusing to give her in marriage to that prince, because she had been betrothed to Shaika Hasan Jalāiar, was the occasion of the Amīr's disgrace and death. Hasan, who had married her, afterwards repudiated her and gave her into the hands of Abū Sa'īd. The prince publicly married her, and for some time was entirely governed by her; but being at last disturbed, and dying a short time after in A.D. 1335, A.H. 736, she was suspected to have poisoned him, and Bāidū Khān, the successor of Abū Sa'īd, put her to death.

Baghuri (بغري), or Baghshūrī, surname of Muhammad bin Is-hāq, an Arabian author who wrote on moral subjects, died in the year A.D. 1280, A.D. 679.

Baghwi (بغوي). *Vide* Abū Muhammad Farāī-ibn-Masa'ūd al-Baghwī.

Bahadur Ali Husaini (Mir) (بهادر علی حسینی میر), chief Munshī of the college of Fort William, author of the *Akhlāq Hindi*, or *Indian Ethics*, translated from a Persian version, also of the *Nasir Benazīr*, a prose translation of the enchanting fairy tale entitled *Sehr-ul-Bayān*, commonly called *Mīr Hasan's Masnawī*. This latter work was written by the request of Dr. Gilchrist in A.D. 1802, A.H. 1217, and published at Calcutta in 1803.

Bahadur Khan Faruqi (بهادر خان فاروقی), succeeded his father, Rājā Alī Khān, in the government of Khāndesh in A.D. 1596, A.H. 1005. When the emperor Akbar a few years afterwards arrived at Māndo, with the avowed intention of invading the Deccan, Bahādur Khān instead of adopting the policy of his father in relying on the honour of Akbar, and going with an army to co-operate with him, shut himself up in the fort of Asīr, and commenced preparations to withstand a siege. When Akbar heard of these proceedings he sent orders to the Khānkhānān 'Abdur Rahīm Khān and the prince Dāniāl Mirzā to continue the siege of Ahmadnagar, while he himself marched to the south and occupied Burhānpūr, leaving one of his generals to besiege Asīr. The blockade of this fortress continued for a length of time, till it surrendered, and Bahādur Khān, the last of the Farūqī dynasty, humbled himself before the throne of Akbar in the year A.D. 1599, A.H. 1008, while the impregnable fortress of Asīr with ten years' provisions and countless treasures fell into the hands of the conqueror.

Bahadur Khan Rohila (بهادر خان روهیله), son of Dariā Khān, was an amīr of high rank in the reign of the emperor Shāh Jahān. He accompanied prince Aurangzib to Qandahār, and died there during the siege, on the 19th July, A.D. 1649, 19th Rajab, A.H. 1059.

Bahadur Nizam Shah (بهادر نظام شاه), the last of the Nizām Shāhī kings of Ahmadnagar in the Deccan. On the death of his father, Ibrāhīm Nizām Shāh, which took place in August, A.D. 1595, Zil-hijja, A.H. 1003, several factions arose in Ahmadnagar, each setting up a nominal sovereign. Miān Manjū who possessed the city, and acknowledged the title of Bahādur Nizām Shāh, then an infant, being besieged by his competitors, invited Sultān Murād, son of the emperor Akbar, then governor of Gujrāt, to his assistance, for which he offered to become tributary to the Mughal power. Sultān Murād embraced the proposal, and arrived before Ahmadnagar with a considerable army. Miān Manjū by this time, having overcome his rivals, repented of his offers, and prepared to oppose the prince. Having committed the city to the charge of Nasīr Khān, his deputy, under the care of Chānd Bībī, great aunt to Sultān Bahādur, he departed to raise levies and implore the assistance of Qutb Shāh of Gōlkanda and 'Adil Shāh of Bijāpūr. Sultān Murād besieged Ahmadnagar, on the 16th December, O.S. 1595, 23rd Rabī II. A.H. 1004, which was gallantly defended. Breaches were made, but were immediately repaired by the heroic conduct of Chānd Bībī, who, covering herself with a veil, headed the troops. At length in the month of March, A.D. 1596, Rajab, A.H. 1004, supplies growing scarce in the camp, and the allies of Bījāpūr and Gōlkanda approaching, Sultān Murād thought proper to accept of some offers of tribute from Chānd Bībī, and raise the siege. Some money was paid, and the districts in Berar belonging to the Nizām Shāhī government were ceded to the Mughals. In the year A.D. 1600, beginning of A.H. 1009, Ahmadnagar was taken by the Mughals, and Bahādur Shāh with all the children of both sexes of the royal family were taken prisoners and sent to perpetual confinement in the fortress of Gwāliar.

Bahadur Shah (بهادر شاه افغان), an Afghān, succeeded his father, Mahmūd Khān, as governor of Bengal in the time of Salīm Shāh, and became independent and reigned five years. He was deposed in A.D. 1549, A.H. 956, and succeeded by another of the nobles of Salīm Shāh, named Sulaimān Qirānī.

Bahadur Shah (بهادر شاه بن مظفر شاه گجراتی), the second son of Muzaffar Shāh II. of Gujrāt. At the time of his father's death, he was absent at Jaunpūr, but when Mahmūd Shāh, his younger brother, ascended the throne of Gujrāt, after the murder of his eldest brother, Sikandar Shāh, Bahādur returned from thence, and having deprived Mahmūd of his kingdom, ascended the throne on the 20th August, A.D. 1526, 15th Zi-Qa'da, A.H. 932. He conquered Mālwā on the 26th February, A.D. 1531, 9th Shabān, A.H. 937, and the king of that place, Sultān Mahmūd II. who was taken prisoner and sent to Champanir, was put to death on the road. In the year A.D. 1536, A.H. 942, Mālwā was taken by the emperor Humāyūn, and Bahādur being defeated was obliged to fly towards Cambay, where, on his arrival, he heard that a fleet, in which there were between 4,000 or 5,000 Europeans, had arrived off the Island of Diu. He immediately repaired thither with a reinforcement of troops, and on his arrival there he ordered his barge and went to visit the admiral with the intention of killing him; but perceiving that he was betrayed he arose and was attacked on all sides by the Portuguese, when a soldier struck him over the head with a sword and threw him into the water, where he was drowned. This event took place on the 14th February, A.D. 1537, 3rd Ramazān, A.H. 943, and has been commemorated in two Persian chronograms, comprising the numerals which form the date of the year when it occurred. Their meaning is this: "The Europeans were the slayers of Bahādur," and "The king of the land became a martyr at Sea." Bahādur Shāh was 20 years of age when he ascended the throne, reigned 11 lunar years, and was slain at the age of 31. After his death his nephew Mīrān Muhammad Shāh was raised to the throne of Gujrāt.

Bahadur Shah I. (بهادر شاه قطب الدين شاه عالم), surnamed Qutb-uddīn Shāh 'Alam, formerly called prince Mu'azzim, was the second son of the emperor 'Alamgīr I. born at Burhānpūr in the Deccan on the 4th October, O.S. 1643, 30th Rajab, A.H. 1053. At the time of his father's death, which took place at Ahmadābād, on the 21st February, O.S. 1707, 28th Ẕi-Qa'da, A.H. 1118, he being then at Kābul, his younger brother, prince 'Azim, was proclaimed sovereign of all India in perfect disregard of the late emperor's will. Prince Mu'azzim, with better reason, assumed the crown at Kābul with the title of Bahādur Shāh; and both brothers prepared to assert their pretensions by force of arms. They assembled very large armies, and met at length between Dhaulpur and Āgra. A bloody battle ensued on Sunday the 8th June, O.S. 1707, 18th Rabī' I. A.H. 1119, in which prince 'Azim and his two grown-up sons, Bedār Bakht and Wālājāh, were killed. Bahādur Shāh reigned nearly five lunar years, and died at Lāhore on Monday the 18th February, O.S. 1712, 21st Muharram, A.H. 1124, in the 71st lunar year of his age. He was buried in the environs of Dehlī, near the tomb of Khwāja Qutb-uddīn, where he had built during his life a mosque entirely of white marble named Motī Masjid. His tomb is also built of the same stone. He received the title of "Khuld Manzil," *i.e.*, "May his mansion be in paradise," after his death. He left four sons, *viz.*, Ma'iz-uddīn Jahāndār Shāh, Azīm-ush-Shān, Rafī-ush-Shān, and Jahān Shāh, among whom a battle ensued, wherein the three latter brothers were killed, and Jahāndār Shāh ascended the throne.

Bahadur Shah II. (بهادر شاه ابولمظفر سراج الدين محمد), the last king of Dehlī, whose title in full was Abū'l Muzaffar Sirāj-uddīn Muhammad Bahādur Shāh, a lineal descendant from Amīr Taimūr, the son of Akbar Shāh II. on whose death he succeeded him on the 28th September, A.D. 1837, 28th Jumāda II. A.H. 1253. He was born on Tuesday the 24th October, A.D. 1775, 28th Shabān, A.H. 1189; and Abū'l Muzaffar is the chronogram of his birth. His mother's name was Lāl Bāī. A stipend or pension of one lakh of rupees monthly was allowed him by the British Government. He was an excellent Persian scholar and an elegant Urdū poet, and Zafar was his poetical name. His Dīwān or Book of Odes was printed some years ago at Dehlī. He was supposed to be the principal instigator of the mutiny of the native troops throughout India in A.D. 1857, and was deposed and tried, but his life was spared. In October, A.D. 1858, he was sent down to Calcutta, from which place he embarked on board H.M. ship *Megara* on Saturday the 4th December, A.D. 1858, for Rangoon, accompanied by two of his wives, a son and a grandson. He died there a few years later, and thus ended the royal race of Taimūr in India. His sons Mirzā Mughal and Mirzā Khwaja Sultān, and a grandson named Mirzā Abū Bakr, who were known to have taken a prominent part in the atrocities attending the insurrection, were captured on the 22nd September, A.D. 1857, at the tomb of Humayūn, and shot on the spot by Major Hodson. During the mutiny in A.D. 1857, Bahādur Shāh had struck a new coin with the following inscription:—

بزر زد سکهٔ نصرت طرازی
سراج الدين بهادر شاه غازی

Sirāj-ud-dīn, that hero bold,
Adorned his triumph with this gold.

Bahadur Singh (بهادر سنگه), the only surviving son of Rājā Mān Singh Kachwaha.

Bahadur Singh Kuchwaha (بهادر سنگه کچواها), brother to Sakat Singh, died of hard drinking in the year A.D. 1621, A.H. 1030.

Bahadur Singh (Rao). *Vide* Rāo Bahādur Singh.

Bahai (بهائی). *Vide* Bahā-uddīn 'Amilī.

Bahar (بهار), poetical name of Tek Chand, which see.

Bahar Bano (بهار بانو), Daulat-un Nisa, and Begam Sultān, daughters of the emperor Jahāngīr. All of them died in their childhood.

Bahar Bano (بہار بانو), daughter of the emperor Jahāngīr; married to Prince Tahmuras, the son of Prince Dāniāl, in their childhood.

Bahar Bano Begam (بہار بانو بیگم), another daughter of Jahāngīr, was married to Tahmūr, a son of prince Dāniāl.

Baha-uddin (بہاء الدین), a learned Arabian, known as a favourite of Sultān Sālah-uddīn (Saladdin) and the historian of that prince's life. He flourished about the year A.D. 1190, A.H. 586. An edition of his work appeared at Leyden in A.D. 1755.

Baha-uddin (بہاء الدین بن شمس الدین), the son of Shams-uddīn, the son of Fakhr-uddīn. His father was the first king of the second branch of the Sultāns of Ghōr. Baha-uddīn was the second king, and is said to have reigned 14 years. Imām Fakhr-uddīn Rāzī, who flourished in his time and died in A.D. 1210, A.H. 606, dedicated the work called *Risāla Haiyat* or book of geometry to him. After the death of Baha-uddīn, his son Jalāl-uddīn succeeded him. He was slain by Sultān Muhammad of Khwārizm, and appears to have been the last of this branch.

Baha-uddin (بہاء الدین حاکم اصفہان), governor of Isfahān, and author of the *Muntakhab-ul-Akhbār*, an abridged history of the patriarchs and prophets, also of Muhammad and his descendants, with a good description of the cities of Mecca and Madina. He flourished about the year A.D. 1271, A.H. 670.

Baha-uddin 'Amili (Shaikh) (بہاء الدین عاملی شیخ), a native of 'Amul in Persia, and son of Shaikh Husain. His poetical name is Bahāī. He is the author of several works, one of which is a Masnawī or poem called *Nān-wa-Halwā* (bread and pudding). He flourished in the time of Shāh 'Abbās the Great, king of Persia; died at Isfahān on Tuesday the 21st August, O.S. 1621, 12th Shawwāl, A.H. 1030, and was buried agreeably to his request at Mashhad. Imād-ud-daula Abū Tālib, the prime minister of Shāh 'Abbās, found the chronogram of the year of his death in the words "Shaikh Bahā-uddīn Wāe." Besides the above-mentioned Masnawī and many Arabic works, he has left a Dīwān and a Kashkōl, or Adversaria.

Baha-uddin Muhammad (بہا الدین محمد جلیل شیخ), Jalal or Jalīl (Shaikh) of 'Amil. This person is mentioned by H. M. Elliot, Esq., in his *Historians of India*, and appears to be the same with the preceding. He was a Persian mathematician, says he, and lived in the reign of Shāh 'Abbās the Great. He was celebrated among his countrymen for a supposed peculiar power which he possessed over the magi and writers of talismans, and was one of the most pious devotees of his time. His works on various subjects are much read in Persia, particularly one entitled *Kashkōl*, or the Beggar's Wallet, being an universal miscellany of literature. The *Jā'ma'-ul-Abbāsī*, a concise and comprehensive treatise on Shia law in twenty books, is generally considered as the work of Bahā-uddīn Muhammad 'Amilī, but that lawyer only lived to complete the first five books, dedicating his work to Shāh 'Abbās. The remaining fifteen books were subsequently added by Nizām Ibn-Husain-al-Sāwaī.

Baha-uddin Naqshband (Khwaja) (بہا الدین نقشبند خواجہ), a famous learned Musalmān, who died on Monday the 1st March, A.D. 1389, 2nd Rabī I. A.H. 791, and was buried at Bukhāra.

Baha-uddin Naqshband (Shaikh) (بہا الدین نقشبند شیخ), a celebrated saint and the founder of an Order of Sūfīs, distinguished by the title of Naqshbandī. He is the author of the *Haiāt Nāma*, an esteemed moral poem. He died at Harafa in Persia, A.D. 1453, A.H. 857. He appears also to be the author of a work on Sūfīism called *Dalīl-ul-'Ashiqīn*.

Baha-uddin Sam (بہا الدین سام), son of Ghayās-uddīn Mahmūd, king of Ghōr and Ghaznī. He succeeded his father in A.D. 1210, A.H. 607, at the age of fourteen years, but was, after three months, defeated by Alā-uddīn Atsiz, son of Jahān Sōz, who reigned four years in Ghōr and Ghaznī, and fell in battle against Taj-uddīn Elduz in A.D. 1214. Bahā-uddīn Sām was, after his defeat, taken captive by the governor of Hirāt, and sent to Khwārizm Shāh, who at the time of the invasion of Chingiz Khān, threw him, along with his brother, into a river, where both were drowned.

Baha-uddin Shirazi (بہا الدین شیرازی), a celebrated Kāzī of Shirāz, who died in the year A.D. 1380, A.H. 782.

Baha-uddin Wald (Maulana) (بہا الدین ولد مولانا), a native of Balkh and the father of the celebrated Jalāl-uddīn Maulawī Rūmī. He flourished and enjoyed distinguished honours in the time of Sultān Muhammad, surnamed Qutb-uddīn of Khwārizm. He was an enthusiastic follower of the doctrine of the Sūfīs, and became so celebrated as a preacher and expounder that people flocked from all parts of Persia to hear him discourse. In the latter part of his life he left his native country and went and dwelt at Qonia (Iconium) in Asiatic Turkey, where he died about the year A.D. 1230 or 1233, A.H. 628 or 631, and his son succeeded him as the head of the sect.

Baha-uddin Zikaria (Shaikh) (بها الدين زكريا شيخ), a Muhammadan saint of Multān, was the son of Qutb-uddīn Muhammad, the son of Kamāl-uddīn Qureshī. He was born at Kōṭkaroṛ in Multān in A.D. 1170, A.H. 565. After his studies he journeyed to Baghdād and became a disciple of Shaikh Shahāb-uddīn Suharwardī. He afterwards returned to Multān, where he became intimate with Farīd-uddīn Shakarganj. He died at Multān on the 7th November, A.D. 1266, 7th Ṣafar, A.H. 665, aged 100 lunar years, and is still considered one of the most revered saints of India. He left enormous wealth to his heirs. His son Shaikh Sadr-uddīn died at Multān in A.D. 1309, A.H. 709.

Baha-uddin (بها الدين) (Badī'-uddīn or Bogo-neddīn), a Muhammadan saint whose tomb is in the neighbourhood of Bukhāra, called Mazāri Bogo-neddīn. During the invasion of the Russians at that place, it is said that a book, written in verse in the Persian language, was found in the tomb of this saint. It is said in this book that in the 82nd year of the Hijrah, A.D. 1865, the Christians will rush upon Tashkand like a river. In the 84th year A.D. 1867, they will occupy Samarkand, and sweep it away like a prickly thorn. In the 88th year, A.D. 1871, the Christians will take Bokhāra, and convert it into a level like the steppe. In the year 90th but one, A.D. 1872, the Khwārizmians will run out of their own accord to meet them like children.

Bahishti (بهشتی), poetical name of Shaikh Ramzān, the son of 'Abdul Muhsin, an author, who died A.D. 1571, A.H. 979.

Bahjat (بهجت), or Behjat, author of a Dīwān which contains chiefly Ghazals, and at the end a very silly Qaseada in praise of Europeans. He was living in Lucknow in A.D. 1797, A.H. 1212.

Bahlol (بهلول), who lived during the reign of the khalīf Hārūn-al-Rashīd, was one of those people who pass amongst the Musalmāns either for saints or madmen. Although surnamed Al-Majnūn, or the Fool, he was possessed of a great deal of wit.

Bahloli (بهلولی), a poet, whose Dīwān was found in the Library of Tīpū Sulṭān.

Bahlol Lodi (Sultan) (بهلول لودي سلطان), a king of Dehlī of the tribe of Afghāns called Lōdī. His father, Mālik Kālā, was the son of Ibrahīm Khān or Mālik Bahrām, governor of Multān. In the year A.D. 1450, A.H. 854, Bahlōl, during the absence at Badāon of Sulṭān Alā-uddīn, son of Muhammad Shāh, took possession of Dehlī. He, however, gave place to the name of the Sulṭān for some time in the khutba; but when that prince promised to cede to him the empire, upon condition that he would permit him to live quietly in the possession of Badāon, Sulṭān Bahlōl immediately threw the name of 'Alā-uddīn out of the khutba and caused himself to be crowned on the 18th January, A.D. 1452, 25th Ẕil-ḥijja, A.H. 855. Bahlōl reigned 38 lunar years, 7 months and 7 days, and died on the 1st July, A.D. 1489, 2nd Sha'bān, A.H. 894. He is buried at Dehlī near the tomb of Nasīr-uddīn Mahmūd, surnamed Chirāgh Dehlī, a Musalmān saint, and was succeeded by his son Nizam Khān, who assumed the title of Sikandar Shāh.

The following is a list of the kings of Dehlī of the tribe of Lodī Afghāns:

Bahlōl Lōdī.
Sikandar Shāh, son of Bahlōl.
Ibrahīm Husain, son of Sikandar, who was the last of this race, and was defeated and slain by Bābar Shāh.

Bahman (بهمن), an ancient king of Persia, better known in history by his title of Ardisher Darāzdast, which see.

Bahmani, name of a dynasty in the Deccan, founded by an Afghān adventurer, 'Ala-ud-din Hasan Gango, (*q.v.*), A.D. 1347, A.H. 748.

Bahman Yar Khan (بهمن یار خان), son of Shāista Khān and grandson of Āsaf Khān, a nobleman of the court of the emperor 'Alamgīr.

Bahram I. (بهرام) (Varanes of the Greeks), the fourth king of the Sasānian race, was the son of Hurmuz (Hormisdas), whom he succeeded to the Persian throne in the year A.D. 273. He was a mild and munificent prince, and much beloved by his subjects. The most remarkable act of his reign was the execution of the celebrated Mānī (Manes), the founder of the sect of the Manichœans.

[*Vide* Mānī. Bahrām reigned only three years and three months, after which he died and left the crown to his son Bahrām II. about the year A.D. 276.]

Bahram II. (بهرام), (some authors term him the fourth of that name), was the son of Bahrām I. whom he succeeded to the crown of Persia in A.D. 276. He reigned 17 years, and after his demise was succeeded by his son Bahrām III. about the year A.D. 293.

Bahram III. (بهرام) succeeded his father, Bahrām II. to the Persian throne about the year A.D. 293, reigned only four months, and was succeeded by his brother, Narsī or Narses.

Bahram IV. (بهرام), the twelfth king of Persia of the Sasānian race, succeeded his brother Shāhpūr (Sapores) (*q.v.*) about the year A.D. 390, and is distinguished from other princes of the same name by his title of Kirmanshāh, which he received from having, during the reign of his brother, filled the station of ruler of the province of Kirmān; and he has perpetuated it by founding the city of Kirmānshāh. He reigned, according to some accounts, eleven years; and to others fifteen. He was killed by an arrow when endeavouring to quell a tumult in his army, and was succeeded by Yezdijard I. who is called Isdigerdes by the Greek authors.

Bahram V. (بهرام) (or Varanes V.), the fourteenth king of Persia of the Sasānian dynasty, who is known, in Persian history, by the name of Bahrām Gōr. He was the son of Yezdijard I. whom he succeeded to the throne of Persia in A.D. 420. The word Gōr signifies a wild ass: an animal to the chase of which this monarch was devoted; and it was in pursuit of one of these that he lost his life; having suddenly come upon a deep pool, into which his horse plunged, and neither the animal nor his royal rider were ever seen again. The first rhythmical composition in the Persian language is recorded to have been the production of Bahrām and his mistress Dilārām. Bahrām visited India, was contemporary with Theodosius the emperor of Constantinople, and ruled Persia eighteen years. He died in A.D. 438, and was succeeded by his son Yezdijard II.

Bahram (بهرام), an author who wrote the History of the Parsīs of Bombay in A.D. 1599, entitled *Qissai Sunjān*.

Bahram Chobin (بهرام چوبین), or Joviān, a general of Hurmuz III. king of Persia, whom he deposed; he reigned eight months, about the year A.D. 590.

[*Vide* Hurmuz III.]

Bahram Mirza (بهرام مرزا), son of Shāh Samā'īl Ṣafawī. He was a good poet and died in the prime of youth in A.D. 1550, A.H. 957.

Bahram Saqqa (بهرام سقه), a poet, was of Turkish extraction and belonged to the Bayāt tribe. It is said that the prophet Khizr appeared to him, and a divine light filled him. He renounced the world and became a water-carrier.

[Vide *Āīn Translation*, i. p. 581.]

Bahram Sarakhsi (بهرام سرخسی), a Prosodian of Sarakhs, a town between Naishāpūr and Marv.

Bahram Shah (بهرام شاه), son of Sultān Masa'ūd III. ascended the throne of Ghaznī by the assistance of Sultān Sanjar his uncle, after his brother Arsalān Shāh, who was put to death in A.D. 1118, A.H. 512. Bahrām Shāh, after a prosperous reign of 35 lunar years, was defeated in A.D. 1152, A.H. 547, by 'Alā-uddīn Hasan Ghōrī, and fled to Lāhore, where he died the same year, and his son Khusro Shāh succeeded him in the government of Lāhore. The poets Shaikh Sa'nāī and Abū'l Majd-bin-'Adam-al-Ghaznawī flourished in the time of Bahrām Shāh.

Bahram Shah (بهرام شاه), surnamed Ma'iz-uddīn, was the son of Sultān Rukn-uddīn Fīrōz. He was raised to the throne of Dehlī after the murder of Sultāna Razia the queen, on Monday the 21st April, A.D. 1240. He reigned little more than two years, and was slain by the instigation of Mahzab-uddīn wazīr, about the 15th May, A.D. 1242, when Sultān 'Alā-uddīn Masa'ūd, another son of Sultān Altimsh, was raised to the throne. Firishta erroneously says that Bahrām was the son of Altimsh and brother of Sultāna Razia.

Bahramand Khan (بهره‌مند خان), son of Mirzā Bahrām, and one of the emperor 'Alamgīr's oldest nobility and his friend. After the death of Rūh-ullāh-Khān, he was raised to the post of Mīr Bakhshī or chief paymaster by the emperor in A.D. 1692, A.H. 1103, and died in the Deccan on the 17th October, O.S. 1702, 5th Jumāda II. A.H. 1114. He was buried at his own request in a small tomb at Bahādurgurh. He was succeeded in his office by Zulfiqār Khān Nasrat Jang, who notwithstanding this appointment continued in the command of the army against the Marhattas in the Deccan.

Bahr-ul Hifz (بحر الحفظ), (or the Sea of Memory,) is the title of Abū Usmān-bin-'Amrū, who wrote a book on the manners and qualities of princes. He died A.D. 869, A.H. 255.

Bahu Begam (بهو بیگم), the mother of Nawāb Asf-ud-daula of Lucknow. She died on the 28th December, 1815. She was one of the "Begams" on whose ill-treatment was based a charge in the impeachment of Warren Hastings.

Baian (بیان), the poetical name of Khwāja Ahsan-uddīn or Ahsan-ullah Khān of Agra, who was living at Dehlī in A.D. 1760, A.H. 1174.

Baiazid I. (Sultan) (بايزيد سلطان), whom we call Bajazet, surnamed Ilderim, or Lightning, succeeded his father, Murād I. (Amurath) in A.D. 1389, A.H. 791, as Sulṭān of the Turks. He caused his elder brother Ya'kūb, his rival for the throne, to be strangled, an act of barbarity which since his time prevailed as a custom at the Turkish court. He conquered Bulgaria, Macedonia, and Thessaly; and after he had made the emperor of Constantinople tributary to his power, he marched to attack Tamerlane in the east. He was, however, totally defeated near Angora on Friday the 21st July, A.D. 1402, 19th Ẓil-hijja, A.H. 804, and taken prisoner; and when the proud conqueror asked him what he would have done with him if he had obtained the victory, Bāiazīd answered that he would have confined him in an iron cage. "Such then shall be thy fate," rejoined Tamerlane, and ordered him to be carried about with his camp in an iron cage. Bāiazīd died on the 8th March, A.D. 1403, 13th Sha'bān, A.H. 805, at Antioch in Pisidia during his confinement in Taimūr's camp. His son Mūsa, who was with his father at the time of his death, brought his remains to Brusa and buried them there. During his (Mūsa's) absence in the camp, his brother Sulaimān had ascended the throne.

Baiazid II. (Sultan) (بايزيد سلطان), emperor of Turkey, succeeded his father Muhammad II. to the throne of Constantinople in May, A.D. 1481, Rabī I. A.H. 886. He extended the boundaries of his kingdom; and obliged the Venetians to sue for peace. His reign was distracted by intestine discord, and he fell by the perfidy of his son Salīm I. who caused him to be poisoned in A.D. 1512, A.H. 918, in the 60th year of his age and 31st of his reign. He was a man of uncommon talents, and did much for the improvement of his empire and the promotion of the sciences.

Baiazid Ansari (بايزيد انصاري), the Afghān Apostle, called Pīr Rōshan, founder of the Sūfī sect called "Rōshania," or "the enlightened." He had established amid the mountains of Afghānistān a temporal power upon the authority of his spiritual character, which enabled him and his successors to disturb the tranquility of the empire of Dehlī, when, under the celebrated Akbar, it had reached the very zenith of its power.

Baiazid Bustami (Khwaja) (بايزيد بسطامي خواجه), the famous ascetic of Bustām, whose original name was Taifūrī; he is therefore sometimes called Bāiazīd Taifūrī-al-Bustāmī. His father's name was 'Isa-ibn-Ādam-ibn-'Isa-ibn-'Alī. His grandfather was a Gabr or magian, but became a convert to Islāmism. These two brothers, Ādam and 'Alī, were, like himself, devout ascetics, but in an inferior degree. He was born in the year A.D. 777, A.H. 160, lived to a great age, and died between the years A.D. 845 or 848, A.H. 231 or 234, but according to Ibn-Khalikān his death took place in A.D. 875 or 878, A.H. 261 or 264. He is said to have been a contemporary of Ahmad Khizroya, who died A.H. 240.

Baiazid Khan (بايزيد خان), Faujdār of Sarhind, who was commanded by the emperor Farrukh-siyar to punish the Sikhs, who had risen in rebellion; he took the field, but was assassinated in his tent when alone at evening prayers, by a Sikh commissioned for that purpose by Banda their chief, and the murderer escaped unhurt. This circumstance took place about the year A.D. 1714, A.H. 1126.

Baiazid (Sultan) (بايزيد سلطان). There is a cenotaph at Chaṭigāon (Chittagong), called the Rauza of Sulṭān Bāiazīd. It is related that he was born at Bustām in Khurāsān, of which country he was king; but abandoning regal pomp and cares for the tranquility of the ascetic life, he came with twelve attending disciples to Chaṭigāon. Their arrival was promptly opposed by the king of the fairies and the attendant genii, who desired them forthwith to depart. Sulṭān Bāiazīd, with feigned humility, entreated to be allowed to remain that night and to occupy only as much ground as could be illumined by a single lamp, called in Bengāli chaṭī or chaṭ; on obtaining their consent, he kindled from his urine a lamp of such radiance, that its light extended to Tīk Naof, a distance of 120 miles, and scorched the terrified genii, who fled from its flame in dismay. In commemoration of this event, the place was named Chaṭigram, in common parlance, Chaṭgāon, signifying the village of the lamp. This insult and breach of confidence led to implacable war on the part of the genii, whom Sulṭān Bāiazīd, in various conflicts, drove from the field; and in his strenuous exertions dropped a ring where the cenotaph now stands—his Karanphūl, or ear-ring, fell in the river, which thence was named the "Karanphūlī"; and a sankh, or shell, dropped from his hand into the other stream, from which it derived the name of Sankhautī. Sulṭān Bāiazīd then became a Gorchela (*i.e.* did penance in the tomb) for 12 years: after endowing it with lands to keep it in repair and defray the expenses of pilgrims and the twelve disciples, he proceeded to Makanpūr, and was succeeded by his disciple Shah, who, in the hope of an eternal reward, performed the penance of standing for 12 years on one leg, after which he also proceeded to Makanpūr; leaving the cenotaph under the charge of Shāh Pīr, an attending disciple of Bāiazīd. This place was therefore in after ages held in great repute, and visited by numerous pilgrims from distant parts. It is situated on a hill, ascended by a flight of steps, inclosed by a wall about 30 feet square and 15 high, with mitred battlements, and a pillar rising two feet above them at each angle, similar to the buildings of the time of Akbar. The tomb, about 12 feet by 9, is in the centre of the area, with some shells and corals deposited at its head.

Baiazid Taifuri-al-Bustami (بايزيد طيفوری البسطامی). *Vide* Bāiazīd Bustāmi.

Baidu Khan (بايدو خان), the son of Turaghāī and grandson of Halākū Khān, succeeded Kaikhatū or Kaijaptū Khān in January, A.D. 1295, Ṣafar, A.H. 694, and enjoyed the crown of Persia only seven months: he was dethroned and slain by his nephew, Ghāzān Khān, the son of Arghūn Khān; who was compelled to attack his uncle and sovereign to preserve himself from destruction. This event took place in October the same year, Ẓil-ḥijja, A.H. 694. In English Histories he is called Batu. In 1235, at the head of half a million of Keptchak Mongols, he conquered the east of Russia, destroying Riazan, Moscow, Vlandimir and other towns.

Baihaqi (بيهقی), surnamed Abū'l Fazl, and whose proper name is Abū Bakr Ahmad, was the son of Husain Baihaqī. He is the author of the works in Arabic called *Sunan Kubra and Sughra* and of one entitled *Sha'b-ul-Imān*, He died in the year A.D. 1066, A.H. 458. His collection of Traditions is also of the highest authority.

Baiju (بيجو), one of the most celebrated songsters of India, besides Nāek, Gopāl, and Fansin.

Baiqara Mirza (Sultan) (بايقرا مرزا سلطان), the son of Umar Shaikh Mirzā, the second son of Amīr Taimūr. Bāiqara succeeded his brother as governor of Persia in A.D. 1394, A.H. 796. His eldest brother, Pīr Muhammad Jahāngīr, was slain in A.D. 1405, A.H. 808. Bāiqara, Mirzā was slain by his uncle Shāhrukh Mirzā in A.D. 1416, A.H. 819; he left a son named Mansūr, who became the father of Sulṭān Husain Mirzā, surnamed Abū'l Ghāzī Bahādur.

Bairam (بيرام), sometimes erroneously written by us for Bahrām. It is the T. name of the planet Mars.

Bairam Beg (بيرام بيگ) was father of Munīm Khān. The latter was a grandee in Humāyūn's Court.

[Vide *Āīn Translation*, vol. i. p. 317.]

Bairam Khan (بيرام خان), styled Khān Khānān, or Lord of lords, was one of the most distinguished officers of the Mughal court. He was a Turkmān and descended from a line of ancestors who served for many generations in the family of Taimūr. Bairām accompanied the emperor Humāyūn from Persia to India, and on the accession of his son Akbar, he was honoured with the title of Khān Khānān and the office of prime minister; and had the whole civil and military powers vested in his hands. When Akbar in A.D. 1558, A.H. 965, thought he was capable of acting for himself, he dismissed Bairām Khan from the wizārat. Bairām at first had recourse to rebellion, but being unsuccessful, was compelled to throw himself on the clemency of his sovereign, who not only pardoned him but assigned to him a pension of 50,000 rupees annually for his support. Bairām soon after took leave of the emperor with the design of making a pilgrimage to Mecca, and had proceeded to Gujrāt in order to embark for Mecca, but was slain by one Mubārik Khān Lohānī, whose father Bairām Khān had slain in battle with his own hand during the reign of the emperor Humāyūn. This event took place on Friday the 31st January, A.D. 1561, 14th Jumāda I. A.H. 968. He was at first buried near the tomb of Shaikh Hisām at Gujrāt, but afterwards his remains were transported to Mashhad and buried there. He is the author of a Dīwān.

Baizawi (Qazi) (بيضاوی قاضی), the surname of Nasir-uddīn Abū'l Khair Abdullāh-ibn-Umar al Baizāwī. He was a native of Baizā, a village of Shīrāz, on which account he is styled Baizāwī. He held the office of Qāzī or Judge of the city of Shīrāz for a considerable time, and died at Tabriz or Tauris in the year A.D. 1286, A.H. 685, or as others say in A.D. 1292, A.H. 691. He is the author of the well-known Commentary on the Qurān called *Tafsīr Baizāwī*, which is also called *Anwār-ul-Tanzīl*, and *Asrār-ul-Tāwīl*. Some say that he is also the author of a history entitled *Nizāmut Tawārīkh*, but the author of this work is said by others to be Abu Sa'īd Baizāwī, which see.

Baisanghar (Mirza) (بايسنغر مرزا), son of Mirzā Shāhrukh, the son of Amīr Taimūr. He was a learned and noble prince, a great protector of letters and learned men. He himself wrote six different hands, composed verses in the Persian and Turkish languages, and constantly had in his employment forty copyists for transcribing MSS. He was born in the year A.D. 1399, A.H. 802, and died before his father in A.D. 1434, A.H. 837, at Herāt, aged 35 lunar years.

Baisanghar (Mirza) (بايسنغر مرزا), son of Sulṭān Husain Mirzā of Herāt. He was killed by Khusro Shāh, king of Qundaz.

Bajazet, name of several Turkish emperors spelt so in English, being a corruption of Bāiazīd, which see.

Baji Bai (باجی بائی), also called Bīja Bāī, which see.

Baji Rao I. (Peshwa) (باجی راؤ پیشوا), the son of Bālājī Rāo Bishwanāth Peshwā, whom he succeeded in October, A.D. 1720. He was the ablest of all the Brāhmaṇ dynasty, and perhaps of all the Marhaṭṭa nation, except Sewājī. He died on the 28th April, O.S. 1740, 12th Ṣafar, A.H. 1153, and left three sons, *viz.* Bālājī Bājī Rāo, who succeeded him as Peshwā; Rāghnuāth Rāo, commonly called Rāghoba, who was at one time much connected with the English, and was the father of the last Peshwā Bājī Rāo II.; and Shamsher Bahādur, to whom (though an illegitimate son by a Muhammadan woman, and brought up in his mother's religion), he left all his possessions and pretensions in Bundelkhand.

Baji Rao II. (باجی راؤ پیشوا), the last Peshwā, was the eldest son of Rāghoba or Rāghunāth Rāo of ambiguous memory. He succeeded Mādho Rāo, the infant Peshwā, who died suddenly in October, A.D. 1795, During the reign of Mādho Rāo he and his brother Chimnājī were confined in the fort of Juneir, near Pūna, and after his death Chimnājī was furtively invested, but he was soon after deposed and Bājī Rāo was publicly proclaimed Peshwā by Daulat Rāo Scindhia on the 4th December, A.H. 1796. In May, A.D. 1818, a proclamation was issued by Government deposing him for rebellion; and the Rāja of Sitāra, Partāp Singh Nārāyan released from confinement, had a part of the Pūna territories assigned for his support, and was vested with the reality of that power of which his ancestors in latter times had enjoyed only the name. Bājī Rāo was compelled to surrender himself to the English, and was pensioned on the 3rd June, A.D. 1818. The pension allowed him by Government was 800,000 rupees per annum. He died at Biṭhūr, near Cawnpore, in December, A.D. 1852, and was succeeded by his adopted son Dhondū Pant, commonly called Nānā Sāhib (*q.v.*), who became a rebel in the disturbances of 1857.

[See Colebrooke's *Mountstuart Elphinstone*.]

Bakhat Singh (بخت سنگه), or Bakht Singh Rāṭhor, son of Ajīt Singh and brother of Abhai Singh, Rāja of Jodhpūr. He was poisoned in A.D. 1752.

Bakhshi 'Ali Khan (بخشی علی خان), whose poetical name was Hashmat, flourished in the time of Nawāb Salābat Jang of Hyderabad, about the year A.D. 1751, A.H. 1164.

Bakhshi Bano Begam (بخشی بانو بیگم), a sister of the emperor Akbar the Great.

Bakhtaiar Beg Gurdi Shah Mansur (بختیار بیگ گرد شاه), Turkman, was an Amīr, and governed (1001) Siwistan.

[Vide *Āīn Translation*, vol. i. p. 474.]

Bakhtaiar Khilji (بختیار خلجی). *Vide* Muhammad Bakhtaiār Khiljī.

Bakhtari (بختری), one of the most celebrated Arabian poets, who died in the year A.D. 823. According to some writers, he was born in A.D. 821, A.H. 208, flourished in the time of the khalīf Al-Musta'īn Billāh, and died in his 63rd year at Baghdād. He is also called Bin-Bakhtarī.

Bakhtawar Khan (بختاور خان), an amīr who served under the emperor Alamgīr. The Sarāe of Bakhtāwarnagar, near Dehlī, was constructed by him in A.D. 1671, A.H. 1082. He is the author of the work called *Mirat-ul-'Alam*, a history of the first part of the reign of 'Alamgīr. He died in A.D. 1684, A.H. 1095.

[*Vide* Nāzir Bakhtaiār Khān.]

Bakhtishu (بختیشوع), name of a Christian physician in the service of Harūn-al-Rashīd.

Bakshu (بخشو), a singer, lived at the Court of Rāja Bikramājit Manṣur; but when his patron lost his throne he went to Rāja Kirāt of Kālinjar. Not long afterwards he accepted a call to Gujrāt, where he remained at the Court of Sulṭān Bahādur, A.D. 1526 to 1536.

[Vide *Āīn Translation*, vol. i. p. 611.]

Baktash Quli (بکتاش قلی), a Musalmān writer of the Persian sect, who wrote a book called *Bostān-al-Khayāl*, or the Garden of Thoughts. (Watkin's Biographical Dictionary.) See also Amīrī, who also wrote a book of that name.

Balaji Rao Bishwa Nath Peshwa (بالاجی راؤ بشو ناتهه پیشوا), the founder of the Brāhman dynasty of Peshwā, was the hereditary accountant of a village in the Kokan. He afterwards entered into the service of a chief of the Jādo family, whence he was transferred to that of the Rāja Sāhū, son of Sambhājī, chief of the Marhattas. His merits were at length rewarded with the office of Peshwā, at that time second in the State. He died in October, A.D. 1720, and was succeeded by his son Bājī Rāo Peshwā.

List of Hereditary Peshwās of Pūna.

Bālājī Rāo Bishwanāth Peshwā.
Bājī Rāo Peshwā, son of Bālājī.

Bālājī Bāji Rāo, son of Bājī Rāo.
Mādho Rāo Bilāl, son of Bālājī, succeeded under the regency of his uncle Rāghunāth Rāo.
Nārāyan Rāo Peshwā, brother of Mādho Rāo.
Rāghunāth Rāo, son of Bājī Rāo Peshwā I.
Mādho Rāo II. posthumous son of Nārāyan Rāo.
Bājī Rāo II. son of Rāghunāth Rāo, proclaimed himself, and was taken by Sindhia.
Chimnājī, furtively invested at Pūna, 26th May, 1796.
Bājī Rāo II. publicly proclaimed, 4th December, 1796. Surrendered to and pensioned by the English, 3rd June, 1818, and Partāp Singh Nārāyan, the Rāja of Sitāra, released from confinement.

Balaji Baji Rao (بالاجی باجی راؤ), also called Bālā Rāo Pandit Pradhān, was the son of Bājī Rāo Peshwā I. and succeeded his father in April, A.D. 1740. He was at Pūna when the battle between the Marhattas and Ahmad Shāh Abdālī took place in January, A.D. 1761, but died in the month of June of the same year, leaving three sons, *viz.*, Biswās Rāo, who was killed in the battle of Pānīpat, Mādho Rāo, and Nārāyan Rāo.

Baland Akhtar (بلند اختر), a brother of the emperor Muhammad Shāh. *Vide* Achchhe.

Balash (بالاش). *Vide* Pālāsh or Pālās.

Balban (بلبن), a king of Dehlī. *Vide* Ghayās-uddīn Balban.

Balbhaddar Singh (بلبهدر سنگه), a Rāja lineally descended from the ancient Hindū monarchs of Audh, who, having 100,000 Rājpūts at his command, considered himself as equal to the Nawāb Wazīr of Lucknow, whose authority he disclaimed. To reduce this Rāja an army was sent about the year A.D. 1780, composed partly of the Nawāb's troops, and partly of the Company's sepoys; but owing to the intrigues of Haidar Beg Khān, the minister of the Nawāb Wazīr Asaf-uddaula, and the native collectors, who extorted large sums from the zamīndārs, this expedition failed of success. During two years he was frequently defeated and pursued; and at length being surprised in his camp, he was killed in endeavouring to make his escape.

Baldeo Singh (بلدیو سنگه), the Jāt Rāja of Bhartpūr, was the second son of Ranjīt Singh. He succeeded to the Raj after the death of his eldest brother, Randhīr Sindh.

Baligh (بلیغ), author of the *Dalāel Zahira*, *Talauwan Qudrat*, and *Makālima*. He was a native of India and was living in A.D. 1772, A.H. 1186.

Balin, erroneously written by some for Balban, which see.

Balqini (بلقینی), *Vide* Bīlqainī.

Balti (بالتی) (*vide* Jodh Baī), the daughter of Rāja Udaia Singh Rāthor, commonly called Motha Rāja; she was married to the emperor Jahangīr and became the mother of Shāh Jahan. She died in A.D. 1619, A.H. 1028.

Balwan Singh (بلوان سنگه), (who was always called by the natives of Āgra as the Kashī-wala Rāja) was the son of the celebrated Chait Singh, Rāja of Banaras. Balwan Singh was born at Gwaliar, and after his father's death, he and his family lived in the city of Āgra for many years on a monthly pension of 2000 rupees. He lost his only son, Kūwar Chakarbatī Singh, on the 17th December, 1871, and after a few days, on the 26th of the same month, he resigned his unusually prolonged life. The only surviving members of this family were the widow of Chakarbatī Singh and his children, a boy aged nine and a girl aged 11 years. Balwān Singh was the author of a Dīwān in Urdū.

Balwant Singh (بلونت سنگه), a Rāja or zamīndār of Banaras. He was the father or brother of the famous Chait Singh who rebelled against the British, and was arrested and deposed by Mr. Hastings in 1781. Balwant Singh succeeded his father Mansa Ram in A.D. 1740, reigned 30 years, died in 1770, and was succeeded by Rājā Chait Singh.

Balwant Singh ((بلونت سنگه), Rāja of Bhartpūr, succeeded his father, Baldeo Singh, in August, 1824; was displaced by one of his cousins, named Durjān Sāl, in March, 1825; but reinstated by the British Government on the 19th January, 1826. Bhartpūr was stormed and taken by the Bengal troops under Lord Combermere, on the 18th January. The British lost during the siege 45 officers killed and wounded, and 1500 men; the enemy lost some thousands, and the usurper Durjān Sāl was seized and sent to Allahābād. His father, Baldeo Singh, was the second brother of Randhīr Singh, the eldest of the four sons of Ranjīt Singh the son of Kehrī Singh, the brother of Ratan Singh, the brother of Jawāhir Singh, the son of Sūrajmal, the son of Chūrāman Jāt, the founder of the principality. Balwant Singh died aged 34 years on the 16th March, 1853, and was succeeded by his infant son Jaswant Singh.

Banana (بنانه), an Arabian poet whose full name is Abū Bakr-bin-Muhammad bin-Banāna. There has been another Bin-Banāna, *viz.*, Abū Nasr-ibn-ul-'Azīz-bin Banāna, who was a poet also, and died at Baghdād in A.D. 1009, A.H. 400.

Banda (بندہ). *Vide* Razī (Maulānā).

Banda (بندہ), a gurū or chief of the Sikhs, and successor of Gurū Gobind. This man obtained great power, and committed great depredations in the province of Lahore, in the reign of Bahādur Shāh I. and while the emperor was in Deccan against his brother Kām Bakhsh, Banda collected his followers, to revenge the death of his predecessor's sons, who were taken prisoners and had been put to death some time before. He committed the greatest cruelties on the Musulmāns, in every advantage shewing no quarter to age or sex, and even ripping up women with child. The emperor found it necessary to march in person against him, and he was besieged in the fortress of Lohgarh, which was taken, but Banda found means to escape, and raise new insurrections. In the reign of the emperor Farrukhsiar, 'Abdus Samad Khān, governor of Kashmīr, was sent against the rebels with a great army. After many severe engagements, he forced Banda to take refuge in a fortress, which was blockaded so effectually as to cut off every supply. The garrison was reduced to the necessity of eating cows, horses, asses, and other animals forbidden by their laws; when at length, having no provision of any sort left, and being reduced to the extremity of famine and disease, they begged for quarter. 'Abdus Samad Khān, having planted a standard on the plain, commanded them to come out and lay their arms under it, which they did. He then divided the meaner sort among his chiefs, who cut off their heads; and threw their bodies into a river near the fortress. Banda and many other captives were sent to Dehlī, through which he was carried in an iron cage upon an elephant, dressed in a robe of gold brocade. The Sikhs bore the insults of the populace with the greatest firmness, and steadily refused the emperor's offers of life if they would embrace the Muhammadan faith. They were put to death, a hundred each day, on the ensuing seven days. On the eighth day Banda and his son were put to death without the city. A dagger was put into his hands, and he was commanded to kill his infant son; but refusing, the child was slain by the executioner, his heart torn out, and forced into the father's mouth. Banda was then put to death by the tearing of his flesh with red hot pincers and other tortures, which he bore with the greatest constancy. This event took place in the year A.D. 1715, A.H. 1127.

Bano Begam (بانو بیگم), the daughter of Shāhnawāz Khān, the son of the Wazīr Asaf Khān, wife of the emperor Alamgīr, and mother of 'Azim Shāh.

Baqai (بقائی), surname of Ibrahīm-bin-'Umar, a learned Musalmān, who is the author of several treatises on ancient philosophers, on divination by numbers, a commentary on the Qurān, etc. He died in the year A.D. 1480, A.H. 885.

Baqai (Mulla) (بقائی ملا), a poet who lived in the time of the emperor Bābar Shāh. He is the author of a poem or Masnawī, which he dedicated to the emperor.

Baqalani (باقلانی), the author of a work called *Ai'jāz-ul-Qurān*, or of the difficult things in the Qurān. See Abū Bakr Bāqalānī.

Baqi Khan (باقی خان), a nobleman of the court of the emperor Shāh Jahān, by whom he was appointed governor of the fort of Āgra. In the 24th year of the reign of the emperor he was raised to the rank of 1500. In the 49th year of the emperor's reign, he still held the governorship of the fort of Āgra, and was raised to the rank of 2000 the following year. He had built in the front of the gate called Hathiapol, which is situated towards the Chauk and the Jama Misjid, a fine bungalow, which was still standing about the year A.D. 1830.

Baqili (بقلی), surname of Abū'l Fazl Muhammad-bin-Qāsim-al-Khwārizmī, who from his learning has the title of Zain-uddīn and Zain-ul-Mashāekh, or the ornament of the doctors. He wrote a book on the prayers of the Musalmāns, on the glory and excellence of the Arabs, called *Salāt-ul-Baqilī*. He died in A.D. 1167, A.H. 562, but according to Hājī Khalfa in A.D. 1170, A.H. 566. There was another Baqilī, also a Muhammadan doctor, who died in A.H. 982.

Baqi Muhammad Khan Koka (باقی محمد خان کوکہ), eldest brother of Adham Khān, the son of Māham Anka, was an officer of 3000 in the time of the emperor Akbar. He died at Garh Katka, where he had a jagīr, in A.D. 1585, A.H. 993.

Baqir (باقر), the poetical name of Muhammad Bāqir Alī Khān, who flourished in the time of the emperor Muhammad Shāh and wrote a Masnawī or poem called *Ramūz-ut-Tāhirīn*, composed in A.D. 1726, A.H. 1139, also another work entitled *Gulshani Asrār*, which he wrote in A.D. 1732, A.H. 1145. He is also the author of a Dīwān, and another poem called *Mirat-ul-Jamāl*.

Baqir Ali Khan (باقر علی خان). *Vide* Bāqir.

Baqir (Imam) (باقر امام). *Vide* Muhammad Bāqir (Imām).

Baqir Kashi (باقر کاشی), whose poetical name is Khirad, was a contemporary of Zahūrī who flourished about the year A.D. 1600, and is the athor of a Dīwān.

Baqir Khan (باقر خاں), a nobleman in the service of the emperor Shāh Jahān. In the latter part of his life, he was appointed governor of Allahābād, where he died in A.D. 1637, A.H. 1047, in which year died also Khān Zamān Bahādur, in Daulatābād.

Baqir Khan (باقر خاں نجم ثانی), surnamed Najm Sānī, an amīr of the reign of Shāh Jahān. He was a very liberal man, fond of literature, and was himself a poet. He died in A.D. 1640, A.H. 1050, but, according to the work *Māzir-ul-Umrā*, in A.D. 1637, A.H. 1047. He is the author of a Dīwān or Book of Odes.

Barahman (برهمن), poetical title of a Brāhman whose name was Chandar Bhān, which see.

Barbak (باربک), the son of Bahlol Lodī, king of Dehlī. *Vide* Husain Shāh Sharqī.

Barbak Shah (باربک شاه), Pūrbī, the son of Nāsir Shāh, whom he succeeded to the throne of Bengal in A.D. 1458. He reigned for a period of 17 years and died in A.D. 1474, A.H. 879.

Barbarassa (باربارسّه), the famous Corsair. Sulaimān, emperor of the Turks, gave him the title of Khair-uddīn, and made him afterwards Pāshā of the sea. He succeeded his brother Aruch, who conquered the kingdom of Algiers, after having killed Salīm the Arabian king. He took Tunis A.D. 1533, A.H. 940, after having driven out the Venetians, but Andrea Doria retook it again A.D. 1536, A.H. 943. After this, he ravaged several parts of Italy, and reduced Yemin, in Arabia Felix, to the Turkish government. Khair-uddīn died at Constantinople in A.D. 1546, A.H. 953, aged 80.

Barbarassa (Aruch) (باربارسّه), a famous pirate. Being called in to assist Salīm, prince of Algiers, against the Spaniards, he murdered that monarch, and took possession of his throne. He afterwards laid siege to Tunis, which he took, and caused himself to be proclaimed sovereign. He was besieged by the Marquis of Gomarez and reduced to the greatest distress. He escaped by a subterraneous passage, but was overtaken with a small number of Turks, the whole of whom died sword in hand in A.D. 1518.

Barbud (باربد), a famous Persian musician, master of music to Khusro Parwez, king of Persia. He composed an air called Aorangī, and invented a musical instrument (a sort of lyre) which bears his name: *i.e.* Bārbud or Bārbut.

Barizi (بارزي), the son of 'Abdul Rahīm, an Arabian author who wrote a commentary on the work called *Asrar-ul-Tanzīl*. He died in A.D. 1337, A.H. 738. This author appears to be the same with Bāzirī, which see.

Barkali (برکلی), the name of two Muhammadan doctors; the one died in A.D. 1553, A.H. 960, and the other in A.D. 1573, A.H. 982. They are sometimes called Birgilī, which see.

Barkat-ullah (Sayyad) (برکت الله سید), styled *Sāhib-ul-Barkāt*, was the son of Sayyad Aweis, the son of Mīr 'Abdul Jalīl, the son of Mīr 'Abdul Wāhid Shāhidī of Bilgarām. His poetical name was 'Ishqī, and as his grandfather's tomb was in Māhara in the district of Āgra, he went and lived in that village till the day of his death, which happened on the 25th July, A.D. 1729, 10th Muharram, A.H. 1142.

Barkayaraq (Sultan) (برکیارق سلطان), the eldest son of Sultān Malikshāh Saljūqī, whom he succeeded in A.D. 1092, A.H. 485. His usual residence was Baghdād. His brother Muhammad ruled over Āzur-baijān; while Sanjar, his third brother, established a kingdom in Khurāsān and Transoxiana, from whence he extended his conquests over the fallen princes of Ghaznī. Barkayāraq reigned twelve years and died in December, A.D. 1104, A.H. 498. His brother Sultān Muhammad succeeded him.

Barmak (برمک), the name of a noble family, originally from Balkh in Khurāsān, and highly celebrated all over the East for their generosity, magnificence, and distinguished patronage of men of genius. One of the most illustrious was governor to the khalīf Harūn-al-Rashīd, and his son Ja'far, afterwards minister to that prince; but having incurred his displeasure, he with several of the heads of the family was put to death. *Vide* Ja'far-al-Barmakī. (The "Barmecide" is familiar to readers of Galland's *Arabian Nights.*)

Baroda (برودا), Rāja of. *Vide* Pelajī.

Barq (برق), poetical name of Muhammad Razā (*q.v.*).

Basasiri بساسيري ("Glutton") was the nickname, and afterwards the surname of Arsalān, who from a slave became Commander-in-Chief of the armies of Bahā-ud-daula, the wazīr of the khalīf of Baghdād. Having quarrelled with him he fled to Egypt and put himself under the protection of Al-Mustanasir Billā, the fifth khalīf of Egypt of the Fatimite dynasty. After some time he came to Baghdād. He took Qāem, the 26th khalīf of the Abbasides, prisoner in Baghdād, deposed him, and caused Mustanasir to be acknowledged the only and legitimate chief of all the Musalmāns. He maintained Mustanasir in the khilāfat for one year and a half, after which Tughral Beg, Sultān of the Saljūqides, put Qāem on the throne of Baghdād again, defeated and killed Basāsīrī A.D. 1059, A.H. 451, and sent his head to Qāem, who caused it to be carried on a pike through the streets of Baghdād.

Bashir-ibn-ul-Lais (بشيرابن الليث), the brother of the arch-rebel Rafa-ibn-ul-Lais, who had revolted against Harūn-al-Rashīd the khalīf of Baghdād in the year A.D. 806, A.H. 190, at Samarqand, and assembled a considerable force to support him in his defection; notwithstanding all Harūn's care, the rebels made in A.D. 807, A.H. 191, great progress in the conquest of Khurāsān. According to Abūl Faraj, in the year A.D. 809, A.H. 193, Bashīr was brought in chains to Hārūn, who was then at the point of death. At the sight of him the khalīf declared, that if he could speak only two words he would say kill him; and immediately ordered him to be cut to pieces in his presence.

Basiti (باسطی), poetical name of a person who is the author of the biography of poets called *Tazkira Bāsitī*.

Basus (باسوس), an Arabian woman, from whom originated a war, called Harb-i-Basūs, which has since become a proverb to express, "Great events from little causes." Two Arabian tribes fought about 40 years because a camel belonging to this woman broke a hen's egg; the owner of the egg wounded the camel with an arrow, and the two tribes were instantly in arms.

Batalmiyusi (بطلميوسی), an Arabian author, who died in A.D. 1030, A.H. 421. He wrote a treatise on the qualities requisite in a secretary and good writer, and another on genealogies.

Batu Khan (باتو خاں), the son of Jūjī Khān, and grandson of Changez Khān. He ruled at Kipchak and was contemporary with Pope Innocent IV.

Bauwab (بوّاب) (or Bouwāb), surname of Abū'l Hasan 'Alī Kāla, who is better known under the name of ibn-Bouwāb. It is he who improved the form of the Arabic Alphabet after Ibn-Maqla. He died in A.D. 1022, A.H. 413, or as some say in A.D. 1032, A.H. 423. After him Yā'kūb, surnamed Mustaa'simī, reduced it to its present form.

Baz Bahadur (باز بهادر) whose original name was Mālik Bāiazīd, succeeded his father Shujāa' Khān to the government of Mālwa in A.D. 1554, A.H. 962, and having taken possession of many towns in Mālwa which were previously almost independent, he ascended the throne under the title of Sultān Bāz Bahādur. His attachment to Rūpmatī, a celebrated courtezan of that age, became so notorious, that the loves of Bāz Bahādur and Rūpmati have been handed down to posterity in song. He reigned about 17 years, after which the kingdom of Mālwa was taken, and included among the provinces of the empire of Dehlī, by the emperor Akbar in the year A.D. 1570, A.H. 978. Bāz Bahādur afterwards joined Akbar at Dehlī and received a commission as an officer of 2000 cavalry. Bāz Bahādur and Rūpmati are both buried in the centre of the tank at Ujjain.

[*Vide* Rupmati.]

Baz Khan (باز خاں), an amīr in the service of the emperor Bahādur Shāh. He was killed in the battle against Azim Shah (*q.v.*) on the 8th June, o.s. 1707, 18th Rabī' I. A.H. 1118, near Dhaulpūr.

Bazil (باذل). *Vide* Rafī Khān Bāzil.

Bazil (باذل), the poetical name of Badr-uddīn, Ismaīl-al-Tabrizī, an Arabian author.

Baziri (بازری), author of a poem entitled *Koukab-al-Darriat* or the Brilliant Star, in praise of Muhammad, who cured him, as he said, of the palsy in a dream. Every line of the poem ends with an M., the initial of the prophet's name, and it is so highly valued that many of the Muhammadans learnt it by heart, on account of its maxims. (Lempriere's *Universal Dictionary* under Bausirri.) Bārizī and Bāzirī appear to be the same person.

Bazmi (بزمی), author of the *Padmāwat* in Persian verse. He was a native of Karkh and resided for some time at Shīrāz. He came to Gujrāt during the reign of the emperor Jahāngīr, and composed the above-mentioned poem in A.D. 1619, A.H. 1028. He was living at Dehlī in the time of Shāh Jahān about the year 1634. His proper name was 'Abdul Shakūr

Bazzaz (بزاز), the author of the *Adāb-al-Mufridāt* or a treatise on the particular conditions and properties of traditions, and some other works on the Muhammadan theology.

Bebadal Khan (بی بدل خان), a poet of Persia who came to India in the reign of the emperor Jahāngīr, and flourished in the time of Shāh Jahān, who conferred on him the title of Bebadal Khān. Under his superintendence the Peacock throne was constructed. Bebadal Khān appears to be the former title of Abū Tālib Kalīm.

Bedar (بیدار), the poetical name of Sanāth Singh, a Hindū, who was living in A.D. 1753, A.H. 1166.

Bedar (بیدار), an author whose proper name was Imām Bakhsh, a native of Ambāla. He is the author of the work called *Tārikh Sa'ādat*, being an account of the progress of the dynasty which ruled over Audh from Shujāa'-uddaula to Sa'ādat 'Alī Khān, to whose name the title is an allusion. It was composed in A.D. 1812, A.H. 1227. He is also the author of several Masnawīs, one of which contains the praises of Nawāb Sa'ādat 'Alī Khān, called *Gulshān-i-Sa'ādat*. He was living in the time of Nasīr-uddīn Haidar, king of Audh.

Bedar Bakht (Prince) (بیدار بخت), son of 'Azim Shāh. He was killed in the battle fought by his father against the emperor Bahādur Shāh on the 8th June, O.S. 1707, A.H. 1119.

Bedar Bakht (بیدار بخت), son of Ahmad Shāh, king of Dehlī. He was elevated to the throne of Dehlī on the 1st September, A.D. 1788, 27th Ẓi-Ka'da, A.H. 1202, when Ghulām Qadir imprisoned Shāh Alam. Bedar Bakht continued to reign until the approach of the Marhattas towards Dehlī, when he fled upon the 12th October, 1788, but was subsequently apprehended and put to death by the orders of Shāh Alam.

Bedil (Mirza) (بیدل مرزا), the poetical name of Saīdaī Gilanī, which see.

Begam Sultan (بیگم سلطان), a lady of rank, whose tomb is to be seen to this day, outside of the gate of Ya'tmād-uddaula's mausoleum in Āgra. From the inscription that is on her tomb, it appears that she died in the time of the emperor Humayūn in A.D. 1538, A.H. 945, and that she was the daughter of Shaikh Kamāl.

Begana (بیگانه), the poetical name of Abū'l Hasan.

Bekasi (Maulana) (بیکسی مولانا), a poet who lived in the time of the emperor Akbar.

Bekasi (Maulana) (بیکسی مولانا), a poet of Shīrāz who was contemporary with Ghizalī, who died in the year A.D. 1111, A.H. 505.

Bekhabar (بیخبر), the poetical name of Mīr'Azmat-ullah, son of Lutf-ullah of Bilgrām. He died in A.D. 1729, A.H. 1142, at Dehlī. He is the author of the work called *Safīnae Bekhabar*.

Bekhud (بیخود), poetical name of Mulla Jāmī Lāhaurī Namdār Khānī, which see.

Bekhud (بیخود), poetical name of Sayyad Hadī 'Alī, son of Sayyad Nāsir 'Alī Sehr, and author of a Dīwān.

Bengal, Sultāns and Governors of. *Vide* Muhammad Baghtaiār Khiljī, and Khān Jahān.

Beni Narayan. A Hindu by birth, but follower of the warlike teacher Sāyyad Āhmad (*q.v.*). He wrote a sort of biographic anthology called *Tazkira-i-Jahān* (published 1812) and many other works in prose and verse. (De Tassy, *Hist. de la litt. hind.* 115.)

Berar (برار راجه), Rāja of. *Vide* Rāghōjī Bhōsla.

Betab (بیتاب), whose proper name is Abbas 'Alī Khān, which see.

Bhagwan Das (Raja) (بهگوانداس راجه), called by Abū'l Fazl Bhagwant Dās was the son of Rāja Bihāra Mal Kachhwāha Ambhar or Amer, now Jaipūr. His daughter was married to the prince Mirzā Salīm (afterwards Jahāngīr) in the year A.D. 1585, A.H. 993, by whom he had a daughter named Sultān-un-nisā Begam, and then a son who became Sultān Khusro (*q.v.*). Bhagwān Dās died five days after the death of Rāja Todar Mal, *i.e.* on the 15th November, A.D. 1589, 19th Muharram, A.H. 998, at Lāhore. After his death, the emperor Akbar, who was then at Kābul, conferred the title of Rāja on his son Mān Singh with the rank of 5000.

Bhagwant Singh (بهگونت سنگه), rānā of Dhaulpūr (1857). He died on the 14th February, 1873.

Bhanbu Khan (بهنبو خان), the son of Zabitā Khān, which see.

Bhartrihari, brother of Rāja Vikram (Bikramjit). His *Century of Sentences* has been translated into English by Prof. Tawney, of Calcutta.

Bhara Mal (Raja) (بہارا مل). *Vide* Bihārī Mal.

Bhartpur (بہرت‌پور راجہ), Rāja of. *Vide* Chūrāman Jāṭ.

Bhaskar Acharya (بہسکر اچاریا), a most celebrated astronomer of the Hindūs, who was born at Bīdae, a city in the Deccan, in the year of Salivāhana, 1036, corresponding with the year A.D. 1114, A.H. 508. He was the author of several treatises, of which the *Līlāwatī* and the *Bījā Ganita*, relating to arithmetic, geometery and algebra, and the *Siromanī*, an astronomical treatise, are accounted the most valuable authorities in those sciences which India possesses. The *Siromanī* is delivered in two sections, the Gōla-Adhyāya, or the Lecture on the Globe, and the Ganita Adhyāya, or the Lecture on Numbers, as applied to Astronomy. The *Līlāwatī* was translated into Persian by Faizī in the reign of Akbar, and an English translation has also been lately made by Dr. Taylor and published at Bombay. Bhaskar died at an advanced age, being upwards of 70 years. Līlāwatī was the name of his only daughter who died unmarried.

Bhau (بہاؤ), a Mahratta chief. *Vide* Sadāsheo Bhāū.

Bhau Singh (بہاو سنگہ), also called Mirzā Rāja, was the second son of Rāja Bhagwān Dās Kachhwāha, Rāja of Amber (now Jaipūr). He succeeded to the rāj after his father's death in A.D. 1614, A.H. 1023, was raised to the rank of 5000 by the emperor Jahāngīr, and died of drinking A.D. 1621, A.H. 1030. Two of his wives and eight concubines burnt themselves on his funeral pyre. Among Jahāngīr's courtiers the Rājas of Amber were the most addicted to drinking. His eldest brother Jagat Singh, and Maka Singh his nephew, had likewise paid with their lives for their drunken habits, but their fate was no lesson for Rāja Bhāū.

Bhim Singh (بہیم سنگہ), rānā of Udaipūr, was living in A.D. 1750.

Bhim (بہیم راجہ), Raja of Gujrāt, in whose time Sulṭān Mahmūd Ghaznawī took the famous temple of Somnāth in A.D. 1027.

Bhim Singh Rathour (بہیم سنگہ راتہور). He usurped the throne of Jodhpūr in A.D. 1793, on his grandfather's death by defeat of Zālim Singh, and died in 1803. He was succeeded by Mān Singh.

Bhoj (Raja) (بہوج راجہ). *Vide* Rāja Bhōj.

Bhori Rani (بہوری رانی), the last of the wives of Maharājā Ranjīt Singh; she died childless at Lāhore on the 5th April, 1872. Her adopted son Kūwar Bhūp Singh distributed large sums of money before and after her death as alms to the poor. The funeral was very grand. Her remains were burnt near the *samādh* of the late Maharājā, and the ashes were sent to be thrown into the Ganges at Hardwār. She drew a pension of 800 rupees per mensem from our Government and held jāgīrs of upwards of 60,000 rupees per annum.

Bhuchchu (بہچو). *Vide* Zarra.

Bhuya (بہویہ میان), a nobleman of the court of Sulṭān Sikandar Lodī, who built the masjid Math in Delhī, but was afterwards assassinated by that prince without any crime, only because people used to assemble at his place.

Bibi Bai (بی‌بی بائی), the sister of Muhammad Shāh 'Adil, king of Dehlī, married to Salīm Shāh Sūr, by whom she had a son named Fīrōz. After the death of Salīm Shāh, when Fīrōz, then an infant, was being murdered by his uncle Muhammad Shāh, she defended her son for some time in her arms, presenting her body to the dagger, but her cruel brother tore the young prince from her embrace, and in her presence severed his head from his body. This event took place in May, A.D. 1554.

Bibi Daulat Shad Begam (بی‌بی دولت شاد بیگم), one of the wives of the emperor Akbar, and the mother of Shakrunnisa Begam, who survived her father, and died in the time of Jahāngīr.

Bibi Marwarid (بی‌بی مروارید), wife of the late Amīr Afzal Khān, died in September, A.D. 1874.

Bibi Zinda Abadi (بی‌بی زندہ ابدی), commonly called Bībī Jind Wadī by the people of Uchcha, was one of the descendants of Sayyad Jalāl. She is buried at Uchcha in Multān. The dome in which she rests is erected of burnt bricks and cemented by mortar. The whole of the edifice is ornamented by various hues, and *lapis lazuli* of the celebrated mines of Badakhshān. The size of this grand building may be estimated at 50 feet high, and the circumference 25.

Bihari Lal (بہاری لعل), a celebrated Hindī poet, called by Gilchrist the Thomson of the Hindus, and much admired among them; he appears to have flourished about the beginning of the 16th century. Being informed that his prince Jaisāh of Jaipūr was so infatuated with the beauty of a very young girl he had married (so as to neglect entirely the affairs of his country, for he never came abroad, having shut himself up to contemplate the fascinating charms of his beauteous, though immature bride), Bihārī boldly ventured to admonish him by bribing a slave girl to convey a couplet, which he had composed, under his pillow; the translation of which is thus given by Gilchrist, "When the flower blooms, what will be the situation of the *tree*, that is now captivated with a *bud*, in which there is neither fragrance, sweets, or colour." This had not only the desired effect of rousing the prince from his lethargy, but excited in his breast a generous regard for the man, whose advice came so seasonably and elegantly disguised. Bihārī received, ever after, a pension from court, with a present of more than one thousand pounds, for a work he published under the name of *Satsaī*, from its consisting of seven hundred couplets.

Bihari Mal (بہاری مل), also called Bharamal and Pūranmal, a Rāja of Amber or Ameir, now Jaipūr, was a rājpūt of the tribe of Kachhwāha. He paid homage to Bābar about the year A.D. 1527, and was on friendly terms with the emperor Akbar, and had at an early period given his daughter in marriage to him, of whom was born the emperor Jahāngīr. Both he and his son Rāja Bhagwān Dās were admitted at the same time to a high rank in the imperial army by the emperor. Bhagwān Dās gave his daughter in marriage to Jahāngīr in A.D. 1585, who was married next year (1586) to the daughter of Rāja Udai Singh, son of Rao Maldeo Rathor.

Bija Bai (بیجا بائی), or Biza Bāī, the wife of Mahārāja Daulat Rāo Scindhia of Gwaliār. After the death of her husband, who died without issue, she elected Jhanko Rāo Scindhia as his successor on the 18th June, 1827. She was expelled by him in 1833, and went over to Jhansī, where she had a large estate. She died at Gwāliar about the middle of the year 1863.

Bijaipal (بجی پال), a famous or fabulous Rāja of Bayāna, regarding whose power, riches, and extent of dominion, many curious tales are still current among the Bhartpūr Jāts, who assert their (spurious) descent from him. In the *Bijaipāl Rasa*, a metrical romance or ballad (written in the Birj Bhākha) the Hindū scholar will find a full and particular account of this great Hindū monarch, who is fabled to have conquered Rāja Jumeswar, the father of Pirthī Rāj, the celebrated chauhān king of Dehlī, and to have ruled despotically over the whole of India. The Karaulī Rāja too boasts his descent from Bijaipāl, and if any faith can be placed in a "Bansāolī or genealogical tree," he has a fair claim to the benefits, real or imaginary, resulting therefrom.

Bijai Singh (بجی سنگھ), son of Rāja Abhai Singh, the son of Mahārājā Ajīt, Singh, Rathor of Jōdhpūr, succeeded to the rāj in A.D. 1752, A.H. 1167. He became infatuated with fondness for a young concubine; after having fought the Mughols for 40 years he organised a confederacy against them in 1787 and was defeated by de Boigne (*q.v.*) at Pātan and Nirta in 1790; his chiefs rebelled, his family were in hostility with each other, and he left at his death the throne itself in dispute. Rāja Mān Singh at length succeeded, in 1804, to the honours and the feuds of Bijai Singh.

Bijai Singh (بجی سنگھ), son of Rāja Bhagwān Dās. *Vide* Rāmjī.

Bikramajit (بکرماجیت), or more properly Vikramāditya, a mythical sovereign of Mālwa and Gujrāt, whose capital was Ujain. His era called the Sambat is still used in the north of India. Bikramājīt died (or ascended the throne) in the Kālī Jug year, 3044, according to Wilford, whose essays in the 9th and 10th volumes of the Asiatic Researches contain information on the history of the three supposed princes of this name and of their common rival Salivāhana. The first Sambat year, therefore, concurs with the year 3045 of the Kālī Jug year, or 57 years before the birth of Christ. This prince was a great patron of learned men; nine of whom at his court are called nine gems, and are said to have been Dhanwantari, Kshapanaka, Amera Siñha, Sanku, Vetālabhatta, Ghatakarpara, Kālidāsa, Virahamihira, and Virāruchi. His real date is still an open question. "To assign him to the first year of his era might be quite as great a mistake as placing Pope Gregory XIII. in the year one of the Gregorian Calendar."—*Holtzmann.*

[Vide *Weber's Sansk-Liter. Eng.* tr., 1882, p. 202.]

Bikramajit (Rajah) (بکرماجت راجه), *Vide* Rae Patr Dās. A Khatre.

Bikrami (بکرامی), the poetical name of Mīr 'Abdur Rahmān Wizārat Khan, brother of Qāsim Khān, the grandfather of Samsam-uddaula Shāhnawāz Khān. He was promoted in the reign of the emperor 'Alamgīr to the Dīwānī of Mālwa and Bījāpūr. He was an excellent poet, and has left a Dīwān composed in a most beautiful style.

Bilal (بلال), the name of the crier, who used to announce to the people when Muhammad prayed. He was an African, and a freed slave of Muhammad. He died in the time of Umar, the second Khalīf after Muhammad, in the year A.D. 641, A.H. 20.

Bilal Kunwar (بلال کنور), the wife of the emperor 'Alamgīr II. and mother of Shāh 'Alam, king of Dehlī. Her title was Zinat Mahal.

Bilqaini (بلقيني), whose proper name was Abū Hafs, is the author of the works called *Mahāsin-ul-Istilāh*, *Sharah Bukhāri*, and *Tarandī*. He died in A.D. 1402, A.H. 805. See Sirāj-uddīn, son of Nūr-uddīn, and Abū Hafs-al-Bukharī.

Binai (Maulana) (بنائي). His father was a respectable architect at Herāt, the birth-place of the poet, and his takhallus or poetical name is derived from Binā or Banna, a builder. He is the author of a work called *Bahrāmwa - Bahrōz*, a story which he dedicated to the Sultān Ya'qūb the son of Uzzan Hasan. His conceit had roused the jealousy of Amīr Alīsher; Binaī tried to conciliate his favour by writing a Qasīda in his praise, but receiving no reward, he therefore substituted the name of Sultān Ahmad Mirzā for that of Alīsher, saying that he would not give away his daughters without dowry. Alisher was so enraged at this, that he obtained a death-warrant against him. Binai fled to Māwarunnahr. He was killed in the massacre of Shāh Isma'īl in A.D. 1512, A.H. 918. He has also left a Dīwān consisting of 6,000 verses.

Bin Ahmad (بن احمد). *Vide* Abū'l Faiz Muhammad.

Binakiti (بناكتى). *Vide* Abū Sulaimān Dāūd.

Binayek Rao (Raja) (بنايک راو راجه), the son of Amrīt Rāo, a Marhatta chief. He died in July, 1853, aged 50 years.

Bin Banana (بن بنانه), surname of Abu Nasr-ibn-ul-'Azīz bin-'Amrū, an Arabian poet who died at Baghdād in A.D. 1009, A.H. 400.

Bindraban (بندرابن), a Hindū author who flourished in the reign of the emperor 'Alamgīr, and wrote a work called *Lubbut-Tawārikh*, a summary history of Hindūstān.

Birbal (بيربل), or Bīrbal, was a Brāhman of the tribe of Bhāt. His proper name was Mahes Dās. He was a man of very lively conversation, on which account he became one of the greatest personal favourites of the emperor Akbar, who conferred on him the title of Rāja and the rank of 5000. He was also an excellent Hindī poet, and was honored with the title of Kabrāe or the royal poet. He was slain, together with Mulla Sherī and other officers of note, in a battle fought against the Yūsafzaī Afghāns of Sawād and Bijor (places between Kābul and Hindūstān) in February, A.D. 1586, Rabī I. A.H. 994. Akbar was for a long time inconsolable for the death of Bīrbal, and as the Rāja's body was never found, a report gained currency that he was still alive among the prisoners, and it was so much encouraged by Akbar, that a long time afterwards an impostor appeared in his name; and as this second Bīrbal died before he reached the court, Akbar again wore mourning as for his friend. Many of Bīrbal's witty sayings are still current in India.

Birbhan, founder of the sect of Sādhs (Hindust. "Quakers") born near Narnaul at A.D. 1640. Date and place of death unknown.

Bir Singh (بير سنگه راجه), a Rāja of the Bundelā tribe of Rājpūts. He was the founder of this family, and from him the family of the Urcha chief is descended. The greater part of his dominions was wrested from him by Rāja Chatar Sāl, who was the last sole possessor of the Bundelkhand province. At that period its capital was Kalanger, but the residence of the Rāja was Pannā, celebrated for its diamond mines.

Birgili (برگلى), surname of Mullā Muhammad-bin-Pīr 'Alī, a celebrated Arabian author, who wrote the *Sharah Arba,īn*, and died A.D. 1573, A.H. 981. He is by some called Barkalī.

Birjis Qadar (برجيس قدر), whose original name was Ramzān 'Alī, was son of Wājid 'Alī, the ex-king of Lucknow. His mother's name was Ma'shūk Begam. At the outbreak, he was created king with the unanimous consent of the rebel soldiery in 1857 at the instance of Barkat Ahmad, Risaladār, late 15th Regiment Irregular Cavalry, who subsequently fell in battle. Birjīs Qādar was then 10 years of age. Before his accession, his uncle Sulaimān Shikoh was much persuaded by the rebels to accept the crown, but refused. Birjīs Qādar was driven out of India and took refuge with his mother at Katmandū in Nepal.

Bir Singh Rao (بير سنگه راو), otherwise written Nar Singh, a Bundela chief suborned by Sultān Salim, eldest son of Akbar, to slay Abul Fazl, the emperor's favourite minister. The Rāo was hotly pursued for his crime but escaped. On Salim's accession he was rewarded.

[*Vide* Jahāngir.]

Bisati Samarqandi (بساطی سمرقندی), a poet of Samarqand who flourished in the time of Sultan Khalīl-ullah, grandson of Amīr Taimūr. He was formerly a weaver of carpets, and had assumed for his poetical title "Hasīrī," but he changed it afterwards to Bisātī. He was contemporary with 'Asmat-ullah Bukhari.

Bishr Hafi (بشر حافي) (*i.e.* Bishr the barefoot), a Muhammadan doctor who was born at Marv, and brought up at Baghdād, where he died on Wednesday the 10th November, A.D. 840, 10th Muharram, A.H. 226. Different dates are given of his death; but it is certain that he died several years before Ahmad Hanbal, and the one given here appears to be very correct.

Bishun Singh (Kachwaha) (بشن سنگه), Rāja of Ambhar or Ameir, was the son of Rām Singh and the father of Mirzā Rāja Jaisingh Sewāī. He died about the year A.D. 1693, A.H 1105.

Bismil (بسمل), the poetical name of Mirzā Muhammad Sha'fi of Naishāpūr, uncle of Nawāb Safdar Jang.

Bismil (بسمل), the poetical name of Amīr Hasan Khān of Calcutta, who was living in A.D. 1845, A.H 1261.

Biswas Rao (بسواس راو), the eldest son of Bālā Rāo Peshwā, the Marhatta chief. He was killed in the battle against Ahmad Shāh Abdālī on the 14th January, N.S. 1761, together with Sadāsheo Bhāū and other Marhatta chiefs.

Bithal Das Gaur (بیتهل داس گور), son of Gopāl Dās, Rāja of Sheopūr. On a spot of 10 bhigas towards Tājganj on the banks of the river Jamna he had built his house and a garden. In the town of Shalighan he was raised to 3000, and was appointed Kiladār of the fort of Āgra. He was afterwards raised to the rank of 5000, and in the year A.H. 1062 went home and there died.

Bo 'Ali Qalandar (بو علی قلندر).

[*Vide* Abū 'Alī Qalandar.]

Boigne (or le Borgne) Benoit, Count de, a Savoyard who, after holding commissions in the French and Russian armies, came to India and entered the East India Company's service at Madras, 1778. After some adventures he entered Sindhia's service in 1784, and trained four regular brigades. In 1796 he returned to Europe with a large fortune, much of which he devoted to public purposes and charity at Chambēri, his native town. He died there on the 21st June, 1830.

[*Vide* Keen's *Fall of the Mughol Empire.*]

Bughra Khan (بغرا خان), surname of Nāsir-uddīn Mahmūd, the second son of Sultān Ghayās-uddīn Balban, king of Dehlī. He was made governor of Lakhnautī in Bengal by his father, at whose death in A.D. 1286, he being then in that province, his son Kaiqubād was raised to the throne of Dehlī.

[*Vide* Nāsir-uddīn Mahmūd.]

Bukhari (بخاري). *Vide* Al-Bukhārī.

Bulbul (بلبل). *Vide* Mirzā Muhammad surnamed Bulbul.

Burandaq (برندق), the poetical name of Maulāna Bahā-uddīn. He was a native of Samarqand, and a sprightly satirical poet; much dreaded by his contemporaries, on account of his wit and caustic humour. He was the especial panegyrist of Sultān Bāiqara Mirzā, the son of 'Umar Shaikh and grandson of Amīr Taimūr. When Prince Bāiqara ascended the throne in A.D. 1394, he ordered that the sum of five hundred ducats (in Turkī bish yūz altūn) should be paid to Burandaq. By a mistake of the Secretary, he received only two hundred; and therefore addressed the following lines to the Sultān:—

"The Shāh, the terror of his foes,
Who well the sound of flatt'ry knows,
The conqueror of the world, the lord
Of nations vanquish'd by his sword,
Gave, while he prais'd my verse, to me
Five hundred ducats as a fee.
Great was the Sultān's generous mood,
Great is his servant's gratitude,
And great the sum; but strange to say!
Perhaps the words in Turkish tongue
Convenient meaning may derive;
Or else my greedy ear was wrong,
That turn'd two hundred into five."

The Sultān was extremely entertained at the readiness of the poet; and sending for him, assured him that the words "*bish yūz altūn*" signified in Turkish a thousand ducats, which he ordered to be immediately paid (*Dublin University Magazine* for 1840). The year of Burandaq's death is unknown. He was contemporary with Khwāja 'Asmat-ullah Bukhārī who died in A.D. 1426, A.H. 829.

Burhan (برهان), a poet of Māzindarān, came to Dehlī and died there shortly after Nādir Shāh had pillaged that city. He is the author of a Dīwān.

Burhan (برهان), the poetical name of Muhammad Hasan, the author of the Persian Dictionary called *Burhān Qāta*.

[*Vide* Muhammad Hasan.]

Burhan 'Imad Shah (برهان عماد شاه), one of the princes of the 'Imād Shāhī dynasty. He succeeded his father, Daria 'Imād Shāh, in the government of Berar when but a child. His minister Taufal Khān became regent; and before the prince was of an age to assume the reigns of his empire, Taufal Khān, assisted by the ruler of Khāndesh and by the Nizām Shāhī court, usurped the government. He eventually confined his sovereign in irons in the fort of Parnāla, and assumed the title of king. In the year A.D. 1568, A.H. 980, Nizām Shāh marched against Taufal Khān, under the pretence of releasing the imprisoned prince from his confinement. He took the fort of Gāwal by capitulation, defeated Taufal Khān and made him prisoner with his son; but instead of placing the captive monarch on the throne of Berār, sent him with the usurper and his son to be confined in one of the Nizām Shāhī forts, where they were all subsequently strangled by the king's order. Thus the family of 'Imād Shāh and that of the usurper Taufal Khān became extinct.

Burhan Naqid (برهان ناقد), a poet who is the author of the poem entitled *Dil Āshōb*, dedicated to the emperor Shāh Jahān.

Burhan Nizam Shah I. (برهان نظام شاه) ascended the throne of Ahmadnagar in the Deccan after the death of his father, Ahmad Nizām Shāh, in A.D. 1508, A.H. 914, in the seventh year of his age. He reigned 47 lunar years and died at the age of 54 in A.D. 1554, A.H. 961, and was buried in the same tomb with his father.

Burhan Nizam Shah II. (برهان نظام شاه), brother of Murtazā Nizām II. ascended the throne of Ahmadnagar in the Deccan on the 15th May, O.S. 1591, 1st Sha'bān, A.H. 999, after deposing and confining his own son Ismā'īl Nizām Shāh, who had been placed on the throne during his absence at the court of the emperor Akbar. He was advanced in years; but notwithstanding his age, gave himself up to pleasures unbecoming his dignity. His reign was marked by an unsuccessful war with the king of Bījāpūr, and a disgraceful defeat from the Portuguese, who had seized the sea coasts of his dominions. He died after a reign of four years and sixteen days, on the 18th April, A.D. 1595, 18th Sha'bān, A.H. 1003, in the 40th year of the reign of Akbar, and was succeeded by his son Ibrāhīm Nizām Shāh. Maulāna Zahūrī dedicated his Sāqīnāma to Burhān Nizām Shāh, containing nearly 4,000 verses.

Burhan-uddin Abu Is-haq-al-Fazari (برهان الدين ابو اسحق), commonly called Ibn-Firkāh, author of the *Farāez-al-Fazārī*, a treatise on the law of Inheritance according to Shāfa'ī's doctrine. He died in A.D. 1328, A.H. 729.

Burhan-uddin Bin Mazah-al-Bukhari (برهان الدين), author of the *Zukhīrat-ul-Fatāwa*, sometimes called *Zakhīrat ul-Burhania*, and of the *Muheet-al-Burhānī*.

Burhan-uddin Ali Bin Abu-Bakr-al-Marghinani (Shaikh) (برهان الدين علی شیخ), author of the *Hidāya Sharah Badīya, or the Lawyer's Guide*, a very celebrated book of Muhammadan Jurisprudence, which during the period that Mr. Hastings governed the British dominions in India, was by his orders most ably translated by Charles Hamilton, Esq., and published in London, in the year A.D. 1791. Burhān-uddīn was born at Marghīnān, in Transoxania in A.D. 1135, A.H. 529, and died in A.D. 1197, A.H. 593. The *Hidāya*, which is a commentary on the Badaya-al-Mubtada, is the most celebrated law treatise according to the doctrines of Abū Hanīfa, and his disciples Abū Yūsaf and the Imām Muhammad. A Persian version of the *Hidāya* was made by Maulwī Ghulām Yehiā Khān and others and published at Calcutta in 1807. He also wrote a work on inheritance entitled the *Farāez-ul-Usmāni*, which has been illustrated by several comments.

Burhan-uddin Gharib (Shah or Shaikh) (برهان الدين غريب شاه), a celebrated Musalmān saint much venerated in the Deccan. He died in A.D. 1331, A.H. 731, and his tomb is at Burhānpūr in Daulatābād, and is resorted to in a pilgrimage by the Muhammadans. He was a disciple of Shaikh Nizām-uddīn Aulia, who died in A.D. 1325, A.H. 725,

Burhan-uddin Haidar Bin Muhammad-al-Hirwi (برهان الدين بن محمد), author of a commentary on the Sirājia of Sajāwandī. He died in A.D. 1426, A.H. 830.

Burhan-uddin Ibrahim Bin Ali Bin Farhun (برهان الدين ابراهيم بن علی بن فرهون), chief biographer of the Māiikī lawyers, and author of the *Dībāj-ul-Mazahhib*. He died in A.D. 1396, A.H. 799.

Burhan-uddin (Qazi) (برهان الدين قاضی), Lord of the city of Sivas in Cappadocia or Caramenia, who died in A.D. 1395, A.H. 798. After his death Bāyezīd I. Sultān of the Turks, took possession of his States.

Burhan-uddin Mahmud Bin Ahmad (برهان الدين محمود بن احمد), author of a *Muhīt*, which, though known in India, is not so greatly esteemed as the *Muhīt-as-Sarakhsī*. The work of Burhān-uddīn is commonly known as the *Muhīt-al-Burhānī*.

Burhan - uddin Muhammad Baqir (Mir) (برهان الدين محمد باقير مير قاضی), Qāzī of Qāshān. He wrote a Dīwān containing about 5,000 verses. He was living about the year A.D. 1585, A.H. 993.

Burhan-uddin (Shaikh) (برهان الدين شيخ), or Sayyad. *Vide* Kutb 'Alam.

Burhan-uddin (Sayyad) (برهان الدين سيد), surnamed Muhaqqiq. He died in the year A.D. 1247, A.H. 645, and was buried at Cæsarea.

Burhan - ul - Mulk Sa'adat Khan (برهان الملک سعادت خان). *Vide* Sa'ādat Khān, and Mirzā Nasīr.

Burzuj (برزوی), a Persian physician who lived under Naushirwān the Just. He was sent by that prince to India to procure a copy of the book called the *Wisdom of all Ages*; which he afterwards translated into Persian. That which now exists is greatly altered from the original version.

Bus-haq (بوسحاق), the abbreviated poetical name of Abū Is-hāq Atma', which see.

Buzarjimehr(بزرجمهر), the celebrated minister of Naushirwān the Just, king of Persia. He is said to have imported from India the game of Chess and the Fables of Pilpay. Such has been the fame of his wisdom and virtues, that the Christians claim him as a believer in the gospel; and the Muhammadans revere him as a premature Musalmān. He lived to a great age, and died in the time of Hurmuz III. son and successor of Naushirwān the Just, between the years A.D. 580 and 590.

Buzarjmehr Qummi (بزرجمهر قمي), a celebrated Persian Prosodian of Qumm, who lived before the time of Saifī, the author of the *Urūz Saifī*.

Buzurg Khanam (بزرگ خانم), the daughter of Saif Khan, by Malika Bāno Begam, the daughter of Asaf Khān Wazīr, and wife of Zafar Khān, a nobleman of the reign of the emperor 'Alamgīr. She died before her husband in the month of May, A.D. 1659, Shawwāl, A.H. 1069.

Buzurg Umaid Khan (بزرگ اميد خان), son of Shāista Khān, an officer of rank in the time of the emperor Alamgīr. At the time of his death, which took place in A.D. 1694, A.H. 1105, he was governor of Behār.

Buzurg Umaid (بزرگ اميد), or Kaia Buzurg Umaid, one of the Ismaīlīs, who succeeded Hasan Sabbāh, the Old Man of the Mountains, in June, A.D. 1124, Rabī II. A.H. 518, and reigned 24 years. After his death his son Kaia Muhammad succeeded him and reigned 25 years.

C

Caragossa. *Vide* Qara Ghuz.

Chaghtai Khan (چغتاء خان), or Qāān, the most pious and accomplished of all the sons of Changez Khān; and although he succeeded, by the will of his father, to the kingdoms of Transoxiana, Balkh, Badakhshān, and Kāshghar in A.D. 1227, A.H. 624, he governed these countries by deputies, and remained himself with his eldest brother, Oqta Qāān, by whom he was regarded with the reverence which a pupil gives to his master. He died seven months before his brother in the month of June, A.D. 1241, Zi-Qa'da, A.H. 638. Qarāchār Nawiān, who was the fifth ancestor of Amīr Taimūr, was one of his Amirs, and, at length, captain general of all his forces. The dynasty that founded the so-called "Moghul, or Mughol Empire" of India was named after Chaghtai.

[*Vide* Keene's *Turks in India*. Chap. i.]

Chaghta Sultan (چغتا سلطان), a handsome young man of the tribe of the Mughols and favourite of the emperor Bābar Shāh. He died at Kābul in A.D. 1546, A.H. 953.

Chait Singh (چيت سنگه), Rāja, son of Balwant Singh, zamīndār of Banāras. He succeeded his father in A.D. 1770. In August, 1781, demands were made upon him, by the Governor-General, for additional tribute to be paid to the Company, as the sovereign power now requiring assistance in its exigency. The Rāja declined, pleading willingness, but inability. He was arrested by Mr. Hastings' order, at Banāras; a revolt took place in his behalf on the 20th August; nearly two companies of Sepoys and their officers were destroyed,—and the Rāja escaped in the confusion. The Governor-General immediately assumed control of the province; and troops were called in to oppose the Rāja, who now headed the numbers flocking to his support. He was defeated at Latīfpūr, in Bundelkhand, where he had taken refuge; and lastly, his stronghold of Bijaigurh was seized, and his family plundered by a force under Major Popham. His post was declared vacant, and the zamīndarī bestowed on the next heir, a nephew of the Rāja, a minor. After these transactions at Banāras, the Governor-General proceeded to Audh, to obtain an adjustment of the heavy debts due to the Company by the Wazīr 'Asaf-ud-daula. The territories of the Begams (one, the mother of Shuja'-ud-daula, the late Nawāb—the other, the mother of the Wazīr) were seized, on a charge of aiding the insurrection of Chait Singh. The Rāja found an asylum in Gwāliar for 29 years and died there on the 29th March, A.D. 1810. *See* Balwant Singh. His estates, with title of Rāja, were presented to his nephew Babū Muhīp Narain, grandson of Rāja Balwant Singh.

[Vide *Warren Hastings;* by Sir A. Lyall, K.C.B.]

Chand (چاند), or Chānd, called also Trikala, from his supposed prophetic spirit, was a celebrated Hindū poet or bard. He flourished towards the close of the twelfth century of the Christian era. He may be called the poet laureate of Prithirāj, the Chauhān emperor of Dehlī who, in his last battle with Shahāb-uddīn Ghōrī, was taken prisoner and conveyed to Ghaznī, where his bard, Chānd, followed him. Both perished by their own hands, after the death of their implacable foe, Shahāb-uddīn. Like the Greek bard, Homer, countries and cities have contended for the honour of having been the place of birth of this the most popular poet of the Hindūs. Dehlī, Qanauj, Mahōba, and the Panjāb, assert their respective claims, but his own testimony is decisive, whence it appears that he was a native of Lāhore. In his *Prithirāj Chauhan Rāsa*, when enumerating some of the heroes, friends and partizans of his hero, he says, "Niddar was born in Qanauj, Siluk and Jait, the father and son, at Abū; in Mundava the Parihār, and in Kurrik Kāngra the Haolī Raō, in Nāgor, Balbhaddar, and Chānd, the bard, at Lāhore."

Chand Saudagar (چاند سوداگر), a Bangali merchant.

Chand (چاند). *Vide* Ṭeik Chand.

Chanda Kunwar (چندا کنور), also called Jindan Koūr; the wife of Mahārāja Ranjīt Singh, of Lāhore, and mother of Mahārāja Dīlīp Singh (*q.v.*). She died at Kensington, 1863.

[*Vide* Griffin's *Ranjīt Singh*, "Rulers of India," also Lady Login's *Sir John Login* and *Duleep Singh*.]

Chanda (چندا ماه لقا), also called Māh-liqā, a dancing girl, or queen of Haidarābād, was a poetess of much taste and merit. She is the author of a Dīwān, which was revised by Sher Muhammad Khān Imān. In the year A.D. 1799, in the midst of a dance, in which she bore the chief part, she presented a British officer with a copy of her poems, accompanied with the following complimentary observations, in the form of the usual gazal:—

Since my heart drank from the cup of a fascinating eye,
I wonder beside myself, like one whom wine bewilders.
Thy searching glances leave nothing unseated;
Thy face, bright as flame, consumes my heart.
Thou soughtest a *Nazar:* I offer thee my head;
Albeit thy heart is not unveiled to me.
My eyes fixed on thy lineaments—emotion agitates my soul,
Fresh excitement beats impatient in my heart.
All that Chandā asks is, that, in either world,
Thou wouldst preserve the ashes of her heart by thy side.

[Garcin de Tassin informs us that there is a copy of her Dīwān in the East India House Library, which she herself presented to Captain Malcolm on the 1st October, A.D. 1799.]

Chanda Sahib (چنداصاحب), surname of Husain Dost Khān, a relation of Dōst 'Ali Khān, Nawāb of Arcot, whose daughter he had married. He had made his way to the highest offices of the government by the services of his sword, and was esteemed the ablest soldier that had of late years appeared in the Carnatic. He cajoled the queen of Trichinopoly, and got possession of the city in A.D. 1736. He was taken prisoner by the Mahrattas on the 26th March, A.D. 1741, and imprisoned in the fort of Sitāra, but was released by the intervention of Dupleix in 1748, and appointed Nawāb of the Carnatic by Muzaffar Jang. He was put to death in A.D. 1752, 1st Sha'bān, A.H. 1165, by the Mahrattas, and his head sent to Muhammad 'Alī Khān, made Nawāb of Arcot by the English, who reigned for over 40 years.

Chandar Bhan (چندر بهان برهمن), a Brahman of Patiāla, well-versed in the Persian language, was employed as a Munshī in the service of the prince Dārā Shikōh, the eldest son of the emperor Shāh Jahān. He is the author of several Persian works, *i.e.*, *Guldasta*, *Tuhfat-ul-Anwār*, *Tuhfat-ul-Fus-hā*, *Majma'-ul-Fuqrā*, one entitled *Chār Chaman*, another called *Manshāt Brāhman* being a collection of his own letters written to different persons, and also of a Dīwān in which he uses the title of Brāhman for his poetical name. After the tragical death of his employer, he retired to Banāras where he died in the year A.D. 1662, A.H. 1073. He had also built a house at Āgra, of which no traces now remain.

Chand Bibi (Sultana) (چاند بی‌بی) was the daughter of Husain Nizām Shāh I. of Ahmadnagar in the Deccan, sister to Murtaza Nizām Shāh, and wife of 'Alī 'Adil Shāh I. of Bījāpūr. After the death of her husband in A.D. 1580, A.H. 988, she had been queen and dowager-regent of the neighbouring kingdom of Bījāpūr during the minority of her nephew Ibrāhīm 'Adil Shāh II. and was one of the most able politicians of her day. The Mughols under prince Murād, the son of Akbar, proceeded in November, A.D. 1595, Rabī' II. A.H. 1004, and besieged Ahmadnagar for some months, while Chānd Sultāna defended the place with masculine resolution. At the same time, there being a scarcity of provisions in the Mughol camp, the prince and Khān-Khānān thought it advisable to enter into a treaty with the besieged. It was stipulated by Chānd Bībī that the prince should keep possession of Berar, and that Ahmadnagar and its dependencies, should remain with her in the name of Bahādur, the grandson of Burhān Shāh. She was put to death by a faction in the year A.D. 1599, A.H. 1008.

Chandragupta (چندرگپتا), called by the Greeks Sandracottus. He seized the kingdom of Magadha, after the massacre of the survivors of the Naida dynasty, whose capital was the celebrated city Patāliputra, called by the Greeks Palibothra. Married a Greek Princess, daughter of Seleucus Nikator, and was grandfather to Asoka (*q.v.*).

Chandu Lal (چندولال رای), a Hindū, who was appointed Dīwān to the Nizām of Haidarābād in A.D. 1808. His poetical name is Shādān. He died in the year A.D. 1863.

Changez Khan (چنگیز خان), also called by us Gengis, Jengis, and Zingis, surnamed Tamūjin, was the son of Yesuki a Khān or chief of the tribe of Mughols. He was born in A.D. 1154, A.H. 549, and at the age of 13 he began to reign, but the conspiracies of his subjects obliged him to fly for safety to Avant Khān, a Tartar prince, whom he supported on his throne, and whose daughter he married. These ties were not binding. Avant Khān joined against Changez, who took signal vengeance on his enemies, and after almost unexampled vicissitudes he obtained, at the age of 49, a complete victory over all those who had endeavoured to effect his ruin, and received from the Khāns of Tartary the title of Khāqān in A.D. 1206, A.H. 602, and was declared emperor of Tartary. His capital was Qarāqurm. In the space of 22 years he conquered Corea, Cathay (part of China) and the noblest provinces of Asia, and became as renowned a conqueror as Alexander the Great. He died on Sunday the 29th August, A.D. 1227, Ramazān, A.H. 624, aged 75 lunar years, leaving his dominions (which extended 1800 leagues from east to west, and 1000 from north to south) properly divided among his four sons, Jūjī, Oqtāī, Chaghtāī and Tūlī Khān.

List of the Mughol emperors of Tartary.

Changez Khān, 1206.
Tūlī Khān, his son, 1227.
Oqtāī, brother of Tūlī, 1241.
Turkīna Khātūn, his wife, regent for 4 years.

Kayūk Khān, son of Oqtāī, 1246.
Ogūlgan-mish, his wife, regent on his death, 1248.
Mangū Khān, son of Tūlī Khān, 1258, died 1259.
After the death of Mangū, the empire of the Mughals was divided into different branches, in China, Persia, in Qapchāq, etc.
Khublāi Khān, the brother of Mangū Khān, succeeded in China, and founded the Yuen dynasty, 1260.
Chaghtāī Khān, son of Changez Khān, founded the Chaghtāī branch in Transoxiana, 1240.
Jūjī, son of Changez Khān, founded the Qapchāq dynasty, 1226.

[*Vide* Halākū Khān, Khublai Khān, etc.]

Char Bagh (چار باغ), name of a garden constructed by the emperor Bābar on the bank of the Jamna, which it is said was also called Hasht Bahisht; it bore all sorts of fruits; no traces of this famous garden are left now.

Chatrapati Appa Sahib (چتراپتی اپا صاحب), Rāja of Sitae, who died in, or a year before, A.D. 1874, whose adopted son was Rāja Rām.

Chatr Sal (چتر سال), or, according to the author of the *Māsir-ul-Umrā*, Satar Sāl, was the son of Chait Singh, chief of the Bundelas or inhabitants of Bundelkhand, of which province he was Rāja. To secure the independence of his posterity against the encroaching power of the Marhattas, he entered into a close alliance with the Peshwā Bājī Rāo I. about the year A.D. 1733, A.H. 1146, and at his demise he bequeathed him a third of his dominions, under an express stipulation that his posterity should be protected by the Peshwā and his heirs. Chatr Sāl died A.D. 1735, leaving two sons, Hirde Sāh and Jagat Rāj. The division of the dominions of Bundelkhand, bequeathed to the Peshwā, comprised the Mahāls of Kālpī, Sirounj, Kūnch, Garra Kotā, and Hirdainagar. Gangadhar Bāla was nominated by the Peshwā as his nāib to superintend the collections. Afterwards the principal leaders in Bundelkhand having fallen in battles, and the ruin of the country having been completed by the subsequent conquest of the Rāja of Panna by Nānā Arjūn, the grandson of Bakhat Singh, a descendant of Chatr Sāl, it hence became the object of Nānā Farnawīs, the Pūna minister, notwithstanding the stipulations by which the former Peshwā obtained from Chatr Sāl one-third of his dominions, to annex the whole of Bundelkhand to the Marhatta States. For this purpose he gave the investiture of it to 'Alī Bahādur, son of Shamsher Bahādur, an illegitimate son of the Peshwā Bājī Rāo, whose descendants became Nawābs of Banda.

[*Vide* Muhammad Khān Bangash.]

Chatur Mahal (چتر محل), one of the Begams of the ex-king of Oudh. One Qurbān 'Alī, who had held a subordinate position, and was latterly a Sharistadār under the British Government, suddenly became a rich man by marrying her. He formed the acquaintance of this young and beautiful woman, and they resolved to be married. But the Begam did not wish the union with a man so inferior to herself to take place where she was known, and so obtained the permission of the Chief Commissioner to leave Oudh on the pretence of making a pilgrimage to Mecca. Once clear of Lucknow, she was joined by Qurbān 'Alī, and made for his home at Bijnaur in Bundelkhand.

Chimnaji 'Apa (چمناجی آپا), the younger son of the Mahratta chief Raghunāth Rāo (Raghōba) was furtively raised to the masnad at Pūna some time after the death of Mādho Rāo II. the son of Narāyan Rāyo II. on the 26th May, A.D. 1796; but was deposed afterwards, and succeeded by his elder brother Bājī Rāo II. who was publicly proclaimed on the 4th December following.

Chin Qalich Khan (چین قلیچ خان). *Vide* Qulich Khān.

Chin Qalich Khan (چین قلیچ خان), former name of Nizām-ul-Mulk Asaf Jāh (*q.v.*).

Churaman (چورامن), an enterprising Jāt who having enriched himself by plundering the baggage of the emperor 'Alamgīr's army on his last march to the Deccan, built the fortress of Bhartpūr, fourteen kōs from Āgra, with part of the spoil, and became the chief of that tribe. The present Rājas of Bhartpūr are his descendants. He was killed by the Imperial army in the battle which took place between the emperor Muhammad Shāh and Qutb-ul-Mulk Sayyad 'Abd-ullāh Khān in November, A.D. 1720, Muharram, A.H. 1133. His son Badan Singh succeeded him.

The following is a list of the Rājas of Bhartpūr:—

Chūrāman Jāt.
Badan Singh, son of Chūrāman.
Sūrajmal Jāt, the son of Badan Singh.
Jawāhir Singh, the son of Sūrajmal.
Rāo Ratan Singh, brother of Jawāhir Singh.
Kehrī Singh, the son of Ratan Singh.
Nawal Singh, the brother of Ratan Singh.
Ranjīt Singh, the nephew of Nawal Singh and son of Kehrī Singh.
Randhīr Singh, the son of Ranjīt Singh.
Baldeo Singh, the brother of Randhīr Singh.
Balwant Singh, the son of Baldeo Singh.
Jaswant Singh, the son of Balwant Singh and present Rāja of Bhartpūr.

D

Dabir-ud-daula Amin-ul-Mulk (Nawab) (دبیرالدوله امین الملک نواب), title of Khwāja Farīd-uddīn Ahmad Khān Bahādur Muslah Jang, the maternal grandfather of Sayyid Ahmad Khān, Munsif of Dehlī. Whilst the British were in Bengal, and the Wakīl of the king of Persia was killed in Bombay in an affray, it became urgent for the British Government to send a Wakīl on deputation to Persia. Dabīr-ud-daula was selected for this high office. On his return, after fully completing the trust, he was appointed a full Political Agent at Ava. After this, in latter times, he held the office of Prime Minister to Akbār Shāh II.

Daghistani (داغستانی), a poet of Dāghistān in Persia, who is the author of a Persian work called *Rayāz-ush-Shu'arā*. [*Vide* Wālih.]

Dahan (داهان), whose proper name is Abū Muhammad Sa'īd, son of Mubārik, better known as Ibn Dāhān-al-Baghdādī, was an eminent Arabic grammarian and an excellent poet. He died in A.D. 1173, A.H. 569.

Dai (داعئ), whose full name is Nizām-uddīn Muhammad Dāī', was a disciple of Shāh Na'mat-ullāh Wālī, and is the author of a Dīwān which he completed in the year A.D. 1460, A.H. 865.

Daqiqi (دقيقي), a famous poet at the court of Amīr Nūh II. son of Amīr Mansūr Sāmānī, by whose request he had commenced to write the *Shāh Nāma*, but before he could finish a thousand verses of the story of Gashtasp, he was slain by one of his slaves. The year of his death is not known, but this event appears to have taken place during the reign of his royal master, who reigned in Khurāsān twenty years, and died in A.D. 997, A.H. 387. His proper name, according to the Aitāshkada, was Mansūr bin-Ahmad.

Dalpat (دلپت), Rāja of Bhojpūr near Buxar, was defeated and imprisoned, and when he was at length set at liberty by Akbar, on payment of an enormous sum, he again rebelled under Jahāngīr, till Bhojpūr was sacked, and his successor Rāja Partāb was executed by Shah Jahān, whilst the Rānī was forced to marry a Muhammadan courtier.

Dalpat Sah (دلپت ساه), the husband of Ranī Durgāwātī, which see.

Damad (داماد), poetical name of Muhammad Bāqir, which see.

Damaji (داماجی), the first Gaeqwār of Baroda. His successor was Pelājī.

Damishqi (دمشقی), an illustrious Persian poet, named Muhammad Damishqī, who flourished in the time of Fazl, the son of Ahia or Yahia, the Barmecide or Barmakī.

Danial Mirza (Sultan) (دانیال مرزا سلطان), the third son of the emperor Akbar. He was born at Ajmīr on Wednesday the 10th September, A.D. 1572, and received the name of Dāniāl on account of his having been born in the house of a celebrated Darwesh named Shaikh Dāniāl. His mother was a daughter of Rāja Bihārī Mal Kachhwāha. After the death of his brother, prince Sultān Murād, he was sent to the Deccan by his father, accompanied by a well appointed army, with orders to occupy all the Nizām Shāhī territories. Ahmadnagar was taken in the beginning of the year A.H. 1009, or A.D. 1600; Sultān Dāniāl died on the 8th April, A.D. 1605, 1st Zil-hijja, A.H. 1013, in the city of Burhānpūr, aged 33 years and some months, owing to excess in drinking. His death and the circumstances connected with it so much affected the king his father, who was in a declining state of health, that he became every day worse, and died not long after. From the chronogram it would seem that the prince Dāniāl died in the year A.H. 1012, or A.D. 1604, a year and six months before his father.

Danish (دانش), poetical name of Mīr Rāzī who died in A.D. 1665, A.H. 1076.

Danishmand Khan (دانشمند خان), whose proper name was Muhammad Shafī or Mullā Shafī, was a Persian merchant who came to Sūrat about the year A.D. 1646, A.H. 1056, from which place he was sent for by the emperor Shāh Jahān. He was soon after raised to the mansab of 3000 and paymastership of the army, with the title of Dānishmand Khān. In the reign of 'Alamgīr he was honored with the mansab of 4000, and after some time to that of 5000, and appointed governor of Shāh Jahānābād, where he died in the month of July, A.D. 1670, 10th Rabī I. A.H. 1081. He used to speak much about the Christian religion. Bernier, the French Traveller, who accompanied 'Alamgīr to Kashmīr in 1664, was attached to his suite, and has mentioned him in his Travels.

Danishmand Khan (دانشمند خان), whose original name was Mirzā Muhammad, and poetical, Ālī, was a native of Shīrāz. In the year A.D. 1693, he was honored with the title of Na'mat Khān, and the superintendence of the royal kitchen by the emperor 'Alamgīr. After the death of that monarch, the title of Nawāb Dānishmand Khān Alī was conferred on him by Bahādur Shāh, by whose order he had commenced writing a Shāhnāma or history of the reign of that emperor, but died soon after in the year A.D. 1708, A.H. 1120.

[*Vide* Na'mat Khān Alī.]

Dara or **Darab II.** (دارا داراب), the eighth king of the second or Kaiānian dynasty of the kings of Persia, was the son of Queen Humai, whom he succeeded on the Persian throne. His reign was distinguished by several wars; particularly one against Philip of Macedon. He reigned 12 years, and was succeeded by his son Dārā or Dārāb II.

Dara or **Darab III.** (دارا داراب) is the celebrated Darius Codomanus of the Greeks. He succeeded his father Dārā II. as king of Persia, and was slain in battle against Alexander the Great in the year B.C. 331. He was the ninth and last king of the 2nd or Kaiānian dynasty of the kings of Persia.

[*Vide* Achaemenes.]

Dara Bakht (Mirza) (دارا بخت مرزا), son of Bahādūr Shāh, the ex-king of Dehlī. His poetical title is Dārā, and he is the author of a Dīwān.

Darab Beg (Mirza) (داراب بیگ مرزا). *Vide* Jōyā.

Darab Khan (داراب خان,) commonly called Mirzā Dārāb, was the second son of Abdul Rahīm Khān, Khān Khānan. After the death of his eldest brother Shāhnawāz Khān in A.D. 1618, A.H. 1027, he was honored with the rank of 5000 by the emperor Jahāngīr and was appointed governor of Berār and Ahmadnagar in the Deccan. He was also governor of Bengal for some time, and on his return to the Deccan the emperor, being displeased with him on some account, ordered Mahābat Khān to strike off his head, which he did, and sent it to the king. This circumstance took place A.D. 1625, A.H. 1034.

Darab Khan (داراب خان), son of Mukhtār Khān Subzwārī, a nobleman in the service of the emperor 'Alamgīr. He died on the 24th June, A.D. 1679, 25th Jumādạ I. A.H. 1090.

Dara Shikoh (دارا شکوه), the eldest and favourite son of the emperor Shāh Jahān, was born on the 20th March, O.S. 1615, 29th Ṣafar, A.H. 1024. His mother, Mumtāz Mahal (*v.* Arjumand), was the daughter of 'Asaf Khān, wazīr, the brother of Nūr Jahān Begam. In the 20th year of his age, *i.e.*, in the year A.D. 1633, A.H. 1043, he was married to the princess Nādira, the daughter of his uncle Sulṭān Parwez, by whom he had two sons, *viz.*, Sulaimān Shikōh and Sipahr Shikōh. In A.D. 1658, during the illness of his father, a great battle took place between him and his brother Aurangzib 'Alamgīr for the throne, in which Dārā being defeated, was at last obliged to fly towards Sindh, where he was captured by the chief of that country and brought to the presence of Aurangzib, loaded with chains, on a sorry elephant without housings; was exposed through all the principal places and then led off to a prison in old Dehlī, where after a few days, in the night of the 29th August, O.S. 1659, 21st Ẓil-ḥijja, A.H. 1069, he was murdered by the order of Aurangzib; his body exhibited next morning to the populace on an elephant, and his head cut off and carried to the emperor, who ordered it to be placed on a platter, and to be wiped and washed in his presence. When he had satisfied himself that it was the real head of Dārā, he began to weep, and with many expressions of sorrow directed it with its corpse to be interred in the tomb of the emperor Humāyūn. Sipahr Shikōh, his son, who was also taken captive and brought with his father, was sent away in confinement to Gwāliar. Sulaimān Shikōh, his eldest son, who, after the defeat of his father had taken refuge in Srīnagar for some time, was subsequently, in A.D. 1670, A.H. 1071, given up by the Rāja of that place to the officers of Aurangzib and conveyed to Dehlī. He was then sent to Gwāliar, where he and his brother Sipahr Shikōh both died within a short space. Dārā Shikōh is the author of the work called *Safīnat-ul-Aulia,* an abridgment of the Life of Muhammad, with a circumstantial detail of his wives, children, and companions, etc., also of a work entitled *Majma' - ul - Bahrain* (*i.e.*, the uniting of both seas), in which he endeavours to reconcile the Brāhmaṇ religion with the Muhammadan, citing passages from the Qurān to prove the several points. In 1656 he likewise, with the same intent, caused a Persian translation to be made by the Brāhmaṇs of Banāras, of the Apnikhat, a work in the Sanskrit language, of which the title signifies "the word that is not to be said;" meaning the secret that is not to be revealed. This book he named *Sarr-i-Asrār*, or *Secret of Secrets*; but his enemies took advantage of it to traduce him in the esteem of his father's Muhammadan soldiers, and to stigmatize him with the epithets of Kafir and Rāfizī (unbeliever and blasphemer), and finally effected his ruin; for Aurangzib his brother made a pretence of that, and consequently had all his bigoted Muhammadans to join him. Anquetil du Perron has given a translation of this work, in two large volumes in quarto, on which a very good critique may be found in the Second Number of the *Edinburgh Review*. There is also a copy of the Persian version of this work in the *British Museum*, with a MS. translation, made by N. B. Halhed. The authorship of other works has been ascribed to this prince. His poetical name was Qādirī. Catrou says that Dārā died a Christian.

[*Turks in India*. Chap. v.]

Dard (Mir) (درد میر) is the poetical name of Khwāja Muhammad Mīr of Dehlī, a son of Khwāja Nāsir who was one of the greatest Shaikhs of the age. Dard was the greatest poet of his time. He was formerly in the army, but he gave up that profession on the advice of his father and led the life of a devotee. When during the fall of Dehlī everybody fled from the city, Dard remained in poverty contented with his lot. He was a Sūfī and a good singer. A crowd of musicians used to assemble at his house on the 22nd of every month. Some biographers say that he was a disciple of Shāh Gulshan, meaning Shaikh Sa'd-ullāh. Besides a Dīwān in Persian and one in Rekhta, he has written a treatise on Sūfīism called *Risāla Wāridāt*. He died on Thursday the 3rd January, A.D. 1785, 24th Ṣafar, A.H. 1199.

List of his Works.

Ālī Nāla-wa-Dard.	Ilm-ul-Kitāb.
Ālī Sard.	Dīwān in Persian.
Dard Dil.	Dīwān in Urdū.

Dardmand (دردمند), poetical name of Muhammad Taqīh of Dehlī, who was a pupil of Mirzā Jān Jānān Mazhar, and the author of a Sāqīnāma and of a Dīwān. He died at Murshidābād in the year A.D. 1762, A.H. 1176.

Daria Ihmad Shah (دریا عماد شاه), the son of 'Alā-uddīn 'Imād Shāh, whom he succeeded on the throne of Berār in the Deccan about the year A.D. 1532, A.H. 939. In A.D. 1543, A.H. 950, he gave his sister Rabia' Sulṭāna in marriage to Ibrāhīm 'Adil Shāh, and the nuptials were celebrated with royal magnificence. In A.D. 1558, A.H. 966, he gave his daughter in marriage to Husain Nizām Shāh, and reigned in great tranquility with all the other kings of the Deccan until his death, when he was succeeded by his son Burhān 'Imād Shāh.

Daria Khan Rohela (دریا خان روهیله), a nobleman in the service of prince Shāh Jahān, who, on his accession to the throne, raised him to the rank of 5000. He afterwards joined the rebel Khān Jahān Lodī. In a battle which took place between him and Rāja Bikarmājīt Bundela, son of Rāja Chhajjar Singh, he was killed, together with one of his sons and 400 Afghāns, A.D. 1630, A.H. 1040. His head was sent to the emperor.

Dariqutni (دارقطنی). *Vide* Abū'l Husain 'Alī-bin-'Umr.

Darimi (دارمی), the son of 'Abdul Rahmān of Samarqand, is the author of the work called *Musnad Dārimī*. He died in the year A.D. 869, A.H. 255. He is also called by some authors Abū Muhammad 'Abd-ullāh-al-Dārimī.

Darki (درکی قمی), of Qumm in Persia, was a contemporary of Shāh 'Abbās. He died in the Deccan and left a Persian Dīwān.

Dasht Baiazi (دشت بیاضی). *Vide* Walī of Dasht Bayāz.

Dastam Khan (دستم خان), son of Rustam Khān Turkistānī, was an Amīr of 3000 in the service of the emperor Akbar. He died in A.D. 1580, A.H. 988, of his wounds which he had received in battle against the three nephews of Rāja Bihārī Mal, who had rebelled against the emperor and were also killed.

Data Ram Brahman (داتا رام براهمن), a poet who wrote beautiful Persian verses.

Dattaji Sindhia (دتاجی سیندهیه), son of Rānājī and brother of Jaiāpā Sindhia, a Mahratta chief who had a cavalry of 80,000 horse under him, and was slain in battle against Ahmad Shāh Abdālī in the month of January, A.D. 1760, Jumāda II. A.H. 1173, a year before the death of Bhāū, the famous Mahratta chief.

[*Vide* Rānājī Sindhia.]

Daud Bidari (Mulla) (داؤد بیدری), a native of Bīdar in the Deccan. When twelve years of age, he held the office of page and seal-bearer to Sulṭān Muhammad Shāh Bahmanī I. king of Deccan about the year A.D. 1368, A.H. 770. He is the author of the *Tahfut-us-Salātin Bahmanī*.

Daud Khan Faruqi (داؤد خان فاروقی) succeeded his brother Mīrān Ghanī to the throne of Khāndesh in September, A.D. 1503,

1st Jumādạ I. A.H. 916, reigned seven years and died on Wednesday the 6th August, A.D. 1510. He was succeeded by 'Adil Khān Farqūī II.

Daud Khan Qureshi (داؤد خان قريشى) son of Bhīkan Khān, was an officer of 5000 in the reign of the emperor 'Alamgīr. In the year A.D. 1670, A.H. 1081, he was appointed governor of Allahābād.

Daud Khan Panni (داؤد خان پنی), son of Khizir Khān Pannī, a Paṭhān officer, was renowned throughout India for his reckless courage, and his memory still survives in the tales and proverbs of the Deccan. He served several years under 'Alamgīr, and when Bahādur Shāh, on his departure from the Deccan, gave the viceroyalty of that kingdom to the Amīr-al-Umrā, Zulfikār Khān, as that chief could not be spared from court, he left the administration of the government to Dāūd Khān, who was to act as his lieutenant. In the reign of Farrukh-siyar, when the Amīr-ul-Umrā Husain 'Alī Khān marched towards Deccan, Dāūd Khān received secret orders from the emperor to oppose and cut him off. Accordingly when the Amīr-ul-Umrā arrived at Burhānpūr, Dāūd Khān, who regarded himself as the hero of his age, prepared to receive him. The engagement was very bloody on both sides; a matchlock ball struck Dāūd Khān, and he fell down dead on the seat of his elephant. This event took place in the year A.D. 1715, A.H. 1127.

Daud Qaisari (Shaikh) (داؤد قيصري شيخ), author of another commentary called *Sharah Hadīs-ul-Arba'īn*, besides the one written by Birgilī. He died A.D. 1530, A.H. 751.

Daud Shah Bahmani (Sultan) (داؤد شاه بهمنی سلطان), the son of Sulṭān 'Alā-uddīn Hasan, ascended the throne of Deccan, after assassinating his nephew Mujāhid Shāh on the 14th April, A.D. 1378, 21st Muḥarram, A.H. 780. He reigned one month and five days, and was murdered on the 19th May, the same year in the mosque at Kulbarga where he went to say his prayers. He was succeeded by his brother Mahmūd Shāh I.

Daud Shah (داؤد شاه گجراتی), a king of Gujrāt, who was placed on the throne after the death of his nephew Qutb Shāh in A.D. 1439, and was deposed after seven days, when Mahmūd Shāh, another nephew of his, a youth of only 14 years of age, was raised to the throne.

Daud Shah (داؤد شاه), the youngest son of Sulaimān Qirānī, succeeded to the kingdom of Bengal after the death of his eldest brother Bāiazīd in the year A.D. 1573, A.H. 981. This prince was much addicted to sensual excesses; and the propensity was rendered more degrading by his inclination to associate with persons of low origin and mean connections, by whom he was induced to attack the frontiers of the kingdom of Dehlī, He had several skirmishes with Munaim Khān, Khān Khānān, governor of Jaunpūr, who was subsequently joined by his master, the emperor Akbar, when an obstinate battle took place on the 30th July, A.D. 1575, 21st Rabī II. A.H. 983, in which Dāūd Shāh was defeated and obliged to retire to a fort on the borders of Kaṭak. After this a peace was concluded, by which Dāūd Shāh was invested with the government of Orisa and Kaṭak, and the other provinces of Bengal were occupied by Munaim Khān in the name of the emperor. The year of this event is commemorated in a Persian Hemistich. After the death of Munaim Khān, which took place the same year at Lakhnauṭī, Dāūd Khān re-took the provinces of Bengal, but was soon attacked by Khān Jahān Turkmān, who was appointed governor, when after a severe engagement Dāūd Khān was taken prisoner, and suffered death as a rebel. From that period, the kingdom of Bengal was subdued, and fell under the subjection of the emperor Akbar. Thus ended the rule of the Pūrbī or independent eastern kings of Bengal.

Daud Tai (داؤد طائي), a Musalmān doctor who was master of several sciences. He had served Abū Hanīfa for 20 years, and was one of the disciples of Habīb Rāī. He was contemporary with Fazail Aiāz, Ibrāhīm Adham and Ma'rūf Karkhī, and died in the reign of the khalīf Al-Mahdī, the son of Al-Manṣūr, about the year A.D. 781 or 782, A.H. 164 or 165.

Daulat Rao Sindhia (دولت راو سيندهيه), son of Anandi Rāo, nephew to Madhoji, by whom he was adopted. Made war against the British, 1803, but was beaten in one campaign; died A.D. 1827.

[*Vide* Doulat Rāo.]

Dawal Devi (داول ديوي), or Dewal Devī.

[*Vide* Kaulā Devī.]

Dawani (دواني), the philosopher, whose proper name is Jalāl-uddīn Muhammad Asa'd Aldawānī, the son of Sā'd-uddīn Asa'd Dawānī. He flourished in the reign of Sulṭān Abū Sa'īd and died, according to Hājī Khalfa, in the year A.H. 908 (corresponding with A.D. 1502.) He is the author of the *Sharah Haiākal*, *Akhlāq Jalālī*, *Isbāt Wājib* (on the existence of God), *Risāla Zaura* (on Sūfiism), *Hāshia Shamsia*, and *Anwār Shāfia*. He also wrote the *Sharah 'Aqāed*, and marginal notes on *Sharah Tajrīd*. The Akhlaq Jalālī is a translation from the Arabic, the original of which appeared in the 10th century under the name of *Kitāb-ut-Tahārat*, by an Arabian author, minister of the imperial house of Boyā. Two centuries after, it was translated into Persian by Abū Nasr, and named *Akhlāq Nāsirī*, or the morals of Nāsir, being enriched with some important additions taken from Abū Sīna. In the 15th century it assumed a still further improved form, under the present designation, the *Akhlāq Jalālī* or morals of Jalāl. This book, which is the most esteemed ethical work of middle Asia, was translated into English by W. F. Thompson, of the Bengal Civil Service, London, 1839.

Dawar Bakhsh (Sultan) (داور بخش سلطان), surnamed Mirzā Bulāqī, was the son of Sultān Khusro. When his grandfather, the emperor Jahāngīr, died on his way from Kashmīr to Lāhore in October, O.S. 1627, Safar, A.H. 1037, 'Asaf Khān, wazīr, who was all along determined to support Shāh Jahān, the son of the late emperor, immediately sent off a messenger to summon him from the Deccan. In the meantime, to sanction his own measures by the appearance of legal authority, he released prince Dāwar Bakhsh from prison, and proclaimed him king. Nūr Jahān Begam, endeavouring to support the cause of Shāhrīār, her son-in-law, was placed under temporary restraint by her brother, the wazīr, who then continued his march to Lāhore. Shāhriār, who was already in that city, forming a coalition with two, the sons of his uncle, the late Prince Dāniāl, marched out to oppose 'Asaf Khān. The battle ended in his defeat; he was given up by his adherents, and afterwards put to death together with Dāwar Bakhsh and the two sons of Dāniāl, by orders from Shāh Jahān, who ascended the throne. Elphinstone in his *History of India* says that Dāwar Bakhsh found means to escape to Persia, where he was afterwards seen by the Holstein ambassadors.

Daya Mal (دیا مل). *Vide* Imtiyāz.

Daya Nath (دیا ناتھ). *Vide* Wafā.

Dayanat Khan (دیانت خان), title of Muhammad Husain, an amīr of 2,500, who served under the emperor Shāh Jahān, and died at Ahmadnagar in the Deccan A.D. 1630, A.H. 1040.

Daya Ram (دیا رام), Paṭṭha, a hero, renowned in the west of Hindūstān for extraordinary strength of body, extraordinary courage, and extraordinary achievements. He was a Gwāla by caste, and flourished in the reign of the emperor Farrukh-siyar. The wonderful feats of this man are sung or recited accompanied by the beat of a *ḍhōl* throughout Hindūstān. A full and affecting account of this hero is given in the *Bengal Annual*, published at Calcutta in 1833, p. 169.

Daya Ram (دیـا رام), a chief of Hātras, tributary to the East India Company, who, about the year A.D 1814, confiding in the extraordinary strength of his fort, showed a spirit of contumacy and disobedience. A train of Artillery was brought against this place from Cawnpore, under Major-General Dyson Marshall; and a few hours of its tremendous fire breached the boasted fortification. Dayā Rām effected his escape by a sally-port, and was never heard of after.

Deo Narain Singh (دیو ناراین سنگھ) (K.C.S.I., Sir, Rāja) of Banāras, died suddenly on the 28th August, 1870.

Dewal Devi (دیـول دیـوي). *Vide* Kaulā Devī.

Dhara (دھـارا), the son of Rāja Todarmal. He was killed in a battle fought against Mirzā Jānī Beg, ruler of Thatta, in November, A.D. 1591, Muharram, A.H. 1000.

Dhola Rao (دھولا راو), the ancestor of the Kachhwaha Rājas of Ambīr or Jaipūr; he lived about the year A.D. 967.

Dhundia Wagh (دھوندیه واگھه), the free-booter, who had for several years with a formidable band, pillaged and laid waste the frontiers of Mysore. This robber assumed the lofty title of king of the two worlds, and aimed, doubtless, at carving out for himself some independent principality, after the example of Haidār 'Alī, in whose service he originally commenced his adventurous career. Subsequently he incurred the displeasure of Tīpū Sultān, who chained him like a wild beast to the walls of his dungeons in Serangapatam, from which "durance vile" he was liberated by the English soldiers after the taking of Serangapatam. He proceeded to threaten Mysore with 5,000 cavalry. The Government of Madras instructed Colonel Wellesley to pursue him wherever he could be found and to hang him on the first tree. His subjugation and subsequent death (in 1800) with the extirpation of his formidable band of freebooters, relieved the **English** Government from an enemy who, though by no means equal to Haidar and Tīpū, might eventually have afforded considerable annoyance.

Dil (دل), poetical name of Zorawar Khān of Sirkar Kol. He is the author of a Dīwān and a few Masnawīs.

Dilami (دلامي) and Sāmānī were two dynasties which divided between them the kingdom of Persia towards the beginning of the 10th century. They both rose to power through the favour of the Khalīfs of Baghdād, but they speedily threw off the yoke. The

Dīlāmī divided into two branches, exercised sovereign authority in Kirmān, Irāq, Fāris, Khuzistān, and Laristān, always acknowledging their nominal dependence on the Khalīfī, and during the whole period of their rule, one of the southern branch of this family was vested with the dignity of Amīr-ul-Umra, or vizīr, and managed the affairs of the Khalifate. Several of the Dīlāmī were able and wise rulers, but Mahmūd of Ghaznī put an end to the rule of the northern branch in A.D. 1029, and the Saljūqs subjugated the southern one in A.D. 1056, by the capture of Baghdād, their last stronghold. Their more powerful rivals, the Sāmānī, had obtained from the Khalīf the government of Transoxiana in A.D. 874; and to this, Ismā'īl the most celebrated prince of the family, speedily added Khwārizm, Balkh, Khurāsān, Sīstān, and many portions of northern Turkistān. Rebellions of provincial governors distracted the Samanida monarchy towards the end of the 10th century; and in A.D. 999 their dominions north of Persia were taken possession of by the Khān of Kāshghar, the Persian provinces being added by Mahmūd of Ghaznī to his dominions. *See* Sāmānī.

Dilawar Khan (دلاور خان), founder of the dynasty of the Muhammadan kings of Mālwa. The Hindū histories of the kingdom of Mālwa go back as far as the reign of Rāja Bikarmājīt, whose accession to that kingdom has given rise to an era which commences 57 years before Christ. After him reigned Rāja Bhōj and many others who are all mentioned among the Rājas of Hindūstān. During the reign of Ghayās-uddīn Balban, king of Dehlī in the year A.D. 1310, A.H. 710, the Muhammadans first invaded and conquered the provinces of Mālwa; after which it acknowledged allegiance to that crown until the reign of Muhammad Shāh Tughlaq II. A.D. 1387, A.H. 789. At this period Dilāwar Khān, a descendant on his mother's side from Sulṭān Shahāb-uddīn Ghōri, was appointed governor of Mālwa, previously to the accession of Muhammad Takhlaq, and he subsequently established his independence. In the year A.D. 1398 A.H. 801, Mahmūd Shāh, king of Dehlī, being driven from his throne by Amīr Taimūr (Tamerlane), made his escape to Gujrāt, and then to Mālwa, where he remained three years, after which, in A.D. 1401, A.H. 804, he, at the instance of the Dehlī nobles, quitted Mālwa, in order to resume the reins of his own government. Dilāwar Khān shortly afterwards assumed royalty and divided his kingdom into estates among his officers whom he ennobled. Dilāwar Khān on assuming independence, took up his residence in Dhār, which place he considered as the seat of his government, but he frequently visited the city of Māndo, remaining there sometimes for months together. He only survived his assumption of the royal titles a few years; for in the year A.D. 1405, A.H. 808, he died suddenly, and his son Alp Khān ascended the throne under the title of Sulṭān Hōshang Shāh. Including Dilāwar Khān eleven princes reigned in Mālwa till the time of the emperor Humāyūn, whose son Akbar eventually subdued and attached it to the Dehlī government. Their names are as follow:

1. Dilāwar Khān Ghōrī.
2. Hōshang Shāh, son of Dilāwar.
3. Sulṭān Muhammad Shāh.
4. Sulṭān Mahmūd I. Khiljī, styled the Great, son of Malik Mughīs.
5. Ghayas-uddīn Khiljī.
6. Nāsir-uddīn.
7. Mahmūd II.
8. Bahādur Shāh, king of Gujrāt.
9. Qadar Shāh.
10. Shujāa' Khān, and
11. Bāz Bahādur, son of Shujāa' Khān.

Dilawar Khan (دلاور خان), a nobleman of the reign of the emperor Shāh Jahān, was the son of Bahādur Khān Rohila. He died at Kābul in the year A.D. 1658, A.H. 1068.

Dildar Aga (دلدار آغا), one of the wives of the emperor Babar, and mother of Mirzā Handāl.

Diler Himmat Khan (دلیر همت خان), original name of Nawāb Muzaffar Jang of Farrukhābād, which see.

Diler Khan (دلیر خان), a Dāūdzaī Afghān, whose proper name was Jalāl Khān. He was the younger brother of Bahādur Khān Rohila, and one of the best and bravest generals of the emperor 'Alamgīr. He held the rank of 5,000, and died in the year A.D. 1683, A.H. 1094, in the Deccan.

Diler Khan (دلیر خان), title of 'Abdul Raūf, the son of 'Abdul Karīm, formerly in the service of the king of Bījāpūr. After the conquest of that country, he joined 'Alamgīr and received the title of Diler Khān and the mansab of 7,000. He died in the reign of Bahādur Shāh in the Deccan, where he held a jāgīr.

Dilip Singh (دلیپ سنگه), Mahārājā, often miscalled by Europeans "Dhuleep Sing," the son of Rāni Chanda Kunwar (*q.v.*). He became titular ruler of the Panjāb A.D. 1843, but was deposed by Dalhousie 1848; became a Christian and settled for some years in England. Married an Egyptian lady, by whom he had issue. Went to India, alleging grievances against the Government, but was not allowed to land. Abjured Christianity and declared himself a foe to the British race. Was living on the Continent in 1890.

[*Vide* Lady Login's book cited above.]

Dilras Bano Begam (دلرس بانو بیگم), daughter of Shahnawāz Khān Safwī, the son of Mirzā Rustam Kandharī, and wife of the emperor 'Alamgīr. She had another sister who was married to Murād Bakhsh, brother of 'Alamgīr.

Dilshad Khatun (دلشاد خاتون), daughter of Amīr Damishq, the son of Amīr Juban or Jovian, and wife of Sulṭān Abū Sa'id Khān. Amīr Hasan Buzurg, after the death of the Sulṭān in A.D. 1335, took possession of Baghdād and married her, but the reigns of government remained in her hands.

Dilsoz (دلسوز), poetical title of Khairātī Khān, a poet who lived about the year 1800.

Din Muhammad Khan (دين محمد خان), the son of Jānī Beg Sulṭān, and 'Abd-ullāh Khān Uzbak's sister, was raised to the throne of Samarqand after the death of 'Abdul Mōmin Khān, the son of 'Abd-ullāh Khān, in A.D. 1598, A.H. 1006. He was wounded in a battle fought against Shāh 'Abbās the Great, king of Persia, and died shortly after.

Diwan (ديوان), a collection of odes. The word is of frequent occurrence in Persian literature.

Diwana (ديوانه), poetical name of Muhammad Jān, who died in the year A.D. 1737, A.H. 1150.

Diwana (ديوانه), poetical name of Rāe Sarabsukh, a relation of Rāja Mahā Narāyan. He wrote two Persian Dīwāns of more than 10,000 verses; most poets of Lucknow were his pupils. He died in A.D. 1791, A.H. 1206.

Diwana (ديوانه), poetical name of Mirzā Muhammad 'Ali Khān of Jahanabad. He was employed at the office of Mr. Colebrooke at Jahanabad.

Diwanji Begam (ديوانجي بيگم). She was the mother of Arjumand Bano Begam Mumtaz Mahal, and the wife of 'Asaf Khān, wazīr. On a spot of fifty bighas of land on the bank of the river Jamna, close to Tājganj, is to be seen her tomb of white marble.

Dost 'Ali (دوست علي), Nawāb of Arkat and a relative of Murtaza Khān. Under him the atrocious seizure of Trichinopoly was perpetrated by Chanda Sahib. He was succeeded by his son Safdar 'Alī, who, after overcoming the effects of poison prepared for him by Murtaza Khān, fell by the poniard of a Paṭhān assassin, hired for the work by the same person. A storm was raised which he had not the courage to encounter; and disguising himself in female attire, he escaped from Arkat to his own fort of Vellore.

Dost Muhammad Khan (دوست محمد ruler of Kābul and Qandahār, was one of the brothers of Fatha Khān, the celebrated wazīr of Mahmūd, ruler of Hirat and chief of the Barakzaī clan. He was the most powerful chief in Afghānistan, and had for some years previous to the restoration of Shāh Shujāa'-ul-Mulk by the British in 1838, ruled that country. He was taken to Calcutta during the war, as related below; but his son Akbar Khān (*q.v.*) defeated and for a time expelled the invaders and killed Shujāa' (*q.v.*). The following is a summary of the Dost's career:—

On the death of this prince, Dost Muhammad again assumed the reins of government. On the base and cruel murder of Fatha Khān by Mahmūd, at the instigation of Prince Kāmrān, his brothers revolted from their allegiance under the guidance of Azīm Khān, the governor of Kashmīr, and drove Mahmūd and his son Kāmrān from Kābul. Azīm Khān in the first instance offered the vacant throne to Shāh Shujāa', but offended by some personal slight withdrew his support, and placed in his room, Aiyūb, a brother of Shāh Shujāa', who was content to take the trappings with the power of royalty. On Azīm Khān's death, his brothers dissatisfied with their position conspired against his son, Habīb-ullāh Khān, and seizing his person, by threats of blowing him from a gun, induced his mother to deliver up the residue of Azīm Khān's immense wealth. Aiyūb's son was killed in these disputes, and he himself, alarmed by these scenes of violence, fled to Lāhore. Dost Muhammad Khān, the most talented of the brothers, then took possession of the throne and became *de facto* king of Kābul. Sher Dil Khān, accompanied by four brothers, carried off about half a million sterling of Azīm Khān's money, and seated himself in Kandahār as an independent chieftain. He and one of his brothers died some years ago; and Kandahār was until lately ruled by Kohan Dil Khān, assisted by his two surviving brothers Rahīm Dil and Mīr Dil. In the year 1839 the British army entered Kābul and placed Shāh Shujāa'-ul-Mulk on the throne on the 8th May, and Dost Muhammad Khān surrendered to the British Envoy and Minister in Kābul on the 4th November, after having defeated the 2nd Bengal Cavalry, who were disbanded for their behaviour in the action of Parwān Darra. He was subsequently sent down to Calcutta, where he arrived, accompanied by one of his sons, on the 23rd May, 1841. He was set free in November, 1842, and returned to Kābul, where he reigned as before till his death, which took place on the 9th June, A.D. 1863, 31st Ẕil-ḥijja, A.H. 1279; his youngest son Amīr Sher Alī succeeded him.

Doulat Khan Lodi (دولت خان لودي), who, according to Firishti, was an Afghān by birth, originally a private Secretary, who after passing through various offices was raised by Sulṭān Mahmūd Tughlaq, and attained the title of 'Aziz Mumālik. After the death of Mahmūd, the nobles raised him to the throne of Dehlī in April, A.D. 1413, Muḥarram, A.H. 816. In March, 1414, 15th

Rabī I. A.H. 817, Khizir Khān, governor of Multān, invaded Dehlī, and after a siege of four months obliged Doulat Khān on the 4th June, 1414, Jamāda I. A.H. 817, to surrender. He was instantly confined in the fort of Fīrōzābād, where he died after two months.

Doulat Khan Lodi (دولت خان لودي), who invited Bābar Shāh to India, was a descendant of the race of that name, who heretofore reigned at Dehlī. He was a poet and a man of learning. He died a short time before Bābar conquered Dehlī, *i.e.* in the year A.D. 1526, A.H. 923.

Doulat Khan Lodi Shahu Khail (دولت خان لودي شاهو خيل) was the father of the rebel Khān Jahān Lodī. He served under Mirzā 'Aziz Kōka, 'Abdul Rahīm Khān Khānān, and Prince Dānial for several years, and was raised to the rank of 2,000. He died in the Deccan A.D. 1600, A.H. 1009.

Doulat Rao Sindhia (Maharaja) (دولت راو سيندهيه مهاراجه), of Gwāliar, a Mahrattā chief, was the grand-nephew and adopted son of Madhojī Sindhia, whom he succeeded to the Rāj of Gwāliar in March, A.D. 1794, A.H. 1208. His violence, rapacity and lawless ambition, were the main causes of the war in 1802 with the confederate Mahrattā chieftains. Hostilities having broken out with the British, Sir Arthur Wellesley (afterwards Duke of Wellington) defeated Doulat Rāo at Assaye in 1803, while Lord Lake drove the Mahrattas from the whole of the Doab. He married Baiza Bāīd, daughter of Sherji Rāo, Ghatgai, reigned 33 years, and died on the 21st March, 1827, 21st Sh'aban, A.H. 1242. He was succeeded by Jhanko Rāo Sindhia.

Doulat Shah (دولت شاه), son of Bakht Shāh of Samarqand, and author of the Biography of Poets called *Tazkira Doulat Shāhī*. He flourished in the reign of Sultān Husain Mirzā of Herāt, surnamed Abūl Ghazī Bahādur, and dedicated the work to his prime minister, the celebrated Amīr Nizām-uddīn 'Alīsher. This work was written in A.D. 1486, A.H. 891, and contains the Lives or Memoirs of ten Arabian, and one hundred and thirty-four Persian poets, with various quotations from their works, and anecdotes of the princes at whose courts they resided. It also gives an account of six poets then residing in Herāt; two of whom were principal ministers of the Sultān; *viz.* 'Alīsher and Amīr Shaikh Ahmad Suhelī. He died in A.D. 1495.

[*Vide* Fāīzī Kirmanī.]

Dundi Khan (دوندے خان روهيله), a Rohila chief, and son of Alī Muhammad Khān, the founder of the Rohila Government. In the partition of lands which were assigned to the chiefs, in the time of Hāfiz Rahmat Khān, Dūndey Khān obtained the districts of Bisaulī, Murādābād, Chāndpūr and Sambhal in Rohilkhand. He died previous to the Rohila war which took place in A.D. 1774, leaving three sons, the eldest of whom, Muhibullah Khān, succeeded to the largest portion of his territories.

Dunyapat Singh (Raja) (دنياپت سنگه راجه). His father died in A.D. 1790, at which time he was only seven years of age. He inherited from his grandfather Rūp Rāe the Chaklas of Kōrā, Fathapūr and Kara, but was dispossessed by the Nawāb Wazīr, and a Nānkar allowance of 24,000 rupees granted to the Rāja on his exclusion. This was subsequently reduced to 7,500 rupees. The original grant amounted to 52,000 per annum, payable from 14 mahāls, but in A.D. 1770, the Nawāb Najaf Khān acquiring unlimited dominion over these provinces, dispossessed his father of eleven of the villages, by which his income was reduced to 20,000 rupees. In 1787 his father was dispossessed of the remaining three villages by Zain-ul-'Abidīn Khān, the 'Amil, but as the Rāja was about to proceed to hostilities, the 'Amil agreed to allow him 10,000 rupees for the first year, and 20,000 thereafter, but failed in the fulfilment of his promise. In A.D. 1792, Zain-ul-'Abidīn died, and was succeeded by his son Bāqar, 'Alī Khān, and from that period up to 1802 the Rāja Duniāpat Singh was allowed 8,000 rupees per annum, which was confirmed by Government in 1805 in perpetuity.

Dupleix, Joseph François, a French officer, governor of Pondicherry. In A.D. 1750 he was elevated to the rank of a Haft Hazārī, or Commander of seven thousand horse, and permitted to bear an ensign, assigned to persons of the highest note in the empire, by Muzaffar Jang, viceroy of the Deccan, after his victory over his brother Nāsir Jang; who fell in battle on 15th December of that year. But the ambitious plans of Dupleix were not approved by the French Government. He was suspended and sent home in 1754; and died in disgrace and poverty Nov. 10th, 1764.

[*Vide* Malleson's *Dupleix*, "Rulers of India," 1890.]

Durduzd (دردزد). *Vide* 'Alī Durduzd of Astrabad.

Durgawati (Rani) (درگاوتی رانی), daughter of Rana Sarika.

[*Vide* Silhaddī.]

Durgawati (Rani) (درگاوتی رانی), the daughter of the Gond Rāja of Mahōba, who was much celebrated for her singular beauty. Overtures had been made for an union with Dalpat Sāh, Raja of Singalgurh (which is situated on the brow of a hill that commands a pass on the road about halfway between Garda and Sangar); but the proposal was rejected on the ground of a previous engagement, and some inferiority of caste on the part of the Garha family, who were of the race of the Chandeil rājpūts. Dalpat Sāh was a man of uncommonly fine appearance, and this, added to the celebrity of his father's name and extent of his dominions, made Durgāwatī as desirous as himself for the union, but he was by her given to understand, that she must be relinquished or taken by force, since the difference of caste would of itself be otherwise an insurmountable obstacle. He marched with all his troops he could assemble, met those of her father and his rival,—gained a victory and brought off Durgāwatī as the prize to the fort of Singalgurh. Dalpat Sāh died four years after their marriage, leaving a son named Bīr Narāyan about three years of age, and his widow as regent during his minority. Asaf Khān, the imperial viceroy at Kaṛa Mānikpūr on the Ganges in the province of Allahābad, invited by the prospect of appropriating so fine a country and so much wealth as she was reputed to possess, invaded her dominions in the year A.D. 1564, at the head of 6,000 cavalry and 12,000 well disciplined infantry, with a train of artillery. He was met by the Rānī at the head of her troops, and an action took place in which she was defeated. She received a wound from an arrow in the eye; and her only son, then about 18 years of age, was severely wounded and taken to the rear. At this moment she received another arrow in the neck; and seeing her troops give way and the enemy closing round her, she snatched a dagger from the driver of her elephant, and plunged it in her own bosom. Her son was taken off the field and was, unperceived by the enemy, conveyed back to the palace at Chūrāgarh, to which Asaf Khān returned immediately after his victory and laid siege. The young prince was killed in the siege; and the women set fire to the palace under the apprehension of suffering dishonour if they fell alive into the hands of the enemy. Two females are said to have escaped, the sister of the queen, and a young princess, who had been betrothed to the young prince Bīr Narāyan; and these two are said to have been sent to the emperor Akbar. In this district of Jabbalpūr the marble rocks and the palace called Madan Mahal are worth seeing. There is some doggrel rhyme about this palace which is not generally known, though of some interest. This building stands on a single granite boulder, and was constructed by the Gond princess Rānī Duragāwatī at the time of the Muhammadan invasion of Central India. Years after the cession of the country to the British, a wag of a Paṇḍit wrote on the entrance door of the palace the following lines:

Madan Mahal kē chhain mē,
Do tāngōn kē bīch,
Gaṛā nau lakh rupī,
Aur sonē kā do īṇt.

Translation—

In the shade of Madan Mahal,
Between two boulders,
There are buried nine lakhs of rupees
And two bricks of gold.

It did not take long for the news of the appearance of this writing on the door to spread abroad, and the very person to fall a dupe to the Paṇḍit's trick was Captain Wheatley, at that time a Political Assistant at Jabalpūr. He mustered some peons and labourers, and having proceeded to the spot commenced digging for the treasure on the part of Government. The native lady, in whose possession were the village lands on which the palace stood, came rushing down to the Agent to the Governor-General and represented that she was being plundered of her treasure by Captain Wheatley. "Paglī" replied Sir Wm. Sleeman, "he is as mad as you are; the Paṇḍit would not have divulged the secret were it of much value." Many years have since elapsed, and many others not possessed of Sir William's wisdom have fallen dupes to the Paṇḍit's poetical trick; and, but for the very durable nature of the martas, there have been enough excavations made in and about the building to raze it to the ground.

E

Egypt, Kings of. *Vide* Moizz-li-dīn-allāh Abī Tamīm Ma'd.

Ekkoji (يكوجى), the founder of the Tanjore family, was the son of Shahjī Bhosla, the brother of Siwājī, but from another consort. The principality of Tanjore was one of the oldest in the Mahraṭṭa confederacy, of which province Ekkojī obtained possession in A.D. 1678.

[*Vide* Letter Y.]

F

Faghfur (فغفور), the general name of the kings of China.

Faghfur Yezdi (فغفور يزدي حكيم), (Hakīm), a physician and poet of Persia, born at Yezd. He is the author of a Dīwān or Book of Odes, and has written several panegyrics in praise of the kings of Persia. He came to India in A.D. 1603, A.H. 1012, and was employed by prince Parwez, and died at Allahābād about the year A.D. 1619, A.H. 1028.

Fahmi Kirmani (Maulana Sadr-uddin Muhammad) (فهمي كرماني مولانا صدرالدين محمد), a poet who is the author of a Masnawī called *Sūrat-wa-Ma'anī*, and also of some Qasīdas, Ghazals, Satires, etc. He died in the year A.D. 1584, A.H. 993, in the fort of Tabrez, during the time it was besieged by the Turks.

Faiq (فايق), or Fāyeq, poetical name of Moulwī Muhammad Fāiq, author of the work called *Makhzan-ul-Fawaed*.

Faiz (فايض), or Fāyez, poetical name of Shaikh Muhammad Fāiz, a pupil of Muhammad Sa'īd Ayāz. He is the author of a short Dīwān, and was probably living in A.D. 1724, A.H. 1136.

Faiz (فيض), the distinguished mystical philosopher and theologist, Mullā Muhsin of Kāshān, commonly called Akhūnd Faiz. He flourished under Shāh 'Abbās II. of Persia, who treated him with great respect. He has written a great number of books, of which *Kitāb 'Asafī*, and *Kitāb Safī* are two Commentaries on the Qurān. He died at Kāshān in the time of Shāh Sulaimān of Persia, and his tomb is a place of pilgrimage.

Faiz (فيض), poetical title of Mīr Faiz 'Alī, an Urdū poet of Dehlī. His father, Mīr Muhammad Taqī, was also an elegant poet, and had assumed the title of Mīr for his poetical name. Both Faiz 'Alī and his father were living at Dehlī in the year A.D. 1785, A.H. 1196.

Faiz (فيض), a pupil of Mirzā Qatīl, and author of a poetical work containing amorous songs in Persia, called *Dīwān Faiz*. He was living in the time of Muhammad 'Alī Shāh, king of Lucknow, about the year A.D. 1840, A.H. 1256.

Faiz (فيض), poetical title of Faiz-ul-Hasan of Sahāranpūr, author of the *Rauzat-ul-Faiz*, a poem composed in A.D. 1847, A.H. 1263.

Faizi (فيضى), of Sarhind. *Vide* Alahdad.

Faizi Kirmani (فايضى كرمانى), a poet who rendered the Tazkira of Doulat Shāh in Persian verses in the time of the emperor Akbar, and altered the division of the original, making ten periods instead of seven.

[*Vide* Lutfullah Muhammad Muhaddis.]

Faizi (Shaikh) (فيضى شيخ), whose proper name was Abū'l Faiz, was the son of Shaikh Mubārik of Nāgor, and eldest brother or Shaikh Abū'l Fazl, prime-minister and secretary to the emperor Akbar Shāh. He was born on the 16th September, A.D. 1547, 1st Shāban, A.H. 954, and was first presented to Akbar in the 12th year of his reign, and introduced his brother Abū'l Fazl six years later. After the death of the poet laureate Ghizālī of Mashhad, about the year A.D. 1572, or some years after, or, according to the *Māsir-ul-Umrā*, in the 33rd year of the emperor, Faizī was honoured with the title of *Malik-ush-Shua'rā*, or king of poets. In history, philosophy, in medicine, in letter writing, and in composition, he was without a rival. His earlier compositions in verse bear his titular name of Faizī, which he subsequently dignified into Faiyāzī, but he survived to enjoy his last title only one or two months, and then met his death. Being desirous of rivalling the Khamsa or the five poems of Nizāmī, he wrote in imitation of them his *Markaz Adwār*, *Sulaiman* and *Bilkais*, *Nal Daman*, *Haft Kiskwār*, and *Akbar Nama*. The story of Nal Daman is an episode of the Mahābhārat, which he translated into Persian verse at the command of the emperor Akbar. He was the first Musalmān that applied himself to a diligent study of Hindū literature and science. Besides Sanskrit works in poetry and philosophy, he made a version of the *Bīja Ganitā* and *Lilāwatī* of Bhaskar Achāryā, the best Hebrew works on Algebra and Arithmetic. He was likewise author of a great deal of original poetry, and of other works in Persian. He composed an elaborate Commentary upon the Qurān, making use of only those 13 out of the 28 letters of the Alphabet which have no dots, and which he named *Sawāta'-ul-Ilhām*; a copy of this extraordinary monument of wasted labour (says Elliot) is to seen in the Library of the East India House. There is also another book of the same description which he wrote and called *Mawarid-ul-Kalam*. Faizī suffered from asthma and died at Āgra on Saturday the 4th October, O.S. 1595, 10th Safar, A.H. 1004, aged 49 lunar years and some months; and, as many supposed him to have been a deist, several abusive chronograms were written on the occasion, of which the following is one—"The Shaikh was an infidel." There is also an Insha or collection of Letters which goes after his name. His mother died in January, A.D. 1590, A.H. 998, and his father in August, A.D. 1593, Zeqa'd, A.H. 1001. He was a profound scholar, well versed in Arabic literature, the art of poetry and medicine. He was also one of the most voluminous writers that India has produced and is said to have composed 101 books. Faizī had been likewise employed as teacher to the princes; he also acted as ambassador. Thus in A.H. 1000 he was in the Deccan, from whence he wrote the letter to the historian Budāoni, who had been in temporary disgrace at Court.

[Vide *Āīn Translation*, i. 490.]

Faiz-ullah Anju (Mir) (فیض الله انجو میر), a Qāzī who presided on the seat of justice in the reign of Sultān Mahmūd Bahmanī, king of Deccan, who reigned from A.D. 1378 to 1397, A.H. 780 to 799. He was a good poet, and a contemporary of the celebrated Khwāja Hāfiz. Once presenting the Sultān with an ode of his own composition, he was rewarded with a thousand pieces of gold, and permitted to retire, covered with honours, to his own country.

Faiz-ullah Khan (فیض الله خان), chief of the Rohelas and Jagīrdar of Rāmpūr, was the son of 'Alī Muhammad Khān Rohela. After the battle of Kutra in A.D. 1774, he retired to the Kamaon hills. By the treaty under Colonel Champion, he had a territory allotted to him of the annual value of 14 lakhs of rupees. He chose the city of Rāmpūr as the place of his residence, and after an uninterrupted and prosperous administration of 20 years, he died in September, A.D. 1794, Safar, A.H. 1209, and was succeeded by his eldest son Muhammad 'Alī Khān. This prince, in the course of a few days, in 1794 was imprisoned and assassinated by his younger brother Ghulām Muhammad, who forcibly took possession of the government. The English, having espoused the cause of Ahmad Alī, the infant son of the murdered prince, defeated and took Ghulām Muhammad prisoner at Bithoura. He was conveyed to Calcutta, where, under pretence of going on a pilgrimage to Mecca, he embarked on board a ship, probably landed at one of the ports in Tīpū Sultān's dominions, and thence made his way to the court of Kābul in A.D. 1797, A.H. 1212, where, united with the agents of Tīpū in clamours against the English, he urged Zamān Shāh, the son of Taimūr Shāh, to invade Hindustān, promising that, on his approach to Dehlī, he should be joined by the whole tribe of Rohelas. The Nawāb Ahmad Alī Khān died about the year A.D. 1839, A.H. 1255. After the death of Ahmad Alī Khān, Muhammad Saīd Khān ascended the Masnad in 1840; after him Muhammad Yusuf Alī Khān succeeded in 1855, who was living in 1872.

Fakhri (فخری), son of Maulana Sultān Muhammad Amīrī of Herāt. He is the author of the *Jawāhir-ul-'Ajāeb*, Gems of Curiosities, being a biography of poetesses. He informs us that with the intention to perform the pilgrimage to Mecca, he came during the reign of Shāh Tahmāsp Husainī to Sindh; the ruler of that country was then Isa Turkhān (who died about the year A.D. 1566, A.H. 974). Ilāhī the poet calls the above-mentioned work *Tazkirat-ul-Nisā*. He is also the author of the *Tuhfat-ul-Habīb*, a collection of Ghazals from the best authors.

Fakhri (فخری), a Persian poet who wrote a Dīwān of 10,000 verses in which he imitated most of the ancient masters, but as he had not much education he was not acknowledged by other poets. He dug a grave for himself outside the Isfahān Gate and made himself a tombstone, and visited his grave every Friday. He was living in A.D. 1585, A.H. 993.

Fakhr-ud-daula (فخرالدوله), title of Abū'l Hasan 'Alī, a Sultān of the race of Bōya, was the son of Sultān Rukn-ud-daula. He was born in A.D. 952, A.H. 341, and succeeded his brother Mowaiyad-ud-daula to the throne of Persia in January, A.D. 984, Sha'bān, A.H. 373. He was a cruel prince, reigned 14 years, and died in August, A.D. 997, Sha'bān, A.H. 387. He was succeeded by his son Majd-ud-daula.

Fakhr-ud-daula (فخرالدوله), a nobleman who was governor of Patna in the reign of Muhammad Shāh, emperor of Dehlī; he held that situation till the year A.D. 1735, A.H. 1148, when it was taken away from him and conferred upon Shujaa'-uddīn Nāwab of Bengal, in addition to that government, and of the province of Urissā.

Fakhr-uddin (فخرالدین), one of the princes of the Druses, who, early in the 17th century, conceived the idea of rendering himself independent of the Porte. He was betrayed, carried a prisoner to Constantinople, where he was strangled by order of Sulṭān Murād IV. in A.D. 1631, A.H. 1041.

Fakhr-uddin Abu Muhammad-bin-Ali az-Zailai (فخرالدین ابو محمد بن علی زیلئی), author of a Commentary on the *Kanz-ul-Daqāeq* entitled *Ta'ba'īn-ul-Haqāeq*, which is in great repute in India, on account of its upholding the doctrines of the Hanafī sect against those of the followers of Shāfa'ī. He died in A.D. 1342, A.H. 743.

Fakhr-uddin Bahman (Malik) (فخرالدین بهمن ملک), third Sultān of the dynasty of Kart or Kard, was the son of Mālik Shams-uddīn Kart II. whom he succeeded to the throne of Herāt, Balkh and Ghaznī in September, A.D. 1305, A.H. 705. He was contemporary with Sulṭān Aljaitū, surnamed Muhammad Khudā Banda, king of Persia, who sent an army against him which he defeated. He died about the beginning of the year A.D. 1307, A.H. 706, and was succeeded by his brother Mālik Ghayās-uddīn Kart I. who died in A.D. 1329.

Fakhr-uddin Ismat-ullah Bukhari (فخرالدین عصمت الله بخاری). He died in A.D. 1426, A.H. 829.

[*Vide* Asmat.]

Fakhr-uddin Junan (Malik) (فخرالدین جونان ملک), eldest son of Sulṭān Ghayās-uddīn Tughlaq Shāh I. On the accession of his father to the throne of Dehlī, he was declared heir-apparent, with the title of Ulagh Khān, and all the royal ensigns conferred upon him. The names of his other brothers were Bahrām Khān, Zafar Khān, Mahmūd Khān and Nasrat Khān. After the death of his father in A.D. 1325, A.H. 725, he succeeded him with the title of Muhammad Shāh Tughlaq I.

Fakhr-uddin Kha'lidi (Maulana) (فخرالدین خالدي مولانا), who was commonly called "Bihishtī," is the author of a work called *Sharah-Farāez*. He was the master of Maulānā Mo'īn-uddīn Jawīnī.

Fakhr-uddin Mahmud Amir (فخرالدین محمد امیر), son of Amīr Yemīn-uddīn Muhammad Mustūfī. He is generally known by his Takhallus or poetical name, Ibn Yemīn, *i.e.* the son of Yemīn-uddīn. According to Dr. Sprenger's Catalogue, he died in A.D. 1344, A.H. 745, and left panegyrics on the Sarabdāl princes and some ghazals, but it is particularly his Qita's which are celebrated.

[*Vide* Amīr Mahmūd.]

Fakhr-uddin Malik (فخرالدین ملک).

[*Vide* Malik Fakhr-uddīn, king of Bengal.]

Fakhr-uddin Mirza (فخرالدین مرزا), the eldest son of Bahādur Shāh II. ex-king of Dehlī. He died before the rebellion, on 10th July, 1856.

Fakhr-uddin (Maulana) (فخرالدین مولانا), son of Nizām-ul-Haq, was styled Saiyad-ush-Shua'rā, or chief of the poets. He is the author of several works, among which are the following: *Nizām-ul-'Aqāed*, *Risāla Marjia* and *Fakhr-ul-Hasn*. He died in the year A.D. 1785, A.H. 1199, aged 73 years, and lies buried close to the gate of the Dargāh of Qutb-uddīn Bakhtyār Kākī in old Dehlī. His tomb is of white marble and has an inscription mentioning his name and the year of his demise. His grandson Ghulām Nasīr-uddīn, surnamed Kālī Sāhib, was a very pious and learned Musalmān; he too was a good poet and died in the year A.D. 1852, A.H. 1268.

Fakhr-uddin Muhammad Razi (Imam) (فخرالدین محمد رازی امام) was a doctor of the Shāfa'ī sect. He surpassed all his contemporaries in scholastic theology, metaphysics and philosophy. He is the author of several instructive works, among which is one called *Hadāyek-ul-Anwar*, a book on different subjects which he dedicated to Sulṭān 'Alā-uddīn Takash, ruler of Khwārizm; and another called *Risāla Haiyat*, or Geometry, dedicated to Sulṭān Bahā-uddīn Ghorī. He was born at Rei on the 26th January, A.D. 1150, 25th Ramazān, A.H. 544, and died at Herāt on Monday the 29th March, A.D. 1210, 1st Shawwal, A.H. 606, aged 62 lunar years. His father's name was Ziyā-uddīn-bin-Umar. The title of Rāzī attached to his name is because he was born at Rei in Tabristan. He is the father of Khwāja Nasīr-uddīn Tūsī.

Fakhr-uddin Sultan (فخرالدین سلطان), also called Fakhra, was the king of Sonārgāon in Bengal, which adjoins the district of Pandūa. He was put to death by Shams-uddīn, king of Lakhnautī, about the year A.D. 1356, A.H. 757, who took possession of his country.

Fakhr-ul Islam (فخرالاسلام برودی), of Barōd, the son of 'Alī. He is the author of the works called *Usūl-ud din* and *Usul Fiqha*, and several other works. He died in A.D. 1089, A.H. 482.

Fakhr-ullah Asad Jurjani (فخرالله اسعد جرجانی). He flourished under the Saljūq princes, and is the author of the love adventures of Wais and king Rāmīn, originally in the Pahlawī language, called *Wais-wa-Ramīn*.

Fakhr-un-nissa Begam (فخرالنسا بیگم), the wife of Nawāb Shujā'at Khān. She is the founder of the mosque called "Fakhr-ul-Masājid," situated in the Kashmīrī Bāzār at Dehlī, which she erected in memory of her late husband in the year A.D. 1728, A.H. 1141.

Falaki (فلکی), takhullus of a Persian poet whose proper name was Abū'l Nizām Muhammad Jalāl-uddīn Shirwānī. He is also commonly styled Shams-ush-Shuā'rā, the sun of the poets, and Mālik-ul-Fuzla, king of the learned. His poems are preferred to those of Khāqānī and Zakīr. Hamd-ullāh Mustaufī calls him the master of Khāqānī, but Shaikh 'Azurī makes mention in his Jawāhir-ul-Asrār that Khaqānī and Falakī both were the pupils of Abū'l 'Alā of Ganja. There has been also another Falakī surnamed Abū'l Fazl, who was an author. Falakī died in A.D. 1181, A.H. 577. His patron was Manochehr Shirwānī.

Fanai (فنائی), poetical name of Shams-uddīn Muhammad-bin-Hamza. He was an author and died in the year A.D. 1430, A.H. 834.

Fani (فانی) (perishable), the poetical name of Muhsin Fānī, which see.

Fani (فاني), the Takhullus of Khwāja Muhammad Mo'īn-uddīn-bin-Muhammad-bin-Mahmūd Dihdār Fānī. He came to India and stood in high favour with Abdul Rahīm Khān the Khān Khānan. He died in A.D. 1607, A.H. 1016, and left several works on Sūfīism, as *Sharah Khutba*, *Hāshia Rāshahāt*, *Hāshia Nafhāt*, *Hāshia bar-Gulshan Rāz*, and *Albayān*. He is also the author of a Dīwān in Persian, and a Masnawī or poem called *Haft Dilbar*, *i.e.*, the seven sweethearts, dedicated to the emperor Akbar.

Faqir (فقیر), poetical name of Mīr Nawāzish 'Alī of Bilgaram. He died in the year A.D. 1754, A.H. 1167.

Faiqr (Mir Shams-uddin) (فقیر میر شمس الدین), of Dehlī, who had also the poetical name of Maftūn. From Dehlī he went to Lucknow in A.D. 1765, A.H. 1179, and is said to have been drowned about the year 1767. He is the author of a Dīwān and also of a Masnawī called *Taswīr Muhabbat*, containing the story of Rām Chānd, the son of a betel-vendor, composed in A.D. 1743, A.H. 1156, and of several other poems.

Farabi (فارابي ابو نصر), commonly called so because he was a native of Fārāb, a town in Turkey. His proper name is Abū Nasr. He was one of the greatest Musalmān philosophers, remarkable for his generosity and greatness of talents, whom we call Alfarabixs. He was murdered by robbers in Syria in A.D. 954, A.H. 313, thirty years before the birth of Abū Sīna. Imād-uddīn Mahmūd and Ahmad-bin-Muhammad were two authors who were also called Fārābī.

Faraburz (فرابرز), the son of Kaikāūs (Darius the Mede), king of Persia.

Faraghi (Mir) (فراغی میر), the brother of Hakīm Fath-ullāh Shīrāzī. He was living in A.D. 1563, A.H. 971, in which year the fort of Ranthanbūr was conquered by the emperor Akbar, on which occasion he wrote a chronogram.

Farai (فراء), whose proper name was Abū Zikaria Yehia, was an excellent Arabic grammarian who died in the year A.D. 822, A.H. 207.

Faramurz (فرامرز), son of Rustam, the Hercules of the Persians. He was assassinated by the order of Bahman, also called Ardisher Darazdast, king of Persia. There is said to have also been an author, named Muhammad bin-Farāmurz, styled Shadīd.

Farasquri (فرسقوری), surname of Muhammad bin-Muhammad-al-Hanīfa, Imām of the mosque named Gouride, at Grand Cairo, who flourished about the year A.D. 1556, A.H. 964, and was an author.

Fard (فرد), poetical name of Abū'l Hasan, the son of Shāh Na'mat-ullāh. He died in the year A.D. 1848, A.H. 1265, and left a Dīwān.

Farghani (فرغانی), commonly called so because he was a native of Farghāna, but his full name is Ahmad or Muhammad-ibn-Kasīr-al-Farghānī, a famous Arabian astronomer whom we know under the name of Alfragan or Alfraganius. He flourished in the time of the Khalīf-al-Māmūn, about the year A.D. 833, A.H. 218, and is the author of an introduction to Astronomy, which was printed by Golius, at Amsterdam, in 1669, with notes.

Farhad (فرهاد), the lover of the celebrated Shīrīn, the wife of Khusro Parwez, king of Persia. The whole of the sculpture at Behstūn in Persia is ascribed to the chisel of Farhād. He was promised, we are told in Persian Romance, that if he cut through the rock, and brought a stream that flowed on the other side of the hill to the valley, the lovely Shīrīn (with whom he had fallen distractedly in love) should be his reward; he was on the point of completing his labour, when Khusro Parwez, fearing to lose his mistress, sent an old woman to inform Farhād that the fair object of his desire was dead. He was at work on one of the highest parts of the rock when he heard the mournful intelligence. He immediately cast himself headlong, and was dashed in pieces. *Vide* Shīrīn.

Farhat (فرحت), poetical name of Shaikh Farhat-ullāh, son of Shaikh Asad-ullāh. He wrote a Dīwān in Urdū and died in the year A.D. 1777, A.H. 1191, at Murshidābād.

Farhat Kashmiri (فرحت کشميري), a poet who was living in A.D. 1724, A.H. 1136.

Farid Bukhari (Shaikh) (فريد بخاری شيخ), commander of the Āgra city guards when Akbar died. Great honours were conferred on him by the emperor Jahāngīr, on account of his services. He received the title of Murtaza Khān, and managed the affairs of the empire till he was rendered unfit for business by a stroke of the palsy, which opened the way for the promotion of Ya'timad-uddaula, the father of the empress Nūr Jahān. He died A.D. 1616, A.H. 1025.

Farid Katib (فريد کاتب). *Vide* Farīd-uddīn Kātib.

Farid or **Farid-uddin Ahwal** (فريد الدين احول) (the squinting), a poet of Persia who was a native of Asfaräen in Khurāsān and contemporary with Imāmī Hirwī. Khwāja Nizām-uddīn Abū Bakr the Wazīr of Azd-uddīn Sa'd was his patron. He died at Isfahān and left a Dīwān containing 5,000 verses.

Farid or **Farid-uddin (Shaikh)** (فريد الدين شکر گنج فريد شيخ), a celebrated Muhammadan saint, who is styled *Shakar Ganj*, on account of his having, it is said, miraculously transmuted dust or salt into sugar. His father's name was Shaikh Jalāl-uddīn Sulaimān, a descendant of Farrukh Shāh of Kābul. He was a disciple of Khwāja Qutb-uddīn Bakhtyār Kākī, and was contemporary with Shaikh Sa'd-uddīn Hamwia, Saif-uddīn Mākharzī, and Bahā-uddīn Zikaria, all of whom died successively a short time after one another. He was born in A.D. 1173, A.H. 569, died on Saturday the 17th October, A.D. 1265, 5th Muharram, A.H. 664, aged 95 lunar years, and is buried at Ajūdhan, a place commonly called Patan or Pāk Patan in Multān. The anniversary of his death is celebrated every year on the 5th of Muharram, when a great crowd of Muhammadans assemble together to pray at his tomb.

Farid-uddin (فريدالدين کاتب), commonly called Farīd Kātib, was a pupil of Anwarī, a good poet and secretary to Sultān Sanjar. When that prince was defeated by the monarch of Qara Khatāi in A.D. 1140, A.H. 535, and fled with a few followers to Khurāsān, Farīd consoled him by composing an ode upon the occasion, in which he says, "that every thing must change, but that the condition of God alone was not liable to vary."

Farid-uddin Attar (Shaikh) (فريد الدين عطار شيخ), surnamed Muhammad Ibrāhīm, was a dealer in perfumes, from which he took his poetical name "'Attar." He afterwards retired from the world, became a disciple of Shaikh Majd-uddīn Baghdādī, and lived to a great age, namely, that of 114 lunar years. He was born at Shādyākh, a village in Naishāpūr in the reign of Sultān Sanjar in November, A.D. 1119, Sha'ban, A.H. 513, and, when at the siege of Naishāpūr, the son-in-law of Changez Khān, the Tartar, was killed, a general massacre of the inhabitants of that place was made by the Mughals, among the number that were slain being Farīd-uddīn. This circumstance took place on the 26th April, A.D. 1230, 10th Jamad II. A.H. 627. He is the author of 40 poems and several prose works, amongst the latter *Tazkirat-ul-Aulia*.

The following are his poems:—

Asrār Nāma.
Ashtur Nāma.
Ausat Nāma.
Besar Nāma.
Bulbul Nāma.
Gul-wa-Khusro or Hurmuz.
Haidar Nāma.
Haft Wādī.
Haqāeq-ul-Jawāhir
Hallāj Nāma.
Jawāhir-ul-zāt.
Khusro Nāma.
Kanzan Makhfia.
Kunt Kauz Makhāfia.
Ilāhī Nāma
Khayāt Nāma.
Kanz-ul-Haqaeq.
Lisān-ul-Ghaib.
Mansūr Nāma.
Miftāh-ul-Fatūh.
Mazhar-ul-'Ajāeb.
Mantiq-ul-Tair.
Mukhtār Nāma.
Musībat Nāma.
Pand Nāma.
Sipāh Nāma.
Wald Nāma.
Wasiat Nāma.

Besides the above, he is also the author of a Dīwān containing 40,000 verses.

Faridun (فريدون), an ancient king of Persia, the son of Abtīn, an immediate descendant of Tahmurs, king of Persia. He had escaped, it is said in a miraculous manner, from Zuhāq, when that prince had seized and murdered his father. At the age of 16 he joined Kāwa or Gāwa, a blacksmith, who had collected a large body of his countrymen; these fought with enthusiasm under the standard of the blacksmith's apron, which was afterwards converted into the royal standard of Persia, called the Durafsh Kāwānī. Zuhāq, after numerous defeats, was made prisoner, and put to a slow and painful death. Faridūn, who was a very just and virtuous king, had three sons, *viz.*, Salm, Tūr, and Iraj, among whom he divided his kingdom; but the two elder, displeased that Persia, the fairest of lands and the seat of royalty, should have been given to Iraj their junior, combined to effect his ruin, and at last slew him, and sent his head to Faridūn. The old man fainted at the sight, and when he recovered he called upon Heaven to punish the base penetrators of so unnatural and cruel a deed. The daughter of Iraj was married to the nephew of Faridūn, and their young son Manuchehr proved the image of his grandfather. When he attained manhood, the old king made every preparation to enable him to revenge the blood of Iraj. A war commenced; and in the first battle Salm and Tūr were both slain. Faridūn soon afterwards died, and was succeeded by Manuchehr. Persian authors assure us that Faridūn reigned 500 years.

Faridun (فريدون), a Turk who wrote a Commentary in the Turkish language on the Ghazals of Hafiz.

Farigh (فارغ), author of the poem called *Masnawi Fārigh*, which he composed in A.D. 1592, A.H. 1000, in which year, he says, Shāh 'Abbās conquered Gīlān, and to whom it was dedicated.

Faris Ecchidiak (فارس), an Arabic poet and litterateur, born about the year A.D. 1796. In religion he was a Syrian Christian. He is the author of several works. When in London he published his revised text of the New Testament in Arabic. His Dīwān in Arabic is highly spoken of by those who have seen it. He was living in 1860.

Fariz (فارض), or Ibn Fāriz, surname of Abū Hafs Sharaf-uddīn Umar bin-al-Asa'dī, bin-al-Murshid, bin-Ahmad al Asa'dī, a very illustrious Arabian poet. He was born at Cairo A.D. 1181, A.H. 577, and died there in the year A.D. 1234, A.H. 632.

Farkhari (فرخاري), a poet who was in the service of Amīr Kaikāūs, and is the author of the story of *Wāmiq-wa-Uzra*, in verse.

Farkhunda Ali Khan (Mir) (فرخنده علی خان میر), Nizām of Deccan. He succeeded his father Sikandar Jāh in the government of Haidarabād in A.D. 1829.

[*Vide* Afzal-uddaula.]

Faroghi Kashmiri (فروغی کشمیری), a poet who died in A.D. 1666, A.H. 1077.

Faroghi (Maulana) (فروغی مولانا), of Qazwīn in Isfahān; he was a dealer in perfumes, but an excellent poet, and lived in the time of 'Abbās the Great.

Farrukhi (فرخی), or Farkhī, a poet who flourished in the time of Sultān Mahmūd of Ghaznī, was a pupil of Unsarī the poet, and a descendant of the royal race of the kings of Sīstān. He is the author of a work called *Tarjumān-ul-Balāghat*, and of a Dīwān in Persian. He wrote several panegyrics in praise of Abū'l Muzaffar, the son of Amīr Nasr and grandson of Nāsir-uddīn, ruler of Balkh.

Farrukh Fa'l (فرخ فال), a son of the emperor Humāyūn by Māh Chūchāk Begam, born at Kābul in A.D. 1555, A.H. 962.

Farrukh-siyar (Muhammad) (فرخ سیر محمد), emperor of Dehlī, born on the 18th July, O.S. 1687, 18th Ramazān, A.H. 1098, was the son of Azīm-ush-Shān, the second son of Bahādur Shāh I. and great-grandson of the emperor Alamgīr. His father was killed in the battle fought against Jahāndār Shāh, his uncle and predecessor. One of Jahāndār Shāh's first acts on his accession to the throne had been to put all the princes of the blood within his reach to death; among those whom he could not get into his power was Farrukh-siyar, who was in Bengal at the time of his grandfather Bahādur Shāh's death. But when the information of his father's death reached him, he threw himself on the compassion and fidelity of Saiyad Husain Alī Khān, the governor of Behār, who warmly espoused his cause, and prevailed on his brother, Saiyad Abdullah Khān, governor af Allahābād, to adopt the same course. By the aid of these noblemen, Farrukh-siyar assembled an army at Allahābād, marched towards Āgra, defeated Jahāndār Shāh, took him prisoner, and having murdered him, ascended the throne in the fort of Dehlī on Friday the 9th January, O.S. 1713, 23rd Zil-hijja, A.H. 1124. The former Amīr-ul-Umrā Zulfiqār Khān and many other nobles and dependants of the late emperor were put to death by the bow-string and other punishments. Rāja Sabhchand, Dīwān to the late Amīr-ul-Umrā, had his tongue cut out: Azīz-uddīn, son of Jahāndār Shāh, 'Alī Tabār, the son of 'Azim

Shāh, and Humāyūn Bakht, younger brother to Farrukh-siyar were deprived of their sight by a red hot iron drawn over their eyes. On Farrukh-siyar's accession, Abdullāh Khān, the eldest brother, was made Wazīr with the title of Qutb-ul-Mulk, and Husain Alī Khān raised to the rank of Amīr-ul-Umrā (Commander-in-Chief) which was the second in the State. The emperor's nuptials with the daughter of Rāja Ajīt Singh of Mārwār were celebrated with unprecedented splendour in the year A.D. 1716, A.H. 1128. Farrukh-siyar had not long enjoyed the throne, when a jealousy arose between him and the Wazīr Qutb-ul-Mulk; and upon the emperor trying to form schemes for the recovery of his independence, he was deposed, blinded and imprisoned by the two brothers. This event took place on the 18th February, O.S. 1719, 8th Rabī' II. A.H. 1131, and not long after he was murdered on the 16th May, A.D. 1719, 9th Rajab, A.H. 1131, following, and buried in the court of the mausoleum of the emperor Humāyūn at Dehlī. He had reigned 6 years 3 months and 15 days. After his deposal the Saiyads set up a prince of the blood to whom they gave the title of Rafī-ud-Darjāt. It was from Farrukh-siyar that the East India Company obtained their Farmān of free trade, with leave to purchase thirty-seven districts in Bengal, besides various privileges; little attention was however paid to it by the Sūbahdār till the English acquired force to give it weight.

Farrukhzad (فرخزاد), a prince of Persia of the Sāsānian race.

[*Vide* Tūran Dukht.]

Farrukhzad (فرخزاد), son of Sultān Masa'ūd I. of Ghaznī, began to reign after the death of his brother Sultān Abdul Rashīd, in March, A.D. 1053, A.H. 444. He reigned 6 years and died in the latter part of the year A.D. 1058, when his brother Sultān Ibrahīm succeeded him.

Farsi (فرسی یا فارسی), or Farasī, surname of Abū'l Fawāris Ibrahīm, a Persian author.

Farsi (فرسی), poetical name of Sharīf Khān Amīr-ul-Umrā, which see.

Faryabi. *Vide* Zahīr-uddīn Fāryābī.

Faryad (فریاد), the poetical name of Lālā Sāhib Rāe, a Kāyeth of Lucknow. He originally had assumed Qurbān, for his poetical name, but latterly changed it to Faryād. He was living in A.D. 1782, A.H. 1196.

Farzada Quli (فرزدا قلی), author of a Catalogue of books in the Arabic, Persian, and Hindī languages, amounting, on a rough estimate, to upwards of 2,000 volumes. From its mentioning the Dīwān of Sanda, it appears that it was written within the last fifty or sixty years. It also mentions the *Mustafā Nāma*, in the metre of the Shāh Nāma, embracing the history of Persia from Muhammad to Tahmasp Shāh Safwī, amounting to 104,000 couplets; also of a Persian translation of the Muqāmāt of Harīzī. *Jour. of the Roy. As. Soc.* No. XI.

Farzadaq (فرزدق), the son of Ghālib, called the master of Arabian poets, was an author, and had the whole Qurān by heart. He died in A.D. 728, A.H. 110, aged upwards of 70 years. He flourished in the reign of Abdul Mālik, the son of Marwan I. who imprisoned him because he wrote a panegyric in praise of Imām 'Alī Zain-ul-'Abidīn, son of Imām Husain, but was released, after the death of the khalīf, by his son Walīd. His Dīwān in Arabic is much esteemed in Hajjāz and Irāq.

Fasihi Ansari (فصیحی انصاری هروی), of Herāt, a Persian poet, who flourished about the year A.D. 1595, A.H. 1004. He never came to India. He died in A.D. 1636, A.H. 1046.

Fasih-uddin Muhammad Nizami Maulana (فصیح الدین محمد نظامی مولانا), author of the *Sharah Jughmīnī.*

Fassi (فسی), surname of Faqīh-uddīn Muhammad-ibn-Ahmad 'Alī-al-Husainī; he was a native of Fass (Fez), on which account he was called Fassī. He was an author and Qāzī of the city of Mecca, and died A.D. 1429, A.H. 833.

Fatha Ali Husaini (فتح علی حسینی), author of the biography called *Tazkirat-ush-Shua'rāe Hindī.* It contains the Memoirs of 108 Hindī and Deccanī authors, with numerous extracts from their works.

Fatha 'Ali Shah (فتح علی شاه), king of Persia, was a Turkman of the tribe of Kājār. He succeeded his uncle 'Akā Muhammad Khān to the throne of Persia in A.D. 1797, A.H. 1212. He had received an excellent education, and possessed some literary accomplishments; was a tolerable poet, and fond of the society of the learned, whom he generously patronized. He reigned nearly 40 years and died in the year A.D. 1834, A.H. 1250. After him Muhammad Shāh, the son of 'Abbās Mirzā and grandson of Fatha 'Alī Shāh, mounted the throne and died in A.D. 1847, when his son Nasīr-uddīn Ahmad Shāh, the present king, succeeded him. It was to the court of Fatha 'Alī Shāh that Sir John Malcolm in 1800 led the magnificent embassy which Lord

Wellesley had despatched from Calcutta, with the view of trumping Bonaparte's cards in the East, and of playing off a Persian ally on our Indian frontiers against an Afghān ill-wisher, the ambitious Zamān Shāh.

Fatha Haidar (فتح حیدر), the eldest son of Tippū Sultān.

Fatha Khan (فتح خان), the son of Sultān Fīroz Shāh Bārbak, king of Dehlī, and brother of Zafar Khān.

[*Vide* Fīroz Shāh Bārbak.]

Fatha Khan (فتح خان), Nawāb of Bhāwalpūr.

Fatha Khan (فتح خان), brother of Dost Muhammad Khān, ruler of Kābul. The celebrated Wazīr of Mahmūd, ruler of Herāt and chief of the Barakzaī clan, whose family drove away the descendants of Ahmad Shāh Abdālī from Kābul.

Fatha Khan (فتح خان), the son of Malik 'Ambar, the Abyssinian chief of Ahmadnagar in the Deccan, who had the Nizām Shāhī dominions under his control for some years. After his father's death in A.D. 1626, A.H. 1035, he succeeded to his authority; but Murtaza Nizām Shāh II. being weary of his control, took him prisoner by treachery, and confined him in the fort of Khybar. Having made his escape, he rebelled, but was again taken, and confined in Daulatābād. He was released in time, and appointed generalissimo by the influence of his sister, mother to Nizām Shāh. He shortly, to prevent another removal from office, confined the Sultān under pretence of insanity, and put to death twenty-five of the principal nobility in one day, writing to the emperor Shāh Jahān that he had thus acted to prevent them from rebelling against him. The emperor in reply commended his attachment, and ordered him to put the captive prince to death, which he did about the year A.D. 1628, A.H. 1038, and placed his son Husain, an infant of ten years, on the throne. Fatha Khān, by offering a present of eight lacs of rupees, and agreeing to pay tribute, was allowed to keep what territory yet remained to the Nizām Shāhī sovereignty. In the year A.D. 1634, A.H. 1044, Fatha Khān was forced to surrender; and the fall of this place put a final period to the Nizām Shahī dynasty, which had swayed the sceptre for 150 years. Husain Nizām Shāh was confined for life in the fortress of Gwāliar, but Fatha Khān was received into favour, and was allowed to retire to Lāhore on a pension of two lacs of rupees, which he enjoyed till his death.

Fatha Naek (فتح نایک), the father of Haidar 'Alī Khān, the usurper of Mysore and Seringapatam. He died in A.D. 1738, and was buried at Kolār, a capital of seven parganas, about 35 miles east of Bangalore.

Fatha-puri Mahal (فتح پوري محل), or Begam, one of the wives of the emperor Shāh Jahān. She was the founder of the Fathapūrī Masjid in Dehlī.

Fatha Shah (فتح شاه پوربی), Pūrbī, succeeded Yūsaf Shāh to the throne of Bengal in A.D. 1482, A.H. 887, and after a reign of about eight years was murdered in A.D. 1491, A.H. 896, by the eunuch Sultān Shāhzāda, who succeeded him.

Fatha-ullah Imad Shah (فتح الله عماد شاه), originally in the service of Sultān Mahmūd Shāh II. Bahmanī, king of Deccan, was made governor of Berar. He became independent about the year A.D. 1484, and died about the year A.H. 1513. His son 'Alā-uddīn 'Imād Shāh succeeded him.

[*Vide* 'Imad-ul-Mulk.]

Fatha-ullah Mustaufi (فتح الله مستوفی), surnamed Fakhr-uddīn, was a good poet and served under Khwāja Rashīd-uddīn, Fazl-ullāh and his son Ghayās-uddin Muhammad, as secretary. He is the brother of Khwāja Hamd-ullah Mustaufī, who died in A.D. 1349.

Fatha-ullah Shirazi Amir (فتح الله شیرازی امیر), one of the most learned men of his time. He came from Shīrāz to Deccan and passed a few years in the service of Sultān Alī Adil Shāh of Bījapūr. After the death of that king, he left Deccan and came to Dehlī in the year A.D. 1582, A.H. 990, and had an honourable office assigned to him by the emperor Akbar, near his person, with the title of Azd-ud-daula. He died on Wednesday, the 3rd Shawwāl, 997 Hijri, the 24th Amardād Mah Ilāhī, in the 34th year of Akbar's reign, corresponding with the 6th August, O.S. 1589, at Sirīnagar the capital of Kashmir, where he had proceeded with his royal master. The emperor was much grieved at his loss; and Shaikh Faizī wrote an appropriate epitaph on the occasion. Fifteen days after his death died also the Hakīm Abū'l Fatha Gīlānī, the brother of Hakīm Hamān, who was then with the king proceeding to Kābul. Sarfī Sāwajī wrote the chronogram of their death.

Fathi (فتحی), a poet of Ardastān, who died in A.D. 1635, A.H. 1045.

Fathi 'Ali Husaini Gurdezi. *Vide* Husaini.

Fatima (فاطمة), the daughter of Muhammad and his wife Khudija. She was born at Mecca five years before her father gave himself out for a prophet, *i.e.*, about the year A.D. 606, and died about six months after him, in the city of Medina on the night of Monday the 23rd November, A.D. 632, 3rd Ramazān, A.H. 11. She was married to Alī, Muhammad's cousin-german, and became the mother of the Imams Hasan and Husain. She passes for a very holy woman amongst the Musalmāns, and is also called by them Batūl, Tāhira, Mathara, and Zahra.

Fatima bint Asad (فاطمه بنت اسد), the daughter of Asah, the son of Hāshim. She was the wife of Abū Tālib and mother of 'Alī.

Fatima Sultan (فاطمه سلطان), one of the wives of Umar Shaikh Mirzā, and mother of the prince Pīr Muhammad Jahāngīr.

Fatimites, or kings of Barbary and Egypt of the Fatimite dynasty.

[*Vide* Muizz-li-dīn-allah and Obeid-ullah Almahdī.]

Fattahi Naishapuri Maulana (فتاحی نیشاپور مولانا), an author who died A.D. 1448, A.H. 852.

[*Vide* Yahia (Mulla).]

Fauji (فوجی), poetical name of Mirzā Muhammad Muqīm; he was born at Shīrāz but came to India in the time of Shāh Jahān, and was attached to the service of his son Shāh Shujā'a in Bengal. After a long residence in India he returned to his father-land, but died in a short time after his arrival there. He was living in A.D. 1649, A.H. 1059, and has left a Dīwān in Persian verse. As he was employed in the army he derived his poetical title from *Fauj*, *i.e.* army.

Faulad Khan (Shidi) (فولاد خان شیدی), an Abyssinian who was at Kotwal in the time of the emperor Muhammad Shāh, about the year A.D. 1737, A.H. 1150, and on whom a satire was written by the poet Sauda. He had built a fine garden in Agrah, of which no traces are to be seen now.

Fauraq (فورق), surname of Abū Bakr Muhammad, bin-Hasan, bin-Fauraq, commonly called ibn-Fauraq, was a great Metaphysician and Schoolman, for which reason he is styled Mutkallim. He was born at Isfahān, and died in the city of Naishāpūr, in Khurāsān, A.D. 1015, A.H. 406.

Fawad Muhammad Pasha (فواد محمد پاشا), a Turkish statesman and litterateur of Constantinople, son of Izzat Mulla, and nephew of Laila Khatūn, a Turkish poetess. He is the author of several works. He was living in A.D. 1870, and has been loaded with distinctions by European sovereigns.

Fayyaz (فیاض). *Vide* 'Abdul-Razzaq of Lāhijān.

Fayyazi (فیضی). *Vide* Faizī (Shaikh).

Fazal Khan (فضل خان), governor or kiladar of the fort of Agra, was turned out by Sūrajmal Jāt, who took possession of the fort and plundered everything he could lay his hands upon.

Fazil (فاضل), a poet who flourished about the year A.D. 489.

Fazl Ali Khan (فضل علی خان), a poet who flourished in the time of the emperor Muhammad Shāh of Dehlī, and was living in A.D. 1739, A.H. 1152.

Fazl Ali Khan (فضل علی خان), whose entire title was Nawāb Ya'timad-ud-daula Zayā-ul-Mulk Saiyad Fazl 'Alī Khān Bahādur Sohrāb Jang, was the prime minister of the king of Audh Ghāzī-ud-dīn Haidar, and was living in A.D. 1829.

Fazl Barmaki (فضل برم کي), brother of 'Jafar-al-Barmakī, the minister of Hārūn-al-Rashīd Khalīfa of Baghdād.

[*Vide* Jafar-al-Barmakī.]

Fazl Haq (فضل حق), the son of Fazl Imām. He wrote prose and poetry as did also his father. His Qasīdas are much esteemed. At the outbreak of 1857, he joined the rebel Nawāb of Banda and others, and was said to have been killed at Narod in an attack made by General Napier on the 17th December, A.D. 1858, A.H. 1274. The *Dehlī Gazette*, May 17th, 1859, mentions, however, that sentence of transportation was passed on the rebels Lonī Singh, ex-Rāja of Mitaulī, and the Maulwī Fazl Haq.

Fazli (فضلی), a poet and author of the Loves of *Shāh-wa-Māh*, a poem containing 12,260 Persian verses, which he completed in the year A.D. 1641.

Fazl Imam (فضل امام), an inhabitant of Khairābād, who wrote prose and poetry, and died in the year A.D. 1828, A.H. 1244.

Fazl Rasul Moulvi (فضل رسول مولوی بداونی), of Badāon, son of Maulvī Abdul Majīd, and author of the works called *Bawārik* and *Tashīh-ul-Masāel.* He was living in A.D. 1854, A.H. 1271.

Fazl-ullah (فضل الله), surnamed Khwāja Rashīd-uddīn, a native of Qazwīn or Hamdan and a Persian historian, who wrote at the desire of his master, the Sultān of Persia, a history of the Mughals, finished in A.D. 1294, to which he afterwards added a supplement. He was beheaded in July, A.D. 1318. His name is spelt in some of our Biographical Dictionaries, Fadl-allah. From the work of Rashīd-uddīn, called *Jāma'-ut-Tawārīkh*, and from other materials, Abū'l Ghāzī, king of Khwārizm, composed in the Mughal language his *Genealogical History.*

[*Vide* Rashīd-uddīn.]

Fazl-ullah Khan Nawab (فضل الله خان), an Amīr of the court of the emperor Babar, who built a mosque in Dehlī in the year A.D. 1529, A.H. 936, which is still standing.

Fazl-ullah Maulana (فضل الله مولانا), Physician to Amīr Taimūr, and the most celebrated and skilful practitioner of the age in which he lived.

Fazuli Baghdadi (فضولي بغدادی), an author who was a native of Baghdād, and died in the year A.D. 1562, A.H. 970, and left us a Dīwān in the Persian and Turkish language.

Fidai Khan (فدائی خان), former title of 'Azim Khān Kōka, which see.

Fidai Mirza (فدائی مرزا), name of a poet.

Fidwi (فدوي), of Lāhore, the poetical name of a poet of the end of the 18th century; was son of a Hindu chandler but converted to Islam by Sābir 'Alī Shāh; became a client of Zābita Khān *(q.v.)* and died at Moradabad about 1780. He is the author of a poem in Urdū entitled *Yūsaf-wa-Zaleikhā* (the Loves of Joseph and Potiphar's wife). Mīr Fatha Alī Shaidā has satirized him in his story of the *Būm* and *Baqqāl.*

Fidwi (فدوی), author of a Persian Dīwān. He flourished in the year A.D. 1649, A.H. 1059.

Fighan (فغان), the poetical title of Ashraf 'Alī Khān, the son of Mirzā 'Ali Khān, and the Kōka or foster-brother of the emperor Ahmad Shāh of Dehlī. He is the author of a Dīwān in the Urdū language, containing about 2,000 verses. He died at Patna in A.D. 1772, A.H. 1186, and was buried there.

Fighani (فغانی). *Vide* Bābā Fighānī.

Fikrat (فکرت), poetical title of Mirzā Ghaiās-uddīn.

Fikri (فکری), poetical title of Sa'īd Muhammad of Herāt. He was a weaver and is therefore called Jāmabāf. He came to India in A.D. 1561, A.H. 969, and gained, through his great talents for making epigrams, the favour of the emperor Akbar. He composed only *Ruba'īs*, and died in A.D. 1565, A.H. 973.

Firaqi (فراقی), poetical title of an author named Abū'l Barkāt, who died in the year A.D. 1507, A.H. 913.

Firdausi or **Firdausi Tusi** (فردوسی یا فردوسی طوسی), the poetical title of Abū'l Kāsim Hasan-bin-Sharaf Shāh, a famous Persian poet, sometimes called the Homer of Persia, whose epic poem, called Shāhnāma, written by order of Sultān Mahmūd of Ghaznī, is justly celebrated. It contains the legendary annals of the ancient kings of Persia, from the reign of the first king, Kaiomurs, to the death of Yezdijard III. the last monarch of the Sāsānian race, who was deprived of his kingdom A.D. 641, by the invasion of the Arabs during the Khilāfat of 'Umar, the second Khālif after Muhammad. It was the labour of 30 years, and consists of 60,000 verses, each of which is a distich. The following circumstances respecting the origin of the poem and the life of the poet are chiefly derived from the preface to the copy of the *Shāhnāma*, which was collated A.D. 1426, A.H. 829, by order of Bāisanghur Mirzā the grandson of Amīr Taimūr. It appears from that preface, that Yezdijard, the last king of the Sāsānian race, took considerable pains in collecting all the chronicles, histories, and traditions connected with Persia and the sovereigns of that country, from the time of Kaiomurs to the accession of the Khusros, which by his direction were digested and brought into one view, and formed the book known by the name of *Siar-ul-Maluk*, or the *Bāstān Nāma*. When the followers of Muhammad overturned the Persian monarchy, this work was found in the plundered library of Yezdijard. In the tenth century one of the kings of the then dynasty, directed Daqīqī (*q.v.*) the poet to versify that extensive work, but the poet only lived to finish a thousand distichs, having been assassinated by his own slave. Nothing further was done till the reign of Sultān Mahmūd, when a romantic accident furnished the Sultān with a copy of the *Bāstān Nāma*, the existence of which was till then unknown to him. From this work, he selected seven stories which he delivered to seven poets to be composed in verse, that he might be able to ascertain the merits of each competitor. The poet Unsarī gained the palm, and he was accordingly engaged to arrange the whole in verse. Firdausī was at this time at Tus, his native city, where he cultivated his poetical talents with assiduity and success. He had heard of the attempt of Daqīqī, and of the determination of the reigning king Mahmūd, to patronize an undertaking which promised to add lustre to the age in which he lived. Having fortunately succeeded in procuring a copy of the *Bāstān Nāma*, he pursued his studies with unremitting zeal, and soon produced that part of the poem in which the battles of Zuhāq and Faridūn are described. The performance was universally read and admired, and it was not long before his fame reached the ears of the Sultān, who immediately invited him to his court. It is related that when Firdausī, on the invitation of the Sultān, reached the capital Ghaznī, he happened to pass a public garden where the three royal poets, Unsarī, Asjadī and Farrukhī were enjoying themselves. The poets observed him approach and at once agreed that if the stranger chanced to have any taste for poetry, which they intended to put to test, he should be admitted to their friendship, and in order to decide as to his merits they settled among themselves to repeat each in turn a hemistich, and leave to Firdausī to complete the fourth, but at the same time satisfied in their own minds that there was no other word in the Persian language that would rhyme with the three which they had taken care to pre-occupy. Firdausī joining them and hearing the proposal, promised to exert his powers. They then commenced each with an extemporaneous line:—

Unsarī ... The light of the moon to thy splendour is weak,
Asjadī ... The rose is eclipsed by the bloom of thy cheek;
Farrukhī ... Thine eyelashes dart through the folds of the Joshan,
Firdausī ... Like the javelin of Geo in the battle with Pushan.

The poets were astonished at the readiness of the stranger, and ashamed at being totally ignorant of the story of Geo and Pushan, which Firdausī related as described in *Bāstān Nāma*. They immediately treated him with the greatest kindness and respect, and afterwards introduced him to Mahmūd, as a poet capable of undertaking the *Shāhnāma*. Mahmūd considered himself never so much honoured as when Firdausī set his foot at Ghaznī; he was never more proud than that Firdausī was by his command, composing, in his faultless verse, a history of the monarchs of Persia, his predecessors. No reward then appeared to him too great to offer, to induce the poet to undertake the task, no promise too splendid to excite him. "Write, unequalled one," cried he, "and for every thousand couplets a thousand pieces of gold shall be thine." Firdausī obeyed, but resolved to accept no reward till he had completed the work he had undertaken, and for thirty years he studied and laboured that his poem might be worthy of eternal fame. In this he succeeded, and presented an elegant copy of his book to Mahmūd, but the patience of the Sultān was exhausted, his enthusiasm was gone, his liberality had faded away, and when the 60,000 couplets of the *Shāhnāma* were ended, there was a pause, which brought to the poet disappointment and to the monarch such everlasting disgrace as has obliterated all his triumphs. Mahmūd received the book, coldly applauded his diligence and dismissed him. Many months elapsed, and Firdausī heard no more of his work; he then took occasion to remind the king of it by the following epigram:

'Tis said our monarch's liberal mind
Is like the ocean unconfined,
Happy are they who prove it so,
'Tis not for me that truth to know.
I've plunged within its waves, 'tis true,
But not a single pearl could view.

Shamed, picqued, and offended at this freedom, the Sultān ordered 60,000 pieces of silver dirhams to be sent to the author, instead of the gold which he had promised. Firdausī was in the bath at the time the money arrived, and his rage and amazement exceeded all bounds when he found himself thus insulted. He immediately distributed the paltry sum amongst the attendants of the bath and the slave who brought it. The excited poet then relieved his mind by a satire full of stinging invective, and caused it to be transmitted to the favourite Wazīr who had instigated the Sultān against him; it was carefully sealed up, with directions that it should be read to Mahmūd on some occasion when his mind was perturbed with affairs of State, as it was a poem likely to afford him entertainment. Firdausī having thus prepared his vengeance, quitted the court and was safely arrived in Māzandarān, where news reached him that his lines had fully answered the purpose he had intended they should do. Mahmūd had heard and trembled, and too late discovered that he had ruined his own reputation for ever. After his satire had been read by Mahmūd, the poet feared to remain too long in one place; he sought shelter in the court of the khalīf of Baghdād, in whose honour he added a 1000 couplets to the *Shāhnāma*, and who rewarded him with the 60,000 gold pieces which had been withheld by Mahmūd. Mahmūd pretended to have discovered that his Wazīr had deceived him in attributing impiety to Firdausī, and he at once sacrificed that favourite, dismissing him with disgrace. Thinking, by a tardy act of liberality, to repair his former meanness, Mahmūd dispatched to Firdausī the 60,000 pieces he had promised, a robe of State, and many apologies and expressions of friendship; but the poet was dead, having expired in his native town full of years and honours, surrounded by his friends and kindred. Firdausī died at Tūs (now called Mashhad) his native country in A.D. 1020, A.H. 411, aged 89 years, but Hajī Khalfa says he died in A.D. 1025, A.H. 416. Besides the *Shāhnāma*, he was the author of other poems called *Abiāt Firdausī*.

Firdausi-al-Thihal (فردوسی التهیہال), a Turkish historian, and author of the Turkish work called *Shāhnāma*, which comprises the history of all the ancient kings of the East. Bayazīd or Bajazet II. to whom the book was dedicated, ordered the author to reduce it from its original bulk of 300 volumes to 80. Firdausī however, felt so mortified at this proposal, that he preferred leaving the country altogether, and emigrated to Khurāsān, in Persia. Firdausī flourished in A.D. 1500.

Firishta (فرشتہ), whose proper name was Muhammad Qāsim, and who was the author of the history called *Tārīkh-i-Firishta*, was born at Astrabād on the borders of the Caspian Sea, between the years A.D. 1570 or 1550, A.H. 978 or 958. His father, a learned man, by name Ghulām 'Alī Hindū Shāh, left his native country when our author was very young and travelled into India. He eventually reached Ahmadnagar in the Deccan during the reign of Murtazā Nizām Shāh I. and was appointed by the Sultān to instruct his son Mīrān Husain in the Persian language, but he soon died after his selection, and Firishta was left an orphan in early youth. After the death of Murtazā Nizām Shāh, in A.D. 1589, A.H. 996, he proceeded to Bījāpūr, and was presented by Dilāwar Khān, minister to Ibrāhīm 'Adil Shāh II: by whose request he wrote the history which goes by his name, in the year 1023 Hijrī (A.D. 1614). The year of his death is altogether unknown. Briggs supposes that it occurred in A.D. 1612, A.H. 1021, making him only 41 years of age. M. Jules Mohl supposes him to have revised his work up to at least A.D. 1623, A.H. 1033, making his age not less than 73, as he supposes him to have been born in A.D. 1550. Firishta styles his work *Gulshan-i-Ibrāhīmī* and *Nauras Nāma*. Its former name is derived from the king to whom it was dedicated; and hence it is frequently quoted under the name of *Tārīkh Ibrāhīmī*. The latter name was given to it in commemoration of the new capital, Nauras, which his patron Ibrāhīm 'Adil Shāh, commenced building in the year A.D. 1599. The first and second books, giving an account of the Dehlī emperors down to Akbar, were translated into English by Colonel Dow in 1768; the history of the Deccan by Captain Jonathan Scott. But the translation of the entire work by General Briggs in four volumes 8vo., 1829, has (according to Elliot) thrown others into the shade, and is by far the most valuable storehouse of facts connected with Muhammadan dynasties of India.

[*Vide* Dowson's *Elliot*, vi. 207.]

Firoz (فیروز), a celebrated Sūfī of Agra, author of a Persian work on Theology called *'Aqāed Sūfia*, written in A.D. 1626, A.H. 1036.

Firoz I. (فیروز) (the Peroses of the Greeks), a king of Persia of the Sāsānian race, was the eldest son of Yezdijard II. He succeeded his younger brother Hurmuz, whom he dethroned and put to death in A.D. 458. He lost his life in a battle against the king of Transoxiana, after a reign of 26 years, in A.D. 484. Balās or Palas or Balasus, his son, succeeded him; and after his death his brother Qubād mounted the throne.

Firozabadi (فیروزابادی), surname of Majd-uddīn Muhammad-bin-'Yaqūb bin-Muhammad, a learned Persian, so called from his birth-place Fīrozābād, a village in Shīrāz. The stupendous work called *Qāmus* or *Qāmūs-ul-Lughāt*, renowned as the most perfect Arabic Dictionary, was written by him. Those who are acquainted with the peculiarities of the Arabic language cannot open this work without feeling amazed at the literary services rendered by this learned man. He died A.D. 1414, A.H. 817.

[*Vide* Majd-uddīn Muhammad-bin-'Yaqūb.]

Firozabadi (فیروزابادی), a learned Musalmān, author of *Al Tanbidh*, or *Tanbiz*, or general information on the Muhammadan law in the 11th century. Lempriere's *Universal Dictionary*.

Firoz Jang Khan (فیروز جنگ خان), the inscription on the gate of the old fort of Patna, dated in the Hijra year 1042 (A.D. 1633), attributes its erection to Fīroz Jang Khān.

Firoz Khan Khwaja Sara (فیروز خان خواجہ سراء), who held the rank of 300 in the time of Shahjahan.

Firoz Mulla (فیروز ملا بن کاؤس), son of Kāūs, chief priest of the Pārsī Qadīmīs of Bombay, author of the *George Nāma*, a history of India from its discovery by the Portuguese to the conquest of Pūna by the English in A.D. 1817, A.H 1233.

Firoz Shah (فیروز شاه), the son of Salīm Shāh, was raised to the throne of Dehlī at Gwāliar after the death of his father when he was only about 12 years old. He had scarcely reigned three months (or only 3 days) when his mother's brother Mubārīk Khān murdered him on the 2nd May, A.D. 1554, 29th Jumāda I. A.H. 961, and ascended the throne with the title of Muhammad Shāh 'Adil. *See* Bībī Bāī.

Firoz Shah Bahmani Sultan (فیروز شاه بهمنی سلطان), king of the Deccan, was the son of Sulṭān Dāūd Shāh. After having deposed and confined Sulṭān Shams-uddīn, he ascended the throne on the 15th November, A.D. 1397, A.H. 800, with the title of Sulṭān Fīroz Shāh Rōz Afzūn. He excelled his predecessors in power and magnificence, and in his reign the house of Bahmanī attained its greatest splendour. On ascending the throne, he appointed his brother Ahmad Khān, Amīr-ul-Umrā, with the title of Khānkhānān, and raised Mīr Faizullah Anjū, his preceptor, to the office of Wazīr-us-Saltanat, with the title of Malik Nāeb. He reigned 25 years 7 months and 15 days, and died on the 25th September, A.D. 1422, 15th Shawwal, A.H. 825, ten days after resigning his crown in favour of his brother Ahmad Khān, who ascended the throne with the title of Sulṭān Ahmad Shāh Walī Bahmanī.

Firoz Shah Khilji Sultan (فیروز شاه خلجی سلطان), surnamed Jalāl-uddīn, son of Qāem Khān, ascended the throne of Dehlī after the murder of Sulṭān Muiz-uddīn Kaiqubād in A.D. 1282, A.H. 688. He reigned about 8 years, after which he was obliged to go down to Kaṛā Mānikpūr in the province of Allahābād to punish his nephew and son-in-law 'Alā-uddīn, the governor of that place, who had rebelled against him. 'Alā-uddīn, hearing of the king's departure from Dehlī, crossed the Ganges and encamped near Mānikpūr upon the opposite bank. When the king reached the landing place, 'Alā-uddīn appeared upon the bank with his attendants, whom he ordered to halt. He advanced alone, met his uncle and fell prostrate at his feet. The king, taking him by the hand, was leading him to the royal barge, when 'Alā-uddīn made a signal to his guards, and one of his officers struck his head off. 'Alā-uddīn caused it to be fixed on the point of a spear and carried through the camp and city. This circumstance took place on the 19th July, A.D. 1296, 17th Ramaẓān, A.H. 695, and 'Alā-uddīn ascended the throne of Dehlī with the title of Sikandar Sānī ("second Alexander"). Fīrōz Shāh was the first Sulṭān of the second branch of the Turko-Afghān dynasty called Khiljī.

List of the Kings of the Khiljī dynasty.

1. Fīrōz Shāh Khiljī.
2. 'Ala-uddīn Khiljī.
3. Shāhab-uddīn Umar.
4. Mubarik Shāh Khiljī, the last of this dynasty, was murdered in A.D. 1321, by Mālik Khusro, a favourite slave, who ascended the throne, but was soon afterwards slain by Ghaias-uddīn Tughlaq Shāh, the first of the 3rd branch of Afghān kings of Dehlī.

Firoz Shah Purbi (فیروز شاه پوربی), a king of Bengal, whose former name was Mālik Andīl, an Abyssinian chief, who after killing the eunuch Sulṭān Shāhzāda, was elevated to the throne of Bengal in A.D. 1491, A.H. 896, with the title of Fīrōz Shāh. He repaired the city of Gour, commonly called Lakhnauṭī, where he gave universal satisfaction to all classes of his subjects. He died in A.D. 1494, A.H. 899.

Firoz Shah Tughlaq Sultan (فیروز شاه تغلق سلطان), called Fīrōz Shāh Bārbak, was the son of Sipahsālār Rajab, the brother of Sulṭān Ghaiās-uddīn Tughlaq, and cousin to Sulṭān Muhammad Tughlaq, whom he succeeded to the throne of Dehlī on the 20th March, A.D. 1351, 21st Muharram, A.H. 752, at Ṭhaṭṭa. He was a just and learned prince. His soldiers and his subjects were equally happy under his administration, nor did anyone dare to exercise oppression in his time. He was himself the author of the work called *Fatāhāt Fīrōz Shāhī*, *i.e.* the conquests of Fīrōz Shāh. In August, A.D. 1387, he abdicated the throne and resigned the reins of government to his son Nasīr-uddīn Muhammad, but the prince giving himself up entirely to pleasure, was soon after expelled and obliged to fly with a small retinue to the mountains of Sirmdur, and Fīrōz Shāh again resumed his full authority. He constructed numerous buildings and canals, as also the fort of Fīrōzabād at old Dehlī, and after a reign of of 38 lunar years and eight months, died on the 21st September, A.D. 1388, 18th Ramaẓān, A.H. 790, aged upwards of 80 years. The words "Wafāt Fīrōz" (the death of Fīrōz) comprise the numerical letters of the year of his demise. He was buried on the banks of the Hauz Khās, a tank built by him in old Dehlī; and was succeeded by his grandson Ghaiās-uddīn (the son of Fatha Khān) who was slain after five months. After him another grandson of the late king, named Sulṭān Abū Bakr, the son of Zafar Khān, was raised to the throne. He had reigned one year and six months, when his uncle Nāsir-uddīn Muhammad Shāh, the son of Fīrōz Shāh, deposed him and ascended the throne of Dehlī in August, A.D. 1390.

Firoz Shah (فیروز شاه), one of the sons of the ex-king Bahādur Shāh II. king of Dehlī, and one of the chief rebels in the outbreak of 1857. He fought the British boldly, and for a time acted with Tantia Topi in 1858; so that the British Government offered a reward of 10,000 rupees for his apprehension. It was reported in 1864 that he had made his appearance in the Seronj Jungles. Some Arabs who arrived at Haidarābād in 1866 reported that they had seen him in Arabia, and supporting himself by begging among the rich merchants. [Since this was written nothing more has been heard of this Prince.]

Fitrat (فطرت), the poetical name of Mīr Mōiz-uddīn Muhammad Mūswī Khān, a mansabdār in the time of 'Alamgīr employed as Dīwān of Sūba Behār. He was a Sayyad and lineal descendant of 'Alī Mūsī Razā. He subsequently chose for his poetical name, Mūswī. He was born in Persia in A.D. 1640, A.H. 1050, and came to India, where he was much esteemed for his talents as a poet and a critic. He is the author of a Tazkira or biography called *Gulshan-i-Fitrat*, also of a Dīwān. He died in A.D. 1690, A.H. 1100.

[*Vide* Mūswī.]

Furati (فراتی). *Vide* Mulla Furātī.

Furqati (فرقتی), whose proper name was Abū Turāb, was a poet. He died in the year A.D. 1617, A.H. 1026.

Fursat (فرصت), poetical title of Muhammad Beg, a poet, who was in the service of Shāh 'Abbās II. and died under Shāh Sulaimān, kings of Persia. He has left a Dīwān of Ghazals.

Fursi (فرسي), poetical title of Husain Alī Shāh, author of the *Nisbat Nāma Shahraiārī*, a history of the Qutbshāhī dynasty of Golkanda in 18,600 verses, from its commencement to Muhammad Qulī Qutbshāh, who died in A.D. 1612, A.H. 1021.

Fuzail Ayaz (فضیل عیاض), a pious Musalmān, whose native country was either Kūfa, Khurāsān, or Samarqand. He received instructions from Imām Ja'far Sādiq, and was the master of Bishr Hafī and Sarī Saqtī. He suddenly fell down and died at the time of prayers at Mecca in January, A.D. 803, Muharram, A.H. 187.

G

Gaj Singh Rathor (گج سنگه راٹور کچهراهه), a Rāja of Mārwār or Jodpūr of the tribe of Raṭhor rājpūts, was the son of Sūraj Singh and the father of Jaswant Singh. He reigned about 18 years and died in the year A.D. 1630, in Gujrāt. The building called Kālā Mahāl at Pīpal Manḍī in Āgrah, was constructed by him. His son Amar Singh killed Salabut Khān. Sulṭān Parwez married Gaj Singh's sister in A.D. 1624, and Sulaiman Shīkoh, the son of Sulṭān Parwez, married the daughter of Gaj Singh in the year A.H. 1065.

Gakkhar (گکهر), a tribe whose residence is amongst the mountains that lie between Bhat and Sindh.

[*Vide* Kamāl Khān Gikhar.]

Ganga Bai (گنگا بائی), Rāni of Jhānsī and widow of Rāja Gangādhar Rāo. At the outbreak of 1857 she joined the rebels, and was the cause of the massacre at Jhānsī. She was killed in the battle of Gwāliar on the 17th June, 1858. She fell with her horse, and was cut down by a Hussar; she still endeavoured to get over, when a bullet struck her in the breast, and she fell to rise no more. The natives hastily burnt her dead body to save it from apprehended desecration by the Firingīs on the night of the 17th and 18th.

Ganna Begam (گنا بیگم). *Vide* Gunna Begam.

Gajpati (گج پتی), a Rāja of Jagdespūr in south Bihār, who, with his brother Bairī Sāl, during the reign of the emperor Akbar, defied the Mughal armies for several years, though the unequal combat led to their destruction.

Garshasp (گرشاسپ), an ancient king of Persia. *Vide* Karshāsp.

Gashtasp (گشتاسپ) was, according to Persian history, the son of Lohrāsp, and the fifth king of the Kaianian dynasty of Persia. In his time flourished Zardasht or Zoroaster, who converted the Persians to the worship of fire. Gashtāsp, it is said, reigned 60 years, and was succeeded by Bahman his grandson, whose father Isfandaiār (*q.v.*) was a great warrior and was killed by Rustam some time before. He is supposed to have been the Darius Hystaspes of the Greek writers.

George Thomas (جارج طامس). The district of Harriana was once the field of the exploits of this famous adventurer. The Jats are a stalwart and brave race, and showed what they could do under his leadership, though when left to themselves they were so divided by factions, that Harriana has always yielded to every adventurer who had been able to attack them. Thus it was overrun by the Mahraṭṭas, under Messrs. Bourquin and Perron, by the Rohillas under Amīr Khān, and another leader, and finally by the British. George Thomas came out to India as a common seaman, and having deserted his ship first took service with Madho Rao Sindhia about the year A.D. 1782. The famous Begam Samru of Sirdhana was then in the zenith of her power, and he left Sindhia to serve her. Shortly after, having collected a body of men, he left her, and marched down to Harriana, and in no time carved out a kingdom for himself. He made the city of Hansi his capital and built a strong fort in it. He built another fort about 20 miles to the south of the town of Rohtak, and called it after his own Christian name Georgegaṛh, which (perhaps from his maritime origin) the natives call Jahājgaṛh, or "ship-castle." After a few years the Mahraṭṭas under Louis Bourquin invaded his territories. He hastened to give them battle, and throwing himself into the small fort of Jahājgaṛh, he fought them for three days, though his force was infinitely smaller than theirs. His cavalry, which was composed principally of Rāughars, having gone over to the enemy, and his Lieutenant, an Englishman of the name of Hopkins, being killed, his troops at length gave way, and he fled on a favourite Arab horse to Hansi, a distance of about 60 miles. Bourquin assaulted the city and Thomas, after a defence of some weeks, gave himself up, and was allowed to join the British Brigade at Anupshahr. Departing thence, in charge of a Capt. Francklin, he died on his way down the river, as he was seeking to return to Europe by way of Calcutta. His great-granddaughter was the wife of a writer on a humble salary (1867) in one of the Government offices in Āgra.

There is a *Life of George Thomas*, written by Francklin, of which a copy is to be seen in the Dehlī Institute Library. [See Keene's *Fall of the Mughal Empire*, part iii. ch. ii. iii.]

Gesu Daraz (گیسو دراز). *Vide* Muhammad Gesu Darāz.

Ghaeb (غایب), a poet who died in A.D. 1750, A.H. 1163.

Ghafil (غافل اکبرابادی), a poet of Āgrah.

Ghairat Khan (غیرت خان), title of Khwāja Kāngār, the nephew of 'Abdullah Khān, Fīroz Jang and son of Sardār Khān. In the year A.D. 1631, he brought the head of Khān Jahān Jodī to Shāh Jahān, and was raised to the rank of 2000 with the title of Ghairat Khān. He died in A.D. 1640, A.H. 1050, at Thatta of which place he was governor. He is the author of the *Jahāngīr Nāma*.

Ghalib (غالب), the poetical title assumed by Muhammad Sa'd, author of a Dīwān which he completed in the year A.D. 1690, A.H. 1101.

Ghalib (غالب), the poetical name of Mīr Fakhr-uddīn, author of a book of Qasīdās which he finished in the 6th year of Muhammad Shāh the emperor of Dehlī, A.D. 1734, A.H. 1136.

Ghalib (غالب), poetical title of Shaikh Asad-ullāh, son of the sister of Shaikh Muhammad Afzal of Allahābād. He died in A.D. 1750, A.H. 1163.

Ghalib (غالب), poetical name of Mirzā Asād-ullāh Khān, author of a Dīwān, and a history of the Mughal emperors of India. He was the son of 'Alī Bakhsh Khān, the brother of Nawāb Ahmad Bakhsh Khān of Fīrozpūr and Lohārī. He died at Dehlī in the month of February or March, A.D. 1869, A.D. 1285.

Ghani (غنی), the poetical name of Mirzā Muhammad Tāhir. He is commonly called Ghanī Kashmīrī on account of his being a native of Kashmīr. He was a pupil of Shaikh Muhsin-Fānī, whom he excelled in his learning and became an elegant poet. He wrote a book of Odes called *Dīwān Ghanī*, and died in Kashmīr two years before his master A.D. 1668, A.H. 1079. It is said that the emperor 'Alamgīr wrote to Saif Khān the governor of Kashmīr to send Ghanī to his presence. Ghanī refused to go, telling him at the same time to inform the emperor that Ghanī had become insane and was not worthy to be sent to his presence. Saif Khān said that he could not call a wise man like him mad; upon which Ghanī immediately really went mad, tore his clothes, and died after three days. He was a young man at the time of his death, having enjoyed a brilliant reputation for poetical excellence for about eighteen years. He sometimes uses Tahīr for his poetical name.

Ghani Bahadur (غنی بهادر), son of Shamsher Bahādur I. and younger brother of 'Ali Bahādur, the Nawāb of Banda.
[*Vide* 'Alī Bahādur.]

Ghanimat (غنیمت), poetical name of Muhammad Akram, author of a short Dīwān and a Masnawī containing an account of the Loves of Azīz and Shāhid, called *Nairang Ishq*, composed in the reign of 'Alamgīr

Gharib (غریب), poetical name of Shaikh Nasīr-uddīn of Dehlī. He is the author of a Dīwān in Persian.

Gharib (غریب), poetical name of Sayyad Karīm-ullah of Bilgrām.

Ghasiti Begam (گهسیتی بیگم و آمنه بیگم), the wife of Shahāmat Jang, and Amina Begam, the mother of Nawāb Sirāj-uddaula, were daughters of Nawāb Mahabat Jang of Bengal; they were drowned in the river, close to Jahāngīrnagar, by order of Mīran the son of Nawāb Ja'far 'Ali Khān, in June, A.D. 1760.

Ghaus Muhammad Khan (غوث محمد خان), whose title is Mohtashim-uddaula, was (1870) Nawāb of Jāwara.

Ghaus-ul-'Alam (غوث العالم), a famous Sūfī. *Vide* Muhammad Ghaus of Gwāliar.

Ghaus-ul-'Azim (غوث الاعظم), a title of the Muhammadan saint 'Abdul Qādir Gīlanī.

Ghauwasi (غواصی یزدی), of Yezd, a poet, whose proper name is Izz-uddīn. He is said to have composed 100,000 verses. This fertile poet, in a work which he wrote in A.D. 1543, A.H. 950, says: "The poetry which I have written amounts to 1,950 books." He made 500 verses a day, and it would appear that he put the *Rauzat-ush-Shohada*, the history of Tabarī, the legends of the Prophets, Kaleila-wa-Damna, and the Medical work called *Zakhīra Khwārizm Shāhī*, and many other works into verse. He died in A.D. 1553, A.H. 960, at an age of more than one hundred years.

Ghayas Halwai (غیاث حلوای), of Shīrāz, was blind and died by a fall from the terrace of a house in the time of Shāh Safī. He is the author of a Dīwān.

Ghayas-uddin (غیاث الدین), author of a Persian Dictionary called *Ghayās-ul-Lughāt*. *Vide* Muhammad Ghayās-uddīn.

Ghayas - uddin Bahmani (Sultan) (غیاث الدین بهمنی سلطان), the eldest son of Sulṭān Mahmūd Shāh I. He ascended the throne of the Deccan in his seventeenth year, after the death of his father in April, A.D. 1397. He had reigned only one month and twenty days, when Lalchīn, one of the Turkish slaves, not being appointed prime minister—to which office he had aspired—put out his eyes with the point of his dagger, and having sent him in confinement to the fortress of Sāgar, placed Shams-uddīn, the late king's brother, on the throne. This circumstance took place on the 14th June, A.D. 1397, 17th Ramaẓān, A.H. 799.

Ghayas-uddin Balban (Sultan) (غیاث الدین بلبن سلطان), king of Dehlī. In his youth he was sold as a slave to Sulṭān Altimsh, who raised him by degrees to the rank of a noble, and gave him his daughter in marriage. On the accession of his son Nāsir-uddīn Mahmūd to the throne of Dehlī, Ghayās-uddīn was appointed his wazīr. After the king's deposal or death in February, A.D. 1266, A.H. 664, he ascended the throne and reigned 20 years. He died in A.D. 1286, A.H. 685, aged 80 years, and was succeeded by his grandson Mōiz-uddīn Kaiqubād, the son of Nāsir-uddīn Baghrā Khān, governor of Bengal, who was then absent in that province.

Ghayas-uddin Kart I. (Malik) (غیاث الدین کرت ملک), fourth king of the race of Kart or Kard. He succeeded his brother Mālik Fakhr-uddīn Kart in A.D. 1307. A.H. 706, reigned more than 21 years over Herāt, Balgh, and Ghaznī, and died in the year A.D. 1329, A.H. 729. He was succeeded by his son Mālik Shams-uddīn Kart.

Ghayas - uddin Kart II. (Malik) (غیاث الدین کرت ملک), the eighth and last king of the dynasty of Kart or Kard. He succeeded his father or grandfather Mōiz-uddīn Husain Kart in A.D. 1370, A.H. 771, and reigned 12 years over Herāt, Ghōr, Sarakhsh, and Naishāpūr, and conquered Tās and Jām. He was a great tyrant, and had several battles with the Sarbadāls of Sabzwār and the chiefs of Jānī Qurbānī. In the year A.D. 1381, A.H. 783, Amīr Taimūr (Tamerlane) conquered Herāt, when Ghayās-uddīn, together with his son and brother, were taken prisoners and put to death. This dynasty lasted one hundred and nineteen lunar years and two months.

Ghayas-uddin Khilji (Sultan) (غیاث الدین خلجی سلطان) succeeded his father Sulṭān Mahmūd Khiljī on the throne of Gujrāt in May, A.D. 1469, Ẕi-Qa'da, A.H. 873. When he had reigned 33 years and arrived at an advanced age, his two sons anxiously looked for his death as an event which would secure to one of them the throne of Malwā; a jealousy arose between the two brothers, who conspired against each other, till Nāsir-uddīn, the eldest, having put his brother, Shujā'at Khān to death on the 22nd October, A.D. 1500, 24th Rabī II. A.H. 906, assumed the reins of government. A few days after, his father was found dead in the Seraglio; and it was supposed that poison had been administered to him by his son.

Ghayas-uddin Mahmud (غیاث الدین محمود), the son of Ghayās-uddīn Muhammad Ghorī, succeeded his uncle Shahāb-uddīn in the kingdom of Ghōr and Ghaznī in A.D. 1205, A.H. 602. He reigned about four years, and was assassinated by the people of Mahmūd Alī Shāh on Saturday night, the 31st July, A.D. 1210, 7th Ṣafar, A.H. 607. He was at first buried at Fīrōz Kōh, but was afterwards transported to Herāt and buried there. He was succeeded by his son Bahā-uddīn Sām, who was after three months defeated by 'Alā-uddīn Atsiz (son of Alā-uddīn Hasan surnamed Jahān Sōz) who reigned in Ghōr and Ghaznī for four years, and fell in battle against Mālik Nāsir-uddīn Husain Amīr Shikār in the year A.D. 1214, A.H. 611. After his death Alā-uddīn Muhammad, son of Abū Alī, cousin of Mālik Ghayās-uddīn Muhammad, was raised to the throne by Tāj-uddīn Eldūz.

Ghayas-uddin Mahmud Ghori (غیاث الدین محمد غوری), the son of Ghayās-uddīn Muhammad Ghorī, and nephew of Shahāb-uddīn Muhammad Ghorī, whom he succeeded to the throne of Ghōr and Ghaznī in A.D. 1206. Mahmūd being naturally indolent, remained satisfied with the throne of Ghōr, and proclaimed Taj-uddīn Eldūz, king of Ghaznī. He died in A.D. 1210.

Ghayas - uddin Muhammad Ghori (غیاث الدین محمد غوری), king of Ghōr and Ghaznī, was the son of Bahā-uddīn Sām, the youngest brother of Alā-uddīn Hasan Ghōrī. He succeeded to the throne of Ghōr and Ghaznī after the death of his cousin Mālik Saif-uddīn, the son of the latter, about the year A.D. 1157, and conferred the government of Ghaznī on his brother Shahāb-uddīn surnamed Mo'iz-uddīn Muhammad; this illustrious general subdued Khurāsān and a great part of India in the name of his brother Ghayās-uddīn, who annexed those countries to his own dominions. Ghayās-uddīn died on Wednesday the 12th March, A.D. 1203, 27th Jumāda I. A.H. 599, and was succeeded by his brother Shahāb-uddīn.

Ghayas-uddin Muhammad (Sultan) (غیاث الدین محمد سلطان), the son of Mālik Shāh of the Saljūk dynasty. In the time of his eldest brother Barkayāraq the empire was divided, Barkayāraq retaining Persia; Ghayās-uddīn Muhammad, Syria and Azurbejān; and Sultān Sanjar, Khurāsān and Mawarunnahr. He reigned about the year A.D. 1095.

[*Vide* Muhammah (Sultān.)]

Ghayas-uddin Purbi (غیاث الدین پوربی) succeeded his father Sikandar Pūrbī on the throne of Bengal in A.D. 1367, A.H. 775, reigned for a period of seven years, and died in 1373. He was succeeded by his son Sultān-us-Salātīn.

Ghayas - uddin Tughlak Shah I. (Sultan) (غیاث الدین تغلق سلطان), king of Dehlī (also known as Ghāzi Mālik). His father Tughlaq was a slave of Sultān Ghayās-uddīn Balban. He ascended the throne of Dehlī after murdering Khusro Shāh on the 26th August, A.D. 1321, 1st Shabān, A.H. 721, reigned three years and some months, and was crushed to death by the fall of a temporary wooden building which his son had raised for his entertainment on his return from Lakhnautī in February, A.D. 1325, Rabī' I. A.H. 725. His son Muhammad Tukhlaq succeeded him. The celebrated poet Amīr Khusro of Dehlī, who lived to the end of this king's reign and received a pension of 1000 tangas monthly, wrote the history of this prince under the title of *Tughlaq Nāma*. Ghayās-uddīn was the first king of the 3rd branch of the Afghān dynasty which is called Tughlaq Shāhi. The following is a list of the Sultāns of this branch:—

1. Ghayās-uddīn Tughlaq I. Mahmūd Shāh Tughlaq, last of this family, expelled by Amīr Taimur.
2. Muhammad Shāh Tughlaq I.
3. Fīroz Shāh Tughlaq.
4. Ghayās-uddīn Tughlaq II.
5. Abū Bakr Shāh.
6. Muhammad Shāh Tughlaq II. Ala-uddīn Sikandar Shāh.
7. Nasrat Khān.
8. Mahmūd Shāh.
9. Ikbal Khān Mahmūd Khān restored A.D. 1405.

Ghayas-uddin Tughlak II. (Sultan) (غیاث الدین تغلق سلطان) was the son of prince Fatha Khān and grandson of Fīroz Shāh Tughlaq. He ascended the throne in place of Fīroz Shāh in Dehlī on the death of his grandfather in A.D. 1388, A.H. 790, but giving loose to his youthful passions, and neglecting the affairs of the State, the chiefs together with the household troops revolted, and put him to death on the 19th February, A.D. 1389, 21st Safar A.H. 791, after he had reigned six months. He was succeeded by his cousin Abū Bakr Tughlaq the son of prince Zafar Khān, the third son of Fīroz Shāh.

Ghazali (غزالی). *Vide* Ghazzālī.

Ghazan Khan (غزان خان), seventh king of Persia of the Tartar tribe and fourth in descent from Halākū Khān, was the son of Arghūn Khān. He succeeded to the crown of Persia after the dethronement of Bāidū Khān his uncle in October, A.D. 1295, Zil-hijja, A.H. 694. He was the second emperor of the race of Changez Khān who embraced the religion of Muhammad, and with him near one hundred thousand of his followers followed their leader into the pale of Islām. He was the first of this race of kings who threw off all allegiance to the Khāqān of Tartary, by directing that the name of that monarch (whom he now deemed to be an infidel) should not in future be struck on the coins of Persia. After embracing Muhammadanism, he took the title of Sultān Mahmūd. He reigned nearly nine years and died on Sunday the 17th May, A.D. 1304, 11th Shawwāl, A.H. 703, at Qazwīn; he was interred in a superb mosque which he had constructed near Tauris or Tabrez. He was succeeded by his brother Aljaitū, who took the title of Muhammad Khudā Banda.

Ghazanfar Khan (غضنفر خان), son of Alawardī Khān I. and brother of Alawardī Khān II. a nobleman of the reign of Shāh Jahān and 'Alamgīr. He was three times at different periods appointed governor of Saharanpūr and afterwards of Thatta in Sindh, where he died on the 1st May, A.D. 1666, 17th Zi-Qa'da, A.H. 1077. His remains were brought to Dehlī and buried there.

Ghazi (غازی), the poetical title of a person who served as Kūrbegī under the prince Sultān Muhammad Muāzzim the son of the emperor 'Alamgīr.

Ghazi (غازی), or Al-Ghāzī, the son of Ortak, the first of the Turkmān Ortakite princes who seized Jerusalem and reigned in

Mardin and Miafarkin in Syria. The following were his descendants :—

	A.D.	A.H.
Husām-uddīn Taimūrtāsh, son of Alghāzī, began to reign . .	1122	516
Najm-uddīn Abū'l Muzaffar Albī or Alpī, son of Taimūrtāsh .	1152	547
Qutb-uddīn Alghāzī, son of Albī.	1176	572
Husām-uddīn Yūlak Arsalan, the son of Qutb-uddīn	1184	580
Mālik Almansūr Nāsir-uddīn Ortak Arsalan, son of Qutb-uddīn	1201	597
Mālik-us-Saīd Najm-uddīn Ghāzī, son of Nāsir-uddīn Ortak	1239	637
Mālik-ul-Mazaffar Qarā Arsalan, son of Najm-uddīn	1255	653
Shams-uddīn Daūd	1291	691
Mālik-al-Mansūr Najm-uddīn Ghāzī	1293	693
Albī Mālik-ul-Adil 'Imād-uddīn 'Alī	1312	712
Mālik-us-Sālah Shams-uddīn Sālah, the last prince of this race	1312	712

Ghazi-uddin Haidar (غازی الدین حیدر), the eldest of the ten sons of Nawāb Sa'ādat 'Alī Khān of Audh. On his father's death, which took place on the 11th July, A.D. 1814, 22nd Rajab, A.H. 1229, he succeeded to his dominions as Nawāb Wazīr, and five years after, assumed, with the concurrence of the British Government, the regal dignity. His coronation took place on Saturday the 9th October, A.D. 1819, 18th Zil-hijja, A.H. 1234, at Lucknow, when he took the title of Abū'l Muzaffar Maiz-uddīn Shāh Zaman Ghazi-uddīn Haidar Pādshāh. On ascending the first step of the throne, the minister delivered to him a crown, studded with diamonds and jewels of great value. He then put it on his head and was congratulated on the occasion by the Resident, who saluted him as king of Audh. Jewels and pearls to the value of 30,000 rupees were then scattered over the heads of the spectators, many of which were picked up by English ladies. Ghazī-uddīn Haidar died after a reign of more than 13 years, on the 19th October, A.D. 1827, 27th Rabī' I. A.H. 1243, aged 58 lunar years, and was succeeded by his son Sulaimān Jāh Nasīr-uddīn Haidar.

Ghazi-uddin Khan I. (غازی الدین خان فیروز جنگ), styled Fīrōz Jang, whose original name was Mīr Shahāb-uddīn, was the son of Kulich Khān Sadr-us-Sudūr, and was raised to the rank of an Amīr with the title of Fīrōz Jang, after his father's death, by the emperor 'Alamgīr in A.D. 1687, A.H. 1098. His son was the famous Nizām-ul-Mulk 'Asaf Jāh whose descendants are known to Europeans as Nizāms of the Deccan. In the reign of Bahādur Shāh he was appointed governor of Gujrāt, and died at Ahmadābād in A.D. 1710, A.H. 1122. His remains were transported to Dehlī, and interred in the yard of the college built by him outside the Ajmīrī Gate.

Ghazi-uddin Khan II. (غازی الدین خان امیر الامرا), Amīr-ul-Umrā, also styled Fīrōz Jang, was the eldest son of the celebrated Nizām-ul-Mulk 'Asaf Jāh. He was elevated to the rank of Amīr-ul-Umrā after the death of Khān Daurān, and departure of Nādir Shāh to Persia, in A.D. 1739, A.H. 1152, by the emperor Muhammad Shāh. Some years after the death of his father, when his brother Nāsir Jang, who had succeeded him, died in the Deccan, he proceeded from Dehlī to regain his possessions in that country, but died on his way at Aorangābād on the 16th October, A.D. 1752, 7th Zil-hijja, A.H. 1165 (new style). His remains were brought to Dehlī and buried there. After his death the office of Amīr-ul-Umrā was conferred on his son Shahāb-uddīn with the title of 'Imād-ul-Mulk Ghāzī-uddīn Khān.

Ghazi-uddin Khan III. (عازی الدین خان امیر الامر), Amīr-ul-Umrā, styled 'Imad-ul-Mulk, was the son of Ghāzī-uddīn Khān Fīrōz Jang, the son of Nizām-ul-Mulk 'Asaf Jāh. His original name was Shahāb-uddīn, but after the death of his father in A.D. 1752, A.H. 1165, he was, by the recommendation of Nawāb Safdar Jang, wazīr, appointed Amīr-ul-Umrā, by the emperor Ahmad Shāh of Dehlī with the title of 'Imad-ul-Mulk Ghāzī-uddīn Khān. This is that Ghāzī-uddīn Khān, who afterwards became wazīr, imprisoned and blinded his master the emperor Ahmad Shāh, and assassinated 'Alamgīr II. His wife was the celebrated Ganna, or Gunna (*q.v.*), Begam, who died in the year A.D. 1775, A.H. 1189. The year of Ghāzī-uddīn Khān's death is unknown, but according to the biography of the poet called Gulzār Ibrāhīm, he was living in A.D. 1780, A.H. 1194, in straitened circumstances. His poetical name was Nizām. According to the work called *Māsir-ul-Umrā*, he went to the Deccan A.D. 1773, A.H. 1187, and received a jāgīr in Mālwa; subsequently he proceeded to Sūrat and passed a few years with the English, and thence on a pilgrimage to Mecca. He composed Persian and Raikhta poetry, and left Arabic and Turkish Ghazals and a thick Persian Dīwān and a Masnawī in which the miracles of Maulāna Fakhr-uddīn are related. Some say he died at Kalpī, A.D. 1800.

[Vide *Jour. As. Soc. Beng.* 1879.]

Ghaznawi (غزنوی). *Vide* Muhammad Khān (Mīr).

Ghazni (غـزنی), Kings of. *Vide* Subaktagīn.

Ghazzal (غزال) (a seller of thread), title of Wāsil-bin-'Atā, a celebrated Musalmān doctor who was thus surnamed.

Ghazzal (غزال). *Vide* Wasil.

Ghazzali (غزالی امام احمد), or Ghazālī (Imam Ahmad), younger brother of Imām Muhammad Ghazzālī. He was a doctor of the sect of Shāfa'ī, and died at Qazwīn in the year A.D. 1123, A.H. 517, but according to Ibn Khallikān in A.H. 520, corresponding with A.D. 1126.

Ghazzali (غزالی امام محمد), or Ghazālī (Imam Muhammad), who is also entitled Hujjat-ul-Islām, is the surname of Abū Hāmid Muhammad Zain-uddīn-al-Tūsī, one of the greatest and most celebrated Musalmān doctors, and author of a treatise on the different classes of science which concern religion, called, *Kīmiāe Sa'ādat*, and many other works such as the *Yākūt-ut-Tawīb*, also called *Tafsīr Jawāhir-ul-Qurān*, *Akāed Ghazzālī*, *Ahia-ul-'Ulum*, and *Tukfat-ul-Filasafa*. He was born in the year A.D. 1058, A.H. 450, in a village called Ghazzāla or Ghazālī, in Tūs, whence he and his brother derived their names of Ghazzālī. He died on the 18th December, A.D. 1111, 4th Jumāda II. A.H. 505, aged 55 lunar years. Some authors say that his name should be spelt Ghazālī and not Ghazzālī, but the following verses from the Mukhbir-ul-Wāsilīn confirm the latter.

احمد انکس که ماه غزالی است
در دو عالم بدرجهٔ عالی است

He is said to have written ninety-nine works, mostly in Arabic, a few in Persian.

Ghazzali (Maulana) (غزالي مولانا), of Tūs or Mashhad, the royal poet. He mentions in one of his Qasīdas named *Rauzat-us-Safā*, that he was born in the year A.D. 1524, A.H. 930. He first came from Mashhad his native country to the Deccan, where being disappointed in his prospects, he went over to Jaunpūr, and was employed for some years by Khān Zamān 'Alī Qulī Khān, governor of that province, during which time he wrote a poem called *Naqsh Badī'a*, for which he received from his patron a piece of gold for each couplet. Afer the death of Khān Zamān, who was slain in battle against the emperor Akbar in A.D. 1568, A.H. 975, he fell into the hands of that monarch, who took him into his service, and conferred on him the title of Mālik-ush-Shua'rā, or the King of poets. He was the first poet that was honoured with this title in India. He accompanied his royal master to the conquest of Gujrāt, and died there of venereal disease, on Friday the 5th December, A.D. 1572, 27th Rajab, A.H. 980. He is buried at Ahmadabād, Gujrāt, at a place called Sarkīj. He is also the author of a Dīwān, and three Masnawīs or poems, containing from 40 to 50,000 verses; their titles are: *Kitāb Asrār*, *Rishahāt-ul-Haiāt* and *Mirat-ul-Kāenāt*.

Ghulam Ahia (غلام یحیی), author of an Arabic work on Logic, which goes after his name. Its marginal notes written by another author are called *Shams-uz-Zuhā*

Ghulam 'Ali (غلام علی), author of the work called *Shāh 'Alam Nāma*, a history of the reign of the emperor Shāh 'Alam, who died in A.D. 1806, A.H. 1221.

Ghulam 'Ali Khan (غلام علی خان), author of the *Lama'āt-ut-Tāhirīn*, a panegyric on the actions of Muhammad, and a number of mystical poems, dedicated to the emperor 'Alamgīr.

Ghulam 'Ali, Mir (غلام علی میر آزاد), a poet whose poetical title is 'Azād, which see.

Ghulam Husain Khan (غلام حسین خان), author of the Persian History of Bengal called *Rayaz-ussalatīn*, which he wrote about the year A.D. 1780, at the request of Mr. George Udney of Mālwa. He was a learned and respectable character, once of great consequence, and afterwards a member of the native court of judicature under the Nawāb 'Alī Ibrahīm Khān.

Ghulam Husain Khan, Nawab Sayyad (غلام حسین خان نواب سید طباطبائی), surnamed Tiba Tibāī, son of Hidāyat 'Alī Khān, Bahādur Asad Jang, author of a Persian work called *Siar-ul-Mutākhirīn* written in the year A.D. 1780, A.H. 1194, and translated soon after into English by a French creole, named Raymond, calling himself "Hāji Mustafa." He is also author of a Poem entitled *Bashārat-ul-Imānat*. He was a client of M. Raza Khān (*q.v.*).

Ghulam Imam Shahid, Maulana (غلام امام شہید مولانا), a poet who is the author of a Persian Dīwān, and of a celebrated Qasīda comprising the dispute between Love and Beauty. His poetical title is Shahed and he is living still, A.D. 1879.

Ghulam Muhammad Khan (غلام محمد خان), present Nawāb of the Karnatic, whose title is Amīr-ul-Hind Wālā Jāh Umdat-ul-Umrā Mumtāz-ul-Mumālik.

Ghulam Muhammad Khan, Nawab (غلام محمد خان نواب). *Vide* Faizullāh Khān.

Ghulam Muhammad (Prince) (غلام محمد), grandson of Tippū Sultān, was installed as a Knight Commander of the Star of India on the 27th February, A.D. 1871. Seventy-two years before he was a prisoner in the hands of the English, and since then a recipient of the highest honours. He died in Calcutta on the night of the 11th August, 1872, aged 78 years.

Ghulam Qadir Khan (غلام قادر خان), son of Zābita Khān, and grandson of Najīb-uddaula, the Rohila chief. This is that traitor who, after extorting as much money as he could from his royal master, the emperor Shāh 'Alam of Dehlī, ordered his Rohilas to pluck out his eyes from their sockets and placed Bedar Bakht, son of Ahmad Shāh and grandson of Muhammad Shāh, on the throne. This tragic scene happened on the 10th August, A.D. 1788, 7th Zil-Qa'da, A.H. 1202. After this, the traitor endeavoured to make his retreat to his own territory Ghousgarh, but was pursued by the Mahrattas who took him prisoner, cut off his ears, nose, arms, and legs, and in this mutilated state he was sent to Dehlī; but died on the road in the month of December the same year, Rabī I. A.H. 1203. His tomb is in Aul, Parganna Furrah, Zila Āgra.

[*Vide* Keene's *Fall of the Mughāl Empire.*]

Ghulam Qutb-uddin Shah (غلام قطب الدین شاه الله ابادی), of Allahābād, whose poetical name is Musībat, was the son of Shāh Muhammad Fākhir. He was an elegant poet eminently learned and accomplished, and is the author of a work called *Nān Qalia* (Cakes and Steaks) which he wrote in answer to a work entited *Nān Halwā* (Cakes and Pudding). He was born on the 29th August, O.S. 1725, 1st Maharram, A.D. 1138, went on a pilgrimage to Mecca, and died there in the year A.D. 1773-4, A.H. 1187-8.

Ghunchacha-i-Umaid (غنچهٔ امید), (*i.e.* a small bud of hope), was one of the wives of Umar Shaikh Mirzā, the son of Sultān Abū Sa'īd Mirzā, and mother of Nāsir Mirzā and Mahd Bāno Begam. She was a native of Andjan.

Gilan Shah. *Vide* Kabūs.

Girami (گرامی), the poetical name of a poet whose Dīwān was found in the Library of Tīpū Sultān.

Girdhar Das (گردهر داس), of Dehlī, author of the history of Rām, entitled *Rāmāyan*, translated from the Sanskrit in A.D. 1722. This is a very celebrated Hindī poem, containing the exploits of the famous demigod Rām, who reigned over India for many years. His capital was at Audh, and his conquests extended to Ceylon, where the chain of rocks which nearly unite that island to the continent is still called Rām's Bridge. Besides this, there are two other *Rāmāyans*, one translated by Tulshī Dās in the Bhākhā dialect, and another by Khushtar in Urdū.

Girdhar Singh (گردهر سنگه), or Girdhar Bahādur, a Rājpūt chief who was governor of Mālwa in the reign of the emperor Muhammad Shāh, and fell in battle against the Peshwā Bājī Rao's officers in A.D. 1729. His nephew, Dayā Rām, who succeeded him, and had opposed a gallant resistance for some time, was defeated by Chimnājī the Peshwā's brother, and lost his life in battle about the year A.D. 1732.

Gobind Guru (گوبند گرو), a chief of the Sikhs.

[*Vide* Gurū Gobind.]

Gopal or Nayek Gopal (گوپل نایک), a celebrated singer of India, who was a native of the Deccan, and flourished during the reign of Sultān 'Alī-uddīn Sikandar Sānī. He was a contemporary of Amīr Khusro, who died in A.D. 1325. It is related that when Gopāl visited the court of Dehlī, he sung that species of composition called *Gīt*, the beauty of which style, enunciated by the powerful and harmonious voice of so able a performer, could not meet with competition:—At this the monarch caused Amīr Khusro to remain hid under his throne, whence he could hear the musician unknown to him. The latter endeavoured to remember the style, and on a subsequent day, sung *Qoul* and *Tarāna* in imitation of it, which surprised Gopāl, and fraudulently deprived him of a portion of his due honour.

Goshyar (گوشیار), an astronomer whose proper name is Abū'l Hasan.

Gouhar Shad Begam (گوهر شاد بیگم), the wife of Mirzā Shāhrukh, the son of Amīr Taimūr. She was slain by Sultān Abū Sa'īd Mirzā for creating disturbances, in A.D. 1457, A.H. 861, at Herāt, where she lies buried on the left bank of a stream called Anjir. The grave is covered by a very high gilt dome. She is said to have been the most incomparable lady in the world. Some erroneously say that she was the daughter of Amīr Taimūr and sister of Shāhrukh Mirzā, and that she never married, but devoted herself to the perusal of the Qurān.

[*Vide* Mohan Lal's Journal.]

Goya (گویا), poetical name of Hisam-uddaula Nawāb Faqīr Muhammad Khān of Lucknow. He is the author of a Dīwān.

Goya (گویا), poetical name of Mirzā Kāmrān, a brother of Jōyā, which see.

Goya (گویا), poetical name of Shaikh Haiāt-ullah of Furrukhābād.

Gujar (گوجر), grandson or son of the daughter of the Peshwā Rāghōjī Bhosla's daughter. He was raised to the masnad of Nāgpūr after the dethronement of 'Apā Sāhib in A.D. 1818.

Gulab Singh (گلاب سنگه), of Jammū (Mahārājā), the independent ruler of Kashmere and the hills, which were made over to him by the British "for a consideration," after the Punjab war (1846). He died 2nd August, A.D. 1857, about three months after the outbreak of the Bengal Army. He was succeeded by his son Ranbīr Singh.

Gulbadan Begam (گلبدن بیگم), a daughter of the emperor Bābar Shāh, sister to Humāyūn and aunt to Akbar Shāh. She was married to Khizir Khān, a descendant of the kings of Kāshghar. Khizir Khān was made governor of Lāhore in A.D. 1555, A.H. 963, and afterwards of Behār, where he died about the year A.D. 1559, A.H. 966.

Gulbarg Begam (گلبرگ بیگم), daughter of the emperor Bābar Shāh; she is also called Gulrang Begam and Gulrukh Begam, which see.

Gulchehra Begam (گلچهره بیگم,) a daughter of the emperor Bābar Shāh, and youngest sister of Humāyūn, by whom she was given in marriage to Abbās Sultān, an Uzbak prince, at Kābul in A.D. 1548.

Gul Muhammad Khan (گل محمد خان ناطق), a poet of Dehlī who died in the year of the Christian era A.D. 1848, A.H. 1264. His poetical name was Nātik, which see.

Gulrukh Begam (گلرخ بیگم), a daughter of the emperor Bābar, who was married to Mirzā Nūr-uddīn Muhammad, a person of respectable family, by whom she had a daughter named Salīma Sultāna Begam, who was married in the beginning of the reign of the emperor Akbar, to Bairām Khān, Khankhānān, after whose death in A.D. 1561, A.H. 968, the emperor married her himself. Gulrukh Begam is called in the *Māsir-ul-Umrā* Gulbarg Begam, and by some Gulrang Begam.

Gulrukh Begam (گلرخ بیگم), a daughter of Kāmrān Mirzā, the brother of the emperor Humāyūn and first cousin to Akbar. She was married to Ibrāhīm Husain Mirzā, the son of Muhammad Sultān Mirzā, a descendant of Amīr Taimūr. Ibrāhīm Husain, who together with his other brothers had created great disturbances in the country, was taken prisoner in A.D. 1573, A.H. 981, and shortly after put to death and his head sent to Akbar, who ordered it to be placed over one of the gates of Āgra. Gulrukh Begam survived him for several years and was living at Āgra in A.D. 1614, A.H. 1023.

Gulshan (گلشن), the poetical name of Shaikh Sa'd-ullāh, a mystical poet, who resided for some years at Dehlī, and left nearly 100,000 verses of Ghazals. He was a disciple of Shāh 'Abdūl Ahad Sarhindī, and made with him a pilgrimage to Mecca. He died A.D. 1728, A.H. 1141.

Gulshani (گلشنی), the poetical title of Shaikh Sa'd-ullāh, which see.

Gunna or Ganna Begam (گنا بیگم), a princess, celebrated for her personal accomplishments, as well as for the vivacity of her wit, and the fire of her poetical genius. Several of her lyric compositions in the Hindūstānī language are still sung and admired, one of which is to be seen in the first volume of the *Asiatic Researches*, p. 55. She was the daughter of Nawāb 'Alī Qulī Khān, commonly called Chhangā or Shash Angushtī (from having six fingers on each hand), a mansabdār of 5000 horse. Gannā Begam was betrothed to Shujā'-uddaula, the son of Nawāb Safdar Jang of Audh, but afterwards married to 'Imād-ul-Mulk Ghāzī-uddīn Khān, wazīr of the empire, and this rivalship is said to have in part laid the foundation of the mortal enmity which afterwards subsisted between that wazīr and Safdar Jang. Adjoining to the village of Nūrābād near Dholpūr, two miles from Cholā Sarāe, is a pretty large garden, the work of the emperor Alamgīr, built in the year A.D. 1688, A.H. 1160, over the gate of which is an inscription bearing the chronogram of the year of its erection, *viz.* "Dida Bāgh Jāmāl." Within this garden is the monument of Gunnā Begam. Her shrine bears the following inscription: "Ah gham Gunnā Begam," which is the chronogram of the year of her death, *viz.* A.D. 1775, A.H. 1189. The poets Sōz, Souda, and Minnat corrected her verses.

Gurdezi Fathi Ali Husaini. *Vide* Husaini.

Guru Gobind (گرو گوبند), the son of Tegh Bahādur, a famous chief of the Sikhs. After the death of his father, who was executed by order of the emperor 'Alamgīr in the year A.D. 1673, having collected his followers, he gave them arms and horses, which till this time they had never used, and began to commit depredations, but he was soon obliged to fly, and two of his sons being taken prisoners, were put to death. Being desirous of returning to his home, he prevailed on some Afghāns to conduct him, disguised as one of their devotees, through the army stationed at Sarhind; and for the remainder of his life kept himself retired, having lost his faculties in grief for his sons. He ordered his disciples to wear blue, and leave their beards and the hairs of their heads unshaved, which they do to this day. He was succeeded by Banda, one of his followers.

[*Vide* Hughes, *Dict. of Islām, in voc.* "Sikhism."]

H

Habib Ajmi, Khwaja (حبیب عجمی خواجه). He was called 'Ajmī or the Persian, on account of his not being able to read the Qurān, or that he could not pronounce the words of it distinctly. He was a pious Musalmān and disciple of Khwāja Hasan Basrī. He died on the 28th August, A.D. 738, 7th Ramazān, A.H. 120.

Habib-ullah (حبیب الله), author of an Arabic work on philosophy called *Bahr-ul-Mantiq*, or the Sea of Logic.

Habib-ullah, Shaikh (حبیب الله شیخ), a celebrated poet of Āgra.

Habib-ullah, Shah or Mir (حبیب الله شاه), a descendant of Shāh Ni'mat-ullāh Walī, and an Amīr in the service of the Bahmanī kings of the Deccan. He was imprisoned, and afterwards put to death in June, A.D. 1460, Sha'bān, A.H. 864, by Sultān Humāyūn Shāh II. Bahmanī, a tyrant, who at the same time cast his brother Hasan Khān, who had rebelled against him, before a voracious tiger, that soon tore the wretched prince to pieces.

Habshi or Habashi (حبشی), a poet who having lost an eye in a scuffle, was asked by Ibrahīm Pāshā, "Where is thine other eye?" and making answer, "It grew tired of stopping at home in the socket, and flew out to see the world?" was imprisoned ten years for his wit in the tower of Hero and Leander, where he daily gave vent to his feelings in such verses as the following:—

I will groan, till every stone in this cold prison-tower shall weep,
I will cry, till earth and sky, and each dark rolling hour shall weep,
I will make, that hearts shall break, and even the dewless flower shall weep,
Yea, for me, the wronged Habshī, both Musulmān and Gabr shall weep!

[So Mr. Beale: We shall perhaps run no great risk of error if we suppose Habshī to have been an Abyssinian domiciled in Egypt.—Ed.]

Hadi (هادی), a khalīf of Baghdād. *Vide* Al-Hādī.

Hadi (هادی), poetical name of Mīr Muhammad Jawād 'Alī Khān, who died in the year A.D. 1800, A.H. 1215, and left a Dīwān in Urdū.

Hafi (حافی), which means barefoot, is the surname of Zain-uddīn Muhammad, an author, who led an austere life, and who always walking barefoot, was thus surnamed.

Hafiz Abru (حافظ آبرو), surnamed Nūr-uddīn-bin-Lutf-ullāh, author of the history called *Tārīkh Hāfiz Abrū*. He was born in the city of Herāt, but passed his infancy in Hamdān, where he received his education. He was fortunate enough to secure the esteem of Amīr Taimūr, who sought every occasion to do him service. After the death of that tyrant, he attended the court of his son Shāhrukh Mirzā, and received from the young prince Mirzā Bāisanghar every demonstration of kindness and regard. To him he dedicated his works under the name of *Zubdat-ut-Tawārīkh Bāisanghar*, which contains a complete history of the world, and an account of the institutions and religions of different people down to A.D. 1425, A.H. 829. He died five years afterwards in the city of Zanjān, about the year A.D. 1430, A.H. 834.

Hafiz Adam (حافظ آدم), a Musalmān devotee and disciple of Shaikh Ahmad Sarhindi, who about the year A.D. 1673, in conjunction with the Sikh Gurū Tegh Bahādur, having collected his followers, levied contributions with the greatest oppression from the inhabitants of his neighbourhood and pretended to royalty. He was banished from the kingdom across the Indus by order of the emperor 'Alamgīr.

Hafiz Halwai (حافظ حلوای), a confectioner and poet of Herāt, who flourished in the reign of Shāhrukh Mirzā, the son of Amīr Taimūr, about the year A.D. 1430, A.H. 834.

Hafiz, Khwaja (حافظ خواجه), whose proper name is Shams-uddīn Muhammad, was the most elegant lyric poet of Persia. He was born at Shīrāz in the reign of Muzaffarians, and was living at the time when Amīr Taimūr (Tamerlane) defeated Shāh Mansūr, the last Sultān of that dynasty. The language of Hafiz has been styled among the Musalmāns "Lisān-ul-Ghaib," the language of mystery. From his frequent celebration of love and wine in his odes he has very appropriately been denominated, by some Orientalists, the Anacreon of Persia. He died in A.D. 1389, A.H. 791, at Shīrāz, where his tomb is yet to be seen at a place called Musalla, and is visited as a sacred spot by pilgrims of all ages. After his death a collection of 569 of his odes was made by Sayyad Qāsim Anwār, entitled *Dīwān Hāfiz*. A few of his poems may be understood in a literal sense; but in general they are figurative, and allude to the Sūfī doctrines; most of them have been at different times translated into some of the European languages. At the head of the English translators stand Sir W. Jones, Messrs. Richardson and Carlyle. [There have been two other Persian poets of the name of Hāfiz, one of them surnamed Halwāī, that is to say, the confectioner, who lived in the reign of Sultān Shāhrukh, the son of Tamerlane, and the other was named Ajāu Rūmī.] Many zealous admirers of Hāfiz insist that by wine he invariably means *devotion;* and they have gone so far as to compose a dictionary of words in the *language*, as they call it, of the Sūfīs; in that vocabulary *sleep* is explained by *meditation* on the divine perfections, and *perfume* by *hope* of the divine favour; *gales* are *illapses* of grace; *kisses* and *embraces*, the rapture of piety; *idolators, infidels*, and *libertines*, are men of the purest religion, and their *idol* is the Creator himself; the *tavern* is a retired oratory, and its *keeper*, a sage instructor; *beauty* denotes the perfection of the Supreme Being; *tresses* are the expansion of his glory; *lips* the hidden mysteries of his essence; *down* on the cheek, the world of spirits who encircle his throne; and a *black mole*, the point of indivisible unity; lastly, *wantonness, mirth*, and *inebriety*, mean religious ardour and abstraction from all terrestrial tnoughts.

Hafiz Muhammad, author of the *Hawī Saghīr*.

Hafiz Rahmat Khan (حافظ رحمت خان), a celebrated Rohila chief. He joined his countrymen during the administration of 'Ali Muhammad Khān, who advanced him to an important station, and Pīlībhīt and Bareily were given to him and Muradābād to another chief named Dūnde Khān. Having attained his office, by military ability and genius, he at length wholly superseded the authority of Sa'd-ullāh-Khān, the son of 'Alī Muhammad Khān, and was advanced to the supreme administration of affairs. He failed in his engagement to pay forty lacs of rupees to Nawāb Shujā-uddaula of Audh for the protection of his country from the ravages of the Marhattas, was killed in a battle fought by the Nawāb by the assistance of the English on the 23rd April, A.D. 1774, 10th Safar, A.H. 1188. His Life has been translated by Elliot.

[*Vide* Strachey; *Hastings and the Rohila war.*]

Hafiz Rakhna (حافظ رخنه) is the name of the person who planted a large garden at Sirhind in the reign of the Emperor Akbar and called it "Bāgh Noulakh." He died in A.D. 1592, A.H. 1000, and a beautiful chronogram was written on the occasion.

Hafiz-uddin Ahmad, Moulwi (حفيظ الدين احمد مولوی), author of the *Khirad Afrōz*, an Urdū translation of the *Ayār Danish*, or Pilpay's Fables, which he translated for the use of the College of Fort William in A.D. 1803, A.H. 1218.

Hafiz - uddin Nasafi - bin - Ahmad (حفيظ الدين نسفى بن احمد), author of the commentaries called *Madāıik-ut-Tanzil* and *Hakāeq-ut-Tanāwīl*, in Arabic. He died in the year A.D. 1310, A.H. 710.

[*Vide* Nasāfī or Al-Nasafa.]

Hafiz-ullah, Shaikh (حفيظ الله شيخ), a relation of Sirāj-uddīn 'Alī Khān Arzū. His poetical name was Asam. He died in the 21st year of the emperor Muhammad Shāh of Dehlī, A.D. 1767, A.H. 1181.

Hafs (حفص). *Vide* Abū Hafs-ul-Bukhārī.

Hafsa (حفصه), a daughter of the Khalīf Umar, and wife of Muhammad, in whose hands Abū Bakr, the successor of the prophet, deposited the original Qurān. She outlived her husband 33 years and died in A.D. 665, A.H. 45.

Haibat Jang (هيبت جنگ), title of Zain-uddīn Ahmad, the youngest son of Hājī Ahmad, and nephew and son-in-law of Alahwardī Khān Mahābat Jang, governor of Bengal. He was the father of Nawāb Sirāj-uddaula, who succeeded Mahābat Jang in the government of Bengal in A.D. 1756.

Haibat Khan (هيبت خان). He is the author of the *Tarīkh Khān Jahān Lodī, Makhzan-i-Afghānī*, containing the history of Khān Jahān Lodī and of the Afghāns. Khān Jahān was a general of great reputation during the reign of the emperor Jahāngīr, but rebelling against Shāh Jahān, was killed in an engagement with the royal troops, A.D. 1631, A.H. 1087. The above work was written in A.D. 1676. There is also an abridgment of this work, by the same author, called *Majmua' Afghānī*.

Haidar (حيدر), a title of 'Alī, the son-in-law of Muhammad.

Haidar (حيدر كليچه يا حيدر كلوج), also called Haidar Kulūj or Haidar Kulīcha, because he was by profession a baker. He was a native of Herāt, and is the author of a Dīwān in Persian and one in Urdū.

Haidar (حيدر), or Mīr Haidar Shāh, a gallant soldier in the service of Nawāb Sarfarāz Khān, governor of Bengal. He put the Dīwān of Walī the Deccani into Mukhammas and interspersed that of Hāfiz with verses of his own. He died at Hūglī in the reign of the emperor Ahmad Shāh, a year or two before or after A.D. 1750, A.H. 1164, aged 100 years. Garcin-de-Tassy thinks that he is the author of a Masnawī entitled *Kissai Chandar Badon and Māhyār*.

Haidar Ali, known to contemporary Europeans as "Hyder Naik," son of a Punjābī adventurer, born in the Deccan about A.D. 1702; distinguished himself in the service of the Maisur (Mysore) State about 1740. Deposed the Rāja and assumed the power of the State twelve years later and ruled for 20 years. His extraordinary efforts and occasional successes against the British are matter of history. Defeated by Sir Eyre Coote at Porto Novo 1781, he died 7th December, 1782. He was succeeded by his son Tīpu (Tīppoo).

Haidar Ali Moulwi (حيدر على مولوى فيض ابادى), of Faizābād, author of the *Muntahī-ul-Kalām* and several other works. He was living in Dehlī A.D. 1854, A.H. 1270.

Haidar Mir (حيدر مير). *Vide* Haidar Mirzā.

Haidar Mirza (حيدر مرزا), who is also called Mīr Haidar and Mirzā Haidar Doghlāt, was the son of Muhammad Husain, and his wife was the aunt of Babar Shāh. He was formerly in the service of Kāmrān Mirzā, brother of the emperor Humāyūn, but being disgusted with his conduct abandoned his standard about the year A.D. 1539, A.H. 946, and joined the emperor, to whom he was afterwards of great service. In A.D. 1540, A.H. 947, he was deputed by the emperor to conquer Kashmīr, which he took in a short time; but as that emperor was soon after expelled from India by Sher Shāh, Haidar became the king of that country. In the year A.D. 1548, A.H. 955, he invaded Little Thibet, and not only succeeded in conquering that country, but subsequently added Great Thibet, Rajora and Pogla to his dominions. He reigned nearly ten years, and was killed by an arrow in a night-attack made upon his camp in A.D. 1551, A.H. 958.

Haidar Khan, Mir (حيدر خان مير), the grandson of Mīr Haidar, who was the author of the *Tarikh Rashīdī*. This person, on plea of presenting a petition, killed Husain 'Ali Khān Amir-ul-Umrā, at the instigation of the emperor Muhammad Shāh, on the 18th September, O.S. 1720, 27th Zi-Qa'da, A.H. 1132, and was himself cut to pieces.

Haidar Malik (حيدر مالك), entitled Raīs-ul-Mulk Chughtāī, author of the most authentic history of Kashmere down to his own time. He was a nobleman in the service of the emperor Jahāngīr, and was living about the year A.D. 1619, A.H. 1028, in which year he accompanied that emperor to Kashmere.

Haidar Muammai, Mir (حيدر معمائي مير), surnamed Rafīsgī Kāshī, a punster who flourished in the time of Shāh Ismaīl II. king of Persia, and wrote a chronogram at his death, which took place in A.D. 1577, A.H. 985. He was distinguished by his skill in making chronograms and enigmas. He came to India in the time of Akbar, and was drowned when returning by sea to Persia. He was in charge of copies of Faizī's works for distribution in Persia, and they were also lost. *Vide* Mīr Haidar.

Haidar Razi (حیدر رازی), a Persian historian who wrote in the 17th century of the Christian Era.

Haidar, Shaikh or Sultan (حیدر سلطان), father of Shāh Ismaīl I. Safwī. He was the son of Sulṭān or Shaikh Junaid, the son of Shaikh Ibrāhīm, the son of Shaikh or Khwāja Alī, the son of the celebrated Shaikh Sadar-uddīn Mūsa, the son of Shaikh Safī or Safī-uddīn Ardibelī, who was the 21st in a direct line from Mūsī Qāzim, the seventh Imām, He was killed in a battle against Ya'kūb Beg the son of Uzzan Husan, at Shirwān in the month of July, A.D. 1488, Sha'ban, A.H. 893.

Hairan (حیران), poetical name of Mīr Haidar 'Alī. He was killed in zillah Bihār, but had the assassin put to death before he expired.

Hairani, Maulana (حیرانی مولانا همدانی), of Hamdān. He is the author of several Masnawīs or poems, viz. *Bahrām-wa-Nahīd.* Dispute between Heaven and Earth, entitled *Manāzira Arz-wa-Samā ;* Dispute between the Candle and the Moth, called *Manāzira Shama'-wa-Parwana ;* and Dispute between the Roasting Spit and the Fowl, named *Manāzira Sīkh-wa-Murgh.* He died in A.D. 1497-8, A.H. 903.

Hairat (حیرت قیام الدین), poetical name of Qayām-uddīn, the author of the biography called *Tazkira Maqālāt-ush-Shua'rā*, which he completed in A.D. 1760, A.H. 1174.

Hairat (حیرت), poetical title of Pandit Ajuddhia Parshad, a native of Kashmere, who resided at Lucknow. He is the author of a small Dīwan and a few Masnawīs. He died A.H. 1234, in the 35th year of his age.

Hairati (حیرتی), a poet of Marv. In reward of a Qasīda which he composed in praise of Shāh Tahmāsp I. Safwī, he obtained the title of Malik-ush-Shua'rā or king of poets. Besides the work called *Bahjat-ul-Mubāhij*, he is the author of a Masnawī to which he gave the title of Gulzār. All his verses amount to about 40,000. He was murdered at Kāshān A.D. 1554, A.H. 962.

Hairati (حیرتی) was the greatest poet of his time. He had studied at Isfahān, and was alive when Taqī Kāshānī wrote his Tazkira A.D. 1585. Though he received a liberal allowance from the Persian Government, owing to his extravagance, it was quite insufficient for his support, and in A.D. 1581, A.H. 989, he came to India being attracted by the prodigality of the Qutb-Shāhi kings of Golkanḍa.

Hajar (حجر), a very great man among the followers of 'Alī, and remarkable for his singular abstinence, piety and strictness of life, his constant purifications according to Muhammadan law, and exactness in observing the hours of devotion. He was put to death in A.D. 666, by order of Mu'āwia I. for speaking reproachfully of him, affronting his brother Zayād, governor of Kūfa, and affirming that the government did not, of right, belong to any but the family of 'Alī.

Hajari. *Vide* Hijrī.

Haji Begam (حاجی بیگم), wife of the emperor Humāyūn.

[*Vide* Hamīda Bāno Begam.]

Haji Khalfa (حاجی خلفه), a celebrated author commonly called Mustafī Hājī Khalfa. He is the author of the work called *Fazlaka*, also of the Biographical Dictionary called *Kashf-uz-Zunūn*, and the work called *Taqwīm-ut-Tawārikh Rūmī.* The latter is a Chronological Table of remarkable events from the Creation of the world to A.D. 1648, A.H. 1058, translated from the Turkish during the reign of Sulṭān Muhammad IV. of Constantinople. The *Kashf-uz-Zunūn* was printed for the Oriental Translation Fund in 1835-50, together with a Latin translation by Professor Fluegel. It appears that Hājī Khalfa formerly bore the title of Kātib Chilpī, and if this is correct, he died in A.D. 1657, A.H. 1067.

[In Chambers' Encyclopædia the month and year of his death are given as September, A.D. 1658, and he is also said to have been the author of the *Tarīkh Kabīr, the Great History*, which is a history of the world from the creation of Adam to A.D. 1655, containing notices of 150 dynasties, principally Asiatic; also a history of the Ottoman empire from A.D. 1591 to 1658, and a history of the maritime wars of the Turks, which has been translated into English.]

Haji Muhammad Beg Khan (حاجی محمد بیگ خان), the father of the celebrated Mirzā Abū Tālib Khān, author of the *Masīr Tālibī*. He was by descent a Turk, but born at 'Abbāsābād in Isfahān. Whilst a young man, dreading the tyranny of Nādir Shāh, he fled from Persia, and on his arrival in India was admitted into the friendship of Nawāb Abū'l Mansūr Khān Safdar Jang. Upon the death of Rāja Nawul Rāe, Deputy Governor of Audh in A.D. 1750, A.H. 1163, Muhammad Qulī Khān, the nephew of the Nawāb, was appointed to that important office, and he (Hājī) was nominated one of his assistants. On the death of Safdar Jang in A.D. 1753, A.H. 116˙, his son Shujā-uddaula became jealous of his cousin Muhammah Qulī Khān, arrested him and put him to death. Hājī fled with a few of his faithful servants to Bengal, where he passed a number of years, and died at Murshidābād in April, A.D. 1769, Ẕil-ḥijja, A.H. 1182.

Haji Muhammad Jan (حاجی محمد جان مشهدی), of Mashhad. His poetical name is Qudsī. He flourished in the reign of the emperor Shāh Jahān, who conferred on him the title of Malik-ush-Shua'ra, or the Royal poet. He is the author of a poem containing the conquests of the emperor, which he named *Zafarnāma*. He died in the year A.D. 1645, A.H. 1055, and after him the title of the royal poet was conferred on Abū Tālib Kalīm. He is also the author of a Dīwān, and an Insha.

Haji Muhammad Kashmiri Maulana (حاجی محمد کشمیری مولانا). One of his forefathers, who was a native of Hamdān, came to Kashmere with Mīr Said 'Alī Hamdānī. Hājī was born in that province, but came to Dehlī in his youth, where he received his education. He was an excellent poet, flourishing in the time of Akbar, and died on Thursday the 22nd September, A.D. 1597, 19th Ṣafar, A.H. 1006, O.S. He was a religious man, and had many disciples, one of whom, named Maulānā Hasan, wrote the chronogram of his death.

Haji Muhammad Khan Sistani (حاجی محمد خان سیستانی). He was at first in the service of Bairām Khān Khānkhānān, after whose dismissal he was honoured with the rank of 3000 by the emperor Akbar. He accompanied Munaim Khān Khānkhānān to Bengal and died at Gour in A.D. 1575, A.H. 983.

Haji Muhammad Qandahari (حاجی محمد قندهاری). He is the author of a history which goes by his name, *viz. Tarīkh Hājī Muhammad Qandahārī.*

Hajjaj-bin-Yusaf-al-Saqafi or **Thaqafi** (حجاج بن یوسف الشقفی), one of the most valiant Arabian captains, who was made governor of Arabia and Arabian Irāq, by Abdulmalik the fifth Khalīf of the Ommaides, after he had defeated and killed Abdullāh-bin-Zubeir, who had taken the title of Khalīfa at Mecca. In the year A.D. 693, A.H. 74, he pulled down the temple of Mecca, which Abdullāh had repaired, placing the black stone on the outside of it again and restoring it to the very form it had before Muhammad's time. He was a great tyrant; it is said of him, that in his lifetime he had put to death a hundred and twenty thousand persons, and when he died had 50,000 in his prisons. He died in the reign of the Khalīf Walīf I. in the year A.D. 714, A.H. 85, aged 54 years.

Hakim I. (حکیم), the poetical title of a person who was a native of Mashhad, and was living about the year A.D. 1688, A.H. 1100. He was an Arabic and Persian scholar, and is the author of a Dīwān and a Masnawī.

Hakim II. (حکیم), the poetical name of Shāh Abdul Hakīm of Lāhore. He is the author of a work called *Mardum Dīda*, compiled at Aurangābād in A.D. 1761, A.H. 1175. It contains an account of those poets with whom the author was acquainted.

Hakim-Ain-ul-Mulk (حکیم عین الملک), of Shīrāz. He was a learned man and a clever writer. He traced his origin, on his mother's side, to the renowned logician Muhaqqiq-i-Dawanī. The Historian Badaoni was a friend of his. Akbar also liked him very much. Hakīm was a poet and wrote under the Lakhalus of Dawanī. He died at Handiah on the 27th Ẕil-ḥijja, A.H. 1003.

[Vide *Āīn Translation*, i. p. 481.]

Hakim Ali (حکیم علی گیلانی), of Gilān, came to India in indigent circumstances, but was fortunate enough to become in course of time a personal attendant and friend of Akbar. In the 39th year of Akbar's reign, he constructed the wonderful reservoir which is so often mentioned by Mughal historians. In the 40th year Alī was a commander of 700 and had the title of Jalinus Uzzamani the 'Galinus of the Age.' He died on the 5th Muḥarram, A.H. 1018.

[Vide *Āīn Translation*, i. p. 466.]

Hakim Muhammad (حکیم محمد). He was half-brother to the emperor Akbar, being born of a different mother.

[*Vide* Muhammad Hakīm.]

Hakim Nur-uddin Shirazi (حکیم نور الدین شیرازی), who appears to have been either grandson or sister's son of Abū'l Fazl, asserts in his preface to the *Hajāt Dara Shikohī*, that he commenced his work in the 14th year of the reign of Shāh Jahān, A.D. 1642, A.H. 1052, the above name of the book gives the year of the Hijra, and brought it to a conclusion in A.H. 1056.

Hakim-ul-Mumalik (حکیم الممالک), title of Mīr Muhammad Mahdī, a physician who held the rank of 4000 in the reign of the emperor 'Alamgīr.

Halaki (هلاکی همدانی), of Hamdān, a Persian poet, though illiterate, wrote a panegyric on the accession of Shāh Isma'īl Safwī II. to the throne of Persia, in the year A.D. 1576, A.H. 984, for which he received a handsome present from the king, while other poets who wrote on the same occasion received nothing.

Halaku Qaan or **Khan** (هلاکو قاآن), also called Īlkhān, was the son of Tūlī Khān, and the fourth successor and grandson of Changez Khān the Tartar. In the reign of his brother Mangū Qāān, king of Tartary, he was detached, in May, A.D. 1253, Rabī' I. A.H. 651, attended by one hundred and fifty thousand horse to subdue Persia, which he soon conquered, after which he extirpated the power of the Isma'īlīs, the descendants of Hasan Sabbāh (*q.v.*), the founder of the sect, and destroyed their strongholds in November, A.D. 1256, Ẕil-qada, A.H. 654. He next intended to march direct to Constantinople, but was persuaded by Nasīr-uddīn Tūsī (whom he had made his prime minister) to turn his arms against Baghdād. He marched against that capital, and after a siege of some months took it in February, A.D. 1258, 4th Ṣafar, A.H. 656. The Khalīfa Mustaa'sim Billāh and his son were seized, and with 800,000 of its inhabitants were put to death. After these successes Halākū was desirous of returning to Tartary to take possession of the government of his native country, which had become vacant by the death of his brother Mangū Qāān; but the great defeat which the general whom he had left in Syria suffered from Saif-uddīn Fīrōz, the prince of the Mamlūks of Egypt, compelled him to abandon his design; and after he had restored his affairs in Syria, he fixed his residence at Marāgha, in Azurbaijan, where he died on Sunday the 8th February, A.D. 1265, 19th Rabī' II. A.H. 663, after a reign of twelve years from his first coming to Persia, and eight years from the death of his brother. During his prosperous reign, the literature of Persia resumed its former flourishing state; and the illustrious Persian Bard Sa'dī of Shīrāz was living in his time. Halākū was succeeded by his son Abā Qāān in the kingdom of Persia.

List of Mughal-Tartar or Īlkhāīn dynasty of Persia.

Halākū Khān, the son of Tūlī Khān, succeeded his brother Mangū Qāān in the kingdom of Persia.
Abā Qāān, the son of Halākū.
Nīkodar or Ahmad Khān, brother of Abā Qāān.
Arghūn Khān, son of Abā Qāān.
Kaikhātū Khān, son of Abā Qāān.
Baidū, grandson of Halākū.
Ghāzān Khān, son of Arghūn Khān.
Aljaitū, the son of Arghūn Khān.
Abū Saīd Bahadur Khān, son of Aljaptū, after whose death the dynasty became dependent.

Halati (حالتی), poetical title of Kāsim Beg, who was born and brought up in Teherān, and spent the greater part of his life at Qazwīn. He flourished in the reign of Shāh Tahmāsp Safwī, and wrote the chronogram of the accession of Shāh Ismaīl II. in A.D. 1576, A.H. 984. He is the author of a Dīwān in Persian.

Halima (حلیمه), the name of Muhammad's nurse, who, it is said, had formerly no milk in her breasts, but immediately obtained some when she presented them to the new born prophet to suck.

Hallaj (حلاج). This word, which properly signifies the person that prepares cotton before it is manufactured, was the surname of Abū Mughīs Husain-bin-Mansūr.
[*Vide* Mansūr Hallāj.]

Hamd-ullah Mustoufi-bin-Abu-Bakr-al-Qazwini, Khwaja (حمد الله مستوفی بن ابو بکر القزوینی خواجه), also called Hamīd-uddīn Mustoufī, a native of Quzwīn, and author of the *Tārīkh Guzīda*, or *Selected History*, which he composed in A.D. 1329, A.H. 730, and dedicated to the minister Ghayās-uddīn, the son of Rashīd-uddīn, author of the *Jāma'-ut-Tawārīkh*, to both of whom Hamd-ullāh had been Secretary. The *Tārīkh Guzīda* ranks among the best general histories of the last eleven years; after the completion of this history, the author composed his celebrated work on Geography and Natural History, entitled *Nuzhat-ul-Qulūb*, *The delight of hearts*, which is in high repute with Oriental Scholars, and which has obtained for him from D'Herbelot the title of le Geographe Persan. Hamd-ullāh died A.D. 1349, A.H. 750. He was the brother of Fakhr-uddīn Fath-ullāh Mustoufī. See also Ahmad-bin-Abū Bakr.

Hamid (حميد), a poet, who is the author of a poem called *Ismat Nāma*, containing the loves of Sātin and Mīna, composed in the year A.D. 1607, A.H. 1016, during the reign of Jahāngīr.

Hamid (حامد), or Abdūl Hāmid Yahia, a celebrated caligrapher, who reformed the Arabian characters in the reign of the Khalīf Muāwia II. of the house of Umaiya. He died in A.D. 749, A.H. 132.

Hamid Ali, Mirza (حامد علی مرزا), or more properly Prince Mirzā Hāmid 'Alī, son of Wājid 'Alī Shāh, the last king of Lucknow. He accompanied his grandmother the Dowager Queen of Lucknow to England to claim his right, in 1856.

[*Vide* Jawād Alī.]

Hamida Bano (حميده بانو), the daughter of Malika Bano, the sister of Mumtāz Mahal, was married to Khalīl-ullāh Khān, who died in A.D. 1662.

Hamida Bano Begam (حميده بانو بيگم), styled (after her death) Mariam Makānī, and commonly called Hājī Begam, was a great-granddaughter of Shaikh Ahmad Jām. She was married in A.D. 1541, A.H. 948, to the emperor Humayūn, and became the mother of the emperor Akbar. She is the founder the Sarāī called Arab Sarā, situated near the mausoleum of her husband at old Dehlī. She had gone on a pilgrimage to Mecca, and on her return brought with her 300 Arabs, for whom she built this place in A.D. 1560, A.H. 968. She died at Āgra on Monday the 29th August, A.D. 1603, 17th Shahrewar, A.H. 1012, aged about 78 years, and was buried in the mausoleum of Humāyūn at Dehlī.

Hamid Kirmani (حامد كرمانی), poetical name of Shaikh Aohad-uddīn Kurmānī.

Hamid-uddin Ali-al-Bukhari (حميد الدين علی البخاری), author of a short Commentary on the Hidāya, entitled the *Fawāed*. He died in A.D. 1268, A.H. 667.

Hamid-ullah Khan (حميد الله خان), author of the *Ahādīs-ul-Khawānīn*, also called *Tārīkh-i-Hamīd*, which contains a history of Chātgawn (Chittagong). Printed at Calcutta in 1871.

Hamid-uddin Mustoufi, Khwaja (حميد الدين مستوفي خواجه).

[*Vide* Hamd-ullāh Mustoufī.]

Hamid-uddin Nagori, Qazi (حميد الدين ناگوری قاضی), a native of Nāgor who held the appointment of Qāzī, and died on the 11th July, A.D. 1296, 11th Ramazān, A.H. 695, and is buried at Dehlī close to the tomb of Khwāja Qutb-uddīn Bakhtiār, commonly called Qutb Shāh. He is the author of the book called *Tawāla-ush-Shamūs*, containing religious contemplations and speculative opinions of the essence and nature of the divinity, etc., etc. The year of his death is taken from an inscription over his tomb.

Hamid-uddin Qazi (حميد الدين قاضی دهلوی), of Dehlī, was the author of the *Sharah Hidāyat-ul-Fiqah* and several other works. He died in A.D. 1363, A.H. 764.

Hamid-uddin Umar, Qazi (حميد الدين عمر قاضي) flourished in the time of Sultān Sanjar, the Saljūkī king of Persia, was a contemporary of the poet Anwarī, and is the author of a Commentary on the Qurān called *Muqāmāt*.

Hammad (حماد), the son of Abū Hanīfa, who was a learned man, and died in the year A.D. 792, A.H. 176.

Hamza, Amir (حمزه امير), the son of Abdul Muttalib, and uncle of Muhammad, who gave him the title of Asad-ullāh, or the lion of God, because of his courage and valour, and put into his hands the first standard he ordered to be made, which was called "Rāet-ul-Islām," the standard of the faith. Hamza, who was also called Abū 'Umar, was killed in the battle of Ohad which Muhammad fought with the Qureshites, of whom Abū Sufiān was chief. After the battle Hinda, the wife of Abū Sufiān, pulled Hamza's liver out of his body and chewed and swallowed some of it. This battle took place in the month of March, A.D. 625, Shawwāl, A.H. 3.

Hamza Bano Begam (حمزه بانو بيگم), daughter of Shāh Jahān by Kandaharī Begam, daughter of Muzaffar Husain Mirzā of the royal race of Shāh Isma'īl Safwī. She was born in the year A.H. 1019.

Hamza Mirza (حمزه مرزا), the eldest son of Sultān Muhammad Khuda Banda, and the grandson of Shāh Tahmāsp I. of the Safwī family of Persia. His father, on account of a natural weakness in his eyes, which rendered him almost blind, had at first entrusted the charge of the empire to his wazīr, Mirzā Sulaimān; when that nobleman was slain, he created his own son, Hamza Mirzā, regent of the empire. This prince, by his valour, extricated his weak father from all his difficulties with which he was surrounded. But this gleam of good fortune soon vanished. This gallant prince was stabbed by a barber, in his own private apartments on the 24th November, A.D. 1586, 22nd Ẕil-ḥijja, A.H. 994.

Hanbal, Imam (حنبل امام), or Ahmad Ibn Hanbal, the son of Muhammad-ibn-Hanbal, was the fourth Imām or founder of one of the four orthodox sects of the Sunnīs called Hanbalites. This sect made a great noise in Baghdād in the reign of the Khalīf Al-Muqtadir in A.D. 929, A.H. 317. Merauzī, chief of the sect, had asserted that God had placed Muhammad on his throne, which assertion he founded upon the passage of the Qurān: "Thy Lord shall soon give thee a considerable place or station." All the other sects of the Musalmāns regard the explication of the Hanbalites as a shocking impiety. They maintain that this *considerable place or station* was the post or quality of a mediator, which they affirm to belong to their prophet. This dispute passed from the schools to the public assemblies. At length they came from words to blows which cost the lives of several thousands. In the year A.D. 935, A.H. 323, the Hanbalites became so insolent, that they marched in arms on the city of Baghdād, and plundered the shops on pretence that wine was drunk in them. Ahmad was a traditionist of the first class, and composed a collection of authenticated traditions called *Masnad*, more copious than those any other person had, till then, been able to form: it is said that he knew by heart one million of those traditions. He was born in the year A.D. 780, A.H. 164, and died on the 31st July, A.D. 855, 12th Rabī' I. A.H. 241, in the reign of the Khalīf Al-Mutwakkil, and was buried at Baghdād. It was estimated that the number of men present at his funeral was 800,000, and 60,000 women; and it is said that 20,000 Christians, Jews and Magians became Moslems on the day of his death. In the year A.D. 835, Ramaẓān, A.H. 220, some time in the month September, he was required by Khalīf Al-Motasim Billāh to declare that the Qurān was created, but would not, and although beaten and imprisoned persisted in his refusal. The eternity of the Qurān, considered as the word of God, is the orthodox Moslem doctrine. [The modern Wahhābis are believed to be partly followers of this teacher. See Hughes' *Dictionary of Islām, in voc.* "Ibn Hanbal."]

Handal Mirza (حندال مرزا), son of the emperor Bābar Shāh and brother of Humāyūn, was born in the year A.D. 1518, A.H. 924. He lost his life in a night attack made by his brother Kāmrān Mirzā on the emperor Humāyūn near Khaibar in the province of Kābul, on the 19th November, A.D. 1551, 21st Ẕi-Qa'da, A.H. 958. He is buried at Kābul close to the tomb of the emperor Bābar Shāh. Humāyūn, out of affection to the memory of Handāl Mirzā, in the same year gave the daughter of that prince, Raqia Sulṭāna, to his son Akbar in marriage.

Hani (حنى), surname of Muhammad-bin-'Alī, a poet who died in the year A.D. 1333, A.H. 733.

Hanifa Imam (حنيفه امام), also called Abū Hanīfa and Imām 'Azim, was one of the four Jurisconsults of Mecca, *viz.* Imām Hanīfa, Imām Hanbāl, Imām Shāfa'ī and Imām Mālik, from whom are derived the various Codes of Muhammadan Jurisprudence. He was one of the most celebrated doctors of the Musalmāns, and chief of the sect of Hanīfites; and though his sect is the principal of the four which they now indifferently follow, he was ill-used during his lifetime. His principal works are: the *Masnad*, *i.e.* the foundation or support, wherein he established all the points of the Musalmān faith; a treatise entitled *Filkalām* or *Scholastic Divinity*; and a catechism called *Mua'llim-ul-Islām, i.e.* the Instructor.

Another of his books is entitled the *Fiqh-ul-Akbar*; it treats of the Ilm-ul-Kalām, and has been commented upon by various writers, many of whom are mentioned by Hājī Khalfa. Some say that the Masnad was written by Imām Hanbāl. By the Shias he is as much detested and censured as by their antagonists he is admired and exalted. For allowing his disciples to drink *nabiz*, which is a wine made of dates, he is accused by the Persians of departing from the clear injunction of the Prophet against all intoxicating beverages. [At the time of his birth some of the "companions" of the Prophet were still living, which adds to his authority among the Sunnī denomination.]

Haqiqat (حقيقت), poetical title of Saiyad Husain Shāh, son of Saiyad Arab Shāh. He accompanied Col. Kydd to Chināpatan in Madras as head Munshī and died there. He is the author of an Urdū Dīwān and seven other works, some of which are named *Tahfat-ul-'Ajam*, *Khazīnat-ul-Amsāl, Sanamkada Chīn* and *Hasht Gulgusht*.

[*Vide* Husain Shāh.]

Haqiri (حقيرى), poetical name of Maulānā Shahāb-uddīn Mua'mmāī.

Harindar Narain Bhup, Maharaja (هرندر نارايں بهوپ مهاراجه), the Rāja of Kūch Behār, who died at Benāres on the 30th May, 1839, and was aged 70 years. He was of the Rajbansī caste, and a follower of Siva, but his style of living was very unlike that of a Hindū. He used to marry without any regard to caste, and entered into the connubial relation with any women he took a fancy to. He did not even spare married women. The number of his wives or rānīs was no less than 1200 !

Hari Rao Holkar (هری راو هلکر), Rāja of Indor, was the cousin and successor of Malhār Rāo III. the adopted son and successor of Jaswant Rāo Holkar. He died on the 24th October, A.D. 1843.

Hariri (حریری), whose full name is Abū Muhammad Qasim-bin-'Alī-bin-Usmān-al-Harirī-al-Basrī, was a native of Basra. He was one of the ablest writers of his time, and is the author of the *Muqāmāt Harīrī*, a work consisting of fifty Oratorical, Poetical, Moral, Ecomiastic, and Satirical discourses, supposed to have been spoken or read in public assemblies; but which were composed by the author at the desire of Anūsherwān-ibn-Khālid, wazīr to Sultān Muhammad Saljūqī. He died at Basra in the year A.D. 1122, A.H. 516. Poets, historians, grammarians and lexicographers look upon the *Muqāmāt* as the highest authority, and next to the Qurān, as far at least as language is concerned. His book has been translated either entirely or partially into nearly every Eastern and European tongue.

Harkaran (هرکرن), the son of Mathura Das, a Kambōh of Multān, was a Munshī in the service of Nawāb Ya'tbār Khān, and is the author of a collection of letters called *Inshāe Harkaran*, or the *Forms of Harkaran*, translated into English by D. Francis Balfour, M.D. The second edition of this work was printed in 1804.

Harun-al-Rashid (هارون الرشید). *Vide* Al-Rashīd.

Hasan (حسن بن سهیل), son of Suhail or Sahl, was governor of Chaldea about the year A.D. 830, under the Khalīf Al-Māmūn, who married Tūrān Dukht his daughter. Some attribute to this Hasan the translation of the Persian book entitled *Jāwedān Khirad* into Arabic.

Hasan (حسن), poetical name of Muhammad Hasan, who flourished in the reign of the emperor Shāh 'Alam of Dehlī.

Hasan Abdal (حسن عبدال), or Baba Hasan Abdāl, a famous saint who was a Sayyad at Sabzwār in Khurāsān. He came to India with Mirzā Shahrukh, son of Anser Taimūr, and died at Qandahār, where his tomb is resorted to by pilgrims. Jahāngīr says in the *Tūzak* that the place Hurasadak is 75 kos from Kashmere.

Hasan 'Ali (حسن علی), the poet laureate in the service of Tīpū Sultān of Mysore. He is the author of a book called *Bhogbal*, or the *Kok Shāstar*. It is a curious but obscene satire on women, said to be a translation or paraphrase from the Sanskrit in Hindī verse. There is another translation of the same book in Persian prose called *Lazzat-un-Nisa*, by Ziyā-uddīn Nakhshabī.

Hasan Askari, Imam (حسن عسکری), or Abū'l Hasan 'Alī-al-'Askarī, was the eleventh Imām of the race of 'Alī, and the eldest son of Imām 'Alī Naqī who was the tenth. He was born at Madīna in the year A.D. 846, A.H. 232, and died on the 6th November, A.D. 874, 22nd Muharram, A.H. 261, aged 28 years. He is buried at Sarmanrāi in Baghdād close to the tomb of his father.

Hasan Basri, Khwaja (حسن بصری خواجه), a native of Basra and a very pious Musalmān, who is said to have possessed all the branches of science, and was noted for self-mortification, fear of God and devotion. He is the author of a Dīwān or book of Odes in Arabic. He was born in A.D. 642, A.H. 21, and died on the 11th October, A.D. 728, 1st Rajab, A.H. 110, aged 89 lunar years, and was buried at Basra.

Hasan Beg (Khani, Badakhshi) (حسن بیگ خانی بدخشی), Shaikh Umari was a good soldier. He was made a commander of 2,500 for his services in Bangash, and was put, towards the end of Akbar's reign, in charge of Kabul, receiving Fort Rohtās in the Panjāb as jagir. Hasan Beg, after making a useless attempt to incriminate others, was put into a cow-hide and in this state he was tied to donkeys and carried through the bazaar. He died after a few hours from suffocation.

[Vide *Āīn Translation*, i. p. 454.]

Hasan-bin-Muhammad Khaki-al-Shirazi (حسن بن محمد خاکی الشیرازی), who came to India in the time of the emperor Akbar and obtained different offices under the government. He is the author of a history also called *Muntakhib-ut-Tawārīkh*, besides the one written by Abdu Qādir Badaonī. He commenced the work before the close of Akbar's reign, *i.e.* A.D. 1610, A.H. 1019, in which year, he tells us, he was appointed Dīwān of Patna.

Hasan-bin-Muhammad Sharif (حسن بن محمد شریف), author of the *Anīs-ul-'Ushshāq*, the lover's companion, containing an explanation of all the metaphors and phrases used by the poets; with numerous quotations from those held in the greatest estimation.

[*Vide* Qhadim.]

Hasan-bin-Sabah (حسن بن صباح). *Vide* Hasan Sabbah.

Hasan Buzurg (حسن بزرگ), also called Sheikh Hasan, Amīr Hasan Īlqānī, and Amīr Hasan Naviān, Kayūkāī, the son of Amīr Īlqān Jalāyer. He was an immediate descendant of Sulṭān Arghūn Khān, king of Persia (whose sister was his mother), and one of the principal chiefs of the Mughals in the reign of Sulṭān Abū Sa'īd. He married Baghdād Khātūn, daughter of Amīr Chobān or Joviān, but the prince being deeply enamoured of her charms, Amīr Hasan, after the death of her father, was forced to resign his consent to him in A.D. 1327, A.H. 728. A few years after the death of Abū Sa'īd, Amīr Hasan married his widow Dilshād Khātūn, went to Baghdād, seized that city, and became the founder of a petty dynasty of princes. His life was passed in contests to establish his authority over the territories of Baghdād, and he died before this object of his ambition was accomplished, in July, A.D. 1356, Rajab, A.H. 757. His son Sulṭān Owes Jalāyer was more fortunate; he not only succeeded in completing the conquest his father had commenced, but carried his arms into Azurbejān and Khurāsān. Sulṭān Owes died in October, A.D. 1374, A.H. 776, and left his government to his second son Sulṭān Husain Jalāyer. This excellent prince, who is also alike celebrated for his benevolence and love of justice, lost his life in an action in A.D. 1382, A.H. 784, with his brother Ahmad, surnamed Īlqānī, a cruel and unjust ruler, whose enormities compelled his subjects to invite Amīr Taimūr (Tamerlane) to their relief in A.D. 1393, and almost the whole of the future life of Ahmad passed in an ineffectual struggle with that conqueror. He fled to Egypt for safety, and when, after the death of Taimūr, he returned to recover his dominions, he was taken and put to death by Qara Yūsaf, a Turkman chief, in A.D. 1410, A.H. 813.

Hasan Ganga. *Vide* Alā-ad-dīn I.

Hasan Imam (حسن امام), the eldest son of 'Alī, the son of Abū Tālib, and Fātima, the daughter of Muhammad; was born on the 1st March, A.D. 625, 15th Ramaẓān, A.H. 3. After the death of his father in January, A.D. 661, Ramaẓān, A.H. 40, he succeeded him as second Imām, and was proclaimed Khalīf by the Arabians, but perceiving the people divided and himself ill-used, he after six months resigned the Khilāfat to Mu'āwia, who assigned to him about 15,000 pounds a year, besides large presents. After this Hasan and his brother Husain retired and lived privately at Madīna, where after a few years he died of poison, administered to him by one of his wives, whom Yazīd, the son of Mu'āwia, suborned to commit that wickedness, on the promise of marrying her afterwards; though instead of a new husband, she was forced to be contented with a good sum of money which Mu'āwia gave her for her pains; for Yazīd was not so mad as to trust himself to her embraces. Hasan's murder took place on the night of the 17th March, A.D. 669 or 670, 7th Ṣafar, A.H. 49. He was buried in Madīna at a place called Baqīa. Hasan is said to have been in person very like his grandfather Muhammad, who, when he was born, spit in his mouth and named him Hasan. He had twenty children—fifteen sons and five daughters. Though his wives were remarkably fond of him, yet he was apt very frequently to divorce them and marry new ones.

Hasan Kashi, Maulana (حسن کاشی مولانا), a poet who was a native of Kāshān. He is the author of many Qāsīdas and Ghazals. The year of his death is not known, but he appears to have flourished about the 8th century of the Hijrī era.

Hasan Khwaja (حسن خواجه). *Vide* Hasan Sanjarī.

Hasan Khwaja (حسن خواجه), a darwesh, the son of Khwajā Ibrahīm. He is the author of a Dīwān of Ghazals, in the last verses of each of which he has mentioned the name of his beloved.

Hasan Kochak, Shaikh (حسن کوچک شیخ), a grandson of Amīr Choubān or Joviān. He was one of the chiefs who, during the period of trouble and confusion which took place after the death of Sulṭān Abū Sa'id, king of Persia, in A.D. 1335, rose to eminence. He fought several battles with Amīr Hasan Buzurg (*q.v.*), and met his death accidentally by the hands of a quarrelsome wife, in December, A.D. 1343, Rajab, A.H. 744.

Hasan Maimandi (حسن میمندی). It is asserted by some that he was one of the ministers of Sulṭān Mahmūd of Ghaznī. This statement is altogether incorrect and unfounded, says Sir H. Elliot, as it is not mentioned by any great historian. But his son who is commonly called Ahmad-bin-Hasan Maimandī was a minister of that monarch. Hasan Maimandī was, during the lifetime of Sulṭān Nāsir-uddīn Subaktagīn, employed as Dīwān or Collector of Revenues at Qasba Bust; but Nāsir-uddīn was led by the secret machinations of his enemies to entertain an unfavourable opinion of him, till he was at last, in consequence of his having been convicted of extortion and fraud to a large amount, hanged by order of that Sulṭān; so that the general notion which prevails that he was the wazīr of Sulṭān Mahmūd, is erroneous.

Hasan, Mir (حسن میر), a Hindūstānī poet of Lucknow, and author of the novel called *Masnawī Mīr Hasan*, containing the loves of Badr-i-Munīr and Benazīr in Urdū verse, which he completed and dedicated to Nawāb 'Asaf-uddaula in the year A.D. 1785, A.H. 1199. It is also called *Sahr-ul-Bayān*. His ancestors were of Herāt, but he was born at Dehlī and went early in life to Lucknow, where he was supported by Nawāb Safdar Jang and his son Mirzā Nawāzish Alī Khān. He is also the author of a Dīwān of about 8000 verses, and of a Tazkira of Urdū poets. He died in A.D. 1790, A.H. 1204. His father's name was Mīr Ghulām Husain Zāhik.

Hasan Mirza (حسن مرزا), son of Mulla Abdur Razzāq of Lahijān. He has left some noble compositions, such as *The True Light on the articles of Faith*, *The Beauty of good Men in their Works*, a pious treatise, and some others. He died in the beginning of the 18th century.

Hasan, Maulana (حسن مولانا), a learned Musalmān who lived in the time of the emperor Jahāngīr and wrote a chronogram on the sudden death of Shaikh 'Alī Ahmad, son of Shaikh Husain Naqshi, in the year A.D. 1609, A.H. 1018.

Hasan Mutkallim, Maulana (حسن متکلم مولانا), a poet and pupil of Maulānā Muzaffar of Herāt. He flourished in the reign of Malik Ghayās-uddīn Kart II. in whose name he composed a book on the art of poetry.

Hasan Rafi (حسن رفیع), a Persian poet.

Hasan Sabbah (حسن صباح), the founder of the dynasty of the Isma'īlīs in Persia. He was styled Shaikh-ul-Jabal, an Arabic title, which signifies "the chief of the mountains." The name by which this ruler and his descendants are indiscriminately known in European history is, "The Old Man of the Mountain." His followers or descendants were also called Hasanī, and the English word "assassin," is supposed to have been formed from a corruption of this term. Hasan Sabbāh was at first a mace-bearer to Sultān Alp Arsalān; but in consequence of a quarrel with Nizām-ul-Mulk, the minister of that prince, he retired to Rai, his native country, and from thence, to Syria, where he entered into the service of a chief of the family of Ismā'il the son of Ja'far Sādiq, and adopted the tenets of that sect. The first object of Hasan was to possess himself of a stronghold; and he succeeded in gaining by stratagem the mountain fort of Alahmūt, situated between Qazwīn and Gīlān. The fort was built by Hasan-bin-Zaid in the year A.D. 860, A.H. 246, and Hasan Sabbāh took it in A.D. 1089, A.H. 482. From this fortress he commenced depredations on the surrounding country, and added several other hill forts to the one he had already seized. That of Rōdbār, which is also near Qazwīn, was next to Alahmūt in consequence. Malik Shāh Saljūkī, the reigning Sulṭān, had sent a force to reduce him, but without any success. In the month of October, A.D. 1092, Ramazān, A.H. 485, Nizām-ul-Mulk, who was then following the royal camp from Isfahān to Baghdād, was stabbed by one of the followers of Hasan Sabbāh who was his personal enemy. Hasan Sabbāh died in A.D. 1124, 26th Rabī II. A.H. 518. Rukn-uddīn, who was the last of this family, and who is better known under the name of Qāhir Shāh or Khūr Shāh, after a weak and ineffectual struggle fell before Halākū. That conqueror not only made him prisoner, but took and dismantled all his strongholds. This event took place in the month of November, A.D. 1256, Ẕi-Qada' A.H. 654. It was his father Alā-uddīn Muhammad who forced Nasīr-uddīn Tūsī to remain with him for some years, till he was released by Halākū Khān. *Vide* Ismaīl and Ismaīlīs. The successor of Hasan was Buzurg Umaid. [Hasan Sabbāh and the minister had both been schoolfellows at Umar Khāyyam (*q.v.*).]

Hasan Salimi (حسن سلیمی). *Vide* Salīmī.

Hasan Sanjari, Khwaja (حسن سنجری خواجه), also called Khwāja Hasan Dehlawī, a celebrated Persian poet of Dehlī, who was a contemporary of the famous Amīr Khusro, and had become at the age of 50 years a disciple of Shaikh Nizām-uddīn Aulia. He died, according to the author of the *Mirat-ul-Khayāl*, in the Deccan in the year A.D. 1307, A.H. 707, and is buried at Daulatābād. He is the author of several works, amongst which is a Dīwān, and one called *Fawāed-ul-Fawād*, a collection of letters written by Nizām-uddīn Aulia to his disciples. Tālib says he died in A.D. 1337, A.H. 738. His father name was Alaī Sanjarī.

Hasan, Shaikh (حسن شیخ), the son of Shaikh Nazar-ullāh. He is the author of a work called *Sarat Istakam*. He died in Mīrat in the year A.H. 1078.

Hasan Khan Shamlu (حسن خان شاملو), governor of Herāt under Shāh Abbās II. and his son Shāh Sulaimān. He died in A.D. 1697, A.H. 1109, and is the author of a Dīwān.

Hasan, Sayyad (حسن سید غزنی), of Ghaznī, a poet who flourished in the reign of Sultān Bahrām Shāh the Ghaznavida, and is the author of a Dīwān. He is also called Sayyad Hasan-al-Husainī. He died on the way while returning from Mecca, in the year A.D. 1170, A.H. 565.

Hasham (هشام بن عبد الملک), the son of Abdūl Malik, and the tenth Khalīf of the house of Umaiya or Ummaides, succeeded his brother Yazīd II. in A.D. 724, A.H. 105. He conquered the Khāqān of Turkistān, and made war against Leo III. the Isaurian. He was always attended by 600 camels to carry his splendid wardrobe. He died after a reign of 19 years 7 months and 11 days in the year A.D. 743, A.H. 125, and was succeeded by Walīd II. son of Yazīd II. In his time lived the celebrated Majnūn, the lover of Lailī.

Hashim (هاشم), a poet who flourished at Burhānpūr in the Deccan in the reign of the emperor Jahāngīr and was a disciple of Shaikh Ahmad Farūqi, commonly called Shaikh Ahmad Sarhindī. He is the author of a Dīwān and several other books, and was alive in A.D. 1646, A.H. 1056.

Hashim (هاشم), the son of Abdūl Manāf, was the father of Abdūl Muttalib, who was the father of Abdullāh and grandfather of Muhammad the prophet of the Musulmāns. He succeeded his father as president of the Ka'ba, and raised the glory of his people to the highest pitch; insomuch that the neighbouring great men and heads of tribes made their court to him. Nay, so great veneration is the memory of Hashim held in by the Arabs, that from him the family of Muhammad among them are called Hashīmites. He died at Ghaza in Syria, and was succeeded by his son Abdūl Muttalib, who became president of the Ka'ba.

Hashimi Kirmani (هاشمی کرمانی), author of a poem or Masnawī called *Mazhar-ul-Āsār*. He died in A.D. 1541, A.H. 948.

Hashmat (حشمت), the poetical name of Mīr Muhtashim Alī Khān, whose ancestors were of Badakhshān, but he was born in Dehlī. He died about the year A.D. 1748, A.H. 1161, and left a Dīwān of 700 verses.

Hashmat (حشمت), the poetical name of Bakhshī Alī Khān, which see.

Hasrat (حسرت), the poetical name of Sayyad Muhammad, who died in the reign of the emperor Muhammad Shāh.

Hasrat (حسرت), poetical name of Mīr Muhammad Hayāt of Patna who had the title of Haibat Qulī Khān. He was for some time attached to the service of Nawāb Shaukat Jang at Purania, and for some time to that of Sirāj-uddaula of Murshidābād. He died in A.D. 1800, A.H. 1215, and left a Dīwān of 2000 verses.

Hasrat (حسرت), poetical appellation of Mirzā Ja'far 'Alī, an Urdū poet who flourished in the latter part of the 18th century, and gave instructions in the art of poetry to Nawāb Muhabbat Khān at Lucknow.

Hasrati (حسرتی). *Vide* Shefta.

Hatifi, Maulana (هاتفی مولانا), the poetical name of Abd-ullāh, the son of Maulānā Abdur Rahmān Jāmī's sister. He was born in Jām, a city of Herāt, and died there in the year A.D. 1521, A.H. 927, and was buried in the village of Kharjard. He was a good poet, and author of several works. Having finished his studies, under the patronage and instruction of his uncle Hātifī, with his permission, secluded himself from the world. When Shāh Isma'īl Safwī fought the Uzbak Tartars in Khurāsān, and slew Shāhībeg Khān their chief in A.D. 1508, A.H. 914, he prevailed on our poet to quit his cell, and come to court. Solely ambitious of rivalling the Khamsa or five poems of Nizāmī, he wrote in imitation of them his *Lailī and Majnūn*, *Khusro and Shīrīn*, *Haft Manzar*, *the Taimur Nāma*, which is also called *Zafarnama*, and in imitation of the Sikandar Nāma, he undertook a heroic poem in praise of his patron, called *Fatūhāt Shahī*, which he did not live to finish. Among the numerous Persian poems on the story of Lailī and Majnūn, that of Hātifī seems universally esteemed the simplest and most pathetic.

Hatim (حاتم طائی), commonly called Hātim Tāī, a famous Arabian Chief of the tribe of Tāī, celebrated for his liberality, wisdom and valour. He flourished before the birth of Muhammad, and his sepulchre may still be seen at a little village called

Anwarz in Arabia. There is an account of his adventures in the romance entitled *Hātim Tāī* in Persian, which has also been translated into Urdū. An English translation of this romance was made by Duncan Forbes, A.M., from the Persian.

Hatim (حاتم اصم), surnamed Al-Asamm, that is to say, the deaf, was a great Musulmān doctor, much esteemed for his piety and doctrine. He was a disciple of Shaqīq Balkhī and master of Ahmad Khizroya. He died A.D. 851, A.H. 237, in the reign of Mutwakkil the Khalīf of Baghdād, and was buried at Balkh in Khurāsān, his native country.

Hatim Kashi, Maulana (حاتم کاشی مولانا), a poet of Kāshān in Persia, who flourished in the reign of Shāh Abbās the Great.

Hatim (حاتم), or Shāh Hātim, poetical name of Shaikh Zahīr-uddīn, a poet who was a contemporary of Walī (*q.v.*). He was born at Dehlī in A.D. 1699, A.H. 1111, and was a soldier by profession. He gave the first impulse to Urdū poetry in Dehlī. In A.D. 1720, A.H. 1132, the Dīwān of Walī was brought to Dehlī and verses of it were on everybody's lips; this induced him and three friends of his, Nāji, Māzmūn, and 'Abrū to apply themselves to Rekhta poetry. Up to the time of Hātim, it would appear that the Dehlī poets wrote in Persian. He is the author of two Dīwāns in Urdū, one in imitation of Walī, and the other in imitation of Sauda and Mīr Taqī. The date of Hātim's death is unknown. His *Dīwān Zuda* appeared in 1750.

Hatim Ali Beg, Mirza (حاتم علی بیگ مرزا). *Vide* Mehr.

Hawas (هوس), poetical title of Nawāb Mirzā Taqī, son of Nawāb Mirzā Alī Khān. He is the author of the story of Lailī and Majnūn in Urdū, and of a Dīwān in which every Ghazal contains the name of Lailī and Majnūn.

Haya (حیا), poetical title of Shio Rāmdās, a Hindū, and brother of Rāja Dayā Mal Imtiyāz. He was a pupil of Mirzā Abdūl Qādir Bedil, and is the author of a Dīwān of about 5000 verses.

Hayat-ullah Ahrari (حیات الله اراری), author of the work called *Hahata Alarfin*, which contains the life of Abrsala. He died in A.H. 1061, and his tomb is in Āgra.

Hayati Mulla (حیاتی ملا), of Gīlān, a poet.

Hazin (حزین مولانا شیخ محمد علی), the poetical name of Maulānā Shaikh Muhammad 'Alī, a Persian of distinction, eminently learned, and accomplished. He fled into Hindūstān from his native country to avoid the persecution of Nādir Shāh in A.D. 1733, A.H. 1146. He was a voluminous author both in prose and verse. He wrote his Memoirs in 1741, eight years after his settlement for life in India, and it contains a variety of personal and historical anecdotes, excellent observations on men and manners, besides an interesting account of his travels, and remarks on many modern literary productions. A translation of this work, entitled *The Life of Shaikh Muhammad Alī Hazīn*, was made by F. C. Belfour, F.R.A.S., and published in 1830. His father's name was Shaikh Abū Tālib of Gīlān, a descendant of Shaikh Tājuddīn Ibrāhīm, commonly called Shaikh Zāhid Gīlānī, who was the spiritual guide of Shaikh Safī-uddīn Ardibelī. He was born at Isfahān on the 7th January, 1692, o.s., 27th Rabī' II. A.H. 1103, was in Dehlī at the time of Nādir Shāh's invasion, and died in 1766, according to Sir Wm. Ouseley, A.D. 1779, A.H. 1180, aged 77 lunar years, at Banaras (where he had built his own tomb some time before his death) equally admired and esteemed by the Musalmān, Hindū and English inhabitants of that place. He is the author of several works in Persian and Arabic.

Hazuq, Hakim (حاذوق حکیم), son of Hakīm Humām, the brother of Abū'l Fatha Gīlānī. He was a noble of the reign of the emperor Shāh Jahān, a physician and a poet, and is the author of a Dīwān in Persian. He died A.D. 1658, A.H. 1068.

Hessing, Colonel John William, of Holland. He came to India and was at first employed by the Nawāb Nizām Alī Khān of the Deccan in the year A.D. 1763, A.H. 1177, and afterwards by Mādho Rāo Sindhia in 1784, after whose death in 1794, he continued in the service of his nephew Daulat Rāo Sindhia, by whom he was appointed a Colonel in 1795, with the command of the fortress and city of Āgra. He died on the 21st July, 1803, and was buried in the Roman Catholic Burial-ground at Āgra, where a splendid mausoleum of red stone was built by his children, with an English inscription on his tomb which is of white marble.

Hidayat (هیدایت), poetical name of Hidayat Khān, the uncle of Nisār-ullāh Khān Firāk. He died in the year A.H. 1215, and left a Dīwān.

Hidayat-ullah (هدايت الله), author of a work on arts and sciences called *Hidāyat-ul-Ramal*, written in A.D. 1601.

Hidayat-ullah Khan (هيدايت الله خان), great grandson of Khān 'Azim Mirzā Koka. He is the author of a history called *Tarīkh Hidayat-ullāh Khān* written in the year A.H. 1659.

Hijri (هجرى), the poetical title of a poet who was a native of Konbān but lived in Bengal. He is the author of a Dīwān in which there is a Qasīda of a most wonderful composition. If you read the first letter of every Misra', you have a Qita' in praise of Nawāb Sayyad Muhammad Riza Khān Muzaffar Jang. Some letters in the Qasīda are written in red, if you read them by themselves, you have a Ghazal, and certain letters in the Ghazal form a Ruba'ī, and certain letters in the Ruba'ī form a Misra'. He was living in A.D. 1766, A.H. 1180.

Hilal Qazwini (هلال قزوينى), an author who died in A.D. 1527, A.H. 934.

Hilali (هلالى استرابادى), of Astarābād, was a Tartar of the tribe of Jughtai or Chughtai, and author of a Dīwān consisting of amorous odes. In his youth he travelled to Khurāsān, and resided at Herāt, where the illustrious Amīr 'Alīsheir conferred on him many favours. He was a Sunnī by religion, and was, by the contrivance of his enemies, who were Shīas, put to death by order of one of the Uzbak chiefs in the year A.D. 1530, A.H. 936, but according to a book called *Tuhfa Shāhī*, in A.D. 1533, A.H. 939. He is the author of the following works, *viz.*, *Shāh-wa-Darwesh*, *Lailī-wa-Majnūn*, *Sifāt-ul-'Ashiqīn*, and a Dīwān.

Hilm (حلم), poetical name of Prince Mirzā Saīd-uddīn, commonly called Mirzā Faiyāz-uddīn, son of Mirzā Rayāz-uddīn *alias* Mirzā Muhammad Jān, son of Mirzā Khurram Bakht, son of Mirzā Jahandar Shāh, son of Shāh Alam, king of Dehlī. He is the author of a Dīwān.

Himmat Bahadur Gushain (همت بهادر گشاين), Dīwān of Ghanī Bahādur, Nawāb of Banda, and one of the Peshwa's (Bājī Rao II.) principal officers in Bundelkhand. He joined the British troops under the command of Lieutenant-Colonel Powell in September, 1803, and gave battle to Shamsher Bahādur, Nawāb of Banda, who was defeated and compelled to retreat with loss. Himmat Bahādur was a powerful commander of a large body of horse, and of a numerous party of Gushāīns or Nagas, a peculiar class of armed beggars and religious devotees of whom he was not only the military leader, but also the spiritual guide. He died at Kalpi in 1804, and his family was provided for by the British Government.

[*Vide* Hunter's *Imperial Gazetteer, in voc.* Kalpi.]

Himmat Khan (همت خان), was the son of Khān Jahān Shāyasta Khān, the son of the wazīr Asaf Khān. He built his house on the banks of the river Jamna in a year with many other buildings such as gardens, reservoirs, baths, etc., etc., of which a bath, a reservoir, a Baolī, etc., etc., are still to be seen. His proper name was Sayyad Muzaffar. Shāh Jahān conferred on him the name of Himmat Khān. In the 19th year of Alamgīr he was appointed governor of Allahābād. In the 24th year of Alamgīr, the appointment of Bakhīgani was conferred on him; and in the 30th year of Alamgīr, he was again appointed governor of Allahābād.

Himu (هيمو), a banian or Indian shop-keeper of the caste of Dhūsar, whom Salīm Shāh, king of Dehlī, had made superintendent of the markets. In the reign of Muhammad Shāh 'Adīl, he was appointed his wazīr, and intrusted with the whole administration of affairs. This person in the beginning of the reign of the emperor Akbar laid siege to Āgra, and having reduced it proceeded to Dehlī which also surrendered, and Tardī Beg, governor of that place, who fled to Sarhind, was seized by Bairām Khān (*q.v.*), the minister of Akbar, and beheaded for abandoning Dehlī, where he might have defended himself. Himū was afterwards defeated and made prisoner in a battle fought at Pānīpat on Thursday the 5th November, A.D. 1556, 2nd Muharram, A.H. 964, and brought into the presence of the king by Bairām Khān, who begged him to kill the infidel with his own hand. Akbar (who was then in his fifteenth year) in order to fulfil the wish of his minister, drew his sword and touched the head of the captive, while Bairām Khān, drawing his own sabre, at a single blow severed the head of Himū from his body.

Hinda (هنده), the daughter of Utba and wife of Abū Sufiān.

[*Vide* Hamzā (Amīr).]

Hindal Mirza (هندال مرزا). *Vide* Handal Mirzā.

Hindu Rao (هندو راو), the brother of Bījā Bāī (*q.v.*), the wife of Mahārājā Daulat Rāo Sindhia. His Kothī or Rekka House on a hillock is well-known at Dehlī. He died in A.D. 1855. [He was fond of the society of Englishmen in India, among whom he was very popular.]

Hira Singh (هرا سینگ), a Sikh Chief and minister of Mahārājā Dilīp Singh of Lāhore. He was murdered with many others about the beginning of January, 1845.

Hirpaldeo (هرپال دیو), the son-in-law of Rāmdeo, Rāja of Deogīr, who by the assistance of the other Rājas of the Deccan, had recovered his country from the Musalmāns, but Mubārik Shāh, the son of Alā-uddīn Khiljī, in the second year of his reign, A.D. 1318, A.H. 718, marched towards the Deccan, took Hirpāldeo prisoner, flayed him alive, and hung his body at the gate of Deogīr which is now called Daulatabād.

Hisam-bin-Jamil (حسام بن جمیل), surname of Abū Sahl-al-Baghdādī, who passed for one of the best traditionists of Musalmānism. He died in A.D. 722, A.H. 104.

Hissan (حسان بن ثابت), the son of Sābit, was a poet and companion of Muhammad. He is the author of a Dīwān in Arabic. When Muhammad overcame his enemies at the battle of Khandaq, Hissān wrote a few verses on that occasion; the prophet was so much delighted, that he gave him Shīrīn the sister of Māria Qabtī, for wife.

Hissan-al-Hind (حسان الهند), that is, the Hissān of India, a title which Mīr Gulām 'Alī Azād assumed.

Holkar. *Vide* Malhār Rāo I. The word means "Ploughman."

Hormisdas. *Vide* Hurmuz.

Hoshang (هوشنگ), second king of the first or Pishdādian dynasty of Persia, was the son of Sayāmak, and grandson of Kyōmurs whom he succeeded. He reigned 40 years and was succeeded by his son Tahmurs, commonly called Deoband, or the Magician binder, a title he derived from the success with which he warred against the enemies of his family.

Hoshang Shah (هوشنگ شاه) (formerly called Alp Khān), was the first Muhammadan king of Mālwa, and the son of Dilāwar Khān Ghorī who was governor of that place from the time of Muhammad Shāh, A.D. 1401, son of Fīroz Shāh Tughlaq, king of Dehlī. After his father's death, which happened about the year A.D. 1405, A.H. 808, taking advantage of the times, he became entirely independent and assumed the title of Sultān Hoshang Shāh. He reigned 30 lunar years, and died on the 17th July, A.D. 1434, 9th Zil-hijja, A.H. 837. He was buried in a stone vault, and a splendid mausoleum of white marble was built over it which is still to be seen at Mando. The date of his death is to be found in the three last words of a tetrastich translated thus by General Briggs.

When death had sealed the Hoshang's fate,
And he prepared to tread on Lethe's shore,
I asked a poet to record the date,
Who briefly said, "Shāh Hoshang is no more."

He was succeeded by his son Sultān Muhammad Shāh, who was poisoned after a reign of one year and nine months by Mahmūd Khān (the son of his Wazīr), who took the title of Mahmūd Shāh and ascended the throne of Mālwa on Tuesday the 15th May, A.D. 1436, 29th Shawwāl, A.H. 839.

List of the kings of Mālwa, whose capitals were Dhār, Mando or Shādiābād.

Dilāwar Khān Ghorī, governor.
Hoshang Shāh Ghorī.
Muhammad Shāh Ghorī (also called Ghaznī Khān).
Mahmūd Shāh Khiljī.
Sultān Ghayās-uddīn Khiljī.
Sultān Nāsir-uddīn Khiljī.
Sultān Mahmūd II. the last of the Khiljīs.

In his time Mālwa was incorporated with the kingdom of Gujrat by Bahādur Shāh (about A.D. 1523).

Hoshdar Khan (هوشدار خان), a title of Hidāyat-ullāh Khān, the son of Irādat Khān Wāzah. He was honoured with this title by the emperor Farrukh-siyar, and after his father's death with that of Irādat Khān and the Faujdārī of Dūhipereya in the province of Mālwa. In the sixth year of Muhammad Shāh, A.D. 1724, A.H. 1136, he attended Nizām-ul-Mulk 'Asaf Jāh to the Deccan, and after the victory over Mubāriz Khān, was appointed Dīwān of the Deccan with the rank of 4000. He was afterwards appointed governor of Kulburga in the Deccan and died in the year A.D. 1744, A.H. 1157. He had many sons, most of whom died in his lifetime. His eldest surviving son, Hāfez Khān, succeeded him in the government of Kulbarga which he held at that time. Shāh-nawāz Khān wrote the *Māsir-ul-Umra*, or *Biography of Nobility*.

Hoshmand Begam (هوشمند بیگم), daughter of Sultān Khusro, married to Prince Hushang, the son of prince Dānial in the year A.H. 1035.

Hujjat (حجت), poetical name of Nāsir Khusro, which see.

Hujjat-ul-Islam (حجت الاسلام), a title of Muhammad Ghazzālī, a celebrated doctor of the Musalmān law.
[*Vide* Ghazzālī.]

Huma (هما), poetical name of Sayyad Imtiyāz Khan, a son of Mo'tmid Khān, and a brother of Sayyad Ahmad whose takhallus was Zamīr. He is the author of a Diwān.

Humai, Queen (همای), was the daughter of Bahman, who is also called Ardisher Darāzdast (Artaxerxes Longimanus of the Greeks). She succeeded her father as queen of Persia, in the fourth century before Christ. She built the city called Simrah, which the author of the *Labb Tawārīkh* says, bore also the name of Simirem, and is the same which is at this day called Jarbadakan. The Persian authors state, that when she ascended the throne, she was pregnant by her own father. Shame led her to conceal this circumstance; and the child, of which she was delivered, was given over to a nurse to be put to death. The life of the child, however, was miraculously preserved; and the unnatural mother first recognised her son when his fortune and valour had advanced him to the rank of a victorious general in her army. Humāi immediately resigned the crown to him, and retired to a private life after she had reigned 32 years. Her son reigned about 12 years, and is called by the Persians Dārā or Dārāb I.

Humam, Hakim (همام حکیم), brother of Hakīm Abū'l Fatha Gīlānī, a well educated and learned man in the service of the emperor Akbar. He was sent by that monarch on an embassy, in company with Sayyad Sadr Jahān, to Abdullāh Khān Uzbak, ruler of Khurāsān, about the year A.D. 1589, A.H. 997. He died in A.D. 1595, A.H. 1004, and left two sons, Hakīm Sādīq and Hakīm Khūshhāl.

Humam (همام), poetical name of Kamāl-uddīn Muhammad bin-Abdul-Wahhāb, styled by Arabshāh, "One of the most illustrious doctors of the member of the Sādāt," that is to say, of the race of Alī. He lived in the time of Amīr Taimūr (Tamerlane) and died in A.D. 1457, A.H. 861. He is author of a Commentary on the Hidāya His proper name is Kamāl-uddīn Muhammad-al-Siwāsī, which see.

Humam Tabrezi, Khwaja (همام تبریزی), a celebrated Persian poet of Tauris or Tabrez, and author of a collection of Rubāīs or quatrain verses called *Rubāyāt Mīr Humām*. He was a contemporary and rival wit of Shaikh Sa'dī. Meeting Sa'dī one day in a bath, Humām, observing Sa'dī to be very bald, presented to him a basin with the bottom upwards; asked him "Why do the heads of the people of Shiraz resemble this?" Sa'dī, having turned the basin with the empty side upwards, replied, "First tell me, why do the heads of the people of Tabrez resemble this?" Many other anecdotes are related of them. Humām died in the reign of Aljaitū, emperor of the Mughals, in A.D. 1313, A.H. 713, and was buried at Tabrez. He is also called Khwāja Humām-uddīn Tabrezī.

Humam-uddin Tabrezi (همام الدین تبریزی). *Vide* Humām Tabrezī.

Humayun (همایون نصیر الدین محمد), emperor of Hindūstān, surnamed Nasīr-uddīn Muhammad, was the eldest son of the emperor Bābar Shāh, was born at Kābul on the night of Tuesday the 7th March, A.D. 1508, 4th Zi-Qa'da, A.H. 913, and his mother's name was Māham Begam. He succeeded his father on the throne at Āgra on the 26th December, A.D. 1530, 6th Jumāda I. A.H. 937, and conferred the government of Kābul, Qandahār, Ghāzni, and the Panjāb on his brother Mirzā Kāmirān; to Mirzā Askarī he gave the government of Sarkār Sambhal, to Mirzā Handāl, Sarkar Alwal, and the government of Badakhshān to Mirzā Sulaimān, the son of Khān Mirzā, the son of Sultān Muhammad, the son of Sultān Abū Saīd. Humāyūn was defeated the first time by Sher Khān (afterwards Sher Shāh) in a battle fought on the banks of the Chaunsā in Behār on the 26th June, A.D. 1539, 9th Safar, A.H. 946, and the second time at Qannoj on the 17th May, A.D. 1540, 10th Muharram, A.H. 967. The capital no longer afforded him a place of refuge; even his brothers became his enemies, and would not grant him shelter in their provinces. He fled from one place to another, subject at times to the greatest hardships; and was at last obliged to quit the kingdom and seek an asylum in Persia, where he arrived in July, A.D. 1544, A.H. 951, and was hospitably and honorably entertained for some time by Shāh Tahmāsp of Persia, who assisted him with troops. During the absence of Humāyūn, which extended to a period of fifteen years, five kings ascended the throne of Dehlī, *viz.* Sher Shāh, his son Salīm Shāh, Muhammad Shāh Adilī, Ibrāhīm Khān, and Sikandar Shāh. Humāyūn having overcome his brothers at Kābul and Qandahār, commenced his march from the former city in the month of January, A.D. 1555, Safar, A.H. 962, towards India. He took the Panjāb, and advancing towards Dehlī defeated Sikandar Shāh on the 22nd June, A.D. 1555, 2nd Shabān, A.H. 962, in a battle fought at Sarhind. Sikandar, after his defeat, fled to the mountains of Sewālik, and Humāyūn having reached Dehlī in triumph; became a second time emperor of Hindūstān. Bairām Khān (*q.v.*), to whose valour and talent the king was principally indebted for his restoration, was rewarded with the first offices in the state with the title of Khān Khānān. The year of this victory was found by Bairām Khān to be contained in the words, "The sword of Humāyūn." Seven months after this victory, on the 21st January, A.D. 1556, as Humāyūn was coming down at the time of evening prayers from the terrace of the Library at Dehlī, he fell headlong down the steps, and died on the 25th January, A.D. 1556. 11th Rabī I. A.H. 963. The words "Alas! my sovereign fell from the terrace," are the English of the line recording the year of his demise. He was buried at Kiloghārī, a distance of four kos from the city of Shāhjānābād on the banks of the river Jumna; and a splendid monument was erected over his remains some years after by his son Akbar, who succeeded him. Humāyūn died at the age of 49, after a reign of 25 years, including the fifteen years of his banishment from his capital. The foundation of his mausoleum was laid in A.D. 1565, A.H. 973, was superintended by Hājī Begam, mother of Akbar, and was finished in 16 years at a cost of 15 lakhs of rupees. Farrukh-siyar, 'Alamgīr II. Dāra Shikōh and other princes are also buried in this mausoleum, where the last of the dynasty took refuge in 1857 (see above, *in voc.* Bahādur Shāh II). Humāyūn, after his death, received the title of Jannat 'Ashiānī.

[For Humāyūn's character *vide* Keene's *Sketch of the History of Hindūstān.*]

Humayun, Amir (همایون امیر), of Isfarāen, a poet who went early in life to Tabrez, and was supported by Qāzī 'Īsa, and Sulṭān Yā'qūb, who called him Khusro Sānī, that is, the second Khusro and Khusro Kōchak. After the death of his patron, he went to Kāshān and died there in A.D. 1496, A.H. 902. He is the author of a Dīwān.

Humayun Shah, Bahmani, Sultan (همایون شاه بهمنی سلطان), surnamed Zālim, or the Cruel, was the eleventh king of the Bahmanī dynasty. He succeeded his father Sulṭān 'Alā-uddīn II. Bahmanī in the year A.D. 1458, A.H. 862, and causing his brother Hasan Khān's eyes to be put out, ascended the throne of the Deccan. According to the will of his father, he conferred the office of Wakīl-us-Saltanat on Khwāja Mahmūd Gāwān, with the title of Malik-ut-Tajjār and the government of Bījāpūr. He was an unjust prince and a great tyrant, on which account he was surnamed "the Cruel." He reigned 3 years 6 months and 6 days, and was murdered with one stroke of a heavy club on the 1st September, A.D. 1461, 28th Ẓi-Qa'da, A.H. 865, during a fit of intoxication, by his own servants, who were wearied out with his inhuman cruelties. He was succeeded by his son Sulṭān Nizām Shāh, then only eight years of age. See above *in voc.* Bahmanī.

Hunain (حنین), surname of Abū Zaid 'Abdur Rahmān Hunain, son of Is-hāq, son of Hunain, was a celebrated Christian physician who translated many books out of the Greek into Syriac and Arabic.

Hurmuz or Hurmuzd I. (هرمزیا هرمزد), the third king of Persia, of the Sāsānian race, was the son of Shāhpūr I. whom he succeeded in A.D. 272. He is the Hormisdas of the Greek authors, and is said to have resembled, both in person and character, his grandfather (*v.* Ardisher Babegān). The mother of this monarch was the daughter of Māhrukh, a petty prince, whom Ardisher had put to death, and whose family he had persecuted, because an astrologer had predicted that a descendant of Māhrukh should attain the throne of Persia. This lady had fled to the tents of a shepherd, where she was seen by Shāhpūr when hunting. This prince became enamoured, and married her privately. His father Ardisher, going one day unexpectedly to his son's house, saw young Hurmuz. He was greatly pleased with the appearance of the child and made inquiries, which compelled Shāhpūr to confess all that had happened. The joy of the old king was excessive. "The prediction of the astrologers," he exclaimed, "which gave me such alarm is, thank God, confirmed, and a descendant of Māhrukh shall succeed to my crown." Hurmuz was a virtuous prince, but reigned only one year and ten days. He died about the year A.D. 273, and was succeeded by his son Bahrām I.

Hurmuz or Hurmuzd II. (هرمزد ثانی), the eighth king of Persia of the Sāsānian race. He succeeded his father Narsī about the year A.D. 303, ruled Persia seven years and five months and died A.D. 310. No events of any consequence occurred during the reign of this prince. At his death he left no son; and the kingdom was on the point of being thrown into confusion, when it was declared that one of the ladies in the harem was pregnant, and that there were certain indications of the embryo being a male. When the child was brought forth, it was named Shāhpūr, and every care was taken to give the young sovereign an education suited to his high duties.

Hurmuz or Hurmuzd III. (هرمزد ثالث), the second son of Yezdijard II. succeeded his father, of whom he was always the favourite, A.D. 456. His elder brother Fīroz, though at first compelled to fly across the Oxus, soon returned to assert his right at the head of a large army, which aided by a general defection of the Persians, who deserted his weak brother, obtained an easy victory, and the unfortunate Hurmuz was, after a short reign of little more than one year, dethroned and put to death A.D. 457.

Hurmuz or Hurmuzd IV. (هرمزد رابع) (the Hormisdas III. of the Greeks) was declared successor to his father the great Chosroes, surnamed Nausherwān the Just, and ascended the throne of Persia A.D. 579. His subjects revolted against him at the instigation of Bahrām Chobīn or Varanes, his general, whom he had offended by sending him a female dress because he had been defeated by the Romans. They confined Hurmuz and put out his eyes to disqualify him from ascending the throne, and soon after put him to death A.D. 590. His son Khusro Purvez having collected a force to oppose Bahrām, who with the intention of taking the government into his own hands was advancing towards Madāin, was defeated, and with great difficulty effected his escape to the territories of the Romans (Greeks), from whose emperor, Maurice, he met with the most friendly and hospitable reception. Bahrām Chobīn took possession of the vacant government, but his rule was short, for within eight months from the period of his taking possession of Madāin, he was defeated by an army of Romans and Persians commanded by Khusro, and fled to Tartary.

Husain (حسین), poetical name of Muzaffar Husain, an author who is also called Shahīd or Martyr. He is the author of the work called *Rayāz-us-Sālikīm*.

Husain Ali Khan Bahadur (حسین علی خان بہادر), second son of Alahwirdī Khān, a nobleman of high rank who served under the emperor 'Alamgīr, and died on the 3rd October, A.D. 1686, 25th Zi-Qa'da, A.H. 1097, a day after the fort of Bījāpūr was taken. See above *in voc.* Alahwirdī.

Husain Ali Khan, Sayyad (حسین علی جان سید), Amīr-ul-Umrā. *Vide* Abdullāh Khān (Sayyad).

Husain-bin-Alim (حسین بن علیم), author of the *Nuzhat-ul-Arwāh*, containing interesting anecdotes of the most celebrated Sūfīs.

[*Vide* Husain-bin-Hasan-al-Hasanī.]

Husain - bin - Hasan - al - Husaini (حسین بن حسن الحسینی), a native of Ghōr and author of several works, viz. *Kanz-ul-Ramūz*, *Sī Nama*, *Nuzhat-ul-Arwāh*, *Zād-ul-Musāfarīn*, *Tarab-ul-Majālis*, *Ruh-ul-Arwāh*, *Sirāt-ul-Mustaqīm*, and of a Dīwān in Arabic and Persian. He died, says Jāmī, in the year A.D. 1317, A.H. 717, and is buried at Herāt. Firishta calls him Amīr Husainī Sādāt and says that he with his father Sayyad Najm-uddīn came to India as merchants and became the disciples of Shaikh Bahā-uddīn Zikaria at Multan, and died at Herāt on 1st December, A.D. 1318, 6th Shawwāl, A.H. 718.

Husain - bin - Muhammad, as - Sa-ma'ani (حسین بن محمد السمعانی), author of the *Khazānat-al Muftiīn*, which contains a large quantity of decisions, and is a book of some authority in India. It was completed in A.D. 1339, A.H. 740.

Husain Dost Sambhali, Mir (حسین دوست سمبهلی میر), son of Abū Tālib of Sambhal. He is the author of a biography of poets called *Tazkira Husainī*, which appears to have been compiled a few years after the death of Muhammad Shāh the emperor of Dehlī, who died in A.D. 1748, A.H. 1161.

Husain Ghaznawi (حسین غزنوی), author of the story of Padmāwat in Persian poetry called *Qissaī Padmāwat*.

Husain Hallaj, Shaikh (حسین حلاج شیخ), the son of Mansūr Hallāj. Many fables have been invented to account for the imprudence of this wise teacher. One of these states, that he observed his sister go out every evening; he followed her; having seen her communicate with the Hūries, and receive from these celestial nymphs a cup of nectar, he insisted on drinking one or two drops that remained of this celestial liquor. His sister told him he could not contain it, and that it would cause his death. He persisted; from the moment that he swallowed it he kept exclaiming "An-ul-Haq!" that is, "I am the truth!" till he was put to death.

[*Vide* Mansūr Hallāj.]

Husaini (حسینی), author of the *Asmāī Husainī* and *Maktūbāt Husainī*.

Husain - ibn - Muin - uddin Maibadi (حسین ابن معین الدین میبدی), author of a work on religion, entitled *Fawātah*.

Husaini Fathi-Ali, a Sūfī of Dehlī, author of a biographical dictionary published 1750-1. Mentioned as still living in 1806 by Qasim of Āgra (*q.v.*).

Husain, Imam (حسین امام), the second son of 'Alī, the son-in-law of Muhammad. He was born at Medina in January, A.D. 626, Shabān, A.H. 4, and was the third Imām of the race of 'Alī. Having refused to acknowledge Yazīd the son of Mu'āwia for the lawful Khālīf, he was obliged to leave Medina and to fly to Mecca, but was overtaken on his way and killed by order of Ubaidullāh-ibn-Zayād, one of Yazīd's captains, on the 10th October, A.D. 680, 10th Muharram, A.H. 61. When his head was brought to Ubaidullāh at Kūfa, he struck it over the mouth with a stick, and treated it with great contempt. He then sent it along with his family, who were made captives, to Damascus, where Yazīd then reigned. The day on which he was killed is still a great day amongst the Musalmāns. He is buried at a place called Karbala in Babylonian Irāq or Chaldea near Kūfa. Some pretend to show that Husain's head was buried near the river of Karbala; others say that there are no other traces of it remaining. However, the first Sulṭān of the race of Boyaides built on that spot a sumptuous monument, which is visited to this very day with great devotion by the Musulmāns. It is called "Gunbaz Faiz," or the dome of grace.

Husain Jalayer, Sultan (حسین جلایر سلطان), grandson of Amīr Hasan Buzurg, succeeded his father Sulṭān Awes Jalāyer to the throne of Baghdād in October, A.D. 1374, A.H. 776, and lost his life in an action with his brother Sulṭān Ahmad, in A.D. 1382, A.H. 784.

[*Vide* Hasan Buzurg.]

Husain Kashi (حسین کاشی), an author, who died in A.D. 1544, A.H. 951.

Husain, Kashmiri (حسین کشمیری), author of the Persian work entitled *Hidāyat-ul-'Amī*, the Guide to the Blind, containing essays on various religious subjects, Sūfī doctrines, etc.

Husain Khonsari (حسین خونساری) was one of the celebrated philosophers of Persia, surnamed from his birth-place Khonsār, a town between Teheran and Kashan. He flourished in the latter part of the 17th century.

Husain Langa I. (حسین لنگا), third king of Multān, succeeded his father Qutb-uddīn Mahmūd Langa in A.D. 1469, A.H. 874. He entered into a treaty of alliance with Sikandar Lodī, king of Dehlī, and died about the year A.D. 904, or according to some, on Sunday the 28th August, A.D. 1502, 26th Ṣafar, A.H. 908, after a reign of 30 or 34 years. He was succeeded by his grandson Mahmūd Khān Langa. Firishta says that the *Tawārīkh Bahādur Shāhī*, which contains the history of this prince, is full of errors, and the author of the *Mirat-Sikandarī* declares it to be absolutely unintelligible.

Husain Langa II. (حسین لنگا), fifth and last king of Multān, was, after the death of his father Mahmūd Khān Langa in 1524, raised to the throne, although a minor. He was only a pageant in the hands of his sister's husband, Shujāa'-ul-Mulk, who assumed the office of protector. Shāh Husain Arghūn, king of Thatta, under the orders of the emperor Bābar Shāh, soon after besieged the place, which was at length, in the year A.D. 1526, A.H. 932, carried by escalade, after a siege of fifteen months. Husain Arghūn having nominated one Lashkar Khan his deputy, returned to Thatta. When Bābar Shāh, during his illness, abdicated the throne in favour of his son Humāyūn, the latter prince gave the Panjāb in jāgīr to Mirzā Kāmrān his brother, who on his arrival at Lāhore sent for Lashkar Khān and made over the district of Kābul to him, in lieu of that of Multān, since which time the kingdom of Multān has continued a province of the empire of Dehlī.

Husain Marwi (حسین مروی). *Vide* Khwāja Husain Marwī.

Husain Maibazi, Muin-uddin (حسین میبذی معین الدین), author of the *Sajanjal-ul-Arwāh*, or *Mirror of Spirits*, a selection from the Persian and Turkī poets. He flourished in the tenth century of the Hijra.

Husain Mashhadi (حسین مشهدی), a Persian poet.

Husain Mirza (حسین مرزا). *Vide* Sulṭān Husain Mirzā.

Husain Muammai, Mir (حسین معمای میر), a celebrated punster who died in the year A.D. 1498, A.H. 904.

Husain Muin-uddin (حسین معین الدین), author of the *Fawātah Saba* on Theology.

Husain Naqshi, Mulla (حسین نقشی ملا), a learned Musalmān of Dehlī. who was a good poet and an excellent engraver in the time of the emperor Akbar. He died on the 16th July, A.D. 1581, 14th Jumādạ II. A.H. 989.

Husain Nizam Shah I. (حسین نظام شاه) ascended the throne of Ahmadnagar in the Deccan in the 30th year of his age, after the death of his father Burhān Nizām Shāh I. in the year A.D. 1554, A.H. 961. In A.D. 1565, A.H. 972, an alliance was formed between him and the three Sulṭāns, *viz.* 'Alī 'Adil Shāh of Bījāpūr, Ibrāhīm Qutb Shāh of Gōlkanḍa and Amīr Barīd of Admadabād Bīdar, against Rāmrāj, Rāja of Bījanagar, who was defeated and slain. Husain Nizām Shāh died eleven days after his return from this expedition, on Wednesday the 6th June, A.D. 1565, 7th Ẓi-Qa'da, A.H. 972, and his son Murtazā Nizām Shāh succeeded him. The death of Nizām Shāh has been commemorated in the following chronogram: "The sun of the Deccan has become obscured."

Husain Nizam Shah II. (حسین نظام شاہ ثانی), a nominal prince of the Nizām Shāhī dynasty.

[*Vide* Fatha Khān, the son of Mālik 'Ambar.]

Husain Sabzwari (حسین سبزواری), a native of Sabzwār, and author of the works entitled *Latāef Wazāef* and *Rāhat-ul-Arwāh*, books on Sūfīism, containing the best means of obtaining salvation and rules for moral conduct.

Husain Sadat, Mir (حسین سادات میر). *Vide* Husain-bin-Hasan-al-Husainī.

Husain Shah (حسین شاہ), of Bengal. *Vide* 'Alā-uddīn Husain Shāh.

Husain Shah Lohani, Pir (حسین شاہ لوهانی پیر), a Muhammadan saint whose tomb is in Mūnghīr, where both Hindūs and Muhammadans make offerings especially on their marriages and other special occasions.

Husain Shah Sharqi, Sultan (حسین شاہ شرقی سلطان), ascended the throne of Jaunpūr after his brother Muhammad Shāh, who was slain in battle about the year A.D. 1452, A.H. 856. He fought several battles with Bahlōl Lodī, the king of Dehlī, and was at last defeated, and so closely pursued that he left his horse and escaped on foot. The army of Dehlī advanced without any other check to Jaunpūr, which fell to the arms of Bahlōl, while Husain Shāh, abandoning his capital, was obliged to content himself with a small tract of country yielding only a revenue of five lakhs of rupees. Bahlōl having delivered over Jaunpūr and its kingdom to his own son Bārbak, enjoined him not to deprive Husain Shāh of the small tract to which he was confined, terming it his family estate. This event took place about the year A.D. 1476, A.H. 881, and the subversion of the Sharqī dynasty may be dated from that year. The reign of Husain Shāh lasted for a period of 19 lunar years. Some years after the death of Bahlōl Lodī (which happened in A.D. 1489, A.H. 894) Husain Shāh incited the prince Bārbak to rise up against his brother Sikandar Lodī, king of Dehlī, and wrest the government out of his hands; but Bārbak was defeated in the first action and retired to Jaunpūr, to which place he was pursued by the king. Jaunpūr fell shortly after, and was added to the kingdom of Dehlī. Husain Shāh was now induced to seek refuge with 'Alā-uddīn Pūrbī, king of Bengal, by whom he was treated with the respect due to his station till his death, which took place in A.D. 1499, A.H. 905. With him the royal line of Jaunpūr was extinguished.

Husain Shah, Sayyad (حسین شاہ سید), author of the story of Bahram Gōr, entitled *Hasht Gulgasht*, which he made into prose from the *Hasht Bahisht* of Amīr Khusro in the year A.D. 1800, A.H. 1215, on the requisition of M. Charles Perron, who served under Daulat Rāo Sindhia.

[*Vide* Hak-īk-at.]

Husain-uddin Husain-bin-Ali (حسین الدین حسین بن علی), who is said to have been a pupil of Burhān-uddīn 'Alī, was the first who wrote a commentary on the Hidāya, entitled the *Nihāya*.

Husain Waez, Maulana (حسین واعظ مولانا), surnamed Kāshifī, was a man of consequence in the time of Sulṭān Husain Mirzā, surnamed Abū'l Ghāzī Bahādur of Khurāsān, and held the office of sacred herald in the city of Herāt till the Hijrī year 910, on the last day of which he expired, *i.e.* on the 3rd June, A.D. 1505, 30th Ẕil-ḥijja, A.H. 910. He is the author of a commentary on the Qurān, commonly called *Tafsīr Husainī*, which he entitled *Mawāhib 'Uliāt*, also of one entitled *Jawāhir-ut-Tafāsīr*. Besides these, he wrote several other works, amongst which are the *Rouzat-ush-Shuhadā*, an excellent history of Muhammad with a minute detail of the battle of Karbala, dedicated to Sulṭān Husain Mirzā in A.D. 1501, an abridgment of which is called *Dah Majlis*. His *Akhlāq Muhsinī* is a very valuable system of Ethics, treating upon worship, prayer, patience, hope, chastity, etc., dedicated to the same Sulṭān A.D. 1494, A.H. 900, the title of which gives the year of its completion. The *Anwār Suhelī*, *Rays of the star Canopus*, is a translation of Pilpay's Fables in Persian, dedicated to Amīr Shaikh Ahmad Suhelī, seal-bearer to the Sulṭān. He calls himself in this book Maulāna Husain-bin-'Alī-al-Waez surnamed Kāshifī. He also made an abridgment of Moulwī Rūmī's Masnawī which he called *Lubb-i-Labāb*. He is also the author of the works called *Makhzan-ul-Inshā*, *Saba Kāshifia* (on astrology), *Asrār Qāsimī*, *Matla-'ul-Anwār*, and of a collection of Anecdotes called *Latāif-ut-Tawāef*. This author is by some writers called Kamāl-uddīn Husain-al-Wāez-al-Kāshifī-us-Subzwārī.

Huzuri, Mir (حضوری میر), son of Amīr Sayyid 'Alī Muhtasib. He lived in the time of Shāh Isma'īl Safwī, and wrote a chronogram on his accession to the throne of Persia in the year A.D. 1576, A.H. 984. He is the author of a Dīwān.

I

Ibn-Abi Tai (ابن ابی طي), author of the work called *Kitāb Ar Rauzatain*.

Ibn-Abu Usaiba, Muwaffiq-uddin Abu'l Abbas Ahmad (ابن ابوعسیبا موفق الدين ابوالعباس احمد), author of the Arabic work called *Ayūn-al-Anbā-fi-Tabqāt-ul-Atibbā*, i.e. Fountains of information respecting the classes of Physicians. This book was translated by the author into Arabic from the Sanskrit at the commencement of the 13th century of our era. In the 12th chapter of this work, he gives an account of all the Physicians who were from India. Of one, whom he calls Kanka-al-Hindī, he says: He was skilful as a philosopher amongst ancient philosophers of India, and one of the greatest of men. He investigated the art of physic, the power of medicines, the nature of compound substances, and the properties of simple substances. He was the most learned of all men in the form of the universe, the composition of the heavenly bodies, and the motions of the planets. An extract from the above work is given in the *Jour. of the Royal As. Soc.* No. 11, by the Rev W. Cureton with remarks by Professor H. H. Wilson. Ibn-Abū Usaiba died in A.D. 1269, A.H. 668.

Ibn-Amin (ابن امیین). *Vide* Ibn-Yamīn or Amīr Mahmūd.

Ibn-'Arabi (ابن عربی), surname of Shaikh Muhī-uddīn Abū 'Abdullāh-bin-Muhammad-bin-'Alī-al-Tāī-al-Hatimī-al-Andalusī, a celebrated doctor of Damascus to whom, the Muhammandans pretend, was dictated or inspired, or sent from heaven, by their prophet in the year A.D. 1229, a book of mystical divinity, called *Fasūs-ul-Hakam.* It contains 27 Hukams or Instructions; each of which is attributed to one of the ancient patriarchs or prophets, excepting the last, which belongs to Muhammad, and is entitled *Hakam Fardiyāt Muhammadiat*. The Musalmān doctors are very much divided as to the merit of this work; for some praise it, and others absolutely reject it as being full of superstition and falsehood. He is also the author of several other works, one of which is called *Fatūhāt Makkia*. He died in A.D. 1240, A.H. 638.—There appears to be another Ibn-'Arabī, who died in Sarmanrae, in Baghdād, in the year A.D. 1040, or A.H. 431, and who was also an author of several works.

Ibn-Arabshah (ابن عربشاه), surname of Ahmad-bin-Muhammad, a native of Damascus, who besides a collection of Tales, wrote several other works in a very polished style, the most celebrated of which is a history of the Life of Amīr Taimūr (Tamerlane) entitled *Ajāeb-ul-Maqdūr*. He died at Damascus in the year A.D. 1450, A.H. 854.

[Also called Arab Shāh (*q.v.*)].

Ibn-'Asir(ابن اثیر). **al-Shaibānī Majd-**uddīn, also called Jazarī, a most celebrated Arabian author, of whom we have several works. He is the author of the Arabian work on Jurisprudence entitled *Jāma'-ul-Usūl*, a work having great authority. Another of his works is called *Kamil-ut-Tawarīkh*. He is also known as Abū'l Sa'ādat, Mubārik-bin-Asīr-al-Jazarī, commonly called Ibn-Asīr. He died A.D. 1209, A.H. 606.

[*Vide* Jazarī.]

Ibn-'Askar(ابن عسکر), an author who wrote the history of Damascus.

Ibn-Babawia (ابن بابویه). *Vide* Abū Ja'far Muhammad bin-'Alī-bin-Bābawia.

Ibn-Batuta (ابن بتوته), the Arab traveller whom Muhammad Tughlaq (*q.v.*) made Judge of Dehlī, was the author of the work called *Travels of Ibn-Batūta*, which has been translated from the Arabic by the Rev. S. Lee, B.D. London, 1829. Ibn-Batūta performed his pilgrimage to Mecca in A.D. 1332, A.H. 732. His work contains few facts concerning Arabia. His whole account of Mecca is, "May God ennoble it."

Ibn-Bauwab (ابن بواب). *Vide* Bauwāb.

Ibn-Dahan (ابن دهانه). *Vide* Dāhān.

Ibn-Darastuya (ابن درستویه), commonly called so, but his proper name is Abū Muhammad 'Abdullāh, the son of Ja'far, a very learned Musalmān who died A.D. 958, A.H. 347, at Baghdād.

Ibn-Dured (ابن درید), author of a dictionary and of a work entitled *Gharīb-ul-Qurān*, which is also called *Jamhira*. He died at Baghdād in A.D. 933, A.H. 321.

Ibn-Fakhr-uddin Anju (ابن فخرالدین انجو), author of the *Farhang Jahāngīrī*. *Vide* Jamal-uddīn Husain Anjū.

Ibn-Farat (ابن فرات), author of the *Geographical Memoirs of Egypt*.

Ibn-Farghani (ابن درغاني), Shaikh Abū 'Bakr Wasiti, a saint, who died about A.H. 320.

Ibn-Fouraq (ابن فورق). *Vide* Fouraq.

Ibn-Ghayas (ابن غیاث). *Vide* Kamāl-uddīn Muhammad (Khwāja).

Ibn-Hajar, Shahab-uddin (ابن حجر شهاب الدین), son of 'Alī 'Usqalānī, an Arabian author who wrote more than a hundred books, among which are *Lisān-ul-Mīzān* and *Asāba*. He died in A.D. 1449, A.H. 853.

[*Vide* Shahāb-uddīn Abū'l Fazl-al-'Usqalānī.]

Ibn-Hajar Yehsami or Yehthami (ابن حجر یہسمی), son of Badr-uddīn, author of the work called *Sawāiq Muhriqa*, and several other books. He died in A.D. 1566, A.H. 974.

Ibn-Hajib (ابن حاجب), an Arabian author of several works. He died at Alexandria in the year A.D. 1248, A.H. 646. He is the author of the two commentaries called *Kāfia* and *Shafia*.

Ibn-Hanbali (ابن حنبلی), surname of Muhammad-bin-Ibrāhīm Hanbalī, author of the *Uddat-ul-Hāsib-wa-Umdat-ul-Masāhib*, a book of Arithmetic. He died A.D. 1563, A.H. 971, and is the author of several other works.

Ibn-Hasham (ابن هشام), the author of the *Sīrat-ul-Rasūl* or *Biography of the Prophet*. His native place was Old Cairo, where he died in A.D. 828, A.H. 213. An abridgment of his work was made at Damascus in A.D. 1307, A.H. 707, by one Ahmad Ibn-Ibrāhīm.

Ibn-Hasham (ابن هشام بن یوسف), son of Yūsaf, author of several Arabic works, among which are *Touzīh*, *Sharah Alfia*, etc. He died A.D. 1361, A.H. 762.

Ibn-Hibban (ابن حبان), whose proper name was Asīr-uddīn Muhammad, the son of Yūsaf. Was the author of several works. He died at Damascus in the year A.D. 1344, A.H. 745.

Ibn-Hilal (ابن هلال), also called 'Alāī, is the author of a work entitled *Minhāj-ul-Tālibīn*, which is also called *Tārīkh 'Alāī*, and is dedicated to Shāh Shujāa' Kirmānī.

Ibn-Houbal (ابن هوبل), a celebrated physician and author, who died in the year A.D. 1213.

Ibn-Houkal (ابن هوکل), an Arabian, and author of the work entitled *Ashkāl-ul-Bilād*, containing maps and geographical description of several countries which he wrote in the year A.D. 977, A.H. 367.

Ibn-Humam (ابن همام), author of a Commentary on the Hidāya, entitled *Fath-ul-Qadīr*, which is also called *Sharah Hidāya*. He died in the year A.D. 1457, A.H. 861. He is also called Humām, which see.

Ibn-Husam (ابن حسام), of Khawāf, surname of Shams-uddīn Muhammad, author of an heroic poem in praise of 'Alī, containing the principal events of his life, his disputes, wars, etc., entitled *Khāwar Nāma*. He died A.D. 1470, A.H. 875.

Ibn-Ibad (ابن عباد), surname of Abū'l Qasim Ismā'īl, Kāfī, who was wazīr and first minister of state to the Sultāns Muwaiyad-uddaula and Fakhr-uddaula of the race of Bōya. He died A.D. 995, A.H. 385, and is said to have left a library consisting of 112,000 volumes, and to have passed for the most generous and most liberal man of his time. He was also styled Kāfī-ul-Kafāt.

Ibn-Imad (ابن عماد), a poet of Khurāsān who flourished in the latter end of the 14th century of the Christain Era. He resided in Shīrāz, and is author of a Dīwān or a love story, called *Dah Nāma*, in Persian.

Ibn-Jinni (ابن جنی), whose proper name was Abū'l Fatha 'Usmām, a learned Musalmān, but blind of one eye. He died at Baghdād A.D. 1002, A.H. 392.

Ibn-Jouzi (ابن جوزی). *Vide* Abū'l Farah-ibn-Jouzī.

Ibn-Kamal Pasha (ابن کمال پاشا), surname of Muftī Shams-uddīn Ahmad-bin-Sulaimān, author of the *Sharah Hadis-al-'Arbain*. He died A.D. 1533, A.H. 940.

Ibn-Khaldun (ابن خلدون), the African philosopher. His name and titles are in Arabic: "Walī-uddīn Abū Zaid 'Abdur-rahman - bin - Muhammad - al - Hazramī - al-Ishbilī," but he is better known by the single patronymic name of Ibn - Khaldūn. His father surnamed Khaldūn was a native of Amazirg or Berber (in Africa), but his wife, descending from a family of the Arabian province Hazramāt, made her son adopt the surname of Al-Hazramī. He was born in Tunis in the year A.D. 1332, and passed his youth in Egypt. He then served a short time under Taimūr, as chief justice at Damascus. He returned to Egypt, where he became Supreme Judge, and died in the year A.D. 1406. His principal and most remarkable work is the history of the Arabs, the Persians, and the Berbers. The whole composition is commonly called *Tarīkh-ibn-Khaldūn*.

Ibn-Khallikan (ابن خلیکان), whose full name is Shams-uddīn Abū'l Abbās Ahmad-ibn - Muhammad - ibn-Abu Bakr-ibn Khallikān, drew his descent from a family of Balkh. This very eminent scholar and follower of Shāfa'ī doctrines, was born at Arbela, but resided at Damascus, where he had filled the place of chief Qāzī till the year A.D. 1281, A.H. 680, when he was dismissed, and from that time till the day of his death he never went out of doors. He was a man of the greatest reputation for learning, versed in various sciences, and highly accomplished; he was a scholar, a poet, a compiler, and an historian. By his talents and writings, he merited the honourable title of "the most learned man," and was an able historian. His celebrated biographical work called the *Wafiāt-ul-Aiyān*, or deaths of eminent men, is considered the acme of perfection. This work was translated from the Arabic by Baron McGuckin De Slane, Member of the Council of the Asiatic Society of Paris, etc., and published in A.D. 1842. The work is in four volumes 4to. and in English. It was printed in Paris for the Oriental Translation Fund of London. This translation is a most valuable work to those who wish to gain a knowledge of the legal literature of the Muhammadans, as the translator has added to the text numerous learned notes, replete with curious and interesting information relating to the Muhammadan law and lawyers. Ibn-Khallikān was born on Thursday the 22nd September, A.D. 1211, 11th Rabī' II. A.H. 608, and died on Thursday the 31st October, A.D. 1282, 26th Rajab, A.H. 681, aged 73 lunar years, in the Najībia College at Damascus and was interred at Mount Kāsiyūn.

Ibn-Khurdadbih (ابن خرداذبه), an historian, who died about the year A.D. 912. [*Vide* Khurdāziba.]

Ibn-Maja (ابن ماجه), whose proper name is Abū Abdullah Muhammad - bin - Yezīd-bīn-Māja-al-Qazwīnī, was the author of a collection of traditions, and of a commentary on the Qurān. The first, which is entitled *Kitab-us-Sunan*, is the sixth book of the Sunna, and is commonly called *Sunan Ibn-Māja*. Ibn-Māja was born in the year A.D. 824, A.H. 209, and died in A.D. 886, A.H. 273.

Ibn-Malik (ابن مالک). *Vide* Abū Abdullāh-ibn-Mālik.

Ibn-Maqla (ابن مقله), wazīr of the khalīf al-Qāhir Billāh of Baghdād, whom, with the consent of other Umras, he deposed and having deprived him of sight raised Al-Rāzī Billāh to the throne. Not long after, his hands and tongue were cut off by the order of Rāzī, because he had written a letter to the Khalīf's enemy without his knowledge, and he died from the injuries in the year A.D. 939, A.H. 327. Ibn-Maqla is the inventor of the present Arabic character which was afterwards improved by Ibn-Bauwāb.

Ibn-Marduya (ابن مردویه), commonly called so, but his proper name is Abū Bakr. He is the author of the work *Mustakharij Bīkhārī* and of a commentary and history. He died A.H. 410.

Ibn-Muallim (ابن معلم). *Vide* Shaikh Mufīd.

Ibn-Qattaa (ابن قطاع علی بن جعفر صقلی المشهوربه), surname of 'Ali-bin-Ja'far Siqillī, an Arabian author, who died A.D. 1121, A.H. 515.

Ibn-Qutaiba (ابن قتیبه), surname of Shaikh al-Imām Abū Muhammad Abdullah-bin-Muslim Dīnwarī, author of the *Ayūn-ul-Akhbār*, and many other works. He died A.D. 889, A.H. 267.

Ibn - Rajab. *Vide* Zain - uddīn - bin-Ahmad.

Ibn-Rashid (ابن رشید), surname of Abū'l Walīd Muhammad-bin-Ahmad, whom the Europeans call Averroes and Aven Rosch, was one of the most subtile philosophers that ever appeared among the Arabians. He was born at Cordova in Spain (A.D. 1149), where his father held the office of high priest and chief judge, under the emperor of the Moors. His knowledge of law, divinity, mathematics, and astrology was very extensive, and to this was added the theory rather than the practice of medicine. On the death of his father, he was appointed to succeed him. Falling under the suspicion of heresy, he was deprived of his posts and thrown into prison, from whence he was at last delivered and reinstated in his office of judge. He wrote a treatise on the art of physic, an epitome of Ptolemy's Almagest, a treatise on astrology, and many amorous verses; but when he grew old, he threw the three last into the fire. He is best known as a translator and expositor of Aristotle; his commentaries were published at Venice A.D. 1489-1560. He was a pantheist, and a despiser of all supposed revelations, as to which his opinions were: that Christianity is absurd; Judaism, the religion of children; and Muhammadanism, the religion of swine. A further edition of his works is that published at Venice 1608. He is said to have died at Morocco in A.H. 595, corresponding with A.D. 1199, though Lempriere in his *Universal Biography* says that he died in A.H. 1206.

Ibn-S'abbagh-al-Shafa$_i$ (ابن صباغ الشافعی), surname of Abū Nasr 'Abdūl Sāīd-bin-Muhammad, author of the *Uddat-ul-'Alim Wāt Tarīq-ul-Sālim.* He died A.D. 1084, A.H. 477.

Ibn-'Sad (ابن سعد), author of the Tabaqāt.

Ibn-Shahab-uz-Zohri (ابن شهاب الظهری), an Arabian author who flourished during the Khilāfat of 'Umar-ibn-'Abdul 'Azīz.

Ibn-Sina (ابن سینا). *Vide* Abū Sīna.

Ibn-Siraj (ابن سراج), whose proper name is Abū Bakr Muhammad, was an Arabian author, and died in A.D. 928, A.H. 316.

Ibn-ul-'Arabi(ابن العربی). *Vide* Ibn-Arabī.

Ibn-ul-Hajar (ابن الحجر). *Vide* Ibn-Hajar.

Ibn-ul-Jazari-bin-Muhammad (ابن الجزری), an Arabian author who died in the year A.D. 1430, A.H. 833.

Ibn-ul-Khashab (ابن الخساب), whose proper name is Abū Muhammad 'Abdullah, was an excellent penman. He died at Baghdād in A.D. 1172, A.H. 567.

Ibn-Uqba (ابن عقبه), surname of Jamal-uddīn Ahmad, author of the *Umdat-ut-Tālib.* He died A.D. 1424, A.H. 828.

Ibn-Uqda (ابن عقده). *Vide* Abū'l 'Abbās Ahmad-bin-Muhammad.

Ibn-ul-Rumi (ابن الرومی), a famous Arabian poet, who was contemporary with Avicenna. He is the author of a Dīwān in Arabic.

Ibn-ul-Warda (ابن الوردا), author of an Arabic history called *Mukhtāsir-Jāma-ut-Tawārīkh*, a valuable general history from A.D. 1097 to 1543.

Ibn-us-Saleh (ابن الصالح), whose proper name is Abū 'Amrū 'Usmān-bin-'Abdur Rahmān-ash-Shahrzūrī, author of a collection of decisions according to the doctrine of Shāfa'ī, entitled *Fatāwā-Ibn-us-Saleh.* He died in A.D. 1244, A.H. 642.

Ibn-Yemin (ابن یمین), a celebrated poet, whose proper name was Amīr Mahmūd, which see.

Ibn-Yunas (ابن یونس), astronomer to the Khalīf of Egypt, who observed three eclipses with such care, that by means of them we are enabled to determine the quantity of the moon's acceleration sinc ethat time. He lived about a century or more after Al-Batanī.

Ibn-Zohr (ابن ظهر). *Vide* Abdul Malik Ibn-Zohr.

Ibn-Zuryk (ابن ظریک), Tanūkī, an author.

Ibrahim (ابراهیم), the patriarch Abraham.

Ibrahim (ابراهیم), an emperor of the Moors of Africa in the 12th century, who was dethroned by his subjects, and his crown usurped by 'Abdul Mūmin.

Ibrahim (ابراهیم), the son of Alashtar, killed in A.D. 690, A.H. 71, in a battle fought between the khalīf 'Abdul Malik and Misaa'b the brother of 'Abdullah, the son of Zubair, whose faithful friend he was.

Ibrahim (ابراهیم), the son of Ibrāhīm Mahrān, a very famous doctor of the sect of Shafa'ī, and author of several works.

Ibrahim Adham (ابراهیم ادهم), a king of Balkh, who retired from the world, became a Dervish and died between the years 875 and 880, aged 110 years. It is said that he saw in a dream a man on the top of a house looking for something. He asked him what he was looking for. The man replied that he had lost his camel. "What a fool you must be" said the king, "to be looking for your camel on the roof of a house!" The man rejoined "and what a fool you must be to look for God in the cares and troubles of a crown!" Ibrāhīm from that day abdicated his throne, and became a wandering Dervish.

Ibrahim 'Adil Shah I. (ابراهیم عادل شاه), Sultān of Bījāpūr, surnamed Abū'l Nasr, son of Ismaīl 'Adil Shāh, succeeded his brother Mallū Adil Shāh on the throne of Bījāpūr in the Deccan in A.D. 1535, A.H. 941. He married the daughter of 'Ala-uddīn 'Imād Shāh, named Rabia Sultāna, in A.D. 1543, A.H. 950, reigned 24 lunar years and some months, and died in A.D. 1558, A.H. 965. He was buried at Kūkī near the tombs of his father and grandfather, and was succeeded by his son 'Alī 'Adil Shāh.

Ibrahim 'Adil Shah II. (ابراهیم عادل شاه), of Bījāpūr, surnamed Abū'l Muzaffar, was the son of Tahmāsp the brother of 'Alī 'Adil Shāh, whom he succeeded in April, A.D. 1580, Safar, A.H. 988, being then only in his ninth year. The management of public affairs was given to Kamāl Khān Dakhanī, and Chānd Bībī Sultāna, widow of the late king, was entrusted with the care of the education of the minor monarch. For some time Kamāl Khān behaved with due moderation in his office; but at length was guilty of some violence towards Chānd Sultāna, who turned her thoughts to means for his destruction. She secretly sent a message to Hājī Kishwar Khān, an officer of high rank, who caused him to be murdered. After this event Kishwar Khān, by the support and patronage of Chānd Bībī, grasped the authority of the State, and ruled with uncontrolled sway till he was assassinated. Akhlās Khān next assumed the regency; but after some time he was seized by Dilāwar Khān, who put out his eyes, and became regent of the empire. He was expelled by the king in A.D. 1590, and his eyes put out and himself confined in A.D. 1592. Ibrāhīm 'Adil Shāh died after a reign of more than 38 years in A.D. 1626, A.H. 1036, and was succeeded by his son Muhammad 'Adil Shāh. The first building of any importance we meet at Bījāpūr is the Ibrāhīm Rauza, the tomb of Ibrāhīm 'Adil Shāh II. On a high-raised platform of stone, separated by a square, in the midst of which is a *hauz* or fountain, stand the *rauza* and mosque opposite each other, and corresponding in size and contour. The tomb is most elaborately ornamented, the walls being covered with inscriptions from the Qurān in raised stone Arabic letters, which formerly were gilt, on a blue ground, though now the colouring has worn away. The mosque also is a beautiful building.

Ibrahim Ali Khan (ابراهیم علی خان), the chief of Malair Kotla, was a minor of about 15 years of age (1872), and was receiving his education in the Wards' School at Umballa.

Ibrahim Ali Khān (ابراهیم علی خان), Nawāb of Tonk, grandson of the famous Pindāri chief Amir Khān. His father Muhammad 'Ali Khān was deposed by the British Government on account of the Lowa massacre in 1867. He was installed as Nawāb of Tonk on the 19th January, 1871, by the British Government.

Ibrahim Astarabadi (ابراهیم استرابادی), an author who translated the Risāla or *Kitāb Hasania* of Abū'l Fatūh Rāzī Makkī from the Arabic into Persian in A.D. 1551, A.H. 958.

Ibrahim Barid Shah (ابراهیم برید شاه) succeeded his father 'Alī Barīd in the government of Ahmadābād Bīdar about the year A.D. 1562, A.H. 970. He reigned seven years and died about the year A.D. 1569, A.H. 977. His brother Qasim Barīd II. succeeded him.

Ibrahim Bayu, Malik (ابراهیم بیو ملک). In the province of Behar there is a hillock called Pīr Pahārī, on the top of which there is a tomb with Persian inscriptions in verse, intimating that Mālik Ibrāhīm Bayū died in the reign of Sultān

Fīroz Shāh on a Sunday in the month of Ẕil-ḥijja, A.H. 753, which corresponds with January, A.D. 1353, but who he was we are not informed.

Ibrahim-bin-Aghlab (ابراهيم بن اغلب), an Arabian captain who was appointed governor of Egypt and Africa by the Khalīf Hārūn-al-Rashīd in A.D. 800, A.H. 184. The descendants of this governor, who settled in Africa, bore the name of Aghlabia or Aghlabites, and formed a dynasty of princes who reigned there till the year A.D. 908, A.H. 296, when they were driven out by the Fatimites.

Ibrahim-bin-Ali (ابراهيم بن علی), author of the work called *Majma'-ul-Ansāb*, or the Genealogy of the different dynasties of Persia, till A.D. 1233, A.H. 630.

Ibrahim-bin-Hariri (ابراهيم بن حريری), author of the *Tārīkh Ibrāhīmī*, an abridged history of India from the earliest times to the conquest of that country by the emperor Bābar Shāh, who defeated Sulṭān Ibrāhīm Hussain Lodī, king of Dehlī, and became the founder of the Mughal dynasty. It was dedicated to Bābar Shāh in A.D. 1528, A.H. 934.

Ibrahim-bin-Muhammad-al-Halabi, Shaikh (ابراهيم بن محمد الحلبی شيخ), author of a Persian work on Theology called *Aqāed Sunnia* and of the *Multāqā-al-Abhār*. This work, which is an universal code of Muhammadan law, contains the opinions of the four chief Mujtahid Imāms, and illustrates them by those of the principal jurisconsults of the school of Abū Hanīfa. He died A.D. 1549, A.H. 956.

[*Vide* Imām 'Alam-bin-'Ata.]

Ibrahim-bin-Nayal (ابراهيم بن نيال), brother of Tughral Beg's mother, a chief who defeated Tughān Shāh I. a prince of the Saljūqian family, in battle, took him prisoner and blinded him. Ibrāhīm was murdered after some time in A.D. 952, A.H. 451, by Tughral Beg, the uncle of Tughān Shāh.

Ibrahim-bin-Saleh (ابراهيم بن صالح), cousin of Hārūn-al-Rashīd. A curious story is given of him in the *Jour. As. Soc.* No. 11, that when he died Mauka-al-Hindī, the philosopher, restored him to life, and that Ibrāhīm lived long after this circumstance, and married the princess 'Alī 'Abbasa, daughter of Al-Mahdī, and obtained the government of Egypt and Palestine, and died in Egypt.

Ibrahim-bin-Walid II. (ابراهيم بن وليد ثانی), a Khalīf of the race of Umaiya, succeeded his brother Yazīd III. in A.D. 744, A.H. 126, and had reigned but seventy days when he was deposed and slain by Mu'āwia II. who ascended the throne in Syria.

Ibrahim Husain, Khwaja (ابراهيم حسين خواجه), a celebrated caligrapher in the service of the emperor 'Akbar, who wrote a beautiful Nastalīq hand. He died in the year A.D. 1593, A.H. 1001, and 'Abdul Qādir Badāonī found the chronogram of his death to be contained in his very name with the exception of the first letter in Ibrāhīm, *viz.* Alif.

Ibrahim Husain Lodi, Sultan (ابراهيم حسين لودی سلطان), ascended the throne of Āgra after the death of his father Sikandar Shāh Lodī in February, A.D. 1510, Ẕi-qa'da, A.H. 915. He reigned 16 years, and was defeated and slain in a battle fought at Panīpat with the emperor Bābar Shāh on Friday the 20th April, A.D. 1526, 7th Rajab, A.H. 932, an event which transferred the empire of Dehlī and Āgra to the family of Amīr Taimūr. From this battle we may date the fall of the Paṭhān empire, though that race afterwards made many efforts, and recovered it for a few years in the time of the emperor Humāyūn.

Ibrahim Husain Mirza (ابراهيم حسين ميرزا), a son-in-law of the emperor Humāyūn, and the second son of Muhammad Sulṭān Mirzā, who had four other sons besides him, *viz.* 1st, Muhammad Husain Mirzā, 2nd, Ibrāhīm Husain Mirzā, 3rd, Masa'ūd Husain Mirzā, 4th, Ulagh Mirzā, who died in A.D. 1567, A.H. 975, and 5th, Shāh Mirzā. They were styled "The Mirzās," and were, on account of their ill-conduct, confined in the Fort of Sambhal by order of the emperor Akbar. When that monarch marched in the year A.D. 1567, A.H. 975, for the purpose of subduing Mālwā, they made their escape and sought an asylum with Chingiz Khān, a nobleman at Baroch. They took Champaner and Sūrat and also Baroch in A.D. 1569, A.H. 977, and created a great disturbance in the surrounding countries. Ibrāhīm Husain was taken prisoner in A.D. 1573, A.H. 981, and shortly after put to death by Makhsūs Khān, governor of Multān, and his head sent to the emperor, who ordered it to be placed over one of the gates of Āgra (*vide* Gulrukh Begam) and caused his brother Masa'ūd Husain Mirzā to be confined in the fort of Gwāliar, where he soon afterwards died.

Ibrahim-ibn-Aghlab (ابراهیم ابن اغلب), a king of Barbary. This country was reduced by the Saracens in the Khilāfat of 'Umar, and continued subject to the Khalīf of Arabia and Baghdād till the reign of Hārūn-al-Rashīd, who having appointed Ibrāhīm-ibn-Aghlab governor of the western parts of his empire, that prefect took the opportunity, first of assuming greater powers to himself than had been granted by the Khalīfs. The race of Aghlab continued to enjoy their new principality peaceably till the year A.D. 910, A.H. 298, during which time they made several descents on the island of Sicily, and conquered a part of it. About this time, however, one Obedullāh surnamed 'Al-Mahdī rebelled against the house of Aghlab, and assumed the title of Khalīf of Qairwān.

Ibrahim, Imam (ابراهیم امام). This Ibrāhīm, who bears the title of Imām, or chief of the religion of Muhammad, is not of the number of the twelve Imāms of the posterity of 'Alī. He was a son of Muhammad, the son of 'Alī, the son of 'Abdullah, the son of 'Abbās, the uncle of the prophet, and eldest brother of the two first Khalīfs of the house of 'Abbās; but was himself never acknowledged as a Khalīf. He was put to death by order of Marwān II. surnamed Himār, last Khalīf of the house of Umayya, in the month of October, A.D. 749, Ṣafar, A.H. 132.

Ibrahim Khan (ابراهیم خان), the son of the celebrated Amīr-ul-Umrā 'Ali Mardān Khān. He was honoured with the rank of 5000 in the second year of the emperor 'Alamgīr, A.D. 1659, and appointed governor, at different periods, of Kashmēre, Lāhore, Bihār, Bengal and other places, and died in the reign of Bahādur Shāh.

Ibrahim Khan Fatha Jang (ابراهیم خان فتح جنگ) was a relation of the celebrated Nūr Jahān Begam, whose mother's sister he had married. When Qasim Khān the grandson of Shaikh Salīm Chishtī was recalled to court from the government of Bihār in the twelfth year of the emperor Jahāngīr, A.D. 1616, A.H. 1025, Ibrāhīm Khān was appointed governor of that province with the rank of 4000. He was killed at Dacca, A.D. 1623, A.H. 1032, in battle against prince Khurram (afterwards Shāh Jahān) who had rebelled against his father Jahāngīr. His wife Rūh Parwez Khānam lived to a great age, and died in the reign of the emperor 'Ālamgīr.

Ibrahim Khan Sur (ابراهیم خان سور), son of Ghāzī Khān, governor of Bayāna, was the brother-in-law of Muhammad Shāh 'Adilī, whose sister he had married. He raised a considerable army and took possession of Dehlī and Āgra on the 28th February, A.D. 1555, 6th Jumada' I. A.H. 962. He had no sooner ascended the throne than another competitor arose in the province of the Panjāb, in the person of Ahmad Khān, a nephew of the late Sher Shāh. He defeated Ibrāhīm Khān in a battle, and the latter retreated to Sambhal, while Ahmad Khān took possession of Āgra and Dehlī, and assumed the title of Sikandar Shāh in May the same year. Ibrāhīm Khān was killed by Sulaimān, king of Bengal, in Orissa in a battle fought in A.D. 1567, A.H. 975, and is buried there. Amongst the incidents of the year A.D. 1555, A.H. 962, was the explosion of the fort of Āgra, when enormous stones and columns were sent flying several *kōs* to the other side of the Jamna, and many people were destroyed. As the whole Fort was called Bādalgaṛh, the date was found in the words "The fire of Bādalgaṛh."

Ibrahim Khawas (ابراهیم خواص), a pupil of Abū 'Abdullah Maghrabī, who died A.D. 911. He was called Khawās, which means a basket-maker.

Ibrahim Qutb Shah (ابراهیم قطب شاه) was the son of Qulī Qutb Shāh I. sovereign of Golkanda. On the death of his brother Jamshid Qutb Shāh, the nobles of the court elevated his son Subhān Qulī, a child seven years of age, to the throne; but as he was unable to wield the sceptre Ibrāhīm was sent for from Bījānagar, where he then resided, and was crowned on Monday the 28th July, A.D. 1550, 12th Rajab, A.H. 957. In the year A.D. 1565, A.H. 972, he, in conjunction with the other Muhammadan monarchs of the Deccan, marched against Ramrāj, the Rāja of Bījānagar, who was defeated and slain, and his territories occupied by the conquerors. In A.D. 1571, A.H. 979, the fort of Rājamandrī was taken from the Hindūs by Rafa't Khān, the general of Ibrāhīm; the following chronogram commemorates the date of its occurrence: "The temple of the infidels has fallen into our hands." Ibrāhīm Qutb Shāh, after a prosperous reign of 32 years, died suddenly on Thursday the 5th June, A.D. 1581, 21st Rabī' II. A.H. 989, in the 51st year of his age, and was succeeded by his son Muhammad Qutb Shāh.

Ibrahim Mirza (ابراهیم مرزا), the son of Bahrām Mirzā and grandson of Shāh Ismāī'l Safwī. His poetical name was Jāhī. He was murdered by order of his grandfather.

Ibrahim Mirza, Sultan (ابراهیم مرزا سلطان), was the son of Shāhrukh Mirzā and grandson of Amīr Taimūr. He was governor of Fars during the life of his father, and died a few years before him in

A.D. 1435, A.H. 839. After his death, his son 'Abdullah Mirzā succeeded him, and was killed in battle against Mirzā Abū Sa'īd his cousin-german in A.D. 1451, A.H. 855.

Ibrahim Mirza (ابراهیم مرزا), a Saffavi of literary tastes; *temp*. Shāh Jahān; his poetical name was Ādham, which see.

Ibrahim Mirza (ابراهیم مرزا), the son of Mirzā Sulaimān of Badakhshān, was born in the year A.D. 1534, A.H. 941. When his father, with the intention of conquering Balkh, went to that country, prince Ibrāhīm accompanied him, and was taken prisoner in battle and put to death by order of Pīr Muhammad Khān, ruler of Balkh, in the month of September, A.D. 1560, Zil-hijja, A.H. 967.

Ibrahim Nayal (ابراهیم نیال). *Vide* Ibrāhīm-bin-Nayāl.

Ibrahim Nizam Shah (ابراهیم نظام شاه) succeeded his father Burhān Nizām Shāh II. in the kingdom of Ahmadnagar Deccan in the month of April, A.D. 1595, Sha'bān, A.H. 1003, and was slain in action against the troops of Ibrāhīm 'Adil Shāh II. of Bījāpūr, after a reign of only four months, in the month of August, A.D. 1595, Zil-hijja, A.H. 1003. Mīān Manjū, his wazīr, raised to the throne one Ahmad a boy, said to be of the Nizām Shāhī family.

Ibrahim Pasha (ابراهیم پاشه), an adopted son of Muhammad 'Ali Pasha of Egypt, was born in A.D. 1789, and gave the first proofs of his gallantry and generalship in A.D. 1819 in quelling the insurrection of Wahābīs. He afterwards made several conquests. In A.D. 1848, when Muhammad 'Ali had sunk into absolute dotage, Ibrāhīm went to Constantinople, and was recognized by the Porte as Viceroy of Egypt; after a short visit to England, on the 9th November, A.D. 1848, he died at Cairo.

Ibrahim Shah Sultan (ابراهیم شاه شرقی سلطان), called Sharaqi, or "Eastern," ascended the throne of Jaunpūr, after the death of his brother Mubārik Shāh in A.D. 1402, A.H. 804. He was famous during his reign for the encouragement he afforded to literature; and we find that in those times of anarchy and confusion which prevailed in Hindūstān, Jaunpūr became the seat of learning; as appears (says Firishta) from several works now extant, dedicated to Ibrāhīm Shāh. He died in A.D. 1440, A.H. 844, after a long reign of upwards of 40 years. He was beloved in life, and he was regretted by all his subjects. His eldest son Mahmūd Shāh Sharqī succeeded him.

Ibrahim Shah Pir (ابراهیم شاه پیر), a Muhammadan saint whose tomb is in the district of Kach thirty miles above Lakpat. Vide *Trans. Roy. As. Soc.*, vol. iii. p. 588.

Ibrahim Shaikh (ابراهیم شیخ), the son of Shaikh Musā, the brother of Shaikh Salīm Chishtī. He served Akbar for several years in the military profession; and, when that emperor was proceeding to Kabul after the death of his brother, Muhammad Hakīm, Shaikh Ibrāhīm accompanied him as far as Thānesar, where he fell sick through excess of drinking and died on the 16th Mehr, in the 30th year of Akbar's reign, corresponding with September, A.D. 1585, Shawwāl, A.H. 992. According, however, to a later work, the *Māsir-ul-Umrā*, he was left behind by the emperor and ordered to take charge of the fortress of Āgra, where he died A.D. 1591, A.H. 999.

Ibrahim, Shaikh, ibn-Mufrij-us-Suri (ابراهیم شیخ ابن مفرج الصوری), author of the history of Alexander the Great and of Khizir in Arabic, called *Kitāb Tarīkh al-Iskandar Zulkarnain-ul-Rūmī-wa-Wazīrat-al-Khizr*. This is one of those substructures of myth upon which Eastern nations have erected a large and romantic edifice of fable, much in the same manner as the tales of chivalry of the Middle Ages, which, though fictitious, were partly attributed to real characters, as in the romances of the Knights of the Round Table and the Peers of Charlemagne.

Ibrahim Shaibani (ابراهیم شیبانی), of Kirman Shāh, a pupil of Abū 'Abdullāh Maghrabī. He lived about the year A.D. 900.

Ibrahim Shirwani, Shaikh (ابراهیم شروانی شیخ), ruler of Shirwān, who reigned about the beginning of the ninth century of the Hijra. Maulānā Kātibī flourished in his time and died in A.D. 1435.

Ibrahim, Sultan (ابراهیم سلطان), the son of Sultān Masa'ūd I. of Ghaznī, succeeded his brother Farrukhzād in A.D. 1059, A.H. 450. He was a pious, liberal and just prince. In the first year of his reign he concluded a treaty of peace with Sultān Sanjar the Saljūkide, at the same time his son Masa'ūd espoused the daughter of Malikshāh, sister to Sultān Sanjar, and a channel of friendship and intercourse was opened between the two nations. He afterwards came to India and took several forts and obtained the title of conqueror by the extent of his victories. Sultān Ibrāhīm had 36 sons and 40 daughters by a variety of women, the latter of whom he gave in marriage to learned and religious men. He died after a reign of more than forty years in A.D. 1098, A.H. 492, aged 76 lunar years, and was succeeded by his son Sultān Masa'ūd II. or III. According to the work called *Tarīkh Guzīda* he reigned 30 years and died in the year A.D. 1088, A.H. 481.

Ibrahim, Sultan (ابراهیم سلطان), emperor of the Turks, was the son of Ahmad (Achmat). He succeeded his brother Murād IV (Amarath) in February, A.D. 1640, A.H. 1049, and spent a great part of his reign in the war of Crete against the Venetians, but without any great success. He was assassinated for his debaucheries and repeated cruelties in A.D. 1649, A.H. 1059. His son, Muhammad IV. succeeded him.

'Ibrat (عبرت), the poetical name of Ahmad 'Alī Khān, cousin of Nawāb Sa'ādat Khān Zulfiqar Jang.

'Ibrat (عبرت), the poetical title of Mīr Zaya-uddīn, a poet, who wrote the first part of the story of *Padmāwat* in Urdū verse, and died; consequently the second part was written by Ghulām 'Alī 'Ishrat, and finished in the year A.D. 1796, A.H. 1211, the chronogram of which he found to contain the words "Tasnif Dosha'ir."

'Ibrat (عبرت), the poetical name of 'Abdul Mannān, which see.

'Ibrat (عبرت), the poetical name of Ahmad, a musician of Dehlī, who from the instructions that he received from Mirzā 'Abdul Qādir Bedil, became an excellent poet. He at first had assumed "Maftūn" for his poetical name, but afterwards changed it for "Ibrat." He was a contemporary of Nāsir 'Alī the poet, and was living about the year A.D. 1688, A.H. 1100.

'Ibrat (عبرت), the poetical title of Mīr Ziyā-uddīn, author of the first portion of the story of *Padmāwat* in Urdū verse. He died about the year A.D. 1795.

[*Vide* Padmāwat.]

Idris or Adris-bin-Hisam-uddin, Mulla (ادریس بن حسام الدین ملا), author of the history called *Tarīkh Hasht Bahisht*, or the Eighth Paradise, containing the Memoirs of the most illustrious characters of the Muhammadan religion, who flourished from A.D. 1451 to 1506.

'Idrisi (ادریسی) (Abū 'Abdullah Muhammad-ibn-'Abdullah Idrīs), also called Sharīf-al-Idrīsī-al-Siqilī, author of a system of Arabian geography, composed in A.D. 1153. He is said to be one of the most eminent Arabic geographers and to have belonged to the royal family of the Idrīsites. He was born at Ceuta or Sibtā (*ad septem*) in the year A.D. 1090. The title of his work is *Nuzhat-al-Mushtaq*, and it has been translated into Latin by several authors.

'Iffat Bano (عفت بانو), daughter of the emperor Jahāngīr. Her mother was the daughter of Saīd Khān of Kashghar. She died at the age of 3 years.

Iftikhar Khan (افتخار خان), title of Sultān Husain, the eldest son of Mīr 'Abdūl Hādī, entitled Asālat Khān Mīr Bakhshī, who died at Balkh in the 20th year of the emperor Shāh Jahān A.D. 1647, A.H. 1057. In the first year of 'Alamgīr, Sultān Husain was honoured with the title of Iftikhar Khān (fr. Arab فخر = "glory"). Some time before his death he was appointed Faujdār of Jaunpūr, where he died in A.D. 1681, A.H. 1092.

Ihsan (احسان), the poetical name of Mirzā Ihsānullāh, commonly known by the title of Nawāb Zafar Khān, who at one time was governor of Kābul when the poet Muhammad 'Alī Sāeb of Persia came to see him there. He died in A.D. 1662, A.H. 1073, and was the author of a Dīwān in Persian.

Ihsan (احسان), the poetical name of 'Abdur Rahmān Khān of Dehlī, who wrote excellent poetry in Urdū, and died some time after the year A.D. 1814, A.H. 1260.

Ihsan (احسان), the poetical title of a Hindū named Chunnī Lāl, who flourished at Āgra in A.D. 1760, A.H. 1174.

Ihtisham Khan (احتشام خان), title of Shaikh Farīd of Fathapūr Sīkrī, the son of Qutb-uddīn Shaikh Khūban (*q.v.*). He served under the emperors Jahāngīr, Shāh Jahān and 'Alamgīr; and was raised to the rank of 3000. He died in A.D. 1664, A.H. 1075.

Ijad (ایجاد), the poetical name of Mīr Muhammad Ihsān, who died in the year A.D. 1721, A.H. 1133.

Ijtihad (اجتہاد), inspired interpretation; authoritative application of texts.

[*Vide* Mujtahid.]

Ikhlas Khan Husain Beg (اخلاص خان حسین بیگ), a nobleman of the reign of the emperor Shāh Jahān who died in the year A.D. 1639, A.H. 1049.

Ikhlas Khan Ikhlas Kesh (اخلاص خان اخلاص کیش) was a Hindū of the tribe called Khattrī of Lāhore. He was well-versed in Persian, and served under the emperor 'Alamgīr, who conferred on him the above title. In the time of Farrukh-siyar (*circ.* 1715) he was raised to the rank of 7,000. He wrote the history of that emperor and called it *Bādshāh Nāma*.

[*Vide* Kishun Chand.]

Ikhwan-us-Safa (اخوان الصفا), "The Brothers of Purity." A society of thinkers and writers about A.D. 990, who lived together in Basra, and produced 51 treatises on science and religion; of which the one best known is on the relations between men and beasts. They arose on the decay of the Mu'tuzilas (*q.v.*).

Ikram Ali (اکرام علی), author of the Urdū *Akhwān-us-Safā*, which he translated from the Persian in the year A.D. 1810, A.H. 1225.

Ikram Khan (اکرام خان), the son of Islām Khān and Lādlī Begam, the sister of Abū'l Fazl, prime minister of the emperor Akbar.

[*Vide* Islām Khān.]

Ikram Khan (اکرام خان), title of Sayyad Hasan, an amīr, who served under the emperor 'Alamgīr, and died in A.D. 1661, A.H. 1072.

Ikram-uddaula (اکرام الدوله), the brother of 'Alī Nakī Khān, the prime minister of Wajid 'Alī Shāh, king of Lucknow, died August, A.D. 1869.

'Ikrima (عکرمه), son of Abū Jahl.

'Ikrima (عکرمه). *Vide* Akrima.

Iksir, Mirza (اکثیر مرزا). *Vide* Aksīr.

Ilahi (الهی), an author who, according to the work called *Khulāsat-ul-Asha'ār*, died in A.D. 1538, A.H. 945.

Ilahi, Mir (الهی میر), name and poetical title of a person who was a descendant of the Sayyads of Rashīdābād in Hamadān. He came to India in the latter part of the reign of Jahāngīr, and served under his son Shāh Jahān. He is the author of a biography called *Khazīna Ganj Ilāhī*, and of a Dīwān containing amorous songs. The author of the *Mirat Jahān* says he died in A.D. 1648, A.H. 1057, but from the chronogram which Ghanī Kashmīrī wrote at his death, it appears that he died in A.D. 1654, corresponding with A.H. 1064.

Ilahi, Shaikh (الهی شیخ), a philosopher of Bayāna, who in the time of Khān, or Salīm Shāh, son of Sher Shāh Sur, made a great stir, by introducing a new system of religion. He called himself Imām Mahdī, who, according to the Shīa tradition, is still living and is to conquer the world. Having raised a great disturbance in the empire, he was in the year A.D. 1547, A.H. 954, scourged to death by order of the emperor.

Ildiguz, Atabak (یلدگز اتابک) was a Turkish slave, sold to Sultān Masa'ūd, one of the Saljūqī princes. He is said to have so completely established himself in the favour of his royal master, that the latter advanced him to the highest stations in the kingdom; and the able manner in which Ildiguz executed every duty that was assigned to him led at last, not only to his being charged with the education of one of the young princes, which gave him the title of Atābak or Atābeg, but to his marriage with the widow of Tughral II. (the brother of Masa'ūd and nephew of Sultān Sanjar), and within a short period he became the most powerful noble of the Persian empire. He died at Hamdān in A.D. 1172, A.H. 568, in the reign of Arsalān Shāh, and left his power and station to his eldest son Atābak Muhammad.

List of the Atābaks of the race of Ildiguz.

Atābak	Ildiguz . . . . . died	1172
,,	Muhammad, son of Ildiguz ,,	1186
,,	Qizal Arsalān, son of Ildiguz, slain	1191
,,	Abū Bakr, son of Muhammad, died	1210
,,	Muzaffar, son of Muhammad; he was defeated by Sultān Jalal-uddīn of Khwarizm, and died some time after. He was the last of the Atābaks of the race of Ildiguz who reigned in 'Azurbaijan	1225

Ilham (الهام). *Vide* Malūl.

Ilmas 'Ali Khan (الماس علی خان), the celebrated rich and powerful eunuch of the Court of Nawāb-Asaf-uddaula. He died in A.D. 1808.

Iltitmish (التمش). *Vide* Altamish.

'Imad-'al-Katib or **Imad-uddin-al-Katib** (عماد الکاتب یا عماد الدین الکاتب), that is, 'Imād the Secretary, was the surname of Muhammad, the son of 'Abdullāh, the son of Samad, also called

Isfahānī. He was a celebrated author, and has written in Arabic the history of Sālāh-uddīn (Saladin) the Sultān of Egypt and Syria, in seven volumes, entitled *Barq-ush-Shāmī*, the Lightning of Syria. He died A.D. 1201, A.H. 597.

'Imad Faqih Kirmani, Khwaja (عماد فقیه کرمانی خواجه), a Muhammad doctor who lived in the time of Shāh Shujāa' of Shirāz. His death is mentioned in the *Jawāhir-ul-Asha'ār* to have happened in A.D. 1391, A.H. 793, but according to the poets Ilāhī and Daulat Shāh he died in the year A.D. 1371, A.H. 773, which appears to be correct. Ilāhī also mentions having seen 12,000 verses of his composition, adding that he is the author of the works called *Muhabbat Nāma* and *Mehnat Nāma*, and also that he wrote in all a *Panj Ganj*, that is to say, five Masnawīs or Poems. It is mentioned in the *Habīb-us-Siar*, that Khwāja 'Imād had a cat that would stand up to prayers with him, and do what he did. This was believed by Shāh Shujāa' to be a miracle of the Khwāja; but Khwāja Hāfiz, who was his contemporary, and would not take it for a miracle, but a trick played by the doctor, wrote a *ghazal* on that occasion; the following is the translation of a couplet from the same: "O thou charming bird, where art thou going; stand still, and be not proud (or think thyself to be safe) because the cat of the saint says prayers." 'Imād Khwāja was buried at Kirman, the place of his nativity.

'Imadi (عمادی), surname of Jamāl-uddīn-bin-Imād-uddīn Hanafī, author of the Arabic work called *Fusūl-ul-'Imādī*.

'Imad Khwaja (عماد خواجه). *Vide* Imād Faqīh.

'Imad Shah (عماد شاه). *Vide* Imādul Mulk, commonly called Fatha-ullāh.

'Imad-uddin (عماد الدین), surname of Qara Arsalān-bin-Dāūd-bin-Sukmān-bin-Artaq. Nūr-uddīn Mahmūd was his son, to whom Sālah-uddīn (Saladin) the Sultān of Egypt gave the city of 'Amid or Qara Amid, A.D. 1183, A.H. 579.

'Imad-uddin Katib (عماد الدین کاتب). *Vide* 'Imād-al-Kātib.

'Imad-uddin (عماد الدین), author of a poem called the *Guldasta* or the *Nosegay*, which he composed in A.D. 1664, A.H. 1075. He was a native of India.

'Imad-uddin (عماد الدین), author of the history of the Saljūkides.

'Imad-uddin Zangi (عمادالدین زنگی), the son of Afsaqar, was one of the Atābaks or ruling ministers under the latter princes of the Saljūkian race. He was the first of that branch that had the government of Musal. He received the governorship of that province in A.D. 1127, A.H. 521, from Sultān Muhammad, the son of Sultān Malikshāh Saljūkī, reigned 19 years, and was murdered by one of his slaves in A.D. 1145, A.H. 540.

The following is a list of the princes of this race:—

	A.D.
'Imād-uddīn Zangī began to rule	1127
Saif-uddīn Ghazī-bin-Zangī, who defeated the French at Damascus	1145
Qutb-uddīn Maudūd, son of Zangī, A.H. 569	1149
Nūr-uddīn Mahmūd, son of Zangī; he reigned at Aleppo and formed another branch; died A.H. 5 9	
Malik Sālah, son of Nūr-uddīn, succeeded his father and reigned at Aleppo; died 1174	
Al-Muizz Saif-uddīn Ghazī-bin-Maudūd	1170
Azz-uddīn Masa'ūd-bin-Maudūd	1180
Nūr-uddīn Arsalān Shāh-bin-Masa'ūd	1193
Malik-ul-Qāhir Azz-uddīn Masa'ūd-bin-Nūr-uddīn	1210
Nūr-uddīn Arsalān Shāh-bin-Qāhir	1218
Nāsir-uddīn Mahmūd-bin-Qāhir	1219
Al-Malik-al-Rahīm Badr-uddīn Lūlū	1222
Al-Malik-us-Sālah Ismā'īl-bin-Lūlū	1259

Halab or Aleppo branch.

'Imād-uddīn Zangī	1127
Nūr-uddīn Mahmūd-bin-Zangī	1145
Al-Malik-us-Sālah Ismā'īl-bin-Nūr-uddīn	1174
'Imād-uddīn Zangī-bin-Qutb-uddīn-bin-Maudūd, delivered Aleppo to Sālah-uddīn (died A.D. 1197)	1181

His son Muhammad reigned at Singara.

'Imad-uddaula (عماد الدوله علی بویه), surnamed 'Alī Buya. *Vide* 'Alī Buya.

'Imad-ul Mulk (عماد الملک) commonly called Fath-ullāh 'Imād Shāh, founder of the 'Imād Shāhī dynasty in the Deccan, was descended from the Kanarese infidels of Bījanagar. Having been taken prisoner in the wars with that country when a boy, he was admitted among the bodyguards of Khān Jahān, commander-in-chief and governor of Berār. In the reign of Muhammad Shāh Bahmanī, through the influence of Khwāja Mahmūd Gāwān, he received the title of 'Imād-ul-Mulk, and was subsequently raised to the office of commander of the forces in

Beṛāṛ. After the murder of his patron Khwāja Mahmūd Gāwān in A.D. 1481, A.H. 886, he retired to his government of Beṛāṛ. On the accession of Sulṭān Mahmūd Bahmanī, he was honoured with the office of wizārat, which he held for some time, but being soon after disgusted with the court, he left it and declared his independence in the year A.D. 1485, A.H. 890. Elichpūr was his capital. He died about the year A.D. 1513, A.H. 919, and was succeeded by his eldest son 'Alā-uddīn 'Imād Shāh.

List of the kings of the 'Imād Shāhī dynasty of Beṛāṛ.

Fath-ullāh 'Imād Shāh.
'Alā-uddīn 'Imād Shāh, son of Fath-ullāh.
Daria 'Imād Shāh, son of 'Alā-uddīn.
Burhān 'Imād Shāh.
Tufal Khān, prime minister of Burhān 'Imād Shāh, who usurped the throne, but was opposed from Ahmadnagar; and the family of 'Imād Shāh and Tufal became extinguished in A.D. 1568.

'Imad-ul-Mulk (عماد الملک), title of the Ghāzī-uddīn Khān who murdered his master 'Alamgīr II. emperor of Dehlī.

[*Vide* Ghazī-uddīn Khān III.]

'Imad Zangi (عماد زنگی). *Vide* 'Imād-uddīn Zangī.

Imam (امام) (lit. "pattern" or "example"), a high priest or head or chief in religious matters, whether he be the head of all Muhammadans, as the Khalīfa or the priest of a mosque, or the leader in the prayers of a congregation. This sacred title is given by the Shīas only to the immediate descendants of 'Alī the son-in-law of the prophet, who are twelve, 'Alī being the first. The last of these, Imām Mahdī, is supposed by them to be concealed (not dead), and the title which belongs to him cannot, they conceive, be given to another. Their doctrine is somewhat mystic; but among the Sunnīs it is a dogma that there must be always a visible Imām or "father of the church." The title is given by them to the four learned doctors who are the founders of their faith, *viz.:* Imāms Hanīfa, Mālik, Shāfa'ī, and Hanbal. Of these four sects, the Hanbalite and Mālikite may be considered as the most rigid, the Shāfa'ite as the most conformable to the spirit of Islāmism, and the Hanīfite as the freest and most philosophical of them all. Two other Imāms, Abū Dāūd-uz-Zāhirī and Sufiān-us-Saurī, were also chiefs of the orthodox sects, but their opinions had not many followers, and after some time were totally abandoned. Ibn-Jarīr-ut-Tabarī, whose reputation as an historian is so familiar to Europeans, founded also a particular sect, which disappeared soon after his death. The following are the names of the twelve Sh'a Imāms of the race of 'Alī:—

Imām 'Alī, the son-in-law of the prophet.
,, Hasan.
,, Husain.
,, Zain-ul 'Abidīn.
,, Bāqir or Muhammad Bāqir.
,, Jafar Sādiq.
,, Mūsī Kāzim.
,, 'Alī Mūsī Raza.
,, Taqī or Muhammad Taqī.
,, 'Alī Naqī.
,, Hasan Askari.
,, Mahdī.

[*Vide* Hughes' *Dictionary of Islām in voc.*]

Imam 'Alam-bin-'Ala-al-Hanafi (امام عالم بن علا الحنفی), author of a large collection of Fatwas in several volumes, entitled *Fatāwā Tātārkhānia*, taken from the *Muhīt-al-Burhānī*, the *Zakhīrat*, the *Khānia* and *Zahīria*. Afterwards, however, a selection was made from these decisions by the Imām Ibrāhīm-bin-Muhammad-al-Halabī, and an epitome was thus formed, which is in one volume, and still retains the title of *Tātārkhānia*.

Imam Bakhsh, Shaikh (امام بخش شیخ). *Vide* Sahābī.

Imam Bakhsh, Shaikh (امام بخش شیخ). *Vide* Nāsikh.

Imam Bakhsh, Moulvi (امام بخش مولوی). *Vide* Sahbāī.

Imam 'Azim, title of Abū Hanīfa.

Imami Hirwi, Maulana (امامی هروی مولانا). He is called Hirwī, because he was a native of Herāt. He was an excellent poet and contemporary with the celebrated Shaikh Sa'dī of Shīrāz, whom, in the opinion of some writers, he surpassed in the Qasīda. He died about the year A.D. 1281, A.H. 680, and has left a Dīwān.

Imam Malik (امام مالک ابن آنس), son of Ānas, one of the four Imāms or Jurisconsults of Mecca. He died on the 28th June, A.D. 795, 7th Rab'ī II. A.H. 179, in the time of the Khalīf Hārūn-al-Rashīd.

[*Vide* Mālik-ibn-Ānas.]

Imam Muhammad (امام محمد مفتی), a Muftī in the reign of Hārūn-al-Rashīd the Khalīfa. He died at Baghdād in A.D. 802,

A.H. 186, and is said to have written 999 works. He was a pupil of Imām Abū Yūsaf, who committed his notes to him, and he (Muhammad) made great use of them in the composition of his works.

[*Vide* Abū 'Abdullād Muhummad-bin-Husain.]

Imam-uddin Amir Katib-bin-Amir Umar (امام الدین امیر کاتب بن امیر عمر), author of a Commentary on the Hidāya entitled *Kifāya*, which he finished in A.D. 1346, A.H. 747. He had previously written another explanatory gloss of the same work, and entitled it the *Ghāyat-ul-Bayān*.

Imdad Ali (امداد علی), the rebel Deputy Collector, who was hanged at Banda, together with the rebel Tahsīldār of Pailānī, Muhammad Muhsin on the 24th April, 1858.

Imtihani (امتحانی), poetical name of Imām-uddīn Beg.

Imtiyaz (امتیاز), the poetical name of Rāja Dayā Mal, whose father was Dīwān of Asad Khān, the Wazīr of 'Alamgīr, and he of Ghazī-uddīn Khān, styled 'Imād-ul-Mulk.

Imtiyaz Khan, Sayyad (امتیاز خان سید خالص), whose poetical name is Khālis, was a native either of Isfahān or of Mashhad. He came to India in the time of the emperor 'Alamgīr, was appointed governor of Gujrāt for some time, and was slain by Khudā Yār Khān in A.D. 1710, A.H. 1122, in Sindh. It is said that Qāsim Alī Khān, the Nawāb of Bengal, was his grandson. He is the author of a Dīwān.

Ina'amullah Khan (انعام الله خان). *Vide* Yeqin.

Inayet Khan (عنایت خان آشنا), whose poetical title is 'Ashnā or Ahsan, and proper name Muhammad Tāhir, was the son of Zafar Khān. He was an excellent poet, and is the author of the work called *Shāh Jahān Nāma*, a history of the emperor Shāh Jahān. Besides the above-mentioned work, he is the author of a Dīwān and a Masnawi. He died in A.D. 1666, A.H. 1077.

'Inayet-ullah, Shaikh (عنایت الله شیخ دهلوی), of Dehlī, author of the work called *Bahār Dānish*, a collection of amusing tales, principally satires on women. Several of these tales were published by Colonel Dow, under the title of *The Tales of 'Ināyet-ullah*, and the whole work was translated in the year A.D. 1799, by Jonathan Scott, in three volumes, octavo.

'Inayet-ullah Khan (عنایت الله خان), the son of Shukr-ullāh Khān, a descendant of Sayyad Jamāl of Naishāpūr. His mother Hāfiz Mariam was tutor of the princess Zeebun Nisā Begam, the daughter of the emperor 'Alamgīr; by her influence her son 'Ināyet-ullāh Khān was raised by degrees to the rank of 2500. In the reign of Farrukh-siyar the rank of 4000 was conferred on him, and in that of Muhammad Shāh, of 7000. He was the author of the work called *Ahkām 'Alamgīrī* and compiler of the *Kalmāt Taiyabāt*. He died A.D. 1726, A.H. 1139.

Indarman Bundela, Raja (اندرمن بندیله راجه), the brother of Rāja Sujān Sindh. He died in the Deccan about the year A.D. 1675, and his zamīndārī of Urcha and the title of Rāja were conferred upon his son Jaswant Singh by the emperor 'Alamgīr.

Insaf (انصاف), the poetical name of Muhammad Ibrāhīm. His father was a native of Khurāsān, but he was born in India. He was a contemporary of Sarkhush, the poet, was living about the year A.D. 1688, A.H. 1100, and died young.

Insan (انسان), the poetical title of Nawāb Asad-ullāh Asad Yār Khān. He held the mansab of Haft Hazārī (7000), in the reign of Muhammad Shāh, and died in April, A.D. 1745, Rabī' I. A.H. 1158. His remains were brought to Āgra and buried there in the cemetery of his ancestors.

Insha or Insha Allah Khan (انشا یا انشاالله خان), a poet and son of Māshā Allāh Khān. He is the author of four Dīwāns of different kinds.

Intikhabi (انتخابی), a poet who was a native of Khurāsān, but was brought up in India. He is the author of a Dīwān.

Intizam-uddaula Khan Khankhanan (انتظام الدوله خان خانان), the second son of Nawāb Qamar-uddīn Khān Wazīr. He was appointed to the rank of second Bakhshī on the accession of Ahmad Shāh to the throne of Dehlī in A.D. 1748, A.H. 1161, and was honoured with the appointment of Wazīr in A.D. 1753, A.H.

1165, after the dismissal of Nawāb Safdar Jang from the office. He was murdered by 'Imād-ul-Mulk Ghāzī-uddīn Khān on the 26th November, A.D. 1759, 5th Rabī' II. A.H. 1173, three days before the assassination of the emperor 'Alamgīr II.

Iqa Pandit (اقا پندت), a Marhatta Brahman who, in the time of Shāh Alam and Madho Rāo Sindhia, held the appointment of the Sūbadarship of the fort of Àgra.

Iqbal Khan (اقبال خان) was the son of Zafar Khān, the son of Fīroz Shāh Tughlaq. He defeated Nasrat Khān and ascended the throne of Dehlī about the beginning of the year A.D. 1400, A.H. 802, and was slain in a battle against Khizr Khān, the governor of Multan, in November, A.D. 1405, 19th Jumāda I. A.H. 808. After his death Sultān Mahmūd Shāh, who was defeated by Amīr Taimūr and had fled to Gujrāt and then to Qanauj, returned on the invitation of Daula Khān Lodī, who commanded at Dehlī, and took possession of the empire.

Iqbal - uddaula Muhsin Ali Khan (اقبال الدوله محسن علی خان), the son of Shams-uddaula Ahmad 'Alī Khān, the son of Nawāb Sa'ādat 'Alī Khān of Lucknow. He sailed for England to claim the throne of Audh in January, A.D. 1838, and after trying in vain to obtain the recognition of his claim from England, determined upon passing the remainder of his days in a life of sanctity in Turkish Arabia. He is the author of the work called *Iqbal Firang*.

Iradat Khan (ارادت خان), the title of Mīr Ishāq or Ishāq Khān, the son of Nawāb 'Azim Khān, who held a high rank in the reign of the emperor Jahāngīr. Irādat Khān held various offices under Shāh Jahān, and in the first year of 'Alamgīr's reign he was appointed governor of Audh, but died after two months in October, A.D. 1658, Zil-hijja, A.H. 1068.

Iradat Khan (ارادت خان واضح), the title of Mirzā Mubarik-ullāh, whose poetical name was Wāzah. His father Is-hāk Khān (who afterwards held the title of Kifāyet Khān) was the son of Nawāb 'Azim Khān. Both his grandfather and father were noblemen of high rank. The former was Mīr Bakhshī to the emperor Jahāngīr, and was afterwards appointed Faujdār of Jaunpūr, where he died in A.D. 1649, A.H. 1059. The latter was the subject of the last article; and his title of Irādat Khān was conferred on his son after his death. In the 33rd year of 'Alamgīr our present subject was appointed Faujdār of Jāgnā, and at other periods of Aurangābād and Māndo in Mālwa. Was equerry to Prince Bedar Bakht (*q.v.*) in the short war of 1707, of which he wrote an account. In the reign of Shāh 'Alam or Bahādūr Shāh I. he was governor of the Doāb, and the intimate friend of Mua'zzim Khān, Wazīr. In the latter part of his days he led a retired life, became a Kalandar, and died in A.D. 1716, A.H. 1128. His abilities as a poet were great, and he left a volume of poems behind him. He is the author of the *Kalmāt Aliāt*, (Sublime discourses), *Mīna Bāzār* and of a history of Aurangzeb's Successors, which latter was translated into English by Jonathan Scott, Esq., in A.D. 1786. After his death, which happened in the time of Farrukhsiyar, his son Mīr Hidāet-ullāh received the title of Hoshdār Khān, held the rank of 4000, and died at Aurangābād A.D. 1744, A.H. 1157.

'Iraqi (عراقی), whose proper name is Fakhr-uddīn Ibrāhīm-bin-Shahryār, was a native of Hamdan in 'Irāq, and a pupil and grandson by the mother's side of the great Shaikh Shahāb-uddīn Suharwardī, author of a host of mystical works highly esteemed by the Sūfīs. 'Irāqī offended his parent and master, in consequence of a love affair, and went to India, where he remained some time, regretting his native country, and uttering his complaints in moving verse. He lived in company with the Shaikh Bahā-uddīn Zikaria of Multan, whom he accompanied on his journey and became his disciple. 'Irāqī, after a long sojourn in India, proposed returning to his own master, Shahāb-uddīn; but the latter had died, and our poet continued his wanderings to Syria, where he expired after a long life of eighty-two years on the 23rd November, A.D. 1289, 8th Zi-Qa'da, A.H. 688, and was buried at Sālahī in Damascus close to the tomb of Shaikh Muhī-uddīn Ibn-ul-'Arabī. His son Shaikh Kabīr-uddīn is also buried there. 'Irāqī is the author of a work called *Lama'āt*.

[*Vide* Fakhr-uddīn 'Irāqī.]

'Irfan (عرفان), poetical name of Muhammad Rizā, the son of Muhammad Jān Irfān, author of the *Kār Nāma*, containing the praises of 'Alī Mardān Khān, the Amīr-ul-Umrā of the emperor Shāh Jahān.

Irtiza 'Ali Khan Bahadur (ارتضا علی خان بهادر), author of the *Farāiz Irtizia*, a concise treatise in Persian on the law of Inheritance, which appears to be the principal authority of that law in the Deccan. It was printed in Madras, but without a date.

'Isa Masih (عیسے المسیح), Jesus Christ.

For Arabic titles of and doctrines regarding, *vide* Hughes' *Dictionary of Islām in voc. Jesus.*

'Isam - uddin Ibrahim - bin - Muhammad Isfaraeni (عصام الدین ابراهیم بن محمد اسفرینی), an Arabian author who died A.D. 1536, A.H. 943; he is the author of the Arabic note-book called *Hāshia Isām-uddīn.*

'Isa-ibn-Musa (عیسیٰ ابن موسیٰ), the cousin-german of the Khalīf Abū Ja'far Mansūr, after whose death in A.D. 775, A.H. 158, he entertained thoughts of setting up for himself at Kūfa, where he then resided; and in order to facilitate the execution of his scheme, fortified himself in that city. But al-Mahdī, the son of Mansūr, being apprised of his defection, sent a detachment of 1,000 horse to bring him to Baghdād; which being done, al-Mahdī not only prevailed upon him to own allegiance to him, but also to give up his right to the succession (he being the next apparent heir to the crown) for 10,000 according to some, and according to others 10,000,000 dīnars.

'Isa Sawaji (عیسیٰ ساوجي), a poet of Sāwa who was a Kāzī. He died in A.D. 896, A.H. 291.

'Isi Turkhan, Mirza (عیسیٰ ترخان مرزا), was a Turkmān and commander-in-chief of Shāh Beg Arghūn, king of Sindh's army, after whose death he took possession of Thatta, of which he was then governor, and assumed the title of king. He reigned 13 years and died in A.D. 1567, A.H. 975, when he was succeeded by his eldest son Mirzā Muhammad Bāqī Turkhān, who during his rule always maintained a friendly intercourse with the emperor Akbar of Dehlī, frequently sending presents, and acknowledging fealty to that monarch. He died after a reign of 18 years in A.D. 1585, A.H. 993, and was succeeded by his grandson Mirzā Jānī Beg.

Isdigertes (یزدجرد). *Vide* Yezdijard.

Isfahani (اصفهانی), author of the *Dānish Nāma*, a system of natural philosophy.

Isfan or Stephen (اسفان) is the name and takhallus of a Christian poet born at Dehlī. His father was a European. He was alive in A.D. 1800, A.H. 1215.

Isfandiyar (اسفندیار), the son of Kishtāsp or Gashtāsp (Hytaspes), the fifth king of the Kayānian dynasty of Persia, was a great warrior, the son of Darius I. and great-grandson of Achaemenes. Isfandiyār answers, in some respects to the Xerxes (Sher Shāh) of the Greeks, and Ahasuerus of the Jews. He is the Kihāyārshā of the Cuneiform inscriptions. [But *vide* Malcolm's *Persia*, where it is shown that, according to native historians, Isfandiyar was never king, but only commander-in-chief of his father's armies. He is said to have been killed by the hero Rustam (*q.v.*).]

Is-haq (اسحاق), the poetical title of Jamāl-uddīn, a cotton-carder of Shīrāz. He was an elegant poet, and has left us a Dīwān called *Aksīr-ul-Ishtihā*, the Elixir of Hunger, full of amorous songs and parodies on the odes of Khwāja Hāfiz, each verse of which contains either the name of a sweetmeat or a dish. He lived in the time of Prince Sultān Sikandar, the son of Umar Shaikh, who much esteemed him. His proper name is Abū-Ishāq, which he uses in poetry by abbreviating it into Bus-hāq.

Is-haq-bin-'Ali (اسحاق بن علی), author of a Dīwān in Arabic, and of a work called *Zuhr-ul-'Adāb.* He died in A.D. 1022, A.H. 413.

Is-haq-bin-Husain or Hunain (اسحاق بن حسین یا حنین), an Arabian author who translated the *Almagest* of Ptolemy from the Greek into Arabic under the title of *Tahrīr-al-Majastī.* This book is to be found in the French National Library. Shīrāzī has written a commentary on this work, and entitled it *Hāl Mushkilāt-al-Majastī.*

Is-haq Khan (اسحاق خان), styled Mō'tamin-uddaula, whose original name was Mirzā Ghulām 'Alī, was a nobleman of high rank, and a great favourite of the emperor Muhammad Shāh of Dehlī. He was a good poet, and used for his political name Is-hāq. He died in the 22nd year of the emperor, A.D. 1740, A.H. 1153, and after his death his daughter was married to Shujā-uddaula, the son of Nawāb Safdar Jang, and the nuptials were celebrated with uncommon splendour, A.D. 1746, A.H. 1159.

Is-haq Maulana (اسحاق مولانا), a learned Musalmān who was born at Uchcha in Multān. In his youth he dedicated himself under the guidance of his uncle Sāyyad Sadr-uddīn Rājū Qattāl, whose sister was his mother. He died in A.D. 1456, A.H. 860, and was buried in the compound of his own house at Sahāranpūr.

Is-haq Mousali (اسحاق موصلی), a celebrated Arabian author, born at Musal. It is related in the *Kitāb Alaghānī* that when he was on a journey he carried with him eighteen coffers full of books, though he declared that if he had not been anxious to make his luggage as light as possible, he would have brought double the quantity.

'Ishq (عشق), poetical title of Shāh Rukn-uddīn, who flourished in the reign of the emperor Shāh 'Alam.

'Ishqi (عشقي), the title of a poet who flourished in the reign of the emperor Muhammad Shāh, and is the author of a Dīwān. He died in A.D. 1729, A.H. 1142.

'Ishqi (عشقي), poetical title of Shaikh Muhammad Wajīh, son of Ghulām Husain Mujrim of Patna. He was for ten years under the English government Tahsīldār of Kharwar; was living in A.D. 1809, A.H. 1224, and is the author of a Dīwān.

Ishrat (عشرت), poetical name of Mirzā 'Alī Rizā, who collected his poems into a Dīwān under Muhammad Shāh in A.D. 1747, A.H. 1160, and died shortly after.

'Ishrat (عشرت), author of the last part of the story of Padmāwat in Urdū verse, which was completed by him A.D. 1796.
[*Vide* Padmāwat and Ibrat.]

'Ishrati (عشرتی), poetical name of a poet who is the author of a small Dīwān. His name is Aka 'Alī of Isfahān; he came to India, and on his return died at Mashhad.

Ishtiyaq (اشتیاق), poetical name assumed by Shāh Walī Ullāh of Sarhind, who was the grandson of Shaikh Ahmad Sarhindī. He was a distinguished theologian and Sūfī. He died in A.D. 1748, A.H. 1161, and left several works. Shāh 'Abdul 'Azīz of Dehlī, the most celebrated Indian theologian in modern times, was one of his sons.

Ishuri or Ishwari Singh (ایسری سنگه), the son of Rāja Jai Singh Sawāī, whom he succeeded to the Rāj of Jaipūr in A.D. 1743. He died in A.D. 1760, and was succeeded by his son Mādho Singh.

Ishuri Parshad Narain Singh Bahadur (ایشري پرشاد نراین سنگه بهادر), Rāja of Benares (1869).

Iskandar (اسکندر), Alexander the Great. *Vide* Sikandar Zulkarnain.

Iskandar Manishi (اسکندر منشی), whom Stewart in his *Catalogue of Tippū Sultān's Library* calls Sikandar Hamnashīnī, is the author of the *Tārīkh 'Alam 'Arāe 'Abbāsī*, a history of the Persian kings of the Safwī dynasty, from Shāh Ismā'īl to Shāh 'Abbās the Great, to whom it was dedicated in A.D. 1616, A.H. 1025.

Islam Khan (اسلام خان), title of Mīr Ziyā-uddīn Husain Badakhshī, whose poetical name was Wālā. He served under the emperor 'Alamgīr, and was raised to the rank of 5000 with the title of Islām Khān. He died in the year A.D. 1663, A.H. 1074, at Āgra, and the chronogram of his death was written by Ghanī Kashmīrī. He was the father of Nawābs Himmat Khān, Saif Khān and 'Abdur Rahīm Khān.

Islam Khan (اسلام خان), the son of Safī Khān and grandson of Islām Khān Mashhadī, was Sūbadār of Lāhore in the time of the emperor Farrukh-siyar, and was raised to the rank of 7000 in the reign of Muhammad Shāh.

Islam Khan Mashhadi, Nawab (اسلام خان مشهدی نواب) (he is by some called Islām Khān Rūmī, but that is a mistake). He was a native of Mashhad, and his original name was Mīr 'Abdus Salām. In the time of Jahāngīr he held the manṣab of 5000, and the Sūbadārī of Bengal; and in the time of Shāh Jahān was raised to the rank of 6000 with the title of Motam-uddaula and held the appointment of second Bakhshigārī and governorship of the Deccan. He afterwards was again appointed governor of Bengal. In the 13th year of Shāh Jahān he was raised to the rank of Wizārat with the title of Jumdat-ul-Mulk. Shortly after he was raised to the rank of 7000, and the Sūbadārī of the Deccan. He was wazīr to Shāh Jahān and held the manṣab of 7000, with the title of Islām Khān. He was some time before his death appointed governor of the Deccan, where he died in the 21st year of the emperor, on the 2nd November, A.D. 1647, 14th Shawwāl, A.H. 1057, and was buried at Aurangābād.

Islam Khan Rumi, "Turk," (اسلام خان رومی), title of Husain Pāshā, son of 'Alī Pāshā. He was governor of Basra, but being deprived of that situation by his uncle Muhammad, he left that country and came to India in A.D. 1689, A.H. 1080, where he was received by the emperor 'Alamgīr with the greatest respect, and honoured with the rank of 5000 and title of Islām Khān. He was killed in the battle of Bījāpūr in the Deccan on the 13th June,

A.D. 1676, 11th Rabī' II. A.H. 1087. He had built his house at Āgra on a piece of ground consisting of four bīgas and seven cottas, and a garden on a spot of three bīgas and nine cottas, on the banks of the river Jamna near the Ghāt called Tajāra close to the fort of Āgra. Byzantine Turks were called *Rumi* in mediaeval India; and officers of that race were often employed in the artillery.

Islam Khan, Shaikh (اسلام خان شیخ), styled Nawāb Ya'tzād-uddaula, was a grandson of Shaikh Salīm Chishtī, and son-in-law of Shaikh Mubārik, the father of the celebrated 'Abū'l Fazl, whose sister, named Lādlī Begam, he had married. He was appointed governor of Bengal by the emperor Jahāngīr in A.D. 1608, A.H. 1017. Nawāb Ikrām Khān was his son, and Qāsim Khān his brother. The latter succeeded him in the government of Bengal in A.D. 1613, A.H. 1022, in which year Islām Khān died. His remains were transported to Fathapūr Sīkrī, where his monument is still to be seen.

Islam Shah (اسلام شاه). *Vide* Salīm Shāh.

Isma'il (اسمعیل), or Ishmael, the son of the patriarch Abraham.

Isma'il (اسمعیل بن امام جعفر صادق), the eldest son of Imām Ja'far Sādiq, from whom the sect of Isma'īlīs or Isma'īlias take their name. They maintain that Isma'īl Ibn Jā'far, who was the eldest son, but died during his father's life, should have succeeded to the dignity of Imām, and not Mūsī Kāzim, who was his younger brother, and became the seventh Imām. For their other opinions see Hughes *in voc. Ismāiliyah.* Hasan Sabbah was of this sect.

[*Vide* Isma'īlīs.]

Isma'il I. Safavi, Shah (اسمعیل صفوی شاه), the son of Sulṭān Haidar, was the first monarch of the Safavī dynasty of kings who reigned in Persia (A.D. 1500). He traced his descent from Mūsī Kāzim the seventh Imām, who was descended in a direct line from 'Alī, the son-in-law of Muhammad. Almost all his ancestors were regarded as holy men, and some of them as saints. The first of this family who acquired any considerable reputation was Shaikh Safī-uddīn, who had settled at Ardible, and from whom this dynasty takes its name of Safwīa or Safavī. His son Sadr-uddīn Mūsa, as well as his immediate descendants, Khwāja Alī, Shaikh Ibrāhīm, Sulṭān Junaid, and Haidar, acquired the greatest reputation for sanctity. Contemporary monarchs, we are informed, visited the cell of Sadr-uddīn. The great Taimūr (Tamerlane), when he went to see this holy man, demanded to know what favour he should confer upon him. "Release those prisoners you have brought from Turkistān," was the noble and pious request of the saint. The conqueror complied; and the grateful tribes, when they gained their liberty, declared themselves the devoted disciples of him to whom they owed it. Their children preserved sacred the obligation of their fathers; and the descendants of the captives of Taimūr became the supporters of the family of Safī, and enabled the son of a devotee to ascend one of the most splendid thrones in the world. Khwāja 'Alī, after visiting Mecca, went on a pilgrimage to Jerusalem, and died at that city. His grandson Junaid, sat on the masnad as a spiritual guide after the death of his father Shaikh Ibrāhīm; and so great a crowd of disciples attended this holy man that Jahān Shāh, the chief of the tribe of the Black Sheep, who at that time ruled Azurbaijān, became alarmed at their numbers and banished him from Ardibel. Junaid went to Dayārbikar, whose ruler, the celebrated Uzzan Hasan, received him kindly, and gave him his sister in marriage. He afterwards went with his disciples to Shirwān, where he was slain in a conflict with the troops of the king of that province in A.D. 1456, A.H. 860. His son Sulṭān Haidar succeeded him, and his uncle Uzzan Hasan, who had now by his overthrow of Jahān Shāh and Sulṭān Abū Saīd become powerful in Persia, gave him his daughter in marriage. The name of this princess, according to Muhammadan authors, was 'Alam Shao', but we are informed by a contemporary European writer that she was called Martha, and was the daughter of Uzzan Hasan by the Christian lady Despina, who was a daughter of Calo Joannes, king of Trebizond. Sulṭān Haidar also lost his life from the wound of an arrow which he received in a battle with the troops of Shirwān Shāh and Ya'qūb Beg in July, A.D. 1488, Shabān, A.H. 893. Sulṭān Haidar had three sons by this princess—Sulṭān 'Alī, Ibrāhīm Mirzā and Shāh Isma'īl. When Isma'īl attained the age of fourteen (his elder brothers having died some years before), he put himself at the head of his adherents, and marched against the great enemy of his family the ruler of Shirwān, called Shirwān Shāh, whom he defeated A.D. 1500, A.H. 906; and soon after, by another victory gained over Alwand Beg, the son of Ya'qūb Beg, a prince of the dynasty of the White Sheep, he became the master of the province of Azurbaijān, and established his residence at the city of Tabrez; and in less than four years became the acknowledged sovereign of the kingdom of Persia. He was born on the 17th July, A.D. 1487, 25th Rajab, A.H. 892, died after a reign of 24 lunar years on Monday the 23rd May, A.D. 1524, 19th Rajab A.H. 930, aged 38 years, and was buried at Ardibel. Muhammadan historians fix the commencement of his reign from the year A.D. 1500. He left four sons—Tahmasp, who succeeded his father, Sam Mirzā, Bahrām, and Ikhlās Mirzā, and five daughters. He composed a Turkish Dīwān in which he uses the Takhallus of Kitabī.

The following is a list of the Safavī kings of Persia :—

1. Shāh Isma'īl Safavī, first son of Sulṭān Haidar.
2. Shāh Tahmasp Safavī I. son of Isma'īl Safavī.
3. Shāh Isma'īl II
4. Muhammad Khudā Banda.
5. Hamza, son of Khudā Banda.
6. Shāh Isma'īl III. son of Khudā Banda.
7. Shāh 'Abbās I. son of Khudā Banda.
8. Shāh Safī, the son of Safī Mirzā, the son of 'Abbās.
9. Shāh 'Abbās II. son of Shāh Safī.
10. Shāh Sulaimān, son of 'Abbās II.
11. Shāh Husain, son of Sulaimān.
12. Shāh Tahmasp II. last of the Safavī dynasty.
    Mahmūd, an Afghān.
    Ashraf, an Afghān.
13. Shāh 'Abbās III. *Vide* Nādir Shāh.

Isma'il II. Safavi, Shah (اسمعيل صفوى ثانى شاه), second son of Shāh Tahmasp I. Safavī, whom he succeeded on the throne of Persia in May, A.D. 1576, Ṣafar, A.H. 984, by the aid of his sister Parī Khānam, who sent for him from the fort of Qahqah, where he had been confined by his father for 18 years. The short reign of this unworthy prince was marked by debauchery and crime. Immediately on his accession, he directed the massacre of all the princes of the blood-royal that were at Qazwīn, except 'Alī Mirzā, whose life was spared; but even he was deprived of sight. His eldest brother Muhammad Mirzā, who had a natural weakness in his eyes, which rendered him almost blind, and was during his father's life employed as governor of Khurāsān, was then at Shīrāz. Orders were sent to murder him and his son 'Abbās, but before they could be executed Isma'īl was found dead one morning in a confectioner's house, supposed to have been poisoned by his sister. His death happened at Qazwīn on Sunday the 24th November, A.D. 1577, 13th Ramaẓān, A.H. 985, after a short reign of one year and six months. He was succeeded by his eldest brother Muhammad Mirzā, who, on his accession to the throne, took the title of Muhammad Khudā Banda.

Isma'il (اسمعيل), **surnamed al-Mansūr,** third or fourth Khalīf of Barbary of the race of the Fātimites, succeeded his father al-Qāem A.D. 945, A.H. 334, and having defeated and slain Yezīd-ibn-Kondat, who had rebelled against his father, caused his body to be flayed, and his skin stuffed and exposed to public view. Al-Mansūr died after a reign of seven years and sixteen days in A.D. 952, 30th Shawwāl, A.H. 341, and was succeeded by his son Abū Tamīm Ma'd, surnamed Mo'izz-uddīn-allāh.

Isma'il 'Adil Shah, Sultan (اسمعيل عادل شاه), of Bījāpūr, surnamed Abū'l Fatha, succeeded his father Yūsaf 'Adil Shāh on the throne of Bījāpūr in the Deccan in A.D. 1510, A.H. 915, and died after a glorious reign of 25 lunar years on Wednesday the 27th August, A.D. 1534, the 16th Ṣafar, A.H. 941, and was buried at Kūkī near the tomb of his father. He was succeeded by his son Mallū 'Adil Shāh.

Isma'il-bin-Hasan (اسمعيل بن حسن), author of the work called *Zakhīra Khwārism Shāh*. He flourished in the reign of Alā-uddīn Takash, Sulṭān of Khwārizm, who died in A.D. 1200, A.H. 596, and was a contemporary of Khaqānī the poet.

Isma'ili or Isma'ilia (اسمعيلى اسمعيليه), sect of Ismaīl-ibn-Jā'far (*q.v.*). Their tenets were held by a man who had through the means of superstition established an influence over the minds of his followers, that enabled them to strike awe into the bosoms of the most powerful sovereigns, and to fill kingdoms with horror and dismay for a period of nearly two centuries. Their ruler, who became the chief of the Assassins, resided on a lofty mountain called Alahmūt, and fate was in his hands; for there was no shape which his followers could not assume, no danger that they could not brave, to fulfil his mandates. These were the Isma'īlīs or Assassins, well-known by the Crusaders, as subjects of the Old Man of the mountain. They were completely extirpated by Halākū, the Tartar king of Persia, in the year A.D. 1256.

[*Vide* Hasan Sabbāh.]

Isma'il Haqqi, Shaikh (اسمعيل حقى شيخ), author of a commentary on the Qurān called *Rūh-ul-Bayān*, and of the *Hadīs-ul-Arba'īn*.

Isma'il Mirza (اسمعيل ميرزا), of Isfahān, an author.

Isma'il Nizam Shah (اسمعيل نظام شاه). His father, prince Burhān Shāh, having been defeated in an attempt to dethrone his brother Murta'zā Nizām Shāh, had fled for protection to the court of the emperor Akbar. On his departure he left behind him two sons, named Ibrāhīm and Isma'īl, who were kept confined in the fortress of Lāhāgurh. On the death of Mīrān Husain Shāh, the younger being raised to the throne of Ahmadnagar by Jamāl Khān in the month of March, A.D. 1589,

Jumādạ I. A.H. 997, took the title of Isma'īl Nizām Shāh. His father Burhān Shāh, having received assistance from the emperor Akbar, marched against his son, but was defeated. However, in a short time after this, he renewed his attempts, and being joined by a great majority of the chiefs and people, attacked Jamāl Khān the king's minister, who was killed in the action on the 27th April, o.s. 1591, 13th Rajab, A.H. 999. Isma'īl, who had reigned little more than two years, was taken prisoner and confined by his father, who ascended the throne of Ahmadnagar with the title of Burhān Nizām Shāh II.

Isma'il Pasha (اسمعیل پاشا), a recent Viceroy of Egypt, the successor of Muhammad 'Alī Pasha, who died in August, A.D. 1849.

Isma'il Samani, Amir (اسمعیل سامانی امیر), the first King of Amīr of the race of Sāmān, called Sāmānī, traced his descent from Bahrām Chobīn, the warrior who contended for the crown of Persia with Khusro Parvez. Sāmān the great-grandfather of Isma'īl, is termed, by the European writers, a keeper of herds, and a robber; but this merely designates the ordinary occupations of a Tartar chief. His father Nasr Ahmad, the son of Asad, the son of Sāmān, was appointed governor of Māwarun Nahr by the Khalīf Mo'tamid in the year A.D. 875, A.H. 261. On his death his son Isma'īl succeeded him. Isma'īl, after his conquest over Amrū-bin-Lais, whom he seized and sent to Baghdād, in A.D. 900, became independent. The power of the dynasty of the Sāmānīs extended over Khurāsān, Seistān, Balkh and the countries of Transoxania, including the cities of Bukhārā and Samarqand. This justly celebrated prince died after a reign of twenty years in A.D. 907, Ṣafar, A.H. 295, aged 60 years, and was succeeded by his son Amīr Ahmad Sāmānī.

The names of the kings of this family, who were called Amīrs, and who continued to reign for a period of 128 lunar years, are as follow:—

1. Amīr Isma'īl Sāmānī.
2. ,, Ahmad Sāmānī.
3. ,, Nasr-bin-Ahmad.
4. ,, Nūh I. son of Nasr.
5. ,, Abdul Mālik.
6. ,, Mansūr I.
7. ,, Nūh II.
8. ,, Mansūr II.
9. ,, 'Abdul Mālik II. the last of this race.

Isma'il, Sayyad-bin-Husain Jurjani (اسمعیل سید بن حسین جرجانی), author of two medical works in Persian, called *Aghrāz-ut-Tibb* and *Khiff-i-'Alāi*, which he dedicated to Alp Arsalān, Sulṭān of Khwārizm.

'Ismat (عصمت). *Vide* Asmat.

Istaghana (استغنا), poetical title of 'Abdul Rasūl.

'Istarushi (عسترشی). *Vide* Muhammad-bin-Mahmūd.

I'tabi (عتابی), a poet, who died in the year A.D. 1614, A.H. 1023.

I'tmad Khan Khwaja Sara (اعتماد خان خواجه سرا), an eunuch and officer in the service of the emperor Akbar. He was stabbed by his servant Maqsūd 'Alī in A.D. 1578, A.H. 916, and was buried at a place called I'tmādpūr, twelve miles from Āgra, which he had founded in his lifetime.

I'tmad Khan (اعتماد خان), title of Shaikh 'Abdūl Qawī, an Amīr of the reign of the emperor 'Alamgīr. He was murdered by a Qalandar in A.D. 1666. A.H. 1077.

I'tmad-uddaula (اعتماد الدوله), title of Khwāja Ayās or Ghayās the father of the celebrated Nūr Jahān Begām, the favourite wife of the emperor Jahāngīr. He was a Tartar and came from Persia to India in the reign of the emperor Akbar. In the time of Jahāngīr, he was raised to the high rank of I'tmād-uddaula, and his two sons to the first rank of 'Umra with the titles of 'Asaf Khān and I'tqād Khān. He died near Kōṭ Kāngrā, where he had accompanied Jahāngīr on his way to Kashmere in February, o.s. 1621, Rabī' I. A.H. 1030. His remains were transported to Āgra and buried on the left bank of the Jamna, where a splendid mausoleum was built over his relics by his daughter Nūr Jahān. It was completed in A.D. 1628, and is still in a high state of preservation. It is said, but it seems not to be true, that she intended to raise a monument of silver to his memory, but was reminded by her architect that one of less covetable material stood a fairer chance of duration. After his death his son 'Abū'l Hasan was appointed Wazīr with the title of 'Asaf Khān. No private family ever made such alliances with royal blood as this Tartar; for his own daughter, his son's daughter and the daughter of his grandson, were married to three successive emperors of Hindūstān; and another daughter of his grandson, to prince Murād Bakhsh, who disputed the throne with 'Alamgīr, and for some days thought himself in possession of it. The place where he is buried was a garden planned by I'tmād-uddaula during his lifetime. There are two tombs of yellow stone under the Rauza, or tomb; one of which is that of I'tmād-uddaula, while the other is said to be his wife's. It has a very large gate towards the east, built of red stone. It has two minars on both sides in the same number as there are two on the side of the Jamna towards the west. There is on the chabūtra towards the Jamna a fish made of stone; if the water runs in and rises as far as its mouth, the whole of Allahābād will be inundated.

I'tmad-uddaula (اعتماد الدوله), title of Muhammad Amīr Khān, the prime minister of the emperor Muhammad Shāh.

[*Vide* Muhammad Amīr Khān.]

I'tmad-uddaula (اعتماد الدوله), son of Muhammad Amīn Khān, Wazīr.

[*Vide* Qamar-uddīn Khān.]

I'tqad Khan (اعتقاد خان), the brother of 'Asaf Khān, Wazīr, and son of I't-mād-uddaula. He was appointed governor of Kashmere by the emperor Shāh Jahān, which situation he held for several years. He died at Āgra in A.D. 1650, A.H. 1060.

I'tqad Khan (اعتقاد خان), the title of Mirzā Bahman Yār, the son of 'Asaf Khān and grandson of I'tmād-uddaula. He was raised to the rank of 4000 in the 25th year of Shāh Jahān, A.D. 1651, A.H. 1061, with the title of I'tqād Khān, which his father held for some time as well as his uncle the brother of 'Asaf Khān. In the 5th year of 'Alamgīr, A.D. 1662, A.H. 1072, the rank of 5,000 was conferred on him. In A.D. 1667, A.H. 1077, he proceeded to Dacca in Bengal, to visit his brother Shāista Khān, who was then governor of that province, and died there in the year A.D. 1671, A.H. 1082.

I'tqad Khan (اعتقاد خان), former title of Zulfiqār Khān Nasrat Jang.

I'tsam-uddin, Shaikh (اعتصام الدين شيخ), author of the *Shagarf Nāma-i-Wilāet*, being the travels of the author in Great Britain and France, some time before or after the year A.D. 1766, A.H. 1180. This work has been translated into English.

Izid Bakhsh, Mirza (ايزد بخش ميرزا). His poetical name was Rasā; he was the grandson of 'Asaf Khān Ja'far Beg, who was Wazīr to Jahāngīr. Izid Bakhsh was at first employed by the prince 'Azim Shāh, and then by his father the emperor 'Alamgīr in the capacity of Munshī. On the accession of Farrukh-siyar, he was disgraced by that emperor for having cast some reflections on his father Azim-ush-Shān on account of the battle which took place between 'Azim Shāh and his brother Bahādur Shāh. By the order of the emperor, the hairs of his mustaches were plucked out one by one, and afterwards he was cruelly murdered. This event took place about the beginning of the year A.D. 1713, A.H. 1125. His tomb is still to be seen in the compound of the Āgra College.

'Izzat (عزت), poetical name of (Shaikh) 'Abdul 'Azīz, which see.

'Izzat (عزت), poetical name of Sangham Lāl, which see.

'Izzat (عزت), poetical title of Jaikishun, which see.

'Izzat (عزت), poetical appellation of Shaikh Wajīh-uddīn.

'Izzat-uddaula Mirza Muhsin (عزت الدوله مرزا محسن), brother of Nawāb Safdar Jang. He was sent to Persia on an embassy to Nādir Shāh after his invasion of Hindūstān, by the emperor Muhammad Shāh.

[*Vide* Najaf Khān and Muhammad Qulī Khān.]

'Izz-uddaula Bakhtyar (عزالدوله بختيار), the son of Mu'izz-uddaula-ibn-Buya. He succeeded to the kingdom of 'Irāq the same day on which his father died, *viz.* Monday the 1st April, A.D. 967, 17th Rabī' II. A.H. 356. The Khalīf-al-Tāya Billāh in the year A.D. 974, gave him his daughter in marriage, on whom a dowry of one hundred thousand dīnārs was settled by her husband. He was a noble prince, and possessed such bodily strength that he could take an enormous bull by the horns and throw him to the ground. A contest which arose between him and his cousin 'Azd-uddaula relative to their respective possessions, caused a breach between them which led to a war, and on Wednesday the 29th May, A.D. 978, they met and fought a battle, in which 'Izz-uddaula was slain, aged 36 years. His head was placed on a tray and presented to 'Azd-uddaula, who is said, on seeing it, to have covered his eyes with his handkerchief and wept.

'Izz-uddin Abdul Aziz-bin-Abdus-Salam Damishqi, Shaikh (عزالدين عبدالعزيز بن عبدالسلام دمشقي شيخ), author of the *Shajrat-ul-Ma'ārif*. He died in the year A.D. 1261, A.H. 660.

'Izz-uddin Husain (عزالدین حسین).

He was created by Sulṭān Ibrāhīm of Ghaznī, Amīr Hājib (Lord Chamberlain), in which station he conducted himself so well, that the king gave him a princess of the house of Ghaznī in marriage. He rose daily in favour and estimation, till Sulṭān Masa'ūd, the son of Ibrāhīm, put him in possession of the principality of Ghōr. By the princess of Ghaznī he had seven sons entitled the seven stars. One of them, Fakhr-uddīn Masa'ūd, became king of Bāmyān. The second was Qutb-uddīn Muhammad, who married his cousin, a princess of Ghaznī, the daughter of Sulṭān Bahrām Shāh. The third was 'Alā-uddīn Hasan, prince of Ghōr, who destroyed Ghaznī (*circ.* A.D. 1152). Izz-uddīn during his life-time paid tribute to the Saljūqs as well as to the Ghaznavides.

'Izz-uddin Khalid Khani (عزالدین خالد خانی), author of the work called *Dalāil Fīrōz Shāhī*, which he translated into Persian by order of Fīrōz Shāh, from a Hindī book which treated on philosophy, astrology and divination.

J

Jabali (جبالی), the son of Ayham, last king of the tribe of Ghassān, who were Christian Arabs. He became a Muhammadan, and afterwards attempted to assassinate Umar, the second Khalīf after Muhammad. He died A.D. 673, A.H. 53.

Jabali (جبالی), surname of Abū 'Alī Muhammad-bin-'Abdul Wahāb, who was the master of the celebrated Abū'l Hasan al-Asha'rī, chief of the sect of the Asharians, and one of the four Imāms of Musalmanism.

Jabali (جبلی), poetical name of Abdul Wāsa, who was born in the mountains of Ghurjistān, hence his takhallus which means mountaineer. He found a patron in Bahrām Shāh of Ghaznī, and served Sulṭān Sanjar Saljūkī fourteen years. He died in A.D. 1160, A.H. 555, and left a Dīwān of Kasīdas.

[*Vide* 'Abdul Wāsa.]

Jabar (جبر), poetical name of Abū Mūsa Ja'far-al-Safī, which see.

Jabila Ram Nagar (جبیله رام نگر), a Hindū chief who was governor of Allahābād, and died there in the commencement of the reign of Muhammad Shāh in A.D. 1720, A.H. 1132. His nephew Girdhar was appointed governor of Audh after his death, and in A.D. 1724, A.H. 1136, the government of Mālwā was conferred on him, and the Sūbadārī of Audh was given to Burhān-ul-Mulk Sa'ādat Khān. Rāja Girdhar died in Mālwā during the invasion of Bājī Rāo Peshwa of the Mahrattas, acting in the name of the Rāja Sāhū, about the year A.D. 1729, A.H. 1142; he was succeeded by Dayā Bahādur his relation, who continued gallantly to resist the enemy, and fell in battle about the year A.D. 1730, A.H. 1143, when Muhammad Khān Bangash was appointed governor of that province.

Jabir (جابر بن عبدالله), the son of 'Abdullah, was a companion of Muhammad and a traditionist. He was present in nineteen battles which Muhammad fought, and died in the year A.D. 692, A.H. 73, aged 94 years.

Ja'far (جعفر), poetical title of 'Asaf Khān, commonly called Mirzā Ja'far Beg.

Ja'far (جعفر), a soldier by profession. He is the author of a Masnawī, which he dedicated to the emperor Shāh Jahān.

Ja'far-al-Barmaki (جعفر البرمکی بن یحیی), son of Ahia or Yahia and grandson of Khālid, the son of Barmak who was originally a fire-worshipper. He succeeded his father Ja'far as wazīr to the

Khalīf Hārūn-al-Rashīd; his grandfather having been wazīr to Abdū'l 'Abbās Saffāh, who was the first of all the Khalīfs who had a wazīr. This wazīr Ja'far, was a great favourite of Hārūn-al-Rashīd who gave him 'Abbāsa, his sister, in marriage, under the condition that he was to have no carnal connection with her, but he transgressed the command, for which the Khalīf ordered his head to be struck off. He also threw his brother Al-Fazl and his father Ahia into prison, and there left them to die. Ja'far was only 28 years old when he was executed, having been in the favour of Hārūn-al-Rashīd for the space of seventeen years. Ja'far was beheaded on Sunday the 29th January, A.D. 803, 1st Ṣafar A.H. 187, his body was gibbetted on one side of the bridge of Baghdād, and his head stuck up on the other. He was the ancestor of the "Barmecides."

Ja'far Ali Khan (جعفر علی خان), commonly called Mīr Ja'far, whom the English placed on the masnad as Nawāb of Bengal, Behar and Orissa, after the defeat and death of Nawāb Sirāj-uddaula, in June, A.D. 1757, Shawwāl A.H. 1170. He was, however, deposed in A.D. 1760, A.H. 1174, on account of alleged negligence in the affairs of his government, and was obliged to retire on an ample pension, when his son-in-law, Mīr Qāsim 'Alī Khān was raised to the masnad. This man after his elevation, intending to drive out the English from Calcutta, was defeated in a battle fought at Udwa Nala on the 2nd of August, A.D. 1763, 22nd Muharram, A.H. 1177, and expelled, and Mīr Ja'far was again placed on the masnad by the English. He died on Tuesday the 5th February, A.D. 1765, 14th Shabān, A.H. 1178, and his son Mīr Phūlwārī, who assumed the title of Najm-uddaula, was elevated to the masnad. Ja'far Alī's cemetery is at Murshidābād, where his Begam and his son Mīran are also buried.

Ja'far Barmaki (جعفر برمکی), see Ja'far-al-Barmakī.

Ja'far-bin-Abu Ja'far-al-Mansur (جعفر بن ابو جعفر المنصور), the Khalīf of Baghdād. His daughter Zubeda was married to Hārūn-al-Rashīd. He died in the year A.D. 802, A.H. 186.

Ja'far-bin-Abu Talib (جعفر بن ابو طلب) was the brother of 'Alī the son-in-law of the prophet. He was killed in a battle fought at Muta in Syria against the Roman army in A.D. 629, A.H. 8.

Ja'far-bin-Muhammad Husaini (جعفر بن محمد حسینی), author of the *Muntakhib-ut-Tawārīkh*, a very judicious abridgment of Oriental history from Adam down to Shāhrukh Mirzā, son of Amīr Taimūr. This work was dedicated to Bāisanghar Bahādur, third son of Shāhrukh, in A.D. 1417, A.H. 820. Many authors have compiled works under this title, one of which was written by Shaikh 'Abdul Qādir Badāonī.

Ja'far-bin-Tufail (جعفر بن طفیل), an Arabian philosopher in the 12th century, author of a romance, called the *history of Hai-ibn-Yokdhan*, in which he asserts that by the light of nature, a man may acquire a knowledge of things and of God.

[*Vide* Lempriere's *Universal Dictionary*, under Jaaphar.]

Ja'far Khan (جعفر خان), entitled "Umdat-ul-Mulk," was the son of Sādiq Khān Mīr Bakhshī, and sister's son and son-in-law of Yemīn-uddaula 'Asaf Khān, wazīr. He held the rank of 5000 under the emperor Shāh Jahān, was appointed prime minister by 'Alamgīr about the year A.D. 1662, A.H. 1073, and died in the 13th year of that emperor, A.D. 1670, A.H. 1081, at Dehlī. After his death the office of wizārat was conferred upon Asad Khān with the title of Asad-uddaula. It seems that after the death of Ja'far Khān his remains were transferred to Āgra, where his tomb is to be seen still standing on the right bank of the Jamna.

Ja'far Khan (جعفر خان), whose first title had been Murshid Qulī Khān, was appointed governor of Bengal by the emperor 'Alamgīr in A.D. 1704, A.H. 1116. He founded the capital of Murshidābād and named it after his original title. He was the son of a Brāhman, converted to Muhammadanism by Hājī Shafīa' Isfahānī. He died in the reign of the emperor Muhammad Shāh about the year A.D. 1726, A.H. 1138, and was succeeded by his son-in-law Shujā-uddīn (also called Shujā-uddaula). The following is a list of his dynasty:—

	A.D.
Murshid Qulī Ja'far Khān	1704
Shujā-uddīn, son-in-law of Ja'far Khān	1726
'Alā-uddaula Sarfarāz Khān	1739
Alahwardī Khān Mahābat Jang . . .	1740
Sirāj-uddaula, grandson of ditto . .	1756
Ja'far 'Alī Khān (dethroned in 1760) .	1757
Qāsim 'Alī Khān, son-in-law of ditto .	1760
Ja'far 'Alī Khān, restored in . . .	1763
Najm-uddaula, son of ditto	1764
Saif-uddaula, brother of Najm-uddaula	1766
Mubarik-uddaula	1769
Nāzim-ul-Mulk Wazīr-uddaula, (died April 28th, 1810)	1796
Sayyad Zain-uddīn 'Alī Khān, son of ditto	1810
Sayyad Ahmad 'Alī Khān	——
Humāyūn Jāh	1824
Mansūr 'Alī Khān, Nasrat Jang . .	1858

Ja'far Khan (جعفرخان بن صادق خان), son of Sādiq Khān, king of Persia of the House of Zend. He was recognised by the principal noblemen in Fars, after the death of 'Alī Murād Khān in 1785, and the people were forward in acknowledging his authority, but unable to resist his enemy 'Aqā Muhammad Khān, who now ventured to embrace a more extensive field for the exertion of his talents, and commenced his march against Isfahān. Ja'far Khān was treacherously murdered in 1788; his head was severed from his body, and cast before the citadel, the sport of children, and the outcasts of the city.

Ja'far Khan (جعفرخان), a nobleman who in the first year of the emperor Bahādur Shāh was appointed governor of Kashmere in the room of Nawāzish Khān A.D. 1707, A.H. 1119. He proved to be a bad governor and a mob set fire to his residence. He died in Kashmere of drink and excess A.D. 1709, A.H. 1121, and according to the record of his death, must be faring badly at present.

Ja'far Nasiri (جعفر نصیری), an author, who completed the work called *Latāif Khayāl*, in A.D. 1742, A.H. 1155, which was commenced by Mirzā Muhammad Sālah.

Ja'far Sadiq (جعفر صادق), or Ja'far the Just. He was the eldest son of Muhammad Bāqir, the grandson of Imām Husain. He is reckoned the sixth Imām; was born at Madina about the year A.D. 702, A.H. 83, and died in the same city under the khilāfat of Abū Ja'far Al-Manṣūr, in A.D. 765, A.H. 148. He was very famous for his doctrine amongst the Musalmāns, was invited to court by Al-Manṣūr, that he might profit by his counsel: Ja'far returned for answer, "Whoever has a view duly to this world, will not give you sincere advice, and he who regards the next, will not keep your company." He was buried in the cemetery of Al-Baqīa at Madina. The same tomb contains the bodies of his father, Imām Bākir, his grandfather 'Alī Zain-ul 'Abidīn, and his grandfather's uncle, Hasan, son of 'Alī. His mother's name was Umm Farwāh, daughter of Kāsim, the son of Muhammad, the son of Abū Bakr Sadīq, the first Khalīf after Muhammad. He is said to be the author of a book of fate called *Fāl Nāma.*

Ja'far Zatalli, Mir (جعفر زٹلی میر). a Sayyad of Nārnoul, contemporary with Mirzā Bedil. He served under prince 'Azim Shāh, the son of the emperor 'Alamgīr, who was slain in battle in A.D. 1707, A.H. 1019, Ja'far was the most celebrated humouristic poet of Hindūstān: his compositions are a mixture of Persian and Urdū. He is the author of a Shāhnāma in Rekhta. He was put to death in A.D. 1713, A.H. 1225, by order of the emperor Farrukh-siyar, on account of a satirical verse he had written on the accession of that emperor to the throne of Dehlī.

Jagat Goshaini (جگت گوشاینی), *Vide* Jodh Bāī.

Jagat Narayan (جگت ناراین), a Hindū poet who wrote some kasīdas in praise of Nawāb 'Asaf-uddaula of Lucknow, who died in A.D. 1797, A.H. 1212.

Jagannath, Raja (جگناتهه راجا), the son of Bhara Mal. He held the rank of 5000 in the time of the emperor Jahāngīr, about the year A.D. 1605, A.H. 1014.

Jagat Singh (جگت سنگه), the son of Makund Singh Haṛa, lived in the time of the emperor 'Alamgīr, A.D. 1659.

Jagat Singh (جگت سنگه), Rāja of Jaipūr or Jainagar, was the son of Rāja Partāp Singh, the son of Madho Singh, the son of Ishurī Singh, the son of the celebrated Rāja Jai Singh Sawāī, who lived in the time of the emperor Muhammad Shāh. Jagat Singh succeeded his father in A.D. 1803, and is said to have been an effeminate prince; though he died without issue, he was succeeded by Rāja Jai Singh, a posthumous son, believed supposititious.

Jagnath Kalanwat (جگناتهه کلاونت), a musician who was employed by Shāh Jahān, who conferred on him the title of Mahā Kabrāj.

Jaghtai (جغتای). *Vide* Chaghtaī Khān.

Jagnath (جگناتهه), brother of Rāja Bhagwān Dās. He distinguished himself in the war with Rāja Partāp Singh. He slew the renowned champion Rām Dās, son of Jahmah.

Jahan. *Vide* Benī Narāyan.

Jahan Ara Begam (جهان آرا بیگم), daughter of the emperor Shāh Jahān, by Mumtāz Mahal, daughter of 'Asaf Khān, wazīr; was born on Wednesday the 23rd March, A.D. 1614, 21st Ṣafar, A.H. 1023. One of the most beautiful examples of female modesty to be found in the annals of woman is recorded of this princess, celebrated in song and history as the heroic, the witty, the generous, the elegant, the accomplished, and the beautiful Jahān Ārā Begam. One night (26th March, A.D. 1644, 27th Muḥarram, A.H. 1054), as she was returning from her father's apartments to the harem, in one of the passages which connect the latter building with the body of the palace, her flowing drapery was unhappily ignited by the flame of a lamp. Her whole dress, which was of the finest muslin, was instantly in flames, and of course her life was in imminent peril; but, knowing that she was then within hearing of many young nobles of the court, she would not raise an alarm, lest they should run to her assistance, and behold her unveiled, or lay their hands upon her in order to extinguish the flames. Heroically enduring all the agonies which fire could inflict, she withheld her cries, and rushed forward until she reached the women's apartments, and there sunk upon the floor, almost lifeless. For a long period, no hopes were entertained of her recovery, but she was ultimately restored to health by an English physician named Gabriel Boughton who was then at Sūrat, and had been sent for by the emperor her father then in the Deccan, although her beauty was cruelly impaired. The emperor, in reward for Dr. Boughton's services, besides other favours, granted him, at his disinterested request, a patent for his countrymen to trade free of customs throughout his dominions. The large masjid of red stone adjoining the fort of Āgra near the Tripolia (now demolished) was built by her (or in her honour) in the year A.D. 1648, A.H. 1058, at a cost of five lacs of rupees. She died in the reign of her brother the emperor 'Alamgīr on the 5th September, A.D. 1680, 3rd Ramazān, A.H. 1092, and lies buried in the yard of the mausoleum of Nizām-uddīn Aulia at Dehlī. The name of Jahān Ārā will ever adorn the pages of history as a bright example of filial attachment and heroic self-devotion to the dictates of duty, more especially when we view it in contrast with the behaviour of her sister Roshan Ārā, who, by aiding the ambitious designs of Aurangzīb, enabled him to dethrone Shāh Jahān. The amiable and accomplished Jahān Ārā not only supported her aged father in his adversity, but voluntarily resigned her liberty and resided with him during his imprisonment in the fort of Āgra. Her tomb is of white marble, open at the top, and at the head is a tablet with a Persian inscription inlaid in black marble letters, to the following effect: "Let no one scatter over my grave anything but verdure, for such best becomes the sepulchre of one who had a humble mind." On the margin is written, "The perishable faqīr Jahān Ārā Begam, daughter of Shāh Jahān, and the disciple of the saints of Chisht, died in the year of the Hijra, A.H. 1092."

Jahan Bano Begam (جہان بانو بیگم), the daughter of Prince Murād, the son of the emperor Akbar. She was married to Prince Parwez, the son of Jahāngīr, by whom she had Nādira Begam, who was married to Dara Sheko, the eldest son of Shāh Jahān.

Jahandar Shah (جہاندار شاہ), surnamed Muhammad Mui'zz-uddīn, was the eldest son of the emperor Bahādur Shāh, and grandson of 'Alamgīr. He was born in the Deccan on Wednesday the 8th April, A.D. 1663, 10th Ramazān, A.H. 1073. The death of his father, which took place in February, A.D. 1712, Muḥarram, A.H. 1124, was followed by the usual struggle among his sons for the crown. The incapacity of Jahāndār Shāh, the eldest, had given a great ascendancy to the second whose name was Azīm-ush-Shān. He was supported by most of the nobility and of the army, but his other brothers joined their interests, and were kept together by the persuasions and false promises of Zulfikār Khān, the Amīr-ul-'Umra. Their concord was of short duration, and lasted only until the defeat and death of Azīm-ush-Shān; after which a bloody battle ensued between the three surviving brothers, two of whom, *viz.*, Jahān Shāh with his son Farkhunda Akhtar, and Rafī-ush-Shān, being killed. The subject of this notice, by the intrigues and support of the Amīr-ul-'Umra, remained undisputed master of the throne, and was crowned at Lāhore on Thursday the 10th April, A.D. 1712, 14th Rābī' I., A.H. 1124, with the title of Jahāndār Shāh. He was in himself a weak man, effeminately careful of his person, fond of ease, indolent, and totally ignorant of the art of government. He made the vast empire of Hindūstān an offering to the foolish whims of a public courtezan, named Lāl Kūnwār, thus vexing the minds of worthy subjects loyal to his family. He reigned only nine months, being defeated in a battle fought near Āgra, and afterwards taken prisoner and murdered in the month of January, A.D. 1713, Zil-ḥijja, A.H. 1124, by order of his nephew Farrukh-siyar (the son of the late Azīm-ush-Shān), who became emperor. His corpse was exposed to public view, and then interred in the platform before the mausoleum of the emperor Humāyūn at Dehlī. His mother's name was Nizām Bāī.

Jahandar Shah, Prince (جہاندار شاہ شہزادہ), the eldest son of the emperor Shāh 'Alam. Born about A.D. 1749. Appointed Regent by Ahmād Shāh Abdāli in 1761, after the overthrow of the Mahrāttās at Pāuipat, he administered the remains of the Empire until his father's restoration in 1771. His private appellation was Jawān Bakht (Mirza). In April, A.D. 1784, on account of the unsettled affairs of his father, he made his escape from Dehlī and repaired to Lucknow, where the British Governor of Bengal, Warren Hastings, had arrived to regulate the concerns between the wazīr, Asaf-uddaula, and the Company. He accompanied Mr. Hastings to Benares, which place he chose for his residence. He had an allowance of five lacs of rupees per annum from the Nawāb wazīr at the earnest request of Mr. Hastings. He died in Benares on the 31st May, A.D. 1788, 25th Shabān, A.H. 1202, after an illness of little more than twenty-four hours; aged about 39 years, and was buried with every honour due to his rank near the tomb of a venerated Muhammadan in Benares. The English Resident and principal people of the city attended his funeral. He left behind him three sons, whom, with the rest of his family, he recommended to the care of the English, under whom they still enjoy a comfortable asylum and allowance at Benares. Garçin de Tassy informs us, that there is a work of his in the Indian House, which has the title of *Bayāz Ināyet Murṣhidzada*. The narrative written by this prince, was translated by Col. Scott, and published in the appendix to Mr. Hastings' Review of the state of Bengal.

[Vide *Fall of the Moghul Empire*.]

Jahangir (جہانگیر), a cousin and husband of Sikandar (*q.v.*) Begam of Bhopal. His ancestor, Dost Muhammad, about the time of Aurangzīb's death, declared himself independent at Bhopal. Jahangir's uncle was the third Nawāb, on whose death his widow was declared Regent by the army, and his daughter Sikandar Begam, heir. She married Jahāngīr who died in the year A.D. 1845.

Jahangir (emperor) (جہانگیر نورالدین محمد), surnamed Nūr-uddīn Muhammad, was the eldest son of the emperor Akbar the Great; was born in the village of Sīkrī on Wednesday the 31st August, A.D. 1569, 17th Rabī' I. A.H. 977, and was named Mirzā Salīm on account of his coming into the world, as supposed, by the prayers of Shai<u>kh</u> Salīm Chishtī, a venerable Shai<u>kh</u> and dervish who resided in the village of Sīkrī, now called Fathapūr Sīkrī in the province of Āgra. His mother, who received the title of Mariam Zammam, was the daughter of Rāja Bihārī Mal Kachhwāhā. After the death of his father, which took place on the 16th October, A.D. 1605, he succeeded him by the title of Nūr-ūddin Muhammad Jahāngīr. He reigned 22 lunar years, 8 months and 15 days from the day of his father's demise; and died in camp on Sunday the 28th October, A.D. 1627, 28th Safar, A.H. 1037, on his way to Lāhore from Kashmere, aged 59 lunar years, 11 months and 12 days; and was interred in the suburbs of Lāhore in the garden of his favourite wife Nūr Jahān Begam. He was succeeded by his son Mirzā <u>Kh</u>urram, who took the title of Shāh Jahān. His favourite Sulṭāna Nūr Jahān, who survived him 18 years, is also buried in the mausoleum. Jahāngīr, after his death, received the title of "Jannat Makānī." It was to this prince that Sir Thomas Roe was sent as ambassador by King James I. Sir Thomas has given a good description of the grandeur of the court of Hindūstān; but very little notice is taken of this embassy in the chronicles of the East. In 1612, Jahāngīr permitted the Company to establish factories at Sūrat, Ahmadābād, and Cambay. Jahāngīr wrote his own memoir in Persian, called *Tūzak Jahāngīrī*, which has been translated by Major David Price, London, 1829, 184 pages 4to. It is also called *Jahāngīr Nāma*.

Jahangir Mirza (جہانگیر مرزا), the eldest son of Akbar Shāh II. king of Dehlī. He was, in consequence of having fired a pistol at Mr. Seton, the Resident at Dehlī, sent as a State prisoner to Allahābād, where he resided in the garden at Sulṭān <u>Kh</u>usro for several years, and died there in A.D. 1821, A.H. 1236, aged 31 years; a salute of 31 guns was fired from the ramparts of the fort of Allahābād at the time of his burial. He was at first interred in the same garden, and subsequently his remains were transferred to Dehlī, and buried in the court-yard of the mausoleum of Nizām-uddīn Aulia.

Jahangir Mirza (جہانگیر مرزا), the eldest son of Amīr Taimūr. He died before his father A.D. 1574, A.H. 776. His son's name was Pīr Muhammad, which see.

Jahangir Quli Khan (جہانگیر قلی خان), son of Khān 'Azim Mirza 'Azīz Kōka, served under the emperors Akbar and Jahāngīr, and died in the fifth year of Shāh Jahān A.D. 1631, A.H. 1041.

Jahangir Quli Khan, Kabuli (جہانگیر قلی خان کابلی), an amīr of the rank of 5000, who was appointed governor of Bengal by the emperor Jahāngīr, in A.D. 1607, A.H. 1016, and died there in A.D. 1608, A.H. 1017.

Jahanian Jahan Gasht, Makhdum (جہانیان جہان گشت مخدوم).

[*Vide* Shai<u>kh</u> Jalāl.]

Jahan Khatun (جہان خاتون), a famous lady, who after the death of her first husband was married to <u>Kh</u>wāja Amīn-uddīn, minister to Shāh Abū Is-haq, ruler of Shīrāz. She is said to have been a very beautiful woman, and a good poet.

Jahan Shah (Prince) (جہان شاہ شہزادہ), the third son of the emperor Bahādur Shāh. He was slain in the battle which took place at Lāhore, after the death of his father, between his brothers in March, A.D. 1712. His mangled body with that of his brother Rafī-ush-Shān and his son, was conveyed to Dehlī and interred without ceremony and pomp in the mausoleum of the emperor Humāyūn, the general receptacle of the murdered princes of the imperial family.

Jahan Shah Turkman (جہان شاہ ترکمان), son of Qarā Yūsaf Turkmān, was the brother of Sikandar Turkmān, after whose death in A.D. 1437, A.H. 841, the government of Azurbejān was conferred on him by Shāhrukh Mirzā, the son of Amīr Taimūr He held it till the death of that prince in A.D. 1447, A.H. 850, after which he conquered most part of Persia, and carried his arms as far as Dayārbikar, and fell in a battle which he fought against Hasan Beg, commonly called Uzzan Hasan, the ruler of that province, on the 10th November, A.D. 1467, 12th Rabī' II. A.H. 872, aged 70 years. He reigned more than 30 lunar years, and as he was slain in battle against Hasan Beg, the chronogram of the year of his death was found to contain the words "Slain by Hasan Beg."

Jahan Soz (جہان سوز), a title of Sulṭān 'Alā-uddīn Hasan Ghorī.

Jahi (جاهی), the poetical name of Ibrāhīm Mirzā (Sulṭān), which see.

Jahiz or **Aljahiz** (جاحظ یا الجاحظ), the surname of 'Abū 'Usmān 'Umar bin-Mahbūb Kana'āna, a man of great learning, but of a very eccentric tendency of mind. He wrote a book on the Commerce of the Arabians early in the third century of the Hijra entitled *Kitāb-al-Nazrat fil Tajārat*, which is frequently quoted by Nawarī. Jāhiz died A.D. 868, A.H. 255, at the age of 96 years.

Jaiapa (جیاپا سیندهیا), Sindhia, succeeded his father Rānoji Sindhia, the founder of the Sindhia family, in A.D. 1750, A.H. 1163, and was murdered in his tent in A.D. 1759, A.H. 1172. He was succeeded by his brother Mādhojī Sindhia.

Jai Chand (جی چند راٹھور), the last Rāṭhōr monarch of Kanauj. He ruled the country from Buxar to Kanauj and reigned about the Sambat year A.D. 1400, A.H. 1343. His favourite residence was near the city of Jounpūr which he had built in A.D. 1359, Sambat 1416. The present city of Jaunpūr was built by Fīrōz Shāh in the year A.D. 1370, A.H. 772, in honour of his uncle Fakhr-uddīn Muhammad Jūnān, the date of which is found in the words "Shahr Jaunpūr." According to Colonel Tod, Jaichand reigned about the 12th century of the Christian era, and one of his grandsons named Seojī, with a few retainers, planted the Rāṭhōr standard in Māṛwār in the year A.D. 1212.

Jai Chand (جی چند), a Rāja of Nagarkot or Kāngra, who lived in the time of the emperor Akbar.

Jaikishun (جی کشن), a Kashmīrī Brāhman whose poetical name was 'Izzat, was the agent of Nawāb Is-hāq Khān.

Jaimal (جیمل), a Rāja, famous in history as "the bravest of the brave." In A.D. 1568 Udai Singh, the son of Rana Sanka or Sanga, and the founder of the capital Udaipūr in Chittōr, came under the displeasure of the emperor Akbar. The recreant chief fled and left the defence of his capital Chittōr to Rāja Jaimal, who was killed by Akbar himself in the course of the siege, A.D. 1568.

Jaipal I. (جیپال اول), son of Hitpāl, Rāja of Lāhore of the Brāhman tribe, who reigned over the country extending in length from Sarhind to Langhan, and in breath from the kingdom of Kashmere to Multān. He was once defeated by Subaktagīn, the Sulṭān of Ghaznī, with great slaughter, and again on Monday the 27th November, A.D. 1001, by his son Sulṭān Mahmūd, when Jaipāl with fifteen of his principal chiefs, being his sons and brethren, were taken prisoners, and 5000 of his troops were slain on the field of battle. He was afterwards released by Mahmūd, but in compliance with a custom which prevailed among the Hindūs, that whatever Rāja was twice overpowered by strangers became disqualified to reign, he ordered a funeral pile to be prepared, and having set fire to it with his own hands, perished therein. He was succeeded by his son Anandpāl.

Jaipal II. (جیپال ثانی راجہ), Rāja of Lāhore, son of Anandpāl, whom he succeeded in A.D. 1013. He was routed in a great battle by Sulṭān Mahmūd in A.D. 1022, on the banks of the river Ravī; the result was the permanent occupation of Lāhore by a Muhammadan governor, and the appointment of a Viceroy of Lāhore by Mahmūd. Jaipāl fled to Ajmīr. This has been considered the foundation of the Muhammadan empire in India.

Jai Singh I. (Raja) (جی سنگھ اول راجہ), of the tribe of Kachhwāhā, commonly called Mirzā Rāja, was the son of Rāja Māhā Singh, the son of Partāp Singh, the son of Rāja Mān Singh. He served under the emperor Shāh Jahān, and was made governor over the conquered provinces of the Deccan about the year A.D. 1664, by the emperor 'Alamgīr. He was recalled to court in A.D. 1666, but died on the road, soon after his arrival at Burhānpūr, 28th Muharram, A.H. 1078. According to *Orme's Historical Fragments of the Mughul Empire*, Jai Singh died at Burhānpūr soon after the pretended revolt of Sulṭān Muazzim, the son of the emperor, and was said to have been poisoned by the procurement of 'Alamgīr. There never was a prince among the Rājpūts equal to him in accomplishments. He was competely learned in Hindī, and understood the Turkish, Persian, and Arabic languages. He left two sons, Rām Singh his eldest, and Kīrat Singh. The former was honoured after his father's death with the title of Rāja, and put in possession of his father's territories. Jai Singh had built several fine edifices at Āgra, of which no sign remains now, but the name and place on which the buildings stood is still called Jaisinghpūra.

Jai Singh II. Sawai (جی سنگه سوائی ثانی), a Rāja of the tribe of Kachhwāhā rājpūts, was the son of Bishn Singh, the son of Kishun Singh, the son of Rām Singh, the son of Mirzā Rāja Jai Singh. He is commonly called Mirzā Rāja Jai Singh Sawāī. He was the zamīndār or Rāja of a considerable territory in the province of Ajmir named Amer, but since the prince founded a new city called Jaipūr the Rājaship has also taken that name. Bishn Singh, the father of Jai Singh and Bijai Singh, died about the year A.D. 1693, Sambat 1750, and after his death the title of Rāja was bestowed on Jai Singh by the emperor 'Alamgīr with the rank of 1500, and subsequently with that of 2000. After the death of that emperor he espoused the cause of 'Azim Shāh, the son of 'Alamgīr, whilst his brother Bijai Singh aided Bahādūr Shāh, who on his accession to the throne conferred the rank of 3000 on the latter. Bijai Singh quarrelled with his brother for the Rāj; and the emperor, not willing to displease either, confiscated their estate, and appointed Sayyad Husain Alī Khān of Bārha, as Faujdār of that place. When the emperor marched to the Deccan to punish his brother Kāmbakhsh, A.D. 1708, A.H. 1120, Jai Singh, with the aid of Rāja Ajīt Singh Rāṭhōr, engaged the Faujdār in battle and having killed him took possession of the province. In the reign of Farrukhsiyar he was honoured with the title of Dhīrāj Rāja Jai Singh, and in the time of Muhammad Shāh with that of Sawāī (*q.d.* "exceptional"). In the year A.D. 1732, A.H. 1145, he was appointed governor of Mālwā. His love of science makes him one of the most remarkable persons of his nation. He built five observatories for astronomical studies, namely, at Dehlī, Banaras, Mathrā, Ujain and Jaipūr, and published a work on astronomy called *Zīj Muhammad Shāhī*. He also erected a Karavānsarai and market in every province of Hindūstān for the convenience of travellers at his own expense. After his death, which took place in September, A.D. 1743, 9th Shabān, A.H. 1156, three of his wives, with many concubines, burned themselves on his funeral pile. He was succeeded by his son Ishurī Singh, after whose death in A.D. 1760 Madho Singh his son succeeded him.

List of Kachhwāhā Rājas of Amer or Jaipūr.

Bhara Mal.	Jai Singh Sawāī.
Bhagwān Dās.	Ishurī Singh.
Mān Singh.	Madho Singh.
Bhāo Singh.	Pirthī Singh.
Mahā Singh.	Partāb Singh.
Jai Singh Mirzā Rāja.	Jagat Singh.
Rām Singh.	Jai Singh.
Bishun Singh.	Rām Singh.

Jai Singh III. (Raja) (جی سنگه ثالث), of the tribe of Kachhwāhā rājpūts and Rāja of Jaipūr, was a posthumous son of Rāja Jagat Singh, who died in A.D. 1818. Jai Singh was murdered by his kāmdār, whose name was Jhota Rām, in the Sambat year 1891, or in January, A.D. 1834, and his infant son Rām Singh succeeded him.

Jai Singh (جی سنگه), or Rānā Jai Singh of Udaipūr, a descendant of Rāna Sanka who lived in the time of the emperor Akbar, succeeded his father Rānā Rāj Singh, A.D. 1680, A.H. 1091.

Jalal Asir (جلال اسیر). *Vide* Asīr.

Jalal 'Azd, Sayyad (جلال عضد سید), a poet who flourished in the reign of Muhammad Muzaffar, ruler of Fars and his descendants. He is the author of a Dīwān.

Jalal Bukhari (جلال بخاری), or Sayyad Jalāl Bukhārī. He came to India from Bukhārā and became a disciple of Shaikh Bahā-uddīn Zikariā of Multān. He resided at Uchcha in Multān and died there. He had three sons, Sayyad Ahmad Kabīr, Sayyad Bahā-uddīn and Sayyad Muhammad. Sayyad Ahmad Kabīr, who succeeded his father as spiritual guide, had two sons, Makhdūm Jahanian, also called Shaikh Jahāl and Shaikh Sadar-uddīn, commonly called Rājū Qattāl.

N.B.—There is some confusion between this man and Shaikh Jalāl.

[*Vide* Shaikh Jalāl.]

Jalal Bukhari, Sayyad (جلال بخاری سید), a descendant of Sayyad Ahmad Kabīr and son of Sayyad Muhammad Bukhārī. He was born in the year A.D. 1594, 5th Jumāda II. A.H. 1003, and was highly respected by the emperor Shāh Jahān, who conferred on him the office of Sadārat (chief justiceship) of all India with the manṣab of 6000. He sometimes amused himself in writing poetry, and had adopted the word Razā for his poetical title. He died on the 25th May, 1647, o.s. 1st Jumādạ I. A.H. 1057, and is buried at Tājganj in Agra. His grandfather Sayyad Ahmad Kabīr lies buried at a place in Dehlī called Bijai Mandil. Jalāl Bukhārī left three sons, *viz.* Sayyad Ja'far, Sayyad Alī styled Razwī Khān, and Sayyad Mūsa, on whom high titles were conferred by Shāhjahān, and his eldest son Ja'far obtained the place of his father.

Jalal (Hakim) (جلال شروانی حکیم), a physician and poet, who was a native of Shīrwān. He flourished in the reign of Muhammad Muzaffar and his son Shāh Shujāa', rulers of Shīraz, both of whom reigned from A.D. 1353 to 1384. He is the author of a poem entitled *Gul-wa-Nauroz*, which he wrote in A.D. 1334, A.H. 734. He is also called Jalāl-uddīn Tabīb.

Jalali or Jalal (جلالی یا جلال), commonly called Sayyad-i-'Alām Jalāl or Jalālī, was a native of Ahmadabād, and his father and spiritual guide was Mīr Sayyad Jalāl bin-Hasan. He is the author of a Dīwān.

Jalali (جلالی), poetical name of Badr-uddīn.

Jalal, Shaikh (جلال شیخ). *Vide* Shaikh Jalāl, commonly called Makhdūm Jahāniān. He was the son of Sayyad Ahmad Kabīr, and grandson of Sayyad Jalāl Bukhārī the first.

Jalal, Shaikh (جلال شیخ تھانیسری), of Thanesar.
[*Vide* Shaikh Jalāl of Thanesar.]

Jalal - uddin Ahmad Afzal - bin - Muwaiyad (جلال الدین احمد افضل بن موید), an author.

Jalal-uddin Aldawani (جلال الدین الدوانی), author of several works.
[*Vide* Dawānī.]

Jalal-uddin Farahani (جلال الدین فرهانی), a poet.

Jalal-uddin Firoz Khilji (جلال الدین فیروز خلجی). *Vide* Fīrōz Shāh Khiljī.

Jalal-uddin Mahalli (جلال الدین محلی), see Jalāl-uddīn Sayūtī. He is sometimes called Jalāl-uddīn Muhammad bin-Ahmad-al-Mahlī.

Jalal-uddin Malikshah (جلال الدین ملکشاه). *Vide* Malikshāh.

Jalal-uddin Khan (جلال الدین خان), the brother of Mahmūd Khān, nawāb of Bijnōr, a rebel of 1857.
[*Vide* Sa'd-ullāh Khān.]

Jalal - uddin Muhammad Akbar (جلال الدین محمد اکبر). *Vide* Akbar.

Jalal-uddin Muhammad-bin-Asa'd Aldawani (جلال الدین محمد بن اسعد الدوانی). *Vide* Dawānī.

Jalal-uddin Purbi (جلال الدین پوربی), king of Bengal, whose original name was Jītmal, ascended the throne of Bengal on the death of his father Rāja Kans in A.D. 1392, A.H. 794. He became a convert to the Muhammadan faith and received the name of Jalāl-uddīn. He ruled with such justice that he became entitled to the appellation of the Nausherwān of the age. He reigned 17 years and died in A.D. 1410, A.H. 812, when his son Ahmad succeeded him.

Jalal-uddin Rumi, Maulana (جلال الدین رومی مولانا), commonly called Maulānā or Maulwī Rūmī, was the son of Bahā-uddīn Wald Balkhī, He is not less esteemed as a poet than as a metaphysician, and is the author of the astonishing work entitled the *Maṣnawī Maulwī Rūmī*. He founded an order of Derwishes or Sūfīs in the city of Conia (Iconium) in Asiatic Turkey. He was born at Balkh on the 30th September, A.D. 1207, 6th Rabī' I. A.H. 604, and died in the time of Abkā Khān on the 17th December, A.D. 1273, 5th Jumādạ II. A.H. 672. He was buried in a monastery at Conia, and his tomb was visited for many centuries by his devout countrymen, who considered his works as the effect of inspiration and only inferior to the Qurān. His Dīwān contains 30,000 verses, and his Maṣnawi more than 47,000. In his Dīwān, instead of his own title, he has inserted the name of Shams Tabrezī his master.

Jalal-uddin Sayuti (جلال الدين سيوطى), son of 'Abdur Rahmān bin-Abī Bakr, an Egyptian author of some merit, who died in A.D. 1505, A.H. 911. He is said to be the author of 400 works, amongst which are the commentary on the *Durr-Al-Munshūr*, and the last half of the *Tafsīr Jalālain*; the author of the other half was Jalāl-uddīn Mahalī, who died in A.D. 1450, A.H. 854. Another work of Sayūtī is called *Lubb-ul-Lubāb*. It is a dictionary of patronymic names, and of others under which the Arabic authors are much more frequently quoted than under their proper names. The confusion under which the Arabs labour to identify men known under different names, has induced them to prepare dictionaries for obviating this difficulty. Sāmānī (or Samnānī) in the sixth century of the Hijra published one, entitled *Fil Ansāb*, in which he does not only explain the sense and origin of these names, but also mentions with regard to every word the true names of the authors who have had them. This work was abbreviated in the succeeding century by Ibn-ul-Asīr, and this extract shortened by Sayūtī. There is another work of Sayūtī called *Kashfus-Salsala-un-Wasfuz Zalzala*, containing an account of all the earthquakes which took place from the year A.D. 713, A.H. 94, to his time. He wrote this work on the occasion of an earthquake in Egypt, with a view of shewing to his countrymen that earthquakes are ordained by God to punish men for their sins. This work was translated from the Arabic by Dr. A. Sprenger. Vide *Jour. As. Soc.* vol. xvii. part ii. p. 741. Sayūtī was also the author of the *Jāma'-ul-Jawāma*, containing a collection of Traditions, of which he afterwards made an abridgment and called it *Jāma'-us-Saghīr*.

Jalal-uddin, Sultan (جلال الدين سلطان), the son of Sultān Muhammad, surnamed Qutb-uddīn, Sultān of Khwārizm.

[*Vide* Muhammad (Sultān).]

Jalayer (جلاير), the name given to a race of kings of Baghdād, the first of whom was Hasan Buzurg, commonly called Hasan Jalāyer (*q.v.*).

Jalinus (جالينوس), "Galen," or Galenus, prince of the Greek physicians after Hippocrates.

Jam Afra (جام افرا). *Vide* Nāsir-uddīn Qabbācha.

Jama Baf (جاما باف). *Vide* Mīr Sayyad Jāma Bāf.

Jamal (جمال), the name assumed by Abū'l Fazl Muhammad, the son of 'Umar, the son of Khālid. He is the author of the *Sarāh*, a dictionary of Arabic words explained in Persian by him, being a translation of a very celebrated Arabic dictionary, entitled the *Sahāh*.

Jamal Faqih, Khwaja (جمال فقيه خواجه), a poet.

Jamali Khalifa (جمالى خليفه), surname of Is-hāq Karamānī, another author of the commentary called *Sharah Hadīs-ul-Arba'īn*. He died A.D. 1526, A.H. 933.

Jamali, Shaikh (جمالى شيخ). *Vide* Shaikh Jamālī.

Jamal Kili, Shaikh (جمال كيلى شيخ), an inhabitant of Qazwīn in Isfahān. He lived in the time of Sultān 'Alā-uddīn the Ismā'īlī, ruler of the fort of Alahmūt, who highly respected him. It is said that he secretly followed the tenets of the Ismā'īlīs, but the people thought otherwise. He died on Monday the 29th September, A.D. 1253, 4th Shawwāl, A.H. 651.

Jamal Khan (جمال خان), a mansabdār, or commander of 5000 horse, in the reign of Shāh Jahān. It is related that the emperor had ordered that all the ladies at court should provide precious stones and bring them to a market-place that he had erected, and there shew their wares publicly to all the noblemen at court, who were ordered to buy them at whatever prices the ladies put upon them; and that the king himself was to be a buyer, to put the greater honour on the new erected market. The ladies obeyed, and took their booths as they thought fit. On the market day the king and the noblemen came to market, and bought the jewels and other trifles the ladies had to dispose of. The king, coming to the booth of a very pretty lady, asked her what she had to sell. She told him she had one large fine rough diamond still to dispose of. He desired to see it, and he found it to be a piece of fine transparent sugar-candy of a tolerable diamond figure. He demanded to know what price she set on it, and she told him with a pleasant air that it was worth a lakh of rupees, or £12,500 sterling. He ordered the money to be paid, and falling into discourse with her found her wit was as exquisite as her beauty, and ordered her to sup with him that night in his palace. She accordingly went and stayed with him three nights and days, and then went back to her husband, whose name was Jamāl Khān. The husband received her very coldly, and told her that he would continue civil to her, but would never live with her again but in the same manner as if she was his sister. Upon which she went to the palace, fell at the emperor's feet, and told him what her husband had said. The king, in a rage, gave orders to carry her husband to the elephant garden, and there have him put to death by an elephant. The poor man was soon apprehended, and as they dragged him from his house he begged to have leave to speak to the king. A friend of his ordered the messengers of death to stop awhile, till he had acquainted the king with the request, which was accordingly done, and he was ordered to be carried into the court of the palace, that the king might hear what he had to say: and being carried thither, the king demanded what he would have. He answered that what he had said to his wife was the greatest honour which he was capable of doing his king, because, after he had honoured his wife with his embraces, he thought himself unworthy ever after to cohabit with her. The king, after pausing a little, ordered him to be unbound, and brought to his own room, where, as soon as he came, the king embraced him, and ordered a royal suit to be put upon him, and gave him command of five thousand horse more, but took his wife into his own harem.—*As. Jour.* vol. xxx. p. 215.

Jamal-uddin Ahmad, Shaikh (جمال الدین احمد شیخ), a celebrated Muhammadan saint of Hansī, and grandfather of Shaikh Qutb-uddīn Manawwar.

Jamal-uddin-Ataullah, 'Amir (جمال الدین عطا الله امیر), nephew of Sayyad Asīl-uddīn 'Abdullah. He is the author of the work called *Rauzat-ul-Ahbāb*.

[*Vide* Atāullāh bin-Muhammad al-Husainī Nishāpūrī.]

Jamal - uddin - bin - 'Abdul Razzaq (جمال الدین بن عبدالرزاق), a celebrated poet of Isfahān, and author of a Dīwān. He is the father of Kamāl-uddīn Ismā'īl and Mu'īn-uddīn 'Abdul Karīm, both of whom were also poets. Jamāl-uddīn died in A.D. 1192, A.H. 588.

Jamal-uddin Hasan bin Yusaf bin-al-Matahhir al-Hilli (جمال الدین حسن بن یوسف), entitled Shaikh al-'Allāma, is called the chief of the lawyers of Hilla. He is the author of the *Khulasat-ul-Aqwāl*. His legal works are very numerous and frequently referred to as authorities of undisputed merit. The most famous of these are—the *Talkhīs-ul-Marām*, the *Ghāet-ul-Ahkām* and the *Tahrīr-ul-Ahkām*, which last is a justly celebrated work. The *Mukhtalif-ush-Shia* is also a well-known composition of this great lawyer; and his *Irshād-al-Azhan* is constantly quoted as an authority, under the name of the *Irshād-i-'Allāma*.

[*Vide* Allāma al-Hilli.]

Jamal-uddin Husain Anju (جمال الدین حسین انجو), son of Fakhr-uddīn Kashmīrī, author of the Persian Dictionary called *Farhang Jahāngīrī*, which he dedicated to the emperor Jahāngīr in A.D. 1605, A.H. 1014. The author of the *Māsir-ul-'Umra* calls him Mīr Jamāl-uddīn Anjū, and says that he is a descendant of the Sayyads of Shīrāz, and came to the Deccan and thence to Āgra A.D. 1585, A.H. 993, in the time of Akbar, who raised him by degrees to the rank of 3000. In the reign of Jahāngīr the rank of 4000 was conferred on him with the title of 'Azd-uddaula.

Jamal-uddin-ibn-Malik (جمال الدین ابن مالک) author of an Arabic work on philosophy, called *Alfia*.

Jami (جامی نور الدین عبدالرحمان), the poetical name of Nūr-uddīn 'Abdur Rahmān, a celebrated Persian poet, the son of Maulānā Muhammad or Ahmad Isfahānī; was born on the 7th November, A.D. 1414, 23rd Shabān, A.H. 817, at a village in Herāt called Jām, from which he derived his poetical name "Jāmī." He was remarkably polite, of a very gentle disposition, and endued with such extensive learning that it was supposed there was not throughout the empire of Persia so complete a master of the language as himself. Even princes who were themselves men of erudition and exalted talents have lavished upon him the most unbounded praises and the highest honours. He was very intimate with Sultān Abū Sa'īd Mirzā of Herāt, who continued the friend of Jāmī so long as he lived. After his death, our poet enjoyed the same favours from his son and successor Sultān Husain Mirzā. He was a contemporary of the esteemed biographer Daulat Shāh, who recorded his fame in the Lives of the Persian poets, called *Tazkira Daulat Shāhī*. Jāmī was the author of more than 44 works. His poem on the Loves of Joseph and Zalikha is one of the finest compositions in the language; it contains about 4000 couplets. He is also the author of the book called *Nafahāt-ul-Ins*, a very celebrated abridgment of the Lives of the Sūfī Shaikhs, translated from the Arabic *Tabkāt-us-Sūfīa*, and dedicated to the celebrated wazīr 'Alīsher in A.D. 1476, A.H. 881. It may be here observed that the celebrated poets, as Hāfiz, Sādī, Jāmī, etc., were professed Sūfīs. The following are the works commonly known composed by Jāmī:—

These together are called Haft Aurang.
1. Silsilat-uz-Zahab, dedicated to Bayazīd II.
2. Salāmān-wa-Absāl.
3. Tuhfat-ul-Ahrār.
4. Sabhat-ul-Abrār.
5. Yūsaf-wa-Zalikha.
6. Lailī-wa-Majnūn.
7. Khirad-nāma.

Sikandar-nāma.
Nafahāt-ul-Ins.
Bahāristān
Fatūh-ul-Haramain.
Khurshed-wa-Māh.
Lawaeh Jāmī.
Shawāhid-ul-Nabūat.

Jāmī died at the advanced age of 81 lunar years, on Friday the 9th November, A.D. 1492, 18th Muḥarram, A.H. 898, mourned by the whole city of Herāt; his funeral expenses were defrayed by Sulṭān Husain, and a magnificent train of the most illustrious nobles accompanied his body to the tomb. 'Alīsher his friend laid the first stone of a monument which he caused to be raised to his memory, and his fame became immortal in the minds of his countrymen. He was also the author of a Tafsīr or commentary of some note. [*Salāman and Absāl* has been translated into English verse by the late Mr. Edward Fitzgerald.]

Jamila (جمیله), the poetical name of a Persian Poet.

Jamil-ibn-Mi'mar (جمیل ابن معمار), a celebrated Arabian poet who lived in the time of the khalīf 'Abdulmālik, and died in the year A.D. 701, A.H. 82. He was contemporary with two other famous poets named 'Umar the son of 'Abdullah and Kathīr Azza. Jamīl was the lover of Shanba, one of those pairs of lovers whose constancy and fidelity the orientals praise in their histories and poems.

Jamil-uddin Kashi (جمال الدین کاشی), author of the history called *Zubdat-ut-Tawārikh*. A work of the same title is mentioned under Shaikh Nūr-ul-Haq of Dehlī.

Jamil-uddin Muhammad Abdul Razzaq (جمال محمد الدین عبدالرزاق). *Vide* Jamāl-uddīn bin-'Abdul Razzāk.

Jamshed (جمشید) (also called Jām) was one of the ancient mythic kings of Persia, and the fourth of the First or Pishdādian dynasty. He is celebrated as the founder of Persepolis, which is to this day called Istakhr and Takht Jamshed. He is said to have introduced the solar year and ordered the first day of it, when the sun entered Aries, to be celebrated by a splendid festival. His country was invaded by Zuhāk, a Turanian king, and the unfortunate Jamshed was obliged to fly before the emperor. He was pursued by the agents of Zuhāk, through Sīstān, India, and China, and was at last seized and carried like a common malefactor before his cruel enemy, who ordered him to be placed between two boards and sawn asunder with the bone of a fish. We are told by Firdausī that his reign lasted 700 years. He is supposed to have flourished 800 years before the Christian era. His goblet, called Jām Jamshed and Jām Jam, was wondrous. A hundred marvellous tales are told of this celebrated cup, which used to dazzle all who looked in it, and has often been employed by the poets to furnish a simile for a bright eye.

Jamshed (جمشید), this title is sometimes given by the Musalmāns to king Solomon the son of David, and they say that his magic ring and throne possessed extraordinary powers, and his control was absolute over genii and men.

Jamshed Qutb Shah (جمشید قطب شاه), son of Qulī Qutb Shāh I. ascended the throne of Gōlkonḍa in the Deccan after the death of his father in September, A.D. 1543, Jumādạ II. A.H. 950. He reigned seven years and some months, and was succeeded by his brother Ibrāhīm Qutb Shāh in A.D. 1550, A.H. 957.

Jan (جان صاحب), or Jān Sāhib, poetical name of Mīr Yar 'Alī, who is the author of a Dīwān.

Janabi (جنابی), the surname of Abū Mūhammad Mustafa bin-Sayyad Hasan-al-Husainī, a celebrated historian and author of a work called *Tārīkh-al-Janābī*, of which the correct name is supposed to be *Bahr-uz-Zakhkhār*, the Swelling of the Sea; it comprises a general history from the beginning of the world to A.D. 1589, A.H. 997. It was originally written in Arabic, and translated by the author into Turkish. Janābī died in A.D. 1591, A.H. 999.

Jan Fishan Khan Bahadur (جان فشان خان بهادر نواب), Nawāb of Sardhānā. A Cabuli of Persian extraction who for his conspicuous loyalty during the mutiny of 1857, was ordered by Government to be rewarded with a pension of 1000 rupees a month in perpetuity to his male heirs, and a grant of confiscated villages of 10,000 rupees per annum to be conferred upon him with remission of one half of revenue for his life, and a quarter for two generations.

Jangez Khan (جنگیز خان). *Vide* Changez Khān.

Jani (جانی). There have been three authors of this name. The first, 'Abū 'Abdullah Muhammad ibn-Mālik Atāī, a native of Damascus; the second, Basar Jānī; and the third, Mansūr-bin'Umar-al-Adīb, a native of Isfahān, who died A.D. 1025.

Jani (جانی), the poetical name of Mirzā Jān, the father of Mirzā Jān Jānān.

Jani Begam (جانی بیگام), daughter of 'Abdul Rahīm Khān, Khān-Khānān, who was married to prince Dāniāl, the son of the emperor Akbar in A.D. 1599, A.H. 1007.

Jani Beg Sultan (جانی بیگ سلطان), son of 'Abdullah Khān Uzbak's sister. His son, Dīn Muhammad Khān, was raised to the throne of Samarqand after the death of 'Abdul Momim Khān, the son of 'Abdullah Khān Uzbak.

Jani Beg Turkhan, Mirza (جانی بیگ ترخان مرزا), ruler of Ṭhaṭṭa, succeeded his grandfather Mirzā Muhammad Bāqī, in the government of Ṭhaṭṭa, the remaining province of Sindh, in A.D. 1584, A.H. 993. Akbar Shāh who before the death of Muhammad Bāqī had gone to Lāhore, and had remained there for some years, expected a personal visit from Jānī Beg; but being disappointed he proceeded to take measures for the subjugation of that country. He therefore in the year A.D. 1591, A.H. 999. directed his commander-in-chief 'Abdul Rahīm Khān, the son of Bairām Khān, to proceed and occupy the place in his name. The first action took place on the 3rd November, A.D. 1591, 26th Muḥarram A.H. 1000, when the Sindhīs were totally defeated. Notwithstanding, daily skirmishes took place between the two armies; at last Mirzā Jānī Beg offered to acknowledge fealty to the emperor and to proceed to the presence. Shortly after 'Abdul Rahīm Khān celebrated the nuptials of his son Mirzā Īrich with the daughter of Jānī Beg, and after the rainy season of the year A.D. 1592, A.H. 1001, accompanied Mirzā Jānī Beg to the presence of Akbar, who created the latter a noble of the realm; and from that date the whole kingdom of Sindh reverted to the sovereignty of the empire of Dehlī. Mirzā Jānī Beg died at Burhānpūr in A.D. 1599, A.H. 1008, and the government of Ṭhaṭṭā was conferred on his son Mirzā Ghāzī.

Jan Janan, Mirza (جان جانان مرزا), son of Mirzā Jān, a learned Musalmān and a good poet, distinguished no less for the grace and spirit of his compositions than for the independent spirituality and anti-idolatrous nature of his sentiments. His poetical name was Mazhar; was born at Āgra about the year A.D. 1698, A.H. 1110, but resided at Dehlī. In the month of Muḥarram or 3rd January, A.D. 1781, 7th Muḥarram A.H. 1195, having expressed his contempt for a superstitious ceremony—the commemoration of the death of Husain—he was shot on the terrace of his own house, by a vindictive partizan of that martyr, and died on the 6th of that month, 10th Muḥarram, A.H. 1195. He was the author of a Dīwān.

Jan Muhammad, Munshi (جان محمد منشی), author of an Inshā or collection of letters which goes by his name.

Jannat Ashani (جنت آشانی), the title given to the emperor Humāyūn after his death.

Jannati (جنتی), a poetical name. [From Jannat = "Paradise."]

Jan Nisar Khan (جان نثار خان), title of Kamāl-uddīn Husain, an Amīr of 3000 under the emperor Shāh Jahān. At the time of his death he was governor of Sīstan, and died there A.D. 1639, A.H. 1049. [The word is the same as Janisary.]

Jan Nisar Khan, Nawab (جان نثار خان نواب), was brother-in-law to the wazīr Qamar-uddīn Khān who had married his sister. He was appointed Chakladār of the districts of Koṛā Jahānābād in the province of Allahābād, and was assassinated by Aṛārū Bhagwant Singh, a zamīndār of that place in A.D. 1731, A.H. 1144.

Jan Nisar Khan, Sayyad (جان نثار خان سید), son-in-law of the wazīr Qamar-uddīn Khān, was put to death, together with several others, by Nādir Shāh, on account of the resistance shewn by them in endeavouring to protect their family in the general massacre. This event took place in March, A.D. 1739, Ẓil-ḥijja A.H. 1151.

Janoji Bhosla (جانوجی بہوسله), the second Rāja of Beṛar, succeeded his father Rāghōjī Bhōsla in A.D. 1749, and died in A.D. 1772. He was succeeded by his younger brother Madhōjī Bhōsla.

[*Vide* Rāghōjī Bhōsla the first Rāja of Beṛar.]

Jansipar Khan Turkman (جان‌سپار خان ترکمان), an Amīr of 4000 in the reign of the emperor Jahāngīr. He was appointed governor of Allahābād in the first year of Shāh Jahān A.D. 1628, A.H. 1037, and died there the same year.

Jansipar Khan (جان‌سپار خان), second son of Mukhtār Khān Sabzwārī, an amīr of the reign of the emperor 'Alamgīr. At the time of his death he held the sūbadārī of Haidarābād, and died there in A.D. 1701, A.H. 1113.

Janubi (جنوبی بدخشان), of Badakhshān, a poet and punster who flourished about the year A.D. 1521, A.H. 927.

Januni (جنونی). *Vide* Junūnī.

Jarbardi (جاربردی), surname of Fakhr-uddīn Ahmad bin-Husan, an author who wrote the *Sharah Shāfia*, and the marginal notes on the *Kashshāf*. He died A.D. 1345, A.H. 746.

Jarir (جریر). *Vide* Jurīr which is the correct pronunciation.

Jarjis (جرجیس), George, and in particular St. George the martyr, very well known in the East, and even by the Muhammadans, who put him amongst the number of the prophets, and confound him with Elias.

Jarj Tamas (جارج طامس). *Vide* George Thomas.

Jarraz (جراز), the surname of Ahmad bin-Ibrāhīm-al-Tabīd-al-Afrīkī, who is often cited under the name of Ibn-Jarrāz. He was a physician and an author, and a native of Africa. He died A.D. 1009, A.H. 400.

Jarullah Zamakhshari (جارالله زمخشری), surname of Mahmūd bin-'Umar-al-Zamakhsharī, the Ma'tzalite of Zamakhshar, a village in Khwarizm. He was the author of an excellent commentary on the Qurān called *Kashshāf*, which he wrote in the name of one of the princes of Mecca. He obtained the surname of Jārullāh (or neighbour of God) on account of his residing for a long period at Mecca. He was born in A.D. 1074, A.H. 467, and died in the place of his nativity in the year A.D. 1142 or 1144, A.H. 537 or 539. He was also the author of many other works, such as—

Kitāb Fasl-dar-Nahr.
Asās-ul-Balāghat-dar-Loghat.
Rabī-ul-Abrār.
Fasūs-ul-Akhbar-wal-Farāez-dar-Ilm Farāez.
Raus-ul-Masāel-dur-Fiqa.
Sharah Abiāt Sebūya.
Mustaqazī-dur-Amsāl 'Arab.
Himam-ul-Arbia.
Sawāer-ul-Islām.
Shakāek-ul-Na'mām-wal-Kistās-dar-urūz.
Mu'ajjam-ul-Hadūd.
Manhāj-dar-Usūl.
Muqaddima-al-Adab.
Dīwān-ul-Tamsīl.
Dīwān-ul-Rasāel.
Dīwān-ush-Shua'rā.

Jassas (جصاص), surname of Shaikh Ahmad bin-'Alī Rāzī, which see.

Jaswant Rae (جسونت رای), a Hindū who was a poet and the author of a Dīwān, a copy of which was found in the Library of Tīpū Sulṭān.

Jaswant Rao Holkar (جسونت راو هلکر), the son of Takojī Holkar, and brother of Kāshī Rāo, whom he succeeded as chieftain of Indor about the year 1802. He made a rapid incursion into the Doab and committed some ravages, but was defeated and pursued by Lord Lake to the Sikh country as far as the Bias in 1803, and all his territories occupied by a British force. The whole was restored to him at the peace. He became insame in 1806, and Tulshī Bāī, his wife, was acknowledged regent. He died on 20th October, 1811, and was succeeded by Malhār Rāo III. his son, by a woman of low birth. Tulshī Bāī, however, continued to act as regent. On the 20th December, 1816, a company of armed men seized Tulshī Bāī, conveyed her forcibly to the neighbouring river of Sīpra, and cutting off her head on the bank, threw the lifeless trunk into the water.

Jaswant Singh (جسونت سنگه), Rāja of Jodhpūr Māṛwār, succeeded to the gaddī after the death of his father Takhat Singh in February, A.D. 1873, A.H. 1289.

Jaswant Singh (جسونت سنگه), son of Balwant Singh Mahārājā of Bhartpūr. He was born on the 28th February, 1851, and succeeded his father on the 16th March, 1853, when he was but two years old.

Jaswant Singh Bundela (جسونت سنگه بندیله), son of Rāja Indarman. He held a suitable rank in the army in the reign of the emperor 'Alamgīr, and died about the year A.D. 1687, A.H. 1099. After his death the zamindārī of Urcha was conferred on Bhagwant Singh his son, an infant of four years, with the title of Rāja, but he dying about the year A.D. 1693, A.H. 1105, there remained no one of the family of Rājas Shujān Singh or of his brother Indarman, to succeed him; upon which the Rānī Amar Kūnwar, grandmother to the deceased prince, placed on the Rāja Udaut Singh, who was descended from Madhukar Sāh, father to Rāja Bīr Singh Deo, which was approved by the emperor, who conferred on him the title of Rāja with a suitable mansab.

Jaswant Singh, Kunwar (جسونت سنگه کنور). *Vide* Parwāna.

Jaswant Singh, Maharaja (جسونت سنگه مهاراجه), the celebrated Rāja of Jodhpūr or Māṛwār, of the tribe of Rāṭhor Rājpūts, who acted so capital a part in the competitions of 'Alamgīr and his brother Dārā Shikōh whose cause he espoused, and was guilty of great impropriety. He was the son of Rāja Gaj Singh and a descendant of Rāo Māldeo. Jaswant Singh, subsequently became one of the best generals of 'Alamgīr, and held the rank of 7000 for several years. He died near Kābul about the 11th December, A.D. 1678, 6th Ẕil-qada A.H. 1089. He had built a fine house at Āgra on the banks of the Jamna, the surrounding walls of which are still standing, and his followers brought his infant children and his women who did not burn with him, towards their native country. Orders were sent by the emperor 'Alamgīr to conduct them to court, where, on their arrival, he insisted on the children being made Musalmāns. Upon this the rājpūt attendants determined to die rather than submit to this order, fled with their charge towards the Rāja's territories, and being pursued by the emperor's troops fought valiantly, and were mostly cut to pieces, but the women and infants arrived safe at Jodhpūr; they were, however, compelled to take refuge in the hills and the woods, and on the death of 'Alamgīr in A.D. 1707, regained their former possession. Ajīt Singh, his son (*q.v.*), was restored to the throne of his ancestors in the year A.D. 1711, by the emperor Farrukh-siyar who married his daughter.

Jat (جاٹ), a tribe of Hindū labourers who made no figure in the Mughul empire, as a nation, till the reign of 'Alamgīr, in whose expedition to the Deccan, they were first heard of as a gang of banditti, under an intrepid leader Chūrāman. They were then so daring as to harass the rear of the imperial army. After the death of that monarch they took advantage of the growing imbecility of the empire, and fortifying themselves, spread their depredations to the gates of Āgra. Mukham Singh, who after the death of Chūrāman commanded the Jāṭs and took upon himself the title of Rāja, but their power increased under Badan Singh and Sūrajmal (*q.v.*).

[*Vide* Chūrāman Jāṭ.]

Jawad 'Ali, Mirza (جواد علی مرزا), or more properly Mirzā Muhammad Jawād 'Alī Sikandar Hashmat Bahādur, son of Amjād 'Alī Shāh, and brother of Wājid 'Alī Shāh, the ex-king of Lucknow. He accompanied his mother, the dowager Queen of Audh, after the annexation of that country to the British possessions in 1856, to England, and died there after the death of his mother, on the 25th February, 1858, aged 30 lunar years. The body of the prince was transferred from London to Paris, to be buried on French soil beside that of the Queen his mother. An immense crowd assembled to witness the procession, attended by Mirzā Hamid 'Alī, the nephew of the deceased.

Jawahir Singh (جواهر سنگه). *Vide* Jouhar.

Jawahir Singh (جواهر سنگه), the Jāṭ Rāja of Ḍīg and Bhartpūr, was the son of Sūrajmal Jāṭ. He succeeded to the Rāj after his father's death in December, A.D. 1763, A.H. 1177, was secretly murdered in 1768, and was succeeded by his brother Rāo Ratan Singh, who did not escape suspicion of having been accessory to his brother's murder. Ratan Singh reigned ten months and thirteen days and was stabbed by a faqīr named Rūpānand, who pretended to transmute copper into gold.

[*Vide* Ratan Singh.]

Jawahir Singh (جواهر سنگه), a Sikh chief who became the minister of Mahārājā Dilīp Singh after the death of Hīrā Singh, and was murdered by the troops at Lāhore on the 21st September, A.D. 1845. Rāja Lāl Singh succeeded him.

Jawahir Singh, Maharaja (جواهر سنگه مهاراجه), son of Dhyan Singh and nephew of Mahārājā Gulāb Singh, ruler of Kashmere.

Jawan (جوان), the poetical appellation of Mirzā Qāzim 'Alī, a Hindūstānī lyric poet, attached to the college of Fort William. He is the author of an Urdū Dīwān and also of a Bārah Māsā, which he composed in A.D. 1802, A.H. 1217. He was alive in 1812.

Jawan Bakht, son of Shāh Alam. [*Vide* Jahānda Shāh II.]

Jawan Bakht, Mirza (جوان بخت مرزا), the youngest son of Bahādur Shāh, the ex-king of Dehlī, who accompanied his father to Rangoon in 1858, where he resided under surveillance at that place till his death in September, A.D. 1884. The British Government sanctioned the grant of a separate pension and an allowance of 250 rupees to his wife Zamanī Begam in A.D. 1873.

Jaweni (جوینی), whose proper name was Abū'l Ma'ālī 'Abdulmalik bin-'Abdullah, was a doctor and a very celebrated metaphysician, who bore the title of "Imām-ul-Haramain." He flourished in the reign of Mālik Shāh the Saljūkide, and professed the doctrine of Shūfa'ī at Naishapūr, where the famous Ghazzālī (*q.v.*) was his disciple. He was the author of several works, amongst which are the two following: *Tārīkh Jahān Kushāe* and *Aqīdat-ul-Nizāmiat*. He died in A.D. 1085, A.H. 478.

Jawera (جویره), one of the wives of Muhammad whom he married in the sixth year of the Hijra A.D. 627. She is said to have been a woman of great beauty, and was brought among the captives after a fight. She died about the year A.D. 670, A.H. 56.

Jawid Khan (جاوید خان), an eunuch and a great favourite of the emperor Ahmad Shāh and his mother, who raised him to the rank of an Amīr with the title of Nawāb Bahādur. Nawāb Safdar Jang, who was much digusted at the influence he had over the emperor, invited him to an entertainment, and murdered him during the banquet. This event took place on the 28th August, O.S. 1752, 28th Shawwāl, A.H. 1165.

Jawini (جوینی). *Vide* Moīn-uddīn Jawīnī.

Jayesi (جایسی). *Vide* Mālik Muhammad Jāyesī.

Jazari (جزری), surname of those who were born at a city called Jazarat-ul-'Umar, situated on the Tigris, to the northward of Nineveh and Mausal. One of the most illustrious amongst the men of letters this city has produced, was Ibn-Asīr ul-Shaibanī Majd-uddīn, who died A.D. 1209, A.H. 606, and of whom we have several works. [*Vide* Ibn-Asīr.]

Jenghis Khan (جنگهیز خان). *Vide* Changez Khān.

Jent Parkas, Lala (جینت پرکاس), author of a poem called *Dastūr Ishq*, containing the story of Sassī and Panūn in Persian verse. It is believed that his correct name is Jōt Parkāsh.

Jhankoji Sindhia (جهنکوجی سیندهیه), son of Jiāpa or Jyāpā Sindhia, was killed in the great battle which took place between Ahmad Shāh Abdālī and the Marhattas on the 14th January, N.S. 1761, at Panīpat.

Jhanko Rao Sindhia (جهنکو راو سیندهیه), also called Mukkī Rāo, on the death of Daulat Rāo Sindhia, was elected by his widow Bājī Bāī as Rāja of Gwāliar, and was put on the masnad on the 18th June, A.D. 1827; but being then only nine years of age, Bājī Bāī acted as regent. He assumed the reins of government in A.D. 1828, reigned 15 years and some months, and died on the 4th February, A.D. 1843, aged 24 years. He was succeeded by his adopted son Jīājī Sindhia the late Rāja of Gwāliar, with whom Bījā Bāī appears to have resided until the time of the mutiny.

Jiaji Rao Sindhia (جیاجی راو سیندهیه), the late Rāja of Gwāliar, whose name in full is, Mahārājā 'Alī Jāh Jīājī Rāo Sindhia, was the adopted son of Jhanko Rāo Sindhia, on whose death he succeeded to the government on the 4th February, A.D. 1843. His installation took place on the 20th January, A.D. 1844, when Lord Ellenborough visited the fort. He was made G.C.B. and a British General, and died in A.D. 1888.

Jiji Begam (جیجی بیگم), the wet-nurse of the Emperor Akbar, and the mother of Mirzā 'Azīz Kōka, who was raised to a high rank by the emperor with the title of Khān 'Azim. She died in the year A.D. 1599, A.H. 1008. The emperor carried her coffin on his shoulders and shaved his beard and moustache.

Jiwan, Mulla (جیون ملا). *Vide* Mulla Jīwan.

Jodha Rao (جودھا راو), Rāja of Mārwār, and a descendant of Seojī, the grandson of the celebrated Jaichand, the last Rāthōr monarch of Kanauj. He, in the year A.D. 1432 founded the modern capital of Jodhpūr, to which he transferred the seat of the government from Mandōr.

Jodh Bai (جودہ بائی) (whose maiden name appears to be Jagat Goshaini and also Bālmatī), was the daughter of Rāja Udai Singh of Jodhpūr or Mārwār, the son of Rāja Maldeo. She was called Jodh Bāī, because she was a princess of Jodhpūr. She was married to Mirzā Salīm (afterwards Jahāngīr) in A.D. 1585, A.H. 994, and became the mother of the Emperor Shāh Jahān, who was born in A.D. 1592, A.H. 1000, at Lāhore. She poisoned herself at Āgra in A.D. 1619, A.H. 1028, and was buried in Sohāgpūra, a village founded by her, where her palace and tomb are still to be seen in a ruinous state.

Jogi, Sultan (جوگی سلطان). *Vide* Muhammad Jogī.

Josh (جوش), poetical title of Ahmad Hasan Khān, who is familiarly called Achchhe Sāhib. He was living in Lucknow in A.D. 1853, A.H. 1269, and was the author of an Urdū Dīwān. He was the son of Nawāb Muqīm Khān, the son of Nawāb Muhabbat Khān, the son of Hāfiz Rahmat Khān (*q.v.*).

Joshish (جوشش), poetical title of Muhammad Hasan or Muhammad Rōshan of Patna, who flourished in the time of the Emperor Shāh 'Alam.

Jot Parkash, Lala (جوت پرکاش لالا), a Hindū Kāyeth and an author. This appears to be the correct for Jent Parkās, which see.

Jouhar (جوهر), the poetical appellation of Jawāhir Singh, a Hindū, who was the pupil of the poet Mulla Nātiq of Naishāpūr. He was the author of a Dīwān in Persian and Urdū, and was living in A.D. 1851, A.H. 1267.

Jouhar (جوهر), the poetical name of Munshī Sewa Rām of Shāhjahānpūr, who flourished in the time of Akbar Shāh II. and was the author of several works in Persian, such as *Jouhar-ul-Talīm*, *Jouhar-ul-Tarkīb*, etc.; the last-named work he wrote in A.D. 1820, A.D. 1235.

Jouhari Farabi (جوهری فارابی), surname of Abū Nasr Ismā'īl bin-Hammād. Although he was a Turk, yet he made such progress in the Arabic language, which he studied in Mesopotamia and Egypt, that he was styled "Imām-ul-Lughāt," or master of the language. He is the author of a very large Arabic Dictionary entitled *Sahāh-ul-Lughāt*, the purity of the tongue. He is often called after this work, "Sāhib-us-Sahāh," or the author of the Sahāh. He is commonly called Fārābī or Fārābī-al-Turkī, because he was a native of Fārāb in Turkistān. He died A.D. 1002, A.H. 393. Some authors say that his death took in A.D. 992, A.H. 382.

Jouhari Zargar (جوهری زرگر), a poet who flourished in the time of Sulaimān Shāh and Arsalān Shāh of the house of Saljūq. He is the author of a poem containing the story of "Amīr Ahmad and Mahastī."

Jounpur (جونپور), kings of. *Vide* Khwāja Jahān.

Jouzi (جوزی). *Vide* Abū'l Faraj ibn-Jauzī.

Juban Choban or **Jovian, Amir** (جوبان امیر), the tutor and general of the armies of Sultān Abū Sa'īd Khān, son of Aljāitū, king of Persia. He was put to death by Mālik Ghayās-uddīn Kart in November, A.D. 1327, Muharram, A.H. 728, by order of the Sultān, because he refused to give him his daughter Baghdād Khātūn in marriage.

[*Vide* Baghdād Khātūn.]

Juber (جبیر), a companion of Muhammad.

Judat (جودت), a poetical appellation.

Jugal Kishor (جگل کشور), an inhabitant of Dehlī whose poetical name was Sarwat. He was wakīl to the Nāzim of Bengal for several years.

Jughtai (جغتای). *Vide* Chaghtai.

Juji Khan (جوجی خان) was the eldest son of Chingiz Khān the Tartar, from whom he had received for his share the wide regions of Qapchāq; but this prince died a few months before his father in A.D. 1226, and left his territories to his son Batū Khān, who conquered Russia and Bulgaria, ravaged the countries of Poland, Moravia, and Dalmatia, and had marched into Hungary in order to attack Constantinople, when death ended his victorious career.

Junaid Baghdadi, Shaikh (جنيد بغدادی شیخ), a celebrated ascetic whose father was a glass-blower, of Nahāwand. He was born and brought up at Baghdād, and became one of the best disciples of Shāfa'ī, but followed the system of Sūfiān Sourī. He made thirty pilgrimages to Mecca, alone and on foot. He died at Baghdād in the year A.D. 911, A.H. 298, and was buried near the tomb of his master and maternal uncle, Sarī Saqtī.

Junaid, Shaikh or **Sultan** (جنيد سلطان), third in descent from the celebrated Shaikh Safī-uddīn Ardibelī, and grandfather of Shāh Ismā'īl I. of Persia, founder of the Safwī dynasty which was extirpated by Nādir Shāh. He was a Sūfī or mystic philosopher, but being expelled from Azurbejān by the Turkmān ruler Jahān Shāh, established himself in Dayarbikar. In the latter period of his life, he went to Shīrwān with his disciples, and was killed in A.D. 1456, A.H. 860, in a conflict with the troops of Amīr Khalīl-ullāh, ruler of that province.

[*Vide* Ismā'īl I. Safwī. The book called *Nukkāt Bedil*, written by Mirzā Bedil, contains his Memoirs.]

Juna Shah (جونا شاه), a brother of Muhammad Tughlaq Shāh, king of Dehlī, who built the city of Jounpūr, which goes after his name.

Jununi (جنونی), author of a poem called *Latāef Shouq*, a collection of entertaining and witty tales, which he composed in the year A.D. 1689, A.H. 1100, and dedicated to the emperor 'Alamgīr, but many were rather obscene.

Jununi, Maulana (خنونی مولانا), a sprightly satirical poet of Herāt who flourished in the time of Amīr Ghayās-uddīn Sultān Husain, son of Fīroz Shāh, about the 9th century of the Hijrī era.

Jurat (جرات), poetical title of Kalandar Bakhsh, a son of Yehia Amān and pupil of Hasrat. He was first supported by Nawāb Muhabbat Khān, but in A.D. 1800, A.H. 1215, he was in the service of prince Sulaimān Shikōh at Lucknow. While still in the prime of life he became blind, but became a good musician and an excellent player on the guitar. It appears that Jurat and his family had the family name of Yehia Mān, because they said that they were descended from Yehia Rāi Mān, who resided in a street at Dehlī which is close to the Chāndnī Chouk, and is still called the Rāi Mān Street. It is also stated that this Rāi Mān was executed by Nādir Shāh. Jurat died in the year A.D. 1810, A.H. 1225. He was the author of an Urdū Dīwān and two Masnawis.

Jurir (جریر), or Abū Hazrā Jarīr ibn-Atiya, was one of the greatest and most celebrated poets. He flourished in the reign of the Khalīf 'Abdulmalik of the house of Umayya, and received from him a handsome salary. He was once rewarded by the prince for a single panegyrical ode, with 100 camels, 18 slaves, and a silver jug. Abū'l Faraj ibn-ul-Jauzī places the death of Jurīr in the year A.D. 729, A.H. 111, aged 80 years.

Jurir-ibn-'Abdullah (جریر ابن عبدالله), a general of the army in the time of 'Umar, the second Khalīfa after Muhammad.

Jurjani (جرجانی), which see.

Jurjani (جرجانی), a native of Jurjān or Georgia. Al-Sayyad-ush-Sharīf Abū'l Hasan (or Husain) 'Alī was thus surnamed because he was born in that country. He was one of the most celebrated Musalmān doctors; was born in A.D. 1339, A.H. 740, and died at Shīrāz A.D. 1413, A.H. 816. There have been several other authors of this surname, as Al-Sharīf-al-Husainī, a son of the first, who was a famous physician and lived in the time of Atsiz, Sultān of the Khwārizmiāns. Also Abū'l Wafa, a mathematican, Abū Bakr bin-'Abdul Kāhir, a grammarian, and Muhammad Jirjānī, a valiant captain of the Sultān of Khwārizm, and governor of the city of Herāt, who was killed in defending that place against Tūlī Khān, son of Changez Khān.

Juya (جویا), poetical appellation of Mirzā Darāb Beg, a poet whose native country was Kashmere. He died in A.D. 1706, A.H. 1118, and is the author of a Dīwān. The poetical name of his brother Mirzā Kāmrān, was Guyā.

K

Ka'b (كعب ابن زهير), or Kaa'b ibn-Zahīr of Mecca, was an Arabian poet, and author of the *Qasāed Bānat Sa'ād*, a poem in Arabic held in the highest estimation, containing a panegyric on Muhammad. A translation of part of it may be found in Sir William Jones's second volume of the *Asiatic Researches*. The author was a Jewish Rabbi, contemporary and opponent of Muhammad, and had written some satirical verses upon him; but afterwards being desirous of a reconciliation with the prophet, he wrote the above poem, which had the desired effect. Some authors say that he died in the first year of the Hijra, that is, A.D. 622, A.H. 1. But, according to Ockley's *History of the Saracens*, "Kaa'b came in the ninth year of the Hijra, and made his peace with Muhammad with a poem in his praise." By this it appears that he was living in A.D. 631. He is said to have assisted Muhammad greatly in the compilation of the Qurān. *Vide* Wilkin's *Biographical Dictionary under Coab*.

Ka'b-al-'Ahbar (كعب العهبر), a famous traditionist of the tribe of Hamyar, who embraced Islāmism in the reign of 'Umar, and died A.D. 652, A.H. 32, during the reign of 'Usmān.

Kabir (كبير), a celebrated Hindī poet, by trade a Musalmān weaver, who, according to the Akbar-nāma, was contemporary with Sikandar Shāh Lōdī, king of Dehlī. Kabīr was a Sūfī or Deist of the most exalted sentiments and of benevolence unbounded. His poems, which are still universally esteemed, inculcate the purest morality, good will and hospitality towards all men, and breathe so fine a spirit of toleration that both Hindūs and Musalmāns contend for the honour of his having been born of their religion. From the disinterested, yet alluring, doctrines his poems contain a sect has sprung up in Hindūstān, under the name of Kabīr Panthī, who are so universally esteemed for veracity and other virtues, among both Hindūs and Musalmāns, that they may be with propriety considered the Quakers of the country. The time of Kabīr's death seems involved in equal obscurity with the manner of his decease and burial. They relate that he lived a long time at Kāsī (Benāras) and Gayā, and sojourned also at Jaganāth, where he gave great offence to the Brāhmaṇs by his conduct and tolerant doctrine. When stricken in years, he departed this life among a concourse of his disciples, both Musalmāns and Hindūs. He is buried at Ratanpūr, where his tomb is said to be seen to this day.

Kabir, Shaikh (كبير شيخ), surnamed Bala Pīr, was the Shaikh Qāsim Qādirī, whose tomb is at Chunār. Shaikh Kabīr died at Qanauj on Monday the 4th November, A.D. 1644, 12th Ramaẕān, A.H. 1054, where a splendid mausoleum was built on his tomb by one of his sons, named Shaikh Mahdī, who died A.D. 1677, A.H. 1088, and is also buried there.

Kabir-uddin (كبيرالدين بن تاج الدين عراقى), son of Tāj-uddīn 'Irāqī, lived in the time of Sulṭān Alā-uddīn, king of Dehlī, and wrote a book on his conquests.

Kabuli Mahal (كابلى محل), a wife of Shāhzahan.

Kachhwaha, the title of the Rājas of Amber or Jaipūr. *Vide* Bharā Mal.

Kafi (كافى), surname of Taqī-uddīn 'Alī bin-'Alī, an Arabian author who died in the year A.D. 1355, A.H. 756. His name is spelt in some of our biographical dictionaries, Cafi.

Kafi or **Kami** (كافى), poetical name of Mirzā 'Alā-uddaula, who flourished in the reign of the emperor Akbar.

[*Vide* Alā-uddaula (Mirzā) and Kāmī.]

Kafi (كافى), whose proper name was Kifāyet 'Alī, was a poet of Muradābād, and author of the *Bahār Khuld*, which is a translation of the *Shimāel*.

Kafi-ul-Kafat (كافى الكفات). *Vide* Ibn-'Ibād.

Kafur, Malik (كافور ملک), a favourite eunuch of Sulṭān 'Alā-uddīn Khiljī, king of Dehlī, probably of Hindū birth, who was raised to the high rank of wazīr. After the kings death the first step which the traitor took was to send a person to Gwāliār, to put out the eyes of Khizir Khān and Shādī Khān, the two sons of the deceased Sulṭān. His orders were inhumanly executed. He then placed Shahāb-uddīn, the king's youngest son (a boy of seven years of age) on the throne, and began his administration; but was assassinated thirty-five days after the king's death, in January, A.D. 1317, A.H. 716, when Mubārik, the third son of the king, was raised to the throne.

Kahaj Tabrezi, Shaikh (كهج تبريزى شيخ), a learned Musalmān who held the office of Shaikh-ul-Islām at Tabrez during the reign of Sulṭān Awis and Sulṭān Husain of Baghdād. He was the author of a Dīwān.

Kahi (كاهى). *Vide* Qāsim Kāhī.

Kaikaus (كيكاوس), second king of the Kayanian dynasty of Persia, was the son of Kaiqubād. He was vain and proud; and appears to have been in continual distress from the unfortunate result of schemes that his ambition led him to form, but which he wanted ability to execute. His life is connected with a thousand fables, which though improper in this place form excellent materials for Firdausī, who has given, in his history of this period, the extraordinary and affecting tale of the combat between Rustam and his unknown son, Suhrāb, who is killed by his father. This part of the Shāh-nāma has been translated in English verse by J. Atkinson, Assistant Surgeon on the Bengal Establishment, and member of the Asiatic Society in 1814. Kaikāūs, when grown old, resigned his crown in favour of his grandson Kaikhusro, the son of Siāwakhsh (corresponds to Cambyses I.; *vide* Achaemenis).

Kaikaus, Amir (كيكاوس امير), grandson of Qābūs, prince of Jurjān, and one of the noblemen who lived at the court of Sulṭān Maudūd, the grandson of Sulṭān Mahmūd of Ghaznī. He is the author of the work called *Qābūsnāma*.

Kaikhusro (كيخسرو), the third king of the Kayanian dynasty of Persia and the grandson of Kaikāūs. He ascended the throne in the lifetime of his father, who resigned the crown in his favour. He had several battles with Afrāsiāb the king of Tūrān, who was at last defeated, taken prisoner, and slain. Soon after these events Kaikhusro resolved to devote the remainder of his life to religious retirement: he delivered over Kābul, Zābulistān and Nīmrōz to Rustam, as hereditary possessions; and resigned his throne to Luhrāsp, the son-in-law of Kaikāūs and his own son by adoption and affection. After these arrangements, he went, accompanied by some nobles, to a spring which he had fixed upon as the place of his repose. Here he disappeared, and all those that went with him were destroyed on their return by a violent tempest. He lived 90 years and reigned 60.

Kaikhusro (كيخسرو), the son of Sulṭān Muhammad Khān, governor of Multan, who was the eldest son of Sulṭān Ghayās-uddīn Balban, king of Dehlī. After his father's death in A.D. 1285 he was made governor of Multān by his grandfather, and after his decease in A.D. 1286 was murdered at Rohtak by Malik Nizām-uddīn, wazīr of Kaiqubād, who ascended the throne as king of Dehlī.

Kaiomurs (كيومرس), the first monarch of Persia, according to all Muhammadan writers. This king is stated to have reclaimed his subjects from a state of the most savage barbarity. They say he was the grandson of Noah, and the founder of the first dynasty of Persian kings, called Pishdādian. His son Siāmak was killed in one of the battles with the barbarians or Devs; and when that monarch carried Hoshang, the infant son of Siāwak, to share in the revenge he meant to take upon his enemies, his army was joined by all the lions, tigers and panthers in his dominions, and the Devs were routed and torn to pieces by the auxiliaries, who had left their native forest to aid the just king. After this victory, Kaiomurs returned to his capital Balkh. He reigned 30 years, and was succeeded by his grandson Hoshang.

The following is a list of kings of the first or Pishdādian dynasty:—

1. Kaiomurs.
2. Hoshang.
3. Tuhmurs, surnamed Deoband.
4. Jamshed, reigned at Persipolis.
5. Zuhāk, surnamed Alwanī.
6. Faridūn, restored by Kawa.
7. Manūchchr.
8. Naudar or Nauzar.
9. Afrāsiāb, king of Turkistān.
10. Zāb, brother of Naudar.
11. Garshāsp.

Kaiqubad (كيقباد), the founder of the second or Kayanian dynasty of the kings of Persia, was a lineal descendant of Manūchchr, according to some accounts he was his great-grandson. This prince had retired to the mountain of Alburz, from which place he was brought by Rustam the son of Zāl and proclaimed king of Persia. He committed the administration of government into the hands of Zāl, whose son Rustam was appointed to lead the Persians against the dreaded Afrāsiāb, who had again passed the Oxus and invaded Persia. In this battle Rustam overcame Afrāsiāb, and afterwards a peace was concluded, by which it was agreed that the Oxus should remain as it had been heretofore, the boundary between the two kingdoms. Kaiqubād lived some time after this in peace: he is said to have reigned 120 years, and to have left four sons—Kaikāūs, Arish, Rūm and Armen. To the former he bequeathed his throne, and enjoined all the others to obey him.

Legendary list of kings of the second or Kayanian dynasty.

1. Kaiqubād.
2. Kaikāūs.
3. Kaikhusro.
4. Luhrāsp.
5. Gushtāsp or Darius.
6. Isfandiar.
7. Bahman or Ardisher Darāzdast (Xerxes).
8. Humai, daughter and wife of Bahman.
9. Dārāb or Dārā, son of Bahman.
10. Dārā, son of Dārāb (Darius overcome by Alexander the Great).

[*Vide* Achaemenes.]

Kaiqubad (كيقباد), surnamed Mu'izz-uddīn, the grandson of Sultān Ghayās-uddīn Balban, whom he succeeded in A.D. 1286, A.H. 685, on the throne of Dehlī in the absence of his father Nāsir-uddīn Baghrā Khān, who was then in Bengal. In the year A.D. 1287, A.H. 686, his father, having heard the state of affairs at Dehlī, marched from Bengal to visit and advise his son. They met on the banks of the Ghāgra at Behār, and the whole scene was so affecting that almost all the court shed tears. On this occasion the celebrated poet Amīr Khusro wrote the poem called the *Kirān-us-Sadain*, or the conjunction of the two planets. Kaiqubād was assassinated in A.D. 1288 through the instigation of the Fīrōz Malik Khiljī, who ascended the throne by the title of Jalāl-uddīn Fīrōz Shāh Khiljī, and became the first Sultān of the second branch of the Turk dynasty called Khiljī.

Kaiuk Khan (كيوك خان). *Vide* Kayūk.

Kakafi (كاكفي). *Vide* Ahmad bin-Idrīs. He is mentioned in some of our Biographical Dictionaries under the name of Cakafī.

Kakafi (كاكفي). *Vide* Ahmad bin-Idris.

Kalb Ali Khan (كلب علي خان), Nawāb of Rāmpūr in 1869-70.

Kalb Husain Khan, Mirza (كلب حسين خان مرزا), Deputy Collector of Etāwah, the son of Ahtarām-uddaula Dabīr-ul-Mulk Kalb 'Alī Khān Bahādur. He is the author of four Dīwāns and a biography called *Shaukat Nādirī*. He was living in A.D. 1864, A.H. 1281.

Kalhana (كلهانه), a Brāhman and author of a history of Kashmere, called *Rājatarangini*. There are four chronicles of the history of Kashmere written in Sanskrit verse; the first by Kalhanā, bringing the history of Kashmere to about 1148 after Christ; the second, a continuation of the former, by Jaūarājā, to A.D. 1412; the third, a continuation of the second, by Srivara, a pupil of Jaūarājā, to A.D. 1477; and the fourth, by Prajyābhatta, from that date to the conquest of the valley by the emperor Akbar. The author of the work, the Pandit Kalhanā, of whom we merely know that he was the son of Champaka, and lived about A.D. 1150, under the reign of Siñha Deva of Kashmere—reports that before entering on his task he had studied eleven historical works written previously to his time, and also a history of Kashmere by the sage Nīla, which seems to be the oldest of all. Kalhanā begins his work with the mythological history of the country; the first king named by him is Gonarda, who, according to his chronology, would have reigned in the year B.C. 2448, and the last mentioned by him is Siñha Deva, about 1150 after Christ.

Kali Das (كالى داس), a celebrated Hindū poet traditionally said to have lived towards the commencement of the Christian era, and to have been one of the nine splendid gems that adorned the court of Rāja Bikarmājīt (Vikrāmaditya). Some say that he flourished in the time of Rāja Bhōj (1040-90 A.D.). He wrote the *Nalodia* for the purpose of exhibiting his unbounded skill in alliteration. In four books, containing on the average fifty-four stanzas each, he has given such illustrations of this art as can never be surpassed. This work has been published in Europe, with a Latin translation by a continental scholar, Ferdinandus Benary. No reason can be imagined why Kālī Dās should again write the history of Nala and Damayanti, after it had been so elegantly written in flowing verse by Vyāsa Deva, except that he intended in this simple story to shew forth his ingenuity in alliteration. He is also the author of the poem called *Kumāra Sambhava*, and of another called *Mahā Nātak*.

Kalim (كليم), the poetical name of Abū Tālib Kalīm, which see.

Kalim-ullah (كليم الله), a title of Moses the prophet.

Kalim-ullah (كليم الله), the last king of the Bahmanī dynasty of Kulbarga or Ahmadābād Bīdar in the Deccan. He was expelled in A.D. 1527 by Amīr Barīd his wazīr, who mounted the throne and took possession of that kingdom.

Kalim-ullah (كليم الله), author of a work called *Kashkol Tasauwaf* an exposition of the mystical phrases of the Sūfīs.

Kali Sahib (کالی صاحب), **surname** of Ghulām Nasīr-uddīn, the son of Maulānā Qutb-uddīn, the son of Maulānā Fakhr-uddīn. Although he was the Murshid or spiritual guide of the king of Dehlī, he preferred the habit of a Derwish. He died in A.D. 1852, A.H. 1268.

Kamal (کمال), a poet of Isfahān.

Kamal (کمال), poetical title of Mīr Kamāl 'Alī of Gaya Mānpūr. He wrote Persian and Rekhta verses, and is the author of a large work called *Kamāl-ul-Hikmat*, on philosophy, and one called *Chahārdah Darūd*, *i.e.* the fourteen blessings, containing an account of the Imāms. He died in A.D. 1800, A.H. 1215, and the chronogram of the Hijrī year of his death is contained in the word Dareghā.

Kamal Ghayas, Maulana (کمال غیاس مولانا شیرازی), of Shīrāz, a poet and physician who flourished in the time of Ibrāhīm Sultān.

Kamal Khan, Gikhar (کمال خان گکهر) prince of the Gikhars, was the son of Sultān Sārang, the son of Malik Kalān II. the son of Malik Kalān I. the son of Malik Khar, who was the founder of the principality of the Gikhars. Their country lies among the mountains between Bhat and Sindh, which formerly belonged to the government of Kashmere. Malik Kalān II. had several battles with Sher Shāh, but was at last taken prisoner and put to death by that monarch, and his son or grandson Kamāl Khān imprisoned in the fortress of Gwāliar. He was, however, after some years released by Salīm Shāh the son of Sher Shāh, but during his confinement his uncle Sultān Ādam had taken possession of the country. In the first year of the reign of Akbar he was introduced to that monarch and was employed in his service. He by degrees rose to the rank of 5000, and was afterwards put in possession of his dominions by that emperor, and Sultān Ādam his uncle taken prisoner and made over to Kamāl Khān, who put him in confinement, where he died. Kamāl Khān, who became tributary to Akbar, died in A.D. 1562, A.H. 970.

Kamal Khujandi (کمال خجندی). *Vide* Kamāl-uddīn Khujandī.

Kamal Qazi (کمال قاضی). *Vide* **Abūl-Fath Bīlgrāmī.**

Kamal-uddin 'Abdul Razzaq, Shaikh (کمال الدین عبدالرزاق شیخ), is the author of several works, among which are the following: *Tafsīr Tāwīlāt*, *Kitāb Istilāhāt Sūfīa*, *Sharah Fasūs-ul-Hikam*, *Sharh Manāzib-ul-Sābirīn*, etc. He was a contemporary of Shaikh Rukn-uddīn 'Alā-uddaula. He died in A.D. 1482, A.H. 887.

[*Vide* 'Abdul Razzāq.]

Kamal-uddin Isma'il (کمال الدین اسمعیل), son of Jamāl-uddīn Muhammad 'Abdul Razzāq, of Isfahān, a celebrated poet of Persia, styled Malik-ush-Shu'ārā, that is to say, king of the poets, and is the author of a Dīwān. In the year A.D. 1237, 2nd Jumāda I. A.H. 635, on the 21st December, when Oqtāī Khān, the son of Changez Khān, invaded Isfahān and massacred the inhabitants of that city, he also fell a martyr. It is said that he was tortured to death by the Mughuls, who expected to find hidden property in his house.

Kamal-uddin Khujandi, Shaikh (کمال الدین خجندی شیخ), was a great Shaikh and lyric poet, and a contemporary of Hāfiz, who, though they never saw each other, much esteemed him, considering him and Salmān Sāwajī as amongst the first poets of their time. He is commonly called Kamāl Khujandī, born at Khujand, a town situated in one of the most beautiful and fertile districts of Persia. After having made the pilgrimage to Mecca he settled at Tabrez, a place which he found extremely agreeable during the reign of the princes of the family of Jalāyer. The principal personages of Tabrez became his pupils, and he led a life of literary ease and enjoyment; but when Tuqtamish Khān surprised Tabrez, Shaikh Kamāl was made prisoner, and was carried to Serai in Kapjāk by order of Mangū Khān the grandson of Changez Khān, where he remained four years, after which he was permitted to return to Tabrez, near which city the Sultān Awes Jalāyer built him a house. Kamāl did not sing the praise of princes in Qasīda, nor did he write Masnawis, but only Ghazals and fragments. He died in the year A.D. 1390, A.H. 792, and was buried at Tabrez. A MS. of the Dīwān of Kamāl, which had been the property of a Sultān, is possessed by the Imperial Library at Vienna, and is a great treasure as a specimen of splendid writing, and also for the superbly executed miniatures which adorn it, illustrating the poems. These pictures are not more than a square inch in size: there are two on each side of the concluding verse; and though so small, represent with the greatest correctness, either allegorically or simply, the meaning of the poet. —*Dublin University Magazine*, 1840.

Kamal - uddin Masa'ud, Maulana (كمال الدين مسعود مولانا شروانی), of Shīrwān, a celebrated logician and author of the marginal notes on the *Sharah Hikmat Āin.*

Kamal-uddin Muhammad-al-Siwasi (كمال الدين محمد السواسی), commonly called Humām and Ibn-Humām, author of a commentary on the *Hidāya* entitled *Fath-ul-Qādir lil 'Ajiz-al-Faqīr.* It is the most comprehensive of all the comments on the *Hidāya,* and includes a collection of decisions which render it extremely useful. He died in A.D. 1457, A.H. 861.

[*Vide* Humām and Ibn-Humām.]

Kamal-uddin Muhammad bin-'Abdul Muna'im Jujari, Shaikh (كمال الدين محمد بن عبدالمنعم جوجاری شیخ), an author who died in A.D. 1484, A.H. 889.

Kamal-uddin Muhammad, Khwaja (كمال الدين محمد خواجه), ibn-Ghayās-uddīn Shīrāzī, was a physician and a poet, and flourished in the time of Sultān Ibrāhīm Mirzā. For his poetical title he used Ibn-Ghayās.

Kamal-uddin Musa bin-Yunas bin-Malik (كمال الدين موسیٰ بن یونس بن ملک), name of an Imām, who was one of the most celebrated Musalmān doctors.

Kamal-uddin Shah (كمال الدين شاه). *Vide* Lutf-ullāh.

Kam Bakhsh (prince) (کامبخش شهزاده), youngest son of the emperor 'Alamgīr, a vain and violent young man, who had received from his father the kingdom of the Deccan, but as he refused to acknowledge the sovereignty of the emperor Bahādur Shāh, his eldest brother, and struck coin in his own name, that monarch, after attempting in vain to win him over by concessions, marched against him with a powerful army to the Deccan, and defeated him in a battle near Haidarābād, where Kām Bakhsh died of his wounds on the same day in the month of February or March, A.D. 1708, Zil-hijja, A.H. 1119. His mother's name was Udaipūrī Muhal, and he was born on the 25th February, A.D. 1667, 10th Ramazān, A.H. 1077.

Kami (کامی), whose proper name is Mirzā Alā-uddaula Qazwīnī, was the son of Mīr Yahya bin-'Abdul Latīf, and is the author of the work called *Nafāis-ul-Māsir,* a Biographical Dictionary of Persian poets. It contains notices of about 350 poets in alphabetical order. Most of them flourished in India during the reign of Akbar, to whom the book is dedicated. It was finished in A.D. 1571, A.H. 979, but there occur much later dates in it. He is supposed by some to have died in A.D. 1563, A.H. 971, and by others in A.D. 1573, A.H. 981, but the latter date appears to be correct. The discrepancy arises from the chronogram of his death, in which the number of the last word is considered by some to be 60 and by others 70, a difference of ten years.

[*Vide* Yahya bin-'Abdul Latīf.]

Kamil (کامل), author of a poetical work, entitled *Chirāghnāma.* It consists of Ghazals all of which rhyme in Chirāgh (lamp), and the first letter of every verse of the first Ghazal is ا or A, of the second ب or B, and so on.

Kamran Mirza (کامران مرزا), second son of the emperor Bābar Shāh, and brother to the emperor Humāyūn, who, after his accession to the throne in A.D. 1530, A.H. 937, conferred on him the government of Kābul, Qandahār, Ghaznī and the Panjāb. He was deprived of his sight by Humāyūn when at Kābul in the year A.D. 1553, A.H. 960, on account of his repeated offences, and continually raising disturbances in the government. The operation was performed by piercing his eyes repeatedly with a lancet. Kāmrān bore the torture without a groan until lemon-juice and salt were squeezed into his eyes, when he called out "O Lord my God! whatever sins I have committed I have been amply punished in this world, have compassion on me in the next." Kāmrān eventually obtained permission to proceed to Mecca, where he resided three years and died a natural death in A.D. 1556, A.H. 964. He left three daughters and one son, named Abū'l Qāsim Mirzā, who was imprisoned in the fort of Gwāliar, and put to death by order of the emperor Akbar, his cousin, in the year A.D. 1565, A.H. 973.

Kamran Shah (کامران شاه), the present ruler of Herāt, is the son of Mahmūd Shāh, the son of Timur Shāh, the son of Ahmad Shāh Abdālī. On the death of his father, Mahmūd Shāh (in A.D. 1829), he succeeded him on the throne of Herāt.

Kapurthala Rajah. *Vide* Nihal Singh.

Karam (کرم), author of the *Harbae Haidarī,* a history of Alī and his son Husain in verse, composed in A.D. 1723, A.H. 1135.

Karim (کریم), poetical name of Mīr Muhammad Kāzim the son of Fikr. He flourished in the time of Kutbshāh of the Deccan, and is the author of a Dīwān.

Karim Khan (کـریـم خـان), the murderer of Mr. W. Fraser, Commissioner of Dehlī. *See* Shams-uddīn Khān (nāwab).

Karim Khan (کریم خان), a Pindarī chief, who surrendered himself to the British Government on the 15th February, 1818, and received for his support the Tālūqa of Burhīapār in the Gorakhpūr district, which was held by his descendants up to the mutiny in 1857.

Karim Khan Zand (کریم خان زند).

The history of Persia, from the death of Nādir Shāh till the elevation of 'Aqā Muhammad, though it occupies nearly half a century, presents no one striking feature, except the life of Karīm Khān, a chief of the tribe of Zand. He collected an army chiefly composed of the different tribes of Zand and Mafī, defeated the Afghāns in several engagements, finally drove them out of the country, and secured to himself the kingdom of Fārs, or the southern division of Persia, while Khurāsān partially remained in possession of the descendants of Nādir Shāh; and the countries bordering on the Caspian Sea were retained by Muhammad Hasan Khān Qājār, ruler of Māzindarān, the great-grandfather of 'Aqā Muhammad Shāh Qājār. Karīm Khān, after subduing his enemies, enjoyed independent power for twenty-six years; and during the last twenty, *viz.* from 1759 to 1779, he had been, without a competitor, the acknowledged ruler of Persia. His capital was Shīrāz. He died at an advanced period of life on the 2nd March, A.D. 1779, 13th Ṣafar, A.H. 1193, being nearly 80 years of age. After his death Zakī Khān assumed the reins of government, and was assassinated two months after. Sādiq Khān, brother of Karīm Khān, took possession of Shīrāz after the death of Zakī Khān, and was put to death on the 14th March, A.D. 1781, 18th Rabī' I. A.H. 1195, by 'Alī Murād Khān, who now became the sovereign of Persia, and died on the 11th January, A.D. 1785, 28th Ṣafar, A.H. 1199. After his death Lutf 'Alī Khān reigned for some years at Shīrāz. He was defeated in 1794 and slain afterwards by 'Aqā Muhammad Khān Qājār, who took possession of the throne of Persia.

Karim - uddin, Professor in Āgra College, published in 1845 an Urdū Anthology which became very popular. It is prefaced by a dissertation.

Karshasp (کرشاسپ), or Garshāsp, the son of Zū, and the last king of the first or Pishdādian dynasty of Persia.

[*Vide* Zū.]

Kart (کرت), kings of the dynasty of. *Vide* Shams-uddīn Kart I.

Kashfi (کشفی), the poetical name of Shāh Muhammad Salāmat-ullāh. He is the author of a Dīwān in Persian, which was printed and published before his death in A.H. 1279.

Kashfi (کشفی), takhullus of Mīr Muhammad Sālah, who flourished in the reign of the emperor Jahāngīr, and is the author of a Tarjīhband called *Majmūa' Rāz*, which he composed in A.D. 1621, A.H. 1030, containing 270 verses. He died in the year A.D. 1650, A.H 1060, at Āgra, and lies buried there.

Kashi, Mulla (کاشی ملا), surname of Kamāl-uddīn Abdū'l Ghanam 'Abdul Razzāq bin-Jamāl-uddīn, a celebrated doctor, placed amongst the Musalmān saints, was author of several works. He died young about the year A.D. 1320, A.H. 720.

Kashi Rao Holkar (کاشی راو هلکر), the eldest of the four sons of Tukājī Holkar, after whose death in A.D. 1797 disputes arose between Kāshī Rāo and his brother Mulhār Rāo, and both repaired to the court of the Peshwā at Pūna, where, on their arrival, Daulat Rāo Sindhia, with a view of usurping the possessions of the family, espoused the cause of Kāshī Rāo, and made a sudden and unexpected attack in the month of September on Mulhār Rāo, whom he slew with most of his adherents. After this, Sindhia pretended to govern the possessions of the Holkar family in the name of Kāshī Rāo, whom he kept in a state of dependence and appropriated the revenue to his own use. A long contest ensued between Daulat Rāo and Jaswant Rāo Holkar, the brother of Kāshī Rāo, and continued till the year A.D. 1802, when Jaswant Rāo appears to have taken possession of Indor, the territory of his father.

Kashifi (کاشیفی), the poetical name of Maulānā Husain bin-Alī, also known by that of Wāez or the preacher. He wrote a full commentary on the Qurān in the Persian language. He was a preacher at the royal town of Herāt in Khurasān. He died in A.D. 1505, A.H. 910.

[*Vide* Husain Wāez.]

Kashmere, kings of. *Vide* Shāh Mīr.

Kasir (کثیر عزا), or Kathīr Azzā, one of the celebrated Arabian poets of the court of the Khalīf 'Abdul Malik. *Vide* Jamīl.

Kathir (کثیر). *Vide* Kasīr.

Katibi (کاتبی ترشیزی), poetical name of Maulānā Shams-uddīn Muhammad bin-'Abdullah-al-Naishāpūrī and Tarshīzī. He wrote a very beautiful hand, on which account he assumed the title of "Kātibī." He came to Herāt in the reign of Bāisanghar Mirzā, and afterwards became one of the best poets of the courts of the prince Sultān Mirzā Ibrāhīm of Shīrwān, in whose praise he once wrote a panegyric, and received from that prince a present of 10,000 dīnars. We have several of his works in the Persian language. In the latter period of his life he fixed his residence at Astrabād, and died there in A.D. 1435, A.H. 839. His works, which contain five poems, are called *Majma'-ul-Bahrain*, the story of Nāsir and Mansūr, which may be read in two different metres; *Dad Bāb*, *Husnwa Ishq* and *Bahrām and Gulandām*.

Kaus. *Vide* Kaikāūs.

Kayuk Qaan (کیوک قاآن), or Kayūk Khān, was the son of Oqtāī Qāān, the son of Changez Khān. He succeeded his father in January, A.D. 1242, A.H. 639, to the kingdom of Tartary, and his uncle Jaghtai or Chaghtai Qāān to the kingdom of Transoxiana, Badakhshān and Kāshghar. He reigned one year, and died about the beginning of A.D. 1243, A.H. 640, when Mangū Qāān, the eldest son of Tūlī Khān, the son of Changez Khān, succeeded him and reigned nine years.

Kazim Ali Khan (کاظم علی خان حکیم). A physician of the Lodi period, who made a garden at Agra on the banks of the Jamna opposite Rām Bāgh. Some traces of this garden still remain called Hakīm ka Bagh. It was made in the year A.D. 1551.

Kazim, Hakim (کاظم حکیم), a physician who had the title of Hāziq-ul-Mulk and was the son of the Mujtahid Haidar Alī Tushtarī Najafī. He is the author of the work called *Farah-nāma Fātima*, which he composed in A.D. 1737, A.H. 1150.

Kazim, Hakim (کاظم حکیم). *Vide* Sāhib.

Kazim Zarbaya (کاظم زربایه), a Persian poet who died at Isfahān in the year A.D. 1541, A.H. 948.

Kerat Singh (کیرت سنگه), second son of Mirzā Rāja Jaisingh. He served under the emperor 'Alamgīr, and after his father's death was honoured with the rank of 3000. He was living in the Deccan A.D. 1673, A.H. 1084.

Kesari Singh (کیسری سنگه), Rāja of Jaipūr who lived in the time of Muhammad Shāh, emperor of Dehlī.

Kesho Das Rathor, Raja (کیشو داس راتهور راجه), who gave his daughter in marriage to the emperor Jahāngīr, by whom he had Bahar Bano Begam.

Khadija (خدیجه), Muhammad's wife. Although this is the correct pronunciation of the name, yet see under Khudyja.

Khadim (خادم), the poetical name of Nazar Beg, a poet. He was a pupil of Muhammad Azfal Sābit, and died some time before the year A.D. 1760, A.H. 1174.

Khadim (خادم), the takhallus or poetical appellation of Shaikh Ahmad 'Alī of Sandīla and son of Muhammad Hājī. He is the author of several works, amongst which is one called *Anīs-ul-'Ushshāq*, an anthology. He flourished about the year A.D. 1752, A.H. 1165.

[*Vide* Hasan bin-Muhammad Sharīf.]

Khaef Kashmiri, Maulana (خایف کشمیری مولانا), a poet.

Khafi (خافی), poetical title of Mīr Abūl Hasan Khān, author of a poem called *Chahār Dervish*.

Khafi Khan (خافی خان), whose original name is Muhammad Hāshim, was the author of the work called *Tārīkh Khāfī Khān*, which is also called *Muntakhib-ul-Lubāb*, an excellent history of Hindūstān, commencing with the invasion of the emperor Bābar Shāh, A.D. 1519, A.H. 925, and continued to the accession of Muhammad Shāh; comprehending the whole of the reign of the emperor 'Alamgīr, also those of Bahādur Shāh, Jahāndār Shāh, Farrukhsiyar, and Rafī-ud-darjāt; all of which, except the first ten years of 'Alamgīr's reign,

Colonel Dow was obliged to pass over, for want of documents. There are few works in the Persian language (says Stewart) so worthy of being translated. The author was a person of good family, who resided at Dehlī during the latter part of the reign of 'Alamgīr, where he compiled his history; but in consequence of the well-known prohibition of that monarch he was obliged to conceal his intentions, and for some other causes did not publish it till the 14th year of the emperor Muhammad Shāh, A.D. 1732, A.H. 1145. The work was well received, and the author was honoured with the title of Khāfī Khān, or the "concealed."

[English extracts may be found in Dowson's *Elliot*, vol. vii.]

Khair - uddin Muhammad, Maulvi (خیرالدین محمد مولوی), author of the history of Jaunpūr.

Khair-un Nisa Khatun (خیر النسا خاتون), a poetess, who was the daughter of the Qāzī of Samarqand, and lived at Khurāsān.

Khaju (خاجو). *Vide* Khwājū.

Khaki (خاکی), author of the *Munāqib-ul-'Arifīn.* This book contains the memoirs of three very celebrated Sūfī Shaikhs, *viz.* Khwāja Bahā-uddīn, Burhān-uddīn, and Jalāl-uddīn. The former of these was reputed a great saint, and was the founder of an Order of Sūfīs, distinguished by the title of Naqshbandī. He died at Harāfa in Persia, A.D. 1453, A.H. 857. The two others were authors of commentaries on the Qurān, and were held in much veneration. The above-mentioned book was dedicated to Bahā-uddīn.

Khaki Shirazi (خاکی شیرازی), author of a Persian Dīwān.

Khaksar (خاکسار), poetical name of Shukr-ullāh Khān, who died in A.D. 1696, A.H. 1108, and has left a Dīwān.

Khaldun (خالدون). *Vide* Khālidūn.

Khalid ibn-Barmak (خالد ابن برمک) was the first of the Barmacides, who acted as wazīr to Abū'l 'Abbās Saffāh. He was the grandfather of Ja'far, wazīr to Hārūn-al-Rashīd. He died in the year A.D. 780 or 782, A.H. 163 or 165.

Khalid ibn-Walid (خالد ابن والید), who became a proselyte to Muhammadanism in A.D. 630, and afterwards so terrible to the Greeks, was called from his courage, the Sword of God. In spreading the doctrines of the Qurān, and the dominion of the prophet, he committed atrocious cruelties, and was at last cut off by the plague in A.D. 639, but according to Ockley's *History of the Saracens* Abū Ubeda died that year, and Khālid survived him about three years, and then died.

Khalid ibn - Yezid ibn - Mua'wia (خالد ابن یزید). He is reported to have been the most learned of the tribe of Quresh in all the different branches of knowledge, and skilled in the art of alchemy. He died in A.D. 704, A.H. 85.

Khalidi (خالدی), surname of Abū'l Faraj, one of the first poets of the court of the Sultān Saif-uddaula Hamdānī. He was a native of Khāldia or Chaldea, consequently he is called Khālidī.

Khalidun (خالدون), or 'Abdul Rahmān bin - Muhammad bin - Khālidūn, surnamed Alhazramī, was an author and Qāzī of the city of Aleppo when Amīr Timur took it, who carried him away to Samarqand as a slave, where he died A.D. 1405, A.H. 808.

Khalif or Khalifa (خلیفه). This Arabic word (which signifies vicar or successor), from which we have formed that of Khalīf or Caliph, is the name of a sovereign dignity amongst the Musalmāns, which comprehends an absolute power, and an independent authority over all that regards religion and political government. Not only the first four immediate successors of Muhammad, but the rulers of the house of Umayya (written by us Ommaides), who reigned in Damascus, and the 'Abbāsides, who reigned in Baghdād, were also called Khalīfas. There were in all 56 Khalīfas, 4 of whom were of the house of the prophet, 15 of the house of Umayya, and 37 of the house of 'Abbās.

Khalif or Khalifas (خلیفه), of the house of Muhammad. *See* Abū Bakr Siddīq.

Khalif or Khalifas (خلیفه امید), of the race or Umayya, who reigned at Damascus.

[*Vide* Mu'āwia I.]

Khalif or Khalifas (خلیفه عباسی), of the house of 'Abbās called 'Abbāsī or Abbāsides, who reigned at Baghdād.

[*Vide* Al-Saffāh.]

Khalil (خلیل), the poetical title of Alī Ibrāhīm Khān, which see.

Khalil (خلیل), the poetical appellation of Mirzā Muhammad Ibrāhīm, whose title was Asālat Khān. He served under the emperor 'Alamgīr, and was living in Patna in A.D. 1690, A.H. 1102. He was a native of Khurāsān, but brought up in India.

Khalil bin-Ahmad (خلیل بن احمد بصری), of Basra, a very learned man who is said to be the first that wrote on the art of writing poetry. He wrote several works and died about the year A.H. 175.

Khalil ibn-Is-haq (خلیل ابن اسحاق), author of a Mukhtasir which goes after his name. This is a work professedly treating of the law according to the Mālikī doctrines, and has been translated into French by M. Perron and published in the year 1849.

Khalil Khan (خلیل خان), a manṣabdār of 5000 of the court of Shāh Jahān, but of a very bad temper. It was he who instigated 'Alamgīr to confine his father Shāh Jahān. He had built a fine house at Agra on the banks of the Jamna, of which some traces are still to be seen.

Khalil, Maulana (خلیل مولانا), a poet of Persia, who flourished in the time of Shāh Tahmāsp Safwī, and was living about the year A.D. 1539, A.H. 946.

Khalil, Sultan (خلیل سلطان), son of Shaikh Ibrāhīm Shīrwānī, ruler of Shīrwān. He reigned about the beginning of the 15th century of the Christian era.

Khalil, Sultan (خلیل سلطان), also called Mirzā Khalīl and Khalīl-ullāh, was the son of Mīrānshāh, and grandson of Amīr Timur, at whose death he, being present with the army at Samarqand, took possession of that country. This prince, who was a person of excellent temper and had many good qualities, might have preserved the power he had acquired, had not his violent love for Shād-ul-Mulk, a celebrated courtezan, whom he had secretly married, diverted him from the cares of government. He had scarcely reigned four years, when he was seized by the chiefs who had raised him to the throne, and sent a prisoner to the country of Kashghar in A.D. 1408, A.H. 811, where instead of endeavouring to effect his release and recover his power, he spent the whole of his time in writing verses to his beloved mistress, who had been exposed, by the reverse of his fortune, to the most cruel indignities. He was at last released by Mirzā Shāhrukh his uncle, who had taken possession of his kingdom, and who not only gave him the government of Rei, Kum and Hamdān, but restored his beautiful mistress to his arms. After this he lived two years and a half and died 6th November, A.D. 1411, 18th Rajab, A.H. 814, aged 28 years, and Shād-ul-Mulk, on the occurrence of this event, acted a part which has given fame to her memory—she struck a poniard to her breast: and the lovers were buried in one tomb in the city of Rei.

Khalil-ullah (خلیل الله), the Friend of God, a title of Abraham the patriarch.

Khalil-ullah Hirwi, Mir (خلیل الله هروی میر), a descendant of Shaikh Na'mat-ullāh Walī.

Khalil-ullah Khan (خلیل الله خان). entitled Umdāt-ul-Mulk, brother of Asālat Khān Mīr Bakhshī, served under the emperor Shāh Jahān, was appointed governor of Dehlī about the year A.D. 1653, A.H. 1063, and was raised to the rank of 6000 in the first year of 'Alamgīr, A.D. 1658, A.H. 1068. He died on the 11th February, A.D. 1662, 2nd Rajab, A.H. 1072.

Khalil-ullah Mirza (خلیل الله مرزا). *Vide* Khalīl Sulṭān.

Khalis (خالص), the poetical name of Imtiyāz Khān of Isfahān, which see.

Khallikan (خلیکان). *Vide* Ibn-Khallikān.

Khamosh (خاموش), poetical name of Rāe Sāhib Rām of Dehlī. He was for some time Tahsīldār under Mr. Jonathan Duncan in Benaras. He has left a large Dīwān.

Khan (خان). This word, which appears to be a corruption of Qāān, is a Turkish title and means powerful lord. The most powerful kings of Turkistān, of Great Tartary and of the Khatāyans have borne this title. Changez, the great conqueror, had no other, and it makes even part of his name, for he is called by the Orientals, Changez Khān. It means the same as Khākān or Qāān.

Khan (خان), the poetical name of Mirzā Sharīf.

Khan 'Alam (خان عالم), title of Mirzā Barkhurdār, son of Mirzā 'Abdul Rahmān Dauldī, a nobleman who served under the emperor Shāh Jahān and was raised to the rank of 5000; he was also in favour under 'Alamgīr (Aurangzeb). In the latter part of his life, he was pensioned by the emperor and received one lac of rupees annually. He had a house and garden in Āgra on the banks of the river Jamna built of red stone touching the northern Burj of the Rauza of Tājganj in a spot consisting of 50 bighas. In the latter part of his life he was raised to 6000 and appointed governor of Bihār.

Khan 'Alam (خان عالم), title of Ikhlās Khān, the son of Khān Zamān Shaikh Nīzām. He served under the emperor 'Alamgīr and was raised to the rank of 5000 in A.D. 1689, A.H. 1100, with the title of Khān 'Alam. In A.D. 1696 the rank of 6000 was conferred on him. After the death of that emperor he espoused the cause of 'Azim Shāh against his brother Bahādur Shāh, and fell in battle A.D. 1707, A.H. 1119. After his death his son was honoured with the same title.

Khanam Sultan (خانم سلطان), a daughter of the emperor Akbar, married to Muzaffar Husain Mirzā, the son of Ibrāhīm Husain Mirzā, in A.D. 1593. [The word is the feminine of Khān, as Begam is of Beg.]

Khan 'Azim (خان عظم). *Vide* 'Azīm Khān.

Khanazad Begam (خانه‌زاد بیگم), the sister of the emperor Bābar, was five years older than he. Another daughter of 'Umar Shaikh was Mehr Bāno, eight years younger than Bābar. Another daughter was Yadgar Sulṭān Begam, whose mother name is Aghā Sulṭān Ghunchichī; the fourth daughter was named Ruqia Sulṭān Begam, whose mother's name was Makhdūma Sulṭān Begam, who was also called Qarā Qūr Begam; the last two daughters were born after the death of their father.

Khanazad Khan (خانه‌زاد خان). *Vide* Khān Zamān Bahādur and Rūh-ullāh Khan.

Khanazad Khan (خانه‌زاد خان), son of Sarbuland Khān, was governor of Peshāwar in A.D. 1723, A.H. 1135. When the government of Allahābad was conferred on his father by the emperor Muhammad Shāh, in A.D. 1732, A.H. 1145, he was deputed to act for him as governor of that province.

Khan Bahadur (خان بهادر), son of Rāja Mittra Jīt of Patna. He is the compiler of the work called *Jāma' Bahādur Khānī*, an epitome of European Sciences in the Persian language, including treatises on astronomy, optics, and mathematics, and copious tables of logarithms for natural numbers, sines, tangents, etc., also of a small octavo volume of Perspective called *'Ilm-ul-Manāzarat*, in the Persian language, which he presented to the Asiatic Society in A.D. 1835, A.H. 1251.

Khan Bahadur Khan. A descendant of Hāfiz Rahmat (*q.v.*) who was sub-judge of Bareli in 1857, and took advantage of the Sepoy mutiny to assume power there. He committed many crimes, but was driven out at the end of the year. The date of his death is uncertain.

Khan Bahadur Khan (خان بهادر خان), the son of Jalāl-uddīn Khān, the son of Hāfiz Rahmat Khān. *Vide* Masrūf.

Khande Rao Gaeqwar (کهاندی راو گه‌قوار), Rāja of Baroda. He died in A.D. 1870, and was succeeded by his brother Malhār Rāo, the deposed (1875) Rāja of Baroda.

Khande Rao Holkar (کهاندی راو هلکر), the only son of Malhār Rāo Holkar I. He was killed in a battle at Dīg against Sūraj Mal Jāt in A.D. 1754, many years previous to his father's death, and left an only son, Malī Rāo, who succeeded his grandfather and died nine months after.

[*Vide* Malhār Rāo I. and Ahlia Bāī.]

Khan Duran I. (خان دوران اوی), whose proper name is Shāh Beg Khān Kābulī, was an Amīr in the time of the emperor Akbar. He received the title of Khān Dourān from Jahāngīr in the year A.D. 1607, A.H. 1016, and was appointed governor of Kābul. He died in Lāhore in the year A.D. 1620, A.H. 1029, aged 90 years.

Khan Duran Khan II. (خان دوران خان ثانی نصرت جنگ), Nasrat Jang, title of Khwāja Sābir, son of Khwaja Hisārī Naqshbandī. He was an officer of state in the service of the emperor Shāh Jahān and held the rank of 7000. He was stabbed one night whilst asleep by a young Kashmerian Brāhman whom he had converted to Muhammadanism, and died after a few days on the 12th July, A.D. 1645, 27th Jumāda I. A.H. 1055, at Lāhore. His remains were transported to Gwāliar and buried there in the cemetery of his ancestors.

Khan Duran III. (خان دوران سیوم نصرت خان), Nasrat Khān, son of Khān Dourān Nasrat Jang. He held the rank of 5000 in the reign of the emperor ʻAlamgīr. In the latter part of his life he was appointed governor of Orissa, which post he held for several years and died there A.D. 1667, A.H. 1077.

Khan Duran IV. (خان دوران چهارم). *Vide* Ābdus Samad Khān Bahādur Jang.

Khan Jahan (خان جهان), title of Husain Qulī Beg, a manṣabdār of 5000 in the reign of the emperor Akbar. He was appointed governor of Bengal after the death of Munaiʻm Khān, about the year A.D. 1576, A.H. 984. He defeated, took prisoner, and slew Dāūd Khān, the ex-king of Bengal, who had again rebelled against the emperor, and sent his head to Āgra the same year. Khān Jahān died at Ṭānḍa in A.H. 1578, A.H. 986, and was succeeded by Muzaffar Khān.

Governors of Bengal.	A.D.
Khān Jahān	1576
Muzaffar Khān	1579
Rāja Todar Mal	1580
Khān ʻAzim	1582
Shāhbāz Khān	1584
Rāja Mān Singh	1589
Quṭb-uddīn	1606
Jahāngīr Qulī	1607
Islām Khān	1608
Qasim Khān	1613
Ibrāhīm Khān	1618
Shāh Jahān	1622
Khānāzād	1625
Mukarram Khān	1626
Fidaī Khān	1628
Qasim Khān Jobun	1628
ʻAzim Khān	1632
Sulṭān Shujaʻ	1639
Mīr Jumla	1660
Shaista Khān	1664
Fidaī Khān	1677
Sulṭān Muhammad ʻAzim	1678
Shaista Khān	1680
Ibrāhīm Khān	1689
Mirzā ʻAzīm-us-Shān	1697

Khan Jahan Barha (خان جهان بارها), title of Sayyid Muzaffar Khān of Bārhā Zilla Muzafarnagar, an officer of the rank of 6,000, who died in the time of the emperor Shāh Jahān at Lāhore, A.D. 1645, A.D. 1055.

Khan Jahan Kokaltash (خان جهان کوکلتاش), whose proper name was Mīr Malik Husain, the son of Mīr Abūʻl Maʻālī Khwāfī. He was a nobleman of high dignity, and being the foster-brother of the emperor ʻAlamgīr, thought himself superior to all the other ʻUmrā. He was appointed governor of the Deccan in A.D. 1670, A.H. 1081, and promoted by that monarch about the year A.D 1674 from the rank of 700 to that of 7000 horse, and the title of Khān Jahān Bahādur Kokaltāsh Zafar Jang. His former title was Bahādur Khān. He died on the 24th November, A.D. 1697, 19th Jumādạ I. A.H. 1109. He seems to be identical with the author of the *Tārīkh Asām* or the *Invasion of Asām.*

Khan Jahan Kokaltash Khan Zafar Jang (خان جهان کوکلتاش خان ظفر جنگ), a title of Alī Murād, a foster-brother of Jahāndār Shāh. In the time of Bahādur Shāh he was honoured with the title of Kokaltāsh Khān, and when Jahāndār Shāh ascended the throne, the rank of 9000 was conferred on him with the title of Khān Jahān Zafar Jang and the office of Mīr Bakhshīgarī. But he did not long enjoy this high station, for he soon after fell in the battle which took place between his master and Farrukh-siyar A.D. 1713, A.H. 1125.

Khan Jahan Lodi (خان جهان لودی), an Afghān probably of obscure birth, but with all the pride and ambition of his nation in India. He is by some said to have been a descendant of Sulṭān Bahlōl Lōdī, and by others of Daulat Khān Lodi Shāhū Khail. He had held great military charges, was raised to the rank of 5000 in the reign of the emperor Jahāngīr, and commanded in the Deccan under prince Parwez at the time of that prince's death. On the accession of Shāh Jahān, he entered into a close intimacy with his late enemies, and seemed to be aiming at independence. He was at last killed, together with his son, in an engagement with the royal troops on the 28th January, A.D. 1631, 1st Rajab, A.H. 1040, and their heads sent as a most acceptable present to Shāh Jahān. An affecting account of his death may be found in the third volume of Dow's History. The *Tārīkh Khān Jahān. Lōdī*, which is also called *Makhzan Alghānī*, contains the memoirs of this chief, written by Haibat Khān in A.D. 1676.

[Vide *Sketch of History of Hindūstān.*]

Khan Jahan Maqbul, Malik (خان جهان مقبول ملک), entitled Kawām-ul-Mulk, was the prime minister of Sulṭān Fīrōz Shāh Bārbak, who ascended the throne of Dehlī in A.D. 1351. He was originally a Hindū by name Kattū. On his conversion to Muhammadanism in his youth, Sulṭān Muhammad, the predecessor of Fīrōz Shāh, changed his name to Maqbūl, and appointed him to the government of Multān. He afterwards became Nāib wazīr under the wazīrship of Khwāja Jahān, whom he at first supported in his attempt to place a son of Sultān Muhammad on the throne, but went over to Sultān Fīrōz on his approach to Dehlī, and was appointed by him wazīr of the kingdom. According to the historian Shamsi Sirāj Afīf, he died in the year A.D. 1374, A.H. 776, but by others in A.H. 772. After his death his son Jahān Shāh was honoured with his place and title of Khān Jahān by the king, who placed as much confidence in him as he had done in his father. He filled the office of prime minister for twenty years.

Khan Khanan (خان خانان). This word is a title of honour, and means Lord of Lords. Bairām Khān and his son 'Abdur Rahīm Khān, both ministers to the emperor Akbar, and several others were honoured with this title. Like the later title, Amir-ul-Amra, it originally implied military command of the highest rank, but became an honorific title in later days.

Khan Mirza (خان مرزا), ruler of Badakhshān, was the son of Sultān Mahmūd Mirzā, the son of Sultān Abū Saīd Mirzā, a descendant of Amīr Taimūr. He died in A.D. 1521, A.H. 927, leaving behind a son of seven years of age named Mirzā Sulaimān. Khān Mirzā was a cousin of the emperor Bābar, who on Mirzā's death appointed his own son Humāyūn to that government.

Khan Mirza (خان مرزا), surname of 'Abdur Rahīm Khān (*q.v.*), Khān Khānān in the time of the emperor Akbar.

Khan Zaman (خان زمان), title of 'Alī Qulī Khān; he and his brother Bahādur Khān were the sons of Haidar Sultān Uzbak, who was an officer of state in the service of the emperor Humāyūn. In the reign of Akbar Shāh, these two brothers, for their good services, were raised to higher ranks and honoured with the post of jāgīrdār of Jaunpūr and the lower provinces. They at last raised a rebellion in the name of the emperor's brother Mirzā Hakīm, which induced the emperor to march against them with a large force; a battle ensued wherein both brothers were slain. This event took place on Monday the 9th June, A.D. 1567, 1st Zil-hijja, A.H. 974, at a place some distance west of Allahābād, which on account of this victory was named Fathapūr. The date of this transaction is commemorated in the words "Fatha Akbar Mubārik," *i.e.* May this great victory be prosperous.

Khan Zaman (خان زمان), title of Mīr Khalīl, second son of 'Azim Khān the brother of 'Asaf Khān Ja'far Beg, and son-in-law of Yemīn-uddaula 'Asaf Khān. He served under the emperor Shāh Jahān for several years, and in the reign of 'Alamgīr was raised to the rank of 5000. At the time of his death he was governor of Mālwā, where he died A.D. 1684, A.H. 1095.

Khan Zaman Bahadur (خان زمان بہادر), whose former title was Khānazād Khān and proper name Mirzā Aman-ullah, was the eldest son of Mahābat Khān, the surname of Zamāna Beg. He was an officer of state in the time of the emperor Jahāngīr, and was appointed governor of Bengal A.D. 1625, A.H. 1033. In the first year of Shāh Jahān, the rank of 5000 was conferred on him with the title of Khān Zamān Bahādur. He was a good poet, and is the author of a work, called *Majmūa*, containing the history of all the Muhammadan kings who reigned in different parts of the world before his time, and of a Dīwān. He died in Daulatābād in A.D. 1637, A.H. 1047, in which year Bāqir Khān also died. His poetical name was Amānī.

Khan Zaman Fatha Jang (خان زمان فتح جنگ) was the title of Shaikh Nizām Haidarābādī. He at first served under Abū'l Hasan ruler of Haidarābād for several years, and then left him and was employed by the emperor 'Alamgīr. In the year A.D. 1689, A.H. 1100, he took prisoner Sambha, the Marhatta chief, together with his wife and children; on which account he was raised to the rank of 7000 with the above title. He died A.D. 1696, A.H. 1108.

Khaqan (خاقان), the title of Changez Khān and his descendants. It means an emperor in the Turkish dialect.

Khaqani (خاقانی), a celebrated Persian poet surnamed Afzal-uddīn Ibrāhīm bin-'Alī Shīrwānī. He was a native of Shīrwān, and the pupil of Falakī the poet. He flourished in the reign of Khāqān Manūchehr, prince of Shīrwān, who conferred on him the title of Khāqānī. He is the author of the book called *Tuhfāt-ul-Irāqīn*, a poetical description of the two provinces of 'Irāq 'Ajam and 'Irāq 'Arab, composed by him while travelling through them on a pilgrimage to Mecca. He is considered the most learned of the lyric poets of Persia, and was called "Sultān-ush-Shu'arā" or king of poets. He is also the author of a Dīwān, according to Daulat Shāh, and the book called *Haft Aqlīm*. He died at Tabrez in the year A.D. 1186, A.H. 582, and is buried at Surkhāb, where, close to his tomb, Zahīr-uddīn Faryābī and Shāh Ghafūr Naishāpūrī are also interred. The chronogram of the year of his death, given in the work *Mukhbir-ul-Wasilīn*, shews that he died in A.D. 1199, A.H. 595.

Kharag Singh, Maharaja (کہرگ سنگہ مہاراجہ), the ruler of Lāhore and the Panjāb, was the eldest son of Mahārāja Ranjīt Singh, whom he succeeded on the 27th June, A.D. 1839, A.H. 1255. He reigned one year and four months, and died on the 5th November, A.D. 1840, A.H. 1256, aged 46 years. He was succeeded by his son Rāja Nau Nihāl Singh, who, after having performed the customary rites at his father's funeral, was returning home, and as he passed the Lāhore gate a part of the building gave way and fell over him, from the effects of which accident he died. This event took place on the 17th November the same year. After his death his mother Rānī Chānd Kūnwar managed the affairs of her country for two months, when her second son Rāja Sher Singh deprived her of that power, and became the sole manager of the government. He reigned about two years and eight months, and was murdered, together with his son Rāja Partāb Singh, by Sardār Ajīt Singh, on the 13th September, A.D. 1843. Rāja Dalīp Singh, the youngest son of Mahārāja Ranjīt Singh, who was only ten years of age, was then raised to the maṣnad.

Khasha (خاشع), the poetical title of a person who is the author of a Dīwān, which he completed in A.D. 1681, A.H. 1092.

Khassaf or **Al-Khassaf** (خصاف). *Vide* Abū Bakr Aḥmad bin-'Umar-al-Khassāf.

Khatib (خطیب), surname of Shams-uddīn Muhammad bin-Ibrāhīm-al-Mālikī, commonly called Khatīb-al-Wazīrī, an author who died in the year A.D. 1486, A.H. 891.

Khattabi (خطابی), surname of Abū Sulaimān Hamīd bin-Muhammad, an author who died in A.D. 998, A.H. 388.

Khatun Jannat (خاتون جنت), *i.e.* the lady of paradise, a title of Fātima, the daughter of Muhammad, and wife of 'Alī.

Khatun Turkan (خاتون ترکان). This name or title means the "Turkish lady," and was always given to princesses of Turkish descent. The wife of Sulṭān Malikshāh Saljūkī bore the ṣame title. She was the mother of Mahmūd, a boy of four years of age, whom she raised to the throne after the death of her husband in A.D. 1092, A.H. 485, but he died soon after, and Barkayārak his eldest brother mounted the throne. The wife of Sulṭān Sanjar was also called Khātūn Turkan. She died in A.D. 1156.

Khawari (خاوری), poetical title of Mīr 'Abū'l Fatha.

Khawas Khan (خواص خان), an amīr in the service of Salīm Shāh, justly renowned for personal courage, strict honour, great abilities in war, and extensive generosity, was long driven about from place to place on account of his fighting against the king in favour of his brother 'Adil Shāh. He at last took protection with Tāj Khān, governor of Sambhal, who to ingratiate himself with Salīm Shāh basely assassinated him about the year A.D. 1551, A.H. 958. His body was carried to Dehlī and there interred. His tomb is frequented to this day, by the devout who number him among their saints.

Khawas Khan (خواص خان), an amīr in the service of the emperor Jahāngīr. He had a jāgīr in Kanauj, and died there in the year A.D. 1521.

Khawind Shah or **Khawand Shah** (خاوند شاه امیر), also called Mīr Khāwand, and Amīr Khān, and Shāh, a celebrated Persian historian, known amongst us by the name of Mirkhond, as he calls himself in the preface of the life of Muhammad, but his true name at length is Muhammad bin-Khāwand Shāh bin-Mahmūd. He is the author of the work called *Rauzat-us-Ṣafā*, the Garden of Purity. He was born towards the close of the year A.D. 1433 or the beginning of 1434, A.H. 836 or 837. His father's name was Sayyad Burhān-uddīn Khāwand Shāh, a native of Māvarunnahr, after whose death he found means to be introduced to the excellent Amīr 'Alīsher, prime minister to Sulṭān Husain Mirzā of Herāt, from whom he experienced every mark of kindness and encouragement, and to whom he dedicated the above work. He died at Balkh after a lingering illness on the 23rd June, A.D. 1498, 2nd Ẕi-Qa'da, A.H. 903, aged 66 years. There is no Oriental work (says Sir H. M. Elliot) that stands higher in public estimation than the *Rauzat-us-Ṣafā*. This work is written in seven books. The author had just completed the 6th book when he died, and his son Khonda Mīr wrote the 7th book, and finished it in A.D. 1523, A.H. 929. [The *Rauzat-us-Ṣafā* was translated by the late David Shea, and published with illustrative notes by the translator, for the Oriental Translation Fund of Great Britain and Ireland in 1832. It is little more than a prose epitome of the *Shāhnāma.*]

Khayal (خیال), the poetical title of Mīr Muhammad Taqī, author of the work called *Bōstān Khayāl*, the Garden of Imagination. He flourished about the year A.D. 1756, A.H. 1170.

Khayali (خیالی بخاری), of Bukhārā, a pupil of Khwāja 'Ismat-ullah, and though he spent the greater part of his life in his native country he was two years at Herāt in the service of Mirzā Ulugh Beg, during whose reign he died and left a Dīwān.

Khazini (خازنی), an astronomer whose proper name was 'Abdul Rahmān.

Khink Sawar (خنک سوار). *Vide* Sāyyad Husain Khink Sawār.

Khirad (خرد), the poetical name of Bāqir Kāshī, which see.

Khitabi (خطابی), the poetical title of Shāh Ismā'īl Safawī I.

Khizr Khan (خضر خان), king of Dehlī. Firishta says that both the authors of the *Tabkāt Mahmūd Shāhī* and the *Tawārīkh Mubārik* style him a Sāyyad or descendant of the prophet. His father Malik Sulaimān was governor of Multān, and he succeeded him in that office. He defeated Daulat Khān Lodī in a battle, and having taken him prisoner ascended the throne of Dehlī on the 4th June, A.D. 1414, 15th Rabī' I. A.H. 817. He died after a reign of seven lunar years two months and two days on the 4th June, A.D. 1421, 17th Jumāda I. A.H. 824, and was succeeded by his son Mubārik Shāh. Khizr Khān did not assume the title of emperor, but professed to hold the empire for Shāhrukh Mirzā the son of Amīr Taimūr, in whose name he struck coins.

The following is a list of the kings of the 4th or Sāyyad Dynasty of Dehlī.

	A.D.	A.H.
Khizr Khān, a Sāyyad . began	1414	817
Mubārik Shāh, son of Khizr Khān	1421	824
Muhammad Shāh, the son of Farīd, the son of Khizr	1434	837
'Alā-uddīn, son of Muhammad Shāh, the last of the Sāyyads, who abdicated in favour of Bahlol Lōdī	1446	849

Khizr Khan, (خضر خان), the son of Sultān 'Alā-uddīn Khiljī. This prince fell in love with Dewal Devī, the daughter of Rāi Karan, Rāja of Gujrāt, and married her. The history of their love is written in a poem, entitled *Ishqia*, by Amīr Khusro.

[*Vide* Kula Devī.]

Khizr Khan Khwaja (خضر خان خواجه), a descendant of the kings of Kāshghar. He served under the emperor Humāyūn, who gave him his sister, named Gulbadan, in marriage, and appointed him governor of Lāhore and afterwards of Behār, where he died about the year A.D. 1559, A.H. 966.

Khizr, Khwaja (خضر خواجه), name of a prophet who, the Orientals say, is still living, and sometimes appears to travellers who have lost their way. He is said to have accompanied Alexander the Great to the dark regions of Zulmāt, where he was told he would find the Water of Life.

Khojam (خوجم), the poetical name of Khwāja Sultān, the author of a poem in Urdū containing the story of Shamshād Shāh, dedicated to Sa'ādat 'Alī Khān, the Nawāb of Lucknow, about A.D. 1798.

Khondamir (خوندامیر), the son of the celebrated Amīr Khawand Shāh (Mirkhond). His full name is Ghayās-uddīn Muhammad bin-Hamīd-uddīn Khond Amīr. He is the author of the history called *Khulāsat-ul-Akhbār*, which is considered to be an abridgment of the *Rauzat-us-Ṣafā*; this book he wrote in A.D. 1498, A.H. 904, and dedicated it to Amīr 'Alīsher his patron. He was born, says Sir H. M. Elliot, at Herāt about the year A.D. 1475, A.H. 880, for he states in the preface to the *Habīb-us-Siar* that when he commenced it in the year A.D. 1521, A.H. 927, he had advanced through seven or eight stages beyond the fortieth year of his life. It was after the name of his patron Karīm-uddīn Habīb-ullah, a native of Ardibel, that he entitled his work *Habīb-us-Siar*. Besides the above mentioned works, he composed the *Māsir-ul-Malūk*, the *Akhbār-ul-Akhiār*, the *Dastūr-ul-Wazra*, the *Mukārim-ul-Akhlāq*, and the *Muntakhib Tārīkh Wassāf*. There are two other works ascribed to him, called *Gharāeb-ul-Asrār* and *Jawāhir-ul-Akhbār*. He was compelled to leave Herāt on account of the disturbed state of the country in A.D. 1527, A.H. 933, and afterwards took a journey to Hindūstān in company with Maulānā Shahāb-uddīn the punster, and Mirzā Ibrāhīm Qānūnī, esteemed the most literary men of the age. On Saturday the 19th September, A.D. 1528, 4th Muharram, A.H. 935, they reached the metropolis of Āgra, and were introduced to the emperor Bābar Shah. They were loaded with presents and directed to remain in future about his person. Khondamīr accompanied the emperor on his expedition to Bengal, and after his death attached himself to his son Humāyūn, in whose name he wrote the *Qanūn Humāyūnī*, which is quoted by Abū'l Fazl in the Akbar-nama. He afterwards accompanied that monarch from Khandesh to Mandū in pursuit of Bahādur Shāh Gujrātī, and in that expedition he died. This event took place in A.D. 1535, A.H. 942, some time after the death of his friend Maulānā Shahāb-uddīn, who died the same year. By his own request his body was conveyed to Dehlī, and was buried by the side of Nizām-uddīn Aulia and Amīr Khusro. The 7th and last book of the *Rauzat-us-Safā* was written by him.

Khub (خوب), the poetical appellation of Kamāl-uddīn Shīstānī, the author of a mystical masnawi in the Gujrātī dialect, composed in A.D. 1578, A.H. 986. He also wrote a Persian translation and commentary on it in A.D. 1582, A.H. 990.

Khuban or **Khubu.** *Vide* Qutb-uddīn Kokaltāsh.

Khub-ullah, Shaikh (خوب الله شيخ), of Allahābād, surnamed Shaikh Muhammad Yahia, was the nephew and son-in-law of Shaikh Afzal of that place, whom he succeeded on the masnad of Irshād, that is to say, as a spiritual guide. He died at Allahābād on Monday the 1st November, A.D. 1731, A.H. 1144, and his son Shaikh Muhammad Nāsir, whose poetical name was Fazlī, succeeded him. Khub-ullah is the author of several works.

Khuda Banda (خدا بنده). *Vide* Muhammad Khudā Banda.

Khuda Banda Khan (خدا بنده خان), son of Amīr-ul-'Umrā Shāistā Khān. In the lifetime of his father he held the Faujdārī of Bahrāich with the rank of 1000, and after his father's death, in A.D. 1694, he was recalled to the presence, and was married to the daughter of Jumlat-ul-Mulk Asad Khān. In the year A.D. 1700, A.H. 1112, he was appointed governor of Bīdar in the Deccan by the emperor 'Alamgīr, and subsequently of Karnatic Bījāpūr. After the death of Rūh-ullah Khān II. in A.D. 1703, he was honoured with the post of grand steward of the household with the rank of 2500 horse. At the time of 'Alamgīr's death, he held the rank of 3000. He espoused the cause of 'Azim Shāh against his brother Bahādur Shāh, and died of his wounds a few days after the battle in June, A.D. 1707, A.H. 1119.

Khudyja (خديجه), or Khadīja, the first wife of Muhammad. She was a widow and dealt in merchandise. She had employed Muhammad for some time to drive her camels, and afterwards married him. Muhammad had several children by her, but all of them died young, excepting three daughters, one of them was Fātima, who was married to 'Alī. After her marriage with Muhammad she lived 22 years, and died at Mecca three years before the commencement of the Hijrī era, and three days after the death of Abū Tālib the father of 'Alī, and uncle of Muhammad, in August, A.D. 619, aged 62 lunar years. Burckhardt informs us that the tomb of Khudyja is still remaining, and is regularly visited by pilgrims. It is enclosed by a square wall, and presents no objects of curiosity except the tombstone, which has a fine inscription in Kufic characters, containing a passage from the Qurān, from the chapter entitled *Sūrat-ul-Kursī*.

Khurdadbih (خردادبه), or Ibn-Khurdāziba, surname of Abū'l Qasim 'Ubaid-ullah bin-Ahmad (or 'Abdullah) Ibn-Khurdāziba. This author has been the object of considerable controversies among the orientalists of Europe. Khurdāziba (the grandfather of our author) was a magician, who was converted to Islām by the Barmacides. Abū'l Qasim (our author) was subsequently appointed to the charge of the post and intelligence department in the provinces belonging to the Jabal (mountain); and ultimately came to the court of the Khalifa Mo'tamid, and became one of his privy counsellors. He is the author of several works, among which are: 1, *Kitāb Adab-us-Samā* (from which Masa'ūdī gives a very interesting extract in his life of Mo'tamid); 2, *Kitāb Jamhūr Ansāb-ul-Fars*, containing the most celebrated Genealogies of the Persians; 3, *Kitāb-al-Masālik-wal-Mumālik*, a geographical work on the roads and kingdoms; 4, *Kitāb-al-Sharāb*, on drink; 5, *Kitāb-ul-Lahwwal-Malāhī*, on playing and amusements; 6, *Kitāb-al-Anwā*, on the stars; and 7, *Kitāb-ul-Nudamā-wal-Julasā*, on courtiers and companions. The *Geography of Ibn-Khurdāziba*, says Sir H. M. Elliot, is the only work which we possess of this author, and of this there is only one copy in Europe. The MS. in question is ancient, bearing the date of A.D. 1232, A.H. 630, but it wants in most instances the diacritical points. It is preserved in the Bodleian Library at Oxford, No. 993. Ibn-Khurdāziba died about the year A.D. 912, A.H. 300.

Khurram Bakht, Mirza (خرم بخت مرزا), the son of Mirzā Jahāndār Shāh, the son of Shāh 'Ālam, king of Dehlī.

Khurram Begam (خرم بيگم), the wife of Mirzā Sulaimān Badakhshī.

Khurram, Mirza (خرم مرزا), original name of the emperor Shāh Jahān (*q.v.*) before he came to the throne.

Khurshed Mirza, Nawab (خورشید مرزا نواب), son-in-law to the late Nawāb Said-'uddaula, eldest son of Nawāb Mumtāz-uddaula, Bahādur, of Lucknow. He died on the 19th January, A.D. 1875. He had a Wasiqa of 1200 rupees per annum, which, it was understood, would be continued to his widow, then a young woman of 20.

Khursindi (خرسندی), a poet of Bukhārā, and author of the *Kanz-ul-Gharāeb*, a commentary in verse on the *Mukhtasir* of Ahmad Mansūrī, which can be read in different metres.

Khushdil (خوشدل), poetical name of Maulvī Mustafa 'Alī Khān.

Khushgo (خوشگو), poetical title of 'Amar Singh of Benares, which see.

Khushgo (خوشگو), poetical name of Bindrāban, a Bania, who was a native of Benares. He is the author of a Tazkira called *Safīnae Khushgo*; the title is a chronogram, and consequently contains the date when he completed it, *i.e.* in A.D. 1734, A.H. 1147. He was a pupil of 'Arzū, who by Khushgo's request in A.D. 1742, A.H. 1155, made some glosses and added a preface to it.

[*Vide* also Amar Singh of Benares.]

Khushi (خوشی), poetical title of a poet.

Khushtar (خوشتر), the poetical name of a poet who was the son of Mirzā Muhammad Afzal Sarkhush.

Khushtar (خوشتر), poetical name of Munshī Jagannāth, a Kāyeth of Lucknow, and author of the *Rāmāyan* in Urdū verse translated from the *Bāhkhā* of Tulshī Dās, in the year A.D. 1852, A.H. 1268.

[*Vide* Tulshī Dās and Girdhar Dās.]

Khushwaqt Rai (خوشوقت رای). He was for many years the agent and intelligencer of the British Government at Amritsar after the treaty with Mahārājā Ranjīt Singh, which was concluded in the year A.D. 1809. Date of death uncertain.

Khusro, Amir (خسرو امیر), one of the most celebrated poets of Hindūstān, who served under several emperors of Dehlī, and wrote 99 poetical works. His father Amīr Mahmūd Saif-uddīn, a Turk of the tribe of Lāchīn, came from Balkh to India and fixed his residence at Patiāla, where Khusro was born in the year A.D. 1253, A.H. 651. Khusro died six months after the death of Nizām-uddīn Aulia, who was his spiritual guide, and was buried close to his tomb at Ghayāspūr in old Dehlī. His death happened in September, A.D. 1325, Ramazān, A.H. 725. Khusro unfortunately lived at a period, says Sir H. M. Elliot, when vice was triumphant throughout Hindūstān. He, however, had the happiness, during the last few years of his life, to see a just prince, Ghayās-uddīn Tughlaq, on the throne, whose virtues he has commemorated in his history called *Tughlaq-nāma*, though he survived him but a few months. The following among his poems are particularly admired by his countrymen, and are thought to rival those of the most esteemed poets of Persia.

1. Tuhfat-ul-Saghīr.
2. Shatt-ul-Hayāt.
3. Ghurrat-ul-Kamāl.
4. Baqia Naqia.
5. Hasht Bahisht.
6. Sikandar-nāma.
7. Risala Nasr.

Besides these there are several other poems, viz. *Nuh Sipehr*, or the nine spheres, a beautiful mystical poem; the *Qirān-us-Sā'dyn*, or the auspicious conjunction, a poem in praise of Sultān Mu'izz-uddīn Kaiqubād, king of Dehlī, and his father Nāsir-uddīn Baghra Khān, king of Bengal, who came to visit him. The *Maqāla*, containing memoirs of the first four Khalīfas, viz. Abū Bakr, 'Umar, Usmān and 'Alī, with a treatise on the Sūfī tenets, written in A.D. 1324, the *Ishqia*, a collection of poems on love subjects; the *Matla'-ul-Anwar*, on the Sūfī doctrines, and his Dīwān, which is held in great estimation in India, containing poems chiefly on mystical theology and divine love: many of them have been set to music, and are chanted by the devotees or Sūfīs; frequently producing extravagant ecstasies, termed by them *wajd*, or spiritual delirium. The Khamsa or the five celebrated books of Amīr Khusro, which contains about 18,000 verses, are the following:

1. Hasht Bahisht.
2. Sikandar-nāma.
3. Panj Ganj.
4. Lailī-wa-Majnūn.
5. Shīrīn-wa-Khusro.

Included in the 99 books which Khusro is said to have written, besides the abovementioned, are the following:

1. Aijāz Khusrowī.
2. Aīna Sikandarī
3. Khizir Khānī.
4. Inshāe Amīr Khusro.
5. Jawāhir-ul-Bahr.

Khusro Malik (خسرو ملک), son of Khusro Shāh, was the last Sultān of the race of Ghaznavides. He ascended the throne at Lāhore after the death of his father in A.D. 1160, A.H. 555, was defeated in A.D. 1184, A.H. 580, by Shāhāb-uddīn Ghorī, then governor of Ghaznī, who took him prisoner and sent him to his brother Ghayās-uddīn to Fīrōz Kōh, where he died after some years.

Khusro Malik. A converted Hindu, who held possession of the throne on the death of Mubārik Shāh Khiljī (*q.v.*). He called himself Khusro Shāh; but after a brief orgy was overthrown and slain by Ghāzi Beg Tughlaq A.D. 1321.

[*Vide* Ghāyas-uddīn]

Khusro Malik (خسرو ملک), the brother-in-law of Sultān Muhammad Shāh I. Tughlaq, whose sister named Khudāwandzāda he had married. He had once formed the project of taking the life of Sultān Fīrōz Shāh, the successor of Muhammad Shāh, by concealing a number of persons in the rooms adjacent to where the king sat, but the king was saved by Dāwar Malik, the son of Khusro Malik, who made a sign to him that danger was to be apprehended, upon which he left the room and took refuge on the top of the house.

Khusro Parwez (خسرو پرویز), the son of Hurmuz III. (or IV.) king of Persia of the Sassanian race. He, by the assistance of the Roman emperor Maurice, after defeating Bahrām Chobīn, his father's general, who had taken possession of the kingdom, ascended the throne of Persia A.D. 591. The moment he was firmly established on the throne he fulfilled in a most faithful manner the engagements he had entered into with his ally, and publicly adopted the emperor Maurice as his father; but when that emperor was slain in A.D. 603 he instantly declared war, on the grounds of avenging his benefactor. His generals invaded the Roman territories; Dara, Edessa, and other strong places on the frontier, were soon subdued; Syria was completely pillaged, Palestine overrun, Jerusalem taken, and the true cross, which had been enclosed in a golden case and buried deep in the earth, is said to have been discovered, and borne in triumph to Persia. His reign of more than 30 years was marked by a success never surpassed by the most renowned of his ancestors. Persia was, however, invaded by Heraclius the Roman emperor, who defeated the troops of Khusro wherever he encountered them, and marched, in one direction, as far as the Caspian, in another to Isfahān; destroying in his progress all his splendid palaces, plundering his hoarded treasures, and dispersing, in every direction, the countless slaves of his pleasure. The subjects of Khusro now lost all regard for a monarch whom they deemed the sole cause of the desolation of his country: a conspiracy was formed against him; he was seized by his eldest son Sheroya or Siroes; his 18 sons were massacred before his face, and he was cast into a dungeon, and soon afterwards died or was put to death in A.D. 628, A.H. 7, after he had reigned 38 years. The glory of the house of Chosroes (Nausherwān) ended with the life of Khusro; his unnatural son enjoyed only eight months the fruit of his crime.

The Muhammadan authors say that Khusro had received an epistle from Muhammad, inviting him to acknowledge Muhammad as the apostle of God. He rejected the invitation, and tore the epistle. "It is thus," exclaimed the Arabian prophet, "that God will tear the kingdom, and reject the supplications of Khusro." The historians of Muhammad, says Gibbon, date this embassy in the seventh year of the Hijra, which commenced the 11th May, A.D. 628. Their chronology is apparently erroneous, since Khusro died in the month of February of the same year (Gibbon, vol. viii. p. 205).

Khusro Shah (خسرو شاه), a descendant of the ancient kings of Badakhshān, whom Bābar Shāh defeated about the year A.D. 1505, and took possession of his country and made it over to his cousin Khān Mirzā.

Khusro Shah (خسرو شاه), surnamed Nizām-uddīn, was the son of Bahrām Shāh of Ghaznī. He succeeded his father at Lāhore in A.D. 1152, A.H. 547, and died there after a reign of seven years in A.D. 1160, A.H. 555. He was succeeded by his son Khusro Malik.

Khusro Shah (خسرو شاه). *Vide* Malik Khusro.

Khusro, Sultan (خسرو سلطان), the eldest son of the emperor Jahāngīr; was born in the month of August, A.D. 1587, Ramazān, A.H. 995, at Lāhore. His mother was the sister of Rājā Mān Singh, the son of Rāja Bhagwān Dās, and after the birth of Khusro she got the title of Shāh Begam. He died in the Deccan on the 16th January, A.D. 1622, 13th Rabī' I. A.H. 1031, aged 36 lunar years, and his remains are said to have been transported to Allahābād, where his monument is to be seen in a garden surrounded by masonry walls, called the garden of Sultān Khusro, or "Khusro-Bāgh" and where his mother Shāh Begam is also buried. The dome over his tomb has a pathetic inscription of several Persian verses, and contains the chronogram of the year of his death in the words "Faiz Lāeq." It is related in the work called *Maāsir Qutb Shāhī* that Khusro was strangled by a man named Razā by the order of Shāh Jahān his younger brother.

Khuzai (خذاعی), a celebrated author, descendant from a tribe of Arabs called Khuzāa

[*Vide* Abū 'Abdullah Muhammad bin-Husain-al-Khuzāī.]

Khuzaima (خزیمه), a companion of Muhammad.

Khwaja Baqi Billah (خواجه باقی بالله), a Muhammadan saint. *Vide* Muhammad Baqī (Khwāja).

Khwaja Hasan (خواجه حسن). *Vide* Sanjarī.

Khwaja Hasan Basri (خواجه حسن بسری). *Vide* Hasan Basrī.

Khwaja Hasan Sadr Nizami (خواجه حسن سدر نظامی), author of the work entitled *Tāj-ul-Maāṣir*, which he dedicated to Sulṭān Qutb-uddīn Aibak, king of Dehlī, about the year A.D. 1208, A.H. 605.

Khwaja Hashim Kashmin (خواجه هاشم کشمین), author of a Persian work entitled *Zubdat-ul-Muqāmat*, containing the (pretended) miracles of Aḥmad Sarhindī, a Muhammadan saint, and others.

Khwaja Husain Marwi (خواجه حسین مروی), a native of Marv in Persia, was an excellent poet. He flourished in the time of the emperor Akbar, and wrote chronograms at the birth of Sulṭān Shāh Murād, second son of the emperor, who was born in the year A.D. 1570, A.H. 978. He put the *Singhasan Battīsī* into Persian verse, but did not complete it. He is the author of a Dīwān.

Khwaja Husain Sanai (خواجه حسین سنائی مشهدی), of Mashhad. He and his father were protéges of Sulṭān Ibrāhīm Mirzā. He flourished about the beginning of the 11th century of the Hijra, left Qaṣīdās and a Maṣnawi called *Sadde Sikandar*.

Khwaja Husain Sanai (خواجه حسین ثنای) a Persian poet, and son of Ghayās-uddīn Muhammad. He came to India in the time of Akbar, died in A.D. 1588, A.H. 996, and left a thick Dīwān.

Khwaja Ibrahim Husain (خواجه ابراهیم حسین). *Vide* Ibrāhīm Husain (Khwāja).

Khwaja 'Imad (خواجه عماد). *Vide* 'Imad Faqīh.

Khwaja Imami (خواجه امامی), author of a story in Persian entitled *Māli Dohafta*. He was a contemporary of Mirzā Qatīl.

Khwaja Jahan (خواجه جهان), honorific name of Malik Sarwar, founder of the race of the kings of the East, or Sharqī dynasty of Jaunpūr. The different rulers who have governed in the provinces of Jaunpūr and Antarbed (territories south of Dehlī lying between the rivers Jamna and Ganges) are styled by historians the Sharqī kings. It appears from the *Tawārīkh Mubārik Shāhī* that Sulṭān Muhammad Shāh, son of Fīrōz Shāh Tughlaq, king of Dehlī, created one of his eunuchs, named Malik Sarwar, his prime minister, and honoured him with the title of Khwāja Jahān; that upon the death of Muhammad Shāh, and on the accession of his son Sulṭān Mahmūd Shāh Tughlaq, a boy of ten years of age, in A.D. 1394, A.H. 796, he was appointed governor of the Eastern provinces of the empire, *viz.* Qanauj, Audh, Kaṛa and Jaunpūr, the latter of which he made the seat of his government. The reign of Mahmūd Shāh was interrupted by serious internal commotions; and Khwāja Jahān taking advantage of these circumstances, and perceiving the weakness of the government arising out of the king's minority, assumed the title of Malik-ush-Sharq (king of the East), founded an independent kingdom at Jaunpūr, and died in the year A.D. 1400, A.H. 802, after a short reign of six years. He was succeeded by his adopted son Malik Wāsil or Qaranfal, who assumed the title of Mubārik Shāh Sharqī, and died in A.D. 1402, A.H. 804. After his death his brother Ibrāhīm Shāh Sharqī succeeded him, and died about the year A.D. 1441, A.H. 845, after a reign of more than forty years. He was succeeded by Sulṭān Mahmūd Shāh Sharqī, who died in A.D. 1452, A.H. 856, and left the kingdom to his son Muhammad Shāh, who was killed in battle about the year A.D. 1458, A.H. 861 or 862, when Husain Shāh, his brother, succeeded him. He had several battles with Bahlōl Lodī, king of Dehlī, and was at last obliged to seek refuge in the court of Sulṭān 'Alā-uddīn, king of Bengal, where he died in A.D. 1499, A.H. 905. There are at Jaunpūr several fine specimens of Pathān architecture—chiefly Mosques—dating from this dynasty.

[For details vide *Imperial Gazetteer*, *in voc.* Jaunpūr.]

Khwaja Jahan (خواجه جهان), an Amīr or Manṣabdār of 5000, who died in the time of Jahāngīr, in the year A.D. 1619, A.H. 1029, at Lāhore.

Khwaja Jahan (خواجه جهان). *Vide* Mahmūd Gāwān.

Khwaja Kamgar (خواجه کامگار). *Vide* Ghairat Khān.

Khwaja Kirmani (خواجه کرمانی), an excellent Persian poet of Kirmānia, surnamed Malik-ul-Fuzlā, or king of the learned. He assumed for his poetical title Khwāja and Khwājū; was contemporary with Sa'dī of Shīrāz and a disciple of Shaikh 'Alā-uddīn Samnānī, whom he outlived, and died some years after A.D. 1345, A.D. 747, for he completed his *Gauhar-nāma* in that year. He has written about 20,000 verses, and one of his poetical compositions is called *Humāe Humāyūn*. Mīr or Amīr Kirmānī and Ahmad Kirmānī were also two Persian poets.

[*Vide* Kirmānī.]

Khwaja Mansur Qarabuqa (خواجه منصور قرابوقه طوسی), a poet of Tūs in Khurāsān who flourished in the reign of Shāhrukh Mirzā, and was employed by the Prince 'Alā-ud-daula. He died A.D. 1450, A.H. 854.

Khwaja Mansur Shirazi (خواجه منصور شیرازی), also called Shāh Mansūr, an excellent accountant who served under the emperor Akbar in the capacity of Dīwān, and afterwards as his wazīr for four years. He was accused of embezzlement by Rāja Todarmal, Bīrbal and others, as he said, on account of his being too strict with them; and was imprisoned and afterwards impaled on the 27th February, A.D. 1581, 23rd Muharram, A.H. 989, on a supposition that he had been carrying on a correspondence with Mirzā Muhammad Hakīm (*q.v.*) half brother of Akbar, who had at that time invested Lāhore.

Khwaja Masa'ud (خواجه مسعود), of Bak. *Vide* Masa'ūd (Khwāja).

Khwaja Masa'ud (خواجه مسعود), a poet who died in the year A.D. 1131, A.H. 525, and left three thick Dīwāns, one in the Persian, one in the Arabic, and one in the Hindūstānī language of that day. He is the earliest Musalmān poet who wrote in Hindūstānī of whom we have any account.

Khwaja Masa'ud (خواجه مسعود), a poet of an illustrious family of Kun, and one of the most celebrated writers of Masnawīs in the last cycle of the greater Persian poets. He chose the admired subject of Yūsuf and Zalekha for one of his poems. He was called to Herāt in the time of the Sultān Husain Mirzā, to celebrate the events of his reign in verse, and appears to have devoted himself to the task in a somewhat voluminous manner, for he wrote 12,000 lines of a poem on the subject dictated; and would, perhaps, have added as many more, had not death put an end to his enthusiasm. He was the author of many admired poems, among others, *A Dispute between the Sun and the Moon*, and *Between the Pen and the Sword*. He flourished about the year A.D. 1480, A.H. 885.

Khwaja Mua'zzam (خواجه معظم), a man of a very mischievous character, was the brother of Hamīda Bāno Begam, and husband of Bībī Fātima, the emperor Akbar Shāh's aunt. He was banished the kingdom several times for improper behaviour, but he soon returned; and when in the year A.D. 1564, A.H. 973, he killed his wife, he was thrown into prison, where, by the command of the emperor, he was put to death in A.D. 1565.

Khwaja Muhammad Athim (خواجه محمد اثم). *Vide* Abd-ul-Samad-Khān.

Khwaja Muhammad Baqi (خواجه محمد باقي). *Vide* Muhammad Baqī (Khwāja).

Khwaja Muhammad Muqim (خواجه محمد مقیم). *Vide* Nizām-uddīn Ahmad.

Khwaja Nasir (خواجه نصیر), author of the works called *Bustān-ul-Kirām* and *Aosāf-ul-Ashrāf*.

Khwaja Nasir (خواجه ناصر), a poet who was a contemporary of Salmān Sāwajī.

Khwaja Nasir (خواجه ناصر), whose poetical name is 'Andalīb, was the father of Mīr Dard the poet.

Khwaja Nizam-ul-Mulk (خواجه نظام الملک), minister of Sultān Alp Arsalān. *Vide* Nizām-ul-Mulk.

Khwaja Parsa (خواجه پارسا), surname of Muhammad bin-Muhammad Hāfiz Bukhārī, author of the book called *Fazl ul-Kitāb fil Muhāzarāt*, containing the memoirs of all the celebrated Sūfī Shaikhs of the Naqshbandī Order; and of several other books. He flourished in the reign of Shāhrukh Mirzā, and died A.D. 1419, A.H. 822.

Khwaja Rustam Khozyani (خواجه رستم خزیانی). *Vide* Rustam (Khwāja).

Khwaja Sadr Nizami (خواجه صدر نظامی), author of the book called *Tāj-ul-Māsir*. He is also called K͟hwāja Hasan Sadr Niẓāmī.

Khwaja Shakir Nasir-uddin 'Abdullah (خواجه شاکر ناصرالدین عبدالله), one of the greatest saints of Turkīstān.

Khwaja Wafa (خواجه وفا), K͟hwāja Sara of Shāh Jahān.

Khwaja Zain-ul 'Abidin 'Ali 'Abdi Beg Nawedi (خواجه زین العابدین علی عبدی بیگ نویدی), of Shīrāz, was for many years Mustaufī or Secretary of State in Persia. He was particularly distinguished as a writer of Masnawī, and composed two K͟hamsas in imitation of Niẓāmī. He is also the author of several other works, one of which is called *Jām Jamshed*, and has left three Dīwāns; the first is called *G͟hurrai G͟hurra*; in this he uses his poetical name of Nawedī, in the second of 'Abdī. He died at Ardibel in A.D. 1580, A.H. 988.

Khwaja Zikaria (خواجه زکریا), son of K͟hwāja Muhammad Ahia, a nobleman of the time of the emperor Jahāngīr.

Khwaju Kirmani (خواجو کرمانی). *Vide* K͟hwāja Kirmānī.

Khwansari or **Khonsari** (خوانساری), poetical name of Mīr Abūl Fatha.

Khwansari (خوانساری). *Vide* Husain K͟hōnsārī.

Khwarizm (خوارزم), kings of. *Vide* Qutb-uddīn Muhammad, son of Anūshtakīm.

Kirmani (کرمانی), a native of Kirmānia. This is the surname of several authors, and amongst others of Ya'kūb bin-Idrīs, who died in the year A.D. 1430, A.H. 833. [*Vide* K͟hwāja Kirmānī.]

Kisai, Hakim (کسائی حکیم), a celebrated poet and physician of Marv in Persia, who was born on Wednesday the 23rd March, A.D. 953, 27th Shawwāl, A.H. 341. The year of his death is not known. There was another Kisāī, whose proper name was Abūl Hasan, who was one of the seven eloquent readers of the Qurān, and died A.D. 796, A.H. 180.

Kishna Raja (کشنا راجه), of Mysore. *Vide* Krishnā Rāja.

Kishn Chand (کشن چند), whose poetical appellation was Ik͟hlās, was the son of Achal Dās K͟hattrī of Dehlī, whose house was the resort of the learned. Kishn Chand, after his father's death, applied himself to poetry, and became the author of a Tazkira or biography, entitled *Hamesha Bahār*, *i.e.* Eternal Spring, which he compiled in the year A.D. 1723, A.H. 1136. It contains, in alphabetical order, an account of about 200 poets who flourished in India from the time of Jahāngīr to the accession of Muhammad Shāh.

[See Ik͟hlās K͟hān Ik͟hlās Kesh.]

Kishn Singh, Kachwaha (کشن سنگه), Rāja of Kishungaṛh, and eldest brother of Rāja Sūraj Singh Rāṭnor, who served under the emperor Jahāngīr, to whom his sister was married. Kishn Singh was slain by his brother Sūraj Singh, A.D. 1615, A.H. 1024, in the 10th year of the emperor Jahāngīr, who was married to his sister, by whom he had Shāh Jahān.

Kishtasp (کشتاسپ). *Vide* Gashtāsp.

Kochak (کوچک), poetical name of Prince Mirzā Wajīh-uddīn, who died in the East, though his remains were brought to Dehlī and buried close to the Dargah of Sulṭān-ul-Mashāek͟h, which is about 6 or 8 miles distant from Dehlī.

Krishn (کرشن), a god of the Hindūs, was in the world in the time of the Kauras and Pandūs, or the 7th century after the commencement of the Kālījug, according to this shlōk: "When something more than 650 years of the Kālījug were expired, then were the Kauras and Pandūs, in whose time the Great War took place."

Krishna Raj Udawar (کرشنا راج اوداور), the lineal descendant of the ancient family of Mysore, whose power Haidar 'Alī K͟hān had usurped in the year A.D. 1761. But after the defeat and death of Tīpū Sulṭān, and the departure of his sons from Seringapatam to Vellore, Mysore was divided between the Niẓām and the English. The English took the southern portion and the city of Seringapatam, by which accession their territory reached from sea to sea. The Niẓām took an equal portion on the north-east. Some districts on the north-west, equal in value to more than half of each of their own portions, were offered by the allies to the Mahraṭṭas, which they refused to take, and they were divided between Niẓām and the English. The remainder was given to Krishnā Rāja, then a child of three years of age, who was raised to the throne of his ancestors on the 30th June, A.D. 1799, and Purania, a Brāhman of great ability and reputation, who had been the chief financial minister of Tīpū, was appointed Dīwān to the young prince by the British Government. He was, in later days, created Knight Grand Commander of the Most Exalted Order of the Star of India. He died on Friday the 27th March, A.D. 1868, aged 72 years. His adopted son, Chamrajaindra Odāwar, was recognized and proclaimed as Mahārāja of Mysore. The young Mahārāja being a minor, the government and administration of the territories of Mysore were, during his minority, conducted under the direction of the Commissioner. The state was made over to Odāwar dynasty A.D. 1881.

Kuar Singh (کنور سنگه), or Kūṇwar Singh, of Jagdīspūr, a rebel of 1857, was killed in battle in May or June, 1858.

Kublai Khan (کبلی خان), great-grandson of Changez Khān. *Vide* Qablai Khān.

Kudsia Begam. *Vide* Udham Bai.

Kukab (کوکب), poetical name of Munshī Mahdī, in the service of Nādir Shāh, author of *Durr-i-Nādira*, *Tārīkh Nādirī*, and a poem entitled *Nādir-nāma*.

Kukab (کوکب), poetical name of a poet who died in the year A.D. 1840, A.H. 1256.

Kula Devi or Kawaldah (کولا دیوی), the beautiful wife of Rāe Karan, Rāja of Gujrāt, which place was taken by Sulṭān 'Alā-uddīn Khiljī in the year A.D. 1297, A.H. 697, and among the captives was Kula Devī, whom the king married. Her daughter Dewal Devī was also taken captive in the year A.D. 1306, A.H. 706. A few days after her arrival, her beauty inflamed the heart of the king's son, Khizr Khān, to whom she was eventually given in marriage. The history of the loves of this illustrious pair is written in an elegant poem called *Ishkia*, composed by Amīr Khusro of Dehlī. Mubārik Shāh, in the second year of his reign, put to death his brother Khizr Khān, who was imprisoned at Gwaliār, and took Dewal Devī to be his wife.

[*Vide* Khizr.]

Kura Mal, Choudhari (کورا مل چودهری), author of the story of Kāmrūp, a poem in Persian verse. He died on the 16th May, A.D. 1848.

Kuthari Bukhari (کوثری بخاری), an author who died in the year A.D. 1475, A.H. 880.

Kya Muhammad (کیا محمد). *Vide* Buzurg Umaid.

Kyjaptu (کیجپتو), second son of Sulṭān Abqa Khān, the son of Halālū Khān, the Tartar king of Persia. He was raised to the throne by the voice of the majority of the Amīrs on the death of his brother Arghūn Khān in March, A.D. 1291, Rabī' I. A.H. 690. The resentment of a personal injury led Bāidū Khān, a grandson of Halākū Khān, to rebel against him, and the unfortunate monarch was, after a short struggle, made prisoner, and put to death in January, A.D. 1295, Safar, A.H. 694. Bāidū Khān succeeded him.

L

Labid (لبید), whose full name is Abū A'qīl Labīd bin-Rabiat, was one of the most distinguished Arabian poets, and one of the seven whose verses constituted the Mua'l-laqāt, a series of prizes suspended in the Ka'ba. He was still an idolater when Muhammad commenced publishing his laws. One of his poems commenced with this verse: "All praise is vain which does not refer to God: and all good which proceeds not from Him is but a shadow;" no other poet could be found to compete with it. At length the chapter of the Qurān, entitled *Barāt*, was attached to a gate in the same temple, and Labīd was so overcome by the verses at the commencement as to declare that they could only be produced by the inspiration of God, and he immediately embraced Islāmism. When Muhammad was apprised of the conversion of Labīd, the finest genius of his time, he was exceedingly delighted, and requested him to answer the invectives and satires of Amra-alkys and other infidel poets who wrote against the new religion and its followers. The following sentence, one of the finest which ever fell from the lips of an Arab, is also attributed to him.—"All is vain which is not of God." Labīd is said to have lived to the age of 140 years, and died at the city of Kūfa in 141 of the Hijra (A.D. 758); but there seems some mistake in the year of his death. *Vide* Ockley's *History of the Saracens*. Labīd is supposed to be the friend and tutor of Amra-alqai, commonly called Kaisand Majnūn, the lover of Laila.

Lachhmi Bai (لچهمی بائي), the wife of Malhār Rāo, Rāja of Baroda, who married her under suspicious circumstances; a child was born in 1874 and it has been recognised as legitimate.

Lachhmi Narayan (لچهمی نارایں), of Benares. He is the author of a biography or Tazkira called *Gul-e-Ra'nā*.

Lachhmi Ram (لچهمی رام), a Hindū who was a poet and had adopted the word "Surūr" (happiness) for his poetical appellation.

Laddardeo (لدردیو), a Rāja of Telangana who became tributary to Sultān 'Alā-uddīn Sikandar Sānī in the year A.D. 1310, A.H. 710.

Ladli Begam (لاڈلی بیگم) was the daughter of Shaikh Mubārik of Nāgōr, and sister to Abū'l Fazl the minister of the emperor Akbar. She was married to Nawāb Islām Khān, who had been governor of Bengal about the year A.D. 1608, A.H. 1017. She died at Āgra, and is supposed to have been buried there in the cemetery of her father, which is now called Rauza Lāḍlī.

Laila, or **Laili** (لیلی), the name of the mistress of the celebrated Majnūn, whose original name was Qais. These two lovers are very famous throughout the East. Laila was the daughter of a neighbouring Chief. She was equally accomplished with her lover; and nothing seemed likely to disturb the happiness which their permitted attachment promised, till the avarice of her father destroyed at once all their hopes. Laila was commanded to think of Qais no more, as she was destined to be the bride of one more rich and powerful; and in spite of the grief and remonstrances of the unfortunate pair, they were separated. Qais became insane from disappointment, and his name was therefore changed to Majnūn (the distracted). Death at length put a period to his miseries, and his faithful mistress soon followed him, leaving her cruel parent to his late and vain remorse, and the memory of these victims of avarice to eternal honour and regret.

Laiq, or **Layiq** (لایق), the poetical name of the author of the poem called *Dastūr Himmat*, containing the story of Kāmrūp in Persian verses, which he dedicated to Himmat Khān Bahādur his patron. He completed this work in A.D. 1685, A.H. 1096, and found the chronogram of that year to be contained in Himmat Khān.

Lais, or **Laith** (لیث) is the proper name of a brazier, who by his valour raised himself to the highest posts in the dominions of Darham, who then reigned in Sajistān. He left three sons, Ya'qūb, A'mrū, and 'Alī, of whom the first, called Ya'qūb bin-Lais, was founder of the dynasty of the Safarides.

Lal (لال), a celebrated Hindu poet; *fl. temp.* Aurangzeb. He wrote a history of Chatr Sāl (*q.v.*) entitled *Chatra Prakāsh*.

Lal (لال), or Lallu, Kābi, a Brahman of Guzrāt in the beginning of the 18th century. Wrote a version of the *Prem Sāgar*.

Lal Chand (لال چند), whose poetical name was Uns, is the author of a Persian Dīwān. He died in the year A.D. 1852, A.H. 1268.

Lal Khan (لال خان), a celebrated songster of India, who died in the fourth year of the emperor Jahāngīr's reign, A.D. 1609, A.H. 1018.

Lal Kunwar (لال کنور), the favourite mistress of Jahāndār Shāh, emperor of Dehlī. This woman had been a public dancer, and her family were of the same discreditable class; yet they were exalted to high stations by the emperor, to the exclusion of the nobles, whom they were also allowed on several occasions to insult with impunity.

Lal Singh (Raja) (لال سنگه راجا), a Sikh chief and paramour of Ranjit Singh's widow, Chānd, or Jindan. After the death of Rāja Jawāhir Singh, the office of prime minister remained vacant for some time and was disposed of by lot to Lāl Singh in November, 1845. Lāl Singh lived at Āgra as a state prisoner for several years; and died at Dehra about A.D. 1870.

Laludin (لالودين), the younger Nawāb of Najībābād, who turned rebel in 1857, and was hanged in April, 1858.

Lama'i (لامعي) (also called Lāma'ī Bukhārī, because he was a native of Bukhāra). His proper name is Mahmūd bin 'Usmān, and he is the author of the works called *Sharaf-ul-Insān*, *Ibrat-nāma*, and *Shama'wa-Parwāna*, in the Turkish language. He died in A.D. 1533, A.H. 940. He was a pupil of Soznī.

Largiran Gun (لرگيرن گون). *Vide* Ahlīa Bāī.

Lashkar Khan (لشکر خان), a nobleman of the court of the emperor Jahāngīr.

Lashkar Khan (لشکر خان), a nobleman of the court of Jahāngīr and Shāh Jahān who held the mansab of 5000. He had built his house near Naīkī Mandī on a spot of 20 bīgas which had a large gate.

Latafat Khan (لطافت خان), favourite eunuch and general in service of Nawāb Asaf-uddaula, viceroy of Audh, sent in command of contingent destined to assist Shāh Alam (*q.v.*) in 1775. He was captured and blinded, by Mirzā Shāfi, in 1783.

Latif-unnisa Begam (لطيف النسيا بيگم), a widow of the late Nawāb Shams-ul-'Umra and Wikār-ul-'Umra's mother, died at Hydarābād Deccan on the 24th August, 1864, at the good old age of 74 lunar years, having survived her husband only sixteen months and thirteen days. She was buried with great pomp in the sepulchre of her husband.

Law, the *Mushir Lās* of native historians, son (or nephew) of the famous financier of the French Regency. Served in Madras and Bengal against Clive, and taken prisoner by Carnac at the battle of Gāya, 15th January, 1761. His son was a distinguished French General under the First Empire; the Marquis de Lauriston represents the family. Date of death unknown.

Lilawati (ليلاوتی). *Vide* Bhaskar Ārchārya.

Lisani (Maulana) (لسانی مولانا), poetical name of Wajīh-uddīn 'Abdullah Shīrāzī, a son of Mīr Muhammad Mushk-farōsh. He died at Tabrez according to Khushgo in A.D. 1583, A.H. 991, and left a Dīwān containing 4000 verses.

Lodi (لودی), a tribe of Pathāns or Afghāns in India. *Vide* Khān Jahān Lodī.

Lonkaran (لنکرن). *Vide* Rāi Lonkaran.

Luhrasp (لهراسپ), the son-in-law of Kaikāūs, and successor of Kaikhusro, king of Persia. He was the fourth king of the Kayanian dynasty, and obliged both the rulers of Tartary and of China to do him homage. In his time Bakht un-Nasar (Nebuchadnezzar), the governor of 'Irāq, took Jerusalem, and carried away into bondage such of its inhabitants as were not put to the sword. Luhrasp is fabled to have reigned 120 years, and was succeeded by his son Kishtāsp or Gashtāsp, who is believed to be the Darius Hystaspes of the Greeks.

Luhrasp (لهراسب), original name of Mahābat Khān, the second son of the celebrated Mahābat Khān Jahāngīrī. He had been governor of Kābul for several years in the time of the emperor 'Alamgīr, but was recalled to the court about the year A.D. 1670, and shortly after ordered to command the army of the Deccan in the room of Mahārāja Jaswant Singh, who was recalled.

Luqman Hakim (لقمان حکيم). A mythical writer, supposed to have written a thousand years before the Christian era, and said to have been contemporary with David the king of Israel. He is held to be the greatest of the Oriental moralists, and held in the highest esteem by the Orientals for his wisdom and virtues; even Muhammad speaks of him in the 31st chapter of the Qurān, which is called *Sūra Luqmān*, with profound reverence. Luqmān's wisdom, like Solomon's, is supposed to have been of divine origin. One day as he was in his room, working at his trade (he was a carpenter), several angels invisibly entered and saluted him. Luqmān, hearing voices, looked around him, but not seeing anyone made no reply. The angels then said: We are messengers from God, thy Creator and ours, who hath sent us to thee to inform thee that He designs to make thee a monarch and his vicegerent on earth. Luqmān answered: If it be the absolute will of God that I shall become a monarch, that will must be accomplished; and I trust that he will grant me grace to execute His commands faithfully; but if the liberty of choice be given me, I should prefer abiding in my present condition; the only favour that I ask from God being, that he would preserve me from offending Him, for were I to offend Him all the dignities of the earth would be but a burden to me. This reply was so agreeable to God that he at once bestowed on Luqmān the gifts of Knowledge and Wisdom to a degree hitherto unparalleled. The Maxims of Luqmān are ten thousand in number; and "any one of these," says an Arabian commentator, "is of much greater value than the whole world." His wisdom and the striking morality of his fables are so like those of Æsop that he is considered by some to have been the original author so called.

Lutf. Literary name of Mirzā Alī Khān (*q.v.*).

Lutf (لطف), the poetical name of Mīr Amman, a Hindūstānī lyric poet, and one of the learned natives formerly attached to the College of Fort William. He is the author of the *Bāgh-o-Bahār*, a simple version of the *Nautarz Murassa* in Urdū, completed in A.D. 1802, A.H. 1217.

Lutf 'Ali Khan (لطف علی خان), the eldest son of Ja'far Khān, king of Persia, whom he succeeded in the year A.D. 1788; had several battles with the troops of Aqa Muhammad Khān Kachār, by whom he was defeated, taken prisoner, and afterwards murdered in A.D. 1795. He was the last prince of the Zand family.

Lutfullah (لطف الله), a Muhammadan gentleman, who was born in the ancient city of Dhārānagar, in Mālwā, on Thursday the 4th November, A.D. 1802, 7th Rajab, A.H. 1217. His father Maulvī Muhammad Akram was a Muhammad of the sacred order, a descendant of Shāh Kamāl-uddīn, who was a great saint of his time in the province of Mālwā, being the spiritual guide as well as general preceptor of Sulṭān Muhammad Khiljī, during a period of 30 years. After his death the Sulṭān built a magnificent mausoleum at the western gate of the city, and endowed therein a shrine to the memory of the holy man; opposite to it he caused to be raised another edifice, surmounted by a superb dome, which was intended as a resting-place for his own mortal remains, and there they still repose. Luṭfullah proceeded to England as secretary to Mīr Ja'far 'Alī the son-in-law of Mīr Afẓal-uddīn, Nawāb of Sūrat in March 1844, and after his return from England he wrote his adventures in 1854, entitled the *Autobiography of Luṭfullah* in English, and dedicated it to Colonel W. S. Sykes, F.R.S., London, and published in June 1857.

Lutfullah Khan (لطف الله خان), son of Sa'dullah Khān, wazīr of the emperor Shāh Jahān. After his father's death in A.D. 1656, A.H. 1066, though he was then only eleven years of age, the manṣab of 700 and 100 sawārs were conferred on him. In the reign of the emperor 'Alamgīr he was raised to a higher rank, and died at the time when that emperor was engaged in conquering the fort of Gandāna in the Deccan. This event took place on the 28th December, A.D. 1702, 18th Shabān, A.H. 1114.

Lutfullah Maulana (لطف الله مولانا), a native of Naishāpūr in Persia. He was an excellent poet and flourished in the time of Amīr Timur. The poet Shaikh Azurī has mentioned him in his work called *Jawāhir ul-Asrār*. He is the author of the *Tārīkh Shāhrukh*, which is an abridgment of the history of Amīr Timur, with memoirs of the first nine years of the reign of his son and successor Shāhrukh Mirzā, to whom he dedicated the work A.D. 1413, A.H. 816, and died the same year.

Lutfullah Muhammad Muhaddis bin-Ahmad (لطف الله محمد محدث بن احمد), author of the work called *'Asmān Sakhun*, a rhymed abridgment of the *Tazkira Daulat Shāhī*. We are informed in the preface that Fāezī Kirmānī rendered the Tazkira of Daulat Shāh in Persian verses in the reign of Akbar and altered the division of the original, making ten periods instead of seven; Luṭfullah, who was a contemporary of Aurangzeb 'Alamgīr, remodelled this version and added two periods more to make the number correspond with the signs of the Zodiac; and in allusion to it, he gave it the above title. It consists of 250 verses; every verse contains the name of a poet.

Lutfullah Sadik. An Ansāri of good family, who held high office under the Emperor Muhammad Shāh (A.D. 1716–48).

Lutf-unnisa Begam (لطف النسا بیگم), the wife of Sirāj-uddaula, Nawāb of Bengal. She was murdered in the time of Nawāb Ja'far 'Alī Khān with several other women of the house of the late Nawāb in June 1760.

M

Madaini (مداینی), a celebrated historian who was a native of Madeïn in Persia.

Madan Pal, Maharaja (مدنپال مہاراجہ), G.C.S.I., of Karaulī, died of cholera on the 17th August, 1869. This event deprived Rājpūtāna of one of the best of her native rulers. The Mahārāja having died without a son, the Government of India recognised Lachhman Pāl, son of his younger brother Birhan Pāl, as successor to the Rāj of Karaulī.

Madari Mal (مداری مل), a Hindū and author of the work *Badāya-ul-Fanūn*, containing forms of letters on different subjects in Persian.

Madar Shah (مدار شاه), a celebrated Muhammad saint whose tomb is at Makanpūr in Qanauj.

[*Vide* Shāh Madār.]

Madhava Rao (مادهو راو), or Mādhōjī Sindhia, Rāja of Gwāliar, was the son of Rānōjī Sindhia. He succeeded his brother Jīāpā Sindhia (A.D. 1759) in the management of his patrimonial inheritance, of which Ujjain was the capital; and by a train of successful operations was enabled to appropriate to himself a considerable part of the province of Mālwā, belonging to the government of Pūna, as well as to extend his domains over a great part of Hindūstān; and to obtain possession of the person and nominal authority of the emperor Shāh 'Alam, of whom he was ostensible minister. He died on the 12th January, A.D. 1794, without male issue, and was succeeded by his grand-nephew and adopted son Daulat Rāo Sindhia. He had built a small fort close to a place called Gazar Tijāra in Āgra, and named it Mādhōgaṛh, the ruins of which were still to be seen about the year A.D. 1830.

[*Vide* Monograph in *Rulers of India* series, Oxford, 1891.]

Madhoji Bhosla (مادهوجی بهوسله), the third Rāja of Beṛar of the Bhosla family, was the son of Baghojī Bhosla I. He succeeded his eldest brother Rānōjī or Jānōjī Bhosla in A.D. 1772, and died at an advanced age on the 29th May, A.D. 1788. He was succeeded by his son Rāghojī Bhosla II. the fourth Rāja of Beṛar of Nāgpūr.

Madho Ram (مادهو رام), a learned Hindū who is the author of a book of letters which goes after his name, called *Inshāe Mādhō Rām*, containing forms of letters on different subjects in Persian.

Madho Rao I. Bilal Peshwa (مادهو راو اول بلال پیشوا), second son of Bālājī Rāo Peshwā, whom he succeeded as nominal Peshwā in A.D. 1761, under the regency of his uncle Raghunāth Rāo. He died in November, A.D. 1770, and was succeeded by his brother Nārāyan Rāo.

Madho Rao II. Peshwa (مادهو راو ثانی پیشوا), of the Marhaṭṭas, also called Sewājī Mādhō Rāo, was the posthumous son of Nārāyan Rāo Peshwā, who was murdered in August, A.D. 1772, by his paternal uncle Raghunāth Rāo, also called Rāghōbā, who usurped the maṣnad. A few months after this event Nārāyan Rāo's widow was delivered of a son, who was named Sewājī Mādhō Rāo, and was raised to the maṣnad, on which he continued until his death, which took place on the 27th October, A.D. 1795, by a fall (supposed to have been intentional) from the terrace of his palace. He was succeeded by Chimnājī Apā, the younger son of the Marhaṭṭa chief Raghunāth Rāo.

Madho Singh Kachhwaha (مادهوسنگه کچهواهه), the son of Rāja Bhagwān Dās and brother-in-law of Jahāngīr.

Madho Singh Kachhwaha (مادهوسنگه کچهواهه), succeeded Ishurī Singh his father to the government of Jaipūr in the year A.D. 1760. He died in A.D. 1778 and was succeeded by his son Pirthī Singh, a minor, who was soon after deposed, and his brother Partāp Singh succeeded to the gaddī the same year, and died in A.D. 1803.

Maftun (مفتون), poetical name of Momin 'Alī, a poet.

Maftun (مفتون), the poetical title of Ghulām Mustafa, a brother of Razī-uddīn Sarūrī, who was usually called Ghulām Murtazā. He is the author of a Dīwān. He died at the age of 30, about the year A.D. 1755, A.H. 1168.

Maghmum (مغموم), poetical name of Rāmjas, a Hindū of Lucknow, and author of an Urdū Dīwān. He was employed by Mumtāz-uddaula (Mr. Johnson), and was living in A.D. 1785, A.H. 1199.

Maghrabi Shaikh (مغربی شیخ), poetical appellation of Muhammad Shīrīn. He was a friend of Kamāl Khujandī, and like him a profound Sūfī. He died at Tabrez A.D. 1416, A.H. 819, and is buried at Surkhāb. Having been given to the most disgusting vices during his lifetime, he is considered as a saint. He is the author of a Dīwān called *Qasāed Maghrabī*, and several other works.

Mahabat Jang (مہابت جنگ). *Vide* 'Alī Wardī Khān.

Mahabat Khan (مہابت خان), whose proper name was Zamāna Beg, was the son of Ghōr Beg, a native of Kābul. He had attained the rank of a commander of 500 under Akbar, and was raised to the highest dignities and employments by the emperor Jahāngīr. He enjoyed a high place in the opinion of the people, and was considered as the most eminent of all the emperor's subjects. In the month of February, A.D. 1626, Jumāda II. A.H. 1035, he seized the emperor's person, because he (the emperor) never consulted him, but followed the advice of his wife Nūr Jahān in all affairs, and carried him to his own tents, where he remained a state prisoner for some time, but was soon released after a severe battle by his wife Nūr Jahān. In the second year of the emperor Shāh Jahān, the government of Dehlī was conferred on him. He died in the Deccan in A.D. 1634, A.H. 1044, and his corpse was conveyed to Dehlī and buried there. After his death his eldest son Mirzā Amān-ullah received the title of Khān Zamān, and his second son Luhrāsp was honoured with the same title of Mahābat Khān. (Vide *infra.*)

Mahābat Khān had his house built on the bank of the river Jamna on a plot of land of 50 bigas in Āgra; though little of it now remains, there are some parts of its ruins still to be seen.

Mahabat Khan (مہابت خان), whose original name is Luhrāsp, was the second son of the celebrated Mahābat Khān of the reign of Jahāngīr, after whose death in A.D. 1634, A.H. 1044, he received this title. He was twice made governor of Kābul, and had the command of the army in the Deccan. He died in A.D. 1674, A.H. 1085, in the reign of 'Alamgīr, on his way from Kābul to the presence. Also mentioned under Luhrāsp, *q.v.*

Mah Afrid (ماہ آفرید), daughter of Fīrōz the son of Yezdijard, the last monarch of the Sasānian dynasty of Persian kings, and mother of Yezīd III. twelfth khalīf of the house of Umayya.

Maham Anka (ماهم انکه), mother of 'Azīm Khān. *Vide* 'Azīm Khān.

Maham Begam (ماهم بیگم), a granddaughter of Shaikh Ahmad Jām. She was married to the emperor Bābar Shāh, and became the mother of Humāyūn. She was living about the year A.D. 1561, A.H. 969, as appears from an inscription on the gate of an old Madrasa (or college) and masjid constructed by her in that year near the fort of old Dehlī called Dīn Panāh. The numerical words of the inscription, from which the year of the buildings is known, are Khair Manazil, or the Mansions of Bliss. She must have been then more than 70 years of age.

Maha Singh (مہا سنگه), the grandson of Rāja Mān Singh Kachhwāhā of Ameir (now Jaipūr), and son of Partāp Singh. He served under the emperor Jahāngīr, and died in A.D. 1617. He was the father of Mirzā Rāja Jai Singh.

[*Vide* Mān Singh.]

Maha Singh (مہا سنگه), a Sikh Rāja of Lāhore, who was the father of Mahārāja Ranjīt Singh. He extended his rule and died in A.D. 1792, when his wife became regent, with Lakhpat Singh minister.

Mah Bano (ماہ بانو), sister of Khān 'Azīm Kōka. She was married to 'Abdul Rahīm Khān, Khān Khānān, son of Bairām Khān, about the year A.D. 1572, A.H. 980, and died A.D. 1597, A.H. 1005.

Mahbub 'Ali Khan (محبوب علی خان). His Highness Āsaf Jah Muzaffar ul-Mulk Nizām-uddaula Nawāb Mīr Mahbūb 'Alī Khān Bahādur Fatha Jang is the Nizām of Haidarābād Deccan.

Mah Chuchak Begam (ماہ چوچک بیگم), one of the wives of the emperor Humāyūn, and mother of the prince Farrukh Fāl, surnamed Muhammad Hakīm.

Mahdi (مہدی), the first khalīf of the Fātimites in Africa. His son, who succeeded him, was named Kāem-bi-amr-ullah.

Mahdi (مہدی), the third khalīf of the house of 'Abbās.

[*Vide* Al-Mahdī.]

Mahdi 'Ali Khan (مہدی علی خان), the grandson of Ghulām Husain Khān, the historian. He resided in Behar in A.D. 1801.

Mahdi 'Ali Khan, Hakim (مہدی علی خان حکیم), prime minister of Nāṣir-uddīn Haidar, king of Audh. The iron suspension bridge over the the Kālīnadī at Khodāganj near Fathagaṛh, which was seven years in progress, was built at his expense for 70,000 rupees, and finished in July, A.D. 1836. He was dismissed from his post in A.D. 1832, which was again restored to him on the accession of Muhammad 'Alī Shāh, in A.D. 1837. After this he lived only a few months and died in December, A.D. 1837.

Mahdi, Imam (مہدی امام), surnamed Abū'l Qāsim Muhammad, the last of the twelve Imāms, who are held in the highest veneration by the Muhammadans. The first of these was 'Alī, and the last Mahdī, the son of Hasan 'Askarī, who was the eleventh Imām. He was born at Sarmanrai in Baghdād on Friday the 29th July, A.D. 869, 15th Sha'bān, A.H. 255, and when he was about four or five years of age his father died. The Shī'as or Shī'ites say that at the age of 10 he entered into a cistern at his father's house, while his mother was looking on, and that he never came out again. This occurred in A.D. 879, A.H. 265. They believe him to be still alive, and concealed in some secret place, and that he will appear again with Elias the prophet at the second coming of Jesus Christ for the conversion of infidels to the Muhammadan religion.

Mahdi Khan, Mirza (مہدی خان مرزا), styled Munshī ul-Mumālik, was the confidential Secretary to Nādir Shāh, and is the author of the *Tārīkh Nādirī*, which is also called *Nādir-nāma*, or the history of Nādir Shāh, and *Tārikh Jahān Kushā*. This work was translated into French by Sir William Jones.

Mahdi, Mirza (مہدی مرزا), author of the work called *Majmūa Mirzā Mahdī*, a chronological table of the remarkable events of the house of Timur, commencing A.D. 1423, with Abū Sa'īd Mirzā (third in descent from Timur, and grandfather of the emperor Bābar Shāh) who reigned over Khurāsān and Transoxiana; and terminating with the emperor Bahādur Shāh, A.D. 1708.

Mahfuz (محفوظ), author of the *Story of Shāh Bedār Bakht*, which is also called *Rashk-i-Chaman*, in Urdū verse dedicated to Ghāzī-uddīn Haidar, king of Audh, in A.D. 1823, A.H. 1238.

Mahip Narayan (مہیپ ناراین), Rāja of Benares. A pottah was granted him by the English on the 14th September, A.D. 1781.

Mahir (ماهر), the poetical name of Mirzā Muhammad 'Alī, a native of Āgra. His father was a Hindū in the service of Mirzā Ja'far Mua'mmāī or the punster, who having no children converted the boy to the Muhammadan religion, adopted him as his own son, and gave him a good education. After the death of Mirzā Ja'far he attached himself to Dānishmand Khān and remained with him till his death, when he retired from the world and died in A.D. 1678, A.H. 1089. He was an excellent poet, and is the author of several works, one of which is called *Gul-i-Aurang*, which he wrote in praise of the emperor Aurangzeb 'Alamgīr on his accession to the throne.

Mahjur (مہجور). *Vide* Muhammad Bakhsh.

Mahmud (محمود ملقب به برهان الشریعت), surnamed Burhān-ush-Shariat, who lived in the seventh century of the Hijra, is the author of the work on jurisprudence called *Wiqāya*, which he wrote as an introduction to the study of the *Hidāya*. This work has been comparatively eclipsed by its commentary, the *Sharh al-Wiqāya*, by 'Abaid-ullah bin-Masa'ud; this author's works combines the original text with a copious gloss explanatory and illustrative. Both the *Wiqāya* and the *Sharh al-Wiqāya* are used for elementary instruction in the Muhammadan Colleges. Other commentaries on the *Wiqāya* exist, but they are of no great note.

Mahmud (محمود), an Afghān chief of Qandahār of the tribe of Ghilzaī, was the son of Mīr Wais, after whose death in A.D. 1715 he succeeded him. He besieged Isfahān in A.D. 1722, and compelled Sulṭān Husain Safwī, king of Persia, to surrender and resign his crown to him. The king went forth with all his principal courtiers in deep mourning, surrendered himself to Mahmūd, and with his own hands placed the diadem on the head of the conqueror. The event took place on the 11th October of the same year, 11th Muḥurram, A.H. 1135. After two years' possession of the sovereign power, he gave orders for the death of the Safwīān princes who were his prisoners, and thirty-nine of them, some grown up, others in their childhood, were barbarously slaughtered. It is said that he became deranged the same night, and not only tore his own flesh, but ate it. Every person that approached him he overwhelmed with abuse, and in this condition died in A.D. 1725. But before his death the Afghāns, being threatened by an attack of the Persian prince, Tahmāsp Mirzā, the son of Sultān Husain, who had fled from Isfahān, elected Ashraf, the cousin of Mahmūd, to be their ruler, who in April, A.D. 1725, 12th Sha'bān, A.H. 1137, murdered Mahmūd, and became the king of Persia.

Mahmud (محمود), the son of Sultān Muhammad Saljūqī. He held the government of Irāq and Azurbejān for several years as deputy to his uncle Sultān Saryar, who gave him his two daughters in marriage named Sītī Khātūn and Māh Malik. He died in A.D. 1131, A.H. 525.

Mahmud (محمود بن عبد الله قان فيروزی), son of 'Abdullah Qān Fīrōzī, is the author of the History entitled *Maāsir Qutb Shahī*, and also of another work of the same description called *Tārikh Jāma ul-Hind*. He served Qulī Qutb Shāh II. for 30 years, and was living at the time of that monarch's death, which happened in A.D. 1612, A.H. 1020.

Mahmud (محمود شبشتری), of Shustar (Shabishtarī), author of a religious book called *Hak-ul-Yekīn*, which is held in great estimation among the Persians.

Mahmud I. Sultan (محمود اول سلطان), emperor of Constantinople, was the son of Mustafa II. and nephew of Ahmad III. whom he succeeded in A.D. 1730, A.H. 1142. His janissaries expected from him the recovery of the conquered provinces, but he lost Georgia and Armenia, which were conquered by Nādir Shāh. Mahmūd died in A.D. 1754, A.H. 1168, and was succeeded by his brother 'Usmān II.

Mahmud II. Sultan (محمود ثانی سلطان), emperor of Constantinople, was the son of Sultān 'Abdul Hamīd, commonly called Ahmad IV. the son of Mustafa III. He was born on the 20th July, A.D. 1785, and ascended the throne after the deposition of his uncle Salīm III. and Mustafa IV. on the 28th July, A.D. 1808. He was of the eighteenth generation from 'Usman I. who founded the dynasty, and the thirtieth sovereign of that family. He died on the 30th June, A.D. 1839, A.H. 1255, and was succeeded by his son 'Abdul Majīd. The reign of Mahmūd has been full of important events. The Greeks, in A.D. 1821, threw off the Ottoman yoke, and after a sanguinary contest were declared independent; and in A.D. 1828 a war with Russia took place, in which the armies of Mahmūd were uniformly defeated, and the Russians were only prevented from advancing to Constantinople by large concessions on the part of the Turks, and the mediation of the European powers. He exterminated the mutinous guards or janissaries at Constantinople; and his fleet was destroyed by the combined Russian, French, and British squadrons at Navarino; whence it was said of him that the Turkish army was ruined by himself, and the Turkish navy by his allies.

Mahmud bin-Faraj (محمود بن فرج), a famous impostor who gave himself out for Moses risen from the dead; but was flogged to death by the order of the khalīf Mutwakkil.

Mahmud Boria, Pahlawan (محمود بوريا پهلوان), a Muhammadan saint of Persia who followed the occupation of a boatman, and is the author of a work called *Kitāb Kanz*.

Mahmud Gawan, Khwaja (محمود گاوان خواجه), styled Malik-ut-Tajjār Khwāja Jahān, was the wazīr of Nizām Shāh Bahmanī, king of the Deccan. In the reign of Muhammad II. the duties of Wakīl-us-Sultānat were conferred on him. His enemies lost no opportunity of poisoning the king's mind, and at last they brought this great man to destruction by contriving an infamous forgery, upon which the king, without investigating the matter, ordered him to be put to death in the 78th year of his age. This event took place on the 5th April, A.D. 1481, 5th Safar, A.H. 886. Mahmūd had great learning and much judgment in composition of prose and verse. A little before his death he had written a poem in praise of his ungrateful master. He is the author of the *Rauzat ul-Inshā* and some poems. Maulānā 'Abdul Rahmān Jāmī corresponded with him, and some of his letters are to be seen in his works.

Mahmud ibn-Masa'ud (محمود ابن مسعود), author of a work called *Zīnat-uz-Zamān*.

Mahmud Khan (محمود خان), nawāb of Bijnor and a rebel of 1857. He was the great-grandson of Zabita Khān the son of Najīb-uddaula Amīr ul-Umra.

[*Vide* Sa'd-ullāh Khān.]

Mahmud Khan Langa (محمود خان لنگا), the fourth king of Multān, son of prince Fīrōz, succeeded his grandfather Husain Langa on the throne in August, A.D. 1502, Safar, A.H. 908. He reigned 23 years. In A.D. 1524, A.H. 931, some time before his death, the emperor Bābar Shāh having conquered the country of the Panjāb proceeded to Dehlī, from whence he wrote an order to Husain Arghūn, governor of Ṭhatta, informing him that he intrusted him henceforward with the directions of affairs in Multān. That chieftain, in consequence, crossed the Indus and marched with a large army to Multān; but before his arrival the king died and was succeeded by his son Husain Langa II.

Mahmud Khwarizmi, Maulana (محمود خوارزمی مولانا), a poet of Khwārizm.

Mahmud, Mulla (محمود ملا), of Jaunpūr, the son of Muhammad Fārūqī, was the author of the work called *Shams Bāzigha*, and of the *Hawāshī Farīd fī Sharah ul-Fawāed*, which he wrote in A.D. 1632, A.H. 1042, and died in A.D. 1652, A.H. 1062.

Mahmud Parsa, Khwaja (محمود پارسا خواجه), a poet who flourished in the time of Prince ʻAlā-uddaula and Sulṭān Abū Saʻīd Mirzā, and died A.D. 1477, A.H. 882.

Mahmud Saʻid, Erchi (محمود سعید), author of the *Tuhfat-ul-Majālis*; he was a contemporary of Shaikh Aḥmad Khaṭṭū, whom he mentions therein.

Mahmud Shah (محمود شاه), one of the sons of Timur Shāh, the son of Aḥmad Shāh ʻAbdālī, who being driven from Kābul by Dost Muhammad Khān, took possession of Herāt, which country he ruled for some years, and after his death in A.D. 1829 his son prince Kāmrān succeeded him.

Mahmud Shah I. (محمود شاه بیقره اول), surnamed Baiqara, the son of Muhammad Shāh and brother of Quṭb-uddīn or Quṭb Shāh, was raised to the throne of Gujrāt after the deposition of Dāūd Shāh in June, A.D. 1459, Shaʻbān, A.H. 863. He caused the city of Ahmadābād to be surrounded by a wall and bastions in A.D. 1847, A.H. 892; and on its completion had the sentence من دخله کان امنا in commemoration of the date of that event, inscribed on one face of the fortification, the meaning of which is, "Whosoever is within is safe." He made two expeditions to the Deccan, reigned 55 lunar years, and died on the 23rd November, A.D. 1511, 2nd Ramaẓān, A.H. 917, in the 70th year of his age. He was buried in Sarkīj or Sarkīch near Ahmadābād in the mausoleum of Shaikh Aḥmad Khaṭṭū. He was succeeded by his son Muzaffar Shāh II.

Mahmud Shah II. (محمود شاه ثانی), whose former name was Nāṣir Khān, was the third son of Muzaffar Shāh II. He was raised to the throne of Gujrāt after the murder of his eldest brother Sikandar Shāh in May, A.D. 1526, Shaʻbān, A.H. 932. He reigned about three months, after which his brother Bahādur Shāh, returning from Jaunpūr, deprived him of his kingdom and mounted the throne on the 20th August the same year, 15th Ẓi-Qaʻda, A.H. 932. Mahmūd Shāh died in A.D. 1527, A.H. 933.

Mahmud Shah III. (محمود شاه ثالث) was the son of Laṭīf Khān the brother of Bahādur Shāh. He was raised to the throne of Gujrāt after the death of Mīrān Muhammad Shāh in April, A.D. 1537, Ẓi-Qaʻda, A.H. 943. In his reign, about the year A.D. 1540, A.H. 947, the fort of Sūrat (Surat), on the shore of the sea, was completed by Khudāwanda Khān, before which time the Portuguese were in the habit of attacking the Muhammadans along that coast. Mahmūd Shāh reigned about 18 years, and was slain on the 16th February, A.D. 1554, 13th Rabīʻ I. A.H. 961, while he was asleep, by one Daulat, at the instigation of Burhān, private chaplain to the king, who hoped by that means to ascend the throne of Gujrāt. The same year died also Salīm Shāh king of Dehlī, and Nizām Shāh Bahrī the Sulṭān of Ahmadnagar in the Deccan. The words, "Zawāl Khusroān," *i.e.* Destruction of Kings, commemorate the date of this event. Mahmūd Shāh was buried in the vault of Sulṭān Mahmūd Baiqara, close to the mausoleum of Shaikh Aḥmad Khaṭṭū and was succeeded by Aḥmad Shāh II.

Mahmud Shah I. Bahmani (محمود شاه بهمنی اول), the fifth Sulṭān of the race of Bahmanī kings of the Deccan, was the youngest son of Sulṭān ʻAlā-uddīn Hasan. He was raised to the throne at Kulbarga after the assassination of his brother Dāūd Shāh in May, A.D. 1378, Muḥarram, A.H. 780, reigned 19 lunar years 9 months and 24 days, and died of a putrid fever on the 20th April, A.D. 1397, 21st Rajab, A.H. 799. He was succeeded by his son Sulṭān Ghayās-uddīn Mahmūd, was a patron of literature, had a taste for poetry, and wrote elegant verses himself. In his reign the poets of Arabia and Persia resorted to the Deccan and were benefited by his liberality. Mīr Faiz-ullāh Anjū, who presided in the seat of justice, once presented him with an ode, was rewarded with a thousand pieces of gold, and permitted to retire, covered with honours, to his own country. In his time the celebrated poet of Shīrāz, Khwāja Hāfiz, determined to visit the Deccan, but was prevented by a train of accidents.

Mahmud Shah II. Bahmani (محمود شاه بهمنی ثانی), the fourteenth Sulṭān of the race of Bahmanī kings of the Deccan, succeeded his father Muhammad Shāh II. on the throne at Ahmadābād Bedar in March, A.D. 1482, Ṣafar, A.H. 887, in the twelfth year of his age. He reigned 37 lunar years, and died on the 18th December, A.D. 1517, 4th Ẕil-ḥijja, A.H. 923. The reign of this prince, though a long one, was passed in troubles and civil wars, and the royal authority fell from the house of Bahmanī. On his death the governors in their respective provinces threw off the small portion of allegiance which they latterly paid to the late king, and proclaimed their independence. He was succeeded by his son Sulṭān Aḥmad Shāh II.

Mahmud Shah I. Khilji (محمود شاه خلجی اول) was the son of Khān Jahān Khiljī styled Malik Mughīs and 'Azīm Humāyūn, the prime minister of Hoshang Shāh, after whose death Mahmūd in conjunction with his father, having succeeded in poisoning his sovereign Muhammad Shāh, the son of Hoshang Shāh, ascended the throne of Mālwā on Tuesday the 15th May, A.D. 1436, 29th Shawwāl, A.H. 839. He reigned 34 lunar years, and died on the 27th May, A.D. 1469, 19th Ẕi-Qa'da, A.H. 873, aged 68 years. The numerals of the two Persian words نشینی جنت give the year of his death. He was succeeded by his son Ghayās-uddīn Khiljī, who reigned 33 years and left his kingdom to his son Sulṭān Nāsir-uddīn. He reigned 11 years and 4 months and was succeeded by his son Sulṭān Mahmūd II. who was defeated and slain by Sulṭān Bahādur Shāh of Gujrāt in A.D. 1531, A.H. 937, and Mālwā incorporated with the kingdom of Gujrāt.

Mahmud Shah II. (محمود شاه ثانی), the third son of Sulṭān Nāsir-uddīn, after whose death he ascended the throne of Mālwā on the 3rd May, A.D. 1511, 3rd Ṣafar, A.H. 917, Mālwā was taken by Bahādur Shāh king of Gujrāt on the 26th February, A.D. 1531, 9th Shabān, A.H. 937, and Mahmūd Shāh taken prisoner with his seven sons and ordered into confinement. He was sent to the fort of Champaner, but died or was murdered on his way to that place, and the kingdom of Mālwā became incorporated with that of Gujrāt. After the death of Bahādur Shāh, one Qādir Khān and after him Shujāa Khān ruled over Mālwā for some years, and after the demise of the latter his son Bāz Bahādur reigned till the year A.D. 1570, A.H. 978, when that kingdom was entirely subdued by the emperor Akbar.

Mahmud Shah Purbi (محمود شاه پوربی) succeeded his father Fīrōz Shāh to the throne of Bengāl in A.D. 1494, A.H. 899. He reigned about one year and was then murdered by Siddī Badr, who succeeded him and assumed the title of Muzaffar Shāh in A.D. 1495, A.H. 900.

Mahmud Shah Sharqi, Sultan (محمود شاه شرقی), ascended the throne of Jaunpūr after the death of his father Sulṭān Ibrāhīm Shāh Sharqī in A.D. 1440, A.H. 844. He reigned about 17 years and died in A.D. 1457, A.H. 862, when his eldest son Bhīkhan Khān succeeded him, and assumed the title of Muhammad Shāh Sharqī.

Mahmud Shah Tughlaq, Sultan (محمود شاه تغلق سلطان), surnamed Nāṣir-uddīn, was the son of Muhammad Shāh, the son of Fīrōz Shāh Tughlaq. He was raised to the throne of Dehlī after the death of his brother Humāyūn Shāh in April, A.D. 1394, Jumādạ II. A.H. 796, at the age of ten years. His minority and the dissensions of the nobles encouraged many of the surrounding chiefs to revolt and become independent. In his time Amīr Timur invaded India, and defeated Mahmūd Shāh in a battle fought, according to Firishta, on the 15th January, A.D. 1399, 7th Jumādạ I. A.H. 801, and according to Sharaf-uddīn Yezdī, on Tuesday the 7th Rabī' II. A.H. 801, corresponding with the 17th December, A.D. 1398, when Mahmūd fled to Gujrāt, and Timur the next day took possession of Dehlī.

On the eighth of Rabī'-us-Sānī, with the sun
In Capricorn, Timur had Dehlī won.

Timur, soon after his conquest of Dehlī, returned to Persia with an immense treasure from India. After the departure of that conqueror Nasrat Khān, son of Fatha Khān, the son of Fīrōz Shāh, took possession of Dehlī, and ascended the throne with the title of Nasrat Shāh. He was succeeded in A.D. 1400 by Iqbāl Khān, after whose death Mahmūd Shāh, who was then at Qanauj, returned and ascended the throne of Dehlī the second time in December, A.D. 1405, 22nd Jumādạ II. A.H. 808. But the governors of provinces no longer acknowledged allegiance to the throne, having established their independence during the civil war. Mahmūd Shāh died on the 4th March, A.D. 1413, 29th Ẕi-Qa'da, A.H. 815, and was succeeded by Daulat Khān Lodī. With Sulṭān Mahmūd the empire of Dehlī was lost to the race of the Turks who were adopted slaves of the House of Ghar.

Mahmud, Sultan (محمود سلطان غزنی), the celebrated king of Ghaznī, was the eldest son of Sulṭān Nāṣir-uddīn Subaktagīn. His father at his death, A.D. 997, A.H. 387, unmindful of the superior right of Mahmūd (who was then employed in the government of Khurāsān), bequeathed his kingdom to Isma'īl, a younger son. Isma'īl attempted to confirm himself in the power to which he was raised, but on the approach of Mahmūd, after a vain attempt at resistance, he was compelled to throw himself upon the clemency of his offended brother. Mahmūd reigned more than 33 lunar years, during which time he made twelve expeditions into India; took Lāhore, Dehlī, Kanauj, and other parts of Hindūstān; many hundred temples of the Hindūs he levelled with the ground; many thousand idols he demolished, and broke to pieces the famous idol of Sōmnāth, the fragments of which he distributed to Ghaznī, Mecca and Medina. He was born on the 15th December, A.D. 967, 9th Muḥarram, A.H. 357, and died on Thursday, the 23rd Rabī' II. A.H. 421, which year and date is inscribed on his tomb at Ghaznī, corresponding with the 30th April, A.D. 1030. On a tombstone of white marble lies the mace of Mahmūd, of such a weight that few men can wield it. He was succeeded by his son Muhammad, who reigned only five months and was deposed and deprived of sight by his brother Masa'ūd, who ascended the throne.

Mahmud, Sultan (محمود سلطان), the son of Muhammad (Sulṭān), the son of Malik Shāh, which see.

Mahmud, Sultan (محمود سلطان غوری), of Ghōr.

[*Vide* Ghayās-uddīn Mahmūd Ghōrī.]

Mahmud Tabrezi (محمود تبریزی), author of the *Miftāh ul-Ya'jāz*, or the Key to Miracles, describing the happiness of those who have obtained the light of Sūfīism and other mysteries. Written in A.D. 1482, A.H. 887.

Mahmud Tistari, Shaikh (محمود تستری شیخ), a native of Tistar, a town in Persia, and author of the poem called *Gulshan-e-Rāz*, which he wrote in A.D. 1317, A.H. 717. He died in the year A.D. 1320, A.H. 720, and was buried at Tistar his native country.

Mahtab Bagh (مهتاب باغ), name of a place or garden, which Shāh Jahān had commenced building on the other side of the Jamna opposite to the Rauza of Tājganj and similar to it, where he intended he should be buried after his death, but 'Alamgīr his son took away all the materials for the construction of some other buildings after his father's death; some of its ruins are still to be seen.

Mail (مایل), the poetical name of Mirzā Quṭb-uddīn, a nobleman of the reign of the emperor 'Alamgīr. He was an excellent poet, but latterly became distracted and died eight days after Mullā Nāṣir 'Alī, in the month of March, A.D. 1697, Ramaẓān, A.H. 1108. His brother Mirzā Nizām-uddīn surnamed Tāla was also an elegant poet.

Maimuna (میمونه), the daughter of Hārith or Hāris, was one of the wives of Muhammad, who married her in the eighth year of the Hijrī, *i.e.* in A.D. 629. This was doubtless another marriage of policy, for Maimūna was 51 years of age and a widow, but the connection gained him two powerful proselytes. One was Khālid, the son of Walīd, a nephew of the widow, who by his prowess obtained the appellation of "The Sword of God." The other was Khālid's friend, 'Amrū, the son of 'As, the same who assailed Muhammad with poetry and satire at the commencement of his prophetic career. Maimūna was the last spouse of the prophet, and, old as she was at her marriage, survived nearly all his other wives. She died many years after him in a pavilion at Sarif, under the same tree in the shade of which her nuptial tent had been pitched, and was there interred. This event took place about the year A.D. 671, A.H. 51.

Maisana (میسنه), the Bedouin bride of the khālīf Mu'āwia I. and the mother of Yezīd, was a daughter of the tribe of Kalab, a tribe remarkable for the purity of dialect spoken in it. She was married to Mu'āwia whilst very young; but this exalted situation by no means suited the disposition of Maisana, and amidst all the pomp and splendour of Damascus she languished for the simple pleasures of her native desert. She was an excellent poetess, and had pleased Mū'āwia's fancy to that degree with some of her verses, that he made her go back into the desert amongst her own relations, and take her son Yezīd along with her that he also might be brought up a poet. This part of his education succeeded, for he was reckoned to excel in that way, though his chief talent consisted in making himself a drunken wretch. Maisana did not revisit Damascus till after the death of Mu'āwia, when Yezīd ascended the throne.

Majahid Shah Bahmani (مجاهد شاه بهمنی). *Vide* Mujāhid Shāh.

Majd Hamkar Farsi (مجد همکرفارسی), also called Majd-uddīn Haibat-ullāh.

[*Vide* Majd-uddīn Hamkar.]

Majd, Maulana (مجد مولانا), author of the work called *Rauzat ul-Khuld*.

Majd-uddaula (مجد الدوله), a Sulṭān of the race of Boya called Boyaites, was the son of Fakhr-uddaula, the brother of 'Azd-uddaula, Sulṭān of Fars and Irāq. He had for a short time governed Khurāsān and assumed a regal state, but was taken prisoner in Rei, by the victorious Sulṭān Mahmūd of Ghaznī in A.D. 1029, A.H. 420. He had been raised by the death of his father in August, A.D. 997, Sha'bān, A.H. 387, when very young, to the government of the city and the surrounding country. During the minority of this prince, all the power was in the hands of his mother. Mahmūd commanded one of his officers to inform the lady that she must submit to his authority, or prepare for war. "Had such a message been sent," replied the heroine, "in the life of my deceased lord, it must have occasioned great embarrassment. That is not the case now. I know Sulṭān Mahmūd; and from his character, am assured he will never undertake an expedition without calculating all the chances. If he attack and conquer a weak woman, where is the glory of such an achievement? If he be repulsed, the latest ages will hear of the shame of such a defeat!" Mahmūd, either swayed by the above reasons or others of more weight, did not prosecute his designs upon Rei till Majd-uddaula was of age and had assumed the reigns of government. He then advanced an army, by the leader of which the prince was deluded to an interview and seized; his treasures and dominions passed into the hands of Mahmūd, who sent him and his family prisoners to Ghaznī.

Majd-uddaula (مجد الدوله), title of 'Abdul Majīd Khān, which see.

Majd-uddin Ahmad ibn-Muhammad Sajawandi (مجد الدين احمد ابن محمد سجاوندی), author of a commentary or Tafsīr called *'Aīn ul-Ma'ānī*. There is another work of the same title on Sūfiism written by Shahāb-uddīn Burhānpūrī.

Majd-uddin Baghdadi (مجد الدين بغدادی), a pupil and disciple of Shaikh Najm-uddīn Kubrā. He is stated to have been a very religious and upright man, and was employed as a physician to Sulṭān Muhammad surnamed Quṭb-uddīn, king of Khwārizm. It is said that he privately got married to the mother of the Sulṭān, who no sooner heard of it than he ordered Majd-uddīn to be thrown into a lake, where he died. This circumstance took place A.D. 1219, A.H. 616, and after a short time the Sulṭān was defeated and his country pillaged by Changez Khān.

Majd-uddin Bilqani (مجد الدين بيلقانی), an author.

Majd-uddin Hamkar Farsi (مجد الدين همكر فارسی), also called Majd-uddīn Haibat-ullāh and Majd Hamkar, *i.e.* Majd the weaver. His poetical title is Majd and Rihī. He was a native of Shīrāz and derived his descent from Anūsherwān. He was in high favour with the Atābak Sa'd Abū Bakr bin-Zangī and a contemporary of Sa'dī. Under Abāqāān, the Tartar king of Persia, he was made governor of Shīrāz, where he died upwards of 90 years of age in A.D. 1287, A.H. 686, and left a Dīwān in Persian. In his time, people used to call him the king of poets.

Majd-uddin Isma'il, Shaikh (مجد الدين اسمعيل شيخ), was Kāzī of Shīrāz in the reign of Shāh Shaikh 'Abū Is-hāq Khwāja Hāfiz, who praises him in one of his odes, and has found the year of his demise to be contained in the words "Rahmat Haq," *i.e.* the mercy of God. He died on Wednesday the 29th July, A.D. 1355, 18th Rajab, A.H. 756.

Majd-uddin Khalil (مجد الدين خليل), a poet who was a contemporary of Khāqānī and wrote poetry in his praise.

Majd-uddin Muhammad bin-Ya'qub bin-Muhammad (مجد الدين بن محمد بن يعقوب بن محمد), commonly called Fīrōzābādī, is the author of the much-esteemed and very copious Lexicon in Arabic called the *Qāmūs*, or *Bahr ul-Muhīt*, "The Ocean," dedicated to bin-Ābbās, prince of Arabia Felix. He died A.D. 1414, A.H. 817. [*Vide* Fīrōzābādī.]

Majd ul-Mulk (مجد الملك), a nobleman of the court of Sulṭān Abqā Khān. He was put to death at the instigation of Shams-uddīn Muhammad, commonly called Sāhib Dīwān, on suspicion of sorcery, in the reign of Sulṭān Ahmad Khān, in August, A.D. 1282, 20th Jumāda I. A.H. 681, and not long after Shams-uddīn had to undergo the same fate.

Majir (مجير). *Vide* Mujīr.

Ma'jiz (معجز). *Vide* Nizām Khān Ma'jiz.

Ma'jizi (معجزی), a poet who was a contemporary of Rukn-uddīn Qabāī, and master of the poet Badr-uddīn Jājurmī.

Majju Khan, Nawab (مجو خان نواب), a chief of the rebels who caused himself to be proclaimed Nawāb of Murādābād, and instigated the people to murder and plunder Europeans, was captured with his son in the latter part of April, A.D. 1858.

Majlisi (مجلسی). *Vide* Muhammad Bākir Majlisī.

Majnun (مجنون). This name was given to a person, whose proper name was Qais, after he had fallen in love with Lailā or Lailī. The meaning of the word is a madman; also a man who is transported by love either divine or profane.

[*Vide* Lailī. Majnūn lived in the time of the khalīf Hashām of the house of Umayya, about the year A.D. 721, A.H. 103.]

Majnun (مجنون), the poetical title of two poets, one of Dehlī and the other of Lucknow.

Majruh (مجروح), takhallus of Munshī Kishun Chand, a Kashmerian, who was living in A.D. 1782, A.H. 1196, at Lucknow.

Majzub (مجذوب), Mirzā Muhammad Majzūb of Tabrez. He is the author of several Masnawīs and also of a Dīwān which he completed in A.D. 1653, A.H. 1063.

Majzub (مجذوب), poetical name of Mirzā Ghulām Haidar Beg, an adopted son of the celebrated poet of India, Souda; was living at Lucknow in A.D. 1800, A H. 1215, and had written two Dīwāns in Urdū.

Majzub (مجذوب), poetical title of Najābat 'Alī Shāh, an Urdū poet who died in the year A.D. 1819, A.H. 1234.

Makhdum Jahanian Jahangasht (مخدوم جهانیان جهان‌گشت). *Vide* Shaikh Jalāl.

Makhdum Sharqi (مخدوم شرقی), author of the *Kitāb un-Nawāfiz.*

Makhfi (مخفی), the poetical title of the princess Zeb un-Nisā Begam, daughter of the emperor 'Alamgīr. She is the author of a Dīwān and of a Tafsīr or commentary on the Qurān. Makhfī was also the takhallus of Nūr Jahān Begam.

[*Vide* Zeb un-Nisā Begam.]

Makin (مکین), poetical name of Mirzā Muhammad Fākhir, a native of Dehlī, who came to Lucknow in A.D. 1759, A.H. 1173. He is the author of a Dīwān. He died in the year A.D. 1806, A.H. 1221.

Maktabi (مکتبی), a school-master of Shīrāz, who is the author of a poem called *Lailī wa-Majnūn*, composed in A.D. 1490, A.H. 895.

Maktub Khan (مکتوب خان), superintendent of the library of the emperor Shāh Jahān.

Makunda Bramhchari (مکندہ برمہچاری), a famous Brāhman ascetic. The Hindūs insist that the emperor Akbar was a Hindū in a former generation. The proximity of the time in which this famous emperor lived has forced them however, to account for this in the following manner:—"There was a holy Brāhman of the above name, who wished very much to become emperor of India, and the only practicable way for him was to die first, and be born again. For this purpose he made a desperate *Tapassia,* wishing to remember then every thing he knew in the present generation. This could not be fully granted; but he was indulged with writing upon a brass plate a few things which he wished more particularly to remember; then he was directed to bury the plate, and promised that he should remember the place in the next generation. Makunda went to Allahābād, buried the plate and then buried himself. Nine months afterwards he was born in the character of Akbar, who, as soon as he ascended the throne, went to Allahābād, and easily found the spot where the brass plate was buried."—(Mill's *British India*, vol. ii. p. 152.) The translation of the inscription on the brass plate is as follows: "In the Sambat year 1598, on the 12th day of the 2nd fortnight of the month of Māgh, I, Makunda Bramhchārī, whose food was nothing but milk, sacrificed myself at Parāg (Allahābād) the grand place of worship, with the design that I should become ruler of the whole world." The above date corresponds with the 27th January, A.D. 1542, and Akbar was born on Sunday the 15th October the same year, being three or four days less than nine months after the above circumstance.

Maldeo Rao (مالدیو راو), a Rāja of Mārwār of the Rāthor tribe of rājpūts, and a descendant of Jodhā Rāo, who founded Jōdhpūr. He acquired a pre-eminence in Rājpūtāna in A.D. 1532, and is styled by Firishta "the most potent prince in Hindūstān." Powerful as he was, however, he was compelled to succumb to the emperor Akbar, and to pay reluctant homage at the court of the Mughal. After his death his son Udai Singh succeeded him.

Malhar Rao Gaekowar (ملہار راو گایکہوار), Rāja of Baroda, succeeded to the Rāja, after the death of his brother Khānde Rāo, on the 29th November, 1870, aged 42. His father was called Mahārāja Khande Rāo Gaekowar, Sona Khaskhail Shamsher Bahādur, G.C.S.I. He is fifth in descent from Pilāji the second Gaekowar, and sixth from Damajī the first Gaekowar. When Sir Seymour Fitzgerald sent a peremptory message directing his brother Khānde Rāo to replace his minion (Dīwān) by some man of character, the Gaekowar fell into so violent a rage that the conflict of passion deprived him of life. At that time Malhār Rāo the new ruler was a prisoner. He had been confined for years on suspicion of having attempted his brother's life, and from his captivity at Padra he was called to a throne by the British government. In Feb. 1873 he was tried for an alleged attempt to poison the British Resident, but the charge was not considered fully proved. He was, however, deposed for obvious maladministration, and interned in Fort St. George, Madras.

Malhar Rao Holkar I. (ملہار راو هلکر).

The Holkar family are of the Dhūngar or Shepherd tribe. The derivation of the name Holkar, or more properly Halkar, is perhaps from Hal a plough, and Kar a labourer; so that it would mean "ploughman." Malhār Rāo, who was the first prince of this family, was an officer in the service of the first Peshwā Bājī Rāo, and was one of the earliest Marhatta adventurers in the expeditions to the northward; he killed Girdhar Bahādur Sūbadār of Mālwā in A.D. 1726 or 1729. The time when he first obtained local authority was in A.D. 1728; the district of Indor was assigned to him by the Peshwa in jāgīr about the year 1733. He was present at the battle of Panipat 14th January 1761, and died in A.D. 1768. The direct line being then extinct, Ahlia Bāī, Khānde Rāo's widow, elected Tukājī Holkar the nephew of Malhār Rāo to the principality. He had four sons, Kāshī Rāo and Malhār Rāo by his wife, and Jaswant Rāo and Etojī by his mistress.

The Holkar Family.

1. Malhār Rāo Holkar I.
2. Mallhī Rāo, grandson of ditto, succeeded under regency of Ahlia Bāī, his mother, and died in A.D. 1767.
3. Tukājī Holkar.
4. Kāshī Rāo.
5. Jaswānt Rāo.
6. Malhār Rāo II.
7. Harī Rāo Holkar.

Malhar Rao Holkar (ملہار راو هلکر), a son of Takojī Holkar, Rāja of Indor, killed in battle against Daulat Rāo Sindhia in September, A.D. 1797.

[*Vide* Kāshī Rāo.]

Malhar Rao Holkar II. (ملہار راو هلکر), the adopted or illegitimate son and successor of Jaswant Rāo Holkar the son of Takojī Holkar. He succeeded his father as Rāja of Indor in A.D. 1811. After the battle of Mahadpūr, a peace was concluded by Government with Malhār Rāo on the 6th January, A.D. 1818. He died in 1834 and was succeeded by Martand Rāo his adopted son, who was soon after dispossessed by Khānde Rāo, who, dying without issue, the East India Company assumed the right of nominating Mulkerjī Rāo.

Malika Bano Begam (ملکه بانو بیگم), the eldest daughter of 'Asaf Khān, wazīr, and sister of Mumtāz Mahal. She was married to Saif Khān surnamed Mirzā Safī, son of Amānat Khān; he was an amīr of 5000, and died in Bengal A.D. 1639, A.H. 1049. Malika Bāno died in A.D. 1640, A.H. 1050, during the reign of Shāh Jahān.

Malika Jahan (ملکه جہان), a princess of Dehlī married to Husain Shāh Sharqī, king of Jaunpūr.

Malika Jahan (ملکه جہان), a wife of the emperor Jahāngīr and daughter of Rawal Bhīm of Jīsalmīr, whose brother's name was Rawal Kalyān.

Malika Zamana (ملکه زمانه), the daughter of the emperor Farrukh-siyar, married to Muhammad Shāh, emperor of Dehlī, in A.D. 1722, A.H. 1135. The year of her death is not known, but she lies buried in a small tomb out of the Kābul gate of Dehlī.

Malik Alashtar (ملک الاشتر), a Saracen chief who served under 'Abū 'Ubaida and subsequently under 'Alī. He was poisoned on his way to Egypt by order of Muāwia I. in A.D. 658, A.H. 38.

Malik Ambar Habshi (ملک عمبر حبشی), an Abyssinian who rose from the condition of a slave to great influence and command in the Deccan. When Ahmadnagar was taken by prince Dāniāl in A.D. 1600, A.H. 1009, Malik Ambar and Rājū Minnān, a Deccan chief, divided the remaining territories between them, leaving to a nominal Sultān, Murtazā Nizām Shāh II. whom they had placed on the throne on the capture of Bahādur Nizām Shāh, only the fortress of Ousa with a few villages for his support. About this period several commotions happening in the Dehlī Government, owing to the rebellion of Sultān Salīm, the death of Akbar, and revolt of Sultān Khusro, successively, Ambar had leisure to regulate his country and levy great armies, and even dared to seize several of the imperial districts. When the authority of the emperor Jahāngīr was established, he sent frequent armies to the Deccan, but Ambar was not to be subdued. He at length gave up the places taken from the Mughals to the Prince Shāh Jahān, to whose interest he became attached, and continued loyal until his death, which took place in the year A.D. 1626, A.H. 1035, in the 80th year of his age. He was buried in Daulatābād, under a splendid dome which he had erected. After his death Fatha Khān his son succeeded him.

Malik 'Aziz (ملک عزیز). *Vide* Malik ul-Azīz 'Usmān, or 'Abū'l Fatha 'Usmān.

Malik Dinar (ملک دینار), a Turk of the tribe of Ghuz. He in A.D. 1187, A.H. 583, dispossessed Bahrām Shāh the last prince of Kirmān of the family of Kādard Saljūqī, and put an end to that dynasty.

Malik Fakhr-uddin (ملک فخرالدین), king of Bengal commonly called Pūrbī. The first Muhammad chief who invaded Bengal was Malik Muhammad Bakhtyār, in the reign of Quṭb-uddīn Eybak, king of Dehlī, A.D. 1191, A.H. 587. Ater him the several governors of that country were appointed from that capital. Malik Fakhr-uddīn was originally a soldier in the service of Qadar Khān, governor of Bengal, whom he put to death in the reign of Tughlaq Shāh about the year A.D. 1338, A.H. 739, proclaimed himself king, and declared his independence of the throne of Dehlī. He reigned two years and five months, when he was defeated, taken prisoner in a pitched battle in A.D 1340, and put to death by Malik 'Alī Mubārik, who had also proclaimed himself king under the title of Alā-uddīn.

Malik ibn-Anas, Imam (مالک ابن آنس امام), one of the four learned doctors of the Sunnīs, who are the founders of their faith. He was born at Madīna in A.D. 714, A.H. 95, and died there in the reign of the khalīf Hārūn al-Rashīd, on Sunday the 28th June, A.D. 795, 7th Rabī' II. A.H. 179, and was buried in the cemetery called Al-Baqīa. He is the founder of the second Sunnī sect, and is sometimes called "Imām Dār ul-Hijrat," from the circumstance of his birth and death occurring at the city of Madīna. In his youth, he had the advantage of the society of Sihl bin-Sa'd, almost the sole surviving companion of the Prophet; and it is supposed that from him he derived his extreme veneration for the traditions. He is the author of the Arabic work called *Muwatta*, being a collection of Traditions, and is always looked upon as next in point of authority to the six Ṣaḥibs.

Malik ibn-Nawera (مالک ابن نویره), the chief of those who refused to pay the Zakāt (or that part of a man's substance which is consecrated to God, as tithes, alms, and the like, and the payment of which is strictly enjoined by the Muhammadan law). He was a person of considerable figure, being the chief of an eminent family among the Arabs, and celebrated for his skill in poetry, as well as his manly qualities and horsemanship. He was murdered by order of Khālid ibn-Walīd in the year A.D. 633, A.H. 12.

Malik 'Imad (ملک عماد), a poet who was a contemporary of Imām Muhammad Ghazzālī.

Malik Imam (مالک امام یعنی ابن آنس). *Vide* Imām Malik or Malik Ibn-Anas.

Malik Jahir (ملک جاحر), also called Nāth Bhanjan. In the well-known town of Mhow in Azimgarh, there is a place which obtains the distinguished title of "Nāth Bhanjan" from the great exploits of a saint called Malik Jāhir, who ejected the evil genius Deo Nāth, together with the original Hindūs, and colonized the place with Muhammadans. The true story is thus related: During the reign of Jahāngīr, king of Dehlī, about A.D. 1609, one Abhimān Singh, a Rājpūt of the Jatran tribe, having separated from his brethren, owing to the inadequacy of the share allotted to him in his hereditary possessions, took service under that monarch, and on his having embraced the religion of Muhammad, Jahāngīr granted to him the whole Zamindārī of Azimgaṛh, under the title of Rāja Abhimān Singh 'Alī Muhammad Naẓir-uddaula Khān. From that period up to the time the Nawāb of Audh resumed the grant, the Muhammadans had the supremacy over the Hindūs, but in A.D. 1801, when the district was ceded to the British, the Hindūs taking courage came and resided there; since then there have always been feuds between the parties.

Malik Mansur (ملک منصور). *Vide* Nūr-uddīn 'Alī.

Malik Mansur Muhammad-bin-'Usman (ملک منصور محمد بن عثمان), third Sulṭān of Egypt of the race of Ayyūb, succeeded his father in November, A.D. 1198, and died in A.D. 1200, when Malik 'Adil Saif-uddīn, the son of Ayyūb, succeeded him and reigned 18 years.

Malik Mo'izz-uddin, Aibak (ملک معز الدین ایبک), a Turkomān slave of the Ayyūbite dynasty, who married the Queen Malika Shajrat ul-Dar, the last of the Ayyūbite family, and reigned in Egypt. He began his reign in A.D. 1250, A.H. 648, and was murdered in A.D. 1257, A.H. 655. His descendants ruled the country for nearly a hundred years.

List of the Mamlūk Sulṭāns who reigned in Egypt and Hamath in Syria, after the Sulṭāns of the Ayyūbite family.

		A.D.	A.H.
Malik	Moizz Azz-uddīn Aibak Turkmanī Sāhahī began to reign	1250	648
,,	Mansūr Nūr-uddīn 'Alī bin-Moizz imprisoned by Muzaffar		655
,,	Muzaffar Kut uz-Moizzī (11 months)		657
,,	Tāhir Rukn-uddīn . . .		658
,,	Sa'īd Muhammad Nāsir-uddīn		676
,,	'Adil Badr-uddīn (4 months)		678
,,	Mansūr Abūl Ma'ālī Qalādūn Sālahī		678
,,	Ashraf Salāh-uddīn Khalīl		689
,,	Nāsir Muhammad bin-Qalādūn (reigned 44 years) .		693
,,	'Adil Kutbagha Mansūrī .		
,,	Mansūr Hisām-uddīn, reigned 2 years, died A.D. 698		
,,	Muzaffar Rukn-uddīn, reigned 10th, died A.D. 709		
,,	Mansūr Abū Bakr (2 months)		
,,	Ashraf Kuchak (8 months)		
,,	Nāsir Ahmad, died A.D. 745		
,,	Sālāh Ismaīl 'Abū'l Fida, the author of an abridgment of *Universal History* down to his time. He succeeded his brother Nāsir Ahmad in A.D. 1344, A.H. 745 . . .		

In process of time, the old Mamlūks grew proud, insolent and lazy; and the Borgites, a new Militia and slaves of the old Mamlūks, taking advantage of this, rose upon their masters, deprived them of the government and transferred it to themselves about the year A.D. 1382. The Borgites also assumed the name of Mamlūks; and were famous for their valour and ferocity. Their dominion lasted till the year 1517, when they were invaded by Salīm I. the Turkish Sulṭān, who defeated them, took possession of their obscure country, and beheaded Tuman Bey the last of the Borgites with 30,000 prisoners.

Malik Muhammad Jaisi (ملک محمد جایسی), a poet who was a native of Jāes and the author of the story of Padmāwat in Hindū verse. He lived in the time of the emperor Jahāngīr.

Malik Nasir Khan Faruqi (ملک نصیر خان فاروقی), son of Malik Rāja, after whose death in April, A.D. 1399, A.H. 801, he also like his father assumed the ensigns of royalty at Khāndesh, and built Burhānpūr. Learned men were invited from all parts, and literature was much promoted. He seized the fort of Asīr from 'Āsā Ahīr, reigned 40 lunar years, and died on the 21st September, A.D. 1437, 20th Rabī' I. A.H. 841. He was buried in the family vault at Tālner by the side of his father, and was succeeded by his son Mīrān 'Adil Farūqī.

Malik Qummi Mulla (ملک قمی ملا), a native of Kumm in Persia. He was an excellent poet, and came to the Deccan in the year A.D. 1579, A.H. 987. He was at first employed by Murtazā Nizām Shāh, and then by Burhān Nizām Shāh, kings of Ahmadnagar. Subsequently he went to Bījāpūr where he was much respected, and the highest honours conferred on him by the king of that place, Ibrāhīm 'Adil Shāh II. He gave his daughter in marriage to Mulla Zahūrī a celebrated poet of that court. Mulla Malik died in A.D. 1616, A.H. 1025, and Zahūrī one year after him. He was called Malik ul-Kalām or the king of Poetry. He is the author of a Dīwān and several Masnawīs.

Malik Raja Faruqi (ملک راجه فاروقی). The first person who assumed independence in the province of Khāndesh was Malik Rāja, the son of Khān Jahān Farūqī, whose ancestors were among the most respectable nobles at the Dehlī court, in the reigns of Alā-uddīn Khiljī and Muhammad Tughlaq. At the death of his father he was very young, and inherited only a small patrimony. About the year A.D. 1370, A.H. 772, he was appointed governor of Khāndesh by Fīroz Shāh Tukhlaq, and had the jāgīr of Tālner conferred on him. After the death of that prince, when Dilāwar Khān Ghorī assumed independence in Mālwā, an intimate connection took place between the latter and Malik Rāja, so much so that Dilāwar Khān gave his daughter in marriage to Malik Nasīr the son of Malik Rāja. He reigned 29 lunar years and died on the 28th April, A.D. 1399, 22nd Shabān, A.H. 801. He was buried at the town of Tālner, and was succeeded by his son Malik Nasīr Khān.

The following are the names of the kings of Khāndesh :—

1. Malik Rāja.
2. Malik Nasīr Khān.
3. Mīrān 'Adil Khān.
4. Mīrān Mubārik.
5. 'Adil Khān I. or 'Alī Shāh.
6. Dāūd Khān.

7. 'Adil Khān II. ('Azim Humāyūn 'Alam Khān).
8. Mīrān Muhammad Shāh.
9. Mīrān Mubārik II.
10. Mīrān Muhammad.
11. Rāja 'Alī Khān.
12. Bahādur Shāh.

Malik Sarwar (ملک سرور). *Vide* Khwāja Jahān.

Malik Shah (ملکشاه جلال الدین), surnamed Jalāl-uddīn, was the third Sultān of the first dynasty of the Saljūqīs or Saljūkides. He succeeded his father Alp Arsalān in December, A.D. 1072, A.H. 465, and reigned twenty years. His right to the crown was disputed by his brother Qādir Beg, also called Qādard (which see), prince of Kirmān; but that chief was defeated and taken prisoner, and afterwards poisoned or put to death. Malik Shāh subdued almost the whole of Syria and Egypt; and being more fortunate than his father, not only conquered Bukhāra, Samarqand and Khwārizm, but received homage from the tribes beyond Jaxartes. Towards the end of his life he moved from Isfahān to Baghdād, with the design of transplanting the khalīf Al-Muqtadī, and fixing his own residence in the capital of the Moslem world. The feeble successor of Muhammad obtained a respite of ten days; and before the expiration of the term, the Sultān was summoned by the angel of death. He died in the 38th year of his age, in the month of November, A.D. 1092, Shawwāl, A.H. 485, a few days after Nizām ul-Mulk his wazīr, who was assassinated by a follower of Hasan Sabbāh. The greatness and unity of the Saljūkian empire expired in the person of Malik Shāh. He invented an era called Tārīkh Malikshāhī or Jalālī (Jalalian Era). This Era, according to Dr. Hyde, commences 15th March, A.D. 1079, corresponding with the 11th Ramazān, A.H. 471. Malik Shāh left four sons—Barkayāraq, Muhammad, Sanjar and Mahmūd, all of whom attained power in their turns. Mahmūd the youngest, was only four years of age when his father died: but the ambition of his mother, the Sultāna Khātūn Turkān, placed the crown upon his infant head. However, she was soon compelled to resign, and after some time they both died, and Sultān Barkayāraq succeeded him.

Malik Sharqi Mirza (ملک شرقی مرزا), an author.

Malik ul-Afzal (ملک الافضل نورالدین علی), surnamed Nūr-uddīn 'Alī, the eldest of the seventeen sons of Sālah-uddīn Yūsaf ibn-Ayyūb. On the death of his father at Damascus in A.D. 1193, A.H. 589, he took possession of that kingdom, whilst his brother Malik ul-'Azīz 'Usmān obtained that of Egypt, and their brother Malik uz-Zāhir continued to hold Aleppo. Damascus was afterwards besieged and taken by his uncle Malik ul-'Adil Saif-uddīn Abū Bakr (the Saphadin of Christian writers). Nūr-uddīn 'Alī, in a poetical address to the khalīf Nāsir, lamented the similarity of his own fate to that of the khalīf 'Alī ibn-Abū Tālib (his namesake) in being thus excluded from his rights by Abū Bakr and 'Usmān: the khalif in his reply consoled him by the assurance that in him he should find the Nāsir (protector) whom 'Alī had sought in vain; but the intercession of the khalif was unavailing to procure the restitution of any part of his territories. In A.D. 1198, however, on the death of his brother, the Sultān of Egypt, Nūr-uddīn became Atābak, or guardian, to his infant nephew Malik ul-Mansūr, and attempted by the aid of his brother, the Sultān of Aleppo, to recover Damascus from his uncle; but the expedition failed, and Saif-uddīn retaliated by invading Egypt, and expelled the young Sultān and his guardian, A.D. 1199. The unfortunate Nūr-uddīn now retired to Samosata, where he died apparently without issue. He was born in June, A.D. 1171, while his father was acting as wazīr to the Egyptians. He died suddenly in February, A.D. 1225, Safar, A.H. 662, and was buried in Aleppo.

[*Vide* Nūr-uddīn 'Alī (Malik ul-Afzal).]

Malik ul-'Aziz 'Usman (ملک العزیز عثمان). *Vide* 'Abū'l Fatha 'Usmān.

Malli or **Mallhi Rao Holkar** (مالی یا ملهی راؤ هلکر), Rāja of Indor, was the son of Khānde Rāo, and grandson of Malhār Rāo I. whom he succeeded in A.D. 1766, and died after a reign of nine months. After his death the original family being extinct, Ahlia Bāī, the widow of Khānde Rāo, elected Takojī to the rāj.

Mallu 'Adil Shah (ملو عادل شاه), of Bījāpūr, succeeded his father Ismā'īl 'Adīl Shāh in August, A.D. 1534, Safar, A.H. 941, and was on account of his shameful vices, blinded and deposed after an inglorious reign of only six months by order of his grandmother, and his younger brother Ibrāhīm was raised to the throne of Bījāpūr in the beginning of the year A.D. 1535, A.H. 941.

Mallu Khan (ملو خان), entitled Qādir Shāh, was the ruler of Mālwā when Sher Shāh took it about the year A.D. 1542, A.H. 949, and made it over to one of his own officers named Shujā'at Khān or Shujā'a Khān Sūr, which see, as also Qādir Shāh.

Maluk Shah (ملوک شاه), the father of the historian Shaikh 'Abdul Qādir of Badāon. He died in A.D. 1561, A.H. 969. He is the author of the work called *Jilāi ul-Khawātir*.

Malul (ملول), the poetical name of Shāh Sharaf-uddīn, a dervish of Murādābād. He wrote two Persian Dīwāns, in which he used the takhallus of Ilhām. He is also the author of a poem called *Haft Mykhāna*, which he composed in A.D. 1777, A.H. 1191.

Malwa (مالوه), kings of. *Vide* Dilāwar Khān.

Mamluk (مملوک). This word signifies, in Arabic, a slave in general; but in particular, it means the Turkish and Circassian slaves, whom the kings of the posterity of Sālah-uddīn (Saladin) had instructed in military exercises, and who at last made themselves masters of Egypt, and are sufficiently known to us by the name of Mamlūks. These Mamlūks reigned in Egypt 275 lunar years, that is to say, from A.D. 1250 to 1517, A.H. 648 to 923, when Salīm I. emperor of the Turks, entirely subdued and exterminated them. The first king of this dynasty was Malik Moizz 'Azz-uddīn Aibak, which see.

Mamnun (ممنون), poetical title of Mīr Nizām-uddīn, a son of Qamar-uddīn Khān Minnat. He flourished in the time of Akbar Shāh II. king of Dehlī, and is the author of two Persian and Urdū Dīwāns. His ancestors were of Sonpat, but he was a native of Dehlī. He was employed by the English Government as a Sadar-us-Sadūr at Ajmer. He died in the year A.D. 1844, A.H. 1260.

Mamun (مامون), the son of Hārūn al-Rashīd. *Vide* Al-Māmūn.

Manbhaoti Begam (من بهاوتي بيگم), one of the concubines of the emperor Akbar. She built at Āgra, on a spot of 40 bighas, a garden, of which no sign remains now.

Mangu Qaan or Khan (منگو قاآن يا منگو خان), emperor of Tartary, was the eldest son of Tūlī Khān, the son of Changez Khān. He succeeded his cousin Kayūk Khān, the son of Oqtāī Khān, over the kingdoms of Tartary and Persia, about the year A.D. 1243, A.H. 640. He died after a reign of sixteen years in A.D. 1258, A.H. 654, and was succeeded in the kingdom of Tartary by his son Qablāī Khān; his brother Halākū Khān became the sole master of Persia.

Mani (مانی), whom we call Manes, was the founder of the sect of the Manichīs or Manicheans. In the reign of Shāhpūr, the son of Ardisher, king of Persia, about the year A.D. 277, a painter, named Mānī, having learned from the conversation of some Christians *that the Redeemer had promised to send a Comforter after him*, formed the wild design of passing for the Paraclete; and, as no opinions are too absurd to be embraced, he soon drew together a multitude of proselytes. Shāhpūr was enraged at this imposture, and wished to punish the author of it; but Mānī found means to escape, and fled as far as the borders of China, having first told his followers that he was going to heaven, and promised to meet them in a certain grot at the end of the year. In this retreat he amused himself with painting a number of strange figures and views, which at the year's end he shewed to his disciples, as a work given to him by angels. He was a very ingenious artist, and had a lively fancy, so that his pictures, which were finely coloured, easily persuaded the credulous multitude, in the infancy of the art in Asia, that they were really divine; they were bound together in a book called *Artang*, which is often alluded to by the Persian poets. Mingling the pure doctrines of Christianity with paganism he taught that there were two principles of all things, coeternal and coeval, that is, God and the Devil, that from the former all good, and from the latter all evil, proceeded. The good being he called the author of the New Testament, the bad of the Old. God, he added, created the soul; the devil, the body. He pretended also to work miracles, and was therefore sent for by Shāhpūr to cure his son, but his pretended power failed him, the child died in his arms, and the disappointed father ordered the prophet to be flayed alive, and his skin stuffed with chaff to be hung at the gates of the capital, where Epiphanius, who refuted his doctrines, saw it. Some say this impostor was put to death in the reign of Bahrām, grandson of Shāhpūr.

Mani (مانی), a poet, who although called Kāsagar Māzandarānī, *i.e.* a porcelain manufacturer of Māzandarān, yet acquired the favour of Muhammad Muhsin Mirzā, a son of Sultān Husain Mirzā, in whose service he was killed by the Uzbeks in A.D. 1507, A.H. 913. He was the author of a Dīwān.

Ma'ni (معنی), the poetical name of Rāi Bijai Mal, a brother of Imtiyāz, was living in A.D. 1760, A.H. 1174, and did military service under Nawāb Shujā'-uddaula.

Manija Begam (مانيجه بيگم), sister of Nūr Jahān Begam.

[*Vide* Qasim Khān Jawenī.]

16

Manik Pal (مانک پال), Rāja of Karaulī. He died in A.D. 1805, and was succeeded by a boy then 13 years of age. In December, A.D. 1817, the Karaulī chief signed a treaty, and put himself under the protection of the British Government.

Manka al-Hindi (منکه الهندی). Ibn-Abu Usaibia, in his work entitled *Ayūn-ul-Anba*, on the physicians of India, says that Manka of India was one of the most distinguished philosophers in the sciences of India, and was well acquainted both with the language of India and Persia. It was he who translated the book of Shānāk the Indian, treating on poisons, from the Hindī to the Persian language. He lived in the days of Hārūn al-Rashīd, and came during his reign from India to Irāq, and attached himself to him.

Manni Ram Seith (منی رام), the great banker of Mathura, died in July, A.D. 1836.

Mannu Lal (منو لال), a Hindū, who is the author of a work called *Guldastār Nashāt*.

Manohar Das (منوهر داس). *Vide* Tousanī.

Mansabdar (منصبدار) (from *manṣab* "elevation" or "post"). The title of an office under the Mug͟hol Empire, the holder of which ranked according to the number of men he was supposed to lead.

[*Vide* Blochmann, *Āīn Translation.*]

Mansa Ram (منسه رام), father of Rāja Chait Singh of Banaras. He possessed originally but half the village of Gangāpūr, by additions to which, in the usual modes of Hindūstān, he laid the foundation of the great zamīndārī of Banaras. He died in A.D. 1740, and was succeeded by his son Balwant Singh.

Man Singh (مان سنگه), a Rāja of Gwāliar who lived in the time of Sulṭān Sikandar Lodī and his son Sulṭān Ibrāhīm Lodī, and died about the year A.D. 1518, A.H. 924. He was a prince of great valour and capacity. His son Bikarmājīt succeeded him in the rājaship and was living at the time the emperor Babar conquered India.

Man Singh (مان سنگه), son or nephew of Rāja Bhagwān Dās Kachhwāhā, ruler of Amer in Ajmer, now called Jaipūr and Jainagar. He was appointed governor of Kābul by the emperor Akbar in A.D. 1587, A.H. 995, and in the next year of Behār, Hājīpūr and Patna; and after the death of his father in A.D. 1589, A.H. 998, he was honoured with the title of Rāja and *manṣab* of 7000, and made governor of Bengal. It is said that he had 1500 concubines, and every one of them had children; but they all died before him. Mān Singh died in the ninth year of the emperor Jahāngīr, A.D. 1614, A.H. 1023, in the Deccan, and sixty of his concubines burnt themselves with his corpse. His second son Rāja Bhāo Singh succeeded him and died of drinking. The eldest son of Mān Singh was Rāja Partap Singh, who died before his father and left a son named Maha Singh, who served under the emperor Jahāngīr, and after the death of his grandfather and uncle was honoured with the title of Rāja. Mān Singh had built a house on the banks of the river Jamna, of which at present towards the river only two broken bastions are to be seen. The Muhalla Mānpanah close to the Jamna Masjid at Āgra is still very well known. He died at Beṛār in A.D. 1617, A.H. 1026. His son Mirzā Rāja Jai Singh served under Shāh Jahān and ‘Alamgīr. He was poisoned by his son Kīrat Singh about the year A.D. 1625. After him his son Rām Singh was reduced to a *manṣab* of 4000; Bishun Singh, reduced to a *manṣab* of 3000, and after him came Jai Singh Sawai, son of Bishun Singh, which see.

Man Singh (مان سنگه), Rāja of Jodhpūr or Māṛwār, was a descendant of Rāja Jaswant Singh Rāṭhorī, the earliest Rāja of this country on record. He succeeded Rāja Bhīm Singh in A.D. 1803 or 1804. Disasters or disappointments either soured the temper or affected the reason of Mān Singh, who became one of the most sanguinary monsters that ever disgraced the gaddī. His death was announced on the 20th September, A.D. 1843. The Māṛwār succession question was settled in favour of Ahmadnagar on the 7th November, 1843, the choice falling not on the young heir of that house, but on his father Tak͟ht Singh, who was unanimously elected, and whose son accompanied him as prince royal. Tak͟ht Singh is a descendant of the Herori Jaswant. Several of the Zanana ladies and three or four slave girls performed *Saṭi*.

Man Singh, Raja (مان سنگه راجه), of Audh. His title was Mahārāja Sir Mān Singh Bahādur Kayam Jung, K.C.S.I. He died at Ajudhia on the 11th October, A.D. 1870. He was Vice-President of the British Indian Association, a post which he held with great success.

Mansur (منصور), a k͟halīf of Bag͟hdād. *Vide* Al-Mansūr.

Mansur (منصور), the son of Bāiqara Mirzā, and father of Sulṭān Husain Mirzā of Herāt.

Mansur (منصور), a poet, who is the author of a Dīwān in which are some Kasīdas in praise of Shāh Abbas II. who died in A.D. 1666, A.H. 1077, and of Abbas Qulī Beg.

Mansur I. Samani, Amir (منصور سامانی امیر), a prince of the race of the Samanides, was the son of Amīr Nūh I. and brother to Amīr 'Abdul Malik, whom he succeeded A.D. 961, A.D. 350. He compelled the Dīlamī ruler of Fars and 'Iraq to pay him an annual tribute of 150,000 dīnars of gold; and the peace by which this tribute was fixed was cemented by his marriage with the daughter of Rukn-uddaula, the reigning prince of that family. Amīr Mansūr died after a reign of 15 lunar years on the 15th March, A.D. 976, 11th Rajab, A.H. 365, and was succeeded by his son Amīr Nūh II. His wazīr Abū 'Alī bin-Muhammad translated into Persian the *Tārīkh Tabarī*.

Mansur II. Samani, Amir (منصور ثانی امیر) succeeded his father Amīr Nūh II. in A.D. 997, A.H. 387, on the throne of Khurāsān. He occupied it for a short period (little more than a year), which was marked with disgrace and misfortune. He was obliged to fly before his rebellious nobles, who afterwards deprived him of his sight and elevated his younger brother, 'Abdul Malik II. to the throne A.D. 998, A.H. 388.

Mansur 'Ali Khan, (منصورعلی خان), Nawāb of Audh.

[*Vide* Safdar Jang.]

Mansur 'Ali Khan, Sayyad (منصور علی خان سید), Nawāb of Murshidābād. He died in 1884.

Mansur Hallaj (منصور حلاج), the surname of Shaikh Husain Hallāj, a celebrated ascetic, who was a native of Baiza, and originally a cotton-carder. The Musalmāns differed in their opinions about the character of this person. Some took him to be a saint, and gave out that he performed miracles; others believed him to be a sorcerer or a juggler, and that he only deceived people with his tricks. He was, however, condemned and sentenced by the khalīf of Baghdād, Maqtadir, and was put to death because he used to proclaim "An-ul-haq," *i.e.* "I am the truth," or in other words, "I am God." When they had taken him to the place of execution, they first cut off both his hands and then his legs; they plucked out his eyes, cut out his tongue, and separated his head from his body. They then burned his mangled corpse to ashes, and threw it into the Tigris. This circumstance took place in the year A.D. 919, A.H. 306, but according to Ibn-Khallikān on the 24th Zi-Qa'da, A.H. 309, corresponding with the 26th March, A.D. 922. Shaikh Husain is commonly called Mansūr Hallāj, though it is the name of his father. He is considered by the Sūfīs to be one of their most spiritual leaders, who, they believe, had attained the fourth or last stage of Sūfiism. An inspired Sūfī is said to have demanded of the Almighty why he permitted Mansūr to suffer? The reply was, "This is the punishment for the revealer of secrets."

Mansur ibn-Alqaem ibn-Almahdi, (منصور ابن القایم ابن المهدی), a prince of Africa who died on Friday the 19th March, A.D. 953, Friday 29th Shawwāl, A.H. 341.

Mansur, Khwaja (منصور خواجه).

Vide Khwāja Mansūr.

Mansur, Shah (منصور شاه). *Vide* Shāh Mansūr.

Manu (مَنُ), the son of Brahmā, the first male according to the Hindūs. Kapila was Manu's grandson, and the author of the *Sankh Shastar*, in which he mentions the *Gīta*, which relates transactions that took place at the end of the Dwāpar and the beginning of the Kaljug. Manu is the supposed author of the work that goes by his name; it is said that it existed in the Satjug according to this shlōk: "When 1010 years of the Satjug were expired, I Manu, at the full moon of the month Bhadr, by the command of Brahmā, finished this *Shastar*." So runs the legend. But the work known to us as the *Institutes of Manu* is a Brahminical *Utopia* of comparatively modern date, probably A.D. 500.

[*See Imp. Gazetteer of India*, vol. vi. c. iv. where the evidence is summarised.]

Manuchehr (منوچهر), one of the legendary kings of Persia of the first or Pishdādiān dynasty, who succeeded Faridūn. He was a good and pious monarch; but the great prosperity which attended his reign was chiefly owing to the wisdom and courage of his prime minister, Sām, the son of Narīmān, whose descendants Zāl and Rustam, even during this reign, obtained a celebrity which has led Persian historians and poets to speak only of those events that are connected with their biography. Manūchehr died after a reign of 120 years, and was succeeded by his son Nauzar, in the latter part of whose reign died Sām, the son of Narīmān. After the death of Sām, Pashang the king of Tūrān invaded Persia with a force of 30,000 men, commanded by his son Afrāsiāb. Two engagements and two single combats took place. Nauzar himself was discomfited by Afrāsiāb, who soon afterwards took him prisoner and slew him. This happened in the seventh year of the reign of that unfortunate monarch. [Such is the record of Mirkhond (*q.v.*).]

Manuchehr (منوچہر). *Vide* Qābūs.

Manuchehr (منوچہر) (prince). He was the son of Shaikh Ibrāhīm, ruler of Shīrwān, who died in A.D. 1417, A.H. 820. His panegyrist was Kātibī, who wrote a chronogram on his death, which happened in the year A.D. 1412, A.H. 815, five years before his father.

Manuchehr (منوچہر). *Vide* Tousanī.

Manuchehr, Malik or **Khaqan** (منوچہر ملک یا خاقان), ruler of Shīrwān, whose panegyrist was Khāqānī the poet. He was a descendant of Bahrām Chobīn, and his title was Khāqānī, hence the takhallus of Khāqānī. Manūchehr reigned about the year A.D. 1180, A.H. 576, of the Christian era.

Manuchehri (منوچہری), who had the sobriquet of Shast Galla. His name was Hakīm Najm-uddīn Ahmad bin-Ya'qūb bin-Manūchehr. He lived at the court of Sultān Mahmūd of Ghaznī and of his two sons Masa'ūd and Muhammad. He acquired much wealth, and hence his sobriquet of Shast Galla, *i.e.* sixty flocks of sheep. He died in A.D. 1090, A.H. 483, and left a Dīwān in Persian.

Manwi, Maulwi (منوی مولوی), an author.

Manzari (منظری سمرقندی), of Samarqand, a poet who was in the service of Bairam Khān at Āgra, and wrote a poem called *Shāhnāmī Khayāl*, which contains an account of the war of Sikandar Shāh Sūr, etc.

Maqanna' (مقنع). *Vide* al-Maqna' or Maqanna.

Maqbul (مقبول), named Maqbūl Ahmad. He is the author of *Nūr-nāma* and *Qāf-nāma*, also of a Masnawī in Urdū called *Dard Ulfat*. He was living at Lucknow in A.D. 1853, A.H. 1270.

Maqna' (مقنع). *Vide* al-Maqna' or Muqanna.

Maqrizi (مقریزی), author of the work entitled *Qitāb us-Sulūh*. He lived about the year A.D. 1229, A.H. 626.

Maqrizi (مقریزی), whose proper name is Taqī-uddīn Ahmad, was an eminent Arabic historian and geographer, born in A.D. 1360, in Maqrīz near Balbec. He early devoted himself to the study of history, astrology, etc. at Cairo, where also he afterwards held the offices of inspector of weights and Imām of different mosques. Some of his works have been translated into French and Latin. He died in A.D. 1442, aged 82 years.

Marghinani (مرغینانی). His proper name was Burhān-uddīn 'Alī bin-Muhammad, but he derived this title from his native country Marghīnān, a city in Māwarun-nahr. He is the author of the *Hidāya* and several other works. His death happened in A.D. 1197, A.H. 593.

[*Vide* Burhān-uddīn 'Alī.]

Maria (ماریہ), one of the wives of Muhammad, by whom he had a son named Ibrāhīm, who died when an infant. She was called Qabtī or Egyptian, because she was sent as a present to Muhammad by Makoukas, king of Alexandria. She died in A.D. 637, A.H. 16.

Mariam (مریم). This word in Arabic signifies Mary, and is only applied to the Virgin Mary. The Qurān, in the chapter called Al-Amrān, or the family of Amrān, and in Sūra Miriam, confounds Mary the mother of Jesus with Miriam the daughter of Amram and sister of Moses and Aaron. In the book called *Al-Sahīb*, there is a tradition that the Apostle of God said: "Among men there have been many perfect; but among women only four:—'Āsia, the wife of Pharaoh, Mary, the daughter of Amrān, Khudyja, the daughter of Khawailid, and Fātima, daughter of Muhammad.'" Employed as an honorific title for Eastern ladies.

Mariam Makani (مریم مکانی), a title of Hamīda Bāno Begam, the mother of the emperor Akbar, which she received after her death. *See* Hamīda Bāno.

Mariam Zamani (مریم زمانی). She was the daughter of Rāja Beharī Māl Kachhwaha, and was married to the emperor Akbar Shāh. Her proper name is not known. She was the mother of the emperor Jahāngīr. She died at Āgra in the time of her son Jahāngīr in A.D. 1623, A.H. 1032, and the mausoleum at Āgra in Sikandra, which was erected by her son over her grave, is called by the people of Āgra, Rauza Mariam.

Ma'ruf (معروف), poetical name of Ilāhī Bakhsh Khān, younger brother of Fakhr-uddaula Nawāb Ahmad Bakhsh Khān, son of Mirzā 'Arif Khān. He died in the year A.H. 1242, and left two Dīwāns in Urdū.

Ma'ruf Karkhi (معروف کرخی). He was by birth a Christian, but being convinced that there are not three Gods as the Christians say, but one, he became a convert to Muhammadanism, and his parents followed his example. He afterwards became a very pious Musalmān; was contemporary with Dāūd Tāī and Ibrāhīm Adham, and became master of Sarī Saqatī. He died in the reign of Māmūn, the son of Hārūn al-Rashīd, on the 31st August, A.D. 815, 20th Muharram, A.H. 200, and lies buried in a place called Karkh in Baghdād. The heart of Ma'rūf (that is to say the letter R, which is the numeral for 200) is the chronogram for the Hijrī year of his demise.

Marwan I. (مروان ابن الحکم), son of Hakam, was the fourth khalīf of the race of Umayya. He was proclaimed khalīf at Damascus after the death of Mu'āwia II. in A.D. 684, A.H. 64. He was also called "Ibn-Tarīd," the son of the expelled, because Muhammad had banished his father Hakam for divulging a secret. He died after a reign of 298 days on the 12th April, A.D. 685, 2nd Ramazān, A.H. 65. He is said by some authors to have been poisoned by his wife, Zainab, the widow of Mu'āwia II. He had married her on condition that her son Khālid should succeed him, but afterwards altering the succession in favour of his own son 'Abdul Malik, young Khālid reproached him with his breach of promise; upon this Marwān calling him bastard, the child complained to his mother, who, to be revenged for this affront, is said to have poisoned Marwān or smothered him with a pillow.

Marwan II. (مروان الحمار), surnamed Himār or "the ass," was the son of Muhammad the son of Hakam, and the fourteenth and last khalīf of the house of Umayya. He was nephew to Marwān I. After deposing Ibrāhīm the son of Walīd II. he ascended the throne of Damascus in A.D. 745, 26th Zil-hijja, A.H. 132, and was defeated and slain on the 5th August, A.D. 750, in a battle fought against Abū'l Abbās al-Saffāh, who was previously proclaimed khalīf by the inhabitants of Kūfa on Friday the 29th November, A.D. 749, 13 Rabī' II. A.H. 132. Marwān, before his accession to the throne, had been governor of Mesopotamia, and had received, by his Georgian warfare, the honourable epithet of the ass of Mesopotamia or Al-Himār, a warlike breed of asses that never fly from an enemy.

Marwan ibn-Hafsa (مروان ابن حفصه), an eminent Arabian poet, on whom the khalīf Mahdī, on one occasion, bestowed the sum of 70,000 dirhams (£1600) as a reward for merit.

Masa'ud I. Sultan (مسعود اول سلطان), son of Sultān Mahmūd of Ghaznī. After cruelly depriving his brother Muhammad of sight, he mounted the throne of Ghaznī A.D. 1030, A.H. 421. He made several incursions into India to maintain the tranquillity of those possessions which his father had subdued. But he had no time to attack others; all his means were required to defend himself from a formidable tribe of Tartars, called Saljūqī, who had, for a considerable time past, made predatory incursions into Khurāsān and other parts of his dominions. He carried on a petty war against different branches of this powerful tribe for some time, and with various success, till he was completely defeated in a great action fought in Khurāsān with Tughral Beg Saljūqī on Friday the 16th June, A.D. 1038, 9th Ramazān, A.H. 429, and was obliged to fly towards Lāhore, which he had resolved to make the future capital of his government. On his march he was deposed by his mutinous army, and his brother Muhammad Makahūl the blind was again placed on the throne. Masa'ūd remained in confinement for several years, and was afterwards assassinated by Ahmad the son of Muhammad Makahūl A.D. 1041, A.H. 433.

Masa'ud II. Sultan (مسعود ثانی سلطان), son of Sultān Maudūd, a child of four years old, was raised to the throne of Ghaznī after the death of his father in December, A.D. 1049, but was soon deposed after a nominal reign of six days, and Abū'l Hasan 'Alī, the son of Sultān Masa'ūd I. was proclaimed emperor.

Masa'ud III. Sultan (مسعود ثالث سلطن), the son of Sultān Ibrāhim, ascended the throne of Ghaznī after the death of his father in A.D. 1098, A.H. 492. He reigned over Ghaznī and Lāhore 16 years; and had for his wife the sister of Sultān Sanjar the Saljūkide, who had made peace with his father. Sultān Masa'ūd died in A.D. 1114, A.H. 508, and was succeeded by his son Sherzād or Shernazād.

Masa'ud IV. Sultan (مسعود رالی سلطان), the son of Sultān Muhammad Saljūqī, and brother of Tughral II. whom he succeeded to the throne of Hamdan. He began to reign about the year A.D. 1134, A.H. 529, and died A.D. 1152, 1st Rajab, A.H. 547. Atābak Eldiguz was his minister.

Masa'ud Ghazi, Salar (مسعود غازی سالار), a celebrated Muhammadan martyr commonly called Ghazī Miyain, whose tomb is at Bahrāich in Audh. He was the son of Sālār Sāhū, and related to Sultān

Mahmūd of Ghaznī; his mother being that monarch's sister. He had forcibly taken possession of a Hindū temple in Bahrāich, upon which the Hindūs surrounded him on all sides; a battle ensued, in which Masa'ūd Ghāzī was slain, and several of his adherents cut to pieces. This circumstance took place on the 15th June, A.D. 1033, 14th Rajab, A.H. 424, at which time he was only 19 years old. To commemorate his martyrdom a festival takes place every year at Bahrāich on the first Sunday in the month of Jaiṭh, which falls exactly on the 29th day after our Easter Sunday, and very seldom on any other day. The festival terminates with the flying of kites.

Masa'ud Hisari, Maulana (مسعود حصاری مولانا), a poet who was living at the commencement of Akbar's reign, and wrote the chronogram of the emperor Humāyūn's death, which took place in A.D. 1556, A.H. 963.

Masa'ud, Khwaja (مسعود خواجه), of Bak, a place near Bukhāra. It is said that he was for some time a king in Māwarun-nahr, but a dervish at heart. He is the author of several works on Sūfīism, one of which is the *Umm al-Nasāeh*. He has also composed a Dīwān, which he called *Nūr ul-Aīn*, the "light of the eye," containing more than 3000 verses.

Masa'ud, Khwaja (مسعود حواجه). *Vide* Khwāja Masa'ūd.

Masa'ud Sa'd Salman (مسعود ساد سلمان), a poet and native of Jurjān. He flourished in the time of Manūchehr, ruler of that country, about the year A.D. 1060, A.H. 452. He is the author of a Dīwān in Arabic and Persian.

Masa'udi (مسعودی), the famous historian who visited India, Ceylon and the coast of China in the year A.D. 915. He is the author of the work entitled *Ma'dan ul-Jawāhir*, Mines of Gems, of which the first part has been well translated by Dr. A. Sprenger The first of his compositions is *Akhbār uz-Zaman*, an enormous work of at least twenty volumes; the second is the *Qitāb ul-Ausath*, being the complement to the *Akhbār*; and the third *Mines of Gems*, or as some call it the *Meadows of Gold*, forming at the same time the extract and the supplement of the two others. He died A.D. 956, A.H. 345. In describing the early discoveries of his countrymen inside the Great Pyramid in Egypt, he says that some of them found in the lower part of the Pyramid a vase containing a quantity of fluid of an unknown quality. They also discoverd in a large hall a quantity of golden coins put up in columns, every piece of which was of the weight of 1000 dinars. In another place they found the image of an old man, made of green stone, sitting upon a sofa, and wrapped up in a garment. Before him were statues of little boys. Having proceeded further they met with the image of a cock made of precious stones and placed upon a green column. Continuing their researches they came to a female idol of white stone and lions of stone on each side. This he says, occurred in the time of Yarid bin-'Abdullah, supposed, says Colonel Howard Vyse, to have been a king of Egypt.

Mas-hafi (مصحفی), an Urdū poet of Lucknow, whose proper name is Ghulām Hamdānī. His native country was Amroha in the district of Murādābād. He died about the year A.D. 1824, A.H. 1240. He is the author of several Dīwāns in Persian and Urdū, and also produced (1795) a *Tazkira*, or biography, of Urdū poets. He also wrote another *Tazkira* for Persian poets, and a historical work, in verse, which he called *Shāhnāma*.

Ma'shuq 'Ali, Maulana Muhammad (معشوق علی مولانا محمد), of Jaunpūr, a learned Musalmān and author of several works in prose and poetry. He died in the year A.D. 1852, A.H. 1268.

Masha-ullah (ماشا الله), the surname of an author who is also styled Al-Misrī, or the Egyptian. It is also the name of a Jew, who was a great astronomer, and lived in the time of the khalīfs Al-Mansūr and Al-Māmūn.

Masih (مسیح), the poetical name of Hakīm Ruknā Kāshī, which see.

Masih (مسیح), whose proper name was Hātim, is the author of the poem called *Qissaia Manūchehr*, containing the story of Manūchehr, which he composed in A.D. 1660, A.H. 1070, and dedicated it to Shāh Jahān the emperor of Dehlī.

Masiha (مسیحا), poetical title of Hakīm Muhammad 'Alī Khān, who is the author of an Urdū Dīwān.

Masihai, Akhund (مسیحائي اخوند), of Kāshān, whose poetical name was Sāhib, a man who possessed every ornament of learning and accomplishment, had been a pupil and son-in-law of Aqā Husain of Khwānsār, and gained the admiration of all mankind by his good qualities and agreeable society. He composed much in verse, and has left elegant compositions in prose. He died at Isfahān in the beginning of the 18th century.

Masihi (مسیحی), a Turkish poet of great repute at Constantinople, who flourished in the reign of the emperor Sulaimān II. styled the Lawgiver. His works are preserved in the archives of the Royal Society. Masīhī died in A.D. 1512, A.H. 918.

Masihi (مسیحی). *Vide* Rukn-uddīn Masa'ūd Masīhī.

Masihi, Mulla (مسیحي ملا), also called Masīhāī, was the poetical name of Sa'd-ullāh, an adopted son of Muqarrab Khān. He was a native of Pānīpat, and flourished in the time of the emperor Jahāngīr. He translated the *Ramāyan*, which contains the battle of Rām Chand with Rāwan the ten-headed monster, from Hindī into Persian verse.

Masir (مسیر), poetical name of prince Mirzā Hamāyūn Kadr, the son of Mirzā Khurshaid Kadr. *Vide* Taskhīr.

Masjidi (مسجدی), poetical title of a poet of Persia.

Masjid Moth (مسجد موث), name of a mosque built by Mīān Bhūya at Dehlī. [*Vide* Bhūya.]

Maslah-uddin (مصلح الدین), proper name of the celebrated Shaikh Sā'dī of Shīrāz. [*Vide* Sa'dī.]

Maslah-uddin al-Lari (مصلح الدین لاری), a native of Lār in Persia, and author of the work called *Mirat ul-Adwār*, the Mirror of the World.

Masruf (مصروف), poetical title of Nawāb Khān Bahādur Khān, the son of Jalāl-uddīn or Zulfiqār Khān, the son of Hāfiz Rahmat Khān of Bareli. He is the author of a Dīwān. He rebelled against the British in 1857, and consequently was obliged to leave his native country and go to Mecca.

Masrur (مسرور), the poetical title of Walī Muhammad Khān, who was governor of Lār under Shāh Tahmāsp II. of Persia.

Mast (مست), the poetical appellation of Zulfiqar 'Alī, which see.

Ma'sum 'Ali Shah, Mir (معصوم علی شاه میر), a celebrated Sūfī teacher, who was a disciple of Sayyad 'Alī Razā, a native of the Deccan. During the reign of Karīm Khān he went from India to Shīrāz, where his followers soon amounted to more than thirty thousand. The orthodox priests took alarm, and prevailed on the mild Karīm Khān to banish the saint from his capital, but his reputation was increased by the act of power which proclaimed him dangerous. After Karīm Khan's death Mīr Ma'sūm, who resided in a small village near Isfahān, deputed his first disciple, Fayāz 'Alī, to teach in that city. That holy person soon died, and was succeeded in his office by his son Nūr 'Alī Shāh: who, though young in years, was (to us the phrase of his historian), "old in piety." The number and rank of Mīr Ma'sūm's followers excited alarm in the priests of Isfahān, who transmitted so exaggerated an account of the vile heresies of the Sūfīs to 'Alī Murād Khān the king, and recommended him so strongly to support the faith, by punishing those whose opinions were alike hostile to true religion and good government, that the monarch, the moment he received their representation, sent orders to cut off the noses and ears of some among the most zealous of the obnoxious sect; and as a further disgrace, to shave the beards of all who had adopted their opinions. The ignorant soldiers intrusted with the execution of this mandate, were not very capable of discriminating between true believers and infidels; and we are assured by a contemporary writer, that many orthodox Muhammadans had their noses and ears cut off and their beards shaved on this memorable occasion.

Mīr Ma'sūm 'Alī and Nūr 'Alī Shāh, after wandering from one place to another, revisited Kirmān, where Mushtāq 'Alī, the most pious of his disciples, was put to death. At Kirmānshāh Nūr 'Alī Shāh was placed in confinement; and Mīr Ma'sūm was murdered when at prayers in the midst of his followers. This sect, however, notwithstanding the efforts of their enemies, continued to increase in numbers; and Nūr 'Alī Shāh, with all who adhered to him, were banished the kingdom. His avowed disciples were at this period about sixty thousand, but many more were supposed to be secretly devoted to him. He is said to have been poisoned at Mausal. It is related that two inhabitants of Kirmānshāh, who were distinguished by an extraordinary appearance of zeal, dressed his dinner on the day that he was suddenly attacked by violent spasms, which in a few hours terminated his existence. Their flight led all to suspect them of having poisoned him. Nūr Alī died at 9 o'clock on the morning of the 3rd June, A.D. 1800, 10th Muharram, A.H. 1215. He expired close to the grave of the prophet Jonas, within a league of Mausal.

Matin (متین), the poetical name of Shaikh 'Abdul Raza bin-'Abdullāh Matīn. He was a native of Isfahān, but of Arabic origin. He came to India in the reign of the emperor Muhammad Shāh, and subsequently went to Lucknow, where he assumed the garb of a dervish and received a pension from Burhān ul-Mulk Sa'ādat Khān. Having lost his pension owing to the change of rulers, he proceeded to Bengal, where he died A.D. 1761, A.H. 1175, and left a Dīwān of 5000 verses.

Matrazi (مطرزی), surname of Muwayyad, the grandfather of Shaikh Nizāmī of Gauja. He was a poet and an author.

Maudud Chishti, Khwaja (مودود چشتی خواجه), son of Khwāja Yūsaf the son of Sama'ān. His father, who died in A.D. 1067, aged 84 lunar years, lies buried at Chisht. Khwāja Maudūd is the founder of a religious sect called Chishtī, of which Khwāja Mo'īn-uddīn Chishtī, whose tomb is at Ajmir, was a follower. Maudūd died on the 8th May, A.D. 1153, 1st Rajab, A.H. 527.

Maudud, Sultan (مودود سلطان), the son of Sulṭān Masa'ūd I. of Ghaznī. He was at Balkh when his father was murdered by Aḥmad the son of the reigning Sulṭān, Muhammad Makahūl; he immediately proclaimed himself king and marched to revenge his father, and having defeated the Sulṭān's army on the banks of the Indus, made Muhammad and his sons prisoners, and put them all to death A.D. 1041, A.H. 433. The dynasty of Ghaznī lost, during the reign of Maudūd, all their possessions in Persia. Maudūd died at Lahore on the 23rd December, A.D. 1049, 24th Rajab, A.H. 441, having reigned upwards of nine years.

Mauji (موجی بدخشانی), of Badakhshān, whose proper name was Muhammad Qasim Khān, is the author of a *Yūsaf Zalekha*, containing 6000 verses. He died at Āgra in A.D. 1571, A.H. 979.

Maulana 'Ali (مولانا علی), the son of Mahmūd Kirmānī, commonly called Shahāb. He is the author of a history entitled *Maāsir Mahmūdi*, which he dedicated to Sulṭān Mahmūd Shāh I. Khiljī, king of Mālwā, who reigned from A.D. 1436 to 1469.

Maulana Hasan (مولانا حسن), a learned Musalmān who died in the time of Sulṭān Salim Shāh of Dehlī in the year A.D. 1549. His tomb, which has a Persian inscription in verse, is still to be seen in the Roman Catholic Burial-ground at Āgra.

Maulana Husain (مولانا حسین) was a disciple of Khwāja Abū'l Wafā, who died in A.D. 1432, A.H. 836. Maulānā Husain is the author of the work called *Maqsad Aqsa* and of the *Sharah Qasīda Burda*.

Maulana Maghrabi (مولانا مغربی). *Vide* Maghrabī.

Maulana Majd (مولانا مجد). *Vide* Majd (Maulānā).

Maulana Nasir (مولانا ناصر). *Vide* Nāṣir Bukhārī (Maulānā).

Maulanae Rum (مولانای روم). *Vide* Jalāl-uddīn Rūmī.

Maulud Muhammad (مولود محمد), author of a Persian work on Physic, called *Bahr ul-Munāfa*, the Sea of Profit, dedicated to Ṭīpū Sulṭān.

Maulwi Rumi (مولوی رومی). *Vide* Jalāl-uddīn Rūmī.

Mauzun (موزون), poetical appellation of Rāja Rām Narāin of Patna, which see.

Mawasi (مواسی), a celebrated poet of Persia, who flourished at the court of Malik Shāh Saljūqī about the end of the eleventh century of the Christian era, and received the designation of Malik ush-Shu'ārā, king of poets, and the dignity of an Amīr. The poet Khākānī made him his model in versification; and so renowned were his odes, that more than a hundred poets endeavoured to imitate his style.

Mazani (مازنی), whose proper name is Abū 'Usmān, was an excellent Arabic Grammarian. He died in A.D. 863, A.H. 249.

Mazani (مزنی), or Al-Mazanī. *Vide* Abū Ibrāhīm Ismā'īl.

Mazdak (مزدک), name of a famous impostor, a native of Persia, surnamed Zandīq, that is to say, the Impious. He lived in the reign of Qubād the father of Nausherwān the Just. He was imprisoned and afterwards put to death by order of the latter.

Mazhar (مظہر), author of a poem containing the story of *Chandar Badan*, which he dedicated to Aurangzīb, emperor of Dehlī.

Mazhar (مظہر), the poetical designation of (Mirzā) Jān Jānān, which see.

Mazhari, Maulana (مظہر مولانا کشمیری), a poet of Kashmere who flourished in the time of Akbar.

Mazhar ul-Haqq (مظهر الحق), poetical name of Abū 'Abdullah Muhammad Fāzil, author of the *Mukhbir ul-Wāsilīn*, a poem containing the chronograms of the most celebrated persons among the Muhammadans. He flourished in the time of the emperor 'Alamgīr and died in A.D. 1696, A.H. 1106.

[*Vide* Abū 'Abdullah Muhammad Fāzil.]

Mazmun (مظمون), the poetical appellation of Shaikh Sharaf-uddīn, a descendant of Shaikh Farīd-uddīn Shakarganj. When he was past forty, he took up his abode in the mosque at Shāhjahānābād called Zīnat ul-Masājid, and led the life of an ascetic. He was a pupil of Mazhar and 'Arzū; the latter called him "Shāi'r-i-Bedāna," because he had lost all his teeth. He died about the year A.D. 1745, A.H. 1158.

Mehr (مهر), poetical title of Mirzā Hatim 'Alī Beg of Āgra, formerly a Munsif of Chunār. He is the author of a Dīwān and a book called *Panjae Mehr*. He was still living at Āgra in A.D. 1873.

Mehr (مهر), poetical name of Nawāb Amīn-uddaula Sayyad 'Aghā 'Alī Khān, a son of Mo'tmid-uddaula 'Aghā Mīr, the ex-Nawāb of Lucknow. He was living at Cawnpore in 1856, and is the author of an Urdū Diwān.

Mehri (مهری), poetical name of an author.

Mehr Nasir (مهر نصیر). *Vide* Mirzā Mehr Nasīr.

Mehrun-nisa Begam (مهر النساء بیگم), fifth daughter of 'Alamgīr. Her mother's name was Aurangabadī Mahal. She was born in August, A.D. 1661, 3rd Ṣafar, A.H. 1072, and married to Prince Ezid Bakhsh, the son of Sulṭān Murād Bakhsh, and died in A.D. 1704, A.H. 1116.

Mehrun-nisa (مهر النساء), daughter of Nūr Jahān by Sher Afgan Khān. She was married to Shahyar, the youngest son of Jahangīr.

Meli (میلی هروی), poetical appellation of Mirzā Muhammad Qulī of Herāt, who came to India in A.D. 1571, A.H. 979, and is the author of a Dīwān.

Mian Mir (میان میر). *Vide* Shaikh Mīr of Lāhore and Shāh Mīr.

Minhaj us-Saraj Jurjani (منهاج السراج جورجانی), a native of Jurjan or Georgia, was an elegant poet and author of the *Tabāqāt Nāsirī*, which he wrote in A.D. 1252, and dedicated to Nāsir-uddīn Mahmūd, king of Dehlī, who reigned from A.D. 1246 to 1266. He is also called Qazī Sadr Jahān Minhāj-uddīn Jurjānī.

[*Vide* Abū 'Umar Minhāj.]

Minnat (منت), poetical name of Mīr Qamar-uddīn Minnat, a native of Dehlī. Warren Hastings conferred on him the title of "Malik-ush-Shu'ārā," or "the king of poets," at the recommendation of the Nawāb of Murshidābād. He visited the Deccan and received 5,000 rupees for a Qasīda or panegyric which he wrote in praise of the Niẓām of Haidarābād. He died at Calcutta in A.D. 1793, A.H. 1208, and left 150,000 verses in Persian and Urdū. Among his compositions is a *Chamanistān* and a *Shakaristān*. He was the preceptor of Gunna Begam (*q.v.*).

Mir (میر). This word is an abbreviation of Amīr, which in Arabic signifies a chief, prince and commander. The Sāyyads of India are also called Mīr.

Mir (میر), the poetical designation of Mīr Muhammad Taqī, a Hindūstanī poet who flourished in the time of the emperor Shāh 'Alam, and whose poetry is mostly Rekhta. He was a native of Akbarābād and nephew to Sirāj-uddīn 'Alī Khān 'Arzū. He is the author of six Dīwāns and a Tazkira or biography of poets. He died at Lucknow, nearly 100 years old (lunar), in the year A.D. 1810, A.H. 1225.

[*Vide* Faiz.]

Mir Akhund (میر اخوند). *Vide* Khāwand Shāh.

Mir 'Alam (میر عالم), title of Mīr Abū'l Qasim, the prime minister of the Niẓām of Haidarābād. This nobleman for upwards of thirty years had taken a lead in the administration of affairs in the Deccan. He died in the month of November, A.D. 1808, and was succeeded by Munīr ul-Mulk.

Mir 'Ali (میر علی), surnamed Dāmād or "the bridegroom" (because he was married to a favourite sister of the great Shāh 'Abbās), was the teacher of a system of philosophy much more pure and sublime than had hitherto been known. His immortal scholar Sadrau has, by his numerous works, proved himself independent of Aristotle in abstract science, though that great philosopher had been hitherto the master of his preceptor and all his predecessors in those branches of learning.

Mir Amman (میرامن), a Hindūstānī lyric poet, whose poetical name was Lutf, which see.

Miran (میرن), surname of Mīr Sādiq, the son of Nawāb Ja'far 'Alī Khān of Bengal. [*Vide* Mīr Sādiq.]

Miran 'Adil Khan Faruqi (میران عادل خان فاروقي), third king of Khāndesh, succeeded his father Malik Nasīr Khān in September, A.D. 1437. He reigned more than three years, expelled the Deccanīs from Khāndesh in A.D. 1440, and was murdered in the city of Burhānpūr on Friday the 28th April, A.D. 1441, 8th Ẓil-ḥijja, A.H. 844. He was buried at Tālner by the side of his father, and was succeeded by his son Mīrān Mubārik Khān I.

Miran Ghani (میران غنی), commonly called 'Adil Khān Fārūqī I. succeeded his father Mīrān Mubārik Khān in May, A.D. 1457, Rajab, A.H. 861, to the government of Khāndesh, which province under his rule attained a degree of prosperity which it had never known under any of its former rulers. This prince added considerably to the fortifications of Asīr, and constructed the strong outwork called Malaigaṛh; he also built the citadel of Burhānpūr, and raised many magnificent palaces in that town. He died after a reign of 48 lunar years on Friday the 8th September, A.D. 1503, 14th Rabī' I. A.H. 909, and was buried at his particular request near the palace of the Daulat Maidān in Burhānpūr. He was succeeded by his brother Dāūd Khān Fārūqī.

Miran Husain Nizam Shah (میران حسین نظام شاه) ascended the throne of Ahmadnagar in the Deccan after the murder of his father Murtaza Niẓām Shāh in June, A.D. 1588, Rajab, A.H. 996. Being of an impetuous and cruel disposition, he began his reign by tyranny and oppression, and was deposed and murdered after a reign of ten months and three days on the 18th March, A.D. 1589, 11th Jumāda I. A.H. 997, and his cousin Ismā'īl Niẓām Shāh, the son of his uncle prince Burhān Shāh (who was then at the court of the emperor Akbar at Dehlī), was raised to the throne.

Miran Mubarik Khan Faruqi I. (میران مبارک خان فاروقی) succeeded his father Mīrān 'Adil Khān Fārūqī in the government of Khāndesh in April, A.D. 1441. He reigned, without undertaking any foreign conquest, or drawing upon himself the hostility of his neighbours, for a period of nearly 17 lunar years. He died on the 17 May, A.D. 1457, 12th Rajab, A.H. 861, was buried at Tālner, and succeeded by his son Mīrān Ghanī, commonly called 'Adil Khān Fārūqī I.

Miran Mubarik Khan Faruqi II. (میران مبارک خان فاروقی) succeeded his brother Mīrān Muhammad Khān in the government of Khāndesh in A.D. 1536, A.H. 943. He reigned 32 lunar years and died on the night of Wednesday the 24th December, A.D. 1566, 6th Jumāda II. A.H. 974, and was succeeded by Mīrān Muhammad Khān Fārūqī II.

Miran Muhammad Khan Faruqi I. (میران محمد خان فاروقی) succeeded to the government of Khāndesh after the death of his father, 'Adil Khān II. in A.D. 1520, A.H. 926, and after the demise of Bahādur Shāh, king of Gujrāt and Mālwā, who was murdered by the Portuguese at Diu in February, A.D. 1537, he (Muhammad Khān) being the son of Bahādur Shāh's sister, was proclaimed by his mother, in concert with the nobles, king of Gujrāt and Mālwā, and was formally crowned at Māṇḍo with the title of Mīrān Muhammad Shāh; but his reign in those provinces was of short duration, for he died suddenly on the 24th April, A.D. 1537, 13th Ẓi-Qa'da, A.H. 943. His body was conveyed to Burhānpūr, and interred in the vault of his father, 'Adil Khān II. His brother Mīrān Mubārik Khān II. succeeded him in the government of Khāndesh, and Mahmūd Shāh (son of Latīf Khān the brother of Bahādur Shāh), to the throne of Gujrāt.

Miran Muhammad Khan Faruqi II. (میران محمد خان فاروقی ثانی) succeeded Mīrān Mubārik Khān II. in the government of Khāndesh in December, A.D. 1566, and died after a reign of ten years in A.D. 1576, A.H. 984. He was succeeded by his brother Rāja 'Alī Khān.

Miran Shah Mirza (میران شاه مرزا), the eldest surviving son of Amīr Taimūr (Tamerlane), was born in the year A.D. 1367, A.H. 769. He had the government of 'Irāq, 'Azurbejān, Dayārbikr and Syria during the lifetime of his father, and after his death he reigned 3 years 3 months and 7 days over those countries, when he was slain in a battle against Qara Yūsaf the Turkmān on the 20th April, A.D. 1408, 24th Ẓi-Qa'da, A.H. 810, aged 41 lunar years 7 months and 10 days. He had several sons, *viz.* Abū Bakr Mirzā, 'Alī Mirzā, Umar Mirzā, who succeeded him, Mirzā Khalīl, Sulṭān Muhammad Mirzā, Mirzā Ayjal and Mirzā Sayūrghamish.

Mir Baqir Damad (میر باقر داماد).

He was called Dāmād because he was the son-in-law of Shāh 'Abbās I. king of Persia. He is the author of the work entitled *Ufq ul-Mubīn*, and the marginal notes on the *Sharah Mukhtasar Usūl*. He died in the year A.D. 1630, A.H. 1040.

[*Vide* Muhammad Baqir Dāmād.]

Mir Buzurg (میر بزرگ), author of a work on Sūfiism called *Durr ul-Ma'rfat*.

Mir Dard (میر درد). *Vide* Dard (Mīr).

Mir Haidar (میر حیدر). *Vide* Haidar (Mīr).

Mir Haidar Rafiqi Mua'mmai (میر حیدر رفیقی معمائی). *Vide* Haidar Mua'mmāī and Rafī-uddīn Haidar Rāfa'ī.

Mir Haji (میر حاجی). The convict

Mīr Hājī, the murderer of Captain Douglas and others during the mutiny at Dehlī, was executed on Tuesday morning the 29th December, A.D. 1868, in front of the Lāhore Gate of the city of Dehlī, facing the apartments which were the scene of the murders for which he suffered death.

He was brought from jail to the place of execution under a strong Police Guard; he mounted the scaffold with a firm step; while the rope was being adjusted he muttered in a low voice, "Brethren, remember your Kalma," and then repeated in the same low tone two or three times, "La illah," etc., soon after which the trap fell, and all was over, almost without a struggle. After hanging the usual time, the body was made over to the friends of the convict.

Mir Husaini (میر حسینی), author of *Zād ul-Musāfirīn*.

[*Vide* Husain bin-Hasan al-Husainī.]

Mir Ja'far (میر جعفر), nawāb of Bengal. *Vide* Ja'far 'Alī Khān

Mir Jumla (میر جمله), title of Mīr Muhammad Amīn of Shāhristān in Persia, came to India in the time of Jahāngīr A.D. 1618, A.H. 1027, and served under him for several years. In the reign of Shāh Jahān, he was raised to the rank of 5000 with the title of Mīr Jumla. He died on the 22nd August, O.S. 1637, 10th Rabī' II. A.H. 1047.

Mir Jumla (میر جمله), title of Mīr Muhammad Saīd the prime minister of 'Abdullah Quṭb Shāh of Golkanḍa. He had formerly been a diamond merchant, and had been known and respected throughout the Deccan for his wealth and abilities long before he attained high station. His son Muhammad Amīn, a dissolute and violent young man, had drawn on himself the resentment of 'Abdullah Quṭb Shāh, and had involved his father in a dispute with the court at Dehlī. Mīr Jumla, in the year A.D. 1656, A.H. 1066, threw himself on the protection of the emperor Shāh Jahān, in whose service he remained; became the chosen counsellor of the prince Aurangzīb, and afterwards one of the most useful instruments of his ambitious designs. On the accession of Aurangzīb 'Alamgīr, he was sent in pursuit of Sulṭān Shujāa' and appointed governor of Bengal. The title conferred on him by 'Alamgīr was Mu'azzam Khān Khān-khānān Sipah Sālār. He held the rank of 7000. In the fourth year of the emperor, A.D. 1662, he went on an expedition against the kingdom of Asām. He marched from Dacca in Bengal about the month of February, and entered Asām by Ghorāghāt; from thence he proceeded with very little opposition to the capital Ghargāon which he took and plundered; but the rainy season setting in soon after, inundating great part of the country, his supplies were cut off by the Assamese, and his troops becoming sickly, it was with great difficulty the army effected its retreat. The unfortunate general fell a victim to the climate a few days after his re-entering Bengal. He died at Khizarpūr in Kūch Behār on the 31st March, A.D. 1663, 2nd Ramazān, A.H. 1073. The history of this expedition was written by Shahāb-uddīn Aḥmad Tālāsh in A.D. 1663, A.H. 1073.

Mir Jumla (میر جمله), title of 'Abdullah, a nobleman and private favourite of the emperor Farrukh-siyar, was promoted for some time to the Sūbadārī of Bihār. In the first year of the emperor Muhammad Shāh, he was appointed to the rank of Sadr us-Sudūr, and died in the 13th year of his reign, about the year A.D. 1731, A.H. 1141.

Mir Khund (میر خواند). *Vide* Khāwand Shāh.

Mir Mannu (میر منو). *Vide* Mu'īn ul-Mulk.

Mir Masum (میر معصوم بہکری), of Bihkar, was an officer of the rank of 1000 in the time of Akbar and Jahāngīr, and an excellent poet. He is the author of a Dīwān, and a Masnawī called *Ma'dan ul-Afkār*, written in imitation of the *Makhzan ul-Asrār*, and of a history of Sindh, called *Tārīkh Sindh*. He died at Bihkar in A.D. 1606, A.H. 1015.

Mir Muhammad Khan Talpur (میر محمد خان تلپور), one of the ex-Amīrs of Sind. He was lately one of the members of the Bombay Legislative Council. He died at Haidarābād (Sind) on the 17th December, A.D. 1870. Much respected, his remains were followed to the family mausoleum by the Commissioner, the Judge, and the Collector, of the district. He lies in the place originally intended for his late father, Mīr Murād 'Alī, who preferred lying out in the open air, where the sun and moon could shed their light on his grave. He died in his 60th year. There now remain only three of the once numerous Talpūr family at Haidarābād, all aged men, at whose death in the course of time the once troublesome family will be extinct. The conquest of their territory and the overthrow of their power, furnish one of the most remarkable and interesting episodes in British Indian history.

Mir Muhammad Munshi (میر محمد منشی), author of a collection of Letters.

Mir Muhammad Sayyad (میر محمد سید), the great Mahdawī of Jaunpūr.

Mir Mu'izzi (میر معزی). *Vide* Amīr Moizzī.

Mir Murtaza (میر مرتضی المدعو بعلم الهدی), surnamed Al-Mad'ū bi-ilm il-Huda. He died on the 25th September, A.D. 1044, 30th Ṣafar, A.H. 436.

Mir Razi (میر رضی), a poet who received a lakh of rupees from a prince of Dehlī for a Ghazal he composed.

Mir Sadiq (میر صادق), commonly called Mīran, was the son of Mīr Ja'far 'Alī Khān, nawāb of Bengal. He was killed by lightning when asleep in his tent on the night of the 2nd July, A.D. 1760, 18th Ẓi-Qa'da, A.H. 1173. He had put to death the Nawāb Sirāj-ud-daula (*q.v.*) and killed several women of his harem with his own hand. Being reproached by the British Resident with the murder of one of the women, he answered, "What, shall not I kill an old woman, who goes about in her litter to stir up people against my father?"

Mir Said Ali. *Vide* Sābir.

Mir Sayyad Jama Baf (میر سید جامه باف), the weaver, was an excellent poet of Persia who came to India in A.D. 1562, A.H. 969, in the time of the emperor Akbar, and died in the year A.D. 1565, A.H. 973. His compositions mostly were Rubāīs, consequently he is sometimes called Mīr Rubā'ī.

Mir Sharaef 'Allama (میر شرف علامه). *Vide* Sharīf Jurjanī.

Mirza (میرزا) is an abbreviation of Amīrzāda, which in Persian signifies the son of a prince or nobleman. It is also written Mirzā, which has been adopted in this work. The descendants of Amīr Taimūr were all called Mirzās till Bābar Shāh, who assumed the honourable title of Bādshāh, and the princes were called Sulṭāns and Salātīn. When used to designate princely rank the word *follows* the name; when it precedes it is a mere prefix of social respect like Mr. or *Monsieur*.

Mirza 'Ali Beg (مرزا علی بیگ). *Vide* 'Alī Beg (Mirzā).

Mirza 'Ali Khan or Lutf. Author of a *Tazkira*, said to be the first ever written in Urdū. Published about 1801, it bears the name *Gulshān-i-Hind*, and contains only 66 articles, but is illustrated by copious extracts. A native of Dehlī, he resided at Patna and Lucknow; but he appears to have died at Haidarābād (De Tassy).

Mirza 'Ali Nawab (مرزا علی نواب). He was executed at Dehlī on Tuesday the 9th July, A.D. 1844, for the murder of two dancing-girls in that city. The Fatwā was given by Maulānā Ṣadr-uddīn Khān Bahādur, Ṣadr-us-Ṣudūr.

Mirza Haidar (مرزا حیدر). *Vide* Haidar (Mirzā), also called Haidar Doghlāt.

Mirza Hasan (مرزا حسن). *Vide* Hasan (Mirzā).

Mirza 'Isa (مرزا عیسی), and Mirzā Inayat-ullah, governors of Tatta in the time of the emperor Shāh Jahān, where they died. Their tombs are magnificent edifices built of yellow marble, beautifully carved, with flowers in bas-relief, and surpassing all the buildings of the place. The inscription gives the year of A.D. 1648, A.H. 1058.

Mirza Jan (مرزا جان), whose poetical name was Jānī, was the father of Mirzā Jān Jānān.

Mirza Jana (مرزا جانا), and Mirzā Ghāzī, two wazīrs who lived in the reign of the emperor 'Alamgīr. Their tombs are in Tatta, and the inscription shows the date to be A.D. 1683, A.H. 1095.

Mirza Jangli (مرزا جنگلی), Nawāb Sa'ādat 'Alī's second brother.

Mirza Khan (مرزا خان), author of the *Tuhfat ul-Hind*, a work on Hindū music, etc., composed under the patronage of 'Azīm Shāh. It contains a minute account of Hindū literature in all, or most of, its branches; he professes to have extracted his elaborate chapter on music, with the assistance of Pandits, from the *Rāgarnarva* or Sea of Passions, the *Rāgdarpana* or Mirror of Modes, etc.

Mirza Mihr Nasir (مرزا مهر نصیر), a physician in the service of Karīm Khān, king of Persia, and author of a Masnawī. Amongst the many poems which have celebrated the charms and delights of the Spring, his Masnawī holds the highest place. He flourished about the year A.D. 1770, A.H. 1184.

Mirza Muhammad (مرزا محمد), surnamed Bulbul, a celebrated lutanist of Persia. It is related by Sir William Jones, that an intelligent Persian repeated to him again and again that he had more than once been present when Mirzā Muhammad was playing to a large company in a grove near Shīrāz, where he distinctly saw the nightingales trying to vie with the musician, sometimes warbling on the trees, sometimes fluttering from branch to branch, as if they wished to approach the instrument whence the melody proceeded, and at length dropping on the ground in a kind of courtesy, from which they were soon raised by the change of the mode.

Mirza Muhsin (مرزا محسن), brother of Nawāb Safdar Jang. His title was Nawāb Izzaf-uddaula, which see.

Mirza Najaf. *Vide* Najaf Khān.

Mirza Nasir (مرزا نصیر), the father of the maternal grandsire of Nawāb Shujā-uddaula. He came into Hindūstān in the beginning of the reign of the emperor Bahādur Shāh the son of 'Alamgīr, by whom he was appointed to an office of trust at Patna about the year A.D. 1708, A.H. 1120, where he died and where his tomb yet remains. He had two sons, the second of whom, Muhammad Amīn, on being apprised of the death of his father, left Persia, and about the year A.D. 1718, visited the court of the emperor Farrukhsiyar. He was appointed by this prince governor of the fort of Āgra; and soon rising to greater honours, he ultimately became the viceroy of Audh, by the title of Burhān ul-Mulk Sa'ādat Khān.

Mirza Nasir (مرزا نصیر), a poet who came to India from Mazindarān in the reign of the emperor Shāh 'Alam the blind. His son Malik Muhammad Khān received the title of Nawāb Samsām-uddaula Malik Muhammad Khān Diler Jang, from Nawāb Zulfikār-uddaula Najaf Khān and after some time died in Jaipūr in A.D. 1804, A.H. 1219.

Mirza Rustam (مرزا رستم), a prince of Qandahār, being driven to difficulties by his own brothers and the Uzbaks, came to the court of Akbar in A.D. 1593, A.H. 1001, and presented the king with the fort of Qandahār, for which the government of Multān was conferred on him, and he was ranked among the Amīrs of the empire. He was the son of Mirzā Sultān Husain the grandson of Shāh Ismā'īl, king of Persia.

Mirza Shafi' (مرزا شفع), nephew of Mirza Najaf Khān (*q.v.*). He contested the succession to his uncle with Afrāsyāb (*q.v.*) on the great Minister's death, and was assassinated before the fort of Āgra by Muhammad Beg Hamadāni in September, 1783.

Misa'ab (مصعب), brother of 'Abdullāh ibn-Zuber, on whose part he was governor of Basra in the time of the Khalīfs Marwān I. and his son 'Abdul Malik. He was killed in a battle fought against the troops of the latter, about the year A.D. 690, A.H. 71, and while 'Abdul Malik was at Kūfa during an entertainment, Misa'ab's head was presented to him; upon which one of the company took occasion to say, "I saw Husain's head in this same castle presented to 'Ubaid-ullah; 'Ubaid-ullah's to Almukhtār; Almukhtār's to Misa'ab; and now at last Misa'ab's to yourself." This observation so affected the Khalīf, that either to avert the ill omen, or from some other motive, he ordered the castle to be immediately demolished. Misa'ab had been 'Abdul Malik's intimate friend before he was Khalīf, but marrying afterwards Sakīna the daughter of Husain, and 'Ayesha the daughter of Talha, by these marriages he was engaged in the interest of two families who were at mortal enmity with the house of Umayya.

Miskin (مسکین), the poetical name of several poets of India.

Miskin Shah (مسکین شاه), a spiritual teacher of the chiefs of Karnāl in the Balāghat districts, Southern Hindūstān, whose mausoleum stands a mile distant from the town of Karnāl. He is the author of a Dīwān.

Mitti (متی), a person of the tribe of Indians called Kalāl, whose profession was to keep watch at the gate of the kings and noblemen of India, and to run before them in their retinue. Some of them were raised even to the rank of 1500. This man was employed by Nūr Jahān Begam, was well educated and became a poet in the time of Jahāngīr. He is the author of a Dīwān.

Mohan Lal (موهن لال), a Hindū who adopted "Anīs" for his poetical name. He was the author of a Tazkira called *Anīs ul-Ahbab*, compiled in A.D. 1783, A.H. 1197. He informs us that when 'Asaf-uddaula the Nawāb of Audh saw the Tazkira of the contemporary poet Hazīn, he ordered him to compile a similar work on Indian poets.

Mohan Lal Munshi (موهن لال منشی), the son of Pandit Budh Singh, the son of Rāja Manī Rām, of Kashmere descent. His father was a resident of Dehlī. He was a student of Dehlī College and accompanied Lieutenant Burnes and Dr. J. G. Gerard in the capacity of a Persian Munshī to Persia in January, 1832, when he wrote a Journal of his Travels entitled *Journal of a Tour through the Panjāb, Afghānistān, Turkistān, Khurasān, and part of Persia*, published in Calcutta in 1834. He was employed as an attaché to the British agency during the first Afghān war, of which he published an account, in which he attributed the outbreak of 1840 to the misconduct of British officers. He died about 1870 at Dehlī, where he resided for the latter part of his life. He became converted to the Muhammadan faith.

Mohan Singh (موهن سنگه), son of Rāo Qaran, murdered by one Muhammad Shāh about the year A.D. 1761. His women burned themselves alive with his corpse.

Moi'zzi (معزی). *Vide* Amīr Moi'zzī.

Moi'zz-ud-din allah Abi Tamim Ma'd (معزلدین الله ابی تمیم معاد), the son of Ismā'īl surnamed Al-Mansūr. He was the 4th Khalīf of Barbary, and the first king of Egypt of the Fatimite dynasty who began to reign in the former country in A.D. 952, 30th Shawwāl, A.H. 361. The greatest achievement performed by this Khalīf was his conquest of Egypt, and the removal of the Khilāfat from Qairwān to that country in A.D. 970, A.H. 361. He subdued all Africa and built the city Al-Qāhira in Egypt, commonly called Grand Cairo, and died after a reign of 24 years in A.D. 976, 19th Rabi' II. A.H. 365.

[*Vide* Muhammad Al-Mahdi.]

List of the kings of the Fatimite dynasty who reigned from A.H. 341 *to* 567 *in Egypt.*

	A.D.	A.H.
Moi'zz-ud-dīn allah Abī Tamīm Ma'd, reigned 24 years	952	341
Al-'Azīz Billāh Abū Nasr Tarār, reigned 21 years	976	365
Hākim-bi-amr allah Abū Mansūr, reigned 25 years	996	386
Tāhir li-āzāz-dīn allah Abū'l Hasan bin-Hakim	1020	411
Mustanasir Billāh Abū Tamīm bin-Tāhir	1036	427
Mustaa'lī Billāh Abū'l Qāsim Ahmad bin-Mustanasir	1094	487
Amar be Ahkām allah Abū 'Alī Mansūr bin-Mustaa'lī	1100	495
Hāfiz-li-dīn allah 'Abdul Majīd bin-Muhammad bin-Mustazehr	1130	524
Al-Zāfir-bi-'Abdullah Ismā'īl bin-Hāfiz	1147	542
Fāez-bi-nasr allah Īsa bin Zāfir	1152	547
'Azid-li-dīn allah bin-Yūsaf bin-Hāfiz, in whose time Egypt was taken by Sālah-uddīn ('Azid died in A.D. 1173)	1158	553

Moi'zz-uddaula (معزالدوله), the brother of 'Imād-uddaula 'Alī Bōya. He was nominated wazīr to the Khalīf Al-Rāzī Billāh in A.D. 936, and held that office during the reigns of Al-Muttaqī and Al-Mustakfī, the latter of whom he afterwards dethroned, and continued through life to exercise absolute authority over Al-Mutīa, the son of the Khalīf Al-Muqtadir, whom he elevated to the throne. He was the youngest of the three brothers. He governed 'Iraq 21 years and 11 months and died at Baghdād on Monday the 1st April, A.D. 967, 17th Rabī' II. A.H. 356. He was succeeded by his son 'Izz-uddaula Bakhtaiār, who was killed in battle in A.D. 968, A.H. 356, by Azd-uddaula, the son of Rukn-uddaula, who succeeded him in the office of wazīr to the Khalīf of Baghdād.

Moi'zz-uddin (معزالدین), title of the emperor Jahāndār Shāh.

Moi'zz-uddin (معزالدین), surname of Qaiqubād the grandson of Sultān Ghayās-uddīn Balban.

Moi'zz-uddin Husain Kart, Malik (معزالدین حسین کرت ملک), the seventh king of the dynasty of Kart or Kard. He succeeded his brother Malik Hāfiz in

A.D. 1322, reigned over Herāt, Ghaznī, etc., about 38 years (some say only 12), and completely subdued the Sarbadāls. He died about the year A.D. 1370, A.H. 771, and was succeeded by his grandson Ghayās-uddīn the son of 'Alī.

Mo'izz - uddin Muhammad Ghori (معزالدين محمد غوری). *Vide* Shahāb-uddīn Muhammad Ghori.

Moi'zz - uddin Muhammad, Mir (معزالدين محمد مير). He was so exquisite a caligrapher that a thousand verses written by him sold for 10,000 dīnārs. He was living about the year A.D. 1585, A.H. 993.

Momin (مومن), **Hakīm Muhammad** Mōmin Khān, a physician and the best poet in his time in Dehlī. He wrote Persian and Rekhta poetry, and has left a Dīwān in Persian and several Masnawīs. He fell from the roof of his house and broke his arm in A.D. 1852, A.H. 1268, and died after a few days.

Momin 'Ali, Shaikh (مومن علی شيخ), a poet whose poetical name was Maftūn.

Momin, Mir (مومن مير استرابادی), of Astarābād, an author.

Mu'ajiz (معاجز), **poetical title of Mu**hammad Niẓām Khān, an Afghān who was an author and died at Dehlī in A.D. 1749, A.H. 1162.

Mu'awia I. (معاويه), **the son of Abū** Sufīan, the son of Harb, and general of the khalīfs 'Umar and 'Usmān. After avenging his master's (Osman's) death, he seized his kingdom A.D. 644, and became the first khalīf of the race of Umayya or Ommiades. He took Rhodes and after destroying the Colossus, he attacked Sicily, and carried devastation to the gates of Constantinople. After besieging in vain the capital for seven years, he purchased peace by an annual tribute. During this siege, the Greek fire is said to have been invented. He died on the 7th April, A.D. 680, New Moon of Rajab, A.H. 60, after having reigned from Hasan's resignation 19 lunar years 3 months and 27 days, and was buried at Damascus his capital, which was made the residence of the khalīfs as long as the house of Umayya continued on the throne. Mu'āwia had embraced the Muhammadan religion at the same time as his father, which was in the year of the victory. Muhammad made him his secretary, and 'Umar gave him the lieutenancy of Syria, which he held during four years of that khalīf's life. 'Usmān continued him in that post during the whole space of his reign, which was about twelve years. For four years more he kept Syria in his own hands by force, whilst he held out against 'Alī. Taken altogether, therefore, he held possession of Syria, either as governor or khalīf, for nearly 40 years. There are different reports about his age; some say 70 years and others 75. He was succeeded by his son Yezīd I.

Khalīfs of the house of Umayya who reigned at Damascus.

1. Mu'āwia I.
2. Yezīd I.
3. Mu'āwia II.
4. Marwān I.
5. 'Abdul Malik.
6. Walīd I.
7. Sulaiman.
8. 'Umar, son of 'Abdul Azīz.
9. Yezīd II.
10. Hashām.
11. Walīd, son of Yezīd II.
12. Yezīd III.
13. Ibrahīm, son of Walīd.
14. Marwān II. the last of the Ommaides.

Mu'awia II. (معاويه), **son of Yezīd I.** and the third khalīf of the race of Umayya. He succeeded his father in September, A.D. 683, A.H. 64, at Damascus, but being of a weakly constitution, and unable to bear the fatigues of government, resigned the crown six weeks after his inauguration, and died soon after without naming a successor. Therefore, as soon as he had made his abdication, the officers of the court proceeded to the election of a khalīf and their choice fell upon Marwān, the son of Hakam. In the meantime 'Abdullah the son of Zuber had been declared khalīf in Arabia, 'Irak, Khurāsān, Egypt, and a great part of Syria.

[*Vide* 'Umar al Maksūs.]

Mu'azzam Khan (معظم خان خانخانان), **Khān Khānān, entitled** Mīr Jumla, which see.

Mu'azzam Khwaja (معظم خواجه). *Vide* Khwāja Mu'azzam.

Mu'azzam, Muhammad (معظم محمد), *Vide* Bahādur Shāh I.

Mu'azzi, Amir (معزی امير), **a nobleman** at the court of Sulṭān Malikshāh Saljūkī. He is the author of a Dīwān in Persian. He was living at the time of the Sulṭān's death, which happened in A.D. 1092.

[*Vide* Amīr Moizzī.]

Mubarik 'Ali Khan (مبارک علی خان نواب), Nawāb of Bengal, Behār and Urisa, placed on the masnad on the 23rd December, A.D. 1824.

Mubarik Shah (مبارک شاه), the son of Khizir Khān, ascended the throne of Dehlī after the death of his father on the 22nd May, A.D. 1421, 19th Jumāda I. A.H. 824. He reigned 13 lunar years 3 months and 16 days, and was murdered on the 18th April, A.D. 1434, 5th Ramazān, A.H. 837, in a masjid where he had gone to say his prayers, by Qāzī 'Abdus Samad, Sadhāran Khattrī and others, who raised Muhammad Shāh, his nephew, to the throne.

Mubarik Shah Khilji (مبارک شاه خلجی), surnamed Qutb-uddīn, ascended the throne of Dehlī (according to Firishta) on the 22nd March, A.D. 1317, 7th Muharram, A.H. 717, after the death of his father Sultān 'Alā-uddīn Khiljī, and the murder of Kāfūr, a slave of the latter, who had aspired to the throne and had raised Shahāb-uddīn 'Umar Khān a boy of seven years of age, the youngest son of the late Sultān to the throne. Amīr Khusro, the celebrated Persian poet who had served three kings before, wrote a book in his name, for which he was remunerated by the king with an elephant load of silver pieces. Mubārik Shāh reigned four years, and was murdered on the 4th April, A.D. 1321, 5th Rabī' I. A.H. 721, by his wazīr, Khusro Malik, a favourite slave to whom he had confided all the powers of the State. This man ascended the throne with the title of Khusro Shāh, but was assassinated five months after by Ghāzī Khān Tughlaq, governor of the Panjāb, who took the title of Ghayās-uddīn Tughlaq Shāh. The house of Khiljī terminated with Mubārik Shāh.

Mubarik Shah Sharqi, (مبارک شاه شرقی), whose former name was Malik Wāzil or Karanfal, was the adopted son of Khwāja Jahān Sharkī, whom he succeeded A.D. 1401, A.H. 803, to the government of Jaunpūr, and perceiving that the kingdom of Dehlī was thrown into disorder and anarchy, he, with the consent of the officers of his government, assumed the royal canopy, and caused coin to be struck in his name under the above title. He died after a short reign of 18 months in the year A.D. 1402, A.H. 804, and was succeeded by his younger brother Ibrāhīm Shāh Sharkī.

Mubarik Shaikh *Vide* Shaikh Mubārik.

Mubarik-uddaula (مبارک الدوله), the youngest of the three sons of Mīr Ja'far 'Alī Khān, Nawāb of Bengal. He succeeded his brother Saif-uddaula in March, A.D. 1770, on the same terms as his brother, *viz.* to receive a pension of sixteen lacs of rupees, and the business of Nāzim to be managed by deputy. He died at Murshidābād in September, A.D. 1793, and was succeeded by his son Nāsir ul-Mulk, Wazīr-uddaula. Mubārik-uddaula is mentioned in Foster's *Travels* as the grandson of Mīr Ja'far and of Mīran. Hamilton says Mubārik-uddaula died in A.D. 1796.

Mubarik-ullah, Mirza (مبارک الله میرزا), a Persian poet.

Mubariz-uddin. *Vide* Muhammad Muzaffar.

Mubariz Khan (مبارز خان), a nobleman who, in the commencement of the reign of Muhammad Shāh of Dehlī, was governor of Haidarābād, and was killed in a battle which he fought at the instigation of the emperor against Nizām ul-Mulk on the 1st October, O.S. 1724, 23rd Muharram, A.H. 1137, and his head sent to court with part of his spoils.

Mubariz ul-Mulk (مبارز الملک), a title of Nawāb Sarbaland Khān.

Mubid (موبد), the takhallus of Zinda Rām of Kashmere. He was a pupil of Mirzā 'Abdul Ghanī Beg Qabūl, and is the author of a Dīwān. He died in A.D. 1759, A.H. 1172.

Mubid Shah (موبد شاه), a Guebre who turned Musalmān and wrote a history of the religions in the time of the emperor Akbar entitled *Dabistān*. The intention of the author appears to have been to furnish to Akbar a pretended historical basis of the religion which this emperor had invented, and which he was desirous to introduce. For this reason, the author commences with a very long chapter on the religion of the Mahābādians, which is a mere web of incoherent fables. Sir William Jones first mentioned this work. Gladwin published its first chapter in the *New Asiatic Miscellany*, together with an English translation. Leyden in the 9th volume of the *Asiatic Researches* translated the chapter on the Illuminati, and the text of the whole work was published at Calcutta in 1809. The Oriental Translation Society also published the whole in English.

Mubtila (مبتلا), takhallus of Shaikh Ghulām Muhī-uddīn Qureshī of Mīrath. He is the author of several works. He was living in A.D. 1807, A.H. 1222.

Mudki Rao (مدکی راو). *Vide* Jhanko Rāo Sindhia.

Mufid, Mulla (مفید ملا). *Vide* Mullā Mufīd.

Mufid, Shaikh (مفید شیخ). *Vide* Abū 'Abdullah Muhammad bin- Muhammad al-Na'mānī.

Mufrid (مفرد), poetical name of Muhammad 'Alī Beg.

Mughal Beg (مغل بیگ), a nobleman of the reign of the emperor Akbar. He is the author of the work entitled *Samrāt ul-Kuds*, commonly called *Tazkira Mashāekh*.

Mughira (مغیره). *Vide* Al-Mughīra.

Mughis-uddin Qazi (مغیث الدین قاضی). He flourished in the reign of Sultān 'Alā-uddīn Khiljī.

Muhabbat Khan, Nawab (محبت خان نواب), whose takhallus is Muhabbat, was also called Muhabbat-ullāh Khān, one of the sons of Hāfiz Rahmat Khān. In composing Rekhta he was a pupil of Mirzā Ja'far 'Alī Hasrat, and in Persian a pupil of Makīn. He resided at Lucknow and received a handsome allowance from the British Government as well as from the nawāb 'Asaf-uddaula. He has written a Masnawī called *Asrār Muhabbat*, containing the loves of *Sīsī* and *Pānū*, at the request of Mr. Johnson, who had the title of Mumtāz-uddaula, and is also the author of a Dīwān. According to a chronogram of Jurat he died in A.D. 1807, A.H. 1222.

Muhammad (محمد) (or Mahomed), the Arabian prophet, author of the *Qurān*, was born on Monday the 20th April, A.D. 571, 10th Rabī' I. at Mecca in Arabia, and was of the tribe of Quresh, the noblest of the country. Arab writers make him to be descended in a right line from Ishmael the son of Abraham; but do not pretend to any certainty in the remote part of his genealogy. He lost his father, 'Abdullah, before he was two years old, and his mother, 'Amina, before he was six; but their attention was supplied by the care of his grandfather, 'Abdul Muttalib, who, at his death, which happened two years afterwards, left him under the guardianship of his son Abū Tālib, with whom he continued till he was twenty-five, when he was placed in the service of a woman named Khudyja, the widow of a rich merchant at Mecca, who sent merchandize into Syria. This woman fell in love with Muhammad, the driver of her camels, and married him. In his frequent journeys through Arabia, he had observed the various sects which divided the opinions of the eastern Christians, and he considered that nothing could so firmly secure to him the respect of the world as laying the foundation of a new religion. In his 40th year he assumed the title of the Apostle of God, and gradually increased his fame and his followers by the aid of pretended visions. When he found himself exposed to danger at Mecca he left the city, and retired to Madīna, where his doctrines found a more friendly reception. This event, which happened in the year A.D. 622, forms the celebrated era of the Muhammadans, called the Hijra or Hijrī, which signifies Separation. At Madīna the prophet erected his standard, and as for thirteen years before he had endeavoured to spread his doctrines by persuasion, he now propagated them by the sword. In the eleventh year of the Hijra the prophet fell sick, and after a confinement of thirteen days he died on Monday the 8th June, A.D. 632, 12th Rabī' I. A.H. 11, aged 63 lunar years. He was buried in the same place where he died, in the chamber of the most beloved of his wives, 'Ayesha, the daughter of Abū Bakr, at Madīna, where his remains are still preserved. It is very remarkable that though Muhammad himself so often declared in the Qurān that he wrought no miracles, yet his followers have ascribed a great many to him. For instance, they affirm that he caused water to flow from his fingers, that he split the moon in two, that the stones, trees, and beasts acknowledged him to be the true prophet sent from God, and saluted him as such; that he went one night from Mecca to Jerusalem, from whence he ascended to heaven, where he saw and conversed with God, and came back again to Mecca before the next morning; with many more miracles equally incredible. Muhammad permitted, by his law, four wives to each of his followers, but did not limit himself to that number; for he observed that a prophet, being peculiarly gifted and privileged, was not bound to restrict himself to the same laws as ordinary mortals. The authors who give him the smallest number of wives own that he had fifteen, four of whom, however, never shared connubial rites. Their names and the year when they died, are as follows:—

	A.D.	A.H.
1. Khudīja, the daughter of Khawylid, died 3 years before the Hijra era, aged 65	619	
2. Sūda, daughter of Zama'a, died	674	54
3. 'Ayesha, daughter of Abū Bakr, died aged 66 .	677	57
4. Hafsa, daughter of 'Umar Khattāb, died . . .	665	45
5. Umm Salma, daughter of Abū Umayya, outlived all Muhammad's wives and died	679	59

	A.D.	A.H.
6. Umm Habība, daughter of Abū Sufyān, died	664	44
7. Zainab, daughter of Jahash, widow of Zaid, Muhammad's slave, died	641	20
8. Zainab, daughter of Khuzyma, died two months after the above	641	20
9. Maimūna, daughter of Harith, died	671	51
10. Jawyria, daughter of Harith	670–5	50–56
11. Safyā, daughter of Hai bin-Akhtab, died	670	50
12. Maria Copti, or the Egyptian, of whom was born Ibrāhīm	637	16

By Khudyja, his first wife, he had six children, two sons and four daughters, *viz.* Qasim and 'Abdullah who is also called Tāhir; and Zainab, Rukia, Umm Kulsūm and Fātima; all of whom died before their father excepting Fātima, who was married to 'Alī and survived her father six months.

Muhammad I. (محمد اول) (or Mahomet I.) Sultān of the Turks, was the son of Bāyezīd I. (Bajazet), whom he succeeded in A.D. 1413, A.H. 816, after an interregnum of eleven years, during which time his brother Sulaimān had taken possession of Brusa. He was a brave and politic monarch, conquered Cappadocia, Servia, Wallachia, and other provinces, and was at peace with Manuel Palœologos, emperor of Constantinople, to whom he restored some of his provinces, and died at Adrianople of a bloody-flux A.D. 1422, A.H. 825, aged 47 years. He was succeeded by his son Murād II. (Amurath).

Muhammad II. (محمد ثانی) (Mahomet II.) emperor of the Turks, surnamed the Great, succeeded his father Murād II. (Amurath) in February, A.D. 1451, Muharram, A.H. 855. His reign was begun with preparations for war; he besieged Constantinople, and conveyed over the land some of his gallies into the harbour, which the Greeks had shut up againt the invaders. Constantinople was taken by him on Tuesday the 29th May, A.D. 1453, 20th Jumāda I. A.H. 857, and in her fall poured forth her fugitive philosophers and learned men to revive literature in the Western world. Muhammad by his victories, deserved the name of Great; and the appellation of Grand Seignor, which he assumed, has descended to his successors. After subduing two empires, twelve tributary kingdoms and two hundred towns, he was preparing for the subjugation of Italy, when a colic proved fatal to him, and he died on Thursday the 3rd May, A.D. 1481, 3rd Rabī' I. A.H. 886, after a reign of 31 lunar years. His death was the cause of universal rejoicings over the Christian world, whose religion he had sworn to exterminate for the tenets of Muhammad. He was of exceeding courage and strength, of a sharp wit, and very fortunate; but withal, he was faithless and cruel; and in his time occasioned the death of 80,000 Christians of both sexes. His son Bāyezīd II. succeeded him.

Muhammad III. (محمد ثالث), emperor of the Turks, succeeded his father Murād III. in January, A.D. 1595, Jumāda I. A.H. 1003, to the throne of Constantinople. He began his reign by ordering nineteen of his brothers to be strangled, and ten of his father's wives to be drowned, whom he supposed to be with child. He made war against Rodulphus II. emperor of Germany, and invaded Hungary with an army of 200,000 men, but his progress was checked by Maximillian the emperor's brother, who would have obtained a decisive victory had not his troops abandoned themselves to pillage. Muhammad, obliged to retire from Hungary, buried himself in the indolence of his seraglio. He died of the plague, after a reign of 9 years, in January, A.D. 1604, Shābān, A.H. 1012, aged 59 years, and was succeeded by his son Ahmad I.

Muhammad IV. (محمد رابع), emperor of the Turks, was the son of Ibrāhīm, whom he succeeded on the throne of Constantinople in A.D. 1649, A.H. 1059. He pursued the war with the Venetians, and after reducing Candia, with the loss of 200,000 men, he invaded Poland. His arms proved victorious, but the disgrace was wiped off by the valour of Sobeski, king of Poland, who the next year routed his enemies at the battle of Choezim. He was deposed in A.D. 1687, A.H. 1098, and sent to prison, where he died in A.D. 1691, A.H. 1102. He was succeeded by his brother Sulaimān II.

Muhammad 'Abd (محمد عبد), author of a Persian work on Jurisprudence called *Asās ul-Islām*, the Foundation of Muhammadanism, and of one called *Fiqha Sunnatf wa-Jamāa't.*

Muhammad 'Adil Shah (محمد عادل شاه), king of Bījāpūr, succeeded his father Ibrāhīm 'Adil Shāh II. in the year A.D. 1626, A.H. 1036. As the armies of the emperor of Dehlī were daily extending their conquests in the Deccan, and he knew that should the country of Ahmadnagar be reduced his own would become the object of attack, he assisted Nizām Shāh against the imperial arms; and more than once suffered for his conduct, being obliged to purchase peace by large contributions. In the year A.D. 1634, A.H. 1044, the armies of the emperor Shāh Jahān invaded the Deccan on three quarters and laid waste the country of Bījāpūr without mercy. After the reduction of Daulatābād and other forts, with most part of the kingdom of Nizām Shāh, Muhammad 'Adil Shāh agreed to pay a considerable tribute to the emperor. He was the last king of Bījāpūr who struck coins in his own name. In the latter part of his reign his vassal Sewājī, the son of Sāhū Bhōsla, by stratagem and treachery obtained great power, and the foundation of the Bījāpūr monarchy became weakened. Muhammad died in November, A.D. 1656, Muharram, A.H. 1067, and was succeeded by his son 'Alī 'Adil Shāh II. His tomb at Bījāpūr, called "Gol Gumbaz," has a dome which measures 130 feet in diameter and which can be seen from 30 miles distance. A beautiful view is seen from the roof; the tomb being at the very end of the city, all the remarkable places present themselves to us, and the eye loses itself in the vast number of cupolas, domes, and minarets crowded together. Conspicuous among these are seen the fair proportions of the Rauza or tomb of Ibrāhīm 'Adil Shah.

Muhammad Afzal (محمد افضل), author of the work named *Madīnat-ul-Aubia*. It gives an account of the creation of the world, and a history of all the prophets prior to the birth of Muhammad.

Muhammad Afzal, Shaikh (محمد افضل شيخ), son of Shaikh 'Abdur Rahīm, a pīrzada and native of Ghāzipūr, who by the command of his murshid or spiritual guide, Mīr Syyid Muhammad of Kālpī, fixed his residence at Allahābād, where he held a school and passed the remainder of his life in teaching Arabic and Persian, and making proselytes. He is the author of several works; was born on the 28th October, O.S. 1628, 10th Rab'ī I. A.H. 1038, and died aged 87 lunar years on Friday the 2nd January, O.S. 1713, 15th Zil-hijja, A.H. 1124. His descendants are still at Allahābād. He used "Afzal" for his poetical name.

Muhammad Akbar (محمد اكبر), the emperor Akbar is sometimes so called.

Muhammad Akbar (محمد اكبر), the youngest son of the emperor Aurangzeb 'Ālamgīr. He rebelled against his father, went to Persia and died there in A.H. 1115.

Muhammad Akbar (محمد اكبر), son of Muhammad Gesū Darāz of Kulbarga. He is the author of a Persian work on Theology entitled *Akāed Akbarī*, containing the principles of the Muhammadan faith.

Muhammad 'Ala-uddin bin Shaikh 'Ali al-Hiskafi (محمد علاء الدين بن شيخ علي الحسكفي), author of the work on Jurisprudence called the *Fatāwā Durr al Mukhtār*, which is a commentary on the *Tanwīr ul-Absār*, containing a multitude of decisions.

Muhammad 'Ali (محمد على), Viceroy of Egypt. Upwards of twelve centuries have passed since Egypt fell under the arms of the successful General of the Khalīf Omar; for a little over five centuries it remained in the possession of the successors of the conqueror; their power was put to an end by the Turkmans in A.D. 1171, and about eighty years afterwards the latter were in their turn expelled by the Mamlūks. The Mamlūks raised one of their own number to the throne, with the title of Sultān, and the dynasty lasted till 1517, when the last of the Mamlūk Sultāns was put to death by the Turkish Sultān Salam, who appointed a Pasha to the government assisted by a council of twenty-four Mamlūk beys or chiefs. This state of things lasted till 1798, when the French under Bonaparte landed in Egypt, and after destroying the Mamlūks were themselves attacked and defeated by the British in 1801. After the departure of the British, the country fell into anarchy till it was restored by Muhammad 'Alī, who by the massacre of the remaining Mamlūks made himself master of the situation. The treaty of London in 1841 made the government of Egypt hereditary in the family of Muhammad 'Alī, and Ismā'īl Pasha was his grandson. Egypt has now ceased to be a province of Turkey. Its ruler has had all the powers of an independent sovereign conceded to him by the Farmān, which dates from the 8th June, A.D. 1873. Muhammad was born in 1769, entered the Turkish army, and in 1799 was sent to Egypt at the head of a contingent to co-operate with the British against the French invaders. Here his fine military qualities rapidly developed themselves, and he at length became the Commander of the Albanian Corps d'armee in Egypt. He was soon afterwards involved in disputes with the Mamlūks, who practically had long ruled Egypt. He was soon after involved in disputes with the Mamlūks who had long practically ruled Egypt. They were at length entirely exterminated in 1820. He declared himself independent of the Porte in 1838, and died on the 2nd August, A.D. 1849. He was succeeded by his son or grandson Ismā'īl Pasha.

Muhammad 'Ali (محمد على), author of an Inshā or collection of Letters.

Muhammad 'Ali Hazin (محمد على حزين). *Vide* Hazīn.

Muhammad 'Ali Khan (محمد على خان), eldest son of Faiz-ullah Khān the Rohela chief of Rāmpūr. He succeeded his father in A.D. 1794.

Muhammad 'Ali Khan (محمد علی خان), Nawāb of the Carnatic, was the son of Anwar-uddīn Khān. After his father's death he was confirmed to the government of the Carnatic by Nawāb Nāsir Jang in A.D. 1750, and placed on the masnad by the assistance of the English. He died, aged 78 years, on the 13th October, A.D. 1795, and his son 'Umdat ul-Umrā succeeded him.

Muhammad 'Ali Khan (محمد علی خان), Nawāb of Tonk, son of the Pindari chief Amīr Khān, succeeded his father to the Gaddī of Tonk in 1834, and was deposed in 1867 on account of the Lawa massacre. His estate came under the immediate control of the Political Department in the end of 1870, when his son Ibrāhīm 'Alī Khān was installed as Nawāb of Tonk.

Muhammad 'Ali Khan, Rohela (محمد علی خان). He succeeded his father Faiz-ullah Khān in September, A.D. 1794, to his jāgir of Rāmpūr.

[*Vide* Faiz-ullah Khān.]

Muhammad 'Ali Mahir (محمد علی ماهر). *Vide* Māhir.

Muhammad 'Ali, Mir (محمد علی میر), of Burhānpūr, author of the *Mirat-us-Safā*. (See *All the Year Round*, vol. xviii. p. 157.)

Muhammad 'Ali Shah (محمد علی شاه), whose former title was Nawāb Nasīr-uddaula, was the son of Sa'ādat 'Alī Khān, Nawāb of Audh. He was placed on the throne of Lucknow by the British, after the death of his nephew Sulaimān Jāh Nasīr-uddīn Haidar, on the 8th July, A.D. 1837, 4th Rabī' II. A.H. 1253, at the age of 70 years, and took the title of Abū'l Fatha Moīn-uddīn Sultān Zamān Muhammad 'Alī Shāh. He reigned exactly five lunar years, and died at Lucknow on Tuesday the 17th May, A.D. 1842, 5th Rabī' II, A.H. 1258, when his son Suryya Jāh Amjad 'Alī Shāh succeeded him.

Muhammad al-Mahdi (محمد المهدی), the first khalīf or king of Barbary of the race of the Fatimites. He began to reign in A.D. 908, A.H. 296, and was supposed to be a descendant of Husain the son of 'Alī and Fātima, whence the race is called Fatimite. His descendants conquered Egypt. He died in A.D. 933, A.H. 321, and was succeeded by his son Kāem Biamr-ullah, who died in A.D. 945, A.H. 334, and was succeeded by his son Mansūr Billāh in A.D. 952, A.H. 341.

[*Vide* Maizli-ud-din-Allah.]

Muhammad Amin (محمد امین), son of Daulat Muhammad al-Husainī al-Balkhī, is the author of the work called *Anfa' ul-Akhbār*, or Useful Chronicle; was in the service of Nawāb Sipahdar Khān, who receives a long and laudatory notice at the close of the work. He concluded it in A.D. 1626, A.H. 1036, and styled it *Anfa' ul-Akhbār* because the Hijrī year A.H. 1036, in which it was completed, is represented by the letters composing those words. He resided chiefly at Ahmadnagar.

Muhammad Amin (محمد امین), author of the work entitled *'Asrār ul-Ma'ānī*, a collection of poems on the conquests of the emperor 'Alamgīr, and a panegyric on several cities of the Deccan, which, previous to its being subdued by his arms, was esteemed the garden of India. He also wrote another work on Theology, entitled *Haqīqat Ilm Ilāhī*.

Muhammad Amin Khan (محمد امین خان), son of Muhammad Sa'īd Mīr Jumla. He served under the emperors Shāh Jahān and 'Alamgīr, and was raised to the rank of 5000. He died on the 6th May, O.S. 1682, 8th Jumāda I. A.H. 1093, at Ahmadābād Gujrāt.

Muhammad Amin Khan (محمد امین خان), entitled Ya'tmād-uddaula, was the son of Mīr Bahā-uddīn, the brother of Nizām ul-Mulk 'Asaf Jāh, and came to India in the reign of 'Alamgīr under whom he served for several years. He was the chief counsellor of the emperor Muhammad Shāh, and was appointed wazīr with the above title after the death of Sayyad Husain 'Alī Khān and the imprisonment of his brother Sayyad 'Abdullah Khān in A.D. 1720, A.H. 1133, but he had scarcely entered on his office when he was taken ill and died suddenly on the 17th January, O.S. 1721, 29th Rabī' I. A.H. 1133. After his death the office of prime minister was only filled by a temporary substitute, being ultimately designed for Nizām ul-Mulk 'Asaf Jāh, who was then in the Deccan.

Muhammad Amin Razi (محمد امین رازی). *Vide* Amīn Ahmad, author of the *Haft Aqlīm*.

Muhammad Amir Khan (محمد امیر خان), of Āgra, author of the *Maulūd Nādirī*, containing the history and miracles of 'Abdul Kadir Gīlānī in Urdū, written in A.D. 1847, A.H. 1263.

[*Vide* Muhammad Qāsim.]

Muhammad Ansar (محمد انصار), author of the work called *Malfūzāt Shaikh Aḥmad Maghrabi*, or the Memoirs of Shaikh Aḥmad Khattū, a very celebrated Sūfī of Gujrāt, whose tomb is at Ahmadābād and who is still held in veneration. It was written in A.D. 1445, A.H. 849.

Muhammad 'Arif, Mirza (محمد عارف ميرزا), a poet who was contemporary with Nāsir 'Alī.

Muhammad Aslam, Qazi (محمد اسلم قاضی), who lived in the time of Shalydan.

Muhammad Atabak (محمد اتابک) *Vide* Atābak Muhammad.

Muhammad 'Azim, (محمد اعظم), an historian who wrote a history of Kashmere in continuation of one written by Haidar Malik. It is amusing to observe, says Sir H. M. Elliot, the extravagant praises which this orthodox historian confers upon 'Alamgīr, whom he infinitely prefers to the noble and enlightened Akbar, of whom he complains that he "treated all his subjects alike!" not favouring the Muhammadans above the Hindūs. Was ever a nobler tribute paid to a ruler?

Muhammad Azim Khan (محمد اعظم خان), ex-amīr of Kabūl. *Vide* Azim Khān.

Muhammad Bakhsh (محمد بخش), whose poetical name is Mahjūr, is the author of a work in Urdū called *Nauratan* or the nine jewels, containing numerous stories, which he completed in the first year of Nawāb Ghazī-uddīn Haidar of Lucknow or A.H. 1230. He is also the author of two other works of the same description, one called *Gulshan Naubahār* and the other *Chār Chaman*.

Muhammad Bakhtyar Khilji (محمد بختيار خلجي) was appointed governor of Bengal by Sultān Qutb-uddīn Aibak about the year A.D. 1203, A.H. 600. He made Lakhnautī the seat of his government.

Governors of Bengal, down to conquest by Akbar.

	A.D.	A.H.
Muhammad Bakhtyār Khiljī	1203	600
Muhammad Sherān Azz-uddīn, slain in battle with the infidels	1205	602
'Alī Murdān 'Alā-uddīn Khiljī slain	1208	605
Husām-uddīn Ghausī slain	1212	609
Nāsir-uddīn bin-i-Shams-uddīn	1227	624
Mahmūd bin-Shams-uddīn, became Sultān of Hindūstān	1229	627
Tughān Khān, governor under Sultāna Rizia	1237	634
Tijī or Tajī	1243	641
Taimūr Khān Qirān	1244	642
Saif-uddīn	1246	644
Ikhtiār-uddīn Malik Uzbak	1253	651
Jalāl-uddīn Khānī	1257	656
Tāj-uddīn Arsalān	1258	657
Muhammad Tātār Khān	1260	659
Moi'zz-uddīn Tughral	1277	676
Nāsir-uddīn Baghrā Khān, son of Ghayas-uddīn Balban, considered first sovereign of Bengal	1282	681
Qadar Khān, viceroy of Muhammad Shāh I. Tughlaq	1325	725
Fakhr-uddīn Sikandar, assumes independence	1340	741
'Alā-uddīn Mubārik	1342	743
Shams-uddīn Muhammad Shāh Iliās Bhangara	1343	744
Sikandar Shāh bin-Shams-uddīn	1359	760
Ghayās-uddīn 'Azim Shah bin-Sikandar Shāh	1368	769
Saif-uddīn Sultān us-Salātīn bin-Ghayās-uddīn	1374	775
Shāms-uddīn bin-Sultān us-Salātīn	1384	785
Kansa, a Hindū	1386	787
Jalāl-uddīn Muhammad Shāh (Chitmal bin-Kansa)	1392	794
Aḥmad Shāh bin-Jalāl-uddīn	1409	812
Nāsir Shāh (descendant of Shams-uddīn Iliās)	1427	830
Bārbak Shāh bin-Nāsir Shāh	1457	862
Yūsaf Shāh bin-Bārbak Shāh	1474	879
Sikandar Shāh	1482	887
Fatha Shāh	1482	887
Shāhzāda Sultān, an eunuch	1491	896
Fīrōz Shāh Habshī	1492	897
Mahmūd Shāh bin-Fīrōz Shāh	1494	899
Muzaffar Shāh Habshī	1495	900
'Alā-uddīn Husain Shāh bin-Sayyad Ashraf	1498	903
Nasrat Shāh bin-'Alā-uddīn Husain, defeated by	1534	940
Farīd-uddīn Sher Shāh	1537	944
Humayūn held court at Gaur also called Jannatābād	1538	945
Sher Shāh, again	1539	946
Muhammad Khān	1545	952
Khizir Khān Bahādur Shāh bin-Muhammad Khān	1555	962
Jalāl-uddīn bin-Muhammad Khān	1561	968
Sulaimān Kirānī	1564	971
Bāyezīd bin-Sulaimān	1573	981
Dāūd Khān bin-Sulaimān, defeated by Akbar's forces under Munaim Khān	1573	981

Muhammad Baqi, Khwaja (محمد باقی خواجه), a Muhammadan saint who died on the 20th October, A.D. 1603, 25th Jumādą II. A.H. 1012, and is buried at Dehlī close to the Qadam Rasūl. Nizām-uddīn Aḥmad has mentioned him in his work called *Karāmāt ul-Aulia*.

Muhammad Baqir (محمد باقر مجلسی), surnamed Majlisī (or the Ornament of Assemblies), the son of Muhammad Taqī, was Shaikh ul-Islām or high priest of the city of Isfahān, and one of the most celebrated Shia lawyers and learned scholars that Persia ever produced in general literature, law and theology. Such was the esteem in which he was held, that Shāh Sulaimān pressed upon him the hand of his daughter, which, strange to say, he declined. One alone of this celebrated man's works, called *Haqq ul-Yeqīn*, which he dedicated to Shāh Husain, extends to fourteen folio volumes. It contains a body of the theology of the Shias, and quotes and refutes the arguments opposed to the opinions advanced, illustrating the whole with evidences of the truth of the Shia doctrines and with numerous traditions. Besides this, he wrote on many other subjects. One of his works, treating exclusively of Hadīs, is called *Bahr ul-Anwār*. He died A.D. 1698, A.H. 1110, aged 72 years.

Muhammad Baqir Damad, Mir (محمد باقر داماد میر). His father Sayyad Mahmūd was styled Dāmād, because he was the son-in-law of Shaikh 'Alī 'Amilī. He was a native of Astrābād in Persia. Muhammad Bākir his son was also styled Dāmād, because he married the daughter of Shāh 'Abbās I. king of Persia. He resided for many years in Isfahān, and is the author of several compilations, one of which is called Utkil Mubun. He died A.D. 1630, A.H. 1040.

[*Vide* Mīr Bāqir Dāmād.]

Muhammad Baqir, Imam (محمد باقر امام), the son of Imām Zain-ul 'Abidīn, was the fifth Imām of the race of 'Alī. He was born on the 17th December, A.D. 676, 3rd Ṣafar, A.H. 57, and died in the month of May or June, A.D. 731, Rabī' I. A.H. 113. His corpse was carried to Madīna and interred at the Baqia cemetery, in the vault wherein was deposited the bodies of his father and his father's uncle; it is placed under the same dome which covers the tomb of 'Abbās. Some authors have stated the day of his death to be 28th January, A.D. 733, which corresponds with the 7th Ẕil-ḥijja, A.H. 114.

Muhammad Beg Khan (محمد بیگ خان). *Vide* Hājī Muhammad Beg Khān.

Muhammad bin-'Abdul 'Aziz (محمد بن عبد العزیز), surnamed Wajūdī, author of the work in Turkī called *Shāhid wa-Ma'nī*. He died in the year A.D. 1612, A.H. 1021.

Muhammad bin-'Abdur Rahman (محمد بن عبد الرحمن), surnamed bin-'Alī Laila, was a very celebrated Musalmān doctor, and Qāzī of the city of Kūfa, where he was born in A.D. 693, A.H. 74, and died in the year A.D. 765, A.H. 148.

Muhammad bin-Abu Bakr (محمد بن ابو بکر), *i.e.* the son of 'Abū Bakr, the first khalīf after Muhammad. He was made governor of Egypt by the khalīf 'Alī, but was taken prisoner soon after in a battle fought against Amrū ibn-ul-'As the deputy of Muāwia I. who killed him, and, inclosing his dead body in the skin of an ass, burned it to ashes in A.D. 657, A.H. 38.

Muhammad bin-Ahmad (محمد بن احمد هروی), of Herāt, author of the *Tarjuma Fatūh 'Arabī*, containing the conquests of the Arabian Tribes and the domestic quarrels of the Muhammadans, commencing from the Khilāfat of 'Abū Bakr A.D. 632, A.H. 11, and continued till the murder of Husain at the battle of Karbala in A.D. 680, A.H. 61. This work is translated from the Arabic, and was written in A.D. 1199, A.H. 595.

Muhammad bin-'Ali (محمد بن علی), author of the Arabic work entitled *Abnāi ul-Janān*, containing the Life of Muhammad and Memoirs of his companions.

Muhammad bin-'Amru at-Tamimi (محمد بن عمرو التمیمی), author of a biographical work on the lives of eminent Shias.

Muhammad bin-Husain (محمد بن حسین), author of an Arabic work on Jurisprudence called *Badāya-ul-Hidāya* and of another in Arabic and Persia entitled *Hayāt ul-Fawād*. He died A.D. 1686, A.H. 1098.

Muhammad bin-Ibrahim Sadr Shirazi Qazi ul-Quzat (محمد بن ابراهیم صدر شیرازی قاضی القضات), who is also called Mullā Sadr, is the author of the marginal notes on the *Ulhyyāt*.

Muhammad bin-Idris, Imam (محمد بن ادریس امام), the founder of the third orthodox sect, who is said to have been the first that reduced the science of Jurisprudence into a regular system, and made a discriminating collection of Traditions. He died A.D. 819, A.H. 204.

Muhammad bin-Is (محمد بن عيس), author of the *Risāla Almua'jjam fee Asha'ār al-'Ajām.*

Muhammad bin-Isa Tirmizi (محمد بن عيسى ترمذى), author of the work called *Jāma' Tirmizī.* It is also called *Sunan Tirmizī* and likewise *Al-'Ilal.* He was a pupil of al-Bukhārī, and died in A.D. 892, A.H. 279.

Muhammad bin-Ishaq-un-Nadim (محمد بن اسحاق النديم), commonly called Abū Ya'qūb al Warraq, author of the *Qitāb ul-Fehrist*, the most ancient record of Arabian literature, written A.D. 987, A.H. 377. This work, though mentioned by Hājī Khalfa, had hitherto escaped the industry of European explorers, but a portion of it (four books) has been found in the Royal Library of Paris, and the remainder in Herr von Hammer Purgstall's collection. By a passage in the *Fehrist*, that learned gentleman has found that the *Thousand and One Nights* (*Arabian Nights*) had a Persian origin. In the eighth book, the author says that the first who composed tales and apologues were the kings of the first dynasty of the Persians; then those of the Arsacides, the third of the four ancient dynasties of Persia; these tales were augmented and amplified by the Sasanides. The Arabs, he then proceeds to say, translated them into their tongue, composing others like them. The first book of this kind was the *Hazār Afsāna*, or *Thousand Tales*, the subject of which the writers explain, mentioning Shahrzāda and Dīnārzāda as the two females who practise the *ruse* upon the king. "It is said," continues the authors, "that this book was composed by Humāe, the daughter of Bahman." The truth is, that the first who had these tales told him at night, was Alexander the Great, in order that he might keep awake and be upon his guard. The kings who came after him made use, for the same purpose, of the *Thousand Tales*, which fill up a thousand nights, and two hundred conversations besides, in the light of the moon, which were related in a number of nights.

[See *Jour. As. Soc.* vol. xxxi. p. 237.]

Muhammad bin-Ismail (محمد بن اسمعيل). *Vide* Muhammad Ismā'īl and Al-Bakharī.

Muhammad bin-Jarir Tabari (محمد بن جرير طبرى), author of several works. He died in A.D. 941, A.H. 330.

Muhammad bin-Khawand (محمد بن خاوند). *Vide* Khāwand Shāh.

Muhammad bin-Mahmud (محمد بن محمود الاستروشى), commonly called Al-Isturūshī, author of the *Fusūl al-Isturūshī*, a work principally restricted to decision, respecting mercantile transactions. He died in A.D. 1227, A.H. 625.

Muhammad bin-Murtaza (محمد بن مرتضى محسن), surnamed Muhsan, author of a Shia law-book called the *Mufatih*, on which a commentary was written by his nephew, who was of the same name, but surnamed Hādī.

Muhammad bin-Musa (محمد بن موسى), of Khwārīzm, author of a work on Algebra called *Aljabr wal-Muqabila.* This work was translated into English by Frederic Rosen.

Muhammad bin-Qasim (محمد بن قاسم) was a cousin of the khalīf Walīd I. and son-in-law of Hajjāj bin Yūsaf Saqafī. By the command of the khalīf in the year A.D. 711, A.H. 92, he marched with a large army to Sindh, and having defeated and killed the Rāja of that country took possession of it on Thursday the 23rd June, A.D. 712, 10th Ramazān, A.H. 93. From amongst the prisoners captured in the fort of Alor, two daughters of the Rāja were sent to Damascus, and the khalīf sent them to his harem, consigning them to the care of his people until their grief should be assuaged. After two months, they were brought to the presence of the khalīf; when they raised the veils from their faces the khalīf was smitten with their beauty, and asked their names; one was called Girpāldeo, the other Sūrajdeo. The khalīf ordered one to his own bed; she said, "O my Lord, I am not fit for the king's service, we have both for three days been with Bin-Qāsim, who after dishonouring us sent us here." The king was highly incensed, and directed that his servants should sieze Bin-Qāsim, sew him up in a cow-hide, and send him to Syria. When Bin-Qāsim received this order, he directed the messengers to do as they were directed. They obeyed the order, covered Bin-Qāsim with a raw cow-hide; after enduring the torture for three days he died. They then put his body into a box, and conveyed it to the khalīf, who, opening it in the presence of the two women, said, "Behold how absolute is my power, and how I treat such servants as Bin-Qāsim." The woman replied, "O king, just men ought not to be precipitate in great affairs, or be too

hasty to act, either upon the representation of friends or foes." The khalīf asked their meaning; they said, "We made this accusation against Bin-Qāsim because of the hatred we bore him, seeing that he slew our father, and through him we lost all our property and possessions, and became exiles from our own country; but Bin-Qāsim was like a father and brother to us, he looked not on us for any bad purpose, but when our object was revenge for the blood of our father, we accused him of this treachery; this end attained, do with us as you will." The Khalīf on hearing this suffered great remorse; he ordered the two women to be tied to horses, and dragged to death, and they buried Bin-Qāsim in the burial place at Damascus.

[See *Jour. As. Soc.* vol. vii. p. i. pp. 305 307.]

Muhammad bin - Qawam - uddin (محمد بن قوام الدین), author of a Persian Dictionary called *Bahr-ul-Fazāel*, the Sea of Excellence.

Muhammad bin-Tahir II. (محمد بن طاهر ثانی) succeeded his father in the government of Khurāsān and was the last of the race of Tāhirians. He was taken prisoner in a battle about the year A.D. 874, A.H. 260, by Ya'qūb bin-Lais, who took possession of Khurāsān. Thus ended the race of the Tāhirians in Khurāsān, who governed that province for upwards of 54 lunar years.

Muhammad bin-Tunish al-Bukhari (محمد بن تنیش البخاری), author of the work called *'Abdullah-nāma*, containing the history of the Uzbak Tartars originally from Dasht Qapchāk, on the northern shores of the Caspian Sea. In A.D. 1194, they invaded Transoxiana under Shāh Beg Khān; and having driven out the descendants of Taimūr, retained possession of that country. The prince, whose memoirs are the chief subject of this work, was 'Abdullah Khān; he was a contemporary of the renowned Akbar, emperor of Hindūstān, with whom he kept up constant correspondence and interchange of ambassadors, and died A.D. 1595, A.H. 1005. This book was dedicated to Nizām-uddīn Kōkaltash.

Muhammad bin-Ya'qub (محمد بن یعقوب), author of the work called *Qāmūs*.

[*Vide* Fīrozabādī.]

Muhammad bin Ya'qub al-Kalini ar-Razi (محمد بن یعقوب الکلینی), who is called the Raīs ul-Muhaddisīn, or chief of the traditionists, is the author of the *Jāma' ul-Kāfī*, which is reckoned one of the books of the *Qutub Arba'*. It is of vast extent, comprising no less than thirty books; and its author is said to have been employed twenty years in its composition. He also wrote several other works of less note, and died at Baghdād in A.D. 939, A.H. 328.

Muhammad bin - Yusaf (محمد بن یوسف هروی حکیم), a physician of Herāt and author of an Arabic Dictionary called *Bahr-ul-Jawāhir*, or the Sea of Jewels, said to be an Encyclopædia or Dictionary of Arts and Sciences.

Muhammad bin-Yusaf (محمد یوسف هروی), of Herāt, author of the *Tārikh Hind*. This work no doubt (says Sir H. M. Elliot) is the same as *Risālae Ajāeb wa-Gharāeb-in-Hindūstān*, since the author of that treatise also bears the name of Muhammad Yūsaf Hirwī. This author appears to have been contemporary with, and to have conversed with, Khwāja Hasan of Dehlī, who was a disciple of Nizām-uddīn Aulia, who died in A.D. 1325.

Muhammad Bukhari, Sayyad (محمد بخاری سید), father of Sayyad Ahmad Jalāl Bukharī. He had many disciples in the time of Shāh Jahān. Close by the western gate of the Rauza of Tajganj is his shrine. He died in the year A.H. 1045.

Muhammad Damishqi (محمد دمشقی), name of an illustrious Persian poet, who lived in the time of Fāzil the son of Ahia the Barmakī or Barmecide.

Muhammad Gesu Daraz, Sayyad (محمد گیسو داراز سید), of Kulbarga in Daulatābād, a famous Muhammadan saint, who was a disciple of Shaikh Nasīr-uddīn Chirāgh, Dehlī. He was born at Dehlī on the 30th July, A.D. 1321, 4th Rajab, A.H. 721. His proper name is Sudar-uddīn Muhammad Husainī, but he was commonly called Muhammad Geisū Darāz, on account of his having long ringlets. He lived at Kulbarga in the reign of the Bahmanī Sultāns, and had the address to engage Prince Ahmad Shāh to become his disciple, and build him a fine house and a superb convent. When this prince ascended the throne, in A.D. 1422, A.H. 825, the credit of the saint became so great, that from the lord to the artificer all made it their glory to follow his instructions;

so that his tomb became a pilgrimage to all sects. He died in the Deccan in the beginning of the reign of Ahmad Shāh in A.D. 1422, and is buried at Hasanābād, commonly called Kulbarga. His tomb is a magnificent edifice covered with a dome, in the middle of an extensive court. During the reigns of the Deccan Sultāns, great sums of money were occasionally offered to his descendants who reposed near the saint, in vows and presents, and many villages were assigned by the kings to defray the expenses of the tomb. He is said to be the author of several works, among which are the *Adāb ul-Murid*, the *Wajūd ul-'Ashiqīn*, containing the whole duty of a Sūfī disciple, etc., and also of a book of Fables in Persian entitled *Asmār ul-Asrār*. His son, named Muhammad Akbar, is the author of the *Aqāed Akbarī*, containing the principles of the Muhammadan faith.

Muhammad Ghaus Jilani, Hazrat Shaikh (محمد غوث جیلانی حضرت شیخ), a celebrated Muhammadan saint whose tomb is at Uchcha of the Jīlānīs in Multān, and round whose shrine this town was built and after whom it was named. He was a descendant of Shaikh 'Abdul Kādir Jīlānī Baghdādī, and came to Uchcha about the year A.D. 1394. The Dāūdputtras have continued to be his murīd or disciples, and the murīd of his successors from the time of their first leaving Shikārpūr.

Muhammad Ghaus Khan (محمد غوث خان). *Vide* Sirāj-uddaula Muhammad Ghaus Khān.

Muhammad Ghaus, Shaikh (محمد غوث شیخ گوالیری), of Gwāliar. His proper name is Hajī Hamīd-uddīn, styled Ghaus-ul-'Alam, one of the greatest saints of India, who is said to have resided for twelve years in the practice of asceticism in the jangal which lies at the foot of the Chunār hills, consuming the leaves and fruits of the forest as his sole food; and so celebrated was he for the fulfilment of his blessings and predictions, that even powerful kings used to come and visit him and pay their respects. He afterwards went to Gwāliar, where he engaged himself in the pursuits of his holy calling and in making proselytes; and managed to content himself with the proceeds of a jāgīr, which yielded a crore of tangas. He was the murshid or master of Shaikh Wajīh-uddīn 'Alw of Gujrāt, and died on the 14th September, O.S. 1562, 14th Muharram, A.H. 970. The chronogram of the year of his death is "Shaikh Auliabūd," *i.e.* Shaikh was a saint. He is the author of several works, among which are the *Jawāhir ul-Khamsa*, and another entitled *Gulzār Abrār* containing the memoirs of all the Sūfī Shaikhs of India with their places of burial and many other particulars. His brother Shaikh Phūl, who served under the emperor Humāyūn, was killed at Āgra, A.D. 1537, A.H. 945, by the adherents of Mirzā Handāl, who had rebelled against his brother. His tomb is on a hill near the fort of Bayāna. They were the descendants of Khwāja Farīd-uddīn Muhammad 'Attār in the seventh generation. Their grandfather's name was Mo'īn-uddīn Qattāl, whose tomb is in Jaunpūr, and father's name Kiyam-uddīn. He lies buried in Zahūrābād, commonly called Kunbra, in Ghazīpūr. A small work entitled *Manākib Ghausia*, containing the adventures of Muhammad Ghaus, was written by Sayyad Fazl-ullah in the year Hijrī 941, 24 years before the death of the saint.

Muhammad Ghaus Zarrin (محمد غوث زرین), of Bijnaur. He lived in the time of Nawāb 'Asaf-uddaula of Lucknow, and is the author of a Chahār Darwesh in Persian.

Muhammad Ghayas-uddin (محمد غیاث الدین), the son of Jalāl-uddīn, the son of Sharaf-uddīn, author of the Persian Dictionary entitled *Ghayās ul-Lughāt*, which he completed after fourteen years' labour in the year A.D. 1826, A.H. 1242, also of the *Miftāh ul-Kunuz*, *Sharah Sikandar-nāma*, *Nuskha Bāgh o-Bahār*, and several poems and Kasīdas, etc. He was an inhabitant of Mustafābād, commonly called Rāmpūr in the Pergunnah of Shāhābād, Lucknow.

Muhammad Ghazzali (محمد غزالی). *Vide* Ghazzālī.

Muhammad Ghori (محمد غوری). *Vide* Shahāb-uddīn Ghorī.

Muhammad Hadi (محمد هادی), a nobleman of the Court of the emperor Jahāngīr, who wrote the last part of the *Tūzak Jahāngīrī*, during the last four years of that emperor's reign; Jahāngīr wrote the first part up to the seventeenth year of his reign, and the second part was written by Matmid Khān.

Muhammad Hakim, Mirza (محمد حکیم میرزا), son of the emperor Humāyūn and half-brother of Akbar, was born at Kābul on the 18th April, A.D. 1554, 15th Jumāda I. A.H. 961. In the reign of his brother, the emperor Akbar, he had the Government of Kābul, of which he remained during his life in undisturbed possession. He had twice invaded the Panjāb; once in A.D.

1566, A.H. 974, and the second time in February A.D. 1581, Muḥarram, A.H. 989, when the emperor found it necessary to proceed himself with an army, and Mirza Muḥammad Hakim was obliged to retreat before him. He died at Kābul in the 30th year of the emperor Akbar, on the 26th July, O.S. 1585, 16th Amardād Ilahī, corresponding with 16th Sha'bān, A.H. 993, aged 32 lunar years. After his death Rāja Bhagwān Dās and his son Mān Singh were sent to Kābul by the emperor to take charge of that province. His mother's name was Māh Chūchak Begam.

Muhammad Hanif (محمد حنيف), also called Muhammad bin-'Alī, was the third son of 'Alī, and because he was not descended from his wife Fatima, as Hasan and Husain were, is not reckoned amongst the Imāms, notwithstanding there were many who after Husain's death secretly acknowledged him to be the lawful khalīf or Imām. He died in the year A.D. 700, A.H. 81.

Muhammad Hasan (محمد حسن دهلوى), of Dehlī, who flourished about the year A.D. 1604, A.H. 1013, is the author of a Masnawī or poem containing the praises of the prophet, of his chaste wives and of great saints.

Muhammad Hasan Burhan (محمد حسن برهان), author of the Persian Dictionary called *Burhān Qāta'*, dedicated to 'Abdullah Quṭb Shāh of Haidarābād and Golkanḍa, A.D. 1651, A.H. 1061.

Muhammad Hashim (محمد هاشم). *Vide* Khāfī Khān.

Muhammad Husain (محمد حسين), author of a Persian work on Theology called *Aqāed Husain.*

Muhammad Husain Khan (محمد حسين خان), the present nawāb of Kalpī; his title is 'Azīm ul-Mulk.

Muhammad Husain Mirza (محمد حسن مرزا). *Vide* Ibrāhīm Husain Mirzā.

Muhammad Husain, Shaikh (محمد حسين شيخ شهرت), whose poetical name is Shuhrat, was an excellent poet and a physician. He was a native of Arabia, but completed his studies at Shīrāz and came to India, where he was employed by the prince 'Azim Shāh as a physician. In the reign of Farrukh-siyar the title of Hakīm-ul-Mumālik was conferred on him. He went on a pilgrimage to Mecca in the time of the emperor Muhammad Shāh, and after his return to India he died in the month of April, A.D. 1737, Ẕil-ḥijja, A.H. 1149, at Dehlī. He is the author of a Dīwān consisting of 5000 verses.

Muhammad Ibn-Alahmar (محمد ابن الاحمر), or more properly Ibn al-Ahmar, one of the Moorish kings of Granada in Spain and founder of the Alhambra, a celebrated fortress or palace which was regarded by the Moors of Granada as a miracle of art, and had a tradition that the king who founded it dealt in magic, or at least was deeply versed in alchemy, by means of which he procured the immense sums of gold expended in its erection. The name of this monarch, as inscribed on the walls of some of the apartments of the Alhambra, was Abū 'Abdullah, but is commonly known in Moorish history as Muhammad Ibn-Alahmar. He was born in Arjona in A.D. 1195, A.H. 591, of the noble family of the Banī Nasar; when he arrived at manly years,. he was appointed Alcayde or governor of Arjona and Jaen, and gained great popularity by his benignity and justice Some years afterwards, on the death of Ibn-Hūd, when the Moorish power of Spain was broken into factions, many places declared for Muhammad Ibn-Alahmar; he seized upon the occasion, made a circuit through the country, and was everywhere received with acclamation. It was in the year A.D. 1238 that he entered Granada amidst the enthusiastic shouts of the multitude. He was proclaimed king with every demonstration of joy, and soon became the head of the Moslems in Spain, being the first of the illustrious line of Banī Nasar that had sat upon the throne. He caused the mines of gold and silver, and other metals found in the mountainous regions of his dominions, to be diligently worked, and was the first king of Granada who struck money of gold and silver with his name, taking great care that it should be skilfully executed. It was about this time, towards the middle of the 13th century, that he commenced the splendid palace of the Alhambra. He retained his faculties and vigour to an advanced age. In his 79th year, he took the field on horseback, accompained by the flower of his chivalry, to resist an invasion of his territories, but was suddenly struck with illness, and in a few hours he died vomiting blood and in violent convulsions.

[*Vide* Yūsaf Abū'l Hājī.]

Muhammad ibn-Husan (محمد ابن حسن). *Vide* Ibn-Husām.

Muhammad ibn-Ishaq (محمد ابن اسحاق), the earliest biographer of Muhammad the Arabian prophet. He died about the year A.H. 151, fifteen years after the overthrow of the Ummiada dynasty.

Muhammad ibn-Jurir ut-Tabari (محمد ابن جریر الطبری), the son of Jurīr, an Arabian author, who died about the year A.D. 942, A.H. 330.

Muhammad ibn-Zikaria al-Razi (محمد ابن زکریر الراضی). *Vide* Rāzī.

Muhammad 'Imad (محمد عماد), who flourished about the year A.D. 1371, A.H. 773. He is the author of the following admired poems: *Misbāh ul-Hidāet*, *Mūnis ul-Abrār*, *Masnawī Kattiat*, and *Muhabbat-nāma*.

[*Vide* 'Imād Faqīh.]

Muhammad 'Imam (محمد عمام).

Vide 'Imām Muhammad.

Muhammad Ishaq (محمد اسحاق), author of the work called *Siar ul-Nabī wa-'Asār Sahāba.*

Muhammad Isma'il Bukhari (محمد اسماعیل بخاری), who is also called Abī 'Abdullah bin-Ismā'īl al-Bukhārī, is the author of the *Sahīh ul-Bukhārī*, a book held in the highest estimation, and considered, both in spiritual and temporary matters, as next in authority to the Qurān. It contains 9,880 traditions, selected from 167,000, recording not only all the revelations, inspirations, actions, and sayings of Muhammad, but also explaining many of the difficult passages of the Qurān. It relates besides many miracles and anecdotes of the ancient prophets and other inspired persons. He was born in the year A.D. 810, A.H. 194, and died in the month of June, A.D. 870, Rajab, A.H. 256. He is commonly called Al-Bukhārī, which see.

Muhammad Isma'il, Moulwi (محمد اسماعیل مولوی), author of the *Sirāt ul-Mustaqim* or *The True Path*, containing an account of the peculiar tenets held by the followers of Sayyad Aḥmad the modern Muhammadan zealot and reformer, with whose name we have recently become familiar. This work is one of the most important of several treatises which have been composed by that sect. The main object of the author in composing it was, in the first instance, probably to shew his own learning; in the next, to justify the claims of Sayyad Aḥmad (of whom he was a constant and confidential adherent) as a devotee, gifted with a surpassing degree of religious capacity and illumination. It makes reference especially, in its explanations and allusions, to the peculiar divisions which prevail in India, among those who aspire to the honours of religious initiation. These are generally numbered as the followers of one or other, of three venerated Pīrs, each of whom has given a name to a distinct school or sect; the first, the "Tarīqa-i-Qādiria," which traces its origin to 'Abdul Qādir Jīlānī. Another, the "Tarīqa-i-Chishtia," so called from its founder Khwāja Mo'īn-uddīn Chishtī, whose tomb is at Ajmer; the third, the "Tarīqa-i-Naqshbandia, derived from a Khwāja Bahā-uddīn Naqshband, a native of Bukhāra. It was one of the peculiar pretensions of Sayyid Aḥmad, that he held himself privileged to be the founder of a school of his own, to which he gave the name of the "Tarīqa-i-Muhammadia." His book was written some time about the year A.D. 1822, and it is to be remarked, as a new feature in the history of efforts for the propagation of Muhammadanism, or for the reform of its corruptions, how extensively the emissaries of this sect have availed themselves of the Press to disseminate their tenets. The *Sirāt ul-Mustaqīm*, the *Taqwīat ul-Iman*, the *Hidāet ul-Mominīn*, and a little tract attached to it, named the *Mūzih ul-Kabīr wa'l Bidaa't*, and two other tracts, entitled the *Nasīhat ul-Muslimīn*, and *Tambīh ul-Ghāfilīn*, have all been printed at private presses in Calcutta or at Huglī.

[*See* Sayyid Aḥmad.]

Muhammad Jani (محمد جانی), author of the work called *Asar Aḥmadī*, a minute history of Muhammad and the twelve 'Imāms, with various anecdotes respecting them.

Muhammad Jogi Mirza (محمد جوگی), son of Shāhrukh Mirzā, the son of Amīr Taimūr. He died A.D. 1444, A.H. 848, two years before his father, aged 43 lunar years.

Muhammad Karim (محمد کریم), the son of prince Azīm-ush-Shān, the son of the emperor Bahādur Shāh. He was murdered by order of the emperor Jahāndār Shāh his uncle, in April, A.D. 1712, A.H. 1124.

Muhammad Kazim, Mirza (محمد کازم مرزا), the son and successor of Mirzā Muhammad Amīn, private Munshī or Secretary to 'Ālamgīr, and author of the history called *'Ālamgīr-nāma.* It is a history of the first ten years of the reign of the emperor 'Alamgīr, to whom it was dedicated in the 32nd year of his reign, A.D. 1689, A.H. 1100. When it was presented to him, he forbade its being continued; and prohibited all other historians or authors from relating the events of his life, preferring (says his panegyrist) the cultivation of inward piety to the ostentatious display of his actions. This monarch, whose reign is admired by the Muhammadans and detested by the Hindūs, after having imprisoned his father, mounted the throne of Dehlī in A.D. 1658, A.H. 1068. At this period the glory of the house of Bābar may be said to have arrived at its zenith. The empire extended from the north-west mountains of Qābul to the southern limits of Chittagong; and the kings of Golkanḍa and Bījāpūr paid tribute. He is also the author of a *Shāh-nāma*, a *Roz-nāma*, or Journal, and another work entitled *Akhbār Hasania*.

Muhammad Khalil - ullah Khan (محمد خلیل الله خان), surnamed Ashk, is author of a history of Amīr Hamzā, uncle of Muhammad, which he professes to have drawn from a compilation made by order of Sulṭān Mahmūd, the Ghaznavide; and observes, "What renders this present history at all times interesting is this: that it informs us of the customs of various nations, and that it instructs us in the art of doing battle, and of taking towns and kingdoms. Accordingly Mahmūd, to avoid the necessity of counsel from any one, had portions of it read to him as a daily observance."

Muhammad Khan Bangash, Nawab (محمد خان بنگش), styled Ghazanfar Jang, a Rohela chief of the tribe of Bangash. He founded the city of Farrukhābād in the name of his patron the emperor Farrukhsiyar. In the reign of Muhammad Shāh, A.D. 1730, A.H. 1143, he was appointed governor of Mālwa, but unable to cope with the Mahraṭṭas on account of their repeated incursions, he was removed in A.D. 1732, A.H. 1145, and appointed governor of Allahābād. Muhammad Khān having planned the reduction of the Bundelas, of whom Rāja Chatursāl was chief, entered that country in A.D. 1733, A.H. 1146, with an army, and took several places; but as he was little acquainted with the roads, Chatursāl, with the assistance of Peshwā Bājī Rāo, surrounded him suddenly with an army. The nawāb, unable to combat a superior force, took refuge in the fortress of Jaitgaṛh, where he was closely blockaded by the enemy for some time, when his son Qāem Jang, having collected an army of the Afghāns, marched to Jaitgaṛh and escorted his father in safety to Allahābād. The imperial ministers, making a pretence of Muhammad Khān's ill-success, removed him from the Sūbadārī. He died in the month of June, A.D. 1743, Jumāda I. A.H. 1156, and was succeeded in his jāgīr by his son Qāem Jang, commonly called Qāem Khān.

The following is a list of the Nawābs of Farrukhābād.

Muhammad Khān, Bangash.
Qāem Jang, son of ditto.
Aḥmad Khān, brother of Qāem Jang.
Muzaffar Jang, son of Aḥmad Khān.
Tafazzul Husain Khān.

Muhammad Khan, Mir (محمد خان میر), commonly called Khān Kalān, was the eldest brother of Shams-uddīn Muhammad Anka Khān. He served under the emperors Humāyūn and Akbar, and was made governor of the Panjāb by the latter, which office he held for several years, and died A.D. 1575, A.H. 983. He was an excellent poet, and has left a Dīwān in Persian, and another in the Turkish language. He was native of Ghaznī, and therefore chose for his poetical name *Ghaznawī*. There is a work on Sūfiism entitled *Burhān ul-Īmān*, either written by him or some other Muhammad Khān.

Muhammad Khan Shaibani (محمد خان شیبانی). *Vide* Shāhī Beg Khān Uzbak.

Muhammad Khan, Sultan (محمد خان سلطان), also called Muhammad Qāān and Khān Shahīd, was the eldest son of Sulṭān Ghayās-uddīn Balban, king of Dehlī, who had appointed him viceroy of all the frontier provinces, *viz.* Multān, Lāhore, Debalpūr and other districts. This prince was blest with a bright and comprehensive genius, taking great delight in learning and the company of learned men. He, with his own hand, made a choice collection of the beauties of poetry, selected from the most famous in that art. The work consisted of 20,000 couplets, and was esteemed the criterion of taste. Among the learned men in the prince's court, Amīr Khusro and Khwāja Hasan bore the first rank in genius and in his esteem. The throne of Persia was at this time filled by Arghūn Khān, the son of Abqa Khān, and grandson of Halākū Khān. Timar Khān Changezī, who was then an Amīr of mighty renown in the empire of the race of Changez Khān, and governed Herāt, Qandahār and other districts, invaded Hindūstān with 20,000 chosen horse. Having ravaged all the villages about Debalpūr and Lāhore, he turned towards Multān. The prince Muhammad Sulṭān, hearing of his designs, hastened to the banks of the river of Lāhore, where both armies drew up in order of battle, and engaged with great fury. The prince, unfortunately, received a fatal arrow in his breast, by which he fell to the ground, and in a few minutes expired. Very few of the unfortunate Muhammad's party escaped from this conflict. Among the fortunate few was Amīr Khusro, the poet, who relates this event at large in his book called *Khizir Khānī*. This event took place on Friday the 9th of March, A.D. 1285, 30th Ẕil-ḥijja, A.H. 683.

Muhammad Khan Talpur (محمد خان تلپور). *Vide* Mīr Muhammad Khān Tālpūr.

Muhammad Khuda Banda, Sultan (محمد خدا بنده), surnamed Aljāilū, a descendant of Changez Khān, succeeded his brother Sulṭān Ghāzān Khān, the son of Arghūn Khān, to the throne of Persia in May, A.D. 1304, Shawwāl, A.H. 703. He is said to have been a just prince, and was the first monarch of Persia who proclaimed himself of the sect of 'Alī. He gave a public proof of his attachment to this sect, by causing the names of the twelve Imāms to be engraven on all the money which he coined. He built the celebrated city of Sultānia in 'Azurbejān or Media, which he made the capital of his dominions, and where he afterwards was buried. The dome over his tomb is fifty-one feet in diameter and is covered with glazed tiles. He died on the 17th December, A.D. 1316, 1st Shawwāl, A.H. 716, after a reign of 13 lunar years, and was succeeded by his son Sulṭān Abū Sa'īd Bahādur Khān.

Muhammad Khuda Banda, Sultan (محمد خدا بنده), surnamed Sulṭān Sikandar Shāh, was the eldest son of Shāh Tahmāsp I.; was born in the year A.D. 1531, A.H. 938, and succeeded to the throne of Persia on the death of his brother Shāh Ismā'īl II. in November, A.D. 1577, A.H. 985. The fortunes of this monarch, who from a natural weakness in his eyes, was incapable of rule, had been for many years upheld by the character of his eldest son, Hamza Mirzā, and his power terminated at the death of that prince, who fell under the blow of an assassin in his own private apartments on the 24th November, A.D. 1586, 22nd Ẓil-ḥijja, A.H. 994. The chiefs of Khurāsān immediately proclaimed 'Abbās, the king's second son, as king of Persia, and in the year A.D. 1588, A.H. 996, marched with him to Qazwīn, the capital of the empire, which they took possession of without opposition, and the unfortunate Muhammad was deserted by every inhabitant of Qazwīn and by his own army.

Muhammad Khusro Khan (محمد خسرو خان), author of a medical work called *Makhzan ul-Adwia*.

Muhammad Lad (محمد لاد), author of the Dictionary called *Muwyyad ul-Fuzlā*.

Muhammad Lari, Mulla (محمد لاری), author of a work which goes after his name, *viz. Tālīf Mullā Muhammad Lārī*.

Muhammad Maghrabi, Maulana (محمد مغربی مولانا). *Vide* Maghrabī.

Muhammad Makahul (محمد مکحول), *Vide* Muhammad (Sulṭān).

Muhammad Ma'sum (محمد معصوم), the son of Shaikh Aḥmad Sarhindī, was born in the year A.D. 1598, A.H. 1007, and died in A.D. 1668, A.H. 1079, aged 72 lunar years.

Muhammad Ma'sum Nami, Amir (محمد معصوم نامی امیر), of Bakkar, was one of the nobles of the court of Akbar. He wrote five Masnawīs or Poems, containing 10,000 verses; one is in the metre of *Haft Paikar*, one in the measure of the *Sikandar-nāma*, one called *Parī Sūrat* is in the measure of *Lailī and Majnūn*, one called *Husn wa-Nāz* is in the metre of *Yūsaf Zalekhā*, and one in the measure of the *Makhzan ul-Asrār*. He also wrote two Dīwāns of Ghazals and two Sākī-nāmas. He once paid a visit to Shāh 'Abbās, king of Persia, accompanied with no less than one thousand followers.

Muhammad Mir, Sayyad (محمد میر). His proper name is Kamāl-uddīn Haidar. He was a native of Lucknow, and translated the *History of Rasselas* from English into Urdū for the Āgra School Book Society, in the year A.D. 1839.

Muhammad Mirza (محمد مرزا), son of Mīrānshāh and grandson of Amīr Taimūr, was a pious prince, and not being ambitious he remained, with his brother Mirzā Khalīl-ullāh ruler of Samarqand; and when that country was taken by Mirzā Shāhrukh his uncle, and made over to his own son Mirzā Ulugh Beg in A.D. 1408, A.H. 811, he passed the remainder of his life with the latter and died about the year A.D. 1441, A.H. 845, recommending his son Mirzā Abū Sa'īd to him.

Muhammad Muhsin (محمد محسن), the rebel Tahsīldār of Pailānī who joined the mutineers in the year A.D. 1857, and was, together with 'Imdād 'Alī the rebel Deputy Collector, hanged at Banda on the 24th April, A.D. 1858.

Muhammad Muhsin of Kashan, Mulla (محمد محسن کاشانی ملا), author of the *Tafsīr Sūfī*.

Muhammad Muqim (محمد مقیم). *Vide* Nizām-uddīn Aḥmad Khwāja.

Muhammad Muzaffar (محمد مظفر), surnamed Mubāriz-uddīn, was the founder of the dynasty of Muzaffarians in Fars. He held a high station at the court of Sulṭān Abū Sa'īd Khān, king of Persia; but after his death, which happened in A.D. 1335, when trouble and confusion began to reign on all sides, he retired to Yazd and took possession of that country. In the year A.D. 1353, A.H. 754, he took Shīrāz from Shāh Shaikh Abū Is-hāq, and having seized him after some time put him to death, and became master of Fars. His son Shāh Shujāa' rebelled against him in A.D. 1359, A.H. 760, deprived him of his sight and ascended the throne at Shīrāz. Muhammad Muzaffar died in the year A.D. 1364, A.H. 765. This dynasty governed Fars 77 years, during which seven princes enjoyed power, *viz.*:

1. Mubāriz-uddīn Muhammad Muzaffar or Muzaffar-uddīn.
2. Shāh Shujāa', son of ditto.
3. Shāh Mahmūd, his brother.
4. Sultān Ahmad.
5. Shāh Mansūr, son of Muzaffar, in whose time Shīrāz was taken by Amīr Taimūr.
   Shāh Ahia.
   Shāh Zain-ul 'Abidīn, the son of Shāh Shujāa'.

The last two only reigned a few months.

[*Vide* Muzaffar.]

Muhammad Nazir (محمد نظیر). *Vide* Khwāja Nāsir.

Muhammad Nazir Ahmad (محمد نظیر احمد), Deputy Collector of Settlements in Jalain, author of the work named *Mirat at Urūs* or the *Bride's Mirror*, an admirable tale of domestic life among the Muhammadans of India, for which a reward of 1000 rupees was conferred on him by the Lieutenant-Governor in A.D. 1870.

Muhammad Parizada (محمد پریزاده), an author whose work is continually studied throughout the Othmānli empire, not only by all the ministers and statesmen of the Porte but likewise by the Greek princes and dragomans.

Muhammad Qasim (محمد قاسم), the original name of the celebrated historian, Firishta.

Muhammad Qasim (محمد قاسم). *Vide* Nāsir-uddīn Qabbācha.

Muhammad Qasim (محمد قاسم), son of Hājī Muhammad Surūrī Kāshānī, and author of the *Farhang Surūrī*, a dictionary of the Persian language, dedicated to Shāh 'Abbās Bahādur Khān, king of Persia, A.D. 1599, A.H. 1008.

[*Vide* Surūrī.]

Muhammad Qasim Khan Badakhshani (محمد قاسم خان موجی), whose poetical name was Maujī, was an officer in the service of the emperors Humāyūn and Akbar. He died in A.D. 1571, A.H. 979, at Āgra, and is the author of a *Yūsaf Zalekha*, containing the loves of Joseph and Potiphar's wife.

[*Vide* Maujī.]

Muhammad Qasim, Mir (محمد قاسم میر), author of the *Ibrat-nāma*, which he wrote after the invasion of Nādir Shāh, about the year A.D. 1739, A.H. 1152.

Muhammad Qasim, Sayyad (محمد قاسم سید), of Danapūr, author of the work entitled *Aijāz Ghausia* in Urdū, which he composed in the year A.D. 1855, A.H. 1271, containing the history and miracles of the celebrated saint of Baghdād, 'Abdul Qādir Gīlānī.

Muhammad Quli Khan (محمد قلی خان), governor of Allahābād, was the son of Mirzā Muhsin, the brother of Nawāb Safdar Jang of Audh. In the year A.D. 1759, A.H. 1172, he, under the royal standard of the prince 'Alī Gohar (afterwards Shāh 'Alam), who had procured from his father, 'Alamgīr II. grants of Bengal, Behār and Urysa, marched towards Patna, where, on his arrival, the place was besieged and the siege was carried on for some days with briskness; but he was obliged to raise the siege and retreat on receiving intelligence that Shujāa'-uddaula (who was his first cousin and the son of Safdar Jang) had treacherously seized Allahābād and possessed himself of that province. On his arrival at Allahābād in A.D. 1761, A.H. 1174, he was seized and imprisoned, and ultimately put to death in the fort of Jalālābād by order of Shujāa'-uddaula, who was jealous of his ambitious views in assisting the prince in the invasion of Bengal, and regarded Allahābād as his right, it having been given only in deputation by his father, Safdar Jang, to Muhammad Qulī Khān, who had refused to surrender it to the son.

Muhammad Quli Qutb Shah (محمد قلی قطب شاه). *Vide* Qulī Qutb Shāh II.

Muhammad Quli Salim (محمد قلی سلیم). *Vide* Salīm.

Muhammad Quresh, Mirza (محمد قریش میرزا), the second son of Bahādur Shāh. His title of succession to the throne of Dehlī was acknowledged by the British Government in 1856; with this condition—that on the king's death he would receive the title of Shāhzada.

Muhammad Qutb Shah (محمد قطب شاه), the fifth Sultān of the Qutbshāhī dynasty of Golkanda, and nephew or brother of Muhammad Qulī Shāh, whom he succeeded in January, A.D. 1612, Zi-Qa'da, A.H. 1020. He was living in A.D. 1620, A.H. 1029. After his death, 'Abdullah Qutb Shāh was raised to the throne of Golkanda.

Muhammad Rafia Waez (محمد رفيع واعظ), a celebrated preacher at Isfahān, was a contemporary of Mirzā Sāeb and Tāhir Wahīd. He is the author of a Dīwān in Persian, as also of a poem containing the battle of Shāh 'Abbās with Elam Khān, ruler of Tūrān, and one called *Abwāb ul-Janān*, a religious book.

Muhammad Rafi-uddin Muhaddis (محمد رفع الدين محدث). *Vide* Rafī-uddīn.

Muhammad Raza (محمد رضا), author of the Arabic work on Theology called *Ashraqāt Alwia*, Heavenly Illuminations, and of another on Jurisprudence entitled *Intikhāb ul-Ahkām*.

Muhammad Raza Khan (محمد رضا خان). He was selected for the office of chief minister by the English, after the death of Jafar 'Alī Khān, Nawāb of Bengal, to the young Nawāb Najm-uddaula, the son of the late Nawāb, in A.D. 1765. Deposed 1772.

Muhammad Sadr-uddin (محمد سدر الدين), surnamed Abū'l Ma'ālī, which see.

Muhammad Salah Kambu (محمد صالح كمبو), author of the *'Amal Sālah.*

Muhammad Salah, Mir (محمد صالح مير) lived in the time of the emperors Jahāngīr and Shāh Jahān about the year A.D. 1628, A.H. 1037. His poetical name wa Kashfī, which see.

Muhammad Salah, Mirza (محمد صالح مرزا). *Vide* Sipahdār Khān.

Muhammad Salah, Mirza (محمد صالح مرزا), author of the *Latāef Khayāb*, or the Beauties of Imagination. It contains extracts from all the poets of any celebrity, with memoirs of the authors; and ought to have been named the Beauties of Poetry, being of the nature of the English compilation of Select Extracts. It was commenced by the author in A.D. 1731, A.H. 1144, and finished by Ja'far Nasīr in A.D. 1742, A.H. 1155.

Muhammad Salah, Shaikh (محمد صالح شيخ), Kamboh, brother to Shaikh Ināyet-ullah, is the author of the book called *Behar Chaman.*

Muhammad Salah, Shaikh (محمد صالح شيخ), author of the *Bahār Sakhun* and the *Tārikh Shāhjahānī*, also of a poem called *Arām Jan*, which he completed in A.D. 1646, A.H. 1056.

Muhammad Saqi (محمد ساقى). *Vide* Mustai'd Khān.

Muhammad Sarbadal (محمد سربدال) was the chief of a kind of vagabonds called Sarbadāls, who had made themselves master of the city of Sabzwār and of some others in Khurāsān. This personage was also called Sayyid Muhammad, and although he was head of a gang of highwaymen or robbers, yet he was much esteemed for his probity.

Muhammad Shafia' (محمد شفيع دهلى), of Dehlī, author of the work called *Mirāt ul-Wāridāt*, or Mirror of Occurrences, a compendious history of the Mughal empire, from the death of Akbar to the invasion of Nādir Shāh. He undertook this work at the request of a nobleman in the reign of Muhammad Shāh.

Muhammad Shah (محمد شاه), the son of prince Farīd-uddīn, the son of Khizir Khān, king of Dehlī. He was placed on the throne after the assassination of his uncle Mubārik Shāh in April, A.D. 1434, Ramazān, A.H. 837. He reigned 12 lunar years and died on the 20th January, A.D. 1446, 22nd Shawwāl, A.H. 849. He was succeeded by his son Sultān 'Alā-uddīn.

Muhammad Shah (محمد شاه), the son of Ahmad Shāh, succeeded his father to the throne of Gujrāt in July, A.D. 1443, Rabī' I. A.H. 847. He reigned eight lunar years 9 months and 4 days, and was poisoned by his wife on the 12th February, A.D. 1451, 10th Muharram, A.H. 855. He was succeeded by his son Qutb-Shāh also called Qutb-uddīn.

Muhammad Shah (محمد شاه), the son of Hoshang Shāh, ascended the throne of Mālwā after the death of his father on the 17th July, A.D. 1434, 9th Ẕil-ḥijja, A.H. 837. He reigned about nine months and was poisoned by Muhammad Khān (the son of Malik Mughīs his prime minister), who ascended the throne under the title of Mahmūd Shāh Khiljī in May, A.D. 1435.

Muhammad Shah (محمد شاه), emperor of Dehlī, surnamed Roshan Akhtar or the Brilliant Star, was the son of the prince Jahān Shāh, one of the three brothers who perished in disputing the crown with their eldest brother Jahāndār Shāh, the son of Bahādur Shāh. He was born on Friday the 7th August, O.S. 1702, 24th Rabī' I. A.H. 1114, and crowned by the two Sayyads after the death of Rafī-uddaula, on the 29th September, A.D. 1719, 25th Ẕi-Qa'da, A.H. 1131 On his accession it was determined that the names of his two predecessors, *viz.* Rafī-uddarjāt and Rafī-uddaula, who reigned about three months each, should be struck out of the list of kings, and that his reign should commence from the death of the emperor Farrukh-siyar. Muhammad Shāh reigned 30 lunar years 6 months and 10 days, and died one month after the battle of Sarhind, which his son fought against Aḥmad Shāh Abdālī. His death took place on Thursday the 16th April, A.D. 1748, 27th Rabī' II. A.H. 1161, at the age of 47 lunar years 1 month and 3 days. He was buried in the court before the mausoleum of Niẓām-uddīn Aulia at Dehlī, and was succeeded by his son Aḥmad Shāh. This emperor may be termed the last of the race of Amīr Taimūr who reigned in Dehlī and enjoyed any power. The few princes of that sovereign's family who were raised to the throne after Muhammad Shāh were mere pageants, whom the nobles of the court elevated or cast down as it suited the purposes of their ambitions.

Muhammad Shah (محمد شاه), king of Persia, was the son of 'Abbās Mirzā, and grandson of Fatha Abū Shāh, whom he succeeded to the throne of Persia in A.D. 1834, and died in A.D. 1847.

Muhammad Shah (محمد شاه), ruler of Badakhshān. He was placed in that high position by Amīr Sher 'Alī of Qābul, to whom he was bound to pay tribute, the amount of which in A.D. 1870 was £8,100 and 500 horses. His predecessor was the intimate friend of 'Abdul Rahmān Khān, the pretender to the Afghān throne, who was opposed by Sher 'Alī in A.D. 1868, but afterwards became Amīr.

Muhammad Shah 'Adil or 'Adli (محمد شاه عادل), an Afghān of the tribe of Sūr, whose original name was Mubāriz Khān, was the son of Niẓām Khān Sūr, the brother of Sher Shāh, and brother-in-law of Salīm Shāh, after whose death in A.D. 1554, A.H. 961, having murdered his son Fīroz, a boy of twelve years of age who had been raised to the throne, he assumed royal dignity with the title of Muhammad Shāh 'Adil. He was illiterate, hated men of learning and kept company with illiterate persons like himself, whom he raised to the highest dignities in the State; among whom, one Hīmū, a Bania or Indian shopkeeper, whom his predecessor Salīm Shāh had made superintendent of the markets, was intrusted with the whole administration of affairs. This naturally created him enemies among the Afghān chiefs, who, having conspired against his life, revolted from his authority. Ibrāhīm Khān Sūr, who had the king's sister for his wife, soon afterwards raised a considerable army, and, getting possession of the city of Dehlī, ascended the throne in A.D. 1555, A.H. 962, and assumed the ensigns of royalty. Muhammad Shāh, finding himself betrayed, fled to Chunār, and contented himself with the government of the eastern provinces. He was slain in a battle fought at Munger with Bahādur Shāh, king of Bengal, A.D. 1556, A.H. 963. The period of his reign at Dehlī was only eleven months.

Muhammad Shah Bahmani I. (محمد شاه بهمنی اول), the second king of the Bahmanī dynasty, was the son of Sulṭān 'Alā-uddīn Hasan Kāngoh Bahmanī, whom he succeeded to the throne of the Deccan in February, A.D. 1358, 19th Ẕi-Qa'da, A.H. 776. He reigned 17 lunar years and died on the 21st March, A.D. 1375. His son Mujāhid Shāh succeeded him.

Muhammad Shah Bahmani II. (محمد شاه بهمنی ثانی), the thirteenth Sulṭān of the Bahmanī dynasty. was the son of Humāyūn Shāh the Cruel, He succeeded his brother Niẓām Shāh to the throne of the Deccan in July, A.D. 1463, in his ninth year; and the affairs of government were conducted, as in the reign of his late brother, by Khwāja Jahān and Khwāja Mahmūd Gāwān, under the direction of the Queen mother. The former was murdered after some time, and the title of Khwāja Jahān was conferred on Mahmūd Gāwān, adding the duties of Wakīl-us-Saltanat to his other functions. Muhammad Shāh reigned nearly 20 lunar years, and died a year after he had caused his minister Mahmūd Gāwān to be put to death, *i.e.* on the 24th March, A.D. 1482, 1st Ṣafar, A.H. 887. His son Mahmūd Shāh II. succeeded him. The year of Muhammad Shāh's death is comprised in a Persian verse, the translation of which runs thus:

Sulṭān Muhammad Shāh, ruler of kings,
When suddenly summoned to yield up his breath,
Abandoned the Deccan and all worldly things,
And *the ruin of the Deccan* recorded his death.

Muhammad Shahid (محمد شهيد), whose garden is still to be seen on the left bank of the Jamna at Āgra, where the swimmers of Āgra assemble after bathing in the Jamna in the rainy season.

Muhammad Shah Sharqi (محمد شاه شرقی) succeeded to the throne of Jaunpūr after the death of his father Mahmūd Shāh Sharqī, in A.D. 1452, A.H. 856, and was killed after five months in a battle which he fought against his brother Husain Shāh Sharqī, who succeeded him.

Muhammad Shah, Sayyad (محمد شاه سید), son of Sayyad Walī of Panduā, author of a collection of documents containing Forms of Letters, Parwanas, instruments or Contracts of Law, etc., entitled *Jāma' ul-Dastūr*, written about the year A.D. 1800.

Muhammad Shah Tughlaq I. (محمد شاه تغلق), whose former name was Malik Fakhr-uddīn Jūnān, succeeded his father Ghayās-uddīn Tughlaq Shāh on the throne of Dehlī in February, A.D. 1325, A.H. 725. He took the fort of Nagarkōt in A.D. 1337, and built several royal buildings and places in Dehlī. It was in his reign that 'Alā-uddīn Hasan Kangōh raised the standard of royalty in the Deccan, A.D. 1347, A.H. 748, where his descendants reigned for several generations. Muhammad Shāh died at Thatta on the banks of the river Sindh on the 20th March, A.D. 1351, 21st Muharram, A.H. 752, after a reign of nearly 27 lunar years. He was succeeded by his cousin Sultān Fīrōz Shāh Bārbak, the son of Sipah Salār Rajab.

Muhammad Shah Tughlaq II. (محمد شاه تغلق ثانی), surnamed Nāsir-uddīn, was the son of Fīrōz Shāh Tughlaq. He was born on the 3rd June, A.D. 1353, 3rd Jumāda I. A.H. 754. He ascended the throne of Dehlī in the lifetime of his father in the year A.D. 1387, but was soon after deposed and expelled by the chiefs. He remained at Nagarkōt till the reign of Abū Bakr Shāh, when he proceeded towards Dehlī with a large army, and after some repulses proving victorious, ascended the throne in August, A.D. 1390, A.H. 792. He was the founder of a fortress in Jalesar, which he called Muhammadābād. He reigned 3 years and 7 months, and died on the 19th February, A.D. 1394, 17th Rabī' II. A.H. 796, and his body was deposited at Dehlī in the same vault with that of his father. He was succeeded by his son Humāyūn, who, on ascending the throne, assumed the name of 'Alā-uddīn Sikandar Shāh, but died suddenly after a short reign of 45 days, and his brother Sultān Mahmūd succeeded him.

Muhammad Sharif Haqqani (محمد شریف حقانی), author of a poem called *Aynak-e-Dil*, which he completed in A.D. 1685, A.H. 1096.

Muhammad Shaikh (محمد شیخ), author of the works called *Jāmi Jahān-nāmā* and the *Nafs Rahmānī*, containing meditation on the unity of God, and rules for solitary devotion.

[*Vide* Shaikh Muhammad.]

Muhammad Sharif, Khwaja (محمد شریف خواجه), a nephew of Maulānā Umaidī. He was wazīr to Shāh Tahmasp Safwī I. and governor of Yezd, Abarkōh and afterwards of Isfahān for several years, and died in A.D. 1538, A.H. 945.

Muhammad Sharif, Mir (محمد شریف میر), author of a Masnawī or poem containing felicitations on the accession to the throne of Lucknow of Ghāzī-uddīn Haidar; it was completed in A.D. 1814, A.H. 1229.

Muhammad Shirin Maulana (محمد شیرین مولانا), commonly called Maulānā Maghrabī, which see.

Muhammad Sufi, Maulana (محمد صوفی مولانا), author of the work called *Maikhāna wa-Butkhāna*, or "the wine shop and idol house." He was a native of Māzindarān, and was residing in A.D. 1725, A.H. 1038, at Ahmadābād in Gujrāt, and afterwards for some time in Qashmīr.

Muhammad, Sultan (محمد سلطان), the last king of the ancient race of the sovereigns of Badakhshān, was taken prisoner in battle by Sultān Abū Sa'īd, a descendant of Amīr Taimūr, and slain together with all his children and relations in A.D. 1466, A.H. 871.

Muhammad, Sultan (محمد سلطان), who was afterwards surnamed Makahūl or the Blind, was the second son of Sultān Mahmūd of Ghaznī. He succeeded his father in A.D. 1030, in the absence of his elder brother Masa'ūd, who after five months deprived him of his sight and placed him in close confinement, where he remained till he was reinstated by the army in A.D. 1038, and his brother Masa'ūd deposed. He reigned at Lāhore for two years, after which he was defeated and put to death by Sultān Maudūd the son of Masa'ūd A.D. 1044.

Muhammad, Sultan (محمد سلطان), was the second son of Sulṭān Malikshāh Saljūkī, after whose death he ruled over Azurbejan, but when his eldest brother Barkayārak died in A.D. 1104, A.H. 498, he seized Baghdād also and assumed the title of Sulṭān. This prince died at Isfahān A.D. 1118, Ẓil-hijja, A.H. 511, and was succeeded by his son Mahmūd, who, however, was soon reduced by his uncle, Sulṭān Sanjar, to the condition of a dependent. Mahmūd died A.D. 1131, 15th Shawwāl, A.H. 525, aged 27 years, at Hamdan after a reign of 14 years.

Muhammad, Sultan (محمد سلطان), surnamed Quṭb-uddīn, succeeded his father 'Alā-uddīn Takash as Sulṭān of Khwārizm in A.D. 1200, A.H. 596. He was defeated by the celebrated conqueror Changez Khān, his country pillaged, and almost all his family made prisoners in A.D. 1218, A.H. 615. He died of a broken heart in March, A.D. 1221, Ẓil-ḥijja, A.H. 617. His son Jalāl-uddīn for a long time bore up against the torrent that had overwhelmed his father, but was at last subdued. He was slain in A.D. 1230, A.H. 627.

[*Vide* Takash.]

Muhammad, Sultan (محمد سلطان), son of Bāisanghar Mirzā.

[*Vide* Bābar (Sulṭān) and Sulṭān Muhammad.]

Muhammad, Sultan (محمد سلطان), the eldest son of Jahāngīr Mirzā. After his father's death, he was named by his grandfather heir of all his dominions, but died before him in A.D. 1404, A.H. 805.

Muhammad, Sultan Mirza (محمد سلطان مرزا), or Sulṭān Mirzā, the son of Awais Mirzā, the son of Bāiqara, the son of Mansūr, a prince of the house of Amīr Taimūr. He accompanied the emperor Bābar Shāh to India, and after his death rebelled against his son the emperor Humāyūn, and though subdued and pardoned, his five sons, *viz.* Muhammad Husain Mirzā, Ibrāhīm Husain Mirzā, Masa'ūd Husain Mirzā, Ulagh Mirzā, and Shāh Mirzā, and three of his nephews took advantage of the general disturbance which took place in A.D. 1566, A.H. 974, and revolted at Sambhal, the government of which had been assigned to Sulṭān Mirzā. At first they were overpowered without an effort and were confined in the fort of Sambhal by order of the emperor Akbar, but when that monarch marched in the year A.D. 1567, A.H. 975, for the purpose of subduing Mālwa, they made their escape to Gujrāt and sought an asylum with Changez Khān, governor of Baroach, where they sowed the seeds of future troubles, which only ended with the subjugation of the kingdoms by Akbar in A.D. 1572, A.H. 980 (*vide* Ibrāhīm Husain Mirzā). Muhammad Sulṭān Mirzā was, on account of his sons' rebellion, confined in the fort of Bayāna about the year A.D. 1567, where he died some years after.

Muhammad Tahir (محمد طاهر). *Vide* Ināyet Khān.

Muhammad Tahir Nasirabadi (محمد طاهر نصيرابادى), author of a biography called *Tazkira Muhammad Tāhir.* He lived in the reign of 'Abbās Shāh I. of Persia.

Muhammad Taqi Imam (محمد تقى امام), also called Muhammad al Jawād, was the ninth Imām of the race of 'Alī, and the son of Imām 'Alī Mūsī Razā, who was the eighth. He was born in the year A.D. 811, A.H. 195, and is said to have been poisoned in A.D. 835, A.H. 220. He was buried at Baghdād near the tomb of his grandfather Imām Mūsī Kāzim, the son of Ja'far Sādiq. His wife's name was Umm ul-Fazl, the daughter of the khalīf Māmūn.

Muhammad Taqi, Mir (محمد تقى مير). *Vide* Taqī (Mīr).

Muhammad Tughlaq Shah (محمد تغلق شاه). *Vide* Muhammad Shāh Tughlaq.

Muhammad Ufi (محمد عوفى), author of a Tazkira or biography called *Labāb ul-Albāb*, and of another work entitled *Jāma, ul-Hikāyāt*. The latter he compiled in A.D. 1228, A.H. 625. He was a native of Marv, which, under the Saljūk princes, was the capital of Persia.

[*Vide* Nūr-uddīn Muhammad Ūfī.]

Muhammad Ufi (محمد عوفى), who flourished in the 16th century of the Christian era, is the author of a biography called *Tazkira Muhammad Ūfī.*

Muhammad Wala (محمد والا), author of the work called *Najm-ul-Hidāet*, containing much good advice, and written according to the Sūfī faith.

Muhammad Walah, Sayyad (محمد واله سيد), author of the *Risāla Dastūr ul-Nazm*, or the art of writing poetry, with specimens of the various measures.

Muhammad Yar Khan (محمد يار خان), the son of Aitmad Khān, nobleman of the time of the emperor 'Alamgīr.

Muhammad Yusaf (محمد يوسف), a native of Qābul, who came to India and was employed in the service of the emperor Akbar. He was a good poet and died in the year A.D. 1562, A.H. 970.

Muhammad Yusaf 'Ali Khan Bahadur (محمد يوسف على خان), the late nawāb of Rāmpūr (1859-1872), who succeeded Muhammad Saīd Khān in 1855.

Muhammad Zahid, Mir (محمد زاهد مير), son of Muhammad Aslam, an author who flourished in the reign of Shāh Jahān and 'Alamgīr, and died in the year A.D. 1690, A.H. 1101.

Muhammad Zaman (محمد زمان), a celebrated punster and poet of Persia, who came to India in the reign of Akbar, but after a few years returned to his native country, where he died some years before or after A.D. 1600.

Muhammad Zaman (محمد زمان). *Vide* Qāsim Khān, Sūbadār of Qābul.

Muhaqqiq Tusi (محقق طوسى), of Tūs, author of the Muiyar ul-Ashār, a book on the art of poetry. He died in the year A.D. 1273, A.H. 672.

[*Vide* Nasīr-uddīn Tūsī.]

Muhi (محى), takhallus of a poet who flourished about the year A.D. 1592, A.H. 1001, and is the author of a Dīwān.

Muhib (محب), poetical name of Sayyad Ghulām Nabī of Bilgrām, who was slain in a battle which took place between Nawāb Safdar Jang and Ahmad Khān, Nawāb of Farrukhābād, on the 5th February, A.D. 1752, 29th Safar, A.H. 1165.

Muhib (محب), poetical name of Shaikh Walī-ullah of Dehlī, who was a pupil of Sauda, and is the author of a Dīwān.

Muhib-uddin Said Hasan al-Yaghawi (محب الدين سيد حسن), surnamed Guz, an author who died in A.D. 1132, A.H. 526.

Muhib-ullah, Qazi (محب الله قاضى), who, in the reign of 'Alamgīr, was appointed Qāzī of Lucknow and afterwards of Haidarābād in the Deccan. On the accession of Bahādur Shāh to the throne of Dehlī, A.D. 1707, A.H. 1119, he was honoured with the Sadārat of all India. He is the author of several works, among which are the *Kitāb Sallam* and *Muslim*.

Muhib-ullah, Shaikh (محب الله شيخ), a pīrzāda of Allahābād who died there in the year A.D. 1648, A.H. 1058. He is the author of a work on Ethics called *'Ibādat ul-Khawās*.

Muhindar Singh, Maharaja (مهيندر سنگه مهاراجا), Rāja of Bhadawar (1870).

Muhip Narayan (مهيپ نارايان), Rāja of Benares, who was living in A.D. 1789, was nephew of Rāja Cheyt Singh and grandson of Rāja Balwunt Singh. The Rāja's daughter was wife of Bābū Dirgbijai Singh, from whom the present Mahārāja is descended.

Muhit (محيط). *Vide* Rāmjas Munshī.

Muhi-uddin (محى الدين), author of a heroic poem called *Tarīkh Najīb-nāma*, in praise of Najīb Khān, styled Najīb-uddaula, an Afghān chief who distinguished himself during the reign of the unfortunate 'Alamgīr II. emperor of Dehlī.

Muhi-uddin (محى الدين), author of the work called *Irshād Yāfa'i*.

Muhi-uddin Abdul Qadir bin-Abi ul-Wafa (محى الدين عبدال قادر بن ابى الوافه). *Vide* 'Abdul Qādir bin 'Abī ul-Wafa Misrī.

Muhi - uddin bin - Arabi, Shaikh (محى الدين بن عربى شيخ), a celebrated learned Muhammadan of Persia, who was born in A.D. 1166, A.H. 561, died in A.D. 1239, A.H. 637, and was buried at Damascus. He is the author of a work in Arabic called *Fatūhāt Makkia*.

[*Vide* Ibn-Arabī.]

Muhi-uddin Tusi, Shaikh (محی الدین طوسی), a native of Tūs, and author of the work called *Kanz ul-'Ashiqīn*, a treatise on divine love; abridged from the *Kīmiā-e-Sa'ādat*. He was a contemporary of 'Umar Mirzā, and was living in A.D. 1408, A.H. 811.

Muhsin 'Ali Khan, Sayyad (محسن علی خان سید), the son of Sayyad Shāh Husain, the son of Sayyad Arab Shāh, was an excellent poet, and is the author of a Dīwān and a biography of Urdū poets called *Sarāpā Sakhun*.

Muhsin Fani (محسن فانی), an excellent poet and author, whose proper name was Shaikh Muhammad Muhsin and poetical title Fānī. He held the appointment of Sadārat of the province of Allahābād for several years in the time of the emperor Shāh Jahān; and when that monarch conquered Balkh in A.D. 1646, A.H. 1056, amongst the spoil which fell into the hands of the emperor belonging to Nazar Muhammad Khān, the ruler of that province, was a Dīwān composed by Muhsin Fānī which he had sent as a present to that ruler with verses in his praise; this annoyed the emperor, and Muhsin was forthwith dismissed from his office. He received, however, a small pension, and passed the remainder of his life at Kashmere, where he died in A.D. 1670, A.H. 1081. His Dīwān contains about 7000 verses.

Muhtadi Billah (مهتدی بالله). *Vide* Al-Muhtadī.

Muhtashim 'Ali Khan (محتشم علی خان). *Vide* Hashmat.

Muhtashim, Maulana (محتسم مولانا), a poet of Kashan and teacher of Fakhrī bin-Maulāna Sultān Muhammad Amīrī of Herāt. He wrote three Dīwāns, viz. *Sabāya*, *Jalālia*, and *Shabābia*, besides a Dīwān of Qasīdas in praise of the Imāms and princes consisting of about 8,000 verses, and a Risāla of Mua'mmas or enigmas and chronograms. There is a Qasīda quoted on the accession of Shāh Ismā'īl Safvī to the throne of Persia, of 66 misras, each of which contains a chronogram for the year A.D. 1576, A.H. 984.

Mu'in Jawini (معین جوینی). *Vide* Mo'īn-uddīn Jawīnī.

Mu'in-uddin (معین الدین), commonly called Bhanbū, the son of Zābita Khān, which see.

Mu'in-uddin (معین الدین) author of *Gang Sa'ādat*, dedicated to the emperor 'Alamgīr.

Mu'in-uddin Chishti Khwaja (معین الدین چشتی خواجی) a celebrated Muhammadan saint whose tomb is at Ajmīr. He was born at Sīstān in A.D. 1142, A.H. 537, came to India and was residing at Ajmīr when Pithaura, Rāja of that place, was taken prisoner and put to death by Shahab-uddīn Ghōrī surnamed Moi'zz-uddīn bin Sām in A.D. 1192, A.H. 633. Mū'in-uddīn died in A.D. 1236, aged 97 lunar years. The inside of the mausoleum is both magnificent and solemn, the floor is paved with pure marble, the walls nicely latticed, the ceiling beautifully white and smooth. In the centre stands the tomb, covered with very valuable brocade. At the head of the tomb is placed a large silver censer, from which the smoke of the burning incense diffuses its fragrance all over the place night and day.

Mu'in-uddin Isfaran, Maulana (معین الدین اسفراری مولانا), author of the *Tārīkh Mubārik Shāhī*.

Muin-uddin Jawini, Maulana (معین الدین جوینی مولانا), a native of Jawīn, and author of the *Nigāristān* (the gallery of pictures), a miscellaneous work upon moral subjects, in prose and verse, which he wrote in imitation of the Gulistān of Sa'dī. There is a beautiful copy of this book, says Sir Wm. Jones, in the Bodleian library at Oxford. He was a contemporary of Shaikh Sa'ad-uddīn Hamwia, who died in the year A.D. 1252, A.H. 650.

Mu'in-uddin Muhammad (معین الدین محمد هروی), of Herāt, an author of several works, among which are *Tārīkh Mūsawī*, a history of the Jews, describing their origin, sufferings in Egypt, etc. The *Rauzat ul-Jannat*, containing a minute description of the city of Herāt, dedicated to Sultān Husain Abū'l Ghāzī Bahādur in A.D. 1493, A.H. 900. The *Mia'rāj ul-Nabūat*, or the Ascent of the Prophet, details some of the grossest falsehoods that human invention ever suggested. Among many shocking circumstances of his journey to heaven, it is related that he saw the souls of his father and mother swimming in the liquid fire of hell; and being about to interpose for them, he was told that if he then interceded for unbelievers, his intercession for the faithful on the Day of Judgment would not be admitted; he therefore left them to their fate. This work was written in A.D. 1486, A.H. 891. He is also the author of the *Rauzat ul-Waezīn*.

Mu'in ul-Mulk Rustam Hind (معين الملک رستم هند), commonly called Mīr Mannū, was the son of Ya'tmād-uddaula Qamar-uddīn Khān, wazīr. He was appointed governor of Lāhore by the emperor Aḥmad Shāh of Dehlī after the battle of Sarhind against Aḥmad Shāh Abdālī, in which his father was killed in A.D. 1748, A.H. 1161. He died suddenly in the year A.D. 1754, A.H. 1167.

Mui'zzi (معزی). *Vide* Moi'zzī.

Mui'zz-li-din-allah (معز الدين الله). *Vide* Moi'zz-li-dīn-ullah.

Mui'zz-uddaula (معز الدوله). *Vide* Moi'zz-uddaula.

Mui'zz-uddin (معز الدين). *Vide* Moi'zz-uddīn.

Mujaddid Alif Sani (مجدد الف ثانی). *Vide* Aḥmad Sarhindī (Shaikh).

Mujahid Shah Bahmani (مجاهد شاه بهمنی) succeeded his father Muhammad Shāh I. Bahmanī on the throne of the Deccan in March, A.D. 1375, Shawwāl, A.H. 776. He was murdered after a reign of three years on the night of the 14th April, A.D. 1378, 17th Ẕil-ḥijja, A.H. 779, by his uncle Dāūd Khān, who ascended the throne by the title of Dāūd Shāh.

Mujib (مجيب شاه), or Shāh Mujīb, author of a history of the loves of Joseph and Potiphar's wife called *Y...f wa-Zalekha*, in Urdū verse, composed in A.D. 1824, A.H. 1240.

Mujid (موجد), the takhallus of a poet who is the author of a Dīwān.

Mujir (مجير بيلقانی), poetical name of 'Abdul Mukārim Mujīr-uddīn of Bīlqān, a town in Azurbejān. He was a pupil of Khākānī, and is the author of a Dīwān. He died in A.D. 1198, A.H. 594. He flourished in the time of Qizal Arsalān, and was a contemporary of Zahīr-uddīn Fāryābī.

Mujir-uddin Bilqani (مجير الدين بيلقانی). *Vide* Mujīr.

Mujrim (مجرم), poetical name of Rahmat-ullāh, who is the author of an Urdū Dīwān.

Mujrim (مجرم), poetical title of Ghulām Husain of Patna, the father of Ishqī, whose proper name was Shaikh Muhammad Wajīh.

Mujtahid (مجتهد), an inspired jurist. The Sunnīs do not recognize the possibility of such existing now, conceiving that inspiration ceased with the first generation after the prophet. The Shī'ahs and Mu'tazilas still believe in this kind of authority.

[*Vide* Hughes, *in voc.*]

Mukalil bin-Sulaiman (مكالل بن سليمان), author of a Commentary on the Qurān. He died in the year A.D. 723, A.H. 105.

Mukarram Khan, Nawab (مكرم خان نواب), governor of Multān in the time of 'Alamgīr.

Mukhlis (مخلص), the poetical name of Rāe 'Anand Rāe, a Khattrī, who was the father-in-law of Tansukh Rāe, and a pupil of Mirzā Bedil. He died in the fourth year of Aḥmad Shāh's reign, A.D. 1751, A.H. 1164. His works contain 50,000 verses. He is also called Mukhlis Hindī, to distinguish him from Mukhlis Kāshī.

Mukhlis (مخلص), the poetical appellation of Mukhlis 'Alī Khān, commonly called Mīr Baqir. He was Nawāb Nawāzish Khān, Shahāmat Jang's sister's son, and is the author of a Dīwān in Urdū.

Mukhlis Kashi (مخلص کاشی), a poet of Persia.

Mukhtar bin-Mahmud bin-Muhammad az-Zahidi Abuar-Rija al-Ghazmini (مختار بن محمود), surnamed Najm-uddīn, is the author of *Quniat ul-Muniat*, a collection of decisions of considerable authority. He died A.D. 1259, A.H. 658.

Mukhtari (مختاری), a Persian poet.

Mukhtar-uddaula (مختار الدوله). *Vide* Murtazā Khān.

Mukim Khan (مقیم خان) held the rank of 700 in the time of the emperor Akbar, and was raised to a high rank in the time of Jahāngīr. He had a home at Āgra on the banks of the Jamna at a place still called Mukīm Khān ka Ghāt.

Muktafi Billah (مکتفی). *Vide* Al-Muktafī.

Mulhim (ملہم), a poet who flourished about the year A.D. 1706, A.H. 1118, and is the author of a Dīwān.

Mulla Ahmad (ملا احمد). *Vide* Aḥmad (Mulla).

Mulla 'Ali al-Hafiz al-Qastamumi (ملا علی الحافظ القستمومی), author of a commentary on the *Hadīs ul-Arbaīn* of *Shaikh Ismā'īl Haqqī.*

Mulla 'Ali Qusanji (ملا علی قوسانجی), who also wrote a Hāshia or marginal notes on the *Kashshaf*, besides the one written by Tuftāzānī. He died about the year A.D. 1405, A.H. 808.

Mulla Firoz (ملا فیروز), a Pārsī priest. The Pārsīs of Bombay entertain the most liberal feelings in favour of science and literature; they possess great wealth, and commercial relation with every part of Asia. The mission sent by them some years ago to Persia at the sole expense of Qans, the father of Mullā Fīroz, the editor of the *Dasatir*, for the purpose of making inquiries relative to the remnant of the Pārsīs in that country, the discovery by Qans while on that mission of a copy of the *Dasatir* in the Pahlawī language, and the English translation of that curious work, published by Mullā Fīroz at Bombay in 1818, shew the spirit and perseverance with which the Pārsīs of Bombay have instituted inquiries connected with the history of their country.

[Vide *Transactions Roy. As. Soc.* vol. iii. App. p. iv.]

Mulla Furati (ملا فراتی), author of a work, entitled the *Qaraq Sawāl*, containing forty questions with the answers of Muhammad, according to tradition.

Mulla Husain Waiz (ملا حسین وایز). *Vide* Husain Waiz (Maulāna).

Mulla 'Imad (ملا عماد), author of a work on Sūfīism in Persian, called *Hāshia Mullā 'Imād.*

Mulla Jami Lahouri Namdar Khani (ملا جامی لاهوری نامدار خانی), whose poetical name is Bekhud, was very well skilled in composing chronograms, and has left a thick Dīwān of Ghazals, etc. He died in A.D. 1675, A.H. 1086.

Mulla Jiwan (ملا جیون امیتھوی), of Amaiṭhī, whose proper name was Shaikh Aḥmad, was the tutor of the emperor 'Alamgīr. He is the author of the commentary on the *Qurān* called *Tafsīr Aḥmadī.* He is also called Mullā Jīān Jaunpūrī, and is said to have died in A.D. 1718, A.H. 1130.

Mulla Khusro (ملا خسرو), author of a law treatise, entitled *Ghurar ul-Ahkām*, and a commentary on the same work called the *Durar al-Hukkām.* Mullā Khusro, who is one of the most renowned of the Turkish jurisconsults, completed his work in A.D. 1478, A.H. 883, and died in A.D. 1480, A.H. 885.

Mulla Malik Qummi (ملا ملک قمی). *Vide* Malik Qummī.

Mulla Mir (ملا میر). He lived in the time of the emperor Akbar. In A.D. 1566, A.H. 974, he constructed a well at Āgra, and Ashraf Khān Mīr Munshī wrote the chronogram of the year of its construction. It is a subtractive one.

Mulla Mufid Balkhi (ملا مفید بلخی), a native of Balkh, was an excellent poet. He came to India and died at Multān in the time of the emperor 'Alamgīr, A.D. 1674, A.H. 1085. He is the author of a Dīwān. A subtractive chronogram on his death was written by Sarkhush.

Mulla Muhsin (ملا محسن). *Vide* Faiz.

Mulla Muqimai (ملا مقیمائی), an author who lived in the time of Shāh Jahān.

Mulla Qasim (ملا قاسم مشهدی), of Mashhad, author of an Insha, or Collection of Letters.

Mulla Shah (ملا شاه), a native of Badakhshān, was a learned and pious Musalmān. He was a disciple of Mīān Shāh Mīr of Lāhore and Murshid or spiritual guide of the unfortunate prince Dārā Shikōh, the eldest son of the emperor Shāh Jahān, who highly respected him and visited him on his tour to Kashmere, where he (Mullā Shāh) had built a place for his residence. He died at Kashmere in the commencement of the reign of the emperor 'Alamgīr, about the year A.D. 1660, A.H. 1070.

Mulla Sharif (ملا شریف), author of a Dīwān, on the loves of *Shīrīn and Khusro*, dedicated to Sulṭān Qulī Quṭb Shāh of Golkonḍa in A.D. 1515, A.H. 921.

Mulla Sheri (ملا شیری). *Vide* Sherī (Mullā).

Mulla Shikebi (ملا شکیبی), an excellent poet who served under 'Abdul Rahīm Khān, Khān Khānān, and was living in A.D. 1592, A.H. 1000.

Mullazada (ملازاده), of Patna, author of an Urdū translation of the novel called *Bahār Dānish*, which he named *Izhār Dānish*.

Mullazada (ملازاده), author of the marginal notes on the *Mukhtasir Ma'ānī wa-Bayān*.

Multan (ملتان بادشاهان), kings of. *Vide* Yūsaf (Shaikh).

Mumtaz (ممتاز), the poetical name of two poets, one of whom is named Maulwī Ihsān-ullāh.

Mumtaz Mahal (ممتاز محل), the favourite wife of the emperor Shāh Jahān, for whom he built the celebrated edifice at Āgra called the Tāj.

[*Vide* Arjumand Bāno Begam.]

Mumtaz Shikoh (ممتاز شکوه), second son of the emperor Shāh Jahān.

Mumtaz-uddaula, Nawab (ممتاز الدوله نواب), the grandson of Muhammad 'Alī Shāh, king of Audh. He was living in A.D. 1868. The Nawāb, during the disorders consequent on the Mutiny of Lucknow, declared his opinions by entering into a contract to give his daughter in marriage to the nominee of the rebels, Birjīs Kadr. For this conduct he was adjudged to suffer the loss of his pension, 700 rupees per mensem.

Munai'm (منعم), poetical name of Nūr ul-Haq, Qāzī of Barelī, who was an excellent Persian poet, and has written upwards of 300,000 verses; among his compositions is a commentary on the Qurān in verse, and Arabic and Persian Qasīdas, several Masnawīs, and three Persian Dīwāns. He was living at Dehli in A.D. 1786, A.H. 1200.

Munai'm Khan (منعم خان), the son of Sulṭān Beg Barlās, a nobleman who had been the emperor Bahādur Shāh's principal officer at Qābul, was, on the accession of that emperor to the throne of Dehlī, appointed his wazīr with the title of Khān Khānān. He proved a capable civil administrator; but, offending the emperor by his conduct in a campaign against the Sikhs in 1710, was disgraced. He died in the early part of the year A.D. 1711, A.H. 1123. He was the author of the work called *Ilhāmāt Munai'mī*.

Munai'm Khan, Khan Khanan (منعم خان خانخانان), a nobleman who was raised to the dignity of prime minister by the emperor Akbar, after the dismissal of Bairām Khān, Khān Khānān in A.D. 1560, A.H. 967, was appointed governor of Jaunpūr after the death of Khān Zamān, where he built the famous bridge on the river Gūmtī in the year A.D. 1567, A.H. 975. He was latterly appointed governor of Bengal after the defeat of Dāūd Shāh, king of that country, in A.D. 1575, A.H. 983. From the period of Muhammad Bakhtyar Khiljī to that of Sher Shāh the city of Gaur, which is also called Lakhnauti, had been the capital of Bengal, after which, owing to its insalubrity, it had been abandoned for Khawāspūr Ṭanḍa. Munai'm Khān, however, admiring the spot, gave orders for its repairs, and made it his residence; but he soon fell a victim to its unhealthy climate, and died there on the 12th October the same year, 9th Rajab, A.H. 983.

Munai'm Shaikh (منعم شیخ), a poet who served under prince Sulṭān Shujāa, governor of Bengal, and was present in the battle fought by that prince against his brother the emperor 'Alamgīr in December, A.D. 1658, after which he was never heard of. For his poetical name, he used his own in his compositions.

Munir Lahori, Mulla (منیر لاهوری ملا), a poet of Lāhore, was the son of Mulla 'Abdul Majīd of Multān. He formerly took the words "Sakhun Sanj" for his poetical title, but afterwards used "Munīr" in his compositions. His proper name was Abū'l Barkāt. He died at Āgra on Saturday the 31st August, A.D. 1644, 7th Rajab, A.H. 1054, and left about 30,000 verses and an Inshā which goes after his name, viz. *Inshā-i-Munīr*.

Munir-uddin, agent of the titular emperor, Shāh 'Alam, at Calcutta, after the battle of Buxar. Died at Benares, 1771.

Munis, Haji (مونس حاجی), author of a Dīwān, which he completed in A.D. 1723, A.H. 1135.

Munna Jan (منا جان). *Vide* Nasīr-uddīn Haidar.

Munni Begam (منی بیگم), a concubine of Mīr Ja'far, Nawāb of Bengal. After his death and the death of his two sons Najm-uddaula and Saif-uddaula, she was appointed guardian to Mubārik-uddaula, the infant son of the late Nawāb, by Warren Hastings, in preference to others whose claims were more plausible. The guardianship was taken away from the Begam in A.D. 1776. She was the mother of Najm-uddaula. She died A.D. 177[illegible], Sha'bān, A.H. 1103.

Munshi (منشی), takhallus of Jaswant Rāe Munshī. He is the author of a Dīwān, and was living in A.D. 1712, A.H. 1124.

Munshi (منشی), poetical title of Munshī Mūlchānd, a Kāyeth and native of Dehlī. He was a pupil of the poet Nasīr, and is the author of some fragments of the *Shāh-nāma* in Urdū. He died about the year A.D. 1822.

Munsif (منصف), poetical title of Fāzil Khān, who is the author of a Dīwān, and was living in A.D. 1704, A.H. 1116.

Muqanna (مقنع). *Vide* Al-Makna or Muqanna.

Muqarrab Khan (مقرب خان). *Vide* Masīhī (Mulla).

Muqtadi Billah (مقتدی بالله). *Vide* Al-Muqtadī.

Muqtadir Billah (مقتدر بالله). *Vide* Al-Muqtadir.

Murad I. Sultan (مراد اول سلطان), whom our English authors call Amurath I. and who is also called Murād Khān Ghāzī and Khwāwandgār Rūm, was the third Sultān of the race of Usmān or Othmān. He succeeded his father Arkhan (Orchan) on the Turkish throne in A.D. 1359, A.H. 760, and was known for his cruelties towards his son and those who espoused his cause. He advanced into Europe, and made Adrianople his capital in A.D. 1360. He was a great warrior and obtained 37 victories, in the last of which he perished, A.D. 1389, A.H. 791, aged 71, by the hand of a soldier. He (or as some say his father) was the first who established the formidable force of the Jānisarīs. His son Bāyezīd I. succeeded him.

Murad II. Sultan (مراد ثانی سلطان) succeeded his father Muhammad I. as Ottoman emperor in A.D. 1422, A.H. 825, and was the first Turk who used cannon on the field of battle. In A.D. 1443, A.H. 847, he resigned the crown in favour of his son Muhammad II. but finding him incapable to hold the reins of government, he abandoned his retirement and defended the famous Sikandar Beg (Scanderbeg), and routed the Hungarians. According to Gibbon, he died on the 2nd February, A.D. 1451, Ẕil-ḥijja, A.H. 854, and was succeeded by his son Muhammad II. who afterwards took Constantinople.

Murad III. Sultan (مراد ثالث سلطان) succeeded his father Salīm II. to the throne of Constantinople in December, A.D. 1574, Shabān, A.H. 982, and to rid himself of all competitors he, at his first coming to the throne, caused his five brothers to be strangled in his presence. This act of cruelty so affected his mother that she destroyed herself. He took from his adversaries the Persians, Armenia, Media, and the city of Tauris, and the fort Gaino from the Hungarians. He died on the 18th January, A.D. 1595, Jumādạ I. A.H. 1003, aged 50 lunar years. At the time of his death such a sudden and terrible tempest arose, that many thought the world would then be dissolved. He was succeeded by his son Muhammad III. Sulṭān Murād is the author of the work called *Fatūhat-us-Siyām.*

Murad IV. Sultan (مراد رابع سلطان), son of Aḥmad I. emperor of Constantinople, succeeded his uncle Mustafa I. who was deposed the second time in A.D. 1623, A.H. 1032. He took Baghdād in A.D. 1637, 30,000 of whose inhabitants he put to the sword, though he had promised them protection. He died on the 8th February, A.D. 1640, A.H. 1049, in the 18th year of his reign, of excessive intoxication, and was succeeded by his brother Ibrāhīm.

Murad Bakhsh, Sultan (مراد بخش سلطان), youngest son of the emperor Shāh Jahān, by whom he was appointed governor of Gujrāt, Ṭhaṭṭa and Bihkar. He was seized and imprisoned in the fort of Gwāliar by the orders of his brother the emperor 'Ālamgīr, after the first battle he fought against his brother Dārā Shikōh, and was subsequently murdered, A.D. 1662, A.H. 1072, at Gwāliar and buried within the fort.

Murad Mirza (مراد مرزا), also called Sultān Murād and Shāh Murād, was the second son of the emperor Akbar. His mother's name was Salīma Sultāna Begam. He was born on Thursday the 8th June, A.D. 1570, A.H. 978, in the house of the venerable Shaikh Salīm Chishtī at Sīkrī. The Hindūs, on account of his being born in the elevated region of Sīkrī, used to call him Pahāri. After this prince's birth the emperor, considering the village of Sīkrī a propitious spot, two of his sons having been born there, ordered the foundation of a city to be laid, which, after the conquest of Gujrāt, he called Fathapūr. This prince was sent by his father to conquer the Deccan in A.D. 1595, A.H. 1004, where he fell sick and died on the 1st May, A.D. 1599, 15th Shawwāl, A.H. 1077. He was at first buried at Shāhpūr, but afterwards his corpse was removed to Dehlī and laid by the side of Humāyūn the prince's grandfather.

Murassa' Raqam (مرصع رقم), title of the author of the *Nautarz Murassa*. *Vide* Tahsīn.

Murauwat (مروت), poetical name of Saghīr 'Alī, a poet, who is the author of a story in Urdū called *Tilismāt Ishq*, composed in A.D. 1792, A.H. 1207.

Murshid Khan (مرشد خان), a poet, who flourished in the time of Jahāngīr, and is the author of a Dīwān.

Murshid Quli Khan (مرشد قلی خان), a nobleman of the time of the emperor Shāh Jahān, who was Faujdār of Muthurā, and was killed there in A.D. 1638, A.H. 1048.

Murshid Quli Khan (مرشد قلی خان), Nawāb of Bengal. *Vide* Ja'far Khān.

Murshid Quli Khan (مرشد قلی خان), Rustam Jang, son-in-law of Shujā-uddīn, governor of Bengal (*q.v.*), by whom he was appointed governor of Katak. Being defeated by Mahābat Jang, Nawāb of Bengal, he fled to the Deccan in the year A.D. 1739, where he died. He was a good poet, and his poetical name was Sarshār.

Murtaza Khan (مرتضی خان سید), a Sayyad, who on the accession of Nawāb 'Asaf-uddaula to the masnad of Lucknow, was appointed by him his nāib or deputy, with the title of Mukhtār-uddaula, but Basant 'Alī Khān, an old khwāja sarā (eunuch) of the nawāb's father, being jealous of the influence he had over the nawāb, resolved to remove him; and for this purpose, having invited him to an entertainment, murdered him, and was himself slain the same day by order of the nawāb. This circumstance took place in the month of March, A.D. 1776, Safar, A.H. 1190.

Murtaza Khan (مرتضی خان), a nephew and son-in-law of Dost 'Alī, the Nawāb of Arkat, under whom the perfidious seizure of Trichinopoly was perpetrated by Chanda Sahib. The nawāb was succeeded by his son Safdar 'Alī, who, after overcoming the effects of poison prepared for him by Murtaza Khān, fell by the poignard of a Pathān assassin hired for the work by the same person. A storm was raised which he had not the courage to encounter, and, disguising himself in female attire, he escaped from Arkat to his own fort of Vellore. Two years afterwards, the youthful son and successor of Safdar 'Alī met the fate of his father, and common report attributed to Murtaza Khān a principal share in the contrivance of this murder also. Such was the man to whom the patronage of Dupleix, who was at that time grievously at a loss for money, was extended, for Murtaza Khān had the reputation of being extremely rich, and was selected by Dupleix as the new Nawāb of Arkat. He was solemnly installed in his new dignity, but finding that his faculties were inadequate to the position, he abdicated and returned to Vellore.

Murtaza Khan (مرتضی خان). *Vide* Shaikh Farīd and Farīd Bukharī.

Murtaza Khan Anju (مرتضی خان انجو), a nobleman of the reign of the emperor Shāh Jahān. At the time of his death, which took place A.D. 1629, A.H. 1038, he was governor of Thatta.

Murtaza, Mir (مرتضی میر), surnamed "Al-Madau bi-ilm ul-Huda. He died in September, A.D. 1046, Safar, A.H. 436.

Murtaza Nizam Shah I. (مرتضی نظام شاه) ascended the throne of Ahmadnagar in the Deccan after the death of his father Husain Nizām Shāh I. in A.D. 1565, A.H. 972, and as he was then in his minority, his mother Khunza Sultāna became for six years chief manager of affairs, after which the Sultān took the affairs under his own management. He reigned about 24 lunar years, and becoming mad, his son Mirān Husain Nizām Shāh shut him up in a warm bathing room, and, shutting fast the doors and windows to exclude all air, lighted a great fire under the bath, so that the Sultān was speedily suffocated by the steam and heat. This circumstance took place about the 15th January, A.D. 1589, 8th Rabī I. A.H. 997. But according to the work of Jāma ul-Hind, he was poisoned by his son on the 5th June, A.D. 1588, corresponding with 18th Rajab, A.H. 996.

Murtaza Nizam Shah II. (مرتضی نظام شاه), a nominal prince and a descendant of the Nizām Shāhī kings of Ahmadnagar, who was raised to the throne by Malik Ambar the Abyssinian and others after the capture of Bahādur Nizām Shāh in A.D. 1600, A.H. 1009. He was put to death about the year A.D. 1628, A.H. 1038, by Fatha Khān, the son of Malik Ambar, who placed his son Husain, an infant of ten years, on the throne. Husain was afterwards confined for life by the emperor Shāh Jahān in the fortress of Gwāliar.

[*Vide* Fatha Khān.]

Musahib, Mirza (مصاحب مرزا), a poet who flourished after the poet Sāeb, whom he imitates, and was probably living in A.D. 1745, A.H. 1158.

Musa ibn-Nusair (موسی), son of Nusair, a Christian captive taken at the siege of Aīn Tamr in Mesopotamia; was born about A.D. 640. He conquered Northern Africa in 709; and three years later overthrew the Visigoths and subjugated Spain. He died in disgrace in Arabia, 717.

Musailima (مسیلمه), commonly called Kazzāb or the Liar, was an impostor who arose in the time of Muhammad in one of the provinces of Arabia, named Hajar. As success in any project seldom fails to draw in imitators, Muhammad having raised himself to such a degree of power and reputation, by acting the prophet, induced others to imagine they might arrive at a similar height by the same means. His most considerable competitors in the prophetic office was Musailima and Al-Aswad. Musailima pretended to be joined in commission with Muhammad, and published revelations in imitation of the Qurān. He sent Muhammad a letter, offering to go halves with him, in these words: "From Musailima the apostle of God, to Muhammad the apostle of God. Now, let the earth be half mine and half thine." But Muhammad, believing himself too well established to need a partner, wrote him this answer: "From Muhammad the apostle of God, to Musailima the liar. The earth is God's; he giveth the same for inheritance unto such of his servants as he pleaseth; and the happy issue shall attend those who fear him." During the few months which Muhammad lived after the setting up of this new imposture, Musailima grew very formidable. Abū Bakr, Muhammad's successor, in the second year of his reign and the 12th of Hijrī (A.D. 633, A.H. 12), sent an army against him under the command of Khālid, the son of Walīd, who defeated and slew him in battle. Al-Aswad set up for himself the very year that Muhammad died; but a party, sent by Muhammad, broke into his house by night, and cut off his head. Musailima and he received the appellation of "The two Liars."

Musannifak (مصنفک), surname of Mulla 'Alā-uddīn 'Alī bin-Muhammad, an Arabian author, who died A.D. 1470, A.H. 875.

Musa, Sayyad (موسی سید). He fell in love with Mohanī, a jeweller's daughter, in the time of the emperor Akbar; an account of whom may be seen in the *Tarikh Badāonī*.

Mushfaqi (مشفقی), a poet who was born at Bukhārā in the year A.D. 1538, A.H. 945, and composed a Dīwān, which he completed in A.D. 1575, A.H. 983.

Mushtaq (مشتاق), the poetical name of Mīr Said 'Alī of Isfahan, who flourished in the year A.D. 1760, A.H. 1174.

Mushtaq (مشتاق), poetical title of Mushtāq Husain, of Āgra. He was the author of a Dīwān, and since he was a pupil of Bahādur Shāh, the last king of Dehlī, in every one of his Ghazals he has mentioned in the last verse the poetical name of the king, *viz.* Zafar.

Mushtaq (مشتاق), poetical appellation of Muhammad Qulī Khān of Patna, a son of Hāshim Qulī Khān. He was a pupil of Muhammad Roshan Joshish, and Darogha of the household of Nawāb Zain-uddīn Ahmād Khān Haibat Jang. He died in A.D. 1801, A.H. 1216.

Mushtaqi (مشتاقی سید). *Vide* Rizkullāh (Shaikh).

Musibat (مصیبت), poetical name of Shāh Ghulām Qutb-uddīn, eldest brother of Shāh Muhammad Afzal of Allahābād. He went on a pilgrimage to Mecca and died there in A.D. 1773, A.H. 1187.

Musi bin-'Uqba (موسی بن عقبه), author of the work called *Kitāb Maghāzī*. He died in A.D. 758, A.H. 141.

Musi Kazim Imam (موسی کاظم امام), was the seventh Imām of the race of 'Alī, and succeeded his father Imām Ja'far Sādiq, who was the sixth. He was born A.D. 745, A.H. 128, and died in the reign of the Khalīf Hārūn al-Rashīd on the 1st September, A.D. 799, 25th Rajab, A.H. 183. He was buried at Baghdād on the west bank of the Tigris, opposite the mausoleum of Abū Hanīfa.

Muslim bin-Amr (مسلم بن عمر), the father of Qutaiba. He was slain in battle along with Misaa'b ibn-Zuber, about the year A.D. 690, A.H. 71.

Muslim bin-Hajjaj Naishapuri (مسلم بن حجاج نيشاپوری), **or Qashmirī,** author of the *Saḥīh Muslim*, a succinct collection of Traditions, and of the *Masnad Kabīr*. He died in the year A.D. 875. A.H. 261. The *Saḥīh Muslim* is considered as almost of equal authority with the *Saḥīh-ul-Bukhārī*, and indeed by some, especially by the African doctors, is preferred to that work. The two collections are constantly quoted together under the name of the Saḥihain or two Saḥīhs. Muslim is said to have composed his work from 300,000 traditions.

[*Vide* 'Abdullah Abū Muslim.]

Muslim ibn-'Uqail (مسلم ابن عقيل), nephew of 'Alī and cousin of Imām Husain, whom he wished to assist against Yezīd, the son of Mu'āwia, but was beheaded along with Hāris on the 8th September, A.D. 680, 8th Zil-hijja, A.H. 60, when their heads were sent as a present to Yezīd by 'Obaid-ullāh ibn-Zayād. This event took place a few days before the death of Imām Husain.

Muslim ibn-'Uqba (مسلم ابن عقبه) was made governor of Medīna by Yezīd, the son of Mu'āwia I. A.D. 682, A.H. 63, to chastise the insolence of the inhabitants of that place, who had rebelled against him, which done, he marched directly with his army towards Mecca, but died by the way in September, A.D. 683, Muḥarram, A.H. 64.

Mustaa'sam Billah (مستعصم بالله), the 37th or last khalīf of the house of 'Abbās. *Vide* Al-Mustaa'sam.

Mustafa (مصطفى), **a title of Muhammad.**

Mustafa I. Sultan (مصطفى سلطان) succeeded his brother Aḥmad I. (Achmet) as emperor of Turkey or Constantinople in A.D. 1617, Zi-Qa'da, A.H. 1025, which was a novelty never before heard of in this kingdom, it being the Grand Seignor's policy to strangle all the younger brothers; however, this Mustafa was preserved, either because Aḥmad, being once a younger brother, took pity on him, or because he had no issue of his own body, and so was not permitted to kill him. It is said that Aḥmad once intended to have shot him, but at the instant he was seized with such a pain in his arm and shoulder that he cried out, "Muhammad will not let him die." He carried himself but insolently and cruelly, and was deposed and sent to prison in A.D. 1618, A.H. 1027, when 'Usmān, his nephew, was raised to the throne. 'Usmān was murdered in A.D. 1621, A.H. 1030, and Mustafa again restored, but was ultimately strangled by his Janisarīs in A.D. 1623, A.H. 1032. He was succeeded by Murād IV.

Mustafa II. Sultan. (مصطفى سلطان), son of Muhammad IV. succeeded Aḥmad II. in A.D. 1695, A.H. 1106, as emperor of Constantinople. He was an able warrior, and after defeating the imperialists at Temswar, he attacked the Venetians, Poles, and Russians. He retired to Adrianople, where he forgot himself in lascivious pleasures, till a revolt of his subjects compelled him to descend from his throne in A.D. 1703, A.H. 1115. He died of melancholy six months afterwards. He was succeeded by his brother Aḥmad III.

Mustafa III. Sultan (مصطفى سلطان), son of Aḥmad III. succeeded his nephew 'Usmān III. as emperor of Constantinople in A.D. 1757, A.H. 1171. He spent his time in his seraglio, and left the government to his favourites. He died on the 21st January, A.D. 1774, A.H. 1187, and was succeeded by his brother Aḥmad IV. also called 'Abdul Hamīd.

Mustafa IV. Sultan (مصطفى سلطان), son of Aḥmad IV. succeeded Salīm III. on the 29th May, A.D. 1807, A.H. 1222, as emperor of Constantinople. He reigned one year, and was deposed and slain in A.D. 1808, A.H. 1223, when Mahmūd II. was raised to the throne.

Mustafa bin-Muhammad Sa'id (مصطفى), **author of the Persian** commentary on the Qurān, entitled *Aqsām 'Ayāt Qurān*.

Mustafa Khan, Nawab, under the name of Shafta, wrote the most considerable of all the Hindūstānī *Tazkiras*. Under the title of *Gulshān-be-Khār*, it was lithographed at Dehlī in 1845, and contains six hundred articles. Shafta was living in A.D. 1868 (Tassy).

Mustai'd Khan (مستعد خان), **sur**named Muhammad Sāqī, was employed as Munshī or secretary to 'Ināyet-ullah Khān, wazīr of Bahādur Shāh, and is the author of the *Māsir-i-'Alamgīrī*, the history of the emperor 'Alamgīr. He had been a constant follower of the court for forty years, and an eye-witness of many of the transactions he records. He undertook the work by desire of his patron, and finished it in A.D. 1710, A.H. 1122, being only three years after the decease of 'Alamgīr.

Musta'in Billah (مستعين بالله). *Vide* Al-Musta'īn Billāh.

Mustajab Khan (مستجاب خان), one of the sons of Hāfiz Rahmat Khān, and author of the work called *Gulistān-i-Rahmat*, being a history of his father. He died in February, A.D. 1833, 2nd Shawwāl, A.H. 1248, aged 74 lunar years.

Mustakfi Billah (مستكفي بالله). *Vide* Al-Mustakfī Billāh.

Mustanasar Billah (مستنصر بالله). *Vide* Al-Mustanasar.

Mustanjad Billah (مستنجد بالله). *Vide* Al-Mustanjid.

Mustarashid Billah (مسترشد بالله). *Vide* Al-Mustarshid.

Mustazahar Billah (مستظهر بالله). *Vide* Al-Mustazhir.

Mustazi Billah (مستضي بالله). *Vide* Al-Mustazī.

Muswi Khan (موسوي خان), an amīr of high rank in the time of the emperor 'Alamgīr. His proper name was Mirzā Moi'zz or Moi'zz-uddīn Muhammad, a descendant of Imām Mūsī Razā. He was a good poet, and had at first assumed Fitrat for his poetical name, but afterwards changed it to Mūswī, to which the title of Khān was added by the emperor. He died in the Deccan in A.D. 1690, A.H. 1101, aged 51 years. [*Vide* Fitrat.] His jagīr at Āgra extended from the Kacheri ghāt to the Dargah of Sayyad near the Rājghāt. The ground contained nearly 300 bighas.

Mutalibi (مطلبي), surname of Muhammad bin-Idrīs al-Shāfa'ī, who was one of the four Imāms, or chiefs of the four orthodox sects amongst the Musalmāns.

Mu'tamid Billah (معتمد بالله). *Vide* Al-Mo'tamid Billāh.

Mu'tamid Khan (معتمد خان), a nobleman of the reign of the emperor Jahāngīr, who wrote the second part (the first part was written by Jahāngīr himself) of the *Ikbāl-nāma Jahāngīrī*, a memoir of that monarch from his accession to the throne in A.D. 1605, A.H. 1014. After the death of Mīr Jumla, A.D. 1637, A.H. 1047, he was appointed Mīr Bakhshī by Shāh Jahān. He died A.D. 1639, A.H. 1049 (*vide* Muhammad Hadī). There is an old masjid still standing in the city of Āgra supposed to have been erected by him.

Mu'tamid Khan (معتمد خان), a nobleman who lived in the time of the emperor 'Alamgīr and in the year A.D. 1661, A.H. 1072, built the Masjid of Gwāliar, which is at the present time in perfectly good order.

Mu'tamid-uddaula Bahadur Sardar Jang (معتمد الدوله بهادر سردار جنگ). He was Dīwān to Salābat Jang of Haidarābād, and died in A.D. 1774, A.H. 1188.

Mu'taqid Khan (معتقد خان), son of Iftikhār Khān, an officer of the rank of 4000 in the time of the emperor Shāh Jahān. He died on the 17th October, O.S. 1651, 12th Zi-Qa'da, A.H. 1061, at Jaunpūr, of which place he was then governor.

Mu'taqid-uddaula (معتقد الدوله), the title of Mān Khān, the brother of Ūdham Bāī, the mother of the emperor Ahmad Shāh of Dehlī, on whose accession to the throne in A.D. 1748, A.H. 1161, he was raised to the rank of 6,000 with the above title.

Mu'tarazzi (معترزى), surname of Nasr bin-'Abdus Sa'īd, also named Burhān-uddīn bin-'Abdul Mukārim. He was one of the most illustrious Arabian grammarians. He died A.D. 1213, A.H. 610.

Mu'tasim Billah (معتصم بالله), khalīf of Baghdād. *Vide* Al-Mo'tasim Billāh.

Mu'tazid Billah (معتضد بالله), khalīf of Baghdād. *Vide* Al-Mo'tazid Billāh.

Mu'tazila (معتزل), a sect of separatists, founded by Wasīl bin-Alā—called Ghazzāl—who taught that the will was free, and that the Qurān was created and not eternal. They flourished at Basra in the 3rd century of the Hijra, and continued to be influential in those parts till the conversion to the Sunnī orthodoxy of Ashān (*q.v.*).

Muti Begam (موتي بيگم), one of the wives of the emperor Shāh Jahān, who built a garden called Mūtī Bāgh on the banks of the Jamna near the Rājghāt at Āgra; no traces of it are to be seen now, but the ground on which it was built is still called Mūtī Bāgh, and some of its land is under cultivation.

Mutia' Billah (مطيع بالله), khalīfa of Baghdād. *Vide* Al-Mutīa' Billāh.

Mutjali (متجلى); poetical name of Sayyad Qutb-uddīn.

Mutnabbi (متنبی), or **Al-Mutnabbi**, surname of Abū Tyyeb Aḥmad bin-Husain, one of the most celebrated of the Arabian poets, born at Kūfa in A.D. 915, A.H. 303. He had acquired an extensive knowledge of pure Arabic, drawn from the best sources, and this he had handed down in his poetical compositions. He flourished about the year A.D. 950, A.H. 339; his father was a water-carrier in Kūfa. His principal patron was Saif-uddaula, prince of Damascus, of the family of Hamdan. The surname of Al-Mutnabbī (the pretended prophet) was given him because he had set up for a prophet in the flat country near Sawāma, where he was followed by a great multitude of the Banū Kalab and other tribes; but Lūlū, governor of Emessa, having marched against him took him prisoner and dispersed his partizans. He kept Mutnabbī in confinement for a long period, and having at length brought him back to the Muslim faith, he set him at liberty. He was attacked by a chief of the tribe of Āsad, at the head of a troop of partizans; a combat took place, in which he was killed with his son Al-Muhassad and his slave Muflik. This event happened in the month of September, A.D. 965, A.H. 354.

Muttaqi Billah (متقی باللہ), a khalīf of Baghdād. *Vide* Al-Muttaqī.

Mutwakkil Ali Allah (متوکل علی اللہ), a khalīf of Baghdād. *Vide* Al-Mutwakkil.

Muwyyad al-Hulla, Shaikh (موید الحلی شیخ). *Vide* Abū'l Qāsim of Hulla.

Muwyyad-uddaula (موید الدولہ), son of Rukn-uddaula, the son of Alī Bōya the Bōyite. He succeeded to a part of his father's dominions in Persia in September, A.D. 976, Muḥarram, A.H. 366. He was taken captive and imprisoned by Hisām-uddaula at Jurjan in January, A.D. 984, Sha'bān, A.H. 373, and his brother Fakhr-uddaula Abū'l Hasan Alī got possession of the empire.

Muwyyad-uddaula (موید الدولہ), the son of Nizām ul-Mulk, the celebrated wazīr of Sulṭān Alp Arsalān and his son Malikshāh. He served as minister to Barkayārak, the son of the latter for some time, and when dismissed by that monarch, he joined his brother Muhammad in an attack upon Barkayārak; but was taken, and put to death by that prince.

Muzaffar or Muzaffarian (مظفر و مظفریان), a dynasty of petty rulers of Fars in Persia. From the period at which the fortunes of the house of Halakū began to decline, *i.e.* after the death of Sulṭān Abū Sa'īd in A.D. 1335, till the conquest of Persia by Amīr Taimūr, the province of Fars was governed by a dynasty of petty rulers, who took the name of Muzaffar from their founder, Mubāriz-uddīn Muhammad, whose title was Al-Muzaffar, or the Victorious, which title he received on his victory over Abū Ishāq, the governor of Shīrāz, in A.D. 1353, A.H. 754. The capital of this family was Shīrāz, which is said to have attained its great prosperity under their rule.

[*Vide* Muhammad Muzaffar.]

Muzaffar (مظفر), the poetical name of a person who flourished about the year A.D. 1690, A.H. 1102. The name of his Murshid or spiritual guide was Alī Amjad, in whose praise he has written some Ghazals.

Muzaffar Husain Mirza (مظفر حسین مرزا) was the son of Sulṭān Husain Mirzā, ruler of Khurāsān, after whose death in May, A.D. 1506, Zil-hijja, A.H. 911, he conjointly with his brother Badī-ūzzamān Mirzā, ascended the throne at Herāt; but they did not enjoy it long, for Shāhī Beg Khān, the Uzbak, defeated them in May, A.D. 1507, Muḥarram, A.H. 913, and took possession of the country. Muzaffar Husain Mirzā, who had gone to Astarābād, died there the same year.

Muzaffar Husain Mirza (مظفر حسین مرزا), of the royal Safwī race of Persia, was the son of Sulṭān Husain Mirzā, the son of Bahrām Mirzā, the son of Shāh Ismā'īl Safwī. He left his jāgīr of Qandahār, and proceeded to India; and on his arrival at the court of the emperor Akbar in August, A.D. 1595, was appointed an amīr of 5000. The Sarkār of Sambhal was assigned to him in jāgīr, and Qandahār (which was made over to the emperor) to Shāh Beg Kābulī. About the year A.D. 1609, Mirzā Khurram (afterwards Shāh Jahān) was married to a daughter of Muzaffar Husain, who received the title of Qandahārī Begam.

Muzaffar Husain Mirza (مظفر حسین مرزا) was the son of Ibrāhīm Husain Mirzā and Gulrukh Begam. He was married to Khānam Sulṭān, the daughter of the emperor Akbar, in A.D. 1593, and was living in A.D. 1600.

Muzaffar Jang (مظفر جنگ), also called Muzaffar Husain Khān, Nawāb of Farrukhābād, whose original name was Diler Himmat Khān. He succeeded his father Aḥmad Khān Bangash in the month of November, A.D. 1771, Sha'bān, A.H. 1185, and received the above title from the emperor

Shāh 'Alam, who was then proceeding to Dehlī from Allahābād. He ceded his territory to the English on receipt of a pension of 108,000 rupees on the 4th June, A.D. 1802. After his death, his grandson Tafazzul Husain Khān succeeded him.

Muzaffar Jang (مظفر جنگ), whose original name was Hadāet Muhīn-uddīn, was the favourite grandson of the celebrated Nizām ul-Mulk, the Sūbadār of Haidarābād. He was the son of that nobleman's daughter, and on his death he collected an army and gave out that his grandsire had in his will not only appointed him to inherit the greatest part of his treasures, but had likewise nominated him to succeed to the government of the southern provinces. Nāsir Jang, his uncle, who had taken possession of his father's wealth, was enabled to keep his father's army in pay; and this was so numerous, that the forces which Muzaffar Jang had collected were not sufficient to oppose him with any probability of success. Muzaffar Jang subsequently went to Arkāt (Arcot), where he defeated and killed Anwar-uddīn Khān, the nawāb of that place, by the assistance of the French, in a battle fought on the 23rd July, A.D. 1749, and was acknowledged the lawful Sūbadār of the Deccan. He was, however, after some months obliged to surrender himself to Nāsir Jang, who kept him in close confinement; but after the murder of Nāsir Jang in December, A.D. 1750, 17th Muharram, A.H. 1164, he was again raised to the masnad by the assistance of the French. His reign was, however, of short duration, for he was not long afterwards assassinated by the same persons who had raised him to power. His death took place on the 3rd February, A.D. 1751, 17th Rabī' I. A.H. 1164, when Salabat Jang, the third son of the old Nizām, was placed on the masnad by the French.

Muzaffar Khan, Nawab (مظفر خان نواب) was the younger brother of Amīr ul-Umrā Khān Daurān Abdus Samad Khān, by whose interest he was appointed governor of Ajmīr in the reign of Farrukhsiyar, and was ordered to march with a numerous army against the Mahratta chief Malhār Rāo Holkar, who had invaded the territories of the Maharāja Jaising Sawāī of Amber (now called Jaipūr). Muzaffar Khān was slain along with his brother in the battle which took place between the emperor Muhammad Shāh and Nādir in the month of February, A.D. 1739, Zi-Qa'da, A.H. 1151.

Muzaffar Khan (مظفر خان), a nobleman who was appointed governor of Āgra by the emperor Jahāngīr in the year A.D. 1621, A.H. 1030. He built the mosque in the city of Āgra called "Kālīn or Kalī Masjid," in the year A.D. 1631, A.H. 1041, which is still standing, but in a ruinous state.

Muzaffar Khan Tirbati (مظفر خان تربتی), a nobleman who was appointed governor of Bengal by the emperor Akbar in A.D. 1579, A.H. 987. In his time Bābā Khān Qāqshāl rebelled against the emperor, took Gaur, slew Muzaffar Khān at Tānda in April, A.D. 1580, Rabī' I. A.H. 988, and became independent for some time.

Muzaffar, Maulana (مظفر مولانا), a celebrated poet of Herāt in Khurāsān, who lived in the time of Sultān Ghayās-uddīn Kart and Shāh Shujāa' of Shīrāz.

Muzaffar Qawami, Maulana (مظفر قوامی مولانا). *Vide* Qawāmī.

Muzaffar Shah I. (مظفر شاه), whose original name was Muzaffar Khān, was the first king of Gujrāt. He was born at Dehlī on the 30th June, A.D. 1342, 25th Muharram, A.H. 743. His family had been elevated from menial stations in the household of the kings of Dehlī. He was, however, appointed governor of Gujrāt in A.D. 1391, A.H. 794, by Sultān Muhammad Tughlaq II. king of Dehlī, in the room of Farhat ul-Mulk, who had rebelled against the king; a battle took place, in which the latter lost his life. In the year A.D. 1396, A.H. 799, Muzaffar Khān caused himself to be proclaimed king under the title of Muzaffar Shāh, and directed coin to be struck in his name. He died after a reign of nearly 20 years, on the 27th July, A.D. 1411, 6th Rabī' II. A.H. 814, in the 71st year of his age, and was succeeded by his grandson Ahmad Shāh the son of Tātār Khān.

Kings of Gujrāt.

1. Muzaffar Shāh I.
2. Ahmad Shāh I. his grandson, the son of Tātār Khān.
3. Muhammad Shāh, surnamed Karīm, the Merciful.
4. Qutb Shāh.
5. Dāūd Shāh, his uncle, deposed in favour of
6. Mahmūd Shāh I. surnamed Baiqara, who made two expeditions to the Deccan.
7. Muzaffar Shāh II.
8. Sikandar Shāh, assassinated.
9. Mahmūd Shāh II. displaced by Bahādur and confined.
10. Bahādur Shāh, who was murdered by the Portuguese.
11. Mīrān Muhammad Shāh Farūqī of Mālwā.
12. Mahmūd II. released from prison.
13. Ahmad Shāh II. a spurious heir, set up by the minister.
14. Muzaffar Shāh III. a suppostitious son of Mahmūd, and the last king in whose time Gujrāt was taken by Akbar.

Muzaffar Shah II. (مظفر شاه) was born on Thursday the 10th April, A.D. 1470, 20th Sha'bān, A.H. 875, and succeeded his father Sulṭān Mahmūd Shāh I. Baiqara on the throne of Gujrāt, in the 41st year of his age, in November, A.D. 1511, Sha'bān, A.H. 917. He reigned nearly 15 years, and died on Saturday the 17th February, A.D. 1526, 3rd Jumāda I. A.H. 932, aged 56 lunar years. He was buried at Sarkīch. His son Sikandar Shāh succeeded him.

Muzaffar Shah III. (مظفر شاه), a supposititious son of Mahmūd Shāh III. named Nathū, was raised to the throne of Gujrāt by Ya'tmād Khān, the prime minister, after the death of Aḥmad Shāh II. in A.D. 1561, A.H. 968. In the year A.D. 1572, A.H. 980, the emperor Akbar was invited by Ya'tmād Khān to occupy Gujrāt as in former times; upon which Akbar advanced on the capital of that kingdom, which he took possession of on the 20th November of the same year, 14th Rajab, A.H. 980, and re-united it to Dehlī as a province of Hindūstān. Muẓaffar Shāh, who had abdicated his throne in favour of Akbar, was sent to Āgra in the first instance, but was subsequently remanded into close confinement, from which he not only made his escape but flying into Gujrāt, collected a respectable force, attacked the viceroy of Quṭb-uddīn Khān, and slew him in action; and after an imprisonment of nearly nine years, re-ascended the throne of Gujrāt. His reign was, however, of short duration; for in the year A.D. 1583, A.H. 991, Akbar having deputed Mirzā Khān KhānKhānān, the son of Bairām Khān to re-take Gujrāt, Muẓaffar Khān was defeated in a pitched battle and fled to Jūnagaṛh; and as he was pursued by Khān 'Azim, he cut his throat with a razor. His head was then cut off and sent to court. His downfall terminated the dynasty of the Muhammadan kings of Gujrāt; ever since which period that kingdom has been considered as a province of Dehlī.

Muzaffar Shah Purbi (مظفر شاه پوربی), whose former name was Siddī Badar, was an Abyssinian slave; he murdered his sovereign Mahmūd Shāh, and ascended the throne of Bengal in A.D. 1495, A.H. 900. He reigned three years, and was killed in a battle fought with his minister Sayyad Sharīf, who succeeded him with the title of 'Ala-uddīn II. in A.D. 1498, A.H. 904.

Muzaffar-uddin (مظفرالدین). *Vide* Sunqar.

Muzaffar-uddin (مظفرالدین). *Vide* Muhammad Muzaffar.

Muzaffar-uddin Zangi (مظفرالدین زنگی). *Vide* Sunqar.

N

Nabi-Effendi (نبی إفندی), a Turkish poet, well acquainted with the classic writers of Greece and Rome. He flourished in the 17th century.

[*Vide* Lempriere's *Univ. Biog.*]

Nadim Gilani (نادم گیلانی), an author who came to India, and was a contemporary of Nazīri of Naishāpūr.

Nadir (نادر), poetical title of Mirzā Kalb Husain, Deputy Collector of Etāwah.

[*Vide* Kalb Husain.]

Nadira Begam (نادره بیگم), daughter of Sulṭān Parwez, the son of the emperor Jahāngīr. She was married to prince Dārā Shikōh, the eldest son of the emperor Shāh Jahān, on the 23rd January, A.D. 1634, by whom she had two sons, *viz.* Sulaimān Shikōh and Sipehr Shikōh. She died of fatigue in May, A.D. 1659, Ramaẓān, A.H. 1069, at Dawar, the country of Malik Jīwan, where her husband had fled along with her after his defeat at Ajmīr. She was buried in the Khanqa of Mian Mīr at Lāhore.

Nadir Shah (نادر شاه), also called Nādir Qulī Khān and Tahmasp Qulī Khān, the greatest warrior that modern Persia has ever produced. He was the son of a shepherd, born in the province of Khurāsān, A.D. 1687, but by selling some of his father's sheep, he collected a number of desperate followers who shared his dangers and the booty gained in plundering caravans. By degrees he saw himself at the head of 6,000 brave adherents, and his assistance was solicited by Shāh Tahmasp II. king of Persia, whose throne was usurped by Ashraf, the chief of the Afghāns. With impetuous valour, Nādir attacked and routed the enemy, and then seated his master on the throne of his ancestors at Isfahān, A.D. 1730. He then pursued the flying Afghāns to Quandahār, and on his return, taking advantage of the odium created by an unfavourable treaty made by Shāh Tahmasp with the Turks during his absence, he deposed the king; and his son, an infant of six months he proclaimed Shāh, by the name of 'Abbās III. This event took place on the 16th August, A.D. 1732, A.H. 1145. In his name, Nādir assumed to himself the sovereign power, and after having recovered all that had been taken from Persia, he concluded a peace with the Ottoman Porte in A.D. 1736. On the death of the young Shāh 'Abbās the same year, he signified his intention of resigning his honours; but the nobles, excited by his private intrigues, invested him with the sovereign power. The historian of Nādir is careful in informing us that the crown of Persia was placed upon the head of the conqueror exactly at 20 minutes past 8 in the morning of the 26th February, 1736, Shawwāl, A.H. 1148. Nādir, now elevated to the height of his ambition, wisely saw that war was the only support of his greatness, and therefore with a numerous army he marched against India in 1739. The Mughol empire was rapidly conquered, 200,000 men were put to the sword, and a booty estimated at one hundred and forty-five millions, in which was the imperial throne set with diamonds of an immense value, called the Peacock Throne, was brought away by him from Dehlī. He latterly became capricious, proud, and tyrannical, and was guilty of such cruelty that the nobles conspired against him and assassinated him on the night of Sunday the 10th May, A.D. 1747, 10th Jumāda I. A.H. 1160, after he had reigned 20 years over one of the most extensive military monarchies of the time. He was buried at Mashhad nine days after his death. His nephew and murderer 'Alī Qulī Khān, who took the title of 'Alī Shāh or 'Adil Shāh, succeeded him. On his accession, he put to death thirteen of the sons and grandsons of Nādir; the only descendant of the conqueror that was spared was his grandson, Shāhrukh, the son of Raza Qulī, who was 14 years of age. He went to Europe and died at Vienna an officer in the Austrian service, known as "Baron von Semlin." 'Adil Shāh was soon afterwards deprived of sight and imprisoned. After him Ibrāhīm his brother reigned for some time in A.D. 1748, Shāhrukh in A.D. 1749, Sulaiman in A.D. 1750, Ismā'īl bin-Sayyad Mustafa from A.D. 1750 to 1759, and after him Karīm Khān Zand and 'Aqā Muhammad Khān Qājār, which see.

Nafis bin-'Iwaz (نفیس بن عوض), author of the Arabic work called *Hall-i-Mūjiz-ul-Qānūn*. He was a contemporary of Mirzā Ulagh Beg.

Naftuya (نفطویه), or Niftūya, was called so, because an offensive smell like naphtha issued from his body. He was an author, and died in A.D. 912, A.H. 300. His proper name is Abū 'Abdullah Ibrāhīm.

Naila (نيلا), the mother of Fīroz Shāh and the daughter of Rāja Mal Bhaṭṭī.

Naishapuri (نيشاپوری), or Naisābūrī, an Arabian author, who took his poetical name from Naishāpūr his birthplace; he is called by European writers Nisaburiensis. He has collected in a little book the grave and witty sayings of Muhammad and his successors, and some of the kings of Persia.

Naiyar and Rakshan (نيار يا رخشن) are the poetical titles of Nawāb Ziyā-uddīn Aḥmad Khān, the son of Nawāb Aḥmad Bakhsh Khān of Fīrozpūr and Lāhore.

Najabat Khan Khan Khanan Nawab (نجابت خان خانخانان نواب), a nobleman of the reign of the emperor 'Alamgīr, by whom he was much respected. His proper name was Mirzā Shujāa; he was the son of Mirzā Shāhrukh, and the grandson of Mirzā Sulaimān of Badakhshān. He was born on the 25th November, A.D. 1603, and died on the 13th December, A.D. 1664, 4th Jumāda I. A.H. 1075, at Ujjain. He held the rank of 5000 at the time of his death.

Najabat, Mir (نجابت مير), author of a poem called *Gulkushtī*, on the art of wrestling, a Sharah of which has been written by Sirāj-uddīn 'Alī Khān 'Arzū; and another by Munshī Ratan Singh of Lucknow.

[*Vide* Najāt (Mīr).]

Najaf Khan (نجف خان), styled Amīr ul-Umrā Zulfiqār-uddaula, was born in Persia of a family said to be related to the Safavī sovereigns of that empire, and in his infancy was, with many of his relations, a prisoner to the usurper Nādir Shāh, who kept all the personages any way allied to the throne in confinement for his own security. At the request of Mirzā Muhsin Khān, the brother of Nawāb Safdar Jang, who was sent on an embassy to Nādir Shāh by Muhammad Shāh the emperor, after his invasion of Hindūstān, Najaf Khān and a sister much older than himself were released. This lady married her deliverer, and Najaf Khān accompanied her and her husband to Dehlī. He was treated with parental affection by Mirzā Muhsin, and at his death attached himself to Muhammad Qulī Khān, his son, the governor of Allahābād, who was shortly afterwards seized and put to death by his first cousin Nawāb Shujā-uddaula, the son of Safdar Jang. Najaf Khān, upon this event, retired with a few followers into Bengal, and offered his services to the Nawāb Mīr Qāsim 'Alī Khān, then at war with the English, who gave him great encouragement. When Qāsim 'Alī took refuge with Shujā-uddaula, Najaf Khān, not choosing to trust himself in the power of the latter, repaired to Bundelkhand, and served Gumāu Singh, one of the chiefs of that country. Upon the flight of Shujā-uddaula, after the battle of Buxar, he offered his services to the English, representing himself as the rightful lord of the province of Allahābād, was received with respectful welcome, and even put in possession of a part of it; but when peace was concluded with the Nawāb Wazīr, the English, alleging the falsehood of his claim, set it aside, and rewarded his attachment with a pension of two lakhs of rupees and strong recommendations to the emperor Shāh 'Alam. The recompense was greater than his services to the English, as he had kept up a correspondence with Shujā-uddaula, whom he would have joined had he been successful in the battle of Korā. From Allahābād he accompanied the emperor Shāh 'Alam to Dehlī in A.D. 1771, and having recovered the city of Āgra from the Jāṭs, he was appointed Amīr-ul-'Umrā with the title of Zulfiqār-uddaula. The Rājas of Jaipūr and several other Hindū princes were his tributaries. He died on the 22nd April, A.D. 1782, A.H. 1169, in the 49th year of his age, leaving no issue, when the succession was disputed by Mirzā Shafi' and Afrāsyāb Khān (*q.v.*). In spite of early intrigues Najaf Khān was an exceptionally efficient man, and gave the Empire some nine years of apparently renewed vigour. He was generally respected.

[Vide *Fall of the Moghul Empire.*]

Najaf Kuli Khan, a follower of the preceding. Died at Kanaund, A.D. 1790.

[Vide *Fall of the Moghul Empire.*]

Najashi (نجاشى). *Vide* 'Abū'l Husain Aḥmad.

Najat, Mir (نجات مير اصفهانى), of Isfahān, whose proper name was Mīr 'Abdul Āl, is the author of a Dīwān. He was a contemporary of Tāhīr Wahīd, who wrote a Preface to that work. He is also, it seems, the author of another poem on the art of wrestling, called *Gulkushtī*. Some of the authors call him Mīr Najābat.

[*Vide* Najābat (Mīr.).]

Naji (ناجى), poetical name of Muhammad Shākir, who lived in the reign of the emperor Muhammad Shāh, and was contemporary with the poets Walī, Hātim, Mazmūn, and 'Abrū.

Najib Khan (نجيب خان). *Vide* Najīb-uddaula.

Najib-uddaula (نجيب الدوله), the title of Najīb Khān, a Rohela chief, and nephew of Bashārat Khān. He came into

Rohelqhand during the administration of 'Alī Muhammad Khān. He was at first appointed to the charge of a very small party, not consisting of more than twelve horse and foot. But his courage and activity soon brought him to the notice of his patron, who entrusted him with a respectable military command, and procured for him in marriage the daughter of Dūndē Khān the Rohela chief. He subsequently espoused the imperial cause, and was honourably received at Dehlī by the wazīr Ghāzī-uddīn Khān, and, being soon afterwards promoted to the command of the army, he attacked Safdar Jang, who had avowedly announced his hostile disposition to the court, and compelled him to cross the Ganges, A.D. 1753, A.H. 1167. On the successful conclusion of this campaign, in which he was wounded, he received from the emperor Aḥmad Shāh the title of Najīb-uddaula. He was created Amīr-ul-'Umrā to the emperor 'Alamgīr II. by Aḥmad Shāh Abdālī on his return to Qandahār, in A.D. 1757, A.H. 1170, but was, soon after that conqueror's departure, deprived of his office by the wazīr Ghāzī-uddīn Khān, who conferred it on Aḥmad Shāh Bangash, the Nawāb of Farrukhābād, as a return for his services. Najīb-uddaula was present in the famous battle fought by Aḥmad Shāh Abdālī with the Marhaṭṭas in January, A.D. 1761, and on his departure to Qandahār, was again restored to his former situation of Amīr-ul-'Umrā, and was entrusted with the care of the city of Dehlī and the protection of the royal family. He governed Dehlī and the few districts yet in possession of the royal family with moderation and justice till his death, which took place in October, A.D. 1770, Rajab, A.H. 1184, when he was succeeded in his dominions by his son Zābita Khān, who continued to protect the royal family, the emperor Shāh 'Alam residing at Allahābād with the English. Najīb-uddaula was buried at Najībādād, a city founded by him.

Najib-uddin Farsi (نجیب الدین فارسی), a poet of Persia who died about the year A.D. 1231, A.H. 628, and left a Dīwān.

Najib-un-Nisa Begam (نجیب النسا بیگم), the sister of the emperor Akbar, and the wife of Khwāja Hasan Nakshbandī.

Najm Sani (نجم ثانی), a famous wazīr of Shāh Ismā'īl Safwī I. whose proper name was Mirzā Yār Aḥmad. He was taken prisoner in a battle fought against the Uzbaks, and put to death on the 12th November, A.D. 1512, 3rd Ramaẓān, A.H. 918, by order of 'Abdullah Khān Uzbak, king of Tūrān.

Najm-uddaula (نجم الدوله), whose proper name was Mīr Phūlwārī, and the eldest son of Mīr Ja'far 'Alī Khān, Nawāb of Bengal, Behār, and Urissa. He succeeded his father in February, A.D. 1765, Sha'bān, A.H. 1178, and the same year the East India Company received from the emperor Shāh 'Alam the appointment of Dīwān of the three provinces of Bengal, and the Nawāb became a mere pensioner. Najm-uddaula died of the small-pox, after a reign of one year and four months, on the 3rd May, A.D. 1766, 22nd Ẓi-Qa'da, A.H. 1179, and was succeeded by his brother Saif-uddaula.

Najm-uddin 'Abru, Shah (نجم الدین آبرو شاه), a poet of Dehlī, who flourished in the reign of the emperor Shāh 'Alam.

Najm-uddin 'Abu Hafs 'Umar bin-Muhammad (نجم الدین ابو حفص عمر بن محمد). *Vide* Nasafī.

Najm-uddin 'Abu'l Hasan 'Ali bin-Daud (نجم الدین ابو الحسن علی بن داود), commonly called Qahqarī, from Qahqar, a place in Chaldea, situated near Basra, where he was born in A.D. 1172, A.H. 568. He was a descendant of Zuber bin-Awām, and a famous jurisconsult, and a good grammarian. He led a very retired and austere life, and was one of the most celebrated professors of the Hanīfian sect, in the college named Ruknia, in the city of Damascus, where he died in A.D. 1274, A.H. 645, aged 77 lunar years.

Najm-uddin Fahdani (نجم الدین فهدانی حافظ), or Kahdanī (Hāfiz), author of an Arabic work entitled *Itahāf ul-Warā bi-Akhbār ul-Qurā.*

Najm-uddin Kubra, Shaikh (نجم الدین کبری شیخ), a celebrated pious Musalmān, who was slain at Khwārizm at the time when the troops of Changez Khān, the Tartar, invaded that kingdom in A.D. 1221, A.H. 618.

Najm-uddin Muhammad 'Umar-al-Samarqandi (نجم الدین محمد عمر السمرقندی), author of a medical work in Arabic, called *Asbāb wa 'Alāmat.*

Najm-uddin Razi (نجم الدين رازی معروف به يدالله), commonly called "Īdullah," or the Hand of God.

Na'man, Mir (نعمان مير), a poet who died at Āgra on the 4th March, A.D. 1648, 18th Ṣafar, A.H. 1058, and was buried there.

Na'mat 'Ali Khan (نعمت علی خان), author of a work called *Shāh-nāma*, containing an account of the Muhammadan kings of India.

Na'mat Khan (نعمت خان علی), whose poetical name is 'Alī, and who afterwards received the title of Dānishmand Khān, Comptroller of the Kitchen to the emperor 'Alamgīr, and a constant attendant on his person. He is the author of a number of excellent poems, one of which is called *Husn wa-Ishq*, but that held in the greatest estimation is a satire on the conquest of Golkonḍa by 'Alamgīr, A.D. 1687, in which the author lashes not only the generals, but even the emperor himself, whose conduct in destroying the Muhammadan kings of Bījāpūr and Golkonḍa, while the Mahraṭṭas and other Hindū chiefs had exalted the standard of defiance, was much disapproved of by many of the zealous Musalmāns. The officers and soldiers were also much disgusted by incessant wars in the Deccan, and the very great hardships they suffered during his campaigns in that country. This book goes by the name of the author, *Na'mat Khān 'Alī*, and has no other name. It is sometimes called *Waqāya Na'mat Khān 'Alī*. He also compiled a very excellent book on Oriental Cookery. The whole of his work is called *Khwān Na'mat*, or the Table of Delicacies. He died in the reign of the emperor Bahādur Shāh, A.D. 1708, A.H. 1120.
[*Vide* Dānishmand Khān.]

Na'mat-ullah (نعمت الله سيد نارنول), a Sayyad of Nārnaul and a pious Musalmān who is said to have performed miracles. He had reared a hawk by whose aid he procured his subsistence for several years. He afterwards proceeded to Akbarnagar, commonly called Rājmahāl, in Bengal, where the prince Sulṭān Shujāa', the son of the emperor Shāh Jahān, then governor of that province, with several of his 'Umrā, became his disciples. He died in the year A.D. 1666, A.H. 1077, at a place called Fīrozpūr, east of Rājmahāl, where he had received a jāgīr from the prince. He was a saint and a poet.

Na'mat-ullah, Khwaja (نعمت الله خواجه), author of the history of the Afghāns or early Abdālīs, an account of which is given in the *Jour. of the As. Soc. of Bengal*, vol. xiv, p. 445. It is called *Tārīkh Afghānī*, translated by Bernhard Dorn, Ph. D., etc.

Na'mat-ullah Wali, Sayyad Shah Nur-uddin (نعمت الله ولی سيد شاه نورالدين), a descendant of Imām Mūṣī Qāzim. He was a learned and pious Musalmān, and an excellent poet. He is said to have performed miracles; was the disciple of Shaikh 'Abdullah Yāfa'ī, but followed the tenets of Imām Shāfa'ī. He is the author of nearly 500 books and pamphlets. He died in the time of Shāhrukh Mirzā, the son of Amīr Taimūr, A.D. 1424 or 1431, A.H. 827, aged 75 years, and is buried at Māhān, a village of Kirmān in Persia. Sayyad was his poetical title.

Nami (نامی), a poet who died in A.D. 1533, A.H. 940.

Nami (نامی). *Vide* Muhammad Ma'sūm Nāmī.

Nami ul-Nami (نامی النامی), surname of 'Abū'l 'Abbās ibn-Muhammad al-Dazamī al-*Massifi*, who was an excellent Arabic poet. He died A.D. 1008, A.H. 399, aged 90 years.

Namkin (نمكين قاسم خان), poetical title of Qāzim Khān, who lived in the time of the emperor Jahāngīr.

Namud (نمود). *Vide* Taskhīr.

Nana (نانا), a corruption of Nānhā, or Nannhā, is the appellation by which Bālājī Rāo Peshwā was commonly known in Hindūstān, and is by most supposed to be a title of State; but, as we are informed, it arose from the nickname given him when a child by his father, Nannhā signifying a little man.

Nana (نانا فرنويس), or Nānhā Farnawīs or Phaṛnawīs, was the Kārkun of Mādhō Rāo Peshwā. His original name was Janardhan, and he rose by the aid of great ability and lack of scruple. Was rival of Madhoji Sindhia, whose great-nephew Daulat Rāo caused the Nāna's fall and ruin. Died about 1797.

Nana (نانا صاحب), or Nānā Sāhib, the nickname of Dhundhūpant of Biṭhūr near Cawnpore. This miscreant was an adopted son of Bājī Rāo II. the ex-Peshwā of Pūnā, who died on the 28th January, A.D. 1853. The pension of the ex-Peshwā, amounting to 8 lakhs of rupees per annum, was not continued to the Nānā, and this appears to have been his principal, if not sole grievance, though he invariably maintained friendly relations with the European residents and indeed on many occasions treated them with apparently cordial hospitality. His residence was at Bithur, situated ten miles from Cawnpore, where he owned an estate left him by his patron the ex-Peshwā, and he was allowed a retinue of 500 infantry and cavalry, with three guns of small calibre, and these troops were of course entirely independent of European authority. On learning the general character of the outbreak of the Bengal army in 1857 he attacked the garrison of Cawnpore, all of whom he destroyed by the help of the vilest treachery; but fled before the avenging force of General Havelock. A proclamation was issued by the Governor-General in March, A.D. 1858, wherein a reward was offered of one lakh of rupees to any person who should deliver Nānā Dhundhūpant of Bithūr to the district officer commanding in any military camp or at any military post; and, in addition to the pecuniary reward, a free pardon was guaranteed to any mutineer, deserter or rebel (excepting the Nawābs of Farrukhābād, Barelī, Banda and Rāja of Mainpūrī) who should so deliver up the Nānā Sāhib. The Nānā was never afterwards heard of authentically, but probably perished in the Nipāl jungles.

Nanak (نانک شاه), or Nānak Shāh, the founder of the sect called Sikhs, was born in the year A.D. 1469. He was the son of a Hindū grain-merchant, and disciple of Sayyad Husain, or as some say of Kabīr, and consequently a sort of Hindū deist, but his peculiar tenet was universal toleration. He maintained that devotion was due to God, that forms were immaterial, and that Hindū and Muhammadan worship were the same in the sight of the Deity. During his travels Nānak was introduced to the emperor Bābar, before whom he is said to have defended his doctrine with great firmness and eloquence. Nānak died in the month of August, A.D. 1539, aged 70 years. After his sect had silently increased for more than a century, it excited the jealousy of the Musalmān government, and its spiritual chief, the Gurū Arjun, was put to death in A.D. 1606, within a year after the decease of the emperor Akbar. This tyranny changed the Sikhs from inoffensive quietists into fanatical warriors. They took up arms under Hargōbind, the son of the martyred Arjun, who inspired them with his own spirit of revenge and of hatred to their oppressors.

The following are the names of the Sikh Gurūs from Nānak.

	A.D.
Gurū Nānak Shāh, the founder of the sect . . .	died 1539
Gurū Angad, who wrote some of the sacred books	died 1552
,, Amardās	,, 1574
,, Rāmdās, who beautified Amritsir . .	,, 1581
,, Arjunmal, he compiled the 'Adi Granth .	,, 1606
,, Hargōbind, who was the first warlike leader	,, 1644
,, Har Rāe, grandson of Hargōbind . . .	,, 1661
,, Har Krishan, son of Har Rāe . .	,, 1664
,, Teigh Bahādur, uncle of Har Krishan .	,, 1675
,, Gobind, son of Teigh Bahādur. He remodelled the Sikh government. He was assassinated by a Pathān soldier in .	,, 1708
,, Banda, put to death by the Musalmāns .	,, 1715
12 Misals of the Sikhs captured Lāhore and occupied the Panjab	
Charat Singh of Sukelpaka misal . .	,, 1774
Maha Singh, his son, extended his rule, and his wife became regent, and Lakhpat Singh her minister	,, 1792
Ranjīt Singh established Lāhore independency in 1805 .	,, 1839 27th June.
[*Vide* Ranjīt Singh.]	

Nandkumar (نندکمار), a Brāhman born about 1720, in the district of Birbham, became Wanu Faujdar of Huglī under Sirāj-ul-daula (*q.v.*) about 1756. All the power of the State had been committed to him without control, in the time of the Nawāb Ja'far 'Alī Khān. He was a treacherous enemy to the English. He was convicted of a forgery, condemned to suffer death, and hanged at the appointed place of execution in Calcutta on the 5th August, A.D. 1775, 7th Jumāda II. A.H. 1189. His treasure and effects were given up to his son Rāja Gūrdās. It is said there were fifty-two lakhs of rupees in money, and about the same amount in jewels and rich goods. In the *Sīyar-ul-Mutakharīn*, it is said that in his house were found counterfeit seals of several eminent persons which he had forged.

[Warren Hastings was long charged with improperly influencing the trial of Nandkumār, but his memory is generally thought to have been cleared by Sir J. F. Stephen, whose book on the subject should be consulted.]

Naqib Khan (نقیب خان), the grandson of Yahia bin-'Abdul-Latīf, which see.

Naqi, Imam (نقی امام). *Vide* 'Alī Naqī (Imām).

Naqi Kamara (نقی کمره), a poet who died in A.D. 1622, A.H. 1031, and left a Dīwān.

Naqshabi (نقشابی), poetical name of a person who is the author of the *Tūtī-nāma*, or Tales of a Parrot. When he flourished or when he died is not known.

Narayan Rao Peshwa (نارایان راو پیشوا), the third son of Balājī Rāo Peshwā, succeeded his brother Madhō Rāo in November, A.D. 1770. He was assassinated by his paternal uncle Raghunāth Rāo, better known by the name Rāghoba, in August, A.D. 1772, and was succeeded by his infant son Sewājī Madhō Rāo. Raghunāth Rāo, failing in his plans, joined the English at Surat.

Nargisi (نرگسی), an author who died at Qandahār, in A.D. 1533, A.H. 937, and has left a Dīwān.

Narsi (نرسی), the Narses of the Greeks, a king of the Sāsānian dynasty, succeeded his brother Bahrām III. A.D. 393, on the throne of Persia, and after a reign of nine years abdicated it in favour of his son, Hurmuz II. and survived that act but a short period.

Narsingh Deo Bundeila, Raja (نرسنگه دیو بندیله راجه), son of Rāja Madhukar Sāh Bundeila, who died in the reign of the emperor Akbar, A.D. 1592, A.H. 1000. He served prince Mirzā Salim (afterwards Jahāngīr) for several years and by his orders slew Abū'l Fazl, the prime minister of his father Akbar, in A.D. 1602, A.H. 1011. In the first year of Jahāngīr he was raised to the rank of 3000, and subsequently to that of 4000. The Hindū temple at Muthura (Muttru), which 'Alamgīr afterwards converted into a mosque, was built by him at a cost of three lakhs of rupees. He died in the year A.D. 1626, A.H. 1036.

Nasafi (نسفی), or al-Nasafī, whose proper name is Abū'l Barakāt 'Abdullah bin-Ahmad, commonly called Hāfiz-uddīn al-Nasafī, is the author of a law-book entitled *Wāfī* and its commentary called the *Kāfī*. He is also the author of the *Kanz ul-Daqāek*, a book of great reputation, principally derived from the *Wāfī*, and containing questions and decisions according to the doctrines of Abū Hanifa, Abū Yūsaf, the Imām Muhammad, Zafar, al-Shāfa'ī, Mālik, and others. Many commentaries have been written on this work; the most famous is the *Bahr ar-Rāeq* by Zain-ul-'Abidīn bin-Nujaim al-Misrī. Nasafī died A.D. 1310, A.H. 710.

[*Vide* Hāfiz-uddīn Nasafī.]

Nasafi (نسفي), surname of Najm-uddīn Abū Hafs 'Umar bin-Muhammad, a celebrated doctor, and author of the *Aqāed al-Nasafī*, a book in Arabic containing the fundamental and principal articles of the Muhammad religion. This work is greatly esteemed by the Musalmāns, who prefer it to many others of the same title. A commentary on the above work was written by Taftazānī. Nasafī died in A.D. 1142, A.H. 537.

Nasai (نسائی). *Vide* Abū 'Abdul Rahmān Nasāī. He was a native of Nasā, a town in Khurāsān.

Nashat (نشاط), the poetical name of Rāe Phuknī Mal, a Hindū, who was Dīwān or Treasurer of 'Alamgīr's wazīr.

Nashati (نشاطی), a poet who died A.D. 1508, A.H. 914.

Nashwan bin-Said Himiri al-Yemani (نشوان بن سعید حمیری الیمنی), author of a work called *Shams-ul-'Ulūm*, or the Sun of Science. He died A.D. 1177, A.H. 573.

Nasibi, Baba (نصیبی بابا), of Gīlān, was a court poet of Sultān Ya'qūb. He died at Tabrez, in A.D. 1537, A.H. 944, and left a Dīwān containing about 5,000 verses.

Nasibi, Mirza Muhammad Khan (نصیبی مرزا محمد خان) came from Persia to Lucknow in the reign of Nasīr-uddīn Haidar; and died in that of Amjad Alī Shāh before or after the year A.D. 1845, A.H. 1261. He is the author of several poems.

Nasikh (ناسخ), Shaikh, Imam Bakhsh, a poet of the present century. His complete works, comprising three Dīwāns, or books of verse, besides chronograms on the deaths of earlier writers, appeared in A.H. 1232-47-54, under the title of *Kitāb-i-Nīsikh*; the collection was to be found in the king of Audh's library. [See *Catalogue* by Sprenger, I. 628.] Died 1839.

Nasim (نصیم), poetical appellation of Paṇḍit Dayā Shankar, who is the author of a story called *Gulzār Nasīm*, in Urdū verse, composed in A.D. 1838, A.H. 1254.

Nasim (نصیم), poetical title of Asghar 'Alī Khān of Dehlī.

Nasim (نصیم), poetical title of Lachhmī Narāyan, Rāja of Benares.

Nasir (نصیر), poetical name of Mīr Nasīr 'Alī of Lucknow.

Nasir (ناصر), poetical name of Nawāb Nāsir Jang, son of Muẓaffar Jang Bangash. He died in A.D. 1813, A.H. 1228, on a day when an eclipse of the sun had taken place.

Nasir (نصیر), poetical name of Shāh Nasīr-uddīn, an Urdū poet, commonly called Miān Kallū. He was a native of Dehlī and the son of Shāh Gharīb. In the latter part of his life, he proceeded to Haidarābād and was employed by Mahārāja Chandū Lāl, in whose service he died about the year A.D. 1840. He has left an Urdū Dīwān, containing more than 100,000 verses, which were collected together after his death by one of his pupils named Mahārāj Singh.

Nasir (ناصر), poetical title of Saādat Khān, the son of Rislat Khān. He is the author of five Dīwāns and a biography.

Nasir (نصیر), takhallus of Nasīr-uddīn Hamdānī, who flourished about the year A.D. 1606, A.H. 1015, in which year he visited Shīrāz. He is the author of a Dīwān.

Nasir (نصیر محمد ناصر خان), the takhallus of Muhammad Nasīr Khān, who is the author of a Dīwān, and was living in A.D. 1807, A.H. 1222.

Nasir 'Ali, Mulla (ناصر علی ملا), a poet of Shāhjahānābād, whose poetical name was 'Alī. He was born at Sarhind, and died at Dehlī in March, A.D. 1697, Ramaẓān, A.H. 1108, and is buried near the mausoleum of Niẓām-uddīn Auliā. He was a fertile poet and has left a Dīwān and a Masnawī.

Nasir Billah (ناصر بالله), a khalīf of Baghdād. *Vide* Al-Nāsir Billāh.

Nasir bin-Khusro, Hakim (ناصر بن خسرو حکیم), the author of the work called *Zadīl Musafarīn*, from which book the compiler of the *Hajat Darakoke Nūr-uddīn Shīrāzī* has so largely borrowed. He was a genuine Kuresh, and must have written under the short reign of al-Wasiq Billāh, the ninth Khalīf of the house of Abbās, who reigned between the year A.D. 840 and 841. Vide *Trans. Roy. As. Soc.* vol. iii. p. 32. 'Alī Raza the 8th Imām, and great-grandfather of Nāsir bin-Khusro, died in the year A.D. 818, A.H. 204.

Nasir Bukhari, Maulana (ناصر بخاري مولانا), a learned Musalmān who lived like a Dervish and wrote poetry on different subjects. He was a contemporary of Salmān Sāwajī, who died in A.D. 1377, A.H. 779.

Nasir Jang, Nawab Nizam-uddaula (ناصر جنگ نواب نظام الدوله) was the second son of Niẓām-ul-Mulk 'Asaf Jāh, whom he succeeded in the government of the Deccan in May, A.D. 1748, Jumāda II. A.H. 1161. He reigned two years and a half, and was slain on the 5th December, A.D. 1750, 17th Muḥarram, A.H. 1164, by a conspiracy of his own servants, supposed to have been favoured by the French, who surprised his camp while he was engaged in quelling a rebellion raised by his nephew, Muẓaffar Jang, who had been imprisoned by him. On his death Muẓaffar Jang was placed on the masnad of the Deccan by the conspirators; but this young prince did not long enjoy his dignity, for he was assassinated almost immediately after his accession by the same persons who had raised him to power. This event took place on the 2nd February, A.D. 1751, 17th Rabī I. A.H. 1164. Nāsir Jang was buried at Burhānpūr near the tomb of his father.

[See *The French in India*, by Colonel Malleson, C.S.I.]

Nasir Khan (نصیر خان), ruler of Haidarābād in Singh, succeeded his brother Mīr Nūr Muhammad Khān in A.D. 1842. He was imprisoned and sent down to Calcutta by the English in A.D. 1843, 6th Rabī' II. A.H. 1261, where he died on the 16th April, A.D. 1845.

Nasir Khan Faruqi (نصیر خان فیروقی). *Vide* Malik Nasīr Khan.

Nasir Khusro (ناصر خسرو), a celebrated physician and poet of Isfahān, whose poetical name was Hujjat. He is the author of several works, among which are the two following, viz. *Rōstāi-nāma* in verse, and

Kanz-ul-Haqaeq in prose. He has also left a Dīwān consisting of 30,000 verses. He was a contemporary of Khwāja 'Abū'l Hasan Jurjānī and the celebrated physician Avicenna. Some say that he was a Deist, and others considered him to be an Atheist, on which account he was persecuted by the Muhammadans, and fled from one city to another, till at last he was obliged to conceal himself among the hills of Badakhshān. Daulat Shāh has given a very interesting account of Nāsir Khusro, in his Tazkira. In 1872 there was discovered among the Elliot papers an Arabic work by Nāsir Khusro, on the buildings and water-works of Jerusalem. He is most precise in his information. It is said, that if this work had been found a little earlier, it might have saved the Palestine Exploration Committee some diggings and considerable outlay. There is also a work of the same kind in Persian, called *The Travels of Nāsir Khusro*, which he wrote in A.D. 1052, corresponding with A.H. 444.

Nasir, Khwaja (ناصر خواجه), a poet who was contemporary with Salmān Sāwajī. [*Vide* Nāsir Bukhārī.]

Nasir Shah Purbi (ناصر شاه پوربی), a lineal descendant of Shams-uddīn Bhangāra, was placed on the throne of Bengal in A.D. 1427, A.H. 831, after the murder of Nāsir-uddīn Ghulām, who had usurped the throne for several days after the death of his master Ahmad Shāh. General Briggs, in his translation, says that he reigned only two years, whereas it appears from Major Stewart's Bengal history, which seems to be correct, that he reigned 32 years, consequently his death must have happened in the year A.D. 1458, A.H. 863. He was succeeded by his son Bārbak. He is also called Nāsir Husain Shāh, as appears from an Arabic inscription on a mosque lately discovered in the district of Hughli in Bengal by the late H. Blochmann, Principal, Calcutta Madrasa.

Nasir, Shaikh (ناصر شیخ اکبرابادی), of Akbarābād, a Musalmān saint who is said to have performed a number of miracles, and was highly respected by the emperor Shāh Jahān. He died on the 7th June, A.D. 1647, 13th Jumāda I. A.H. 1057, and was buried at Āgra.

Nasir-uddaula (نصیرالدوله), Nizām of the Haidarābād State, succeeded his father Sakandar Jāh on the 23rd May, A.D. 1829, and died in May, A.D. 1857. His son ascended the masnad with the title of Nawāb Afzal-uddaula.

Nasir-uddin (نصیرالدین), title of Ahmad Shāh, the present king of Persia. [*Vide* Ahmad Shāh.]

Nasir-uddin (نصیرالدین), author of the Arabic work on Jurisprudence called *Fatāwī Ibrāhīmī*.

Nasir-uddin (نصیرالدین), king of Persia. *Vide* Nasīr-uddīn Shāh.

Nasir-uddin Haidar (نصیرالدین حیدر), king of Audh, was the son of Ghāzī-uddīn Haidar, whom he succeeded on the throne of Lucknow on the 30th October, A.D. 1827, 28th Rabī' I. A.H. 1243, with the title of Sulaimān Jāh Nasīr-uddīn Haidar. He reigned ten years, and died, poisoned by his own family, on the 7th July, A.D. 1837, 3rd Rabī' II. A.H. 1253, in which year died also William IV. king of England, and Akbar II. king of Dehlī. Nasīr-uddīn Haidar was succeeded by his uncle Nasīr-uddaula, who took the title of Abū Muzaffar Mōī-uddīn Muhammad 'Alī Shāh, and Munna Jān the illegitimate son of Nasīr-uddīn Haidar was sent to the fort of Chunār, where he died on the 15th January, A.D. 1846, 16th Muharram, A.H. 1262.

Nasir-uddin Khilji, Sultan (ناصرالدین خلجی سلطان), was the son of Sultān Ghayās-uddīn Khiljī, king of Mālwā. He ascended the throne of that kingdom a few days before the death of his father, which happened on the 25th October, A.D. 1500, 27th Rabī' II. A.H. 906. He reigned eleven years and four months; and, having previously declared his third son Mahmūd as his successor, died about the year A.D. 1511, A.H. 917.

Nasir-uddin Mahmud (نصیرالدین محمد چراغ دهلی), also called, by Firishta, Nasīr-uddīn Mahmūd Awadhī, surnamed Chirāgh Dehlī, or the Candle of Dehlī, a celebrated Muhammad saint, who was a disciple of Shaikh Nizām-uddīn Auliā, whom he succeeded on the masnad of Irshād, or Spiritual Guide, and died on Friday the 16th September, A.D. 1356, 18th Ramazān, A.H. 757. He is buried at Dehlī in a mausoleum which was built before his death by Sultān Fīrōz Shāh Bārbak, one of his disciples, and close to his tomb Sultān Bahlōl Lōdī was afterwards buried. He is the author of a work called *Khair-ul-Majālis*.

Nasir-uddin Mahmud (ناصرالدین محمد بغرا خان); surnamed Baghrā Khān, governor of Bengal, was the son of Sultān Ghayās-uddīn Balban, and the father of Mōizz-uddīn Kaiqubād, who was, during the absence of his father in Bengal, made king of Dehlī. When Sultān Ghayās-uddīn Tughlaq, in A.D. 1324, marched in person towards Bengal, he was then living, and came from Lakhnautī to pay his respects, bringing with him many valuable presents. He was confirmed in his government of Bengal, and permitted to assume the ensigns of royalty. He died in the time of Muhammad Tughlaq Shāh.

[*Vide* Baghrā Khān.]

Nasir-uddin Mahmud, Sultan (ناصر الدین محمد), son of Sultān Shams-uddīn Altimsh, succeeded his nephew Sultān 'Alāuddīn Masa'ūd Shāh in June, A.D. 1246, to the throne of Dehlī. He reigned 20 years, was imprisoned, and died on the 18th February, A.D. 1266, when Ghayās-uddīn Balban succeeded him.

Nasir-uddin Muhtashim (ناصرالدین محتشم) is the person in whose name Khwājā Nāsir-uddīn Tūsi wrote the work entitled *Akhlāq Nāsiri.*

Nasir-uddin Murtaza (ناصرالدین مرتضی), author of several works, one of which is called *Risāla Misbāh ilm Nahv.* He died in A.D. 1213, A.H. 610.

Nasir-uddin Qabbacha or Fattah (ناصرالدین قباچه یا فتاح), ruler of Sindh. It is related in several histories, such as the *Khulāsat ul-Hikāet*, the *Haj-nāma*, and the *History of Hājī Muhammad Qandahāri*, that the first establishment of the Muhammadan faith in the country of Sindh took place in the time of Hajjāj bin-Yūsaf, governor of Basra, at the time when Walīd, the son of the Khalīf 'Abdulmalik, was ruler of the provinces of both 'Irāqs. Hajjāj deputed Mahmūd Husain in the year A.D. 706, A.H. 87, with a select army into Mikrāu, and he subdued that country and made converts of many of the inhabitants called Ballochīs. He afterwards deputed Budmīn to conquer Dībāl (modern Thatta on the Indus). Budmīn failed in his expedition, and lost his life in the first action. Hajjāj, not deterred by this defeat, resolved to follow up the enterprise by another. In consequence, in the year A.D. 712, A.H. 93, he deputed his cousin Imād-uddīn Mūhammad bin-Qāsim, the son of Aqīl or Uqail Thaqafī or Saqafī, with six thousand soldiers to attack Dībāl, and he in a short time conquered the place, and Rāja Dāhir, the ruler of Dībāl, was slain in battle. After the death of Muhammad bin-Qāsim, a tribe who trace their origin from the Ansārīs established a government in Sindh; after which the zamīndārs, of the tribe of Sūmara, usurped the power, and held independent rule over the kingdom of Sindh for the space of 500 years. About A.H. 737 the dynasty of Sūmara was subverted, and the country subdued by another native dynasty called Sūmana, whose chief assumed the title of Jām. During the reigns of these dynasties in Sindh, the Muhammadan kings of India Proper, such as those of Ghaznī, Ghōr and Dehlī, invaded Sindh, and, seizing many towns, appointed Muhammadan governors over them. Among these rulers, Nāsir-uddīn Qabbācha asserted his independence, and caused the public prayers to be read in his name as king of Sindh. Nāsir-uddīn was one of the Turkish slaves of Shahāb-uddīn Muhammad Ghōrī, who made him governor of Uchcha in Multān about the year A.D. 1203, A.H. 600. He espoused the daughter of Sultān Qutb-uddīn Aibak, viceroy, and afterwards king of Dehlī, after whose death in A.D. 1210, A.H. 607, having seized many of the towns subjected to the Sindh government, he reduced the territory of the Sūmanas to the small tract of country around Thatta, and, renouncing his allegiance to the throne of Dehlī, became independent. Besides Sindh, his kingdom embraced the provinces of Multān, Kohrām and Sursatī. He was twice attacked by Tāj-uddīn Elduz of Ghaznī, but he successfully repelled both these invasions. In A.D. 1225 Shams-uddīn Altimsh, king of Dehlī, made several attempts to remove him from his government, and even marched for that purpose as far as Uchcha, when Nāsir-uddīn, having no hopes of eventually repelling the arms of the Dehlī monarch, placed his family and personal attendants with his treasure, in boats, and endeavoured to occupy a contiguous island; when a storm coming on, the boat foundered, and every one perished. This usurper ruled in Sindh and Multān for a period of 22 years. In the latter end of the reign of Muhammad Tughlaq of Dehlī, Sindh owned allegiance to that monarch; nevertheless, occasionally taking advantage of local circumstances, the Sindhīs contrived, for a considerable period, to shake off their allegiance. The first of the family of which we have any account was Jām Afrā.

The following is a list of the Jām dynasty of Sūmana, originally Rājputs.

A.H.			A.D.
737—740	1.	Jām Afrā, reigned 3 years and 6 months from A.D. 1336, and	died 1339
754	2.	Jām Chōban, his brother, reigned 14 years . . .	,, 1353
769	3.	Jām Banī, son of Jām Afrā, reigned 15 years .	,, 1367
782	4.	Jām Timmājī, son of Jām Afrā, reigned 13 years .	,, 1380
793	5.	Jām Salāh-uddīn, converted to Muhammadanism	,, 1391
796	6.	Jām Nizām-uddīn, his son	,, 1393
812	7.	Jām 'Alīsher, his son . .	,, 1409
,,	8.	Jām Giran, son of Timmājī, died on the 2nd day after his accession.	
827	9.	Jām Fatha Khān, son of Iskandar Khāh	,, 1423
854	10.	Jām Tughlaq, his brother, invaded Gujrāt, reigned 27 years, and was succeeded by his kinsman Jām Mubārak, who was deposed after a reign of 3 days	,, 1450

A.H.		A.D.
856	11. Jām Sikandar, son of Fatha Khān, reigned 18 months	died 1452
,,	12. Jām Sanjar, a descendant of the former kings of Sindh, was elected in 1452, reigned 8 years . . .	,, 1460
894	13. Jām Nizām-uddīn, commonly called Jām Nanda, was contemporary with Hasan Langa, king of Multān, reigned 30 years	,, 1489
927	14. Jām Fīrōz, his son, reigned about 33 years, when Shāh Beg Arghūn, governor of Kāndahār in A.D. 1520, marched to conquer Sindh, and occupied the whole country, even to the possession of Thatta . . .	,, 1520
930	15. Shāh Beg Arghūn, reigned 3 years	,, 1523
966	16. Shāh Husain Arghūn . .	,, 1554
982	17. Mahmūd of Bakkar, reigned till A.D. 1572, when the emperor Akbar annexed Sindh to the empire.	

Nasir-uddin Qazi Baizawi (ناصرالدين قاضى بيضاوى), the son of Imām Badr-uddīn Umar bin-Fakhr-uddīn 'Alī Baizāwī.

[*Vide* Baizāwi.]

Nasir-uddin Shah (ناصرالدين شاه), king of Persia, was born in A.D. 1831, and was the eldest son of Muhammad Shāh, the eldest son of 'Abbās Mirzā, so well known for his partiality to the English, and the great-grandson of Fatha 'Alī Shāh. Nāsir-uddīn ascended the throne after the death of his father, on the 4th September, A.D. 1848, in his 19th year. He visited Russia, London, France, Germany, etc., in A.D. 1873, and again in 1889.

Nasir-uddin Tusi, Khwaja (نصيرالدين طوسى خواجه), the famous philosopher and astronomer who was employed by Halākū Khān, the grandson of Changez Khān, to form the Ilkhānī Tables, etc. He was the son of Imām Fakhr-uddīn Muhammad Rāzī, was born at Tūs in Khurāsān on Saturday the 3rd March, A.D. 1201, 11th Jumāda I. A.H. 597, and though a somewhat over-zealous Shīa, was one of the best, and certainly the most universal scholar that Persia ever produced. He wrote on all subjects, and some of his works are to this day standard books in Persian Universities. He was a fair Greek scholar, and made a new translation of Euclid into Arabic, wherein he proves most of the propositions, sometimes in two, three, and four ways, wholly different from the demonstrations of the Greek author. He likewise translated the *Almajisti*, and wrote a volume of learned explanatory notes upon it. He also wrote several works on geometry, astronomy, philosophy, theology, and dissertations on miscellaneous subjects. During the Mughal persecutions he wandered among the mountains of Khurāsān, and was taken captive by Alauddīn Muhammad, a descendant of Hasan Sabbah, who forced him to remain with him for several years and employed him as his wazīr. It was during his captivity that he wrote the most celebrated of all his treatises, a well-known and excellent little work on moral philosophy, which he styled *Akhlāq Nāsirī*, or the Morals of Nasīr, in compliment to Nasīr-uddīn 'Abdul Rahīm, governor of the fortress of Dez; but the flattery did not procure him his liberty, he remained in that mountainous region till he was released by Halākū Khān in November, A.D. 1256, A.H. 654. It was Nasīr-uddīn that persuaded Halākū to march against Baghdād, which was taken in A.D. 1258. The *Akhlāq Nāsirī* is a translation in Persian of the *Kitāb-ut-Tahārat fil Hikmat Amalī*, an Arabic work by Abū Alī Muhammad of Mecca. There are two other works on Sūfiism which he wrote, one called *Aosāf-ul-Ashrāf*, the Praises of the Virtuous, and the *Bahar-ul-Maānī*, the Sea of Truth. He is also the author of a work entitled *Khillāfat-nāma Ilāhī*, and another work on Prosody called *Māsr-ush-shohra*. Nasīr-uddīn died in the reign of Abākāan, the son of Halākū, on the 24th June, A.D. 1274, 18th Zil-hijja, A.H. 672, and was buried at Baghdād near the tomb of Imām Mūsī Qāzim. His brutal severity towards Ibn Hājib, a helpless captive, is an everlasting stain on the otherwise illustrious character of this distinguished man.

[*Vide* Al-Mustaasim Billāh.]

Nasr (نصر), commonly called Nasr Badakhshī, is the poetical name of Mirzā 'Abū Nasr of Badakhshān, who was an author, and died in A.D. 1668, A.H. 1078.

Nasrabadi (نصربادى). The full name of this author was Muhammad Tāhir; he was born at Nasrabād (which is in the district of Isfahān) about the year A.D. 1616, A.H. 1025, and is the author of the biography called *Tazkira Nasrābādī*, which he wrote in the year A.D. 1672, A.H. 1083, and added about nine biographies ten years after.

Nasr Ahmad (نصر احمد), a grandson of Sāmān. He was appointed governor of Bukhārā by the Khalīf Mo'tamid Billāh in A.D. 875.

[*Vide* Ismā'īl Sāmānī.]

Nasr 'Asim (نصرعاصم) was the first who introduced the diacritical marks in the Qurān, by order of the Khalīf 'Usmān.

Nasrat (نصرت), the poetical title of Dilāwar Khān, who is the author of a Dīwān. He died in A.D. 1726, A.H. 1139.

Nasrati (نصرتی), a celebrated poet of the Deccan, who is the author of a heroic poem in Hindī and the Dakhinī dialect, called *'Alī-nāma*, which contains the conquests or wars of Sulṭān 'Alī 'Adil Shāh of Bījāpūr. This prince, to whom the work was dedicated, was assassinated in A.D. 1580, A.H. 938. Nasratī is also the author of two other poems, called *Gulshan Ishq* and *Guldastae 'Ishq*; the former is the tale of Rāja Manohar and the princess Chintāwatī, and the latter contains a variety of odes and amatory poems, also dedicated to his patron the Sulṭān, and written between the year A.D. 1560 and 1570.

Nasrat Jang (نصرت جنگ). *Vide* Khān Dourān Nasrat Jang.

Nasrat Khan (نصرت خان). *Vide* Khān Dourān Nasrat Jang.

Nasrat Shah (نصرت شاه), the son of Fatha Khān, the son of Fīrōz Shāh Tughlaq. The throne of Dehlī, which was vacated by Sulṭān Mahmūd Shāh on the invasion of Amīr Taimūr in A.D. 1399, was taken possession of by Nasrat Shāh on that conqueror's return to Persia. He reigned eleven months, and was defeated in a battle by his cousin Eqbāl Khān, the son of Zafar Khān, who succeeded him in A.D. 1400. The Sūbahs had rendered themselves independent in their own governments, during the misfortunes and confusions of the empire. Gujrāt was seized upon by Khān 'Azim Zafar Khān; Mālwā by Dilāwar Khān; Qanauj, Audh, Kaṛa and Jaunpūr by Sulṭān-ush-Sharaq Khwāja Jahān; Lāhore, Dībālpūr, and Multān by Khizir Khān; Samāna by Khalīl Khān; Bayāna by Shams Khān; Mahōba by Muhammad Khān bin-Malikzada Fīrōz, and so on.

Nasrat Shah (نصرت شاه), who is called, by General Briggs, Nasīb Shāh, succeeded his father 'Alāuddīn in the government of Bengal in A.D. 1524, A.H. 930. When Ibrāhīm Lodī fell in battle with Bābar (*q.v.*) the latter ascended the throne of Dehlī in A.D. 1526, A.H. 932, when many of the adherents of the Lodī dynasty sought protection at the court of Bengal. Among others the prince Mahmūd (brother to Ibrāhīm Lodī) also took refuge there, and his sister became the wife of the king. Nasrat Shāh died in A.D. 1538, A.H. 945, and Mahmūd, who was then one of his ministers, succeeded in usurping his throne. About this period Sher Khān, who afterwards ascended the throne of Dehlī, attacked and defeated Mahmūd in action, and eventually expelled him from Bengal, whence he fled to the court of Dehlī, where, representing his grievances, the emperor Humāyūn marched with an army and took the kingdom of Bengal from Sher Khān, whom he defeated in a general action. Sher Khān, rallying his defeated troops in the year A.D. 1542, A.H. 949, succeeded in re-conquering Bengal. On his death, and after the accession of his son Salīm Shāh to the throne of Dehlī, the province of Bengal was made over to Muhammad Khān Afghān, one of the officers of his court, on whose death his son declared his independence, and proclaimed himself king under the title of Bahādur Shāh.

Nasr bin-Ahmad Samani (نصر بن احمد سامانی). *Vide* Nasr Sāmānī.

Nasr Samani, Amir (نصرسامانی امیر), the third Sulṭān or Amīr of the race of Sāmān or Samanides, was eight years old when he succeeded his father Amīr Aḥmad on the throne of Bukhārā and Khurāsān, A.D. 914, A.H. 301. He enjoyed a long and prosperous reign, and died at Bukhārā, A.D. 943, Rajab, A.H. 331, leaving all his territories in peace. He was succeeded by his son Amīr Nūh I. Rōdakī the poet lived in his time.

Nasr-ullah (نصرالله بن عبدالحمید بن ابی المعالی), the son of 'Abdul Hamīd bin-Abī ul-Ma'ālī, a poet who flourished in the reign of Bahrām Shāh of Ghaznī, in whose name he wrote the book called *Kallela Damna*, or Pilpay's Fables, which he translated from the Arabic into Persian.

[*Vide* 'Abū'l Ma'ālī, the son of 'Abdul Majīd.]

Nasr-ullah (نصرالله), king of Bukhāra, who died in the year A.D. 1860. He was a great tyrant, a greater probably never ruled a people. When on his death-bed, and so weak as to be scarcely able to make himself understood, he directed one of his wives to be brought into his room. The poor lady's brother had recently been in rebellion, and the news of his defeat and capture reached the tyrant when on his deathbed. Unable to glut his eyes with the sight of their execution, he wreaked his vengeance on his own wife, because she was sister to the rebel chief. She was beheaded before his eyes, now about to close in death. Laden with every crime that could burden the conscience of a responsible king, Nasr-ullah died, leaving the throne to his son and successor Muẓaffar-uddīn.

Nasr-ullah bin-'Abdullah al-Akhmi Alazhari (نصرالله بن عبدالله), a celebrated poet who died in the year A.D. 1173, A.H. 569. He is also called Qalakas and Alaaz al-Iskandarī.

Natiq (ناطق نیشاپوری), a poet of Naishāpūr, who came to India, and was the master of Jawāhir Singh the poet.

Natiq (ناطق), the poetical name of Gul Muhammad Khān of Dehlī. One of his works is called *Jawhar ul-Muazzim*. He died in A.D. 1848, A.H. 1264.

Nawai (نوائی), the poetical name of Amīr Alīsher.

Nawai, Mulla (نوای ملا خراسانی), of Khurāsān. He came to India and found a patron in prince Daniāl, the son of Akbar, and died at Burhānpūr in A.D. 1610, A.H. 1019. He is the author of a Dīwān.

Nawal Rae, Raja (نول رای راجه), a Kāyeth of the Saksena tribe in the service of Nawāb Safdar Jang; was by degrees raised to higher rank with the title of Rāja, and was appointed his deputy to settle the affairs of the province of Farrukhābād, which was seized by the Nawāb after the death of its ruler, Nawāb Qāem Jang. Nawal Rāe was slain in a battle fought against Aḥmad Khān, the brother of the late Nawāb, on the 3rd August, A.D. 1750, 10th Ramazān, A.H. 1163.

Nawal Singh (نول سنگه راجه), the Jāṭ Rāja of Bhartpūr, who succeeded his brother Rāe Ratan Singh after the death of Kehri Singh, his nephew, about the year A.D. 1769, A.H. 1183, and died in the year A.D. 1776, at the time when the fort of Ḍīg was besieged by Nawāb Najaf Khān. After his death his nephew Ranjīt Singh, the son of Kehrī Singh, the son of Sūrajmal Jāṭ, succeeded him.

Nawawi (نوی بن شرف), the son of Sharaf, whose proper name was Abū Zikariā Yehia; is the author of several works on different subjects. One of his works is called *Tahzīb-ul-Asmāe*, a biographical dictionary of Illustrious Men, another the *Fatāwā-an-Nawāwi*, a collection of decisions of some note. He also composed a smaller work of the same nature, entitled *'Uaiūn-al-Masāel al-Muhimmat*, arranged in the manner of question and answer. He died A.D. 1278, A.H. 676.

Nawazish Khan (نوازش خان), author of the *Gulzār Dānish*.

Nawedi (نویدی), a poet who is the author of a Dīwān. He was living in A.D. 1645, A.H. 1055. This person appears to be another Nawedī besides the one whose proper name was Khwāja Zain-ul-'Abidīn, which see.

Naweri (نویری), an historian who wrote the Life of Sulṭān Bibars, the sovereign of Egypt. He died in A.D. 1331, A.H. 732.

Nazar (نضر بن شمیل), son of Shumīl, whose proper name is Abū'l Hasan Nazar, was an author of several works. He died at Marv A.D. 820, A.H. 204.

Nazari, Hakim (نزاری حکیم). *Vide* Nizārī (Hakīm).

Nazar Muhammad Khan (نذر محمد خان), ruler of Balkh. He was defeated by the emperor Shāh Jahān, and his country taken possession of by that monarch in A.D. 1646, A.H. 1056.

Nazar Muhammad Khan (نذر محمد خان), Nawāb of Bhopāl, succeeded his father Wazīr Muhammad in March, A.D. 1816.

Nazim Hirwi (ناظم هروی), a poet of Herāt, who is the author of a Dīwān and a *Yūsaf Zalekha*, which he completed in the year A.D. 1648, A.H. 1058.

Nazim-ul-Mulk, Nazir-ul-Mulk (ناظم الملک ناظر الملک), Wazīr-uddaula, the son of Mubārik-uddaula, the Nawāb of Bengal, whom he succeeded 28th September, A.D. 1793, and died in April, A.D. 1810. He was succeeded by his son Zain-uddīn 'Al Khān.

Nazir (نظیر), the poetical title of a poet of Āgra, whose proper name was Shaikh Walī Muhammad. He was the author of a poem or Dīwān containing Persian, Urdū, and Hindī verses on different subjects. He has besides composed a *Tarjīhband* in Urdū on the *Pand-nāma* of Sa'dī. He supported himself by teaching, and his poetry is much esteemed by the bazar people of Āgra. He died at Āgra on Monday the 16th August, A.D. 1830, 26th Ṣafar, A.H. 1246, and was buried at Tājganj.

Nazir Bakhtyar Khan (ناظر بختیار خان), a man of letters who led a private life near Farīdābād, within a few miles of Āgra, and is the author of a work called *Mirat 'Alam*, or the Mirror of the World. This work contains the history of the first ten years of the emperor 'Alamgīr. He is also called Bakhtāwar Khān, which see.

Naziri (نظیری نیشاپوری), poetical title of Muhammad Husain of Naishāpūr. He came to India, where he found a patron in 'Abdul Rahīm Khān KhānKhānān. In A.D. 1603, A.H 1012, he made the pilgrimage to Mecca, and after his return he paid a visit to his patron and then settled in Aḥmadabād, Gujrāt, where he died in A.D. 1613, A.H. 1022. He is the author of a Persian Dīwān.

Nekodar (نیکودار), surname of Aḥmad Khān, king of Persia, which see.

Neko Siar, Sultan (نیکو سیر سلطان), son of Muhammad Akbar, the youngest son of 'Ālamgīr Aurangzeb.

Nigahi (نگاهی), of Arān, near Kāshān, is the author of a poem or Masnawī called *Mukhtār-nāma*, of about 30,000 verses in the metre of the *Shāh-nāma*, and one called *Mehr-wa-Mushtarī*, in imitation of Assār's Masnawī.

Nihal Singh (نیہال سنگه), Rāja of Kapūrthala. He died in the year A.D. 1852, having made his last will and testament, in which he left the throne, with nearly the whole of his kingdom, to his eldest son, Randhīr Singh, and to his two younger sons, Bikrama Singh and Suchait Singh, he assigned a jagīr of one lakh each, in case they disagreed with their brother. The Government of India was made the executor of the will. After the Rāja's death his eldest son, Randhīr Singh, ascended the gaddī. His youngest brother, Suchait Singh, fell out with him, and asked the British Government to execute his father's will in regard to him. Lord Dalhousie at once ordered the separation of a jāgīr of one lakh from the Kapūrthala Rāj, according to the provisions of the will. The other brother, Bikrama Singh, was a worthy man, and much attached to the British rule. Like his royal brother, he performed important services to the English Government in 1857, and was rewarded for them with a jāgīr in Audh and titles besides. He received his jāgīr of one lakh in Kapūrthala in 1868.

Nirpat Rae (نرپت رای), a Hindū who was in the service of Sarhindī Begam, the wife of Shāhjahān. He also built a garden at Āgra on a spot of 28 bīghas.

Nirpat Singh (نرپت سنگه), Rāja of Panna.

Nisar (نثار دهلوی), of Dehlī, a poet who is the author of a Persian Dīwān.

Nisari (نثاری), poetical name of a person who is the author of the work called *Chahār Gulzār*.

Nisbati (نسبطی تهانیسری), of Thānesar, a poet who has left a Dīwān in Persian.

Nizam (نظام), the poetical name of 'Imād-ul-Mulk Ghāzī-uddīn Khān III.

Nizam of Astrabad (نظام استرابادی), an extremely pious man, who died in A.D. 1515, A.H. 921, and left, besides a Dīwān, a Masnawī, which bears the title of *Bilqais and Sulīmān*, and contains the story of Solomon and the Queen of Sheba.

Nizam Ahmad (نظام احمد), author of the work called *Rāhat-ul-Qulūb*, Delight of Hearts, containing the sayings of Shaikh Farīd-uddīn Shakarganj, a Muhammadan saint who is buried at Ajodhan, a place commonly called Paṭan in Mulṭān.

Nizam 'Ali Khan (نظام علی خان نواب), Nawāb or Niẓām of Haidarābād in the Deccan, was the son of the famous Niẓām-ul-Mulk 'Asaf Jāh. He deposed and imprisoned his brother Salābat Jang on the 27th June, A.D. 1762, 4th Ẓil-ḥijja, A.H 1175, and assumed the government of the Deccan; but his power was much curtailed by the Marhaṭṭas, who obliged him to resign a great part of his territories and pay a tribute for the remainder. He made Haidarābād the seat of his government, reigned 42 lunar years, and died on the 17th August, A.D. 1802, 16th Rabī' II. A.H. 1217. He was succeeded by his son Nawāb Sikandar Jāh.

Nizam Bai (نظام بائی), the mother of the emperor Jahāndar Shāh, and wife of Bahādur Shāh.

Nizam Dast Ghaib (نظام دست غیب), a poet.

Nizam Haji Yemani (نظام حاجی یمنی), author of the *Latāef Ashrafī*, which explains the origin of the Sūfīs, their tenets, customs, dress, mystical phrases, moral obligations and every other particular of their sect. Dedicated to Sayyad Ashraf Jahāngīr Sāmānī, A.D. 1446, A.H 850.

Nizami (نظامی), the surname of 'Abū Majd bin-Yūsaf Al-Mutrazī, was one of the most illustrious poets of Persia.

Nizam ibn al-Husain al-Sawai (نظام ابن الحسين الساوي), author of the three last portions of the *Jāma Abbāsī*.

[*Vide* Bahā-uddīn Muhammad (Shaikh).]

Nizami Ganjawi, Shaikh (نظامی گنجوی شیخ), also called Nizām-uddīn Ganjawī, a very celebrated poet who was a native of Ganja. He is the author of the poem called *Sikandar-nāma*, the history of Alexander the Great, which is one of the most celebrated Romances of the East, and is written in admirable poetry. The number of works attributed to Nizāmī amount to nine or ten, among which are the five following poems called the Khamsa, or the five books, viz.:—

1. *Makhzan-ul-Asrār*, the Magazine of Mysteries, which he dedicated to Bahrām Shāh.
2. *Lailī-wa-Majnūn*, dedicated to Khāqān Manūchehr, ruler of Shīrwān.
3. *Khusro-wa-Shīrīn*
4. *Haft Paikar* } dedicated to Qizal Arsalān, for which he received from that chief fourteen villages free of rent.
5. *Sikandar-nāma*, which was his last work, and which he finished on the 15th October, A.D. 1200, 4th Muharram, A.H. 597, and died the same year, aged 84. This book, it seems, he had dedicated to Tughral III. Saljūqī, some years before his death, for Tughral died in A.D. 1194. Some authors say that Nizāmī died in A.D. 1209, A.H. 606.

To Nizāmī is accorded the palm for the best poem on the loves of Khusro and Shīrīn; to Jāmī, for those of Yūsaf and Zalekha; and to Hātifī, for the *most* musical, *most* melancholy version of the sad tale of Lailī and Majnūn. Nizāmī's Dīwān contains nearly 20,000 verses on all subjects.

Nizami 'Uruzi (نظامی عروضی سمرقندی), of Samarqand, was a pupil of Amīr Mu'izzī, who lived in the time of Malikshāh. He is the author of a poem entitled *Waisa-wa-Rāmīn*, and of another work in verse called *Chahār Maqāla*.

Nizam Khan Ma'jiz (نظام خان معجز), a poet, who is the author of a Dīwān in Persian.

Nizam, Mirza (نظام مرزا), a poet who died in A.D. 1629, A.H. 1039, and is the author of a Persian Dīwān.

Nizam Saqqa (نظام سقه) is the name of a person who was a water-bearer, and saved the emperor Humāyūn from being drowned in the river Chounsā after his first defeat by Sher Shāh, near Patna. It is said that the emperor, after his return to Āgra, rewarded this man by allowing him to sit on the throne for half a day and then honoured him with the dignity of an Amīr.

Nizam Shah Bahmani (نظام شاه بهمنی), son of Humāyūn Shāh the Cruel, whom he succeeded on the throne of the Deccan in September, A.D. 1461, A.H. 865, when only 8 years of age, the queen-mother acting as regent. Mahmūd Gawān, who now held the government of Berar, was appointed wazīr, and Khwāja Jahān assumed the office of Wakīl-us-Saltanat and was made governor of Tilangāna. By the happy co-operation and unanimity of these two personages and the queen-mother, a woman of great abilities, the injuries occasioned by the tyranny of the late king were soon repaired. Nizām Shāh died suddenly on the night of his marriage, being the 29th July, A.H. 1463, 13th Zi-Qa'da, A.H. 867, after a reign of two years and one month, and was succeeded by his brother Muhammad Shāh II.

Nizam, Shaikh (نظام شیخ), one of the authors of the *Fatāwā 'Alamgīrī*, a work on jurisprudence. Of the collections of decisions now known in India, none is so constantly referred to, or so highly esteemed, as this work. It was compiled by Shaikh Nizām and other learned men, and commenced in the year A.D. 1656, A.H. 1067, by order of the emperor 'Alamgīr, by whose name the collection is now designated. It was translated into Persian by order of 'Alamgīr's daughter, Zeib-un-Nisa.

Nizam, Shaikh (نظام شیخ). His poetical name was Zamīrī, which see.

Nizam-uddaula (نظام الدوله), Nawāb of Haidarābād. *Vide* Nāsir Jang.

Nizam-uddaula, Nawab (نظام الدوله), a variant of the name of Najm-ud-daula (*q.v.*), eldest son and successor of the unfortunate Mīr Ja'far, whom he succeeded as titular Nawāb Nāzim of the Eastern Provinces, or Bengal.

Nizam-uddin Ahmad, Khwaja (نظام الدین احمد خواجه), author of the *Tabqāt Akbarī*, which is also known as *Tārīkh Nizāmī*, a general history of India, dedicated to the emperor Akbar about the year A.D.

1593, A.H. 1002. He was the son of Khwāja Muhammad Muqīm of Herāt, who was one of the dependants of the emperor Bābar Shāh, and who, at the latter part of that king's reign, was raised to the office of Dīwān of the household. After the death of Bābar, when Gujrāt was conquered by Humāyūn, and the provinces of Aḥmadābād was entrusted to Mirzā 'Askarī, Khwāja Muqīm was appointed wazīr to the Mirzā. He accompanied Humāyūn to Āgra, after that monarch's defeat by Sher Shāh at Chounsā. The Khwāja subsequently served under Akbar. His son Niẓām-uddīn, in the 29th year of Akbar's reign, was appointed Bakhshī of Gujrāt, to which office he continued for a long time. He died on the 28th October, A.D. 1594, 23rd Ṣafar, A.H. 1003, on the banks of the Rāwī, and was buried in his own garden at Lāhore. The following chronogram by 'Abdul Qādir Badāonī, translated by Mr. H. M. Elliot, records the date of his death: "Mirzā Niẓām-uddīn has departed in haste; but with honour has he gone to his final doom. His sublime soul has fled to the celestial regions, and Kādirī has found the date of his death in these words, 'A jewel without price has left this world.'"

Nizam-uddin Ahmad (نظام الدین احمد بن محمد صانع), son of Muhammad Sālah, author of a work called *Majmūa'-us-Sanāyạ*, or Collection of Arts, containing some beautiful poetical inventions, compiled in the year A.D. 1650, A.H. 1060, and published in the Lithographic Press at Lucknow in A.D. 1845, A.H. 1260. He is also the author of the work called *Karamat-ul-Aulia*, containing a minute detail of the (pretended) miracles performed by the twelve Imāms and other saints of the Muhammadan faith, written in A.D. 1657, A.H. 1067.

Nizam-uddin Aulia, Shaikh (نظام الدین اولیا شیخ), styled Sulṭān-ul-Mushāekh. He was one of the noblest disciples of Shaikh Farīd-uddīn Shakarganj, and a most celebrated saint among the Musalmāns. He was born at Badāon in October, A.D. 1236, Ṣafar, A.H. 634, and died at Dehlī on Wednesday the 3rd April, A.D. 1325, 18th Rabī' I. A.H. 725, where he lies buried, and his tomb, which is in Ghayās-pūr, is visited by the Muhammadans to this day. Amīr Khusro, the poet, was one of his disciples. Sayyid Aḥmad, the father of Niẓām-uddīn, is buried at Badāon.

Nizam-uddin Ganjawi (نظام الدین گنجوی). *Vide* Niẓāmī Ganjawī.

Nizam-uddin, Mir (نظام الدین میر). *Vide* Mamnūn.

Nizam - uddin Sihali, Maulana (نظام الدین سهالی مولانا), son of Quṭb-uddīn, is the author of the *Sharah* or marginal notes on the *Sadra*, and *Shams Bāzighā*, etc., etc. He died in A.D. 1748, A.H. 1161.

Nizam-uddin Sikham, Amir (نظام الدین سخم امیر), a poet who was a contemporary of Amīr Alīsher, and a panegyrist of Mirzā Sulṭān Aḥmad of Samarqand.

Nizam-ul-Mulk (نظام الملک), a justly celebrated minister of Sulṭān Alp Arsalān, second king of the Saljūkides, and afterwards of his son Malikshāh; to his virtue and ability is attributed the success and prosperity of their reigns. After an administration of 30 years the fame of the wazīr, his wealth and even his services, were transformed into crimes. This venerable statesman, at the age of 89 years, was dismissed by his master, accused by his enemies, and stabbed by an assassin, who was a follower of Hasan Sabbāh, the Old Man of the Mountain, on Friday night the 15th October, A.D. 1092, Ramaẓān, A.H. 485, at a place called Nahāwand. His body was carried to Isfahān, where he was interred with great pomp. It is said that the assassin was suborned against him by Malikshāh, who was fatigued to see him live so long. The Sulṭān survived him 35 days only. Niẓām-ul-Mulk appears to be the author of the work entitled *Siar-ul-Malūk*. [Niẓām and Hasan Sabbāh had both been school-fellows of the poet Uman Khāyyām (*q.v.*).]

Nizam-ul-Mulk (نظام الملک آصف جاه), entitled 'Asaf Jāh, whose original name was Chīn Kulich Khān, was the son of Ghāzī-uddīn Khān Jang, a favourite Turkman officer of the emperor 'Alamgīr, under which monarch he also distinguished himself. In the reign of the emperor Farrukh-siyar, he held the government of Morādābād and was afterwards appointed governor of Mālwā, which province he restored to a flourishing condition, but the reputation he acquired rendered him an object of jealousy to the two brothers, Sayyad 'Abdullah Khān and Husain 'Alī Khān, who wished to remove him to another quarter less favourable to his interest than the frontier of the Deccan; but Niẓām-ul-Mulk, not willing to quit his post, excused himself, and resolved to seek an independent power in the Deccan. The disturbed state of that country gave him a pretence for raising troops, and turned his attention to the conquest of the Deccan. By intrigue and money he obtained possession of the fort of Asīrgaṛh about the year A.D. 1717, and procured the junction of several officers of the province.

He was pursued from Hindūstān by the force under Dilāwar Khān and another under Ālam 'Alī Khān, both of whom he defeated and slew in battle in April, A.D. 1720, and at last remained without a rival in the Deccan. In the reign of Muhammad Shāh, after the death of the two Sayyads, he was invited to court by that emperor; and on his arrival at Dehlī, the high office of prime minister was conferred on him, but Niẓām-ul-Mulk, being soon disgusted with the state of things at court, sent in his resignation, and marched off for the Deccan, and though he continued to send honorary presents on fixed occasions to the emperor, he thenceforth conducted himself, in other respects, as an independent prince, and governed the provinces of the Deccan for 30 years with great ability and success. He was present in the battle which took place between Muhammad Shāh and Nādir Shāh, but soon returned to the Deccan; and the present Niẓāms of Haidarābād are his descendants and successors. He died on the 22nd May, A.D. 1748, 4th Jumādạ II. A.H. 1161, thirty-seven days after the death of the emperor Muhammad Shāh, at a very advanced age, and was buried at Burhānpūr near the tomb of Shāh Burhān-uddīn Ghārīb. He left behind him six sons, *viz.* Ghāzī-uddīn, Nāsir Jang, Salābat Jang, Niẓām 'Alī, Basālat Jang and Mughal 'Alī, and was succeeded in the government of the Deccan by the second, Mīr Aḥmad surnamed Nāsir Jang, who was present at Burhānpūr when his father died; the eldest, Ghāzī-uddīn Khān, then residing at Dehlī in the office of Amīr-ul-'Umrā. Nāsir Jang was assassinated in December, A.D. 1750, and Muẓaffar Jang, a grandson of Niẓām-ul-Mulk, was placed on the throne and soon afterwards assassinated, in February, A.D. 1751. Salābat Jang, by the influence of the French, was then proclaimed and reigned until A.D. 1761, when he was imprisoned, and in A.D. 1763 put to death by his brother Niẓām 'Alī, who assumed the administration, and reigned till 6th August, A.D. 1803, when he died, and was succeeded by his eldest son, Mirzā Sikandar Jāh. Sikandar Jāh died on the 23rd May, A.D. 1829, and was succeeded by his son Mīr Farkhunda 'Alī Khān, the late Niẓām (1858). Niẓām-ul-Mulk appears to have been the author of a Dīwān, which was found in the Library of Tīpū Sulṭān, called *Dīwān 'Asaf Niẓām-ul-Mulk*.

[Vide *Sketch of the Hist. of Hindūstān.*]

Nizam-ul-Mulk Bahri (نظام الملک بحری), the father of Aḥmad Niẓām Shāh Bahrī, who was the first king of the Niẓām Shāhī dynasty. Niẓām-ul-Mulk was originally a Brāhman of Bījānagar, but, being taken prisoner in his infancy by the army of Sulṭān Aḥmad Shāh Bahmanī, was made a Musalmān, and was educated as one of the royal slaves. He finished his education under the same tutor with the king's eldest son, Sulṭān Muhammad, and became eminently learned in Persian and Arabic literature. On the accession of Sulṭān Muhammad II. to the throne of the Deccan, in A.D. 1463, he was raised to the rank of a thousand and the charge of the royal falconry was entrusted to him, on which account he was called Bahrī, *i.e.* a falconer. By degrees he rose to the highest honours and was appointed governor of Tilangāna. On the death of Muhammad Shāh, in A.D. 1482, he by his will became first minister to his son Sulṭān Mahmūd II. who added Bīr and other districts to his jāgīr. This he committed to his son Malik Aḥmad, who took up his residence at Khaibar and employed himself diligently in the affairs of his government, and after his father's death set up a separate dynasty in the Deccan called Niẓām Shāhī, the capital of which was Aḥmadnagar. Niẓām-ul-Mulk, who had the sole power of the administration in his hands, latterly paid little or no regard for the king's authority, and was murdered by the orders of the Sulṭān about the year A.D. 1486, A.H. 891, or some time afterwards.

Nizam-ul-Mulk Mahmud (نظام الملک محمود), the son of Abī Sa'īd Junaidī, a general and wazīr of Shams-uddīn Altamsh, king of Dehlī. He died in the reign of Sulṭāna Razia, on the mountains of Sirmor, where he had taken refuge from his enemies about the year A.D. 1238.

Nizam-ul-Mulk Muhammad (نظام الملک محمد), the son of 'Alī Sayyad Junaidī, to whom the *Jāmạ-ul-Hikayat* is dedicated, was the general of Shams-uddīn Altamsh, king of Dehlī. He was living in A.H. 622.

Nizari, Hakim (نزاری حکیم قهستانی), of Qohistān, a man of talents, but given to gaieties and pleasure, particularly to wine. He travelled much, and during his travels he met Sa'dī and other distinguished men. Towards the end of his life he retired from the world and lived by agriculture. He died in A.D. 1320, A.H. 720, and left, besides a Dīwān, two Masnawīs.

Nudar or **Nuzar** (نودر), an ancient king of Persia of the Pishdadian dynasty. [*Vide* Manūchehr.]

Nuh I. Samani, Amir (نوح سامانی امیر), the fourth king of the Samānian dynasty, succeeded his father Amīr Nasr to the throne of Khurāsān and Bukhārā in A.D. 942, A.H. 331, and died in A.D. 954, A.H. 343. His son 'Abdulmalik succeeded him.

Nuh II. Samani, Amir (نوح سامانی امیر دویم), seventh king of the Samānian dynasty, surnamed 'Abū'l Qāsim, succeeded his father Amīr Mansūr I. in

March, A.D. 976, Rajab, A.H. 365. His reign was marked by extraordinary vicissitudes of fortune. He was contemporary with Subaktagīn, a chief of high reputation, who had established a principality at Ghaznī. He died in A.D. 997, Rajab, A.H. 387, and was succeeded by his son Mansūr II.

Nunihal Singh (نونهال سنگه). *Vide* Kharag Singh, ruler of the Pānjab.

Nuras Bano Begam (نورس بانو بیگم), the wife of Shahnawāz Khān, wazīr. She was living in September, A.D. 1659, Muharram, A.H. 1070.

Nur 'Ali Shah (نور علی شاه), a leader of the Sūfī sect and disciple of Ma'sūm 'Alī Shāh, is supposed to have been poisoned, and died on the 3rd June, A.D. 1800, 10th Muharram, A.H. 1215, close to the grave of the prophet Jonas, within a league of Mousal.

[*Vide* Masūm 'Alī Shāh.]

Nuri (نوری قاضی نور الدین اصفهانی تخلص به), poetical appellation of Qāzī Nūr-uddīn of Isfahān, who died in A.D. 1592, A.H. 1000, and left a Dīwān.

Nuri (نوری), a poet who is the author of the *Maulūd Nūria* in verse, which he dedicated to Sultān 'Abū'l Muzaffar Ya'kūb Bahādur Khān, commonly called Ya'kūb Beg. He died in the year A.D. 1482, A.H. 887.

Nuri (نوری). *Vide* Nūr-uddīn Safaidūnī.

Nur Jahan Begam (نور جهان بیگم), the favourite Sultāna of the emperor Jahāngīr, was the daughter of the wazīr I'tmad-uddaula, whose tomb is at Āgra. She had attracted the notice of the prince Sultān Salīm (afterwards Jahāngīr). The Prince was, at the suggestion of his father, the emperor Akbar, sent on service; while, in order to withdraw the lady from the attentions of the prince, she was married to Sher Afgān Khān, a young Persian lately come into the service, to whom Akbar gave a jāgīr in Bengal. After the death of his father, Jahāngīr appointed Qutb-uddīn Khān, his foster-brother, the son of Shaikh Salīm Chishtī, as governor of Bengal. Qutb-uddīn Khān, on his arrival at Burdwān, was slain by Sher Afgān Khān, who was himself despatched by Qutb-uddīn's attendants. Nūr Jahān was seized and sent as a prisoner to Dehlī, and was at first placed by the emperor among the attendants of his mother, but he subsequently married her in the sixth year of his reign, A.D. 1610, A.H. 1019, changed her name, which was Mehr-un-Nisā, into Nūr Jahān (the light of the world), and raised her to honours such as had never before been enjoyed by the consort of any king in India. From this period her ascendancy knew no bounds; the emperor took no step without consulting her, and on every affair in which she took an interest, her will was law. A circumstance so uncommon in an Asiatic government is thus recorded on the coins of that period:—"By order of the emperor Jahāngīr, gold acquired a hundred times additional value by the name of the empress Nūr Jahān." Her father, Mirzā Ghayās or Ayas, was made prime minister with the title of I'tmād-uddaula; and her two brothers were raised to the first rank of 'Umrā, by the titles of Ya'tqād Khan and 'Asaf Khān. One of the accomplishments by which she captivated Jahāngīr, is said to have been her facility in composing extemporary verses. After the death of her husband, she was treated with much respect and allowed a stipend of £250,000 a year. She survived Jahāngīr eighteen years, and died aged 72 in A.D. 1645, A.H. 1055, at Lāhore, where she was buried in the mausoleum of her husband close to his tomb, some say near the tomb of her brother 'Asaf Khān on the banks of the Rāwī, at Lahore. Hugh Murray, in his *History of British India*, p. 230, by his erroneous assertion, that she was buried in the mausoleum at Āgra called the Tāj Mahal, has misguided many others. Even so late as the year A.D. 1858, the author of the *History of the Indian Revolt*, page 109, says that "this was the mausoleum of Shāh Jahān and his favourite wife Nūr Jahān." [Some further particulars may be found in the *Turks in India*, by the present Editor.]

Nur Manzil (نور منزل), name of a garden in Āgra, built by the emperor Jahāngīr, which is now called Bāgh Dahra. There is a large well in the garden, so large that it is more like a tank.

Nur Muhammad (نور محمد سید بداونی), a Sayyad of Badāon, was a learned and pious Musalmān of the sect of Naqshband. He died on the 3rd August, A.D. 1723, 11th Zi-Qa'da, A.H. 1135.

Nur-uddin Ahmad, Shaikh (نورالدین احمد شیخ), surnamed Qutb 'Alam, which see.

Nur - uddin 'Ali, Malik Mansur (نورالدین علی ملک منصور), the second Sultān of the dynasty of Tartar or Baharite Mamlūks in Egypt, was placed on the throne by the Amīrs after the assassination of his father Malik Moi'zz 'Azz-uddīn Aibak, A.D. 1257, A.H. 655, at the age of 15. His short reign of two years was troubled by continual feuds among the Mamlūk chieftains, and attempts on the part of the Ayyūbite princes of Syria to recover the lost sway of their family in Egypt; and the apprehension of an irruption of the Mughals under Halākū, who had taken Baghdād and destroyed the Khilāfat, showed the necessity of substituting a ruler of matured years and experience. The Amīr Qutuz accordingly assumed the reigns of government, A.D. 1259, A.H. 657, and no more is heard of Nūr-uddīn.

[*Vide* Malik Moi'zz 'Āzz-uddīn.]

Nur - uddin 'Ali, Malik - ul - Afzal (نورالدین علی ملک الافضل), the eldest of the seventeen sons of Sālah-uddīn; born A.D. 1170, A.H. 556. In the partition of his father's extensive dominions, which followed his death in A.D. 1193, Damascus and Southern Syria with Palestine fell to the lot of Nūr-uddīn; but in the dissensions which soon followed, he was stripped of his kingdom by his uncle Saif-uddīn 'Abū Bakr (the Saphadin of Christian writers), and his brother 'Usmān made Sultān of Egypt, A.D. 1196.

[*Vide* Malik-ul-Afzal.]

Nur - uddin Arsalan Shah, Atabak (نورالدین ارسلان شاه اتابک), a prince of Mousal and Mesopotamia, of the family of Zangī, and grand-nephew of the famous Nūr-uddīn, Sultān of Aleppo and Damascus. He succeeded his father, Azz-uddīn Masa'ūd, A.D. 1193, A.H. 589 (the year of the death of Sālah-uddīn). During a reign of 18 years he established in some measure the declining power of his house, and compelled the minor princes of his family to acknowledge his supremacy as lord paramount. He died A.D. 1210, A.H. 607, regretted by his subjects as a mild and beneficent ruler. His son Azz-uddīn, after a reign of between seven and eight years, was succeeded by an infant son bearing the title of Nūr-uddīn Arsalān II. who survived him only a few months.

Nur-uddin bin-Lutf-ullah (نور الدین بن لطف الله), better known as Hāfiz 'Abru, which see.

Nur-uddin Mahmud, Malik-ul-'Adil (نورالدین محمود ملک العادل), one of the most celebrated and powerful of the Muhammadan rulers of Syria in the age of the Crusades, born A.D. 1117, A.H. 511, was a younger son of 'Imād-uddīn Zangī, the second of the dynasty of the Atābaks of 'Iraq and Syria. At the death of his father, who was murdered by his own Mamlūks at the siege of Jabbār, A.D. 1146, A.H. 541, Nūr-uddīn, hastening to Aleppo with the signet of the deceased prince, secured the possession of that city and of his father's Syrian dominions; while Mesopotamia, with Musal for a capital, fell to the lot of the elder brother Saif-uddīn; and the feeble attempts of Alp Arsalān, a prince of the house of Saljūq, to assert his ancestral claims to the dominion of these provinces were easily frustrated by the combined power of the two brothers. The earliest exploits of the reign of Nūr-uddīn were in continuance of the Holy War which his father had assiduously waged against the Latin Christians of Palestine. Josceline de Courtenay, whose capital of Edessa had been taken by Zangī a few years previous, was signally repulsed in an attempt to recover it, and the Christian inhabitants, who had aided the enterprise, were put to the sword without mercy by command of Nūr-uddīn, who even levelled the fortifications of the town to prevent it ever again becoming a bulwark to the kingdom of Jerusalem. The recovery of this important fortress was the avowed object of the second Crusade, undertaken A.D. 1148, A.H. 543, under Louis VII. of France and the emperor Conrad; but of the mighty hosts which they led from Europe, only a miserable and dispirited remnant escaped the arrows of the Saljūqī Turks in their march through Anatolia to Palestine, the project of retaking Edessa was abandoned as hopeless, the siege of Damascus, which was attacked by the crusading monarchs in conjunction with Baldwin III. of Jerusalem, was foiled when on the eve of success by the address with which the minister of the Muslim prince Mujīr-uddīn fomented the mutual jealousies of the Christian leaders; and this vast armament, which if properly directed might have overwhelmed the rising power of Nūr-uddīn, only served by its failure to extend and confirm it. Resuming the offensive immediately after the departure of the Crusaders, he invaded the territory of Antioch, and in a pitched battle (27th June, A.D. 1149) routed and slew the prince Raymond, whose head was sent as a trophy to the Khalīf at Baghdād; and though he sustained a severe defeat in the following year from his ancient opponent Josceline de Courtenay, who surprised his camp, this disgrace was amply compensated by the captivity of that active leader, who was soon afterwards seized, while hunting, by a marauding party of Turkmans, and died in confinement, while the remaining dependencies of Edessa, the fortress of Aintab, Tellbasher, Ravenden, etc., fell almost without resistance into the power of Nūr-uddīn, whose dominions now included the whole of Northern Syria. Mujīr-uddīn was still the nominal ruler of Damascus and the southern portion, but the government was entirely in the hands of his wazīr Mo'īn-uddīn Anār, whose daughter Nūr-uddīn had married; and after the death of this able minister the inhabitants, alarmed at the capture of Ascalon by Baldwin III. in A.D. 1153, and dreading an attack from the Christians, voluntarily offered their allegiance to Nūr-uddīn (1154) as the price of his protection. The weak Mujīr-uddīn resigned his power, and sought an asylum at the court of the Khalīf of Baghdād, which then seems to have been the usual retreat of deposed princes; while Nūr-uddīn, the circuit of whose realms now encompassed on all sides by land the Latin territories in

Palestine, and extended to the frontiers of the Fatimite possessions in Egypt, fixed his capital at Damascus, which he raised from the ruinous state in which it had been left by an earthquake, and adorned with mosques, fountains, colleges, and hospitals. The death of Baldwin III. in A.D. 1162, released Nūr-uddīn from the ablest of his antagonists, his brother and successor, Almaric, or Amaury, being far inferior to Baldwin, both in prowess and abilities. Mesopotamia, ruled by the Sulṭān's nephews, acknowledged his supremacy as head of the family; he was now, by his officers, absolute master of Egypt; his name was recited with that of the Khalīf Mustazī of Baghdād in all the mosques throughout his dominions, and even in the holy cities of Mecca and Medina, which Tūrān Shāh, brother of Sālah-uddīn, had made dependencies of Egypt. But the power and glory of Nūr-uddīn had now attained their highest pitch, and the three remaining years of his life were unmarked by any memorable achievement, and disquieted by the forebodings of the future downfall of his house by the ambition of Sālah-uddīn, who, though still ostensibly acting as his lieutenant, and making public professions of loyalty and obedience, had in fact become independent master of Egypt, and eluded or disregarded all the orders of his nominal sovereign. Nūr-uddīn was preparing to march into Egypt to reduce or expel his refractory vassal, when an attack of quinsy terminated his life at Damascus after a prosperous reign of 27 years on the 26th May, A.D. 1173, 21st Shawwāl, A.H. 569. His son Malik-us-Sālah Ismā'īl, a youth 11 years old, succeeded to the titular sovereignty of his extensive dominions, but was speedily stripped by Sālah-uddīn of Damascus and the greater part of Syria, and died 8 years afterwards, reduced to the sovereignty of Aleppo and its dependencies.

Nur-uddin Muhammad, Mirza (نورالدین محمد مرزا), son of 'Alā-uddīn Muhammad, the son of Khwāja Husain. He was married to the daughter of the emperor Bābar, named Gulrukh Begam, by whom he had Salīma Sulṭāna Begam, who was married to Bairām Khān.

Nur-uddin Muhammad Ufi (نورالدین محمد عوفی), the author of the *Jāma'-ul-Hikāyāt*, a collection of historical anecdotes. This work he wrote and dedicated to Niẓām-ul-Mulk Mahmūd, a general of Shams-uddīn Altimsh, king of Dehlī, about A.D. 1230.
[*Vide* Muhammad Ufī and Sadr-uddīn Ūfī.]

Nur-uddin Safaiduni, Mulla (نورالدین سفیدونی ملا), entitled Nawāb Tarkhān, was a native of Jām in Herāt and brought up at Mashhad. He was a favourite companion of the emperor Humāyūn; and as the Pargana of Safaidūn had been conferred on him as jāgīr, he was consequently called Safaidūnī. He cut a canal from the river Jamna to Karnāl in the year A.D. 1569, A.H. 977, and named it "Shaikhū Nahr, in honour of the prince Sulṭān Salīm, who was born in that year and was nicknamed by his father the emperor Akbar, Shaikhū Bābā. He was an excellent poet and has left a Dīwān or book of odes. His poetical title was Nūrī.

Nur-uddin, Shaikh (نورالدین شیخ), an historian who wrote the history of Kashmere in Persian called *Tārīkh Kashmīr*, which in after times was continued by Haidar Malik and Muhammad 'Azim.

Nur-uddin Shirazi (نورالدین شیرازی).
Vide Hakīm Nūr-uddīn Shīrāzī.

Nur-ul-Haq (نورالحق قازی بریلی), Qāzī of Barelī. *Vide* Munai'm.

Nur-ul-Haq, Shah or Shaikh (نورالحق شاه), surnamed Al-Mashraqī, Al-Dehlawī and Al-Bukhārī, was the son of Shaikh 'Abdul Haq bin-Saif-uddīn of Dehlī. He is the author of the *Zubdat-ut-Tawarīkh*, which is an enlarged edition of his father's history, and was composed in order that by improving the style and supplying omissions, he might render it worthy the acceptance of his patron, Shaikh Farīd-uddīn Bukhārī, with whom he was connected by marriage, and who under the title of Murtaza' Khān managed for some time the affairs of the empire in the reign of the emperor Jahāngīr. He has also written a Sharah on the *Sahīh Bukhārī* and *Muslim*. He died in the reign of the emperor 'Alamgīr, A.D. 1662, A.H. 1073.

Nur-ullah Shustari, Mir (نورالله شوستری میر), who is sometimes called Nūr-ullah bin-Sharīf-ul-Husainī-ush-Shūstarī, was a nobleman at the court of the emperor Akbar. He is the author of the work called *Majālis-ul-Mominīn*. This great biographical work is a mine of valuable information respecting the most notable persons who professed the Shia faith. The author has given an entire book or section (the fifth Majālis) to the lives of the traditionists and lawyers, and has specified the principal works by each learned doctor at the end of their respective histories. Nūr-ullah was a zealous Shia and suffered in the year A.D. 1610, A.H. 1019, for his religious opinions in the reign of Jahāngīr.
[*Vide* Sūfī.]

Nur-un-Nisa Begam (نورالنسا بیگم), the daughter of Ibrāhīm Husain Mirzā by Gulrukh Begam. She was married to prince Mirzā Salīm afterwards Jahāngīr.

Nubat Khan, Nawab (نوبت خان نواب), an officer of the reign of the emperor Akbar, whose mausoleum is in old Dehlī close to the seraglio of Shāh Jahān. It was built in the year A.D. 1565, A.H. 973, and is called "Nīlī Chhatrī" on account of its having a blue canopy at the top. It is now in a ruinous state.

Nusherwan (نوشیروان عادل), surnamed 'Adil or the Just (Chosroes of the Greeks), was the son of Qubād, king of Persia, at whose death, A.D. 531, he ascended the throne of that kingdom. The accounts given by Eastern and Western authors of the successes of this king in his invasions of the Roman empire, differ but very little. Some of the former have falsely asserted that he took an emperor of the Romans prisoner; and they have all, with a partiality that, in national historians writing of this monarch, seems almost excusable, passed over the few reverses which his arms sustained. But the disgraceful peace which the emperor Justinian purchased at the commencement of the reign of Nusherwān, the subsequent war, the reduction of all Syria, the capture of Antioch, the unopposed progress of the Persian monarch to the shores of the Mediterranean, his conquest of Iberia, Calchos, and the temporary establishment of his power on the banks of the Phasis and on the shores of the Euxine, are facts not questioned by his enemies. They, however, assert, that his genius as a military leader, even when his fortune was at the highest, was checked by Belisarius, who was twice sent to oppose his progress; and whose success, considering his want of means and the character of the court he served, was certainly wonderful. In all the negotiations which took place between the emperor Justinian and Nusherwān, the latter assumed the tone of a superior. His lowest servants were treated, at the imperial court, in a manner calculated to inflame the pride and raise the insolence of a vain and arrogant nation; and the impressions which this conduct must have made were confirmed by the agreement of the Roman emperor to pay 30,000 pieces of gold, a sum which could have been of no importance to Nusherwān, but as it showed the monarch of the Western world in the rank of one of his tributaries. In a second war with the Roman emperors Justin and Tiberius, Nusherwān, who though 80 years of age, still led his armies, experienced some reverses of fortune; but the perseverance and valour of the aged sovereign were ultimately rewarded by the conquest of Dara and the plunder of Syria, A.D. 572. He died after a prosperous reign of 48 years about the year A.D. 579, and was succeeded by his son Hurmuz IV.

Muhammad, who was born during the reign of Nusherwān, A.D. 571, used to boast of his fortune in being born when so just a king reigned. This is great praise, and from a source that cannot be suspected of flattery.

Nusherwan Kirmani (نوشیروان کرمانی), an author who translated the *Ardai Virāf-nāma*, originally written in the Zend, into the modern Persian. Another translation was made by Zaratash Bairām in Persian prose and one in verse. This work was translated into English by Mr. J. A. Pope and published in London in 1816.

[*See* Ardai Virāf.]

Nuzar (نوذر), an ancient king of Persia. *Vide* Manūchehr.

Nuzhat (نزهت), poetical name of Muhammad 'Azīm of Dāmghān, a poet, who is the author of a Dīwān. He died A.D. 1724, A.H. 1137.

O

Oqtai Qaan or **Khan** (اقتاء قاآن), the eldest surviving son of Changez K͟hān, whom he succeeded to the dominions of Tartary and Northern China, being crowned as K͟hāqān or emperor A.D. 1227, A.H. 624. He died by excess of wine seven months after his brother Chug͟htāi, about the month of January, A.D. 1242, A.H. 639. He was of a mild and generous disposition, and governed his conquered subjects with impartiality and justice. As a warrior, he was brave but prudent, and as a sovereign, equitable and benevolent. He was succeeded by his son Kayūk K͟hān.

List of the K͟hāqāns of Tartary.

	A.D.
Oqtāi Qāān, eldest son of Changez K͟hān, began	1227
Kayūk K͟hān, son of Oqtāi Qāān . .	1242
Mangū Qāān, eldest son of Tūlī K͟hān	1243
Qablāi K͟hān, son of Mangū Qāān, succeeded to the kingdom of Tartary in A.D. 1259, and died in A.D. 1294. His brother Halākū K͟hān, after the death of his father, succeeded to the kingdom of Persia (*vide* Halākū K͟hān)	1259

Oodham Bai (اودهم باي), a Ḥindū lady, married to the emperor Muhammad Shāh. She was the mother of the emperor Aḥmad Shāh. On the accession of her son to the throne, she received the titles of Nawāb Bāī, Nawāb Qudsia, and Sāhiba Zamānī, and her brother Mān K͟hān was raised to the rank of 6000 with the title of Mo'taqid-uddaula.

Orkhan (اورخان), the son of Othmān or Osmān, the son of Amīr Tug͟hral. After his father's death he made himself Sulṭān of the Turks at Brusa in A.D. 1327, A.H. 727, by the destruction of his elder brothers. He added largely to the territories of his father, and formed a body of infantry, afterwards formidable to Europe—the Yenicherī or Jannisārīs. He died about the year A.D. 1359, A.H. 760, and was succeeded by his son Mūrād I. (Amarath).

P

Padmawati (پدماوتی), daughter of the Rāja of Ceylon, who was carried off forcibly by Ratan Sain, Rāja of Chittor, and taken away from him by Sulṭān 'Alā-uddin, when he conquered Chittor about the year A.D. 1303, A.H. 703. Her story called *Qissae Padmāwat* has been written in Persian poetry by Husain of Ghaznī, and there is also a version in the Bhākha language in verse, by Malik Muhammad Jāesī. There is another in Persian prose by Rāe Gobind Munshī, who wrote it in A.D. 1652, A.H. 1062, and called it *Tukfat-ul-Kulūb*, which is also a chronogram for that year. In the year A.D. 1796, A.H. 1211, another translation into Urdū verse was written by two poets, the first part by Mīr Ziyā-uddīn 'Ibrat, and the last by Ghulām 'Alī 'Ishrat.

Palas or **Palash** (پالاس) (the Valens of Roman history) succeeded his father Fīroz I. on the throne of Persia A.D. 484. He reigned four years, and was succeeded by his brother Qubād.

Panahi (پاناهی), a celebrated poet and artist, who, says 'Ashik, "broke the pencil of the Frank painters, and by painting a single rose-leaf could metamorphose Winter into Spring."

Parhez Bano Begam (پرهیز بانو بیگم), daughter of Shāh Jahān by Kandharī Begam. She died in the year A.D. 1675, A.H. 1086.

Parsaji (پرساجی), also called Parsārān Bhosla, the son of Rāghojī Bhosla, succeeded his father in the government of Berār or Nāgpūr in March, A.D. 1816, but being an idiot, he was soon afterwards strangled by Mūdhajī surnamed 'Apā Sāhib, who was acknowledged by the English.

Parsaram Bhao or **Bhosla** (پرسارام بهاؤ). *Vide* Parsājī.

Partab or **Partap Pal** (پرتاپ پال), present Rāja of Karoulī.

Partap Singh (پرتاپ سنگه), Rāja or Rānā of Udaipūr, was the son of Udai Singh, the son of Rānā Sanga. Partāp Singh, who is still idolized by his countrymen for the heroism with which he repelled the attacks of the Mughals, and preserved the germ of national independence in his wild fastnesses, reigned in A.D. 1614, and recovered the greater portion of his dominions before Akbar died. He founded the capital of Udaipūr.

Partap Singh (پرتاپ سنگه), eldest son of Rāja Mān Singh, the son or nephew of Rāja Bhagwān Dās Kachhwāhā of Amber. He died before his father. and left a son named Maha Singh, the father of Mirzā Rāja Jai Singh.

Partap Singh (پرتاپ سنگه), Rāja of Jaipūr. He succeeded his father Mādho Singh in A.D. 1778, joined the confederacy organised by Bijai Singh, Raṭhore (*q.v.*), and shared his overthrow 1790; made peace in consequence, and died in A.D. 1803, when he was succeeded by his son Rāja Jagat Singh. Don Pedro de Silva was employed by Partāp Singh as a physician, at the time when Colonel Polier visited Jaipūr in search of the Vedas of the Hindūs, about the year A.D. 1788. His son or grandson Augustine de Silva, who received a pension from the Rāja of Bhartpūr, died in the year A.D. 1856; his son Joseph de Silva settled at Āgra, and the pension was continued to him. After the death of Jagat Singh, who died without issue, Rāja Jai Singh III. posthumous, believed supposititious, succeeded him A.D. 1818.

Partap Singh Narayan (پرتاپ سنگه نارائن), Rāja of Sitāra, the son of Rāja Sāhū, commonly called Abba Sāhib, and grandson of Rāghojī Bhosla. He was closely confined by the Peshwa Bājī Rāo. After the dethronement of Apā Sāhib, he was released from confinement and formally enthroned by the English on the 11th April, A.D. 1818, and a part of the Pūna territories assigned for his support. On the 25th September, A.D. 1819, a treaty was concluded between the British Government and the Rāja, ceding to him the districts he subsequently possessed. He violated his treaty, was deposed in 1839, and died at Benares in A.D. 1847. He left only one daughter, but was reported to have adopted Balwant Singh Bhosla as her son. His next brother having died without issue in 1821, the third brother, Shāhjī *alias* Appa Sāhib, succeeded in A.D. 1839, and died 5th April, A.D. 1848, leaving no issue.

Parwana (پروانه), poetical name of Kūnwar Jaswant Singh, a son of Rāja Benī Bahādur. He died in A.D. 1832, A.H. 1248.

Parwiz, Sultan (پرويز سلطان), second son of the emperor Jahāngīr. His mother's name was Sāhib Jamāl, daughter of Khwāja Hasan, uncle of Zain Khān Koka. He was born at Kābul about the year A.D. 1590, A.H. 998, and died at Burhānpūr in his 38th year on the 28th October, A.D. 1626, 6th Ṣafar, A.H. 1035. At a place called Sulṭānpūr near Āgra, on a spot of 450 bīghas, he had built many splendid buildings now in ruins.

Pashang (پشنگ), an ancient king of Tūrān, and father of Afrāsiāb.

Payam (پيام), the poetical name of Mīr Sharaf-uddīn, who died at Agra in the year A.D. 1753, A.H. 1166.

Payami (پيامى), the poetical name of 'Abdul-Salām. He lived during the reign of Akbar.

[Vide *Āīn Translation*, i. 601. ; and Sprenger, p. 119.]

Pelaji or **Belaji** (پيلاجي), the second Gaikowār and Rāja of Baroda. In A.D. 1721, he laid the foundation of the future greatness of Baroda on the firm foundation of a most sagacious policy. He was murdered by the Rāja of Jaudpūr while engaged in the congenial occupation of lifting some of the Rāja's property. He was succeeded by his son Damajī, who was an unworthy representative of his illustrious sire. He had the audacity to declare open war against the Peshwa while the Peshwa was unencumbered with any other quarrels, and as the result of this unequal contest he lost half of his possessions, and was forced to hold the other half himself as a fief from the Peshwa. Syajī, the son of Daurojī, was a fool, and Anand Rāo was a fool, that is, not fools in the conventional and uncomplimentary sense of the word, but literally fools—persons of weak intellect. But they were the heirs to the throne, and it was sought to make them the victims of an usurpation. The British Government was horrified at this iniquity, and they stepped in to prevent it. Afterwards, when the British were engaged in their fresh struggle with the Peshwa, Baroda sided with us. The Marhaṭṭa confederacy was broken up, and in the final settlement the Gaikowār received a large accession of territory. Anand Rāo died in A.D. 1819, and was succeeded by Saiajī Rāo. Since then we have maintained what was called by the term of the treaty our *alliance* with Baroda.

Peroses (پيروسيس), of the Greeks. *Vide* Fīroz.

Perron, General (پيرون جنريل), a French adventurer who came to India as a ship's carpenter, and was employed by Niẓām 'Alī Khān of Haidarābād under the celebrated Raymond. When on the 1st September, A.D. 1798, a treaty was concluded between the English and the Nawāb, Perron with his French troops were discharged from his service and employed by Daulat Rāo Sindhia the Gwāliar Chief. When M. de Boigne, who had the command of the districts of Koel, Alīgurh etc., left India, Perron was appointed General and succeeded him, and continued in command till Lord Lake on the 29th August, A.D. 1803, took these places, and General Perron, being defeated, went over to Lake. He subsequently returned home to France.

[Vide *Fall of the Mughol Empire.*]

Persia (پارسى). For ancient kings of Persia of the 1st or Pishdādian dynasty, *vide* Kaimurs.

For ancient kings of the 2nd or Kayānian dynasty, *vide* Kaiqubād.

The ancient kings of the Greek dynasties founded after the death of Alexander the Great by his generals, who were called by the Persians Ashkānians and Ashghānians or Arsacidæ of the Greeks, are not given in this work.

For the ancient kings of Persia of the Sāsānian race called by the Persians Malūk-ut-Tawāef or Petty Kings, *vide* Ardisher Bābagān and Sassan.

The princes of the present dynasty are Kajār Turks; it was founded by Akā Muhammad (*q.v.*). *Vide* also Karīm Khān Zand. For the Safani dynasty, *vide* Ismail I.

Peshwa (پيشوا). *Vide* Bālājī Rāo Bishwanāth Peshwa.

Phul, Shaikh (پهول شيخ), a brother of the saint Muhammad Ghaus of Gwāliar, which see. He is also called Phūl Shahīd. His tomb is on a hill near the fort of Bayana.

Piari Banu (پيارى بانو), the second wife of Prince Shujāa', son of the emperor Shāh Jahān. She bore him three daughters and two sons. She was so famed for her wit and beauty, that songs were made and sung in her praise in Bengal; and the gracefulness of her person had even become proverbial. After her husband's melancholy death in Arracan she dashed her head against a stone and died, and two of her daughters poisoned themselves, while the third was married to the Rāja of that place.

Pindar Razi (پندار رازی), a poet of Rei whose proper name is Kamāl-uddīn, and who lived at the court of Sulṭān Majd-uddaula, son of Fakhr-uddaula, about the year A.D. 1009, A.H. 400, and wrote poetry in Arabic, Persian and the Dīlamī language.

Pir Ali Hajwiri, Shaikh (پیر علی هجوری شیخ), a native of Hajwīr, a village in Ghaznī, and author of the work called *Kashf-ul-Mahjūb*. He died about the year A.D. 1064, A.H. 456, and is buried at Lāhore.

Pir Badar (پیر بدر), a celebrated Musalmān saint, whose tomb is at Chitagānw in Bengal and is evidently of great antiquity. There is a stone scraped into furrows, on which, it is said, Pīr Badar used to sit; there is also another bearing an inscription, which from exposure to the weather, and having on it numerous coats of whitewash, is illegible. There is a mosque near the tomb, with a slab of granite, bearing an illegible inscription, apparently from the Qurān. At a short distance is the Masjid of Muhammad Yāsīn with an inscription conveying the year of the Hijrī 1136. (A.D. 1724).

Pir Muhammad (پیر محمد جهانگیر) was the eldest son of Jahāngīr Mirzā and grandson of Amīr Taimūr. He was sent to India some time before his grandfather, *viz.* in the year A.D. 1397, A.H. 799, and had already taken possession of Multān when his frandfather invaded it. He was a brave prince and his grandfather had bequeathed his crown to him, but he was at Qandahār when his grandfather died; and Khalīl Sulṭān, another grandson, who was present with the army, obtained the support of several powerful chiefs, and the possession of Samarqand, the capital of the empire. A contest took place between these princes, which terminated unfavourably for Pīr Muhammad, who was put to death by the treachery of his own minister six months after the death of his grandfather, A.D. 1405, A.H. 808.

Pir Muhammad (پیر محمد). *Vide* Aghar Khān.

Pir Muhammad, Mulla, of Shirwan (پیر محمد ملا شروانی), an officer who held the rank of 5000 in the time of the emperor Akbar. He was drowned in the river Narbada in pursuit of Bāz Bahādur, king of Mālwā, A.D. 1561, A.H. 969.

Pir Muhammad Shah (پیر محمد شاه), a Pīrzāda or Mutwallī of the Dargāh at Saloun, who died in A.D. 1688, A.H. 1099.

Pirthi Raj (پرتهی راج), the Chauhān Rāja of Ajmere and Dehlī who, in his last battle with Shahāb-uddīn Ghorī in A.D. 1192, was taken prisoner and conveyed to Ghaznī, where he stabbed himself, or was put to death. He is also called Pithoura. He was sung by the poet Chand (*q.v.*).

Pirthi Raj Rathor (پرتهی راج راتهور), a Hindū chief who held a high rank in the service of the emperor Shāh Jahān, and died in the Deccan A.D. 1656, A.H. 1066. After his death his brother Rām Singh and his son Keisrī Singh were raised to suitable ranks.

Pirthi Singh (پرتهی سنگه). *Vide* Mādho Singh Kachhwāha.

Pithura (پتهورا). *Vide* Pirthī Rāj the Chauhān Rāja.

Pran Sukh (پران سک), a learned Hindū, of the Kāyeth caste, who is the author of an Inshā or specimens of letter writing, entitled *Inshāe Rāhat Jāt*, written in the reign of the emperor Muhammad Shāh and completed in the year A.D. 1750, A.H. 1163.

Prithi Raj (پرتهی راج). *Vide* Pirthī Rāj.

Puranmal (پورنمل راجه), Rāja of Amber (now called Jaipūr). He is also called Bihārī Mal, which see.

Purbahae Jami (پوربهاء جامی), a poet, who was a native of Jām, a village in Herāt. He flourished in the reign of Arghūn Khān and was contemporary with Humām Tabrezī.

Purdil (پردل), a poet who flourished in the time of 'Alamgīr, and is mentioned in the *Mirat-ul-Khayāl*.

Pur Hasan Asfaraini (پور حسن اسفراینی), a very pious Musalmān who was a native of Asfarāen. He was a disciple of Shaikh Jamāl-uddīn Zākir, a contemporary of Shaikh Razī-uddīn Alī Lālā, and a good poet, and has left a Dīwān consisting of Persian and Turkish ghazals. In his Persian poems, he uses for his poetical appellation his own name, viz. Pūr Hasan, and in his Turkish compositions, Hasan Ughli.

Q

Qaan. *Vide* Khān.

Qablai Quan (قبلاء قاآن), or Khān, more properly Qawaila Qāān, Grand Khān of the Mongols and Emperor of China, was the son of Mangū Khān, emperor of Tartary, and great-grandson of Chingiz Khān. He succeeded his father about the year A.D. 1259, A.H. 655, and founded the Yueen dynasty in China. Being ordered by his father Mangū, then Khakan of the Mongols, to subjugate Corea and China, he entered China with an immense army in A.D. 1290, drove out the Tartars of the Kin dynasty and took possession of North China. In 1279 he completed the ruin of the Song dynasty by invading and subduing Southern China, so that his dominion now extended from the Frozen Occean to the Straits of Malacca and from Corea to Asia Minor—an extent of territory the like of which had never before, and has seldom since, been governed by any one monarch. The rule of the Mughuls, hitherto severe and barbarous, changed its character in the reign of this prince, who adopted entirely the manners of the Chinese, and who is regarded, even by that people, as one of the best and most illustrious of their emperors. He died in A.D. 1294, A.H. 693. English readers will recognise the "Khubla Khān" of S. T. Coleridge.

[*Vide* Yule's *Marco Polo.*]

Qabul (قبول), the poetical appellation of Mirzā 'Abdul Ghānī Beg of Kashmere, who was a Sūfī and a pupil of Jōyā, the brother of Gōyā. He died in A.D. 1726, A.H. 1136.

Qabus (قابوس), a prince of the house of Shamgīr, or Dashmagīr, whose capital was Rei, and afterwards Jurjān in Khurāsān. Shamgīr was succeeded by his son Bīstūn, of whom nothing particular is related. But the next of this family, Qābūs, whose title was Shama'-ul-Mulk, or "the candle of the kingdom," is celebrated for his extraordinary wisdom and learning. He was, by the instigation of his son Manūchehr, slain by his own mutinous officers A.D. 1012, A.H. 403, whose excesses he had probably desired to restrain. He was succeeded by his son Manūchehr, who submitted to the power of Sulṭān Mahmūd of Ghaznī; but that monarch not only continued him in his family possessions, but gave him his daughter in marriage. He died A.D. 1070, A.H. 463, and was succeeded in the government of Jurjān by his son Gīlān Shāh. Qābūs is the author of several works, one of which is called *Kamāl-ul-Balāghat.*

Qadard (قادرد), the son of Ja'far Beg Dāūd, and brother of Alp Arsalān of the race of Saljūk. He was installed by Tughral Beg, his uncle, in A.D. 1041, A.H. 433, and became the first Sulṭān of the Saljūk dynasty of Kirmān, where he reigned 32 years and died of poison in A.D. 1072, A.H. 465, by order of Malik Shāh.

The following is a list of the Sulṭāns of Kirmān of the race of Saljūk.

	A.D.	A.H.
Qādard, the son of Ja'far Beg Dāūd . . . . . began	1041	433
Sulṭān Shāh, the son of Qādard .	1072	465
Tūrān Shāh, brother of Sulṭān Shāh	1074	467
Īrān Shāh, son of Tūrān Shāh, a tyrant who was slain in 1100 .	1096	489
Arsalān Shāh, son of Kirmān Shāh, reigned 42 years . . .	1100	494
Mughīs-uddīn Muhammad, son of Arsalān	1141	536
Tughral Shāh, son of Muhammad	1156	551
Bahrām Arsalān and Tūrān Shāh, sons of Tughral, dispute succession	1169	565
Muhammad Shāh, son of Bahrām Shāh, who after the death of his father and two uncles ascended the throne of Kirmān, was dispossessed by Malik Dīnār, a Turk of the tribe of Ghuz, in A.D. 1187, A.H. 583. Thus ended the Saljūk dynasty of Kirmān of the race of Qādard.		

Qadar Khan (قادرخان). *Vide* Qadr Khān.

Qadir (قادر), the poetical title of Shaikh 'Abdul Qādir Badāonī. *Vide* 'Abdul Qādir.

Qadir (قادر), the poetical appellation of Wazīr Khān, an inhabitant of Āgra, who was in great favour with 'Alamgīr and his two successors. He died in A.D. 1724, A.H. 1136, and is the author of a Dīwān.

Qadir (قادر), the poetical name of Shaikh 'Abdul Qādir, who was employed as Munshī by Prince Muhammad Akbar, son of 'Alamgīr. He is the author of a Dīwān.

Qadir or **Qadiri** (قادر یا قادری), the poetical name of 'Abdul Qādir of Badāon.

Qadiri (قادری), the poetical title of Prince Dārā Shikōh, the eldest son of the emperor, Shāh Jahān.

Qadir Billah (قادر بالله). *Vide* Al-Qādir Billah.

Qadir Shah (قادر شاه), of Mālwā. After the occupation of Mālwā by the emperor Humāyūn, that monarch had left his own officers in the government of that kingdom, but shortly after his return to Āgra Mallū Khān, one of the officers of the late Khiljī government, retook all the country lying between the Narbada and the town of Bhilsa, after a struggle of twelve months against the Dehlī officers; whom having eventually subdued, he caused himself to be crowned in Manḍo, under the title of Qādir Shāh of Mālwā. He reigned till the year A.D. 1542, A.H. 949, when Sher Shāh took Mālwā, and conferred the government on Shujaa' Khān, his minister and relative.

Qadr Khan (قدر خان), king of Khutan, who was a contemporary of Sultān Mahmūd of Ghaznī. He was living between the years A.D. 1005 and 1024. It is related of him that he was very fond of music, and that four bags were constantly placed round his sofa, and as he listened to the song he cast handfuls of gold and silver to the poets.

Qael (قایل), poetical name of 'Abdullah, a Persian poet.

Qaeli or **Qabili** (قایلی), of Sabzwār, is the author of a biography or Tazkira of poets. He died in A.D. 1548, A.H. 955.

Qaem (قایم), poetical appellation of Qāem Khān, who held the post of captain in the service of Wazīr Muhammad Khān, Nawāb of Tōnk, the son of Amīr Khān. He is the author of an Urdū Dīwān, which he completed and published in A.D. 1853, A.H. 1270.

Qaem-bi-amr-ullah (قایم بامرالله) was the son of Madhī, the first Khalīf of the Fatimites in Africa. He rebuilt the city of Massilah in Africa in the year A.D. 927, A.H. 315, and called it Muhammadia.

Qaem Billah (قایم بالله), Khalīfa of Baghdād. *Vide* Al-Qāem Billah.

Qaem Jang or **Qayum Jang** (قایم جنگ), the son of Muhammad Khān Bangash, Nawāb of Farrukhābād, whom he succeeded in June, O.S. 1743, Jumāda I. A.H. 1156. He made war by the instigation of the Wazīr, Nawāb Safdar Jang, with the Rohelas of Kaṭer, now called Rohilkhanḍ, after the death of their chief, 'Alī Muhammad Khān, but was defeated and slain on the 10th November, O.S. 1749, 10th Ẕil-ḥijja, A.H. 1162, and his estates confiscated by the wazīr. The principal servants of the deceased were sent prisoners to Allahābād; but his mother was allowed to keep the city of Farrukhābād and twelve small districts for the support of the family, as they had been conferred on it in perpetuity by the emperor Farrukh-siyar. The conquered country was committed to the care of the wazīr's deputy, Rāja Nawāb Rāe, who was soon afterwards slain in battle against Aḥmad Khān, the brother of Qāem Jang, who took possession of the country.

Qahir Billah (قاهر بالله). *Vide* Al-Qāhir Billah, Khalīfa of Baghdād.

Qahqari (قهقری). *Vide* Najm-uddīn Abū'l Hasan. In some of our Biographical Dictionaries his name is spelt Cahcari.

Qaisar (قیصر), a poet of the tribe of Shāmlū, who is commonly called Qaisar Shāmlū.

Qaisar (قیصر), poetical name of Prince Khurshaid Qadr, the son of Mirzā Asmān Qadr, the son of Mirzā Khurram Bakht, the son of Prince Mirzā Jahāndār Shāh, the son of Shāh 'Alam, king of Dehlī.

Qaisari Kirmani (قیصری کرمانی), a poet of Kirmania.

Qalandar (قلندر), author of the work called *Sirāt-ul-Mustaqīm*, which he composed in A.D. 1405, A.H. 808, and dedicated to Abū'l Muzaffar Husain Shāh bin-Mahmūd Shāh bin-Ibrāhīm Shāh of Jaunpūr.

Qalanisi (قلانیسی), surname of Abdullah bin-Muhammad, an Arabian author, who died in A.D. 1121, A.H. 515.

Qamar-uddin Khan, Wazir (قمرالدین خان وزیر), whose original name was Mīr Muhammad Fāzil, was the son of Ya'tmād-uddaula Muhammad Amīn Khān, wazīr, and was himself appointed to that office, with the title of Ya'tmād-uddaula Nawāb Qamar-uddīn Khān Bahādur Nasrat Jang, by the emperor Muhammad Shāh, after the resignation of Nizām-ul-Mulk Asaf Jāh, in A.D. 1724, A.H. 1137. He was sent under Prince Aḥmad on the invasion of Aḥmad Shāh Abdālī to oppose him, but was killed by a cannon ball, while at prayers in his tent, during the battle of Sarhind on the 11th March, O.S. 1748, 11th Rabī' I. A.H. 1161.

Qamar-uddin, Mir (قمر الدين مير), whose poetical title is Minnat, which see.

Qambari (قنبری نیشاپوری) or Qanbarī, a poet of Naishāpūr, flourished in the time of Sulṭān Bābar, who died A.D. 1457, A.H. 861.

Qandahari Begam (قندهاری بیگم), the first wife of the emperor Shāh Jahān. She was the daughter of Muzaffar Husain Mirzā Safwī, of the royal house of Persia, who was the son of Sulṭān Husain Mirzā, the son of Bahrām Mirzā, the son of Shāh Ismā'īl I. of Persia. When Akbar Shāh, in the third year of his reign, made over Qandahār to Shāh 'Abbās, king of Persia, the latter conferred the government of that province on his nephew Sulṭān Husain Mirzā, after whose death his son Muzaffar Husain succeeded him. His three brothers came to India in the 38th year of Akbar (A.D. 1592), and Muzaffar Husain followed them afterwards, was received by the emperor with the greatest kindness, and honoured with the rank of 5000 and the jāgīr of Sambhal. His sister Qandahārī Begam was married in September, A.D. 1610, Rajab, A.H. 1019, to Prince Khurram (afterwards Shāh Jahān), the son of the emperor Jahāngīr, and received the title of Qandahārī Begam, because she was born at Qandahār. The year of her death is unknown. She lies buried at Āgra, in the centre of a garden called Qandahārī Bāgh. The building over her tomb, which is in the vault, is converted into a dwelling place; it is a beautiful edifice, and now belongs to the Rāja of Bhartpūr.

Qaplan Beg (قپلان بیگ), of the Qushchī family, was born in India and served under Khān-Khānān in the Deccan with great distinction, and was in high favour with Jahāngīr. He is the author of a Dīwān and a Maṣnawi; the latter is called *Māh Dost*, which celebrates the loves of Rustam and Rūdāba.

Qara Arsalan (قرا ارسلان) (which signifies, in Turkish, a black lion), surnamed 'Imād-uddīn, was the son of Dāūd, the son of Sukmān bin-Artak. Nūr-uddīn Mahmūd was his son, to whom Sālah-uddīn (Saladin) gave the city of 'Amid or Qara 'Amid in Mesopotamia A.D. 1183, A.H. 597. His name is to be found in some of our Biographical Dictionaries under Cara Arslan.

Qarachar Nawian (قراچار نویان), name of the wazīr and son-in-law of Changez Khān.

Qara Ghuz (قرا غز), a Beglarbeg of Natolia, whom our historians call Caragossa. He was impaled near Qara Hisār by Shāh Qulī in the reign of Bāyazīd II. emperor of the Turks.

Qara Khan (قرا خان). *Vide* Sadr-uddīn bīn-Ya'kūb.

Qarak Shah (قرک شاه). *Vide* Shāh Qaṛak.

Qara Muhammad Turkman (قرا محمد ترکمان). The Turkmāns of Asia Minor were divided into two great tribes, the Qara Koinlū and Aqa Koinlū, *i.e.* the tribes of "Black and White Sheep," from their carrying the figures of these animals in their respective standards. Qara Muhammad, the founder of the first dynasty, left his small territories, of which the capital was Van, in Armenia, to his son, Qara Yūsuf, who though possessed of considerable power was compelled to fly before the sword of Timur. When that conqueror died, he returned from Egypt, and was victorious in an action with Sulṭān Aḥmad Jālāyer Ilkānī, the ruler of Baghdād, whom he made prisoner and put to death in A.D. 1410, A.H. 813. After this success he collected an army of 100,000, and was preparing to attack Sulṭān Shāhrukh, the son of Amīr Timur, when he was suddenly taken ill and died near Tabrez in A.D. 1411, A.H. 814. He was succeeded by his son Sikandar Turkmān, who was defeated by Shāhrukh in A.D. 1421, A.H. 824. Sikandar after this had several battles with Shāhrukh, but was at last slain by his son Qubād A.D. 1437, A.H. 841, when Shāhrukh added Rei to his own possessions, and gave Tabrez to Jahān Shāh, the brother of Sikandar. Jahān Shāh, after a long reign of 30 lunar years, fell in one of the first actions he fought with Uzzan Hasan, chief of the Turkmāns of the White Sheep, in November, A.D. 1467, Rabī' II. A.H. 872.

Qarari (قراری), a Persian poet. *Vide* Abul Fath Gīlānī.

Qara Yusuf (قرا یوسف). *Vide* Qara Muhammad.

Qarmat (قرمط), or Qarmaṭa, a famous impostor, named Abū Zar, who in the year A.D. 891 became the head of a sect called Qarmaṭī or Karamatians, which overturned all the principles of Muhammadanism. He came from Khozistān to the villages near Kūfa, and there pretended great sanctity and strictness of life, and that God had enjoined him to pray fifty times a day; pretending also to invite people to the obedience of a certain Imām of the family of Muhammad; and this way of life he continued till he had made a very great party, out of whom he chose twelve apostles to govern the rest, and propagate his doctrines. Afterwards, his courage failing him, he retired to Syria, and was never heard of any more. This sect began in the Khilāfat of Al-Mo'tamid; they multiplied greatly in Arabian Irāq or Chaldea, and maintained perpetual wars against the Khalīf. In the year A.D. 931, they besieged and took the city of Mecca, filled the well Zamzam with dead bodies, defiled and plundered the temple and carried away the black stone; but they brought it again in A.D. 950, and fastened it to the seventh pillar of the portico, giving out that they had both taken it away, and brought it back again, by express order from heaven. This sect was dissipated by degrees, and at last became quite extinct.

[*Vide* Abū-Zarr Qarmaṭī.]

Qarmati (قرمتی), or Qaramatian, a follower of Qarmaṭ, which see.

Qasim (قاسم اکبر ابادی), of Āgra, author of the *Zafar-nāma Akbarī*, or book of the victory of Akbar Khān, the son of Dost Muhammad Khān, which he completed in A.D. 1844, A.H. 1260. It is a poem and contains an account of the late wars in Kābul by the British.

Qasim (قاسم), the poetical name of Hakīm Mīr Qudrat-ullāh, who is the author of a Tazkira or Biography of poets.

Qasim Ali Khan, Mir (قاسم علیخان میر), commonly called Mīr Qāsim, was the son-in-law of Mīr Ja'far 'Alī Khān, the Nawāb of Bengal. The English, deceived by his elegance of manners and convinced of his skill in the finances of Bengal, raised him to the maṣnad in the room of his father-in-law in A.D. 1760, A.H. 1174. He, in the latter years of his government, retired to Munger, and, actuated by a keen resentment against the English for their extensive encroachments on his authority and the commerce of his country, formed the plan of throwing off their yoke and annihilating their influence in Bengal; but was deposed and defeated, in a battle fought on the Odwa Nāla on the 2nd August, A.D. 1763, 22nd Muḥarram, A.H. 1177, and the deposed Nawāb Ja'far 'Alī Khān was again placed on the Maṣnad. Qāsim 'Alī, incensed to madness at these reverses, fled from Munger to Patna, and there cruelly ordered the massacre of the English in his power: there were fifty gentlemen, Messrs. Ellis, Hay, Lushington, and others, and 100 of lower rank. On the 5th October they were brought out in parties, and barbarously cut to pieces, or shot under the direction of a German, named Samrū or Sombre. Munger fell to the English early in October. Patna was stormed on the 6th November, and the Ex-Nawāb Qāsim 'Alī fled to the wazīr of Audh, with his treasures and the remnant of his army. On the 23rd October, A.D. 1764, Major Carnac fought the celebrated battle of Buxar, completely routing the wazīr Shuja-uddaula's army. The following day the Mughul emperor Shāh 'Alam threw himself on the protection of the British, and joined their camp with the imperial standard of Hindūstān. The British army advanced to overrun Audh. The wazīr refused to deliver up Qāsim 'Alī, though he had seized and plundered him. Qāsim 'Alī made his escape at first into the Rohela country, with a few friends and some jewels, which he had saved from the fangs of his late ally, the wazīr, and found a comfortable asylum in that country; but his intrigues rendered him disagreeable to the chief under whose protection he resided, he was obliged to leave it, and took shelter with the Rānā of Gohad. After some years' residence in his country he proceeded to Jōdhpūr, and from thence came to try his fortune in the service of the emperor Shāh 'Alam about the year A.D. 1774, A.H. 1188, but was disappointed, and died shortly afterwards in A.D. 1777, A.H. 1191, at Kotwal, an obscure village near Dehlī, unpitied even by his own family. With Qāsim 'Alī ended, virtually, the powers of the Sūbadārs of Bengal.

[Vide *Fall of the Mughol Empire*; also Broome's *History of the Bengal Army*.]

Qasim Ali Khan, Nawab (قاسم علیخان نواب), uncle to the Nawāb of Rāmpūr. He was living in Bareli in 1869, and his daughter was murdered on the 22nd December of that year.

Qasim Anwar, Sayyad (قاسم انوار سید), surnamed Ma'īn-uddīn Alī, a great mystical poet, called from his knowledge and writings the "diver into the sea of truth," the "falcon of the transcendent plains," the "profound knower of the world of spirits," the "key of the treasury of secrecy," etc. He was born at Tabrez; and was a member of a considerable family of the tribe of Sayyad, descended from the same stock as the Prophet. In his youth he dedicated himself, under the guidance of Shaikh Sadr-uddīn Mūsā Ardibelī, to the contemplative life and deep study of the Sūfīs. He then journeyed to Gīlān, where he soon acquired great fame; and subsequently went into Khurāsān. During his residence at Herāt he obtained such celebrity, and was surrounded by so many princes and learned men, his followers, that Mirzā Shāhrukh (the son of Amīr Timur), moved by jealousy of the Sayyad, and attentive to the danger of the increase of the Sūfī creed, commanded him to retire from the capital. In order to mitigate the harshness of this command Bāisanghar, the son of Shāhrukh, a learned and noble prince, took upon himself to make it known to the Sayyad, which he did in the most humane manner, inquiring of him, in the course of conversation, why he did not follow the counsel contained in his own verse. The Sayyad inquired in which verse, and Bāisanghar immediately quoted the following:—

" Qāsim, cease at once thy lay ;
Rise and take thy onward way ;
Other lands having waited long,
Worthy thy immortal song ;
Give the bird of paradise
What the vulture cannot prize;
Honey let thy friends receive,
To thy foes the carrion leave."

The Sayyad thanked him, and immediately set out for Balkh and Samarqand, where he remained for a time. He afterwards, however, returned to Herāt, where, as before, he was constantly followed by great and powerful men. His death occurred in the village of Kharjard in Jām, near Herāt, where a garden had been bought for him by his disciples, in which he greatly delighted. This event took place in the year A.D. 1431, A.H. 835, and his tomb was erected in the very garden which he so much enjoyed. Amīr Alīsher afterwards piously endowed it. A book of Odes is the only work he has left behind, in which he uses Qāsim for his poetical name.

Qasim Arsalan (قاسم ارسلان مشهدی), of Mashhad, a poet who was a descendant of Arsalān Jāzib, a general of Sultān Mahmūd of Ghaznī. He flourished in the time of the emperor Akbar, and was in great favour with that monarch. He died in A.D. 1587, A.H. 995, and has left a Dīwān.

Qasim Barid Shah I. (قاسم برید شاه) was the founder of the Barīd Shāhī dynasty in the Deccan. He was a Turkish or Georgian slave, became by degrees the wazīr of Mahmūd Shāh II. king of the Deccan, and assumed such power as to take upon himself the entire government of the kingdom. He treated the king as a mere pageant, and about the year A.D. 1492, A.H. 898, by the advice of 'Adil Shāh, Nizām Shāh and 'Imād Shāh, became entirely independent, and, leaving to the king only the town and fort of Ahmadābād Bīdar, read the public prayers and coined money in his own name. After having ruled his estate for a period of twelve years, during the lifetime of his sovereign, he died in the year A.D. 1504, A.H. 910, and his son Amīr Barīd succeeded him in office, and assuming still greater power deprived Mahmūd Shāh of what little power had been left him by his father. Seven princes of this family have reigned since their establishment in the capital of Ahmadābād Bīdar; their names are as follow:—

	A.D.
Qāsim Barīd I . . . . . began	1492
Amīr Barīd	1504
Alī Barīd ; first who assumed royalty .	1542
Ibrāhīm Barīd Shāh	1562
Qāsim Barīd Shāh II	1569
Alī Barīd Shāh II	1579
Amīr Barīd Shāh II	1602

Qasim Barid Shah II. (قاسم برید شاه) succeeded his brother Ibrāhīm Barīd Shāh to the government of Ahmadābād Bīdar in A.D. 1569, A.H. 977, and died after a reign of three years in A.D. 1572. He was succeeded by his son Mirzā 'Alī Barīd II. who was deposed after a reign of 27 years by his relative Amīr Barīd II. who ascended the throne in A.D. 1609, and was the last of this dynasty.

Qasim Beg Halati (قاسم بیگ حالتی). *Vide* Hālatī.

Qasim Diwana (قاسم دیوانه), a poet who was probably alive in A.D. 1724, A.H. 1136, and is the author of a Dīwān.

Qasimi (قاسمی). His proper name is Maulānā Majd-uddīn, a poet of Khwāf in Khurāsān. He is the author of the work *Rauzat-ul-Khuld*, which he wrote in imitation of the *Gulistān of Sa'dī*.

Qasimi (Dervish) (قاسمی تونی), of Tūn in Persia, who went about like a dervish and wrote poetry. He lived in the 9th century of the Hijra.

Qasim Kahi, Maulana (قاسم کاهی مولانا), a Sayyad, whose proper name was Najm-uddīn and surname Abū'l Qāsim. He was a pupil of 'Abdul Rahmān Jāmī; he accompanied Mirzā Kāmrān, the brother of the emperor Humāyūn, on a pilgrimage to Mecca from Herāt, and after the death of that prince in A.D. 1557, A.H. 964, he came to India in the reign of the emperor Akbar. For a long period he remained with Bahādur Khān, the brother of 'Alī Qulī Khān, at Benāras, and after his demise he came to Āgra, where he passed the remainder of his life, and died there on the 17th April, A.D. 1580, 2nd Rabī' II. A.H. 988, aged 110 lunar years. He was buried at Āgra at a place called Madār Darwāza. Maulānā Qāsim Arsalān, another poet, and Shaikh Faizī wrote the chronograms of his death. 'Abdul Qādir Badāonī calls him an atheist and a disgusting cynic.

Qasim Khan (قاسم خان), Sūbadār of Kābul in the reign of the emperor Akbar Shāh. He was murdered by one Muhammad Zamān, who gave out that he was the son of Shāhrukh Mirzā. He had held possession of Badakshān for some years, but after his defeat by 'Abdullah Khān Uzbak, he came to Kābul and was confined by Qāsim Khān, whom he murdered about the year A.D. 1600, and was consequently put to death by Muhammad Hāshim, the son of Qāsim Khān.

Qasim Khan Jawini, Nawab (قاسم خان جوینی نواب), was a nobleman of the court of the emperors Jahāngīr and Shāh Jahān, and held the rank of 5,000. He was a native of Sabzwār and was married to Manija Begam, the sister of Nūr Jahān, consequently he was sometimes in jest called by the officers of the court "Qāsim Khān Manija." He is the author of a Dīwān, and his poetical name is Qāsim. He succeeded Fidāī Khān in the government of Bengal in the first year of Shāh Jahān, A.D. 1628, A.H. 1037. He slew about 10,000 Portuguese (men and women) and drove the rest from Huglī, of which place he took possession, but died three days afterwards, A.D. 1631, A.H. 1041. He had built a very grand house at Āgra, on 10 bighas of land, and on 20 bighas of land the garden was built, of which no traces now remain.

Qasim Khan, Shaikh (قاسم خان شیخ فتحپوری), of Fathapūr Sīkrī, entitled Muhtashim Khān, brother of Islām Khān. He was a noble of the rank of 4,000 in the reign of the emperor Jahāngīr, who appointed him governor of Bengal after the death of his brother in A.D. 1613, A.H. 1022. He invaded Asām, and his troops were mostly killed in a night attack by the Asāmīs, on which account he was recalled to court. He died not long afterwards.

Qasim Qadiri, Shaikh (قاسم قادری شیخ), also called Shāh Qāsim Sulaimānī, a Musalmān saint whose tomb is at Chunār. His son Shaikh Qabīr, commonly called Bālā Pīr, is buried at Qanauj, where he died in the year A.D. 1644, A.H. 1054. The shrine of Shāh Qāsim Sulaimānī at Chunār is the only notable Muhammadan endowment in the Mirzāpūr District supported from the income of rent-free lands and a Ma'āsh Rozīna pension.

Qasim Shah (قاسم شاه). *Vide* Shāh Qāsim.

Qasim Shirazi (قاسم شیرازی), a native of Shīrāz, and author of the *Timurnāma*, a very beautiful poem on the conquest of Amīr Timur.

Qasim Sulaimani (قاسم سلیمانی). *Vide* Qāsim Qādirī.

Qasim Tibbi (قاسم طیبی), author of an Inshā.

Qassab (قصاب), the poetical name of an author.

Qastalani (قسطلانی), the surname of Ahmad bin-Alī al-Khātīb. He is so called because he was born at Qastalā. He is the author of several works, among which is the history called *Mawāhib Ladīna* or *Mawāhib-ud-Dunnī*, an accurate history of the first forty years of Muhammad, being the period before his assuming the prophetic character. He died in the year A.D. 1517, A.H. 923. Besides him there were other authors of this surname, *viz.* Ahmad-bin-Muhammad al-Qastalānī, who died A.D. 1527, A.H. 933, Ahmad bin-Ibrāhīm bin-Yahya-al-Yazdī-al-Qastalānī, and Mulla Maslah-uddīn Mustafā Qastalānī, who died A.D. 1495, A.H. 901. They were all born at Qastalā, a city in Persia.

Qatil, Mirza (قتیل مرزا), the poetical name of Mirzā Muhammad Hasan. He was a native of Dehlī, and a Hindū of the tribe of Khattrī, but became a convert to Muhammadanism. He was an excellent Urdū and Persian poet, and died at Lucknow in the time of Ghāzī-uddīn Haidar, then nawāb of that country, A.D. 1817, A.H. 1232. He is the author of several works, amongst which are:—*Nuskha Shairat-ul-Amānī*, dedicated to Mīr Amān 'Alī, *Nahr-ul-Fasāhat*, a Persian grammar, *Chahār Sharbāt*, and a Dīwān.

Qatran (قطرن). *Vide* Qitrān.

Qawami Matarzi (قوامی مطرزی), a great poet who was a native of Mutarāz, a city in Persia, and is an author. He was a brother of Shaikh Nizāmī Ganjwī.

Qawami Maulana Muzaffar (قوامی مولانا مظفر), a celebrated poet.

Qawam-uddin Hasan, Haji (قوام الدین حسن حاجی), wazīr to Shāh Shaikh Abū Is-hāq, ruler of Shīrāz. He was a man of great liberality, and one of the patrons of the celebrated Persian poet Khwāja Hāfiz, who has praised him in many of his odes. He died, during the siege of Shīrāz by Mubāriz-uddīn Muhammad Zafar, on Friday the 12th April, A.D. 1353, 6th Rabī I. A.H. 754.

Qawam-uddin Khwaja (قوام الدین خواجه), surnamed Sāhib Ayār, was the wazīr and favourite companion of Shāh Shujāa', the son of Mubāriz-uddīn Muhammad Zafar, commonly called Muẓaffar Shāh, who took Shīrāz in A.D. 1353. He was put to the rack and beheaded by Shāh Shujāa' in August, A.D. 1363, Zi-Qa'da, A.H. 764.

Qawela Qaan (قویلا قاآن). *Vide* Kiblai Qāan.

Qaza (قضا), poetical name of Muhammad Hafīz-ullāh K͟hān.

Qazib-ul-Ban (قضیب البان), surname of Shaik͟h Muhīn-uddīn 'Abdul Qādir bin-Sayyad Muhammad, an Arabian author who died in A.D. 1630, A.H. 1040.

Qazi Khan (قاضی خان). He is commonly called by this name, but his full name is Imām Fak͟hr-uddīn Hasan bin-Mansūr-al-'Uzjandī-al-Farg͟hānī. He died in A.D. 1195, A.H. 592. He is the author of a work entitled *Fatāwa Qāzī K͟hān*, a collection of decisions which is held in the highest estimation in India. Yūsuf bin-Junaid, generally known by the name of Ak͟hī Chalabī-at-Tūkātī, epitomised this work and compressed it into one volume.

Qazwini (قزوینی), author of the *Ajāeb-ul-Mak͟hlūkāt*. *Vide* Zikaria bin-Muhammad bin-Mahmūd.

Qitran (قطران بن منصور اجلی), or Qutrān bin-Mansūr Ajlī, a celebrated poet of Tabrez, was contemporary with the poet Rashīd Watwāt. He is the author of a poem called *Qaus-nāma*, which he dedicated to Amīr Ahmad or Muhammad bin Amīr Qammāj, ruler of Balk͟h, who was contemporary with Sulṭān Sanjar.

Qizal Arsalan (قزل ارسلان) (which means the red lion), was the second son of Atābak Eldiguz. He succeeded his brother Atābak Muhammad in the office of prime minister to his nephew Sulṭān Tug͟hral III. A.D. 1186, A.H. 582, and in combination with Nāṣir, the reigning k͟halīf of Bag͟hdād, seized and imprisoned Tug͟hral, and resolved to usurp the name as well as the power of a monarch. But the day before that fixed for his coronation he fell by a blow of an assassin, A.D. 1191, A.H. 587, and was succeeded by his nephew Atābak Abū Bakr, the son of Atābak Muhammad.

Qizal Bashi (قزل باشی). This is a Turkish word and means "red-headed."

Qizal Bash Khan (قزل باش خان), an amīr of 4000, who served under the emperor Shāh Jahān, and died in the year A.D. 1648, A.H. 1058.

Qizal Bash Khan (قزل باش خان همدانی), of Hamdān, whose proper name was Muhammad Razā, came to India in the reign of the emperor Bahādur Shāh, and was honoured with the title of Qizalbāsh K͟hān. He subsequently served under Mubāriz K͟hān, governor of Haidarābād, and after his death under Niẓām-ul-Mulk 'Asaf Jāh, and died at Dehlī in the year A.D. 1746, A.H. 1159. He was a good musician and knew the Indian and Persian systems of musical compositions. His poetical name is Umaid.

Qubad (قباد) (Cavades of the Greeks), was the son of Fīrōz I. king of Persia of the Sassanian race, and the successor of his brother Palāsh. We are told that when his brother Palāsh came to the throne Qubād, who had aspired to it, fled towards the territories of the K͟hāqān, or king of Transoxiana; and as he passed Naishāpūr he spent one night with a beautiful young lady of that city, who, when he returned four years afterwards accompanied by a large army, presented him with a fine boy, the fruit of their casual amour. He was delighted with the appearance of the child; and as he was contemplating him, he received accounts that his brother Palāsh was no more, and that the crown of Persia awaited his acceptance. This intelligence reaching him at such a moment made him conclude that fortune already smiled on his son, whom he, from that day, treated with the greatest favour, and gave the infant prince the name of Nusherwān (*q.v.*). Qubād succeeded his brother in A.D. 488, and carried on a successful war against the Roman emperor Anastasius; and died, after a long reign of 43 years, in A.D. 531. His son Nusherwān succeeded him.

Qubadi (قبادی), surname of Shīs bin-Ibrāhīm, an Arabian author, who died in the year A.D. 1202, A.H. 599.

Qudrat (قدرت), the poetical name of Shāh Qudrat-ullah of Dehlī, a Persian and Urdū lyric poet, and author of the work called *Nataej ul-Afkār* and a Dīwān. He was living at Murshidābād in A.D. 1782, A.H. 1191. He was one of the most fertile Persian poets; his Dīwān consists of 20,000 verses. He died in A.D. 1791, A.H. 1205, at Murshidābād.

Qudrat (قدرت), the poetical name of Shaik͟h Qudrat-ullah of Bhopal.

udrat-ullah, Shaikh (قدرت الله شیخ), Superintendent of Stamps at Bhopal, and author of several works in Persian and Urdū, which were published by him in the year A.D. 1863, A.H. 1280, at Bhopal.

List of Books composed by him.

Poetry.

Of Ghazals, called . . .	Dīwān Qudrat.
Of Panegyrics or Kaṣīdas	Agwān Qudrat.
Poems	Gulzār Qudrat.
Ditto.	Izhār Qudrat.
Malcolm's History . . .	Mājrī Qudrat.
Mutiny of 1857.	Tamāshāe Qudrat.
Promiscuous pieces . . .	Kīmiyāe Qudrat.

Prose.

On Miracles	Ajāebāt Qudrat.
On Medicine	Mujarribat Qudrat.
Letters	Rukkāt Qudrat.
Stories	Hikāyāt Qudrat.

Qudsi (قدسی). *Vide* Hājī Muhammad Jān Qudsī.

Qudsi Ansari (قدسی انصاری), of Isfahān, whose proper name is Shaikh 'Abdul Karīm, was a celebrated learned and pious Musulmān of Isfahān. He died on the 3rd February, A.D. 1615, 14th Muḥarram, A.H. 1024.

Qudsia Begam (قدسیه بیگم), daughter of 'Asaf Khān, wazīr, the son of the celebrated Yatmād-uddaula, wife of the emperor Shāh Jahān, niece to the empress Nūr Jahān Begam, and mother of the emperor 'Alamgīr.

[*Vide* Arjumand Bano Begam and Mumtāz Mahal.]

Qudsia Begam. *Vide* Udham Baī.

Quduri (قدوری), surname of Abūl Husain Ahmad bin-Muhammad, a celebrated Musalmān doctor of Baghdād, of the Hanīfa sect, who died A.D. 1036, A.H. 428. He is the author of the *Mukhtasir-ul-Qudūrī*, which is one of the most esteemed of the works which follow the doctrines of Abū Hanīfa, and is of high authority in India. It is a general treatise on law, and contains upwards of 12,000 cases. A well-known commentary on the *Mukhtasir ul-Qudūrī* is entitled *Al-Joharat ul-Naiyarat*, and is sometimes called *Al-Joharat ul-Munīrat*.

Qulich Khan (قلیچ خان), title of 'Abid Khān, who came to India in the reign of Shāh Jahān, and was raised to the rank of 4,000. He was killed by a cannon ball at the siege of Golkanda, on the 8th February, A.D. 1686, 24th Rabī I. A.H. 1097. He is the father of Ghāzī-uddīn Khān Fīrōz Jang I. and grandfather of the celebrated Nizām ul-Mulk 'Asaf Jāh of Haidarābād (*q.v.*).

Qulich Khan (قلیچ خان), of Andjān, of the tribe of Jānī Kurbānī, was an amīr of 4000, who served under the emperors Akbar and Jahāngīr from the years A.D. 1572 to 1611, A.H. 980 to 1020. His poetical name was Ulfatī.

Qulich Khan Turani (قلیچ خان تورانی), an amīr who served under the emperors Jahāngīr and Shāh Jahān; was raised by the latter to the rank of 5000, and appointed governor of Kābul and Kandāhār. He died A.D. 1654, A.H. 1064.

Qulini (قلینی). *Vide* Muhammad bin-Ya'qub.

Quli Qutb Shah I. Sultan (قلی قطب شاه اول سلطان). This prince was the founder of the sovereignty of Golkanda (Golconda). His father Quṭb ul-Mulk was originally a Turkish adventurer who came to try his fortune in the Deccan and embraced the service of Muhammad Shāh Bahmanī. By degrees he was promoted to high rank; and in the reign of Mahmūd Shāh obtained the title of Quṭb ul-Mulk and the Tarafdārī or government of Telingāna. In A.D. 1493, A.H. 899, he received orders to besiege the fortress of Jāmkonda, and as he was reconnoitring was killed by an arrow from the walls. After his death his office and titles were conferred by the king on his son Sulṭān Qulī with the territory of Golkanda, part of Telingāna, in jāgīr. On the decline of Bahmanī authority, when 'Adil Shāh and others assumed royalty, he also in the year A.D. 1512, A.H. 918, styled himself Sulṭān of Telingāna, under the title of Qulī Quṭb Shāh. He was a chief of great abilities and ruled the country for a period of 50 years; 18 of which he governed Telingāna in the name of Mahmūd Shāh, and reigned as king 32 lunar years, at the end of which he was assassinated by a Turkish slave supposed to have been bribed by his son and successor, Jāmshed Quṭb Shāh. His death happened on Sunday the 2nd September, A.D. 1543, 2nd Jumāda II. A.H. 950. The kings of the Quṭb Shāh dynasty who reigned at Golkanda, are as follows:—

1. Qulī Quṭb Shāh.
2. Jāmshed Quṭb Shāh.
3. Ibrāhīm Quṭb Shāh.
4. Muhammad Qulī Quṭb Shāh.
5. Muhammad Quṭb Shah.
6. 'Abdullah Quṭb Shāh.
7. Abū'l Hasan.

Quli Qutb Shah II. Sultan (قلی قطب شاه سلطان), who is also called Muhammad Qulī Quṭb Shāh, was the son of Ibrāhīm Quṭb Shāh, upon whose death in June, A.D. 1581, Rabī' II. A.H. 989, he ascended the throne of Golkanda in his twelfth year. In the beginning of his reign he was engaged in war with 'Adil Shāh of Bījāpūr, with whom he concluded peace in the year A.D. 1587, giving him his sister in marriage. The air of Golkanḍa not agreeing with his constitution, he founded a city at about eight miles distance, which he called Bhāgnagar, after his mistress Bhāgmatī, a celebrated courtezan; but being afterwards ashamed of his amour, he changed it to Haidarābād. Shāh 'Abbās, emperor of Persia, courted his alliance, by asking his daughter in marriage for one of his sons; and Quṭb Shāh, esteeming connection with so august a monarch as an honour, complied with the request. He was much esteemed for his abilities and encouraged literature; he also is the author of the work called *Kulliāt Quṭb Shāh*, a very copious volume, containing Hindī, Dak͟hanī, and Persian Poems, on a variety of subjects. He was the fourth Sulṭān of the Quṭb Shāhī dynasty and reigned 31 years. He died on Saturday the 11th January, A.D. 1612, 17th Ẕi-Qa'da, A.H. 1020, and having no son was succeeded by his brother Muhammad Quṭb Shāh.

Qummi (قمی). *Vide* Malik Qummī.

Qumri (قمری), poetical name of Sirāj-uddīn.

Qusi (قوسی), poetical name of Majd-uddīn 'Alī, an author.

Qutb 'Alam (قطب عالم), a celebrated Muhammadan saint, whose original name is Shaik͟h or Sayyid Burhān-uddīn, but he is commonly known by the former; he was the grandson of Mak͟hdūm Jahāniān Sayyid Jalāl Buk͟hārī. He chose Gujrāt for his place of residence, and died there on the 9th December, A.D. 1453, 8th Ẕil-ḥijja, A.H. 857. His tomb is at Batūh, six miles from the city of Ahmadabād in Gujrāt. There is a slab kept at the door of his mausoleum, which some say is stone, others think it would be wood or iron. His son, named Shāh 'Alam, was also a pious Musalmān and is likewise buried at Gujrāt.

Qutb 'Alam (قطب عالم), another Musalmān saint, whose proper name is Shaik͟h Nūr-uddīn Ahmad. He was born at Lāhore, and died in the year A.D. 1444, at Pinḍūa in Behar, where he is buried. Shaik͟h Hisām-uddīn, whose tomb is at Kaṛa Mānikpūr, and who is also considered a saint, was one of his disciples.

Qutb Shah (قطب شاہ), a title of the kings of Golkanḍa. *Vide* Muhammad Quṭb Shāh and Qulī Quṭb Shāh.

Qutb Shah (قطب شاہ), a king of Gujrāt. *Vide* Quṭb-uddīn (Sulṭān.)

Qutb Shah (قطب شاہ), a celebrated Muhammadan saint of Dehlī. *Vide* Quṭb-uddīn Bak͟htiār.

Qutb-uddin (قطب الدین), a grandson of Shaik͟h Salīm Chishtī.

Qutb-uddin 'Abdul Karim ibn-'Abdul Nur (قطب الدین عبدالکریم بن عبدالنور) is the author of the work called *Sharah Saḥīḥ Buk͟hārī*, and of a history of Egypt entitled *Tārīk͟h Misr*. He died in the year A.D. 1333, A.H. 733.

Qutb-uddin Aibak (قطب الدین ایبک), king of Dehlī, originally a slave of Shihāb-uddīn Muhammad G͟hōrī, prince of G͟hōr and G͟haznī, who raised him to high rank in his army, and in the year A.D. 1192, A.H. 588, after his victory over Pithaura, the Rāja of Ajmer, left him as his deputy in India. The same year Quṭb-uddīn conquered Mirath and Dehlī and extended his conquest as far as Bengal. After the death of Shihāb-uddīn in A.D. 1206, A.H. 602, his nephew G͟hayās-uddīn Mahmūd, who succeeded him, sent Quṭb-uddīn all the insignia of royalty, a canopy, a crown and a throne, and conferred on him the title of Sulṭān. On the 27th June the same year, 18th Ẕi-Qa'da, A.H. 602, Quṭb-uddīn, having invested himself with sovereign power, ascended the throne and made his residence the capital of Dehlī. His reign, properly speaking, lasted only four years, though he enjoyed all the state and dignities of a king for upwards of twenty years. He died at Lāhore by a fall from his horse in A.D. 1210, A.H. 607, and was succeeded by his adopted son, Sulṭān 'Arām Shāh. The Jāma' Masjid in old Dehlī, which is famous under the name of Qūwat ul-Islām, and stands close to the Quṭb Mīnār, was formerly a Hindū temple. Quṭb-uddīn first converted it into a masjid, commencing the Mīnār as its *Mazina*, and afterwards Shams-uddīn Altimsh and 'Ala-uddīn K͟hiljī made some additions to it. The following is a list of the Sulṭāns of the Slave (or Turk) dynasty of G͟hōr who reigned at Dehlī.

	A.D.	A.H.
1. Quṭb-uddīn Aibak, of the first Turk dynasty . . began	1206	602
2. 'Arām Shāh, son of Quṭb-uddīn	1210	607
3. Shams-uddīn Altimsh . . .	1210	607
4. Rukn-uddīn Fīrōz, son of Altimsh	1236	633
5. Sulṭāna Razia, daughter of Altimsh	1236	634
6. Bahrām Shāh, son of Altimsh	1240	637
7. 'Ala-uddīn Masa'ūd, son of Fīrōz	1242	639
8. Nāṣir-uddīn Mahmūd, son of Altimsh	1246	644

		A.D.	A.H.
9.	Ghayās-uddīn Balban (a slave of Altimsh)	1266	664
10.	Kaiqubād, grandson of Altimsh (last of the branch)	1286	685
11.	Jalāl-uddīn Fīrōz Shāh Khiljī, first Sultān of the second branch of the Turk dynasty called Khiljī, which see	1288	688

Qutb-uddin Allama, Maulana (قطب الدین علامہ مولانا), a learned Muhammadan poet who was contemporary with the celebrated Shaikh Sa'dī of Shīrāz, and is the author of several works, among which are the *Tuhfa Shāhī*, *Sharah Kulliāt Qānūn* and *Sharah Miftāh ul-'Ulūm*. He died at Tabrez on Sunday the 7th February, A.D. 1311, 17th Ramazān, A.H. 710.

Qutb-uddin Bakhtiar Kaki Khwaja (قطب الدین بختار کاکی خواجہ), a celebrated Muhammadan saint of Dehlī, commonly called Qutb Shāh, and sometimes called Ūshī from his native country Ūsh near Andjān in Persia. He died at old Dehlī on the 27th November, A.D. 1235, 14th Rabī' I. A.H. 633. His tomb is still conspicuous in that district, and is visited by devotees. He is the author of a Dīwān. Shaikh Farīd-uddīn Shakar Ganj was one of his disciples.

Qutb-uddin Khan (قطب الدین خان), brother of Shams-uddīn Auka, entitled 'Azīm Khān. He was an amīr of 5,000 in the reign of the emperor Akbar; was made governor of Bahroch, and was treacherously slain by Sultān Muzaffar, king of Gujrāt, in A.D. 1583.

Qutb-uddin Khan Kokaltash (قطب الدین خان کوکلتاش), whose original name was Shaikh Khūban or Khūbu, was the son of Shaikh Salīm Chishtī's sister, and foster-brother of the emperor Jahāngīr, who raised him to the rank of 5000. He was made governor of Bengal in A.D. 1606, A.H. 1015, and was killed at Bardwān by Sher Afkan Khān, the former husband of Nūr Jahān Begam, in A.D. 1607, A.H. 1016. His remains were transported to Fathapūr Sīkrī and buried there.

Qutb-uddin Mahmud bin-Muhammad Shirazi (قطب الدین محمود بن محمد شیرازی), author of the *Ghurrat-ut-Tāj* (Splendour of the Crown) and several other works. He died A.D. 1310, A.H. 710.

Qutb-uddin Mahmud Langa (قطب الدین محمود لنگا), second king of Multān of the tribe of Langa, who having secured the person of Shaikh Yūsuf, his predecessor and son-in-law, sent him to Dehlī and ascended the throne of Multān in the reign of Sultān Bahlōl Lodī. He reigned for a period of sixteen years and died much lamented in A.D. 1469, A.H. 874. He was succeeded by his son Husain Langa.

Qutb-uddin Muhammad (قطب الدین محمد), the son of Anūshtakīn, the cup-bearer of Sultān Sanjar Saljūqī. He was installed by the Sultān about the year A.D. 1140, and became the first king of Khwārizm of the race called Khwārizm Shāhī. The following is a list of the kings of this race:—

1. Qutb-uddīn Muhammad.
2. Atsiz, the son of Qutb-uddīn Muhammad
3. Alp Arsalān, the son of Atsiz.
4. Sultān Shāh, the son of Alp Arsalān.
5. 'Ala-uddīn Takash Khān, his brother.
6. Sultān Muhammad, son of Takash. He was defeated by Changez Khān in A.D. 1218.
7. Jalāl-uddīn, the son of Sultān Muhammad, and last king of this race, slain A.D. 1230.

Qutb-uddin Muhammad Ghori (قطب الدین محمد غوری) was the son of 'Izz-uddīn Ghōrī (*q.v.*). He married the daughter of Sultān Bahrām Shāh, king of Ghaznī, and having founded the city of Fīrōzkoh in Ghōr, made it his capital, and assumed all the dignities of a sovereign. At length he was induced to attack Ghaznī. Sultān Bahrām (*q.v.*), obtaining intimation of his intentions, contrived to get him into his power, and eventually put him to death. This is the origin of the feuds between the houses of Ghōr and Ghaznī. Saif-uddīn Sūrī, prince of Ghōr, brother of the deceased, raised an army to revenge his death, with which he marched direct to Ghaznī, which was evacuated by Bahrām, who fled to India. After some time Saif-uddīn was betrayed into the hands of Sultān Bahrām by the inhabitants of Ghaznī. The unhappy prince had his forehead blackened, and was seated astride on a bullock with his face towards the tail. In this manner he was led round the whole city; after which, being first put to torture, his head was cut off and sent to his uncle Sultān Sanjar Saljūqī, while his wazīr, Sayyad Majd-uddīn, was impaled. This took place about A.D. 1159, soon after which Bahrām was defeated and expelled by Saif-uddīn's brother, Ala-uddīn Hasan (*q.v.*).

Qutb-uddin Munuwar, Shaikh (قطب الدين منور شيخ), a Muhammadan saint of Hānsī, who was a grandson of Shaikh Jamāl-uddīn Aḥmad. He lived in the time of Sulṭān Fīrōz Shāh Bārbak, king of Dehlī. He was a contemporary of the celebrated saint Shaikh Nāṣir-uddīn Chiragh Dehlī, both of whom were disciples of Shaikh Niẓām-uddīn Aulia, and both of whom died the same year. Nāṣir-uddīn died on the 16th September, A.D. 1356, 18th Ramaẓān, A.H. 757, and Quṭb-uddīn on the 22nd November, A.D. 1356, 26th Ẓi-Qa'da, A.H. 757. The former lies buried at Dehlī and the latter at Hānsī.

Qutb-uddin Sultan (قطب الدين سلطان), also called Quṭb Shāh, was the son of Muhammad Shāh, king of Gujrāt. After the death of his father in February, A.D. 1451, Muḥarram, A.H. 855, he ascended the throne of Gujrāt, reigned more than eight years, and died on the 25th May, A.D. 1459, 23rd Rajab, A.H. 863. He was buried in the vault of his father, Muhammad Shāh, and was succeeded by his uncle Dāūd Shāh, who reigned only a few days and was deposed.

Qutbul-Mulk (قطب الملک), the father of Qulī Quṭb Shāh I. which see.

Qutbul-Mulk (قطب الملک), the title of 'Abdullah Khān (Sayyīd), which see.

Qutlagh Nigar Khanam (قتلغ نگار خانم), daughter of Yūnas Khān, king of Mughalistān, and sister to Mahmūd Khān, a descendant of the famous Changez Khān. She was married to 'Umar Shaikh Mīrzā, and became the mother of Bābar Shāh, king of Dehlī. She died at Kābul on the 4th June, A.D. 1505, 1st Muḥarram, A.H. 911.

Qutlamish (قتلمش), a descendant of Saljūqī, was taken prisoner by Malikshāh Saljūqī.

[*Vide* Sulaimān bin-Qutlamish.]

Qutlaq Khan (قتلق خان), the title of Atābak 'Abū Bakr bin-Sa'd bin-Zangī.

Qutran (قطران). *Vide* Qitrān.

Qutrib (قطرب), an author who was a contemporary of Seboya the poet, and received this title from him, but his original name is Muhammad. He is the author of several works. He died A.D. 821, A.H. 206.

Qutyba (قتيبه), the son of Mushnī ibn-Amar, was governor of Khurāsān in the reign of Khalīf 'Abdulmalik. He was slain in the time of Sulaimān, son of 'Abdulmalik, in September, A.D. 715, Ẓil-ḥijja, A.H. 96.

R

Raba'a Basri (رابعہ بصری), a very celebrated pious lady of Basra, who had a good knowledge of all the traditions. She is said to have constructed a canal from Baghdād to Medina, was a contemporary of Sarī Saqtī, and died A.D. 801, A.H. 185.

Rabit (رابط), poetical name of Moulwī Abdul Ahad.

Rafa'i (رافعی), whose proper name was Imām-uddīn, is the author of the *Tadwīn* and several works in Persian.

Rafa'i (رافعی شیخ محی الدین حسین), surnamed Shaikh Muhī-uddīn Husain. He died about the year A.D. 1422 or 1427, A.H. 825 or 830.

Rafai, Sayyad (رافعی سایید), was an inhabitant of Dehlī and lived for a long time in an old mosque which he repaired. He died about the year A.D. 1867, A.H. 1233.

Rafi or **Rafia'** (رفیع مرزا حسن بیگ), the poetical name of Mirzā Hasan Beg, who was employed as secretary to Nazar Muhammad Khān, the ruler of Tūrān. He came to India about the year A.D. 1646, A.H. 1056, in the reign of the emperor Shāh Jahān, who conferred on him the mansab of 500. He died in the time of 'Alamgīr.

Rafi Khan Bazil, Mirza (رفیع خان باذل مرزا), author of the work called *Hamlae Haidarī*, containing the wars of Muhammad, and the first four Khalīfas, viz. Abū Bakr, 'Umar, 'Usmān and 'Alī, in heroic verse consisting of 40,000 verses. He was a native of Dehlī and a descendant of Ja'far *Sarond* Mashhadī. For some years he had the command of the fort of Gwāliar in the time of 'Alamgīr, after whose death he lived in retirement at Dehlī, where he died A.D. 1711, A.H. 1123. He is also the author of a Dīwān of Ghazals. His poetical name is Bāzil.

Rafi-u'ddarjat (رفیع الدرجات), the son of Rafī-ush-Shān and grandson of Bahādur Shāh. He was raised to the throne of Dehlī by the two Sayyads, viz. 'Abdullah Khān and his brother Husain 'Alī Khān, after the dethronement of the emperor Farrukhsiyar on the 18th February, A.D. 1719, 8th Rabī II. A.H. 1131, but died in little more than three months of a consumption at Āgra on the 28th May the same year, 19th Rajab, A.H. 1131, when another youth of the same description, younger brother to the deceased, was set up by the Sayyads under the name of Rafī-uddaula Shāh Jahān Sānī, who came to the same end in a still shorter period. Both were buried in the mausoleum of Khwāja Qutb-uddīn Kākī at Dehlī. After their death the Sayyads pitched on a healthier young man as their successor, who ascended the throne by the title of Muhammad Shāh.

Rafi-uddaula (رفیع الدولہ), younger brother of the emperor Rafī-uddarjat, which see.

Rafi-u'ddin (رفیع الدین), a poet who is the author of a very curious and entertaining Dīwān or collection of poems. He was a native of Hindūstān, and probably of that province which is called the Deccan. He served in a military capacity, and attached himself to the person of the illustrious emperor Akbar, whom he first met at Kashmere in the year A.D. 1592, and received from that monarch the reward of his poetical labours. His Dīwān, which he commenced writing in the kingdom of the Deccan, was brought to a conclusion A.D. 1601, A.H. 1010. It contains about 15,000 distichs.

Rafi-u'ddin Haidar Rafa'i Mua'mmai, Amir (رفیع الدین حیدر رفعی معمائی امیر), is said to have composed more than 12,000 verses of chronograms, etc. but did not collect them. He was living in A.D. 1585, A.H. 993. This person appears to be the same as Mīr Haidar Rafīyī Mua'mmāī.

Rafi-uddin Lubnani (رفیع الدین لبنانی), native of Lubnān, a village of Isfahān. He was contemporary with the poets Asīr-uddīn Admānī, Sharaf-uddīn Shafrowa, and Kamāl-uddīn Ismā'īl. He is the author of a Dīwān.

Rafi - uddin Shaikh Muhammad (رفیع الدین شیخ محمد), surnamed Muhaddis or Traditionist, who died A.D. 1547, A.H. 954, and was buried in the Hawelī of Asaf Jāh at Āgra.

Rafi-u'sh-Shan (رفیع الشان) (prince), son of the emperor Bahādur Shāh, killed in battle against Jahāndār Shāh, his brother. [*Vide* Jahāndār Shāh.]

Rafi-u's-Sauda, Mirza (رفیع السودا مرزا). *Vide* Saudā.

Rafi Waez (رفیع واعظ), a poet who is the author of a Dīwān. *Vide* Muhammad Rafī Wāez.

Rafizi Mua'mmai (رفیعزی معمائی). *Vide* Mīr Haidar Rafīqī.

Raghib (راغب), poetical title of a poet of Shīrāz, whose proper name is Kalb Husain Beg.

Raghoba (رگهوبا). *Vide* Raghunāth Rāo.

Raghoji Bhosla I. (رگهوجی بهوسله) was nominated Senā Sahib Sabha, or general of the Marhaṭṭa confederacy, in A.D. 1734, received a sanad from the Peshwā and became the first Rāja of Berār or Nāgpūr in A.D. 1740, in which year a great revolution took place in the Marhaṭṭa government. The Rāja of Sitāra, Rāmrāja, a weak prince, being upon the throne, it was concerted between the two principal officers of the State, Bājī Rāo the Peshwā, and Rāghojī Bhosla, the Bakhshī or Commander-in-Chief, to divide the dominions of their master. In consequence of this arrangement, the former assumed the government of the western provinces, continuing at the ancient capital of Pūna; the latter took the eastern, and fixed his residence at Nāgpūr, a principal city in the province of Beṛār; whilst Rāmrāja was confined to the fortress of Sitāra, the Peshwā administering the government in his name. Hence the distinction between the Marhaṭṭas of Pūna and Beṛār. Rāghōjī was the son of Vimbojī, who was killed in Audh during the lifetime of his father Parsojī, who was Bakhshī under his brother Sāhojī, the son of Sambhojī, the son of Sivājī, the founder of the Marhaṭṭa empire. Rāghōjī Bhosla died A.D. 1749 or 1753, and transmitted his government to his son Jānojī, who, dying in A.D. 1772, left his inheritance to his nephew and adopted son Rāghōjī Bhosla II. the son of his younger brother Madhūjī. This occasioned a contention between Jānojī's brother Sāmojī and Madhūjī. The former claimed the government in the right of priority of birth, and the latter as father and guardian of the adopted child. They were accordingly engaged in hostility until the death of Sāmojī or Sabhojī, who was killed in an engagement with his brother on the 27th January, A.D. 1775. From that period the government of Beṛār was held by Madhojī or Madhūjī Bhoslā.

Bhosla Rājas of Nāgpūr or Beṛār.

Rāghōjī Bhosla I.	died	1753
Jānojī or Rānojī	,,	1772
Madhojī	,,	1788
Rāghōjī Bhosla II	,,	1816
Parsojī (strangled by Apā Sahib) .	,,	1816
Mūdojī (Apā Sahib) was acknowledged by the English in 1816, and	deposed	1818
Partāp Singh Nārāyan, grandson of Rāghōjī Bhosla, put on the gadi . .		1818
Rāghōjī Bhosla III.		1853

Raghoji Bhosla II. (رگهوجی بهوسله) succeeded his father, Madhojī Bhosla, in the government of Beṛār or Nāgpūr in May, A.D. 1788, and died on the 22nd March, A.D. 1816, when his son Parsojī succeeded him.

Raghoji Bhosla III. (رگهوجی بهوسله), Rāja of Beṛār. He died in A.D. 1853, not only without heirs but without any male relations who could support a legitimate claim to the Rāj; thereupon the Governor-General quietly annexed that large country to the Company's dominions.

Raghunath Shah (رگهوناتهه شاه), of the Mandla district, who was a direct descendant of the eldest branch of the Gond dynasty, was executed in A.D. 1857 for rebellion, and his estates confiscated. Fifteen years later the Government gave his widow, Mare Kūṇwar, a compassionate allowance of 120 rupees per annum.

Raghunath Rao (رگهوناتهه راؤ), commonly called Raghōba, a Marhaṭṭa chief who was at one time much connected with the English. He was the son of Bājī Rāo Peshwā I. and father of the last Peshwā Bājī Rāo II. and paternal uncle of Mādhō Rāo Peshwā II. He usurped the Peshwāship after the death of Nārāyan Rāo, youngest son of Bālājī Rāo Peshwā. On the death of Bālājī Rāo, who left two sons, Mādhō Rāo and Nārāyan Rāo, both minors, the power of the state was for some years wielded by his brother Raghunāth as regent. Mādhō Rāo was enabled to take the reins of government into his own hands after some time, but died in A.D. 1772, and was succeeded by his brother Nārāyan Rāo. He was soon afterwards murdered in consequence of a plot which Raghobā had formed against him. Raghobā was acknowledged Peshwā after his death;

but it appeared soon afterwards that the widow of Nārāyan Rāo was with child. The ministers proclaimed the event during Raghobā's absence. He was defeated and fled to Surat.

Rahia (راحيه), one of the earliest professors of Muhammadanism, although he was not present at the battle of Badar. Muhammad used to say of him, that of all men he had ever seen Rahia did most resemble the angel Gabriel. He died in the year A.D. 670, A.H. 50.

Rahim Beg, Mirza (رحيم بيگ مرزا), of Sardhāna, author of a small work on Persian and Arabic poetry entitled *Makhzan Shuārā*, which he composed in the year A.D. 1852, A.H. 1268. It is also called *Wasīlat-ush-Shuārā*.

Rahim-uddin Bakht, Mirza (رحيم الدين بخت مرزا), and Mirzā Muhsin Bakht (princes of Dehlī and grandsons of Shāh Alam), who came to Āgra from Benares when the Duke of Edinburgh came to Āgra in A.D. 1870.

Rahmat-ullah (رحمت الله), author of the history of the martyr Malik 'Umar, who is buried at Bahrāich. He composed this poem 750 years after the death of the saint.

Rai Gobind Munshi (راى گبيند), a Kayeth, who is the author of the story of Padmāwat in Persian, entitled *Tuhfat-ul-Kulūb*, which he wrote in the year A.D. 1652, A.H. 1062.

Raiha (رايحه), poetical name of Mīr Muhammad 'Alī of Sayālkōt, who died in A.D. 1737, A.H. 1150.

Rai Indarman (راى اندرمن), a Hindū, by caste a Bais of Hisār, and author of a work called *Dastūr-ul-Hisāb*. He was living in A.D. 1768, A.H. 1182.

Rai Lonkaran (راى لون كرن), Rāja of Pargana of Sambhar, lived in the time of the emperor Akbar, and died in the 11th year of Jahāngīr, A.D. 1615, A.H. 1024. He was a good Persian scholar, and used to compose verses; his poetical name was Tusanī. He was succeeded in his territories by his son Manōhar Dās, whose poetical title, some authors say, was Tusanī and not his father's. He fought on the Imperial side in the battle of Goganda, A.D. 1577.

[*Vide* Noer's *Kaiser Akbar*.]

Rai Maldeo (راى مالديو). *Vide* Maldeo Rāi.

Rai Phukni Mal (راى پهكنى مل). *Vide* Nashāt.

Raiq (رايق), author of the biography called *Tazkira Rāiq*, an abstract of which was made by Sirāj-uddaula Muhammad Ghaus Khān Nawāb of the Karnatik in A.D. 1842.

Rai Rai Singh (راى راى سنگه), son of Rai Kaliān Mal Rathor, a descendant of Rāi Maldeo and zamīndār of Bikaner in the time of the emperor Akbar. Rāi Kaliān Mal, with his son, served under that monarch for several years, and received his niece in marriage. Rāi Singh subsequently gave his daughter in marriage to Sultān Salīm, who, on his accession to the throne, conferred on him the rank of 5000. Rāi Singh died in the year A.D. 1612, A.H. 1021.

Rai Rayan Raja Bikarmajit (راى رايان راجه بكرماجيت) was the title of a Brāhman named Sundardās, who at first served under the Prince Shāh Jahān in the capacity of a Munshī. He afterwards rose by degrees to higher dignities and received the above title from the emperor Jahāngīr. When Shāh Jahān rebelled against his father, Bikarmājīt, who was then with the prince, fell in the battle which took place between the troops of the prince and his father about the year A.D. 1621, A.H. 1030.

Rai Sarjan Hara (راى سرجن هاڑا), Rāja of Ranthanbūr in the province of Āgra, lived in the time of the emperor Akbar. After his death Rāo Bhoj Hārā succeeded him.

Rai Shew Das (راى شيو داس), a Khattrī who was appointed deputy to Rāja Jai Singh Sūbādar of Āgra in the time of Muhammad Shāh. He built a fine garden at Āgra on the banks of the Jamna, which still goes after his name, Bāgh Shew Dās.

Rai Tansukh Rai (راى تنسكه راى), a Hindū whose poetical name was Shauq, was the son of Rāi Majlis Rāi, who was Nāeb of the Dīwān Khālsa of Āgra. He is the author of a Tazkīra of Persian poets called *Safīnat-ush-Shauq*, and also of a small Dīwān of 1000 verses. He was living at Āgra in A.D. 1756, A.H. 1170.

Raja (راجه), poetical title of Rāja Balwān Singh, son of Rāja Cheyt Singh of Benares. He was a pensioner of the British Government, and used to reside at Āgra; he is the author of a Dīwān in Urdū.

Raja Ali Khan, Faruqi (راجه علی خان فاروقي) succeeded his brother Mīrān Muhammad Khān II. in the government of Khāndesh in A.D. 1576. At this period the princes of Hindūstān, from Bengal to Sindh including Mālwā and Gujrāt, had been subdued by the victorious arms of the emperor Akbar; and Rāja 'Alī Khān, in order to avoid so unequal a contest, dropped the title of king, which his brother had assumed, and wrote a letter to Akbar, begging that ne might be considered as his vassal and tributary. In order to convince him of his sincerity, he sent him many rich and valuable presents. After the death of Burhān Niẓām Shāh II. king of Aḥmadnagar in the year A.D. 1596, A.H. 1004, the prince Mirzā Murād and Mirzā Khān Khān Khānān, the son of Bairām Khān, marched for the purpose of subduing the Deccan. Rāja 'Alī Khan accompanied them, and was killed with many officers of distinction by the explosion of a powder tumbril, in the famous battle fought between Khān Khānān and Suheil Khān, general of the Aḥmadnagar forces. His death happened on the 26th January, A.D. 1597, 18th Jumāda II. A.H. 1005, after he had reigned 21 years. His body was carried to Burhānpūr, where he was buried with due honours. He was succeeded by his son Bahādur Khān Farūqī.

Rajab Salar (رجب سالار), brother of Tughlaq Shāh, and father of Sulṭān Fīrōz Shāh, king of Dehlī. His tomb is in Bahrāich.

Raja Kans Purbi (راجه کنس پوربی), a Hindū zamīndār, who succeeded in placing himself on the throne of Bengal after the death of Shams-uddīn II. Pūrbī in A.D. 1386, and became the founder of a new dynasty. He reigned seven years and died in A.D. 1392, A.H. 795, and was succeeded by his son Jītmal, who became a Musalmān, and assumed the name of Jalāl-uddīn.

Raja Ram (راجه رام), the brother of Sambhājī the Marhaṭṭa chief, by another mother. He succeeded his brother in July A.D. 1689. On his accession Sambhājī, in April 1680, was seized and sent to reside in one of the forts of the Karnatic, with a decent appanage, but without any power in the government, and there he continued to reside till the death of his brother (July A.D. 1689), when he was acknowledged his successor. In his time the fortress of Sitāra was taken by 'Alamgīr on the 21st April, A.D. 1700, 13th Ẓil-Qā'da, A.H. 1111, but before it fell Rāja Rām died of the smallpox the same year at Jhinjī. He was succeeded by his son Karan, who survived him but a few days, when another son of his, named Seiwa, an infant only two years old, was put on the masnad under the guardianship of Rām Chānd Paṇḍit and regency of his mother, Tārā Bāī. But when, after the death of 'Alamgīr, Rāja Sāhū or Sāhjī II. was released from confinement, he was put aside, and Sāhjī was crowned at Sitāra in March, A.D. 1708.

References to the line of Rājas.

Rājas of Beṛār or Nāgpūr, *vide* Raghojī Bhosla I.
,, of Chittor and Nāgpūr, *vide* Rānā Sanka or Māldeo Rāo.
,, of Gwāliar, *vide* Rānojī Scindhia.
,, of Jaipūr or Jainagar, *vide* Bihārī Mal or Sandhal dewa.
,, of Mālwā or Indor of the Holkar family, *vide* Malhār Rāo I.
,, of Mārwār of Jodhpūr, *vide* Jodhā Rāo and Maldeo Rāo
,, of Bhartpūr, *vide* Chūraman Jāṭ.
,, of Sitāra, *vide* Sāhjī.
,, of Indor, *vide* Malhār Rāo Holkar I.

Raj Indar Goshain (راج اندرگوشائین), chief of a sect of Hindū ascetics who used to go about stark naked. He had under his command an army of those people, and was employed by Nawāb Safdar Jang. He was killed in a campaign between Ghāzi-uddīn III. (*q.v.*) and Safdar Jang in the time of the emperor Aḥmad Shāh, who had dismissed Safdar Jang from his office and given it to Nīlizam-uddaula. His death took place on the 20th June, A.D. 1753, 17th Shābān, A.H. 1166.

Raj Singh Kuchhwaha, Raja (راج سنگه کچهواها), son of Rāja Askaran, brother of Rāja Bihārī Mal. Served under the emperors Akbar and Jahāngīr, and died in the year A.D. 1615, A.H. 1024.

Raj Singh, Rana (راج سنگه رانا), of Chittor and Udaipūr, succeeded his father Rānā Jagat Singh, A.D. 1652, A.H. 1062, and was honoured by the emperor Shāh Jahān with the rank of 5000. In his time the fort of Chittor was demolished by order of the emperor 'Alamgīr. He died in the 24th year of that monarch, A.D. 1680, A.H. 1091, and was succeeded by his son Rānā Jai Singh. He is said to have been the writer of a remarkable letter to the Emperor 'Alamgīr (Aurangzeb) preserved by Col. Tod.

[*Vide* Tod's *Rājasthān*.]

Raju Qattal (راجو قتال), surnamed Sayyad Sado-uddīn, a Musalmān saint and brother of Makhdūm Jahāniān Jahān Gasht Shaikh Jalāl. He is the author of the *Tuhfat-un-Nasayeh*, which contains much good advice, though written according to the Sūfī School. His tomb is at Uchcha in Multān, where he died in the year A.D. 1403, A.H. 806.

Rajwara (راجواره), name of a place at Āgra built by several Rājas, such as Rāja

Jaswant Singh, Rāja Jai Singh, Rāja Mān Singh, Rāja Bharath, Rāja Bohar Singh, Rāja Beattal Dās son of Rāja Gopāl Dās, Rāja Dwārka Dās and others. They built their house at Āgra at a place which is now called Mauza Rājwāra.

Ramai or **Rami** (رامي). *Vide* Sharaf-uddīn Rāmī.

Ram Charan Mahant (رام چرن مهنت), the founder of the Rām-sanehī sect, was a Rāmāwant Bairāgi, born A.D. 1719 in a village in the principality of Jaipūr. Neither the precise period, nor the causes which led him to abjure the religion of his fathers, now appear; but he steadily denounced idol-worship, and suffered, on this account, great persecution from the Brāhmans. On quitting the place of his nativity in A.D. 1750, he wandered over the country, and eventually repaired to Bhīlwāra, in the Udaipūr territory, where, after a residence of two years, Bhīm Singh, Rānā or prince of that state, was urged by the priests to harass him to a degree which compelled him to abandon the town. The chief of Shāhpūra offered the wanderer an asylum at his court, where he arrived in the year A.D. 1767, but he does not seem to have settled there permanently until two years later, from which time it may be proper to date the institution of the sect. Rām Charan expired in April, A.D. 1798, in the 79th year of his age, and his corpse was reduced to ashes in the great temple of Shāhpūra. Rām Charan composed 36,250 Sabds or hymns, each containing from five to eleven verses. He was succeeded in the spiritual directorship by Rāmjan, one of his twelve disciples. This person died at Shāhpūra in A.D. 1809, after a reign of 12 years 2 months and 6 days. He composed 18,000 Sabds. The third hierach, Dulhā Rām, succeeded him and died in A.D. 1824. He wrote 10,000 Sabds, and about 4000 Sakī, or epic poems, in praise of men eminent for virtue not only of his own faith, but among Hindūs, Muhammadans, and others. After him Chatra Dās ascended the gaddī, and died in A.D. 1831. He is said to have composed 1000 Sabds, but would not permit their being committed to paper. Nārāyan Dās, the fourth in descent from Rām Charan, succeeded him, and was living in A.D. 1835.

[See *Jour. As. Soc. of Bengal*, Vol. 4, page 65.]

Ramdeo (رامديو), a Rāja of Deogīr (now Daulatābād), became a tributary to Sulṭān 'Alā-uddīn Sikandar Sānī, and died in the year A.D. 1310, A.H. 710.

Ramin (رامين), a lover, the name of whose mistress was Waisa. Their story, entitled *Rāmīn and Waisa*, has been written in Persian poetry by Niẓāmī 'Urūzī.

Ramjas Munshi (رام جس منشي) whose poetical name was Muḥīṭ, was a Khattrī by caste, and his father Lālā Gangā Bishun, whose poetical title was 'Ājiz, resided at Lāhore, but Muḥīṭ was born in Dehlī. He obtained an appointment in the Customs Department at Benares, which gave him 1200 rupees a year. He is the author of several Masnawīs, such as *Muḥīṭ-i-'Ishq*, *Muḥīṭ-i-Dard*, *Muḥīṭ-i-Gha'm*, etc. He also translated some books on mysticism from the Sanskrit, as *Muhiṭ-ul-Ḥaqāik*, *Muḥīṭ-ul-Asrār*, *Gulshān-i-Ma'rifat*, *Muḥīṭ Ma'rifat*, etc.

Ramji (رامجي), son of Rāja Bhagwān Dās, the uncle of the celebrated Rāja Mān Singh. He, together, with his two brothers. Bijai Rām and Sayām Rām, was crushed to death under the feet of an elephant, by order of the emperor Jahāngīr in the early part of his reign.

Ram Mohan Rai (رام موهن راى), afterwards Rāja Rām Mohan Rāi, a Brāhman of a respectable family in Bengal, was early celebrated for his precocious genius, high linguistic attainments, and other natural gifts, which in his after life procured for him the reputation of a reformer. Among several other reforms, the degenerate state of Hindūism demanded his earliest attention, and he, with his wonted zeal and assiduity, took upon himself to introduce a reform, which at the risk of his purse and reputation he succeeded in a great measure in effecting among his former co-religionists. His object was to reconstruct and varnish the old Hindūism, and not to abandon it altogether, as some of the modern reformers propose. He picked up morals and precepts from the Vedas, Dussanas, and Upanishads, which he thought most appropriate and instructive; but never accepted them as revelations. He likewise borrowed rules and precepts from other religions, but more particularly from Christianity. His originality of mind, his natural logical powers, his mastery of mental and moral philosophy, and above all his ardent desire to establish the true knowledge of God among his countrymen, made him discard all the prevailing religions of the world as revelations. When in England, the Rāja always attended the Unitarian church and much approved of its doctrines. He embarked for England and arrived at Liverpool on the 8th April, A.D. 1831, and died at Stapylton Grove near Bristol, while on a visit to that country, for the purpose of giving information and promoting the interests of his countrymen, by advocating a more liberal intercourse with India. After his death his followers in Bengal strictly adhered to the faith, and multiplied in number by thousands. The works of Sir W. Hamilton and Bishop Berkeley have also become their guides in points of philosophy. In a word the Brahmists are neither idolaters, as considered by some, nor infidels, as supposed by many. Rāja Rām Mohan translated the Upanishads of the Yajur-Veda, according to the Comment of Sankar Āchārya, into English, establishing the unity and incomprehensibility of the Supreme Being, whose worship alone can tend to eternal beatitude. A translation of the *Vedanta* (an abridgment of all the sacred writings) in Hindūstānī and Bengalī, was made by this Hindū philosopher and philanthropist. The Rāja also published an abstract of it in English. His tomb is in Arno's Vale cemetery in Bristol.

Ram Narain, Raja (رام نارایں). He was deputy governor of Bīhār in the time of Mīr Ja'far 'Alī Khān, the Nawāb of Bengal, and was driven out of Patna by the Shazādo Alī Gauhān (*vide* Shāh Alam) in 1760. Mīr Qāsim 'Alī, on his accession to the masnad in A.D. 1760, A.H. 1174, having detected embezzlements of large sums from the revenues, the jāgīrs, and pay of the troops, confiscated his effects. About seven lakhs of rupees in money and goods were found in his house, and nearly the same sum was recovered from persons to whom it had been entrusted by himself and his women. He was then kept in confinement with several others on suspicion. In August, A.D. 1763, Muḥurram, A.H. 1177, a few days before Mīr Qāsim 'Alī's defeat by the English on the banks of the Undwa nala, he commanded these persons to be put to death, and Rāja Rām Nārāyan was drowned in the Ganges with a bag of sand tied round his neck. Rām Nārāyan was a Persian scholar and wrote poetry in Persian and Urdū, having adopted the word *Mauzūn* for his poetical name.

Ramraj (رامراج), a Rāja of Bījānagar or Bijaiānagar, who was slain in battle against the four Muhammadan princes of the Deccan. This celebrated action took place on the banks of the Kṛishṇa river on Friday the 25th January, A.D. 1565, 20th Jumāda II. A.H. 972. It cost Rāmrāj his life, and ended in the defeat of the Hindū army with the loss of nearly one hundred thousand men. Rāmrāj, being defeated, was taken prisoner and brought before Husain Niẓām Shāh, who ordered his head to be struck off, and caused it to be placed on the point of a long spear to be displayed to the army; and afterwards kept at Bījāpūr as a trophy.

Ramraja (رامراجه) succeeded Sāhjī II. as Rāja of Sitāra in December, A.D. 1749. He was the adopted son of Sāhjī and grandson of Tārā Bāī. He died on the 12th December, A.D. 1777, having a short time before his death adopted Abba Sāhib, the son of Trimbakjī Bhosla. This adopted son was formally enthroned under the title of Sāhū, but was always kept a close prisoner by the Peshwā.

Ram Singh (رام سنگه), name of the Rāja of Koṭā and Būndī (A.D. 1858).

Ram Singh Hara (رام سنگه هاڑا) and Dalphat Rāo Bundela, two Hindū chiefs who served under the emperor 'Alamgīr in the military capacity, and were both killed at the same instant by a cannon shot in the battle which ensued between 'Azim Shāh and his eldest brother Bahādur Shāh, on the 8th June, A.D. 1707, 18th Rabī' I. A.H. 1119.

Ram Singh I. (رام سنگه راجه), Rāja of Jaipūr. He was honoured, after the death of his father, Rāja Jai Singh I. by the emperor 'Alamgīr in A.D. 1666, with the title of Rāja, and put in possession of his father's territories. His son, Bishun Singh, succeeded him after his death about the year A.D. 1675.

Ram Singh Munshi (رام سنگه منشی), author of a collection of letters entitled *Gulshan Ajāeb*, written in A.D. 1716, A.H. 1128.

Ram Singh Rathor (رام سنگه راٹهور), son of Abhai Singh, Rāja of Jodhpūr. He poisoned Bakhat Singh, his uncle, and usurped the throne. At his death, A.D. 1773, disorganization prevailed in Māṛwār, promoted by the Marhaṭṭas (who then got footing in Rājpūtāna), and by the evils generated by its feudal institutions. At Tonga, however, the Raṭhors defeated De Boigne, the celebrated general of Sindhia; but they were crushed at the subsequent battles of Pāṭan and Mairta under their reigning prince Bijai-Singh.

Ram Singh Sawai II. (رام سنگه سوائي), late Rāja of Jāipūr, son of Jai Singh III. was born a few months before the death of his father, whom he succeeded in January, A.D. 1834. He became a member of the Governor-General's Council in A.D. 1869.

Rana Amar Singh (رانه امر سنگه), the son of Rānā Partāp Singh of Chittor. He rebelled against the emperor Jahāngīr for some time, but was at last compelled by force of arms to acknowledge fealty to the throne of Dehlī. The emperor ordered to be cut in marble the images of Amar Singh and his son Qaran, which, when finished and brought to him, he took to Āgra and placed in the garden seat called Jharokha Darshan, where the people assembled every morning to pay their respects to the emperor. Amar Singh died in A.D. 1619, A.H. 1029, but the statues were made while he was living.

Rana Karan (رانا کرن), son of Amar Singh, the son of Rānā Partāp Singh, the son of Rānā Udai Singh, the son of Rānā Sankā. He succeeded his father Amar Singh in the rāj of Udaipūr, A.D. 1619, and died in the first year of the reign of Shāh Jahān, A.D. 1678, when his son Rānā Jagat Singh succeeded him, and was honoured by the emperor with the title of Rānā and rank of 5000. Jagat Singh died A.D. 1652, and was succeeded by his son Rāj Kūnwar, who received the title of Rānā Rāj Singh.

Rana Mal (رانا مل), a Rāja of Bhatner who lived in the reign of Sulṭān Ghayās-uddīn Tughlaq. His daughter, named Naila, was married to Sālār Rājab, the brother of the Sulṭān and father of Sulṭān Fīroz Shāh Tughlaq.

Rana of Jhansi (رانا جهنسى). *Vide* Gangā Bāī.

Rana Raj Singh of Chittor (رانا راج سنگه). *Vide* Rāj Singh (Rānā).

Rana Sanga or Sanka (رانا سانكا), Rāja of Chittor. His son Udai Singh is the founder of the state now known by the name of its capital Udaipūr (formerly called Mewar). The Udaipūr chief is, in the estimation of all the Hindū dynasties of India, *par excellence* the head, without a rival and free from stain. It is true that the independence of the "great Rānās of Chittor" was assailed by the Moguls, and that they succumbed to circumstances; but they never acknowledged a superior in birth or descent. The family dates back upwards of a thousand years. Chittor was captured by Akbar (*q.v.*), but the conquest was but a barren slaughter: it was in A.D. 1614, in the reign of the emperor Jahāngīr, that the house was first compelled by force of arms to surrender that complete independence it had then maintained for eight hundred years, and to acknowledge fealty to the throne of Dehlī. In A.D. 1512 we first hear of the renowned Rānā Sangā of Chittor. His army consisted of 80,000 horse, supported by 500 war elephants. Seven Rājas of the highest rank, and 113 of inferior note, attended his stirrup in the field. The Rājas of Jaipūr and Mārwār served under his banner, and he was the acknowledged head of all the Rājpūt tribes. In A.D. 1527 he espoused the cause of the dethroned dynasty of Dehlī. All the princes of Rājpūtāna ranged themselves under his banner, and he advanced with 100,000 men to drive Bābar across the Indus. The encounter took place at Biana, where the advanced guard of the Moguls was totally routed by the Rājpūts. Bābar eventually put Rānā Singh to flight, 16th March, A.D. 1527, and he soon afterwards died (A.D. 1528). In A.D. 1568 Udai Singh, the son of Rānā Sangā, came under the displeasure of Akbar. He fled and left the defence of his capital, Chittor, to Rāja Jaimal, who was killed by Akbar himself. His death deprived the garrison of all confidence, and they determined to sell their lives as dearly as possible. The women threw themselves on the funeral pile of the Rāja, and the men rushed frantically on the weapons of the Moguls, and perished to the number of 8000. In A.D. 1614 Partāp Singh was Rāja. He had recovered the greater portion of his dominion before Akbar died. In A.D. 1678, Aurangzīb marched against Udaipūr and succeeded in subjugating it, but the alienation of the Rājpūts from the Moguls was now complete, and never changed. The great boast of the chiefs of Udaipūr is, that their house never gave a daughter to the Mogul *zanāna*. Jaipūr and Jodhpūr did so, and gloried in these imperial alliances as conferring additional dignity on their families.

List of the Rānās of Mewar or Udaipūr since the foundation of the Mughol Empire.

Rānā Sankā	died	1528
,, Udai Singh, son of Rānā Sānkā	,,	
,, Partāp Singh, son of Udai Singh	,,	1594
,, Amar Singh, son of Partāp Singh	,,	1619
,, Karan, son of Amar Singh, embellished Udaipūr	,,	
,, Jagat Singh, son of Rānā Karan, tributary to Shāh Jahān	,,	1652
,, Rāj Singh, son of Jagat Singh	,,	1680
,, Jai Singh, son of Rāj Singh		
,, Amar Singh II.		
,, Sangram Singh		
,, Jagat II. pays chouth to the Marhattas	,,	1752
,, Partāp Singh	,,	1755
,, Rānā Rāj Singh	,,	1762
,, Rānā Ursi	dep.	}
,, Rānā Rāj Singh	pretender	}
,, Rānū Hamīr	,,	1778
,, Bhīm Singh	,,	1828
,, Yuwān Singh	,,	1838
,, Sardar Singh (of Bagor)	,,	1842
,, Swanip Singh	,,	1861
,, Sambhu Singh	,,	1874
,, Sujjan Singh	,,	1884
,, Fateh Singh		

Ranas of Chittor of Udaipur (رانا). *Vide* Rānā Sankā.

Ranbir Singh, Maharaja (رنبير سنگه مهاراجه), ruler of Kashmere, son of Mahārāja Gulāb Singh, whom he succeeded about the month of July or August, A.D. 1857.

Ranchhor Das (رنچهورداس), a learned Kāyeth of Jaunpūr, and author of a work on the art of writing prose and poetry, entitled *Daqāeq-ul-Inshā*, which he wrote in the year A.D. 1732, A.H. 1145.

Randhir Singh (رندهیر سنگه), **the** Jāt Rāja of Bhartpūr, was the eldest son of Ranjīt Singh, whom he succeeded. After his death, his brother Baldeo Singh ascended the Masnad of Bhartpūr.

Randhir Singh, Raja (رندهیر سنگه), of Kapūrthalla, was the son of the Alūwal chieftain near Jalandhar, in the Panjāb, who claimed equal rank with Mahārāja Ranjīt Singh, but whose fortune diminished as that of his rival increased. During the disturbances of A.D. 1857, he rendered excellent service to the State in and around Jalandhar, for which he was rewarded, though with no very liberal hand. He married a Christian wife.

Rangin (رنگین), takhallus of Sa'ādat Yār Khān, who is the author of a poem called *Mehr-wa-Māh*, a story of the Sayyad's son and the jeweller's daughter, who lived at Dehlī in the reign of Jahāngīr. He is also the author of several Dīwāns and also of a curious Dīwān in Urdū, rather indecent, in which he has brought in all the phrases of the women of the seraglio of Dehlī and Lucknow. He died in October, A.D. 1835, Jumāda II. A.H. 1251, aged 80 years.

Ranjit Singh (رنجیت سنگه), **the** Jāt Rāja of Bhartpūr, was the son of Kehrī Singh, the brother of Ratan Singh and Jawāhir Singh, the sons of Sūrajmal Jāt, the founder of the principality. He succeeded his uncle Rāja Nawāb Singh in A.D. 1776, A.H. 1190. He was despatched by Scindhia to raise the siege of Āgra, near which a bloody battle was fought on the 16th June, A.D. 1788, 12th Ramazān, A.H. 1202, in which Ismā'īl Beg was completely defeated, with the loss of all his cannon, baggage, and stores. He was succeeded by his son Randhīr Singh.

Ranjit Singh, Maharaja (رنجیت سنگه مهاراجه), the Sikh ruler of the Panjāb and faithful and highly-valued ally of the British Government, was the son of Mahā Singh, and appeared as a leader, first in 1779; and obtained investiture as Chief of Lāhore from the Afghān ruler Zimān Shāh in A.D. 1799. At his death, which happened on the 27th June, 1839, minute guns corresponding with the years of the deceased were fired from the ramparts of the forts of Dehlī, Āgra, Allahābād and all the principal stations of the army. Four of his Rānīs and seven slave girls burnt themselves with his corpse. He was succeeded in the Rāj by his eldest son, Kharag Singh.

The following are the names of his successors.

	A.D.
Kharag Singh, son of Ranjīt Singh, died 5th November	1840
Nounihāl Singh, son of Kharag Singh, died 17th November	1840
Rānī Chanda Kūnwar, widow of Kharag Singh, died	
Sher Singh, brother of Kharag Singh, murdered	1843
Dalīp Singh, a son of Ranjīt Singh, in whose time the Panjāb was annexed to the British Government, A.D. 1846. He was baptized 8th March, A.D. 1853, and is now living in England.	

Ranoji Bhosla (رانوجی بهوسله). *Vide* Jānōjī Bhōslā.

Ranoji Sindhia (رانوجی سیندهیه), the founder of the Sindhia or "Sindhāa" family of Gwāliar was born at Patīlī near Pūna, and served first under a chief, who commanded the bodyguard of Bājī Rāo, the first Peshwā. From this inferior station he gradually rose, and afterwards accompanied the Peshwā in the expedition which was undertaken at the close of the reign of Rāja Sahūjī against the province of Mālwā. This province was afterwards divided into three parts, of which the first was allotted to Bājī Rāo the Peshwā; the second to the Rāja of Sitāra; the third to the family of Holkar. As a reward for the services which Rānōjī rendered in the expedition against Mālwā, the Peshwā granted a considerable portion of the shares belonging to himself and to the Rāja of Sitāra to Rānōji; which grant was afterwards confirmed in jāgīr to his descendants, now the Rājas of Gwāliar. He died in A.D. 1750, and left five sons, viz. Jaiāpā, Jotība, Dattājī, Madhōjī and Jokaji. Jaiāpā succeeded his father and was assassinated in his tent in A.D. 1759; his brother Mādhōjī succeeded him, and although illegitimate was confirmed in the jāgīr by Mādhō Rāo Peshwā. He was the most powerful of the native princes of that day. He died at Pāna in A.D. 1794, and was succeeded by his grandnephew and adopted son Daulat Rāo Scindhia, then only 13 years of age; the latter married the daughter of Sherji Rao Ghatkai, and died on the 21st March, A.D. 1827.

List of the Sindhia family, now Rājas of Gwāliar.

	Began	died
Rānōjī Sindhia, the first of the race	1724	1750
Jīāpā, son of Rānōjī	1750	1759
Mādhojī or Mahājī Sindhia, brother of Jīāpā	1759	1794
Daulat Rāo Sindhia, son of Anand Rāo and adopted son of Mādhojī (who fixed his camp at Gwāliar in 1817) . . .	1794	1827
Bājī Bāī, his widow, who adopted Jhankōjī and acted as regent	1827	
Jhankōjī, assumed the reins of government	1833	1843
Jaiājī Sindhia, adopted son of Jhankōjī	1843	1886
Jaiājī, was succeeded by his son Mādhojī, or Mādhava Rāo .	1876	

Rao Amar Singh (راو عمار سنگه), whose daughter was married to Sulaimān Shikoh.

Rao Bahadur Singh (راو بهادر سنگه), a petty Rāja of the Doāb of the Gūjar tribe of Rājpūts and ruler of Ghāshera and Koel, nominally dependant on Dehlī. The Nawāb Safdar Jang in one of his contests had been deserted by Rāo Bahādur Singh, whose punishment was entrusted by the emperor to Sūraj Mal Jāṭ, with the grant of all the lands and castles he might wrest from his opponent. He performed the duty triumphantly. Bahādur Singh was killed in the siege of Ghāshera, which with Koel acknowledged the sovereignty of the Jāṭ prince. These events occurred in A.D. 1753, and form an episode in the *Sujān Cherittra*, a heroic poem.

Rao Dalip or Dalpat Rao Bundela (راو دلیپ). *Vide* Rām Singh Hāṛā.

Rao Jodha, Rathor (راو جدهر), of Jodhpūr. He had 23 brothers, who had separate fiefs. He founded Jodhpūr, and removed from Mandor about the year A.D. 1458.

Rao Maldeo (راو مالديو). *Vide* Māldeo Rāo.

Rao Raj Singh Rathor (راو راج سنگه راتهور). He commanded the advanced body of the army of the emperor 'Alamgīr in the Deccan. He died about the year A.D. 1675, A.H. 1086.

Rao Ratan Singh (راو رتن سنگه), a Rāja of Bhartpūr. *Vide* Ratan Singh.

Rao Ratan Singh Hara (راو رتن سنگه هاڑا), son of Rāo Bhōj Hāṛā, the son of Rāo Sarjan Herāt, Rāja of Būndī. He succeeded his father in the Rāj about the year A.D. 1607, A.H. 1016. The rank of 5,000 was conferred on him by Jahāngīr with the title of Sarbaland Hāṛā, and subsequently with that of Rāmrāj. He died A.D. 1630, A.H. 1040.

Rasa (رسا), poetical name of Mirzā Eizid Bakhsh, which see.

Rashid (رشید), or Ibn Raschid or Averroes. *Vide* Ibn-Rashīd.

Rashid (رشید) (Pasha), a celebrated Turkish Statesman, was born at Constantinople about A.D. 1802. Though a Turk, he was one of the most enlightened men of his time, and was well versed in foreign languages, general literature and science. He died 7th January, A.D. 1858. He was 55 years of age, and filled the position of grand wazīr at the time of his death. He was known to Europeans as Redschid Pasha.

Rashidi of Samarqand (رشیدی سمرقندی), or of Balkh, surnamed Watwāt, a poet celebrated for his ready wit and smallness of stature. He was a descendant of 'Umar Khattāb and a native of Balkh, but brought up at Samarqand. He flourished in the time of Sulṭān Atsiz, son of Khwārizm Shāh, one of the Sulṭāns of Khwārizm. He was a contemporary of Anwarī, and was in the fort of Hazār Asp while besieged by Sulṭān Sanjar, in whose service Anwarī was. During the siege the two poets wrote very severe satires against the parties of each other, which they exchanged by means of arrows; but the fort being at length taken, Watwāt was made prisoner. He was, however, released at the intercession of Anwarī, and they both became intimate friends. He was called Watwāt, which is the name of a small animal, on account of his being of a small stature and thin in body. He died in the year A.D. 1182, A.H. 578, in the time of Sulṭān Shāh, the son of Arsalān, the son of Atsiz, aged 97 years, at Jurjānia in Khwārizm. He is the author of the *Misbāh Sharīf*, an extensive collection of poems on various subjects, and different metres also of several other works, one of which is called *Hadāeq-us-Sehr*. He is also called Rashīd-uddīn Abdul Jalīl Watwāt 'Umarī. His Dīwān contains 15,000 verses.

Rashid Mehrban (رشید مهربان), a man who was the leading Zoroastrian inhabitant of Yezd in Tehran, and enjoyed the confidence of the Shāh of Persia. He was assassinated by the Musalmāns at Yezd on the 28th November, 1874.

Rashid-uddin Amir (رشید الدین امیر), whose full name is Fazl-ullāh Rashīd-uddīn ibn-'Imād-uddaula, Abū'l Khair-ibn-Mawaffiq-uddaula. He was author of the *Jāma'-ut-Tawārīkh*, or collection of histories, which he completed in A.D. 1310, A.H. 710, and deposited in the mosque constructed by him at Tabrez. He was born in the city of Hamdān in A.D. 1247, A.H. 645, was by profession a physician, and it was probably from skill in the science of medicine that he procured office under the Tartar Sulṭāns of Persia. He passed part of his life in the service of Abā Khān, king of Persia. At a subsequent period Ghāzān Khān, who was a friend to literature, appointed him to the post of wazīr in A.D. 1298, A.H. 697, in conjunction with Sa'd-uddīn, who became his enemy. Rashīd-uddīn was maintained in his office by Aljāitū, surnamed Khudā Banda, the brother and successor of Ghāzān Khān, and was treated by him with great consideration and rewarded with the utmost liberality. Rashīd-uddīn, in his first rupture with Sa'd-uddīn, was compelled in self-defence to denounce him, and to cause him to be put to death. Amīr 'Alī Shāh Jūbān, a person of low origin, was appointed Sa'd-uddīn's successor at Rashīd-uddīn's request, but they soon fell out, and shortly after the death of Aljāitū, who was succeeded by his son Sultān Abū Sa'īd, Amīr 'Alī Shāh was so far successful in prejudicing the Sultān against the old minister, that he was removed from the wizārat in A.D. 1317, A.H. 717. A short time afterwards he was recalled, but it was not long before he again lost favour at court, and was accused of causing the death of his patron, Aljāitū Khan. It was charged against him that he had recommended a purgative medicine to be administered to the late king, in opposition to the advice of another physician, and that under its effects the king had expired. He was condemned to death, and his son Ibrāhīm, the chief butler, who was only 16 years old, and by whose hands the potion was said to have been given to the king, was put to death before the eyes of his parent, who was immediately afterwards cloven in twain by the executioner. His head was borne through the streets of Tabrez, and proclaimed by the public crier as the head of a Jew. Rashīd-udddīn was 73 years old when he died, and his death occurred on the 19th July, A.D. 1318, 13th Jumāda I. A.H. 718. His eldest son, Ghayās-uddīn, was subsequently raised to the same dignities as his father, and met with an equally tragical death. Besides the *Jāma'-ut-Tawārīkh*, Rashīd-uddīn composed several other works, such as the *Kitāb-ut-Tauzīhat*, *Miftāh-ut-Tāfāsīr*, and the *Risālat-us-Sultāniat* (*vide* Fazl-ullāh). The body of Rashīd-uddīn was buried near the mosque which he had constructed in Tabrez, but by a strange fatality it was not destined to repose quietly in this its last asylum. Nearly a century after his death, the government of Tabrez, together with Azurbaijān, was given by Taimūr to his son Mīrānshāh. This young prince, naturally of mild disposition, had become partially deranged in consequence of an injury of the head occasioned by a fall from his horse, and one day, during a temporary access of madness, caused the bones of Rashīd-uddīn to be exhumed, and they were finally deposited in the cemetery of the Jews.

Rashid Billah (راشد باللّٰه), a Khalīfa of Baghdād. *Vide* Al-Rashīd Billāh.

Rashid-uddin Watwat (رشید الدین وطواط). *Vide* Rashīdī Samarqandī and Watwāt.

Rashk (رشک), poetical name of 'Alī Aosat, who is the author of a dictionary and three Urdū Dīwāns, the last of which he composed in A.D. 1845, A.H. 1261.

Rasikh (راسخ), the poetical appellation of Mīr Muhammad Zamān of Sarhind. He was a Sayyad, and a respectable officer in the service of prince 'Azim Shāh, the son of the emperor 'Alamgīr. He was an excellent poet, and died in the year A.D. 1695, A.H. 1107, at Sarhind.

Rasikh (راسخ), the poetical title of Ghulām 'Alī of Patna, a Dervish, who died in A.D. 1824, A.H. 1240, and has left an Urdū Dīwān.

Ratan Singh (رتن سنگه), also called Rāo Ratan Singh, was the second son of Sūrajmal Jāt. He succeeded his brother Jawāhir Singh in the Rāj of Bhartpūr in A.D. 1768, A.H. 1182, and was not long afterwards murdered by a low assassin named Rūpa Nand, who pretended to be a transmuter of metals, and whom the Rāja had threatened with death. Ratan Singh reigned ten months and thirteen days, and left an infant son named Kehrī Singh, during whose minority internal commotions, occasioned by contests for the regency, contributed to the success of Najaf Khān (*q.v.*) with whom the Jāts were then at war. Kehrī Singh dying was succeeded by his uncle Nawal Singh, the brother of Ratan Singh.

Rathor (رتهور), a tribe of Rājpūts or Rājas, who reigned in Jodhpūr (Mārwār). *Vide* Māldeo.

Raughani (روغنی), a jester in the service of the emperor Akbar. He is the author of a Dīwān consisting of 3,000 verses. He appears to have died in Kābul in the country of the Kāfirs in A.D. 1573, A.H. 981. The following chronogram on his death expresses the estimation in which he was held by his contemporaries: "H; has given his life in Kāfiristān like a dog."

Rayah (رایح), poetical name of Mīr Muhammad 'Alī, a Persian poet.

Rayazi of Herat (ریاضی هروی), an author and poet who flourished in the time of Shāh Ismā'īl I. Safwī. He left a Masnawī of 8,000 verses, containing an account of the reign of Sultān Husain Mirzā of Herāt, and had begun a poem on the exploits of Shāh Ismā'īl, but did not finish it. He died in A.D. 1515, A.H. 921.

Rayazi of Samarqand (ریاضی سمرقندی), an author who died in A.D. 1479, A.H. 884.

Raymond, General (رایمند), a French chief in the service of the Niẓām of Haidarābād. He distinguished himself in the battle of Kurdla, 1795. He died in the middle of the year A.D. 1798, and was succeeded by General Perron. But the force was broken up, and a contingent substituted under British officers.

[*Vide* Malleson's *Final French Struggles* where a high testimony is borne to Raymond's character.]

Raza, Imam (رضا امام). *Vide* 'Alī Mūsī Razā

Raza Quli Mirza (رضا قلی مرزا), the eldest son of Nādir Shāh. He was blinded by his father in A.D. 1741, A.H. 1154.

Razi (راضی), poetical title of Fasāhat Khān, who flourished about the year A.D. 1700, A.H. 1112, and was the author of a Dīwān and a Masnawī.

Razi (راضی), takhallus of Muhammad bin-Zikaria, who assumed the poetical name of Rāzī, because he was a native of the city of Rāi. He was one of the first physicians of the Khalīfa Muqtadir Billāh, and a great philosopher and astronomer. He died in the year A.D. 922, A.H. 311, and is the author of several works, one of which is called *Al-Hāwī* or *Al-Hāwī fi'l Tibb*, which he wrote from the Sanskrit.

Razi (راضی), poetical name of Mīr 'Askarī entitled 'Aqil Khān, the wazīr of the emperor 'Alamgīr.

[*Vide* 'Aqil Khān (Nawāb).]

Razia Sultana (رضیه سلطانه), a queen of Dehlī. *Vide* Sulṭāna Rāzīa.

Razi Billah (راضی بالله). *Vide* Al-Rāzī Billāh.

Razi, Maulana (رضی نیشاپوی), of Naishāpūr, a poet, whose proper name is Razī-uddīn Muhammad, and who, instead of writing his takhallus in his Dīwān, usually writes Banda (the slave). He died in A.D. 1202, A.H. 598, and was the author of a work on Jurisprudence, entitled *Muhīt*.

Razi, Shaikh (رضی شیخ). *Vide* Shaikh Razī.

Razi-uddin 'Ali Lala (راضی الدین). *Vide* 'Alī Lālā.

Razi-uddin Muhammad-bin-'Ali Shatibi (رضی الدین محمد بن علی شاطبی), an Arabian author, who died A.D. 1285, A.H. 684.

Razi-uddin Naishapuri (رضی الدین). *Vide* Rāzi (Maulana) Rāzī-uddīn Muhammad.

Reinhardt. A French adventurer. *Vide* Shamru.

Rihai (رهائی), poetical name of a poet, who is the author of a Dīwān. He died in A.D. 1572, A.H. 980.

Rihi (رهی), poetical name of Majd-uddīn Hamkar Fārsī, which see.

Rihi (رهی), author of a collection of poems on religious subjects entitled *Durr-i-Aqāed*.

Rijai (رجائی), poetical name of Hasan 'Alī, a native of Herāt, who died in the year A.D. 1558, A.H. 965.

Rind (رند), poetical name of Sayyad Muhammad Khān, son of Mirzā Ghayās-uddīn Muhammad Khān, Bahādur Nasrat Jang, who died in the year 1813, A.H. 1228, at Lucknow. Rind is the author of a Dīwān in Urdū. He was living in A.D. 1850, A.H. 1267.

Rind (رند پوتیکا), poetical name of Jānī Mānkī Lāl, a Kayeth of Dehlī. He is the author of a small Dīwān in Persian, which he published in the year A.D. 1851.

Rizq-ullah, Shaikh (رزق الله شیخ), whose poetical name is Mushtāqī, was the uncle of Shaikh 'Abdul Haq bin-Saif-uddīn of Dehlī, and brother of Shaikh Nūr-ul-Haq's grandfather, Shaikh Nūr-ul-Haq being the son of 'Abdul Haq. Rizq-ullāh is the author of a history called *Wāka'āt Mushtāqī*, written by him in the reign of Sulṭān Sikandar. He was a Persian as well as a Hindī poet. In Persian compositions he used Mushtāqī for his poetical title, and in Hindī, Rājan; and he is also the author of a work in Hindī which he called *Jot Niranjan*. He was born in the year A.D. 1495, A.H. 901, and died in A.D. 1561, A.H. 969. He had eight brothers, all of whom were men of learning.

Roshan 'Ara Begam (روشن ارا بیگم), the youngest daughter of Shāh Jahān. She died about the year A.D. 1669, A.H. 1080, and is buried at Shāhjahānābād in her own garden, called the Garden of Roshan 'Arā.

Roshan - uddaula Rustam Jang (روشن الدوله رستم جنگ), whose proper name was Zafar Khān, was a nobleman of the reign of Muhammad Shāh. He is the founder of the Sonahrī Masjid (golden mosque) at Dehlī, situated near the Kōtwālī Chabūtra, and built in the year A.D. 1722, A.H. 1134. Another mosque or college, called the Masjid of Rōshan-uddaula, situated in the vicinity of Kāzīwara at Dehlī, which he had inlaid all over with gold, was built by him in A.D. 1725, A.H. 1137. This is that college, on the roof of which Nādir Shāh took post, and from whence he gave orders to slaughter the inhabitants of that city. Rōshan-uddaula died in the 14th year of Muhammad Shāh, A.D. 1732, A.H. 1145.

Roshan-uddaula, Nawab (روشن الدوله), brother to the late Nizām of Haidarābād, died of apoplexy on 27th July, A.D. 1870.

Roz Afzun, Nazir (روز افزون ناظر خواجه سرا), a celebrated Khwāja Sarā or eunuch of the emperor Muhammad Shāh. The garden called Bāgh Nāzir at Shāhjahānābād, Dehlī, was built by him in the year A.D. 1748, A.D. 1161.

Roz Bihan Shaikh (روز بهان شیخ), surname of Abū Muhammad ibn-Abī Nasr-al-Baqilī, a learned and pious Musalmān, who is the author of the commentary on the Qurān called *Tafsīr Arāesh*, *Safwat-al-Mashārib*, and several other works. He died in July, A.D. 1209, Muharram, A.H. 606.

[*Vide* Abū Muhammad Rōz Bihān.]

Rudaki (رودکی), a celebrated Persian poet and musician who flourished in the reign of Amīr Nasr, the son of Ahmad Sāmānī; and though born blind, soon attained, from the superiority of his genius, the highest rank at the court of that liberal ruler. History, indeed, gives no instance of a poet so honoured. His establishment was raised by Nasr to a level with that of the proudest nobles; and we may conjecture the style in which Rudakī lived, when assured that he was served by two hundred slaves, and that his equipment was conveyed, when he attended his patron in the field, by four hundred camels. He turned the Arabic translation of *Pilpay's Fables* into modern Persian verse in A.D. 925, A.H. 313, and received from his royal master a reward of 40,000 dirhams. He is the first who wrote a Dīwān or book of Odes in Persian. His original name is Farīd-uddīn 'Abū 'Abdullāh, but he assumed the title of Rudakī from Rudak, the place of his birth in Samarqand or Bukhārā. His death happened in the year A.D. 954, A.H. 343.

Ruhani, Amir (روحانی امیر), a most learned poet and philosopher. He was a native of Samarqand and a pupil of Rashīdī. He fled from Bukhārā after that city was taken by Changez Khān about the year A.D. 1226, A.H. 623, and sought protection at Dehlī in the reign of Sultān Altimsh, where he wrote many excellent poems.

Ruhi (روحی), poetical name of Sayyad Ja'far of Zānbīrpūr. He died in the year A.D. 1741, A.H. 1154.

[*Vide* Sayyad Ja'far.]

Ruhi Baghdadi (روحی بغدادی), a Turkish poet of celebrity. His satires are very forcible and striking, and his manner not unlike that of Juvenal.

Ruhul Amin Khan, Shaikh (روح الامین خان شیخ), son of Qāzī Muhammad Sa'īd of Bilgram. He was related to Shaikh Alāh Yār Khān, whose sister he married. He was an excellent poet and wrote a poem containing 7,000 verses. He held the rank of 6,000 with a jāgīr and 2,000 sawārs. He acted as deputy to Nawāb Sipahdār Khān, and after his death to Nawāb Mubāriz-ul-Mulk Sarbaland Khān, Sūbadār of Allahābād. He was subsequently made governor of 22 mahāls in the Panjāb in the time of Muhammad Shāh, and was killed in battle against Nādir Shāh at Karnāl on Tuesday, 13th February, A.D. 1739, 15th Zi-Qa'da, A.H. 1151.

Ruh-ullah Khan (روح الله خان), an Amīr who held the high office of Mīr Bakhshī or Paymaster-General, in the reign of the emperor 'Alamgīr. He died in the Deccan in the 36th year of the emperor, on the 8th August, A.D. 1692, 5th Zil-hijja, A.H. 1103. After his death his son Khānazād Khān, who was grand-steward of the emperor's household and treasurer of the privy purse, was also honoured with the title of Rūh-ullāh Khān II. and died about the year A.D. 1703, A.H. 1115.

Rukn Kashi, Hakim (رکن کاشی حکیم), a physician and poet who adopted Masīh for his poetical name. He was a respected attendant at the court of Shāh Abbās the Great, king of Persia, but having taken offence on some cause or other, he came to India and passed some years in the service of the emperor Akbar and his successors, Jahāngīr and Shāh Jahān, during whose reign he went on a pilgrimage to Mecca and returning from thence to Persia he died there some years afterwards in A.D. 1646, A.H. 1056, or, as some authors say, about the year A.D. 1656, A.H. 1066, and left nearly 100,000 verses. His nephew Rahmat Khān, also called Hakīm Ziyā-uddīn, son of Hakīm Qutba, served under Shāh Jahān and 'Alamgīr, and died about the year A.D. 1664, A.H. 1075.

Rukn-uddaula (ركن الدوله) was the brother of 'Imād-uddaula 'Alī Bōya, the founder of the race of the Bōyaites, whom he succeeded on the throne of Fars and 'Irāq, A.D. 949, A.H. 328. He was lord of Isfahān, Rei, Hamdān and all Persian 'Irāq, and father of the three princes 'Azd-uddaula, Muwayyad-uddaula and Fakhr-uddaula, between whom he shared his possessions, which they governed with the greatest ability. He continued to reside in 'Irāq after the death of his brother, and gave over the charge of the affairs of Fars to his eldest son, 'Azd-uddaula. Besides 'Imād-uddaula he had another brother, Moiz-uddaula, younger than himself, who was wazīr to the Khalīf Al-Rāzī Billāh and his three successors. Rukn-uddaula died at Rei on Friday night, the 15th September, A.D. 976, 18th Muharram, A.H. 366, and was buried in the mausoleum which bears his name at Shīrāz. He is said to have reigned 44 lunar years 1 month and 9 days, viz. he governed Persia during the life of his brother more than 16 years, and after his death he reigned nearly 28 years. He was succeeded by his son Muwayyad-uddaula.

[*Vide* 'Alī Bōya.]

Rukn-uddaula (ركن الدوله), a minister of the Nizām of Haidarābād, who was put to death by his master about the year A.D. 1794. His subserviency to the views of the Marhattas has generally been considered one of the chief causes which induced the Nizām to put him to death.

Rukn-uddaula Ya'tqad Khan (ركن الدوله اعتقاد خان), whose original name was Muhammad Murād, was by birth a Kashmerian, and native of the same place as Sāhiba Niswān, mother of Farrukh-siyar. He was introduced by her to the emperor, whom he persuaded that he could easily effect the destruction of the two brother Sayyads without coming to open war, or causing confusion in the State. Farrukh-siyar, gratified by his flatteries, suddenly promoted him to the rank of 7000 with suitable jāgīrs and the title of Rukn-uddaula. The district of Murādabād was taken from Nizām-ul-Mulk and, being with additional lands created into a Sūbadārī, was conferred on him, but after the dethronement of Farrukh-siyar in A.D. 1719, A.H. 1131, by the Sayyads, he was disgraced, put under strict confinement, his fortune confiscated and severe tortures were also inflicted upon his person, to compel a disclosure of his wealth. He died during the reign of Muhammad Shāh.

Rukn-uddin Dabir (ركن الدين دبير), author of the *Shamāel Atkia*, a record of the excellencies of the saints, and of the wonders and miracles performed by the Almighty; with an eulogium on Muhammad, dedicated to Burhān-uddīn Sūfī.

Rukn-uddin Firoz, Sultan (ركن الدين فيروز سلطان), the son of Sultān Shams-uddīn Altimsh, king of Dehlī, at whose death he ascended the throne on the 1st May, A.D. 1236, Shabān, A.H. 633, but was after six months deposed by the nobles, and his sister Sultāna Razia was placed on the throne on the 19th November the same year. Rukn-uddīn died in confinement some time afterwards.

Rukn-uddin Masa'ud Masihi, Maulana (ركن الدين مسعود مسيحى مولانا), author of the Arabic work on the practice of Medicine called *Zābitat-ul-Ilāj*. He was also a good poet and was living about the year A.D. 1585, A.H. 993.

Rukn-uddin Qabai (ركن الدين قبائي), a poet who was a pupil of Asīr-uddīn Asmānī. He was a native of Qabai in Turkey, and contemporary with the poet Ma'jizī.

Rukn-uddin Shaikh (ركن الدين شيخ), surnamed Abū'l Fatha, a Muhammadan saint, was the son of Shaikh Sadr-uddīn 'Arif and grandson of Shaikh Bahā-uddīn Zikaria of Multān. He lived in the time of Sultān 'Alā-uddīn Sikandar Sānī about the year A.D. 1310, A.H. 710, and was a contemporary of Nizām-uddin Aulia. Shaikh Jalāl, who is commonly called Makhdūm Jahānian, as well as Shaikh 'Usmān Syyāh, were his disciples.

Rumani (رمانى), a learned Musalmān, whose proper name was Abū'l Hasan 'Alī-bin-Īsā. He died A.D. 994, A.H. 384. [The word (="Roman") was an epithet often applied during the Middle Ages to natives of the Eastern Empire.]

Runaq (رونق), poetical name of Rām Sahāe, a Hindū, who was an excellent Persian poet.

Runaqi (رونقى), a poet of Hamdān who died in A.D. 1622, A.H. 1031.

Rupmati or **Rupmani, a Hindū poetess,** the favourite of Bāz Bahādur of Mālwā (*q.v.*). On the defeat and flight of her protector she committed suicide to escape the addresses of Adham Khān (*q.v.*). Her story will be found in *Sk. of the Hist. of Hindūstān.*

Rup Singh, Raja (روپ سنگه راجه) gave his daughter in marriage to Muhammad Muazzim, the son of 'Alamgīr, in the year A.D. 1661, A.H. 1072.

Ruqayya (رقیه), a daughter of Muhammad. She was at first married to 'Utba, the son of Abū Lahab, Muhammad's uncle, and after being divorced by him was married to 'Usmān, the son of Affān. She died about the month of March, A.D. 624, A.H. 2, a few days after the battle of Badar.

Ruqia (رقیه سلطان). *Vide* Sultāna Ruqaya.

Ruqia Sultana Begam (رقیه). *Vide* Sultāna Ruqaya.

Ruqta (رقته), name of a place built by the emperor Akbar about ten kōs from Samoghar, where all his Begams and relations had built their houses as far as Gaughat. This was a park or pleasure-ground.

Rustam (رستم), a legendary hero of Persia, whom some Persian historians call Rustam Dāstān and Rustam Zābulī, because he was a native and governor of Zābulistān. This personage, who was the greatest and most famous of all Persian heroes, is said to have been the son of Zāl or Zālzar, and grandson of Sām, the son of Narīmān. He was killed in a battle fought against Bahman, the sixth king of the dynasty of the Kayānians. [Rustam possibly represents a rebellion of the southern provinces.]

Rustam 'Ali, Maulana (رستم علی مولانا), son of 'Alī 'Asghar of Qanauj. He is the author of the commentary on the Qurān called *Tafsīr Saghīr*. He died in A.D. 1764, A.H. 1178.

Rustam Bastami, Khwaja Nizam-uddin (رستم بسطامی خواجه), an author who died in A.D. 1431, A.H. 834.

Rustam Qadd Khoziani, Khwaja (رستم قد خوزیانی خواجه), a poet who was a native of Khōziān, a village in Bastām, and flourished about the year A.D. 1408, A.H. 811. He was a panegyrist of Sultān 'Umar, son of Mīrānshāh, ruler of Khurāsān, and a contemporary of Shāhrukh Mirzā. In the *Mirat-ul-Khayāl* he is also said to be contemporary with Ibn-ul-Arabī, but this cannot be correct, for Ibn-ul-Arabī died in A.D. 1240, A.H. 638, and Sultān 'Umar and Shāhrukh lived in the early part of the ninth century of the Hijra.

Rustam Zaman Khan (رستم زمان خان). *Vide* Alah Yār Khān.

Ryazi (ریاضی). *Vide* Rayāzī.

S

Sa'adat (سعادت), poetical name of Mīr Sa'ādat 'Alī, a resident of Amroha and pupil of Shāh Wilāyet-ullāh. He is the author of a poem called *Sailī Sakhion*, containing the story of two lovers who lived in the time of Nawāb Qamar-uddīn Khān, wazīr.

Sa'adat 'Ali Khan, Nawab (سعادت علی خان نواب), surnamed Yeman-uddaula, was raised to the masnad of Audh at Lucknow by Sir John Shore, Governor-General, after the death of his brother Nawāb 'Asaf-uddaula, and the dethronement of that Nawāb's adopted son Wazīr 'Alī Khān, on the 21st January, A.D. 1798, 4th Shabān, A.H. 1212. He died, after a reign of nearly 17 years, on the 11th July, A.D. 1814, 22nd Rajab, A.H. 1229, and was succeeded by his son Ghāzī-uddīn Haidar, who was afterwards crowned king of Audh. In the treaty with Sa'ādat 'Alī Khān, the annual subsidy was fixed at 76 lakhs of rupees and the English force in Audh at 10,000 men. The fort of Allahābād was also surrendered to the English. Twelve lakhs of rupees were to be paid to the English as compensation for the expense of placing him on the masnad, and he was restrained from holding communication with any foreign state, employing any Europeans, or permitting any to settle in his dominions, without the consent of his British ally.

Sa'adat Khan (سعادت خان برهان الملک), styled Burhān-ul-Mulk, whose former name was Muhammad Amīn, was originally a merchant of Khurāsān. He is the progenitor of the nawābs and kings of Audh. His father, Nasīr Khān, came to India during the reign of Bahādur Shāh, and after his death Muhammad Amīn came also. At the commencement of the emperor Muhammad Shah's reign he held the faujdārī of Bayāna, and was in the year A.D. 1724, A.H. 1136, appointed governor of Audh with the title of Sa'ādat Khān, in the room of Rāja Girdhar, who was appointed governor of Mālwā. He afterwards received the title of Barhān-ul-Mulk and was present in the battle with Nādir Shāh, dying on the night previous to the massacre of Dehlī by that monarch, *i.e.* on the 9th March, A.D. 1739, 9th Zil-hijja, A.H. 1152; he was buried at Dehlī in the mausoleum of his brother Sayādat Khān. His only child was a daughter, who was married to his nephew Abū'l Mansūr Khān Safdar Jang, the son of Sayādat Khān, who succeeded him in the government of Audh.

List of the Nawābs and Kings of Lucknow.

Burhān-ul-Mulk Sa'ādat Khān.
Abū'l Mansūr Khān Safdar Jang.
Shujā-uddaula, son of Safdar Jang.
'Asaf-uddaula, son of Shujā-uddaula.
Wazīr 'Alī Khān (deposed as spurious).
Sa'ādat 'Alī Khān, son of 'Asaf.
Ghāzī-uddīn Haidar, son of Sa'ādat 'Alī Khān, who was made king of Audh by Lord Hastings.
Nasīr-uddīn Haidar, son of ditto.
Muhammad 'Alī Shāh, brother of Ghazī-uddīn Haidar.
Amjad 'Alī Shāh, son of Muhammad 'Alī.
Wājid 'Alī Shāh, the son of Amjād 'Alī Shāh, the last king of Audh, in whose time that country was annexed to the British Government (1856).

Sa'adat-ullah Khan (سعادت الله خان), a regular and acknowledged Nawāb of the Karnatic, who, having no issue, adopted two sons of his brother, appointing the elder, Dost 'Alī, to succeed him in the Nawābship, and conferring upon the younger, Bākir 'Alī, the government of Velore; he likewise directed that Ghulām Husain, the nephew of his favourite wife, should be Dīwān or prime minister to his successor. Having reigned from the year A.D. 1710 to 1722, A.H. 1122 to 1135, he died much regretted by his subjects. According to the *Māsir-ul-Umrā*, he held the Nawābship of the Karnatic from the time of 'Alamgīr to the year A.D. 1732, A.H. 1145. Dost 'Alī and his son Hasan 'Alī were killed in battle against the Mahrattas on the 20th May, A.D. 1740. His son Safdar 'Alī succeeded him, but was poisoned by his brother-in-law Murtaza 'Alī and died on the 2nd October, A.D. 1742. After his death Murtaza 'Alī was acknowleged Nawāb of the Karnatic; but in March, A.D. 1744, Nizām-ul-Mulk, the sūbadār of the Deccan, having appointed one of his officers, named Anwar-uddīn, Nawāb of Arkot, he (Murtaza 'Alī) was deposed.

Sa'adat Yar Khan (سعادت یار خان), son of Muhammad Yār Khān, the son of Hāfiz Rahmat Khān, the Rohela chief, is the author of a work called *Guli Rahmat*, being a history of his grandfather Hāfiz Rahmat, written in 1833. This work is an abridgment of the *Gulistān Rahmat*, written by Mustaza Khān, his uncle.

Sa'adat Yar Khan (سعادت یار خان), son of Muhkan-uddaula Tahmāsp Beg Khān Ya'tkād Jang Bahādur.

[*Vide* Rangīn.]

Sabahi (صباحی), the poetical name of Akhund Masīhā.

Sabat (ثبات), the poetical name of Mīr Muhammad 'Azīm, the son of Mīr Muhammad Afzal Sābit, born at Allahābād in A.D. 1710, A.H. 1122. He died in A.D. 1748, A.H. 1161, and left a Dīwān of about 4,000 verses.

Sabiq (سابق), poetical appellation of Mirzā Yūsaf Beg, a poet whose brothers were mansabdārs in the service of the emperor 'Alamgīr: he himself was a dervish and died in A.D. 1687, A.H. 1098.

Sabir (صابر), poetical name of Mīr Said 'Alī, a famous musician, who wrote a work in Persian containing instructions on music, *temp.* Shāh 'Alam.

Sabir (صابر), poetical title of Shāh-zāda Mirzā Qādir Bakhsh of Dehlī. He is the author of a Dīwān in Urdū.

Sabir (صابر). *Vide* Shahādīn Adīb Sābir.

Sabit (ثابت), the poetical title of Mīr Muhammad Afzal of Dehlī, who died in A.D. 1738, A.H. 1151, and left a Dīwān in Persian of 5,000 verses.

Sabit (ثابت), poetical title of Khwāja Hasan, an Urdū poet, who is the author of a Dīwān. He died in A.D. 1821, A.H. 1236.

Sabit-bin-Qirra (ثابت بن قره), who translated Euclid and several other works into Arabic from the Greek, and died in the year A.D. 901, A.H. 288.

Sabr (صبر), poetical title of Mīr Husain 'Alī of Lucknow, a pupil of Asghar 'Alī Khān Nasīm of Dehlī.

Sabri (صبری), also called Roz Bihān, a Persian poet of Isfahān.

Sabuhi (صبوحی), a poet in the service of the emperor Akbar. He died in the year A.D. 1564, A.H. 972.

Sabzwari (سبزواری), a native of Sabzwār and author of the *Sawāna Sabzwārī*, which contains a description of the city of Daulatābād in the Deccan, with a particular account of all the Sūfīs and holy men that are buried in its vicinity, written in A.D. 1318, A.H. 718.

Sadafi (صدفی), a poet who flourished in the time of Muhammad Shāh. He is the author of a Dīwān which is usually called *Dīwān Sadafī*, but the true title given by the author is *Rāz-ul-'Arifī*.

Sadasheo Bhao (سداشیو بهاؤ), a Mahratta chief, son of Chimnājī and nephew of the Peshwā Bālājī or Bājī Rāo. He was slain in battle against Ahmad Shāh Abdālī on the 14th January, A.D. 1761, 6th Jumāda II. A.H. 1174. After his death several pretenders started up, calling themselves the Bhāo. In 1779 one appeared in Benares and began to levy troops and raise disturbances in the city, upon which he was seized and confined in the English garrison at Chunar, from whence he was released by Mr. Hastings in 1782.

Sada Suk (سدا سوک), son of Bishun Parshād, the son of Gulāb Rāe, a Kāyeth of Allahābād and author of a work on the art of writing prose and poetry entitled *Murassa Khurshaid*, which he wrote in A.D. 1802, A.H. 1217. He also wrote a book of Anecdotes in Urdū.

Sa'd-bin-'Abdullah-al-Asha'ri (سعد بن عبدالله الاشعری), or Ibn-ul-Farāez, author of a treatise on the law of Inheritance, entitled *Ihtijāj-ush-Shia*. He died A.D. 913, A.H. 301.

Sa'd-bin'-Sharif Jaunpuri (سعد بن شریف جونپوری), author of a Persian work called *Dastūr-ul-Musallīn*.

Sa'd-bin-Zangi, Atabak (سعد بن زنگی اتابک). *Vide* Sunqar, or Sanqar.

Sa'di (سعدی دکهنی), of the Deccan, who is the author of some verses which are erroneously ascribed to Sa'dī of Shīrāz.

Sa'd-ibn Ahmad (سعد ابن احمد), Qāzī of Toleda. He died A.D. 1069, A.H. 462.

Sa'did-uddin Gazaruni (صدید الدین گازرونی), author of an Arabic work on Medicine called *Almughnī*.

Sa'did Usi (صدید اوسی), an excellent poet, author of the *Jāmą-ul-Makiat*.

Sadiq (صادق). His proper name is Sādiq 'Alī, and he is the author of the *Chahār Bāgh Haidarī*, dedicated to Nawāb Ghāzī-uddīn Haidar of Lucknow, who died in A.D. 1827, A.H. 1243. It contains selections from ancient authors rather than original poetry.

Sadiq (صادق), the poetical name of Mīr Ja'far Khān, grandson of Said Muhammad Qādirī. He is the author of a work called *Bahāristān Ja'farī*. He was a native of Dehlī, where he died some years before A.D. 1782, A.H. 1196, and was buried in the same vault wherein his grandfather was interred, and which is over the nala of Bairām Dai in Dehlī.

Sadiqi (صادقی), poetical name of Sādiq Beg, of the tribe of Afshār. He is the author of a Dīwān and a Tazkira or Biography of poets in Turkī.

Sadiq Khan (صادق خان), the son of 'Aqā Tākir, whose poetical name was Waslī, grandson of Muhammad Sharaf Hajrī, and nephew and son-in-law of Ya'tmād-uddaula Tehrānī. He held a high rank in the time of Akbar and Jahāngīr, and died on the 7th October, A.D. 1630, 9th Rabī' I. A.H. 1040, in the reign of the emperor Shāh Jahān.

Sadiq Khan (صادق خان) was a spiritual guide of the emperor Akbar the Great. He died in A.D. 1597, A.H. 1006. To the left of the road, about half way between Sikandra and Āgra, are some tombs in the fields; one with an adjacent hall of 64 pillars is believed to be the resting-place of this saint.

[*Vide* Keene's *Āgra Guide*, p. 44.]

Sadiq Khan (صادق خان), brother of Karīm Khān, king of Persia. He took possession of Shīrāz after the death of Zakī Khān; reigned nearly two years, and was murdered on the 14th March, A.D. 1781.

[*Vide* Karīm Khān Zand.]

Sa'diq Muhammad Khan (صادق محمد خان ازادها زهی ازاده), a mansabdār of 4000; died A.D. 1597, A.H. 1005, buried at Dholpūr. He was a Persian, cousin to Nūr Jahān, one of whose sisters he married. He was esteemed one of Akbar's best officers.

Sa'di, Shaikh (سعدی شیرازی شیخ), of Shīrāz, a celebrated Persian poet, whose full appellation was Shaikh Maslah-uddīn Sa'dī-al-Shirāzī. He was born at Shīrāz about the year A.D. 1175, A.H. 571, and died in A.D. 1292, A.H. 691, aged 120 lunar years. During his youth he served as a soldier both against the Hindūs and the Crusaders; by the latter he was taken prisoner, and obliged to work at the fortifications of Tripoli, whence he was liberated by a person who gave him his daughter in marriage; but the lady was of so bad a temper that the poet complained he had exchanged his slavery for a worse bondage. He was a great traveller, and made the pilgrimage to Mecca fourteen times. He was a disciple of the venerated Sūfī, 'Abdul Qādir Gīlānī, or, at least, adopted his opinion. His tomb is still to be seen in the neighbourhood of Shīrāz. Besides the Gulistān and Bostān, he is the author of a large collection of odes and sonnets. There is likewise a short collection of poetical pieces attributed to him called *Al-Khabīsāt* or the book of Impurities. The author, however, seems to have repented of having written these indecent verses, yet endeavours to excuse himself on account of their giving a relish to other poems, "as salt is used in the seasoning of meat." His works, all of which are held in high estimation, are the following:—

A Preface.	Rubā'yāt.
Majālis Khān.	Fardiāt.
Resala Sāhib Dīwān.	Ghazaliāt.
Gulistān.	Mukaltiāt.
Bostān.	Murakkabāt.
Pand-nāma.	Al-Khabīsāt.
Qasāed Arabī.	Tarjiāt.
Qasāed Fārsī.	Kitāb-al-Badāya.
Marāsī.	Kitāb Tyyobāt.
Mulamma'āt.	Al-Khawātīm.
Muzahhabāt.	

A very good edition of Sa'dī's works was published in Calcutta by Mr. Harrington, with an English Preface containing memoirs of the author and many interesting anecdotes; and Mr. Gladwin translated some of his works, including the *Gulistān*. From the late Mr. E. B. Eastwick, C.B., we have another English version of the *Gulistān*. Jamī calls Sa'dī *the Nightingale of the Groves of Shīrāz*.

Sadr Jahan (صدر جهان), a learned Muhammadan who lived in the time of Sultān Qulī Qutb Shāh, king of Golkanda, who reigned from A.D. 1512 to 1543, A.H. 918 to

949. He is the author of a Persian work called *Marghūb-ul-Kulūb*, a history of that king.

Sadr Jahan, Qazi (صدر جهان قاضی). *Vide* Minhāj-us-Sirāj.

Sadr Jahan, Mir (صدر جهان میر), a well educated and learned Musalmān, a native of a village near Lucknow. He was an officer of 4000 in the service of the emperor Akbar, in the 31st year of whose reign, A.D. 1585, A.H. 993, he was sent on an embassy, together with Hakīm Humām, to 'Abdullah Khān Uzbak, ruler of Tūrān, whose father, Iskandar Khān, had died at that time. He lived 120 years, and at the time of his death, which took place in A.D. 1611, A.H. 1020, he was so much emaciated by old age, that there was nothing left in him but bones.

Sadr-uddin Ardibeli (صدر الدین اردبیلی). *Vide* Sadr-uddīn Mūsa.

Sadr-uddin bin-Ya'qub, Mulla (صدر الدین بن یعقوب ملا), author of a collection of decisions in Persian entitled *Fatāwā Qarā Khānī*, which was arranged some years after his death by Qarā Khān, in the reign of Sultān 'Alāuddīn.

Sadr-uddin Muhammad (صدر الدین محمد), son of Zabardast Khān, and author of the work called *Irshād-ul-Wazrā*, written in the reign of the emperor Muhammad Shāh.

Sadr-uddin Muhammad (صدر الدین محمد), surnamed Abū'l Ma'ālī, which see.

Sadr-uddin Muhammad bin-Ishaq Qunawi (صدر الدین محمد بن اسحاق قونوی), a native of Iconium and an author, who died in A.D. 1273, A.H. 672.

Sadr-uddin Muhammad, Mir (صدر الدین محمد میر), author of the *Jawāhir-nāma*, a book on Arts and Sciences.

Sadr-uddin Musa, Shaikh (صدر الدین موسیٰ شیخ), the son of Shaikh Safī-uddīn, the celebrated founder of the Safwī kings of Persia.

[*Vide* Shaikh Safī and Ismā'īl Shāh I. Safwī.]

Sadr-uddin Sayyad 'Ali Khan (صدر الدین سید علی خان), son of Sayyad Nizām-uddīn Ahmad Husaini. He was the best Arabic poet of his time, and is the author of the following works: *Qitāb Badīq'*, *Salafat*, and *Sharah Sahīfa Kāmila*.

Sadr-uddin, Shaikh (صدر الدین شیخ), the son of Shaikh Bahā-uddīn of Multān. He died in A.D. 1309, A.H. 709, at Multān and is buried there.

Sadr-uddin, Ufi Maulana (صدر الدین عوفی مولانا), author of the *Jāma'-Hikāyāt*. He is also called Nūr-uddīn Muhammad Ufī, which see.

Sa'd-uddin (سعد الدین), a Turkish historian, was born in 1536, and died at Constantinople in 1599. His history entitled the *Taj-ul-Tawārīkh* (the Crown of Histories), a work held in high estimation by scholars, gives a general account of the Ottoman empire from its commencement in 1299 till 1520. He also wrote the *Sālīm-nāma* or History of Salīm I. which is chiefly a collection of anecdotes regarding that prince.

Sa'd-uddin Hamwia (سعد الدین حمویه), entitled Shaikh-ul-Mashāeq, is the author of several works, one of which is called *Sajanjal-ul-Arwāh*, The Mirror of the Soul, and another entitled *Qitāb Mahbūb*, the Beloved book. He died in the year A.D. 1252, A.H. 650.

Sa'd-uddin of Dehli (سعد الدین دهلوی), author of the works called *Sharh Kans-ul-Daqāiq* and *Sharah Manār*. He died in A.D. 1486, A.H. 891.

Sa'd-uddin of Kashghar (سعد الدین کاشگهر), the spiritual guide of Jāmī. He died A.D. 1456, A.H. 860.

Sa'd-uddin Tuftazani, Mulla (سعد الدین تفتازاني ملا). *Vide* Tuftāzanī.

Sa'd-ullah Khan (سعد الله خان), the son of the Rohela chief 'Alī Muhammad Khān, whom he succeeded to the Rohela territories in A.D. 1749, A.H. 1162, but retired with a pension of eight lakhs of rupees annually from Hāfiz Rahmat Khān, and died in the year A.D. 1761, A.H. 1175, at Aonla. His brother 'Abdullah Khān was killed in the battle which took place between Hāfiz

Rahmat Khān and Nawāb Shujā-uddaula, A.D. 1774, A.H. 1188. After his death his brother Faiz-ullāh Khān succeeded him in the Rohela territories of Rāmpūr.

Sa'd-ullah Khan (سعد الهه خان), whose title was Khān 'Alam, was sent as ambassador to the king of Persia by the emperor Shāh Jahān. He died in the year A.D. 1631, A.H. 1044.

Sa'd-ullah Khan (سعد الهه خان), the brother-in-law of Mahmūd Khān, Nawāb of Bijnour and Munsif of Amroha. He, together with Jalāl-uddīn Khān, the Nawāb's brother, was tried and convicted by court-martial, and shot by order of General Jones on the 23rd April, 1858, at Kote Khādir, within eight miles of Najībābād, on account of their rebellion.

Sa'd-ullah Khan Wazir (سعد الهه خان وزير), surnamed 'Allāmī Fahhāmī, and entitled Jumlat-ul-Mulk, was the most able and upright minister that ever appeared in India. He makes a conspicuous figure in all the transactions of the emperor Shāh Jahān, and is constantly referred to as a model in the correspondence of the emperor 'Alamgīr during the long reign of that monarch. He died on the 9th April, A.D. 1656, 22nd Jumāda II. A.H. 1066, aged 48 lunar years. After his death the mansab of 700 and 100 Sawars was conferred on his son Lutf-ullāh Khān, a boy of 11 years of age.

Sa'd-ullah Kirmani (سعد الهه كرمانى), author of the work called *Fatūhāt Mīrānshāhī*, containing an account of the conquests made by Mīrānshāh, the son of Amīr Taimūr.

Sa'd-ullah, Shaikh (سعد الهه دهلوى شيخ), of Dehlī, a descendant of Islām Khān, who was wazīr to one of the kings of Gujrāt; and as he was a disciple of Shāh Gul, whose poetical name was Wahdat, a descendant of Shaikh Ahmad Mujaddid, consequently he lived like a dervish, and assumed the title of Gulshān for his poetical name. He died at Dehlī on the 13th December, A.D. 1728, 21st Jumāda I. A.H. 1141.

Safavi (صفوى), a Persian dynasty. *Vide* Ismā'īl I.

Safavi Khan (صفوي خان), a descendant of the royal house of Persia of the Ṣafavī family. He held a high rank in the service of the emperor 'Alāmgīr, and was killed in the battle which took place between the two brothers 'Azim Shāh and Bahādur Shāh on the 8th June, A.D. 1707, 18th Rabī I. A.H. 1119.

Safdar 'Ali Khan (صفدر على خان), Nawāb of Arkaṭ, son of Dost 'Alī, murdered by his brother-in-law Murtazā 'Alī Khān, of Vellore, on the 2nd October, A.D. 1742.

Safdar Jang (صفدر جنگ), Nawāb of Audh, whose proper name was Mirzā Muqīm and surname Mansūr 'Alī Khān, was the son of Sayādat Khān, and nephew and son-in-law of Burhān-ul-Mulk Sa'ādat Khān, whom he succeeded in the government of Audh, after paying two crores of rupees to Nādir Shāh in the beginning of the year A.H. 1152, or April, A.D. 1739. He was appointed wazīr in A.D. 1748 on the accession of the emperor Ahmād Shāh (in the room of Nizām ul-Mulk, who had died that year), and assumed the whole administration of the imperial authority for several years. He was, however, dismissed from the wizārat in A.D. 1752, A.H. 1166, and died on his way to Audh at Pāparghāṭ on the 17th October, A.D. 1754, 17th Ẕil-ḥijja, A.H. 1167. He was buried for some time at Gulāb Bāṛī in Faizābād, his seat of government, but afterwards his remains were conveyed to Dehlī and interred in the vicinity of the Dargāh of Shāh Mardān, where a splendid mausoleum was built over his tomb. He was succeeded in the government of Audh by his son Nawāb Shujā-uddaula.

Saffah (صفاح). *Vide* Al-Saffāh.

Safia (صفيه), daughter of a Jew of Khaibar, whom Muhammad married after the battle of Khaibar. She was one of the most beloved wives of the prophet, whom she survived for forty years of widowhood. She died about the year A.D. 670, A.H. 50.

Safi Khan (صفى خان), son of Islām Khān Mashhadī, a nobleman who served under the emperors Shāh Jahān and 'Alamgīr.

Safi Mirza (صفى ميرزا), the son of Shāh 'Abbās I. He was murdered at the instigation of his father, who hated him, about the year A.D. 1611, A.H. 1020.

Safir of Faryab (سفير), poetical name of a poet of Fāryāb.

Safi, Shah (صفى شاه), king of Persia. *Vide* Shāh Ṣafī.

Safi, Shaikh (صفی شیخ). *Vide* Shaikh Ṣafī.

Safi-uddin Muhammad (صفی الدین محمد), son of Husain Wāez. He is the author of a book called *Rishhāt*, which is a chronogram for A.H. 909, in which year it was completed (A.D. 1503). It contains the sayings of his Murshid or spiritual guide Obeid-ullāh Ahrār, who resided at Samarqand.

[*Vide* 'Alī Wāez.]

Safi-uddin, Shaikh (صفی الدین شیخ). *Vide* Ismā'īl Shāh Safwī and Shaikh Safī.

Safshikan Khan (صف شکن خان), title of Muhammad Tāhir, a nobleman of the rank of 3000, who served under the emperor 'Alamgīr and died A.D. 1676, A.H. 1085.

Saguna Bai Saheb (سیگونه بائي صاحب), Rānī of Sitāra and widow of the late Mahārāja of Sitāra Chatrapatī Appa Saheb, who died about the year A.D. 1874.

Sahabi (سحابی), poetical name of a poet who wrote in Persian, and is the author of a Dīwān.

Sahar (سحر), poetical title of Sayyad Nāsir 'Alī, who died in A.D. 1833, A.H. 1249.

Saharawi (صحراوی). *Vide* Abū'l Kāsim Al-Saharāwī.

Sahba (صهبا), whose original name was 'Abdul Bāqī, was a poet who flourished about the year A.D. 1653, A.H. 1063, in the time of the emperor 'Alamgīr.

Sahbai (صهبائي), poetical name of Maulwī Imām Bakhsh, Professor in the Dehlī College. He translated the Arabic work called *Hadāeq-ul-Balāghat* into Urdū, and is the author of several Persian and Urdū works, including a poetical Intikhāb, or anthology, lithographed at Delhī 1842. He was living in A.D. 1854, A.H. 1271.

Sahban (سحبان), the son of Wāil Kheyāī, who lived in the time of Harūn-al-Rashīd. Shaikh Sādī, in his *Gulistān*, says that Sahbān Wail has been considered as unrivalled in eloquence, insomuch that if he spoke before an assembly for the space of a year he did not repeat a word twice, and if the same meaning occurred he repeated it in a different form.

Sahib (صاحب), the poetical appellation of Hakīm Kāzim, commonly called *Masīh-ul-Bayān*. He was a physician and also a poet, and held the rank of 500 in the reign of 'Alamgīr. He died, two or three years before Mirzā Sāeb the poet, about the year A.D. 1667, A.H. 1077, and left two or three Dīwāns. He imitated Jalāl-uddīn Rūmī and wrote several masnawīs or poems, *viz. Aīna Khāna, Parī Khāna, Malāhat Ahmadī, Sabāhat Yūsafī, Gul Muhammad*, and *Aufās Masīhī*.

Sahib (صاحب). *Vide* Masīhāī (Akhānd).

Sahib (صاحب) (Aloysius Reinhardt), a son of Shamrū or Sombre, who had the title of Mazaffar-uddaula Mumtāz-ul-Mulk Nawāb Zafaryāb Khān Bahādur Nasrat Jang. He sometimes held (says an author) assemblies of poets in his house, and is said to have been a pleasant man, but a great scoundrel. He was a pupil of Khairātī Khān Dilsōz. He died in the prime of life, and was buried at Āgra in the small Catholic Church built by his father. He was grandfather of the late Dyce Sombre.

Sahiba Zamani (صاحب زمانی), daughter of the emperor Muhammad Shāh. She was sought in marriage by 'Alamgīr II. but she refused him. Her mother, Malika Jahān, claimed the protection of Ahmad Shāh Abdālī against 'Alamgīr's designs upon her daughter, and he carried them both to Kābul in A.D. 1757, and some time afterwards espoused Sāhiba Zamāni himself.

Sahib Balkhi (صاحب بلخی), a poet of Balkh who wrote panegyrics in praise of some of the kings of Badakhshān. He flourished in the 9th century of the Hijra.

Sahib Jamal (صاحب جمال), wife of the emperor Jahāngīr and a relative of Zain Khān Koka. She was the mother of Sultān Parweiz.

Sahib Qiran (صاحب قران). This is the title the Orientals, as well as Arabs, Persians and Turks, have given to Amīr Taimūr (Tamerlane), because he was born in a particular planetary conjunction.

[*Vide* next article but one.]

Sahib Qiran (صاحب قران), the poetical title of Sayyad Imām 'Alī of Bilgram, who became distracted in A.D. 1813, A.H. 1228, and wrote indecent and satirical poetry. He came to Lucknow in the time of Nawab 'Asaf-uddaula.

Sahib Qiran Sani (صاحب قران ثانی), or Sāhib Qirān the Second, a title of the emperor Shāh Jahān, the first being Taimūr or Tamerlane, the founder of the family. The word means "nearness" and is used in Astrology to express a planetary conjunction. Taimūr and his descendant, the builder of the Tāj, were both born when Jupiter and Venus were "in the same house."

[*Vide* Shāh Jahān.]

Saḥji (or **Sahuji Bhosla I.**) (ساهجی یا ساهوجی), a Marhaṭṭa chief who rose to considerable rank in the time of Malik Ambar, an Abyssinian chief of Aḥmadnagar. He afterwards entered the service of the king of Bījāpūr and was continued in his jāgīr, which had fallen to that state in the partition of the Aḥmadnagar territory. He was subsequently employed on conquests to the southward, and obtained a much more considerable jāgīr in the Mysore country, including the towns of Sira and Bangalore. When at a great age he was killed by a fall in hunting, about the year A.D. 1664. He was the father of the celebrated Sewājī, who, though the son of a powerful chief, began life as a daring and artful captain of banditti, ripened into a skilful general and an able statesman, and left a character which has never since been equalled or approached by any of his countrymen. Sāhjī, in consequence of some dispute with his first wife, separated from her and married Toka Bāī, by whom he had Ekōjī, who afterwards became king of Tanjore.

List of the family of Sewājī or Rājas of Sitāra.

	A.D.
Sāhjī, Sūbadār of the Karnātik under 'Alamgīr, bestows jāgīrs on his sons —Tanjore on Ekōjī—and dies . .	1664
Sewājī, his son commences predatory expeditions	1647
——— plunders Surat, and assumes the title of Rāja	1664
——— establishes a military government A.D. 1669, and dies	1680
Rāja Rām, set up by minister, imprisoned at Rāegarh	1680
Sambhājī assumed the sovereignty A.D. 1680—executed at Talāpūr	1689
Santa, usurped power—murdered . .	1698
Rāja Rām again proclaimed, A.D. 1698, at Sitāra, and died . . .	1700
Tārā Bāī, his wife, assumed regency .	1700
Sewājī II. son of Sambhājī, nicknamed Sāhūjī, released on 'Alamgīr's death, and crowned at Sitāra in March, 1708, and died in	1749
Rām Rāja, nominal successor—power resting with minister or Peshwā, died 12th December	1777
Sabū, surnamed Abba Saheb, the adopted son of Rām Rāja, succeeded	1777
Partāp Singh, the son of Sabū, reinstated at Sitāra by the British, 11th April	1818

[*Vide* Grant-Duff's *History of the Marhaṭṭas.*]

Saḥji (Saḥuji or **Sau Bhosla II.)** (ساهجی ساهوجی یا ساو), the son of Sambhājī, the Marhaṭṭa chief, after whose death in A.D. 1689, 15th Muḥarram, A.H. 1101, he (though then an infant) was acknowledged as Rāja, and his uncle Rāja Rām nominated to be regent during his minority; but when subsequently the infant Rāja fell into the hands of 'Alamgīr and was confined, Rāja Rām proclaimed himself Rāja on the ground of the captivity of his nephew. In his time the fort of Sitāra was taken by 'Alamgīr on the 21st April, A.D. 1700, 13th Ẓi-Qa'da, A.H. 1111, but, before it fell, Rāja Rām had died of the small-pox at Jhinjī, and had been succeeded by his son Sewā, a child of two years, under the regency of his mother Tārā Bāī, the widow of the deceased. After the death of 'Alamgīr, Sāhjī was released from confinement by 'Azim Shāh, and was acknowledged by the Marhaṭṭas as their principal chief, and crowned at Sitāra in March, A.D. 1708. During his reign the Marhaṭṭas, having overrun and plundered almost every part of Hindūstān, excepting Bengal, extended their territories from the Western Sea to Ūrisa, and from Āgra to the Karnātik, forming a tract of nearly one thousand miles long by seven hundred wide. Sāhu had lost the old Marhaṭṭa vigour during his long captivity; and his minister, the Peshwā Bālājī Bishwanāth, gained such an ascendancy over the mind of his master as to persuade him to delegate the exercise of all authority and power in the state to himself. During the latter part of his reign Sāhjī shut himself up in Sātāra, and his person and government were almost forgotten. Sāhu died (some time after the death of Niẓām-ul-Mulk) about the month of December, A.D. 1749, after a reign of 50 years. He was succeeded by his adopted son, Rām Rāja, the grandson of Tārā Bāi, power resting with the minister or Peshwā. Before his death he entrusted the Peshwā with the sole management of the Marhaṭṭa empire, and directed that Kolhāpūr, then governed by Sambhājī, the son of Rāja Rām, should be always considered as an independent kingdom. The headship of the Marhaṭṭa tribes passed permanently to the Peshwās from this time.

Sahu (ساهو), **also called Abba Sāheb,** was the son of Trimbakjī Bhosla, and adopted the son of Rām Rāja, whom he succeeded on the masnad of Sitāra on the 12th December, A.D. 1777. He was always kept a close prisoner. After his death, his son Partāp Singh succeeded him.

Saib Mirza (صایب مرزا), the poetical name of Mirzā Muhammad 'Alī of Tabrez, a celebrated poet of Persia, who, in the latter part of the reign of the emperor Jahāngīr, came to India as a merchant. He became intimate with Zafar Khān, a nobleman of the court, who, being appointed governor of Kashmere in those days by Shāh Jāhān, took him along with him to that country. From Kashmere he returned to Isfahān, where he was honoured with the title of Malik-ush-Shu'ārā, or the king of poets, by Shāh Abbās, king of Persia. He wrote Ghazals in an entirely new style, and may therefore be considered as the founder of the new school. He died in A.D. 1669, A.H. 1080, and was buried at Isfahān. His Dīwān in Persian contains 80,000 verses.

Saib Mirza (صایب مرزا), a Hindūstānī poet and author of the *Mirat-ul-Jamāl*, or the Mirror of Beauty, a very eccentric work, containing a distinct poem in praise of each of his mistresses' features, limbs, and perfections.

Saidai Gilani (سیدائي گیلانے) came to India in the time of Jahāngīr, and as he was very clever and of great abilities, he was made a Darogah of the Zargār Khāna or goldsmith's shop, and received the title of Bedil. He is the author of a Diwān, *Nukat Bedil*, *Rukaat Bedil* and *Chahar Ansur*. He died about the year A.D. 1116.

Sa'id-bin-Mansur (سعید بن منصور), author of the works called *Sunan* and *Suhd*. He died in A.D. 842, A.H. 227.

Sa'id-bin-Masa'ud of Shiraz (سعید بن مسعود شیرازی), author of the *Tarjuma Maulūd*, a complete history of Muhammad, translated from the Arabic about the year A.D. 1358, A H. 759.

Sa'id-bin Muhammad (سعید بن محمد), author of the works called *Minhāj-ul-'Abidīn* and *Sa'īd-nāma*, which contain moral and philosophical treatises on the virtues, vices, passions, rewards, punishments, etc.

Sa'id-bin-Musayyab (سعید بن مسیب), son-in-law of Abū Hureira. He was one of the seven Fiqhas of Madīna, made forty pilgrimages to Mecca, and died in A.D. 713, A.H. 94.

Sa'id-bin-Zand (سعید بن زند) was the last of those ten companions who had a positive promise of paradise from Muhammad. He died in the year A.D. 671, A.H. 51.

Sa'id Hirwi (سعید هروی), a poet who was a native of Herāt and contemporary with Qāzī Shams-uddīn Tibsī.

Sa'id Khan, Hakim (سعید خان حکیم), a physician of Kaem who lived in the time of Shāh 'Abbās II. of Persia, and is the author of a Dīwān.

Sa'id Khan Muhammad (سعید خان محمد), Nawāb of Rāmpūr in 1858.

Sa'id Khan Qureshi (سعید خان قریشی), whose proper name was Shaikh Muhammad, was a native of Multān. He was a good poet and a wit, and was employed by the prince Sultān Murād Bakhsh, son of Shāh Jahān, at the time when he was governor of Gujrāt; and afterwards by prince Dārā Shikōh, after whose death he was employed by the emperor 'Alamgīr. He died in November, A.D. 1676, Ramazan, A.H. 1087, at Multān, where he was buried in a monument which he had built whilst living. He is the author of a Dīwān.

Sa'id Muhammad Kirmani (سعید محمد کرمانی), author of the *Siar-ul-Aulia*, containing the memoirs of all the principal Sūfī Shaikhs and saints. Written in A.D. 1594, A.H. 1003.

Saifi of Bukhara, Mulla (سیفی بخاری ملا). He is the author of two Dīwāns, one of Ghazals, and the other for the use of tradespeople.

[*Vide* the following article.]

Saifi of Naishapur (سیفی نیشاپوری), a poet who flourished in the reign of Alāuddīn Takask of Khwarizm. There are several other poets of this name, such as Saifī of Bukhāra, Amīr Hājī Saif-uddīn Saifī, a nobleman at the court of Amīr Taimūr, etc. One of them is the author of a small work on the art of writing poetry, called *Urūz Saifi*, which he wrote in the year A.D. 1491, or A.H. 896. This work was translated into English in A.D. 1872, by H. Blockmann.

Saif Khan (سیف خان), a nobleman of the reign of the emperor 'Alamgīr, who was appointed governor of the Sūba of Āgra in September, A.D. 1659, A.H. 1070.

Saif Khan (سیف خان), the brother of Zain Khān Kōka.

Saif Khan (سیف خان بن ابراهیم خان), son of Ibrāhīm Khān, Fatha Jang, governor of Bengal, by a sister of the empress Nūr Jahān, named Malika Bāno Begam. His aunt the empress, having no sons by Jahāngīr, adopted Saif Khān as her own, and he was from his tender years brought up at court by the empress. He was subsequently made governor of Bardwān, where, after some years, as he was riding on an elephant through the street, a child was accidentally trodden to death. The parents loudly demanded an exemplary punishment on the driver. Saif Khān refused their request and ordered them to be driven away. They made their complaint to the emperor, who ordered Saif Khān to make them ample amends for their loss; but Saif Khān threw them into prison, which coming to the ears of the emperor, he sent for Saif Khān at Lāhore, and for his disobedience had him trodden to death in the presence of the child's parents.

Saif Khan Koka (سیف خان کوکه), eldest brother of Zain Khān Kōka, who was raised by the emperor Akbar to the rank of 4000. He was killed in battle against Muhammad Husain Mirzā at Aḥmadābād Gujrāt in the year A.D. 1572, A.H. 980.

Saif-uddaula (سیف الدوله), a prince of Hamdān who reigned about the year A.D. 967, A.H. 356.

Saif-uddaula (سیف الدوله), whose proper name was Mīr Najābat 'Alī Khān, was the second son of Mīr Ja'far 'Alī Khān, governor of Bengal, Behar and Ūrisa. He succeeded his brother Najm-uddaula, who died of small-pox in May A.D. 1766, Ẕil-ḥijja, A.H. 1179, and assumed the title of Saif-uddaula. A pension was granted to him by the English, and the office of Nazim managed by deputy. He lived after this three years and ten months, and died on the 10th March, A.D. 1770, 8th Ẕi-Qa'da, A.H. 1183. He was succeeded by his younger brother, Mubārik-uddaula, a minor.

Saif-uddaula (سیف الدوله). This man, who was a faithful follower of Mirzā Najaf Khān, was a Hindū Rājpūt called Raṭhor, a native of Bikaner. Having been in service at Allahabād under the brother of the late wazīr, father of Muhammad Qūlī, he became a Muhammadan about the year 1866, and was appointed to the charge of districts returning 20 lakhs a year, with the title of Saif-uddaula.

[*Vide* Keene's *Moghul Empire*, p. 110.]

Saif-uddaula or Saif-uddin (سیف الدوله), son of 'Alā-uddīn Hasan Ghōri, whom he succeeded in the kingdom of Ghōr and Ghaznī A.D. 1156, A.H. 551, and made over the latter province to his cousin Ghayās-uddīn Muhammad, the son of Sām. He was slain in a battle he fought against the Ghizān Turkmans A.D. 1163, A.H. 558, after a reign of seven years, and was succeeded by his cousin Ghayās-uddīn.

Saif-uddin Asfarikati (سیف الدین اسفراکاتی), a poet who was a native of Asfarīkat, a town in Māwarunnahr. He flourished in the time of one of the Sulṭāns of Khwārizm, named Alp or Apal Arsalān, who reigned after Atsiz and died in A.D. 1166, A.H. 561. Saif-uddīn has left a Dīwān containing 12,000 verses.

Saif-uddin Lachin, Amir (سیف الدین لاچین امیر), a Turk of the tribe of Lāchīn, came to India about the year A.D. 1253, A.H. 651, and served under several emperors of Dehlī. He is the father of 'Azz-uddīn 'Alī Shāh, Hisām-uddīn Aḥmad, and of Abū'l Hasan, who is commonly called Amīr Khusro, the celebrated poet of Hindūstān.

Saif-uz-zafar Naubahari (سیف الظفر بنجر نوبهار), author of a work called *Durr-ul-Majālis*, containing anecdotes of various persons from the earliest ages to the time of Abū Sa'id Abū'l Khair, who died in A.D. 1048, A.H. 440, together with a description of heaven and hell. He is also called Sayūf Zafar Naubahārī.

Sajawandi (سجاوندی). *Vide* Sirāj-uddīn Muhammad bin-'Abdur Rashīd-al-Sajāwandī.

Sajjad, Mir (سجاد میر), an Urdū poet of Āgra, who was a pupil of Shāh Najm-uddīn 'Abrū.

Sakha (سخا), poetical name of Zāhid 'Alī Khān, an author.

Sakhawi (سخاوی), author of the *History of the Qāzīs of Egypt*.

Sakhi Sarwar (سخی سرور), a Muhammadan saint. *See* Sulṭān Sakhī Sarwar.

Sakhun (سخن), a poet of Āgra, named Mīr Abdus Samad, who died in A.D. 1727, A.H. 1140.

Sakina (سکینه), daughter of Imām Husain. After her father's death she was married to Misaab, the brother of 'Abdullāh, the son of Zubeir.

Sakina Bano Begam (سکینه بانو بیگم), sister of Mirzā Muhammad Hakīm, half-brother to the emperor Akbar. She was married to Shāh Ghazī Khān, the nephew of Nokīb Khān.

Sakkaki (سکاکی). This word, which is in Arabic, signifies a cutler, was the surname of Abū Ya'qūb Yūsaf bin-Abū Bakr, who was also called Sirāj - uddīn - al - Khwārizmī. He was a great author and master of Zāhidī. One of his works is called *Misbāh-ul-Ulūm.* He was born in A.D. 1160, A.H. 555, and died in the year A.D. 1229, A.H. 626.

Salabat Jang (صلابت جنگ), the third son of Nizām-ul-Mulk 'Asif Jāh, was placed by the French on the masnad of the Deccan after the assassination of Muzaffar Jang, his nephew, which took place on the 3rd February, A.D. 1751, 17th Rabī' I. A.H. 1164. The Marquis de Bussy, a French General, was created by him a nobleman of the empire, and the Northern Sircars granted in jāgīr to his nation. Bussy continued to conduct the affairs of the Deccan till, by the intrigues of Nizām 'Alī, brother to Salābat Jang, his counsellor, Haidar Jang, being assassinated on the 12th May, A.D. 1758, 3rd Ramazān, A.H. 1171, and the English who had patronized Muhammad 'Alī Khān in the province of Arkāt growing powerful, he was obliged to return to the French territories to the assistance of his countrymen. Nizām 'Alī, being without a rival, deposed and imprisoned Salābat Jang on the 26th June, A.D. 1762, 4th Zilhijja, A.H. 1175, and assumed the government. Salābat Jang remained in confinement till his death, which happened on the 29th September, A.D. 1763, 20th Rabī' I. A.H. 1177.

[*Vide* Malleson's *French in India.*]

Salabat Khan (صلابت خان), a nobleman, who held the office of Mīr Bakhshī or Paymaster-General in the time of the emperor Shāh Jahān. He was stabbed in the presence of the emperor by a Rājpūt chief, named Amar Singh Rāthor, the son of Gaj Singh, on the evening of Thursday the 25th July, A.D. 1644, 30th Jumāda I. A.H. 1054, in the fort of Āgra. His tomb is still to be seen in the vicinity of Āgra. Amar Singh was pursued and cut down near one of the gates of the fort, which goes after his name, Amar Singh Gate.

Salabat Khan (صلابت خان), a nobleman, who on the accession of the emperor Ahmad Shāh to the throne of Dehlī in A.D. 1748, A.H. 1161, was raised to the rank of Mīr Bakhshī or Paymaster-General with the title of Zulfikār Jāng.

Saladin. *Vide* Sālah-uddīn Yūsaf, the son of Ayyūb.

Salah (صالح), author of the Masnawī or poem called *Nāz wa Nayāz,* which he composed about the year A.D. 1523, A.H. 930.

Salah bin-Mubarik-al-Bukhari (صالح بن مبارک), author of the *Muqāmāt Khwāja Bahā-uddīn,* containing the memoirs of the celebrated Shaikh Bahāuddīn, founder of the Naqshbandī Order.

Salah, Mir (صالح میر کشفی), styled Kashfī, was the son of 'Abdullāh Miskīn. He died in the year A.D. 1650, A.H. 1060, at Āgra, and lies buried there.

[*Vide* Kashfī.]

Salah-uddin Yusaf (صالح الدین یوسف), the son of Ayyūb (the same who is called by Christian writers Saladin), a celebrated Sultān of Syria and the first king of Egypt of the Ayyūbite family, equally renowned as a warrior and legislator. He was of Kurd extraction, and born at Tahrait, in Mesopotamia, about A.D. 1137. He rose in the service of the Fātimite Khalīfs of Egypt, and conducted operations against the Syrians under Nur-ul-din (*q.v.*), on whose death he became Sultān of Egypt and Syria. He had all the qualities of his position, and the influence of his amiable character prevailed against the united efforts of the chief Christian potentates of Europe, who carried on gratuitous attacks against him, under the false appellation of Holy Wars. In A.D. 1187 he overthrew the Crusaders at Tiberias, and followed up the victory by capturing Jerusalem, their capital. He was, however, no mere soldier, as some of his public works, still extant, are enough to show. He reigned over Egypt and Syria from A.D. 1173 to A.D. 1193, A.H. 568 to A.H. 588, and in the year following he died at Damascus, leaving seventeen sons, who divided his extensive dominions. He was succeeded by his son Malik-ul-'Azīz 'Usmān in the government of Egypt, but as none of his successors possessed the enterprising genius of Sālah-uddīn, the history of Egypt from that time to the year A.D. 1250 affords nothing remarkable. At this time the reigning Sultān, Malik-al-Sālah, was dethroned and slain by the Mamlūks, a kind of mercenary soldiers, who served under him. In consequence of this revolution the Mamlūks became masters of Egypt, and chose a Sulṭān from among themselves.

[*Vide* Mamlūk.]

Sulṭāns of Egypt of the Ayyūbite family.

		A.D.
Sālah-uddīn Yūsaf bin-Ayyūb	died	1194
Malik-ul-'Azīz 'Usmān, son of Sālah-uddīn	,,	1197
Malik Mansūr Muhammad bin-'Usmān	,,	1200
Malik 'Adil Saif-uddīn Abū Bakr bin-Ayyūb	,,	1218
Malik Kāmil Muhammad, son of Saif-uddīn	,,	1237
Malik 'Adil Abū Bakr bin-Kāmil	,,	1239
Malik Sālah Ayyūb Najm-uddīn bin-Kāmil; he was slain in battle with the Franks	,,	1249
Malik Muazzim Tūrān Shāh bin-Sālah	,,	1250
Malika Shajrat-uddurr, a slave girl of Malik Sālah; she reigned three years, and	,,	1255
Malik Ashraf Mūsa bin-Yūsaf, reigned five years.		

Malik Moizz 'Azz-uddīn Aibak, a Turkoman slave or Mamlūk of the Ayyūbite dynasty, married the queen Malika Shajrat-uddurr, and ascended the throne of Egypt. His descendants ruled for nearly one hundred years, and were called the Mamlūkites.

Salamat 'Ali (سلامت علی), the city Munsīf of Allahābād, who became a rebel and was hung in June, A.D. 1857, at that station.

Salamat 'Ali Khan, Hakim (سلامت علی خان حکیم), of Benares, author of a treatise on Music, who lived about the commencement of the 19th century.

Salami or Salmi (سلمی). This word, which signifies a native of Baghdād, was also the surname of Abū'l Hasan Muhammad bin-Obeid-ullah, who was one of the most illustrious Arabian poets of his time. He lived at the court of 'Azd-uddaula, a Sulṭān of the dynasty of the Bōyaides, who reigned at Fārs and 'Irāq from A.D. 975 to A.D. 983.

Salar Masa'ud Ghazi (سالار مسعود غازی). *Vide* Masa'ūd Ghāzī (Salār).

Salghar (سلغر), from whom the Atābaks of Fārs were descended, was a Turkish general in the service of the Saljūqī kings, and was entrusted with the charge of one of the princes of that race and appointed to the government of Fārs and some adjoining provinces. Salghur managed not only to keep his government during his life, but to transmit it to his descendants, seven of whom held Fārs as governors, *viz.*:—

1. Maudūd, the son of Salghur.
2. Fazlān-Shubān-Karra, who received the government from Alp Arsalān, rebelled, but was subdued by Nizām-ul-Mulk, the prime minister of the Sulṭān.
3. Rukn-uddaula.
4. Atābak Jalāl-uddīn Jawālī.
5. Atābak Kuraja, who built a college at Shīrāz, and a palace called Takht Kuraja.
6. Atābak Mankūs.
7. Būzāba, who is said to have been a just and wise governor. After the death of Būzāba, who was the last of these governors, Atābak Sunqar, the great-grandson of Salghur, succeeded in A.D. 1148, and became a powerful ruler.

[*Vide* Sunqar and Muẓaffar.]

Salhahan or Salivahana (سالہاهن) is said to have been the son of a potter and to have lived at Patar on the Godavarī. His era is still in use in the Deccan; its date is A.D. 78.

Salibi or Thalibi, Imam (ثالبی), author of the *Tarīkh Ghadr-us-Siar* and *Tārīkh Arāes*.

Saliha Bano (صالحه بانو), the daughter of the Kāsim Khān and wife of the emperor Jahāngīr, who gave her the title of Bādshāh Mahal.

Salik (سالک), poetical title of Shāh Ibrahīm.

Salik Qazwini and Salik Yezdi (سالک قزوینی سالک یزدی). These two poets, one from Qazwīn and the other from Yezd, flourished in the time of the emperor Shāh Jahān, and both died in the reign of 'Alamgīr. Sālik Qazwīnī died in A.D. 1699, A.H. 1080, and the other, one year after him.

Salim (سلیم حاجی محمد), author of a Dīwān, which he completed in A.D. 1701, A.H. 1082. His proper name is Hājī Muhammad Aslam.

Salim (سلیم), the poetical title of Muhammad Qulī, who came to India from Persia during the reign of Shāh Jahān and was employed by Islām Khān, wazīr. He was the author of a Dīwān and also of a Masnawī, which he wrote in Persia, and in which he describes Lahijān. But when he came to India he altered the heading and called it a description of Kashmere. He died in the year A.D. 1647, A.H. 1057.

Salim (سلیم میر محمد), Mīr Muhammad Salīm of Patna, a merchant who died at Murshidābād in A.D. 1781, A.H. 1195, and left a Masnawī in Urdū.

Salim I. Sultan (سالیم سلطان), emperor of the Turks of Constantinople, and the greatest monster of that monstrous race, was the second son of Bāyezīd II. whom he defeated in a battle, and after poisoning him and murdering eight of his brothers or nephews, ascended the throne of Turkey on the 6th April, A.D. 1512, 18th Safar, A.H. 918. He subverted the Mamlūks of Egypt, bringing it—with Palestine, Syria and Arabia —under the yoke of the Turks. He invaded the kingdom of Persia; subdued and slew Aladeules, the mountain king of Armenia, and reduced his kingdom to the form of a Turkish province. He repressed the forces of the Hungarians by a double invasion; but, when intending to turn all his forces upon the Christians, he was suddenly seized with a cancer on his back, of which he died on Friday the 21st September, A.D. 1520, 6th Shawwal, A.H. 926, on the very spot where he had formerly unnaturally assaulted his aged father. He was succeeded by his son Sulaimān I. surnamed "The Magnificent."

Salim II. Sultan (سلیم سلطان), succeeded his father Sulaimān I. surnamed "The Magnificent," as emperor of the Turks in September, A.D. 1566, Safar, A.H. 974. He was an idle and effeminate emperor; but his deputies took from the Venetians the isle of Cyprus, and from the Moors the kingdom of Tunis and Algiers. Over this emperor the Christians were victorious in that famous sea-fight called the battle of Lepanto, when he lost above 35,000 men besides his fleet. Devoting his time to the enervating pleasures of his seraglio, he died, little respected, on the 9th December, A.D. 1574, Shaban, A.H. 982, aged 52, and was succeeded by his son Sultān Murād III.

Salim III. Sultan (سلیم سلطان), son of Mustafā III. was born in A.D. 1761, and succeeded to the throne of Turkey on the death of his uncle Ahmad IV. in April, A.D. 1789. He began his reign with a war with Catherine II. of Russia, in which peace was purchased by great sacrifices of territory. At a later period Egypt was invaded by the French; but they were defeated, and compelled to quit the country, by the English, in 1801. A revolt of the Jannisarīs deposed Salīm on the 28th July, A.D. 1807, Jumāda I. A.H. 1222, and raised Mustafā IV. to the throne; but he was deposed after a reign of one year, and Mahmūd II. made emperor A.D. 1808.

Salim Chishti, Shaikh (سلیم چشتی شیخ), of Fathapūr Sīkrī, surnamed Shaikh-ul-Islām, a Muhammadan saint, who during his life was greatly revered by the emperor Akbar. It is said that by his prayers the king was blessed with several children. His father Bahā-uddīn was a descendant of Shaikh Farīd Shakarganj. He was born at Dehlī in A.D. 1478, A.H. 883, was a disciple of Khwāja Ibrāhīm Chishtī, and resided on a hill close to the village of Sīkrī about 20 miles from Āgra. By the liberality of the emperor, he was enabled to build a splendid Masjid or mosque on the hill, called the Masjid of Fathapūr Sīkrī, which was completed in A.D. 1571, A.H. 979, at a cost of 5 lakhs of rupees. He died a few months after its completion on the 13th February, A.D. 1572, 27th Ramazān, A.H. 979, aged 96 lunar years, and was buried on the top of the hill, where his tomb is to be seen to this day. He was one of the chief saints of Hindūstān, and some of his sayings have been found worthy of commemoration. After his death his son Badr-uddīn succeeded him to the gaddī. His pedigree runs thus: "Shaikh Salīm Chishtī, the son of Bahā-uddīn, the son of Shaikh Sulaimān, the son of Shaikh 'Adam, the son of Shaikh Mūsā, the son of Shaikh Maudūd, the son of Shaikh Badr-uddīn, the son of Shaikh Farīd-uddīn of Ajūdhan, commonly called Shakarganj." Twenty-four times Salīm Chishtī is said to have gone on a pilgrimage to Mecca and returned again. His bread was made of singhāras (water-nuts) that were produced in the reservoir of Sīkrī. His son Qutb-uddīn was killed in Bengal by Sher Afkan, first husband of Nur Jahān. His grandson Islām Khān, the son of Badr-uddīn, was raised by the emperor Jahāngīr to the rank of an Amīr and was appointed governor of Bengal in A.D. 1601, A.H. 1017.

[*Vide* Islām Khān.]

Salim Shah Sur (سلیم شاه سور), more properly called Islām Shāh, was the younger son of the emperor Sher Shāh. His elder brother, 'Adil Khān, being absent at his father's death, Jalāl Khān (as he was then) ascended the throne in the fortress of Kalinjar on the 29th May, A.D. 1545, 17th Rabī' I. A.H. 952, and assumed the title of Islām Shāh, which by false pronunciation was turned to that of Salīm Shāh. He reigned nine years and became afflicted with a fistula, of which he died at Gwāliar A.D. 1554, A.H. 961, in which year also died Mahmūd Shāh, king of Gujrāt, and Burhān Nizām Shāh, king of Ahmadnagar. In commemoration of the remarkable circumstance of these monarchs dying almost at the same time, Maulānā 'Alī, the father of the celebrated historian Firishta, wrote a short epitaph, in which the words "the ruin of kings" exhibit the Hijrī year A.D. 961. The remains of Salīm Shāh were conveyed to Sahsarām and buried close to his father's tomb. Salīm Shāh was succeeded by his son the prince Fīroz, then 12 years of age, who was placed on the throne by the chiefs of the tribe of Sūr, at Gwāliar. He had not reigned three days (some say three months) when Mubāriz Khān, the son of Nizām Khān Sūr, at once the nephew of the late Sher Shāh and brother-in-law of Salīm Shāh, assassinated the young prince, and, ascending the throne, assumed the title of Muhammad Shāh 'Adil.

Salima Bano Begam (سلیمه بانو بیگم), the daughter of Sulaimān Shaikh, the son of Dāra Shaikh, was married to Prince Muhammad Akbar, Aurangzeb's fourth son. Their offspring was Nekusīyar, who was proclaimed emperor at Āgra and imprisoned by Rukn-uddaula.

Salima Sultana Begam (سلیمه سلطانه بیگم). The mother of this lady was Gulrukh Begam, the daughter of the emperor Bābar Shāh, who gave her in marriage to Mirzā Nūr-uddīn Muhammad, by whom she had Salīma. Salīma was married to Bairām Khān Khān Khānān in A.D. 1558. The marriage took place at Jalandhar with the consent of the emperor Akbar, who was present at the nuptials. After the death of Bairām Khān in 1561, she became the wife of the emperor, by whom she had a daughter named Shāhzāda Khānam and a son named Sultān Murād. She was well-versed in Persian and had a good genius for poetry. She died in the reign of the emperor Jahāngīr A.D. 1612, A.H. 1021.

Salimi or Hasan Salimi, Maulana (سلیمی حسن مولانا), a poet who died and was buried at Sabzwar, in the year A.D. 1450, A.H. 854. He has left a Dīwān.

Saljuq (سلجوق). *Vide* Saljūqī.

Saljuqi (سلجوقی), a dynasty of Tartar kings who derive their name from Saljūq, a chief of great reputation, who had been compelled to quit the court of Bīghū Khān, the sovereign of the Turks of Qapchāk. Saljūq, who had proceeded with his tribe to the plains of Bukhārā, embraced the religion of Muhammad and acquired the crown of martyrdom in the war against the infidels. His age of an hundred and seven years surpassed the life of his son Mikāīl. Saljūq adopted the care of his two grandsons Tughral and Ja'far, the eldest of whom, at the age of 45 years, was invested with the title of Sultān in the royal city of Naishāpūr. It is said that Mikāīl became known to Sultān Mahmūd of Ghaznī, and was greatly honoured by that monarch. It is related that on Mahmūd asking the ambassador of their chief what force they could bring to his aid: "Send this arrow," said the envoy, presenting one of two which he held in his hand, "and 50,000 horse will appear!" "Is that all?" exclaimed Mahmūd. "Send this," he said, presenting the other, "and an equal number will follow." "But suppose I was in extreme distress," observed the monarch, "and want your utmost exertions?" "Then," replied the ambassador, "send my bow, and 200,000 horse will obey the summons!" The proud conqueror heard with secret alarm this terrifying account of their numbers; and we are told that he anticipated the future overthrow of his empire. Tughral Beg and his brother served for several years under Sultān Mahmūd. In A.D. 1036, A.H. 429, the former resisted Sultān Masa'ūd, the son of Mahmūd, and received investiture as Sultān of Khurāsān from the Khalīfa of Baghdād. *Vide* Tughral Beg, who was the first king of the Saljūk dynasty of Persia. Kadard was the first of the Saljūq dynasty who reigned in Kirmān; Sulaimān or Qutlamish, the first Sultān of the Saljūq dynasty who reigned in Rūm or Anatolia.

Salman (سلمان), a poet who died in A.D. 1530, A.H. 937.

Salman, 'Aqa (سلمان آقا), also called Mirzā Hisābī, is the author of a commentary on the Preface of the Gulistān of about 3000 lines. He devoted himself to Sūfiism and wrote a treatise thereon. He also compiled an Arabic commentary on Qūsanjī's Persian treatise on astronomy; another work of his is called *Ausāf-ul-Bilād* He was living in A.D. 1585, A.H. 993.

Salman Farsi (سلمان فارسی), or the Persian. Is said to have been a native of a small place near Isfahān, and that on passing one day by a Christain Church he was so much struck by the devotion of the people, and the solemnity of the worship, that he became disgusted with the idolatrous faith in which he had been brought up. He afterwards wandered about the East, from city to city, and convent to convent, in quest of a religion, until an ancient monk, full of years and infirmities, told him of a prophet who had arisen in Arabia to restore the pure faith of Abraham. He then journeyed to Mecca, and became a convert of Muhammadanism. This Salmān rose to power in after years, and was reputed by the unbelievers of Mecca to have assisted Muhammad in compiling his doctrines. He died at Madāin in Persia in A.D. 653, A.H. 33.

Salman Sawaji (سلمان ساوجی), a celebrated Persian poet, native of Sāwa, surnamed Jalāl-uddīn Muhammad, who flourished in the time of Amīr Shaikh Hasan Jalāyer, also called Hasan Buzurg, and his son Sultān Aweis, rulers of Baghdād. In the latter period of his life he became blind, and having retired from the world died in the year A.D. 1377, A.H. 779. He is the author of a poem entitled *Jamsheid-wa-Khursheid*, and of the *Firāq-nāma*, and several other works, and also of a Dīwān.

Sam (سام), the son of Narīmān, and grandfather of Rustam, the celebrated hero of Persia.

[*Vide* Zāl and Manūchehr.]

Saman (سامان), the great-grandfather of Ismā'īl Sāmān, the first king of the Samānides. His grandson Nasr Aḥmad was appointed governor of Bukhārā by Mo'tamid, the Khalīfa of Baghdād, in A.D. 874, A.H. 261.

[*Vide* Ismā'īl Samānī.]

Samani (سامانی), a dynasty of Muhammadan kings who reigned over Transoxiana, holding its court at Bukhārā. Its power extended over Khwārizm, Māwar-un-Nahr, Jurjān, Sīwastān and Ghaznī. This dynasty continued to reign in Bukhārā for a period of 128 years, when it became extinct by the death of its last prince, 'Abdulmalik II. in A.D. 999, A.H. 389. The first king of this race was Ismā'īl Sāmānī, great-grandson of Sāmān, a robber-chief, from whom this dynasty took its name.

Samani or **Samnani** (سامانی), an Arabian author who, in the 6th century of the Hijrī, wrote a dictionary of the names of all the Arabian authors, entitled *Fi'l Ansāb*, which in the succeeding century was abbreviated by Ibn-al-Asīr, and this extract again shortened by Sayūtī.

[*Vide* Jalāl-uddīn Sayūtī.]

Samanini (ثمانینی), commonly called so, but his proper name is Abū'l Qāsim 'Umar, and his father's name Sābit. He was an excellent Arabic grammarian and died in A.D. 1050, A.H. 442.

Sama-ullah, Shaikh (سماء الله شیخ), or Samā-uddīn, one of the great Mashāekhs of India, and brother of Shaikh Isḥāq. He lived in the time of Sulṭān Bahlōl Lodī, and died according to 'Abdul Haq in A.D. 1496, A.H. 901, and lies buried on the banks of the Hauz Shamsī at Dehlī.

Sambhaji (سمبهاجی), the son of Sewājī Bhosla, the Marhaṭṭa chief and second Rāja of Sitāra. He was at Parnāla when his father died, and a faction endeavoured to secure the succession to Rāja Rām, a son of Sewājī by another wife. But Sambhājī, supported by the greater part of the troops, who had been the companions of his contests with the forces of the emperor 'Alamgīr, established his sovereignty. He behaved with great cruelty to his opponents, imprisoned Rāja Rām, and reigned nine years. He succeeded his father in April, A.D. 1680, generally spent his time in female society and excessive drinking, and possessed no talents for government. He listened to the advice of no one, having a conceited opinion of his own abilities, and chose for his favourite Kab Kalās or Kālūsāh, a Brāhman, with whom he acted such scenes as made him hateful to the world. He was taken prisoner together with his minion by the officers of the emperor 'Alamgīr, who ordered them to be executed. Sambhājī's eyes were first destroyed with a hot iron, his tongue cut out, and he was at last beheaded along with his favourite. This event took place in July or August, A.D. 1689, A.H. 1100. His son Sāhjī, also called Sāo or Sāhū, an infant, was acknowledged Rāja by the Marhaṭṭas, but he was soon afterwards taken prisoner by 'Alamgir and confined till the death of that monarch, when he was released.

[*Vide* Sāhjī II.]

Sambhu Singh (سمبهو سنگه), Maharana of Udaipūr and Mewar, who was invested a G.C.S.I. on the 6th December, A.D. 1871, and died on the 7th October, A.D. 1874, at the early age of 27. He succeeded to the gaddī of Mewar by adoption in 1862. His elevation was great and sudden, as his father, a brother of the late Rāna Sarūp Singh, had fallen under suspicion of conspiring to gain his way to the throne by poisoning the invalid Sarūp; and, while the father died under the hands of assassins in a prison within the walls of the palace, the son, along with other members of the family, suffered for several years the most cruel persecution.

Samdik Phra Paramidr (سامڈیک فری پرمیڈر), king of Siam, who came to Hindūstān in the beginning of 1872, and was received in Calcutta, Lucknow, Bombay, etc., with all the honours due to high rank.

Sam Mirza (سام مرزی), the son of Shāh Ismā'īl I. He is the author of the work called *Tuhfa Sāmī*, being a biography of the contemporaneous poets of Persia, compiled in A.D. 1550, A.H. 957. His poetical name is Sāmī.

Sammugarh (ساموگره), a place near Āgra founded by the emperor Akbar. It was the scene of Aurangzeb's victory over his brother Dara 20th or 30th May, 1658.

Samnani (سمنانی), one of the chief followers of the Sūfī sect. He died in A.D. 1325, A.H. 736, six years before Khwāja Kirmānī.

[*Vide* Ata-uddaula Samnānī.]

Samrat Jagannatha (شمرات جگناتهه), a Brāhman, who made a version of Euclid's Elements by order of Sewāī Jai Singh, Rāja of Jaipūr, in Sanskrit and called it *Rekhi Ganita.*

Samru or **Sombre** (سامرو). *Vide* Shamrū.

Samsam-uddaula (صمصام الدوله), title of Shāhnawāz Khān, which see.

Samsam-uddaula (صمصام الدوله), the son of Mirzā Nasīr, who came to India from Māzindaran in the reign of the emperor Shāh Alam. Samsām-uddaula, whose original name was Malik Muhammad Khān, received the title of Nawāb Samsām-uddaula Malik Muhammad Khān Dilair Jang from Nawāb Najaf Khan. He died in Jaipūr in A.D. 1804, A.H. 1219.

Samsam-uddaula or **Samsam Jang** (صمصام الدوله صمصام جنگ), the son of Samsām-uddaula Shāhnawāz Khān, who received the same title after his father's death. Both of them held distinguished positions in the court of the Nizām of Haidarābād.

[*Vide* Shāhnawāz Khān.]

Sam Sultan Bahadur (سام سلطان بهادر), a native of Gujrāt, and author of the *Tārīkh Bahādur Shāhī.*

Sana' (صانع), poetical name of Shaikh Nizām-uddīn Ahmad, commonly called Basī Miān. He flourished about the year A.D. 1738, A.H. 1151.

Sanai, Husain (ثنای حسن). *Vide* Khwāja Husain Sanāī.

Sanai, Shaikh (ثنائي شيخ), commonly called Hakīm Sanāī, a celebrated poet and native of Ghaznī, who flourished in the reign of Bahrām Shāh, son of Masa'ūd Shāh of Ghaznī. He is the author of several poems. His last work, which he dedicated to Bahrām Shāh, is called the *Hadīqa*, or *Hadīqat-ul-Haqāeq*, the Garden of Truth, a very beautiful poem on the unity of God and other religious subjects, said to contain 30,000 verses. This book he finished in A.D. 1131, A.H. 525, in which year he is supposed to have died, aged 62 years. He is also the author of a small work containing about 280 verses, entitled *Ramūz-ul-Anbia wa Kanūz-ul-Aulia*, and of a Dīwān.

Sanai, Maulana (ثنائي مولانا), author of a poem entitled Bāgh Iram.

Sana-ullah, Maulana (ثنا الله مولانا), Qāzī of Panīpat, flourished about the year A.D. 1539, A.H. 946, and is the author of the commentary called *Mazharī* and other works, one of which is called *Saif-ul-Maslūf.*

Sandhal Deo (ثندهال ڏيو), one of the Rājas of Amīr, now called Jaipūr; after him reigned Gokul or Kantal, and after him reigned Pūjandeva or Pajūrji about the year A.D. 1185. He married the daughter of Prithi Rāja. After him Malesi; after him the following Rājas reigned in succession:—Bījaljī, Rajdeo, who was defeated by Mahmūd II. A.D. 1251, Kīlan, Kantal, who built the city of Amīr, Jūnsi, Udaikaran, Nar Singh, Banbir, Udhirao, Chandarsen, Prithiraj, murdered by his son Bhīm, Askaran; after him reigned Bharamal, also called Pūranmal and Biharīmal, which see.

Sangham Lal (سنگهم لال), a Hindū whose poetical name was Izzat. He was a pupil of Mirzā Jān Jānān Mazhar, and was living at Āgra in A.D. 1760, A.H. 1174.

Sangram Shah (سنگرام شاه), Rāja of Kharakpūr in South Bihār, defied the Mughal armies in the time of Akbar, lost his life in a struggle, and his son and successor were forced to become converts to Islām.

Sanjar, Mir (سنجر مير), also called Shāh Sanjar Bījāpūrī, was the son of Mīr Haidar Kāshī the punster. He was an excellent poet and flourished in the time of Sultān Ibrāhīm 'Adil of Bījāpūr. He died in A.D. 1612, A.H. 1021, and left a Dīwān.

Sanjar Shah (سنجر شاه), the son of Tughan Shāh II. He was contemporary with Takash Khān, who married his mother and adopted him; but when he rebelled against him, Takash blinded him.

Sanjar, Sultan (سنجر سلطان), the third son of Sultān Malikshāh Saljūqī. He held at his father's death, A.D. 1092, the government of Khurāsān, and took little concern in the troubles that ensued on that event; but after the death of his brother, Sultān Muhammad, he may be deemed the actual sovereign of Persia. He forced Bahrām Shāh, a monarch of the race of Ghaznī, whose capital was Lāhore, to pay him tribute; and Alāuddīn, prince of Ghōr, who had defeated Bahrām Shāh and taken Ghaznī, yielded in his turn to the superior fortune of Sanjar, by whom he was defeated, made prisoner and tributary to the house of Saljūq. But Sanjar, after a long reign marked by singular glory and success, was destined to experience the most cruel reverses of fortune. In the year A.D. 1140, A.H. 535, he advanced far into Tartary to attack Gour Khān, the monarch of Qara Khatā, and suffered a signal defeat, in which almost his whole army was cut to pieces, his family taken prisoner, and all his baggage plundered. He next marched, A.D. 1153, A.H. 547, against the Turkman tribe of Ghuz, who had withheld their usual tribute of 40,000 sheep: an action ensued, in which he was defeated and taken prisoner. During his long confinement of four years, his dominions were ruled by his favourite, Sulṭāna Khātūn Turkān, at whose death in A.D. 1156, A H. 551, Sanjar made an effort to escape and was successful; but he lived only a short time after he regained his liberty, for he died on Friday the 24th May, A.D 1157, 11th Rabī‘ II. A.H. 552, in the 73rd year of his age, and was buried in Marv. The Saljūq dynasty in Khurāsān ceased with his existence, and the greater part of his kingdom fell into the possession of Khwārizm Shāh Atsiz ibn-Muhammad ibn-Anushtakīm, the grandfather of Takash Khwārizm Shāh. The poets of his court were Adīb Sābir, Rashīd Wātwāt, Abdul Wāsa, Jabalī, Farīd Kātib, Anwarī, Malik ‘Imād Zauzanī, and Sayyad Husain of Ghaznī.

Sanqa (سنقا). *Vide* Rānā Sānqā.

Sanqar (سنقر). *Vide* Sunqar.

Saqafi (ثقفی), or Thaqafī, whose original name is Abū Īsā, was an excellent Arabic grammarian and author. He died in A.D. 766, A.H. 149.

Saqqa (سقه بخاری), or Dervish Saqqā of Bukhāra. He died in A.D. 1555, A.H. 962, and is the author of a Dīwān.

Saqqa Bardwani (سقه بردوانی), author of a Dīwān found in the library of Tipū Sulṭān.

Saraj-uddin (سراج الدین). *Vide* Sirāj-uddīn.

Sarakhsi or **Al-Sarakhsi** (سرخسی). *Vide* Abū Bakr Muhammad-al-Sarakhsī.

Sarbadal (سربدال), a tribe of Afghāns of Sabzwār. *Vide* ‘Abdul Razzāq.

Sarbaland Khan (سربلند خان), an Amīr of the time of the emperor ‘Alamgīr, who held the rank of 4000 and died in the year A.D. 1679, A.H. 1090.

Sarbaland Khan (سربلند خان), entitled Nawāb Mubāriz-ul-Mulk, was governor of Patna in the time of Farrukh-siyar, and was recalled to court about the year A.D. 1718, A.H. 1130. In the reign of the emperor Muhammad Shah he was appointed governor of Gujrāt, A.D. 1724, A.H. 1137, but in A.D. 1730, A.H. 1143, was removed from his government on account of his consenting to pay the Marhaṭṭas the Chouth or part of the revenue of that province, and Rāja Abhay Singh, the son of Ajit Singh Raṭhor, was appointed to succeed him. Sarbaland Khān made some opposition to his successor, but was defeated and prevented from coming to court by the emperor. He was, however, after some time appointed governor of Allahābād, A.D. 1732, A.H. 1145, when he deputed his son Khānazād Khān to command, himself residing at court. He died in A.D. 1745, A.H. 1158.

Sardar Singh (سردار سنگه), present Rāja of Bikaner (1857).

Sarfaraz Khan, Nawab (سرفراز خان نواب), entitled ‘Alā-uddaula, was the son of Nawāb Shuja-uddaula or Shuja-uddīn, governor of Bengal, whom he succeeded on the 13th March, A.D. 1739, 13th Ẕil-ḥijja, A.H. 1151. He reigned one year and two months, and was slain in an attack made by Alahwardī Khān Mahābat Jang on the 29th April, A.D. 1740, 13th Ṣafar, A.H. 1153. The cause of this murder is thus recorded: " ‘Alā-uddaula having accidentally met the niece of his wazīr, Mahābat Jang, a young lady who bore the repute of being the most beautiful woman of the age, first commanded and then entreated her to withdraw her veil, that he might enjoy one look at her face. The modest damsel, overwhelmed with confusion and terror, entreated the prince's pardon, and, pleading eloquently for her honour, declined to gratify his curiosity; but he, being charmed with her exquisite grace and the delicious tones of her voice, was fired with a hasty determination and himself withdrew the veil. He gazed in ardent admiration on her lovely countenance for a few seconds; then, dropping the drapery, he asked forgiveness for his rudeness, and, paying the beauty some princely compliment, passed on. The unhappy girl fled in tears to her father, ‘Atāullāh, and to her uncle the wazīr, and with mixed indignation and shame declared the sad tale of her disgrace, and immediately afterwards destroyed herself with poison. Suffice it to say that the prince became their victim within a few hours."

Sarfi Sawaji (صرفی ساوجی), a poet named Shaikh Yaqūb, who flourished in the time of the emperor Akbar, and wrote a chronogram on the death of Amīr Fath-ullāh Shīrāzī and Hakīm Abū'l Fatha Gīlānī, both of whom died in A.D. 1589, A.H. 997. He was a native of Sāwa in Persia and came to India, where he died in A.D. 1595, A.H. 1003, and left a Dīwān.

Sarfoji (سرفوجی), Rāja of Tanjore, a descendant of Ekkojī, the brother of the celebrated Sīwājī, the Marhatta chief. By the treaty of the 25th October, A.D. 1799, the English Government decided between two rival claimants to place Sarfojī upon the masnad, on condition that he transferred the management of his territory to the British, consenting to receive in lieu of its revenue an annual payment of £118,350. The absolute sovereignty of the fortress and city of Tanjore itself were at the same time guaranteed to the prince. Sarfojī died in A.D. 1832, and was succeeded by his only son Sīwājī, who reigned 23 years, and died on the 29th October, A.D. 1855, leaving no legitimate son to succeed him. The surviving family consisted of the following persons, viz.: the Queen Dowager, 16 wives, 2 daughters, 2 sisters, 6 natural sons, 11 natural daughters, and 54 collaterals.

Sarhindi Begam (سرهندی بیگم), one of the wives of Shāhjahān, who built a garden at Āgra, no traces of which are left now.

Sari Saqti (سری سقتی), a celebrated Musalmān saint, called Saqtī because he formerly dealt in metals, but afterwards became a disciple of Marūf Karkhī. He was the uncle of Shaikh Junaid as well as his master. The following anecdote is related on good authority: Sarī Saqtī said that for thirty years he never ceased imploring divine pardon for having once exclaimed "Praise be to God;" and on being asked the reason he said: "A fire broke out in Baghdād, and a person came up to me and told me that my shop had escaped, on which I uttered those words, and even to this moment I repent having said so, because it showed that I wished better to myself than to others." He died on Wednesday the 9th August, A.D. 870, 6th Ramazān, A.H. 256, and was buried at Baghdād. Some authors say that he died three years before that period.

Sarkhush (سرخوش), the poetical name of Muhammad Afzal, who was born in A.D. 1640, A.H. 1050, flourished in the time of the emperor 'Alamgīr. He wrote a biography of the poets of his own time, entitled *Kalmāt-ush-Shu'ārā*, the letters of which, if taken according to their numerical values, will give the year in which it was produced, viz. A.D. 1682, A.H. 1093. He was a good poet, and had the good fortune to become acquainted with almost all men of talents of his day. He died at the advanced age of 76 years, about the year A.D. 1714, A.H. 1126, and left, besides the above-mentioned work, four Masnawīs or poems, viz. *Husn-o-Ishq*, *Nūr-i-'Alī*, *Sāqī-nāma*, and *Shāh-nāma Muhammad 'Azim*.

Sarmad or Muhammad Sarmad (سرمد) Qazī of Seringapatam in the time of Tīpū Sultān, by whose request he translated into Persian a work in the Dakhanī dialect, and called it *Khulāsa Sultānī*.

Sarmad (سرمد), the poetical name of an Armenian merchant who came to India in the reign of the emperor Shāh Jahān. In one of his journeys towards Thatta, he fell so passionately in love with a Hindū girl that he became distracted and would go about the streets stark naked. He was well versed in the Persian language and was a good poet. In the beginning of the reign of 'Alamgīr he was put to death on account of his disobeying the orders of that emperor, who had commanded him not to go about naked. This event took place about the year A.D. 1661, A.H. 1072. Some say that the real cause of his execution was a Rubāī which he had composed, the translation of which is: "The Mullas say that Muhammad entered the heavens; but Sarmad says that the heavens entered Muhammad." His tomb is close to the Jama Masjid at Dehlī.

Sarmadi (سرمدی), takhallus of Muhammad Sharīf of Isfahān. He died A.D. 1606, A.H. 1015.

Sarsabz (سارسابز), poetical name of Mirzā Zain-ul-Abidīn Khān, son of Nawāb Salar Jang. He is the author of a Dīwān.

Sarshar (سرشار), the poetical name of Murshid Qulī Khān Rustum Jang, son-in-law of Nawāb Shujā-uddīn, of Bengal. He was living in the time of Nawāb Ala Virdi Khān.

Sarup Chand (سروپ چند), a Hindū who is the author of a history called *Sāhīh-ul-Akhbar*.

Sarup Singh, Rana (سروپ سنگه رانا), ruler of Udaipūr (1857), died A.D. 1862.

Sarwar (سرور), poetical name of 'Azim-uddaula Nawāb Mīr Muhammad Khān Bahādur, a son of 'Azim-uddaula Abū'l Qāsim Muzaffar Jang. He died in A.D. 1834, Shawwāl, A.H. 1250, and left besides the Tazkira called *Umda-i-Muntakhiba*, a thick Dīwān.

Sarwat (سروت). *Vide* Jugal Kishōr.

Sassan, grandfather of Ardisher Bābagān, the founder of the Sassanian dynasty, who ruled Persia for four centuries, during which the empire was kept at its fullest strength and extent; and was probably the best and longest of Oriental powers.

[*Vide* Ardisher.]

Sata (ساتع), takhallus of a poet.

Satesh Chandar Rae Bahadur (ستیش چندررای بهادر), Mahārāja of Nadea, the great-grandson of Rāja Kishan Chandar Rae, who aided the English in despoiling Sirāj-uddaula, died November, A.D. 1870.

Sauda (سودا). His real name was Mirzā Muhammad Rafīa, to which he subsequently added his poetical title of "Soudā," and is now commonly known by the appellation of Mirzā Rafīūs Saudā. He was a native of Dehlī but resided at Lucknow, and his Dīwān and Qasāed contain a variety of poems on various subjects; also Idyls, Elegies, and other miscellaneous pieces in Hindūstānī verse. These volumes are held in the highest estimation all over India. They include a number of encomiastic poems on the Nawāb 'Asaf-uddaula of Lucknow, and many other persons of high rank and power both at Lucknow and Dehlī, not the least remarkable of which is an eulogy on the well-known Mr. Richard Johnson. The satires of this poet are also numerous and admirable; but having created him many enemies, to avoid the consequences of their anger, he feigned himself insane, and took the poetical name of Saudā, or madman, but he is frequently known by the appellation of Malik-ush-Shuarā, or king of the poets. He died at Lucknow in the year A.D. 1781, A.H. 1195, aged 70 years. 'Asaf-uddaula of Lucknow gave him a stipend of 6000 rupees a year. He was a pupil of Sirāj-uddīn 'Alī Khān 'Arzū.

Saudai, Baba of Abiward (سودائي بابا ابیوردی), a poet who had formerly assumed Khāwarī for his poetical title, but as he used to go about the streets without turban or shoes, people gave him the title of Saudāī, *i.e.* distracted, which he subsequently used in all his compositions. He lived in the time of Shāhrukh Mirzā. He died A.D. 1448, aged 80 years.

Sayadat Khan (سیادت خان), brother of Islām Khān, a nobleman of the reign of Shāh Jahān; he died in the month of July, A.D. 1659. He was the father of Fazl-ullāh Khān.

Sayadat, Mir Jalal-uddin (سیادت), a son of Mīr Jamāl-uddīn Muhhadis. He flourished about the year A.D. 1670, A.H. 1081, and is the author of a Dīwān.

Saydi, Mir (صیدی میر), a poet of Persia, who in A.D. 1654, A.H. 1064, came to India in the reign of Shāh Jahān. It is said that in one instance he received a present of 5000 rupees from Jahān 'Arā Begam, the daughter of the emperor, and in another one lakh for his poems. He died in A.D. 1672, A.H. 1083, and is the author of a Dīwān containing 4000 verses.

Sayuf Zafar, Naubahari (سیوف ظفر نوبهاري). This is his correct name; however, *see* under Saif-uz-zafar Naubahārī.

Sayuti (صیوطي). *Vide* Jalāl-uddin Sayūtī.

Sayyad (سید). The Sayyads who are also called Mīrs, are the descendants of 'Alī, the son-in-law of the prophet.

Sayyad Abdullah (سید عبدالله), son of Sayyad 'Abdul Kādir Gīlānī, the great saint of Baghdād. His tomb is in the city of Tatta in Sindh.

Sayyad Ahmad (سید احمد), brother of the celebrated Sayyad Jalāl Bukhārī. He was left in charge of Gujrāt by Dārā Shikōh in A.D. 1659. His elder brother's name was Sayyad Jafar Khān. His tomb is near Tājganj at Āgra.

Sayyad Ahmad (سید احمد بریلی), of Bareilī, who raised a religious war with the Sikhs in the Panjāb and was killed at Balākot. He began life in an indifferent school for the character of reformer and saint, which he ultimately assumed, as a sawār serving with Amīr Khān's free-booting horse in Mālwā. Quitting that service, he repaired to Dehlī, and became a disciple of Shāh 'Abdul 'Azīz, a very celebrated devotee of the city; the fame of whose knowledge and piety has been widely extended throughout that side of India. It is frequently said by the natives, that it was from Shāh 'Abdul 'Azīz that Sayyad Ahmad derived the peculiar opinions which he subsequently promulgated, and the design which he adopted of preaching a religious war. It is at least certain that the chief of his first disciples and the most constant associates of all his fortunes were two near relatives of 'Abdul Azīz, one his nephew, Maulwī Muhammad Ismā'īl, author of the *Sirāt-ul-Mustaqīm*, the other his son-in-law (and also partially a contributor to the book), named Maulwī 'Abdul Hai. By that school Muhammad Ismā'īl is generally esteemed to have been a man of much talent and learning. The extreme honour which he and his brother Maulwī paid to Sayyad Aḥmad, who was himself nearly illiterate, had a powerful effect in attracting towards him the respect of the vulgar. They rendered him almost menial offices, running, it is said, with their shoes off, by the side of his palankeen, when he moved out with his servants. From his first leaving Dehlī he assumed the character of a religious teacher, and commenced to spread his religious doctrines. The general spirit by which these were animated (identical nearly with that of the tenets of the Arabian Wahābīs, of whom the sect of Sayyad Aḥmad may perhaps be accurately termed an Indian imitation) was the ardent profession of Muhammadanism in its primitive simplicity and fervour, and the utter rejection of all idolatrous or superstitious innovations, whencesoever derived. The manner in which they were at first actually received was, however, highly favourable. When Sayyad Aḥmad at last came down to Bengal, he had got together many followers and had established an extensive reputation. He arrived in Calcutta with a considerable retinue towards the end of A.D. 1821, and immediately a great majority of the Muhammadans of the place, of all ranks and stations, flocked to become, or to profess themselves, his disciples. In the early part of A.D. 1822 he proceeded with his friends, the two Moulwīs, to Mecca, from whence he returned in October of the next year, having touched for a few days at Bombay, where, with reference to the shortness of his stay, his success in gaining numerous followers was nearly as remarkable as in Calcutta. In December, A.D. 1823, he again started for Upper India. The next important event of his career, his commencing a religious war in the Lāhore territories, did not occur till after a considerable interval, though the enterprise was one in which he had long openly announced his intention to engage. Its date is given in the *Targhīb-ul-Jihād*, or *Incitement of Religious War*, a little treatise written in Hindūstānī during the continuance of the struggle by a Maulwī of Qanauj with the view, as its name purports, of rousing the Faithful to rally round the standard which had been raised in the Panjāb. "The tribe of Sikhs," says the indignant Maulwī, "has long held sway in Lāhore and other places. Their oppressions have exceeded all limits. Thousands of Muhammadans they have unjustly killed, and on thousands have they heaped disgrace. The 'Azān, or summons for prayer, and the killing of cows, they have entirely prohibited. When at length their insulting tyranny could no longer be borne, Sayyad Aḥmad, going to the direction of Kābul and Qandahār, roused the Muhammadans of those countries, and, nerving their courage for action in the service of God, some thousands of believers became ready at his call to tread the path of God's service; and on the 21st December, A.D. 1826, 20th Jumāda I. A.H. 1242, the Jihād against the Kāfir Sikhs began." The events of this war were watched with a natural interest by the Muhammadan population of India generally, whether followers of Sayyad Aḥmad or not. Many of the inhabitants of our Western provinces went in bodies to range themselves under his standard; and his emissaries gathered large contributions of money and jewels, even from our own distant Presidencies, and from the principal Muhammadan towns of the Deccan. The prominent occurrences of the war, the perseverance with which it was kept up, the temporary and occasional successes which Sayyad Aḥmad met, and his ultimate death in battle, are well known. With his death the struggle appears to have entirely ceased.—*Jour. As. Soc. of Bengal*, vol. i. p. 450. [This story is chiefly interesting as an instance of what may be done in India by an ardent fanatic.]

Sayyad Ahmad Kabir (سيد احمد كبير), grandfather of Sayyad Jalāl Bukhārī, and a Musalmān saint, whose tomb is in Bijaimandil, near the tomb of Shāh Muhammad Khayālī at Dehlī.

Sayyad Ahmad, Sir, K.C.S.I. (سيد احمد منصف دهلى), Munsif of Dehlī in the British Government service, was the son of Sayyad Muhammad Muttaqī Khān Bahādur, and author of the work called *Asār Sanādīd*, containing a description of old Dehlī and Shāhjahānābād, and also of another work, entitled *Silsilat-ul-Malūk*. The native place of his ancestors is Arabia. They removed afterwards to Herāt, and during the reign of Akbar the Great they came into India. Ever since that period they have enjoyed titles and dignity. Under the British Sayyad Ahmad has been made Khān Bahādur and K.C.S.I. His greatest work is the Anglo-Muhammadan College, Aligarh; and he will have a place in Indian history as the greatest Muhammadan Reformer of modern times. His *Life* appeared in 1885, written by Lieut.-Col. Graham. [See also Dowson's *Elliot*, vol. viii.]

Sayyad 'Ali or **Sayyad 'Ali Hamdani** (سيد على همدانى), a famous Sayyad who fled to Kashmere from his native city of Hamdān, where he had incurred the wrath of Amīr Taimūr. Seven hundred Sayyads are said to have accompanied his flight to Kashmere in the reign of Sultān Quṭb-uddīn. He arrived in that province in A.D. 1380, A.H. 782. He remained at Kashmere six years and named it the "Garden of Solomon" (Bāgh Sulaimān). He died at Paklī whilst on his return to Persia. His son Mīr Muhammad-Hamdānī, also a fugitive, brought in his train three hundred Sayyads to Kashmere, where he remained twelve years. These two immigrations of fugitive Sayyads fixed the religion of the country, and were doubtless the chief cause of the religious persecutions which ensued in the following reign.

Sayyad 'Ali bin-Shahab-uddin Hamdani (سید علی بن شہاب الدین همدانی), author of the *Tazkirat-ul-Malūk*, treating upon religion, articles of faith, duty of kings to their subjects, etc.

Sayyad 'Ali Shirazi (سید علی شیرازی), the saint of the Jokhia Sindhi tribe. His tomb is in Tatta. The inscription bears the date A.D. 1776, A.H. 1190.

Sayyad Husain (سید حسین خنک سوار), commonly called Khink Sawār. It is mentioned in the *Akbar-nāma* that Sayyad Husain came to India with Shahāb-uddīn Ghōrī, who, after his conquest of India in A.D. 1192, A.H. 588, left him behind as governor of Ajmīr, where he died some years afterwards, and was buried on the hill where the fort of Ajmīr then stood. He is now venerated by the Muhammadans as a saint.

Sayyad Husain or Mir Husain (سید حسین), a celebrated Muhammadan of Ghaznī, who died at Herāt in December, A.D. 1317, Shawwāl, A.H. 717, aged 117 lunar years. He is the author of works called *Nazhat-ul-Arwāh* and *Kanz-ul-Ramūz*.

Sayyad Husain, Makhdum (سید حسین مخدوم), a contemporary of Shaikh Nizām-uddīn Aulia, and author of the work called *Siar-ul-Aulia*.
[*Vide* Wajīh-uddīn Mubārik Kirmānī.]

Sayyad Husain Shahid, Amir (سید حسین شہید امیر), a Muhammadan saint or martyr, who was slain on the 9th May, A.D. 1538, 9th Zil-hijja, A.H. 944, in the time of the emperor Humāyūn, and is buried at a place called Nāikī Mandī at Āgra, where his tomb is to be seen to this day bearing a Persian inscription in verse.

Sayyad Ismail Shah (سید اسمعیل شاه), commonly called Pir Chattar, a Muhammadan saint, whose tomb is situated about two thousand paces out of the western gates of the city of Broach on the northern bank of the Narbada. The tomb is said to be upwards of three hundred years old. It is built of the ordinary form in a small enclosure. It is shaded by a Khizni tree, which grows by the side of the eastern wall out of the enclosure. In the middle of the tomb is a reservoir about 5 feet 4 inches by 1 foot 8 inches, and in depth about 1 foot 2 inches. In the midst of the water there rises, about one inch above it, a small island, or the inner tomb, of 4 feet by 1. This miraculous reservoir is always full to the brim of very cold water. Hundreds of visitors go to the shrine every Thursday, and drink a tumbler full of the water, but it never diminishes nor increases.

Sayyad Ja'far (سید جعفر زمبیرپوری) of Zamīrpūr or Zambīrpūr, was a descendant of Sayyad Namat-ullah Walī. His poetical name was Rūhī. He died on the 30th October, A.D. 1741, 1st Ramazān, A.H. 1154, and is buried at Zambīrpūr, a place situated thirty miles from Lucknow.

Sayyad Ja'far Khan (سید جعفر خان), the eldest son of Sayyad Jalāl Bukhārī and brother of Sayyad Ahmad. After his father's death he sat on the masnad of Irshād as a spiritual guide. He lived in the time of the emperor 'Ālamgīr.

Sayyad Jalal Bukhari (سید جلال بخاری). *Vide* Shaikh Jalāl.

Sayyad Jalal Bukhari (سید جلال بخاری), son of Sayyad Muhammad Bukhārī and a descendant of Sayyad Ahmad Kabīr, a very proud and learned Musalmān who held the rank of 6000 in the reign of the emperor Shāh Jahān. He was born on the 11th February, A.D. 1595, 11th Jumāda II. A.H. 1003, and died in A.D. 1647, A.H. 1057, and is buried near the gate of the city of Dehlī. Some say his tomb is near Tāj-ganj at Āgra.

Sayyad Kabir, Sayyad (سید کبیر سید). His tomb is still to be seen at Āgra near a place called Sultānganj, and, from the inscription on the tombstone, we learn that he died in A.D. 1609, A.H. 1018.

Sayyad Muhammad (سید محمد), a poet whose poetical name was Rind. *Vide* Rind.

Sayyad Muhammad or Said Muhammad (سید محمد), author of an Arabic work on Theology called *Asrār 'Ulūm*.

Sayyad Said (سید سعید), Sultān of Oman and Imām of Muskat, who, at the age of 16, ascended the throne in A.D. 1803. The connection of the British with Muskat commenced in the beginning of the present century, when, in conjunction with the then Imām, Sayyad Saīd, the English were engaged in suppressing the Wahabī pirates who infested the Persian Gulf and the Indian Ocean. Sayyad Saīd lived to a great age, and filled the throne of Muskat for about fifty years. He died in A.D. 1856, and was succeeded by his son Thowaynī, who was murdered by his son Salīm. The old Imām left several sons, one of whom received as his share the kingdom of Zanzibār, and the other, Sayyad Turkī, another chiefship.

In the year A.D. 1868, one Azan bin-G͟hais, aided by the other potentates, having attacked and driven the Sulṭān from the throne, occupied it himself. Sulṭān Salīm fled to Bandar Abbās, where he is now. The new ruler, Azan bin-G͟hais, was no doubt connected with the Wahabīs and supported by them.

Sayyad Sharif Jurjani (سید شریف جرجانی). *Vide* Sharīf Jurjānī.

Sayyad Tehrani (سید طهرانی), author of a Dīwān found in Tīpū Sulṭān's Library.

Seodasheo Bhao, Marhaṭṭa general, son of Chimnājī, younger brother of the second Peshwā, Bāji Rāo I. When his cousin, son of Bāji, succeeded to the Peshwāship, Seodasheo Bhāo became commander-in-chief, and after minor successes easily persuaded his cousin to undertake the conquest of Hindūstān after the murder of the emperor 'Alamgīr II. (*q.v.*). Defeated and killed at Pānīpat, January, 1761.

[*Vide* Ahmad Shāh.]

Seoji or **Shioji** (سیوجی), a grandson of the renowned Jaichānd, the last Rāṭhor monarch of Qanauj. He with a few retainers migrated in the year A.D. 1212, and planted the Rāṭhor standard in Māṛwār. His successors in process of time, by valour, and by taking advantage of the times, enlarged the state, and in A.D. 1432 Jōdhā Rāo of Māṛwār founded the modern capital of Jōdhpūr, to which he transferred the seat of government from Mandōr. The name of Māṛwār is a corruption of Mārūwār, also called Mārū-deis, or "the region of death." Anciently, and properly, it included the entire western desert, from the Satlaj to the ocean.

Sewaji or **Siwaji** (سیواجی), a celebrated chief of the Bhōsla family and founder of the Marhaṭṭa States in the Deccan, of whose origin we have the following account. Bhīm Sen, rānā of Udaipūr, the first in rank among the Hindū princes, had a son named Bhāg Singh by a concubine of a tribe very inferior to his own. On the death of his father, Bhāg Singh finding himself despised and neglected by his relations, the Sisodhia rājpūts, who from the low caste of his mother regarded him only as a bastard, and not of their tribe, became weary of the indignities shewn him; and moved from Udāipūr to K͟hāndesh, where he embraced the service of a Zamīndār, named Rāja 'Alī Mōhan. He afterwards retired into the Deccan, where he purchased a tract of land near the present Marhaṭṭa capital of Pūna, and settled upon it as Zamīndār, in which situation he died. Bhāg Singh had four sons, two of whom, Mallūjī and Bambūjī, being of an enterprising spirit, entered into the service of Jādho Rāe, a Marhaṭṭa chief of distinguished rank at the court of Bahādur Niẓām Shāh. Mallūjī had a son named Sāhjī or Sāūjī, who married the daughter of Jādho Rāe, and thus the Bhōsla family became incorporated with the Marhaṭṭas, and are commonly esteemed as such in Hindūstān. Sāhjī, after the death of his father, left Aḥmadnagar with his followers and entered into the service of Ibrāhīm 'Adil Shāh, king of Bījāpūr, who gave him a jāgīr in the Karnatic, with a command of ten thousand horse. Soon after this, in May, A.D. 1627, his son Sewājī, afterwards so celebrated in the Deccan, was born, from the daughter of Jādho Rāe Marhaṭṭa. Sāhjī, having disagreed with his wife, sent her, with the infant Sewājī, to reside at Pūna, of which and the vicinity he had obtained a grant. Sewājī, though neglected by his father, was properly educated, and at the age of seventeen excelled in every accomplishment. Military fame was his first passion; and the government of Bījāpūr being now weakened by intestine divisions and the encroachments of the Mug͟hals, he had soon an opportunity of signalizing himself among other rebels. He raised banditti and plundered the neighbouring districts, and having now taken possession of the jāgīr, raised more troops, successfully levied contributions on several Zamīndārs, and much extended the limits of his territories. At this crisis the prince Aurangzeb, governor of the imperial territories in the Deccan, was meditating the overthrow of his brother Dārā Shikōh, the favourite son of the emperor Shāh Jahān, who was now in a dangerous state of health. For this purpose he was preparing an army to march to Āgra; and, observing the enterprizing genius of Sewājī, sent him an invitation to his service. Sewājī, pretending to be struck with horror at the rebellion of a son against a father, received the prince's messenger with indignity, drove him from his presence, and ordered the letter he had bought to be tied to the tail of a dog. Aurangzeb for the present stifled his resentment, but never would forgive Sewājī's insolence, and hence may be dated his tedious war in the Deccan, and finally the ruin of the Mug͟hal empire by the Marhaṭṭas. Aurangzeb having left the Deccan in A.D. 1658, A.H. 1068, Siwājī resolved to turn the inactivity of the imperial troops, and the weakness of the Gōlkanḍa and Bījāpūr princes, to the utmost advantage. He took the strong fortress of

Rājgarh, which he fixed upon as the seat of his government. The Bījāpūr government having in vain desired his father Sāhjī (who disclaimed all connection with him) to repress the excesses of his son, at length sent against him a considerable force under a general named Afzul Khān. Sewājī with artful policy invited him to come and receive his submission. Afzul Khān advanced without opposition to his tent, when he was stabbed by the treacherous Zamīndār in embracing him. Upon a signal given, the Marhattas rushed from an ambuscade, attacked the unsuspecting army of Bījāpūr, which, deprived of their chief, was quickly defeated. Sewājī plundered their rich camp, and by this victory became master of all Kōkan, the Zamīndārs of which flocked to acknowledge his authority, to save their possessions. The strong fortress of Sitārā and other places also opened their gates to receive him. In the course of only three years Sewājī became a powerful prince, his authority being acknowledged over almost the whole coast of Mārwār. He built palaces and erected fortifications in every part of his country; gave much trouble to the emperor 'Alamgīr; reigned more than twenty years, and left a character which has never since been equalled or approached by any of his countrymen. He died on the 14th April, A.D. 1680, 24th Rabī' I. A.H. 1091, but, according to Elphinstone's *History of India*, on the 5th April the same year, aged 53 years representing the difference between old and new styles. His funeral pile was administered with the same sacrifices as had been devoted the year before to the obsequies of the Mahārāja Jaswant Singh of Jodhpūr; attendants, animals, and wives, were burnt with his corpse. He was succeeded by his son Sambha or Sambhājī.

Shabib (شبیب بن یزید بن نعیم), the son of Yezīd, the son of Naīm, was a Khārajite. It is related that his father, Yezīd, was sent by 'Usmān the Khalīf to assist the Syrian Muhammadans against the Greeks in the twenty-fifth year of the Hijra. The Musalmāns obtaining the victory, the Christains were exposed for sale. Among the captives Yezīd espied a beautiful maid, whom he bought and married. She proved with child of Shabīb, who was born on the 10th of the month of Zil-hijja, being the day on which the pilgrims killed the sacrifices at Mecca. Yezīd opposed Hajjāj, the governor of Mecca, for a long time, and was at last drowned in a river. His body being drawn out, his head was cut off and sent to Hajjāj. This happened in A.D. 696, A.H. 77.

Shadad (شداد), poetical title of Rāe Chandra Lāl, an Amīr in the service of the Nizām of Haidarabād.

Shaddad (شداد), the Adite, was the son of 'Adand, the first king of the 'Adites, a race of ancient Arabs; the smallest of their tribe is said to have been 60 cubits high, and the largest 100 cubits. 'Ad had two sons, Shadīd and Shaddād; on the death of their father, they reigned conjointly over the whole earth. At length Shadīd died, and his brother Shaddād ruled after him. Shaddād was fond of reading the ancient books, and when he met with descriptions of Paradise and of the world to come, his heart enticed him to build its like upon the earth. A pleasant and elevated spot being fixed upon, Shaddād despatched one hundred chiefs to collect skilful artists and workmen from all countries. He also commanded the kings of Syria and Onnus to send him all their jewels and precious stones. Forty camel-loads of gold, silver and jewels were daily used in the building, which contained a thousand spacious quadrangles of many thousand rooms. In the areas were artificial trees of gold and silver, whose leaves were emeralds, and fruit clusters of pearls and jewels. The ground was strewed with ambergris, musk and saffron. Between every two of the artificial trees was planted one of delicious fruit. This romantic abode took 500 years in the completion. To this paradise he gave the name of Irām. When finished Shaddād marched to view it, and when he arrived near, divided two hundred thousand youthful slaves, whom he had brought with him from Damascus, into four detachments, which were stationed in cantonments prepared for their reception on each side of the garden, towards which he proceeded with his favourite courtiers. Suddenly was heard in the air a voice like thunder, and Shaddād, looking up, beheld a personage of majestic figure and stern aspect, who said, "I am the Angel of Death, commissioned to seize thy impure soul." Shaddād exclaimed, "Give me leisure to enter the garden," and was descending from his horse, when the seizer of life snatched away his impure spirit, and he fell dead upon the ground. At the same time lightnings flashed, and destroyed the whole army of the infidel; and the rose-garden of Irām became concealed from the sight of man.

This paradise, though invisible, is still supposed to be standing in the deserts of Aden, and sometimes, though very rarely, God permits it to be seen.

Crighton, in his *History of Arabia*, says that "The whole fable seems a confused tradition of Belus and the ancient Babylon; or rather, as the name would import, of Benhadad, mentioned in Scripture as one of the most famous of the Syrian kings, and who, we are told, was worshipped by his subjects."

Shadid (شدید), an author, whose proper name is Muhammad bin-Farāmurz.

Shadid, Qazi (شدید قاضی), an eminent Musalmān doctor and author, who died in the year A.D. 1447, A.H. 851.

Shadman, Sultan (شادمان سلطان), a poet who had assumed the title of Sulṭān on account of his being a descendant of the royal race of Gihkars, whose territory was between the countries of the Panjāb and Hasan Abdal. He flourished in the reign of the emperor Shāh Jahān, and is the author of a Dīwān. He wrote some beautiful verses in praise of the peacock throne on its completion in the year A.D. 1635, A.H. 1044, for which he was very handsomely rewarded by the emperor. He died in the reign of 'Alamgīr A.D. 1668, A.H. 1079.

Shad-ul-Mulk (شاد الملک یا سعد الملک), a celebrated courtezan, whom Sulṭān Khalīl, the grandson of Amīr Taimūr, had secretly married, and at last lost his kingdom on her account.

[*Vide* Khalīl (Sulṭān).]

Shafa'i (شافعی), poetical appellation of a poet. *Vide* Hanīfā (Imām).

Shafa'i Hakim (شفائي حكيم), poetical title of Sharaf-uddīn Hasan, a physician and poet who is the author of several Masnawīs, one of which is called *Namakdān Haqīqat*, the Salt-cellar of Truth. He died in A.D. 1628, A.H. 1037.

[*Vide* Sharaf-uddīn Hasan Shafāī.]

Shafa'i, Imam (شافعی امام), surname of Abū Abdullah Muhammad bin-Idrīs, who was thus surnamed from Shafīa, one of his forefathers, who was a descendant of 'Abdul Mutallib, grandfather of Muhammad. It is from that origin that the Sunnīs give to this doctor the title of Imām-ul-Mutallibī, as well as that of 'Arif Billāh, or learned in God. He was born at Ghaza, a city of Palestine, on the very day that Abū Hanīfa died, A.D. 767, A.H. 150, and eventually became the founder of the third of the chief Sunnī sects. He died in Egypt on Friday the 20th January, A.D. 820, 30th Rajāb, A.H. 204, aged 54 lunar years. He is the author of several works, and is said by all Sunnī writers to have been a learned and virtuous man, who laboured to arrange the traditions so as to render them useful as a code of laws. In his youth he was a pupil of Mālik ibn-'Aus. His followers were at one time very numerous in Khurāsān; but at present his opinions are rarely quoted, either in Persia or India. He is reputed to have composed two collections of traditions, namely the *Masnad* and the *Sunan*. Besides the works on the traditions, he is said to have composed a most excellent treatise on jurisprudence called *Al-Fiqh-ul-Akbar*; but it has been questioned whether he was the author.

Shafari (شفاری), one of the three authors who composed the poems entitled *Lamaāt-ul-Arab*.

Shah Abbas I. (شاه عباس). *Vide* Abbās (Shāh I.).

Shah Abbas II. (شاه عباس). *Vide* Abbās (Shāh II.).

Shahab-uddin (شهاب الدين), author of a medical work in Persian called *Asrār Atibba*.

Shahab-uddin Abu'l Fazl Ahmad-al-'Usqalani (شهاب الدين ابوالفضل احمد العسقلانی), author of a work on Traditions, entitled *Bulūgh-al-Marām*, an abridgment of which, called *Muntakhib Bulugh-al-Marāni*, was printed at Calcutta with an interlinear Urdū translation. 'Usqalānī died in A.D. 1448, A.H. 852.

[*Vide* Ibn-Hajar.]

Shahab-uddin Adib Sabir (شهاب الدين اديب صابر), a celebrated poet at the court of Sulṭān Sanjar Saljūqī. He was a contemporary of Anwarī and Rashīdī, and was drowned in the river Jaihūn by order of Sulṭān Atsiz of Khwārizm, who was an enemy of Sulṭān Sanjar. When Atsiz raised in Khwārizm the standard of revolt against Sanjar, the latter sent Adīb as a spy to the court of Atsiz that he might continually keep him informed of the intentions of his enemy. It so happened that Atsiz despatched an assassin who was to murder Sanjar on Friday. Adīb sent the intelligence of the plot and portrait of the assassin in advance to Sanjar. The plot was thus frustrated, but Adīb paid with his life for his fidelity to his former patron. Atsiz ordered that his hands and feet be tied, and that he be thrown into the Oxus. This happened in A.D. 1152, A.H. 546. He has left a Dīwān of Kasīdas called *Qasāid Adīb Sābir*.

Shahab-uddin Ahmad (شهاب الدين احمد), son of Muhammad Maqdisī of Jerusalem, author of the *Sharah Lāmia Shatibia*. He died A.D. 1328, A.H. 728. There appears to be another Shahāb-uddīn, the son of Yūsaf Chilpī, who is said to be the author of the above work. He died in the year A.D. 1355, A.H. 756.

Shahab-uddin Ahmad (شهاب الدين احمد), author of the *Fatāwā Ibrāhīm Shāhī*, which was composed by order of Ibrāhīm Shāh of Jaunpūr in the ninth century of the Hijra.

Shahab-uddin Ahmad bin-Mahmud-al-Siwasi (شہاب الدین احمد بن محمد السواسی), author of a most celebrated Commentary on the Sirājia of Sajāwandī. He died A.D. 1400, A.H. 803.

hab-uddin Ahmad bin-Yahia (شہاب الدین احمد بن یحیٰ), an Arabian author who died in A.D. 1317.

Shahab-uddin Ahmad Talash (شہاب الدین احمد تالاش), author of the *Tārīkh Mulk Asham*, which contains the account of an expedition undertaken against the kingdom of Asām in the 4th year of the reign of 'Alamgīr, A.D. 1661, by Muazzim Khān Khān Khānān, written in 1663.

[*Vide* Mīr Jumla.]

Shahab-uddin Burhanpuri (شہاب الدین برھانپوری), author of the Fountain of Truth, called *Ayn-ul-Maānī*, an essay on the knowledge of God, etc., written in the year A.D. 1518.

[*Vide* Majd-uddīn Aḥmad.]

Shahab-uddin Burlusi (شہاب الدین برلسی), author of a work on Sūfīism called *Durr-ul-Ghaūwās.*

Shahab-uddin, Maulana (شہاب الدین مولانا), author of the marginal notes on the Qurān called *Hashia Shahāb Hifāchī.*

Shahab-uddin, Mua'mmai (شہاب الدین معمائي), or the Punster. He accompanied the emperor Bābar Shāh to India; was a good poet, and wrote a book of enigmas, on account of which he received the title of Mua'mmāī or the Punster. He died in the reign of the emperor Humāyūn, A.D. 1535, A.H. 942, and Khūndamīr, the historian, found the year of his death in the words "Shahāb-ul-Sāqib," or Shahāb the Sublime.

Shahab-uddin Muhammad Ghori (شہاب الدین محمد غوری), surnamed Moizz-uddīn Muhammad Sām. He was appointed governor of Ghaznī in A.D. 1174, A.H. 570, by his elder brother, Ghayās-uddīn Muhammad, Sulṭān of Ghōr and Ghaznī. He defeated and took prisoner Khusro Malik, the last prince of the race of the Ghaznavides, A.D. 1186, A.H. 582, and subdued Khurāsān and great part of India. He fought two battles with Pithoura, the Rāja of Ajmīr, who was made prisoner and put to death along with Khānde Rāe, king of Dehlī, in A.D. 1192, A.H. 588. His brother Ghayās-uddīn died in A.D. 1203, A.H. 599, when he succeeded to the throne and reigned over Ghōr, Ghaznī and India three years. He was murdered by the Gihkars on his way to Ghaznī on the 14th March, A.D. 1206, 2nd Shabān, A.H. 602, after he had reigned 32 years from the commencement of his government over Ghaznī, and three from his accession to the throne. His remains were taken to Ghaznī and buried there in a new vault which had been built for his daughter. He was succeeded by his nephew Ghayās-uddīn Mahmūd, the son of Ghayās-uddīn Muhammad.

Shahab-uddin, Qazi (شہاب الدین قاضی دولتابادی), of Daulatābād, author of the Commentary on the Qurān called *Bahr Mauwāj*, in Persian. He received the title of Malik-ul-'Ulmā, "king of the learned," from Sulṭān Ibrāhīm Sharqī of Jaunpūr, and died in the year A.D. 1437, A.H. 842. He is also the author of the work entitled *Munāqib-us-Saādat.*

Shahab-uddin Suharwardi (شہاب الدین سہروردی شیخ), generally called Shaikh Maqtūl and Qatīl-ullāh, because he was put to death by the famous general Sālah-uddīn (Saladin) of Aleppo, for having more philosophy than religion. According to the work called Haft Aklīm, he was starved or put to death at Aleppo in A.D. 1189, A.H. 585, aged 36 or 38 years. He is the author of the Commentaries called *Sharah Hayākal* and *Sharah Ayzāh*. In the 4th vol. of *Hājī Khalfā*, p. 236, he is said to be the author of another work called *Akl Surkh.*

Shahab-uddin Suharwardi, Shaikh (شہاب الدین سہروردی شیخ), the son of Abū Najīb, was born at Suharward in January, A.D. 1145, Rajab, A.H. 539. He was a pious Shaikh, most assiduous in his spiritual exercises and the practice of devotion. He is the author of several works, among which is one called *Awārif-ul-Maārif*, also called *Awārif-ul-Haqāeq.* He died on the 26th September, A.D. 1234, 1st Muharram, A.H. 632, in his 93rd year, at Baghdād, where he was buried. There is another work in Arabic found in the Library of Tīpū Sulṭān, entitled *Hikmat-ul-Ashrāq,* of which he is said to be the author.

Shahab-uddin, Sultan (شہاب الدین سلطان), the son of Sulṭān 'Alā-uddīn, whom he succeeded on the throne of Kashmere, A.D. 1356, A.H. 757. He turned his attention to foreign conquest, and during the succeeding ten years subdued Thibet, Kāshghar, Badakhshān and Kābul. He then, according to the historian Haidar Malik, invaded Hindūstān with an immense army, and is said to have worsted Fīrōz Shāh, king of Dehlī, in a pitched battle on the banks of the Satlaj, the result of which was to cause that potentate to acknowledge his supremacy. Shahāb-uddīn then returned to Kashmere, where his religious zeal led him to destroy the idol temples at Bijbihārī and elsewhere. He died after a reign of 19 years, A.D. 1376, and was succeeded by his brother Quṭb-uddīn, during whose reign the famous Sayyad 'Alī Hamdānī arrived at Kashmere.

Shahab-uddin 'Umar (شهاب الدين عمر), son of Sultān 'Alā-uddīn Sikandar Sānī, king of Dehlī.

[*Vide* Kāfūr and 'Alā-uddīn.]

Shahadat (شهادت), poetical name of Mirzā Sālah of Balkh, who died in A.D. 1742, A.H. 1155.

Shah 'Alam (شاه عالم), king of Dehlī, whose original name was 'Alī Gauhar, was the son of the emperor 'Alamgīr II. by Zinat Mahal, surnamed Bilāl Kūnwar; and was born on the 15th June, A.D. 1728, 17th Ẕi-Qa'da, A.H. 1140. In the year A.D. 1758, A.H. 1172, fearing he might be made a prisoner by 'Imād-ul-Mulk Ghāzī-uddīn Khān, the minister of his father, he left Dehlī to try his fortune in Bengal, the Nawāb of which province, Sirāj-uddaula, had been deposed by the assistance of the English, and Mīr Jafar set up in his room. He was in Behār when he received the intelligence of the murder of his father, and, having assumed the imperial authority, he ascended the throne on the 25th December, A.D. 1759, 4th Jumāda I. A.H. 1173, with the title of Shāh 'Alam. After the defeat of Shujā-uddaula, his prime minister, at Buxar, on the 23rd October, A.D. 1764, 26th Rabī' II. A.H. 1178, and his flight to the upper province, the king followed the English to Allahābād, where he granted the East India Company the Sanad of the Dīwānī of Bengal, dated 12th August, A.D. 1765, 24th Ṣafar, A.H. 1179, on the Company agreeing to pay the emperor 24 lakhs of rupees annually from the revenues of the three provinces, viz. Bengal, Behār, and Orissa. This important business being settled by Lord Clive, he returned to Calcutta, leaving General Smith to attend the emperor, but in fact to rule him; for the General resided in the fortress, and his majesty in the town; and the sound of the imperial naubat in the fort being disagreeable to General Smith, he forbad the band to play, nor did the servants of the emperor dare to disobey the disgraceful order. Shāh 'Alam continued to reside at Allahābād under the protection of the English till the year A.D. 1771, A.H. 1185, when, growing weary of his retirement, he proceeded to Dehlī, where he arrived on the 25th December the same year, but not long afterwards fell into the power of Ghulām Kādir Khān, a Rohila chief, who put out his eyes on the 10th August, A.D. 1788, Ramaẓān, A.H. 1185. Shāh 'Alam, after this event, re-assumed the throne, and died on the 19th November, A.D. 1806, 7th Ramaẓān, A.H. 1221, aged 81 lunar years. Shāh 'Alam's poetical name was Aftāb. He was a good poet, and has left a Dīwān called *Dīwān-Aftāb*, in Persian and Urdū verse. His remains were deposited close to the tomb of Bahādur Shāh, adjoining the Motī Masjid, near the Dargāh of Quṭb Shāh.

[*Vide* Keene's *Fall of the Mughal Empire.*]

Shah 'Alam (شاه علم), a celebrated Muhammadan saint, was the son of Quṭb 'Alam, which see.

Shah 'Ali, Hazrat (شاه على حضرت), a pious Sayyab, who is the author of several works on religion in Persian, Arabic, and Gujrātī. He died at Aḥmadābād Gujrāt in A.D. 1565, A.H. 973, and was buried there.

Shah 'Ali Muhammad (شاه على محمد), author of the *Tajjalliāt Rahmānī*, an explanation of the Sūfī tenets and mystical phrases, etc.

Shahbaz Banda Nawaz (شاهباز بنده نواز), author of two books called *Ishq-nāma* and *Sārdat-nāma*, containing essays on divine love, the soul, future state, etc.

Shahbaz Khan Kambu (شاهباز خان كمبو), a descendant in the sixth generation of Hājī Jamāl, who was a disciple of Shaikh Bahā-uddīn of Multān. He passed the first part of his life as a Dervish or mendicant, but was afterwards employed by the emperor Akbar, and raised to the dignity of an Amīr. He was appointed governor of Bengal in A.D. 1584, A.H. 992, and died in the 44th year of the reign of that monarch, A.D. 1599, A.H. 1008, aged 70 years. He was buried at Ajmīr, near the mausoleum of Khwāja Mo'in-uddīn Chishtī. His liberality and the money he expended was so great, that it made the people think that he had in his possession the Philosopher's Stone.

Shah Begam (شاه بيگم), the mother of Sulṭān Khusro, the son of the emperor Jahāngīr. *Vide* Khusro (Sulṭān).

Shah Begam (شاه بیگم). This was the title conferred by Jahāngīr on his first wife, who was the daughter of Bhagwān Dās, the son of Rāja Behārī Mal. She was married to prince Salīm (afterwards Jahāngīr) in A.D. 1584, A.H. 993, and became the mother of Sulṭān Khusro, who was born in A.D. 1587, A.H. 995. When Jahāngīr rebelled against his father Akbar, and was living independently at Allahābad, he gave himself up more than ever to debauchery. He had always entertained a peculiar dislike for his eldest son, Sulṭān Khusro, whose own levity and violence seem to have given him reasons for his displeasure. Some circumstance in their disputes so affected Khusro's mother that she swallowed poison (opium) in A.D. 1603, A.H. 1012, and died at Allahābād, where she was buried in a place called Sulṭān Khusro's garden, where her son Sulṭān Khusro also was afterwards buried.

Shah Begam (شاه بیگم), a daughter of Muhammad Muqīm, brother of Shāh Beg Arghūn, governor of Qandahār and afterwards king of Sindh. She was married to Qāsim Kōka, who was killed in the wars of the Uzbaks. On the conquest of Qandahār by Bābar Shāh, she was taken away to Kābul.

Shah Begam (شاه بیگم), mother of Khān Mirzā, of Badakhshān, traced her genealogy to Alexander the Great.

Shah Beg Arghun or **Urghun** (شاه بیگ ارغون), king of Sindh and founder of the Arghūn family, was the son of Mirzā Zunnūn Beg Arghūn, the commander-in-chief and head of the nobles at the court of Sulṭān Husain Mirzā, king of Khurāsān, and governor of Qandahār and the provinces of Shāl, Sitūnak and Arghūn. Mirzā Zunnūn met his death in attempting to resist an invasion under Muhammad Khān Shaibānī Uzbak. After his death the government of Kandahār devolved on his son Shāh Beg Arghūn. When the emperor Bābar Shāh invaded the province of Qandahār, Shāh Beg, unable to resist him, retreated towards Sindh, and having overcome Jām Fīrōz, the last king of the Samāna dynasty, A.D. 1521, A.H. 927, he settled himself as king in that country. His reign was, however, but of short duration, for he died two years and some months after the conquest, in the year A.D. 1524, A.H. 930, and his eldest son, Shāh Husain Arghūn, succeeded him.

Shah Dai-ullah, Shirazi (شاه داعی الله شیرازی), a pupil of Shāh Namat-ullāh Walī. He was a mystical poet and a great saint. His tomb, which is at Shīrāz, is a place of pilgrimage.

Shah Ghulam Azim (شاه غلام عظیم), son of Shāh Abul Maālī, the son of Shāh Ajmal of Allahābād. He is the author of two Dīwāns and a Masnawī.

[*Vide* Afzal.]

Shah Girami or **Mirza Girami** (شاه گرامی), a poet who lived in the dress of Kalandar and Dehlī, and died in the year A.D. 1743, A.H. 1156.

Shah Gul (شاه گل). *Vide* Wahdat.

Shah Hatim (شاه حاتم), surname of Shaikh Zahīr-uddīn, a Hindūstānī poet. *Vide* Hātim.

Shah Husain Arghun (شاه حسین ارغون), king of Sindh, succeeded his father, Shāh Beg Arghūn, in A.D. 1524, A.H. 930. He reigned 32 years, and died in A.D. 1555, A.H. 962. After his death the government of Sindh was divided between two rivals, Mahmūd, the governor of Bakkar, and Mirzā Īsa Turkhān, governor of Thaṭṭa, who both assumed the title of king, and between whom frequent dissensions arose, and battles were fought. The emperor Akbar on coming to Lāhore reduced the whole of the province of Bakkar exclusive of the fort, till at last Mahmūd was willing to give it up, and Akbar deputed Geisū Khān to receive it, but Mahmūd died before his arrival, A.D. 1574, A.H. 982, after a reign of 20 lunar years, and Akbar thus became possessed of Upper Sindh, and put an end to the hopes of the race of Mahmūd. Īsa Turkhān, who took possession of Thaṭṭa after the death of Shāh Husain, died after a reign of 13 years in A.D. 1567, A.H. 976.

Shah Husain Safwi (شاه حسین صفوی) succeeded his father, Shāh Sulaimān, king of Persia, in A.D. 1694, A.H. 1134. In the year A.D. 1722 Mahmūd, an Afghān chief of Qandahār, besieged Isfahān and compelled Sulṭān Husain to surrender and resign his crown to him. This circumstance occurred on the 23rd October the same year, A.H. 1135, and the unfortunate Sulṭān was confined in a small palace, where he remained seven years, when a reverse of fortune, which threatened their downfall, led his enemies, whose chief was Ashraf, the successor of Mahmūd, to put an end to his existence. This melancholy event took place in November, A.D. 1729, A.H. 1142. The Safwian family may be said to have actually terminated with Sulṭān Husain. His son Tahmasp assumed the title of king, and struggled for a few years with his fate, but a weak, effeminate, and debauched youth was unsuited for such times; and he only merits a place in history as his name furnished a pretext for the celebrated Nādir Shāh to lay the foundation of his great power.

Shah Husain Sayyad (شاه حسین سید). *Vide* Haqīqat.

Shahi (شاهی), poetical title of Prince Mirzā Nūr-uddīn, the son of Mirzā Khān Bakht, the son of Mirzā Sulaimān Shikoh.

Shahi Beg Khan Uzbak (شاهی بیگ خان اذبک), also called Shaibānī Khān, who, after he had conquered Transoxiana, invaded Khurāsān, took Herāt in A.D. 1507, A.H. 913, and extinguished the principal branch of the house of Taimūr. He was, however, defeated and slain in a battle against Shāh 'Ismā'īl I. Safwī, in A.D. 1510, A.H. 916, when his skull was overlaid with gold, and made into a drinking cup by that monarch. After his death Taimūr Sultān succeeded him and Jānī Beg Sultān and 'Abdullāh Khān divided Bukhārā between themselves. The Uzbaks were Tartars who came from the borders of Russia, where they had been governed by a race of princes descended from Shaibānī, the grandson of Changez Khān; but they derived their name from Uzbak, the seventh of their race, who introduced the Muhammadan religion among them. The last prince of this tribe was Burgū Khān, who was slain by Shāh Bakht, upon which the Uzbaks quitted their ancient habitation, and conquered Khurasān, Khwarizm, etc.

Shahid (شاهد). *Vide* Ghulām Imām Shahīd.

Shahidi (شاهدی), poetical name of Mīr 'Abdul Wāhid of Bilgrām, which see.

Shahidi Qummi (شاهدی قمی), an author, who was a native of Qumm, and died in A.D. 1529, A.H. 935.

Shahi, Mir or Amir (شاهی میر), poetical name of 'Aqā Malik, son of Jamāl-uddīn Fīrozkohī. His mother was the sister of Khwāja Muwyyad, a chief of the race of Sarbadāls of Sabzwār. He was himself a native of Sabzwār and a very learned man. He wrote a beautiful hand, and was a good musician and painter. He flourished in the time of Baisanghar Mirzā and Sultān Bābar, and died at Astrabād in A.D. 1450, A.H. 854, aged more than 70 years. He was buried at his own request at Sabzwār. He is the author of a biography of poets called *Majmūa-ush-Shuarā*, and of a Dīwān entitled *Dīwān Shāhī*.

Shah Jahan (شاه جهان), emperor of Dehlī, surnamed Shahāb-uddīn Muhammad Sāhib Qirān Sānī, was the third son of the emperor Jahāngīr. He was born at Lāhore on the 5th January, A.D. 1593, 29th Rabī' I. A.H. 1000, and named Mirzā Khurram. His mother, Balmatī, was the daughter of Rāja Udai Singh, son of Rāja Maldeo, of Jodhpūr, and sister to Rāja Sūraj Singh. At the time of his father's death he was absent in the Deccan, but the throne was secured for him by his father-in-law, 'Asaf Khān, the wazīr, the brother of Nūr Jahān Begam. He marched towards Lāhore on hearing of the throne being at his disposal, and began his reign 4th February, A.D. 1628, 8th Jumāda II. A.H. 1037. He was the most magnificent prince that ever appeared in India. The most striking instance of his pomp and prodigality was his construction of the famous peacock throne. It took its name from two peacocks fashioned splendidly in sapphires, emeralds, rubies, and other appropriate jewels, which formed the chief ornament of a mass of bullion and precious stones that dazzled every beholder. Tavernier, a jeweller by profession, reports that it cost nearly six millions and-a-half sterling. His greatest splendour was shown in his buildings. He founded a new city at Dehlī, called after him Shāhjahānābād, but of all the structures erected by him there is none that bears any comparison with the Tāj Mahal at Āgra, a mausoleum of white marble decorated with mosaics, which for the richness of the material, the chasteness of the design, and the effect at once brilliant and solemn, is not surpassed by any edifice, either in Europe or Asia. Tāj Mahal is a corruption of Mumtāz Mahal (Arjumānd Begam, *q.v.*), the name of Shāh Jahān's favourite wife, whose sepulchre it forms. Shāh Jahān reigned thirty years, but was deposed and confined in the fort of Āgra by his son 'Alamgīr Aurangzeb on the 9th June, A.D. 1651, 17th Ramazān, A.H. 1068, and died at Āgra, after an imprisonment of 7 years and 10 months, on Monday night, the 23rd January, A.D. 1666, 26th Rajab, A.H. 1076, aged 76 lunar years 3 months and 17 days, and was buried in the Tāj close to his wife's tomb. There were living at the time of his imprisonment four of his sons and four daughters. Of the sons the eldest was Dārā Shikōh, the second Sultān Shujāa, the third 'Alamgīr, and the fourth Murād Bakhsh; but 'Alamgīr, who succeeded his father, murdered two of his brothers, viz. Dārā and Murād, and the third, Sultān Shujāa, died in Arracan, or was murdered by the Rāja of that country. His daughters were Arjuman 'Arā, Gaitī 'Arā, Jahān 'Arā, and Dahr 'Arā (or Roshan 'Arā).

Inscription on a gold coin of Shāh Jahān of great size and value, struck in A.H. 1064.

OBVERSE.

سکه برمهردوصد مهری زد از لطف اله
ثانئ صاهب قربن شاه جهان دین پناه
روی زر باد از نقش سکه اش عالم فروز
تاشود از پرتو خورشید روشن روی ماه

REVERSE.

از صدق ابوبکر شد ایمان انسور
اسلام قوی دست شد از عدل عمر
دین تازه شد از شرم و حیا عثمان
از علم علی یافت ولایت زبور

[Vide *Turks in India*; also S. Lane-Poole's *Catalogue of Mughal Coins.*]

Shah Jahan Begam of Bhopal (شاه جاهان بیگم) succeeded to the principality of Bhopāl on the death of her mother, Sikandar Begam, on the 30th October, A.D. 1868. Her Highness in A.D. 1871 married her prime minister, Muhammad Sādik Hasan Khān, by the advice or consent of the Supreme Government. He was her second husband. She commanded that in future he should be addressed thus: Motamid-ul-Muhārn Muhammad Sādik Hasan Khān Sahib Bahādur, second minister of the State of Bhopāl.

Shah Jalal (شاه جلال), a Muhammadan saint of great sanctity, whose tomb is in Sylhet. This shrine has a large number of attendants to minister at it, and the pigeons and other birds which flock there are held as sacred as the birds within the temple of Mecca.

Shah Karak (شاه کرک), a celebrated Muhammadan saint, who is buried at Kaṛa, a city in the province of Allahābād, and whose tomb is still held sacred by the Musalmāns. It is mentioned by Firishta, that the day before the assassination of Sulṭān Jalāl-uddīn Fīroz, in A.D. 1296, Sulṭān 'Alā-uddīn visited the holy man, who, rising from his pillows repeated the following extempore verses: "He who cometh against thee shall lose his head in the boat, and his body shall be thrown into the Ganges;" which, they say, was explained a few hours afterwards by the death of the unfortunate king, whose head fell into the boat upon this occasion. Shāh Kaṛak died between the years A.D. 1296 and A.D. 1316.

Shah Madar (شاه مدار), a celebrated Muhammadan saint, whose proper name was Badī-uddīn. He was a disciple of Shaikh Muhammad Taifūrī Bastāmī, and is the founder of the sect called Madāria in India. Many curious anecdotes are related of him. He died on the 20th December, A.D. 1434, A.H. 838, aged 124 years, and is buried at Makanpūr in Qanauj, where a great assembly is held every year at his tomb. He was a contemporary of Qāzī Shahāb-uddīn Daulatābādī, who lived in the time of Sulṭān Ibrāhīm Sharqī of Jaunpūr.

Shah Mahmud of Isfahan (شاه محمود اسفهانی). *Vide* Shāh Shujāa.

Shah Mansur (شاه منصور), last Sulṭān of the dynasty of the Muẓaffarians, was the son of Shāh Muhammad Muẓaffar. He reigned in 'Irāq and Fars after Shāh Zain-ul-'Abidīn, whom he deprived of sight, and took possession of Shīrāz. He was defeated by Amīr Taimūr, who put him to death on Thursday, the 22nd May, A.D. 1393, 10th Rajab, A.H. 795.

Shah Mansur (شاه منصور). *Vide* Khwāja Mansūr.

Shah Mir (شاه میر), also called Mīān, whose proper name was Shaikh Muhammad, was a descendant of the Khalīf 'Umar, and a very pious Musalmān. He is reckoned amongst the Muhammadan saints. He was born at Shīstan A.D. 1550, A.H. 957, came to Lāhore, where he resided 60 years, and died there on Tuesday, the 11th August, A.D. 1635, 7th Rabī' I. A.H. 1045, aged 88 lunar years. He is buried at a place called Hāshimpūr, near Lāhore. He had numerous disciples, one of whom was Mullā Shāh, the spiritual guide of the prince Dārā Shikōh, the eldest son of the emperor Shāh Jahān. He is the author of the work called *Ziyā-ul-Ayūn*, or the Light of the Eyes, containing the rules for propriety of conduct through life.

Shah Mir (شاه میر), first Muhammadan king of Kashmere. The original inhabitants of Kashmere appear to have been the followers of Brahmā. The period of the first establishment of the Muhammadan faith in that country took place during the reign of Rāja Seina Dēva, about the year A.D. 1315, A.H. 715, when a person called Shāh Mīr, coming to Kashmere in the habit of a Dervish, was admitted into the service of that prince. Upon the death of the Rāja he was appointed prime minister to his son and successor, Rāja Ranjan. When this Rāja died Anand Dev, who succeeded him, also made Shāh Mīr his minister. The whole of this family not only gained great ascendancy over the Rāja, but also over the minds of the people, till the Rāja, becoming jealous of their power, forbade them in court. This exclusion drove Shah Mīr into rebellion, when, having occupied the valley of Kashmere with his troops, most of the officers of the Rāja's government also joined him. This insurrection soon brought the Rāja to the grave, and in the year A.D. 1327, A.H. 727, he died of a broken heart, leaving his widow regent. Shāh Mīr, after some years, married Kaula Devī, the wife of the Rāja, who embraced the Muhammadan faith, an event which secured to him the country which he had before nearly usurped. It is related by another author, that when preparations for the marriage commenced, the devoted princess, despairing and ignorant, surrounded by her train of maidens, advanced into the presence of the usurper and, upbraiding him for his ingratitude and treachery, stabbed herself before him. Thus perished, by her own hand, the last Hindū sovereign of Kashmere, and Shāh Mīr, who is considered the first Muhammadan king of that country, ascended the throne under the title of Sulṭān Shams-uddīn in the year A.D. 1341, A.H. 742. He died in A.D. 1344 or A.D. 1349, A.H. 745 or A.H. 750, and was succeeded by his son Jamshid.

List of the Muhammadan Kings of Kashmere.

1. Sulṭān Shams-uddīn Shāh Mīr.
2. Jamshid, son of Shāh Mīr, reigned 14 months, and was expelled by his younger brother, 'Alā-uddīn 'Alīshir, and slain.
3. 'Alā-uddīn 'Alīshir, son of Shāh Mīr, reigned 13 years.
4. Shahāb-uddīn, son of 'Alā-uddīn, reigned 19 years, and died A.D. 1376.
5. Quṭb-uddīn, brother of Shahāb-uddīn, during whose reign the famous Sayyad 'Alī Hamdānī arrived in Kashmere. He reigned 15 years.
6. Sikandar, surnamed Butshikan, who destroyed all images and subverted the Hindū religion, was the son of Quṭb-uddīn, and a contemporary of Amīr Taimūr. He reigned about 25 years.
7. 'Alī Shāh, the son of Sikandar, reigned nearly 7 years.
8. Zain-ul-'Abidīn, brother of 'Alī Shāh, reigned 52 years, and died about the year A.D. 1474.
9. Haidar Shāh, son of Zain-ul-'Abidīn, reigned little more than a year, and was killed by a fall from his palace.
10. Sulṭān Hasan, son of Haidar Shāh, reigned 12 years in excess and drunkenness.
11. Muhammad Shāh, a child of seven years of age, son of Hasan Shāh. He had several battles with Fatha K͟hān, and after a reign of 11 years was imprisoned by his uncle.
12. Fatha K͟hān, who took the title of Fatha Shāh, reigned 10 years.

Muhammad Shāh re-ascended the throne in A.D. 1596, and reigned two months, and then Fatha Shāh one year, after which Muhammad Shāh ascended the throne the third time, and was deposed after a reign of 19 years. He was once more raised to the throne, and died in A.D. 1533 after an interrupted reign of 50 years.

Ibrāhīm, the son of Muhammad, reigned five years.

Mubārik Shāh, also called Nāzuk and Barbak, son of Ibrāhīm, ascended the throne and, after a reign of three months, was expelled by the army of the emperor Humāyūn, who, being defeated by Sheir Shāh in A.D. 1541, had fled his country, and had retreated to Lāhore, whence he sent an army under the command of Mirzā Haidar Dog͟hlāt, who, invading Kashmere, conquered that province, and reigned there 10 years.

Mirzā Haidar Dog͟hlāt, after a reign of nearly 10 years, was killed in a night attack in A.D. 1551, A.H. 958. After his death the leading men divided the country into three principalities among themselves, though for form's sake Nāzuk, the son of Ibrāhīm, was again seated on the throne, and was again deposed the second time, by his brother.

Ibrāhīm II. was placed on the throne by Daulat Chak, and after a short time was deposed and blinded, and his brother

Ismā'īl was raised to the throne in A.D. 1556. He reigned nearly two years, and was succeeded by his son

Habīb, who ascended the throne and reigned three years, after which he was imprisoned by G͟hāzī Chak.

G͟hāzī Chak declared himself king and assumed the title of G͟hāzī Shāh, and reigned four years, when, being attacked by a leprosy, he abdicated the throne in A.D. 1563.

Husain Shāh, his brother, mounted the throne, reigned six years, and was compelled to abdicate in favour of his brother 'Alī K͟hān in A.D. 1569.

'Alī Shāh ascended the throne in A.D. 1569, and in the year A.D. 1572 Mullā Ishqī and Qāzī Sadr-uddīn came as ambassadors from the court of Dehlī, the result of which was that Akbar was proclaimed emperor of Kashmere in the public prayers; and 'Alī Shāh, at the request of Akbar, sent his niece, the daughter of his brother Husain Shāh, to be married to the prince Salīm. In the year A.D. 1578, 'Alī Shāh was killed by a fall from his horse, after a reign of nine years, and was succeeded by his son

Yūsaf Chak, who proceeded to the court of Akbar in 1586, and his son

Yaqūb Chak succeeded to the throne in consequence of his father's detention at the court of Dehlī. In the year A.D. 1587, A.H. 995, Akbar appointed Muhammad Qāsim K͟hān, Amīr-ul-Bahr (Admiral), to march and subdue Kashmere. Yaqūb was defeated and at last seized and sent to Dehlī in 1588, where Akbar enrolled Yūsaf Shāh and his son Yaqūb among the nobles of his government. Each of them received estates in the province of Behār, and from that period the kingdom of Kashmere has been a province of Dehlī.

Shah Muhammad, Khalifa (شاه محمد خليفه), author of the book called *Inshāe Jāma-ul-Qawānīn*, commonly called *Inshāe Khalīfa*, containing forms of letters.

Shah Murad (شاه مورد). *Vide* Murad Mirzā.

Shahnawaz Khan (شاهنواز خان), son of 'Abdul Rahīm Khān KhānKhānān. His daughter was married to prince Shāh Jahān. He died in the year A.H. 1028.

Shahnawaz Khan (شاهنواز خان), a nobleman of the reign of the emperor Shāh Jahān, was the son of 'Asaf Khān, wazīr, and father-in-law of the emperor 'Alamgīr, and of his brother prince Murād Bakhsh; though the author of the *Māsir-ul-Umrā* says that he was the son of Mirzā Rustam Qandahārī. He was appointed governor of Gujrāt in the room of the prince Murād Bakhsh, who was imprisoned by order of his brother 'Alamgīr in July, A.D. 1658. When Dārā Shikōh, through various adventures, after his flight from Multān, came to Ahmadabād Gujrāt, Shāhnawāz Khān, his maternal uncle, was then in that city, and his daughter, the wife of Murād Bakhsh, was in his palace. Her bitter supplications against 'Alamgīr, the impending murderer of her husband, prevailed on him to join the cause of Dārā, for whom he levied an army, and marched with him towards Ajmīr, where on their arrival a bloody battle ensued between the armies of Dārā and 'Alamgīr, on Sunday, the 13th March, A.D. 1659, Jumāda II. A.H. 1069, which ended in the defeat and flight of Dārā and death of Shāhnawāz Khān, who fell by the lance of Dileir Khān. He was buried by the orders of 'Alamgīr in the mausoleum of Khwāja Mo'īn-uddīn Chishtī at Ajmīr.

Shahnawaz Khan (شاهنواز خان), a nobleman of Shāh 'Alam's court, author of the book called *Miraat-i-Aftāb-numai*, a work on the history of modern Dehlī.

Shahnawaz Khan (شهنواز خان سمس الدوله), entitled Samsām-uddaula. The original name of this nobleman was 'Abdul Razzāk; he was descended from the family of Sadāt of Khawāf in Khurāsān, but his great-grandfather Amīr Kamāl-uddīn left Khawāf, and came to Hindūstān in the reign of the emperor Akbar, when he was admitted amongst the nobles of the court of Āgra. Mīrak Husain, the son of Kamāl-uddīn, held a situation in the service of the State, in the reign of Jahāngīr. The son of Mīrak Husain, Mīrak Mo'īn-uddīn, commonly called Amānat Khān, was in great favour with Shāh Jahān, and rose to the first rank. He retained also the patronage of 'Alamgīr, was appointed by him to various important governments, as those of Lāhore, Multān, Kābul and Kashmere. Amānat Khān was the ablest man in the court, and a great favourite of 'Alamgīr. When the emperor resided in Upper India, he bestowed the Sūbadārī of the Deccan on Khān Jahān Bahādur Kokaltāsh about the year A.D. 1670, A.H. 1081, and Amānat Khān was appointed Dīwān of the Deccan, or Paymaster-General, and Historiographer. He had four sons of eminent character: the first, 'Abdul Qādir Dayānat Khān, was the keeper of the Privy Purse; the second, Mīr Husain Amānat Khān, was the public treasurer and governor of Sūrat; after his death the latter post was assigned to his elder brother; the third son was Mīr 'Abdul Rahmān Wizārat Khān, who was promoted to the Dīwānī of Mālwā and Bījāpūr; he was an excellent poet and composed a Dīwān under the poetical title of Bikrāmī; the fourth son, Qāsim Khān, was Dīwān of Multān. Mīr Hasan 'Alī, the son of Qāsim Khān, was the father of Nawāb Samsām-uddaula Shāhnawāz Khān. He was born on the 10th March, A.D. 1700, 29th Ramazān, A.H. 1111, at Lāhore, but repaired to 'Aurangābād at an early age, and took up his abode with his relations and kinsmen who resided there before him. He was engaged first by Nizām-ul-Mulk 'Asaf Jāh, under whom, and his son Nāsir Jang, he served as Dīwān of Berār for several years. In the time of Salābat Jang he was raised to the rank of 7000 with the title of Samsām-uddaula. On the 12th May, A.D. 1758, 3rd Ramazān, A.H. 1171, the day on which 'Abdul Rahmān Haidar Jang, the counsellor of Monsieur Bussy, the French general, was assassinated by the instigation of Nizām 'Alī, the brother of Salābat Jang, he also was murdered in the confusion, together with his youngest son, Mīr 'Abdul Nabī Khān, but his two other sons, Mīr 'Abdur Salām and Mīr 'Abdul Hai, escaped. The remains of the father and son were interred in the tomb of their ancestors in the southern part of the city of 'Aurangābād. The chronogram of this event gives the following: "We have been murdered by 'Abdul Rahmān." Shāhnawāz Khān is the author of the work called *Māsir-ul-Umrāe Taimūria*, containing the memoirs of the nobility who served in Hindūstān and the Deccan under the house of Taimūr. It was commenced by him, but he left it unfinished, and in the turbulent scenes which attended his death the manuscript was scattered in various directions, and was considered as lost; some short time afterwards Mīr Ghulām 'Alī Azād, a friend of his, collected the greater portion of the missing leaves, and restored the work to its entire form with a few additions, amongst which was the life of the author. At a subsequent period again, his son Mīr 'Abdul Hai Khān, who had received the title of Samsām-uddaula Samsām Jang after his father's death, completed the work in the form in which it now occurs, in the year A.D. 1779, and died on the 28th April, A.D. 1782, 15th Jumāda I. A.H. 1196.

Shah Nur (شاه نور), a celebrated Dervish and saint who died on the 2nd February, A.D. 1693, and was buried in the vicinity of 'Aurangābād, where his tomb is still visited by the Muhammadans.

Shah Nur Ashhari (شاه نور اشهری), a famous poet, who was a pupil of Zahīr-uddīn Fāryābī, and flourished in the reign of Sulṯān Muhammad Khwārizm Shāh, son of Takash. He died at Tabrez in A.D. 1204, A.H. 600.

Shah Qasim (شاه قاسم), a pious and learned Musalmān, who died in the year A.D. 1584, A.H. 992, and Khwāja 'Abdul Razā wrote the chronogram of the year of his death.

Shah Qudrat-ullah (شاه قدرت الله). *Vide* Qudrat.

Shah Quli Khan Mahram (شاه قلی خان محرم), a nobleman of the court of the emperor Akbar. He held the rank of 5000, and was sent with prince Sulṯān Salīm to Ajmīr, accompanied by Rāja Mān Singh, to chastise the Amīrs under the Rāja of Udaipūr in A.D. 1598, A.H. 1007. The emperor Jahāngīr says, in his Memoirs, that in the first year of his reign, A.D. 1605, he gave the daughter of Mirzā Handāl, named Sulṯān Begam, in marriage to Shāh Qulī Khān Mahram, but his death is mentioned in another work, viz. *Māsir-ul-Umrā*, to have taken place in the month of December, A.D. 1600, 18th Azar, A.H. 1009, at Āgra.

Shahristani (شهرستانی). *Vide* 'Abū'l Fatha Muhammad-ash-Shāhristanī.

Shahrukh, Mirza (شاهرخ مرزا), the son of Razā Qulī and grandson of Nādir Shāh. His father's (Razā Qulī) mother, Fātima Sulṯān Begam, was the daughter of Shāh Sulṯān Husain Safwī. Shāhrukh was raised to the throne some time after the death of his grandfather, but was soon afterwards seized and deprived of sight. He retired to Mashhad, which province he was allowed to hold in his possession till the time of his death, which happened at Dāmghān in A.D. 1796. His death was the consequence of the tortures that had been inflicted upon him by 'Aqā Muhammad, king of Persia, who by this act extorted from him many precious stones of great value which had once belonged to Nādir Shāh.

Shahrukh, Mirza (شاهرخ مرزا), was the fourth son of Amīr Taimūr, and held the government of Khurāsān at his father's death, which took place in February, A.D. 1405. After the imprisonment of Sulṯān Khalīl, his nephew, ruler of Samarqand, A.D. 1408, A.H. 811, he marched from Khurāsān to take possession of his dominions. His authority was immediately acknowledged, not only in Samarqand, but over all Transoxiana. He was brave and generous, but not an ambitious prince; and during a reign of 42 years we hear of no wars in which he was engaged, except with the Turkmān tribes of Asia Minor, whose power Taimūr had overcome, but not destroyed. Mirzā Shāhrukh was born at Samarqand on the 21st July, A.D. 1377, 14th Rabī' I. A.H. 779, and died at Fishāward in the province of Rei, on the Persian new year's day, viz. Sunday, the 12th March, A.D. 1447, 25th Zil-hijja, A.H. 850, aged 71 lunar years. He reigned 42 years, during which the conquests of his father in India seem to have remained in subjection to his authority. At his death he left five sons, viz. Mirzā Ulagh Beg, Ibrāhīm Mirzā, Mirzā Bāisanghar, Sayūrghamish, and Muhammad Jūgī. He was succeeded by his son Mirzā Ulagh Beg.

Shahrukh Mirza (شاهرخ مرزا), a descendant of Amīr Taimūr, was the son of Ibrāhīm Mirzā, the son of Mirzā Sulaimān, ruler of Badakhshān. His mother's name was Muhtarim Khānam. About the year A.D. 1575, A.H. 983, he forcibly took possession of Badakhshān from his grandfather, and reigned there about 10 years, after which, in A.D. 1585, A.H. 993, that province was conquered by 'Abdullāh Khān Uzbak, and Shāhrukh compelled to fly to India, where he was kindly received by the emperor Akbar, who gave him his daughter Shakar-un-Nisā Begam in marriage in the year A.D. 1593, A.H. 1001, and raised him to the rank of an Amīr of 5,000, In the time of Jahāngīr the rank of 7,000 was conferred on him. He died at Ujjain in A.D. 1607, A.H. 1016, and was buried there.

Shahruk Mirza or **Mirza Shahruk** (شارک مرزا مرزا شارک), who had a jāgīr in Gujrāt, was murdered by his younger brothers in the year A.H. 1032.

Shahryar (شهریار), a king of Persia of the Sassānian race, who reigned in Persia a few months in A.D. 629. *Vide* Shirōya.

Shahryar, Sultan (شهریار سلطان), the youngest son of the emperor Jahāngīr, was married to a daughter of Nūr Jahān Begam by her former husband, Sher Afghān Khān. On the death of Jahāngīr in A.D. 1627, A.H. 1037, this prince, who was then at Lāhore, seized the royal treasure, brought over the troops, and forming a coalition with the two sons of his uncle, the late prince Daniāl, marched out to oppose 'Asaf Khān, the wazīr, who had released prince Dāwar Bakhsh, surnamed Bulāqī, the son of Sulṯān Khusro, from prison, and proclaimed him king. The battle ended in Shahryār's defeat. He fled, but being given up by his adherents, was imprisoned and blinded. He was, after three months, put to death, together with Dāwar Bakhsh and the two sons of Daniāl, named Tahmur and Hoshang, by order of Shāh Jahān (*q.v.*). Shahryār was famous for the beauty of his person as also for his mental imbecility, on which latter account he was called "Nāshudani" (the Inefficient), answering to the O. E. "Niddering."

Shah Sadr (شاه سادر), a Muhammadan saint, whose tomb is situated at the foot of a large mountain of Siwistān, at the distance of about 300 yards from the village of Lakki in Sindh, which belongs to the Sayyads of that place. This famous saint, says Lutf-ullah in his Autography, originally came from Arabia, and brought thousands of infidels to the light of Islām from the darkness of idolatry in Sindh. The year of his death is not known, but his tomb was built here by order of Nādir Shāh, king of Persia, in A.H. 1155. Tradition states that Nādir in a dream was invited by this saint to come to Amarkote, where he was to find a very large treasure. Nādir, having acted upon the visionary command, discovered the treasure promised to him, and received a very large amount as a tribute from the Amīrs of Sindh. Nādir then bestowed a large sum of money upon the Sayyads of the village, and directed them to have the edifice built over the remains of the saints. This they carried into execution, and an inscription at the door of the shrine, of which translation follows, gives the date of its completion:—

> "I inquired of intellect the year of its date.
> "Inspiration informed me, It is the Paradise of the members of the sacred house." A.D. 1742, A.H. 1155.

All Sayyads of Sindh that are called Lakki Sayyads are, I am informed (says Lutf-ullah), the descendants of this saint, whose parentage ascends up to the Imām 'Alī Naki. I am therefore inclined to think that the word Lakki is a corruption of Naki, which is the name of the tenth Imām.

Shah Safi (شاه صفی), grandson of Shāh Abbās the Great, king of Persia. His father's name was Safī Mirzā and his original name Bahrām Mirzā. He succeeded his grandfather in January, A.D. 1629, Jumāda I. A.H. 1038, and took the title of Shāh Safī. He was a capricious tyrant; and every year of his rule presented the same horrid and disgusting scene of barbarous cruelty. All the princes of the blood royal, and almost every minister, or general of family or character, were either put to death, or deprived of their eyes, by command of this monarch. He reigned nearly 14 years, died in May, A.D. 1642, Ṣafar, A.H. 1052, and was succeeded by his son, Abbās II.

Shah Sharaf-uddin (شاه شرف الدین), a Muhammadan saint, who died in the year A.D. 1379, A.H. 781, and is buried in Behār, where his monument is still standing and is visited by the Muhammadans. There is an inscription in the Kūfī character over the entrance to the dargāh, which however time has rendered illegible with the exception of the date of the death of the saint, and of the erection of the tomb in A.D. 1569, A.H. 977. The dargāh is held in great veneration by the Muhammadans, who at the 'Urs or anniversary of the death of the saint, assemble from all parts of the country, it is said to the number of 50,000. He is also called Makhdūm-ul-Mulk Shāh Sharīf-uddīn and Shaikh Sharīf. The emperor Sikandar Shāh, the son of Bahlōl Lodī, went to visit his tomb about the year A.D. 1495, A.H. 900.

[*Vide* Sharaf-uddīn Aḥmad 'Ahia Manerī.]

Shah Sharif or Sharif-uddin (شاه شریف). *Vide* Shāh Sharaf-uddīn.

Shah Shujaa' (شاه شجاع), Sultān of the Muẓaffarians, whose capital was Shīrāz. It is said that this prince was in such a manner plagued by a malady called Jūu'l Baqar, or canine hunger, that he could not satisfy his hunger, neither on his journey, nor when he was at rest. He deprived his father, Muhammad Muẓaffar, of his sight in A.D. 1359, and held the reins of government in his own hands. His brother Shāh Maḥmūd of Isfahān besieged Shīrāz in 1364, took possession of that country, and died before his brother in A.D. 1375, 9th Shawwāl, A.H. 776, after a reign of 16 years. Shāh Shujāa' died on Sunday the 9th October, A.D. 1384, 21st Shabān, A.H. 786. He was succeeded by his son Zain-ul-'Abidīn, who, on the approach of Amīr Taimūr to Shīrāz, retired to Tishtar, where his uncle, Shāh Mansūr, seized him and deprived him of his sight. Shīrāz was bestowed by Amīr Taimūr on Shāh Ahia, the son of Muẓaffar, but it was soon afterwards taken by Shāh Mansūr, in whose possession it remained till it was retaken by that conqueror in A.D. 1393, A.H. 795. There is a garden near Shīrāz called Haft-tan, which contains the remains of Shāh Shujāa', and has on one side of it a small building ornamented with a variety of pictures.

Shah Shujaa' or Shuja'-ul-Mulk (شاه شجاع یا شجاع الملک), king of Kābul, was the youngest son of Taimūr Shāh, the son of Aḥmad Shāh Abdālī. He was sent to Kashmere by his brother Muhammad Shāh and imprisoned in the fort of the Kōh-i-Mārān in A.D. 1812, from which place he was released in 1814 by Ranjīt Singh and detained at Lāhore as a prisoner, till his escape to the British territories. He was placed by the British Government on the throne of Kābul on the 8th May, A.D. 1839, and was murdered by his nephew, a son of Zamān Shāh, on the 2nd May, A.D. 1842. He is the author of a biographical sketch of his own life, written at Lūdhiana in 1826-27. This work was translated by Lieut. Bennet, of the Artillery, and published in the *As. Jour.* vol. xxx. p. 6, under Asiatic Intelligence.

[*Vide* Keene's *History of India*, ii.]

Shah Sub-han (شاہ سوبان), a Muhammadan saint, who died in A.D. 1200, A.H. 596.

Shah Sufi (شاہ صوفی), a Muhammadan saint, whose shrine is at a village called Sūfīpūr, in the Pargana of Fīrozābād in Āgra. It is related by the Khādims of the dargāh that in the reign of the emperor Akbar, Shāh Sūfī, a faqīr of some celebrity, wandered from Isfahān to India, and took up his hermitage among the Jamna ravines near the city of Chandwār, then the county town of the Pargana of the same name, and which, from the remains which still cover the surrounding country for miles, ruined mosques, dilapidated octagon mausolea, fallen entrance gates, and such like works of costly strength, must have been an important post in a fiscal and military point of view. All the time from which the fable of Shāh Sūfī's miracles commence, Rāja Chandarsen was the lord of the fort of Chandwār, and a troublesome tributary of the Dehlī court. Non-compliance with the royal demands for payment of revenue brought upon the Rāja the investment of his fort by the army of Akbar, who is said to have commanded his forces in person, and to have prosecuted his attack with no approach to success for a period, which the credulous or imposing Khādims of the establishment have exalted into a term of ten years. In the language of Oriental metaphor, the emperor is said to have planted a mango tree on the commencement of the siege, and to have eaten the fruit of it ere his success was secured. This success he owed to the anchorite of the ravines, Shāh Sūfī. During a severe land storm the lamps of the entire camp were put out, and the light of the Shāh's hut alone glimmered in the surrounding darkness. This extraordinary fact led to the Shāh's being visited by some of the courtiers. The miraculous character of the event being much commented on by visitors, the Shāh acknowledged himself to be under the special favour of heaven; and in the end the conversation turned upon the difficulties of the siege, and the grateful sense of the hermit's interference which the sovereign would entertain in the event of its being brought to a close by his holy means. The Shāh promised the required aid, and declared that the fort should be captured by a fixed day. Thus much for the emperor. In respect to the Rāja, the Shāh acted effectually upon his superstitious fears; told him that the fort was destined to fall; and proffered his own miraculous powers to secure for the Rāja a safe and honourable retreat for himself, family, and valuables. The whole were accordingly passed invisible through the besieging camp, and the Rāja quitted Hindūstān for the eastward. In return for this valuable service, the emperor bestowed half of an hamlet of Chandwār on the Shāh. The place assumed the name of Sūfīpūr, and has since been inhabited by the descendants of the Shāh. The decease of Shāh Sūfī took place soon after the grant was made, and he was buried on the brow of a deep ravine, a handsome tomb being erected over his remains. The mausoleum is still in good order, and forms a picturesque object in the midst of the desolation of the Jamna ravines in the vicinity of Chandwār and Fīrozābād. Its pretty dome and minarets, commanding as they do the heights of the Jamna ravines, often lead the voyagers on the river to visit the shrine of the saint, and landwards the building is an object of interest and beauty, which (says Mr. Mansel, Collector of Āgra, in a letter to the Commissioner of Revenue at Āgra, 29th May, 1839, No. 125) all would regret to see lost to the country. There are several dālāns, a handsome gate, and a small mosque comprised within the building, and the whole is kept in occasional good repair by the outlay of part of the funds of the grant. The fable of the whole is palpable. Indeed, the Rāja, who, under the name of Chandarsen, was ousted from Chandwār, lived, it is supposed by those best acquainted with the annals of Fīrozābād, in the reign of 'Alā-uddīn, and his descendants were the party who fell under the displeasure of Akbar.

Shah Sulaiman Safwi (شاہ سلیمان صفوی), the son of Shāh Abbās II. king of Persia, whom he succeeded on the 26th August, A.D. 1666, 5th Rabī' I. A.H. 1077. He reigned over Persia 29 years, and died A.D. 1694, A.H. 1106. He was succeeded by his son Shāh Husain Safwī.

Shah Tahir Junaidi (شاہ طاہر جنیدی) also called Dakhanī, was the youngest brother of Shāh Jafar. He came to India in the time of the emperor Humāyūn, and went afterwards to the Deccan, and was appointed minister to Burhān Nizām Shāh I. of Ahmadnagar. He was of the Shia sect, and succeeded in converting his sovereign to the Shia persuasion in the year A.D. 1537, A.H. 944, and induced him to exchange the white canopy and scarlet pavilion for the green standard assumed by the followers of 'Alī. Shāh Tāhir died in the Deccan A.D. 1545, A.H. 952. He was an excellent poet and is the author of several works.

Shah Taqi or **Shaikh Taqi** (شاہ یا شیخ تقی), a Muhammadan saint, who died between the years A.D. 1413 and A.D. 1421, and is buried at a place called Jhūsī in the province of Allahābād, where a great crowd of Musalmāns assemble every year and make offerings on his tomb.

Shah Turkman (شاہ ترکمان), a Musalmān saint who died in February, A.D. 1241, 24th Rajab, A.H. 638, and lies buried in Shāhjahānābād (Dehlī) at a place called Dargāh Shāh Turkman.

Shah Wali Muhammad (شاہ والی محمد), a saint whose dargāh is in Āgra.

Shah Wali Ullah (شاہ ولی الله). *Vide* Ishtiyāq.

Shahzada Khanam (شاهزاده خانم), a daughter of the emperor Akbar by Salīma Begam. She was living in the commencement of the reign of her brother Jahangīr.

Shahzada Sultan (شاهزاده سلطان). *Vide* Sulṭān Shāhzāda.

Shah Zaman (شاه زمن). *Vide* Zaman Shāh.

Sha'ib (شعیب), the name of Jethro, the father-in-law of Moses.

Sha'ib (شعیب), the title of a poet of Isfahān, who wrote the poem called *Wāmik and Uzra*.

Shaibani (شیبانی), an author whose proper name was Abū Amrū Is-hāk. He died at Baghdād in the year A.D. 828, A.H. 213.

Shaibani Khan, (شیبانی خان). *Vide* Shāhī Beg Uzbak.

Shaida (شیدا), poetical appellation of Mīr Fatha 'Alī of Lucknow, author of the story of the Owl and the Grocer, entitled *Būm-o-Baqqāl*. He was contemporary with Fidwī, author of an Yūsaf and Zaleikha in Urdū.

Shaida, Mulla (شیدا ملا), title of a poet who flourished in the latter part of the reign of Jahāngīr and commencement of the emperor Shāh Jahān. He was one of the Sheikhzādas of Fathapūr Sīkrī, and a contemporary of the poets Tālib Kālīm, Qudsī, Hakīm Hāzik, and Nawāb Islām Khān wazīr. His works contain more than 50,000 verses. He has left a Masnawī of 12,000 verses in the style of the *Mukhzan-ul-Asrār* of Nizāmī. He died in A.D. 1652, A.H. 1062, in Kashmere, and was buried there. He also had a home at Āgra.

Shaikh 'Alai (شیخ علائی), a philosopher of Bayana, who made a great stir in the world in the reign of Sulṭān Salīm Shāh by introducing a new system of religion. He called himself Imām Mahdī, who is believed to be the last of the prophets. This impostor raised great disturbances in the empire, and converted some thousands by force and persuasion. After being twice banished by the king, he returned and kindled fresh troubles, for which he was scourged to death at Āgra, by order of the king, A.D. 1548, A.H. 955. He remained firm to his doctrine in the agonies of death; but his religion was not long maintained by his disciples.

[Vide *Āīn Translation* (Abū'l-Fazl's Biography).]

Shaikh 'Alam (شیخ عالم), who wrote a book on the Music of India, and called it *Mādhoānal* or *Mādhō Nāek*, after the name of the musician who first wrote it in Hindī.

Shaikh 'Ali (شیخ علی), author of the *Jawāhir-ul-Samania*.

Shaikh Buhlul (شیخ بہلول), the brother of the saint Muhammad Ghaus of Gwāliar. He was put to death in Āgra by Mirzā Handal, the brother of the emperor Humayūn, about the year A.D. 1539, A.H. 945. His tomb is on a hill near the fort of Baiana.

Shaikh Farid Bhakari (شیخ فرید بہکری), a native of Bhakar, and author of the work called *Zakhīrat-ul-Qāwānīn*, which he composed in the time of the emperor Shāh Jahān, A.D. 1650, A.H. 1060.

Shaikh Farid Bukhari (شیخ فرید), a nobleman, who, in the first year of Jahāngīr, was raised to the rank of 5000, with the title of Murtazā Khān, and appointed Paymaster-General of the army. He died in the year A.D. 1616, A.H. 1025.

Shaikhi 1st (شیخی), a poet, on whom Murād I. had conferred a wazīrship. The following amusing anecdote of this poet is recorded by an author. In the early part of his career Shaikhī suffered much from a complaint in the eyes, and, being very poor, he was so inconsequent as to open a shop for the sale of eye-water. The price was an asper a bottle. One day, however, a stranger, passing by and observing the bloodshot eyes of the poet, stopped to purchase a bottle, and in paying for it laid down two aspers. "I charge but one asper," said Shaikhī, "do you not know that?" "Certainly I know it," said the stranger, "and therefore you see I give you a second." "Give me a second!" replied Shaikhī angrily, "for what?" "To enable you to buy one of your own bottles, my friend," replied the other coolly, "and cure yourself?" The poet shrugged his shoulders and shut up his shop. He flourished about the year 1395.

Shaikhi 2nd, a Turkish poet, who was contemporary with Aḥmadī.

Shaikh Ibrahim (شیخ ابراهیم), an uncle of the poet Hazīn. He is the author of the *Rāfa'-ul-Khilāf*, which contains glosses on various works, and of the *Kāshif-ul-Ghawāshi*, being glosses on the Kashshāf as far as the 49th Sūra, and of a commentary on Euclid. He died at Lāhijān in A.D. 1707, A.H. 1119.

Shaikh Jalal (شیخ جلال), surnamed Makhdūm Jahānian Jahāngasht; a celebrated saint of Multān, the son of Sayyad Aḥmad Kabīr, the son of Sayyad Jalā'l Bukhārī. He was the disciple of Shaikh Rukn-uddīn Abū'l Fatha, grandson of Shaikh Bahā-uddīn Zikaria. He is said to have travelled all over the world, and is on that account called Jahāngasht. He made seven pilgrimages to Mecca, and brought from there a stone bearing the footmark of the prophet, which he made over to Sulṭān Fīrōz Shāh Tughlaq, who became one of his disciples. Shaikh Jalāl was born on the 8th February, A.D. 1308, 14th Shabān, A.H. 707, and died on Wednesday, the 3rd February, A.D. 1384, 10th Ẓil-ḥijja, A.D. 785, aged 78 lunar years; he was buried at Uchcha in Multān. The Persian inscription is engraved on the gate of his mausoleum, which is annually visited by the pilgrims of distant countries. It is a popular belief that a fool can get restored to perfect sense by eating the earth of his tomb. He is the founder of the sect of Malang and Jalālia Faqīrs in India, and is the brother of Sayyad Rājū Qattāl. His memoirs were written by one of his disciples and is called *Kitāb Kutbī*.

[*Vide* Thomas, *Chronicles of the Paṭhān Kings*, p. 94, *note*.]

Shaikh Jalal of Thanesar (شیخ جلال بخاری), a celebrated pious Musalmān who lived in the time of the emperor Akbar, and died on the 10th January, A.D. 1582, 14th Ẓil-ḥijja, A.H. 989, and lies buried at Thānesar.

Shaikh Jamali, Maulana (شیخ جمالی مولانا), was a native of Dehlī and an excellent Persian poet. He at first took for his poetical title Jalālī, but subsequently at the request of his *murshid*, Shaikh Samā-uddīn, changed into Jamālī. From Dehlī he proceeded on a pilgrimage to Mecca, and on his return he came to Herāt in the time of Sulṭān Husain Mirzā, where he resided for several years, and became acquainted with the celebrated Maulwī Jāmī. He is the author of the work entitled *Siar-ul-'Arifīn*, or Lives of the Pious, as also of a Dīwān. He died in the time of the emperor Hūmāyūn, A.D. 1535, A.H. 942, and lies buried at old Dehlī, where his tomb is still to be seen. His son, Shaikh Gadāī Kambōh, served under Bairām Khan for several years, rose to a suitable rank, and died in A.D. 1568, A.H. 976.

Shaikh Jun or Jiwan bin-Abi Sa'id-al-Makki (شیخ جون), author of the *Nūr-ul-Anwār fī Sharh-al-Manār*, a law treatise.

Shaikh Mir (شیخ میر), a nobleman and one of the best generals of 'Alamgīr, whose cause he espoused and was killed in the last battle which took place between that emperor and his eldest brother, Dārā Shikōh, at Ajmīr, on Sunday the 13th March, A.D. 1659, 29th Jumāda II. A.H. 1069. He was buried by the orders of 'Alamgīr close to the tomb of Khwāja Mo'īn-uddīn Chishtī at Ajmīr.

Shaikh Mir of Lahore (شیخ میر). He is also called Shāh Mīr, and is said to have been a pious Musalmān and spiritual guide of Mullā Shāh. He died in August, A.D. 1635, A.H. 1045, and is buried at Lāhore.

[*Vide* Shāh Mīr.]

Shaikh Mubarak of Nagor (شیخ مبارک ناگوری), father of Shaikh Faizī and Abū'l Fazl, the celebrated wazīr of the emperor Akbar. He is the author of the Commentary on the Qurān called *Munba-ul-Ayūn*, and of another work entitled *Jawāmạ-ul-Kalām*. He was born in the year A.D. 1505, and died at Lāhore on the 5th August, A.D. 1593, 17th Ẓil-Qa'da, A.H. 1001, and was buried at Āgra, where, in the same compound, it is supposed Faizī, Abū'l Fazl, and Ladlī, their sister, were buried. His father's name was Shaikh Mūsā, who was a Turk by birth.

Shaikh Mufid (شیخ مفید). *Vide* Abū 'Abdullāh Muhammad bin-Muhammad-al-Namānī.

Shaikh Muhammad (شیخ محمد), author of a work on Sūfiism, in Persian, called *Chehal Risāla*, or Forty Chapters.

[*Vide* Muhammad (Shaikh).]

Shaikh Muwyyad (شیخ موید). *Vide* Abū'l Qāsim of Hulla.

Shaikh Nizam (شیخ نظام). *Vide* Niẓām (Shaikh).

Shaikh Razi (شیخ رضی), son of Hasan, author of the Sharah on the Kāfia and Shāfia of Ibn-Hājib. He died in A.D. 1287, A.H. 686.

Shaikh Saduq (شیخ صدوق), also called Abū Jafar Muhammad bin-'Alī Babawia. *Vide* Babawia.

Shaikh Safi or **Safi-uddin** (شیخ صفی), the celebrated founder of the sect of Sūfīs in Persia, from whom were descended the royal Safwī family. He dwelt in Ardibail, in Media, and died there. His son Shaikh Sadr-uddīn Mūsa was held in such high estimation that he was honoured by a visit from the great conqueror, Amīr Taimūr. That monarch was so much pleased by the Shaikh's conversation that, at his request, he released all the prisoners taken in Asia Minor and Turkey. Many of the captives were persons of wealth and family, who afterwards enriched their benefactor by costly presents and acknowledged him as their tutelar saint. Their respect, and that of their descendants, was continued to him and his posterity. Shaikh Safī died at Ardibeil on the 7th August, A.D. 1335, 17th Ẓil-ḥijja, A.H. 735.

Shaikh Sharif (شیخ شریف). *Vide* Shāh Sharaf-uddīn.

Shaikh Taqi (شیخ تقی). *Vide* Shāh Taqi.

Shaikh Yusaf (شیخ یوسف). *Vide* Yūsaf (Shaikh).

Shaiq (شایق), poetical name of Yūsaf Beg, a poet of Dehlī, who passed a retired life, although his other brothers were mansabdārs in the service of the emperor 'Alamgīr. He died A.D. 1687, A.H. 1098.

Shaiq (شایق), poetical name of Mīr Ghulām 'Alī bin-Sayyad Fatha 'Alī Razawī Jālisī. He flourished under Ghāzī-uddīn Haidar, king of Audh, who reigned at Lucknow from A.D. 1814 to A.D. 1827, A.H. 1229 to A.H. 1243. He is the author of a Dīwān.

Shaiq (شایق نذیر الدین حسن), poetical name of Nazīr-uddīn Hasan, son of Shāh Ghulām Muhī-uddīn Aweisī. He is the author of a work called *Masdar Fayūz*, a grammar to learn the Persian language, which he wrote at Bareili in the year A.D. 1815, A.H. 1230, when in the service of Nawāb Aḥmad Yār Khān.

Shaista Khan, Amir-ul-Umra (شایسته خان امیر الامرا). His original name was Abū Tālib, or Mirzā Murād. He was the son of 'Asaf Khān, wazīr, and grandson of 'Itmād-uddaula (*q.v.*). After the death of his father, A.D. 1641, he was appointed wazīr by the emperor Shāh Jahān. The large Jamạ Masjid which stood (till 1857) on the banks of the Jamna river to the west of the fortress of Allahābād, was built by him in the time of Shāh Jahān and completed in the year A.D. 1646, A.H. 1056. His son Khudābanda Khān also held a high rank in the time of 'Alamgīr, and was appointed Faujdār of the Karnatic Bījāpūr, and subsequently, after the death of Ruh-ullah Khān, he held the post of grand steward of the household. Shaista Khān was appointed governor of Berār by Shāh Jahān in A.D. 1638; and in A.D. 1652 to the more important command of Gujrāt. In A.D. 1656 he was employed by 'Alamgīr (Aurangzeb), at that time viceroy of the Deccan, to serve as lieutenant to his eldest son, Sulṭān Muhammad, in the war of Golkanḍa. In the contentions of Shāh Jahān's sons for the throne in A.D. 1658, he served with Dārā Shikōh, whom he betrayed by giving intelligence and guides to Aurangzeb. He was appointed in July, A.D. 1659, governor of the Deccan in the room of Muhammad Muazzim, the son of the emperor 'Alamgīr, who was recalled to the presence, and in A.D. 1666 as governor of Bengal. He kept his court at Dacca, and by his injustice provoked a war with Job Charnock, Governor of the factory of the East India Company at Golāghāt, near Hughlī. He died in the reign of 'Alamgīr on the 31st May, A.D. 1694, 16th Shawwāl, A.H. 1105, aged 93 lunar years. Some traces of his Rauza and garden are still to be seen at Āgra on the banks of the Jamna.

Shaista Khan, Nawab (شایسته خان نواب), the son of Asaf Khān, the prime minister.

Shakar-un-Nisa Begam (شاکر ان نسا بیگم), the daughter of the emperor Akbar, who gave her in marriage to Mirzā Shāhrukh, son of Ibrāhīm Mirzā. She is buried in the mausoleum of Akbar at Sikandra in Āgra. Her mother's name was Bībī Daulat Shāh.

Shakir (شاکر), the poetical name of Niẓām-ul-Mulk 'Asaf Jāh.

Shakir (شاكر), the poetical name of 'Abdur Rahmān, author of the poetical work called *Gulistān Musarrat*, which he also named *Hadāek-ul-Maāni*. He wrote this book at Lucknow during the reign of Amjād 'Alī Shāh in A.D. 1845, A.H. 1261, and finished it in the time of Wājid 'Alī Shāh.

Shali (شالی), author of a Dīwān, which goes after his name, *Dīwān Shāhlī*.

Shama'ul-Mulk (شمع الملک), title of the ruler of Jurjān, named Qābūs.

Shamgar (شمگر). *Vide* Qābūs. He is called Shamgīr by Daulat Shāh.

Shamru, Samru or **Sombre** (شمرو), whose real name was Walter Reinhardt, a person of obscure parentage in the Electorate of Treves. He entered early as a common soldier the service of the French, taking for his *nom-de-guerre* Summer, which his comrades, from his saturnine complexion, turned into Sombre, and the Indians, by corruption, Samrū and Shamrū. At length he repaired to Bengal, and enlisted in one of the Swiss Companies then employed at Calcutta; but at the end of eighteen days deserted to the French at Chandarnagar, where he became a serjeant. Deserting this post he fled into the Upper Provinces, and was for some time a private trooper in the cavalry of Safdar Jang, father to Shujā-uddaula. This service he quitted and led a vagabond life in different provinces; but in A.D. 1760 was with the rebel Faujdār of Purnia Khādim Husain Khān. Upon his being expelled from Bengal, Shamrū left him and entered into the service of Gregory, an Armenian, then in high favour with Nawāb Qāsim 'Alī Khān and distinguished with the title of Gūrgīn Khān. From him he had the command of a battalion of Sepoys, and afterwards obtained from the nawāb the addition of another. In this station he massacred the English captives at Patna in A.D. 1763. Some time previous to the battle of Buxar he treacherously deserted Qāsim 'Alī with his corps, and embraced the service of the Nawāb Shujā uddaula, who had gained him over by bribes. Upon the nawāb's defeat at Buxar he was entrusted with the protection of the Begams, and remained with nawāb till he made peace with the English, when, fearful of being delivered up to them, he retired to Āgra, and entered into the pay of the Jāt Rāja Jawāhir Singh; but quitted him for the service of the Rāja of Jaipūr, who soon dismissed him on a remonstrance from the English General. He then again served the Jāts; quitted them once more, and came to Dehlī, from whence he followed the fortunes of Nawāb Najaf Khān, in whose service he died. Such are the outlines of the fortunes of this man, who had some merit as a soldier, but wholly obscured by a treacherous and blood-thirsty disposition. His corps was continued after his death in the name of his son and a favourite concubine, who received for their maintenance the sum of 65,000 rupees per month. He died, or was murdered, in the year A.D. 1778, A.H. 1192, at Āgra, where his tomb is to be seen in the Roman Catholic burial-ground, with a Persian inscription in verse, mentioning the year of his death and his name.

[*Vide* next article.]

Shamru Begam (شمرو بیگم), the celebrated princess of Sardhana, whose native title was Zeb-un-Nisa, was the wife, or rather concubine, of Shamrū or Sombre. She held an extensive jagīr at Sardhana, and died on the 27th January, A.D. 1836, 8th Shawwāl, A.H. 1251, aged 88 lunar years. She was buried in the church of Sardhana, of which she was the founder. She was one of the oldest and most sincere allies of the English. At her death she left upwards of six lakhs of rupees to various charitable and pious purposes, and gave instructions for founding a college for young men, to serve on the apostolic mission of Thibet and Hindūstān. Captain Mundy, in his *Journal of a Tour in India*, says that the history of her life, if properly known, would form a series of scenes such as, perhaps, no other female could have gone through. Colonel Skinner had often, during his service with the Marhattas, seen her, then a beautiful young woman, leading on her troops to the attack in person and displaying, in the midst of carnage, the greatest intrepidity and presence of mind. The Begam contracted a lawful marriage in A.D. 1793. Her first lord, Reinhardt, who bought her when a young and handsome dancing girl, married, and converted her to the Roman Catholic religion. Her second husband was a French adventurer, a soldier of fortune named Levassoult, who commanded her small army. It is of this man that the following anecdote is related, which is wondrous strange, if it be true. Skinner used to say that her husband had become possessed of wealth, power, and a numerous army; of these his ambitious wife coveted the undivided possession, and she then accomplished her purpose. A mutinous disposition, on the subject of pay, having manifested itself among his body-guard, the Begam, then about twenty-five, exaggerated the danger to her husband, and got intelligence conveyed to him that the rebels had formed a plan to seize and confine him, and to dishonour his wife. They consequently arranged to escape together from the fury of the soldiery; and at night started secretly from their palace in palankeens. Towards morning the attendants, in great alarm, announced that they were pursued; and our heroine, in well-feigned despair, vowed that, if their escort were overcome, she would stab herself to the heart. The devoted husband, as she expected, swore he would not survive her.

Soon afterwards the pretended rebels came up, and after a short skirmish drove back the attendants, and forced the bearers to put down the palankeens. At this instant Levassoult heard a scream, and his wife's female slave rushed up to him and exclaimed that her mistress had stabbed herself to death. The husband, true to his vow, instantly seized a pistol and blew out his brains. His tomb is at Sardhana. [So wrote Mr. Beale, but the Begam's collusion has never been proved.]

[Vide *Fall of the Moghul Empire.*]

Shamshir Bahadur I. (شمشیر بهادر), an illegitimate offspring of the Peshwā Bājī Rāo Marhatta by a Musalmān concubine named Mastānī, who brought him up in the Muhammadan religion. He was severely wounded in the famous battle which took place between the Marhattas and Ahmad Shāh Abdālī in January, A.D. 1761, and got to Dīg, where Sūrajmal Jāt had his wounds treated with the greatest care, but he died soon afterwards, and was buried at Dīg.

Shamshir Bahadur II. (شمشیر بهادر), Nawāb of Banda, was the eldest son of 'Alī Bahādur, the son of Shamshir Bahādur I. the son of Bājī Rāo Peshwā. He succeeded to the territories of his father in Bundelkhand about the year A.D. 1802, but subsequently a pension or stipend of four lakhs of rupees annually was granted him in perpetuity by the British Government. He died on the 30th August, A.D. 1823, 24th Zil-Qa'da, A.H. 1238, and was succeeded by his brother Zulfiqār 'Alī Khān.

Shamshir Khan (شمشیر خان), a nobleman, at whose request a prose abridgment of the *Shāh-nāma* of Firdausī was made by Tawakkul Munshī in A.D. 1652, A.H. 1063.

Shams Shahab 'Afif (شمس شهاب عفیف), the son of Malik Sad-ul-Mulk, who was Amaldār of Abūhar and Dibālpūr in the reign of Sultān Ghayās-uddīn Tughlaq. He was born the very day that Sultān Fīroz Shāh came into the world, *i.e.* in the year A.D. 1309, A.H. 709, and was the grandfather of Shams Sirāj Afīf, the author of the *Tārīkh Fīroz Shāhī.*

Shams Siraj 'Afif (شمس سراج عفیف), the grandson of Shams Shahāb Afīf, was an historian who flourished in the reign of Sultān Fīroz Shāh Bārbak, king of Dehlī, who reigned from A.D. 1351 to 1388. He is the author of the entire history of that monarch, called *Tārīkh Fīroz Shāhī*, in which he relates that when that emperor built the city of Fīrozābād, adjoining to that of (old) Dehlī, in the year A.D. 1354, A.H. 755, he (the author) was then 12 years of age, and that the red stone pillar in the Koshak of Fīrozābād, near the mosque or Jama Masjid, was brought by that emperor in the same year, with great expense and labour, from a place called Naweira, in the vicinity of Sitaura, near Khizirābād, a city situated at the foot of a mountain, ninety cōs distant from (old) Dehlī, where it then stood. The whole length of this pillar, says the author, was 32 gaz, eight of which the king ordered to be buried in the earth or sunk in the building, and the remaining 24 to be above the surface. This pillar was called by the emperor, Mīnar Zarīn, *i.e.* the Golden Minar. The second pillar which the emperor set up within his hunting-place, called Shikārgāh Fīroz Shāh, was brought from Mīrath, and was somewhat smaller than the one just mentioned. This pillar is now called the Lāth of Fīroz Shāh. These two pillars were, even at that period, as they are still, believed by the Hindūs to have been the walking sticks of a famous hero of antiquity named Bhīm Sen. The characters engraved round these two pillars the most intelligent and learned men of all religions were not able to decipher. They have now been shown to have been made by Asoka. The author was living at the time of Tamerlane's invasion of India in A.D. 1398, A.H. 801, whom he has mentioned in his work.

[*Vide* Dowson's *Elliot*, iii. p. 269.]

Shams Tabrizi (شمس تبریز). *Vide* Shams-uddīn Muhammad Tabrīzī.

Shams Tibsi (شمس طبسی). *Vide* Shams-uddīn Tibsī (Qāzī).

Shams-uddin Ahmad (شمس الدین احمد), author of the *Khulāsat-ul-Munākib*, containing the lives of ten celebrated Sūfī Shaikhs.

Shams-uddin Ahmad Khan (شمس الدین احمد خان), a descendant of the Sayyads of Naishāpūr. He held the rank of 5000 in the reign of the emperor Akbar, and died in A.D. 1591, A.H. 999.

Shams-uddin 'Ali Khan (شمس الدین علی خان), author of the *Muntakhib-ul-Hasnāt*, which contains the history of the eighth Imām, *viz.* 'Alī Razā bin-Mūsa, also called 'Alī Mūsī Razā, who died A.D. 818, and whose tomb is at Mashhad (formerly called Tūs) in Khurāsān, and is still an object of pilgrimage to the Persians; also memoirs of his descendants. This work was translated from the Arabic of Abū Jafar.

Shams-uddin-al-Shafa'i (شمس الدين الشافعی), author of the Arabic work called *Ayūn-ul-Asar*; containing the wars and conquests of Muhammad, his successors and companions, interspersed with various anecdotes of his generals.

Shams-uddin Altimsh, Sultan (شمس الدين التمش سلطان), a king of Dehlī, whose original name was Altimsh. In his childhood he was bought from a merchant by Sulṭān Quṭb-uddīn Aibak, king of Dehlī, who afterwards gave him his daughter in marriage. He expelled 'Arām Shāh the son of Quṭb-uddīn, from the throne of Dehlī, A.D. 1210, A.H. 607, and declared himself king, with the title of Shams-uddīn. He defeated and imprisoned Tāj-uddīn Ildūz, king of Ghaznī, who came to Lāhore with a large army in A.D. 1215. He besieged for a whole year the fortress of Gwāliar, and took it in A.D. 1233; and, after a reign of 26 years, died on the 30th April, A.D. 1236, A.H. 633. His son Sulṭān Rukn-uddīn Fīroz succeeded him. It is supposed that the Quṭb Mīnār in old Dehlī, which is now commonly called the Lāṭh of Quṭb Sāhib, because it stands close to the dargāh of the celebrated saint Khwāja Quṭb-uddīn Bakhtyār Kākī, was built or completed by Sulṭān Shams-uddīn Altimsh some time before the year A.D. 1236. A part of it was injured by lightning, and was repaired and completed on the 26th October, A.D. 1501, 13th Rabī' II. A.H. 907, by Fatha Khān Masnad 'Alī, in the reign of Sulṭān Sikandar Shāh Lodī.

Shams-uddin Bahmani, Sultan (شمس الدين بهمنی سلطان), the son of Sulṭān Mahmūd Bahmanī. He was placed on the throne of the Deccan on the 14th June, A.D. 1397, 17th Ramaẓān, A.H. 799, after the dethronement of his brother Ghayās-uddīn by Lālchīn, who was now honoured with the title of Malik Nāib, or regent. Shams-uddīn had reigned only five months and seven days, when Fīroz Khān, the son of Sulṭān Dāūd Shāh, having deposed him, sent him, together with Lālchīn, to confinement, and ascended the throne, with the title of Fīroz Shāh Rōzafzūn, on Thursday the 15th November, A.D. 1397, 23rd Ṣafar, A.H. 800.

Shams-uddin bin-Mubarik (شمس الدين بن مبارک), author of the *Sharah Hikmat-ul-Ain.*

Shams-uddin Faqir, Mir (شمس الدين فقير مير), a native of Dehlī, and author of the work called *Hadāiq-ul-Balāghat*, or Garden of Eloquence, a treatise on the rhetoric, poetry and rhyme of the Persians.

Shams-uddin Kart I. Malik (شمس الدين كرت ملک), also called Malik Shams-uddīn Muhammad Kart, the son of Abā Bakar Kart, was the founder of the dynasty of Kart or Kard, a tribe of Turks. He commenced his reign in the year A.D. 1268, A.H. 666, over Herāt, Ghōr, Ghaznī and Kābul. His mother was the daughter of Malik Rukn-uddīn Ghōrī, who, before his death in A.D. 1245, A.H. 643, had named him to be his successor, and which was subsequently confirmed by Mangū Khān and Halākū Khān, kings of Persia. His descendants continued to reign over those countries for 119 lunar years and two months, till they were extinguished by Amīr Taimūr (Tamerlane) in A.D. 1381. He was a contemporary of Abaqā Khān, king of Persia, and died at Tabrīz in January, A.D. 1278, Shaban, A.H. 676, after a reign of ten years, and was succeeded by his son Malik Shams-uddīn II.

Kings of the dynasty of Kart or Kard.

1. Malik Shams-uddīn Muhammad Kart I.
2. ,, Shams-uddīn II. his son, also called Rukn-uddīn.
3. ,, Fakhr-uddīn Bahman, his son.
4. ,, Ghayās-uddīn Kart, his brother.
5. ,, Shams-uddīn Kart III. his son.
6. ,, Hāfiz, his brother.
7. ,, Moi'zz-uddīn Husain, his brother.
8. ,, Ghayās-uddīn, the son of 'Alī and grandson of Moi'zz-uddīn, the last king of this race.

Shams-uddin Kart II. Malik (شمس الدين كرت ملک), second king of the dynasty of Kart, was the son of Shams-uddīn Kart I. whom he succeeded in January, A.D. 1278, A.H. 676. He was a contemporary of Abaqā Khān, the Tartar king of Persia, and reigned about 28 years over Herāt, Ghaznī, Balkh, etc. He died on Thursday the 2nd September, A.D. 1305, 12th Ṣafar, A.H. 705, and was succeeded by his son Malik Fakhr-uddīn Bahman.

Shams-uddin Kart III. Malik (شمس الدين كرت ملک), the fifth Sulṭān of the dynasty of Kart, who reigned over Herāt, Balkh, Ghaznī and Kābul. He succeeded his father, Ghayās-uddīn Kart, in A.D. 1329, A.H. 729, reigned ten months and died in A.D. 1330, A.H. 730. He was succeeded by his brother Malik Hāfiz, who was slain in 1332. After him Moi'zz-uddīn Husain, his brother, ascended the throne.

Shams-uddin Khan (شمس الدين خان نواب), the nawāb of Fīrozpūr, was the son of Nawāb Ahmad Bakhsh Khān, a jagīrdār of Pargana Fīrozpūr and Lohārī. It was at his instigation that Karīm Khan, one of his confidants, murdered Mr. W. Fraser, the British Commissioner of Dehlī, on the evening of the 22nd March, A.D. 1835, for which act Karīm Khān was hanged on the 26th August following, and subsequently the nawāb, being found guilty after a full investigation of the case, was executed on the 8th October of the same year at Dehlī. Nawāb Shams-uddīn was the Jagīrdār of Fīrozpur, the town of a large district of the same name, situated at a distance of sixty miles to the south-west of Dehlī. He enjoyed a revenue variously estimated at from three to ten lakhs of rupees a year. The actual cause of his animosity towards Mr. Fraser, and the reason which induced him to instigate his murder, will, perhaps, ever remain a mystery. The supposition is that Mr. Fraser had, in the faithful discharge of his duty, apportioned to Amīn-uddīn and Ziya-uddīn, the younger brothers of the nawāb, a part or whole of Lohārī, an extensive estate, to which the latter considered himself the most entitled.

Shams-uddin Khawafi, Khwaja (شمس الدین خوافی خواجه), the son of an Amīr of Khawāf, in Khurāsān, by name Khwāja 'Alā-uddīn. Shams-uddīn held a high rank in the service of the emperor Akbar, and was appointed Dīwān of the Panjāb in A.D. 1599, A.H. 1008, but died after a few months at Lāhore.

Shams - uddin Muhammad (شمس الدین محمد), author of the works called *Bakhtyār-nāma* and *Sindbād-nāma*.

Shams-uddin Muhammad Anka Khan (شمس الدین محمد عنکا خان). *Vide* 'Azim Khān.

Shams - uddin Muhammad Assar (شمس الدین محمد عصار). *Vide* Assār.

Shams - uddin Muhammad - bin - Abdullah - al - Ghazi, Shaikh (شمس الدین محمد بن عبدالله الغزی), author of the *Tanwīr-ul-Absār*, which he composed in A.D. 1586, A.H. 995, and enriched with a variety of questions and decisions. It is considered to be one of the most useful books, according to the Hanafī doctrines, and has been frequently commented upon. The most noted of these commentaries is one written by the author himself, entitled *Manh-al-Ghaffar*.

Shams-uddin Muhammad bin-Hamza (شمس الدین محمد بن حمزه), surnamed Fanārī. He was an author, and died in the year A.D. 1431, A.H. 834. He wrote a commentary which is considered one of the best glosses on the *Sirājia* of Sajāwandī.

Shams-uddin Muhammad bin-Killai (شمس الدین محمد), author of the *Farāez-ul-Fāriqia*, a treatise on the Law of Inheritance, according to Shāfaī's doctrine. He died in A.D. 1375, A.H. 777.

Shams-uddin Muhammad ibn-Nasar (شمس الدین محمد ابن نصر), author of the work called *Mujma-ul-Bahryn*. He lived in the time of Tāj-uddīn Eldūz.

Shams - uddin Muhammad Kuswi, Khwaja (شمس الدین محمد کوسوی خواجه), a descendant of Shaikh Ahmad Jām. He died on Saturday the 31st March, A.D. 1459, 26th Jumāda I. A.H. 863, and is buried near the Jama Masjid at Herāt, close to the tomb of Faqīh Abū Yezīd Marghazī.

Shams-uddin Muhammad Sahib Diwan (شمس الدین محمد صاحب دیوان) held the office of Dīwān and prime minister in the reign of Halākū Khān and his son Abāqā Khān, the Tartar kings of Persia. In the first year of the reign of Arghūn Khān, the son of Abāqā Khān, he was accused by his enemies of causing the death of the king's father by poison, and was executed at Qara Bāgh of Tabrez, on Monday the 16th October, A.D. 1284, 4th Shabān, A.H. 683. He was a good poet, and is the author of the work called *Risāla Shamsia dar ilm Mantaq*, a work on the science of Logic. His brother Alā-uddīn, surnamed Atā Malik, is the author of a history entitled *Jahān Kushā*.

Shams - uddin Muhammad Tabrizi, Maulana (شمس الدین محمد تبریزی مولانا), commonly called Shams Tabrīzī, a celebrated Muhammadan of Tabrīz. He was the master of Jalāl-uddīn Maulwī Rūmī, who wrote a book of odes in his name, entitled the *Dīwān of Shams Tabrīzī*. He was murdered by 'Alā-uddīn Mahmūd, the son of the Maulwī, and thrown into a well, A.D. 1247, A.H. 645. He is considered by the Sūfīs to be one of the most celebrated martyrs of their sect. He was, they say, sentenced to be flayed alive, on account of his having raised a dead person to life. We are told that, after the law had been put into force, he wandered about, carrying his own skin, and solicited some food to appease his hunger, but he had been excommunicated as well as flayed, and no one would give him the slightest help. After four days he found a dead ox; but he could not obtain fire to dress it. Wearied out with the unkindness of men, he desired the sun to broil his meat. It descended to perform the office; and the world was on the point of being consumed, when the holy Shaikh commanded the flaming orb to resume its station in the heavens.

Shams-uddin Purbi I. (شمس الدین پوربی), surnamed Bhangeira. His proper name was Khwāja Iliās. He ascended the throne of Bengal after the assassination of 'Alā-uddīn Pūrbī, about the year A.D. 1343, A.H. 744. For 13 years he resisted with success the forces of the king of Dehlī, who could never succeed, during the whole of that period, in making any impression upon him. He died, after a reign of 16 years, A.D. 1358, A.H. 760, and was succeeded by his son Sikandar Shāh Pūrbī.

Shams-uddin Purbi II. (شمس الدین پروبی) ascended the throne of Bengal after the death of his father Sulṭān-us-Salātīn, A.D. 1383, and died, after an inglorious reign of three years, A.D. 1386, A.H. 788. He was succeeded by Rāja Kans Pūrbī.

Shams-uddin Tabrizi (شمس الدین تبریزی). *Vide* Shams-uddīn Muhammad Tabrīzī.

Shams-uddin Tibsi, Qazi (شمس الدین طبسی قاضی), one of the learned men of Khurāsān, and an excellent poet, who attended the court of Niẓām-ul-Mulk, wazīr to Sulṭān Jalāl-uddīn Malikshāh. He died about the year A.H. 473.

Shams-ul-'Umra, Amir Kabir Nawab (شمس الامرا امر کبیر نواب), a nobleman or Amīr-ul-'Umrā of the court of the Niẓām of Haidarābād. He was born in A.D. 1780, and survived three successive Nizāms. The first was Niẓām 'Alī Khān, by whom the nawāb was originally appointed commander of the household troops, during the troubled periods of Tīpū Sulṭān's reign. On Niẓām 'Alī's death in A.D. 1803, the nawāb lived to see Mīr Akbar 'Alī, *alias* Sikandar Jāh, raised to the masnad, and subsequently, on the decease of this prince in 1830, saw him succeeded by Nāsir-uddaula, the late Niẓām, from whom he received the title of Amīr Qabīr, in acknowledgment of his services to the State. As a geometrician he stood unrivalled, and the compilation styled after himself, *Shams-ul-Handisa*, besides other works published by him on the Arts and Sciences, distinguish him as an author. He died on the 10th April, A.D. 1863, when he had just completed the 83rd year of his age, and was the oldest nobleman then living in Haidarābād. He left two sons, and both worthy of him. The elder of the two has inherited his father's vast estates and his official titles. The younger received most of his father's immense wealth during his lifetime, and many jagīrs since his death.

Shams-un-nisa Begam (شمس النسا بیگم), the daughter of Hakīm Kamar-uddīn Khān of Benāres, but her place of residence was at Lucknow. She is the author of a small Dīwān, and was living in the year A.H. 1272.

Shani (شانی), a poet who flourished in the reign of Shāh Abbās I. king of Persia, and died in the year A.D. 1614, A.H. 1023. He is sometimes called Maulana Shānī Taklū.

Shapur (شاپور), a poet of Teherān, who died A.D. 1638, A.H. 1048. His tomb is at a place called Surkhab, in Tabrīz. He had the title of Malik-ush-Shoārā, or king of poets.

Shapur or **Shahpur I.** (شاپور) (the Sapores of the Greeks), the second king of Persia of the Sasanian dynasty, was the son of Ardisher Bābigān. He began to reign about the year A.D. 240, and carried his arms into the Roman territories, gaining many important victories over that nation, whose emperor, Valerian, he made prisoner at the battle of Edessa, and flayed him alive. According to Persian historians Shāpūr reigned 31 years, and died about the year A.D. 273. He was not only a good general but a wise and beneficent ruler of his country. He was succeeded by his son Hurmuz I. the Hormisdes of the Greeks. Shāpūr conquered Armenia and Georgia, which he added to the empire.

Shapur II. (شاپور), surnamed Zū'l Aktāf, was the son of Hurmuz II. king of Persia, and was born A.D. 310, a few months after the death of his father, on which account the Persian historians say that his reign was a few months longer than his life. He died A.D. 381, aged 71 years. During his long reign he raised his country to a state of the greatest prosperity; having defeated all his enemies, and extended the limits of his empire in every direction, adding Georgia, Armenia, and other provinces to the empire. He was succeeded by his son, Ardisher II.

Shapur III. (شاپور), the son of Shāpūr II. and the uterine brother of Ardisher II. whom he deposed, and mounted the throne of Persia, A.D. 385. This prince, who is described as virtuous and beneficent, reigned over Persia only five years. He was killed by the fall of his tent, the pole of which struck the monarch as he slept.

Shaqiq Balkhi (شقیق بلخی), a celebrated pious Musalmān. He died on the 20th January, A.D. 791, 9th Ramaẓān, A.H. 174, in the reign of the Khalīf Hārūn-al-Rashīd, and was buried at Khatlān.

Sharaf-ibn-Shams-uddin (شرف ابن شمس الدین), author of the *Sharaf-nāma*, a Persian History of the Dynasties which have governed in Kurdistān. It was translated into English by Professor Charmoy.

Sharaf Jahan, Mirza (شرف جہان مرزا), an author whose father, Qāzī Jahān, held a high appointment at the court of Shāh Tahmasp Safwī, but, being suspected of being a Sunnī, he was deprived of it. Sharaf Jahān died in A.D. 1561, A.H. 968.

Sharaf Qazwini (شرف قزوینی), a poet who was a native of Qazwīn, and is the author of a Persian dīwān. He came to the Deccan in the reign of Quṭb Shāh, in whose service he died.

Sharaf-uddaula (شرف الدوله), a nobleman of the reign of the emperor Muhammad Shāh. He is the founder of the Masjid situated in the Darība Bāzār at Dehlī, which he built in the year A.D. 1723, A.H. 1135.

Sharaf-uddaula, Nawab (شرف الدوله نواب), ex-prime minister of Audh, was a native of Kashmere. His ancestors were "Rafūgurs" or shawl-darners. At an early age he travelled to the Deccan, where he obtained employment under the Niẓām. He did not, however, remain long at Haidarābād; the reputed splendour of the court of Lucknow brought him to Audh, where he found he had an uncle, the celebrated Maulwī Ahia, the residency Wakīl during the reign of Nāsir-uddīn Haidar. On the accession of Muhammad 'Ali Shāh to the throne in A.D. 1839, Maulwī Ahia was advanced to the post of prime minister, *vice* Hakīm Mahdī, deceased, and Sharaf-uddaula was appointed residency Wakīl, *vice* his uncle promoted. Maulwī Ahia dying soon afterwards, Sharaf-uddaula succeeded him as prime minister. He held the office up to the time of Muhammad 'Alī Shāh's death, which took place in May, A.D. 1842, when Amjād 'Alī Shāh succeeding to the throne, he nominated his favourite, Amīn-uddaula, to the premiership, obliging Sharaf-uddaula to retire. By the Resident personally the nawāb was so much esteemed that, after he lost office, he (the Resident) deemed him the fittest man in Lucknow to manage the very responsible and important concerns of the Husainabād Imāmbārah, of which he induced the king to make him Wasīqadār, or stipendary. Sharaf-uddaula was known by everyone to be the most sincerely attached friend the British had in Audh. He was, therefore, looked upon with much jealousy and rancour by all the courtiers, but especially by Nawāb 'Alī Naqī Khān, the father-in-law and prime minister of Wājid 'Alī Shāh, the last king. Viewing him always as his rival, 'Alī Naqī often contemplated his ruin, and at one time, in league with Nawāb Wasī 'Alī Khān, one of the famous abominables of the court of Lucknow, he would have compassed his end, as he had succeeded in getting the king to issue an order of banishment against Sharaf-uddaula, with his whole family, but for the timely interference of the Resident, who had the order revoked. During the early part of the rebellion (in 1857) the insurgents surrounded his house, insisting that he should become prime minister of the rebel government. He refused, and tried to excuse himself in every way, but they forcibly installed him in the office, which he knew he only nominally held, since Mammū Khān was the ruling spirit with the Begam. On the arrival of General Havelock's force for the relief of the Lucknow garrison, he was in the Keisar Bāgh and received a bullet in the shoulder. When the final grand attack was made on the city by the Commander-in-Chief, which caused the Begam and her party to remove to the Mūsa Bāgh, Sharaf-uddaula took advantage of the confusion and skulked behind, and endeavoured to steal out of the city, when he was recognized by some Sepoys, who bound him with cords, took him to Maulwī Aḥmad-ullāh Shāh, who, after starving him for four days, had him put to death.

Sharaf-uddin Ahmad Ahia Maniri, Shaikh (شرف الدین احمد احیا منیری شیخ), a celebrated saint of Behār. He and his eldest brother, Shaikh Jalāl-uddīn, were the disciples of Shaikh Najm-uddīn Firdausī. Sharaf-uddīn was a contemporary of Shaikh Niẓām-uddīn Aulia. He resided at Behār, and is the author of the works called ***Maʿdan-ul-Maʿānī*** and ***Mukātibāt Ahia Manīrī***; the latter contains the whole duty of a Ṣūfī in a series of 250 letters addressed to his disciples and friends. He died in the year A.D. 1379, A.H. 781, and his tomb (an exact delineation of which has been given by Mr. Daniel) stands near the junction of the river Sōn with the Ganges, and is still the resort of devout Muhammadans. He is called Manīrī, because he resided in a town called Manīr, near Patna. The tomb of his father, Shaikh Ahia or Yehia, is in the town of Manīr.

[*Jour. As. Soc. of Bengal*, vol. xiv. pt. i. pp. 138–140. *See* also Shāh Sharaf-uddīn.]

Sharaf-uddin 'Ali Yezdi, Maulana, (شرف الدين على يزدى مولانا), a learned man, and author of several works. He lived at the court of Sulṭān Ibrāhīm, the son of Shāhrukh Mirzā, at whose request he wrote, in a beautiful style, the *Zafar-nāma*, also called *Tārikh Sāhib Qirānī*, a history of the celebrated conqueror Amīr Taimūr (Tamerlane), whose dominions extended from the borders of China to the shores of the Mediterranean. This work was finished in four years and dedicated to Shāhrukh Mirzā, A.D. 1425, A.H. 828. It has been translated by P. De la Croix, and the heads of it may be found in Gibbon's sixth volume of the *Decline of the Roman Empire*. Sharaf-uddīn may be considered as the panegyrist of Taimūr, while the work of Aḥmad-ibn-Arabshāh is a coarse satire on that conqueror. He is also the author of the *Sharb Burda*. Sharaf-uddīn, who used Sharaf for his poetical name, died about the year A.D. 1446, A.H. 850.

Sharaf-uddin Ashrafi Samarqandi (شرف الدين اشرفى سمرقندى), a poet of Samarqand, who died in the year A.D. 1199, A.H. 595.

Sharaf-uddin Hasan Shafai of Isfahan (شرف الدين حسن شفائي اصفهانى). He is the author of the following Masnawīs or poems, viz.: *Namakdān Haqīqat*, *Mehr-o-Muhabbat*, and *Dīda Beidar*. He died in the year A.D. 1628, A.H. 1038.

Sharaf-uddin Husain, Mirza (شرف الدين حسين مرزا), the son of Khwāja Mo'in, who was of the race of Khwāja Shākir Nāsir-uddīn 'Abdullah, one of the greatest saints of Turkistān. Sharaf-uddīn Husain was the son-in-law of the emperor Humāyūn, and was governor of Ajmīr. He, with another chief named Abū'l Maālī, had revolted at Nāgor, before the Uzbak rebellion took place in Mālwā, about the year A.D. 1561, A.H. 969, had defeated the emperor Akbar's troops, and advanced towards Dehlī. They were afterwards driven back in their turn, and forced to seek safety, the latter beyond the Indus, and the former to Aḥmadābād, in Gujrāt, where he joined the Mirzās at Barouch, in the year A.D. 1568, A.H. 976.

Sharaf-uddin Panipati (شرف الدين پانى پتى). *Vide* Abū 'Alī Qalandar.

Sharaf-uddin Rami, Maulana (شرف الدين رامى مولانا), author of a Dīwān and the *Hadāeq-el-Ḥaqāeq*, which treats on metric and poetic compositions, and has been written in imitation of, or competition with, Rashīd-uddīn Watwāt's *Hadāek-us-Sehr*. He flourished in the reign of Shāh Mansūr, and died A.D. 1393, A.H. 795.

Sharaf-uddin Shafrawa (شرف الدين شفروه), a poet of Isfahān, who flourished in the reign of Tughral III. and was contemporary with the poet Mujīr. He is the author of the work called *Itbak-uz-Zahab*, which he wrote in imitation of *Itwak-uz-Zahab* of Zamakhsharī.

Sharaf-uddin, Shah (شرف الدين شاه). *Vide* Shāh Sharaf-uddīn.

Sharifi Maulana (شريفى مولانا), a native of Balkh, who was a physician, poet, and a good musician. He has written several panegyrics in praise of the king of Badakhshān.

Sharif Jurjani, Mir or **Sayyad** (شريف جرجانى مير), whose full name is Sayyad Sharīf 'Alī bin-Muhammad, is the author of the *Hāshia Kashshāf* and *Hashia Tafsīr Anwār-ut-Tauzīl*, also of an Arabic work on philosophy called *'Adāb-ul-Sharīf*, and the marginal notes on the *Sharah Matla-ul-Anwār*, and on the *Mawākif Azdia*, a work on Jurisprudence in Arabic. He also wrote a Commentary on the *Sirājia* of Sajāwandī, which he named *Sharīfia*. He was born in A.D. 1339, A.H. 740, and died in July, A.D. 1413, 6th Rabī' II. A.H. 816.

Sharif Khan Amir-ul-'Umra (شريف خان امير الامرا), son of Khwāja Abdus Samad, a nobleman of the reign of the emperor Jahāngīr, who in the first year of his reign conferred on him the rank of 5000 and appointed him governor of Haidarābād, in the Deccan, where he died after some years. He was an excellent poet and has left a Dīwān. His poetical name was Farsī.

Sharif Muhammad (شريف محمد), author of the Persian work on Jurisprudence called *Fatāwa Faerōz Shāhī*, dedicated to Fīrōz Shāh, king of Dehli.

Sharif-uddin Muhammad Abdullah-al-Mousali-al-Basri (شريف الدين محمد عبدالله الموصلى), author of a Dīwān, which he called *Dīwān Murtazā Alī*.

Sharm (شرم). *Vide* Shams-un-Nisa Begam.

Shatab Rai, Raja (شتاب رای راجه), was by caste a Kāyeth, and a native of Dehlī; in his youth he served 'Aqā Sulaimān, the favourite dependant of Samsām-uddaula, son of Khān Daurān, Amir-ul-'Umrā to the emperor Muhammad Shāh. Upon the death of Samsām-uddaula, he obtained the office of imperial Dīwān at Patna. Attaching himself to the English in the several revolutions, he became their chief adviser in their connections with the country powers. He was an able statesman, and understood completely the direction of finance: under orders from the Court of Directors Warren Hastings held an enquiry into his official conduct, 1772, when Shatāb was completely exonerated. He died about the year A.D. 1777, A.H. 1187.

Shayurghamish, Mirza (شیورغمش مرزا), a son of Shāhrukh Mirzā.

Sher Afgan or **Afkan** (شیرافگن خان), a Turkman nobleman of high lineage and great renown, was the first husband of the celebrated Nūr Jahān Begam. He served in the wars of Akbar with extraordinary reputation, and had a jāgīr at Bardwān, where he was slain, A.D. 1607, A.H. 1015, in an encounter with the Governor, Quṭb-uddīn. His original names were Asta Fillo and 'Alī Kulil Beg, but having killed a lion, he was dignified with the title of Sher Afgan Khān or the Destroyer of Lions. The emperor Jahāngīr married the widow some years afterwards, which gave rise to a legend of the emperor having caused his death.

Sher 'Ali Afsos, Mir (شیرعلی افسوس میر). *Vide* Afsōs.

Sher 'Ali Khan, Amir of Kabul (شیرعلی خان), the youngest son of Dost Mohammad Khān.

Sheri Maulana (شیری مولانا), a poet who flourished in the reign of the emperor Akbar. When the fortress of Chittor was taken by that monarch in December, A.D. 1567, Jumāda II. A.H. 975, and the fort of Rinthanpūr on the 22nd March, A.D. 1569, 3rd Shawwāl, A.H. 976, in which year the fort of Āgra was also completed, Sherī was then living, and wrote the chronogram of all three. He was slain, together with Rāja Bīrbal and other officers of note, in a battle fought against the Yūsafzaī Afghāns of Sawād and Bijūr in February, A.D. 1586, Rabī' I. A.H. 994. The author of the *Māsir-ul-'Umrā* says that he was the nephew of Khwāja Jahān Hirwī, a nobleman of the court of Akbar, who died in November, A.D. 1574, Shaban, A.H. 982, and that Sherī died in A.D. 1581, A.H. 989. He is the author of a Dīwān.

Sher Khan Lodi (شیرخان لودی), the son of 'Alī Amjād Khān Lodī, who died on the 13th November, A.D. 1673, 14th Shaban, A.H. 1084. Sher Khān is the author of a Tazkira or biography of poets called *Mirat-ul-Khayāb*, or the Mirror of Imagination, which he wrote in the year A.D. 1691, A.H. 1102, in the reign of the emperor 'Alamgīr. It contains an account of the most celebrated poets and, besides, it treats on almost every science cultivated by the Musalmāns: music, medicine, cosmography, oneiroscopy, talismans, etc.

Sheroya (شیرویه), the Siroes of the Greeks, was the son of Khusro Parwez, or Chosroes, king of Persia, whom he threw into a dungeon and subsequently murdered, A.D. 628, A.H. 7. He reigned only eight months, and died A.D. 629, A.H. 8. At the death of Sheroya, an ambitious noble raised Ardisher, the infant son of that prince, to the throne; but another noble of the name of Shahryār, disapproving this measure, marched from the province which he governed, seized Madāin, put Ardisher to death after he had reigned five months, and usurped the crown, which, however, he held only a few days, having been slain by the adherents of the royal family. These not being able to discover any heir male of the house of Sasān, elevated Tūrāndukht, the daughter of Khusro Parwez, to the throne.

Sher Shah (شیر شاه), a native of Hissar. His original name was Farīd. His father, Hasan, was an Afghān of the tribe of Sūr, and a native of Roh beyond Peshāwar, who had received from Jamāl Khān, the governor of Jaunpūr, the districts of Sahsarām and Ṭānda in jāgīr for the maintenance of 500 horse. Farīd was for some time in the service of Muhammad Lohānī, king of Behār, and on his killing a tiger, received from him the title of Sher Khan. He defeated the emperor Humāyūn once at Behār on the 26th June, A.D. 1539, 9th Ṣafar, A.H. 946, and the second time on the 17th May, A.D. 1540, 10th Muḥarram, A.H. 947, at Kanauj, when he pursued him through Āgra and Lāhore to Khūshāb; from whence Humāyūn eventually retreated towards the Indus. Sher Khān by this victory became the sovereign of Dehlī, assumed the title of Sher Shāh, and ascended the throne on the 25th January, A.D. 1542, 7th Shawwāl, A.H. 948. In the 5th year of his reign he moved towards Kalingar, one of the strongest forts in Hindūstān. The batteries were advanced close to the walls, a breach was made, and a general assault was ordered, when a shell, which was thrown against the fort, burst in the battery in which the king stood. The explosion communicating to a powder magazine, several gunners were blown up, and the king so much scorched that his recovery was hopeless. In this position he encouraged the prosecution of the attack, and continued to give his orders till in the evening news was brought him of the reduction of the place. He then cried out,

"Thanks to the Almighty God!" and expired. His death happened on the 24th May, A.D. 1545, 12th Rabī' I. A.H. 952. His corpse was conveyed to Sahsarām, the family estate, where it was buried in a magnificent sepulchre, which is still to be seen standing in the centre of a reservoir of water, built during his own life. Tradition adds that, during his reign, such was the public security that travellers rested and slept with their goods by the highways without apprehension of robbery. He was succeeded by his son Salīm Shāh.

Sher Singh (شیر سنگه), ruler of the Panjāb, was the second son of Kharag Singh, the son of Ranjīt Singh. After the death of his eldest brother, Nau Nihāl Singh, which took place on the 17th November, A.D. 1840, his mother, Rānī Chānd Kūnwar, managed the affairs of his country for two months, when Sher Singh, her second son, deprived her of that power and became the sole manager. On the 13th September, A.D. 1843, the royal palace was taken by a powerful body of troops, and Sher Singh and his son Partāp Singh were murdered by Sardār Ajīt Singh. Every child and all of Sher Singh's and Partāp Singh's wives were brought out and murdered; amongst the rest, one of Sher Singh's sons, only born the previous evening. After Sher Singh's death, Rāja Dalīp Singh, the youngest son of Mahārāja Ranjīt Singh, was placed on the Masnad.

[*Vide* Kharag Singh.]

Sherzad, Sultan (شیرزاد سلطان), son of Sultān Masaūd III. of Ghaznī, whom he succeeded in A.D. 1114, A.H. 508, and was murdered after one year by his brother Arsalān Shāh, who ascended the throne A.D. 1115, A.H. 509.

Shia or **Shia'** (شیعه). Those Muhammadans who assert the rights of 'Alī, are called Shias or Shiites or Sectaries, whilst those who consider the first three Khalīfas preceding 'Alī as the rightful successors of Muhammad, are called Sunnīs or Sannites or Traditionists. The animosity which exists between the Shias and Sunnīs fully equals that of the Protestants and Papists of former times. It was owing to their dissensions that Baghdād was taken, and the Khilāfat overturned. The Turks and Arabs are Sunnīs; the Persians and most of the Muhammadans of India are Shias. A complete history of the Shias will be found in a work called *Majalis-ul-Mominīn*. The Shia doctrines were adopted by the Persians at the foundation of the Safwī dynasty in A.D. 1500, A.H. 905, and from that period until the present time have prevailed as the national religion and law of Persia, notwithstanding the violent efforts to substitute the Sunnī creed made by the Afghān usurper Ashraf and the great Nādir Shāh.

Shibli (شبلی). *Vide* Abū Bakr Shiblī.

Shidi (شیدی), an African.

Shidi Foulad Khan (شیدی فولاد خان). *Vide* Foulād Khān Shīdī.

Shikeibi, Maulana (شکیبی مولانا), a poet of Persia, whose proper name is Muhammad Razā. He came to India in the reign of the emperor Akbar, and died in the time of Jahāngīr, A.D. 1614, A.H. 1023.

Shimbhu (شمبهو), a Brāhman, who is the author of a *Zafar-nāma*, or book of victory, containing a poetical account of the military career of General Lake.

Shinasi (شناسی), title of a poet who died in the year A.D. 1627, A.H. 1037, and is the author of a work called *Fazl-nāma*.

Shio Ramdas (شیو رامداس), a poet whose poetical title was Hayā, which see.

Shirazi (شیرازی), an author who wrote a commentary on the *Tahrīr-ul-Majastī* of Is-hāq bin-Husain, and named it *Hall Mushkilāt Majastī*.

Shirin (شیرین). This word, which signifies in Persian, sweet, charming or agreeable, is the name of a lady well known throughout the East. Some call her Mary, and others Irene. The Greeks only describe her as a Roman by birth, a Christian by religion; but she is represented as the daughter of the emperor Maurice in the Persian and Turkish romances, which celebrated the love of Khusro for Shīrīn, and of Shīrīn for Farhād, the most beautiful youth of the East. This celebrated beauty has been accused of giving those affections, which a monarch so anxiously sought, to the lowly Farhād, in whose breast her beauties kindled a flame, which deprived him of reason and life. We are told that the son of Khusro, after putting his father to death, sought the favours of his father's mistress, who appeared to consent, but desired to take one look at the remains of his father. The murdered body of her former lover was shown to her, and she immediately put an end to her existence by stabbing herself.

[*Vide* Farhād.]

Shorish (شهورش), a poet, whose proper name is Gholām Husain and who is the author of a biography of Urdū poets. He died in A.D. 1781, A.H. 1195.

Shoukat of Bukhara (شوکت بخاری), a poet who died at Isfahān in A.D. 1695, A.H. 1107, and left a Dīwān in Persian. His proper name is Muhammad Is-hāq.

Shouq (شوق), the poetical name of Mīr Muhammad Bakīr, father of Mīr Muhammad 'Atā Husain Khān Tahsīn.

Shouq (شوق), the poetical name of Maulwī Kudrat-ullāh, who has left a Dīwān and a Biography of poets called *Tabkat-ush-Shoara*.

Shouq (شوق), the poetical name of Rāe Tansukh Rāe, which see.

Shouqi (شوقی), a poet of Tabrīz, but he is usually called Hirwī, *i.e.* of Herāt. He left the service of Sām Mirzā, son of Shāh Tahmasp Safwi, and went with the emperor Humāyūn to Kabul, where he died in A.D. 1546, A.H. 953.

Shouqi, Amir (شوکی امیر), a nobleman and poet, who lived in the time of the emperor Shāh Jahān. His proper name was Mīr Muhammad Husain. He died in A.D. 1634, A.H. 1044.

Shuhrat or **Shahrat** (شہرت), the poetical title of Nawāb Hakīm-ul-Mumalik. *Vide* Muhammad Husain (Shaikh.)

Shujaa' Khan or **Shujaa't Khan** (شجاع خان), a relative of Sher Shāh, king of Dehlī, who conferred the government of Mālwā on him after the expulsion of Mallū Khān entitled Qādir Shāh in A.D. 1542, A.H. 949. He governed Mālwā for a period of 12 years, and died in A.D. 1554, A.H. 962. After his death his eldest son, Malik Bāyezid, assuming the title of Bāz Bahādur, took the reigns of government in his own hands.

Shujaa', Sultan (شجاع سلطان). *Vide* Sulṭān Shujāa.

Shujaa't Khan, Nawab (شجاعت خان نواب), a nobleman in the service of the emperor 'Alamgīr (*vide* Fakhr-un-Nisa Begam). He was a mansabdār of 4000 in the time of Shāh Jahān. He had a house at Āgra, of which no trace now remains.

Shuja-uddaula, Nawab (شجاع الدوله نواب), who played a conspicuous part in the early history of British India, was the son of Mansūr 'Alī Khān Safdar Jang, governor of Audh. His original name was Jalāl-uddīn Haidar; he was born in the year A.D. 1731, A.H. 1144, and after the death of his father succeeded to the government in October, A.D. 1753, Ẕil-ḥijja, A.H. 1167. He was present in the famous battle which took place between Aḥmad Shāh Abdālī and the Marhaṭṭas in January, A.D. 1761; was appointed wazīr to the emperor Shāh 'Alam; was defeated at Buxar by the English on the 23rd October, A.D. 1764, 26th Rabī' II. A.H. 1178, and died at Faizabād, the seat of his government, in the midst of his victories and highest prosperity, on the 29th January, A.D. 1775, 24th Ẕi-Qa'da, A.H. 1188. By his own subjects he was sincerely beloved, and the sons of Hāfiz Rahmat Khān, whose country he had seized, wept at his death. He was buried at a place called Gulāb Bāṛī in Faizābād, and was succeeded by his eldest son, 'Asaf-uddaula. For a legendary account of his death see Keene's *Fall of the Mughal Empire*, p. 117.

Shuja-uddin (شجاع الدین نواب), nawāb of Bengal, also called by some Shujā-uddaula, was a native of Burhānpūr, and a descendant of a Turkish tribe of Afghāns in Khurāsān. During 'Alamgīr's campaigns in the Deccan he married Zeb-un-Nisā, the daughter of Murshid Qulī Jafar Khan Sūbadār of Bengal, and accompanied him to that province. Jafar Khan, who died in the year A.D. 1726, A.H. 1138, left at his death the succession to his government to his grandson 'Alā-uddaula Sarfarāz Khān; but Shujā-uddīn, his father, having more interest at the court of Dehlī than his son, procured the Sūbadārī for himself, and in the year A.D. 1735, A.H. 1148, the province of Behār also was conferred on him by the emperor Muhammad Shāh. Shujā-uddīn was celebrated for his clemency, justice, and good qualities. He died after 12 years' government of Bengal on the 13th March, A.D. 1739, 13th Ẕil-ḥijja, A.H. 1151, just at the time when Nādir Shāh was at Dehlī. As there were only a few days remaining for the commencement of the Hijrī year, A.D. 1152, at his death. He was succeeded by his son 'Alā-uddaula Sarfarāz Khān, a young prince whose character as a moral and religious man stands high on the pages of native history.

Shuja-ul-Mulk, Shah (شجاع الملک شاه). *Vide* Shāh Shujāa.

Shukr-ullah (شکر الله), author of the history called *Bahjat-ut-Tawarīkh*.

Shukr-ullah Khan I. Nawab (شکر الله خان نواب), a nobleman in the service of the emperor Aurangzeb, who died about the year A.D. 1698, A.H. 1110.

Shukr-ullah Khan II. Nawab (شکراللہ خان نواب), son of Shukr-ullāh Khān I. was an Amīr in the service of the emperor Aurangzeb 'Alamgīr. He was appointed governor of Mewāt in A.D. 1702, A.D. 1114.

Siamak (سیامک), the son of Qayomurs and the father of Hoshang, the second king of the Pishdadian dynasty of Persia.

Siawakhsh (سیاوخش), son of Kaikāūs, king of Persia of the Kayānian dynasty. He was murdered by Afrāsiāb, king of Tūrān.

Sibuya (سیبویه), an author who received this name on account of his keeping an apple (sib) in his hand, and smelling it often, but his proper name was Abū Bashar 'Umar. He died in A.D. 796, A.H. 180, aged 32 years.

[*Vide* Qutrib.]

Sidi or **Sayyad Maula** (سیدی مولا), a venerable sage, in a mendicant dress, who travelled from Jurjān towards the east and, arriving at Dehlī, set up a great academy and house of entertainment for travellers and the poor of all denominations. Though he was very religious, and brought up in the Muhammadan faith, yet he followed some particular tenets of his own, so that he never attended public worship. He kept no women nor slaves for himself, and lived upon rice only; yet his expenses in charity were so great that, as he never accepted any present, men were astonished whence his finances were supplied, and actually believed that he possessed the art of transmuting other metals into gold. He made nothing of bestowing two or three thousand pieces of gold to relieve the wants of any noble family in distress. In short, he displayed more magnificence in his feasts than the princes themselves. He expended daily upon the poor 1000 maunds of flour, 500 maunds of meat, 80 maunds of sugar, besides rice, oil, butter and other necessaries in proportion. He latterly began to bestow titles and offices upon his disciples, and to assume a tone and manner sufficiently indicative of his design on the throne. One of his followers, dissatisfied with the part assigned to him, went privately to the king (Jalāluddin Fīroz Khiljī) and disclosed the plot. The king caused him to be apprehended and trodden to death by an elephant. This event happened in the year A.D. 1291, A.H. 690, and is accounted one of the most deplorable events that took place in the reign of that monarch, for many believed Sidi entirely innocent of the charge.

Sidi 'Ali Kapudan (سیدی علی کپدان) or Captain of the fleet of Sulṭān Sulaimān I. emperor of Constantinople. He is the author of the work called *Mirat-ul-Mumālik*, or Mirror of Countries, containing a description of his journey overland from the Indian shores to Constantinople; and of the *Muhīt*, that is the Ocean, a Turkish work on Navigation in the Indian Seas. This work the author finished at Aḥmadābād, the capital of Gujrāt, in December, A.D. 1554, Muḥarram, A.H. 962. It was translated by the Baron Joseph von Hammer, Professor, Oriental Languages, at Vienna, and communicated through the *Jour. As. Soc. of Bengal*, in 1837.

Sihl or **Sehl bin-Sa'd** (سهل بن سعد), one of the companions of Muhammad.

Sijaj (سجاج), a false prophetess contemporary with Musylima, another impostor. She was a Christian of extraordinay talents and eloquence, and, being prompted by an aspiring ambition, she announced herself a prophetess and, uttering her string of rhapsodies in rhyme, declared that they came inspired from above. Struck by her success, Musylima thought it advisable to temporize with her, and accordingly, having sent agents, invited her to a private conference, Sijāj consented and came to an interview; she was deceived, and, having forfeited all pretensions to that purity which is the highest attribute of her sex, she fell from her proud pre-eminence and became a mere debased and contaminated woman. She subsequently enrolled herself amongst the proselytes of the Qurān.

Sikandar, Alexander the Great (سکندر ذوالقرنین), called by Muhammad in the Qurān, Zū'lqarnyn the Two-Horned Man; probably by reason of his head being figured as Ammon, with the Ram's Horns, on coins and medals. Eastern commentators have been at a loss to decide who is intended, but generally agree that he was a being favoured of, and who believed in, the true God; that, guided by the prophet Khizir, he reached the land of Darkness, near the Fountain of Life, but he could not obtain permission to take a draught of the Eternal Spring. He died B.C. 327, at the age of 33 years. He conquered Darius, king of Persia, in B.C. 331, and in 327 he he proceeded to invade India. He crossed the Indus without opposition. He was afterwards opposed by a Rāja who is called by the Greek Poros, whose army was utterly routed.

[*Vide* Shea's *Translation of Mirkhond.*]

Sikandar (سکندر), poetical name of Khalīfa Sikandar, who used to write beautiful Marsias in the Pūrbī, Mārwārī, and Panjābī language, and is the author of a poem containing the story of the Fish, the Ferryman and king Dilkhwār.

Sikandar 'Adil Shah (سکندر عادل شاه), the last of the kings of Bījāpūr. He succeeded his father, 'Ali 'Adīl Shāh II. when an infant, about the year A.D. 1672, A.H. 1083, but never acquired any real power, being the tool of his nobility. In the year A.D. 1686, 4th Ẕi-Qa'da, A.H. 1097, on Monday the 13th September, Bījāpūr was taken, the young prince made prisoner, and the kingdom with its remaining dependencies was reduced to the Mughal yoke by the emperor 'Alamgīr. He died after three years' imprisonment.

Sikandar (Prince) (سکندر شاهزاده), the son of 'Umar Shaikh Mirzā, the son of Amīr Taimūr, after whose death he had several battles with his two brothers, Pīr Muhammad and Mirzā Rustam, and took possession of Fars and Isfahān, which they had received as inheritance from their grandfather; on which account his uncle Shahrukh Mirzā, having defeated him in a battle, put out both his eyes. This circumstance took place in A.D. 1414, A.H. 817.

Sikandar Begam (سکندر بیگم), the ruler of Bhopāl. She was born in A.D. 1816. Her father was one of the Paṭhān or Afghān soldiers of fortune, who, after the death of the emperor Aurangzeb, declared himself independent in Bhopāl. On his death his wife was declared Regent by his troops, and his daughter Sikandar Begam heir. She married her cousin Jahāngīr, in spite of her mother, upon condition that her husband swore to leave her the direct and visible control of all affairs. Her husband, Jahāngīr, died in A.D. 1845. She was publicly presented with the Grand Cross of the Star of India at the Durbar at Āgra. She died on the 30th October, A.D. 1868. Her Highness had conducted the administration of her principality since the year 1847, when she was first appointed Regent, with ability and success until the day of her decease. Her eldest daughter, Shāhjahān Begam, succeeded her.

Sikandar Jah (سکندر جاه نواب), nawāb or Niẓām of Haidarabād, succeeded his father, Nawāb Niẓām 'Alī Khān, to the Masnad of the Deccan on the 16th August, A.D. 1802, 16th Rabī' II. A.H. 1217, and died on the 23rd May, A.D. 1829, 19th Ẕi-Qa'da, A.H. 1244, after a reign of 28 lunar years and some months. He was succeeded by his son Mīr Farkhunda 'Alī Khān, who took the title of Nasīr-uddaula.

Sikandar Khan Uzbak (سکندر خان اذبک), a descendant of the royal house of that tribe, also called Sikandar Khān of Kāshghar. He accompanied the emperor Humāyūn to India, and was created a nobleman by that monarch. He accompanied Mirzā Haidar, who took possession of Kashmere in A.D. 1543, and died at Lucknow in the reign of the emperor Akbar on the 18th September, A.D. 1572, 10th Jumada I. A.H. 980.

Sikandar Munshi (سکندر منشی), Secretary to Shāh Abbās I. king of Persia. He is the author of the *Tārikh 'Alam Arāe Abbāsī*, a history of that monarch, in three books, which he dedicated to him in A.D. 1616, A.H. 1025.

[*Vide* Iskandar Munshī.]

Sikandar Qadr, Mirza (سکندر قدر), the son of Prince Khurshaid Kada. *Vide* Taskhīr.

Sikandar Shah (سکندر شاه), king of Gujrāt, succeeded his father, Muẓaffar Shāh II. in February, A.D. 1526, 19th Shabān, A.H. 932, and after a reign of only three months and seventeen days was assassinated on the 30th May the same year. After his death his younger brother, Nasīr Khān, was raised to the throne under the title of Muhammad Shāh II.

Sikandar Shah Lodi, Sultan (سکندر شاه لودی), whose original name was Niẓām Khān, was the son of Sulṭān Bahlōl Lōdī, whom he succeeded in July, A.D. 1489, Shabān, A.H. 895. He was the first Musalmān king who made Āgra his capital. In his time a violent earthquake took place, when many houses were thrown down and several thousands of inhabitants lost their lives. This happened on Sunday the 6th July, A.D. 1505, 3rd Ṣafar, A.H. 911. It was in his reign that the Hindūs first commenced reading Persian. He reigned 21 lunar years and some months, and died at Āgra on Sunday the 17th February, A.D. 1510, 7th Ẕi-Qa'da, A.H. 915. Colonel Dow and General Briggs, in their translation of *Firishta*, say that Sikandar Shāh died in the year of the Hijrī 923, corresponding with A.D. 1517, and that he reigned 28 years and some months; this is evidently a mistake, for the words "Tārī Shud" show the year of his death to be A.H. 915, consequently the period of his reign was only 21 years. He was succeeded by his son Ibrāhīm Ḥusain Lōdī. Sikandar Lōdī in his time had built a small fort at Āgra on the right bank of the Jamna, and called it Badalgarh. The emperor Akbar, in the 10th year of his reign, *viz.* in A.H. 972, having demolished this fort laid the foundations of another fort of redstone, which was completed in the course of eight years, superintended by Qasim Khān Mīr Bahar. This fort had three gotis and two windows, and cost 36 lakhs of rupees. It was accidentally burned down in the time of Shāh 'Alam and Madho Rao Sendhia.

Sikandar Shah Purbi (سکندر شاه پوربی). He was raised to the throne of Bengal after the death of his father, Shams-uddīn Bhangeiṛa, about the year A.D. 1358, A.H. 760. He had not long entered on his rule before his country was invaded by Fīroz Shāh Tug͟hlāq, king of Delhī, who was, however, induced to retreat on Sikandar Shāh promising to pay an annual tribute. He reigned in peace for a period of nine years and died in A.D. 1367, A.H. 769, when he was succeeded by his son Ghayās-uddīn Pūrbī.

Sikandar Shah Sur (سکندر شاه سور). His original name was Aḥmad K͟hān Sūr, a nephew of Sher Shāh. He ascended the throne of Dehlī after defeating Sulṭān Ibrāhīm Sūr in a battle fought in May, A.D. 1555, Jumādạ II. A.H. 962. He had not long enjoyed his good fortune, however, when he was obliged to repair to the Panjāb to oppose the emperor Humāyūn, who, having returned from a long exile, was now advancing to recover his dominions. He engaged Bairām Khān, the general of the army near Sarhind, was defeated on the 22nd June, A.D. 1555, 3rd Shabān, A.H. 962, and fled to the Sewālik Mountains, from whence he was afterwards expelled by the emperor Akbar, A.D. 1557, 27th Ramaẓān, A.H. 964. He sought refuge in Bengal, where he died after two years.

Sikandar Shikoh Mirza (سکندر شکوه), a cousin of Bahādur Shāh II. king of Dehlī. He was executed for the murder of his wife in July, A.D. 1838.

Sikandar, Sultan (سکندر سلطان), king of Kashmere, surnamed But Shikan, or Destroyer of Idols, was the grandson of Shāh Mīr Darweish, who introduced the Muhammadan religion into Kashmere. Sikandar, with the assistance of his mother, succeeded his father, Sulṭān Quṭb-uddīn, A.D. 1393, A.H. 796, his authority being acknowledged by all the nobles and other officers, and became one of the most powerful kings that ever reigned in Kashmere. Various magnificent temples and images of the Hindūs did this Sulṭān lay in ruins; which conduct obtained him the glorious title of But Saikam, or Iconoclast. He reigned 22 years and 9 months, and died in A.D. 1416, A.H. 819. In his time Tamerlane invaded India, and presents passed between him and Sikandar. He was succeeded by his son Sulṭān 'Alī Shāh.

Sikandar Turkman (سکندر ترکمان). *Vide* Qarā Muhammad.

Silhaddi (سلهدی), a Rāja of Raisīn, who was made prisoner by Bahādur Shāh of Gujrāt, and was forced to become a Muhammadan in the year A.D. 1531, A.H. 938, after which, when the fort of Raisīn was surrendered by his brother Lachhman to the king, Rānī Durgāwatī, the daughter of Rana Sanka, Rana of Chittor and wife of Rāja Silhaddī, with a heroic fortitude, invoking curses on the heads of those who should not revenge her cause, set fire to a pile with which she had caused the female apartments to be surrounded, containing seven hundred beautiful women. She then plunged into the flames, and they were all consumed. Silhaddī and Lachhman (his brother), with one hundred of their blood-relations, now putting on their armour, rushed impetuously on the Gujrāt troops, and bravely met their fate the same year.

Simi Naishapuri (سیمی نیشاپوری), a very learned Musalmān of Naishāpūr. It is said that in one night and day he composed 3,000 verses. He flourished in the time of Prince 'Alāuddaula (the son of Bāisang͟har Mirzā), who reigned at Herāt A.D. 1447.

Sina, Abu Sina or **Avicenna** (سینا). *Vide* Abū Sina.

Sindbad Hakim (سندباد حکیم), author of a Dīwān or book of Odes, which he completed in the year A.D. 1374, A.H. 776, and dedicated to Shāh Mahmūd Bahmanī.

Sindh (سنده), Medieval history of. *Vide* Nāsir-uddīn Qabbācha.

Sindhia (سیندهیه). A distinguished Marātha family. For Rājas of the Sindhia family, *vide* Rānōjī Sindhia, Mādho Rāo, Daulat Rāo, Shanko Rāo, etc.

Sipahdar Khan (سپهدار خان), whose proper name is Mirzā Muhammad Sālah, was a native of Tabrīz, and his ancestors were reckoned among the nobles of that country. In the year A.D. 1592, A.H. 1000, he left Persia for Hindūstān in company with K͟hwāja Beg Mirzā, son of Maṣūm Beg Safwī. On his arrival in India he obtained the honour of an interview with the emperor Akbar. Mansabs suitable to his dignity, as well as the government of Gujrāt, were conferred on him time after time. When, after the death of prince Murād in A.D. 1599, A.H. 1007, prince Daniāl went to the Deccan and captured the fort of Aḥmadnagar, the capital of Niẓām Shāh, the government of that country was conferred upon K͟hwāja Beg Mirzā and Sipahdār K͟hān.

Sipahdar Khan (سپهدار خان) was the second son of K͟hān Jahān Bahādur, the foster-brother of the emperor 'Alamgīr. He was raised to the rank of 3000 by that monarch, A.D. 1691, A.H. 1103, with the government of the province of Allahābād, which he held for several years. His brother Himmat Khān was killed by an arrow in an action with the Marhattas about the year A.D. 1698, A.H. 1110, and soon afterwards their father, Khān Jahān Bahādur, died in the imperial camp.

Sipehr Shikoh (سپہر شیکوه), third son of Dara Shikoh. He was confined in the fort of Gwāliar by 'Alamgīr who, in his 16th year, A.H. 1085, sent for him from Gwāliar, and married him to his daughter Badr-un-Nisa, of whom was born prince 'Alī Tabar.
[*Vide* Sulaiman Shikoh.]

Siraj (سراج), takhallus of Sirāj-uddin Husain of Aurangābād, who is the author of the *Dīwān Muntakhib*, containing extracts from no less than 680 poets, and which he completed in A.D. 1756, A.H. 1169.

Siraj Qummi (سراج قمی), a poet who was a native of Qumm, in Persia, and contemporary with Salmān Sāwajī.

Siraj-uddaula Muhammad Ghaus Khan (سراج الدوله محمد غوث خان), titular Nawāb of Arkot, whose poetical name was 'Azim, the author of the work called *Tazkira Subh Watan*, being a biography of the poets of the Karnatik, compiled in A.D. 1842, A.D. 1258. It is an abstract of the *Tazkira of Rāeq*, also called *Guldasta Karnatik.*

Siraj-uddaula (سراج الدوله نواب), Nawāb of Bengal, formerly named Mirzā Mahmūd, was the eldest son of Zain-uddīn Ahmad, styled Haibat Jang, the nephew and son-in-law of Alahwardī Khān Mahābat Jang, governor of Bengal. On the death of his grandfather Mahābat Jang, which happened on the 10th April, A.D. 1756, 9th Rajab, A.H. 1169, he succeeded him in the government of that province, and immediately taking offence at the English, for their protection to a native officer said to have escaped from Dacca with treasure, he attacked Calcutta, carried it on the 20th June the same year, and allowed his officers to shut up 146 European prisoners in a small military prison room called the "Black Hole," of which number 123 perished during the night. Mr. Drake, the governor of Calcutta, escaped on board a ship with a few Englishmen and retired to Madras. At that time Colonel Clive commanded the Company's forces in the province of Arkot. It was agreed by the government of Madras that he should repair with a force to Bengal and endeavour to regain the factory of Calcutta. Colonel Clive and Admiral Watson left Madras with 900 Europeans and 1500 Sepoys. They reached Falta on the 20th December, re-took Calcutta on the 2nd January, A.D. 1757, A.H. 1170, and forced Sirāj-uddaula into a treaty, offensive and defensive, on the 9th February following. Clive subsequently made a secret treaty with Mīr Ja'far, an officer of the nawāb, and advanced in June towards Murshidābād, the nawāb's capital. On the 23rd June, A.D. 1757, Clive fought the battle of Plassy against 18,000 horse and 50,000 infantry, and, aided by the treachery of Mīr Ja'far, routed the nawāb's troops. Sirāj-uddaula fled, but in a few days was seized and cruelly assassinated on the 4th July, A.D. 1757, 15th Shawwāl A.H. 1170, by order of Mīran, the son of Mīr Ja'far. Thus perished Sirāj-uddaula in the 20th year of his age and the 15th month of his reign. On the 29th June Mīr Ja'far was raised to the masnad, and from that date the influence of the British may be said to have become paramount in Bengal. His tomb is not far from that of Mahābat Jang.

Siraj-uddin (سراج الدین), son of Nūr-uddīn, author of the *Sharah Bukhārī* and *Sharah 'Umda.* He died in A.D. 1401, A.H. 804. [*Vide* Bilqainī.]

Siraj-uddin 'Ali Khan (سراج الدین علی خان عرزو), whose poetical title is 'Arzū, was a native of Akbarābād (Āgra), and a descendant of Shaikh Muhammad Ghaus of Gwāliar. He was an excellent poet and an officer of rank in the time of the emperor Farrukh-siyar. He is the author of several works, among which is a Dīwān and a biography entitled *Majmūa-ul-Nafāes*, which is also called *Tazkira 'Arzū*, containing the memoirs of the Indian poets who have written Persian, Hindūstānī and Deccanī poems. 'Arzū, in A.D. 1734, A.H, 1147, met at Dehlī the poet Hazīn, who had just come from Persia. The jealousy between the two poets induced 'Arzū to write a treatise entitled *Tambīh-ul-Ghāfilīn*, in which he points out the errors in Hazīn's poems. He died at Lucknow on the 27th January, A.D. 1756, 23rd Rabi' II. A.H. 1169, and was buried there for some time, but afterwards his remains were removed to Dehlī by his nephew Muhammad Husain Khān. Beside the above-mentioned works he is the author of the following:

Mōhibat Uzma.
'Atia Kubrā.
Sirāj-ul-Lughāt.
Chirāgh Hidāet.
Gharāeb-ul-Lughāt.
Khayābān.
Mustilāhāt-ush-Shuarā.
Jawāb Yatarāzāt Munīr.
Sharah Kasāed 'Urfī.
Sharah Sikandar-nāma.
Sharah Mukhtasir-ul-Maānī.
Sharah Gulkushtī Mīr Najāt.
Nawādir-ul-Alfarz, a Hindūstānī Dictionary.

Siraj-uddin Husain (سراج الدين حسين). *Vide* Sirāj.

Siraj-uddin Muhammad bin-'Abdur Rashid-al-Sajawandi (سراج الدين محمد بن عبدالرشيد آل شيزاوندى), author of the *Sirājia*, which is sometimes called *Farāez as-Sajāwandī*. This book is of the highest authority on the law of inheritance amongst the Sunnīs of India. It has been commented upon by a vast number of writers, upwards of forty being enumerated in the *Kashf-uz-Zunūn*. The most celebrated of these Commentaries, and the one most generally employed to explain the text, is the *Sharīfia*, by Sayyad Sharīf 'Alī bin-Muhammad-al-Jurjānī. The original text of the *Sirājia*, together with that of the *Sharīfia*, was published in Calcutta in A.D. 1829. A Persian translation of the *Sirājia* and *Sharīfia* was made by Maulwī Muhammad Rāshid, by order of Warren Hastings, and published in Calcutta in A.D. 1812. The most celebrated Commentaries on the *Sirājia*, next after the *Sharīfia*, are: that by Shahāb-uddīn Aḥmad bin-Mahmūd-as-Siwāsī; one by Burhān-uddīn Haidar bin-Muhammad-al-Hirwī; another by Shams-uddīn bin-Hamza-al-Fanārī; and lastly, a Persian Commentary entitled *Al-Farōez-at-Tājīfī Sharh Farāez-as-Sirājī*, by 'Abdul Karīm bin-Muhammad-al-Hamdānī.

Siraj-uddin Muhammad bin-'Umar Halabi (سراج الدين محمد), an author who died in A.D. 1446, A.H. 850.

Siraj-uddin Sawai, Maulana (سراج الدين ساوئي مولانا), one of the celebrated poets of Sāmāna, a city in the province of Dehlī. He is the author of the work called *Khiljī-nāma*. When Sulṭān Jalāl-uddīn Fīroz Khiljī, before his accession to the throne, was governor of Sāmāna, the poet was ill-treated by some of his people, and, as the Sulṭān took no notice of it then, he wrote the above-mentioned book, in which he satirized the governor and the Khiljīs. However, the Sulṭān, after his accession to the throne of Dehlī in A.D. 1289, sent for the poet, and he, having tied a rope round his own neck, presented himself like a criminal before the king, who embraced him and made him one of his principal confidants. The poet afterwards wrote several panegyrics in praise of the Sulṭān.

Siraj-uddin, Shaikh (سراج الدين شيخ), a celebrated Muhammadan saint whose relics are deposited on an island in the river Krishna, near the town of Kursī, in the district of Rāebāgh Bījāpūr, in southern Hindūstān.

Siraj-uddin 'Umar (سراج الدين عمر), who, after the death of his brother Zain-ul-'Abidīn Nujaim, completed the work called *Bahr-ar-Rāeq* about the year A.D. 1562, A.H. 970, and wrote another but inferior commentary on the *Kanz-ul-Daqāeq*, entitled the *Nahr-ul-Fāeq*.

Sirati (سيرتى), a poet who wrote Kasīdas, of which some are panegyrics on Sadiq Khān and his son Jafar Khān Rāzī, kings of Persia, the latter of whom was murdered in A.D. 1785, A.H. 1199.

Soz (سوز), the poetical name of Sayyad Muhammad, who flourished in the reign of the emperor Shāh 'Alam, and is the author of a small Dīwān in Urdū. He became a Dervish or religious mendicant, and lived to the age of 80. He died in A.D. 1797, A.H. 1212. Another Soz is mentioned in the *Mirat-ul-Khayāl*, who lived in the time of 'Alamgīr. He was a native of Bukhārā and was brought up in India.

Sozan (سوزان), poetical appellation of Nawāb Aḥmad 'Alī Khān Shoukat Jang, son of Nawāb Iftikhār-uddaula Mirzā 'Alī Khān, and nephew of Nawāb Sālār Jang. He lived in the time of Nawāb 'Asaf-uddaula of Lucknow, and is said to have been a good Urdū poet.

Sozani, Hakim (سوزنى حكيم), surnamed Shams-uddīn Muhammad of Samarqand, a Persian poet who derived his origin from Salmān Fārsī, one of the first companions of Muhammad. Some authors say he was a native of the city of Nakhshab, and others pretend of Samarqand. It is said that when he was a student at Bukhārā, he conceived so great a friendship for the apprentice of a needle-maker that he himself learned that profession, and he therefore assumed the takhallus of Sozanī (Sozan means a needle). He is considered the best humoristic poet of his time, and is the author of a poem called *Qasāed Sōzanī*, or elegies, written in a very devout style, containing nearly 8000 verses. During his youth he was a great debauchee; but when advanced in years he became very devout, made the pilgrimage of Mecca, and died in A.D. 1173, A.H. 569, at Samarqand, aged 80 years. One of his friends declared that he had appeared to him after his death (in a dream) and said that God had forgiven all his sins for the sake of one of his verses, in which, expressing his humility and contrition, he says, "O Lord, I offer unto Thee an oblation, not to be found in Thy treasury. Accept thou my sins, my poverty, my repentance and my nothingness."

Subaktagin (سبکتگین ناصر الدین), surnamed Nāsir-uddın, a man of Turkish descent (according to the *Tābākāt-i-Nasiri* descended from Yuzdujird, the last Persian king of the Sasanian dynasty), who, according to some historians, was purchased as a slave by Alaptagīn Sulṭān of Ghaznī. The latter, perceiving in him the promise of future greatness, raised him by degrees to posts of confidence and distinction; and his character obtained him the support of all the adherents and officers of that prince. He was raised to the throne of Ghaznī after the death of Abū Is-hāk, the son of Alaptagīn, A.D. 977, A.H. 367. He enlarged its dominions, and became the first of a family, called Ghaznawī, and by us Ghaznavides, which outshone, at one period, the glory of the proudest dynasties of Asiatic monarchs. He conquered a part of India, which, when connected with his former possessions of Ghaznī and Kābul, gave him a kingdom that extended from Khurāsān to the Panjāb. Subaktagīn reigned 20 lunar years, and died in August, A.D. 997, Shaban, A.H. 387, aged 56, near Balkh, from which place his remains were conveyed to Ghaznī for interment. He was succeeded by his son, the celebrated Sulṭān Mahmūd. Including Subaktagīn sixteen kings of his race reigned at Ghaznī and Lāhore. Their names are as follows:—

List of the Ghaznavide dynasty of Persia and India, including Khurāsān, Mawar-un-nahr, Bukhārā, etc. Capital, Ghaznī.

1. Nāsir-uddīn Subaktagīn.
   Ismaīl appointed successor, but displaced by his brother.
2. Sulṭān (Yemin-uddaula Abū'l Qāsim) Mahmūd.
3. Muhammad, his son, deposed instantly and blinded.
   Muhammad, restored and again deposed.
4. Masa'ūd I. another son, deposed and killed.
5. Maudūd, son of Masa'ūd.
6. Masa'ūd II. reigned only six days.
7. Abū'l Hasan 'Alī, son of Masa'ūd I.
8. Abdur Rashīd, son of Mahmūd.
9. Farrukhzad, son of Masa'ūd.
10. Ibrāhīm, his brother.
11. Masa'ūd III. son of Ibrāhīm.
12. Sheizād.
13. Arsalān Shāh.
14. Bahrām Shāh, fled to Lāhore.
15. Khusro Shāh, ruled at Lāhore.
16. Khusro Malik, ruled at Lāhore.

Kings of the family of Ghōr.

Alā-uddīn Hasan Ghorī.
Malik Saif-uddīn.
Ghayās-uddīn Muhammad Ghorī.
Shahāb-uddīn Muhammad Ghorī.
Tāj-uddīn Eldūz.

Subhan Bakhsh, Maulwi (سبحان بخش، مولوی), author of a modern history of jurisprudence, or rather of jurists, in Urdū, compiled from the works of Ibn-Khallikān and Sayūtī, entitled *Tarjuma Tārikh-al-Hukmāe wa Tazkirat-al-Mufassirīn.* It was published at Dehlī in A.D. 1848.

Sub-hani Maulana (سبحانی مولانا), a poet whose native country was Najaf Ashraf, commonly called Kūfa, from which place he never stirred all the time of his life. He lived at the same period in which Shaikh Faizī and Zahūrī flourished, and wrote nothing but Rubāīs in the Persian language on different subjects, of which 12,000 were collected after his death.

Sub-hi (صبحی), a poet who served under Sulṭān Shujāa, the son of Shāh Jahān.

Suchet Singh (سچت سنگه), a Sikh chief, who joined the rebels after the murder of Māhārāja Sheir Singh, was attacked by Hīra Singh, near Lāhore, his force dispersed and himself killed about the 6th April, 1844. On hearing of the death of this chief, no less than 95 females of his family sacrificed themselves at Lamba.

Suda (سوده), daughter of Zamaa, the second wife of Muhammad. He married her after the death of his first wife, Khudyja, and before his marriage with Ayesha, the daughter of Abū Bakr. She died in A.D. 674, A.H. 54, forty-three years after the death of Muhammad.

Sudi (سودی), a Turkish poet who wrote a commentary on the *Dīwān-i-Hāfiz* in the Turkish language. The names of Shorī, Sayyad 'Alī, Lamaī, Surūrī and Shamaī occur also as commentators on *Hāfiz*; but Sūdī excels all as an enlightened and accurate critic, not only on account of his eminent success in correcting the exuberances of this fanciful and extravagant mode of interpretation, but of the singular happiness with which he has illustrated the ambiguous and more obsolete allusions of the poet.

Sufi (سوفی), a sect among the Muhammadans. Kāzī Nūr-ullah of Shustar, a Persian author of very high reputation for his piety and judgment, has given an excellent account of the Sūfīs and their doctrine in the *Majālis-ul-Mominīn*, a treatise on the Shia faith. "The Sufis" (he there says) "are of two classes: those who desire human knowledge and pursue it in the accustomed way, observing the common ordinances of religion, are called Mutakallam (advocates or observers); those who practice austerities and strive to purify their souls, are called Sūfīs." This word literally means *pure, clean.* The celebrated Moulwī Rūmī has the following play upon it in one of his lines: Sūfī na Shawad Sāfī tā dar narasad jamī "The Sūfī will not be pure till he takes one cup." This is said to have a mystical meaning.

Sufi, Mulla Muhammad Sufi of Amol, (صوفی ملا محمد), author of a *Sāqī-nāma*, which he composed in the year A.D. 1592, A.H. 1000.

Sufian Suri (صفیان ثوری), whose proper name was Abū 'Abdullah, was born at Kūfa in A.D. 713, A.H. 95. He was a master of the highest authority in the Traditions and other Sciences. He died in the time of the Khalīfa Al-Mahdī, about the A.D. 777, A.H. 160, and is buried at Basra, where he had concealed himself in order to avoid accepting the office of Qāzī.

Suhyli Khurasani (سهیلی خراسانی), whose full name is Amīr Shaikh Aḥmad Suhylī, also called Niẓām-uddīn Aḥmad Shykham, was seal-bearer to Sulṭān Husain Mirzā of Herāt. The work called *Anwār Suhylī* was dedicated to him by Husain Wāez. He is the author of a Dīwān. His death took place in A.D. 1501, A.H. 907.

Sulaiman (سلیمان), a Khalīf of the house of Umayya, and son of 'Abdulmalik. He succeeded his brother Walīd I. in Syria, A.D. 714, A.H. 96, and died, after a reign of three years, in A.D. 717, A.H. 99.

Sulaiman (سلیمان), the son of Bāiazīd I. (Bajazet) was proclaimed emperor of the Turks in A.D. 1402, A.H. 805, at the time when his father was taken captive by Amīr Taimūr. He displayed great valour, but his glory was tarnished by his excessive love of pleasure. He was dethroned and murdered in A.D. 1410 by his brother Mūsa, who in his turn was defeated and assassinated by another brother, Muhammad I. who ascended the throne in A.D. 1413. This Sulaimān is not reckoned among the Turkish Sulṭāns.

Sulaiman II. Sultan (سلیمان سلطان ثانی), emperor of Turkey, who succeeded his brother Muhammad IV. in A.D. 1687, A.H. 1098, was a very indolent prince. He died in the year A.D. 1691, A.H. 1102, and was succeeded by his brother Aḥmad II.

Sulaiman Badakshi, Mirza (سلیمان بدخشی مرزا), ruler of Badakhshān, was the son of Khān Mirzā, the son of Sulṭān Abū Sa'īd Mirzā, a descendant of Amīr Taimūr. When his father, Khān Mirzā, died in the year A.D. 1521, A.H. 927, he was then only seven years old, consequently that province fell into the hands of the emperor Bābar, who was then in Kābul; he appointed his son Humāyūn to take charge of that country; but when Bābar conquered Dehlī in A.D. 1526, A.H. 932, he, after four years, restored that kingdom to Mirzā Sulaimān, in whose possession it remained till the year A.D. 1575, A.H. 983, when it was usurped by his grandson Shāhrukh Mirzā, the son of Ibrāhīm Mirzā, who intended to assassinate him. Mirzā Sulaimān was obliged to fly to India, where, on his arrival, he was received by the emperor Akbar with the greatest affection and kindness. He subsequently made a pilgrimage to Mecca and returned to India in A.D. 1587, A.H. 995, where, after two years, he died (at Lāhore) on Saturday the 12th July, A.D. 1589, 8th Ramaẓān, A.H. 997, aged 77 lunar years.

Sulaiman Baiza (سلیمان بیضا), an author.

Sulaiman bin-Ahmad (سلیمان بن احمد), author of the book called *Umdat*, a Turkish work on Navigation in the Indian Seas, written in the year A.D. 1511, A.H. 917, and five others of the same description called the *Fawāed*, the *Hawia*, the *Tuhfat-ul-Fahūl*, the *Minhāj*, and the *Qilādat-ul-Shamūs*.

Sulaiman bin-Ahmad Tahrani (سلیمان بن احمد طهرانی), author of the *Muajjam Kabīr*, *Muajjam Ausat*, *Muajjam Saghīr*, *Dalāel-ul-Nabūat*, and many other works. He died in A.D. 971, A.H. 360.

Sulaiman bin-Qutlamish (سلیمان بن قتلمش), by the aid of Malikshāh, who took his father prisoner, Saljūqī became the first king of the Saljūq dynasty of Rūm, or Anatolia, whose capital was Iconium. He began his reign in A.D. 1077, A.H. 470, reigned eight years, and destroyed himself through fear of Takash, or Turtash, the son of Alp Arsalān. After him there was an interregnum of seven years, from A.D. 1085 to 1092, when his son Dāūd ascended the throne.

Kings of the Saljūq dynasty who reigned in Iconium.

1. Sulaimān bin-Kutlamish.
2. Daūd, son of Sulaimān, having gained a victory over his enemies, ascended the throne in A.D. 1092, and died in A.D. 1107.
3. Qulich Arsalān, his brother, who, in a battle with Atābak Jāwalī, fell into a canal with his horse and was drowned, A.D. 1116.
4. Masa'ūd, son of Qulich Arsalān, died in A.D. 1156.
5. 'Azz-uddīn Qulich Arsalān, son of Masa'ūd. He destroyed the first Crusade army and died in A.D. 1188.
6. Quṭb-uddīn Malikshāh, son of 'Azz-uddīn, deposed in A.D. 1192.
7. Ghayās-uddīn Kaikhusro, son of 'Azz-uddīn, deposed in A.D. 1200.

Ghayās-uddīn Kaikhusro, restored A.D. 1203.
8. Rukn-uddīn Sulaimān, son of 'Azz-uddīn Qulich Arsalān, deposed in A.D. 1203.
9. Qizal or Qulich Arsalān, son of Rukn-uddīn, deposed by Ghayās-uddīn Kāikhusro in A.D. 1203.
10. 'Azz-uddīn Kaikāūs bin-Kaikhusro began to reign in A.D. 1210 and was deposed in A.D. 1219.
11. 'Alā-uddīn Kaiqubād bin-Kaikhusro, poisoned in A.D. 1236 or 1239.
12. Kaikhusro, son of Kaiqubād. He was invaded by the Mughal princes, descendants of Changez Khān.
'Azz-uddīn Kaikāūs, restored and reigned in nominal conjunction with his brothers Rukn-uddīn and 'Alā-uddīn, sons of Kaikhusro, A.D. 1245.
13. Rukn-uddīn Qulīch Arsalān, son of Kaikhusro, began in A.D. 1257.
14. Ghayās-uddīn Kaikhusro, son of Rukn-uddīn, began A.D. 1267.
15. Masa'ūd bin-'Azz-uddīn Kaikāūs, died in A.D. 1308, A.H. 708. He was the last of this race.

Sulaiman Qadr, Mirza (سلیمان قدر), a prince, the son of Mirzā Khurshaid Qadr, the son of Mirzā Asmān Qadr. Their poetical titles were Taskhīr, Kaisar and Namūd.

[*Vide* Kaisar.]

Sulaiman Qirani (سلیمان قرانی) was made governor of Bengal after the deposition of Bahādur Shāh Afghān in A.D. 1549, A.H. 956, but threw off his allegiance to the throne of Dehlī after the death of Salīm Shāh, king of Dehlī, A.D. 1554, A.H. 961. During his rule he subdued the province of Orissa; and, notwithstanding he was virtually independent, he used frequently to send valuable presents to the emperor Akbar. He reigned for a period of 25 lunar years, and died in A.D. 1572, A.H. 981. His eldest son, Bāiazīd Khān, succeeded him, but was murdered one month afterwards, and Dāūd Khān, his younger brother, ascended the throne with the title of Dāūd Shāh.

Sulaiman Shah (سلیمان شاه), the son of Muhammad Malikshāh, the Saljūkide. He was much addicted to pleasure and wine, and resigned his crown to Arsalān Shāh, the son of Tughral II. He was killed in A.D. 1159.

Sulaiman Shah (سلیمان شاه), king of Persia. [*Vide* Shāh Sulaimān.]

Sulaiman Shikoh (سلیمان شکوه), the eldest son of the prince Dārā Shikōh, the son of the emperor Shāh Jahān. He was born on the 5th April, A.D. 1635, 26th Ramazān, A.H. 1044. After the defeat and assassination of his father in A.D. 1659, A.H. 1069, he was seized and brought to Dehlī by the officers of 'Alamgīr from Sirīnagar, where he had taken refuge, and imprisoned by that emperor, along with his brother Sipehr Shikōh, in the fort of Gwāliar, where they both died one after the other and were buried in the fort. Sulaimān had a house built at Āgra close to his father's palace.

Sulaiman Shikoh, Mirza (سلیمان شکوه مرزا), the son of the emperor Shāh 'Alam and brother of Akbar Shāh II. king of Dehlī. He died on the 24th February, A.D. 1838, 29th Zil-Qa'da, A.H. 1253, at Āgra, and was buried in the mausoleum of Akbar the Great at Sikandara, in Āgra. His tomb is of white marble and has a Persian inscription mentioning his name and the year of his death. He has left a Dīwān in Urdū.

Sulaiman Sultan (سلیمان سلطان), surnamed the Magnificent, was the son of Salīm I. whom he succeeded as emperor of the Turks in September, A.D. 1520, Shawwāl, A.H. 926. His reign was splendid. He defeated the Mamlūks in Egypt, and made peace with Shāh Ismā'īl I. Safwī, king of Persia, after which he carried his arms against Europe and took Belgrade. In 1522 he attacked Rhodes and took it, and then invaded Hungary and defeated the Hungarians at Mohatz in 1526. The conquest of Buda was followed by the siege of Vienna, but, after twenty unsuccessful assaults, he retreated with the loss of 80,000 men. In 1534 he made war against Shāh Tahmāsp Safwī, and invaded Tauris and Persia, but suffered a defeat. Later, he was disappointed in his attack on Malta. He died on the 4th September, A.D. 1566, Ṣafar, A.H. 974, having lived 76 solar years and reigned 46. He was a prince more just and true to his word than any other of his predecessors, but a great terror to all Christians. His son Sulṭān Salīm II. succeeded him.

Sultan Ahmad bin-Masa'ud (سلطان احمد), author of the Arabic work called *Asmāi-ul-Rijāl*.

Sultan Ahmad Jalayer (سلطان احمد جلیار). *Vide* Hasan Buzurg.

Sultan Ahmad Mirza (سلطان احمد مرزا). Aḥmad Mirzā (Sulṭān).

Sultan 'Ali Khurasani (سلطان علی خراسانی), author of the Persian work on Medicine called *Dastūr-ul-Ilāj*, which he wrote in A.D. 1334, A.H. 734, and dedicated to Sulṭan Abū Sạid Bahādur Khān.

Sultan 'Ali Mashhadi (سلطان علی مشہدی), a native of Mashhad. He was not so much distinguished as a poet as he was a caligrapher. He was in caligraphy a pupil of Maulānā Azhar, who was a pupil of Ja'far, and Ja'far was a pupil of Maulāna Mīr 'Alī, the inventor of the Naskhta'līq. Maulānā Sulṭān 'Alī lived at the court of Mirzā Bāiqara, and found a patron in Amīr 'Alīshir. He was upwards of 63 years of age in A.D. 1550, A.H. 957.

Sultan Husain Mirza (سلطان حسین مرزا), surnamed Abū'l Ghāzī Bahādur, was the son of Mirzā Mansūr, the son of Mirzā Bāiqara, the son of Mirzā 'Umar Shaikh, the son of Amīr Taimūr. After the death of Sulṭān Abū Sa'īd Mirzā, he contrived to make himself master of Khurāsān, and ascended the throne at Herāt on the 24th March, A.D. 1469, 10th Ramaẓan, A.H. 873. The great victories which this prince gained over the numerous competitors for the throne, as well as over the Uzbaks, obtained him the title of Ghāzī, or victorious. The court of this prince boasted of many eminent men. The celebrated historian Khandamīr was his subject, and Amīr 'Alīshir his wazīr. He reigned in Khurāsān 38 lunar years and 4 months, and died, according to the Tābkāt Akbarī, on the 10th May, A.D. 1506, corresponding with the 16th Ẓil-ḥijja, A.H. 911, aged 70 years, and was buried at Herāt. He was succeeded by his two sons Badīu'zzamān Mirzā and Muẓaffar Husain Mirzā, who reigned conjointly for some time over Khurāsān. The former in the year A.D. 1507, A.D. 913, was driven from his dominions by Shāsī Beg Khān Uzbak; and his brother, who usurped the throne and reigned a short time at Herāt, afterwards shared the same fate. Sulṭān Husain Mirzā is the author of the work called *Majālis-ul-Ishq*, a very entertaining work, containing a variety of stories, principally on the subject of love. He had a turn for poetry, and composed a Dīwān in Turkī. His poetical name was Husainī.

Sultan Husain Safwi (سلطان حسین صفوی). *Vide* Shāh Husain Safwī.

Sultan Ibrahim (سلطان ابراهیم). *Vide* Ibrāhīm (Sulṭān).

Sultan Khusro (سلطان خسرو). *Vide* Khusro (Sulṭān).

Sultan Mahmud (سلطان محمود). *Vide* Mahmūd (Sulṭān) of Ghaznī.

Sultan Mahmud Mirza (سلطان محمود مرزا), the son of Sulṭān Abū Saīd Mirzā, who was sovereign of the greater part of Mawar-un-nahr and Badakhshān. His takhallus or poetical name was Zillī.

Sultan Mirza (سلطان مرزا). *Vide* Muhammad Sulṭān Mirzā.

Sultan Muhammad (سلطان محمد بن عالمگیر), the eldest son oı the emperor 'Alamgīr. He died, 30 years before his father, on the 5th December, A.D. 1676, 8th Shawwāl, A.H. 1087, in the fort of Gwāliar, where he was confined by his father, and was buried near the mausoleum of Quṭb-uddin, called Quṭb Shāh, at Dehlī.

Sultan Muhammad (سلطان محمد بن مرزا بایسنغر), the son of Mirzā Bāisanghar, the son of Mirzā Shāhrukh, the son of Amīr Taimūr. He was defeated in a battle against his brother Bābar Sulṭān, taken prisoner and put to death in January, A.D. 1452, Ẓil-ḥijja, A.H. 855.

Sultan Muhammad Saljuqi (سلطان محمد بن جلال الدین ملکشاه), the son of Sulṭān Jalāl-uddīn Malikshāh. He succeeded his brother Barkayāraq in December, A.D. 1104, A.H. 498, and after a reign of about 13 years died in A.D. 1118, A.H. 511.

[*Vide* Muhammad (Sulṭān).]

Sultan Murad (سلطان مراد). *Vide* Murad Mirzā.

Sultan Parwez (سلطان پرویز). *Vide* Parwez Sulṭān.

Sultan Sakhi Sarwar (سلطان ساخی سروار), a Muhammadan saint. His shrine is situated at the mouth of the Sierī Pass, leading in the direction of Kāndahar, and is built at the *Dāmanphār*. Though not much reverenced in the Dehrājat it is said that from 180,000 to 200,000 pilgrims, both Musalmāns and Hundūs, from the Panjāb and Sindh visit it annually. In February, March, and April disciples assemble in large numbers, and the fair is over in April.

Sultan Shah (سلطان شاه), son of Alp Arsalān, Sulṭān of Khwārizm. Some time after his father's death, which took place in A.D. 1162, A.H. 557, he was defeated in several battles by his elder brother, Alā-uddīn Takash, and obliged to fly to the forests, where he died from hunger and distress, about the year A.D. 1193, Ramaẓān, A.D. 589.

Sultan Shahzada (سلطان شهزاده), an eunuch of Fatha Shāh, king of Bengal, whom he murdered, and ascended the throne A.D. 1491, A.H. 896. He reigned only a few months and was assassinated the same year by Malik Andīl, who succeeded him and took the title of Fīrōz Shāh Pūrbī.

Sultan Shujaa' (سلطان شجاع بن شاهجهان), second son of the emperor Shāh Jahān, was born at Ajmīr on Sunday the 12th May, A.D. 1616, 4th Jumāda I. A.H. 1025, and married to the daughter of Mirzā Rustam Safwī, brother of Muzaffar Husain Mirzā, of the royal house of Persia. He was appointed governor of Bengal by his father, which country he governed with justice and clemency till the accession of his brother the emperor 'Alamgīr and the defeat of Dārā Shikōh in A.D. 1658, when he marched with a powerful army towards Dehlī. He was defeated by 'Alamgīr on the 5th January, A.D. 1659, 19th Rabi' II. A.H. 1069, at a place called Khajūa, about thirty miles west of Allahābād, and pursued by Mīr Jumla and Sulṭān Muhammad, the eldest son of 'Alamgīr, to Bengal, from which place he was obliged to seek refuge in Arakan, where, two years afterwards, A.D. 1660, A.H. 1071, he was put in a boat with all his family and sunk in the river by order of the Rāja of that country.

Sultan-ul-Nisa Begam (سلطان النسا), eldest daughter of the emperor Jahāngīr, and sister of Sulṭān Khusro. Her mother was the daughter of Rāja Bhagwān Dās, and she was born in the year A.D. 1586, A.H. 994. After the death of her brother Sulṭān Khusrau, she erected a tomb for herself close to his grave at Allahābād, but died at Āgra and lies buried there in the mausoleum of the emperor Akbar.

Sultan-us-Salatin Purbi (سلطان السلاطين) was elevated to the throne of Bengal on the death of his father, Ghayās-uddīn Pūrbī, A.D. 1373, A.H. 775. This prince was benevolent, merciful and brave. He died, after a reign of ten years, A.D 1383, A.H. 785, and was succeeded by his son Shams-uddīn II. Pūrbī.

Sultan Walad (سلطان ولد), son of the celebrated Maulwī Rūmī. He is the author of a beautiful poem on the Sūfī doctrines, etc., written in imitation of the Masnawī of his father, A.D. 1291, A.H. 690, and also of a Dīwān, and another work called *Walad-nāma*, containing an account of his father and grandfather.

Sultana Begam (سلطانه بیگم), a daughter of the emperor Bābar Shāh.

Sultana Begam (سلطانه بیگم), a daughter of Mirzā Handāl, the brother of the emperor Humāyūn. She was married to Shāh Qulī Mahram. Her sister named Ruqia Sulṭāna (*q.v.*) was married to the emperor Akbar.

Sultana Razia (سلطانه رضيه), daughter of Shams-uddīn Altimsh, king of Dehlī. She was raised to the throne after the deposition of her brother Rukn-uddīn Fīrōz in November, A.D. 1236. She was deposed in November, A.D. 1239, and confined in the fort of Bitahnda, from which place she made her escape and contrived to raise an army with which she marched towards Dehlī; but was defeated and put to death by her brother Bahrām Shāh, who ascended the throne. The reign of Sulṭāna Razia lasted 3 lunar years 6 months and 6 days. Her tomb is still to be seen in old Dehlī.

Sultana Rukia or Ruqia (سلطانه رقيه), the daughter of Mirzā Handal (*q.v.*), the son of the emperor Bābar, was the first or chief wife of the emperor Akbar, by whom he had no children. Consequently when Shāh Jahān was born to Jahāngīr, his grandfather Akbar made him over to her to be brought up by her. She was also the patroness of Nūr Jahān; and died at Āgra in January, A.D. 1626, Jumāda I. A.H. 1035, aged 84 lunar years.

Sunna (سنا). This word is used generally to signify all the traditions, both of the sayings and doings of the Prophet, and the term Hadīs is employed in the same comprehensive sense. The distinction between the Hadīs (sayings) and the Sunan (doings) is not attended to by doctors of the Muslim law; both are generally authoritative.

Sunni (سنی). Those Musalmāns who assume to themselves the appellation of orthodox, and uphold the succession of the Khalīfas Abū Bakr, Umar, and Usmān, and deny the right of supremacy, either spritual or temporal, to the posterity of 'Alī, are called Sunnīs. They are divided into an infinity of sects, but of these there are only four principal ones, which are called after their founders.

[*Vide* Imām and Shia.]

Sunqar or **Sanqar** (سنقر), son of Maudūd, one of the Atābaks of Fars, who is better known by his title of Atābak Muzaffar-uddīn, was the great-grandson of Salghar, the founder of this dynasty. He succeeded Būzāba, the last governor of Fars of this family, and threw off all dependence upon the Saljūqī Sultāns about the year A.D. 1148, A.H. 543. He made his residence the city of Shīrāz, which afterwards became the capital of his family. He died in A.D. 1161, A.H. 556, and was succeeded by his brother

Muzaffar-uddīn Zangī, who, after a peaceful reign of 14 years, left the government to his son Takla in A.D. 1175, A.H. 571.

Takla, who acquired fame by employing, as his wazīr, the victorious Khwāja Amīn-uddīn of Gāzarūn, reigned 20 years, and at his death, which happened in A.D. 1195, A.H. 591, the government of Fars fell to his brother

Atābak Sa'd bin-Zangī, who made a successful attack upon Isfahān. The memory of Atābak Sa'd is to this day held in great respect at Shīrāz. He surrounded that city by a wall, and built the Jām'a Masjid, or chief mosque, which still remains a monument of his piety and munificence. He reigned more than 30 lunar years, and died about the year A.D. 1226, A.H. 623. He was succeeded by his son

Atābak Abū Bakr, also called Abū Nasr, a son every way worthy of his father. He gave an extraordinary proof of his foresight in his early conciliation of Changez Khān, to whom he sent a mission and some valuable presents. The conqueror received the advance with favour, conferred the Turkish title of Kutlaq Khān upon him; and the province of Fars, through the wisdom of its prince, was exempted from that destruction which fell on all those in its vicinity. In his time lived the celebrated Sa'dī of Shīrāz, who wrote the *Gulistān* in his name. Abū Bakr died at Shīrāz in A.D. 1260, 5th Jumāda II. A.H. 658, after a long and prosperous reign of 34 years, and left his government to his son. Daulat Shāh says he died in A.H. 667.

Atābak Sa'd II. who, at the time of his father's death, was with the army of Halākū Khan, the grandson of Changez Khān, hastened to take possession of his inheritance, but was seized with an illness, which terminated his existence before he could reach his capital. His infant son

Atābak Muhammad was placed upon the masnad; and the rule devolved upon the child's mother, Khātūn Turkān; but her authority received a great shock in the death of her son, who, two years and a half after his advancement, fell from the terrace of his palace, and was killed on the spot, A.D. 1262, A.H. 660. After his death

Muhammad Shāh, a chief of the family of Salghar, was elevated to the dignity of Atābak, but Khātūn Turkān, after eight months, being displeased with his conduct, seized him and sent him prisoner to Halākū Khān; while she elevated his brother Saljūq Shāh to the government.

Saljūq Shāh, with a view of confirming his power, married Khātūn Turkān; but afterwards, in a fit of intoxication, ordered one of his slaves to strike off her head. Some officers of the emperor Halākū Khān, who were present, expressed their feelings at this horrid act and were instantly put to death. When Halākū heard of these proceedings, he immediately ordered the execution of his brother Muhammad. Saljūq, dreading the vengeance of the emperor, fled to Kāzarūn: but was seized and put to death, A.D. 1263, A.H. 661.

Īsh, the daughter of Atābak Sad, who reigned one year, was married to Mangū Taimūr, the son of Halākū, which put an end to this family, which lasted 120 lunar years.

Supkaran or **Subhkaran Bundela** (سبہکرن بندیله), a Rājpūt, who was an Amīr of 2500 in the service of the emperor 'Alamgīr. He died at Bahādurgarh in the Deccan about the year A.D. 1678, A.H. 1089, and was much lamented by all who knew him. Many of his women buried themselves upon the funeral pile with his corpse. He was a soldier unequalled, had in repeated battles won the prize of valour, and was in general successful. After his death his son Dalpat Rāo was exalted to the rank of 500 by the emperor.

Suqman bin-Ortak (سقمان بن ارتک), first king of the princes of the Turkmān Ortakites, who reigned at Amid and Khaifa. The following is a list of this race:—

	A.D.	A.H.
Suqmān bin-Ortak	1097	490
Ibrāhīm bin-Suqmān	1104	498
Rukn-uddīn Dāūd	1128	522
Fakhr-uddīn Qarā Arsalān bin-Dāūd	1149	544
Nūr-uddīn Muhammad bin-Qarā Arsalān	1166	562
Qutb-uddīn Suqmān bin-Muhammad	1185	581
Malik-us-Salāh Nāsir-uddīn Mahmūd	1200	597
Malik-ul-Masaūd bin-Mahmūd .	1221	618
Malik-ul-Kāmil, nephew of the celebrated Sālah-uddīn (Saladin). He took Amid	1231	629

Surajmal Jat (سورجمل جات), Rāja of Bhartpūr, was the son of Badan Singh Jāt, whom he succeeded to the Rāj a few years before A.D. 1750, A.H. 1163. His younger brother, Partap Singh, built the fort of Kumbhīr or Kumīr. After the departure of Ahmad Shāh Abdālī from India to Qandahār, Sūrajmal, taking advantage of the weakness of the empire, made himself master of all the countries that were dependent on Āgra, and ultimately of the town itself and many other important places; but fell in battle with the Rohela chief Najīb-uddaula in December, A.D. 1763, A.H. 1177. His son Jawāhir Singh succeeded him.

Suraj Singh, Raja (سورج سنگه راجه), son of Udai Singh Rathor, the son of Rāe Maldeo. After the death of his father, A.D. 1594, A.H. 1002, he was raised by Akbar to a suitable rank, and served under that emperor and his son Jahāngīr for several years. The mansab of 5000 was conferred on him by the latter. He died in the Deccan, A.D. 1619, A.H. 1028, and Rāja Gaj Singh, his son, succeeded him, and, as his father was uncle to the emperor Shāh Jahān on the mother's side, he was in a short time raised to the rank of 5000. Gaj Singh died on the 6th May, A.D. 1638, 2nd Muharram, A.H. 1048. His son Amar Singh killed Salābat Khān Mīr Bakhshī in A.D. 1624, A.H. 1054, and was himself cut to pieces at one of the gates of the fort of Āgra, now called Amar Singh Gate.

Surdas (سورداس), son of Bābā Rāmdās, a Hīndū poet and an excellent musician, who flourished about the 16th or 17th century. He is the author of the work called *Sūr Sāgar*, in Hindī, etc.

Surur (سرور), poetical name of Mirzā Rajab 'Alī Beg of Lucknow. He is the author of a Dīwān and several other works and of a beautiful story in Urdū called *Fisāna Ajāeb*, which he completed in the first year of the reign of Nasīr-uddīn Haidar, A.D. 1828, A.H. 1244.

Surur (سرور), the poetical name of Lachhmī Rām.

Sururi (سروری), poetical name of Hājī Muhammad, a poet, who died in A.D. 1561, A.H. 969. He was the son of a shoemaker, and had so excellent a memory that he knew more than 30,000 verses by heart. He composed a dictionary called *Mujma-ul-Furs*, and a book in which he explains the difficult words of Nizāmī and other poets. He also wrote a Commentary in the Turkish language on the Dīwān of Hafiz.

[*Vide* Muhammad Qāsim, son of Surūrī.]

Sururi (سروری), poetical appellation of Razī-uddīn, a brother of Maftūn. He is the author of several Persian poems, besides which he has composed from ten to twelve thousand Urdū verses. He was alive in A.D. 1796, A.H. 1211.

Suryya Jah (ثریا جاه). *Vide* Amjad 'Alī Shāh, king of Audh.

Swami Bhopat Rae (سوامی بهوپت رای), a Khattrī who resided at Patan, near Jammū, in the Panjāb. He translated, from the Sanskrit into Persian, the *Prabodh Chand* (*Chandrodaya*) *Nātak*, a very curious work on Theosophy, and dedicated it, as well as several other treatises on Sūfīism, to Narāyan Chand.

T

Taban (تابان), the poetical name of Mīr 'Abdul Hai, of Dehlī, a youth whose extraordinary beauty was the theme of contemporary poets, and of whose personal charms it is related that they were the envy of the other sex and the admiration of all who beheld him. He was slain at an early age in consequence of having himself formed a very unbecoming attachment. His odes are held in high estimation for delicacy and elegance of sentiment, and even the poet Sauda was among the number of his admirers. He lived in the time of the emperor Muhammad Shāh.

[*See* Gilchrist's *Hindūstānī Grammar.*]

Tabari (طبری), a celebrated historian of Tabaristān, and author of the *Tārīkh Tabarī*. He was a famous Imām of Baghdād, and the Livy of the Arabians. He finished his *General History* in A.D. 914, A.H. 302. At the request of his friends he reduced his work of 30,000 sheets to a more reasonable size. He died A.D. 922, A.H. 310.

[*Vide* Abū Jafar-at-Tabarī, and Abū Alī, the wazīr of Mansūr.]

Taba Taba (طبا طبا), a poet whose proper name was Mīr Rafī-uddīn Husain, a Sayyad, who, being of the Tabātabā tribe, used it as his poetical name. He was living in A.D. 1601, A.H. 1010.

Tabiat (طبیعت), poetical name of Shaikh Saif-uddīn Muhammad, a poet who lived in A.D. 1742, A.H. 1155.

Tadbir (تدبیر), poetical title of Prince Sikandar Kadr.

Tadrawi or **Tazrawi Ab-hari** (تدروی), a nephew of Nargisī. He came from Rome to India, died there A.D. 1567, A.H. 975, and was buried at Āgra. He is the author of a memoir or Masnawī called *Risāla Hasan-o-Yūsaf Muhammad Khān.*

Tafazzul Husain Khan (تفضل حسین خان), the rebel Nawāb of Farrukhābad. He was the grandson and successor of Muzaffar Jang, also called Muzaffar Husain Khān. This man, a British protegé, caused, or sanctioned, the murder of sixty-two Englishmen, women, and children, during the insurrection of 1857, under circumstances of the most cold-blooded atrocity. After months of unavailing pursuit, Major Barrow, Commissioner of the district of Audh, to which he had fled, offered him his life, provided he had himself committed no murders. The Nawāb surrendered, was tried, found guilty, and sentenced to death. The Governor-General, however, while fully coinciding in the verdict, held that the word of a British officer must be maintained, declared the criminal exempt from the punishment of death, on the condition that he should immediately quit the British territory for ever. If, ran the order, he accept this condition, he will be conveyed to the frontier as a convict, under a military guard, and there set at liberty. If he refuse the condition, it was added, or, if having accepted it, he shall break it, or attempt to break it, now, or at any future time, the capital sentence pronounced upon him will be carried out. The Nawāb elected to be sent to Mecca. Accordingly on the 23rd May, A.D. 1859, he was taken to the Magistrate's office under a European guard, and there fettered. He was allowed to see his children but not his wife. Two hundred men of the Fathagarh Levy were ordered to guard him to Bombay, on his way to Mecca.

Tafta (تفتہ), poetical name of Munshī Hargopāl of Sikandarābād, by caste a Kāyeth. He is the author of a Persian Dīwān, which he completed and published in the Lithographic Press at Āgra in A.D. 1851, A.H. 1267, and of a parody on the verses of the *Gulistān* in verse, entitled *Tazmīn Gulistān*, published in A.D. 1858, A.H. 1274.

Taftazani or **Tuftazani** (تفتازانی), which is sometimes erroneously written Tughtāzānī, is the surname of an author, who was called so from his birth-place, a city in Khurāsān. His proper name is Mulla Sad-uddīn Masaūd bin 'Umar. He is the author of the Commentaries on the *Maāzid*, *'Aqāed* and *Kashshāf*; and also of the *Sharah Sharaf Zanjānī*, *Mutouwal*, which he dedicated to Malik Husain Kart, and *Mukhtasir Talkhīs*, dedicated to Jānī Beg. There is another work, entitled *Sharah Hallāj*, which is also attributed to him. In the latter part of his life he served under Tamerlane and died at Samarqand. According to the *Muntakhib-*

ut-Tawārīkh he was born in A.D. 1322, A.H. 722, and died on the 10th January, A.D. 1390, 22nd Muharram, A.H. 792, but, according to Hājī Khalfa, in A.H. 791.

Taghallub (تغلب), a learned and pious Musalmān, whose proper name was Abū'l Abbās Ahmad. He was the Imām of the inhabitants of Kūfa, and died at Baghdād in the year A.D. 903, A.H. 290.

Tahawi or Al-Tahawi (طحاوی). *Vide* Abū Jafar bin-Muhammad Tabāwī.

Tahir (طاهر), the grandson of Amrū bin-Lais, which see.

Tahir and Ghani (طاهر غنی), poetical names of Mirzā Muhammad Tāhir, commonly called Ghanī Kashmīrī, which see.

Tahir I. or Tahir ibn-Husain-al-Khuzai' (طاهر ابن حسین الخذاعی), surnamed Yeminain (Ambidexter). He was one of Al-Māmūn's ablest supporters and one of the greatest generals of his age. He defeated and slew 'Alī ibn-Isā in battle, A.D. 811, A.H. 195, and sent his head as a present to the Khalīf Al-Māmūn, his employer, who amply rewarded Tāhir for his services. And when that prince was residing at Marv, the capital of Khurāsān, he revolted against his brother Al-Amīn, the Khalīf of Baghdād, and despatched Tāhir with an army to attack him at Baghdād, which place he took in A.D. 813, Safar, A.H. 198, and, having slain Al-Amīn, sent his head to Khurāsān, that it might be presented to Al-Māmūn, his brother, who conferred the government of Khurāsān upon Tāhir and his descendants with almost absolute and unlimited power. Tāhir died on Saturday the 15th November, A.D. 822, 24th Jumāda II. A.H. 207, at Marv, and his son Talha was appointed wazīr in his room. The following is a list of his descendants:

Tāhir I. died A.D. 823, A.H. 207.
Talha, his son.
'Abdullāh, son of Tāhir, died A.D. 845, A.H. 230.
Tāhir II. son of 'Abdullāh.
Muhammad, son of Tāhir II. and last prince of this race.

Tahir II. (طاهر ابن عبدالله), great-grandson of Tāhir I. and son of 'Abdullāh, whom he succeeded in the government of Khurāsān in the reign of Al-Mustain Billāh, and died a natural death. He was succeeded by his son Muhammad, the last prince of this race.

Tahir Abiwardi (طاهر ابیوردی), a poet who flourished in the time of Sultān Bāisanghar.

Tahir-al-Azaz din Allah (طاهر ال لاعز دین الله), son of Hākim Abū Mansūr, succeeded his father, A.D. 1020, on the throne of Egypt. He reigned 15 years, and left his crown to a son under seven years of age, named al-Mustanasar Billāh. Tāhir died in A.D. 1036, A.H. 427.

Tahir bin-Ahmad-al-Bukhari, Imam Iftikhar-uddin (طاهر بن احمد البخاری), author of a work on Ilm-ul-Fatāwā, or science of decisions, entitled the *Khulāsat-ul-Fatāwā*, a select collection of decisions of great authority. He was also the author of the *Khazīnat-ul-Waqiāt* and the *Kitāb-an-Nisāb*, on which books the *Khulāsat* was grounded, and to which many subsequent collections are indebted for numerous valuable cases. He died A.D. 1147, A.H. 542.

Tahir Billah (طاهر بالله). *Vide* Al-Tāhir Bi-amrullah, a Khalīf of Baghdād.

Tahir Bukhari (طاهر بخاری), a very pious Musalmān of Bukhārā, and an excellent poet, who flourished in the reign of Sultān Bābar of Herāt.

Tahir Muhammad bin-Imad-uddin Hasan bin-Sultan 'Ali bin-Haji Muhammad Husain Sabzwari (طاهر محمد بن عماد الدین حسن). He is the author of the history called *Rauzat-ut-Tāhirīn*, the Garden of the Immaculate. It is a general history and was commenced in A.D. 1602, A.H. 1011, three years before the death of Akbar, and concluded in A.D. 1606, A.H. 1015. Sir H. M. Elliot, in his *Historians of India*, calls it the *Rauzat-us-Safā*. This is evidently a mistake, for that book was written by Mīr Khāwand Shāh, who died in A.D. 1498.

Tahir Wahid, Mirza (طاهر وحید مرزا), son of Husain Khān Qazwīnī, commonly called Wākaa Nawīs, the news-writer, was one of the greatest poets of the age. He was historigrapher of Shāh Abbās II. and afterwards wazīr to Shāh Sulaimān, kings of Persia. Mirzā Sāeb, who died in A.D. 1669, was one of his contemporaries. Tāhir Wahīd is the author of a Dīwān containing 60,000 verses, and of a history of the Safwī kings of Persia. One of his works, which he wrote in A.D. 1656, A.H. 1066, is called *Mirat-ul-Ai'jaz*, and one, which contains letters written by him for the king of Persia, goes after his name, and is called *Tāhir Wahīd.* He died in A.D. 1696, A.H. 1108.

Tahmasp I. Shah Safavi (طهماسپ شاه صفوی), king of Persia, was born on Wednesday the 22nd February, A.D. 1514, 26th Ẕil-ḥijja, A.H. 919, and succeeded his father, Shāh Ismā'īl I. to the throne of Persia, on the 24th May, A.D. 1524, 19th Rajab, A.H. 930, when he was ten years of age. The reign of this prince owes much of its celebrity to the truly royal and hospitable reception he gave to the emperor Humāyūn (*q.v.*), A.D. 1543, when that monarch was forced to fly from India, and to take shelter in his dominions. All the means of the kingdom were called forth to do honour to the royal guest; and they were as liberally furnished to replace him upon his throne. Shāh Tahmāsp died at the age of 64 after a reign of more than 53 lunar years, on Tuesday the 15th May, A.D. 1576, 15th Ṣafar, A.H. 984. His fourth son, Ismaīl Mirzā, succeeded him. According to his own request he was buried at Mashhad.

Tahmasp II. Shah Safavi (طهماسپ شاه صفوی), king of Persia, was the son of Sulṭān Husain. He assumed the title of king of Persia after the confinement of his father by Mahmūd the Afghān chief, and struggled a few years with his fate; but a weak, effeminate, and debauched youth was unsuited for such times; and he only merits a place in history as his name furnished a pretext for the celebrated Nādir, or Tahmāsp, Qulī Khān to lay the foundations of his great power. He was confined at Sabzwār in Khurāsān, and put to death by Razā Qulī Khān, the son of Nādir Shāh, who was then absent on his expedition to India in A.D. 1739, A.H. 1151.

Tahmasp Quli, Mirza (طهماسپ قلی مرزا), a Turk, and an excellent poet, who flourished in the time of the emperor Shāh Jahān, and wrote a beautiful chronogram consisting of nineteen verses in Persian on the marriage of the emperor's eldest son, Dārā Shikōh, each hemistich of which gives the year A.D. 1633, A.H. 1043.

Tahmurs (طهمرث), commonly called Deoband or the Magician binder, a title which he derived from the success with which he warred against the enemies of his family. He succeeded his father, Hoshang, and was the third king of Persia of the first or Pishdadian dynasty. He governed Persia 30 years, and was succeeded by his nephew, the famous Jamshed.

Tahsin (تحسین), poetical name of Mīr Muhammad 'Atā Husain Khān, of Lucknow, who lived in the court of Nawāb Mansūr 'Alī Khān, Safdar Jang, and had the title of Murassa Raqam. His father, Mīr Muhammad Bākir, whose poetical name was Shauq, was also a learned man and a poet. Tahsīn is the author of the works called *Zawābit Angreizī*, *Tawārīkh Qāsimī*, *Inshāe Tahsīn*, and of the *Nautarz Murassa*, an Urdū version of the Four Darweishes, which he wrote in the commencement of the reign of Nawāb 'Asaf-uddaula, about the year A.D. 1775.

[*Vide* 'Atā Husain Khān.]

Tahsin 'Ali Khan (تحسین علی خان خواجه سرا), an eunuch of Nawāb 'Asaf-uddaula, of Lucknow. He died in the time of Nawāb Sa'ādat 'Alī Khān, in August, A.D. 1813, Shabān, A.H. 1228.

Taimur (تیمور). *Vide* Amīr Taimūr.

Taimur Shah (تیمور شاه), the eldest son of Aḥmad Shāh Abdālī, succeeded his father to the throne of Qābul and Qandahār in A.D. 1772, A.H. 1186, after murdering Shāh Walī Khān, his father's wazīr, who intended to crown his son-in-law, prince Sulaimān, a younger brother of Taimūr. He reigned 20 years over Qābul, Qandahār, and Khurāsān, and died 17th May, A.D. 1793, 7th Shawwāl, A.H. 1207, aged 47 years. He left several sons, *viz.* Humāyūn Shāh, Zamān Shāh, Mahmūd Shāh, Shāh Shuja'ā, Fīroz Shāh, Abbās, and Ayyūb. On Taimūr's death a powerful faction, headed by his favourite wife and supported by Pāinda Khān, entitled Sarfarāz Khān, the head of the Barakzaī family, placed Shāh Zamān upon the throne, at Qābul; Humāyūn, the elder brother, proclaimed himself king of Qandahār, and Mahmūd became the ruler of Herāt.

Taimur Sultan (تیمور سلطان), the successor of Shaibānī Khān, the chief of the Uzbaks, after whose death in A.D. 1510, A.H. 919, he took possession of Samarqand, and Jānī Beg Khān and 'Abdullāh Khān divided Bukhārā between themselves.

Tajalli (تجلی), poetical title of 'Alī Razā, an encomiast of 'Aqā Husain Khwānsārī. He is the author of a poem called *Mʿrāj-ul-Khayāl*. He died in A.D. 1677, A.H. 1088.

Tajara Begam (تاجارا بیگم), the mother of Wājid 'Alī, the ex-king of Lucknow, who proceeded to England after the annexation of Audh to the British possessions; and died in France in A.D. 1857.

[*Vide* Jawad 'Alī.]

Taji (تاجی), poetical appellation of Mīr Muhammad Husain, the native country of whose forefathers was Andjān, in Persia. He flourished in the time of 'Alamgīr, and is the author of a Dīwān.

Tajrid (تجريد), a poet who is the author of a Dīwān.

Taj-uddin 'Abdul Wahhab bin-as-Sabki (تاج الدين عبدالواهب بن اسبکی), author of the *Tabaqāt-ash-Shāfi'at*. There are numerous biographical collections treating of the lives of the principal followers of Shāfa'ī, besides the one just mentioned, which have similar titles; but the most noted is by Tāj-uddīn. He died in A.D. 1369, A.H. 771.

Taj-uddin Abu Ja'far bin-Sukman (تاج الدين ابو جعفر بن صقمان), an author who died in A.D. 1118, A.H. 512.

Taj-uddin Abu'l Fazl (تاج الدين ابوالفضل بن طاهر), son of Tāhir, ruler of Sīstān, also called Nīmrōz, which country he received from Sultān Sanjar Saljūqī, some time about the year A.D. 1150, A.H. 545. The following is a list of his descendants, who reigned in Sīstān till the invasion of Changez Khān:

1. Tāj-uddīn 'Abū Ja'far.
2. Shams-uddīn Muhammad, son of Tāj-uddīn, who, along with his sister, was slain by his own subjects.
3. Tāj-uddīn Harb, son of 'Izzul Mulk, who is said to have reigned 60 years.
4. Bahrām Shāh, son of Tāj-uddīn, in whose time lived Abū Nasr Farāhī, the author of the *Nisāb-us-Subiān*.
5. Nasrat-uddīn, son of Bahrām, who was killed in battle against his brother Rukn-uddīn.
6. Rukn-uddīn, son of Bahrām, who was slain at the time of the invasion of Changez Khān.
7. Shahāb-uddīn, son of Tāj-uddīn, slain in battle.
8. Tāj-uddīn, who defended himself for two years in the fort of Sīstān, which was at last taken and every soul put to the sword by the troops of Changez Khān.

Taj-uddin Yalduz (تاج الدين يالدوز), king of Ghaznī. It is related that Shahāb-uddīn Muhammad Ghōrī, who had no children excepting a daughter, took pleasure in educating Turkish slaves, whom he afterwards adopted. Four of these slaves, besides Qutb-uddīn Aibak, became great princes, of whom Tāj-uddīn Yaldūz was one. On the death of Shahāb-uddīn, in A.D. 1206, A.H. 602, the Turkī officers espoused the cause of his nephew, prince Mahmūd, the son of Ghayās-uddīn Ghōrī; but Mahmūd, being unambitious and naturally indolent, felt satisfied with the throne of his ancestors at Ghōr, and proclaimed Yaldūz king of Ghaznī, content to receive homage from that chief. Yaldūz had several battles with Qutb-uddīn Aibak, king of Dehlī, and some time after that king's death recruited his army and marched towards India with a view to conquer that country, but was defeated near Dehlī by Shams-uddīn Altimsh in A.D. 1215, A.H. 611, and, being taken prisoner, was imprisoned in Badāon, where, according to some accounts, he died a natural death, but, according to others, he was poisoned. The whole length of his reign was nine years. A list of the Sultāns of the Slave Dynasty of Ghōr, who reigned in India, is given under Qutb-uddīn Aibak.

Taj-uddin Gazruni (تاج الدين گازرونی), author of the *Bahr-i-Sa'ādat*, the Sea of Felicity, a Persian work containing Essays on the goodness of God, the Creation of the world, on Virtue and the necessity of observing the moral duties, proved by various quotations from the Qurān.

Taj-uddin Sangreza (تاج الدين سنگریزه), a Persian poet, who lived in the time of Ghayās-uddīn Balban, king of Dehlī, about the year A.D. 1274, A.H. 670.

Taj-uddin 'Umar bin-'Ali (تاج الدين عمر بن علی فقهی), surnamed Fiqahī, an Arabian author, who died in the year A.D. 1331, A.H. 731.

Taj-ul-Mulk (تاج الملک), whose original name was Malik Tājū, was appointed wazīr by Khizir Khān, king of Dehlī, in the first year of his reign, A.D. 1414, A.H. 817, with the above title. He died on the 13th January, A.D. 1421, 8th Muharram, A.H. 824, and his eldest son, Sikandar, succeeded him in the office of wizārat under the title of Malik-ush-Sharq.

Takash or Taksh (تکش), surnamed 'Alā-uddīn Sultān of Khwārizm, the son of Alp Arsalan, the son of Atsiz, a descendant of the prince of that country, who had been cupbearer to the celebrated Sultān Sanjar, king of Persia. He defeated and slew Tughral III. Saljūqī in a battle, A.D. 1194, A.H. 590. At his death, which happened 4th July, A.D. 1200, 19th Ramazān, A.H. 596, he left his kingdom to his son Sultān Muhammad, surnamed Qutb-uddīn, whose reign was, at its commencement, splendid and successful; but his fortune fell before that great destroyer of the human race, Changez Khān, by whom he was defeated, his countries pillaged, and almost all his family made prisoners. He died of a broken heart, A.D. 1220, A.H. 617. His son Jalāl-uddīn, who was the last of this dynasty of kings, long bore up against the torrent that had overwhelmed his father, but was at last subdued. He was slain A.D. 1230.

Takash or **Turtash** (تکش), which see.

Takhallus (تخلص), the poetically-assumed title, or pen-name, of a Persian writer; of which many instances appear in this work. It was originally, perhaps, adopted from motives of caution, to conceal identity; but it became a fashion, adopted even by royal authors.

Takhat or **Takht Singh** (تخت سنگه), Rāja of Jodhpūr Mārwār, who was raised to the gaddī after the death of his father, Rāja Mān Singh, in November, A.D. 1843. He died on the 12th February, A.D. 1873, and was succeeded by his eldest son, Jaswant Singh, to whom he had resigned the reins of government some months before his death.

Takla (تکله), a king of Fārs. *Vide* Sunqar.

Takuji Holkar (تکوجی هولکر), the nephew of Malhār Rāo Hōlkar I. was elected and placed on the masnad of Indor by Ahlia Bāī, the widow of Khande Rāo, son of Malhār Rāo, in A.D. 1768, on the death of her father-in-law. He reigned 30 years, and died on the 15th August, A.D. 1797, leaving two legitimate sons, Kashī Rāo and Malhār Rāo, and two illegitimate sons, Ithojī and Jaswant Rāo. After the death of Takūjī his eldest son, Kāshī Rāo, succeeded him; but the country was usurped by Daulat Rāo Scindhia for some time, and afterwards made over to Jaswant Rāo.

Takuji Holkar (تکوجی هولکر), Rāja of Indor, was raised to the gaddī in A.D. 1844.

Tala' (طالع), the poetical name of Mirzā Nizām-uddīn, brother to Mirzā Qutb-uddīn Māel. He was an excellent poet, and flourished in the time of the emperor 'Alamgīr, and was living about the year A.D. 1696, A.H. 1108.

Talaiha ibn-Khawailid (طليحه ابن خويلد), one of the false prophets who pretended to prophecy like Muhammad, and imitated him from ambitious motives, saying that inspiration came down to him from heaven. He was received into favour by the Saracens in A.D. 638, A.H. 17, by saving the life of Sarjabīl ibn-Hasanī in a battle against the Greeks, and was subsequently employed by the Khalīf 'Umar in his wars against the Persians.

Talash (تالاش), the poetical name of Shahāb-uddīn Ahmad, which see.

Talha (طلحه بن طاهر), the son of Tāhir, the general of the Khalīf al-Māmūn. He succeeded his father in the government of Khurāsān in A.D. 822, A.H. 213, and, after a reign of six years, died a natural death in A.D. 828. His son 'Alī was killed the same year in a battle against the rebels at Naishapūr.

Talha ibn-'Obeidullah (طلحه ابن عبيدالله). He, together with Zubeir and 'Ayesha, the widow of Muhammad, were 'Alī's irreconcilable and implacable enemies. The Kūfians, Egyptians, and the greater part of the Arabians were for 'Alī. A part of the Basorians favoured Talha, but the rest supported Zubeir. He was killed with Zubeir in a battle against 'Alī, at Basra, with an arrow by Marwān, the then secretary of 'Alī, A.D. 656, A.H. 36.

Talib 'Amuli (طالب آملی), a celebrated poet of 'Amul, in Persia, who came to India in the reign of the emperor Akbar, and lived till the time of the emperor Jahāngīr, and was honoured by that monarch with the title of "Malik-ush-Shu'ārā," or the king of poets, A.D. 1619, A.H. 1028. He died in A.D. 1625, A.H. 1035, aged nearly 100 years, in Kashmīr, and left a Dīwān of 14,000 verses.

Talib Jajurmi (طالب جاجرمی), author of a poem called *Manāzira Gōlī-o-Chougān*, or Dispute between the Bat and the Ball, which he dedicated to Sultān 'Abdullāh, the son of Sultān Ibrāhīm, the son of Shāhrukh. He died in A.D. 1450, A.H. 854, and is buried close to the tomb of Khwāja Hāfiz at Shīrāz.

Talib Kalim (طالب کلیم). *Vide* Abū Tālib Kalīm.

Talmasani (تلمسانی), a poet.

Tamanna (تمنا), author of a small Dīwān in Urdū.

Tamas (تامس). *Vide* George Thomas.

Tamerlane or **Timurlang** (تمرلنگ). *Vide* Amīr Taimūr.

Tana Shah (تانا شاه). *Vide* Abū'l Hasan Qutb-shāh.

Tanha (تنها), poetical title of 'Abdul Latīf Khān, who is the author of a Dīwān.

Tanha (تنها), poetical name of Muhammad 'Alī.

Tansen (تانسین), a celebrated Hindī musician or singer who flourished in the time of Akbār, and was employed by him. He was originally in the service of a Rāja named Rām Chand, and was sent to court at the special request of the emperor. He died in the 34th year of that monarch's reign, A.D. 1588, A.H. 996.

The musicians in India, both vocal and instrumental, ever since the Musalmān conquests, who have been highly esteemed, and whose names are handed down to posterity with much respect by different authors, are as follows: Gopāl, Amīr Khusro the poet, Baijū, Bhāno, Panḍwā, Bakhshū, Lohang, Sulṭān Husain Sharqī of Jaunpūr, Rāja Mān of Gwāliar, founder of the Dhurpad, in whose time also lived the four following, *viz.* Chārjū, Bhagwān, Ḍhondhī, and Ḍālū; Tānsein, Subhān Khān, Sūrgayān Khān of Fathapūr, Chānd Khān, and his brother Sūraj Khān, Tāntarang Khān the son of Tānsein, Madan Rāe, Rāmdās and his son Sūrdās, a blind moral poet and musician, Bāz Bahādur, Munḍia, Mīān Panḍ, Mīān Dāūd Mullā Is-hāq, Shaikh Khizir, Shaikh Beichū, Hasan Khān Ṭeinī, Sūrat Sein and his brother Lālā Deibī, Mirzā 'Aqil, Mīān Shōrī, Ghulāmī, Lāl Khān, Nīlam Prakāsh, and the *Bīn* players, Fīrōz Khān and Naubat Khān.

Tantia Topi (تانتیا توپی), a famous rebel chief of 1857. He was captured in the jungles of Perone on the 7th April, 1859, and hanged on the 18th. It is said that before his death he solemnly affirmed that he was the instigator of the Cawnpore massacre, and that the Nānā, who had sworn to protect the Europeans, was angry with him for his conduct and never saw him afterwards. If this confession was made, it was evidently with the view of saving the Nānā, when it could no longer injure himself. In his confession Tāntiā described himself as a Brāhman of high caste, a native of Pūna, which place he had left about 30 years before for Central India, where he became an Artillery soldier (Tōpi). He next obtained employment in the Nānā's establishment at Biṭhūr in connection with the Treasury, and was so employed in 1857, when the Mutiny broke out. He also said that he commanded the rebel army of 8000 men which attacked Colonel Greathed's column on the parade ground at Āgra, on the 10th October, 1857. He declared he was aware of the arrival of the column from Dehlī before he opened fire on the encampment that morning, and did not suppose he had only the Agra brigade to deal with, as we imagined. He was deceived, however, after the action had commenced, by seeing a reinforcement of European redcoats coming up (Greathed's men being dressed in Khākhi), for whose appearance and apparent numbers (for they were reported to be 2500 men) he could not account; but supposing them to be new arrivals from down-country, he immediately retreated; otherwise he would have held his ground, and not have allowed Colonel Greathed to win so easy a victory. Tāntiā also mentioned that the largest force he ever commanded was at the battle of the Betwa, when he had under him 22,000 fighting men, and 130 pieces of ordnance of various calibre.

[*Vide* the Appendix to Malleson's 3rd vol.]

Tanuqi (طانوقی), surname of Abū'l 'Alā, one of the most celebrated Arabian poets of the tribe of Tānūq, which has produced many clever men.

Tapish (تاپش), the poetical name of Munshī Ghulām Muhammad Khān, editor of the newspaper called *Audh Akhbar*.

Taqi Aohadi (تقی اوحدی), a Persian poet who came to India and was living at Āgra in A.D. 1614, A.H. 1023. He is the author of a Diwān.

Taqi, Imam (تقی امام). *Vide* Muhammad Taqī.

Taqi Kashani (تقی کاشانی). *Vide* Taqī-uddīn Muhammad Kāshānī.

Taqi, Mir (تقی میر), a Persian and Urdū poet, who is the author of six Dīwāns and several other works. He was a native of Āgra and died at Lucknow in A.D. 1810, A.H. 1225. His father's name was Muhammad Muttaqī. His poetical name is Mīr, which see.

Taqi-uddin Muhammad bin-Ahmad bin-'Ali Hasani Fasi (تقی الدین محمد بن احمد بن علی), author of the work called *Shafa-ul-Gharām*. He died A.D. 1428, A.H. 832.

Taqi-uddin Muhammad Kashani (تقی الدین محمد کاشانی), son of Sharaf-uddīn 'Alī Husainī Zikrī. He was born at Kāshān about the year A.D. 1539, A.H. 946, and is the author of a biography called *Khulāsat-ul-Ashaār, wa Zubdut-ul-Afkār*, compiled in the year A.D. 1585, A.H. 993.

Taqi-uddin Sabaqi (تقی الدین سبقی), son of Abdul Kāfī. He is the author of more than 150 works on different subjects. He died A.D. 1349, A.H. 750.

Taqi-uddin Tamimi (تقی الدین تمیمی), author of a biographical treatise giving an account of the Hanafī lawyers, arranged in alphabetical order, entitled *Tabaqāt us-Saniat fī Tarājim-ul-Hanafiat*. He died A.D. 1596, A.H. 1005.

Tara Bai (تارا بای), the wife of Rāja Rām, the brother of Sambhajī, the son of Seiwājī Bhosla, the Marhaṭṭa chief of Sitāra. After the death of her husband in March, A.D. 1700, she ruled as regent in the name of her son Seiwā, a child of two years, over the territories acquired by Seiwājī. But on 'Alamgīr's death in A.D. 1707, when Sāhū, the son of Sambhajī, was released by 'Azim Shāh, he (Sāhū) quickly made himself master of Sitāra and imprisoned Tārā Bāi.

Tara Begam (تارا بیگم), one of the wives of the emperor Akbar. She had a garden in Āgra consisting of 40 bīgas of ground, now in ruins.

Tarbiat Khan (تربیت خان), a nobleman of 4000 who served under the emperor 'Alamgīr as Mīr 'Atash, or Commander of Artillery. After the death of that monarch, he espoused the cause of his son 'Azim Shāh, and was killed in the battle against Bahādur Shāh, A.D. 1707, A.H. 1119. He had built a house at Āgra on a piece of ground called Tajāra, or Majāra, outside the fort opposite to the Amar Singh gate of the fort.

Tarbiat Khan Barlas (تربیت خان برلاس), title of Shafī-ullāh Khān, a native of Persia, who came to India and served under the emperors Shāh Jahān and 'Alamgīr. At the time of his death he held the rank of 4000, and was governor of Jaunpūr, where he died A.D. 1685, A.H. 1096.

Tari (تاری), poetical title of Mullā 'Alī Muhaddis.

Tarkhan or **Nawab Tarkhan** (ترخان نواب). *Vide* Nūr-uddīn Safaiduni (Mullā).

Tarki (ترکی), the first Sulṭān or emperor of, and his descendants. *Vide* Usmān or Uthmān.

Tarmadi, Tarmizi or **Tirmizi** (ترمدی). *Vide* Tirmizī, which is the correct name.

Tasalli (تسلی), the poetical name of Ibrāhīm of Shīrāz, who came to India and was living in A.D. 1623, A.H. 1032. He is the author of a Dīwān.

Tashbihi (تشبیہی). *Vide* Akbar 'Alī Tashbīhī.

Tashkparizada (تاشکپری زاده), surname of Mullā Aḥmad bin-Mustāfa, a celebrated Arabian, who died A.D. 1560, A.H. 968.

Tasir (تاثیر), the poetical title of Mirzā Muhsin, who is the author of a Dīwān. He flourished about the year A.D. 1718, A.H. 1130.

Taskhir (تسخیر), poetical title of Prince Mirzā Sulaimān Qadr, the son of Mirzā Khurshaid Qadr. *Vide* Qaisar.

Taslim (تسلیم), title of Muhammad Hāshim of Shīrāz. He came under 'Alamgīr to India, and is the author of a Diwān. He was living in A.D. 1697, A.H. 1109.

Tatar Khan (تاتار خان), adopted son of Tughlaq Shāh and prime minister of Sulṭān Muhammad Shah Tughlaq. He is the author of a Commentary on the Qurān, entitled *Tafsīr Tātār Khānī*, and of another work on Muhammadan Law, called *Fatāwī Tātār Khānī*. He died in the reign of Sulṭān Fīroz Shāh Bārbak.

Tatar Khan (تاتار خان), of Khurāsān; a mansabdar of 1000 under Akbar. He was Governor of Dehlī, and died there A.D. 1588, A.H. 986.

Tatar Khan (تاتار خان), son of Muẓaffar Shāh I. king of Gujrāt, and father of Aḥmad Shāh I.

Taufal Khan (توفل خان), prime minister. *Vide* Burhān 'Imād Shāh.

Taufiq. Viceroy or Khedive of Egypt; died A.D. 1892.

Taufiq, Mulla (توفیق ملا کشمیری), of Kashmere, a Persian poet.

Tauli Khan (تولی خان), the fourth son of Changez Khān. On the death of his father, A.D. 1227, he succeeded to the kingdoms of Persia, Khurāsān, and Qābul, and died three years afterwards. He left several sons, among whom the two eldest, *viz.* Mangū Khān and Halākū Khān, were the most famous.

Taurandukht (توران دخت), daughter of Khusro Parwiz. She was elevated to the throne of Persia some time after the death of her brother Sheroya, A.D. 631. We are told by Persian historians that this queen restored the sacred cross, which had been borne away from Jerusalem by Khusro Parwiz; and by that act, acquired great power with the Roman emperor. But this is evidently erroneous; for there is no doubt that the emperor Heraclius, when he returned from Persia, carried that precious relic to Constantinople, which was deemed a more splendid trophy of victory than all his spoils and conquests. Taurāndukht ruled Persia only one year and four months. She was succeeded by her cousin and lover, Shāh Shanandá. He had reigned only one month when he was deposed, and 'Azrarm or Arzamīdukht, another daughter of Khusro Parwiz, was raised to the throne, A.D. 632. This princess, who was alike distinguished by her sense and beauty, resolved to take the whole management of the affairs of the kingdom into her hands. She would not even appoint a wazīr. But the fatal passion of a Persian noble defeated all her designs. Farrukh Hurmuz, the governor of Khurāsān, fell violently in love with her, or perhaps, with her dominions. He proceeded to court and made his love known to his royal mistress; she refused her hand, and he was soon afterwards murdered through her instigation. As soon as his melancholy fate was known to his son Rustam, he collected a large army, and marched from Khurāsān to Madain. The queen was unable to oppose him; and the young chief revenged his father by putting her to a cruel death. After her demise, Farrukhzād, the son of Khusro Parwiz by a female singer of Isfahān, was raised to the throne; but before he had reigned a month, his days were terminated by poison. Such were the events which immediately preceded the reign of Yezdijard III. and the fall of the Persian monarchy.

Tauran Shah (توران شاه), surnamed Mulik-ul-Muazzim, was the brother of the famous Salāh-uddīn, who had appointed him as his lieutenant in Damascus. He died at Alexandria on the 1st July, A.D. 1180, 5th Ṣafar, A.H. 576.

Tauran Shah, Khwaja (توران شاه خواجه), surnamed Jalāl-uddīn, was wazīr of Shāh Shujāa, ruler of Shīrāz, and died on the 3rd April, A.D. 1385.

Tausani (توسنی), the poetical name of Manōhar Dās, who, though a Hindū, was also called Muhammad Manōhar and Mirzā Manōhar. He flourished in the reign of the emperor Akbar. The name of his father was Lōnkaran (Salt Manufacturer). He was Rāja of Sambhar.

[*Vide* Rāe Lōnkaran.]

Tausi Maulana (طوسی مولانا), a poet of Khurāsān, who flourished in the reign of Bābar Sulṭān, after whose death he went over to Azurbaijan in the time of Jahān Shāh, and died there A.D. 1487, A.H. 892.

Tauti Begam (توتی بیگم), one of the wives of the emperor Akbar. She had built a garden in Āgra called Tota Bāgh; there is also a tank in Āgra which is called Tota ka Tāl.

Tauti, Maulana (طوطی مولانا ترشیزی), of Tarshish, a learned Musalmān and a good poet. He flourished in the time of Bābar Sulṭān and died at Herāt in the year A.D. 1462, A.D. 866. As Tautī means in Persian a parrot, consequently Amīr 'Alīsher found the year of his death to be contained in the word "Khurūs," which means a cock.

Tawakkul bin-Isma'il bin-Haji Ardibeili (توکل بن اسمعیل), author of the work entitled *Safwat-us-Safā*, containing the history of the celebrated Ṣhaikh Ṣūfī, the founder of the sect of Sūfīs in Persia, and from whom were descended the royal Safwī family, written in A.D. 1397, A.H. 800.

Tawakkul Munshi (توکل منشی), author of the work called *Shāh-nāma*, *Shamsher Khānī*, a prose abridgment of the celebrated *Shāh-nāma* of Firdausī, written in A.D. 1652, A.H. 1062. A translation of this was again made in Urdū verse by a poet in the reign of the emperor Shāh Akbar II. A.D. 1810, A.H. 1225.

Taya' or **Tai Billah** (طایع باالله), a khalīf of Baghdād. *Vide* Al-Tāya' Billāh.

Tayyabi (طیبی), author of the *Hāshia Kashshāf* and *Sharah Mashkūt-ul-Masābīh*. He died in A.D. 1342, A.H. 743.

Tazkira (تذکره), "Memoir," from ذکر. The title of many biographical works in Persian and Urdū.

Tazrawi (تذروی). *Vide* Tadrawī.

Tegh Bahadur (تیغ بهادر), a gūrū or chief of the Sikhs, who, having collected his followers, levied contributions from the inhabitants of his neighbourhood, in conjunction with Hāfiz 'Adam, a Musalmān devotee, and his votaries. He was put to death as a dangerous heretic in the 17th year of the emperor 'Alamgīr's reign, A.D. 1673, A.H. 1084. His body was divided into four parts and hung in the city.

Tek Chand (ٹیک چند), whose takhallus is Chānd, was the son of Balrām, a Hindū of Sarhind. He is the author of the *Guldastae Ishq*, Nosegay of Love, a Masnawī or poem, containing the story of Kāmrūp, in Persian verse. He flourished in the time of 'Alamgīr.

Tek Chand, Munshi (ٹیک چند), whose poetical title is Bahār, was a Hindū, by caste a Khattrī, and author of a work entitled *Bahār Ajam*, a voluminous dictionary of Persian idioms, and another called *Nawādir-ul-Musādir*. The former work he completed in the year A.D. 1739, A.H. 1152. He also wrote another work called *Abtāl Zarūrat*.

Thatta, Rulers of (ٹھٹ تہہ). *Vide* Nāsir-uddīn Qabbācha.

Thomas, George. *Vide* George Thomas

Thomas, John, a Hindūstānī poet, probably son of the preceding. Known in literature as "Khān Sahib."

Tippu Sahib (ٹیپو صاحب). *Vide* Ṭīpū Sulṭān.

Tipu Shah or Tippu (ٹیپو شاہ), a celebrated Muhammadan devotee of Arkaṭ, from whom the famous Ṭīpū Sulṭān, the sovereign of Mysore, was named. His Mausoleum still continues a favourite resort of the pious, and Haidar 'Alī Khān, the father of Ṭīpū Sulṭān, had a particular veneration for him. Ṭīpū, or Ṭippū, in the Canarese language signifies a tiger.

Tipu or Tippu Sultan (ٹیپو سلطان), the son of Haidar 'Alī Khān of Mysore. He was born in the year A.D. 1749, and succeeded his father in December, A.D. 1782, as ruler of Mysore. During the American war he joined the French against the English; but after the breaking out of the French Revolution he was exposed alone to the fortunes of the war. In A.D. 1790 he was defeated in Travancore, and, yielding to the British arms, he consented, in A.D. 1792, to make peace with Lord Cornwallis by delivering up his two sons as hostages, and paying, besides part of his dominion, above three millions sterling. His intrigues with the French, and his machinations to destroy the English power, renewed the war in A.D. 1799. He was attacked by the British in his very capital, and was killed whilst bravely defending himself on the ramparts on the 4th May, A.D. 1799, 28th Ẕil-Qa'da, A.H. 1213, aged 52 years. He was buried in the mausoleum of his father in the garden named Lāl Bāgh. Ṭīpū, though oppressive and capricious, patronized the arts, and his fondness for literature was displayed in the collection of books found in his palace, consisting of various works in the Sanskrit language of the 10th century, translations of the Qurān, MSS. of the history of the Mughal victories, and historical memoirs of Hindūstān, all of which were deposited in the Library of Calcutta, and a catalogue of them was written by Captain Stewart, and published. Ṭīpū Sulṭān is the author of two books, or collections of letters, one entitled *Farmān-banām 'Alī Rāja*, and the other *Fath-ul-Majāhidīn*. A part of the latter has been translated and published by Mr. B. Crisp, of Bengal.

Tirandaz Khan (تیرانداز خان), a slave of the emperor Akbar Shāh the Great, was raised to high rank and received the title of Khān. He built his house on a spot of ground, consisting of six bīgas, in Āgra, towards the south of the house of Islām Khān Rūmī. He was raised to the rank of 2000 and appointed governor of Aḥmadabād by the emperor Shāh Jahān.

Tirmizi (ترمیزی), also called Hakīm-al-Tirmizī. This was the title or surname of Abū 'Abdul āh Muhammad bin-'Alī, an author and philosopher of Tirmiz, in Persia, who died in the year A.D. 869, A.H. 255.

Todar Mal or Torar Mal (توڈر مل), the celebrated minister of finance, or Dīwān of the emperor Akbar Shāh, was a Hindū of the tribe of Khattrī of Lāhore. He was appointed Sūbadār of Bengal in A.D. 1580, A.H. 988, and died at Lāhore in the 36th year of the reign of that monarch, on Monday the 10th November, A.D. 1589, 11th Muḥarram, A.H. 998. Abū'l Fazl describes him as entirely devoid of avarice and quite sincere, but of a malicious and vindictive temper, and so observant of the fasts and other superstitions of the Hindūs as to draw down upon him reproof even from Akbar.

Tufail (طـفـيـل), the name of Alī's nephew.

Tughan Khan (طغان خان), the Muhammadan governor of Bengal in A.D. 1243. He invaded the principality of Jahāzpūr, in Urysa, and was defeated by its Rāja, who pursued him into Gour, his metropolis; but reinforcements from Audh compelled the Rāja subsequently to retreat.

Tughan Shah I. (طغان شاہ), a prince of the Saljūqian family, whose seat of government was Naishāpûr. This prince is said to have been defeated in his younger days in a battle fought against Ibrāhīm bin-Nayāl, who took him prisoner and blinded him. After some time his uncle Tughral Beg seized Ibrāhīm, murdered him, and restored the titular kingdom to his cousin Tughān Shāh. The poet Arzaqī lived in his time and wrote several panegyrics in his praise.

Tughan Shah II. (طغان شاہ), a prince of the Saljūq dynasty, who ascended the throne of Persia after the death of Sulṭān Sanjar and, after several battles, was defeated and slain by Ṭakash, the Sulṭān of Khwarizm, and died in A.D. 1185, A.H. 581.

Tughan Taimur Khan (طغان تیمور خان), a descendant of the Mughal kings of Persia and ruler of Jurjān. After the death of Sulṭān Abū Saīd and Arpa Khān he conquered several provinces of Khurasān and subdued the Sarbadāls of that place. He was at last slain by Khwāja Ahia Kiratī, chief of the Sarbadāls, on Saturday the 14th December, A.D. 1353, 16th Ẕi-Qa'da, A.H. 754.

Tughlaq (تغلق), a slave of Sulṭān Ghayās-uddīn Balban. His son, after murdering Khusro Shāh, ascended the throne of Dehlī and assumed the title of Ghayās-uddīn Tughlaq in A.D. 1321.

Tughlaq Shah (تغلق شاه). *Vide* Ghayās-uddīn Tughlaq Shāh and Muhammad Tughlaq Shāh.

Tughrai (طغرائی), surname of Hasan Abī Ismā'īl of Isfahān, a celebrated wazīr of the king of Mousal, Sulṭān Mas'aūd Saljūqī. He was called Tughrāī on account of his excellence in the species of writing styled Tughrā, and also had the title of "Honours of Writers," but is better known in Europe by his admired Arabic poem, entitled *Carmen Tughrāī*. Being taken prisoner in a battle where his sovereign was defeated by his brother Mahmūd, A.D. 1120, A.H. 514, he was put to death by that prince's wazīr, who hated him for his great abilities. A collection of the poems of Tughrāī has been made, the most celebrated of which is that called *Lāmạ-ul-'Ajam*.

Tughrai (طغرائی), title of Amīr Yemīn-uddīn, of Alashhad, a poet, and author of the *Kulliāt Tughrāe Mashhadī*, a collection of poems, odes, elegies, etc., which also contains the following prose works, all of which are entertaining novels, *viz. Mirat-ul-Maftuh, Kanz-ul-Mạānī, Majmūạ-ul-Gharīb, Chashmae Faiz*, and *Anwār-ul-Mubārak*. He died at a place called Fareomud in A.D. 1324, A.H. 724. There is an Insha supposed to have been written by him entitled *'Inshae Tughrāī*. He was contemporary with the Tartar king of Persia, Muhammad Khuda Banda, and his son Abū Saīd.

Tughrai, Mulla (طغرائی ملا), an author who lived in the middle of the 11th century of the Hijrī.

Tughral Beg (طغرل بیگ) (the Tangrolipix of the Greeks) was the son of Mikāīl, the son of Saljūq, and the first Sulṭān of the Saljūqides. Tughral Beg and his brother Ja'far Beg Dāūd were in the service of Sulṭān Mahmūd of Ghaznī. After defeating Sulṭān Mas'aūd I. son of Sulṭān Mahmūd, in a battle fought in A.D. 1038, A.H. 429, he assumed the title and state of a sovereign at Naishāpūr. He subdued 'Irāq, took Baghdād, and by its reduction became master of the person of the Khalīfa al-Qāem Billāh, who invested him as Sulṭān of Khurāsān, appointed him vicegerent or vicar of the holy prophet, and the lord of all Muhammadans. He gave his sister in marriage to the khalīf, and his nephew Alp Arsalān afterwards married the daughter of the khalīf al-Muqtadī. The Saljūq family divided into three branches and settled in Hamdān, Kirmān and Rūm, or Anatolia. Tughral Beg died, after a reign of 25 lunar years, A.D. 1063, A.H. 455, aged 70 lunar years, and, as he had no issue, he was succeeded by his nephew Sulṭān Alp Arsalān, the son of Abū Ja'far Dāūd. The following are the names of the Sulṭāns of the Saljūq dynasty of Irān or Persia:

1. Tughral Beg, the son of Mikāīl, the son of Saljūq.
2. Alp Arsalān, nephew of Tughral Beg.
3. Malikshāh, the son of Alp Arsalān.
4. Barkayāraq, the son of Malikshāh. In his reign the empire was divided, he retaining Persia; Muhammad, his brother, Syria and Āzarbaijān, and Sulṭān Sanjar, Khurāsān and Māwarun-nahr.

Tughral II. (طغرل), also called Tughral Sulṭān, of the race of Saljūq, was the son of Sulṭān Muhammad, the son of Alp Arsalān. He was raised to the dignity of Sulṭān by his uncle Sulṭān Sanjar, A.D. 1132, A.H. 525, after the death of his brother Sulṭān Mahmūd, and, after a reign of three years, died in October, A.D. 1134, Muharram, A.H. 525, aged 25 years. His brother Mas'aūd succeeded him.

Tughral III. (طغرل), a Sulṭān of the Saljūqian family, was the son of Arsalān Shāh, the son of Sulṭān Muhammad, the brother of Sulṭān Sanjar. After the death of Sulṭān Sanjar, A.D. 1157, A.H. 552, Persia continued, for a period of forty years, to be distracted with the wars of different branches of the Saljūqian dynasty. The last who exercised power was Tughral III. who succeeded his father, Arsalān Shāh, in January, A.D. 1176, Jumādạ II. A.H. 571, and, after a reign of ten years, was seized and imprisoned by his uncle and wazīr, Qizal Arsalān, who resolved to usurp the throne, but fell by the hand of an assassin in A.D. 1191, A.H. 587, and the kingdom was restored to Tughral. He was, however, after some years, defeated in a battle, taken prisoner and executed by Takash, ruler of Khwārizm, A.D. 1194, A.H. 590, and his head sent to Nāsir, the khalīfa of Baghdād. With this prince terminated the Saljūqian monarchs of Persia, who had governed that country from the commencement of the reign of Tughral I. to the death of Tughral III.—158 years.

Tughtazani (تغتازانی). *Vide* Tuftazānī.

Tulshi Bai (تلشی بائی), the widow of Jaswant Rāo Holkar. *Vide* Jaswant Rāo Holkar.

Tulshi Das (تلشی داس), a Brahmān and a celebrated poet among the Hindūs. He is the author or the *Ramāyan* in the Bhā<u>kh</u>a dialect. He flourished in the reign of the emperors Akbar and Jahāngīr, was originally an inhabitant of Rājapūr, near Chitarkōṭ and Tarhuwān; but went about as an ascetic from one place to another, and died at Benares on the 24th October, A.D. 1623. In the Bhā<u>kh</u>a, or pure Hindī, there are still extant many elegant poems, songs, etc., the productions of Hindu poets, *viz.* Kab Gang, Tulshī, Bihārī, Girdhar, Lālach, Sūrdās, Kabīr, Nāuhak; and to these we may add the names of Malik Muhammad Jāyesī, Aḥmad Wahāb, Muhammad Afzal, Amīr <u>Kh</u>ān, etc., as they composed in both dialects. Girdhar Dās is the author of another *Ramāyan*.

[*Vide* Girdhar Dās.]

Tuqtamish Khan (تقتمش خان), ruler of Dasht Kapchāk, whom Amīr Taimūr defeated in A.D. 1395.

Turkan Khatun (تـرکان خاتـون), a daughter of Sulṭān Jalāl-uddīn of <u>Kh</u>wārizm. She was given in marriage by Halākū <u>Kh</u>ān to Malik Shāh, son of Badr-uddīn Lūlū, prince of Mausal.

Turkan Khatun (ترکان خاتون), wife of Sulṭān Jalāl-uddīn Malikshāh.

Turkman (ترکمان), the poetical name of a person whose father was a native of Shīrāz, but he was born in India, and was living about the year A.D. 1690, A.H. 1102.

Turtush (ترتش), a brother of Malikshāh the Saljūqian, against whom he rebelled, and was compelled to save himself by leaving the kingdom. This appears to be the same person called by Ibn-<u>Kh</u>allikān, Turtush the son of Alp Arsalān, who took prisoner Atsiz, a Sulṭān of <u>Kh</u>wārizm, and put him to death on the 21st October, A.D. 1078, 11th Rabī' II. A.H. 471. Turtush was slain in a battle fought against his nephew Barkayaraq, on Sunday the 25th February, A.D. 1095, 17th Safar, A.H. 488, aged 30 years.

Tutash (تتش). *Vide* Turtush.

U

'Ubid (عبيد), a poet who lived in the time of Sultān Ghayās-uddīn Tughlaq Shāh, and was buried alive on account of his having raised a false report that the king was dead, and that a great revolution had taken place at Dehlī. This event took place in the second year of the king's reign, A.D. 1322, A.H. 722.

'Ubid Khan (عبيد خان), ruler of the Uzbaks, was contemporary with Shāh Tahmāsp I. Safwī, king of Persia, who in a battle defeated his troops, and gave them a signal overthrow in A.D. 1527, A.H. 935.

'Ubid-ullah (عبيد الله), sovereign of the Uzbaks. This monarch was the nephew of the celebrated Shāhī Beg Khān, the conqueror. He commenced his reign about the year A.D. 1542, A.H. 949.

'Ubid-ullah Ahrar Naqshband (عبيد الله احرار نقشبند), a celebrated learned Musalmān and saint of Khurāsān, among the number of whose disciples Maulwī Jāmī was one. He died in the month of February, A.D. 1491, Rabī' II. A.H. 896, and is buried at Samarqand. Amīr Alīsher, the celebrated wazīr of Sultān Husain Mirzā, who much respected him, found the chronogram of the year of his death in the words "Khuld Barīn."

'Ubid-ullah-al-Mahdi (عبيد الله المهدى), a chief of Barbary, in Africa, who, in A.D. 910, A.H. 298, rebelled against the king of that country, of the race of Aghlab, and assumed the title of Khalīf of Qairwān (the ancient Cyrene, and residence of the Aghlabite princes). To give the greater weight to his pretensions, he also took the surname of al-Mahdī, the director. According to some, also, he pretended to be descended in a right line from 'Alī, the son of Abū Tālib, and Fātima, the daughter of Muhammad; for which reason the Arabs called him and his descendants Fātimites. He likewise encouraged himself and his followers by a traditional prophecy of Muhammad, that at the end of 300 years the sun should rise out of the West. Having at length driven the Aghlabites into Egypt, where they became known by the name of Maghrabians, he extended his dominions in Africa and Sicily, making Qairwān the place of his residence. He sent several of his generals at different times to conquer Egypt, but they were always defeated and obliged to fly to Qairwān. Al-Mahdi reigned in Barbary 24 years, and was succeeded by his son Abul Qāsim, who then took the surname of al-Qāyem Mahdī.

'Ubid-ullah bin-Masa'ud (عبيد الله بن مسعود), author of a Commentary on the *Wiqāya*, a work on jurisprudence, entitled *Sharh Wiqāya*. He is also the author of the *Nikāya*, which is sometimes called *Mukhtasir-al-Wiqāya*, being in fact an abridgment of that work. 'Ubid-ullah died A.D. 1349, A.H. 750.

[*Vide* Mahmūd, surnamed Burhān-ash-Sharīat.]

'Ubid-ullah ibn-Qais (عبيد الله ابن قيس), a distinguished Arabian poet, who commemorated the death of Misaa'b, the son of Zubeir, who was on terms of friendship with him, and had fought in his cause in the year A.D. 690, A.H. 71.

'Ubid-ullah ibn-Zayad (عبيد الله ابن زياد) was appointed governor of Kūfa by the khalīf Yezīd in the room of al-Namān, A.D. 679, A.H. 60. He beheaded Muslim, Husain's cousin, and his troops surrounded Husain at Karbala, who, having desperately engaged his troops, was after long resistance cut to pieces with all his men in October, A.D. 680, Muharram, A.H. 61. In the reign of 'Abdulmalik, 'Ubid-ullah was sent to Kūfa with leave to plunder it for three days; but, before he reached that city, al-Mukhtār, then ruler of that place, sent his forces against him under the command of Ibrāhīm, the son of Alashtar, when, after a sharp engagement, 'Ubid-ullāh's forces were beaten, and himself killed in the camp. Ibrāhīm, having cut off his head, sent it to al-Makhtār, and burned his body. This circumstance took place in August, A.D. 686, Muharram, A.H. 67.

'Ubid Zakani (عبيد زاكانى), a celebrated jester and poet, was contemporary with the poet Salmān Sāwajī. He composed several ludicrous verses on Jahān Khātūn, the wife of Khwāja Amīn-uddīn, wazīr of Shāh

Abū Is-hāq, ruler of Shīrāz. He is the author of the work called *Risāla dar ilm Bayān*, which he dedicated to the king, and also of a Dīwān. He died in A.D. 1370, A.H. 772.

Udaipuri Begam (اودیپوری بیگم), the favourite wife of the emperor 'Alamgīr, and the mother of the prince Kāmbakhsh, whom his father cherished with the utmost tenderness as the son of his old age. She was living in A.D. 1686. She is believed to have been a Sisodia from Jodhpur.

Udai Singh (اودی سنگه رانا), Rānā of Chittor, was the son of Rānā Sanka, the emperor Bābar's competitor, but a man of feeble character. In his time the fort of Chittor was taken by the emperor Akbar in March, A.D. 1568, Shaban, A.H. 975. His son, Rānā Partāp, founded the new capital called Udaipūr, which is still occupied by his descendants. Rānā Partāp Singh died A.D. 1595, A.H. 1004, and Amar Singh his son succeeded him, and died in the 14th year of Jahāngīr, A.D. 1620, A.H. 1029.

Udai Singh Rathouri (اودی سنگه راتهوری), commonly called Mota Rāja, was the son of Rāe Māldeo, of Jodhpur Mārwār. He served under the emperor Akbar, and in the year A.D. 1586, A.H. 994, gave his daughter, named Bālmatī, in marriage to Sultān Salīm (afterwards Jahāngīr), by whom he had Shāh Jahān. He was raised to high rank, and Jodhpur, his native country, given him in jāgīr. He died A.D. 1594, A.H. 1002, and four of his wives burned themselves with his corpse. After his death his son Sūraj Singh succeeded him.

Udham Bai, also called Kudsia Begam, a Hindū princess, mother of the emperor Ahmad Shāh (*q.v.*). She laid out the garden on the banks of the Jumna, often mentioned in connection with the siege of Dehlī in 1857 as the Kudsia Bāgh.

Ugarsen (اوگرسین راجه), a Rāja who is said to have reigned at Āgra several centuries before the time of Sultān Sikandar Lodī. After him Āgra became a village of Bayana, the name of the Rāja of which place was Bīn.

Ulagh Beg Mirza or **Ulugh Beg** (الغ بیگ مرزا), a prince celebrated for his knowledge in Astronomy, was the son of Mirzā Shāhrukh, the son of Amīr Taimūr. He reigned at Samarqand for 40 years during the lifetime of his father, whom he succeeded in March, A.D. 1447, A.H. 851. He was a prince who made peaceful studies the chief object of his life, and had entirely neglected the art of war. He assembled all the astronomers of his kingdom, and the celebrated Tables which are known by his name, viz. *Zīj Ulagh Beg*, were the result of his labours. He is said to have had very large instruments for making his observations, particularly a quadrant as high as the church of Santa Sophia at Constantinople, which is 180 Roman feet. His fate was cruel: he was defeated, taken prisoner, and put to death by his son Mirzā 'Abdul Latīf, on the 27th October, A.D. 1449, Ramazān, A.H. 853. It is a consolation to know that this unnatural prince enjoyed the power he had attained by so monstrous a crime only for the short space of six months: he was slain by his own soldiers. Ulagh Beg's Catalogue of fixed stars, rectified for A.D. 1434, was published by Hyde, at Oxford, in A.D. 1665, in 4to. with learned notes.

Ulfati (الفتی), poetical name of Qulich Khān of Andjān, which see.

'Umar-al-Maksus (عمر المکسوس), the favourite master of the khalif Mu'āwia II. who, after his father's death, consulted him whether he ought, or not, to accept the khilāfat. His master told him that if he thought himself able to administer justice duly to the Musalmāns, he ought to accept it; but otherwise he ought not to charge himself with it. This khalif had scarcely reigned six weeks, when he found himself too weak to sustain the weight of the government, and resolved to lay it down. This he did, and had no sooner renounced the khilāfat but he shut himself up in a chamber, from whence he never stirred till he died, not long after his abdication, of the plague, according to some, and according to others of poison. The family at Umayya was so greatly irritated at his proceedings that they vented their resentment upon the person of 'Umar-ul-Maksūs, whom they buried alive, because they supposed that it was by his advice that Mu'āwia deposed himself. This circumstance took place in the year A.D. 683, A.H. 64.

'Umar bin-'Abdul Aziz (عمر بن عبد العزیز), grandson of Marwān I. was the ninth khalif of the house of Umayya. He succeeded Sulaimān at Damascus in September or October, A.D. 717, A.H. 99, and died after a reign of two years and some months, in February, A.D. 720, A.H. 101, at Dyr Samān. He was succeeded by Yezīd II. This khalīf ('Umar 'Abdul Azīz) was eminent above all others for temperance and self-denial, insomuch that, according to the Muhammadan faith, he was raised to Muhammad's bosom, as a reward for his abstinence in an age of corruption.

'Umar bin-'Abdul Aziz (عمر بن عبد العزیز) was an eminent Musalmān, who died in the year A.D. 742, A.H. 124.

'Umar bin-'Abdul Aziz bin-Maja (عمر بن عبدالعزیز بن ماجه), commonly called Husām-ush-Shahīd, author of a most esteemed Commentary. He was killed A.D. 1141, A.H. 536.

[*Vide* Abū Bakr Aḥmad bin-'Umar-al-Khassāf.]

'Umar bin-'Abdullah (عمر بن عبدالله), a famous Arabian poet, who flourished in the time of the khalīf 'Abdulmalik.

[*Vide* Jamīl.]

'Umar bin-Khattab (عمر بن خطاب), one of the favourite companions and father-in-law of Muhammad. He succeeded Abū Bakr Sadiq as second khalīfa after Muhammad in August, A.D. 634, Jumāda II. A.H. 13. He spread his conquests over Syria and Phœnicia, and took Jerusalem after an obstinate siege in A.D. 637, A.H. 16. His generals extended his conquests over Persia and Egypt, and increased the worshippers of Muhammad. The fall of Alexandria under his power was marked by the destruction of its celebrated library, but he restored the canal between the Nile and the Red Sea. During his reign the Muhammadans conquered 36,000 towns, destroyed 4,000 Christian temples, and built 1,400 mosques. He was the first who was called "Amīr-ul-Mominīn," or the Lord of the Believers, and this title was ever afterwards used by all succeeding khalīfs. He was married seven times, and one of his wives was Umm Kulsūm, the daughter of 'Alī. He was stabbed on Wednesday the 3rd November, A.D. 644, 25th Zil-hijja, A.H. 23, by a Persian slave named Fīrōz, whilst saying his morning prayers in a mosque, and died three days afterwards, aged 63 lunar years. He reigned 10 years 6 months and 8 days, and was succeeded in the khilāfat by 'Usmān, the son of 'Affān. Waring, in his *Tour to Shīrāz*, mentions that while he was at Shīrāz (A.H. 1802), the Persians (who are Shias) celebrated the death of the khalīf 'Umar. "They erected a large platform, on which they fixed an image, disfigured and deformed as much as possible. Addressing themselves to the image, they began to revile it for having supplanted 'Alī, the lawful successor of Muhammad; at length, having exhausted all their expressions of abuse, they suddenly attacked the image with stones and sticks, until they had shattered it into pieces. The inside was hollow, and full of sweetmeats, which were greedily devoured by the mob who attended the ceremony."

'Umar-ibn-'Ubed (عمر ابن عبید), the son of Bāb; disciple of Wāsil-ibn-Alā, and, with him, joint founder of the Mu'tazila sect or school in the eighth century A.D. He lived at Basra.

[*Vide* Mu'tazila.]

'Umar Khan Khilji (عمر خان خلجی), the youngest son of Sulṭān 'Alā-uddīn Khiljī, a boy of seven years of age, was raised to the throne of Dehlī, after the death of his father, by Malik Kāfūr the eunuch, in December, A.D. 1316, Shawwāl, A.H. 716. Malik Kāfūr was assassinated after 35 days, and soon afterwards 'Umar Khān was deposed by his brother Mubarak Khān, who ascended the throne in January, A.D. 1317, A.H. 716.

'Umar Khayam (عمر خیام). He was originally a tent-maker, and hence his *takhallus* of Khayām. He is held to be one of the most remarkable of Persian poets, unprecedented in regard to the freedom of his religious opinion. The Voltaire of Persia, his works gave great offence to the priests, but are, nevertheless, highly esteemed by general readers, apparently with justice, as the animation and brilliancy of his style are unquestionable. His hatred of hypocrisy and the tricks of false devotees appears his crime in the eyes of the supposed pious; his tolerance of other creeds was looked upon with equal suspicion and dislike. He was born at Naishapūr, and devoted much of his time to the study of astronomy, of which science he was a distinguished professor; but it is said that, instead of his studies leading him to the acknowledgment of the Supreme Being, it prompted his disbelief. The result of his reflections on this important subject is given in a poem of his, much celebrated under the title of *Rubāyāt-i-'Umar Khayām*. He was the friend of Hasan Sabbāh, the founder of the sect of the Assassins, and, it has been stated on unwarranted conjecture, assisted him in the establishment of his diabolical doctrine and fellowship. Great allowance must, evidently, be made for the prejudices of Muslem historians, who would, of course, neglect nothing calculated to cast odium on one so inimical to their superstitions. 'Umar Khayām seems particularly to direct his satire against the mysticisms of Mawāsī, the most exalted poet of his time, though inferior in this extraordinary and incomprehensible style to the later followers of the same school, Attār and the great Mulla. However reprehensible his mockery would be if really directed against religion in general, it scarcely deserves the severity it met when we consider that it was the abuses he attacked and the absurdities he ridiculed; and as for the incongruities introduced into his poems, and his professed love of pleasure, he is only following, or rather pointing out as absurd, the contradictions of the mystic poets which are difficult enough to reconcile to the understanding, whether allegorical or not. The following will give an idea of the true spirit of 'Umar Khayām:

"Ah! ye who long that, in time's coming night,
Your names should shine in characters of light,
Let not this duty ever be forgot—
Love well your neighbour; do him no despite."

"Ah! strive your best no human heart to wring,
Let no one feel your anger burn or sting;
Would you be wrapped in everlasting joy,
Learn how to suffer, and cause no suffering."

A famous paraphrase of the Quatrains by Mr. Edward Fitzgerald has been published by Quaritch of London. Though most charming as poetry, this version fails to give a correct idea of the original, which is a mere collection of disjointed and inconsistent epigrams, and by no means the continuous meditations of the English poet. A more faithful, though less artistic, version has appeared in Trübner's *Oriental Series*; made by Mr. E. H. W. Whinfield. 'Umar Khayām was contemporaneous with Hasan Sabbāh, Nizām-ul-Mulk, wazīr of Malikh-shāh, and Mawāsī the poet. Khushgo in his Tazkira has recorded the year of 'Umar Khayām's death A.D. 1123, A.H. 517, and this appears to be correct. Wajid 'Alī, in his *Matla-ul-Ulūm*, says that he died in A.D. 1121, A.H. 515.

'Umar Mahrami (عمر مہرامی), author of a work called *Hujjat-ul-Hind*, written in A.D. 1645.

'Umar Mirza (عمر مرزا), one of the sons of Mīrānshāh, the son of Amīr Taimūr. He was defeated and wounded in a battle fought against Shāhrukh Mirzā, and died after a few days in May, A.D. 1407, A.H. 809.

'Umar Sahlan (Qazi Mir) Sawaji (عمرسہلان قاضی ساوجی), author of a work on the Science of Logic and Philosophy called *Masābir Nasīrī*, which he dedicated to Nasīr-uddīn Mahmud, the wazīr of Sultān Sanjar.

'Umar Shaikh Mirza (عمر شیخ مرزا), second son of Amīr Taimūr. He was governor of Persia during the lifetime of his father, and was killed in battle in A.D. 1394, A.H. 799, aged 40 years. Bāiqara Mirzā who succeeded him was one of his sons.

'Umar Shaikh Mirza (عمر شیخ مرزا), one of the eleven sons of Sultān Abū Sa'īd Mirzā, the son of Sultān Muhammad, the son of Mīrānshāh, the son of Amīr Taimūr. He was the father of Bābar Shāh, king of Dehlī; born at Samarqand in the year A.D. 1456, A.H. 860, and held the government of Andijān during the lifetime of his father, which, with the united principality of Farghāna, he continued to govern after his death, which took place in A.D. 1469, A.H. 873. He died after a reign of 26 lunar years and 2 months, on Monday the 9th June, A.D. 1494, 4th Ramazān, A.H. 899, by the fall of a scaffold upon which he stood to see his pigeons fly, aged 39 lunar years. His son Bābar, then in his eleventh year, was advanced to the throne by his nobles, and assumed the title of Zahīr-uddin.

'Umdat-ul-Mulk (عمدت الملک), a title of Nawāb Amīr Khān.

'Umdat-ul-Umra (عمدة الامرا), the eldest son of Muhammad 'Alī Khān, the Nawāb of the Karnātik. He succeeded his father in October, A.D. 1795, and died on the 15th July, A.D. 1801. On his death the English resolved to take the functions of government into their own hands. 'Alī Husain, the next heir, refused to comply. The English, in consequence, raised 'Azim-uddaula, the nephew of the deceased nawāb, to the nominal throne, on condition that he renounced the power of government in their favour.

Umid (امید), the poetical name of Mirzā Muhammad Raza, whose title was Kizalbāsh Khān, which see.

Umidi Maulana (امیدی مولانا), one of the best poets of his time, born at Tehrān, a province of Rei. Najm Sānī, Mīr 'Abdul Bāqī and Khwāja Habīb-ullāh, who were nobles in the service of Shāh Ismā'īl Safwī, were his intimate friends; but Shāh Kawām-uddīn Nūr Bakhshī, who was also one of the courtiers, and was his enemy, murdered him one night in the year A.D. 1519, A.H. 925.

Umm Habiba (ام حبیبہ), one of the wives of Muhammad. She was the daughter of Abū Sufiān, the father of Mu'āwia I. and died in A.D. 664, A.H. 44.

Umm Habiba (ام حبیبہ), daughter of Rabia', and fourth wife of 'Alī, by whom she had one son, named 'Umar.

Umm Hanna (ام حنی), a daughter of Abū Tālib, and sister of 'Alī, the son-in-law of Muhammad.

Umm Jamil (ام جمیل), daughter of Harb, sister of Abū Sufiān, and wife of Abū Lahab. Because she fomented the hatred which her husband bore to Muhammad, a passage in the Qurān, chap. cxi. was revealed against them.

Umm Maqri (ام مقری), one of the principal Muhammadan saints, born at Ghaznī; who acquired such great reputation by his sanctity that Sultān Mahmūd often went to consult him, and refused to sit down in his presence out of respect for his virtues. He lived about the year A.D. 1000.

Umm Salma (ام سلمہ), daughter of Abū Umayya and wife of Muhammad. She outlived all the wives of that prophet, and died in A.D. 679, A.H. 59.

Ung or **Ang** (انگ), which see.

Uns (اُنس), poetical name of Munshī Lālchānd. *Vide* Lālchānd.

'Unsari (عنصری), commonly called Abū'l Qāsim 'Unsarī, a native of Balkh, and one of the learned men who lived at the court of Sultān Mahmūd of Ghaznī. He was a pupil of Abū'l Farah Sanjarī and master of the poets Asjadī and Farrukhī. He is esteemed to hold the first rank, as to genius, in that age; for besides being one of the best poets he was a great philosopher, versed in all the known sciences and all the learned languages of those times. Four hundred poets and learned men, besides all the students of the university of Ghaznī, acknowledged him for their master. Among the works of 'Unsarī there is an heroic poem upon the actions of Sultān Mahmūd. The king one night in a debauch having cut off the long tresses of his favourite slave, Ayaz, was much concerned in the morning for what he had done. 'Unsarī accosted him with some extempore lines on the occasion, which so pleased the king that he ordered his mouth to be thrice filled with jewels. He wrote a Dīwān consisting of 30,000 couplets, and died, according to Daulat Shah, in the reign of Sultān Masa'ūd I. the son of Sultan Mahmūd, A.D. 1040, A.H. 431. Dr. Sprenger, in his *Catalogue of Persian Books*, says, page 15, "that 'Unsarī died in A.D. 1049, A.H. 441."

Unsi (اُنسی), a poet, whose proper name was Muhammad Shah. He died in A D. 1565, A.H. 973.

'Uqail (عقیل), the brother of 'Alī, the the son of 'Abū Tālib, who, not being entertained by his brother according to his quality, joined Mu'āwia, A.D. 660, A.H. 40, who received him with open arms, and assigned him large revenues. His son Muslim, who espoused the cause of his uncle Husain, was beheaded by 'Ubed-ullāh ibn-Zayād in the reign of Yezīd.

'Urfi, Maulana (عرفی مولانا), a native of Shīrāz and an excellent poet. His proper name is Jamāl-uddīn, but he is better known by his poetical title, 'Urfī. He first came to the Deccan, and thence to Āgra, where he passed a few years in the service of Hakīm Abū'l Fathā Gīlānī, after whose death, in A.D. 1589, A.H. 997, 'Abdul Rahīm Khān, Khān Khānān introduced him to the emperor Akbar, who, finding him to be a well learned man, and a good poet, employed him among his own officers. Not long afterwards he died, in the year A.D. 1591, A.H. 999, aged 36 years, at Lāhore, where he was buried; but as he had expressed his wish in one of his odes that his remains should be transported to Najaf Ashraf, where 'Alī is buried, his bones were accordingly, after some years, sent to that place by Mīr Sābir Isfahānī and re-interred there. He is the author of several works, of which his Dīwān and Qasāed are most esteemed; and were, even during his lifetime very popular, and sold in every street.

'Urian (عریان), poetical name of Mirzā Asad.

'Usmar, Osman or **Othman** (عثمان), the first Sultān of the Turks, was the son of Amīr Tughral, who died in A.D. 1288, A.H 687. His grandfather Sulaimān was a native of Balkh, which country he left on the invasion of Changez Khān in A.D. 1414, A.H. 611, and went to Rome, where he was drowned. 'Usmān served under Sultān 'Alā-uddīn Kaikubad, one of the Saljūqian Sultāns of Iconium in Karamania. He had received a grant of land in the direction of ancient Phrygia, where he took Brusa from the Greek emperor, and laid the foundation of that power called after him Ottoman or 'Usmania, and on the destruction of the Sultānate of Iconium in A.D. 1299 by the Mongols succeeded in obtaining possession of a portion of Bithynia. According to the work *Haft Aklīm*, the first year of his reign is fixed A.D. 1289, A.H. 688, and that he reigned 38 lunar years and died in A.D. 1327, A.H. 727, and was buried at Brusa. His son Orkhān succeeded him.

List of the Emperors of Turkey of the 'Usmān or Ottoman Family.

'Usmān or Osmān.
Orkhān, son of 'Usmān.
Murād I. son of Orkhān.
Bāyezīd I. son of Bāyezīd.
Sulaimān, son of Bāyezīd.
Muhammad I. son of Bāyezīd.
Murād II. son of Muhammad.
Muhammad II. son of Murād.
Bāyezīd II. son of Muhammad II.
Salīm I. son of Bāyezīd.
Sulaimān I. surnamed the Magnificent, son of Salīm.
Salīm II. son of Sulaimān.
Murād III. son of Salīm II.
Muhammad III. son of Murād III.
Ahmad I. son of Murād III.
Mustafā I. son of Murād III.
'Usmān I. son of Ahmad I.
Murād IV. son of Ahmad I.
Ibrāhīm, son of Ahmad I.
Muhammad IV. son of Ibrāhīm.
Sulaimān II. son of Ibrāhīm.
Ahmad II. son of Ibrāhīm.
Mustafā II. son of Muhammad IV.
Ahmad II. son of Muhammad.
Mahmūd I. son of Mustafā II.
'Usmān II. son of Mustafā II.
Mustafā III. son of Ahmad III.
Ahmad IV. son of Ahmad III.
Salīm III. son of Mustafā III.
Mustafā IV. son of Ahmad IV.
Mahmūd II. son of Ahmad IV.
Abdul Majīd, son of Mahmūd II.

'Usman, Osman or Othman I. (عثمان), son of Aḥmad I. (Achmet), succeeded his uncle, Mustafā I. (who was deposed in 1618), on the Turkish throne, and, being unsuccessful in his wars against Poland in 1621, was by the Jannisārīs slain in an uproar, A.D. 1622, and Mustafā was again restored; but not for long, for the same hands that raised him to the throne again plucked him down, in A.D. 1623, and raised Murād IV. to be their king.

'Usman II. (عثمان), brother of Mahmūd I. (or, as some call him, Muhammad V.), whom he succeeded to the throne as emperor of Constantinople in A.D. 1754, A.H. 1168. He renewed, under severe penalties, the Muhammadan law that his subjects should drink no wine. He died after a short reign in A.D. 1757, A.H. 1171, aged 59 years, and was succeeded by Mustafā III. his nephew.

'Usman (عثمان بن عفان), the son of 'Affān, the son of 'Abū'l 'As, the son of Umayya, was one of the favourite companions of Muhammad. He succeeded 'Umar as third khalīf after Muhammad, in November, A.D. 644, Muḥarram, A.H. 24, and was murdered, after a reign of nearly twelve years, in his own house at Medina by 'Al Ghāfikī and several others on the 30th June, A.D. 665, 18th Ẕil-ḥijja, A.H. 35, aged 82 years. His corpse lay unburied for three days; at last it was removed, bloody as it was, and buried in the same clothes as he was killed in, without so much as being washed, and without the least funeral solemnity. The dissensions which arose on the death of the Prophet, with regard to the succession to the Khilāfat, were revived with renewed fury when, on the murder of 'Usman, the noble and unfortunate 'Alī succeeded to the dignity of Amīr-ul-Mominīn; and they eventually caused the division of Islām into two great parties or sects, called respectively the Sunnīs and the Shias, who differ materially in the interpretation of the Qurān, and in admitting or rejecting various portions of the oral law. The hatred entertained between these rival sects has been the cause of constant religious wars and persecutions scarcely to be surpassed in the history of any nation or creed, and still separates the followers of Muhammad into two classes by a barrier more insurmountable than that which divides the Roman Catholic from the Protestant.

'Usman bin-Isa bin-Ibrahim Sadiq (عثمان بن عیسوی), author of a collection of traditions in Arabic called *Ghāet-ut-Touzīh*.

'Usman Mukhtari (عثمان مختاری), a poet who flourished in the reign of Sulṭān Ibrāhīm of Ghaznī, and was a contemporary of Shāikh Sanāī, the poet.

'Usqalāni (عسقلانی), an author. *Vide* Shahāb-uddīn Abū'l Fazl Aḥmad.

'Utba (عتبه), the son of Abū Lahab. He was married to Rukyya, third daughter of Muhammad, but repudiated her afterwards. It is said that he was torn to pieces by a lion, in the presence of a whole caravan, when on a journey to Syria.

'Uzaeri Razi (عضایری رازی), one of the learned men, and poet of the court, of Sulṭān Mahmūd of Ghaznī, whose poetical performance as a panegyrist are esteemed very good, for one of which he received a present of 4000 dirhams from the Sulṭān. He is called Assaberi Rāzī in the *Dictionary of the Religious Ceremonies of the Eastern Nations*. He was a native of Rei, consequently the word Rāzī is fixed to his name.

Uzbak (اذبک), a tribe of Turks.

Uzlat (عذلت), the poetical name of Sayyad 'Abdul Walī, the son of a very learned and pious man named S'adullāh, in whom Aurangzeb had very great confidence. After the death of his father he went down to Murshidābād and was supported by Alahwardī Khān. After the demise of his patron, in A.D. 1756, he went to the Deccan, where he died, and left a Dīwān.

Uzzan Hasan (أذن حسن) (or Hasan the Long), who is also called Hasan Beg, was the founder of the tribe of Turkmans called Aqqoinlos, or the White Sheep. After he had extirpated his rival, Jahān Shāh, the son of Qarā Yūsaf, in A.D. 1467, and put all his relations to death, he engaged in a war with Sulṭān Abū S'aīd Mīrzā, king of Persia, who fell into his hands and was slain, A.D. 1449. Uzzan Hasan from this event became sovereign of a great part of the dominions of the house of Taimūr. After he had made himself master of Persia he turned his arms in the direction of Turkey; but his career of greatness was arrested by the superior genius of the Turkish emperor, Muhammad II. from whom he suffered a signal defeat, which terminated his schemes of ambition. He died, after a reign of eleven years, at the age of seventy, on the 7th December, A.D. 1477, A.H. 882. Catherine Commenus, who is called by the Persians, Carum Commeniah, was married to him. She had a daughter named Martha, married to Shaikh Haidar, father of Shāh Ismā'īl Safwī, first monarch of the Safwīan dynasty of Persia. Uzzan Hasan was succeeded by his son Y'aqūb Beg.

V

Victoria Gaurama, Princess (وکتوریا گـاورامـا). The Princess Victoria Gaurāma, the daughter of his Highness Prince Bīr Rājindar Wadēr, ex-Rāja of Kurg (Coorg), a small principality of Hindustān, situated near the Mysore country; its greatest length is about seventy miles, and the mean breadth about twenty-two miles. Haidar 'Alī contrived, in the middle of the last century, to get possession of Kurg by treachery; but in 1787 the young Rāja Bīr Rājindar, his prisoner, escaped from confinement, through the aid of several of his subjects, and succeeded in establishing himself in his dominions. At his death, in 1808, he left the succession to an infant daughter, to the exclusion of his brother, to whom of right it belonged, according to ancient usages; but the young princess soon afterwards abdicated in favour of her uncle, with the sanction of the British Government.

The Princess Victoria Gaurāma was born in February, A.D. 1841. The melancholy circumstance of the death of the mother, two days after the birth of the child, seems to have led to increased affection for his offspring on the part of the father, who, from his own previous convictions in favour of Christianity, determined that his favourite daughter should be brought up in the principles of the Christian faith. From this period the Rāja entertained an anxious desire to visit Europe, in order that, when she had arrived at a suitable age, she might be introduced into European society; and thereby receive such impressions as would promote a feeling favourable to Christianity. Accordingly, in the early part of A.D. 1852, the prince quitted India for England, leaving at the city of Benares the rest of his family, consisting of eleven children, with their mothers. On his arrival in England the object of his visit was made known to the Queen, who at once most kindly and graciously consented to become sponsor to the young princess. The baptismal ceremony was performed by the Archbishop of Canterbury in the private chapel of Buckingham Palace on the 30th June, A.D. 1852, in the presence of Her Majesty, the Prince Consort, and numerous other members of the Royal Family: the princess received the prefix of "Victoria" to her Indian name of "Gaurāma," by which she had been called after one of the pagan divinities of her country. She married a British officer named Campbell.

The princess is said to have become a good scholar under the care of those charged with her education. Her personal appearance was exceedingly interesting and intelligent, and the complexion of her skin but little darker than that which Europeans call a deep brunette. Her portrait, which Winterhalter painted by command of Her Majesty, is at Buckingham Palace.

[Vide *Art Journal*, vol. iii. p. 293.]

Vikramaditya (ویکرامادیتیا), commonly called Bikramājīt, which see.

W

Waez (واعظ). *Vide* Husain Wāez, and Muhammad Rafī Wāez.

Wafa (وفا). *Vide* Ayn-ul-Mulk Hakīm.

Wafa (وفا), poetical name of Mirzā Sharaf-uddīn 'Alī Husainī of Qumm. He came to India in A.D. 1749, A.H. 1162, and is the author of a short Dīwān.

Wafa (وفا), poetical name of Dayānāth, a Kashmīrī of Barelī. He is the author of a poem called *Gul wa Bulbul*, the Nightingale and the Rose, which he composed in A.D. 1847, A.H. 1263.

Wafai (وفای), title of a poet.

Wahab or **Wahhab** (وهاب), the son of 'Abdul Manāf, was the father of 'Amina, the mother of Muhammad.

Wahdat (وحدت), poetical name of Shaikh Jamāl-uddīn, the great-grandfather of Shaikh Muhammad Hazīn. He is the author of several works, *viz. Elucidation of the Miracle of the Morāj, or Ascent of the Prophet*; *An Explanation or Commentary in Persian on the Kulliāt of the Qānūn*, which he wrote at the desire of Khān Aḥmad Khān, king of Gilān; *An Epistle or Treatise on the Confirmation of a Necessary Being*; *A Treatise on the Solution of Obscurities in the Section of Surds or Solids*; an extensive *Commentary on the Fisūs or Gems of Faryābī*, and a Dīwān containing 2000 couplets.

Wahdat (وحدت), poetical name of 'Abdul Ahad, who was familiarly called Shāh Gul, a son of Shaikh Muhammad Sa'īd and grandson of Shaikh Aḥmad Sarhindī. He resided mostly in the Kōṭila, near Dehlī, and is the author of a Dīwān. He died in A.D. 1714, A.H. 1126.

Wahid (واحد). *Vide* Tahir Wahīd.

Wahidi (وحیدی), poetical title of Wahīd-uddīn, which see.

Wahidi (واحدی), poetical name of 'Alī, son of Aḥmad, which see.

Wahid-uddin Tabrizi (وحیدالدین تبریزی), a poet of Persia, whose poetic title is Wahīdī. He is the author of a treatise written professedly upon versification.

Wahmi (واهمی), poetical appellation of Hājī Tahmāsp Qulī, a poet who flourished in India between the years A.D. 1637 and 1647, A.H. 1047 and 1057.

Wahshat (وحشت), poetical title of Shaikh 'Abdul Wāhid, who was a descendant of Imām Muhammad Ghazzālī. He was an excellent poet, born and brought up in Qasba Thānesar. He flourished in the reign of 'Alamgīr, and is the author of a Dīwān.

Wahshi Yezdi, Maulana of Yezd (وحشی یزدی مولانا), author of the Masnawī or poem called *Nāzir wa Manzūr*, which he completed in the year A.D. 1559, A.H. 966, and of another poem called *Farhad and Shīrīn*, in the metre of Niẓam's *Khusro and Shīrīn*, and several other works. He died in A.D. 1584, A.H. 992.

Wa'il Khuza'i (واعل خزاعی), an Arabian poet in the time of Harūn-al-Rashīd and his son Māmūn. He was contemporary with Imām 'Alī Mūsī Raza, and is the author of a Dīwān in Arabic wherein he praises the charms of his beloved Salmī.

Wajid 'Ali (واجد علی), author of an Urdū Grammar, entitled *Guldastae Anjuman*, which he wrote and published at Āgra in the year A.D. 1849, and another work called *Matla-ul-Ulūm*.

Wajid 'Ali Shah (واجد علی شاه), the last king of Audh, was the son of 'Amjad 'Alī Shāh, after whose death he ascended the throne at Lucknow, in A.D. 1847, A.H. 1263. In his time Audh was annexed to the British Government, on the 7th February, A.D. 1856. His poetical title is Akhtar, and he is the author of three Dīwāns and three Masnawīs in Urdū. This ex-king died in Calcutta, pensioned by Government.

Inscription on his coin.

سکه زه بر سیم و زر از فضل و تامیر الهه
ظل حق واجد علی سلطان عالم بادشه

Wajih-uddin Ahmad Maghrabi (وجیه الدین احمد مغربی), commonly called Shaikh Aḥmad Khaṭṭū, which see.

Wajih - uddin Mubarak Kirmani (وجیه الدین مبارک کرمانی), a Sayyad and a disciple of Niẓām-uddīn Aulia. He was commonly called Sayyad Khūrd, or the little Sayyad. He is the author of the work called *Siar-ul-Aulia*.

[*Vide* Sayyad Husain (Makhdūm).]

Wajih-uddin, Shaikh (وجیه الدین شیخ), of Gujrāt, a disciple of Shaikh Muhammad Ghaus of Gwāliar. He was a learned man, is the author of several works, and his poetical name was Alwī. He died on the 30th November, A.D. 1589, 1st Ṣafar, A.H. 998, and was buried in Aḥmadabād Gujrāt.

Waqidi (واقدی), surname of Muhammad bin-'Umar, an author who wrote in Arabic the work called *Tabaqāt Wāqidī*, containing the history of the conquests of Syria by the generals of 'Umar during the years A.D. 638-9. He died in the year A.D. 824 or 834, A.H. 209 or 219. Ibn-Jauzī relates that Wāqidī, who dwelt at Baghdād, when removing to the eastern bank of the Tigris, required 120 camels to convey his books.

[*Vide* Abū Abdullāh Muhammad ibn-'Umar-ul-Wāqidī.]

Waqif (واقف), the poetical name of a poet whose proper name is Nūr-al-Ayn. He was a native of Paṭiāla, of which place his father was a Qāzī. He was contemporary with the poet 'Arzū, and died about the year A.D 1776, A.H. 1190. He is commonly called Wāqif Lahorī, and his Dīwān contains about 800 Persian Ghazals.

Wala (والا), poetical name of Islām Khān, which see.

Walad (ولد). *Vide* Sulṭān Walad, who is also called Maulānā Walad.

Walah (واله), poetical name of Said Muhammad, author of a poem called *Dastūr-ul-Nazm*.

Walah (واله), poetical title of 'Alī Qulī Khān of Dāghistan. He is the author of a Tazkira entitled *Rayāz-ush-Shu'ārā*. It is an universal biographical dictionary of Persian poets, and contains about 2500 articles. He came to India in A.D. 1734, A.H. 1147, where he composed the above work in A.D. 1748, A.H. 1161, and died nine years afterwards, in A.D. 1757, A.H. 1170. He was the father of Gunna Begum, which see.

Walajah (والاجه), a title of Muhammad 'Alī Khān, nawāb of the Karnatik, who died in A.D. 1795, aged 87 years.

Walajah, Prince (والاجه شهزاده), son of 'Azim Shāh. He, along with his brother Beidār Bakht, was killed in the battle fought by his father against the emperor Bahādur Shāh, his eldest brother, in A.D. 1707.

Wali (والی), poetical name of Najaf 'Alī Beg, an author.

Wali (والی), poetical name of Shāh Walī-ullāh, a native of Gujrāt, but who passed the greatest part of his life in the Deccan. He was living in the time of the emperor 'Alamgīr, and is the first poet who wrote a Dīwān in Urdū. A copy of this book was brought to Dehlī in A.D. 1720, A.H. 1132, which induced many poets of that city to apply themselves to Urdū poetry.

[*Vide* Hātim.]

Wali, of Dasht Bayaz (ولی دشت بیاض), a place in Khurāsān. He was contemporary with Mirzā Muhammad Qulī Mailī, who came to India in A.D. 1571, A.H. 982. Walī is the author of a Persian Dīwān.

[*Vide* Walī (Maulānā).]

Walidad Khan and Ahmad 'Ali Khan (ولیداد خان), rebel leaders in Bulandshahr (N.W. Provinces) during the troubles of 1857.

Wali, Maulana (ولی مولانا دشت بیاضی), a famous poet of Dasht Bayāz, in Khurāsān, who was a contemporary of Maulāna Zamīrī, and was put to death by order of Taimūr Sulṭān Uzbak, who had taken possession of Khurāsān in the reign of Sulṭān Muhammad Khudā Banda, king of Persia, who reigned from A.D. 1577 to 1588, A.H. 985 to 995. He is the author of a Persian Dīwān.

[*Vide* Walī of Dasht Bayāz.]

Wali Muhammad, Hazrat (ولی محمد حضرت نارنولی), of Narnoul, a Musalmān saint, who died on the 13th November, A.D. 1647, Shawwāl, A.H. 1057.

Wali Muhammad Khan Uzbak (ولی محمد خان اذبک), king of Tūrān, was the son of Jānī Beg Khān by 'Abdullāh Khān Uzbak's daughter. He was raised to the throne of Tūrān after the death of his brother, Bāqī Beg Khān, and visited Shāh Abbās, king of Persia, in A.D. 1611, A.H. 1020. He reigned six years, and was killed in battle about the year A.D. 1612.

Wali Qalandar (والی قلندر), a poet who lived in the time of Bāisanghar Mirzā.

Wali Ram (ولی رام), a Hindū, who was usually called Banwālī Dās, is the author of a Masnawī.

Wali-uddin 'Abu 'Abd-ullah Muhammad bin 'Abdullah-al-Katib, Shaikh (ولی الدین ابو عبدالله شیخ), author of the *Mishqāt-ul-Masābīh*, a new and augmented edition of the *Masābīh* of al-Baghwī, which he completed in A.D. 1336, A.H. 737. It is a concise collection of traditions, principally taken from the Six Books or Sahīhs, and arranged in chapters according to subjects. This collection was translated by Captain Matthews in A.D. 1809.

Wali-ullah, Maulwi Shah (ولی الله مولوی شاه دهلوی), of Dehlī, author of the commentary on the Qurān in Persian, entitled *Fath-ul-Rahmān*.

Wali-ullah Husaini, Maulwi Muhammad (ولی الله حسینی مولوی محمد), author of a commentary on the Qurān, called *Nazm-ul-Jawāhir*, which he wrote in A.D. 1821, A.H. 1236.

Walid (ولید بن عتبه), the son of 'Utba, was made governor of Medina by Mu'āwia I. but was removed from the government of that city by Yezīd I. in favour of Amrū, the son of Saīd, who was then governor of Mecca.

Walid I. (ولید بن عبدالملک), seventh khalīf of the house of Umayya. He succeeded his father, 'Abdulmalik, in Syria, A.D. 705, A.H. 96, and died, after a reign of nine years and some months, about the year A.D. 714. Spain was conquered in his time by his generals. He was succeeded by his brother Sulaimān.

Walid II. (ولید بن یزید), son of Yezīd II. succeeded his uncle Hāshim in Syria as eleventh khalīf of the race of Umayya in A.D. 743, A.H. 126. He reigned little more than a year, and was slain in A.D. 744, when his son Yezīd III. succeeded him.

Wamiq (وامق), the celebrated lover of Azrā. The poet Farkhārī has written a poem on their love adventures.

Waraqa (ورقه), a lover, the name of whose mistress was Gulshāh.

Waraqa bin-Naufat (ورقه بن نوفت), a cousin of Khudyja, the wife of Muhammad. In the days of ignorance he learned the Christian religion, translated the gospel into Arabic, gave himself up to devotion, and opposed the worship of idols. He became a convert to Muhammadanism about the year A.D. 611, lived to a great age, becoming blind towards the end of his life.

Warusta (وارسته لاهوری), a poet of Lāhore, who is the author of a work called *Jung Rangārang*, being a collection of verses of all the poets who have written on different matters. He was living in A.D. 1766, A.H. 1180.

Wasfi (وصفی). *Vide* Abdullāh Tirmizī.

Wasili (واصل). *Vide* 'Alā-ud-dīn (Sayyad).

Wasili (واصلی), poetical appellation of Mīr Imām Wardī Beg, who is the author of a Dīwān, and was living at Lucknow in A.D. 1780, A.H. 1194.

Wasil-ibn-'Ata (واصل ابن عطا), the master of Amr-ibn-Waid, with whom he seceded from the school of Al-Hassan al-Basri, in the 8th century, A.D. The name of M'utasila was given to them by Katāla ibn Diāma, the Sadusi (*q. v.*).

Wasil Khan of Kashmere (واصل خان کشمیری), author of the *Mahārāj-nāma*, in the preface of which he praises Nawāb 'Asaf-uddaula, Mahārāja Nirmal Dās, and Lāla Hulās Rāe.

Wasiq or **Wathiq Billah** (واثق بالله), a khalīfa of Baghdād. *Vide* Al-Wāsiq.

Wasiq Mulla (واثق ملا), name of a poet.

Wasli (وصلی), the poetical title of 'Aqa Tāhir, the father of Sādiq Khān.

Wasti (واسطی), poetical title of Mīr 'Abdul Jalīl Bilgramī, which see.

Watwat (وطواط), the nickname of the poet Rashīdī, which see. It is also the surname of Muhammad bin-Ibrāhīm, the son of Ahia, the son of 'Alī-al-Kātibī, an Arabian author.

Wazah (واضح), the poetical title of Mirzā Mubārik, styled Irādat Khān, the grandson of Nawāb 'Azim Khān, of the time of Jahāngīr. He took instructions in the art of poetry from Mīr Muhammad Rāsikh, and became an excellent poet; but in the latter part of his life he led a retired life, became a Qalandar, and died in A.D. 1716, A.H. 1128. [*Vide* Irādat Khān.]

Wazah (واضح), poetical name of 'Aqā 'Alī Asghar, who was originally a manufacturer of gold thread. He was living in A.D. 1720, A.H. 1132, and is the author of a Dīwān.

Wazir (وزیر), the poetical title of Khwāja Wazīr, son of Khwāja Faqīr of Lucknow. He died in A.D. 1854, A.H. 1270, and is the author of a Dīwān in Urdū.

Wazir (وزیر), poetical name of Shaikh Wazīr, author of two Dīwāns, Persian and Urdū.

Wazir 'Ali Khan (وزیر علی خان), for a short time Nawāb of Lucknow, was the adopted son of Nawāb 'Asaf-uddaula, on whose death, in September, A.D. 1797, he was raised to the masnad of Audh at Lucknow, but after a short interval, grounds for disputing the authenticity of his pretensions having been established, he was deposed on the 21st January, A.D. 1798, by Sir John Shore, and Saādat 'Alī Khān, the brother of the late Nawāb, was placed on the masnad. Wazīr 'Alī was sent to Benares, where he murdered Mr. Cherry, the Political Agent, on Monday the 14th January, A.D. 1799, 8th Shāban, A.H. 1213. He at first fled to Butwal, and afterwards took refuge with the Rāja of Jaipūr, a powerful independent chief, who refused to give him up unless under a stipulation of his life being spared. To this it was thought prudent to accede, and, being accordingly given up to the British in December following, he was brought down to Calcutta and confined at Fort William in a bomb-proof, divided by iron-gratings in three parts; the longest, in the centre, was occupied by Wazīr 'Alī, and the other two by sentries, one English and one native. After many years captivity, he was transported to a more suitable prison, in the palace built for Tipū Sultān's family in the fort of Vellore, where the females of his family subsequently joined him, and there he died. Lord Teignmouth, in the Life of his father, states that Wazīr 'Alī died in rigorous confinement in Fort William, but this appears to be a mistake. His death took place in the month of May, A.D. 1817, Rajab, A.H. 1232, after 17 years 3 months and 4 days' confinement, and was buried at Kāsī Bāghān, close to a tomb of one of the sons of Tipū Sultān. He was then in his 36th year. His mother was the wife of a Farrash. The expenses of his marriage in A.D. 1795 amounted to 30 lakhs of rupees, while 70 rupees were sufficient to defray all the cost of his funeral in A.D. 1817; a strange reverse of fortune.

Wazir Khan (وزیر خان), surname of Muhammad Tāhir, an officer of the rank of 5000, who served under the emperor 'Alamgīr. In the latter years of his life he was appointed governor of Mālwa, where he died in A.D. 1672. His nephew, Rāfī Khān, is the author of the *Hamlae Haidarī*.

Wazir Khan (وزیر خان), an Amīr of the Court of the Emperor Shāh Jahān, by whom he was raised to the rank of 5000 into the title of Wazīr Khān, and the Sūbadarship of the Panjāb. He built a splendid masjīd at Lāhore in A.H. 1044, which is still in good preservation. His proper name was Hakīm Alīm-uddīn.

Wazir Muhammad, Nawab of Bhopal (وزیر محمد), an ally of the British Government, died in March, A.D. 1816, and his son, Nāzar Muhammad Khān, succeeded him.

Wazir-uddaula (وزیر الدوله), title of Wazīr Muhammad Khān, the Nawāb of Tonk, the son of Nawāb Amīr Khān, the Pindara Chief. He died in June, A.D. 1864.

Wazir-uddaula (وزیر الدوله). *Vide* Nāzir-ul-Mulk Wazīr-uddaula.

Wikar-ul-Umra (وکرال عمرا), the son of Shams-ul-Umra, Nawāb of Haidarabād, Deccan.

Wisal (وصال), the poetical name of Mirzā Kōchak of Shīrāz, author of a *Farhād wa Shīrīn*.

Wisali (وصـــالـی), poetical name of Sayyad 'Alā-uddīn, a modern poet of Khurāsān, who was settled in Audh. He is the author of an *Elegy on the Imāms*.

[*Vide* 'Alā-uddīn (Sayyad).]

Wis Karani (ویس کرانی. *Vide* Aweis Qaranī.

Wizarat Khan. (وزارت خان), whose proper name is Mīr Abdur Rahmān, was the second son of Amānat Khān Mīrak, an excellent poet. His poetical name was Bikramī. He flourished in the time of the emperor 'Alamgīr, and has left a Dīwān.

[*Vide* Bikramī.]

X

Xavier Hieronymo, a Catholic Missionary who came from Goa to Dehlī in the reign of the emperor Jahāngīr. He is the author of a religious work in Persian, entitled the *Mirror of Truth*, which he dedicated to the emperor in the year A.D. 1609, and which has been preserved in the Library of Queen's College, Cambridge. A reply to this book was written a few years after its appearance by Aḥmad ibn-Zain-ul-'Abidīn Alalwī, to which he gave the title of *The divine rays in refutation of Christian error*, a copy of which is also preserved in the same College. This work was written by the author in the month of November, A.D. 1621, Muḥarram, A.H. 1031.

Y

Yadgar Muhammad, Mirza (یادگار محمد مرزا), the son of Mirzā Muhammad, the son of Mirzā Bāisanghar, the son of Mirzā Shāhrukh, the son of Amīr Taimūr. After the death of Mirzā Bāisanghar, his grandfather, he succeeded him as governor of Khurāsān in A.D. 1434, and held that situation till the death of Sulṭān 'Abū Saīd Mirzā, who, being taken prisoner by a competitor, was made over to Yādgār Muhammad in A.D. 1469, A.H. 873, who slew him. After his death Sulṭān Husain Bāiqara took possession of Herāt, with whom Yādgār Muhammad had several battles; but was at last slain in a night attack on the 25th August, A.D. 1470, 27th Ṣafar, A.H. 875. He was the last of the descendants of Shāhrukh Mirzā, and is said to have written excellent poetry.

Yadgar Nasir, Mirza (یادگار ناصر مرزا), brother of the emperor Bābar Shāh. When the emperor Humāyūn, after his return from Persia, marched in person in the year A.D. 1546, A.H. 953, to reduce Badakhshān, Yādgār Nāsir, having attempted to stir up a sedition in the royal army, was, upon conviction, sentenced to death, though he was uncle to the emperor.

Yafa'i, Imam (یافعي امام), a Muhammadan doctor, whose proper name was 'Abdullah bin-Asa'd. He was a native of Yāfa', in Syria, from which he was called Yāfa'ī. He is also called Quṭb Mecca and Yāfa'ī Nazal-ul-Haramyn. Shāh Na'matullah was one of his disciples. He is the author of several works in Arabic, among which are *Durr-ul-Nazm fī Munāfa-ul-Qurān*, *Rauzat-ul-Rayāzīn fī Hikāet-ul-Sālahīn*, *Khulāsat-ul-Mufākhir fī Munāqib-ush-Shaikh 'Abdul Qādir*, and the *Mirat-ul-Janān fī Hawādis-uz-Zamān*, the latter containing Memoirs of all the Muhammadan Generals and other illustrious characters, from the commencement of the Hijrī era, A.D. 622, to the year A.D. 1300, a very interesting work. Yāfa'ī, according to some, died in A.D. 1354, and according to others, in A.D. 1366, A.H. 755 or 767, but the latter date appears to be correct. He is sometimes called 'Abdullah bin-'Abdul Yāfa'ī.

Yafith, Hazrat (یفیث حضرت), the third son of the patriarch Noah, from whom the Turkmāns claim to be descended.

Yahia-bin-'Abdul Latif-al-Husaini of Kazwin, Amir (یحیی بن عبد اللطیف الحسینی امیر), author of the *Lubbut Tawārīkh*, which he composed in A.D. 1541, A.H. 948. Hājī Khalfa gives his name as Ismā'īl-bin-'Abdul Laṭīf, and in the *Māsir-ul-Umra* he is called Mīr Yahia Husainī Saifī. He was patronized by Shāh Tahmāsp Safwī, but his enemies, envious of his good fortune, endeavoured to poison his patron's mind against him, and at last prevailed so far as to induce the king to order him, together with his son Mīr 'Abdul Laṭīf, to be imprisoned. The latter, however, made his escape, but Mīr Yahia died in prison after one year and nine months' imprisonment in A.D. 1555, A.H. 962, aged 77 years. His second son, Alā-uddaula, known by the poetical name of Kāmī, is the author of the work called *Nafāis-ul-Māsir*. His eldest brother, Mīr 'Abdul Laṭīf, who had fled to Gīlān, came afterwards to Hindūstān with his family some time after Akbar had ascended the throne. By him he was received with great kindness and consideration, and was appointed his preceptor. He is said by some authors to have died at Sīkrī in A.D. 1563, A.H. 971, but the author of the *Māsir-ul-'Umra* writes that his death took place in A.D. 1573, A.H. 981, and that Qāsim Arsalān found the chronogram of his death to be "fakharālyas." His eldest son, Ghayās-uddīn 'Alī, was also endowed with an excellent disposition, and served Akbar for a long period. In the 26th year of Akbar's reign, A.D. 1581, he was honoured with the title of Naqīb Khān, by which he is now best known. In the time of Jahāngīr he attained still further honours, and died at Ajmir in A.D. 1614, A.H. 1023. He was buried there in a marble tomb within the area of Mo'in-uddīn Chishtī's mausoleum, where his wife also lies buried by his side. Naqīb Khān was one of the compilers of the first portion of the *Tārikh Alfī*, and the translator of the *Mahābhārat*, though this honour is usually ascribed to Faizi. He left a son named Mīr 'Abdul Laṭīf, who was a person of great worth and ability and attained high honours, but died insane.

Yahia bin-'Abdur Rahman (یحیی بن عبدالرحمان), author of the Arabic work on Theology called *Ayn-ul-Ilm*, the fountain of science, and one entitled *Afzal-uz-Salāt*, a collection of Traditions.

Yahia bin-'Abul Mansur (يحيى بن ابوالمنصور), one of the greatest astronomers that lived in the time of the Khalīf Al-Mansūr.

Yahia bin-Ahmad-al-Hilli or **Hulli** (يحيى بن احمد الحلى), who was celebrated for his knowledge of traditions, is well-known amongst the Imāmia sect for his works on jurisprudence, and is the author of the *Jamạ-ush-Sharāyạ* and the *Madkhal dar Usūl Fiqh*, which are in the greatest repute. He died A.D. 1280, A.H. 679.

Yahia bin-Aktam (يحيى بن اكتم) was Chief Justice during the Khilāfat of Al-Māmūn. He died in the reign of the Khalīf Al-Mutwakkil, A.D. 856, A.H. 242.

Yahia bin-Khalid (يحيى بن خالد), Grand Wazīr of Harūn-al-Rashīd, whose son Ja'far-al-Barmakī was put to death by order of that khalīf, A.D. 803, A.H. 187.

Yahia bin-Ma'az Razi (يحيى بن معاذ رازى), a very learned Muhammadan, who died on the 9th August, A.D. 871, 18th Ramaẓān, A.H. 257, and was buried at Naishāpūr.

Yahia Kashi, Mir (يحيى كاشى مير), one of the celebrated poets of the reign of the emperor Shāhjahān. On the completion of the palace and city of Shāhjahānābād in the year A.D. 1648, A.H. 1058, he wrote a chronogram, for which he was rewarded by that monarch with 5000 rupees. He died in the year A.D. 1654, A.H. 1064.

Yahia Maniri (يحيى منيرى), a celebrated saint, who is buried at Manīr.

[*Vide* Sharaf-uddin Aḥmad Ahia Manirī.]

Yahia, Mulla of Naishapur (يحيى ملا نيشاپورى). His poetical name is Fattāhī. He is the author of a Dīwān and of the Persian work called *Shabistān Khayāl*, "the Chamber of Imagination." He flourished in the reign of Shāhrukh Mirzā, and died A.D. 1448, A.H. 852.

Ya'jaz (يعجاز), the poetical name of Shaikh Muhammad Sa'īd, a native of Āgra and an excellent poet. He was living about the year A.D. 1691, A.H. 1102, in the reign of the emperor 'Alamgīr, and was employed in the service of Nawāb Mukarram Khān, Nāzim of Multān. He was a contemporary of the poet Sarkhush, who has mentioned him in his biography called *Kalmat-ush-Shu'āra*.

Yalduz (يلدوز). *Vide* Tāj-uddīn Eldūz.

Ya'mali of Herat (يعمالى هراتى), a poet who is the author of a Persian Dīwān.

Yamin-uddin Amir (يمين الدين امير), entitled Malik-ul-Fuzla, or prince of the learned, was the father of Amīr Mahmūd, commonly called ibn-Yamīn.

[*Vide* Amīr Yamīn-uddīn; also Tughrāī.]

Yamin-uddin, Amir (يمين الدين امير نزلابادى), a poet who was a native of Nazlābād in the province of Baihaq in Persia. He was contemporary with the poets Kātibī and 'Alī Shahāb. He is the author of several Masnawīs, viz. *Miṣbāh-ul-Kulūb*, containing dialogues between the Candle and the Moth; *Mishkāt-ul-Tālibīn*, dialogues between Wisdom and Love; and the story of *Fatha and Fathūh*.

Yamin-uddin Tughrai of Mashhad (يمين الدين طغرائي). *Vide* Tughrāī Mashhadī.

Yaqin (يقين), the poetical name of Ina'ām-ullāh Khān, an Urdū poet, who has left a Dīwān or collection of vernacular poems, principally on love subjects. He was the son of Azhar-uddīn Khān Bahādur Mubārak Jang, a grandson of the Mujaddid Alif Sānī, or Reformer of the second thousandth year, and a pupil of Mirzā Jānjānān Mazhar, who was so fond of him that he wrote most of his poetry in his name; he was killed at the age of 25 years, in the time of Aḥmad Shāh, about the year A.D. 1750, A.H. 1163, by his own father, because he brought disgrace on his family. His Dīwān is very celebrated.

Ya'qub Beg or **Sultan Ya'qub** (يعقوب بيگ), the son of Uzzan Hasan, whom he succeeded in A.D. 1477, A.H. 882, and became the king of the Turkmān tribes called Aqqoinlū, or the White Sheep. After his death he was succeeded by his son Alwand Beg, who was defeated about the year A.D. 1500, A.H. 996, by Shāh Ismā'īl I. Safwī.

Ya'qub bin-Idris (يعقوب بن ادريس). *Vide* Kirmānī.

Ya'qub bin-Lais Saffar, Amir (يعقوب بن ليث صفارى امير). He is also called Yakūt. He was the first who rebelled against the Abbasides, and was the founder of the dynasty of the Safārī, or Safārides, which signifies a pewterer. He raised himself from the humble station of a coppersmith to the rank of a sovereign in Sīstān, and having obtained the possession of Khurāsān and Tabaristān in A.D. 874, A.H. 260, from Muhammad, the son of Tahir II. whom he took prisoner, he was declared rebel by the Khalīf Mo'tamid, in consequence of which he marched with a powerful army towards Baghdād in the year A.D. 878, A.H. 265, but died on the road after a reign of 11 years. He was succeeded by his brother Amrū bin-Lais.

[*Vide* Lais.]

Ya'qub, Sultan (يعقوب سلطان). *Vide* Ya'qūb Beg.

Yaqut (ياقوت). *Vide* Ya'qūb bin-Lais.

Yari, Maulana (یاری مولانا), an author.

Yar Muhammad Khan, Mir (یار محمد خان میر), the son of Mīr Murād 'Alī, former ruler of the Haidarābād portion of Sindh. He is a brother of Muhammad Khān, who, being dispossessed and kept for some time a prisoner on the annexation of Sindh under Sir Charles Napier, was allowed to return, and afterwards lived at Haidarābād as a private gentleman upon a pension from Government.

Yazdi (یزدی), author of a treatise concerning divine love, called *Risālat fī bayān Muhabbat.*

Yazdijard I. (یزدجرد), surnamed Al-'Athim or Al-'Asim, the Sinner (the Isdigertes of the Greeks), whom some authors term the brother, and others the son, of his predecessor, Bahram IV. whom he succeeded to the throne of Persia, A.D. 404. This monarch is represented by Persian historians to have been a cruel prince, and, we are told, the nation rejoiced when he was killed by the kick of a horse. He died after a reign of 16 years, and was succeeded by his son Bahram V.

Yazdijard II. (یزدجرد), (the second Isdigertes of the Greeks), succeeded his father, Bahram V. to the throne of Persia, A.D. 438. He was a wise and brave prince, and reigned 18 years.

Yazdijard III. (یزدجرد), the son of Shahryār and grandson of Khusro Parwez, was raised to the throne of Persia after the dethronement of the queen Arzamī Dakht, A.D. 632. He is the Isdigertes III. of the Greeks, and a contemporary of 'Umar, the Khalīf of Arabia. This prince, who appears to have been as weak as he was unfortunate, sat upon the throne only nine years; that being the period from his elevation to the battle of Nahawand, which decided the fate of Persia, and which, from its date, A.D. 641, fell under the dominion of the Arabian Khalīfs. For a period of ten years afterwards this monarch was a fugitive, and possessed no power whatever. He first fled to Sīstān, then to Khurāsān, and lastly to Marv, where he was murdered A.D. 651, A.H. 31. He was the last sovereign of the house of Sāsān, a dynasty which ruled Persia for 415 years. It is from the commencement of his reign that the Persian Era, which is in use to this day in Persia, is called after him the Era of Yezdijard. It began on Tuesday the 16th June, A.D. 632, 20th Rabī' I. A.H. 11, being only eight days after Muhammad's death.

Yazid (یزید بن ابو سفیان), the son of Abū Sufiān. He died by the plague that raged in Syria in the year A.D. 639. The mortality both among men and beasts was so terrible that the Arabs call that year "'Am-ul-ramada," or the year of destruction. By this pestilence the Saracens lost 25,000 men, among whom were Abū 'Obeida, general of the Saracen army at Syria, Sarjabīl, ibn-Hasana, formerly Muhammad's secretary, and Yazīd ibn-Sufiān.

Yazid I. (یزید بن معاویه), the son of Mu'āwia and the second Khalīf of the house of Umayya. His inauguration was performed at Damascus on the same day that his father died, *viz.* on the new moon of the month of Rajab, corresponding with the 7th April, A.D. 680, 1st Rajab, A.H. 60. He was a man of considerable taste and refinement, an eloquent orator, and an admired poet. Some specimens of his composition, which are still extant, display no ordinary powers of mind. The first and the last lines of the ode with which the bard of Persia, the celebrated Hāfiz, opens his magnificent Dīwān, are borrowed from Yazīd. It was once sarcastically asked of Hāfiz, "How could a distinguished poet like yourself stoop to borrow from Yazīd, who was not only an usurper but also the murderer of Imām Husain?" He answered, "Which of you, seeing a dog running away with a diamond, would not stop the brute, and rescue the jewel from its unclean mouth?" By Persian authors Yazīd is never mentioned without abomination, and ordinarily this imprecation is added to his name, "La'nat-ullāh," that is "the curse of God be upon him;" in reference not to his vices, but to the death of Husain, the son of 'Alī, whom he first of all attempted to destroy by poison, and afterwards caused to be killed, with all his family, on the plains of Karbala. Under his khilāfat the Musalmāns conquered all Khurāsān and Khwārizm, and put the territories of the princes of Samarqand under contribution. The motto of his seal was "God is our Lord." Yazīd died on the 31st October, A.D. 683, 4th Rabī' I. A.H. 64, in the 39th year of his age, after he had reigned 3 years and 8 months, and was succeeded by his son Muāwia II. His mother's name was Maisana, a Bedouin of the tribe of Kalabī. Yazīd was a debauchee, and is represented by some Moslem writers as an atheist.

Yazid II. (يزيد بن عبدالملک), the ninth Khalīf of the race of Umayya, was the son of the Khalīf 'Abdulmalik. He succeeded 'Umar, the son of 'Abdul Azīz, in A.D. 720, A.H. 101, in Syria, and died after a reign of four years, A.D. 724, A.H. 105. His brother Hashām succeeded him.

Yazid III. (يزيد بن وليد), the twelfth Khalīf of the house of Umayya, succeeded his father, Walīd II. in Syria, A.D. 744, A.H. 126, and died the same year, after he had reigned six months. He was succeeded by his brother Ibrāhīm.

Yunas bin - Abdur Rahman - al - Yuktaini (يونس بن عبدالرحمان), a celebrated Shia traditionist. Amongst other works, he wrote the *'Ilal-al-Hadīs*, the *Ikhtilāf-al-Hadīs*, and the *Jāma-al-Kabīr*. He is said to have made forty-five pilgrimages to Mecca, and fifty-four 'Umrats when he merely visited the sacred city, and to have written the surprising number of 1,000 vols., controverting the opponents of the Shia doctrines. He died at Madīna in A.D. 823, A.H. 208.

Yusaf of Ahmadabad (يوسف احمد ابادى), author of an Arabic work on Theology, called *Aqāed Yūsaf*.

Yusaf (يوسف), author of a collection of letters called *Badāyu'l Insha* or wonders of letter-writing. It is also called *Inshāe Yūsafī*.

Yusaf Abu'l Haji (يوسف ابوالحاجى), one of the Moorish kings of Granada, and the finisher of the celebrated palace of the Alhambra. He ascended the throne of Granada in the year A.D. 1333, and his personal appearance and mental qualities were such as to win all hearts. He established schools in all the villages, with simple and uniform systems of education; he obliged every hamlet of more than twelve houses to have a mosque, and prohibited various abuses and indecorums that had been introduced into the ceremonies of religion and the festivals and public amusements of the people. His attention was also directed towards finishing the great architectural works commenced by his predecessors, and erecting others on his own plans. The Alhambra, which had been founded by the good Muhammad ibn-Alahmar, was now completed. He constructed the beautiful gate of Justice, forming the grand entrance to the fortress, which he finished in A.D. 1348. He likewise adorned many of the courts and halls of the palace, as may be seen by the inscriptions on the walls, in which his name repeatedly occurs. In the year A.D. 1354, as he was one day praying in the royal mosque of the Alhambra, a maniac rushed suddenly from behind, and plunged a dagger in his side. He was borne to the royal apartments, but expired almost immediately. The murderer was cut to pieces and his limbs burnt in public, to gratify the fury of the populace.

Yusaf Adil Shah (يوسف عادل شاه), whose original name was Yūsaf 'Adil Khān, was the founder of the 'Adil Shāhī dynasty of Bījāpūr. He was a nobleman in the service of Muhammad Shāh II. Bahmanī, king of the Deccan. When the Sulṭān left this world, and dissensions began to prevail in the kingdom, most of the foreign officers and soldiers attached themselves to Yūsaf 'Adil Khān, who, seeing the ministers of Sulṭān Mahmūd II. the successor of the late king, bent on his destruction, withdrew himself from Aḥmadābād, with his family and followers, to his government of Bījāpūr, and, resolving to become the founder of a kingdom, he began to add to his territories by conquest. In the year A.D. 1489, A.H. 895, he, with the assent of Malik Aḥmad Bahrī, assumed the title of Shāh, and read the khutba of Bījāpūr in his own name. Yūsaf 'Adil Shāh died at Bījāpūr in A.D. 1510, A.H. 916, of a dropsical disorder, after he had reigned with great prosperity 21 years, in the 75th year of his age, and was succeeded by his son Ismā'īl 'Adil Shāh.

List of the kings of the 'Adil Shāhī dynasty.

	A.D.
Yūsaf 'Adil Shāh, supposed to be the son of Murād II. of Anatolia; purchased for the bodyguard at Aḥmadābād from a merchant. He began to reign	1489
Ismā'īl 'Adil Shāh, son of Yūsaf . .	1510
Mallū 'Adil Shāh, son of Ismā'īl, reigned six months	1534
Ibrāhīm 'Adil Shāh I. son of Ismā'īl	1535
'Alī 'Adil Shāh I. son of Ibrāhīm .	1557
Ibrahīm 'Adil Shāh II. son of Tahmāsp, the son of 'Alī 'Adil Shāh .	1579
Muhammad 'Adil Shāh, son of Ibrāhīm II.	1626
'Alī 'Adil Shāh II. son of Muhammad	1660
Sikandar 'Adil Shāh, the last king of Bījāpūr	1672

Yusaf 'Ali Khan (يوسف على خان), Nawāb of Rāmpūr. His Highness was one of the few princes who were faithful to the British Government in the troublous times of A.D. 1857, when the whole of the North West Provinces was in a state of revolt and insurrection. Lord Canning rewarded him with liberal grants of land worth a lakh per annum, whilst Her Majesty was pleased to confer on him the Star of India. He died at his capital in Rohilkhand on the 21st April, A.D. 1865, 24th Ẕi-Qa'da, A.H. 1282.

Yusaf Amiri, Maulana (یوسف امری مولانا), a Persian poet, who flourished in the time of Shāhrukh Mirzā and wrote panegyrics in praise of his son Bāisanghar Mirzā.

Yusaf bin-Muhammad (یوسف بن محمد), author of a medical work called *Fāedat-ul-Akhbār.*

Yusaf bin-Junaid (یوسف بن جنید), generally known by the name of Akhī Chalabī. *Vide* Qāzī Khān.

Yusaf bin - Hasan - al - Muqaddasi (یوسف بن حسن المقدسی), author of a portion of the *Tabaqāt-al-Hanbaliat.* He died in A.D. 1466, A.H. 871.

[*Vide* Abū'l Husain bin-Abū Yalī.]

Yusaf Hamadani (یوسف همدانی), a celebrated learned Musalmān of Hamadān, who died in the year A.D. 1141, A.H. 536.

Yusaf Khan (یوسف خان), governor of Sindh, who lived in the time of the emperor Shāh Jahān. In his time (says Mūnshī Lutf-ullah) he built an Īdgah, in Tatta, a splendid mosque, where all true believers gather together twice a year and perform the divine service. Its inscription is in beautiful large Nastalik characters, as follows:—

"Yūsaf Khān, the powerful lord, erected this place of worship as high as his fortune. The year of its finishing is found by cherubion —the temple of Makka for the virtuous." A.D. 1633, A.H. 1043.

There are upwards of 400 mosques in the city of Tatta (says Lutf-ullah), but almost all of them are going to decay. There is also a Grand Mosque (Juma Masjid) begun by Shāh Jahān, in A.D. 1647, A.H. 1057, and finished by Aurangzeb in A.H. 1072. The edifice is a magnificent one, about 200 yards long by 30 broad, built of baked bricks and mortar. The whole site is roofed with 100 domes, every one of them painted in a different style from another. The inscriptions carved round the great arch of stone, and those upon the two Lata stones, are excellently done in large letters. In short, the whole scene presents a picture of beauty and solemnity to the spectator.

Yusaf Khan, Mirza (یوسف خان), a Mansabdar of 2500 in the 30th year of Akbar, and subsequently governor of Kashmere. Later still served with distinction under Abū'l Fazl in the Deccan. Died Jam. II. A.H. 1010; was a native of Mashhad, of the Sāyyid tribe.

Yusaf, Mir (یوسف میر استرابادی), of Astrabād, who was living in A.D. 1580, A.H. 988, and wrote a chronogram on the death of the poet Kāsim Kāhī, who died that year.

Yusaf Muhammad Khan (یوسف محمد خان), Commander of Five Thousand under Akbar, whose foster-brother he was. Died from the effects of drink, A.H. 973.

Yusaf Muhammad Khan, (یوسف محمد خان), author of a history of the reign of Muhammad Shāh, emperor of Dehlī, called *Tarīkh Muhammad Shāhī.*

Yusaf, Maulana of Naishapur (یوسف مولانا نیشاپور), is the first person who wrote a book on the art of writing poetry in Persian; he flourished about two hundred years after Khulīl bin-Ahmad of Basra, who had also written on the same subject in Arabic.

Yusaf Shah Purbi (یوسف شاه پوربی), the son of Bārbak Shāh, whom he succeeded to the throne of Bengal in A.D. 1474, A.H. 887. He reigned eight years, and died in A.D. 1482. His son Fatha Shāh succeeded him.

Yusaf, Shaikh (یوسف شیخ), first king of Multān. The introduction of the Muhammadan faith into Multān, says Firishta, first took place in the latter part of the first century of the Hijra, about the year A.D. 700, by the conquest of that country by Muhammad Kāsim, after whom, until the reign of Sultān Mahmūd of Ghaznī, no account is to be traced of its history. Mahmūd conquered Multān from the infidels; but on the decline of the Ghaznī power, the inhabitants succeeded in expelling the Muhammadans, and establishing a separate government. From the period of its subjugation by Muhammad Ghōrī it remained tributary to Dehlī until the year A.D. 1443, A.H. 847, when the governor of that province, like most others of the kingdom at the same period, declared independence, after which time several princes reigned in succession. The first of these was one Shaikh Yūsaf, a man of learning, wisdom, and high character, of the tribe of Qureish, whom the inhabitants of Multān selected to be ruler over the people of Multān and Uchcha, when the public prayers were read and money coined in his name. Shaikh Yūsaf had reigned but two years when his father-in-law, Rāe Sehra, of the tribe of Langa, having seized him, sent him under a guard to Dehlī, and mounted the throne under the title of Quṭb-uddīn Mahmūd Langa. Abū'l Fazl in the '*Ayīn-i-Akbarī*, assigns seventeen years for the reign of Shaikh Yūsaf.

Muhammadan kings of Multān.

	A.D.
Shaikh Yūsaf, who established an independent monarchy, began . . .	1443
Rāe Sehra or Quṭb-uddīn Mahmūd Langa.	1445
Husain Langa I.	
Mahmūd Khān Langa . . . . A.D.	1502
Husain Langa II. who began A.D. 1524, was overcome by Shāh Husain Arghūn, and subsequently Multān became a province of the empire under the emperor Humāyan.	

Yusaf, Shaikh of Gujrat (یوسف شیخ گجراتی), author of the *Tazkirat-ul-Atqiyā*.

Z

Zabita Khan (ضابطه خان), a Rohela chief and son of Najīb-uddaula Amīr-ul-Umrā. After the death of his father in October, A.D. 1770, Rajab, A.H. 1184, he continued to protect the royal family at Dehlī till the return of the emperor Shāh 'Alam from Allahābād in December, A.D. 1771, Ramaẓān, A.H. 1185, when he was convicted of having been deficient in respect to the royal authority while the emperor resided at Allahābād, and having abused his trust by corrupting the ladies of the harem, especially the princess Khairunnisa, the king's sister. His territories were seized, and he was compelled to make his escape to Shujā-uddaula, the nawāb of Audh. But not long afterwards, the Marhaṭṭas obliged the emperor to confer on Zābita Khān the rank of Amīr-ul-Umrā, and to restore him the grant of almost all the districts of which he had, only a few months before, been deprived of by their assistance. Zābita Khān died A.D. 1785, and was the father of that traitor, Ghulām Qādir Khān, who subsequently blinded the emperor Shāh 'Alam. His second son, by name Mo'īn-uddīn Khān, commonly called Bhanbū Khān, received a pension of 5000 rupees from the British Government, and after his death a pension of 1000 rupees monthly was granted to his two sons, Mahmūd Khān and Jalāl-uddīn Khān. The elder rebelled in A.D. 1857, and being subsequently arrested died in Meerut jail.

Zaer or **Zayer** (زاير), poetical name of Shaikh Muhammad Fākhir, of Allahābād, who died in A.D. 1751, A.H. 1164.

Zafar (ظفر), the poetical name of Abū Zafar Sirāj-uddīn Bahādur Shāh, the ex-king of Dehlī. *Vide* Bahādur Shāh.

Zafar (ظفر), poetical title of Ṭīkā Rām a Hindū.

Zafar Khan (ظفر خان), the original name of (Nawāb) Roshan-uddaula, which see.

Zafar Khan (ظفر خان), son of Sulṭān Fīroz Shāh Bārbak, was murdered by Khān Jahān, the prime minister, in A.D. 1385, A.H. 787.

Zafar Khan (ظفر خان), the title of Khwāja Ihsān-ullāh, a nobleman of the reign of the emperor Shāh Jahān, and father of Ināyet Khān, who was the author of the work called *Shāh Jahān-nāma*. Zafar Khān held the rank of 3000, and died at Lāhore A.D. 1662, A.H. 1073. His poetical name was Ihsān, which see.

Zafaryab Khan. Title of Aloysius Reinhardt, son of Gen. Reinhardt, commonly called Shamru Sāhib. A poet and patron of authors.

[*Vide* Shamru.]

Zagatai, Jagatai. *Vide* Chagatāī (Khān), which is more consonant to the Turkish pronunciation.

Zahid (زاهد), whose proper name is Mirzā Zāhid-uddīn, the son of Mirzā Kam Bakhsh, the son of Mirzā Sulaimān Shikoh, the son of Shāh Alam, king of Dehlī. He is the author of a Dīwān.

Zahid, Shaikh (زاهد شيخ گيلاني), of Gilān, a pious Musalmān, who resided in Ardibail, a city in Azurbaijān, about 25 miles to the east of Taurus or Tabrez, and was the father-in-law of the celebrated Shaikh Safī or Safī-uddīn Ardibeilī. He died A.D. 1335, A.H. 735.

Zahidi (زاهدی), a learned Muhammadan, who wrote excellent Commentaries on the Qurān in Arabic as well as in Persian, called *Tafsīr Zāhidī*. He died in A.D. 1260, A.H. 658.

Zahik (ضاحک), the poetical name of Mīr Ghulām Husain, the father of Mīr Hasan, of Lucknow. He is the author of an Urdū Dīwān, and every Ghazal of his are full of jokes.

Zahir Faryabi (ظهير فاريابی). *Vide* Zahīr-uddīn Fāryābī.

Zahir Kirmani (ظهير کرمانی), author of a poem called *Majma-ul-Bahryn*, containing the story of Manōhar, composed in the year A.D. 1749, A.H. 1162.

Zahir-uddaula Bahadur (ظهير ملک), (Prince) of Arkot, son of Azīm Jāh Bahādur. He succeeded to the Masnad after the death of his father in January, A.D. 1874.

Zahir-uddin Abu Bakr Muhammad bin-Ahmad-al-Bukhara (ظهير الدين ابو بکر محمد بن آحمد البخاری), who died in A.D. 1222, A.H. 619, is the author of the *Fatāwa-az-Zahīria*, a collection of decisions.

Zahir-uddin Faryabi (ظهير الدين فاريابی), a native of Fāryāb, was an excellent poet and the pupil of Rashīdī. He flourished in the reign of Tughral III. Saljūqī and Atābak Kizal Arsalān. He died at Tabriz A.D. 1201, A.H. 598, and is buried close to the tomb of Khāqānī at Surkhāb in Tabriz. He is the author of a Dīwān. Some authors say that the style of his poetry is far better than Anwarī's. Another poet has written that "Should you come across with the Dīwān of Zahīr Fāryābī, steal it, though you find it in the Qaba."

Zahir-uddin 'Isa, Shaikh (ظهير الدين عيسیٰ), a son of Shaikh Ahmad Jām and author of a work called *Ramūz-ūl-Haqāeq*.

Zahir-uddin Makhdum (ظهيرالدين مخدوم), an Arab, Egyptian, or subject of the Turkish empire, who is thought to have been despatched to assist the Muhammadan princes of Malabar against the Portuguese, and to have, during his stay in India, composed an historical account of Malabar in the Arabic language, which terminates with the Hijrī year A.H. 987, corresponding with the year of our Lord 1580.

Zahir-uddin Marghashi (ظهير الدين مرغشی), author of the *Tarīkh Tabaristān*.

Zahir-uddin, Mir (ظهيرالدين), son of Mīr Khalib-ullah of Yazd, came from Persia to Lāhore *temp.* Jahāngīr, and rose to high employ.

Zahuri, Mulla (ظهوری ملا ترشيزی), a native of Tarshish, a city of Sabzwār, in Persia. His proper name is Nūr-uddīn. After completing his studies he came to the Deccan in the reign of Ibrāhīm 'Adil Shāh II. of Bījāpūr, and passed the remainder of his days in his service. He dedicated his *Sāqī-nāma*, a celebrated poem, containing 4000 verses, to Burhān Nizām Shāh II. of Ahmadnagar, who made him a present of seven elephants loaded with valuables. He is also the author of several other works, among which are the *Mīna Bazār*, *Ruqaat Zahūrī*, *Seh Nasr*, a Dīwān, *Risāla Nauras*, *Khwān Khalīl*, and *Gulzar Ibrāhīm*. The last three he dedicated to his patron, Ibrāhīm 'Adil Shāh. Zahūrī died one year after his father-in-law, Mulla Malik Qummī, *i.e.* in A.D. 1617, A.H. 1026, aged more than 90.

Zaid bin-Haria (زيد بن حارث), of the tribe of Kalb, was the emancipated slave of Muhammad, who married his divorced wife Zainab. (*See* the following article.) Zaid was killed in an attack on the Greeks at Muta in Syria, A.D. 629, A.H. 8.

Zaid bin-Sabit Abu Sa'd (زيد بن ثابت), one of Muhammad's secretaries, to whom he dictated the Qurān. He wrote that copy which was used by the Khalīfs or Imāms at the command of 'Usmān, the son of Affān, the third Khalīf after Muhammad. He died about the year A.D. 665, A.H. 45; some say that he died in A.D. 673, A.H. 54. He is the earliest authority on the *Ilm-al-Farāez* and may be called the father of the law of inheritance. Muhammad is reported to have said to his followers—"The most learned among you in the laws of heritage is Zaid;" and the Khalīfas 'Umar and 'Usmān considered him without an equal as a judge, a jurisconsult, a calculator in the division of inheritances, and a reader of the Qurān.

Za'ifa Khatun (ضعیفه خاتون), sister to Sultān Sanjar, married to Malik Tāj-uddīn Abū'l Fazl, a descendant of the royal family of Amrū bin-Lais.

Zainab (زینب بنت جحش), the daughter of Jahash and the wife of Muhammad. She was formerly married to Zaid, the emancipated slave of the prophet. Towards the end of the fifth year of the Hijrī, A.D. 626, Muhammad, going into the house of Zaid, did not find him at home; but happening to espy his wife, he could not conceal the impression made upon him, but cried out, "Praise be to God, who turneth men's hearts as he pleaseth!" Zainab heard him, and told it to her husband when he came home. Zaid, who had been greatly obliged to Muhammad, was very desirous to gratify him, and offered to divorce his wife. Muhammad pretended to dissuade him from it, but Zaid, easily perceiving how little he was in earnest, actually divorced her. Muhammad thereupon took her to wife, and celebrated the nuptials with extraordinary magnificence, keeping open house upon the occasion. She died nine years after the death of Muhammad, in the year A.D. 641, A.H. 20.

Zainab (زینب بنت خزیمه), the daughter of Khuzyma, was also one of the wives of Muhammad, and died two months after the preceding one, in the year A.D. 641, A.H. 20.

Zainab (زینب), a daughter of Muhammad married to Abū'l 'As. This man, who was an unbeliever, was taken prisoner in the battle of Badar, and the prophet would fain have drawn his son-in-law to him, and enrolled him among his disciples, but Abū'l 'As remained stubborn in unbelief. Muhammad then offered to set him at liberty on condition of his returning to him his daughter. To this he agreed, and Zaid, the faithful freedman of the prophet, was sent with several companions to Mecca to bring Zainab to Medina, where after her arrival, Abū'l 'As was released.

Zain Khan (زین خان), son of Khwāja Maksud, of Herāt. A connection of Akbar and Jahāngīr, and Mansabdār of 4500, afterwards promoted to 5000: an accomplished soldier and literary man. He died from the effects of drink in A.D. 1010.

Zain Khan Koka (زین خان کوکه), the foster-brother of the emperor Akbar. He was the son of Khwāja Maqsūd Hirwī; his mother, whose name was Pīchah Jān, was employed as an Anaga or nurse on Akbar in his childhood, consequently Zain Khān was called Kōka or foster-brother to Akbar, who raised him in course of time to the rank of 4500. Subsequently his uncle Khwāja Hasan's daughter was married to Sultān Salīm, and became mother of Sultān Parwez. In the year A.D. 1586, A.H. 994, Zain Khān was despatched with a considerable detachment against the Afghāns of Sawād and Bijour, but he was defeated, and Khwāja Arab Bakhshī, Rāja Bīrbal, Mulla Sherī, and many other persons of distinction, with 8000 men, were killed in the action. In A.D. 1588 he was appointed to the government of Kābul. He died at Āgra on the 6th Mehr, A.H. 1009, corresponding with the 19th September, A.D. 1600. He is said to have been the best musician of the time of Akbar, but a bad poet. He played chiefly Hindī tunes. (The same as Zain Khān, *q.v.*)

Zain-uddin Ahmad 'Ali Khan (زین الدین علی خان), succeeded Nāzir-ul-Mulk Nawāb Nāzim of Bengal at Murshidābād in April, A.D. 1810.

Zain-uddin 'Ali-al-Sai'li (زین الدین علی السیلی), commonly called the second Shahīd, author of a valuable and voluminous commentary upon the Sharāyạ-al-Islām, entitled the *Masālik-ul-Afhām*.

Zain-uddin bin-Ahmad (زین الدین بن احمد), commonly called Ibn-Rajab, is the author of the *Sharah Tirmizī*, *Sharah Bukhārī*, and *Tabaqāt Hanābila*. He died in A.D. 1393, A.H. 795. He is sometimes called Zain-uddīn Abdul Rahmān bin-Aḥmad. [*Vide* Abū'l Husain.]

Zain-uddin Muhammad Hafi, Shaikh (زین الدین حافی), an excellent poet and author, who flourished in the reign of the emperor Humāyūn. He was called Hāfī on account of his walking barefoot.

Zain-ul-'Abidin (زین العابدین), metropolitan of Seringapatam, and author of the work called *Muwayyad-ul-Jahidīn*, a poem consisting of 52 odes or hymns, one of which was ordered to be chanted in the mosques throughout the kingdom of Mysore every Friday. They are in sixteen different kinds of metre, and were compiled by order of Ṭipū Sulṭān to rouse the zeal of his Muhammadan subjects against the Hindūs and the Christians.

Zain-ul-'Abidin 'Ali Abdi (زین العابدین علی ابدی). *Vide* Khwāja Zain-ul-'Abidīn 'Alī Abdī.

Zain-ul-'Abidin Ibrahim bin-Nujim-al-Misri (زين العابدين بن نجيم) author of the Commentary on the *Kanz-ul-Daqāiq*, entitled *Bahr ar-Rāiq*, which he left incomplete at his death, but it was finished by his brother Sirāj-uddīn 'Umr, who also wrote another and inferior Commentary on the same work, entitled *Nahr-ul-Fāiq*. Zain-ul-'Abidīn died in A.D. 1562, A.H. 970. The *Ashbāh wān Nazāir* is also an elementary work of great reputation by Zain-ul-'Abidīn, also the *Fatāwa az-Zainia*, which contains decisions, and were collected by his son Aḥmad about A.D. 1562.

Zain-ul-'Abidin, Imam (زين العابدين امام), surnamed Alī Asghar, was the son of Imām Husain, and the fourth Imām of the race of Alī. His mother's name was Salafa or Shahr Bāno, said to be the daughter of Yezdijard III. king of Persia. She was one of the captives when Persia was conquered, and sold to 'Alī, who gave her to his son Husain. It is said that the Khalīf Walīd I. suspecting him of a design upon the Khilāfat, said to him, alluding to his mother having been exposed for sale as a slave, "You are unworthy to reign, as being the son of a slave." The Imām answered, "Hagar, the mother of Ishmael, the son of Abraham, was a slave, yet Muhammad was descended from her." The Khalīf blushed and was silent. He was born in A.D. 657, A.H. 37, and died in the reign of the Khalīf Walīd I. in the month of October, A.D. 713, Muḥarram, A.H. 95. He was buried in the cemetery called Baqīr in Medina, close to his uncle Imām Hasan's tomb.

Zain-ul-'Abidin, Sultan (زين العابدين سلطان), son of Sulṭān Sikandar, ascended the throne of Kashmere, after taking prisoner his brother 'Alī Shāh in a battle, in 1423. This prince improved the country more than any of his predecessors. He built bridges, towns and forts, and erected at Naushahra a noble palace, twelve stories high, each story of fifty rooms. He also enlarged and beautified the city of Srīnagar, his capital. He died in A.D. 1474, after a reign of 52 lunar years, and was succeeded by his son Haidar Shāh, who, after reigning little more than a year, was killed by a fall from his terrace, A.D. 1475, and was succeeded by his son Sulṭān Ḥasan.

Zakaria (زكريا). *Vide* Bahā-uddīn Zikaria.

Zakaria bin-Muhammad Ansari of Egypt (زكريا بن محمد انصارى مصرى), an author, who died A.D. 1520.

Zakaria bin-Muhammad bin-Mahmud-al-Kamuli-al-Qazwini (زكريا بن محمد بن محمد الكمولى القزينى), a native of Qazwīn, and author of the *'Ajāeb-ul-Makhlūqāt*, or the Wonders of the Creation, which he completed in the year A.D. 1363, A.H. 764. There are several copies of this work to be found in the public libraries of London, and in private collections, some of them containing beautiful and correct drawings of all the beasts, fishes, birds, trees, and even monsters, described in the book; and the account of metals and gems, a subject that has attracted great public attention of late, contains in particular much curious information.

Zakaria Khan (زكريا خان), the son of Abdus Samad Khān, styled Saif-uddaula Bahādur Jang. He held the government of Lāhore at the period of Nādir Shāh's invasion of India, A.D. 1739, A.H. 1151, and died in the year A.D. 1745, 12th Jumāda II. A.H. 1158. His eldest son succeeded him in the government, with the title of Shāhnawāz Khān.

Zakhmi, Hazrat (ذخمى حضرت), author of a Persian Dīwān.

Zakhmi (زخمى), takhallus of Fakhr-uddaula Dabīr-ul-Mulk Rāja Ratan Singh Bahādur. He was a native of Lucknow, where he was Minister of Finance. He died in A.D. 1850, A.H. 1266, and left a considerable Library at Barelī. A few years before his death, *viz.* in A.D. 1846, he had embraced the Muhammadan faith.

Zaki (ذكى همدانى), a poet of Hamdan, who lived in the time of Shāh Tahmāsp Safwī, and died about the year A.D. 1621, A.H. 1030. He is the author of a Dīwān.

Zaki (ذكى), poetical name of Jaʿfar 'Alī Khān of Dehlī, who lived in the time of the emperor Shāh 'Alam.

Zaki or Safi-uddin Zaki Maraghai (ذكى), but he was simply called Zakī. He was a poet, and died in A.D. 1210, A.H. 607.

Zaki Khan (ذكى خان), who usurped the throne of Persia after the death of Karīm Khān in March, A.D. 1779, but was assassinated after two months.

[*Vide* Karīm Khān.]

Zal (زال), also called Zālzar, the son of Sām and grandson of Narīmān. He was the father of Rustam, and these three personages, *viz.* Sām, Zāl and Rustam, pass for the most famous heroes of Persia; they belong to the reigns of Manūchehr, Bahman and Afrāsiāb. It was Zāl who drove Afrāsiāb, king of the Turks, out of Persia, and put the crown on the head of Zū or Zab, son of Tahmāsp, a descendant of one of the kings of the Pishdādian dynasty. This same Zāl was put in prison by Bahman, son of Isfandiār; but he made his escape, and married Rūdāba, daughter of Mehrāb, governor of Kābulistān, who became the mother of Rustam. Unfortunately, however, he fell into the hands of Bahman again, who put him to death.

Zalali Hirwi (زلالی هروی), a poet who was a native of Herāt, and who died in the year A.D. 1525, A.H. 931.

Zalali Khwansari, Mulla (زلالی خوانساری ملا), who is sometimes called Hakīm Zalālī, was a native of Khwānsār. He was a pupil of Mirzā Jalāl Asīr, and is the author of the following seven Masnawīs or poems, viz. *Sulaimān-nāma, Shīala Dīdār, Maikhāna, Husn Gulūtoz, Azur wa Samundar, Zarra wa Khursheid,* and *Mahmūd Ayāz*, which was his last composition, and which he commenced in A.D. 1592, A.H. 1001, and completed in 23 years, in A.D. 1615, A.H. 1024, but died before he could arrange it. This was done in India, and Mulla Tughrāī wrote a preface to it.

Zalali Shirazi (زلالی شیرازی), an author, who died in A.D. 1541, A.H. 948.

Zalim Singh (ظالم سنگه), the present Rāja of Koṭa.

Zamakhshari (زمخشری). *Vide* Jār-ullāh.

Zaman Shah (زمان شاه), king of Kābul and Qandahār, was the son of Taimūr Shāh and grandson of the celebrated Aḥmad Shāh Abdālī. He ascended the throne of Kābul after the death of his father in A.D. 1793, A.H. 1207. He advanced to Lāhore in A.D. 1796, A.H. 1210, and threatened to visit Dehlī, but soon retreated to his own dominions, the tranquility of which had been disturbed by the rebellion of one of his brothers. He was blinded by his younger brother, Mahmūd Shāh of Herāt, about the year A.D. 1800, and confined in the Bālā Hisār. When, in the year A.D. 1839, the British Government placed Shāh Shujāa on the throne of Kābul, Zamān Shāh was proclaimed king by the Afghāns in January, A.D. 1842.

Zamani, Yezdi (زمانی یزدی), a Persian poet, who died in A.D. 1612, A.H. 1021.

Zamir (ضمیر), the poetical name of Sayyad Hidāet 'Alī Khān, styled Na'sīr-uddaula Bakhshī-ul-Mulk Asad Jang Bahādur, a relative of Alah Wardī Khān Mahābat Jang, Nawāb of Bengal. He held for some time the Sūbadārī of Patna, where he died in the beginning of the reign of Shāh 'Alam, and is buried at Husainābād.

Zamir (ضمیر), poetical name of Sayyad Aḥmad, the brother of Sayyad Imtiyāz Khān Humā.

Zamir (ضمیر), poetical name of Narāyan Dās, a Hindū.

Zamiri, Maulana (ضمیری مولانا), a celebrated poet of Persia, who flourished about the year A.D. 1538, A.H. 945, in the time of Shāh Tahmāsp Safwī. He is the author of the following six poems, viz. *Naz wa Nayāz, Wāmiq wa Azra, Bahār wa Khizān, Lailī wa Majnūn, Sikandar-nāma,* and *Jannat-ul-Akhiyār*. He also wrote two Dīwāns of Qasīdas called *Sahāef Yamāl* and *Isdāf Lāal*. He died in A.D. 1565, A.H. 973.

Zamiri, Maulana (ضمیری مولانا), the poetical name of Shaikh Niẓām, who was the son of Shaikh Sulaimān's sister. They were both inhabitants of Bilgrām, and both were employed in the service of the emperor Humāyūn after his conquest of India the second time. Shaikh Sulaimān died in the reign of the emperor Akbar, on the 1st September, A.D. 1589, 1st Ẕi-Qa'da, A.H. 997, and Maulānā Zamīrī, who was an excellent poet, died at Safaidūn, A.D. 1594, A.H. 1003, and Nawāb Mubarak, Khān of Dehlī, found the chronogram of his death to consist of the words "Ah! Ah! Niẓām."

Zamzam (زمزم), a famous well at Mecca, which the Muhammadans pretend was made from the spring of water which God shewed to Hagar and Ishmael, whom Abraham had driven from his house and obliged to retire to Arabia.

Zangi Shahid (زنگی شهید), a Muhammadan saint, whose Dargāh is in Āgra towards the gate of the Hatheapul.

Zardasht (زردشت), the celebrated Persian Magian Zoroaster, who has been conjecturally dated between 1000 and 550 B.C. The religion of the first Persians appears to have been the worship of the planets; but in the reign of Darius Hystaspes or Gashtasp, the adoration of fire and the elements was introduced by Sapetman, called "Zardasht," and continued to be the religion of the State until its conquest by the Muhammadans. The fugitives known as Gabrs and Parsīs still follow this faith. The doctrines and practices of this system are collected in a work called *Avesta*, or *Zand Avesta*, being written in the Zand language. The *Zand Avesta* was translated into French by Anquetil Du Perron, and subsequently much studied and elucidated by Rask, Barnouf and other Continental scholars. [Zardasht (corr. of Zarathushtra) was perhaps a title rather than a name, and applied to different men at various periods.]

Zarra (ذرہ), the poetical name of Mirzā Bhuchchū of Dehlī or Lucknow, who has left a Persian Dīwān, which he completed in A.D. 1774, A.H. 1188.

Zarra (ذرہ), the poetical title of Mirzā Rāja Rām Nāth, who served under the emperor Shāh 'Alam the blind. He chose the takhallus of "Zarra," *i.e.* atom or dust, in reference to "'Aftāb," the poetical appellation of his patron the king.

Zeb-un-Nisa Begam (زیب النسا بیگم), a daughter of the emperor 'Alamgīr, born on the 5th February, A.D. 1639, 10th Shawwāl, A.H. 1048; was well versed in Persian and Arabic, had the whole Qurān by heart, wrote a beautiful hand, and is the author of a commentary on the Qurān entitled *Zeb-ul-Tafāsīr*. She was also a good poetess, and has left a Dīwān in Persian. Her poetical name was Makhfī. She died, unmarried, in the year A.D. 1709, A.H. 1113. Her tomb was close to the Kabulī gate at Dehlī, but was demolished when the Rājpūtana Railway was constructed.

Zila'i (زیلعی), the son of Yūsaf, a learned Musalmān and author, who died A.D. 1361, A.H. 762.

Zilli (ظلی), poetical name of Sultān Muhammad Mirzā, which see.

Zinat Mahal (زینت محل), the wife of Bahādur Shāh, king of Dehlī, who was still living in A.D. 1873 in British Burma as a State prisoner.

Zinat-un-Nisa Begam (زینت النسا بیگم), a daughter of the emperor 'Alamgīr. She died in A.D. 1710, A.H. 1122, and is buried in the yard of the mosque called Zīnat-ul-Masājid, in Dehlī. This mosque, which is built of red stone, was erected by her, and is situated on the banks of the Jamna at a place called Dariāganj in Shāhjahānābād.

Zingis Khan (ظنگیس خان). *Vide* Changez Khān.

Zinut Mahal (زینت محل), the title of Bilāl Kūnwar, the mother of Shāh 'Alam, king of Dehlī.

Zitali (زٹلی), (Chatterer). *Vide* Jāfar.

Ziyad (زیاد), supposed to be an illegitimate son of Abū Sufiān by a woman named Abia. He was Mu'āwia's brother by the father's side, and was publicly acknowledged by him to be his brother. He was reckoned one of the companions of Muhammad, although he was born in the first year of the Hijrī, A.D. 622, and was but 11 years old when Muhammad died. In Alī's reign he was made lieutenant of Persia; this office he discharged much to his own credit, and to the advantage of the people. He was a man of incomparable parts and singular greatness of spirit. Besides the lieutenancy of Baṣra, Mu'āwia gave Ziyād those of Khurāsān, Sajistān, India, Bahrein and Ammān. He died of the plague on his fingers, on the 22nd August, A.D. 673, 3rd Ramazān, A.H. 53, in the 53rd (lunar) year of his age, and was buried near Kūfa. A little before his death he gathered the people together and filled both mosque and street and castle with them, in order to impose upon them by oath the renunciation of the line of 'Alī; but the plague had just seized him, and the accident was afterwards looked upon by all as a providential deliverance.

Ziyai Barani (ضیاء برنی). *Vide* Ziyā-uddīn Baranī.

Ziyai Burhanpuri (ضیاء برهانپوری), author of a Persian Dīwān.

Ziya-uddin Ahmad Khan, Nawab (زیاوالدین خان), the son of Nawāb Ahmad Baksh Khān, of Fīrozpūr and Loharī. His poetical name is Nyyar and Rakhshān. He succeeded to his father's estate on the 1st January, A.D. 1870.

Ziya-uddin Barani (ضیا الدین برنی), also called Ziyāi Baranī, flourished in the reign of Sultān Muhammad Shāh Tughlaq and Fīroz Shāh Tughlaq, kings of Dehlī, and is the author of the history called *Tarikh Fīroz Shāhī*, which gives an account of eight kings from the first year of Sultān Ghayās-uddīn Balban, A.D. 1266, to the sixth year of Sultān Fīroz Shāh Tughlaq, A.D. 1356, A.H. 757, at which period our author was 74 (lunar) years of age. His uncle Malik 'Alā-ul-Mulk was Kotwāl of the city of Dehlī in the reign of Sulṭān Alā-uddīn Khiljī, and his father, who held the title of Muwayyad-ul-Mulk, was appointed in the first year of that monarch, A.D. 1296, to the Nayābat of Baran or Baran Shahr, now called Bulandshahr, which city appears to have been the birthplace of our author, on which account he calls himself in the above-mentioned history Ziyāe Baranī. Baran is also the name of a Pergunnah in Bulandshahr.

Ziya-uddin Ghazanfar, Maulana (ضیا الدین غضنفر مولانا) was born at Qumm, but educated at Kāshān. Besides many Qasīdas and Ghazals, etc., he left a Masnawī, called *Pīr wa Jawān*, of about 3000 verses. He was living about the year A.D. 1585, A.H. 993.

Ziya-uddin, Ibrat. *Vide* Ibrat.

Ziya-uddin Khujandi (ضیا الدین خجندی), a poet who died in A.D. 1225, A.H. 622.

Ziya-uddin Nakshabi (ضیا لدین نخشی), author of the *Tūtī-nāma*, or Tales of a Parrot in Persian, and also of a story called *Gulreiz*, containing the story of prince M'asūm Shāh and the princess Naushāba. He is also the author of a treatise entitled *Lazzat-un-Nisā*.

[*Vide* Hasan 'Alī, the poet laureate.]

Ziya-ullah, Sayyad (ضیا الهه سید), an author, who died in A.D. 1691, A.H. 1103.

Zohak (ضحاک). *Vide* Zuhāk.

Zouq (ذوق), poetical title of Shaikh Muhammad Ibrāhīm, of Dehlī, an Urdū poet, who passed the greatest part of his life in the service of Akbar II. king of Dehlī, and was living about the year A.D. 1837.

Zouqi Ardastani (ذوقی اردستانی), a poet, who died in A.D. 1635, A.H. 1045.

Zouzani (زوزنی), whose full name and title is Al-Qāzī-al-Imām Sayyad Abū 'Abdullah-al-Zouzanī, was the author of the *Sharah Qasāed-ul-Saba'-al-Mua'llaqā't*, an esteemed Commentary in Arabic on the seven celebrated poems which were written in letters of gold, and suspended to the door of the temple of Mecca, previous to the mission of Muhammad. Their authors were Amri-al-Kais, Tarafa, Zaheir, Labīd, Antar, Amrū, and Harath. These poems have been so elegantly translated by Sir William Jones, that, had he never published anything else, they would have stamped his fame as a man of taste, a good poet, and an excellent Oriental scholar.

Zu or **Zab** (زو یا زب), a descendant of the ancient kings of Persia, whom Zāl, the father of Rustam, raised to the throne of Persia, and drove Afrāsiāb, king of the Turks, who had conquered it, out of that kingdom. Zū died after he had conquered Fars, and was succeeded by his son Karshāsp. This prince, who was soon set aside as incompetent by Zāl, is considered by Persian authors as the last of the first, or Pishdādian, dynasty; who, according to their own computation, governed Persia 2450 years. The names of twelve kings only of their race have been preserved. After Karshāsp, Kaiqubād, who is the first king of the second, or Kayānian, dynasty, was proclaimed king of Persia.

Zubari (زبری), the son of Muslim, an Arabian author, who died in A.D. 742, A.H. 124.

Zubdatun-nisa (زبدة النساء), the fourth daughter of the emperor 'Alamgīr. Her mother's name was Nawāb Bai. She was born on the 26th Ramazān, A.H. 1061, and was married to one of Dara Shikoh's sons. She died a few days before her father, in the same month and year, A.H. 1118.

Zubeda Khatun (زبیده خاتون), the wife of Hārūn-al-Rashīd. She was the daughter of Abū Ja'far, the son of the Khalīf Al-Mansūr, and mother of the Khalīf Al-Amīn. Her chastity was ample, her conduct virtuous. She died at Baghdād in June, A.D. 831, Jumāda I. A.H. 216. She is said to have built the city of Tabrīz, in A.D. 806, A.H. 190.

Zuber (زبیر بن بکار), the son of Bakkār, a Kazī, of Mecca, and author of the *Kitāb Sunan* and *Kitāb Akhbār Madīna*. He died in the year A.D. 870, A.H. 256.

Zuber ibn-al-Awam (زبیر ابن الاوام), was the father of 'Abdullah ibn-Zuber, and an enemy of Alī. He was slain by Amrū ibn-Jarmuz, A.D. 656, and his head carried to 'Alī, who not approving this act of his, Amrū drew his sword and ran himself through.

Zuhak or **Zohak** (ضحاک), or Azdahāk, a tyrant of Persian mythology, who overcame Jamshid, king of Persia, in a battle, and became the king of that country. There are various accounts of the descent of Zuhāk. Some say he was an Arabian, but descended from Qaiomurs (*q.v.*); others trace his descent to Shaddād, and term him a Syrian; and it has even been conjectured that he was the Astyages of the Greeks. All agree in one fact, that he was of a cruel and sanguinary temper. He is described as having had two dreadful cancers on his shoulders, which the Persian fabulists have changed into snakes, whose hunger nothing could appease but the brains of human beings: two of his subjects were slain daily to furnish the horrid meal, till the manly indignation of Kāwa or Gāwa, a blacksmith of Isfahān, whose two sons were on the point of being sacrificed, relieved the empire from this tyrant, and raised Farīdūn, a prince of the Pishdādian dynasty, to the throne. The fable perhaps indicates an ancient subjugation of Persia by a Median or Arab tribe who used the serpent, a dragon, for their standard. There is a ruin near Bāmiān called by the people "The Castle of Zohāk."

Zujjaj (زجاج), whose proper name was Abū Ishāq Ibrāhīm bin-Muhammad, was the author of several works. He died at Baghdād in the year A.D. 923, A.H. 311, when he was upwards of 80 years old.

Zuka (ذکا), poetical name of Mīr Aulād Muhammad, of Bilgrām, a nephew of Mīr Ghulām Alī 'Azād. He was living in A.D. 1761, A.H. 1175.

Zukah (ذوکاه), poetical name of Khub-chand Kayeth, of Dehlī, author of a biography of poets in Urdū.

Zulfiqar 'Ali (ذوالفقار علی), whose poetical name was Mast, was the author of a Tazkira entitled *Rayāz-ul-Wifāk*, containing the biography of the poets of Calcutta and Benares who wrote Persian verses; it was completed in A.D. 1814, A.H. 1229, at Benares. He is also the author of several other works.

Zulfiqar 'Ali Khan (ذوالفقار علی خان), Nawāb of Banda, was the son 'Alī Bahādur, ruler of Bundeilkhand. He succeeded his brother Shamshīr Bahādur on the 30th of August, A.D. 1823, 22nd Zil-hijja, A.H. 1238. He was succeeded by 'Alī Bahādur Khān.

Zulfiqar Jang (ذوالفقار جنگ), a title of Salābat Khān.

Zulfiqar Khan (ذوالفقار خان), a nobleman of the reign of the emperor Shāh Jahān. He is the father of Asad Khān, whose son also held this title. He died in A.D. 1659, Muharram, A.H. 1070.

Zulfiqar Khan, Amir-ul-Umra (ذوالفقار خان امیر الامرا نصرت جنگ), styled Nasrat Jang, whose former title was Y'atkād Khān, was the son of Asad Khān, a nobleman, of the reign of 'Alamgīr; he was born in A.D. 1657, A.H. 1067, and held several appointments under that emperor. On the accession of Bahādur Shāh in the year A.D. 1707, A.H. 1119, the title of Amīr-ul-Umrā was conferred on him with the government of the Deccan. It was by his aid and intrigues that Jahāndār Shāh, after the death of his father, Bahādur Shāh, overcame all his brothers and ascended the throne of Dehlī, when he was appointed to be chief wazīr; but after the defeat of that emperor in the battle against Farrukh-siyar, he was taken up and strangled, by order of the latter, as a punishment for his conduct. His head, with that of the late emperor Jahāndār Shāh, who had also been put to death in prison, was carried on poles, and their bodies, hanging feet upwards across an elephant, were exposed in the new emperor's train when he made his triumphant entry to the palace at Dehlī. This event took place in January, A.D. 1713, Zil-hijja, A.H. 1124. The aged minister, Asad Khān, Zalqiqar Khān's father, was compelled to attend the procession, accompanied by the ladies of his family as spectators of their own disgrace. Asad Khān, who, in hopes of making peace with the new emperor, had persuaded his son to visit him, and had thus put him in his power, with tears in his eyes wrote the following chronogram on his death: نمود ابراهیم المیل را قربان (Abraham sacrificed Ishmael). Mehr-un-Nisa Begam, the daughter of Yemīn-uddaula 'Asaf Khān was his mother, and Shaista Khān, the son of 'Asaf Khān, was his father-in-law.

Zulfiqar Khan Turkman (ذوالفقار خان ترکمان), an officer who served under Shāh Jahān and died in A.D. 1647, A.H. 1057.

Zulfiqar of Sabzwari (ذوالفقار سبزواری), a Sayyad, and a great poet, who flourished in the reign of Sultān Muhammad of Khwārizm, about A.D. 1200.

Zulfiqar-uddaula (ذوالفقار الدوله), a title of Najaf Khān.

Zulqadar (ذوالقدر), the poetical name of Mirzā Muhammad Mīhsia, a Turk of the tribe of Zulqadar, the meaning of which in the Turkish language is an archer that never misses his aim. This title he assumed for his takhallus. He flourished about the year A.D. 1688, A.H. 1100, and is the author of a Dīwān.

Zulqarnyn (ذوالقرنين), master of two horns, a title of Alexander the Great, probably based on coins representing him in the character of Ammon.

[*Vide* Sikandar]

Zunnun or Zu'l Nur Misri (ذوالنون مصری), surnamed Abū'l FazlTūb ān, son of Ibrāhīm, a celebrated Muhammadan saint of Egypt, whose merits were great in number, and who is said to have performed many miracles, and to have been the founder of the sect of Sūfī in Egypt, where he was held in the greatest estimation. It is related in the *Nafahāt* that at his death, when they were carrying him for burial, a large flock of birds, of a kind that was never seen before, overshadowed his coffin to the grave. He died in February, A.D. 860, Zi-Qa'da, A.H. 245, and a chapel was built over his tomb in Egypt, where a number of other holy men are buried. The work called *Latāef ul-Akhbār* contains the Memoirs of this famous saint.

NOTE.

In the article on 'Alamgir I. (Aurangzeb), at page 49, the statement of Mr. Beale that the emperor's children were all the issue of one mother seems to demand correction. According to the latest investigations the two elder Mirzās—Muhammad, who predeceased his father, and Mu'azzam, who succeeded to the throne—were the offspring of a Hindū mother, while Kāmbakhsh was the son of a Georgian from the Zenāna of the eldest brother of the emperor, the ill-fated Dārā. The Persian lady named by Beale was the mother of three, or at most of four of the emperor's offspring. Beale himself partially neutralises his error at page 46, article Akbar, Prince. (Vide *Aurangzeb* by Stanley Lane-Poole : "Rulers of India" series; 1893.)

CORRIGENDA

Page 96, column 1, line 2 from bottom, *for* H.M. Elliot, Esq., *read* Sir H.M. Elliot.

Page 172, column 1, line 12 from bottom, *for* 952 *read* 1058.

THE END